The Mush Hole
Life at two Indian Residential Schools
compiled by
Elizabeth Graham

Heffle Publishing
Waterloo, Ontario

© Heffle Publishing, 1997
Waterloo, Ontario

ISBN 0-9683179-0-1

Canadian Cataloguing in Publication Data

Main entry under title:

   The mush hole : life at two Indian residential schools

Includes bibliographical references and index.
ISBN 0-9683179-0-1

   1. Mohawk Institute (Brantford, Ont.)--History.
2. Mount Elgin Indian Residential School (Muncey, Ont.)--History. 3. Indians of North America--Canada--Residential schools. 4. Indians of North America--Canada--Interviews. 5. Indians of North America--Education--Canada--History. I. Graham, Elizabeth, 1941-

E96.5.M88 1997   371.829'970713   C98-900003-6

Preface

How history is written depends on the perception of a narrator living in a particular cultural group, era and geographical location. The history of the Mohawk Institute and Mount Elgin Indian Residential Schools is the result of the interaction of various cultural groups over a time period of 140 years. These schools, that were thought by their founders to be a good solution to the "Indian problem", can now be viewed quite differently with post-modern value systems and hindsight. Aboriginal Peoples who may initially have welcomed the schools as a mechanism for coping with the intruding society, naturally rejected the concept of an "Indian Problem" that would be solved by eliminating Indians from the equation, and resisted assimilation. In researching the history of two residential schools and talking to people whose lives were profoundly affected by their experiences at the schools, it is impossible to remain dispassionate and refrain from some implicit historical judgement. In recognition of the different biases and value systems of the various protagonists, the history of these two schools is presented through the words of these protagonists, to provide readers from various cultural and interest groups with the tools to interpret this history according to their own context and background. *Voice-over* is an analytical commentary on the schools from my own perspective as an anthropologist with experience of boarding-schools.

This is a resource book not only for historians and anthropologists, but also for Natives exploring both personal histories and that of their communities. The stories told in the book may encourage other former students in their healing process. The book is intended to be useful to anyone interested in Native Studies and who wants to learn more about residential schools. Administrators could learn how the imposition of policies by the dominant group and insufficient funding, turned a solution into the problem: rather than equipping Native children with the professional and economic skills to lead their communities as originally intended, the schools played a significant role in the process by which Native communities were deprived of their culture, and the power and resources to take charge of their lives. I make no apology for stubbornly resisting advice to direct the book to a particular market, and thereby make it shorter, because I want to provide people with the opportunity to read the original documents. I believe we can only understand the present by exposing the prejudices that people were up against in the past. Although this means including some documents that contain extremely offensive and hurtful material, a real understanding of attitudes can be lost in preinterpreted history and this understanding of the history of Aboriginal-White relations in Canada is urgently needed. Readers can read texts and interpret sub-texts for themselves and add their own perspective to my analysis. This approach places the onus on the reader to do more work, however, those who simply wish to get an overview of the subject can read Voice-over and follow up particular topics. The *School Life and Times* section includes many dates so that readers can refer easily to the documents in *Voice of Authority*. These documents and the personal stories in *Voice of Experience* are arranged in chronological order for each school. The subject index will help readers explore matters of interest and topics that may not be discussed in detail in *Voice-over*.

I owe much gratitude to all the people who told me their stories and accepted me into their homes and their lives, and greatly enriched my life. I would particularly like to thank Vena Missauba, Karen Hill and Lorna McNaughton for their friendship, help and kindness.

Many thanks to: Laird Christie for suggesting this research topic, reading the manuscript, and for his help and advice over the years. Sheila Staats at the Woodland Cultural Centre for her support and reading the manuscript; Tom Hill at the Woodland Cultural Centre, Barry Hill, Karen Hill and CKRZ Radio; Vena Missauba, Edward Groat and Sara English for lending materials; E. Palmer Patterson, Mathias Guenther, Charlotte Granskou for reading and commenting on *Part One: Voice-over*; Archivists Wendy Pickard at Indian Affairs, Ruth Wilson at United Church Archives, Ontario Archives, Anglican Church Archives, National Archives of Canada, Guildhall Library, London; Donald Smith for putting me in touch with Enos Montour and sending items of information; my husband, John Graham, for his moral and financial support.

Contents

Part One: Voice-over
by
Elizabeth Graham

3. Thomas Moore as he appeared when he entered the
Regina Indian Industrial School

4. Thomas Moore, after tuition at the
Regina Indian Industrial School

Voice-over

The Mohawk Institute in Brantford, Ontario opened as a residential school in 1834 and closed in 1970, and Mount Elgin at Muncey near London, Ontario operated from 1850-1946. Reports and letters from Government and Church archives, newspaper articles and the experiences of 60 former students as told by them, have been collected here as a documentary history of two Indian residential schools.

The schools are examined in two major contexts. Firstly, their context within the wider society is significant because the schools were controlled by Church and/or State and management policies towards these schools reflected national policies. The history of these two schools is a microcosm of the history of the changing images of what the wider society has perceived throughout the 19th and 20th centuries as the **"Indian problem"**. The schools were founded to solve the "Indian problem" through "civilization". "Civilize" is (still) defined in the Oxford English Dictionary as "to bring out of a barbarous or primitive stage of society to a more developed one," and there was no doubt in the minds of policy-making 19th century Englishmen that their society was the highest form of development. As perceptions of the so-called "Indian problem" changed over the years, so did the solutions. The schools were always part of these solutions but their roles changed over the decades, and these changes are examined.

Several themes emerge from exploration of the internal context of the schools. These institutions were designed to implement 'civilization' or total culture change. A residential school removes children from their homes and places them in a community where they can be educated and moulded into shape. An institution of this kind for Native children provides almost experimental conditions for would-be civilizers bent on total culture change. The mechanisms for achieving total culture change and the relationships of power and control within the institutions are examined. The experiences of the former students provide a picture of life at the schools and insight into the impact of the institutions on the lives of the children who went there, with discussion of such concerns as discipline and abuse, the food, education, living conditions and health.

Voices

This work consists of three Parts, each representing a 'Voice'. Part One: **Voice-over** is an analytical editorial essay with an overview of the subject. **Voice-over** introduces my methodology, and outlines and analyses various topics. This section combines both introduction and conclusions to highlight what I consider to be the significant aspects of Parts Two and Three. The two schools are analysed in the context of institutions attempting to wield total power, and the consequent uses and abuses of power. Part Two: **Voice of Authority** comprises a resource collection of documents which primarily represent the administration. Part Three: **Voice of Experience** contains the memoirs of former students. Because of the cultural differences the three Voices are kept separate to minimize confusion as to who is speaking to an issue. To further the aim of clarity, I have deliberately used the first person to express my personal opinions. Rather than claiming ownership of the subject by writing a concluding chapter with my observations, the book ends with the **Voice of Experience**, to give the former students the last word.

This work is organized as representing three Voices, but there are in fact as many Voices as there are individuals and interest groups speaking. **Voice-over** expresses the Voices of the author as anthropologist and as a former boarding school resident.

Although the **Voice of Authority** narrative does contain correspondence from parents and children to the authorities, most of the authors had an official position in one or more hierarchies. Principals, for example, were responsible to both church and government and responsible for children and used their Voice in several contexts. Most principals saw themselves as government/church representatives vis-à-vis the children, but occasionally a principal would reverse this. The majority of the communications are official and unfortunately, without personal diaries we do not hear the human Voice. The authorities themselves were sometimes at odds. Both in the early years and the last years at Mt. Elgin there was considerable controversy between the United Church and the government. When the NEC was negotiating a new lease for the Mohawk Institute in 1945, both Church and government were involved with their own political agendas. Personnel involved included four levels of government from the Indian agent to the Minister of Mines and Resources, the Synod of Huron represented by the Bishop, and the Missionary Society of the Church of England in Canada, all in negotiation with the Governor and Treasurer of the NEC. The sub-texts in this narrative emerge with an appreciation of the varying and sometimes conflicting political positions of the occupants of this category over a period of 140 years.

Within the **Voice of Experience** category each experience was unique. Although former students were glad to have the opportunity to meet other Native children from across Ontario, to a certain extent they retained a community identity, and an individual identity, as their Indian identity was taken away. What comes through from all the former students who have spoken is their resilience and humour. There are a number of former students who hated their school, ran away frequently and suffered much from physical punishment and confinement and the bullying that occurred, attributing their troubles in life, such as alcoholism, imprisonment, lack of parenting skills, inability to love, to the trauma of the residential school.

There are many people who liked their school. Many appreciate that they were given opportunities in life that their economic circumstances would have denied them otherwise. Many people formed friendships that lasted them through their lives giving them a 'family'. Some found a home better than the abusive foster home or family they came from. Others accepted that this was the only home they had, and made the best of it. There were good days and bad days.

The Voices take their identity from their position in a system of power relations. The ordering of this system depends on the perspective of the participants. The schools were seen by members of the dominant society as solutions to the "Indian problem", but from a Native perspective any problems were caused by non-Natives. Although administrators assumed that they should have total control over the students and expected gratitude, or subjection, from Native people in return, Native parents and Councils frequently expressed the belief that the schools were founded for the benefit of the Aboriginal communities and should be serving their interests and providing proper education, food and health care etc.. From a Native perspective the closing of the Mohawk Institute in 1970 was just another instance of the DIA reneging on its responsibility to the Six Nations. The *Before* and *After* photographs on page one of Thomas Moore at the Regina Indian Industrial School illustrate more effectively than any words the opposite perspectives on the value of "civilization".

Ways and Means

In this history of two residential schools, there is a twofold aim. One is to provide a chronological presentation of the historical records that people can look at and say: "That was what happened." The other is to present the historical records so that the reader can examine the social implications. The construction of the social patterns underlying events may be seen as a subjective exercise. Both approaches however, do involve subjective interpretation of events. The interaction concerns more than one cultural group, and several interest groups. Readers identifying with these groups will have different points of view and reference in their interpretations of what actually happened. Oral history from former students shows how events and incidents can be perceived very differently by the various parties and individuals involved.

There are various methodological problems in ethnohistorical studies. Doing ethnohistory is a unilateral exercise. The process of selection of documentary material by an ethnohistorian may be subject to critical self-analysis, but cannot involve 'dialogue' with the subjects. More often than not information on any one issue or incident is one-sided or incomplete.

Another problem is that all material that survives in archives has been selected by persons and for reasons unknown. There is a temptation to give the material significance because it is there, when it could just be happenstance that letters of complaint are more prevalent at certain periods. Was the material selected according to criteria that were important at the time? Who selected it? Is it what they considered important? Was there someone cautious who put everything away? Are the records representative of what was actually received?

Readers concerned with assessing the validity of the evidence should keep in mind that the material in the archives consists mainly of correspondence and reports received and sent by government officials or the school principals accountable to government, and much of it has an 'official face'. Reports and letters from school officials are constructed for their political context, either to make the writer look good, and show that they are spending government money wisely, or sharing things with government that could not be made public. The principal of Mt. Elgin wrote in 1945:

> *There are a great many things about conditions around this building, and conditions under which little children have to live, which if printed and publicized would cause such a furore of indignation that someone would have to take cognizance of it, and that immediately.*[1]

What I select from archives as relevant to the topic is also a subjective choice, and also partly contingent on my own experiences at two boarding schools in England from 1952-1960. These experiences provide a useful analytical contrast, as the schools catered not only to ordinary middle-class people like me, but also to aristocracy and royalty. Having experience of boarding school life at another point in the social spectrum gives me a perspective of what is general to boarding schools. However, this sense of common experience initially hampered my analytical ability because of a tendency to identify, and to assume that because I suffered it too, it is 'normal' rather than noteworthy to be obsessed by food, or to take my experience as the standard in matters of discipline or restrictions on personal freedom. With this mind set, it was more difficult for me to look at rules and discipline objectively, especially when in my case we accepted them knowing implicitly that we would end up with a relatively privileged position in society. Later in this essay I look at Foucault's explanation of the process by which institutions such as schools gain the right to control their inmates. Because I, along with the people who attended the Mohawk Institute and Mt. Elgin, have been subject to this process, at first I automatically assumed it was natural that they believed "We deserved the punishment if we broke the rules." Similarly, although we did not like the rules and frequently broke them, knowing the risks involved, we did not question the right of the administration to make and enforce these rules. Until I began to do this research, I too accepted without question the right of the school to make rules constraining my freedom, when for example, our parents who paid substantial fees and drove long distances to see us, were not allowed to take us out to dinner on a Saturday night but had to return us to the school by 6 p.m. However, although I have a certain level of understanding and empathy about residential school life, which is useful for analytical purposes, the circumstances were vastly different, and I cannot claim real understanding of the emotional and physical conditions these children experienced and in many cases suffered.

The transcribed documents are presented with very little editing. Verbal flourishes and courtesies have been removed, and repetitive information in the annual reports, in which some sections remained unchanged for several years, has been taken out. Spelling and typographical errors (*A more filthy place morlats never entered*!)[2], and layout are retained. Of course the selection is edited. Readers may feel that the selection was not edited enough! Details of finances, reasons for admission and discharge, health care, menus, farm management etc. are included where available, to show the reader first hand not only the actual conditions, but also to illustrate the priorities and attitudes held by the administration, and the bureaucratic context in which decisions had to be made. The relative amount of money spent, or the amount of time devoted to a project, and the proportion of a report devoted to a certain subject, all tell us something about its importance. Some very trivial matters are included to illustrate the bureaucratic control and the kinds of details principals had to be concerned with. I have also included selections of the details of the farm work and building construction and maintenance to show exactly how much work the children did, and to show the variety of projects principals were involved in. Drains and toilets may not usually be considered the stuff of which history is made, but the state of the plumbing and sanitation tells us a good deal about the attitudes of the administration to their charges. This detail also portrays the fuller picture to enrich our understanding of the history of life at the schools.

The records include a considerable amount of personal information. This kind of study involves an extremely difficult decision whether or not to include names at the considerable risk of hurting people still living or the surviving families. There are two rationales for keeping names: one is that many people want to trace their own personal and family history and increase their understanding of who they are and where they have come from. The other rationale is that to accept that Aboriginal people must have responsibility for their future, members of the wider society should be aware of, and face up to the reality of, the past and how it has shaped the present. The social situations inflicted on Aboriginal people that led to the existence and persistence of the residential schools were situations that little children had to live through. The attitudes and rigid treatment the children had to face because they were Indian and poor, and the sheer hard work they had to do, happened to real people, many of whom are still trying to come to terms with the experience. Changing the names would "fictionalize" the experiences and diminish the impact of what can be learned from them. However, I have taken out names, or separated names from information from this century that is personal with regard to families, or could hurt the reputation of the people concerned. Of course, this is also a subjective judgement. For example, I do not consider that there is any stigma attached to being named in RCMP truancy reports, but rather that it shows a spirit of resistance. Several individuals named in the truancy reports were interested and amused by the record.

The **Voice of Experience** section consists of the stories of individual students told first hand. The range of reactions and experiences of the former students is varied, and again it is important to present them with minimal editing, so that an editorial opinion is not imposed on the stories. The sample of people represented here consists of people who were willing to talk to me and were contacted through newspaper advertisements, the phone-in radio show at CKRZ in Ohsweken, and word of mouth. 36 former students from the Mohawk Institute, and 31 from Mt. Elgin were interviewed and several others spoken to. Seven of the people interviewed did not wish to have their interviews printed. 26 came originally from Six Nations, 2 from New Credit, 10 from Muncey, 14 from Oneida, 4 from Walpole Island, 1 from Sarnia, 3 from Kettle Point, 1 from Stony Point, 2 from Christian Island, 2 from Moraviantown. At the time of the interviews 11 people lived off-Reserve, 3 divided their time between the Reserve and the U.S., and the remainder lived on a Reserve.

The interviews were extremely informal. The following questions were asked, but not in any particular order: When did you go there? How long were you there? Why did you go there? Did you like/ hate it? Did you speak your Native language? What did you think of the principal? What did you think of the staff and teachers? Did you get an education? Did you learn any skills that were useful to you afterwards or helped you get a job? How did you get on with the other children? What did you think of the food? What did you think of the discipline? Did you run away? Was there sexual abuse?

Most of the interviews were taped; the tapes were then transcribed, any questions or discussion with the interviewer edited out, and personal information about other students taken out. Extraneous speech patterns such as - um, like, you know, eh?, which occur very frequently in speech, were mostly taken out because they are too distracting to the eye in written conversation. Readers should note however, that transcribed conversations and monologues do read very differently from neatly contrived literary works. In real speech people do not finish sentences, frequently use parentheses and skip trains of thought. After receiving the transcript, some contributors asked me to edit their stories. Interviews that were not taped rely on written notes. These do not always reflect the dialect and speech style of the contributor because initially I was not aware that I was translating into my own use of grammar while writing the notes. In some cases where other people were present, their remarks were edited out. In many cases contributors were reading the records and making comments, which sometimes seem out of context. If a lot of conversation was edited out, the order of comments was adjusted for coherence, but generally, a natural and spontaneous series of reminiscences is preferred, to capture the essence of what was memorable, how it is remembered, and how people feel about it now.

Because there are discrepancies between students in their versions of events, or between official reports and students' experiences, the questions arise - who do we believe and what is the truth? Events impact on individuals in different ways and one person may find an experience devastating and another person might forget all about it. Memories are selective and the memories of people who were only young children when they were taken to a strange institution may have their own reality. As one person says when she remembers her sister (who remembers getting 3 on each hand) getting 24 swats with a strap: *"I was only 4½ - maybe I said 1, 2, 24!"*[3] But that was her experience. Fifty years later that memory is still with her, and that is what is important. As an anthropologist I am primarily interested in the experience of the people involved in a version of events, rather than trying to establish validity or "truth", which I am not in a position to judge. I share with the author of *Old Boys*, an oral history from former students at Upper Canada College, the premise that *"because an interview subject has chosen to remember an event in a certain way, the recollection is the truth for him."*[4]

Plans - Promises - Pressures

Missionary societies starting their work in Ontario during the 1820s and 1830s, envisioned viable Native communities taking their place within the wider society. Contemporary philosophy espoused a belief in natural laws of progress, and missionaries believed they could help the natural progress along and 'elevate' Aboriginal peoples to the 'level' of 19th century European society through 'civilization'. The schools were a vital component in this process, to train Native teachers and religious leaders, who would in turn instruct their people. Both took boys and girls:

...the boys to be taught, in connection with a common English education, the art of farming and useful trades, and the girls instructed in reading, writing, domestic economy, sewing, knitting and spinning, so as to qualify them to be good wives and mothers...to select from these schools the most promising boys and girls, with a view to giving them superior advantages, so as to qualify them for missionaries and school teachers among their brethren...[5]

Although the possibility of the government opening a central manual labour school was proposed by the Lieutenant Governor of Upper Canada, Sir John Colborne, in 1830,[6] the four residential manual labour schools that did open in Southern Ontario were operated by missionary societies. During the 1820s John Brant solicited help from the New England Company (NEC) for the schools at Six Nations. The NEC opened a Mechanics Institute at the school in the Mohawk Village in 1830, taking boarders into the Institute

in 1834, and they also opened a boarding school at Mud Lake in 1842. The NEC was a protestant missionary society based in England, with the mission that: *"The first duty of the New England Company...is to civilize heathen natives...their second duty is to christianize them."*[7] The missionaries employed by the NEC at the Mohawk Institute were all Church of England/Anglican clergy.

Methodist missionaries were also active. Peter Jones (Kahkewaquonaby), the famous Methodist missionary whose father was Welsh but who was raised in his mother's Mississauga Native community, wrote in 1838:

I am now trying to get the Wesleyan Missionary Committee in London to establish a central manual labour school...I feel very anxious to see an institution of this kind established amongst us, for I am fully persuaded that our children will never be what they ought to be until they are taught to work and learn useful trades, as well as to learn to read and write.[8]

The Wesleyan Methodist Missionary Society worked closely with the Government to try and establish central manual labour schools. The Wesleyan Methodist Missionaries at Alnwick started taking boarders into the Mission House in 1839. Peter Jones wrote again in 1842:

...I am very anxious to see manual labour schools established among our people, that the children may be properly trained and educated to habits of industry...all the Indians with whom I have conversed highly approve of the project. They are ready and willing to give up

their children to the entire control and management of the teachers...unless something be done in this way, the Indians will for ever remain in their half-civilized state, and continue to be a burden to the British Government and the missionary societies...I see no reason why they may not be raised in their condition, so as to become useful subjects of our Great Mother the Queen, and an ornament to society...[9]

At the meeting in 1846 between the Superintendent of Indian Affairs, Captain Anderson, and representatives of the Indian Tribes of Upper Canada, Anderson told the Chiefs:

Manual Labour Schools will be established for the education of your children, and the Land to which you may now, with the consent of the Government, remove, the Government will secure by written documents, to you and your posterity forever...That you shall devote one-fourth of your annuities, which many of you promised me last fall that you would do, for a period of from twenty to twenty-five years, to assist in the support of your children of both sexes, while remaining at the Schools. It is to be hoped, by that time, that some of your youth will be sufficiently enlightened to carry on a system of instruction among yourselves, and that this proportion of your funds will, therefore, no longer be required after that period...It has been determined that your children shall be sent to the schools, where they will forget their Indian habits, and be instructed in all the necessary arts of civilized life, and become one with your White brethren. In these schools, they will be well taken care of, be comfortably dressed, kept clean, and get plenty to eat.[10]

The Rev. William Case, founder of Wesleyan Methodist Indian missions, told them it was the:

...wishes of the Queen and her Government...that you congregate in larger communities; abandon your roving habits: enter the business of farming: consent to the establishment of Boarding Schools, on the scheme of Manual Labour, and with the Government Grants, apply a portion of your annuity for a term of years, to carry this important plan into effect. The Government wish you to be religious, industrious and happy...we see no reason why the Red man should not be as comfortable, respectable and happy as the White man. We know not why your young men should not be so educated as to be able to transact your affairs as well as your White brothers. You may, indeed, live to see some of your sons Doctors, Attorneys and Magistrates. This is a thing not at all impossible. You have already lived to see your Warriors become Ministers of the Gospel, Interpreters, Teachers of your Schools. These you now see standing before you...[11]

Security on their lands was a strong incentive for the Indians to agree to these proposals as it was not long since Sir Francis Bond Head had been around and tried - *"he persuaded, and even threatened"*[12] - to get the Indians to cede all their land and move to Manitoulin Island.

The response of a Chief from the Mohawks of the Bay of Quinte illustrates the kind of choice facing the Indians:

This is our only hope to prevent our race from perishing, and to enable us to stand on the same ground as the White man. Let us then sound the shell, and summon the Red man from the woods; let us give up the chase of the Deer and the Beaver; it is unprofitable. The White man's labour is fast eating away the forest, while the sound of his Axe in summer and his Bells in winter is driving the game far away from their old haunts; it will soon be all gone. Brothers, we understand that one of the chief objects the Indian Department has at present is to improve our young people by means of Boarding Schools, at which they will not only be taught book and head knowledge, but also learn to work with their hands; in fact, to make our boys useful and industrious Farmers and Mechanics, and our girls good Housekeepers...[13]

Of the 12 assembled Chiefs two voted against the proposals and two abstained.[14]

Lord Elgin said in 1846:

...it is certain that their, (the Indians') truest interest require that habits of independence, and self-help should be fostered among them, and that the period of tutelage, as much as possible, be curtailed...I attach, however, more importance to the establishment of Industrial Boarding Schools for the children of both sexes, than to any other measure of this class...I trust that it may soon be in my power to report that these useful establishments have been multiplied in the Indian Settlements, without cost to the Government.[15]

Combined with the obvious motives of providing education, there were pragmatic aspects in the Government's agenda - the Government would not only save money on direct support, but the issue of gunpowder would be stopped and the money saved spent on schools. This plan in turn provided a rationale for settling the Indians in a few communities, making them manageable and freeing up more land for white settlers.

With these pressures from government and missionaries, and in particular the tireless Peter Jones who raised funds in England and Scotland as well as Canada, there was considerable support in the 1830s and 1840s from Native people for manual labour schools.

The Indian parents have repeatedly acknowledged and mourned over their want of government and knowledge in training up their children in the way they should go, specially in teaching them habits of industry; and I have often heard them say that they would gladly consign them over to the care of suitable teachers for a certain number of years.[16]

The result of these plans was the building of two schools by the Methodist Church, Alderville in 1848, and Mt. Elgin at Muncey near London, which was to be maintained by annuities of the Ojibwa at Muncey, New Credit, Sarnia, assisted by the Wesleyan Missionary Society. The Central Manual Labour School that was to be built at Owen Sound by the Government was abandoned after the Credit Indians found that the site for their community was in fact unfit for agriculture. Frequent changes of Governor General also delayed consent for building Mt. Elgin, and it was not until Lord Elgin became interested that the arrangements were completed. Peter Jones wrote in 1848:

> ...the contract for our School here is given out; and the buildings are to be finished by the 1st of September next. The main building is to be built of brick, and is calculated to board and lodge one hundred children, besides the manager and teachers. This building, with a stable and other out-buildings, such as a house for the farmer, barns, sheds, etc, which are not included in the above contract. The money I collected in England and Scotland is to be laid out entirely on the School here...supported by the funds of the Indians here and the River Credit people, whose annual grants amount to about 220l...We expect to obtain aid from the St. Clair Indians, who receive a large annuity from the Government; and what will be lacking will be made up by the Wesleyan Missionary Society...[17]

The opening of Mt. Elgin in 1850 was the culmination of more than ten years of work by Peter Jones and the Methodist Missionary Society. The schools that survived in Southern Ontario were the Mohawk Institute and Mt. Elgin. Alderville closed in 1859 and Mud Lake closed in 1870.

School Life and Times

Administration

Principals and Policies

Founding of the schools

The Mohawk Institute was founded 20 years before Mt. Elgin, but both schools were founded by Missionary Societies with the aim of "civilizing" Native peoples and producing ministers and teachers who would act as agents of "civilization", and teaching farming and trade skills useful in Native communities. Initially both schools were supported in principle by Christian Native groups, with Mt. Elgin receiving financial support from several bands. Both schools were opened in locations central to the communities they were to serve. The Mohawk Institute was situated in the Mohawk Village. Six Nations people had been settled on the Grand River since 1784, depending on horticulture, hunting and fishing for subsistence, but their land base had gradually been sold. The government moved the Six Nations to their present Reserve on the south side of the river in the 1840s, leaving the Mohawk Institute several miles from the Reserve and later to become engulfed by Brantford. Mt. Elgin was located on the River Thames on the Caradoc Reserve shared by the Munsees who were Delaware people who had also come from the U.S. at the close of the American Revolutionary War, and the Chippewa of the Thames. The Oneida people came from the U.S. in 1840 and settled across the River Thames from Muncey. Although there was geographical contiguity, culturally the schools and the communities were worlds apart, a situation the missionaries were determined to change by "civilizing" the children.

Mohawk Institute

The New England Company's missionary, the Rev. Robert Lugger, hired a schoolmaster for the newly built day school at the Mohawk Village (now Brantford) in 1828. In 1830 Lugger, without informing the NEC in advance, decided to open a Mechanics Institution for teaching handicrafts. Lugger also planned to board and clothe some orphan children. In 1831 Lugger built two large rooms for teaching girls spinning and weaving, and two for teaching the boys tailoring and carpentry, and a mechanic shop. By 1834 the missionaries, Lugger, Nelles and Richardson, finding that the Indians were still suspicious of all whites as intruders, decided that the best way to remedy this was *"the instruction of a number of youth of both sexes in the arts, habits and customs of civilized life, who may hereafter act as instruments in the hands of the Company, for the complete civilization of Indians generally..."*[18] A boarding school was opened to ten boys and four girls, to be taught farming and gardening, as well as the trades of blacksmith, carpenter, waggon and sleigh-maker, and cabinet maker. After Lugger's death in 1837, a missionary from the Reserve, the Rev. Abraham Nelles, was put in charge.

Nelles commented that initially there had been some difficulty getting 14 children to come,[19] but in 1838 more girls were added, and in 1840 the building was expanded to take 40 children. There was a waiting-list, and by 1842 there were 30 applicants for two vacancies. There was support from the Chiefs of the Six Nations who hoped that their young people would learn agriculture and benefit by getting farms when they left the Institute.[20] In 1859 the Institute was rebuilt to hold 60 students. The NEC acquired a farm in 1860, and in 1864 gave up teaching trades to concentrate on farming. By 1868 the number of children had increased to 90.

During the early period of Nelles' superintendency the mood was positive and plans for expansion were always in the works, and individual success stories in education were frequent. After 1840 there were no reports of truancy. There was evidence that Mr. and Mrs. Nelles took a personal interest in the students.[21] During Nelles' time the instruction was carried on in English, but the children were allowed to speak Indian amongst themselves. Towards the end of Nelles' era reports were not as positive - visitors finding that the children were learning by rote, management of the farm was haphazard, the buildings were uncomfortable, and the food and sanitary conditions left much to be desired.[22] However, the students still believed that the school existed so that they could get an education.[23] The NEC Committee became frustrated with Nelles' lack of communication and thought that the school and farm were run inefficiently. On Nelles' retirement their top priority was to find someone efficient to take over as a full-time principal. The aim of the Committee was to supplement the education at the day schools and *train Indian youths for useful employments in life.*[24]

Mt. Elgin

The cornerstone of Mt. Elgin was laid with much ceremony on July 17th 1849, and the school was opened in May 1850 with 30 boarders and a number of day students. The Rev. Samuel Rose took over the principal's job from the Rev. Samuel D. Rice in 1851. Rose saw his task as:

...to save from utter extinction the remnant of a once noble, but now deeply degraded and long neglected race...From this class is to spring a generation, who will either perpetuate the manners and customs of their ancestors, or being intellectually, morally and religiously elevated, take their stand among the improved, intelligent nations of the earth, act their part in the great drama of the world's doing; or through want of the necessary qualifications, to take their place and perform their part, be despised and pushed off the stage of action and cease to be!"[25]

Rose's attitude, though demonstrating the blatant ethnocentrism of the time, seeing radical culture change or 'civilization' as the desirable and only means of survival, was nonetheless realistic in that social context in which First Nations were in grave danger of being eliminated.[26] A spirit of optimism prevailed, a wing was added to the building, and by 1853 there were 42 students. By 1855 Rose had to reject applicants daily but he was desperate as the money from the Indian annuities promised by the Indian Department for repairs and expansion to the building, and the money promised the graduates to set up on farms and title to their land had not come through. Rose believed that *"One of the primary objects...of the Industrial Schools is, the raising up among the Indians, on Indian lands, of a class of industrious and intelligent people, who would prove a blessing to their*

race, and a credit to the government..."[27] He was experiencing problems with truancy. Rose resigned in 1857. The Rev. James Musgrove took over and was enthusiastic about the students leaving who were qualified as teachers.

The Special Commissioners' Report published in 1858, looked at the role of the Alderville and Mt. Elgin schools and described the *"benevolent experiment"* as *"to a great extent a failure"*[28] and suggested withdrawing the funds from Indian annuities, closing the schools down and turning Mt. Elgin into an Indian Orphan Asylum. By 1862 the Indians were not happy with the school either and did not want to continue their funding. Although it was called an industrial school farming was the only mechanical art taught, and it did not provide enough benefits to compensate for losing their children.[29] Musgrove died in 1863 and the school closed. In 1867 the school was reopened with 4 boarders under the care of the Rev. and Mrs. R. E. Tupper, but within a few months had nearly 50 scholars. Workshops were built for teaching carpentry and shoemaking. Tupper was soon complaining that the work was hindered by the lack of support from the Indian Department which had undertaken to assist toward the board and clothing of fifty scholars, but in 1869 cut this number to thirty.[30] The Rev. James Gray took over in 1871 and the Rev. Ephraim Evans in 1873. The Rev. Thomas Cosford became principal in 1875. He was shocked by the condition of the buildings and put a great deal of energy into putting the buildings and the farm in shape. He, along with all the former principals reiterated that the government should raise the number of pupils they supported, and that *"these scholars must become our native agents as missionaries, teachers, local preachers, exhorters, leaders, etc. to carry on their work among their people..."*[31] Cosford denounced the Government for its lack of support and for trying to shut down the Institute. He remained at the Institute until 1881, and assessed the contribution of his incumbency in terms of the 'intellectual development and spiritual attainments' of the pupils.[32]

Our Aim...is to educate and elevate the Indian youth of our country, that they become instrumental in the elevation and salvation of their own people.[33]

Although there was a succession of principals in this period and the school was closed from 1863 to 1867, they did not lose sight of the goal of education for the children.

After the Indian Act

After years of legislation to control Aboriginal peoples, the Indian Act of 1876 entrenched their position as wards of the government. The government gained more control over the Mohawk Institute with annual per capita grants. An amendment to the Indian Act in 1894 paved the way for compulsory education, and the government required the schools to accept children from other Reserves, and orphans. The period at the end of the 19th century was one of prosperity for both schools as farming was very profitable.

Mohawk Institute

The NEC brought Robert Ashton, a schoolmaster from an Industrial school in England, to be the first full-time Superintendent in 1872. In his first report Ashton expressed his horror at the insanitary conditions of the buildings which were in very poor shape; they lacked bedding and clothing, the food was bad and the children dirty and undisciplined. His idea of the aim of the school was very different from Nelles', and he complained bitterly that the boys had been taught that they had no right to be set to work against their will, and that they did not like to work, but looked on the school as a boarding house where they could do as they pleased, and go out or go home whenever they liked. Worst of all, Nelles had made a speech to the boys in his presence telling them that they no longer had to work in the fields once the harvest was in, as the object of their coming to the school was to be educated, and Isaac Barefoot had agreed with Nelles that the parents also believed that their children came to be educated only, and not to work unless they liked. Well, Ashton anticipated no difficulty in getting them to work heartily. In his judgement the school had been run in a very sloppy way, so he proceeded to set up a strict system of discipline. The boys were organized in military style, with squads forming a company with corporals and sergeants who acted as monitors.[34] Ashton also drew up a comprehensive system of rules. Prison cells for solitary confinement were set aside for offenders. Other regulations Ashton instituted in 1873 were qualifications for admission, censorship of mail, and a requirement of speaking English except on half-holidays. By 1876 the use of English was compulsory at all times.[35]

However, concomitant with the compulsory use of English came success in the school system. During the 1880s Ashton encouraged students to go to high school, and he set up scholarships for teachers. By the time Ashton had been at the school twenty years, 20 boys and 25 girls had become Indian school teachers and 15 others had obtained professional standards. To prevent students from leaving after a short time at the school, Ashton brought in a policy that applicants had to sign up for two years, during which time no holidays were allowed.[36]

The aim of the institute as expressed by the NEC in 1879 was *"to impart such an education as shall fit its pupils for teachers amongst their own people, at the same time training them in the arts and practices of civilized nations."*[37]

In 1885 the DIA made a grant for current expenses and the school began to accept students from other Reserves. In 1891 an addition was built to hold more pupils, and the DIA started making an annual per capita grant. By 1894 the school had started to admit orphans and neglected children and Martin Benson from the DIA described the chief aim of the Institute as *"to impart a practical education to the children."*[38]

In 1903 the main building and some of the barns, the play-house where the boys were sleeping, and a neighbouring farmer's barn were destroyed by fires set by some of the boys. At this time Benson wondered whether the school should be rebuilt if the Six Nations Indians did not appreciate the benefits. Government and NEC officials believed that the fires had been started by pupils who resented the strict discipline, and with reason: the school was run like a reformatory, and the over-discipline was causing great frustration and discontent among the students. The subject of prison cells in the play-house for runaway students, complaints from parents and negative comments from visitors about the discipline and food, occupied correspondence with the DIA between 1903 and 1913. Former pupils of the Mohawk Institute were reported as reluctant to send their own children there because the discipline was too strict. At a Warriors' Meeting the Indian agent was told that the boys' education was not as good as that of the girls, and that the boys could learn farming just as well at home. The school was rebuilt in 1904 to hold 125 students.[39]

Robert Ashton retired in 1911, having taken Holy Orders in 1903, and was succeeded by his son, A. Nelles Ashton. Nelles Ashton was described as cruel by a former student, and he was taken to court by a parent in 1914 and fined $400 for the treatment of three girls who had run away, and on their capture had been placed in solitary confinement, their hair cut off, and one girl, 13 years old, whipped on her bare back with a rawhide whip.[40]

Mt. Elgin

At Mt. Elgin the Rev. W. W. Shepherd took over as principal in 1881. At that time the object of the Institute was described by a visitor as:

...to give its pupils a good common English education, and instruct them in agriculture and other industrial pursuits. The boys are taught farming...carpentry, cabinet work, shoemaking, etc., and the girls sewing, knitting, spinning, and general housework.[41]

Alexander Sutherland expressed the opinion in 1883 that:

Experience convinces us that the only way in which the Indians of this Country can be permanently elevated and thoroughly civilized, is by removing the children from the surroundings of Indian home life...[42]

There were 50 students but Shepherd believed they could take double that number and they had many applications. During the 1880s the number increased gradually and jumped to 90 in 1890. Shepherd worked very hard to make the Institution self supporting through the farm and the Government grant. After a decade the income from the farm and shops and Indian Department was enough to cover all expenses and improvements. The 1890s were a time of prosperity, high attendance, and a new building was built, and enrolment increased to over 100. Shepherd's enthusiasm peaked in 1900 with the jubilee report. After this time he found there was not enough land, expenses were higher, the shops were not bringing in much income and not really saving the school money in supplying needs. By 1902 the institution was experiencing financial problems with a deficit for the first time. Martin Benson reported that to make ends meet, the boys were being worked too hard on the farm, and the Department was receiving numerous complaints of the ill-treatment of pupils. There were problems with parents over health. In fact Benson questioned the value of the system *"...there is little use in our educating an Indian if, in our endeavour, we spoil a horn and fail to make a spoon. That our schools have failed in their object is generally admitted..."*[43] Shepherd had a fatal accident in 1903 and was succeeded by the Rev. T. T. George.

George's regime from 1903-1909 was another period of complaint, discontent, and truancy. Within a year George had accumulated a deficit of about $3500. There were conflicts with parents over care of a sick child, complaints about scabies and parental contact. There were complaints about the severe discipline - that George whipped the girls, and complaints about the food, and some parents did not want to send their children back to the school. Three fires were set in 1907 and 1908.[44]

World War I to World War II

At both schools the period between the wars was more settled. Duncan Campbell Scott was in charge of education from 1909 as Superintendent of Education and from 1913-32 as Deputy Superintendent General of Indian Affairs. Scott believed in assimilation: *the further development of the race toward its ultimate goal, that is, its absorption by the ordinary civil life of the country,*[45] and his view influenced policy for twenty years, with a stifling effect on any ambition for students to become leaders or even teachers. By the 1930s money was very tight; the physical condition of the buildings deteriorated, and every decision was made with economy in mind. Admission to the schools was restricted to orphans or destitute children. The 1943 Young Report on the Education of Indian children in Western Ontario concluded that residential schools had outlived their usefulness as educational institutions, but that they were still needed to deal with the problem of orphans and needy children. Mt. Elgin was closed in 1946.

Mohawk Institute

In 1914, with the outbreak of war, Nelles Ashton joined the Services, leaving his sister, Mrs. Ann Boyce, as acting principal. She followed the system of discipline set up by her father, though she maintained that she was not as strict.[46]

In 1915 another Englishman, the Rev. Cyril M. Turnell, was appointed principal. His first actions were to relax discipline, to feed the children whole milk and extra butter, and to allow the children living nearby to go home for a short holiday in the summer. He also met with the Six Nations Chiefs in Council to discuss the Institute. There was no truancy between October 1917 and June 1918.[47] In

1918 the NEC dismissed Turnell from his position and reappointed Boyce. Duncan C. Scott, whose 'vision was narrow'[48] but who nevertheless wanted the schools to be run humanely, was opposed to this move, describing Turnell's appointment as in the best interests of the Institute.[49]

Mrs. Boyce tried hard to run the school efficiently. She had been trained as a nurse and was most interested in the physical condition and appearance of the buildings and grounds, and the farm. The boys and girls both had to work hard, the girls doing painting and light farming and gardening as well as all the indoor work, but Boyce reported that they made an effort to provide amusements and recreation for the children, with concerts, outings and other treats. The educational standards were not a priority for the principal. There were incidents of truancy. The detailed reports give a good idea of the day-to-day running of the institution, and particularly how important and time-consuming the farm work and property maintenance were.[50]

Mrs. Boyce married the boys' master, Sidney Rogers, in 1922 and he took over as principal. One student thought Mr. Rogers was nice - he would take the girls sledding or for rides in his truck - while Mrs. Rogers was cross but grew great flowerbeds![51] The principal reported that many of the children preferred to stay at school during the Christmas holidays because it was more fun.[52] However, the official reports and perceptions were often very different from the experience of the students:

They took us kids down [to the Ohsweken Fair]...I don't know if it was any use them taking us down there because we never got any money. What's the use of going to the fair with your hands empty? I asked the fellow who was making hot dogs if he would give me one, and he fixed 'er up and handed it over to me, and he put his hand out and wanted money. I said "I told you to give it to me - that's what I asked for", and he took it back. They never gave you a cent and then they took you down there in a waggon. What good is that going to do you when you're starving to death?

Christmas time come around too, and this here Rogers come up in the dormitory where we slept, and he just had a few peanuts with shells on them, and he just throwed them around, and you had to pick your own and somebody would step on your fingers and you didn't even get very much. That was all we got - that was supposed to be Christmas.[53]

Conditions on the Reserve were bad at that time and many parents could not afford to have their children home. The buildings were extensively renovated in 1922-3, and management went on much as before, with the introduction of team sports like lacrosse, a Cadet company, Girl Guides, a boys' band, and much success in track and field competitions. These activities brought the school into the Brantford community and according to the principal, inspired some school spirit. Despite this there were incidents of bullying.[54] Pauline Johnson's sister, Evelyn, attacked the

Institute in the newspaper and suggested that it should provide a first-class education, and teach trades and nursing and domestic science. She said students were running away in droves.[55] Indeed there were many reports of truancy during the period, and even one incident where some students tried to attack the principal with clubs.[56] Rogers came into conflict with the local Indian Superintendent, there were rumours that he was drinking excessively, and when he bought a farm to run as a riding school and used Institute labour and equipment, he was fired by the DIA, who also did not appreciate that the school farm was not profitable and was running up a deficit.[57]

The Rev. Horace Snell, who took over as principal in 1929, did not make many changes in the way things were run, and does not seem to have put as much personal energy into the job.

"Snell was a very intelligent guy...he would take us out for a walk in the evening and he'd explain the stars in the sky, and sometimes when he had the energy, he would recite things for the kids...He used to do a wonderful job of preaching."[58]

"My biggest complaint about him was his lack of caring ...he didn't put enough into the job that he had there."[59]

The experiences the boys had depended a lot on the boys' master. The DIA was concerned about the food, truancy and the discipline. There was concern that the boys were going to the dump to scrounge food, an anonymous letter was received saying that the children didn't have warm clothes for winter. In 1938-9 inspectors found the building and the washrooms dirty, and a report in 1942 stated that the whole atmosphere in the school was depressing and the rooms were bleak and unattractive.[60] *"Mr. Snell is an old man and has never been a good administrator at any time. He never appears to have a good grip on his finances."*[61] After he left Snell was described by the Indian agent as *"sadly lacking in every quality to make the Institute a happy home for children."*[62]

Mt. Elgin

The Rev. S. R. McVitty became principal of Mt. Elgin in 1909. McVitty commented on the feeling of unrest, frequent truancy and dissatisfaction of the parents that he found when he took over the school, and described the previous regime as chaos and the school as practically a penitentiary.[63] McVitty was a good manager and had the school self-sustaining again by 1913. Enos Montour described him as *"calm and dignified."*[64] Another former student described the school as a nice place because she liked McVitty and his family. Students who were at the school in the late 1920s found that McVitty could wield the strap vigorously. The aims for the childrens' future he expressed in 1909 show their limited prospects:

It is my conviction that the aim of the school should be to fit boys and girls for farm and domestic work (not by any means for office work or even teachers unless in

very few cases) and just as soon as they are well fitted to earn their own living let them go out to good homes and do so...they would early take their place in the nation's life and be a real help to those who so much need farm and domestic helps.[65]

There were some complaints from parents about harsh treatment, lice, the food and overwork during 1914-1915, but McVitty defended himself:

...the pupils of this school are furnished better food, better clothing, better sleeping accommodation, and do less work than the average white child in the province of Ontario. Since taking charge of the School I have never knowingly done, or permitted to have done to any child in the School what I would not be willing to have done to a child of mine under similar circumstances.[66]

Changing government policy made administration of the school more difficult, and in 1929 McVitty complained:

In compliance with your request...we have opened our school to a crowd of very young and inefficient children, in fact, telling the Indian Agents to pick out the needy ones. This means that our school staff has to be increased, not only to do the work that older pupils would do, but to nurse and care for the little ones who cannot take care of themselves...[67]

In 1925 the school was filled to capacity.

McVitty believed it hampered the girls in their search for domestic work if they had too much education and he tried unsuccessfully to get proper domestic science training for the senior girls.[68] In 1929 McVitty hired the Rev. Oliver B. Strapp, a missionary from Oneida, as vice-principal to run the school. An article in the London Free Press extolling the work at Mt. Elgin contained the headline *"Present Undertaking Is To Fit Him [Redman (sic)] Into Customs of White Brother"* saying *"Boys and girls alike are being fitted for the duties that confront the adult British citizen."*[69]

McVitty resigned in 1934 after 25 years and he summed up his work:

...we have earnestly endeavoured to give or furnish our pupils with food, clothing, lodgings, nursing, teachers, recreation, vocational training and religious instruction fully equal to if not better than that enjoyed by the children of the great working and middle class white people of the Province of Ontario. I felt that anything less would be unworthy and anything more would be unjust. This standard of equality has been heartily endorsed by the multitudes of white people who visit us from time to time and I am pleased to add by the Indian people themselves who without any solicitation on our part keep the school filled to its doors.[70]

Strapp's regime from 1934 to 1944 was marked by truancy. Many students say of Strapp: *"He sure lived up to his name!"* A former teacher described him as a *"maniacal despot"* who imposed impossibly stringent rules *"to get the Indianness"* out of the students.[71] When the students were leaving the school for their summer holidays one year Strapp told them *"Come back clean you savages."*[72] There were complaints from truants and also from parents about poor food and harsh treatment, and Strapp also clashed with the local Medical Officer of Health over the diet. Many former students only came in contact with him when they were getting the strap, though two former students described incidents in which they expected to get the strap but found Strapp constructive and reasonable. Several parents swore out complaints before a Justice of the Peace in 1943 to try and get Strapp removed - he did leave in 1944 but went to another Residential School in Brandon, Manitoba. The physical condition of the buildings was appalling. Attempts were made by the principal and the architect and inspectors to get improvements, but the Department pleaded lack of funds and only carried out repairs and renovations when there was mortal danger.[73]

The administration was finding that the improvement in conditions on the Reserves during the war led to fewer older students at the school to do the work, and there was competition with the parents for the labour of the children. Parents found it difficult to get their children discharged as the schools had become dependent on the students. The students were there to maintain the operation of the residential school. Or, as the Young Report stressed, *"profit rather than educational policy becomes the object of this work."*[74] Strapp wrote:

...the mother thinking that they are now old enough to do some work and they could therefore perhaps be of use at home. While they were younger she was quite satisfied to have us look after them and now they are old enough to make a contribution to the life of the school she would like to have them at home...it is imperative that we should have a percentage of pupils old enough to carry on the work of the school...[75]

In 1944 the Indian agent inspected the school and found all the fire escapes barred to prevent truancy. The whole place was shabby. The Rev. S. H. Soper had just taken over as principal and was finding it exceedingly difficult to make ends meet with the deplorable conditions at the school. He wrote many desperate pleas to the Department for supplies and financial help. In 1945 he wrote:

After I pay salaries I have just 20 cents a day from the grant to feed and clothe and warm and light the children. On top of that we have to pay all farm equipment repairs and transportation...These wee children have to earn that...In time past when big boys and big girls came to the school this was possible. Today when we have 45 children under ten and only 3 who are sixteen, three fifteen and five thirteen it is an impossibility...It is impossible for babies of this age to feed, clothe and wash for themselves. I cannot afford to employ help.[76]

The number of students dropped to 65 in 1944, rising to around 100 for the last years. Mt. Elgin closed in 1946.

Post-World War II

The documentary record presented in this book is not representative of the existing record, for is period much of the material in government archives restricted. The Mohawk Institute was the only Indian Residential School in Southern Ontario. The NEC withdrew all funding and although the principal was appointed by the Anglican Church the school was under the control of the DIA. The post war austerity period coincided with the poor condition of the school. It was not until the 1960s that some modernization was undertaken. The Mohawk Institute closed in 1970.

Mohawk Institute

In 1943 the DIA's lease from the NEC expired and the NEC suggested that the DIA should take over the school and they would support the Mohawk Chapel and a Chaplain. The Church of England in Canada did not want to lose control and offered to run the school. In 1945 Snell was retired as Principal and battle was joined between the DIA and the Bishop of Huron over the right to appoint the new Principal. The Bishop insisted that the lease must contain an amendment in which the Principal would be appointed by the Church, even though in fact since 1872 there had been nearly 50 years on and off during which the principal had been a layperson. These negotiations and administrative bungles are reported in detail in **Voice of Authority** as a prime example of political agendas overriding the interests of the children at the Institute.[77]

A candidate recommended by the Government to replace Snell was Joseph C. Hill, principal of a Six Nations Day School, who not only had an outstanding record as a teacher, but had spent two years at the Ontario Agricultural College, had business experience, leadership experience with young people on the Reserve, and was seemingly the ideal candidate. His wife, as a graduate of Home Economics, had the qualifications to be Matron. But he was an Indian, a member of the United Church, and not a clergyman or the Bishop of Huron's nominee. Unspeakable to us now was the Bishop of Huron's use of a racist justification to take control and appoint a principal while blatantly ignoring historical fact and professional qualifications. He wrote:

...the supervision of a staff of teachers and other officers in the School, always a difficult matter as experience has shown, is likely to be much more successful in hands other than those of an Indian, however well qualified he might be."[78]

The government caved in rather than risk the threatened "embarrassment".[79] So, the Rev. W. J. Zimmerman, an Anglican parish priest whose qualifications were that he had run children's camps and was born on a farm, was appointed.

By the end of 1945 the DIA had control of the school, and the Anglican Church, having won the right to select the Principal, withdrew its offer of financial support.[80] The government had however failed to move the school in the direction the Director of Indian Affairs, Hoey, envisioned ..."*the Principal of the school should be an agricultural college graduate with pedagogical training and experience both in classroom work and farm management...*"[81]

Recommendations made by the Local Council of Women soon after Zimmerman's arrival are listed here to point up just how many things the school lacked: trained domestic science teachers in homemaking, child care, home nursing, dietetics and nutrition; trained instructors to teach boys woodwork, handcrafts, farming and trades; the teaching of music and art; a well-equipped library; a quiet, supervised study room; proper, modern classroom equipment, and laundry training and equipment; installation of physical education facilities and a sports director; a supervised recreation room for boys and girls; installation of better toilet facilities for all children; more dormitory accommodation and teacher supervision at night; a trained dietitian to plan balanced diets; regular dental and medical care, an infirmary, clothing for all children, bedding, mattresses, dishes and cutlery.[82]

More and more children were being accepted from other Reserves - and as time went on more and more children came from broken homes, or were orphans. In 1948 the Bishop of Huron wrote:

The Institute has become a School mainly for underprivileged children...The Church is profoundly interested in making the Mohawk Institute an important asset in our vexed Indian problem.[83]

In 1955 there were 185 students.

Most first-hand reports portray Zimmerman as strict and authoritarian - his life intersecting with the children usually in the area of punishment.

The principal came right down at lunchtime and gave us a strapping, right in front of everybody. He used to jump up with all his might...you could see the shape of the strap on your arm after he'd get through, then it would be swollen and purple.[84]

The work Zimmerman did behind the scenes as an advocate for the children in dealing with government, social agencies and home conditions, was not visible to the children. For example, he reportedly intervened to rescue two boys whose mother had unknowingly signed adoption papers which the welfare agent told her were medical forms. A staff member said in 1966:

Nothing has ever been too much trouble for the Canon where Mohawk Institute children's welfare was involved, such as taking a sick child to Lady Willingdon hospital at 2 a.m. He is usually seen going about his work with a smile and is seldom ruffled.[85]

During Zimmerman's time a new school block with a gymnasium, and improved kitchen facilities were built. Relaxing of rules on dress, communication between boys and girls, dances, Sunday dinner with brothers and sisters, camping trips to Christian Island, and a broadening of extra-curricular activities, eased living conditions for the children.

The farming operation was closed in 1963.

By 1965 the school's purpose was described as "*to provide hostel accommodation for children requiring special care and attention or those who cannot receive an education while residing at home.*"[86] Most needy children in Southern Ontario were placed in foster homes by the Children's Aid Societies.

The school closed in 1970 because the majority (96) of children were coming from the north and it was decided to build schools for them on their Reserves. Only 23 children from Six Nations were at the school.

Comment

In May 1920 McVitty wrote an article about his work:

...we were under no illusion what ever as to the difficulties of the task awaiting us - the business management of a thousand acre farm, the purchase and sale of all the live stock connected therewith, the judicious expenditure of approximately $25,000 per annum for wages, food, clothing, fuel, light and many other things incidental to the life of the school. Add to these the final responsibility for the health, happiness and discipline of at least 120 boys and girls always in residence, the selection of suitable officers and teachers, and the blending of all these varied interests into something like a happy and suitable community life, and we have a job quite big enough to tax the energies of any one man.[87]

The job was certainly taxing and very few principals were equal to the whole task, and most concentrated on certain aspects, losing sight of the original aims of the schools. To do this job, apart from Robert Ashton, who was later ordained, and a period of 'dynastic succession', or nepotism at the Mohawk Institute with A. Nelles Ashton, Mrs. Boyce and Major Rogers, the principals were all Ministers of religion, none of them were qualified for **all** the facets of the job, most of which were far removed from being a Minister.

Although the personalities of the individual principals had a profound effect on the running of the schools at any time, the pattern of events was remarkably similar at both schools as external factors changed. The first principals were optimistic, though of course their mission was to eradicate Indian culture. Education was important and the schools were there for the students. Before the turn of the century, increasing accountability to the Department of Indian Affairs produced principals whose concerns were efficient management rather than the happiness of the students. After the turn of the century there was discontent at both schools, fires were set, and the volume of complaints from parents increased. From World War I until the 1930s there was continuity and reasonably good management, but in the 1930s the principals were strict and lacked vision and were not liked by the children. In the case of some principals, such as Zimmerman and Snell, children who attended school during the early stages of a principal's tenure liked the principal better than those who were there at the end, suggesting that principals tended to lose their initial zeal, or become old and tired. To the children the principal was the supreme authority who administered punishment, and more personal, friendly relationships were rare.

There was also a difference between the official face presented by principals and that face presented to the children. *"Zimmerman was nice when there was other people around, but when you was there by yourself you were the bottom of the barrel...He was strict...If he didn't like you he'd let you know."*[88] There are several incidents reported in which principals said one thing to outsiders or parents but after they left went back on their word. One student ran away from Mt. Elgin during Soper's time because a teacher was picking on him unfairly. His father took him back:

We had a discussion about it with Mr. Soper...and my Dad said that I had come back willingly...and I shouldn't get punished or get the strap...and Mr. Soper agreed. Twenty minutes after my Dad left I got the strap...he was a Minister and gave his word that he wouldn't give the strap, but he did, and it took a little bit off of his shine as far as I was concerned.[89]

Staff

Mohawk Institute

The Mohawk Institute was started with one teacher for ten children, who also worked as a mechanic. Instructors in carpentry, shoemaking, blacksmithing, and a wheelwright were added during the 1830s. The superintendent was not a full-time principal in those days. In 1840 with the increased number of children, a full-time teacher was needed at the Institute, and a family of three were hired. During this time the agent, Richardson, mentioned the importance of teachers having qualities of kindness and fondness for children.[90] By the 1840s the superintendent was cutting down the number of trades teachers to save money.

In 1869 the NEC decided to employ an Indian, and former pupil Isaac Barefoot was hired to teach the girls. He taught the boys from 1873-1876. Ashton was hired as a full-time principal in 1872. In 1887 another ex-student, Susan Hardy, was hired as a teacher and she taught generations of children in the senior school until her retirement in 1935. From 1869 on there were 2 academic teachers, but an ever-increasing enrolment of students.

By 1918 the principal was complaining of the difficulty in keeping staff because they were not getting enough money. Turnell paid out of his own pocket for a teacher to come in and give a weekly course in domestic science.[91] In 1921 they hired a junior teacher who was not qualified, but very enthusiastic. The reports during the 1920s show the frequent turnover in academic and non-academic staff for one reason or another.

Henrietta Hill and Vera Duncan were hired as sewing teachers in 1898 and 1908. More ex-pupils were taken on the staff in the 1920s. Business College graduates Elsie Clause and Carrie Crowe were hired as temporary staff, one as a sewing-teacher, and the other doing housekeeping jobs. Floretta Elliott was hired as a sub-officer in 1923.

During the 1930s the boys' master was an important figure to the boys. Kenneth Kidd (the archaeologist) who was boys' master for a year or so, made life-long friendships with some of the students, another individual took an interest in sharing his inventions with the boys, but he was very untidy and lax in discipline and he got in trouble from the DIA for not supervising the boys properly. Another of the boys' masters was accused of unmercifully beating a boy who had thrown a stone at a younger boy.[92]

In 1948 the principal was still fighting the problem of low salaries and the difficulty of getting manual training teachers. He tried to get more classroom teachers so they could have small classes and decent salaries. The DIA took over direct payment of the staff in 1949, and wanted the teachers to do extra supervisory work, but this did not go over well. In 1955 a supervisor to organize recreation was appointed to look after the children in the summer and a PT Instructor was hired in 1958. The DIA recommended employing personnel with cheerful dispositions, who could establish a good atmosphere in the school and give the children care and affection.[93] By 1961 there were 5 classroom teachers. Zimmerman and the regional education office wanted 6 supervisors, plus part time Manual Training and PT Instructors, and a teacher-counsellor on call. In 1961 Zimmerman asked Sara English, who had been at the school as a student, to join the staff as a housemother. During her three years on the staff she made many changes to humanize the school, and was a staunch advocate for the children.[94] There were 35 staff members by 1966.

Mt. Elgin

The school started in 1851 with one male and one female teacher, but by 1856 the principal was complaining that he could not get teachers because there was not enough pay.[95] In 1868 there was only one teacher, and in 1888 one teacher assisted by advanced pupils. In 1893 the staff consisted of 4 farm instructors, 2 teachers, foreman in carpenter and shoe shops, matron and cook.

In 1913 there were 3 teachers, a music teacher, domestic science teacher, sewing-room mistress and laundress, farm instructor, stock-man, mechanic and engineer. The mechanic, John Kapayo, who had been a student at Mt.

Elgin, was on the staff for 21 years. In 1914 a trained nurse was hired. The principal in 1915 said there were not enough pupils to justify having 3 teachers.[96]

In 1920 a nurse was hired who wanted to give the Senior girls a course. In 1926 the school Inspector reported that another qualified teacher was needed for the 140 children, and that there had been too many changes of teachers in the primary classes that year. The principal thought that two teachers were enough (1928) as the class room work was not the most important part of the training as *"In the case of the Indian 'a little learning is a dangerous thing'."*[97] The Inspector reiterated his view in 1928, that 2 teachers could not adequately deal with 148 pupils, especially as many came who could not speak English. In 1929 the principal asked for more staff to look after the large number of younger children the school was accepting.[98]

Comment

At both schools two main difficulties throughout their history were getting qualified teachers for the low amount they were paid, and getting them to stay. With the exception of Miss Hardy, who taught for 50 years, there was often a high turnover rate amongst the staff. The academic teachers were a minority of the staff and the teacher/pupil ratio very low. Besides Isaac Barefoot and Susan Hardy as teachers, several Native former pupils were hired as staff members at the Mohawk Institute. Mt. Elgin had one long-term Native staff member, a former student, and occasional Native staff but no Native teachers. However, the Native teachers who were hired had themselves been educated at the residential school and did not represent Native culture.

The children's experiences with the staff were similar to that in any school. There were some teachers at both schools that the former students thought were good teachers, and liked and respected, others that they found mean. The teachers seem to have been more popular than other staff members and most of the comments about the classroom teachers from former students interviewed are positive. A frequent comment was that the schools soon got rid of any staff members who were nice to the children.

Regrettably it was not possible to include the perspective of staff members. Most staff members are no longer alive, and the staff members I was able to contact did not wish to participate in this project.

Finances

Mohawk Institute

The school was founded and funded wholly by the New England Company until 1891. There was not an unlimited fund and even before the Mechanics Institution opened Lugger complained about the inadequacy of funds.[99] Periodically during the 1830s and 1840s there was talk of 'savings', 'expansion when they could afford it', 'the high cost of the school', 'retrenchment'. After 1860 the purchase of the farm helped to defray expenses, but there were no funds for expansion after the new school was built in 1858, and the NEC asked the principal for economical management.[100]

In 1872 an attempt was made to get the Six Nations parents to contribute from their interest money to the school.[101] Ashton made a considerable outlay on the farm and by 1874 it was showing a profit. In the following years (apart from a loss in 1876), profits varied from $200 to the best in the history of the farm in 1903, $2,258.

In 1891 the DIA started making an annual per capita grant to the school, and in 1905 the NEC had to get assistance from the DIA to rebuild the Institute and put in a proper water supply.

In 1918 the NEC tried to sell the school to the DIA but Scott refused to negotiate by mail, threatening to withdraw the government grant, and the NEC said their officers were too busy to come to Canada. By 1920 the NEC was complaining that the bills were high and restricted their grant. The NEC was in financial straits and there was a rumour that they were giving up the school and the grant would be cut so drastically that enrolment would have to be limited to 75.[102] The NEC leased the school to the DIA in 1922 for 21 years. In 1921 the DIA had increased the per capita grant to $80.00 because the NEC had withdrawn most of its financial assistance. This was to be paid out of the general vote for Indian Education as the Bands did not want to pay. By 1929 there was a deficit. In 1930 the NEC tried to sell the Mohawk Institute to the DIA but the DIA could not afford it. The NEC was paying $1000 and offered to pay the principal's stipend.[103]

When the lease expired in 1943 there was disagreement between the Anglican church and the DIA and the lease was not renewed. The NEC lost its money during the war and discontinued the grant, though the school and 9 acres of land remained its property.[104] In 1947 the DIA increased the per capita grant by $20. In 1949 the Bishop of Huron said that the Church could not give money and the Government grant must be increased.[105] The DIA took over the school completely, but budget problems remained.

In 1960 many improvements were needed, and Zimmerman was finding it difficult to work within the budget. Working within the government bureaucracy meant juggling various departments - trying to get running shoes from the educational budget, sanitary napkins from National Health and Welfare, skates from the school balance etc.

By 1962 the boys were in school all day and could not work on the farm and hired labour was too expensive. The farm was discontinued in 1963.

Mt. Elgin

The school was founded with money raised by Peter Jones and with the support of the Methodist Church. The Chippewa of the Thames, New Credit and Sarnia Bands contributed voluntary annuities. The DIA arranged to pay insurance and a per capita grant for students, while the Church was to pay all the other expenses, which were supposed to be defrayed eventually by the farm.[106]

By 1855, with the building addition, the principal was already in need of more money, and by 1856 waiting for the Department to pay the $3,660, he was in debt and desperate. In 1863 the Bands withdrew their support as no mechanical arts were being taught.[107]

In 1883 proceeds from the farm and the grant from the church covered the expenses for the first time. The farm was very successful in 1891, and for several years covered not only expenses but also improvements. In 1901 the returns from the farm were the largest in history. But by 1902 the principal said they could not carry on with the government grant of $60 per capita. The farm was not large enough to pay its way and the boys had to work too hard to pay for the school. The Methodist Missionary Society did not support the school, though it made up any deficit. In 1904 Benson said that Shepherd had sacrificed the interests of the school to make both ends meet.[108]

After McVitty took over the school was once again self-sustaining from 1911-1913, and he described the success as marvellous. By 1925, however, there was a need to increase the per capita grant as the expenses had not been covered by revenue from the farm and the grant since the end of the war, and the large Reserve was exhausted. By 1934 there were no funds to do more than minimal repairs. In 1936 there was a lack of funds to implement the doctor's recommendations.[109]

In 1938 there was an increase in the per capita grant, but by 1944 the school was facing an increasing deficit, and in 1945 the financial situation was desperate. Superv te that it was impossible to feed, clothe, warm and l at the children on 20 cents a day. He deplored the fact at the school was supposed to earn money from working the farm with tiny children.[110]

Comment

The financial situation was difficult at both schools, right from the very beginning, apart from a 20-25 year period of profitable farming at the end of the 19th century. Most plans and schemes to carry out the original and continuing intentions of the school were wrecked on financial rocks. The policy at both schools for many of their years was to make the farm carry the school, and the children were needed to work the farm. Lack of money affected the quality of health care, the food, recreation, quality of staff, sanitary conditions, etc. etc. etc. Principals had to spend time they might have devoted to the children, worrying about making the books balance and running the farm.

Because financial responsibility was split between Church and government there was the additional tendency on the part of each to try to make the other take more responsibility, or neither wanted to pay.

If financial backing had been sufficient to achieve the goals of the schools in the first place, they might have been successful in terms of their original mission to provide a generation of teachers, ministers and farmers who would take charge in their communities (though we should keep in mind that the desirability of their mission of culture change is obviously a matter of opinion) and their roles might have disappeared a hundred years earlier.

The Learning Process - Admission to Discharge

Admission

Mohawk Institute

The first children to board at the school were taken only from Six Nations, with the majority being Mohawks, and this remained the rule until 1860 when Nelles admitted 5 children from Muncey. Attendance at a day school and good conduct were the prerequisites for admission, but Nelles said he often deviated from the rule and admitted *"ignorant and even heathen children."*[111] In 1870-1 the NEC decided that admission would be restricted to children attending the day schools on the Reserve who passed a competitive exam before the Board of Missionaries. By the 1870s children who had been examined and obtained a certificate of fitness were chosen first from the day-schools on the Reserve. Then children from other districts could be

admitted with permission from the NEC and a certificate of fitness. The qualifications for admission were:- aged 10-17, and possessing a good character, ability to read the 2nd book of lessons, and a fair knowledge of the simple rules of arithmetic.[112]

In 1893 the big change came when orphaned and destitute children were admitted. By 1902 "pagan" children had the first claim plus destitute, neglected, deserted children, or those from large families or living in a "vicious environment." By 1948 it was described as a school for underprivileged children coming either from broken homes or with anti-social tendencies.[113]

In the 1960s Children's Aid Societies began finding foster homes for children, and enrolment dropped. Students came from 27 different groups and/or places.[114] Children deemed in need of care were brought in from as far north as Mistassini to make up the numbers.

Mt. Elgin

The school originally took students from Muncey, New Credit and Sarnia Bands which funded the school, plus Walpole Island and Oneida. In 1883 Shepherd wanted to have an entrance exam to screen students. In 1888 students seeking admission had to be able to read in the Second book and work the simple rules of arithmetic. By 1929 McVitty was complaining about the number of needy students.[115]

During the 1930s the school was continually receiving applications from Indian agents from at least 18 Reserves.[116] All pupils were sent to the school because the agent judged their home conditions unsatisfactory, or at least one parent was dead. Many of the children were very young. Strapp was often unwilling to discharge older pupils, either because he needed a rcentage of pupils old enough to carry on the work, or because they were short of their grant earning number.[117] In 1944 the principal complained that if the agents regarded the school as a Children's Aid Shelter they could not do the work. They needed more students and older students, or they could not finance it at all.[118]

Comment

Initially, admission to the schools was a privilege restricted to children from certain Reserves. Gradually the area was expanded. At both schools there was a period in the 1870s and 1880s when children had to be able to read and do arithmetic at a certain level to be admitted. In the 1890s the admission of orphan and destitute children changed the character of the schools. By the 1930s admission was virtually restricted to needy children. Both schools were full and had a waiting list during most of their history - at first because parents wanted to send their children to the schools, and latterly because of the number of needy children as determined by the Indian Agents.

At both schools the majority of the alumni interviewed went because their parents died or separated, or were too poor to keep them. At least 5 of the students say they wanted to go or their parents chose to send them there. Three of the students said that they were forced to go by the Indian agent or Children's Aid Society, having a different perception of their home conditions from the authorities. Most of the students believe their parents sent them to the school because economically they had no choice.

Education

Mohawk Institute

At first the curriculum was confined to reading in the Bible, writing, and arithmetic, and the level achieved was described in 1837 as good compared to country schools in England, and in 1841 as better than the district school.[119] Geography was added in the 1840s and history in 1859. By this time Lesson Books were being used.

The NEC's policy during the 1860s was to fund students who wanted to get a higher education off the Reserve. In 1867 three students were sent to Brantford Grammar School, and by 1870 there were 7 students getting higher education. An exam for admission was proposed, so that students would know more coming into the school and would only have to stay three years rather than five.

In 1872 the scholars were described as having "proficiency not understanding" in reading.[120] The NEC discussed raising the standard of education provided at the school so that there would be no need to send children out for higher education.[121] Consequently support for higher education was withdrawn without the concomitant raising of the standards. A visitor observed that the instruction was not equal to schools for white children.[122]

Ashton arranged the children in divisions to take weekly turns in attending school in the mornings while the other division did farm or domestic work, and instituted mixed classes. By 1876 Ashton had improved the educational

standards so that the junior classes reached the level previously attained by the senior classes. Ashton's aim was to come in line with Provincial standards of education. During the 1880s several students went to high school and Ashton worked hard to train pupils as teachers. In 1885 ten scholarships were set up for training teachers, and in that year 8 students passed the Entrance exam for high school. In 1887 seven students attended the Brantford Collegiate.

In 1893 Ashton lamented that the standards had to be lowered with the admission of orphans and neglected children.[123] Later, a few would get to Entrance. There were usually up to 6 children going to high school and boarded at the school. By the end of the century 1 or 2 students a year passed the Entrance exam.

In 1911 typing and stenography were added to the curriculum. In 1921 a class in telegraphy was started. In 1923 the School Inspector reported that the junior school was not progressing because of the high staff turnover. Rogers did not report on education and did not want to hire a well-qualified teacher who would only be interested in the classroom and not the general life of the pupils. In 1926, 6 passed their Entrance. By 1928 there were 3 boys at the Collegiate, but several girls who had passed the Entrance were boarded in Brantford. In 1929 there were 6 boys and 1 girl at the Collegiate.

By the 1950s there were some Grades going to school all

day. In 1953 there were about 14 pupils attending high school, and in 1955 the DIA suggested the children would make better progress at local schools. The DIA then decided to try and integrate Grades 7 and 8 only, but the school board refused to take only part of the Mohawk children.[124] A new school block was opened in 1958. The number of academic classroom teachers was increased to 5 from 3, and by 1961 the number of pupils attending Brantford schools was 40. In 1962 an official commented that the future educational needs of the students would be better served through complete academic training, and students in all Grades started to attend school the whole day. There were 15 high school students in 1962. In the mid-sixties there were so many students from Quebec that two French class rooms were set up.

4/36 of the former students interviewed went to high school while at the school, and at least 11 more have gone on and taken courses on their own initiative. None attribute their success in life to the education they received at the Mohawk Institute. Although one person appreciated the opportunity to go to high school, he was not put in the course he wanted. Some appreciate the discipline they learned which enabled them to achieve their own success.

Mt. Elgin

The original curriculum consisted of reading, scriptures, writing, geography, and arithmetic. In 1856, history, algebra and agricultural chemistry were added to the curriculum. In 1868 the progress was described as the same as in the best white schools.[125] By 1881 the principal reported that some of the students were so anxious to learn that they studied in their leisure time,[126] and in 1884 the first students are reported to have passed the Entrance exam, with 9 students obtaining teacher's certificates by 1886.

In 1886 an industrial system of two days in school and one out, was adopted. Vacations started. In 1887 the principal commented that they were finding it expensive and difficult to send children to high school from Mt. Elgin.[127] The subjects taught were the same as the public schools in the province. In 1890 the vacation was limited to three months in the summer. School was added on Saturday afternoons, plus an hour of preparation in the evenings. A plan was made that students who were going to train as teachers could remain at Mt. Elgin until they got their third-class certificates and would have their expenses paid while

attending the model school. 20 pupils got their teacher's Certificates in 8 years. In 1897 the holidays were shortened to 6 weeks. In 1889 only one student passed the Entrance which was the lowest number in years. In 1904 and 1905, 3 students passed the Entrance exam.

By 1910 a half-day system of school was in effect. In 1911, Ferrier had a plan for Mt. Elgin to run a class to train teachers to teach in Indian schools, but this was vetoed by the DIA. A Model class was added in 1912 with 4 students to be trained as teachers, under the supervision of the head teacher.[128] From 1912 to 1932 between 5 and 8 students passed the Entrance exam annually. In 1936 Strapp wanted to get an examination centre at the school so students could take their Entrance exam in familiar surroundings.[129]

Mt. Elgin was so far from a high school, that although students were taken to Entrance, only one of the former students interviewed went directly on to high school. This was arranged by the school but she had to take a live-in domestic job and work her way through school.[130] Some would like to have gone, but they could not afford it, and for most it simply was not considered an option.

Comment

At both schools the curriculum in the early years depended heavily on reading the Bible in English and some arithmetic. Gradually the curriculum was expanded until it came into line with Provincial standards in the 1880s. Pride in the educational work of the schools and plans to train teachers reached their peak in the final decades of the 19th century. For most of their existence the schools were run on an industrial system with school only half-a-day, but measured against the day schools on the Reserve the residential schools did well. Realistically, the students interviewed probably had more opportunities for education than most other students on the Reserves, and some acknowledge that fact. However, measured against the original aims to provide an education and train teachers and professionals, the schools failed to deliver their promise. Although it was possible for students to go on to higher education, particularly at the Mohawk Institute, most of them were quite old by the time they got to Entrance for high school, and money was a problem. The encouragement did not outweigh the difficulties, and only 5/67 of those interviewed went directly to high school.

Manual Training and Work

Mohawk Institute

The school started out as a boarding school to provide a program of manual training. The trades for boys included carpentry, cabinet-making, waggon-making, shoe-making, blacksmithing, and initially, tailoring. Girls were to learn

spinning and weaving. When the Reserve moved to the south side of the Grand River in the 1840s and economic conditions changed, the manual training programme gave way to farming.

For both boys and girls over the years the manual training

program tended to lose out to the necessity of putting the children to work. As early as 1837 some of the girls and their parents, backed by Mrs. Nelles, were advocating that the senior girls would learn more if they had proper training in domestic skills and were not just expected to do the menial work.[131]

In 1848 Agriculture was added to the program. By the 1860s the manual training program was abandoned and the boys all did farm work. The girls spun the yarn and made all the socks.

By 1872 the older boys were taking turns working with the farmer, while the small boys looked after pigs, cows, and milking. Some boys refused to work, saying they were there for the education. The girls made all the clothes, and did the knitting. Nelles said they were doing too much work.[132]

Ashton came in expecting the boys to work, but he complained that he could not get the boys to apprentice for carpentry as it was too confining and they preferred farming.[133] The girls made all the clothes, sewing and knitting, besides keeping the clothes and linen repaired. They also did all the cooking, cleaning and most of the laundry, and the bread-making.

In 1877 carpentry was reinstated and a foreman hired. In the following years Ashton complained that 2 apprentices left before finishing their course (1886), and in 1891 that he could not get the lads to stay at school long enough to learn a trade.[134]

The work day was long. In summer the children rose at 5.30 a.m. and one division worked from 7 - 12 noon and from 5 - 6 p.m. with school in the afternoon, while the other division worked in the afternoon and went to school in the morning(1894).[135]

In 1907 there were complaints from parents that the boys were kept at the school too long, to do farm work rather than attend school.[136]

In 1921 a manual training instructor was hired, and taught the boys to repair, build and upholster furniture, and overhaul machinery. But an inspector commented in 1923 that although they did a lot of practical work there was no systematic instruction in the principles of manual training, household science, or agriculture.[137]

The reports from 1922-29 give a detailed account of all the work the students did - all the farm projects, building repairs and painting, sewing, not to mention all the regular chores on the farm and in the house. In 1929 the Department wanted the girls to learn milking.

In 1929 Snell hired a mechanic as boys' master to save money getting mechanics from the city, and in 1936, he maintained that the boys got manual training doing repairs with the boys' master and they were also making models.[138]

In 1939 a teacher was hired for manual training and a shop equipped for carpentry, forging, woodwork, farm mechanics. But by 1944 the girls were getting training in house-work and sewing, while the boys had little vocational training as they could not get a qualified teacher. So in

1946 the Local Council of Women recommended trained domestic science teachers, and woodwork, farming, and trades instruction for boys.[139] Shortly afterwards a manual training teacher was hired who started out by repairing desks as Zimmerman wanted the boys to do something practical, but by 1948 he was also doing academic teaching and not spending so much time on manual training. In 1949 Zimmerman reported that the boys were responding to manual training and a program for the girls was needed.[140] Ten years later he was again trying to get a manual training instructor two nights a week for a "much-needed program."[141] Then in 1961 the Home Economics and Industrial Arts positions were cut back to pay for 5 classroom teachers and the vocational training needs were being studied. In 1962 the Education Supervisor in Toronto recommended that the school hire a Manual training instructor 1½ days a week. In 1963 the farm was closed.

The school was always meant to provide manual training, but only provided proper training on occasions. The moving of the Reserve to the south side of the river in the 1840s removed the market for goods made at the school. The long apprenticeship for trades such as carpentry discouraged most students at the end of the 19th century. Difficulties finding suitable teachers, and general lack of interest scuppered the programme at other times, but the records do not really explain why the programme always failed.

None of the former students interviewed benefitted particularly from a manual training or domestic science training programme. One appreciated the opportunity to make things with the boys' master. They certainly worked - doing all the chores in the farm and household and garden. Domestic experience enabled many of the girls to get jobs, and do them well and earn a living, or helped them in raising their families.

Mt. Elgin
This school was also called an Industrial school but opened in 1850 as a farm. The girls made all the clothes as early as 1851. A work day starting at 5 a.m. had the students working at least 5½ hours a day and also attending school for 5½ hours, plus evening school and sewing. By 1855 the boys were doing nearly all the labour on the farm.

Carpentry and shoemaking were added in 1869, and new workshops built. These shops were successful during the 1870s. In 1884 some boys complained that they had to do too much work when they wanted an education; when they complained to the principal they were discharged.[142] During the 1880s the boys produced first-class items - shoes, boots and cabinets which should have made a profit, but by 1887 there was no market for the manufactured goods and most of the work was done to supply the Institution. By 1898 they were ready to give up shoe making.

A government official commented in 1902 that the boys were *"not only working but being worked."*[143]

In 1907 George wanted to add manual training as a special department of class work. McVitty said in 1909 that *"pupils have been kept in school longer than necessary simply for the work they could do,"*[144] and that this caused resentment. He added a steam plant in 1910 to lighten the laundry load for girls. In 1913 blacksmithing was added. At this time the work day went from 6-6.45 am; 7.45-11.45 am; 5.30-6 pm, adding up to 5¼ hours a day, in addition to school work. In 1914 a parent complained that the children had to do too much work.

In 1928 the school inspector commented that there was not enough diversity in the practical work they did and that they needed instruction similar to a Technical school. The response to the Department's request in 1929 that girls learn milking was that this had been discontinued for a couple of years as most girls went on to be domestics in city homes.

In 1932 the principal wanted a Domestic Science Department for the senior girls who had their Entrance, but who did not have the technical training for worthwhile jobs as housekeepers. By 1935 there was a Domestic science program with lectures and practical work under the supervision of a graduate dietitian. The boys did practical work in farming and gardening and manual training. In 1937 a pupil complained he had to do too much work.[145]

In 1938 there was another attempt to revive the manual training program, and tools were bought and an instructor hired, yet in 1939 the Indian agent said they needed an extensive manual training program. A weaving course was started for the girls. In 1942 Strapp asked for electric sewing machines so that girls would be prepared for work in city homes. By 1944 Soper was deploring the amount of work the children had to do to keep the school going, and how young the children were, asking the DIA to tell him what repairs they would pay for, and which had to be earned by the labour of 10 and 11 year old boys. Young children had to bring in the harvest, yet for vocational plans they needed older children.[146]

Of the alumni interviewed only two men mentioned receiving and appreciating some manual training, but they all did farm work. All of the women cleaned, cooked and the sewing and did laundry, and most appreciated this as stood them in good stead when they had their own households.

Comment

At both schools, organized manual training programmes to teach specific skills such as carpentry, blacksmithing, shoemaking etc. came and went sporadically. There were long intervals in between these efforts in which the children learned through practical experience, which meant that the children did all the work to run and maintain the schools. Some details of building maintenance have been retained in **Voice of Authority** to illustrate the kinds of work children did, such as painting and carpentry, in addition to the farming and domestic work. The former students scrubbed floors, prepared, cooked, and served all the meals, did the dishes, washed the sheets and clothes, made the clothes, tended gardens, milked cows, tended chickens, ploughed the fields, harvested the crops etc. etc., as young teenagers. Clyde Peters describes taking the tractor by himself and spending his days preparing all the fields for the spring planting, at the age of sixteen. The photographs on p.353 and p.428 of boys farming and gardening, illustrate just how small some children were. At times the students and parents complained, government officials complained, principals complained. The harsh reality was that the children's labour was needed for the schools to carry on, as Soper pointed out.

Most of the alumni interviewed appreciated learning how to work hard and do things right, even if the specific skills learned were not useful in choosing a career. Independent farming was beyond the means of those who learned farming skills, for example. Many of the women appreciated the domestic skills they learned. There were relatively few complaints about overwork, and some actually found that the work relieved the boredom of their everyday lives.

Careers

Mohawk Institute

The first students to leave were set up in trades such as carpentry and blacksmithing and as wheelwrights. By 1859 the emphasis had changed and four school teachers and five catechists had graduated.

By 1872 ex-students were being 'sought as servants' but the students themselves were not keen. Of pupils who left between 1881 and 1885, only one girl was in service to a white family. Actively working in their professions in 1887 were 17 teachers, 2 clergy, 2 physicians, 1 civil engineer, 2 civil service clerks, and several in trades (carpenters and blacksmiths), others farmers and wives of farmers.[147] By 1891 people needed employment as farmhands and

domestics because of increasing material needs, and there was a marked increase in the number of girls working as domestics away from home.

Between 1872 and 1892 20 boys and 25 girls became teachers; 5 boys and 10 girls were teaching in 1892, and 11 were in other professions. Ashton did try to keep the boys in school but they did not like the apprenticeship system and the commitment to one trade for 6 or 7 years.[148] By 1895 most boys were working on farms on leaving - even those who learned trades. By the turn of the century girls were much sought after as domestic servants and Mrs. Ashton found jobs for them. Between 1910 and 1913 more than half the girls did domestic work and more than half the boys did farm work after they left the school.

In 1922 there were 4 girls taking courses in telephone, telegraphy, and high school. From 1922-29 there was no specific information, but in 1931, Ferrier's history of the school[149] named as many 'successful graduates' could be contacted. He heard from 50 boys and 38 girls from a 60-year period. Their occupations, of which several individuals had had more than one, included:

Boys: clergy-4, teacher-15, farmer-10, interpreter-2, bookkeeper-1, clerk in Indian Dept-2, reporter-1, storekeeper-1, blacksmith-3, fought in war-8, councillor-6, carpenter-4, factory-3, office-3, construction foreman-1, runner (Tom Longboat)-1, fruit farmer-2.

Girls: teacher-24, Indian Dept-1, governess-2, nursing-3, office-9, Institute for blind-2, domestic-2 plus many. Ten girls had worked at the Mohawk Institute - three as teachers, others as sewing, music, housekeeping, and junior officers.

Of the former students interviewed most of the men had a variety of jobs including steelwork, a stint in the armed services, factory work, machine work, farming, trucking, one man went into engineering and one into politics, two became Ministers. Most of the women were busy with families, combined with various jobs in domestic service, business offices or stores, three do social and health care work, one has her own tree service, one became a Minister.

When I came out of the Service, I went back to school to get my high school education, I stayed there for a couple of years. I went to welding school - earning money was more important. I found out later the recommendation they gave me was "a very good farmer".[150]

Mt. Elgin

Although one aim of the school was to produce teachers and ministers, the specific aim for graduates in 1853 was to get them to settle on farms, and they were promised money and land.[151] By 1857, two boys were teachers and two others had qualified.

In 1881 many of the girls were servants, though reportedly they did not like to stay long in positions away from home, others were teachers. By 1882 there were many teachers, ministers, and farmers, and the boys were in great demand as farm labourers. They were offered such high wages that they did not want to stay in school to train as teachers and earn less money. Between 1885 and 1891, 15 pupils got teaching certificates and most of them had taught or were teaching. In 1892, there was 1 mechanic who was also a teacher but preferred his trade, 1 pursuing higher studies. Of the 17 who got teacher's certificates in the previous few years, half were working as teachers, others got higher pay working in the St. Clair tunnel and then on lake steamers. At least 20 were working for white men near their Reserve.

By 1902 there were about 25 school-leavers each year, most of whom were encouraged by the school to go out to service among white people. Towards the end of the war in 1917, there was a great demand for farm help and pressure to allow the senior pupils out in the summer to work on farms. Eighty graduates from Mt. Elgin volunteered for active service in the war.

Of the former students interviewed the mens' occupations included a trucker, a carpenter, a heavy machine worker, one went to trade school later. Eleven of the women did domestic work to begin with, one became a furrier, two worked in factories, one went to business school.

Comment

Originally the schools encouraged the boys to go back to the Reserve and set up in trades (blacksmith, shoemaker, wheelwright etc.) or farm, and girls were meant to set up households and teach by example. They were all discouraged from working for whites. A lack of land or title to land made farming difficult. In the last part of the 19th century there was an emphasis on producing teachers, and in the final two decades success was measured by the number of teachers and other professionals, and both schools had many graduates teaching in Reserve schools all over Ontario. Male graduates found they could earn more money as labourers, because they were qualified to teach on Reserves only and the Department did not pay its Indian teachers much money. By the beginning of the 20th century more graduates were going into service among white people, and they had no trouble finding jobs. During the 1920s at the Mohawk Institute an attempt was made to teach girls some business skills - typing and telegraphy, but at Mt. Elgin McVitty's emphasis was on domestic work. Many male graduates fought in the two world wars. During the latter years at both schools training at the schools was confined to domestic work for girls and farming for boys, who picked up other skills doing jobs fixing up the schools.

The founders of the schools believed in civilization but equality of opportunity. The school trained children for careers that would enable the graduates to assist people in their communities to live on an equal footing with non-Native settlers. As Reserve lands shrank and First Nations were increasingly marginalized, assimilation into a working class became the norm. Teachers could only work on Reserves, funding for post-secondary education disappeared, education was no longer the first priority, manual training programs no longer trained students for specific skills. Of those interviewed, all attended the schools in the 20th century, and only those who did domestic work, farming or had families were directly prepared for life after they left school. Despite the lack of encouragement, some of the former students interviewed later pursued careers in engineering, health care, social work, the ministry, business, etc. but did so on their own, picking up qualifications along the way. None of them became teachers.

Residential School Life

Language

Mohawk Institute

The first students at the school spoke no English and one of the first tasks was to teach the children enough English for them to learn to read and write. Lugger's plan had been to make the children speak nothing but English so they could understand what they learned, but this was not put into practice at first.[152] In the 1860s some classes of children volunteered to speak only English. However, in 1872 a visitor was told that the boys spoke Indian entirely amongst themselves and did not wish to speak English.[153]

Teaching was always in English, but it was not until 1872, when Ashton became principal, that children were not allowed to speak in their Native language, even amongst themselves. Ashton found that the children were not learning English, or were learning Mohawk from the other children[154] and their school work improved markedly when the children were made to speak English all the time.

Although the issue of language disappeared from the reports it revived in the 1960s with the importation of Cree children who did not speak English and whose second language was French. Being robbed of their language still remains a major concern of the former students, whether or not they ever spoke their Native language. Many had parents or grandparents at the school who lost their language. Eight of the former students interviewed could speak their Native language when they went there. Only one can speak her Native language now with any fluency, and she had to relearn her language after she returned home because her mother-in-law spoke no English. All were punished, threatened with punishment, or feared punishment if they spoke Indian. *"I spoke Cayuga when I went there but if you tried to speak to someone in your own language you'd always get the strap or something - they figured we were talking about them."*[155] Punishments ranged from being strapped to being thrown in the clothes press. An incident described in the late 1960s shows that the staff still felt threatened by students speaking in a language they could not understand:

> *...a couple of girls ran away and we all had to stand in a circle and I remember the House Mother swinging this Cree girl around and she was yelling at her in Cree....we all had to line up and go in the office...and she was asking us "What did she say?" but we didn't know what she said - we didn't speak the language...*[156]

Mt. Elgin

The school was committed to teaching the children to read and write English. The early reports did not contain any discussion of language. Evans' comment in 1873 that the religious condition would be more satisfactory if they had an Ojibwa-speaking leader, suggests that the children were far from fluent in English and he was not averse to using the Native language to communicate religious ideas to the children. The school inspector in 1884 commented that the big difficulty was *"to reach the pupils' minds thru the English language"* and that *"For the most part the Indian tongue is used in the playground, and by the teacher to give explanations"*[157] but he was probably referring mainly to the day schools. A decade later the inspector reported some fluency and understanding in English. In 1901 the principal mentioned that letters home had to be written in English, and in 1906 wrote that all conversations between visitors and the children had to be in English.[158]

Enos Montour wrote that in 1911 most of the children spoke English well, newcomers haltingly.[159] In 1917 the Inspector recommended that Grade 1 pupils should be in school full time - half the day being spent with a monitor who would train the pupils to speak English.

Children were punished for speaking their Native language -*"I got the strap a lot of times for speaking my language."*[160] Fifteen of the former students interviewed spoke their Native language when they went to the school. Seven managed to keep their language by speaking it among themselves. The majority of the people, i.e. five, who retained their language were from Oneida- a close-knit community which was just across the river from the school - and the children had a group of friends to talk to.

Comment

'Civilization' required teaching Native people to speak English, and indeed, at the beginning Native people who sent their children to the residential school did so to enable their children to get an English education so that they would not be cheated in their dealings with white people. However, teachers found that the children had difficulty learning in English when they were allowed to speak their Native languages amongst themselves. Administrations not only viewed Native language as an impediment to learning, however, but as signifying 'heathenism' and 'savagery', which had to be eradicated. Nelles was an exception because he was able to read the church liturgy in Mohawk and had been involved in the publication of a Mohawk Prayer Book, but after his time the use of Native language was banned at the Mohawk Institute.

Only 8/67 of the former students interviewed can speak their Native language now, but all of them feel a deep sense of loss, saying that losing the language, whether individually or collectively, and the associated loss of their culture, was the worst thing about the schools. *"That was the only thing I had against them was they took away our language."*[161]

Crime and Punishment

Mohawk Institute

Discipline was not a concern in the reports during Nelles' superintendency. There were some problems with truancy in the 1830s but the children settled down by 1838. There was another episode of truancy in 1840 when the school was expanded and some new pupils who were not used to the school ran home.[162] However, when Ashton took over he was appalled by what he viewed as the slack discipline and introduced a comprehensive system of rules, rewards and punishments, with Good Conduct Badges and the Black List. This system, although modified in later years, not only set the tone for the rigid discipline system maintained throughout the existence of the school, but provided a model for other residential schools. Four main classes of crimes were theft, absconding, direct insubordination and gross breach of discipline. Every offence of each individual was marked on a board so everybody could see a child's record at a single glance. A prison cell was built. During this time only the principal ordered or administered corporal punishment.[163] Ashton mentioned some truancy in 1874, 1885, and in 1891, though he remarked that there had not been any truancy for a year before that.

After the turn of the century the school was burned down by dissatisfied students and officials of both the DIA and the NEC commented on the strict discipline. In 1908 an inspector from the NEC reported that the school was like a reformatory. The concern of the Six Nations Council that children ran away because of the poor food and indignities they suffered, culminated in charges being laid against the principal and he was found guilty in 1914 of excessive punishment.[164] At this time Duncan Campbell Scott described the rules as antiquated and too severe. The punishment reports that Mrs. Boyce sent in showed that all the girls were planning to run away, and they illustrate the rigid discipline system. Some of the offences that were noted for posterity, which ranged from idleness, impudence and carelessness, to stealing apples and truancy, appear to us now to be trivial, and the reaction of Martin Benson of the DIA was that the pupils were disciplined to death.[165]

It was not until 1915, when Turnell became principal, that discipline was relaxed. The prison cell was taken out and the cat-o'-nine-tails abolished. Students had to put their own arm out to get the strap and could only be hit on the hand.[166] After Boyce took over again, and then Rogers, there were many truants. In 1922 10 students ran away, and Evelyn Johnson complained to the newspaper in 1923 that more than 20 children had run away in the summer, saying they were hungry.[167] More truancy occurred in 1923 and two boys with clubs defied the principal openly, but the principal found that the introduction of Girl Guides led to better discipline and a developing esprit de corps, except for a problem with the Jesse James gang among the girls. The

Honour system among the boys was working and took care of bullying.[168] In 1926 there was some petty theft among the girls, and two girls were dismissed for teaching younger girls to steal. Another problem was boys meeting girls in the dormitory.[169]

In 1929 Snell commented that he got the students themselves to punish theft by putting offenders "through the lines". The pupils were cooperating in the prevention of truancy. There was an "epidemic" of truancy, but the number decreased in January 1930 with the cold weather. There were several cases in 1930 and 1931 and the DIA were concerned with the number. By 1938 Snell reported that truancy had almost ceased.[170]

By 1934 the DIA was concerned with the lax discipline. In 1937 a boy accused the boys' master of excessive punishment. In 1938 Snell commented that he resorted to corporal punishment on rare occasions, but he was later alleged by eyewitnesses to have beaten a girl so badly that she had a seizure.[171]

On discovering that some of the boys were engaging in homosexual relations, and theft, Zimmerman asked the DIA if he could *"spank their posterior ends."*[172] The official reply was that he should only use the regulation strap - on the hands. Despite the DIA's injunction there are many reports of physical punishment experienced by students who were beaten on their buttocks.

I ran away one time...Mr. Zimmerman bent us over this chair and took our trousers down and just whaled us. You get the strap when you're half frozen - it's a killer.[173]

In 1949 25 girls ran away, and after they were brought back 10 left again.

Of the former pupils interviewed 16/36 ran away, and of these 7 never went back. Reasons for running away varied from going along with someone else, to a desperate desire to get away. *"The only thing I could think about was how to get out of there - to escape."*[174] Many ran away frequently and were brought back - *"The first day I was there I ran away - I ran away about a hundred times."*[175]

31/36 of the former students interviewed got the strap and some, both boys and girls, were beaten on their bare buttocks. Offences for which students can remember getting the strap included: throwing yarn across the sewing room instead of getting up and handing it, running in the hall on her first day at the school, being in the dormitory at the wrong time, having a 'dirty neck' (actually a birthmark), wrongly accused of breaking into the barn, new children playing in the barn unaware that it was off limits, mouthing a teacher, a boy talking to his sister, speaking their Native language, doing bad drawings and wasting paper, slapping someone, throwing inkballs, giving brother soup (theft), pushing salt cellars around on the table, late to bed because he was tied up by the other boys, losing a towel, stealing turnips, stealing apples, talking in the dormitory after lights out, late for school because he was working for a farmer overtime, sleeping in church, singing funny words to a hymn, talking in school, throwing up and making a mess, having a head injury and unconscious in a cupboard and missing school, throwing a rotten potato in the storage room, and truancy.

Mt. Elgin

Truancy was the only aspect of discipline that made the reports during the 1800s, with mentions of truancy in 1855, in 1873 that there had been no absconding for 10 months, and in 1874 that there had been no recurrence of the frequent abscondments. George was accused by some parents in 1906 of stripping girls, which he denied, and whipping them, which he admitted.[176] In 1908 there was a report that children from Gibson were beaten too much. A fire was set in the barn by a boy who did not want to stay, and some girls set a fire in the kitchen. A fire destroyed the boys' lavatory and gym. The DIA was concerned and asked the Indian agent to find out what caused the pupils to take this means of avenging their real or imaginary wrongs.[177]

McVitty took over and in 1910 he described punishment as *"our strange work."*[178] In 1912 he said reports and punishments were almost unknown. But there were incidents: in 1914 a parent complained that her daughter was harshly strapped, and there was the stone in the thresher case in 1915, in which a boy was punished and parents complained and the Chippewa council complained of cruel over-punishment, which McVitty denied.[179]

In 1920 there were problems with local people getting the children to steal from the school, and some students stole from the village shop and were sent to trial.[180]

In 1925 it was mentioned that truancy was rare, and in 1926 the inspector said that discipline was nearly perfect.

McVitty was reasonable...but he used to use that strap on the girls something terrible. They used to have to go in the prayer room, and I seen him strapping those girls...[181]

Strapp took over from McVitty in 1934 and by 1936 the DIA was concerned by the large number of truants. The RCMP reported that truants said they were not getting enough to eat, and were made to eat foods they didn't like.[182]

In 1937 22 students ran away and again the DIA was concerned; in 1939 there was more truancy. There was an incident in which two girls assaulted a classmate. From 1939-41 there was more truancy. In 1940 a girl was found forcing younger ones to steal. In 1943 Moses Seneca from Muncey, who did not like the conditions at the Institute, got several children and their parents/guardians to swear out complaints against Strapp.[183]

18/31 of the former students interviewed ran away. Two left and never went back. Reasons ranged from wanting to escape, grievance with a teacher, to wanting to see their

parents, to boredom. Some used to sneak hon˙˙ ˙o the Reserve but be back in time for supper, many wo˙˙ ˙sneak out to dances or the store.

22/31 of the students interviewed got the strap and ˙˙other refused to take the strap. Three boys and two gir˙ were beaten on the buttocks - one girl refused to 'bend ˙ver'. Offences for which the strap was given included: tru˙cy, smoking, talking after lights out, riding horses after hours, singing funny words to a hymn, giving apples from ˙e storeroom to friends, poking another girl with a pencil in school, being in the main hall, not eating all of a meal, late for school, sassing the teacher, speaking their Native language. Some cannot remember the offence.

Comment

At both schools the rules were comprehensive and strict. Everything was done according to bells at specified times.

You had five minutes when the first bell would ring, to get up and put your clothes on, to run two flights of stairs and be downstairs and stand in line. Five minutes to wash your hands and face, brush your teeth, comb your hair and stand in line again. They'd be standing at the bottom of the stairs to make sure you were down there when the second bell rang, or up you would go to get the strap.[184]

Students would line up and march to school and meals, work, to take baths etc. At any particular time each student was supposed to be in a particular place in the building or grounds. Certain areas were designated as 'in bounds'. Boys were not allowed on the girls' side and vice-versa. Brothers and sisters were only allowed to meet at specific regulated times. In many periods silence was mandatory in the dining-room:

Chester and I were sitting together in the dining-room and we couldn't speak a word of English. We were talking back and forth and laughing, and suddenly this woman, Miss Barnett, hit us BANG! BANG! with a ruler right on the head. It wasn't really our language that they were after, it was to be quiet. You couldn't talk in the dining-room when you were eating ...Everybody had to stand up and our seats went back together. Everybody stood up, and faced the way they were going to go, and they marched out.[185]

Students were expected to work hard and be polite. Any appropriation of school property such as food or clothing was regarded as theft - even windfall apples, but the students became expert at taking food and not getting caught *"I don't know that it was stealing - it was a matter of survival."*[186]

Truancy was frequent in most eras, and was treated as a significant crime. Although many did run away to get away, there were some who just ran away to go with their friends, or for something to do.

The lists of offences committed for which the former students were strapped show a broad range from trivial to serious, and illustrate how every aspect of the childrens' lives was ordered by the rule system.

Punishments included corporal punishment using a strap or whip; solitary confinement, cutting off hair, the blacklist and removal of privileges, walking around the playground, being tied on a rope and walking around a pole, cleaning up the playground, cancelling leave of absence, extra work, scrubbing the walls, scrubbing the floor with a toothbrush, being sent to bed, standing out in the hall, cancelling visiting privileges of parents or siblings, dismissal. The punishments used at the Mohawk Institute were more severe in most periods than at Mt. Elgin.

Food

Mohawk Institute

The first report about the food was in 1868 when a NEC visitor reported that the dinner consisted of Irish stew with scraps of meat, water to drink, and that meat was served three times a week. Another visitor in 1872 reported that there were no stores on hand and the meal consisted of soup. Meat was served every second day; for tea they had porridge. Milk was served "if we have it." Two mothers who visited in 1873 described the food as "excellent", according to the NEC report.[187]

A menu for 1895 showed that the students had porridge for breakfast every day and also for supper five times a week, hence the nickname of 'mush hole' for the school. Meat was served four times a week.[188]

In 1913 the Six Nations Council decided to investigate complaints that the children were poorly fed, getting skim milk, bad meat, and porridge with worms in it. Duncan C. Scott ordered whole milk to be served, but if this was done it did not last long, as two years later when Turnell became principal he had to make the change back to whole milk again, and he doubled the butter ration.[189]

In 1923 the school stopped making butter. The reports from 1922-29 describe treats on holidays. At Christmas they would kill pigs, and the children would get nuts, candy, oranges. During the summer better meals were served with occasional treats of ice cream and fruit.

In 1924 enough eggs were being produced to feed the pupils eggs more than once a week. A newspaper reported that the children received a fare more substantial and toothsome than city children generally get. In 1925 the Indian agent reported a meal of liver, potatoes, turnips, and buns, with plentiful quantities.[190] Another meal in 1930 was described as consisting of an abundance of liver and gravy. After a report in 1936 that the meals were not appetizing or bountiful the DIA instructed the principal to improve the quality and quantity, to serve whole milk and more eggs.[191]

Zimmerman wrote to the DIA in 1947 worrying about the problem of serving good meals within his budget, and relating the food to truancy,[192] and indeed students who were there when Zimmerman took over from Snell commented on the improvement in the food. By the 1950s there were again many complaints about the food. The food service was revamped and a new kitchen built in 1961. The highlight of one student's time at the school was being allowed to go for second helpings one time when visitors came.

Two of the former students interviewed really liked the food. Others found that the best thing about it was:- *"It wasn't the best but you got three meals a day. We got enough to sustain us, but probably not enough to satisfy us."*[193] *"The food was good - I didn't mind it because I had three meals a day there...Even if it was kinda wormy and ugly that was better really than what we had at home sometimes."*[194] Many others thought the food was awful and cannot eat 'mush' to this day. The majority complained that they were hungry. Most could not understand why they did not get eggs, whole milk, butter and meat when the farm was stocked with chickens and cows etc, and apples from the large orchard, and most commented on the superior meals eaten by the staff.

Mt. Elgin

As early as 1884 there were complaints about tainted meat and stale bread. In 1902 Benson from the DIA mentioned numerous complaints and said that while the meals were plentiful they were not at all inviting. In 1908 a parent complained that the pupils did not get enough to eat and that the same food was put on the table until it was eaten, except when visitors were expected when they got good meals. The agent investigating this complaint described dinner as consisting of potato pie, gravy, a small piece of meat, 2 slices of bread, no butter, water. They only provided milk if there was enough. Seconds of potato pie were allowed. The Indian agent said the complainant's daughter told him later that the food was good and she was never hungry.[195]

McVitty in 1911 said the food was good, and Ferrier described the children as well-fed. In 1914, however, another parent described the food and meat as not fit to eat. In 1921 McVitty said that the children got all the whole milk they desired for breakfast, and skim milk at dinner and supper.[196]

In 1932 McVitty described an abundance of excellent food such as whole milk, butter, eggs, meat, bread and a superabundance of fresh vegetables being served daily, but the Indian agent reported that the pupils had one egg at Easter for the previous 4 years and none at all in 1932. Meals on January 12th 1933 consisted of the usual porridge for breakfast, a beef stew for lunch with rice for dessert and macaroni for supper. McVitty said in 1934 that they tried to provide food equal to that of middle class whites. In 1934 the doctor reported that a well-balanced ration was provided, but he was sceptical about the eggs, saying that even if they didn't get eggs the children were in fine physical condition. In 1935 the agent reported that dinner consisted of roast beef and vegetables, rhubarb pudding, bread butter and milk. A big problem was the lack of a refrigerator to store fresh meat. A parent complained to the Indian agent a year later that there was not enough to eat and it was not up to home standard. The meal when the parent visited, and this was confirmed by the staff, consisted of milk, dry bread, 4 small potatoes, diced carrots and butterscotch pudding. The daughter said they got meat once in three weeks, but the Dietitian said it was twice a week. The agent and the doctor agreed that additional meat and butter should be given, if only for the psychological effect.[197]

An October 1936 menu indicates that they had meat twice a week and porridge every day for breakfast. At this time the doctor and dietitian drew up a special menu with extra food for underweight children. This diet was never implemented but extra milk was given. There was still no refrigerator in 1937 and complaints that there was not enough meat. The meal served on the 1939 visit of the agent contained potato soup, peanut butter, fruit cake, bread.[198]

In 1942 there was a Departmental enquiry into food in residential schools and the school had to provide the menus for several weeks. When these menus were shown to several students who were there at the time they expressed amazement and disbelief at the amount of meat and the desserts they were supposed to have had. Parents complained in 1943 about mouldy, stale bread, wormy cereals, sour milk, and that the children were hungry.[199]

Although two of the former students interviewed thought the food was good and some described it as sufficient, many did not think much of the food. *"The only time we had a good meal was when guys came from Ottawa to visit the school."*[200] The staff at Mt. Elgin had a separate kitchen and the girls who worked there ate well. Many remember the undercooked soya beans, the vegetables they disliked, the dry bread and lack of meat. Stealing food was a frequent occupation - students who worked in the kitchen with access to the store rooms would occasionally manage to help themselves to such delicacies as raw oatmeal, brown sugar and cream, peanut butter or raw vegetables and apples.

Comment

Preoccupation with food comprises a large part of the documentary record, and a very large part of the memories of individuals, so that almost everything seems to be about food. Residential schools were known as the "mush hole" by their inmates because of all the porridge they were served. Former students still identify themselves as "mush hole kids". Enos Montour devotes two chapters of his book to food and the theme runs through many chapters.[201]

Officials evaluated the condition of the schools based on the food, a child was removed from Mt. Elgin by his father because of the food, children ran away because of the food. The 1914 court case at the Mohawk Institute came about when the girls ran away because they were fed porridge with worms in it, and bad meat. Long lists of truants from Mt. Elgin are recorded for 1937-41. The RCMP commented that truants complained that *"they were not receiving enough to eat and made to eat foods that they were not accustomed to and did not like and could not eat."*[202]

Zimmerman reported in 1947:

One of the boys said the other day that one of the things which keeps him at the school is the good food. He plainly stated that if there was a return to the former meals as served a number of years ago he would not stay. I am spending a great deal of time on this matter of food."[203]

The only offences many students ever committed involved stealing food, often to give to someone else.

The quality of the food gave great cause for complaint. The children received skim-milk, which until recent decades was considered pig food, no butter, and very little meat. In both White and Native cultures, fat and meat were the valued foods. Salt pork was a longed-for Native food associated with home; "Loaf 'n' Lard" in Enos Montour's time was the food the students would get from the village as a treat when they had some cash. The first thing Turnell did on being made principal at the Mohawk Institute, was to feed the children whole milk and extra butter - he also relaxed discipline and allowed the children living nearby to go home for a short holiday in the summer, and met with the Chiefs in Council to discuss the Institute. These actions "broke all the rules" and Turnell lasted only three years!! Time and again outsiders would come in and recommend that the children should be given whole milk, not skim, as part of a general revamping of conditions at the schools. This process exemplifies the whole pattern of the history of these schools. Sporadically there would be an attempt to do something that would be good for the children and give the schools a new lease on life, but soon they slipped back into the old ways because of the necessity for economy.

Food was also important in the internal power structure among the students. Enos Montour described the trauma of the small boy who had traded away his Sunday Cake in advance for the immediate gratification of a piece of Loaf 'n' Lard, when Sunday came and he was forced to "send it" to the larger boy.[204] The Indian agent at Muncey in the 1930s suggested that the kitchen children took the food of the smaller children and played favourite to their friends. Many of the boys said they would never have survived if they had not had a friend in the kitchen. Trading food was still going on vigorously in the 1950s at the Mohawk Institute:

We'd go in the middle of the night and...picked apples...There was a pretty decent dessert - date turnover. It was generally on Friday that we had that dessert so we had the dates all scheduled to make a deal with someone. Everybody was bargaining every which way they could "I'll give you two apples now for that dessert." If you didn't pay your dessert you were in for a licking from the guy you made the deal with. It was hard to give it up.[205]

Health

Mohawk Institute

In 1843 a boy left because he was scrofulous, otherwise there were no reports on health until the early 1870s when there were outbreaks of measles and scarlet fever. After Ashton arrived, during the 1870s, several children left because of ill health and several died soon after they left. The first reported death was in 1876, and another in 1880, but Ashton was proud of an 11 year period before 1892 with no deaths. There were episodes of measles, scarlet fever and flu. In 1895 a child died of a brain infection, and between 1898 and 1903 11 children died of illnesses such as typhoid (2), TB (2), heart disease (1), brain infections (2), respiratory diseases (2).

The first report of children being sent to hospital was in 1911, with a typhoid case and appendicitis. In 1913 a child died of heart trouble in hospital. There is not much information on health until Mrs. Boyce, who was a nurse, took over the school, to be faced with an influenza epidemic in 1918 in which all the children were sick and one girl died. Sore eyes were another complaint, flu, measles, mumps, german measles, chicken pox in the 1920s, sore throats, erysipelas, uremic poisoning. In 1921 with an outbreak of scarlet fever, a hospital was opened in the school and a special nurse hired. In 1922 one girl was sent to hospital to have her tonsils and adenoids removed.

After an outbreak of flu in 1923, there was a period of 8 months when they did not have to call a doctor, though some children were having dental problems seen to. In 1924 two serious cases were sent to hospital. During the fatal illness of a child with tubercular meningitis, four doctors held free consultations to help the school doctor. In 1925 there was an epidemic of accidents, but all were reported as being promptly attended to, and also cases of pneumonia which were carefully looked after, otherwise this was a period of relatively good health.

From 1928 on there was an increasing number of tonsillectomies performed, 2 in 1929, 3 in 1929, and 24 in 1930. In 1929 a diabetic girl who had previously been in hospital, and who had been sent to bed with a cold was found in a coma and died in hospital. There were outbreaks of measles, chicken pox and one case of polio. A clinic to check eyes, throat and teeth was held.

The Local Council of Women said in 1946 that the school needed more medical care, but Zimmerman maintained that there was a Doctor on call, a trained nurse on staff, and sick children were taken to Lady Willingdon Hospital on the Reserve, or Brantford hospital, and they held regular dental clinics. The doctor reported that over 3 months, 40 children were hospitalized: 36 tonsils and adenoids; 2 rheumatic fever, 2 Interstital Karatitis, and there were several cases of impetigo.[206]

By 1960, Zimmerman was asking for a registered nurse.

Mt. Elgin

The first report of children dying was in 1873 when, although the general health was good, 2 girls died of pulmonary disease. In 1874 and 1875 health was unusually good. In 1889 one girl died. In 1892 it was not necessary to call a doctor and Shepherd made the point that a death in 1896 at the school, was only the third in 15 years. Another death occurred in 1901.

In 1902 a parent complained that her daughter was very sick after a vaccination, but the principal did not tell them or call a doctor. The principal said that he did call the doctor.[207] During the next few years there were some fatal cases of TB, most of whom were sent home before they died. Other problems included a death from spinal meningitis, erysipelas, diphtheria, a complaint from a parent whose boy had sore eyes; syphilis; a measles epidemic in 1907 with one fatality.

In 1908 a parent complained that his daughter had incipient pulmonary TB and should be sent home for proper care, however the school doctor said she was in good health and that remaining at school would be more beneficial to her health. The girl had had to stay in a room with another girl with TB and fetch the matron if necessary. One child died of pneumonia followed by pulmonary TB, two were discharged with TB; there were also complaints of scabies, but only one case was found and the school blamed the home. Other parents whose son had TB complained that they had to go to the school to nurse the child every second night and relieve the matron. The school had a different perspective saying that the parents insisted on coming but they smoked so much they were asked to leave. They took the child home and when he died they blamed the Institute, saying they had a doctor who could have cured him.[208]

By 1910 health was so good that the doctor was not called during the year, and the following year the doctor's bill was only $35. The record for 1912 was marred by a scarlatina outbreak brought from home, and in 1913 a child died of pneumonia. Complaints of head lice were frequent in 1915, the home blaming the school and vice versa. During the rest of McVitty's tenure health was fairly good and in 1931 he said it was almost perfect.

From 1934 on there were lots of medical reports in the records, including cases such as a nasty impetigo-like skin condition, trachoma, and frequent tonsilectomies: 15 in 1935, 11 in 1936, 11 in 1937. By 1936 the trachoma had improved, the impetigo subsided and general health was excellent. 15 children were underweight - 6 of them new pupils. In 1937 there was one case of scarlet fever, and 18 of flu. In 1938 there was a complaint from a parent whose child was sick with arthritis but the doctor had only made three visits in three months. However, the doctor said it was more like twelve times, and did not think it would be good to release her to deplorable home conditions. In the case of another child with a kidney infection whose parents wanted him home where he would not have to work, the doctor maintained that the sick child would be better at school with rest, a warm bed and shelter, a proper diet, trained nurse. However the 4 year old boy who fell out of the window and died, had been in bed after an ear infection and was left alone in the dormitory. In 1942 a former teacher complained of the lack of dental care. Dental service was provided after this, and in 1945 the doctor tried to get another dental and throat clinic.[209]

Comment

Health care is an important aspect of any residential institution, and the schools usually had a resident nurse and provision for a visiting doctor. Although many students found the nurses kind in times of illness, one student described being strapped for making a mess and being made to clean up her own vomit, and two Mohawk Institute students describe being afraid to go for help when they suffered head injuries.[210]

Health care also suffered in times of economy and dental and eye checkups would be stopped. The three letters in 1941 about a 50 cent cost to repair a pair of glasses, illustrate the bureaucratic red tape involved in any

decision.[211]

The health of the children was another arena for protest by the parents. Because the administrators believed the schools were more sanitary and comfortable than the students' homes, they took responsibility in illness, and they frequently failed to notify parents that their children were sick, and that worried the parents. The lack of communication fostered an adversarial atmosphere. One principal commented that if the mother had stayed away the girl would have been all right in a short time. Parents said the children picked up lice at school, and the school said they got them at home, and scabies. Parents occasionally managed to take control. A former student tells how her father only saved her brother from dying of pneumonia by forcing his way past the principal, going to the dormitory to visit his son and insisting that his son be taken to hospital.[212] Another managed to inform her neighbour that her son was ill and unattended, and the parents took him away to hospital where he was operated on for appendicitis.[213]

These incidents juxtaposed with the official reports indicate that perception of the quality of health care was not the same for principals, parents and children. These two schools had better health records than some of the schools out West at the turn of the century, where Dr. Bryce reported in 1907 that in 15 schools an average of 25% of the pupils had died since their founding, and in others 67% were dead. Bryce was shocked by the total lack of ventilation in the schoolrooms and dormitories, and by the practice of admitting and keeping children with tubercular diseases for fear of lowering the per capita grant. Ferrier commented that children were caged in unventilated rooms at Mt. Elgin in 1906, saying it was more a matter of good fortune than of a good policy that there was not a complete break-down in health.[214] Statistics may be more favourable for these two schools as it was probably easier for them to send sick children home to die as the Reserves were closer.

Recreation

Mohawk Institute

The missionaries' report in 1872 mentioned separate playgrounds and hours set apart for recreation during which the children played games of their choice, but no special gymnastics were provided. During Ashton's time recreation hours were an hour at noon and two hours in the evening in the summer and one in winter. The boys had a playground with swings and horizontal bars, and the girls had swings and croquet. There was a field where the boys played football, cricket and baseball. A Bugle band and a Cadet Corps for the boys were started.

The principals' reports during the 1920s describe outings and entertainments, picnics and corn-roasts, truck-rides, sleighing-parties. Another boys' band was started, and a

Hawaaiian orchestra, Guides and Brownies for the girls. They bought a cheap victrola and Books of Knowledge to occupy the children and improve discipline. They also tried out sports between boys and girls to prevent clandestine meetings. In 1925 a powerful radio with a speaker in one classroom was purchased. In 1928 a Barn dance was held. Running was important during this time, with several boys (notably Norman Lickers, Miles Isaacs) winning local races.

Brownies and Girl Guides were restarted when Zimmerman came, but in 1946 there were no recreational facilities, not even seats or tables in the boys' playroom, and the inspector commented in 1948 on the sense of depression and that children wandered about without any purpose in their free time, and they should have a staff person to direct physical education and games.[215]

In 1949 Cadets were started again and the Local Council of Women bought a movie projector. In 1957 the principal started taking the children to camp on Christian Island in the summers. A gymnasium was built with the new school block in 1958 and the DIA recommended the addition of a sports and social recreation program to improve the morale of the school. In 1958 Zimmerman was still asking for a Phys.Ed. instructor for after-school activities to improve morale.[216] The Native housemother persuaded the principal to allow the girls to invite the boys to supper on Saturday nights in their newly painted and refurnished playroom, where they danced to records the girls were allowed to buy. By 1966 there were baseball and hockey teams, Girl Guides, Sea Cadets and Cubs.

Former students mostly complain that there was no recreation provided. The girls were confined to the playground outside and played ball and hide-and-seek, and occasionally they were taken to the show. Boys were freer in most periods. In the 1930s and 1940s boys could get odd jobs near the school and if they had money could go to the show on Saturdays. The playrooms had nothing in them and the children had to make their own fun. The boys' playroom at the Mohawk Institute only contained steam pipes and in the 1950s bullies would make smaller boys hang from the hot pipes until they burned. Fighting was another occupation for both boys and girls.

Mt. Elgin

The first mention of recreation at Mt. Elgin was in 1910. In winter they had outdoor walking, skating, tobogganing and sleigh-riding. Indoor games included fort, crokinole, checkers, bean-bags, and other parlour games. In summer there was swinging, basket and baseball, also hunting and fishing, in season.

In 1920 McVitty said that amusements did not receive so large a place in their program, though there were several hours allowed for recreation each day.[217]

Some of the girls enjoyed singing in a choir and putting on entertainments. Generally, recreation had a low priority for many years. In 1945 Soper wrote:

The long winter evenings are coming. We have no games equipment. We need a moving picture projector. Just think of having one hundred and twenty children to amuse seven nights a week for ten months of the year. We need equipment." [218]

Some former students say they had fun - but they made it themselves playing games that required little equipment - hopscotch, sledding etc.

I had lots of fun. We played ball, did sports, and in the summer time we'd go swimming in Mud Creek. Wintertime we went sliding. I learned how to ice skate, how to roller skate, play ball, wheelbarrow racing. We ran. I learned how to ride horses there.[219]

Comment

Apart from the 1920s at the Mohawk Institute, when there seem to have been some outings and entertainments planned for the children, and an attempt to set up a constructive recreation program in the late 1950s and 1960s, organized recreation was not significant at either school. Attention to this might have made all the difference to the atmosphere, morale, and happiness of the children at both schools. The playrooms were empty rooms and students had to make their own fun - though this did not mean they did not have any. However, because of the lack of toys, games and organized activities, the children had to use their own resources. At the Mohawk Institute in the 1940s and 1950s this often meant that some of the games played in the playroom had malicious overtones. Playing 'house' with children from dysfunctional families could be a problem if a domineering person was playing mother.[220] Fighting, and bullying games, which have been described as torture by witnesses, resulted from the lack of things to do. Children ran away for something to do.

Buildings and Living Conditions

Mohawk Institute

The first major expansion was in 1840 when the boys helped build an addition to hold 40 children. In 1858 a new building held 60. By 1861 Nelles wanted to expand but the NEC did not have the money. An addition to hold 70 was built in 1865, and during the 1860s accommodation was increased to 90, with a new school house built in 1869. The bedrooms were described as fresh in 1872, but the boys' class/play/washroom as little better than a cellar.[221]

Ashton's arrival in 1872 heralded repairs and a new laundry was installed in 1874. In 1875 a large addition was built with a cupola. In 1886 a superintendent's residence

was built, freeing up more dormitory space. Improvements in 1891 included a boys' playhouse and hot and cold showers. In 1903 the whole school was burned down, and was rebuilt in 1904 - with a new cupola.[222]

In 1915 the principal proposed enlarging the building to hold 200, but this was not done. By the end of the war in 1918, with a new principal, a great many repairs were needed and were started in 1919. In 1922 the whole building was renovated with a new dining room and new lavatories and bath. Between 1922-9 there was constant painting, plastering etc. and in 1924 a playhouse was built for the girls. In 1925 the school grounds were even beautified. In 1931 new dormitories were constructed and fire escapes all painted. The principal's flat was redecorated.

In 1939 the building was totally redecorated. The Indian agent commented that the work would create a much more favourable impression of the Department's efforts on behalf of the Indians with visitors, but it was not kept clean afterwards. By 1942 the structure was described as not in first class shape with a bleak and unattractive atmosphere, though in 1944 the building was reported in good condition except for the boys' playroom. An Inspector in 1948 said the dormitories and playroom left a sense of depression, and the sanitary conditions were bad, even degrading.[223]

A new school block of classrooms and gymnasium was built in 1958, and in 1961 a new kitchen and food service were installed.

Mt. Elgin

Five years after the opening of Mt. Elgin a new wing was added, but by 1856 repairs were needed to the building. It was enlarged to hold 80.

In 1869 workshops were built. Cosford, commenting on the bad conditions of the buildings when he arrived, said that it was no wonder one of his predecessors and two principals' wives had died there. He made many repairs.[224]

In 1884 a new boys' playhouse was built, and the schoolroom improved. In 1888 a new barn was built, but a fire in the playhouse in 1889 gave rise to a plan to enlarge the building. In 1890 a new recreation hall was built.

In 1896 a new building (with a tower) was built and the old building remodelled in 1899. In 1902 Shepherd described the buildings as comfortable, magnificent, stately, and splendid, but Benson reported that the buildings needed repairs, there were no bathing facilities, and the out-buildings were shabby. By 1905 the boys' lavatory and the laundry needed repair, and in 1906 improvements were made to the kitchen for convenience, which were important for the privacy, welfare and comfort of the girls, but ventilation was poor. In 1907 the boys' lavatory and gymnasium burned down, and in 1908 a barn was burned down by an unhappy student, and some girls set fire to the kitchen.[225]

Electric light was installed in 1911, and some repairs improved the sanitation. In 1913 two large wings were added providing additional accommodation. The barns were accidently burned down in 1915. McVitty spent a considerable amount of his time overseeing repairs.

In 1934 when the doctor reported that they needed improved ventilation and sanitation, two plans were drawn up - one to make the plant 'worthy of Government and Church', another the barest minimum to carry on at all. It was reported that the laundry could collapse, the sanitary arrangements were antiquated and inadequate, the dormitory ventilation was notoriously poor.[226] The lack of funds meant that repairs were only made where there was real danger.

In 1937 a long list of needed repairs was made - the pupils' bathroom was anything but sanitary, the ventilation

and lighting were poor, plaster and painting were needed. However, the Departmental Architect said replanning was impossible and impracticable and that they needed a new building. A building which had been planned for 75 held 154. It was a fire hazard. Things went from bad to worse. In 1938 more repairs were needed and a walk-in refrigerator was needed.[227]

By 1939 the agent said they needed more space and Strapp said they needed a new building. In 1940 it was reported that toilets were urgently needed as the odour was terrific. When Hoey inspected in 1942 he reported that it was *"one of most dilapidated structures I have ever inspected."*[228] The washrooms were filthy, the kitchens were literally alive with cockroaches. The farm, on the other hand, was a model of efficiency. Hoey said that officials would not tolerate such conditions for 24 hours. Dorey described the condition of the school as deplorable, and said that repairs were essential if the school was to be carried on as the building was condemned from a sanitary point of view. By 1944 the building was still described as dilapidated, while the farm buildings were in first-class condition. The school needed major repairs - it was depressing, dark, dingy, dirty, untidy and smelly.[229]

Comment

Many details of construction and maintenance of the buildings have been included in the selection of documentary records to show their significance in the life of the school. The kinds of projects for which funds were made available represent attitudes. Occasionally improvements were made for the comfort of the children, sometimes funds were available for beautification, sometimes for paint jobs to make a good impression on visitors. Shame at what visitors might think was a compelling reason for change, but at other times there had to be mortal danger and threats of lawsuits before repairs were made. There seems to be a process in the life of an institution where the building itself, rather than its occupants, comes to represent the institution. Jean Manore comments on the building of churches in the late 19th century as monuments to the glory of God,[230] and similarly the school buildings can be seen as monuments to their purpose. The outward magnificence symbolized grand ideas of the munificence of Church or Government, but the condition in which the buildings were maintained represented the value society put on their use at various times and how the occupants were viewed. At both schools there was steady expansion and additions to the physical plant through until the 1890s. Both schools were rebuilt around the turn of the century, the Mohawk Institute sporting a cupola, and Mt. Elgin a tower. Thereafter there were periods of maintenance, but generally the buildings became run-down, and Mt. Elgin was eventually pulled-down. It is significant that Mt. Elgin, housing needy children, was not closed down as recommended in the 1943 Young Report because it was not effective as an **educational** institution, but only when it was decided that the buildings themselves could not be renovated - the buildings represented the Institution. The Mohawk Institute was given a new lease on life in the late 1950s.

Burning down the school is a fantasy indulged in by a myriad of school-children, and was acted-out on several occasions by incendiary students also believing that the buildings represented the institution. Unfortunately for them, buildings can be replaced.

Parents, Children and Community Relations

Mohawk Institute

School attitudes to parents

The premise on which residential schools were founded was that children could be 'civilized' much faster and more effectively if they were taken away from their parents. In the 1870s the NEC report referred to *"obstruction on the part of parents"*[231] as frequently being an impediment to the elevation of young Indians, or children *"relapsing into the lower life of their parents,"*[232] and the difficulty of interesting the parents in the education of their children.

In 1902 Ashton mentioned some parents who wanted their children discharged and who had *"as usual in such cases, made many lying statements."*[233] Milligan referred to children not taking jobs as domestics because of the *"interference of relatives."*[234]

In 1914 Mrs. Boyce complained that the parents were undermining discipline. The punishment reports contain many negative comments about parents: *"The parents influence is often very bad," "If the mother would uphold the discipline of the school, there would be much less trouble with the children," "The mother visits children every month and stirs up trouble by her rude and impertinent behaviour," "Some of the parents...aid and abet their children in their misbehaviour."*[235]

By the end of Turnell's appointment in 1918 he said the parents were backing up the school authorities and making sure their children attended school. After Mrs. Boyce returned she referred to children returning from their homes in a filthy condition, with scabies and rashes, or not wishing children to go home to an immoral home.[236] In 1922 Rogers did not let any children go home for Christmas as he said they always came back with trouble, and some were always disappointed by parents who did not come to get them.[237]

In 1924 a mother was described as impudent and critical of food and clothing, and abusive. But by 1925 Rogers commented that more parents and relatives were appreciating the school, offering help rather than criticism, but in 1926 when a grandmother wanted a boy home, Rogers commented that the relatives just wanted his interest money.[238]

In 1929 Snell wrote to the Parents in appreciation of their cooperation which helped the school to run smoothly. Zimmerman in 1947 blamed truancy partly on parents who neglected to visit. He said holidays were bad for girls as their parents allowed them unlimited freedom.[239] A student who wrote to her mother complaining about the treatment she was getting at the school had her letter stopped and she was told she would be punished if she ever did anything like that again.[240]

Attitudes of parents

Several parents complained about the school in 1837. Some objected to their girls performing household duties, when they should be taught properly, but by 1839 it was reported that parents were more and more contented with the treatment their children received. In 1844 they were showing eagerness to obtain admission for their children. By 1864 it was reported that many parents who had been at the school wanted to send their own children there. The Six Nations Council praised Nelles for his work.[241]

Ashton was told on his arrival that parents had the prevailing idea that their children were there to be educated, not to do work unless they wanted to.[242]

In 1907 the Indian agent said he had numerous complaints from parents about their children being kept at the school to work, that the interest money was going to Ashton when it should go to the children to buy clothing,[243] and in 1908 Webster noted that the Indians on the Reserve had *"little admiration for the education"*[244] at the Mohawk Institute.

In 1913 two parents brought a lawsuit against Nelles Ashton, and the Six Nations Council complained about the children being treated as if they were criminals, and having bad food. At the same time there were 80 children on the waiting list.[245]

In 1937 a parent complained that her son had been mistreated, but the school denied any over-punishment and the DIA said they could not find a single complaint about harsh treatment in the records.[246]

Attitudes to children:

In 1837 the NEC agent reported that it would be advisable to allow three shrewd intelligent girls to be treated like boarders at a white school, despite a previous report which described *"naturally indolent dispositions."*[247] Although Nelles referred to the children as *"little untutored savages,"*[248] in 1844 it was reported that the children showed as much aptitude in acquiring knowledge as white children. Nelles valued kindness and personal attention. The Indian agent in 1876 described the children as having natural defects which caused them to become wayward - a tendency that should be nipped in the bud.[249]

A. Nelles Ashton on cross-examination in court about the severity of his punishment said *"it was all a question of who was being dealt with."*[250]

Snell wrote that he wanted the children to be happy and contented so he would like to hear any criticisms, but *"Of course children often make unfounded complaints..."*[251]

The Bishop of Huron described the children admitted during the 1950s as mostly difficult, subnormal and incorrigible,[252] and Zimmerman said that many of the students presented difficult educational problems.[253] Zimmerman was anxious to provide the children with a sense of dignity, with proper clothes etc. Officials of the DIA mentioned that the children needed affection, cheerfulness, and needed to feel that they were needed and wanted.[254] One student going to a staff member for help when she first got her period was met with the comment *"Damn bleeding Indians anyway."*[255]

Attitudes of children

The childrens' views are hardly represented in the documentary literature. In 1903 some boys set fire to the Institute because they resented the discipline. In the early 1920s Mrs. Boyce sent in two letters from girls who had left or were on holiday, saying they were lonely and would rather be at school, and reported in 1923 that some old pupils visited and spoke highly of the school.[256]

The feelings the former students interviewed had about the school are very varied, frequently ambivalent, and each experience was individual. *"I literally hated that place,"*[257] *"I enjoyed it there,"*[258] *"I wouldn't send my cat or my dog to that place,"*[259] *"After a while I really started liking it there."*[260] Of 36 former students interviewed: 5 liked it, 19 were positive on balance, but there was some good, some bad, 12 hated it. Two people refused to give interviews because they liked the school and did not want to participate in a project they perceived as negative.

Mt. Elgin
School Attitudes to parents

In 1901 Shepherd mentioned that all correspondence was closely censored and letters had to be written in English - distrusting both parents and children. In response to a parent complaining that they were not informed of their daughter's illness Shepherd said that their judgement was that if the Mother had stayed away the girl would have been all right in a short time. His attitude was that they did their best but it seemed as if they would never be appreciated by those for whom they had done the most.[261]

I expect rumors and vile fabrications from members of Bands, whose desires concerning their children I have been unable to grant, but these, I expect all who know the Indian character will accept only when verefied...[262] wrote George, who in 1906 also commented that parents were free to visit except when there was reason to believe that their visits were a bad influence causing discontent and truancy. He

also tried to persuade parents to leave their children at the Institute for the holidays, or they had to sign an agreement to return them at the proper time.[263]

In 1908, fires were set. The Indian agent from Brantford sent to look into the situation thought the parents were causing much of the trouble, as the Reserve was so close and the parents hanging around a lot, and blamed a discontented parent for inciting his daughter to set a fire.[264]

In 1911 McVitty and the other missionaries recommended that children should not be allowed to go home to parents living immorally. In 1914 they said again that homes should be clean, sanitary, right-living if the children were to be allowed home.[265] During 1914 McVitty had a controversy with a parent, whom he described as *"Possessed of an evil spirit,"*[266] and in 1915 he said that the holidays were conducive to great evil, the children returning seemingly possessed. The agent said that often the children came back loaded with vermin.[267]

In 1938 there were parents who wanted their children home, but the school was suspicious of their motives. One mother was described as abusive with the principal, and her actions called *"interference."*[268]

Attitudes of parents

Parents supported the school with voluntary annuities at first - and in 1852 Rose described turning away disappointed parents almost every week. The financial support was withdrawn by 1863 because the parents felt that the children did not benefit enough from the instruction to compensate for the long separation of parents and children.[269]

In 1902 a parent complained when his daughter was made to work in the laundry after a vaccination and became ill and they were not informed. Martin Benson mentioned complaints reaching the Department of ill-treatment of pupils.[270] In 1906 parents complained about the excessive punishment of children. In 1908 parents from Gibson complained that their children were beaten, made to work when sick, given bad food, and were cold in winter, and they refused to send any more children. The Indian Department received many complaints from parents about the treatment of their children. A parent complained that children were punished by making them work when they should be in school, they did not get enough to eat, children had to nurse sick children, parents were not informed when their children were sick, children got lice at the school. A parent complained in 1914 that her children came home with lice and poor clothes, the food was bad and they did too much work.[271]

In 1938 parents complained that their sick daughter was not getting proper care, but Strapp refused to discharge her, saying the family was on relief and their morals questionable. Five parents/guardians swore out complaints against Strapp and his treatment of the students in an attempt to have him dismissed.[272]

School Attitudes to children

Rose described the children as affectionate and promising, but he was extremely culturally biased, believing that the children's habits were evil and irreligious, and convinced that the only way to save the *"long neglected, deeply degraded and decimated race"* was to educate the children, saying: *"to break up their indolent, irregular, and vicious propensities, is an arduous task...."*[273]

Although McVitty talked of the home-like atmosphere of the school in 1912, and a mutual sympathy between staff and children, Enos Montour's poignant account of the extreme loneliness suffered by a small boy in 1911 for a real home-like atmosphere, illustrates the gulf between the two perspectives.[274] In 1920 McVitty wrote:- *"we love them all...they are lovable."*[275]

Strapp was described by one student as not liking Indians - they felt they were nobodies.[276] Another student said poignantly *"I think they forgot we were human."*[277]

Attitudes of children

In 1857 James Musgrove reported that the boys leaving the school made speeches with gratitude for the benefits and advantages they had received, but in 1884 five boys complained that they were spending too much time working rather than getting an education, and the food was bad.[278]

Enos Montour (1911-1915) expresses the ambivalence many people feel:

For, though Institution life has many hardships, there come in later life (Senior years), days that are just about perfect...They were indeed happy days. Their Senior days came after years of drudgery, rough knocks and anonymity.

"You know, Angus," said Brown Tom, "I'll kinda hate to leave this old place. It's been rough but kind underneath. I think they meant well by us, don't you? But I sure hated it, that first night four years ago. I was that lonely I coulda howled to the moon."[279]

Five of the former students interviewed liked Mt. Elgin: *"It was a wonderful school, and it was a good Christian school."*[280] Five definitely did not like it, and most had some good and some bad experience and were philosophical: *"That school was better than starving to death,"*[281] *"If we hadn't gone there, what would have happened to the lot of us?"*[282] *"That was the only home I ever knew - you...make the best of it."*[283]

Community

Relationships between the Reserve communities and the two schools were good at the outset. The Mohawk Institute was situated in the Mohawk Village and Lugger and Nelles were both missionaries in the community besides being superintendent of the Mohawk Institute. Nelles enjoyed a good relationship with the Chiefs of the Six Nations who appreciated his work.[284] After the Reserve Community moved to the south side of the Grand River, contact between

community and school was more difficult to accomplish. The New England Company's missionaries on the Reserve were members of a board overseeing the school. Ashton's policies of English-speaking only, stopping free and easy movement between reserve and school, and requiring a minimum of two years continuous attendance, accentuated the separation between school and community. At the same time Ashton extended the influence of the school on the community - he was head of a school board and supplied nearly all the teachers at Six Nations for a number of years. There were complaints from Six Nations parents in 1907 that Ashton was taking interest money which should be spent on the children.[285] Nelles Ashton's relationship with the Council over discipline and the food was bitter. Turnell tried to build a bridge between the School and the Six Nations Council but his tenure was too short to have much impact. In 1920 the Council appointed a committee to visit the school regularly, but Mrs. Boyce said they never went. The restriction of visiting hours and the expense involved discouraged parents from visiting. Some children spent so many years at the school without going home that they did not really remember where they came from. After the 1920s most interaction between school and the communities the children came from occurred through the Indian agent. A visit from the Council in 1962 was the first in many years and was the first time many of the Members had returned to the school since they were students there.[286]

Mt. Elgin was situated right on the Caradoc Reserve and partially funded by Native communities for a few years. The opening ceremonies involved participation by the local Bands, Peter Jones being anxious to include his fellow Indians. Thereafter, ceremonial occasions involved the controlled participation of local communities, but active involvement by individuals was usually seen as interference. George got the parents in several communities upset, and McVitty was very concerned with restoring good relations between school and communities, though he himself was accused by the Council of the Chippewa of the Thames in 1915 of mistreating children. Children at Mt. Elgin came from as many as 20 communities, but most contact with these communities was through the Indian agent. Occasionally parents appealed to the Band Council to try to get something changed, as in 1938 when a Chief from Muncey intervened in the case of a sick child. It was a community member from Muncey who collected the complaints against Strapp in 1943. Joblin's survey of the reserves in 1943 for the Young Report was an attempt to get the opinions of community members on the schools.[287]

For most of the schools' existence community involvement was a token effort, and although the administrations preferred to be on good terms with the Band Councils, they did not want to recognize the Band Councils' rights to any say on school matters. To preserve the privacy of individuals the Indian Agents' correspondence with the schools about children has not been reproduced in the original letter form in the main text, but the information indicates the control wielded by the agent over families in the communities, and that direct communication was rare.[288]

Comment

At both schools the principals and the parents frequently had very little respect for each other. The children were in the schools in the first place because their homes were not considered suitable, either culturally, economically or morally, though some principals complained that some parents did not take enough interest in their children. The documents probably contain more direct evidence of parents' dissatisfaction with the schools in the form of complaints about the food, health and harsh treatment, whereas inference of satisfaction has to be drawn from the applications for admission and waiting lists that existed in most periods. Principals were often condescending or hostile in their attitudes to parents, dismissing parents' right to know what was going on as interference or impudence. Much of the parents' frustration with the schools came as a result of a lack of communication, especially when parents were not informed that their children were sick.[289] There are several stories of parents sticking up for their children and threatening the principal both verbally and physically.[290] For many parents this was the only way they could deal with the principal, as other forms of intervention were seen as interference and blocked. However, many of the parents supported the school and the discipline, as in the case of the girl whose mother whipped her because she refused to take her punishment.[291] Some children would not tell their parents about their punishments because the parents would probably be angry and punish them again.

Children who could count on parental support and visits could generally cope with the school better than those who came from difficult family situations. The majority suffered feelings of abandonment and extreme loneliness when they entered the school, even if they came to like or tolerate it later. Many suffered from the lack of affection, love and family life. For many it was not the school per se that they did not like, but the confinement. Some tell how they waited for hours for their parents to come and take them out on Saturdays even if they were not really expecting them. Many children did not get out on Saturdays or even go home for holidays and some were confined at the school for as many as eight or nine years.

You know what the hardest time was? When it came time to leave for the summer holidays and no-one came there. I used to look out the window and look out the

window, waiting for someone to come. But it never happened to me. I was very disappointed. I never really blamed anyone.[292]

The move from family life to institutional life was a big adjustment for the children, and this was exacerbated by the move from one culture to another. The schools opened during a time of extreme culture change as missionaries persuaded Native groups with a shrinking land base to settle in farming communities and adopt European lifestyles.[293] The children were from Iroquois, Ojibwa, Delaware, and Cree-speaking groups, coming from as many as 27 different community groups, spanning generations from pre-Victorian to post-war 20th century society. This spectrum of culture variation and change precludes any generalization about "traditional" cultural systems and a meaningful discussion of culture conflict within the bounds of this book. The first generation of students had to face great cultural differences in language, food, clothing, confinement, discipline and the exercise of authority by individuals who were not family members, education, and work, and following generations also experienced considerable changes in lifestyle, language and authority structures etc.

So although an understanding of how the children felt about the schools is one of the most significant aspects of this book, it is a very individual matter and defies generalization. It cannot be stressed enough that the variety of experience is too important to summarize and can only be fully appreciated by reading all the Voices of Experience. A wide range of experiences is portrayed spanning a period from 1911 to 1969 and it is obviously impossible to provide a scientific sample in a study of this kind. The extremes of experience may not be represented as some people did not want to be interviewed because they really liked the school but thought the book was designed to denounce the schools, and some people who had bad experiences or suffered sexual abuse were understandably not prepared to talk about them and share them in this public forum. Some people simply preferred to keep their privacy. However, in the light of the common popular negative perceptions of Indian Residential Schools, the somewhat surprising finding is the range and mixture of feelings, from anger and trauma, through indifference, ambivalence and tolerance, to extremely positive and grateful, with roughly 75% of the former students interviewed expressing at least some positive sentiments about their experience. Many people are very bitter, but many are amazingly forgiving and do not wish to assign blame for things over and done with.

The Uses and Abuses of Power

Abuse

The term "abuse" - 'to make a bad or wrong use of', 'to mistreat', is widely used these days, and the definition of what actually is abusive has changed considerably since the founding of the schools. The most drastic change of view is in the judgement of the whole premise on which the schools were founded, changing a culture. Although the policy of 'civilization' was implemented with good intentions it had disastrous results. It was a racist destructive policy that is seen to-day as "cultural genocide," depriving people of their culture, identity, and self-respect. The whole socio-political situation that led not only to the existence of residential schools, but to their continuation for a hundred years after losing sight of the original purpose of the schools, could with hindsight, be thought of as the major form of abuse. The definition of abuse has also expanded to include not only deliberately cruel or abusive actions, but the consequences of actions, and failure to act or care. Within the schools various kinds of abuse occurred.

Although within the contexts of the various times it was not unusual for children to receive corporal punishment at school or at home, whether Native or not, personally I consider all forms of physical punishment abusive. I was at two boarding schools between 1952 and 1960 and there was no corporal punishment, nor was there any in my brother's school in the same period. It did not have to be that way.

Punishment

Any system requiring total power needs rules and the consequence of breaking the rules is punishment. The punishments used would not necessarily all be considered abusive.

Physical abuse as discipline, or corporal punishment, was used freely in most periods, but who administered it, and why, varied. Some principals were very free with their use of the strap, others restrained. Some allowed their staff to wield the strap. A seven-year old girl on her first day at school got the strap for running in the hall - she didn't know it was wrong. Another girl poked a class mate with a pencil and got a strapping. Truants invariably got a strapping - sometimes tied down and beaten on their bare buttocks, with a strap or a whip, sometimes strapped on the hands in front of the whole school.

I only just got there, and Ashton was going to give my brother a strapping. He done it right in the schoolroom. And when he strapped them, he strapped them right down to the bare butt with the cat-o'-nine-tails. He had to lay on the bench and I'm sitting there and every time he brought the strap down I cried all the harder because he was whipping my brother.[294]

There is no doubt that corporal punishment was administered abusively, even by the social standards of bygone eras. These standards were not always so different from our own. For example, when Nelles Ashton was convicted in 1914 for ordering a whipping for a young girl, Duncan C. Scott said *"I do not believe in striking Indian children from any consideration whatever."*[295] At my school in the 1950s there was no corporal punishment, but at the Mohawk Institute in the same period the strap was used by any staff member to punish all kinds of offences. From both schools there are many first hand accounts of vindictive punishment which often consisted of more than the regulation four strokes on the hand. Children were left with arms cut, swollen, and purple up to their elbows or shoulders. Some, both boys and girls, were beaten on their bare buttocks. Former students experienced principals and other staff members lashing out at random with the strap, hitting and even kicking them, strapping them until they cried, or apparently enjoying administering punishment.

I think the real terrible thing that happened for me - There was this young woman and she went up into the dormitory during the day when you weren't supposed to be up there. She went there for privacy because she was having her period, and the nurse caught her and reported her to the principal. The principal came down and he strapped her until she had an epileptic seizure. The children tried to protect her but we couldn't, because he was starting to strap her and lick her and he just kept on, and the girls were standing around and one of the girls pulled the strap from his hand from behind and kicked it, and all the girls tried to kick it away, and he shoved everybody aside knocking girls down. So everybody ran out of the lavatory and into the playroom, and that's when he got the strap and came after everybody and started strapping everybody wherever he could swing the strap. And then he got to her, because the children backed away - nobody wanted to get hit, and she was left alone, and he strapped her and strapped her until she had this seizure. And the next time at line-up, the principal's wife came down and told the girls not to talk about what had happened. She said if we talk about it one to another, or...to anybody, and if they find out, we would get worse.[296]

Emotional Abuse

Even more destructive than the strap to the identity of the children was the emotional abuse suffered - extreme loneliness, the lack of caring, the lack of love. Emotional abuse runs the gamut from subtle cruelty through rigid rules, to a lack of sensitivity and awareness that small children might have feelings. The fear that many lived in constantly - not only of the staff, but of the bigger children, had a devastating effect on them. Loneliness was compounded by the fact that many of the children were too young to understand the reason why they were separated from their parents and placed in the school. There is no doubt that the economic conditions on the Reserves in the Depression, and the breakdowns in family life that occurred all with more increasing frequency in the 20th century, sometimes led to home conditions that were dreadful, but the children were often very young and did not always understand, or know what was happening to them. Even with good home conditions there can be acute home-sickness at residential school. Frequently parents did not have enough money to visit, or the children did not have clothes to go home in for holiday visits, and had to stay at the schools during the holidays.

When I first went there I cried and I cried and I cried, but it didn't help any. One day you're a baby, the next day you're a man - you look after yourself.
I often say "I have no heart."[297]

Brothers and sisters were virtually separated from the only family they had:

I couldn't even go and talk to my sister. They'd want to know what you were talking about. "We were just talking." They'd say "Go to the principal," and I'd get the strap just for talking to my sister.[298]

The only communication between many brothers and sisters had to be furtive meetings over the fence, except for brief visits permitted once a month or so. A student tells how she was not told when her brother was sick, and when she went back to the school for an extra year to be with her brother, she did not know for two weeks that he had actually gone away.[299] What insensitivity or cruelty keeps children from the only family they have? Sunday family suppers were instituted in the 1960s at the Mohawk Institute so siblings could get together once a week.

The **Voice of Experience** section of the book contains horrendous stories of people who were sick or injured and who got punished for making a mess, or were afraid to go for help to the staff - again at the Mohawk Institute in the 1940s and 1950s.

We used to play hide and go seek, and I jumped over the pile of leaves we used to hide in under the porch, and I hit my head on the brick. I had this big cut in my head, and I bled and bled and bled and I passed out. When they finally found me they saw I was laying in my blood, and they carried me to the lavatory and and they used my towel to wash out my hair. We couldn't get the blood out of the towel, and there was a high fence there and I hid my towel over there, because I didn't want to report that I had gotten hurt. I was afraid of the strap so I threw my towel over there. I got the strap for losing my towel.[300]

I remember getting the flu and getting sick and almost delirious from the fever, and throwing up, but still being forced to get up out of my bed and clean up the mess I made, and got strapped for making a mess.
I had fallen and probably had concussion after bumping my head. I remember crawling into a great big cupboard that was in the girls' playroom, and I lost a day and I got punished for not being accounted for, and I got the strap...[301]

A former student tells how they had to line up by their numbers at Christmas and were given new pyjamas or a nightgown. She remembers that these were then collected again at the end of the day and given to the 'poor children'.[302] Is it not an abuse of power to use Christmas gifts to send the message to the children that they were expected to be grateful to the school that they were better off than the poor children? Similarly another student tells of being given a toy at a Christmas party in Brantford and having it taken from him when he got back to the school because "he did not need it."[303] Bedwetters were humiliated by being made to wear their wet sheets. A student who was very successful at the school commented:

We never got a pat on the back even for anything that we did. Nobody said: "That's a nice job you're doing - Gee that was great".[304]

Cultural Abuse

Residential schools were designed to change culture. The abusive aspect of culture change is that Native cultures were denied any validity or value, and children faced with such attitudes as Rose's, which denied them a culture, were given no choice but to change:

We do not get them before they have been educated in all that is evil; until immorality and irreligion have gained a complete ascendancy, and habits and practices the most demoralizing and enervating have been formed controlling every power or faculty of body and soul.[305]

A hundred years later Jennie Blackbird tells us:

The thing that shocked me most was when I was told I could not speak my Native language. I was birthed into this language, yet was told I was being rude. This really pierced me...My inner emotions could not accept this, but I could not express myself enough in the English language, to say what was in my heart[306]

This student was even more unhappy because deprived of any voice, she was unable to express her feelings on being told this. She, and hundreds of others over the years, were robbed of their individual means of expression and identity, leading to a group loss of culture. This was a devastating, irreparable loss to several generations.

Sexual Abuse

None of the former students that I interviewed were sexually abused at the schools. However there are people who witnessed one of the staff abusing boys at the Mohawk Institute in the 1960s.[307]

I can remember laying in bed wondering when it was my turn at night. One of the housefathers was gonna come around, and I was wondering when it was my turn to take me down that aisle and back. My turn came but I never went. I wouldn't get out of that bed, and I kicked and screamed and cried, and the guy just left.[308]

Zimmerman himself was shocked by finding homosexual abuse among the boys in the dormitory, and some of the former boys confirm that this went on though it did not happen to them personally.

There is a certain amount of speculation about incidents in the 1940s, and I have been told of girls running away and coming to one person's house bleeding and distressed. I was told of a girl who was raped around the turn of the century and had a child who grew up at Six Nations. I have heard of sexual abuse, but although I have been urged to "tell the truth" about what went on, I regret that I am not in a position to do this without first-hand information.

All except three or four former students in the late 1920s who heard various stories, state categorically that they never heard of any sexual abuse at Mt. Elgin.

Bullying

Fighting was commonplace among the boys in all periods and occasionally among girls. Although there was some bullying and fighting at Mt. Elgin, bullying was particularly prevalent during the 1940s and '50s at the Mohawk Institute. There were gangs who would beat up on the younger children, boys and girls would be put through the mill, boys would be made to undergo various tortures such as being made to hang on to the steam pipes in the basement, towels wrapped around their necks until they passed out,[309] younger children would be forced to steal for the older ones.

Physical Living Conditions

The attention paid to proper food and health care and comfort etc. can be said to express and reflect the attitudes held by members of the wider society towards the Aboriginal children and their status. Lack of attention to proper health care and providing a good diet can also be abusive. Certainly they were perceived as such by hungry children who spent their days tending cows, pigs and chickens, or preparing meals, and never got eggs or cream,

or meat that they remember.

The food was bad. We had mush every morning with worms - we only ate down to the bugs! We never had any eggs though they had thousands of chickens. We did have a bun every Sunday, but when I first went there I never got my bun, because I had traded it away and always owed it to someone. We had whole milk once a year and we never got any meat. The officers ate good though. The girls would cook a roast for the officers and we'd steal it. Christmas was the only time we got meat - then we got chicken. We became good peach and pear pickers at night.[310]

The children's low status was also indicated by the sanitary conditions which frequently showed no concern for individual privacy and dignity. This is another form of surveillance. At Mt. Elgin, as late as the 1940s, they literally put the boys into the shit to clean out the cesspit. Like the use of skim milk, the state of the sanitary arrangements was like a thermometer indicating the level of caring for the children at that particular period.

Many students complain that they did not have warm clothes or adequate footwear for winter. They did not have warm bedclothes.

It seems quite inhumane that they could have allowed children to be so ill-fed and so ill-dressed.[311]

Dental care was inadequate most of the time:

...we didn't have...toothpaste and toothbrush. There was some powder that you clean the basin with...I wanted nice clean teeth...so I cleaned my teeth with it and rinsed my mouth real good, and I felt really good about it. Maybe that's why I don't have any teeth today![312]

The condition of the buildings was another important reflection of status with renovations and expansion in times of optimism when the work was considered important. In the 1940s at Mt. Elgin, although the girls were for ever cleaning the building, they could not stay ahead of the physical condition of the delapidated buildings, and the filthy, insanitary bathroom facilities, kitchens literally alive with cockroaches, while at the same time the farm buildings were described as being in A1 condition. This reflects attitudes to children who were orphans or from troubled or poor homes. Throughout the literature there are reports of depressing conditions, depressed children. Buildings were burned down in times of dissatisfaction.

The Schools - Ends of a Spectrum

"All runaways were, as a matter of policy, made severe examples of at Dotheboys Hall, inasmuch as in consequence of the limited extent of its attractions there was but little inducement, beyond the powerful impulse

of fear, for any pupil provided with the usual number of legs and the power of using them, to remain.[313]

Does Dickens' 1839 description of Nicholas Nickleby's school, Dotheboys Hall, ring true for the Mohawk Institute of the 1900s and 1950s, or the roasting of Tom Brown in *Tom Brown's Schooldays* (1857)[314] compare with hanging little boys on the steam pipes? Although these are fictional works the similarities invite the question: how did the Mohawk Institute and Mt. Elgin compare with other residential schools? How did they differ because they were Indian residential schools? How did they compare with other Indian Residential Schools? To answer these questions properly would require a comprehensive analysis of the whole spectrum of residential schools - schools for rich and poor, manual labour schools and industrial schools, training schools, reform schools, boys' and girls' schools, Indian residential schools in the U.S. and Canada - all within their social and chronological frames of reference. Among the variables that would have to be considered in a comparative study of other Indian Residential Schools are geographic locations, different cultures, time periods, churches, children, value systems etc. etc. Such an analysis is beyond the scope of this 'microhistory'.[315]

However some observations can be made about schools at the ends of the social spectrum, in a comparison of Crichel with the Mohawk Institute and Mt. Elgin. Crichel was an independent school, while the Mohawk Institute and Mt. Elgin were controlled by the state. The Mohawk Institute and Mt. Elgin can be lumped together for comparative purposes, because, as outlined in this essay, the similarities in policies and operation of the schools far outweigh the differences. The Mohawk Institute and Mt. Elgin were run by different churches, for different periods of time, but even the individual principals show similarities in their attitudes to discipline, and competence in running the schools. The general patterns of restrictions on language, admission of students, the food and discipline, the education, failures of manual training programs, career prospects and living conditions are all similar during the periods that the schools coexisted. Students at Mt. Elgin were not so likely to go to high school and the Mohawk Institute produced more teachers in the 1800s, and hired more Native Staff members, but most differences are idiosyncratic rather than systemic, and pertain to the particular administration and personality of the principal. There was less bullying and fighting amongst Mt. Elgin boys, but bullying was most prevalent at the Mohawk Institute during the 1950s after Mt. Elgin closed. Sexual abuse was also reported at the Mohawk Institute in the 1960s.

The techniques discussed in the next section, that were used by institutions aiming for total power - bells, training, uniforms, rules superseding parents' rights, the right to punish infringements of the rules, confinement or boundaries - were similar but the degree of rigidity in the application of these techniques varied. At Crichel our lives were also governed by bells telling us when to get up, eat, pray, go to class, rest, play lacrosse, sleep. Punctuality and orderliness - no running in the hall - were required but we did not have to line up and march and you could be late three times

before punishment. There was a uniform of grey skirts and sweaters but the style and colour of blouse and socks was our choice. Our clothes were our own. There were boundaries but with permission we could go outside these bounds. The girls of the Mohawk Institute and Mt. Elgin could never go outside the playground unsupervised.

The schools all assumed the right to make rules and administer punishments, but the absence of corporal punishment sets Crichel apart from the Indian residential schools. However in this respect Crichel and our 'brother' school, Bryanston, differed from Upper Canada College and most English boys' boarding schools where corporal punishment, often viciously executed, existed until the 1970s. Punishments at Crichel included runs, extra work, standing in the hall, confinement within bounds. Expulsion, the most drastic recourse, was not exercised during my time at Crichel, and lacking much value as a threat was not a very effective punishment option for the Indian residential schools, although difficult students were dismissed occasionally. Going 'out of bounds' without permission was the most serious crime at Crichel. We used to get permission to go out for a bicycle ride but would find a river and swim, to experience the thrill of breaking the rules without getting caught, just as some children at the Mohawk Institute and Mt. Elgin would go out at night, and found many other ways to break the rules and secretly challenge the power of the system.

Although admission to the Mohawk Institute and Mt. Elgin was voluntary and required qualifications in the early days, towards the end of the 19th century the government took control of admission through its agents, and children became pawns of the system. Admission to Crichel was entirely voluntary but children had to pass an entrance exam. The educational standards at Crichel were high and students were prepared for the University entrance exam, though in practice girls either went to Oxford or Cambridge or to secretarial school while waiting for marriage, and preparation for career options was limited. Until the 1950s most of the Native children only went to school half-a-day and very few went to high school or university. The children at the Mohawk Institute and Mt. Elgin had to grow the food on the farm, cook, sew and clean. We did no work beyond making our beds. At the Indian residential schools recreational activities were limited, but at Crichel we had many extra-curricular cultural and sporting activities. The Staff shared the characteristic that they tended to be people who did not fit in in other schools, but there were separate teachers for different subjects, and no one teacher had as much power over the students.

Although parents are considered a necessary evil in any residential school, as a private school Crichel was dependent on fees or donations from parents. Because parents could remove their children and fees from the school if they did not like the treatment, private schools had to treat parents and children with some respect. At the Indian residential schools parents were excluded from decision making processes initially because they were Indian and Indianness was to be rooted out. Later social class became a factor. Because Indian parents did not pay directly they had very little power beyond the value they held for their children in matters of love, food and health, as discussed above. By the 20th century children were steered into a servant class and spent half their time doing the work of the school, and education was not a top priority. When Zimmerman tried to ensure that girls who were going to high school had decent clothes to wear he asked for an allowance comparable to that of the Grandview Training School. This illustrates where the Mohawk Institute was situated on the social scale.

Much of the quality of treatment the children of the Mohawk Institute and Mt. Elgin received - low standards of education, the hard work, the poor quality of the food, the rigid discipline, the confinement, the lack of recreation etc can be ascribed to their lower class and/or orphaned status, and powerless position in the system. While higher social class did not necessarily guarantee better treatment in boarding schools, it did determine the ultimate rewards. 17th and 18th century parents tended to believe that children possessed original sin which had to be beaten out of them.[316] Indian children were seen as having not only original sin but as being 'contaminated' by their Indianness - their language and culture had to be beaten out of them. This is a fundamental difference which non-Natives can understand intellectually but not adequately - these children were different because they were Native children and were not only denied their culture but made to feel like nobodies - that it was *evil* or *rude* to be who they were. As English residential schools, and schools like Upper Canada College, became institutions for the upper and aspiring middle classes, children were beaten to teach them to conform to their society but they were guaranteed a secure social position in the 'old boys network'. Indian children forced to renounce their society for the wider society, frequently ended up without a place in either society or an identity.

Solving the "Indian Problem"

The founders of the Mohawk Institute and Mt. Elgin, who equated civilization with salvation, had benevolent intentions. They envisaged a plan of self-help for Native communities in which Native students would acquire education, manual labour, agricultural and domestic skills, become teachers and Ministers, and solve the "Indian problem" by becoming the agents of civilization in their own communities. With the Indian Act of 1876 and the image of Indians as government wards in the latter part of the 19th Century, dependency was fostered. The "Indian problem" was to be solved through assimilation of Indians into a lower dependent class and the vision of education changed to the training of domestic servants and hired hands. With the legacy of the Reserve system, which marginalized Indians and kept the majority in poverty, the image of Indians as true "problem" with no direct relevance for Canadian society became prevalent after World War I. The schools became shelters for orphans and needy "problem" children, who had no place in their society.

These processes occurred with very little discussion of policy over the years. Management of the schools was discussed - who was going to run the schools and how. Why the schools were founded was clear, but why they remained in existence was not a topic that concerned the administration to a great degree. Even the Special Commissioners' Report in 1858 and Benson's comments in 1902, both describing residential schools as failing in their objectives, did not lead to real consideration of the question of whether the schools should continue to exist. The Young Report of 1943 on Indian Education in Western Ontario, looked carefully at the role of Mt. Elgin and pointed out that the residential schools were planned as Vocational Schools but were being used as orphanages. The report recommended closing the residential school and opening a senior school in its place that would give an academic education qualifying students to go to local high schools, proper vocational training with an emphasis on training rather than profit, and voluntary enrolment with a complete change of atmosphere so that Indian parents and children would want to attend the school. Joblin hoped that the vision of the report would *lead to a new day in Indian Education...all over Canada.*[317] This did not happen.

As it was, as both schools moved away from the original purpose of providing an education and manual training for the students, as a result of a shortage of funds and burgeoning bureaucracy, the running of the institution became the major purpose of the institution. The students were working for the school. The kind of domestic and farm work they were doing for the school became the kind of work they were qualified to do. To paraphrase Kennedy's exhortation, they were being asked "Ask not what your school can do for you, ask what you can do for your school." The solution had become the problem.

We shall turn now to examine the process in which this reversal of goals occurs, and how having 'created the monster', survival of the institution becomes the goal, through the method of achieving total power of the institution over its members.

The Quest for Total Power - Schools and Prisons

Separating children from parents is what boarding-schools do, but at Indian Residential Schools the goal of eradicating "Indianness" was added to the process. The schools excluded the Native culture by removing the children from their homes, restricting their holidays, and not allowing them to communicate with their parents in their Native language. After 1872 students could not even speak their Native language amongst themselves. Visits and conversations between brothers and sisters were forbidden or severely restricted. Parents were often described as 'interfering'. The administrators of the schools even saw themselves as **protecting** the children from their parents - parents were considered a bad influence or immoral, with dirty, unhealthy houses; sick and dying children would be more comfortable at the Institute. When the majority of students came from broken homes or were orphans, the parental factor was further diminished.

This exclusion not only worked to keep parents out, but to keep students in. The schools came to resemble prisons with prison-cells in the schools, fire-escapes locked, and truancy as the major crime and the major problem.

In *Discipline and Punish* Michel Foucault wrote that: *"Prisons resemble factories, schools, barracks, hospitals, which all resemble prisons."*[318] The aim for 'total power' on the part of the authorities, and the techniques used to achieve it, are similar in these institutions. To achieve total power the right of the authorities to hold total power must be accepted by everyone in the system. Foucault asks:- "How were people made to accept the power to punish, or quite simply, when punished, tolerate being so"?[319] Foucault looks at Jeremy Bentham's model of the Panopticon as the ideal prison - a central tower from which every aspect of the institution is visible. The inmate sees the tower from which he is being spied upon and never knows whether or not he is being watched at any one moment, but he must always believe that someone might be observing him and so he has to constantly monitor his own behaviour so as not to be caught unawares. Surveillance thus becomes permanent in its effects even though it may not actually be continuous. This visibility and permanent and total surveillance has the effect that the inmate takes over from the watchers the responsibility for his behaviour, becoming both watcher and watched, *"he becomes the principle of his own subjection."*[320] Through surveillance school children, as well as prisoners, become the principle of their own subjection, and it is possible to control behaviour with the economical use of power. Foucault specifies some of the techniques used to manage power economically in these institutions - timetables, uniforms, discipline, training.

The schools all depended on a rigid timetable. The children's lives were very structured. Bells marked the course of the day, telling the children where they should be

and what they should be doing at each moment, ensuring that they were under surveillance for most of the day.

The wearing of uniforms, while removing the identity of individuals so that they could be controlled more effectively, gave them an outward identity as members of the school - another technique designed to engineer the internal acceptance of the rules.

At the Mohawk Institute the hierarchical system of military discipline instituted by Ashton in the 1870s, was also another form of surveillance. Lining up and marching to the dining-room, the class-room, the chapel, to work etc. trained the children to 'keep in line' literally. The strict rules of conduct comprised another technique which left little room for individuality.   The compulsory use of English also removed the children's 'Indian identity' and gave them a 'school identity'. At the same time it was part of the total surveillance, extended to include the parents when they intruded into the school sphere and were forced to communicate with their children in English, so that the content of their communication could be monitored.

Numbers were used to identify the children. Although this removes their original identity even further, and it might seem that all individuality is lost in this kind of system, Foucault argues that one function of discipline and punishment is in fact to give individuals a separating identity within the carceral, rather than allowing them to form a homogeneous mass, which would have a potential for gaining power. Children at the residential schools were differentiated by the discipline system - particularly Ashton's military-type hierarchy at the Mohawk Institute. Punishment records from 1913 at the Mohawk Institute also show how children were differentiated by the number of punishments they received. The deeds that were classified as misdeeds or offences, which to the reader may seem quite trivial, illustrate the extent of surveillance on all aspects of behaviour, with details of each child's misbehaviour recorded in punishment books, or displayed on a notice board.

Corporal punishment is a flagrant invasion of personal dignity - the intent is to cause humiliation as well as pain. Humiliation destroys dignity and value of self, and consequently identity.   Control through humiliation is a deliberate appropriation of self-respect, and this intrusion into an individual's identity is, in a sense, another form of surveillance. However, in the play-room subculture of the Mohawk Institute the children did not allow themselves to cry if they received the strap, but had to "tough-it-out."

I was up in the dorm where I wasn't supposed to be and I was helping the other children make beds and I got caught. So this supervisor gave me the strap and there was about seven of us girls and she gave the strap to my wrist, and I didn't cry. I vowed to myself I wasn't going to cry. So she said "Get to the end of the line." She strapped two and she got to me, and she strapped me up to the elbow, and I still didn't cry. "I'll get to you later." So she strapped all the rest of them and it was just me up there and she strapped me up to my shoulder, and it was really red, and it was just all swollen, just a dreadful sight. And I got downstairs determined I wasn't going to cry, and my sister saw it and she started to cry. That's when I started to cry. [321]

This refusal to cry and be broken, which is mentioned time and again by the former students, allowed them to retain their dignity/identity, but sometimes at great cost in terms of physical punishment.

Both prisons and schools have areas where overt surveillance by the officials is lacking. However, it is taken over by the inmates, who have absorbed the principles by which they accept subjection and use them on their weaker fellow inmates. Prison brutality, and bullying in the residential schools fill in this gap. Students from the 1950s actually complain of a lack of surveillance by officials, which allowed the older/bigger children to bully the younger ones quite mercilessly, with physical tortures and beatings, taking food, and making them steal for the old ones. This is in fact a very efficient extension of surveillance, with the authorities not needing to use power directly, and has the effect of maintaining the hierarchy which differentiated the children, preventing them from uniting against the administration. Snell was one principal who used this technique overtly, and as Lorna describes, she only came belatedly to the realisation of what she was doing when they helped to punish their peers by putting them 'through the mill' in the playroom after they had run away. [322]

Most students did accept the right of the administration to make and enforce the rules, making observations such as: *"Of course you got the strap when you needed it,"* [323] *You made it bad for yourself or you made it good...If there was a reason you'd get a strapping for it...it must have been my fault,"* [324] *"If I was punished it was my own fault,"* [325] *"You got a licking if you needed it."* [326] However, there were individuals who refused to accept punishment:

Miss Hardy said "Put your hands up." "Nope." She said "I said put your hands up." "Nope." Saturdays our parents could come and take us out, but this day, when my mother and Dad got there, Miss Hardy told my mother I couldn't go out, and my mother turned to the principal and says "What has she done?" So the principal told her and said she won't take a licking. My mother says "Have you got the strap handy"? She laid me across her lap, pulled my skirt up and she walloped my butt with the strap. [327]

So the principal took the strap out of the desk, and I went to the opposite side of the room. I thought "Boy, you're going to have to catch me before you do it." So he says "Come over here and hold your hands out." I says "If you can catch me you'll strap me...!!!" I'd wait till he came close and then I'd just jump on the desk

and on to the other one. He chased me for a good half hour until he got so tired. [328]

Others had relatives who confronted the principal:

One time my Uncle came with this car and took us for a ride to my grandmother's. When we got back Strapp was standing there and he pulls out his strap. He was going to start on me but Uncle Don said "Don't you ever touch that kid." [329]

My Dad caught Strapp hitting my sister. We just happened to come in the front door and he said "Where's your sister?" I said "That's her hollering in there." He went in there and pushed him down. He said "Don't ever touch my children again." That's why nothing happened to us after we run away. [330]

In most eras there was considerable truancy, but ironically, there was more truancy during periods when strict discipline prevailed and there was more of a need for the inmates to challenge the total power of the school administration. 34/66 of the people interviewed had run away at least once, some many times. Compared with a figure of zero truants from my school, 50% is a significant number, representing a considerable challenge to school authority. Physicial confinement was a problem for many of the children who could not adjust to this curtailment of their freedom, especially when they did not know when they would ever get out..

There were other arenas in the struggle for power in which the administration was not always able to gain total control over the students, food and health.

Basil Johnston writes about the school at Spanish:

Food was the one abiding complaint because the abiding condition was hunger, physical and emotional. Food, or the lack of it, was something that the boys could point to as a cause of their suffering; the other was far too abstract and therefore much too elusive to grasp. But food was a reality that the boys could understand; However, it was more than a full stomach that the boys craved when they complained about the mush...actually a protest against abuse and maltreatment... [331]

Food symbolizes status and can be an expression of power: rich people eat differently from poor people. At my school teachers ate at a separate table and got better food. In the residential schools, where staff had their own dining-room and at Mt. Elgin a separate kitchen, the quality and quantity of the food served definitely expressed a status difference and concomitantly a power differential. Staff got butter, students did not. Staff got roasts of meat, students did not. The boys from the Mohawk Institute used to sneak out to the town dump to get food (albeit candy) thrown out by a local factory, to supplement their rations. Going to the dump for food symbolizes their low status, however, it also empowered the boys who were temporarily outside the school surveillance. Possession of food was also one of the forms of currency in power relations among the students.

Older children would take the younger ones' food or force them into trading or stealing food. At my school the authorities capitalized on the relationship between food and power with the prefect system, which extended the authority and surveillance system of the administration. Prefects had to ensure that people were in the right place at the right time, ring the bells, punish minor infractions and report gross breaches of discipline. The reward for this work was a small kitchen and supplies of milk and bread. This was an enormous privilege and favours could be dispensed by inviting other girls to share toast and coffee. Before I was appointed as prefect the headmistress asked: "Are you willing to sacrifice your popularity for the good of the school?" I was prepared to be bribed by the prospect of access to the power elite and the kitchen, unaware of the total extent of my subjection!

Why do we find that so many of the complaints from parents were about the food and state of health? Parents who were excluded from school life, and were powerless to speak on academic and vocational matters, could intrude their parental role into the school world only by complaining on these grounds on which they still held value. In Native culture and family life food played a cohesive role through sharing, rather than the institutional role marking differences in status. Food held a value for the children which expressed their feelings about home life, which could not be taken away from them, and which became a symbol of resistance and a focus of power for the oppressed. Students would run away and go home to their parents.

The children would run away because they didn't like being confined - they were lonely for their parents. They didn't get any love in the school, and they didn't get enough to eat - no matter how poor their home they wanted to get back home for food and love.[332]

Zimmerman's comment in 1947 linking food and truancy, shows that he was catching on to this chink in the armour of total power and trying to provide good food. Periods when the food was acceptable and truancy non-existent were, however, few and far between.

Children who went to residential school in the 1930s came from poor homes - because of the Depression their parents could not afford to keep them at home. Grateful for three meals a day and clothes, they accepted the discipline: *"We did a lot of work - but I think it was good for us - it was discipline."*[333] *"We learned to work,"*[334] and found it stood them in good stead for the rest of their lives. In the 1950s, after welfare came in and improved financial conditions somewhat on the Reserve, children coming from broken homes, and orphans, did not like the food and did not accept the discipline.

Children who did complain were dismissed as ungrateful trouble-makers. Although a former student laments *"I just wished someone would come and do something about the school,"*[335] there was not very much that parents or children could do to change the system.

Celia Haig Brown (1988), J. R. Miller (1996), and Basil Johnston (1988) have pointed out the resistance displayed by children at Indian Residential Schools and their parents. There is plenty of evidence in the following pages of resistance to the rules - smuggling food, stealing apples, speaking Native languages when they were out of earshot of the staff, going out at nights, truancy, arson etc., but the right of the administration to make the rules was accepted to a large extent by the students who acknowledged that they deserved to be punished if they broke the rules. However, the widespread truancy demonstrates that many individuals did not accept that they had to be part of this system. Students who absconded did not 'become the principle of their own subjection,' but removed themselves from the sphere of surveillance. The schools failed to achieve total surveillance and power.

Footnote

Policies governing Native peoples have been formulated by officials who apparently see history as a linear development of progress and social evolution. A Nietzschean cyclical model might be more appropriate. The Rev. Mr. Lugger remarked in 1828:

There is an Indian Department paid by the government at home, whose support would appear to depend, not on the civilization of these poor creatures, but on their continuance in their present state...[336]

In 1997 the DIA still depends on maintaining the status quo, and the RCAP report shares the opinion Rev. Abraham Nelles expressed in 1844:

The Indians generally can manage their own affairs;

they might perhaps make a better use of their money themselves, than agents appointed to act for them.[337]

We have come around in a circle. The wider society has viewed Native peoples as raison d'etre for the Indian Department; next "to be helped become equals"; then to be assimilated into the lower class. Excluded from the political system, Native peoples are still irrelevant to the wider society but raison d'etre for the Indian Department. Agencies outside government are still trying to get help for Native communities to enable them to be self-supporting and take their place in Canadian society as equals. Awareness that we have been here before could influence choices made this time around, to move history onto a different path.

Part Two: Voice of Authority
Mohawk Institute

5. Mohawk Institute

THE

⟨◦MOHAWK◦⟩⟨◦INSTITUTION◦⟩

(Indian Industrial and Normal School,)

BRANTFORD,   :   ONTARIO.

Will Re-Open on Saturday, Aug. 29th, 1885.

———

Thirty boys and thirty girls are admitted from the Tuscarora Reserve, and fifteen boys and fifteen girls from any Indian Reserve in the Dominion.

Pupils are boarded, educated and clothed free of charge. Those who are fitted, if desirous, may be apprenticed to various trades or be trained for school teachers

Ten deserving pupils are maintained at the Colleg. iate Institute, Brantford, to obtain third and second class Provincial Certificates.

Candidates for admission must be between the ages of 11 and 17 years, and able to read fairly in the Third Reader and work correctly the simple rules in arithmetic.

Applications, stating age and qualifications, must be addressed to the Rev. Robt. Ashton, Superintendent, Box 18, Brantford, before August 20th.

N. B.—Pupils whose names are upon the register of the Instisution, must return on the day the school opens OR NOT AT ALL.

6. Notice

1827 - 1872
Lugger 1827-1836 - Nelles 1836-1872

1. **31 October 1827   NEC Report**
The Rev. Mr. Lugger...a member of the University of Cambridge, in priests' orders, of good moral character. The first of his dispatches from Brantford...he mentions his having been received by the Indians with the greatest respect and attention, and having been addressed by the chiefs:

   Father, we thank the Great Spirit for having sent you to us, and giving you and your family a safe voyage to this place. We hope you will be a blessing to our people. We thank the good Society, who have thus shown such kindness to poor Indians. We pray for you, that you may enjoy a long life and live amongst us for many years in health and happiness.

2. **26 May 1828   NEC Report**
...alludes also to Mr. Lugger's taking...a white man to teach the Indians at £50 per annum, which he considers important to the teaching of Indian children in the English language.

3. **13 June 1828   NEC Report**
...Referring to Mr. Lugger's suggestions respecting a white man to teach the boys English, and a woman to teach the girls in the Mohawk school...the Company were disposed to make the experiment for one year.

4. **3 April 1929   NEC Report: Lugger**
...I have purchased the agricultural implements, and have clothed the boys and girls in the Mohawk School, and although their civilization must be a slow and laborious work, I have no doubt of its ultimate success.

5. **14 May 1829   NEC Report: Lugger**
The four school houses and the lots of land, of 100 acres, granted to each, are exclusively the property of the Company, and a deed will shortly be executed to confirm the same to them for ever; the Indians having granted it in general council to the government for the New England Company.

6. **16 July 1829   NEC Report: Lugger**
...our schools are all prospering...In the Mohawk and Oneida schools the first classes can already read well in the New Testament; indeed, the attainments of the children surpass my most sanguine expectations...

7. **1 November 1829   NEC Report: Lugger**
...I have been on a visit to Sir John Colborne, at York, and I had subsequently the honour of a visit for six days from His Excellency.   Sir John has been appointed superintendent to all the Indians of that province, and has personally made himself acquainted with all their concerns.   He examined the scholars in English, reading the New Testament, repeating the Lord's Prayer, Commandments, Creed, and Hymns, and saw their writing, attended church on the Sunday...it was the intention of Mr. Brant and himself to draw on the Treasurer for the sum allowed by the Company, for the purpose of advancing the children in various handicraft works, and for the residences...

8. **8 July 1830   NEC Report**
...(what Mr. L.[Lugger] terms) the Mechanics Institution for teaching the Indians all sorts of handicraft trades, would very soon be in operation; but, that considerable difficulty was experienced from the inadequacy of funds. Mr Lugger then refers the Company to Mr Richards, who had lately attended the quarterly examination of the Mohawk children, when he expressed himself highly satisfied, and surprised at such attainments under so short a period of education...

9. **1830   NEC Report: Treasurer to Lugger**
...You mention the Mechanics Institution, and when it is completed, there will be nothing left of the £600. It does not appear from the correspondence with the Company, that any direction for such an expenditure was contemplated, or indeed, that any such establishment was on foot. On a drawing, which has been received from a private friend (Mr. Richards, I think) there is a building under that title. The Company are desirous to know the particulars of this, as relates to the building itself, as well as the objects to which it is directed, and also the period of the correspondence which authorized it, as it has escaped the notice of the Company, if it existed.

10. **19 November 1830   S.P.G.F.P. Resolution**
...the services of Mr. Nellis...transferred to the New England Company...

11. **10 March 1831   NEC Report: Lugger**
Our Mohawk and Oneida Schools have decreased rather in number of late, from the extreme severity of the winter, ...Messrs. Brant, Nellis, and myself, have conferred together, and for a short time, have thought it will be likely to answer a better end to put in native teachers in these two schools, and to appropriate the surplusage, together with what can be saved out of the allowance for general purposes, to take up a number of poor orphan Indian children to board and clothe, by which means we have more entirely their time and attention, and shall be able to effect twice as much in one half the period...

12. 29 April 1831 NEC Report
...Mr. Lugger gives an account of a further advance in the formation of the Mechanics' Institution. There were then four large rooms, in two of which girls might be taught spinning and weaving, and in the other two, the boys tailoring and carpentering; besides an additional building for a mechanic shop. The Governor, Sir John Colborne, had visited the place, approved what had been done, and induced Mr. Lugger to indulge some expectation he might further the undertaking by some pecuniary aid...the sum of £100 was allotted by the Company for the...Institution, accompanied with a promise of considerable support, when the extent of the expense, and the real probablility of success, should be better ascertained...

13. 1831 NEC Report
...[Lugger] had, the last week, ridden 80 miles, preached (through interpreters) in five different languages, and attended two councils...These matters he considered more immediately to concern him as a Minister of God, than Mechanics Institutes, which...he would not neglect, but was apprehensive he had undertaken more than he was equal to...wish for the assistance of a lay agent...every building, then erected for the Company, was paid for...
...the Treasurer...desire for fuller and more frequent accounts of what was done, and for correct estimates of what was intended to be done, before any thing fresh should be undertaken...

14. June 1833 NEC Report: Lugger
Mohawk Village..36 Scholars...The upper class read well in the Bible, repeat Scripture, Hymns, Catechisms, (Dr. Watts,) write a good round hand, cypher as far as division, and say all the tables...as to understanding what they learn that is quite out of the question, and will be for years, until they are taken from their families and obliged to speak nothing but English, as I had purposed and planned for the proposed Institution...

15. July 1833 NEC Report
...a resolution was passed to increase the annual allowance for...the Grand River...The Lay Agency was offered to Mr. W. Richardson...at £100 per annum...

16. 26 April 1834 NEC Report
...separate advices were received from Mr. Lugger, Mr. Nellis, and Mr. Richardson, agreeing in recommending particular attention to the selecting some of the Indian children of each sex for particular instruction, and affording them the advantage of education, and in proposing to adapt part of the building erected for a Mechanics' Institute to that purpose...Mr. Nellis particularly expresses his opinion that while the ground-work of improvement must be laid amongst the young,

that can be but imperfectly done if they are left to live and grow up at home.

17. 8 September 1834 NEC Report: Lugger Nellis Richardson
The NEC have...done much for their improvement, by building schoolhouses, appointing teachers...but still in many instances the Indians show themselves insensible to these advantages, and continue irresolute and suspicious, and look upon all whites as intruders...no measure would tend so much to remove their prejudices, as the instruction of a number of the youth of both sexes in the arts, habits and customs of civilized life, who may hereafter act as instruments in the hands of the Company, for the complete civilization of Indians generally...They will therefore, use the building already erected for this purpose and select 10 boys and 4 or 6 girls, for instruction from the Six Nations Indians, to be boarded, lodged and taught, keeping the school open for as many day scholars as can be accommodated and instructed. A respectable man, with a small family, has been engaged as a teacher who has been employed already as a teacher among the Mohawks. The expense of such an establishment they compute at £320 p.a. To this school a garden will be attached in which the children will be taught to labour. When the boys are sufficiently advanced, they will be taught different branches of trade... the expense...wages and tools of a blacksmith, carpenter, waggon and sleigh-maker, and cabinet maker...estimate £380...deduct articles manufactured and sold. These trades...selected, not only as the most useful but because some of the Indians had shown a taste for these employments. The next object ...should be the introduction of an agricultural system.

18. 27 February 1835 NEC Report: Treasurer
...to approve of the establishment of a central School, and the appointment of a blacksmith and carpenter for instructing the young Indian scholars in those trades...the expense might be gradually diminished by a sale of the produce of the artificers' labour,
May 23d.- By subsequent advices it appears progress was making...wishes were expressed that the number of children might be increased from fourteen to fifty...

19. 1 March 1836 NEC Report
[Nelles]...The progress of the children at the Institution he describes as very gratifying. They have been visited by many persons of respectability, some clergymen, who expressed satisfaction and delight.
...July. Ill health obliged Mr. Lugger, in the month of May, to leave home...Mr. Nellis, during his absence, the charge...In July, he returned...but so little improved in health that he was compelled to apply for further leave of absence...the boys at the Institution were making

considerable progress, and promised fair to do credit to the benevolent designs of the Company.

Aug...he determined to quit Canada for England...he expired at Devonport, on the 10th of March following.

20. January 1837 NEC Report: Nellis
At the Institution, 18 children; three...are day scholars...

21. NEC Report
...soon after the death of the Rev. Mr. Lugger...the Rev Abraham Nelles, the Company's then second or assistant Missionary at the Tuscarora village, was appointed to succeed to the office lately held by Mr. Lugger, at a salary of £200 per annum...

22. 1837 NEC Report
The Company's Schools...The proficiency of the scholars who were examined in reading, writing, and arithmetic, was encouraging, and...should be deemed satisfactory; some could add, subtract, and multiply, saying the multiplication table correctly; more could write English legibly, read distinctly, and answer questions in the catechism as pertinently as...children in country schools in England...At the Institute, besides the younger children, there were four youths acquiring facility in the practice, if not in the principles of carpentry, there were three grounding themselves in the rudiments of shoemaking, and two acquiring with ardour the art of blacksmiths. There cannot be a doubt, either of the practicability or of the expediency of increasing the number of pupils...the inmates at the Institute are lodged, fed, and clothed, at the Company's expense. To supply them with support after quitting that establishment, would be founding a kind of fellowships for them, a plan which could not be carried to any extent, without entailing a heavy expense, and detracting from other more valuable services. Besides, it might produce on their naturally indolent dispositions, an unfavourable effect, and instead of promoting, retard their endeavours to find situations, where they could turn their acquirements at once to the benefit of their countrymen and their own profit. It is, however, deserving the consideration of the Company, whether it might not have a beneficial effect, if some of the young artificers, who showed themselves best qualified to become useful workmen, were assisted in the purchase of tools or other articles required to commence their trades.

23. 15 October 1837 NEC Report
...appointment of the Rev. Mr. Nellis...Both schools and Institution have fallen off from what probably they once were, and are in many respects short of what they ought to be. They have suffered much since Mr. Lugger's departure, for want of more active special superintendence ...In the conduct of the Institution, there is need of some alteration; complaints have been made by several of the

parents of the scholars, which we have taken much pains to investigate...

24. 18 November 1837 Richardson to Busk
Mr. Nellis and myself have visited the Institution, with a view of making known the instructions committed by you to paper for our guidance...and it is our intention to make out, and put up at the Institution, such rules and regulations...in conformity with those instructions...

We have engaged the shoemaker for five days in the week, as...by allowing him time to work for his own advantage, much loss and inconvenience accrues...There is no grant for a shoemaker, but I hope that from the saving, or deduction from the carpenter's salary, together with other little savings, I shall be enabled to make up his salary. Application must...be made for an extension of grant for payment of the blacksmith, as a very egregious error was made in the estimate...and if a wheelwright is engaged, it will be necessary that an appropriation be made for his wages, provided the benefits arising from the articles manufactured are appropriated to the education and instruction of a greater number of children. In talking...with Mrs. Nellis...she is a strong advocate for the instruction of girls at the Institution, under the impression that they might become very useful in the education of children in their respective neighbourhoods; but this can only be effected by granting to them exemption from those duties which may be called menial...the principal objection, as well on their part as on the part of their parents, is to the performance of household duties; and although it is very desirable that they should perform those duties in order to acquire a knowledge of them, it is a question whether it would not be better to waive this branch of instruction at first, and to endeavour to qualify them for higher duties. Three of the girls who have left the Institution are shrewd and intelligent, and, if you are not opposed to it, probably it would be advisable to take them back under a promise of exemption from the duties to which they object, and allow them to be treated, in other respects, as boarders at a white school are treated.

25. 12 February 1838 NEC Report
[Richardson]...progress making at the Mechanics' Institute...addition of a shoemaker and a wheelwright...the expenses of which would require some addition to former grants. Laments that there is much more trouble and difficulty in managing the female than the male scholars, but is very desirous of completing the education of at least a few, that they may be qualified to instruct the younger children...The disturbed state in which the country has been, still prevents the receipt of any material sums from the sale of any of the articles manufactured...

26. 28 April 1838 NEC Report: Treasurer
...coincides in the opinion...as to the expediency of

instructing in the Institute, some young female Indians, and recommends admitting four or six of that sex...

27. 3 July 1838 NEC Report
Mr. Richardson complains again of the difficulty of collecting the amount of the sales which had been made of goods manufactured at institution...The boys at the Institution are happy and contented; not one of them has attempted to depart from the school for a long time...

28. 1 September 1838 NEC Report
[Nelles}...the addition of six girls to the Institute had been made in July; that they seemed to be contented and promised to profit by the instructions given them, as much as the boys. Amongst these young people, a good state of health generally prevailed, but lately a few cases of fever and whooping cough had occurred.

29. 1 February 1839 NEC Report
[Nelles]...Sir G. Arthur had been present at the service of the Mohawk church, and expressed himself much pleased...with the examination afterwards, at the School, of about 30 Indian children...The Institution is conducted now with more satisfaction to the Indians, the girls are behaving with propriety, and making as much improvement as can be expected for the time...

30. 1839 NEC Report
...At the Institute the new Overlooker had entered on his duties and was proceeding satisfactorily - Mr. Nelles much recommends an increase in the number of children as he regards this Institute as the most useful part of the Company's establishment.
...much of the amount of articles sold from the manufacture of the artisans at the Institution remains outstanding; ascribes this irregularity also to the state of the province, and recommends the making of cheaper articles in future, and selling them only for ready money.

31. 28 August 1839 NEC Report: Treasurer to Richardson
...expresses...the approbation of the Company of the alterations that had been made in the Overseer, and some other particulars at the Institution, of his scheme of selling in future for ready money, and of manufacturing chiefly cheap articles, which may best suit the early civilized habits of the Indians...The Company would also be desirous, when they can afford it, to enlarge the accommodation at the Institution...

32. 29 August 1839 NEC Report: Treasurer to Nelles
...communicating the assent of the Company to the enlargement of the Mohawk Institution...enquiring after the condition of the school...enquires what became of the Indians who had been instructed under the Company's care after they had left the Institution, and how far he

thought it might be expedient and practicable to furnish them with any subsequent assistance by the supplying them with tools or otherwise.

33. 11 October 1839 NEC Report: Nelles
...The alterations which have been made at the Institution are very satisfactory, and the proficiency of some of the boys in the trades they are learning very respectable...

34. 1839 NEC Report
...It has been gratifying also, to discover sufficient encouragement, to extend the accommodation at the schools and the Institution at the Mohawk village and to have been able, whilst the number of scholars was nearly doubled, so to alter the arrangements there, as greatly to increase the means of comfort and instruction to them all. It has been additionally gratifying, to find both the youths and their parents becoming every day, more and more contented with the treatment received; more sensible of the expediency of closer attention and stricter discipline; more inclined and better qualified, to take a juster view of the importance of the knowledge imparted.

35. 5 December 1839 NEC Report
[Richardson]...furnishes an estimate of the expence of boarding and clothing forty Indian children, thirty boys and ten girls...viz. for board, at the rate of sixpence a head per day £365; for clothing £148 15s., making together the sum of £513 15s. currency.

36. 24 February 1840 NEC Report: Treasurer
...the estimate of boarding Indian children in Canada, compared with keeping adults in England, appears so high, that the Committee...hope...considerable reduction may be found practicable; still they are not deterred from wishing the experiment to be made by increasing the number at the Institute to forty, as soon as proper subjects offer. That the alterations and extension proposed at the Mohawk institute be immediately set about by the workmen and apprentices there; and that, when ready for the reception of the twenty additional scholars, and twenty proper subjects for additional scholars offer, they be admitted, and set to learn some of the different trades. That a new agreement be made with Smith, the superintendent at the Institution for their board on the best terms practicable, and that they be supplied with the clothing requisite also in the most economical way.

37. 29 February 1840 NEC Report: Treasurer
...it is agreeable to learn that there is no want of fit subjects to be introduced as scholars at the Institute;

38. 1 April 1840 NEC Report: Richardson
...the work to be performed in the alteration and extension

of accommodation at the Institute, will be placed in a state of progress so soon as the weather becomes sufficiently settled to admit of the cartage of timber from the woods... the buildings may be got ready for admission of the increased number of children on the 1st July. Smith and Rennet, assisted by the apprentices who are being taught the trade, would be employed, and thereby save to the Company any advance in money for that portion of the labour, which would come under the head of carpentering.

39. 31 March 1840 Nelles [see p.215]
...John Thomas...William English...Isaac Doxtater... Baptiste Gibson...only attend school occasionally for a few days, to keep up with what they already know; and devote the remainder of their time to the trades they are learning, the two former carpenters, the two latter blacksmiths.
...The improvement of the children generally...is satisfactory. The First class has been very careless in their writing: well pleased with the cleanly manner in which their writing, and cyphering books are kept.

40. 3 April 1840 NEC Report
[Nelles]...perused with satisfaction the Treasurer's communication...which authorizes the alterations at the Institute, preparatory to taking an additional number of scholars. Mr. Nelles will urge the completion of this work with as much expedition as possible, that they may be prepared to commence the next half-year with forty children; they had had some opportunity of judging of the expence of clothing the girls, and were of opinion it costs more than £2. each per annum. Mrs. Nelles had always purchased every thing for them, and attended herself to the cutting out, &c. to prevent waste or abuse; and, from the closest calculation they could make, each girl would cost about £3. per year. Mr. Nelles could not speak so confidently respecting the boys, as he had had nothing to do with furnishing their clothes until the last half-year; but thought they might be furnished for about the same price as the girls, independent of shoes, which are made in the Institution. The girls are required to make as much of the clothing as possible, and are also learning to knit. Mrs. Nelles intends introducing the spinning wheel among them this summer, so that in a year or two...they should be able to reduce the expence of clothing considerably.

41. 26 May 1840 NEC Report
...Mr. Nelles and himself [Richardson] had entered into an arrangement with Mr. Smith to devote his own time to the instruction, - the time of his wife and daughters to the care and management, and to provide the board of 40 children, and a servant (in order that his wife and daughters might devote more of their time and attention to the instruction of the girls in sewing, spinning, knitting and other useful occupations for a female), for the sum of

£500...p.a...he had reason to hope that nothing would occur to prevent the new arrangement from commencing on the 1st July, the alteration in the buildings at the Institution being in a state of progress towards completion.

42. 26 August 1840 NEC Report: Nelles
...the Institution with forty children, is now fairly in operation. They had less difficulty in training the "little untutored savages" to habits of regularity and obedience than he anticipated. The example of those they had previously instructed was very influential.

43. 26 October 1840 NEC Report
[Nelles}They found that with the increased number of children at the Institution, Smith could not properly superintend it, while he had to follow his trade, and feared therefore another change would be necessary. They had had a good deal of trouble with some of the new scholars, and several had run away and gone home; some were immediately sent back by their parents, others they had had to send for; he trusted they were more settled now; they had had time to get over that restlessness which children, he believed, always felt when first taken away from their homes. They were obliged to dismiss three for bad conduct last week; he regretted in the case of one boy, Isaac Doxtater, who had been there some time and was learning the blacksmith's trade, in which he had made considerable proficiency; he had become very disobedient and unsettled and others were evidently following his example. His father intended building him a shop; he was quite able to do such work as Indians require, and would improve himself; indeed the knowledge he had gained would fit him to be very useful among his people, if he turned it to proper account...Mr. Nelles begged to be informed whether the Company would authorize him to promise to those boys who learned trades any assistance in furnishing them with tools, to enable them to carry on their respective trades, when they returned home. He thought it would be a strong motive for their continuing at the Institute until they had thoroughly acquired the trade, and without some such assistance some of them might not be able to pursue their calling and would either become idle, or hire themselves out among white people, which should, as far as possible, be prevented, by affording them every facility and inducement to settle, as mechanics, among their own people.

44. 24 November 1840 NEC Report: Richardson
...there have been no attempts, on the part of either boys or girls, to leave the school, since the dismissal of Doxtater, and two girls noticed in his last...they seemed to conduct themselves with much greater satisfaction to Mr. Nelles and himself...it would be advisable to make a change at the Institute...to find some persons willing to undertake the board of children. It became every day

more apparent that Smith could not, with profit to the Company, or advantage to the children, discharge the duties of mechanic and a provider for the Institute, and the family were not so efficient as they might be...a separation of the two departments would be desirable.

45. 1 March 1841 NEC Report: Richardson
We have at length found two persons to take charge of the Institution, upon the same conditions as the family of Smith took it, say £400 perannum, to commence on the first day of July. These persons, Mr and Mrs Hay, are elderly professed members of the Church of England, and without a family, the only one about them claiming kindred being a young man who was brought up and educated under their direction, and is engaged by us to take charge of the Mohawk school, with the understanding that he shall board with the children, and take charge of them at all times. The whole time, in fact, of the three will be given to the uses of the Company for the £400, and usual allowance to the young man as teacher. The family of Smith has always been very kind to the children, but they are not the proper persons to discharge the duties of an Establishment, of this nature...Smith will remain as the waggon maker at the salary of £100 per annum, or, otherwise at so much per diem for the days he may work. The latter arrangement would be preferable... as he will then be paid for such time only as he may be in the shop; a similar arrangement to the one with Rennet, the cabinet maker, who loses all the time he is absent, whether from sickness or otherwise.

46. 30 June 1841 NEC Report: Richardson
The elder boys at the Institute are beginning to appreciate the advantages which they derive from the munificence of the New England Company, but the younger ones are very careless and indifferent; however, there is much progress amongst all, and it is pleasing to witness the occupations of the boys in the several tribes. One boy can make a very good waggon, another can make articles of furniture, four others can make shoes, and two others are progressing in the blacksmithing; and it is sincerely to be hoped, that after they shall have left the school, their attention will not be drawn away from the desirable object of becoming trades-people amongst their separate tribes.

I sincerely hope that the change...will prove the means of much saving and expense in the clothing of the children, which has been much increased by the inattention of Mr. Smith to this particular, owing...to the occupation of his time in the workshop.

47. 6 August 1841 NEC Report: Nelles
Mr and Mrs. Hay have entered upon their duties...since the beginning of July; so far they promise well...I am every day more convinced of the usefulness of the

establishment. We have now several boys who will leave it, during the present year, very respectable mechanics. I had a public examination of the school the last of June, when the persons present expressed themselves much surprised and pleased at the improvement of the children, both in the school and the mechanical department. Mr. Rucey who is one of the board of education for this district assured me the examination was more creditable than that of the district school...

48. 19 August 1841 NEC Report: Richardson
...a visible change for the better is apparent at the Institution, from the circumstance, in some measure, of Mrs. Hay having no family, and possessing, at the same time, a fondness for children. Matters will also go on better in the workshop, particularly the carpenters and waggon shop, as the attention of Mr. Smith will not be diverted from his work.

49. NEC Report
...scholars at the Institution...some of them have made such progress in the knowledge taught them there as to be nearly qualified to quit it with advantage..."You will, of course, endeavour...to keep an eye upon their conduct when they are released from the discipline of the school, and come to move without restraint amongst their own countrymen. No more pleasing return for the expence and attention which the Institution has cost can be made than to find that the youths there educated retain the habits of sobriety and diligence, which they may have acquired, and beneficially employ the arts in which they have been instructed for their own maintenance, and the benefit and improvement of their nation.

50. 8 December 1841 NEC Report: Richardson
The tools furnished to John Obey and William English are now in use by those boys who still continue at the Institute; and I shall be very grateful if they can be persuaded to remain until the spring. They are becoming very useful in the waggon and cabinet shops, and they are good boys and I hope will succeed in their trades after having departed from the protection of the Company.

51. 6 January 1842 NEC Report: Nelles
The Institution is...in a more efficient and prosperous condition than at any former time. Two of the larger boys have just left it. They return home qualified to follow their respective trades. I shall do all in my power to encourage them to make a good use of the advantages they have enjoyed. If a little assistance could be promised towards enabling them to commence business, it might be of great use. If...lumber and nails to finish a workshop could be promised to any boy, who, with the assistance of his friends, would erect such a building, it would be an inducement to them to exert themselves, and probably a

little in the way of materials to begin work with, in some instances could be of service. If having learned a trade, they have a shop to work in, and tools to work with, they will be very likely to follow their trade at all events it will be their own faults if they do not. As a proof that the Institution is in better favour with the Indians...there are about 30 applicants for the two vacancies; we had some difficulty at first in getting 14 children in it.

52.   19 March 1842 NEC Report: Richardson
...during the past several months, the improvement of the boys and girls has gone forward steadily and satisfactorily, amongst those of the boys who are being taught trades, two have become almost perfect. John Obey as a waggon maker, and William English as a cabinet maker, and three or four of those who are being taught shoe making, and it is my intention to bring before the chiefs a plan for having such of the boys who become perfect located in a convenient place to prosecute their several trades. This will be the only method of inducing them to profit by the acquirements they will have attained...

53.   6 April 1842 Six Nations Indians to Sir Charles Bagot
...We would in conclusion, add that the New England Company have manifested a most friendly disposition towards us, in the erection of churches at the Mohawk and Tuscarora villages, the appointment of ministers, to instruct us in our spiritual welfare, in the erection of school houses, and appointment of schoolmasters to instruct our youth, as well as in the ordinary branches of education as in the arts of trade: and therefore we trust that the portions of land set apart for the Churches, Glebes and schoolhouses will be confirmed to the Company by deed from the Government...

54.   15 April 1842 NEC Report: Treasurer to Nelles
...desirous, at the critical period of these youths quitting the Institution, that they should receive such assistance as the Company...can afford. The supplying of such among them as had acquired competent skill in the arts they had been taught, and had manifested a sober and industrious disposition, with tools, was approved of, and there seems no objection to add occasionally to these tools, such a supply of lumber, or nails, or materials, as may appear to yourself and Mr. Richardson expedient to enable them to commence a regular trade...prudence requires that the amount should not be left undefined, and I am requested to name the sum of £10 as a limit which, whether for tools, or for iron, or for lumber, or for leather, or...should not, in the case of any one boy, be exceeded...

55.   10 June 1842 NEC Report: Nelles
So few boys have as yet gone out from this Institution, and those few have been so short a time away, that we can hardly judge of their success among their own people.

I am most anxious that they should follow, in their respective neighbourhoods, the arts they have learned at the Institution, and...nothing shall be wanting on my part to encourage the youths who have been instructed here, in habits of industry, sobriety, and religion. The assistance which the Company is willing to afford them will be very important in establishing them in their trades when they return home.

56.   27 June 1842 NEC Report: Richardson
I am glad to perceive that the Company have authorized the expenditure of money in establishing the boys who have left, or may hereafter leave the Institute, after having become perfect in their trades. One of the two boys who left some little time ago, John Obey, evinces a disposition to profit by the opportunities he has had, and is preparing to carry on the wheelwright trade at the Tuscarora Village in which he must receive every encouragement and assistance connected with his trade; a blacksmith is necessary, and Baptiste Gibson is progressing towards perfection. William English, I am sorry to say is not possessed of the same spirit of emulation as John Obey, and unless he can be removed from the same immediate neighbourhood of his family, he will do little good.

57.   24 January 1843 NEC Report: Nelles
...the Institute continues much as when I last wrote about it; what I have most to regret is that we are not able to receive into it all the children who apply for admittance; there are in it, at present, 25 boys and 11 girls...Two boys, who had been instructed in shoe making, left the Institute at Christmas being furnished with tools and leather.

58.   22 May 1843 NEC Report: Richardson
The advantages of variety of instruction combined, are observable to a most pleasing extent in John Obey, who, since his departure from the Institute, has erected a workshop, in which he employs his time in the manufacture of waggons, sleighs, tables, bedsteads, chests, etc. William English, who was taught the trade of cabinet making, is not doing so well, but it may be that his disposition to idleness is more inherent than in the case of Obey, who always evinced stronger efforts than English to attain a proficiency. The two lads, Baptiste Gibson and William Joseph, apprentices to the blacksmith trade, are progressing in a most satisfactory manner, affording a reasonable expectation that they will cooperate with Obey in the manufacture of waggons and sleighs, and in making themselves generally useful in the branches appertaining to their trade. Of the several boys who are being taught shoemaking, a brother of John Obey promises to become a master of the trade, and, if industrious after leaving the Institute must necessarily benefit not only himself, but his friends, who are respectable and industrious people. One of the boys, Joseph Lutbridge, has been for some time

labouring under the disease of scrofula, and, as little prospect appeared of a cure, we acceded to the proposal of his friends to remove him, and he departed last week. It is possible he may recover under the effects of herbs made use of by the Indians, and, if so, he will be readmitted, if his friends desire it, but he is now almost perfect in shoe-making, and may prosecute the trade at home, and to enable him to do so, he will be supplied with tools and materials.

59. 3 August 1843 NEC Report
...the land of the Mohawk Institute was granted to the Company...as per Richardson's petition.

60. 17 August 1843 NEC Report: Nelles
The Institute is doing well. Several children of Pagan parents have been admitted.

61. 10 January 1844 NEC Report: Richardson
There are now three apprentices, two in the carpenter's and one in the blacksmith's shop, who will shortly be advanced sufficiently to admit of their leaving the Institute, but until it is known where the principal settlement of the Indians will be, it would not be advisable to permit them to leave; when the period, however, does arrive, it will be advisable to erect a suitable building, in which the two trades of waggon-making and blacksmithing can be carried on, and I shall look with much anxiety to the hope that they will prosecute their respective trades with energy.

62. 22 February 1844 NEC Report: Nelles
Of those who have left the Institution...two have erected...frame houses for their parents. John Obey, who, both before and since his leaving the Institute has conducted himself with great propriety, was doing very well, and...making considerable profit by his trade until this winter, when it pleased God to afflict him very severely with sickness; he has been confined to his house for several months, but is rather better now, and I trust he may be restored to health. William English left the Institute about the same time...but I quite despaired of ever seeing him turn to any good account the education he had received, as he was for some time very idle and careless, but he has become much more industrious, and works a good deal at his trade. I think all who have learned trades work a portion of their time at them. Though some may appear to adopt the indolent careless habits of their friends when they return home I feel sure the instruction they receive will be a benefit to them when those, perhaps, who have assisted in imparting it will not be here to observe it. I think we should not estimate the advantages conveyed to the Indians by any immediate good which may be visible, but by the influence beneficial, we must hope, which will be exerted upon the

brethren by those who are trained upon habits of regularity, industry, and piety...nothing would do more towards improving the condition of these people than an establishment such as the Institute, could it be conducted on a larger scale, and have a farm attached to it, its usefulness would be greatly magnified. The number of children in the Institute is 43, and seven day scholars...

63. 10 June 1844 Six Nations Indians to NEC
Henry Brant and 40 Chiefs Onondaga Council Fire
We, the Chiefs, Sachems and Warriors of the Six Nations of Indians...would feel themselves destitute of gratitude, if they did not, upon all ocassions, express, in the warmest manner, their sense of the many advantages which they have derived from the firm, unsolicited and untiring zeal with which your Society have uniformly advocated and maintained the cause of the poor Indians...lands comprising the Eagle's nest and Ox Bow...have been reserved and set apart by the Government...that those of our youth who are educated at your Institute, may hereafter, upon their assimilating themselves to the habits of the whites, receive each a farm for their good conduct...The Chiefs are now anxious that 300 acres of the flats, in front of your Institute may be set apart for a farm...that their youth...may be taught agriculture. We wish the land to be held by the same tenure that the Society hold their other lands...

64. 19 July 1844 NEC Report
[Nelles]...The Six Nation Indians had surrendered to the Government, all their lands except 20,000 acres...in January 1841...no compulsory measures would be taken to remove the Indians from the North side of the river, but they must go...the mechanics institution might remain where it is; it would be desirable that more land should be attached to it, in the cultivation of which the children might be employed...With respect to the Company exercising any control over the Indian funds, I think the Indians themselves would have a good deal to say about their own funds, and would not like other persons to interfere, particularly the Pagan Indians, who do not approve of the Company's plans for civilization...The Indians generally can manage their own affairs; they might perhaps make a better use of their money themselves, than agents appointed to act for them. The mechanics' institution has increased from 14 (1838) to 20, and from 20 to 40 boarders, (July, 1840). With a view to retrenchment, Mr. Nelles thinks that one carpenter, the cabinet maker...might be dispensed with.

65. 23 July 1844 NEC Report
...Indian children leaving the Institution do not usually seek employment amongst white people; Mr. Nelles has discouraged it, thinking it better they should turn their attention to agriculture, amongst their own people.

66.   23 July 1844 NEC Report: Nelles

The Mohawk Institution was opened as a boarding school, with fourteen children, in 1835 or 36;   this was the number at the school in 1837, when I was placed in charge of the Mohawk station;   the number was increased to twenty in 1838, by the addition of six girls;   and in 1840, the Company allowed the number to be increased to forty: since that time, there have been between forty and fifty children in constant attendance;   of those who were first admitted into the institution, some were very young, - others were too old to receive much benefit, and after remaining for some time, they left it, and others were taken in their place.

The children that have left the institution, so far as I can recollect, are the following. -

---Norton, who did not remain long, but is a very sober and industrious young man.

Isaac Doxtator, remained until he had acquired a tolerable fair knowledge of the blacksmith's trade, but in consequence of his bad conduct at the school he was dismissed;   he has not followed his trade since, and is intemperate.

Jacob Johnson, was dismissed on account of an infirmity which rendered him a disagreeable companion for the other children;   he is a steady well-behaved young man.

William English, remained at the institution until he learned the trade of a carpenter;   on his return home, he appeared idle, he has improved much since he married, and now works at his trade;   he has done a great deal towards finishing a frame house for his father - he promises well.

John Thomas, learned the trade of a wheelwright;   on his return home he immediately commenced working at his trade. I have no doubt he would become a respectable mechanic, had he not been laid up during the greater part of the last winter with a severe attack of rheumatism;   he is now getting better: he is one of our most promising young men.

John Hill, Sen., learned the trade of a shoemaker;   he works occasionally at his trade, at other times on land, for his mother, who is a widow.

John Staats, learned the shoemakers' trade.   I do not think he has worked much at his trade since he left the institution, but he is a very industrious lad, and works very well on his father's farm, who is one of the most industrious Indians we have;   he has cleared upwards of thirty acres on the South side of the river.

Nelson Hess, did not remain long;   he learned the carpenters' trade, partially, - he is idle.

Hannah Green, was not very long at the institution;   she is a very exemplary young woman, and does a great deal of needlework, for sale.

Ann John, left the institution well instructed in housewifery, but...married badly, and is not doing well.

Christian Hill, had the same advantages with the above Ann John, but is making a much better use of them;   she lives with her mother, who is a widow, and is a very good girl.

Ellen Smith, has only left the institution a short time;   she is the best educated of any of the girls we have had, and promises to do well.

Nancy Green, was taken away by her parents, to be sent to an institution which the baptists promised the Indians: I believe she has since married a black man.

Catherine John, Betsy Tunis, John John Bearfoot. - I have not had an opportunity of knowing how they go on, as they reside far down the river...there are several who will leave the institution this year;   and every year some will go out and make room for others.

The institution may now be said to be only fairly in operation;   and the benefits, which we may hope it is likely to confer on the Indians, just commencing.   All who remain sufficiently long, receive a common English education: the boys are instructed in figures, sufficiently to enable them to keep accounts, and transact any business which their situation and calling may render necessary. Though some of the boys do not apply themselves to their trade immediately on their return home, I have no doubt, but in most instances, they will, at some future time, shew the advantages of the education they have received.

67.   1 October 1844 NEC Report

Mr. Nelles thinks the services of the cabinet maker at the Institution may be dispensed with;   the age of the eldest apprentice to the wheelwright is about 20, he would not have sufficient influence to fill up the place of that mechanic.   The £125 salary of the blacksmith is high; another blacksmith might be procured for £100 a year;   the blacksmith has been in the Company's service for four or five years.   The collections should be more;   very long credit is given in our country;   there are a good many waggons on hand;   it is a great pity the number of children at the institution is not greater, - the boarding of the children is the least expense...On the south side of the river there would be greater difficulty in disposing of the articles manufactured at the Institution, - it would be necessary to have a market at Brantford...Mrs. Hay was a very excellent person;   Mrs. George Richardson, I thought, would not be equal to the instruction of the children and to the housekeeping.   Some of the girls who have left the Institution would be equal to assist as seamstresses. Peter Smith, the interpreter, employs Indian boys on his farm.   There would be risk in letting boys loose from the institution to attend to agricultural pursuits. I do not think the Indians leaving the institution would devote themselves exclusively to following their trades, they would cultivate their lands also.

68. Commissioners' Report

Among the evidences of their desire for advancement is ...their eagerness to obtain admission for their children into the Boarding School of the New England Company at the Mohawk Village, near Brantford. A few years ago, there was difficulty in procuring Scholars for this School; now there are fifty applications, in addition to the fifty already there.

Besides the Boarding School...in which the scholars are taught handicrafts, and are instructed...upon the system adopted in Schools for Whites of industry...The mode of teaching is the same as that among Common Schools for the Whites, and the Text-Books...are those recommended by the Provincial Board of Education, videlicet: - the Bible, Mavor's Spelling Book, English Reader, Daboll's Arithmetic, Murray's Grammar and a Geography. The instruction is carried on altogether in English. The children show as much aptitude in acquiring knowledge as the Whites. At the New England Company's School fifteen boys are under instruction in the several trades of Waggon-maker, Blacksmith, Carpenter and Shoe-maker. The girls, (twelve in number,) are taught House-keeping, Needle-work, Spinning and Knitting.

69. NEC Report

In the year 1844...the boarding school at the Mechanic's Institute...numbered between 40 and 50 children, boys and girls, and there were many instances of Indian youths who, on leaving the Institute, and being supplied with tools and materials for work, followed their respective trades with considerable success among their own people

70. NEC Report

In consequence of the decease of the Superintendent of the Institution, the Company sent out Mr. Richard Edward Clark, in 1846, as Superintendent, and on the death of the lay-agent (William Richardson), in 1847, this office also was in 1848 conferred on Mr. Clark at a salary of £150 a year, on the understanding that he should instruct the boys in the Institution in the art and practice of agriculture, and should superintend the farming operations, the Company having resolved to instruct the Indians in agriculture, in addition to giving them a good English education, and teaching them mechanical trades.

In December, 1848, the Company, on the recommendation of Mr. Clark, allowed the carpenter and blacksmith to take the Company's workshops at the Institution for a year at a small rent, on condition of each of them teaching four boys his trade.

Illness in a few years obliged Mr. Clark to resign first one and then the other of his offices, and the lay agency was thenceforth in abeyance.

The Institution which had prospered at first, became for a time in a less satisfactory state...

In February, 1852, the Company recommended that the elder boys at the Institution should not be wholly removed from the school to the workshops, but engaged part of their time in each.

In July, 1853, Mr. Nelles wrote that there were about 40 adults residing in the mission, who had been brought up at the Institution; the greater number married, and settled on land which they cultivated, and some followed the trades they had been taught at the Institute. More commodious buildings were necessary for extending the Institution, as the Company agreed with Mr. Nelles in desiring to do.

In August, 1856, Mr. Nelles reported that the Institution building was in very bad repair, and recommended that a new and larger building should be erected, and the old building converted into workshops. Accordingly the Company erected a new building in a better position on the ten-acre lot, near the Mohawk parsonage, to accommodate a larger number of children, as well as the master and mistress.

The new building was completed and occupied in April, 1858. In September, 1858, Mr. Nelles wrote that he had increased the number of pupils to fifty-five, and would probably make it sixty, which would be as many as the building would accommodate without some additions.

In June, 1859, a Government license was received for occupying the 200-acre lot, so long as the Company kept up a manual labour school for the use of the Six Nations Indians. Both Mr. Nelles and Mr. Elliot reported the progress of the children to be much more satisfactory in the Institution than in the day schools.

71. 1859 NEC Report

...an application from Mr. Nelles...for permission to increase the number of children at the new Institution to 60...the Company...cheerfully acceded to Mr Nelles's recommendation...

72. 9 February 1859 NEC Report: Nelles

...It is satisfactory to observe an increasing desire on the part of the Indians to have their children educated...This improved state of feeling among the Indians is probably chiefly brought about by the influence of those who have been educated at the Company's schools, of whom four are now engaged as School Teachers, five as Catechists, besides many others who render much useful assistance both to Mr. Eliot and myself, by their advice and example. There are still many drawbacks to the advancement of the Indians in civilized pursuits and habits ...we...expect that a constant though gradual improvement will continue to take place among these people.

73. 14 June 1859 NEC Report: Nelles, Elliot

There is a great difficulty in securing regular attendance at the day schools; but at the New England Company's Institution, where the children are boarded and educated, their progress in learning is much more satisfactory. Four of the school teachers at present employed are Indians, who have been educated at this Institution; and another, through the liberality of the Company is pursuing his studies with a view to entering the ministry.

74. **30 June 1859 Institution Report [see p.215]**
...The School opens precisely at 9 a.m. with prayer. We dine at a quarter past 12, and are again in the school-room at 1 p.m. The school closes with scripture-reading, catechism, and prayer, at 4 p.m.

75. **31 December 1859 Institution Report [see p.216]**
...They sing and read in the English language with tolerable ease and freedom; but it is a difficult thing to induce them to practise English among themselves when alone. They generally read and speak English in an under voice, requiring much patience and great attention on the teacher's part...

76. **3 August 1859 NEC Report: Nelles**
On the 25th June I received...a Licence of Occupation of the Farm intended by the Indians to be attached to the Mohawk Institute...I had...previously taken possession of a portion of the land, and have some very promising crops upon it, -turnips, potatoes and spring wheat, - and also have a field of 20 acres now preparing for fall wheat...when we have the farm properly in use, we will be able to raise a large proportion of the provisions used at the Institution. But in the mean time a considerable outlay must be made to render it at all available. By long neglect the place is greatly out of repair, the fences that are upon it are bad, and much of the land has never been fenced at all...I have purchased some materials for fencing; much more is needed...A barn is also needed...For...fencing and stocking the farm, £200 at least will be required...

77. **20 September 1859 NEC Report: Treasurer to Nelles**
...I am authorised to advance £200...or such part thereof as...necessary to 'fence and stock the farm'...

78. **January 1860 NEC Report: Nelles to Treasurer:**
That the number of children at the Mohawk Institution during the last half-year has been more than we have ever had before, being 62; at the same time the expenses have not been more than usual, on account of our having produced on the farm a portion of the provisions used; and I have no doubt that when the farm shall be got into good order we will be able to maintain the present number, and perhaps increase it, without any additional grant from the Company.

During the last summer the articles produced on the farm were 1,000 bushels of potatoes, and as many turnips, besides other vegetables, upwards of 200 bushels of wheat, and about 200 bushels of oats and pease. The girls have made all the socks used, and spun yarn to make 150 yards of cloth...

79. **12 July 1860 NEC Report: O'Meara**
...I went through the rooms, both of the male and female departments, and was very much pleased with the order and neatness of everything about them. I had an opportunity also of examining the pupils with reference to their general progress, under the care of the excellent schoolmaster...and have to report that it was very satisfactory. I was particularly struck with their proficiency in arithmetic, which is a branch of knowledge that more than any other is calculated to test the degree of mental improvement which the Indians had attained.

The buildings appear to me to be very commodious and suitable for the purpose for which they are intended; but I think that a good-sized school-house close to the building, is much needed - the one that is at present in use being that belonging to the old institution, and at a considerable distance from the new building. Much benefit is likely to result from the acquisition of the farm...The land is good, and its produce will enable the Company to maintain many more children, with the same outlay, than would otherwise have been possible; and at the same time a means of practical instruction will be furnished in the branch of industrial education most needed by the Indians...I was much gratified by seeing on the farm a fifteen acre field of full wheat, which was far superior...to any that I had seen...till I arrived at the institution...Mr. Nelles has exercised a wise discretion in discontinuing the other branches of industrial education... The instruction in the trades...discontinued would...benefit the individual to whom it was imparted, but would produce no effect on the Indians as a community...as employment in them would only be furnished in the more populous towns of the white settlement, at a distance from the habitations of their Indian friends.
...I accompanied Mr. Nelles to a distant settlement of Indians...in the carriage with us was one of the young men who are being educated at the institution, with whom I was very much pleased...This young man remains at the institution the greater part of his time; but as he has a widowed mother and her family to support, he goes home occasionally to till his farm in the wilderness, on which they almost entirely depend for subsistence...I was much pleased to see the order in which he had his fields, which showed that, even while receiving instruction, he was applying to the most practical purpose the knowledge that was being communicated to him, and the habits of industry in which he was being trained.

I visited and examined several of the day-schools...I was struck with the difference between the schools which are taught by Indian-speaking masters, and those the teachers of which do not understand the language of their pupils. In the former the pupils evidently understood what they were learning, so as to be able to give an intelligent account in their own language of the lesson that they were reading or learning in English; which was by no means the case in those of which the masters and pupils had no common medium of communication.

80. 13 August 1860 NEC Report: Nelles
...I...am convinced that the most, if not the only effectual way of imparting a useful education is by taking the children entirely under our own control, as is done at the Mohawk Institution; and therefore I hope the Company will not think me unreasonable in indulging the hope that I may see the Institution enlarged so as to accommodate a much larger number of children...An addition to the present building would be necessary before any great increase in the number of children could take place...With respect to the application of the Munsey Indians to have some of the children received into the Mohawk Institution, I do not think that with our present accommodation it would be expedient to take more from a distance than we now have; but if the establishment could be enlarged so as to enable us to take the greater number of pupils, I am of opinion that it would be attended with the best results to admit a limited number of children from among those tribes who have not the advantages of education at home, and I should be glad to see the privilege extended to others as well as to the Munsey Indians...At the earnest solicitations of the Indians and their missionary, I have been induced to take a few children from a distance, and at the present time I have five from Munsey Town...

81. 29 October 1860 NEC Report: Treasurer to Nelles
...The Committee agrees with you in thinking it extremely desirable to extend the Institution. I...regret..that the want of funds must prevent our carrying out the plan...for the present. A large sum has lately been expended on the building; the consequent increased accommodation has added considerably to the annual expense...

82. January 1861 NEC Report: Nelles to Treasurer
...the expenditure for the last half-year, notwithstanding some unusual extras, has been considerably less than usual; the reduction has been chiefly in the account for boarding, occasioned by the farm having produced much of the provisions used...The Mohawk Institution has never been in more efficient operation than it is at present. During the past year ten of the oldest pupils left it, most of them sufficiently instructed to transact any ordinary business...I enclose two notes received from Indians. Isaac Powless, the writer of one of them, was educated chiefly at it; after he left it, he was sent for a short time, at the expense of the Company, to a White School, and is, perhaps, the best educated Indian we have; he is married, and is a prosperous farmer. The other, Isaac Barefoot, has been, so far, entirely educated at the Mohawk Institute. He has been employed for some time in teaching one of our schools, but at present is at the Normal School in Toronto, where I have sent him to be better qualified for a School Teacher. Many others who left the Institution are his equals in attainments, and I have satisfaction in being able to say they are generally

exemplary in their conduct.
...I regret...that it is not at present convenient for the Company to extend the Institution...by an outlay of £350 or £400 in building, the number of children could be increased to eighty, or perhaps more, with very little, if any additional annual expense to the Company...

83. 19 December 1860 Isaac Powless to Nelles
I received a note from you in July last, informing me that you cannot promise to continue that allowance which you have been giving to me, but at the same time you would not like to lose my services, so far as would not interfere with my other duties. Common courtesy and my respect for you compel me to reply to your note in writing, which I have till now neglected. I may say that I never asked it of you from the first, and your withdrawing it now has not in the least weaken* my attachment to do or to perform the duties which you have thought proper to impose upon me, - on the contrary, I feel thankful for the opportunity I have of doing good in the position I am placed by the mercy of God. I am not unmindful of the many privileges which I have received in my early days, and I do feel it to be my duty to set forth those privileges which I have enjoyed by doing all the good I can towards my fellowmen in my own humble way.

I trust, therefore, Rev. Sir, that you will not consider as imposing any severe burden upon me, when you allow me to go on with those duties I have been doing for nothing; for I do not think that I am making any sacrifice, for the reason above stated.

I might say more to the same effect; but enough has been said, I think, to show the principle and the motive upon which I act.

84. 14 January 1861 Barefoot to Nelles
...I arrived safely in Toronto on Thursday last. In the following afternoon I presented my application to the several Officers of the Department, and obtained admission without undergoing an examination into the Senior or First Division. It was not my intention to have entered into that Division; however, I shall try it for a few weeks or so, and ascertain whether my circumstances will permit me to keep pace with my fellow-students, and if so, I shall continue in it; but if I find it trespassing beyond the limits of my circumstances or abilities, I shall come down into the Junior or Second Division.

I hope you are all well, and I shall be very happy to receive your favour by a response when time and convenience shall permit you. I am thankful to say I am in good health for the time being...We shall begin business to-morrow, and I sincerely trust that the Supreme Being...may in His infinite goodness bestow a blessing upon my efforts...in propagating civilization and enlightenment amongst my fellow country people.

85. 3 April 1861 NEC Report: Treasurer to Nelles

...it is very satisfactory to learn that the farm has contributed many articles required at the Institution; I sincerely trust that the assistance to our income may continue. It shows that the farm is working satisfactorily, and reduces the additional expenditure caused by the enlarged Institution.

I need not call your attention to an economical management, and feel sure it will suffice to mention that the increase in the expenditure is already rather more than the Company contemplated...

86. 14 May 1861 NEC Report: Nelles to Treasurer

You may rely upon the strictest attention being paid to your suggestions on the subject of economy, so far as the efficiency of our Establishment will allow.

87. NEC Report

In January, 1862, Mr. Nelles reported that there were sixty-five children in the Institution during the preceding half-year.

In August, 1863, Mr. Nelles again recommended the enlargement of the Institution, and in the December following he was requested to furnish the Company with a sketch of the ground floor, showing the proposed addition to the building...the following April the Company authorized the proposed addition to the building, which it was stated would then accommodate 100 children...

In 1864, Mr. Nelles and, at his request, his then Assistant Missionary, Rev. Robert James Roberts, bore testimony to the great usefulness of the Institution, and the desire of young Indian fathers and mothers to place their children where they had themselves been educated.

The Company, in 1864, bought thirty-two acres adjoining the Institution.

Mr. Nelles informed the Company, in August, 1865, that the addition to the Institution building was completed, and in the October following he wrote that he had admitted ten new pupils to the Institution, making the total number there seventy.

In February, 1866, Mr. Nelles recommended that the number of pupils should be increased to eighty; in June following the Company gave their sanction to this addition, and in March, 1867, Mr. Nelles wrote that since the summer vacation there had been eighty pupils at the Institution.

In the year 1867, three of the most promising boys boarding at the Institution, attended the Grammar School at Brantford at an expense of 1 dollar each per month, to be taught the higher branches of education. One young Indian, John Jacobs, who had acted as a schoolmaster among Indians, became a student in Huron College, to prepare for the ministry. The original grant for John Jacobs as a college student in the year 1867, was 50 dollars per annum for three years; this grant was afterwards increased at the recommendation of the Bishop, to £50 per annum for three years, from 1st July, 1868.

In November, 1867, Mr. Nelles wrote that the Institution could conveniently accommodate ten more pupils, and might be made to accommodate twenty more. In June 1868, the Company sanctioned the admission of ten new pupils, and in the following August Mr. Nelles wrote that the children would shortly return to the Institution, after a short vacation, and that he would then complete the number of pupils to ninety, as authorized. In October, 1868, Mr. Nelles recommended the increase of the salary of Mr. Bouslaugh and wife (the superintendent and matron at the Institution) from 320 dollars to 400 dollars a year, and in April, 1869, received instructions to pay them the increased amount.

88. 1868 NEC Report [see p.217]

...attendance at the day schools and good conduct there a *sine qua non* before admittance to the Institution, which is much sought for by the Indians. At present most of the children are quite ignorant, many even of English, when they enter the Institution, and therefore Mr. Nelles likes to keep them there for five years, a much longer time than would be necessary if they had been efficiently taught in the day schools, when perhaps half that time would suffice; and therefore, double the number of children could be educated in the period of five years, without enlarging the present building. Besides, it is to the day schools that the education of the greater part of the Indians must be entrusted, so their efficiency is very important. The best and cheapest teachers for them would be Indians brought up at the Institution; and perhaps sent afterwards for a year to a good school for teachers, like the Normal School in Toronto.

...Boys School...The Boys of this Class are making a great effort to master the English Language by denying themselves the use of their own language.

...The greater number of Boys in this class understand but little English, but like the other Boys, they promise to give up talking Indian, till they have learnt to speak English with more ease and fluency.

These Girls, like the little Boys, are at present scrupulously avoiding the Indian Language, in order to learn English. Both Boys and girls talk more English among themselves than they ever did before...

The expenditure of the Mohawk Institution for 1868 amounted to £729, of which £426 were laid out in the boarding account, and £189 in the clothing account.

89. Autumn 1868 NEC Report:Lister

We entered first the boy's school-room, where there were about forty children, all healthy looking, and evidently half of them of mixed blood. The boys read with tolerable mechanical correctness, but most of them did not seem to wish to ask the meanings of words they did not understand. With one or two exceptions they never read after leaving school, but then they are not tempted at the Institute to do so by entertaining story books. About 10 boys did sums in reduction fairly well, but nearly all had to be told the rule first. The present set of boys are rather young; however, 13 left the school last year, with a thorough knowledge of arithmetic, at least up to the rule of three and decimals.

The dormitories seemed very clean and well ventilated, but there were only 16 beds for 37 boys so some contained three boys apiece. The girls were at dinner when I went to their side of the house. The meal consisted of a kind of Irish stew of very fine potatoes, meal, scraps of meat and bread. The drink was water; meat is given three times a week...the girls schoolroom and found there about 40 children and the teacher who seemed to manage them well. The girls were certainly more advanced than the boys, 8 of them read quite correctly and did difficult sums in compound division and subtraction.

90. 25 February 1869 NEC Report

...Lister...visited the Institution, and found it on the whole very well managed...he recommended that pupils for admission to the Institution should be chosen from the regular attendants at the day schools on the Reserve, and that the instruction given at the day schools should be improved, so that pupils going from these schools to the Institution need not remain there so long as at present. He also recommended that each pupil should have a separate bed. Accordingly Mr. Nelles was in June, 1869, authorized to provide a sufficient number of iron bedsteads to allow every pupil to have a separate bed.

91. 12 May 1869 NEC Report: Nelles

I concur in Mr. Lister's opinion as to admitting children to the Institution, and have acted in accordance with it when practicable, but I have often deemed it expedient to act otherwise, as in the case of the children of Pagan parents; and in localities where there is no school, I admit from time to time at the Institution children without previous instruction.

92. 5 June 1869 NEC Report: Nelles

Mr. and Mrs. Bouslaugh...thank the New England Company for...increasing their income...it is well deserved.

"It is scarcely correct "that most of the children when they enter the Mohawk Institution are quite ignorant," but it is true that many of them on their entrance are even unacquainted with English. One of the principal objects of the Institution is to teach them English, which is not their mother tongue. Yet...not a few children have been admitted here for instruction, able to speak English as well as many English children themselves. My rule as to

admission at the Institution...has always been that the children must have some previous instruction before their entrance. But my study has ever been for the benefit of the Indians in general...I have often deemed it expedient to deviate from my rule, and admit ignorant and even heathen children, and have never regretted doing so.

93. 30 June 1869 NEC Report

...Thomas Griffith, teacher...reported...for the half year ending the 30th of June 1869, there were in that seminary 47 male pupils and 42 female pupils, altogether 89.

In the male department, the ages of the head class were, one pupil, 19, and two pupils, each 15 years old. These three scholars had gone through a course of arithmetic as far as cube root, as well as courses of algebra, book-keeping etc.

The ages of the second class consisted of one pupil of 20, two of 18 and one of 17 years old; these youths had been learning the fifth book, English history, grammar, geography, and arithmetic as far as compound proportion and fractions.

There were 13 male pupils in the third class, their respective ages varied from 12 to 18, and their subjects of instruction comprised the fourth book, second lesson, grammar as far as the conjugation of the verb; arithmetic to compound rules and fractions, geography, the Catechism and Testament reading.

Seven pupils were in the fourth class; their ages varied from 12 to 14 years, and they were learning the third book, page 20; arithmetic as far as compound addition, the Church catechism etc.

The fifth class included 14 pupils, of ages varying from 10 to 18. their subjects were spelling, reading in the second book, page 24; writing in large hand, learning multiplication table and simple Catechism, and ciphering as far as simple addition.

The sixth class, of six pupils, were reading the first book, page 20, and their ages varied from 9 to 12.

In the Girls' School there were 11 in the first class, of ages varying from 11 to 16. They were reviewing the Fifth Book of Lessons, reading English history, and studying geography and grammar; they learnt arithmetic as far as the compound rules and fractions, and the Explanatory Catechism; they read in the Testament, and learnt needlework, spinning etc.

The second girls' class comprised six pupils, of ages varying from 11 to 16. They read the Fourth book, page 281; learnt the first principles of grammar, arithmetic as far as the compound rules, and the Explanatory Catechism...read in the Testament and did needlework.

A third class of girls comprised 10 pupils, of ages varying from 10 to 16. They read in the Third book, page 50; learnt arithmetic as far as simple multiplication and division, and the Church Catechism; they also read in the Testament, and were instructed in needlework.

Eight female pupils were in the fourth class, of ages from 11 to 16. They were reading the Second book, page 91; they learnt arithmetic - simple addition, subtraction, and multiplication table; they also learnt Catechism, first steps, and were taught needlework.

The fifth class of girls included seven pupils, of ages...from 9 to 14. They were reading the First book, page 32, and were taught needlework.

94. 30 June 1869 NEC Report: Nelles

...in addition to the Johnsons, I have selected from the children of the Mohawk Institute, Susannah Carpenter and Nelles Monture to be sent to the Hellmuth Colleges. The former has been in the Institution for three or four years, and is a fair English scholar, and well acquainted with the Mohawk language; her age is fourteen years, she is the daughter of Joseph Carpenter, who has been interpreter in the church for many years, and is a man of excellent character. Monture is a Delaware, a boy of good ability and character, fifteen years of age...

In choosing children for a higher education, I would like to be informed whether I am to confine my selection to the children of Indian parents, or include the children of white men who are married to Indian women, and whether it shall be a necessary qualification that the child should speak the Indian language.

95. 3 July 1869 NEC Report: Treasurer to Nelles

...you and the Rev. A. Elliot advise the employment of an Indian at the Mohawk Institution, not only to teach English, but also to be an interpreter to the children; this the New England Company willingly accede to, and they are further desirous that the interpreter should be an assistant to you, and that he should receive a salary not exceeding £60 a year.

96. 30 August 1869 NEC Report: Nelles

I am much pleased to hear that the Company has acceded to our suggestion of employing an Indian teacher at the Mohawk Institution...the most Eligible person is Isaac Barefoot, a Mohawk Indian, who has taught one of the Company's schools for several years. He is a good scholar and a good teacher, having spent some time in the Normal School at Toronto...Isaac Barefoot was, in September 1869, appointed teacher in the Mohawk Institute with a salary of £60 per annum.

97. 23 November 1869 NEC Report

Nelles...suggested that a school-house should be built with two apartments, one for boys and one for girls, as he found more room required for the dormitories. The girls were each provided with a separate bed, but there was not room in the Institution to give each boy a separate bed. If a school-house were built, there would be ample room for at least a hundred beds.

98. 21 December 1869 NEC Report

The Special Committee...granted £60 to Canon Nelles towards building a new school-house.....

99. 31 December 1869 NEC Report

Barefoot...teacher in the girls' department...reports for the half year ending the 31st of December 1869...the upper class of girls (25) were reading the Third book in the new series, studying grammar and history, practising composition, writing and ciphering in simple interest weights and measures, simple division and subtraction.

A younger class of girls (8) are described by I. Barefoot as reading the Third book of the old series, page 10, studying Watt's Catechism, writing, and ciphering in simple division and subtraction.

Four girls are mentioned by Isaac Barefoot as reading the Third book, old series, page 10, studying Catechism, writing, and ciphering in simple rules.

One girl as reading the Second Book, page 6.

Three girls as reading the First book, old series, page 33. And four girls as reading the First book, old series, page 14.

In the report from Mr. Griffith for the half year ending the 31st of December 1869, the teacher remarks that in January 1867, a class of 17 or 18 boys, of this school, underwent a creditable examination in the presence of Mr. Gilkison, the local Indian Superintendent, and of some other gentlemen, who expressed themselves extremely well pleased with the boys' proficiency.

Alexander Smith, the first name on this class list, is the only one remaining in 1869 of the above-mentioned class, and he was afterwards away for above a year, but returned in the spring of 1869, and worked hard to prepare himself for the profession of a teacher. He is described by Mr. Griffith as "certainly a talented young man." He is now a teacher in a day school in the reserve. The others boys of the same class are reported by Mr. Griffith as "generally sober, steady, industrious young men, promising fairly to take their places in respectable society."

100. 6 January 1870 NEC Report: United States Consul

...the Indian school-house...is a plain, substantial three-storey building of brick, pleasantly situated on a farm...At the time of my visit the number of children in attendance, including both sexes, was eighty-two...None are admitted before the age of ten. The writing of several was very good, and their examinations in spelling were highly creditable. There is no attempt to confer more than a plain English education, but provision is made for consecutive advancements to higher schools, if the proficiency attained seems to justify them. The farmer of the establishment carefully instructs the boys in the work of the farm at all seasons of the year, taking a limited number with him into the fields and barns on all suitable occasions, and allotting specific work to each of them, subject to his inspection...

In addition to the common branches of education the girls are instructed in the ordinary household work of the farm...spinning and sewing by hand and on the machine. ...the influence exerted by the school has had a very beneficial influence on the farm and homes of these Indians.

...Here no attempt is now made to teach the mechanical arts, although at one time this was done. The project was not abandoned because the Indian youths manifested an insufficient aptitude for such acquirements; they preferred the independent life of farmers to that of confined and systematic mechanics.

101. 5 February 1870 NEC Report: Nelles

The expenses of this half year are more...on account of the addition of bedsteads and bedding for the institution, and also preparing the three Indian children for the Hellmuth Colleges, which was done with as much regard to economy as possible, Mrs Nelles having personally attended to getting the girls ready...the two girls (who made my house their home chiefly during their Christmas vacation) have made very creditable improvement during the short time they have been there...Ojibway Settlement...the school...under the charge of Isaiah Joseph, a Tuscarora Indian, who was educated at the Mohawk Institution, and is quite competent for the situation...

102. 19 March 1870 NEC Report: Treasurer to Nelles
...that the Company would be glad to hear of "the Manual Labour School", near him.

103. 9 April 1870 NEC Report: Nelles
...The number of children sanctioned by the Company, namely, ninety, is complete, and their improvement satisfactory. The health of the children generally has been good, but a case of measles has just appeared, and I fear it will spread through the school...There are applications from seven or eight young persons, both boys and girls, to be sent to superior schools.

104. 12 April 1870 NEC Report: Gilkison to Treasurer
...I had the gratification of being present last evening at your Institute, where the children, to the number of near ninety, were assembled in the boys' school-room...The children looked well and cheerful, singing the several hymns and songs with much harmony and effect...

105. 25 June 1870 NEC Report: Treasurer to Nelles
...asking who did duty on Sunday at the Mohawk Village Church, and who read the service to the pupils in the Mohawk Institution on Sunday?...requested some account of what is done in the 200 acres set apart for a "Manual Labour School," near the Mohawk Institution, and added that some time had elapsed since the Company had heard particulars of the "Manual Labour School for the Six Nations' youth."

106. 15 July 1870 NEC Report: Nelles
...there have been no services in the old Mohawk Church for some time; it is at present undergoing repairs, and when finished will be used on Sundays for the children at the institution. In my absence on Sundays, Mr. Griffith, the teacher, reads service for the children and lectures them; he is quite competent, having been a Scripture reader before he came to this country...the Manual Labour Farm...managed by Mr. Bouslaugh, who teaches the large boys general farming, the boys in turns assisting him in the work. Occasionally, and particularly in harvest time, other labourers have to be employed. The farm is now tolerably well stocked, and produces a considerable part of the provisions used in the establishment. Some of the young men who have left the institute were excellent ploughmen and had a fair knowledge of general farming,

which I consider of great importance to them when they return to the reserve.

107. NEC Report
In September, 1870, the Company's Commissioner, the Hon. A.E. Botsford, visited the Company's Missions on the Grand River...

108. December 1870 NEC Report: Botsford
...That the pupils to be admitted at the Mohawk Institution should be selected from the day-schools on the Reserve in proportion to the average attendance at each school respectively, according to proficiency and good conduct, the Chairman of the Board and the Missionary in charge of the school to hold a competitive examination for that purpose. This mode of selecting the applicants for admission to the Institution will prove a great incentive to the Indian parents to send their children regularly to the day-schools, and will render unnecessary so long an attendance at the Institution as five years, which is required if the pupils are not previously instructed in the elementary branches, and thus enable a greater number of Indian children to enjoy the advantages of the Institution, as a course of three years...would amply suffice.
...It is capable of accommodating ninety boarders, the superintendent and his wife. It is proposed to build a school-room attached to the main institution, sufficiently large to accommodate the boys on the first flat, and the girls to occupy the upper storey. This addition, if sanctioned by the Company, will afford room for one hundred pupils, as the present school-rooms can be appropriated for sleeping apartments; this arrangement will also relieve the present over-crowded dormitories. The estimate of the probable cost of this addition, Mr. Nelles informed me, is being prepared; I think it will not exceed one hundred and seventy-five pounds sterling. It is well worthy the favourable consideration of the Company. Every part of the Institution is kept in good order, and the pupils are neatly and comfortably clothed. The branches taught are spelling, reading, writing, arithmetic, grammar, geography, composition, and in a few instances, drawing.

The girls are taught, in addition to these studies, to sew, knit, wash, and do other housework. The Institution is well supplied with the Canadian series of school-books (old and new), Lovell's "General Geography", with maps and illustrations, blackboards, maps, and Sangster's "Elementary Arithmetic," designed for the use of Canadian schools.

Isaac Barefoot, a Mohawk, who was educated at the Institution, and afterwards passed through a course of instruction at the Normal School, Toronto, is the teacher and catechist of the girls department. He is a very methodical and intelligent instructor. There were thirty girls present, and some of the specimens of composition were very creditable. After I had examined the classes, we went into the small reception-room...furnished with a harmonium, and the girls sang a hymn with much skill.

I then examined the boys' department, which is taught by Thomas Griffith, who has been in the Company's employment nearly nineteen years, having previously taught a day-school on the Reserve, a most estimable man. The first classes passed a good examination in reading, spelling, arithmetic, and grammar. Mr. Griffith stated that some of his best scholars had not returned since the vacation. There were forty boys present, some of them rather too young to be admitted at the Institution, requiring to be taught the very first rudiments, thus occupying the time of the teacher which could be more profitably devoted to his other pupils. This objection applies to the girls' department, though not to the same extent, and will be removed if the suggestion I have previously made, of selecting from the day-schools, be adopted. There are on the registers forty-four boys, and forty-eight girls.

Mr. Griffith in his return makes the following interesting remarks, viz:- It is no uncommon question for visitors to ask me if Indian children have equal capabilities for receiving instruction as white children, and from a long experience I can only answer in the affirmative. The Indian language is the only hindrance to their improvement in English literature. When both whites and Indians are taught together at the same school, the white children seldom have much to boast of in advance of the Indian, and very often the Indians are superior. We have sent some of our boys to Brantford Common and Grammar Schools, from time to time, and every one of them was a credit to this Institution. Those who are at the Hellmuth College, London, at present, are remarkable for good behaviour and proficiency in their studies. It is true they are slow in getting along at first, but we should not expect too much of the children of the forest, who have everything to learn and a great many bad habits to get rid of. If they can only master the English language, all else that is learned by people generally comes very easy to them. There are many of them at present well taught, and it is reasonable to hope that the day is not far distant when they will be able to dispense altogether with the white man's help.

...Mr. Griffith performs the duty of Catechist to the pupils of the Institution; on Sundays reads the Church Service, and gives them religious instruction. As to the number of young Indians receiving assistance from the Company to enable them to complete their education...The Indian children...assisted by the New England Company in obtaining a superior education are Albert Anthony, at Huron College; Beverley Johnson and Nelles Monture, at Hellmuth College; Charlotte Johnson, Susannah Carpenter, and Jemima Maracle, at the Ladies' Hellmuth College; and George Hill, at a medical college at or near Belleville...

Mr. and Mrs. Nelles devote much of their time in superintending and watching over the interests of the Institution, and are both of them loved and respected by all the scholars, whose welfare and comfort are looked after by Mrs. Nelles as if they were members of her own family. She frequently has the girls at the parsonage, and to her example and teaching are mainly to be attributed the gentle and correct demeanour of the girls. I have only to add my testimony to that of others as to the excellent management of this Institution, and to the great benefit it has conferred on the Indian race.

The cost of keeping up the Institution for a year, including salaries, except that of the Rev. Canon Nelles, is about $5750, or $64, about thirteen pounds sterling, for each scholar; this includes boarding, clothing, as well as all other expenses, but does not show the product of the Manual Labour Farm used in the Institution. I have suggested to Mr. Nelles that he had better in future keep a farm account, showing the quantity of produce raised and how disposed of.

MANUAL LABOUR FARM

Consists of the 200 acre lot previously referred to, the Babcock lot, 33 acres, and about 20 acres of...the "Mohawk Mission" Glebe...and is farmed by the Superintendent Bouslaugh. Most of the land is under very good cultivation...Mr. Bouslaugh takes a certain number of the boys at the Institution to work on the farm in turn for a week or less at a time, as the exigency of the work may require; teaching them to plough, sow, make hay and other occupations of the farm. The boys have also a certain number of horses, cows, etc., to take care of when they are kept in the barn. This arrangement is so managed as not to interfere much with their studies while it is calculated to give them a fair knowledge of agricultural operations, and instil habits of industry.

There are several good barns and sheds on the farm, which are well filled with wheat, oats and peas. The products of the farm not consumed in the Institution are sold, and the proceeds credited to the fund appropriated to its maintenance. There is an old building on the Babcock lot which is rented. The old institute buildings near the Mohawk church have become dilapidated and entirely valueless, and should be pulled down, to prevent any vagrant person getting into them...the young Indians were formerly taught trades in these buildings, but this branch of instruction has for some time been abandoned; the result not seeming to justify the expense. The resident Indians on the Reserve did not employ the mechanics thus taught, and the few who followed their trade were employed as journeymen by the whites in...Brantford.

109. June 1871 NEC Report

The Committee...postponed till next year the consideration of the applications of George Powless, Isaiah Joseph, and Daniel Simon, who had been pupils at the Mohawk Institution, and were then teachers of schools in the Grand River Reserve, for aid in obtaining the education necessary to qualify them for the ministry of the Church of England, the Company not then having any funds available for the purpose.

110. 31 October 1871 Roberts Journal
Abraham Van Every, a Christian Onondaga...received some education at the Mohawk Institute; he has a good log house and a frame barn. His farm is well cultivated ...best farmer in his tribe...a wish to have his oldest girl sent to a higher school (now at Mohawk Institute)

111. 9 December 1871 NEC Report: Nelles
...the Bouslaughs left the Institution on the 1st October, partly on account of Mrs. Bouslaugh's health, but chiefly I believe with the prospect of improving their condition. Mr. and Mrs. Griffith are in charge at present, and I would recommend that they succeed the Bouslaughs if they wish to do so, and that a first-class male teacher be provided for the boys in place of Mr. Griffith. I think such an one may be secured for about £70...

On the 18th December, 1871, the Committee...expressed their approval of Mr. and Mrs. Griffith remaining in charge of the Institution as superintendents, for the present, and their opinion that the successor of Mr. Bouslaugh must be qualified to superintend not only the Mohawk Institution, but also the Manual Labour School, which the Committee wish to be kept up in a thoroughly efficient state.

The Committee also resolved and advised Canon Nelles that the admission of pupils to the Mohawk Institution should for the future be by selection made from the children attending the day schools on the Reserve, on the recommendation of the missionaries, and under competitive examination; and that the Company would determine the number of pupils to be admitted and the date of admission to the Institution; also the number of pupils to be selected from each school section, according to the quarterly reports of school attendance furnished by each missionary.

The Committee at the same time instructed Mr. C.J. Blomfield...to make inquiry and report as to the Manual Labour School and the instruction there given, stating whether in his opinion better instruction in working trades could be given to the boys in the Mohawk Institution; and to inquire and advise the Committee as to a fit and proper person for the appointment of Superintendent of the Institution and the Manual Labour School.

112. 5 February 1872 NEC Report
...Rev. James Chance...in which he thus expresses his views as to the past state of inefficiency of the Mohawk Institution, and the higher purposes which it should serve.
"I have nothing officially to do with the Mohawk

Institution; but as many of the children of this district are being taught there, I feel deeply interested in its welfare; and in my opinion (without intending to say anything which could be in any sense whatever considered derogatory to the present Chief Superintendent, who is so universally esteemed), it should be made to answer a higher purpose than it now accomplishes. The least-qualified teacher there should be equal to Mr. Barefoot, who holds a first-class certificate from the Normal School in Toronto; and the Institution should give, except in a few instances of rare talents, a finishing education to the children. There has been an undue demand for higher education, which I think has been too much encouraged, to the depreciation of the value of education on the Reserve and at the Mohawk Institution..."

The following letter from Isaac Barefoot, formerly a pupil and then a teacher at the Institution, was received February 19th, 1872:-

I beg to send you a copy of an address from the Indians to the Rev. A. Nelles. The Indians requested me to have it published, and a copy of the paper sent to you, and would have done so, but Mr. Nelles did not wish to have it published. The Rev. Canon Nelles is by no means anxious to have reported far and near every circumstance that occurs to show how highly he is esteemed by his people the Indians. It is on this account that his sterling worth and kindness to the Indians are not so much commented on by the public press.

Our Indian Hymn-book has been at length completed...I undertook the translation of the book most cheerfully, if by that means I can in some measure, however small, testify my gratitude to the New England Company for the incalculable benefits they have conferred upon me in educating me and making me what I am. I only trust that I may be enabled to spend and be spent in their service, and endeavour all I can to promote their praiseworthy work among my people.

The address referred to was as follows:-

Reverend and dear Father Nelles, -It is difficult for us sufficiently to express the pleasure which we feel in being enabled, by the goodness of God our Creator and Preserver, to meet you on this occasion; to see you in good health and spirits; and to wish you and Mrs Nelles, whom we have great reason to look upon as a mother to us and to our children who receive instruction at the Mohawk Institution, many happy returns of the approaching festival of the Nativity of our Lord...

It is pleasing to us to speak of the goodness of the New England Company to the people of the Six Nations, evinced by their continually extending to them the means of civilization and religion; and particularly of our lasting obligations to them for the munificent support of the Mohawk Institution, for the education of our children under your long-tried superintendency and management.

It is not a little gratifying to us to hear the kind friends of the Indians from distant parts say, when they occasionally visit the institution that in their opinion it is far superior to any other establishment for the education of the Indian children in America.

We feel assured that this prosperity is mainly owing to your love for our people, and the skill which you have acquired in the education of our children, by your long and constant residence among us; and it is delightful for us to infer that your exertions for our benefit are appreciated by the New England Company, from their employing you for so long a period as their chief missionary and agent...John S. Johnson, Chairman.

113.   1 March 1872 NEC Report: Nelles
Since I have been relieved from all duty on the Reserve, and my services confined to the Mohawk Institution, I beg to report that I visit that school almost daily, as does Mrs. Nelles also; and I hope, by devoting more time to it, to render it more efficient than it has hitherto been. I have divine service in the old Mohawk Church every Sunday morning, where, in addition to the children, about forty or fifty white people assemble. In the afternoon we have Sunday school in the Institution, Mrs Nelles taking charge of the girls...Mrs. Nelles takes the general supervision of the female department, and personally attends to purchasing all articles of clothing and directs the making of them.

At present the school is much interrupted by the scarlet fever, which...has broken out among the children at the institution. At first, I thought of closing the school; but the fear of spreading the disease among the Indians on the Reserve prevented me doing so. There have been about thirty cases; as yet none has proved fatal, and with two or three exceptions, all are getting better. Small-pox is also prevalent in the neighbourhood; but as the children have been vaccinated, I trust it will not get into the school. I have not seen or heard anything of Mr. Blomfield; I will be happy to afford him any information in my power when he comes.

114.   14 February 1872 NEC Report: Nelles
In my letter of the 15th instant, I omitted to inquire what I am to do with respect to a successor to Mr. Bouslaugh...I would also like to be informed whether the Company desire Mr. Griffith to take charge of the school again. I think it would be beneficial if a first-class teacher were employed. Mr. Griffith...is willing to retire, but, in consideration of his long services, would expect a small annuity or perhaps a year's salary.

115.   2 March 1872 NEC Report: Blomfield
...The accommodation appears insufficient for the number of pupils, and I can endorse the recommendation of Mr. Nelles, in which Mr. Roberts also concurs, that a school-house should be erected with room below for boys, and

above for girls, the cost of which will probably be about £200. The children (many of them) had only just recovered from scarlet fever, and I noticed that the building was insufficiently heated even for children in good health. The bedrooms were clean, but I cannot say that the rooms generally had any appearance of comfort. I had not an opportunity of giving an opinion on the food supplied. Both the boys and girls have obtained considerable proficiency in arithmetic, write fairly, and read tolerably easily, although not apparently with much understanding. There, however, their education seems to stop, and I am inclined to think that the children learn more at the common schools. Hardly any history or geography is taught at the Institution, and nothing approaching to an education has ever been given there. No daily religious instruction appears to be given, for I gave Mr. Nelles an opportunity of telling me if such were the case; from another quarter, however, I learnt that the Sunday school there is to be commended.

To my mind, the Company could not lay out its money to better advantage and satisfaction to both giver and recipient, than by raising the character of this institution, so that it shall become one of the recognized educational establishments of the province. I learn that the Company yearly expends a considerable sum of money in sending promising pupils to the first colleges in the province. The money that is devoted in this way would go far towards giving a higher education in the Institution. The evil of the present plan, as pointed out by Mr. Nelles, is, that the scholars return home unfitted for the life there, having mixed with educated and refined people. A good education among their own people would raise the young gradually and together to a higher scale of social life, and the next generation might in intelligence, education, and industry be fully on a par with the 'white' people; the Mohawk Institution might be made a lasting and noble testimonial to the philanthropy of the New England Society...

One first-class head master should...be appointed, who should have entire charge of the children and the Institution. Mr. Nelles has, I understand, practically been superintendent, and has catered for the children, but he would no doubt be gladly relieved of a responsibility which should properly be thrown on the head master, under instruction from the Company, and possibly some supervision on this side. There should, I consider, be a formal examination of the children twice a year, at which the other teachers should be invited to be present...

It appears very doubtful whether it would be judicious in the company to go to any considerable expense in teaching trades. The expenditure would be difficult to check, and the Indians do not often follow the trade to which they may have been trained. I would advise only the establishment of a carpenters' shop, as this will be useful in connection with the farm; and a knowledge of carpenters' work is useful to any man in this country. The Company might authorize instruction in some trade hereafter, if it can be shown to be advantageous to the children, and with a guarantee that it will not involve too great expense. The girls might be taught sewing, as now, and any other work of that nature which should cost the Company little or nothing...I would give any boy an opportunity of learning farming, provided it did not interfere with his education. But he can always gain some knowledge of this at his own home.

...On reference to your letter, I see the Manual Labour School mentioned as in existence. I could see or hear nothing of it further than that it had been tried at considerable expense with unsatisfactory results. I arrived at the conclusion that it had not been given a fair trial, and that money had not been used to the best advantage of the Company or those who should have derived benefit therefrom. In any case, however, I believe money required for such a purpose can be expended with far greater effect in giving a higher education, which Mr. Nelles is also anxious to see.

116. NEC Report

On receipt of this report...the Rev. Canon Nelles...was reminded that he had not furnished the Committee with any information in reference to the Manual Labour School, either as to the number of pupils receiving instruction, or as to the trades taught therein. The four missionaries at the Company's stations on the Grand River were requested to meet and confer upon the question whether the appointment of a Superintendent for the Mohawk Institution, in succession to Mr. Bouslaugh, was then necessary, and the measures to be adopted to render the Institution really efficient, and report to the Committee, collectively or individually, what they recommended to be done. Canon Nelles was informed that if Mr. Griffith retired from teaching the boys school at the Mohawk Institution, the Company would give him one year's salary as a gratuity. The Canon was also requested to inquire for a first-class certificated teacher from the Normal School at Toronto, to fill the situation of superintendent if required...Canon Nelles was also requested to inform the Committee in what manner the Manual Labour Farm, the Mohawk Mission School Lot, and the land bought of Babcock were then occupied, and to what uses they were devoted; and also as to the course of instruction given to the pupils at the Mohawk Institution in farming and in carpentering, and other trades, if any such were given, and in all other respects. The foregoing Report of Mr. C. J. Blomfield on the Mohawk Institution having been maturely considered...it was resolved "That, inasmuch as the wish of the Committee to render the Mohawk Institution thoroughly efficient might occasion a considerable increase of expenditure...the Committee requested the Auditors to

consider and report of the best means of providing for such probable increase of expenditure.

117. 13 March 1872 NEC Report: Roberts Journal

...visit...a young girl who appears to be dying of consumption...expressed a wish to have a book. She has been at the Mohawk Institute, and though young, she can read very well.

118. 2 April 1872 NEC Report: Clerk to Nelles

...to direct your attention to the Manual Labour School - our request, more than once repeated, for detailed information as to this school has not received your attention. I am to repeat the Committee's request that you will in your next inform them of the number of pupils who are receiving instruction, and the trades which each is being taught, and by whom.

...They will also thank you to report to them particulars of the course of instruction now given to the pupils at the Mohawk Institution in farming, and also in carpentering and other trades, if any be given, and in all other respects.

With respect to the Mohawk Institution, it would be uncandid not to mention to you that the information received by the Committee from all quarters has established in the minds of the Committee the fact that the Institution does not at present, and has not for some considerable time been productive of that amount of benefit to the Indian people which the Company has long been desirous it should afford. The Company very earnestly desires to raise its character, so that no pupil of Indian race need be sent to the higher schools and colleges of the Dominion for the completion of his education; they conceive it to be their duty to raise the Institution to this state of efficiency...

One question before your meeting will be whether a successor to Mr. Bouslaugh is necessary; if so, whether he should be a first-class certificated teacher from the Normal School at Toronto.

Should Mr. Griffith retire from teaching the boys' school at the Institution, the Company would be willing to give him a year's salary, as a gratuity...

119. 6 April 1872 NEC Report: Nelles

...With respect to Margaret Van Every, I have to inform you that she was not refused a longer continuance at the Mohawk Institution. Previous to the summer vacation she became very self willed and stubborn; so much so, that both the matron and teacher complained of her ill-conduct; and when she was spoken to by Mrs. Nelles, she said she did not intend to remain at the Institute, as Mr. Roberts had promised to send her to a better school. When the children returned to school, Margaret did not come back, and I supplied her place by taking her cousin. Some weeks after the school reopened, she came to see her sister, and then told the mistress that she was not coming back any more, as she was soon to be sent to college; how her father understood that she could not remain any longer I do not know. She was neither a good child nor a good learner.

When the pupils remain sufficiently long at the Institute, they receive an education which is quite adequate for the ordinary requirements of the Indians. At the same time I agree with the Committee in the desirability of making the Mohawk Institution more efficient...I think it very important that a schoolhouse should be erected separate from the main building; this would give additional sleeping compartments, which are much needed. I enclose an estimate of the probable expense of a brick building, to accommodate 100 children...

I very much regret that there should have been any mistake with respect to your communication of October 6th last. I did not understand that the Committee desired an immediate and special report, but that at the end of the half-year, as had been usual, I should give the information desired, which I trust you have received ere this. I may not have entered sufficiently into details, but I did not suppose the Committee would care to hear that once a week Mrs. Nelles and myself spend an evening with the children at the Institute; or how she spent about six weeks getting up two Christmas trees for their amusement; or that the girls from college spend their vacations chiefly at the parsonage, where their wardrobes undergo inspection and refitting or the many little difficulties among the children I am constantly called upon to settle.

In my last, I did not speak of the farm; at this season of the year very little can be done...that since Mr. Bouslaugh left in October last, I have had Robert Park engaged, as Mr. Griffith does not understand anything about farming. About thirty acres of land was put in with wheat last fall; in consequence of unusually dry weather, it was not possible to plough or prepare much land for spring crops, which will cause additional work to be done this spring. A good team of horses is much needed on the farm; the work for the last few years has been chiefly done by my teams...I enclose letters from the two Indian girls at Hellmuth College...

120. NEC Report

At the same time Canon Nelles sent an estimate of the cost of building a new school-house for the Mohawk Institution to accommodate 100 pupils...It amounted to 1390 dollars, or about £285.

On the 2nd April, 1872, the Committee wrote to the Rev. Jas. Chance...expressing...their entire agreement with him that the teaching at the Mohawk Institution should be of a much higher character than it had for some time been...the education given on the Reserve and at the Institution should be sufficient for all classes of Indian pupils, and that the practice of sending them to the highest

schools and colleges in the Dominion should as a general rule be discontinued; and that, for teachers, the Toronto Training School is the best preparation.

121. 16 April 1872 NEC Report: Blake

...my knowledge of the Indians generally is quite limited...in the main the education obtained at your schools and institutions is all that is really useful, but I do, at the same time, think that a higher education of suitable persons to be teachers and ministers among their own people is very desirable. I believe that those that have most experience in the work of missions, have found that native preachers are, almost without exception, the most successful, and more especially is this the case when English speaking ministers have to preach though an interpreter...it has been found that suitable native preachers can teach their own people better than any man who cannot speak their own language.

Levi Bomberry wishes to preach the Gospel to his countrymen. His talents for this work are much in advance of those of Indians generally; he is thought to be a very promising young man for this work. He has been offered a good salary for an Indian, viz $300 per annum, to act as an interpreter. This he has refused in order that he might fit himself to preach the Gospel to his countrymen.

At the school where Bomberry has been he is thought to be above the average of white pupils, and in character and spirit he is all that can be required.

P.S.Private: Had I time I would like to say something relating to the education of the Indians, especially on the Grand River...where I am most acquainted with them. I believe that if workshops were established, such as blacksmiths' shops, waggon-making, and other mechanical work, it would be of very great service to those people; many of those people are capable of learning trades that would be of great use to them. There should also be more attention paid to their agricultural education. The Company have a large farm which, if properly worked, which might be done with the labour of the pupils, and be of great service to them, would be a source of profit to the Company...I had better say but little about this matter, as I might come in contact with my good friend Mr. Nelles, who is probably doing his best for your interest.

122. 2 May 1872 NEC Report: A. Stewart

...Bomberry attended the Mohawk Institute...for four or five years, and the course at that school being limited and having been completed by him. He is still desirous of a higher education, which may fit him for becoming a useful teacher and preacher amongst his own people.

On making his acquaintance I became deeply interested in his welfare, and accordingly took upon myself to place him as a student in the Canadian Literary Institute...with the strong hope that your Company would kindly grant him the assistance asked for...

The benefit arising to himself will be the same as the benefit which...any man receives from having a thoroughly trained and well-educated mind. The benefit arising to his race generally will...be great...Our greatest hope respecting this work lies in selecting young men from the Indians themselves, who, being of the right spirit and receiving the advantages of an education, will be best capable of elevating their race, morally, intellectually, and spiritually. Bomberry gives evidence of being a man of the right stamp, and is moreover able to speak readily in five Indian dialects...such a person as Bomberry cannot obtain at these schools [Indian] (including the Mohawk Institute), even the literary training which he requires...

123. 8 May 1872 NEC Report: Barefoot to Treasurer

The Rev. Canon Nelles has conveyed to me the sentiments of the Company, which they very kindly express with reference to what I have done towards getting out an Indian Hymn-book for our people, which is very much needed. The Company may rest assured that I shall always cheerfully do all I can to further any means calculated to elevate the Indians in their temporal, social, and religious state. I hope I shall ever remember what the Company have so kindly done for me, and strive to show my gratitude to them by my conduct.

124. NEC Report: Deliberations of the Committee

...the best mode of rendering the Institution thoroughly efficient for the purpose of supplementing the education at the different day schools on the Reserve, and training the Indian youths of both sexes for useful employments in life, might be to send out from this country a lay Instructor at the Institution, if a suitable person could be found...One result of their individual inquiries was a private letter from Captain Brookes, the Superintendent of the Middlesex Industrial School at Feltham, to one of the members of the Committee, speaking highly of Mr. Robert Ashton, who had been since 1861, an efficient Schoolmaster, and was then acting as second Clerk at that Institution...he had had much experience as a schoolmaster, and had given instruction in the usual indoor studies, and also out of doors, in gardening, digging, etc., but not in carpentering, or other trades.

On the 13th May, 1872, the Committee informed Canon Nelles that they desired him to forward Monthly Reports of the proceedings at the Mohawk Institution and Station, and to render accounts of his receipts and payments for the Institution and the farm...

In January, 1872, the Committee had received...from Levi Bomberry...an application for assistance to obtain higher education...accompanied by applications from four of the chiefs, and from Mr. W. Watkins, Mayor of Brantford; the Hon Oliver Blake, Senator of Canada, and the Rev. Alexander Stewart, Superintendent of the Baptist

Churches and Congregations in the Reserve. This application, however, was not supported by the Rev. R. J. Roberts, on the ground of the health of the applicant and for other reasons. The Committee therefore did not entertain the application, but thought the opportunity favourable for obtaining from the gentlemen who had recommended it their general views on the subject of improving the education given at the Mohawk Institution, so as to supply all the wants of the Indians...

125. 16 May 1872 NEC Report: Nelles, Elliot, Chance, Roberts

...with reference to a successor to Mr. Bouslaugh...in our opinion it is necessary that one should be appointed. He should be a practical farmer, and married, so that his wife could take charge of the housekeeping department, and look after the general interests of the establishment.

Report of the Board of Missionaries...5th June 1872

1. Q.-What is the present number of pupils in the Mohawk Institution (male and female), and their ages?

A.- The number of the pupils...is 90 - 45 males and 45 females; the ages of the former range from 9 years to 20, and of the latter from 10 to 17. Some few have recently, for several reasons, gone away for a time on leave of absence.

2. Q.- Have they sufficient accommodation in point of lodging, warming, ventilation, and comfort, and have they all separate beds?

A.- The accommodation in point of lodging is not sufficient. The ventilation and heating are defective, and require improvement according to modern approved plans. A commodious room, which will fully serve all the purposes of an hospital for the sick, is much needed. They have separate beds.

3. Q.- Are they properly supplied with food, as to quantity and quality?

A.- The supply of food is abundant as to quantity, and good, comparatively, as to quality; much superior to Indian fare generally. However, if the Company's funds are adequate to an improvement in the boarding at the Institution, it would no doubt be acceptable.

4. Q.- What provision is made for their recreation and exercise?

A.- The boys and girls have their separate playgrounds, and certain hours in the day are set apart for recreation and exercise, which are occupied in playing at different games, according to the different tastes and predilections of the children, but no special gymnastics are provided.

5. Q.- Is the school-room accommodation sufficient and suitable divided for the several classes, and the supply of desks, forms, maps, books, etc., adequate?

A.- No. A new school-room, built, arranged, and furnished on some good modern plan is much needed. ...the rooms...now occupied for school purposes would be then available for sleeping accommodation. The supply of books and maps is adequate for present requirements.

6. Q.- What progress have the present pupils individually made in the different subjects in which they have been instructed? How many classes are there, and how many in each class?

A.- As no standard of education for admission into the Institution has been hitherto fixed, and since the proficiency of candidates has not been tested by an entrance examination, no accurate knowledge of individual progress can be ascertained beyond that conveyed by the reports supplied...by the teachers. By comparing...the attainments of the children at the Institution with those...attending the day schools, the former seem to have made favourable progress. In the boys' school there are five classes with a range of four to twelve in each class. In the girls' school there are seven classes, and a range from one to eleven in each.

7. Q.- In what respects is the education at the Mohawk Institution superior to that obtained in the day schools of the reserve?

A.- The education imparted...is superior to...the day schools in respect to its character and extent. The Institution professedly supplements the education given in the day schools, and by the advantage of boarding which it affords it secures that regular and punctual attendance so essential to satisfactory progress.

8. Q.- What religious instruction is given, and is it confined to the Sunday school, or is it given daily in the Mohawk Institution; and are pupils allowed to be absent in case their parents object to such teaching?

A.- The religious instruction given in the Mohawk Institution is in accordance with the...creeds and Articles of the Church of England. It is not confined to the Sunday school, but is given in some measure daily. There are children at the Institution belonging to several denominations of Protestants, there are some Roman Catholics and some pagans, but, happily, no objection to the religious teaching has ever yet been made by any.

9. Q.- What standard of education will the day schools of the reserve supply to the best scholars before they are admitted to the Institution?

A.- The standard of education in those schools is very low - much lower than it ought to be...but the present standard of education certainly embraces the subjects of reading, writing, and arithmetic mentioned in the following suggestion:-

10. Q.- It is suggested that acquirements at the day schools should certainly embrace - 1. Reading English easily and with understanding; 2. Writing fairly; 3. Some proficiency in Arithmetic. And that a knowledge of these three subjects should be required previous to admission into the Mohawk Institution.

A.- It is exceedingly desirable that the education of candidates for the Institution should...include...Reading, English (say Second Book National series) with some fair understanding, Writing a legible hand, and a good knowledge of the first rules of Arithmetic.

11. Q.- At the Institution the elementary education obtained at the day school should be supplemented and extended to higher branches of a good practical nature, so as gradually to raise all the young who go there to a higher scale of social life. How can this be best accomplished?

A.- This suggestion meets a hearty and universal concurrence, and may be fully and satisfactorily carried out by teachers specially qualified...

12. Q.- Modern History, down to our own day, will be more valuable than Ancient History: Geography, Geology, Mineralogy, Biology, Chemistry, Electricity, Steam, etc. etc. Cannot all these subjects be made interesting and familiar to the pupils?

A...when we consider the relation which Ancient History bears to Modern, the former cannot be altogether dispensed with, as a knowledge thereof in some degree is essential to the full and proper understanding, and due appreciation of Modern History. An answer to the direct question may be given in the affirmative, providing the teachers are supplied with the necessary apparatus.

13. Q.- Carpentering and smiths' work must be of use for all boys in the Dominion. Cannot some other manual labours also be advantageously taught?

A.- The arts or occupations here mentioned would be unquestionably useful, but they cannot be advantageously taught at the Institution. However, as many of the Indians (like the white people) are not disposed to farming, and as some are physically incapable of following that occupation, it may be very beneficial to the Indians to have some of their children apprenticed from time to time to learn some useful arts or trades in the adjacent towns or neighbourhood, according to their different tastes or predilection and aptitude for learning.

14. Q.- Why may not farming, gardening, draining, road-making, and boring wells, engineering, etc., claim attention?

A.- The first four occupations here mentioned are already taught at the Institution as far as practicable; the others may be more advantageously taught elsewhere.

15. Q.- Sewing and knitting, mending and making clothes, must be of use to almost all. Why should they not be taught in the schools, and why not also at the Institution?

A.- These useful arts are already taught in those schools presided over by female teachers, and also at the Institution.

16. Q.- Should not cooking and household work be taught to all the girls at the Institution?

A.- Most certainly, and it has been so effectually taught that girls from the Institution have been eagerly sought after as servants by some of the most respectable people at Brantford...

18. Q.- The acquisition and study of other languages, ancient and modern, besides English, will probably not be desirable, at any rate, for the present?

A.- This depends upon the object which the Institution is expected to accomplish - whether it is to be a finishing school, and what will be considered the standard of a finished education for the Indians.

19. Q.- How can the desire of the New England Company be best accomplished that admission to the Mohawk Institution should be by merit; and the proficiency of candidates should be tested by an entrance examination, comprising the reading of English, writing, and arithmetic in all cases, without exception?

A.- By the establishment of a Board of Examiners, consisting of all the Company's missionaries, who shall examine all candidates for admission into the institution, and who shall grant admission only according to a certain standard of proficiency, and providing the candidates present to the Board testimonials of good conduct from their teachers or superintendents.

20. Q.- Why should not some instruction be given as to health, and general views be given on physiology, so as to enable the Indian children to become acquainted with the structure of the human body, and the injurious effects of alcoholic liquors?

A.- Instruction on these important subjects is given to some extent at the Institution; it may, however, be desirable for the missionaries to supplement the efforts of the teachers by giving lectures occasionally on those subjects, adapted to the understanding of the children...

22. Q.- What will be the requisite salary for a Toronto certificated teacher at the Mohawk?

A.- From five to six hundred dollars.

---

126. 18 May 1872 NEC Report:Nelles

1. "TIME TABLE FOR THE MOHAWK INSTITUTE SCHOOL.
OPEN SCHOOL WITH READING A CHAPTER OF THE BIBLE AND PRAYER. CLOSE...WITH SINGING A HYMN AND PRAYER"

A.M.	Monday Div.I	Div.II	Tuesday Div. I	Div.II	Wednesday Div.I	Div.II	Thursday Div. I	Div.II	Friday Div.I	Div.II
9-9.30	Reading	Preparation	Spelling	Preparation	Reading	Preparation	Spelling	Preparation	Reading	Preparation
9.30-10	"	"	"	Recitation	"	"	"	"	"	"
10-10.30	Grammar	Recit.per Mon.	Geography	per Monitor	Grammar	Recit.per Mon.	Geography	Recitation	History	Recitation
10.30-10.45				Recess	15 Minutes					
10.45-11.30	Arithmetic	Recitation.	Writing	Recitation	Arithmetic	Recitation	Writing	Recitation	Arithmetic	Recitation
11.30-12	Mental Arith	"	Dictation	Preparation	"	Preparation	Dictation	Preparation	"	" "
P.M.										
1-1.30	Arithmetic	Recit.per Mon.	Arithmetic	Recitation	Arithmetic	Recitation	Arithmetic	Recitation	Arithmetic	Recitation
1.30-2	" Review	"	" Review	per Monitor	" Review	Per Monitors	"	"	"	"
2-2.30	" "	Preparation	" "	"	"	Preparation	"	Preparation	"	Preparation
2.30-2.45				Recess	15 minutes					
2.45-4	Human Physiology		History	Recitation	Physiology	Writing	Drawing	Recitation	Catechism	Writing or Tables

2. LIST OF WORK GIRLS WEEKLY

I.	III	V
Mary Ann Cusick	Mary Ann Powless	Rebecca Miller
Christina John Sr.	Phebe Snake	Eliza Snake
Mary Jane Butler	Avis Johnson	VI
Lucy Douglass	Sarah Splicer	Charlotte Hope
II	IV	Charlotte Hill
Julia Carryer	Louisa Clench	Catherine Vanevery
Julia Jonathen	Charlotte Powless	Esther Martin
Sarah Jane Davis	Charlotte Johnson	
Martha Jamieson	Christina John Jr.	

3. 17 May 1872 NEC Report: from Visitor's Book
"I have been much gratified by my visit to the Mohawk Institution...the neatness and clearness of the writing and ciphering of the pupils, which compares very favourably with that which I have been accustomed to see in the English elementary schools. Henry Newman, M.A. Balliol College, Oxford, England..

---

127. 18 May 1872 NEC Report: Nelles:

...On the subject of the Manual Labour School, there seems to be some misunderstanding. There has been no such school for many years. It was found that the benefit to the Indians was not what it was expected to be, and by no means adequate to the expense incurred, and the Company directed the teaching of trades should be dispensed with.* The Indians have plenty of land, and the boys when they leave school and settle in life generally turn their attention to farming. Of all the Indian youths who were taught trades at the Institution, only two work at their trade on the Reserve, and they do so only part of the time...The farmer takes two or three of the largest boys, in turn, to work with him and to teach them.

A few of the boys refuse to work, saying they come to the Institution to learn their books and not to work, but generally they are willing to work very well. As far as possible some employment is provided for the small boys; after school hours some attend to the pigs, some bring the cows from pasture, others assist to milk and do any light work about the place that is necessary...

...the girls...in addition to their studies in school, they are, and have always been, taught all useful housekeeping as well as spinning, knitting, sewing, mending, darning, etc.

All the clothes worn by the children at the Institution, except the boys' winter coats, have always been made by the girls, under the instruction and with the assistance of a sewing woman. The knitting for all the children has also been mostly done by the girls, but I think they have too much of this sort of work to do, and would recommend that a knitting-machine be purchased...cost about $60...when Mr. and Mrs. Bouslaugh left...not being able...to find...suitable persons to take their place, I put Mr. Griffith and his wife in charge of the establishment...I could not expect the services of both for the sum Mr. Griffith received as schoolmaster, and considered it right to give them the same that was given to the Bouslaughs when they first came to the Institution...Mr. Griffith could not satisfactorily perform both duties, particularly when the scarlet fever broke out, and I employed Carryer to take his place in the boys' school for the month of December. Carryer has continued teaching until last week ...Mr. Griffith will attend to school as far as possible until the changes contemplated shall have been made...it is almost impossible to get a first-class certificated teacher ...for less than 600 or 500 dollars at the least...

*The Committee find no trace of any such direction.

128. 30 June 1872 Institution Report Griffith [see p.218]
Boys School...Indian children learn to read and spell as quick as white children, but it takes them a long time before they become good readers, as they cannot speak English words plain, not understand what they read, therefore they read very little more than their lessons.

...Their speaking Indian so much among themselves when at play, or when out of school, is one of the greatest hindrances to their progress at school. We do what we can to induce them to talk English, *without compulsion*. The boys are taught to be practical farmers in an unostentatious way. In winter they help to tend the farm stock, and as soon as spring opens they see the preparations for spring and summer work. Then each boy of competent age and strength, when there is work to do, is called on in his turn to give a helping hand. Some of these boys at present manage a plough, cultivator, seed-drill, and even a mowing-machine, very cleverly, equal, perhaps, to some of our most experienced farmers' sons.

I may also remark of the girls that they certainly compare favourably with their white neighbours in an industrial point of view. As I look over the work they have put through their hands, during the last 15 months, since I took charge of this place, I am astonished. I may here mention some of the work.

Boys Clothing: smocks and coats, 155; pants, 212; shirts, 193; socks, 140. Girls' Clothing: dresses, 205; chemises, 104; skirts, 43; petticoats, 46; stockings, 105; aprons, 14; sheets, 87; pillow slips, 74; bed-ticks, 22; towels, 37; 2 suits, 2 pairs of drawers, 2 nightdresses: and all this work is said to be done well and in good taste.

129. 6 June 1872 NEC Report: Clerk to missionaries:
...wished them to form a Board, under the presidency of Canon Nelles...education given at the Mohawk Institution, the Manual Labour School...advisability of admitting the Indian boy, John Nahwakezhik (who had accompanied the Rev. James Chance from Garden River)...[admitted January 1873], and also the advisability of sending the young Indian, James Powless, to the Normal School at Toronto, for one year, with the view of fitting him to become a school teacher on the Reserve.

130. 30 July 1872 NEC Report: Nelles
I have been prevented forwarding to you the enclosed sooner by the serious illness of R. Park, the principal hand on the Institution farm. In consequence of the difficulty of getting labourers at this season of the year, I have been obliged to be with the boys during the harvest...have just secured the wheat and barley crops - 20 acres of each...

My duties now are of such a routine nature that a daily report must be a repetition of the same employments almost every day. I have Divine service every Sunday morning, and in the afternoon a short service and Sunday school at the Institution. During the week I visit the Institution almost daily, and since Bouslaugh left I have had to superintend the work on the farm. I also make all the purchases for the establishment...

131. NEC Report: Martland notes of verbal statement
Canon Nelles came...and in reply to his inquiries informed him that the Manual Labour school has not been found to answer, and had been given up many years ago. ...Mr. Bouslaugh...late Superintendent of the Institution, and his wife, had left in October 1871 and since then the Institution had been without a Superintendent and a Matron, and the farm without a farmer.

The boys...had done the ploughing and harrowing on the 200 acres of farm land this year, under the direction of Canon Nelles and a hired man. Mr. Martland asked if any farm books were kept, and was told in reply by Canon Nelles that was a matter between himself and the Committee.

At the time of Mr. Martland's visit the boys were not at work upon the farm, but the children were seen by him in the Institution.

The farm was in excellent condition, and the fences (snake fences) in good order.

On entering the Institute Mr. Martland went first upstairs, and the day being a very fine one found the windows all open, and the bedrooms beautifully clean and fresh, and the beds all in order, but no other furniture or utensils of any kind in the bedrooms. In the girls' department he was shown a room called the Lavatory, but on asking to see the wash-basins, etc., was informed there were none, and was told that the Indian children were dirty in their habits, and if supplied with basins, etc.

would use them improperly; they were therefore supplied instead with tubs and pails.

Mr. Martland was favourably impressed with Mr. Griffith, the teacher of the boys' school, but found it very difficult to get any information either from him or Canon Nelles; the latter objecting that he had brought no credentials. On going down stairs Mr. M was shown the room in which the boys had their classes, and in which they sat in evening, and in which also, in the winter time, they washed. The room was very little better than a cellar in an ordinary house; not so good as a laundry. He was told that in summer the boys washed in a shed close by, in which he saw one tub and one pail. He asked about the privies, but could get no answer.

He was, with difficulty, allowed to go into the kitchen; some girls were there making soup from beef; there were no stores. He went into the larder but found nothing whatever in it.

...Mr. M was informed that for breakfast the pupils had bread and butter, and sometimes potatoes, but that they did not like potatoes. For dinner, meat was given every second day, but they were very fanciful, and would not eat mutton. At tea time they had porridge. Mr. Martland asked what drink was given to the children at breakfast and tea time...Canon Nelles replied "Milk, if we have it".

In the school-room Mr. Martland found the boys were taught by Mr. Griffith without any assistant; there were four or five classes. In the girls school Mr. Martland found an Indian teacher, Isaac Barefoot. The religious instruction given seemed to be the reading of a chapter from the New Testament, without comment. The writing from copy-heads was very good indeed. In reading, they pronounced English words well - up to three words of three syllables - but did not seem to understand the meaning of what they read.

The boys told Mr. Martland that they spoke Indian entirely amongst themselves, and they said that they did not wish to speak English.

In geography the girls went through the towns and counties of Ontario, but did not know the capital. In history, the children answered by rote, they knew Victoria was the Queen, but could not explain how she became so. Mr. Martland informed the boys that he was going to England, and asked them to tell him how he should get there. They supposed, they said, by railway.

Mr. Martland wished to have a conversation with some of the older boys, but this Canon Nelles prevented.

Mr. Griffith seemed a very kind master, but one of the old school. The Indian teacher, Barefoot, seemed constrained, and frightened to speak to Mr. Martland before Canon Nelles. Barefoot teaches in English. The children seemed well fed.

The boys' dormitories are rather overcrowded, the mattresses are of straw, and are shaken out, Mrs. Griffith informed Mr. Martland, 'perhaps every three months.'

Mr. Martland gave it as his opinion that the children in the Institution are not equal, in point of instruction, to the children in the common schools for white children in Canada, and he believes that the Indian children generally are by no means wanting in intelligence.

132. NEC Report

The Company may not be aware that Isaac Barefoot had a certificate from the Normal School at Toronto (grade B of the 1st class), which is only one grade less than the highest that could be given at the time.

133. 15 August 1872 Gilkison to Supt. Gen. DIA

...a proposal to procure from the parents and guardians of the children attending the Institute of the Company near this, their several shares of monies, so as to contribute towards the expense of thier board, lodging and education; a suggestion of my own made several years ago (but not acted upon)...that the Indians of the Six Nations should, if possible, be induced to cultivate the practice of <u>giving</u> towards education, which the liberality of the Company rendered unnecessary...The Six Nations have been spoiled or pampered by the Company, so much so, that the most trifling contribution, even...a load of wood, has been denied, but I am in hope's of a change; and if the present proposition can be carried into effect <u>amicably</u>, it will be a good commencement...My view is to <u>persuade, not force</u> the Indians, to comply with the request of the Company...

134. 30 August 1872 NEC Report: Nelles

With respect to the Manual Labour School...I may have been in error in saying that the trades were discontinued to be taught by direction of the New England Company...

135. 10 September 1872 NEC Report

The Committee considered the important question of the appointment of a Superintendent of the Mohawk Institution, and the duties which should devolve upon such Superintendent; and they determined that he should have the control and be responsible for the management of the Institution, Manual Labour School and Farm; and that upon him should devolve the due execution of the directions of the Company, or Special Committee, in relation thereto, and that his salary should be £125 per annum, for the services of himself and his wife, in addition to the residence of himself and family at the Institution, with rations and fuel...the Committee appointed Mr. Robert Ashton to be such Superintendent...

136. 12 September 1872 NEC Report: Clerk to Nelles

On the 2nd instant I advised you of certain changes in the management of the Mohawk Institution which were in the contemplation of the New England Company...to bring the Institution to a state of greater efficiency and usefulness to the Indian races on the Reserve.

...the Committee resolved to appoint a Superintendent of the Institution...proceeded to appoint Mr. Robert Ashton...accompanied by his wife and two young children, will...leave England...on the 15th October next, and the Committee will be obliged by your preparing for his reception...and by your rendering him, on his arrival, every assistance of which he may stand in need.

...Mr. Ashton should thus have the entire control of the Institution, School, and Farm, and that the Board of Missionaries should act as visitors, conducting periodical examinations, and reporting to the Committee from time to time upon its state and condition...

Mr. Ashton, on entering upon his very responsible duties in a country entirely new to him, will have a difficult task to perform, and the Committee rely with confidence that he will receive...the most cordial and active support and co-operation.

137. 9 October 1872 NEC Report
Rules and Regulations for the Superintendent

1. The Superintendent shall have the control, and be responsible for the management of the Institution, Manual Labour School, and Farm, and upon him shall devolve the due execution of the directions of the Company, or Special Committee, in relation thereto.

2. The School Teachers at the Institution shall be independently recommended to the Company by the Superintendent, and the Board of Missionaries, and be appointed by the Company.

3. Vacancies in the Institution will be filled up from the Day Schools on the Indian Reserve, from candidates who have been examined by the Board of Missionaries, and have obtained a certificate of fitness for admission. Other Indian children may be admitted on permission being granted by the Special Committee of the Company, and having passed an examination by the Board of Missionaries and obtained the necessary certificate of fitness.

4. The Superintendent is to keep a list of all the children in the Institution, showing the dates of their admission, their age when admitted, the names and occupations of their parents, and from what school on the Reserve or elsewhere they came; together with a note of the state of knowledge at the time of admission.

5. He is also to keep a list of the children as they leave the Institution; to keep up a communication with them, and to chronicle their progress in life, as far as is practicable, for four years afterwards.

6. He is to forward every quarter to the Special Committee a report on the actual state of the Institution, in the form required by the Committee.

7. He is to provide for the daily board of the establishment according to a dietary sanctioned by the Special Committee; also to be responsible for the cleanliness and good order of the dormitories and other rooms inhabited by or used by the children...advance with all diligence the industrial, moral, and religious education of the establishment; and is expected to interest himself in all that may conduce to the real good of those that are placed under his care. He will conduct family Prayer night and morning with the children, and attend with them Public Worship every Sunday.

8. All the accounts connected with the Institution, Farm, and Manual Labour School are to be kept by the Superintendent.

9. He is to send to the Committee at least two months before the expiration of each quarter an estimate of all expenses (including the salaries and wages of all the officers and servants of the Institution, Manual Labour School, and Farm) for that quarter; and at the end of every quarter to send to the Committee an accurate and detailed account, with vouchers, of the expenditure...

138. 1872 NEC Report: Nelles
...promises gladly to cooperate in any way it might be thought best to carry out the wishes of the Company, but expressed his regret that he could not give his "cordial concurrence" with respect to the amount of salary that the Committee proposed giving to him. In consideration of being relieved of much labour and responsibility, he stated he had no objection to relinquish part of his income.

139. 4 November 1872 NEC Report: Alexander Stewart
1. That the school-houses be improved...

2. That the teachers of the common schools be required to hold certificates of qualification...

4. That the Mohawk Institution be dispensed with, inasmuch as the standard of education there is no higher than it should be in the common schools...

5. That a high-school be established in a central position on the Reserve...That there be one active superintendent, whose aim it shall be to conform the educational system amongst the Indians to the character of the very excellent educational system which exists throughout the rest of Ontario.

140. NEC Report
The Clerk...replied to this letter...10th December, 1872:
...The Committee have...engaged in earnest endeavours to carry out the improvements suggested by you...on the Grand River Reserve, and in the Mohawk Institution, and they are glad to find that your experience leads you to confirm their views. They observe, however, that you recommend the removal of the Institution to a more central site; in this...there are very grave difficulties, and unless you are able to furnish them with very urgent reasons for taking this step other than the Committee are at present aware of, they do not see any sufficient reason for encountering the great expense and the other inconveniences which would attend the removal of it.

1872 - 1914
Robert Ashton 1872-1911 - A. Nelles Ashton 1911-1914

1. 28 November 1872 Blomfield

We walked over to the Mohawk Institute where we were cordially welcomed by Mr. and Mrs. Ashton...Mr. Ashton seemed determined to introduce discipline in the Institution, which had hitherto been neglected. He complained of the extremely filthy habits of the boys, which had evidently been unchecked, if not fostered. This...was entirely corroborated by Mr. Martland...Poor Mrs. Ashton was bewailing the loss of her little girl's hair, necessitated from having been too near one of the Indian children; a shocking condition of things for any school. As to the food, Mr. Ashton says there was no lack of meat, but it was cooked to shreds, and allowed to get luke-warm by dinner-time, and even the young Indians would not eat it. Matters of this kind, however, will doubtless soon be put straight by Mr. Ashton, who also expressed an intention to work the farm properly in the interest of the Company. The farm is a very valuable one, which should not only supply all vegetables required for the Institution, but should bring in no inconsiderable net revenue...

...I saw Barefoot, the Indian master, who was not there last February. The old regime, I believe, is more congenial to his taste than the new, and I imagine from his manner that Mr. Ashton may expect a good deal of trouble with him. Mr. Ashton will probably have to go through a probationary period of plotting, as I understand his predecessors have done...

2. 20 November 1872 R. Ashton to NEC

...I arrived at and took charge of this Institution on the 30th October, 1872...It is very pleasantly situated, and from the public road has the appearance of being a newly and substantially built brick building, with a wooden verandah six feet wide right across the front and level with the first floor. On passing the gate, however, from the general appearance of neglect and untidiness, I began to think the whole place deserted.

The building is about 250 yards from the road...The first 100 yards is a tolerable road (for Canada); the next a rough grass plot; and the remaining fifty yards...is used as a play-ground by the girls, and drying-ground for linen, but is little else than a wilderness of sand and rubbish - the former being over one's ankles...

The arrangement and condition of the building is anything but good. The older portion has, in fact, never been finished - there not being a single sash-line to any of the windows, and consequently, they cannot be opened at the top; and at the bottom, if opened at all, must be propped up with whatever may happen to be at hand - the result is very bad ventilation...I may say none at all - this being particularly apparent in the girls' school-room...

The accommodation for the officers of the Institution is very limited...one room in the girls' dormitory should be set apart for the triple purpose of a meeting-room for the Board, reception-room for visitors to the Institution, and parents visiting their children; the latter at present consider any room free to them - mine included. It might also serve the purpose of an office for myself.

It has been the custom here for all the officers - superintendent included- to take their meals together in the kitchen, where all kinds of work were going on at the same time. I certainly prefer taking my meals with my family alone, but have for the present fallen in with the custom of having a common table for convenience' sake, but it is now laid in the girls' work-room instead of the kitchen, that being the only available room.

The only means of ingress and egress for the girls is through the front door, consequently no part of the house is free from their incursions; and strangers visiting the Institution must be at once struck with the apparent want of order and discipline; as should they arrive during hours of recreation, they will find themselves at once surrounded, and their progress barred, by groups of girls whose curiosity overruns all sense of politeness. Neither is there any room into which such visitors may be shown. As already stated, the room marked 'Board-room' is furnished, and occupied by Mr. and Mrs. Griffith.

Furniture. - I enclose a correct statement of such house furniture and effects as...belong to the Company...the totals...show how utterly inadequate they are to the requirements. Of the 89 iron bedsteads, 16 are broken, and at present unfit for use...they are of cast-iron, and made to fold up, most of them are too large, and consequently crowd the dormitories. They are easily broken in moving them to clean the rooms. There are only 75 bed-ticks, 70 pillows, 85 blankets, 74 quilts, 72 counterpanes, to make which large ones have been cut into two, instead of getting them a convenient size at once; now they are too small to cover the beds. Only 107 sheets; they use but one on each bed, the remainder being in the wash, so that each child sleeps with a blanket next to it, or lies on the bed itself; 10 table-cloths, 12 towels, three yards long, are all we have for use. It is...easy to account for the several cases of ophthalmia...None of the sheets, blankets, etc., are nearly large enough for the beds. This gives the dormitories an uncomfortable and untidy appearance...

The heating and cooking arrangements are very defective. In the kitchen is a very large stove, consuming a great quantity of wood to little purpose, as the oven will not bake anything, consequently all the food has to be boiled. Mr. Griffith tells me that they have never been able to bake with it...

There is no bath on the place, and no means at present of making one; so that, excepting in summer, when the boys can go to the river, they never bathe. To give any child a hot bath now it would be necessary to use a washing-tub, and to heat the water over the stoves. Something should be done to correct this at once, as the children on returning from their homes after the holidays are often in a very filthy condition. Until I can offer some suggestion on this subject I will see that every boy and girl has at least a hot sponge-bath once a week.

The dormitories are clean and tidy; the dining-room and kitchen in good order, but deficient in cooking utensils, etc. The school-rooms are in very good order, but the desks and forms are rough home-made benches, quite unfitted for the purpose, and to one accustomed to a well-fitted school-room present a most unsightly appearance...

Outside the building all is disorder, rags, old shoes, wood, bones, paper, slops, etc, being strewed in all directions, so that to walk within ten feet of the building is, or was, quite unpleasant. I had upwards of a cartload of such rubbish removed from under and around the front verandah alone. There are no paths or gardens; nothing, in fact, to make the place look comfortable. The girls play in the front and the boys at the back of the building, and not the slightest attempt has ever been made to make the place attractive, or even neat.

Drains must have been considered quite superfluous, as there is only one, and that is from the scullery, and discharges itself within thirty yards of the building. Slops and dirty water of all kinds are thrown outside the doors or out of the windows, whichever happens to be most convenient. Even the pumps, of which there are three quite close to the house, have no drains for the waste water, it being allowed to run all over the yard, so that the amount of mud and filth brought indoors is abominable.

All the refuse and sweepings are thrown just outside the doors, or over the verandahs, there being neither dust-holes nor dust-heaps to receive them, and no one considers it necessary to do more than throw it into the first place they come to. This is certainly not the way to train children in the habits and practices of civilized life, at least not to my 'old country notions'.

There are four closets, rough wooden structures, at distances varying from thirty to sixty or more yards from the building; three of them grace the view from my window, and are also visible to any one approaching the front entrance. Those used by the boys and girls were, on my first visit, (it being a warm day) quite unapproachable to any one afraid of catching a fever; as they are open behind, and all the soil exposed to sight and the action of sun and air. In inquiring when they were cleaned out, I was informed that the soil was drawn back with hoes, 'now and then', and 'once in a while' it was carted away and left to 'blow about', but never used as manure; in fact, it is useless for that purpose, as instead of paper the

children use pieces of wood - no one ever thinking it their duty to teach them differently. I am correcting this as fast as possible; but the setting in of winter has put a stop to all out-of-door work; however I have adopted the earth-closet system as far as present circumstances will allow. There are at present 41 boys and 32 girls; two of the latter are absent with leave just now...

Several of the boys might be called young men - four or five are steady young fellows and always willing to go to work with the horses; these generally find their own clothes, and are therefore of little actual cost to the Company - the value of their work being equal to if not greater than the cost of their food. I cannot give so favourable an account of the majority, for they are the idlest and most disobedient boys I ever saw; they will not do a stroke of work but just when it pleases them. I had to keep them all out of school one week to hurry in the harvest, but they had no idea of work, and when I attempted to show some, the others took the opportunity to slip off and I had to fetch them back again; if I left the field for a few moments they would do nothing until I returned. No one has attempted to maintain discipline amongst them. In whatever room they may happen to be, they spit and blow their noses over the floor - no one here took any notice of it, but since I have pointed out to them how disgusting it was, they are leaving it off; some of them have even written up in the school-room and sitting-room, 'No spitting'.

The girls are more industrious and are constantly employed at house or needle work.

On my arrival many of the children were without shoes and socks - the girls from choice - and the boys because they had none to wear. Some of them find all or portions of their clothing, the remainder are clothed here, but no rule exists as to how long garments ought to wear. Some girls have had as many as seven dresses this year; some of the dresses were certainly common prints, but two should have worn longer than that. The girls have very neat and good linsey dresses for best wear, and more are being made for every day. The boys mostly dress at the Company's expense in grey tweed suits, some of the most recent issue being of a good stout quality. No boy, however, has a second pair of trousers or boots...

The boys have been <u>taught</u> that they have no right to be set to work of any kind against their will; it has been the practice to coax a boy to do any little thing required of him. They have a natural dislike to work of all kinds, and appear to look on this school as a boarding house where they are at liberty to do as they please, and to go out or go home whenever they like. Mr. Nelles evidently concurs in their opinion respecting work; for even after I had had a conversation with him about it, and told him that it was the wish of the Company that every boy should do his share of manual labour, he made the following remarks to the boys in my presence on the night we celebrated our Harvest Home: -'That now the harvest is gathered in or nearly so, there will be no further necessity for keeping any of you from school to work in the fields; and as the object of your coming here is that you may be educated', etc. etc. - 'but now at harvest time, when there is a press of work, it is right that you should render what assistance you can, else the crops would spoil on the ground'.

I considered this too pointed, and in replying told the boys what I considered was expected of them.

The next morning I sounded Mr. Barefoot on this subject, and he quite agreed with Mr. Nelles, and said that the prevailing idea among the boys' parents was that the children came here to be educated only, and not to work unless they liked. He added that most of the boys on leaving here follow farming, but that the manner of working this farm was so slovenly, they could learn how to farm better at home. Still, he thought, the girls ought to be made to work. He evidently reasons as an Indian, after all, - the woman may work while the man takes his ease. At present, the boys do nothing but play marbles from 6.30 to 9 a.m. I, however, anticipate very little difficulty in getting them to work heartily. I have commenced by drilling them; this they like amazingly and take the greatest possible pains to do it well. I am also teaching them to sing.

...The staff of officers and servants is as follows:

Mr. Griffith, schoolmaster.
Mrs. Griffith, acting assistant matron and needle woman.
Mr. Barefoot, schoolmaster
Mr. Park, farm man.
Kitchen maid
Dairy maid.
Mrs. Money, laundry woman and to assist in kitchen.

The last-named woman I dismissed on the 13th, instant, as I detected her in conveying a piece of meat from the Institution that was given to her to put in the soup. I shall try to do without filling up the vacancy.

Mr. Griffith is...a most faithful and hard-working servant of the Company, but is getting too old for his present post. He is very kind to the children, and understands the treatment of all their minor ailments, and...often saves the expense of a doctor. He has little control over the boys out of school. He devotes his whole time to the Institution, and is very handy about the place.

Mrs. Griffith is now acting as assistant matron and work-room woman. The last assistant matron left about a month since.

Mr. Barefoot, the girls' teacher, is a married man; but his wife is at present residing with her friends. She was recently a pupil here. He tells me he has been led by Mr. Nelles to consider his appointment as only temporary, in consequence of proposed changes, and that he has no regular engagement, but considers himself at liberty to leave at the end of any quarter without previous notice. He has been trying for another appointment. On inquiring what he considered his duties here, he said that he had only to instruct the girls in school from 9 to 12 a.m., and from 1.30 to 4 p.m. from Monday to Friday, and that anything else he might do is altogether voluntary on his part. He does no duty from Friday night until Monday morning, but goes to the Reserve, where he holds an appointment as interpreter to Mr. Chance. I consider this arrangement most objectionable, as every person engaged in an institution of this kind should devote his whole time to the work, and when not engaged in actual teaching should take a fair share in looking after the pupils out of school. Of course he could not look after the girls, and consequently renders another officer necessary, but he could take some share in the oversight of the boys, and not leave it all to Mr. Griffith. If one teacher is excused these duties, the other should be, but this would render an additional staff necessary. He is quite willing that his duties should be re-arranged, but if called upon to resign his office of interpreter he would expect an advance of salary equal to the emolument he relinquishes. He also wishes to have a private residence provided for him; but in my opinion every officer should reside on the spot, and do all in his power to instruct the pupils in habits of cleanliness and industry.

Mr. Park looks after the horses and stock, and attends to cultivating the land. He is a very superior man; is most attentive and hard-working. He is just the man to make an excellent industrial trainer for the boys.

The Farm...is all under cultivation, and in very good order...there is not a single root except potatoes on the farm. No vegetables of any kind have ever been grown for the house; we are even now compelled to purchase onions for flavouring the soup.

3. 23 December 1872 NEC Report: Committee
...deeply deplore the untidy and neglected state of things ...most pressing of the wants...furniture, of bedding, towelling, and similar matters, they leave to your discretion...grant of fifty pounds...Among the most urgent would seem to be the sewerage to carry the soil and waste water to a distance from the house...to some part of the land, where it would be useful as manure.

Also, a proper provision of bath accommodation for the Indian children, that their persons may be kept clean and a habit of cleanliness introduced. Would it be practicable, without encountering large expense, to have warm water laid on for bath and other purposes, as part of an improved system of warming the premises, which might... be made not only more efficient but more economical?

The ventilation of the rooms by means of windows that will open at the top.

Your account of the condition of the iron bedsteads surprises us, as they were supplied as recently as 1869... Be good enough to state whether the broken ones are capable of repair...

...as to Mr. Barefoot. The present arrangement of his duties must necessarily be most unsatisfactory, and they would be glad to have the benefit of your suggestions as to his future employment, and the duties which should be assigned to him.

In dealing with him and others of the present establishment...it will be desirable to proceed cautiously, so as not to lead to an impression that great changes, hostile to their interests, were in contemplation, and...to keep on good terms with all the missionaries...

You will...have to form a kitchen-garden for the supply of vegetables for the household. It is quite amazing to the Committee that such a state of affairs as you describe should have been permitted by your predecessor.

4. NEC Report: Six Years Summary
1. REGULATIONS

This Institution is maintained and managed solely by the New England Company, and is established for the purpose of civilizing the Indians and advancing the Christian Religion among them, and imparting a good education, combined with all kinds of useful industrial training, to the youth of both sexes of the Six Nations and other tribes of Indians.

Its aim is to impart such an education as shall fit its pupils for teachers amongst their own people, at the same time training them in the arts and practices of civilized nations.

The boys and girls occupy separate and distinct portions of the Institution, and each pupil is provided with a separate bed, and food and clothing of the best description.

Rules relating to Pupils

1. Vacancies in the Institution are principally filled up from the day-schools on the Indian Reserve from candidates of any religious denomination, who have been examined by the School Board of the Six Nations Indian Reserve, and have obtained a certificate of fitness for admission. Other Indian children may be admitted on permission being granted by the Company, and having obtained the necessary certificate of fitness from the missionary or school-teacher of the district in which they reside. In the latter case, application for admission should be made to the Superintendent at the Institution.
2. The qualifications for admission are, that the candidate must be between the ages of 10 and 17 years, of good character, and must be able to read the 2nd book of lessons, and possess a fair knowledge of the simple rules of arithmetic.
3. The school terms are from the last Saturday in August to the 31st of January, and from the 1st of February to the Saturday next before the 20th of July.
4. No girls or small boys will be permitted to leave the Institution unless fetched away by some responsible person, or the parents have signified to the Superintendent in writing that they desire their children to proceed home alone. Girls will not be permitted to go out, not even to visit friends, unless wearing the distinctive dress of the Institution, so that they may be easily recognized.
5. No holidays other than those stated above can be allowed, except in cases of sickness.
6. Whenever it is desirable that pupils should return to their homes during the school terms, in consequence of the sickness or death of relatives, a note to that effect must be presented to the Superintendent, signed by either the minister or doctor of the district in which the pupil resides.
7. Pupils leaving the Institution without the sanction of the Superintendent, must be returned by their friends within forty-eight hours, or they will be considered as dismissed from the Institution. In the event of the pupil not returning within the time specified, all articles of clothing, etc., the property of the Institution, must be immediately returned to the Institution.
8. It is expected that all pupils entering the Institution during any term, will remain until its completion; and that those who wish to continue to avail themselves of its advantages will return punctually at the appointed time.
9. If by any reason a pupil is prevented from returning on the day the school opens, the parents must communicate the reason to the Superintendent within ten days, or such pupil's name will be removed from the books...
10. In cases where pupils have been absent from the Institution from any cause for a period not exceeding two calendar months, on seeking re-admission they must present the Superintendent with a certificate of character from the missionary of the district in which they reside.
11. Each pupil in the Institution will receive on an average not less than 28 hours' schooling per week, exclusive of Sundays. In addition, the girls will receive instruction in sewing, knitting, and all kinds of domestic work; the boys in farming, gardening, and such other useful occupations as may be from time to time deemed advisable.
12. The Superintendent is empowered to expel any pupil from the Institution who shall grossly misconduct him or herself; or who, through continued disregard to the rules of the school, shall render such expulsion desirable.
13. All necessary articles of winter and summer clothing are provided for the use of pupils at the Institution only; but parents are required to supply their children with clothing for use elsewhere.
14. Pupils are at liberty to write to or receive letters from their relations and friends as often as they wish, but in order to guard against improper correspondence, all communications must be addressed to the care of the Superintendent, who will open and peruse the same should he deem it advisable.

Rules respecting Visitors

1. Visitors are at liberty to inspect any part of the

Institution during the school term, between the hours of 10 a.m. and 4 p.m., excepting on Thursdays and Saturdays, when the Institution is open for inspection between the hours of 10 and 12 a.m. only.

2. Visitors are invited to question or address the pupils, as it will tend to overcome their extreme shyness.

3. It is desired that visitors will, before leaving the Institution, inscribe their names and addresses in the visitor's book, together with any remarks they may desire to make.

4. Pupils may receive visits from their friends any Saturday between the hours of 10 a.m. and 4 p.m. Such visits to take place in the room set apart for that purpose.

5. All visitors must enter the Institution by the front door. On no account can any one be permitted to enter the kitchen or other parts of the Institution, without permission.

2. The Superintendent's Annual Reports on the Mohawk Institution for the years 1873-8, presented to the Special Committee of the New England Company.

REPORT FOR 1873

...the general conduct of the pupils, and of the boys especially, has steadily improved, and...they now meet my utmost expectations, many of them exhibiting an amount of industry, obedience, and carefulness I never expected them to attain in so short a time.

This result is owing to the excellent manner in which Mr. Barefoot and Miss Fisher have seconded my endeavours and the hearty zeal they have displayed in anticipating my wishes and carrying out my instructions for the good of those entrusted to their charge.

The educational progress of pupils has been satisfactory, considering the very unsettled state of the school, and the irregular attendance during the early part of the year. Now, however, that good order has been established, and both pupils and their friends begin to understand that the changes introduced are to their advantage, a spirit to regard the rules of the Institution is exhibiting itself, and the children appear as cheerful and contented as can be expected of them. Since it has become a rule that the pupils in the Institution should speak English at all times, excepting on their half-holidays, they have made greater progress in their studies, and appear far more intelligent; whilst by accustoming themselves to speak English when at play, fluency of expression is being rapidly acquired.

As an instance of the advantages attending the compulsory use of English, especially at recreation time, I must point out Catherine Gibson, who was admitted in April, 1871; but in April, 1873, she could neither speak nor understand a word of English, and barely knew the alphabet, and being an Onondaga did not understand Mohawk, the language generally spoken here. Now she can well understand and speak English very fairly and is progressing rapidly in reading.

When children who were not Mohawks came to the Institution they had two languages to acquire - Mohawk and English; the former being used amongst themselves and at play-time, was very well learned; the latter used only when speaking to an officer of the school, was very imperfectly understood, and soon forgotten. Some of the elder boys who left in the spring had been here over seven years, yet some could barely make themselves understood in English; now we have neither boys nor girls who cannot speak English far better than those referred to.

In such subjects as Scripture, geography, grammar, etc., very little progress has been made...as until a better acquaintance with the English language was attained, it was utterly impossible to exercise the reasoning faculties of the pupils, they could repeat their lessons by rote, without in the least understanding what they said.

For the last four months I have myself instructed the whole school in Scripture history...The religious knowledge of the pupils is still, in my opinion, lamentably deficient; and as they are unaccustomed to answer questions it is very difficult to instruct them.

It has afforded me great pleasure to instruct the pupils in singing as they take great pains, and make excellent progress.

Some of the elder girls are learning to play the harmonium, but the small one belonging to the Institution is getting past use.

The farming operations have not been attended with the success I could have wished. Much of the land has been overworked, and some considerable portion allowed to get into a most filthy condition.

The Indian corn crop was an entire failure...Twenty acres of fall wheat yielded only 150 bushels, and twenty acres of barley the same quantity...left the farm deficient in feed and litter, and will necessitate the feeding of hay to the stock that might otherwise have been sold...

The potato crop was the best in the neighbourhood...In anticipation of a failure in this crop I grew a large quantity of white beans.

The "flats," comprising 90 to 100 acres, will afford excellent pasturage...A moveable fence is now in progress for this part of the farm...

To render the farm profitable it will require considerable outlay for the next two or three years; and an additional labourer should be regularly employed, as much waste is caused by want of proper supervision and care...To gain the full benefit of the boys' work, and to properly instruct them, one man is altogether inadequate for so large a farm...

The sum of $146.75 was realized during three months of the year by the sale of milk and letting pasturage. The sums...may be considerably increased when the fences are in good order...

Five large pig-sties were erected during the year from materials taken from the old Institution buildings, the remainder of the expenses being charged to farm repairs.

The year has not passed without severe trial, difficulties and disappointments...

REPORT FOR 1874

Three girls and five boys left the Institution without permission, and, not returning within the required period, their names were removed from the Register. The former left because I refused to let them leave the Institution for their homes unless accompanied by some responsible person. They had each been upwards of <u>seven</u> years in the Institution. Four of the boys had been but a very short time in the school, and one had absconded four or five times.

Conduct of Pupils

I do not think it would be possible to select a school of boys whose conduct would be so uniformly good as that of the boys in this Institution.

The girls are not so well conducted; they are extremely self-willed and frequently quarrel amongst themselves. This arises from the fact that Indian girls are too soon treated as women, and allowed to do just as they think fit, when at home.

Educational Progress

The educational progress has been most satisfactory. When I first came here the pupils showed a great deficiency of capacity for mental exertion, and it was all but impossible to obtain an intelligent answer to the most simple question. The teachers have laboured most zealously to exercise the mental powers of their pupils, and to raise the standard of English speaking amongst them. The classes are still very deficient in arithmetic; I have found this the weak subject with all Indian children. This arises from the fact, that until a child understands the English language fairly, it is an absolute impossibility to explain to him the principles of numbers.

Industrial Training

I have failed in inducing any of the boys to offer themselves for apprenticeships to trades; one boy wishes to be a carpenter, but would not consent to be bound for longer than <u>six months.</u> As most of the lads on leaving here will take to farming, we shall endeavour to make the training in that branch of industry as thorough as possible.

We experience great difficulty in obtaining desirable persons for training girls in kitchen and laundry work. The emigrant class supplies most of the domestics in this country, but they are not fitted for an institution of this kind; a better class of persons must be found if possible, and they should take a position above that of ordinary domestics. Nothing will induce Indian girls to become servants; they will not remain steadily in a situation if they obtain one. The Missionaries are all compelled to employ white girls entirely, as Indian girls will not remain with them more than a week or two.

<u>All the clothing</u>, including boys <u>coats and pants</u>, has been made by the girls; they have also knitted all the socks, stockings, comforters, and clouds, in addition to keeping clothing and house linen in thorough repair...large outlay in clothing is owing to...supplying pupils with all necessary articles of apparel. The greater part of the extra clothing purchased will last for years.

5. **31 March 1874   NEC to Chance**

...in the case of any prolonged absence of a pupil...the Superintendent should, before re-admitting such Pupil, confer with the Missionary of the District in which the Pupil has been residing, who will thus be able to learn...the cause of such absence. Such absence may be occasioned by something in the Institution which is distasteful to the Indians, and which the Superintendent and Committee should be apprized of and the missionary may be able to explain to the Parents and remove any cause of dissatisfaction, or any prejudice operating against the Institution in the Indian mind.

6. **27 May 1875   Venning to Ashton**

The Committee observe that in your reply to the remark of one of the Chiefs that the Company enjoyed the proceeds of the Institute Farm derived from Indian labor you stated it was but a trifle and not worthy of mention by them...it would be well for you to tell them that such profits of the farm, when there are any, are spent by the Company upon the Institute and...defray expenses a trifle. As the Company spends <u>all</u> its income upon the Indians it is absurd to speak of profit to the Company. The profit goes wholly to themselves. The Committee do their responsible and heavy work quite without any remuneration.

7. **1875, 1876   NEC Reports: R. Ashton**
    REPORT FOR 1875

...twenty-six pupils...have left. Of the latter three boys and one girl absconded; one boy and two girls left through ill-health. The boy...died of consumption, and the other had disease of the spine. Of the discharged pupils, nine had been less than one year in the Institution; of these, eight belonged to the Tuscarora Reserve.

The conduct, manners, intelligence, and contentment of the pupils generally, and of the girls in particular, have immensely improved during the year. For this...result I am indebted to the employment of a superior class of persons, who, whilst instructing girls in domestic duties, could command their respect and enforce obedience and order. The whole of the cooking, cleaning, and most of the laundry work is now done by the girls under instruction, and in short time they will be able to bake the greater part of the bread required.

The introduction of girls from other Reserves, and especially from the Bay of Quinte, has also been instrumental in improving the manners of the girls, as their greater intercourse with white people, and better acquaintance with the English language places them far in advance of their kindred of the Tuscarora Reserve. They more fully appreciate the advantages of the Institution, and...evince greater readiness in doing as they are bidden. ...the educational standard of the Institution is steadily advancing, whilst the individual progress of each pupil is satisfactory.

Both the teachers evince a lively interest in their work, and the energetic efforts of Miss Fisher in the junior school are productive of the best results; the pupils passing from her classes to the senior school compare most favourably with the others in the intelligence and accuracy displayed in their work.

The committee were pleased to sanction the admission of a few young and ignorant children to form a practising class for pupils under special training for teachers. I have not...availed myself of the permission to form this class... owing to the disappointments I have met with in failing to induce the most advanced scholars to place themselves under special training. They profess a desire to become teachers, but fail when their energies are put to the test, or else, believing themselves to be more competent than they really are, they persuade their friends to allow them to leave the Institution, thinking they will be able to obtain situations as teachers at once; this latter idea has arisen from the fact that they know that the majority of teachers in Indian schools are less qualified than themselves, and, with the natural incredulity of Indians, they refuse the guidance of those best fitted to direct them. After the summer vacation I selected the two most advanced girls, and, with the approbation of their friends, placed them in training for teachers; at first they displayed great zeal and application, but within a month expressed a wish to change. I used all possible means to induce them to persevere; they did so till the end of the term, and then left the Institution altogether.

When all teachers in Indian school are subjected to an examination similar to that conducted by the Company's Missionaries, or are required to hold certificates of qualification, Indian youths will exercise as much zeal in seeking the attainments as they now display in obtaining the emoluments of teachers.

Table VI.[see p. 210] shows the present condition of the 87 pupils, who have left the Institution during my superintendency...it is a most imperfect return compared with similar reports from Institutions maintained amongst white people, but allowance must be made for Indian character and customs, which prevent children seeking any regular employment, and hence both young men and young women may generally be said to reside with their friends, working a little here and there, until they marry and have homes of their own.

To accurately test the results of the training given in this Institution, it will be necessary to closely watch the lives of past pupils for years, and to ascertain from the condition of their homes, farms, and children, how far we succeed in inculcating good principles and establishing proper habits.

I sincerely trust the Company will shortly be able to grant sums for the improvement of the accommodation of the Institution. Under present circumstances I could not recommend the admission of more than eighty-two pupils, without incurring great risk in the possible event of any outbreak of sickness. On the boys' side of the house there is really no available accommodation for the sick...

I have endeavoured to follow closely the instructions of the Committee in the matter of the expenditure, undertaking nothing which involved a large outlay and promising only a remote return...a liberal outlay is necessary before any moderately fair returns can be expected, as the work and expense attending the raising of such crops we get is excessive; and as each year the grass crop fails, we are compelled to feed the cattle with the straw that ought to be converted into manure...

...the year has been productive...most marked results in the general improvement of the discipline, and character of the pupils, and the public reputation of the Institution.

All the officers are becoming well accustomed to their work and, without exception, combine a high sense of the importance of their responsibilities with a zealous discharge of their duties.

REPORT FOR 1876

...an increased attendance of 6 over...last year.

Of those discharged I am happy to say that none absconded; one boy, however, died of inflammation of the lungs, and one girl died of consumption a few months after leaving here. 13 have been less than one year in the Institution, 5 from 1 to 2 year, 2 from 2 to 3 years, 2 from 4 to 5 years, 1 from 6 to 7 years, 1 from 7 to 8 years. The majority leaving after being so short a time in the Institution evidences the lamentable want of control on the part of parents, and their indifference as to the future well-being of their children.

It is encouraging to notice the improvement that has taken place in the habits, intelligence, and appearance of the pupils during the past year, and to find that they perform their allotted tasks cheerfully and well, generally striving to merit the approbation of their instructors, all of whom take the deepest interest in promoting the good of those entrusted to their charge.

The educational progress has been more marked than in former years...At the examination held by the Board of Missionaries...the highest form of the Senior School passed a written examination from papers prepared for the examination of teachers on the Reserve...

I consider that the attainments of the pupils in the highest class in the Junior School very nearly equal to the most advanced class in the Institution when I entered upon my duties here, whilst they are able to make far more use of what they do know. This results from the compulsory use of the English language at all times.

The school has lost the services of Mr. Isaac Barefoot, who for four years had charge of the Senior School, and was for many years a zealous and painstaking officer of the Company, and to me a most valued assistant. He is now studying for the ministry. Miss Fisher, as teacher in the Junior School, continues to discharge her duties to my entire satisfaction, and as she will have completed her fourth year of service on the 1st of May next, I would recommend that her salary be advanced $25 per annum, from that date, as a mark of the Company's approbation...

8. 25 August 1876   Gilkison

Mr. Ashton...reports 83 pupils in course of instruction, who, while there, are supported and clothed at the expense of the Company, and taught the ordinary branches and vocal music; the boys work a farm of 300 acres; the girls, the house-work, including baking of bread and making the clothing of the pupils.

From what may be called natural defects, Indian children, in general, not being brought up with a due sense of propriety and obedience, become wayward; but the Institute, to some extent, proves a corrective to those who are happily there...far greater benefits would be conferred could the Institute be enlarged...arrangements such as to admit children at the earliest age...

9. 1877   NEC Report: R. Ashton

Although no deaths took place at the Institution, 4 girls died of consumption within three months after leaving.

...The general conduct of the pupils both at work and school has been all that could reasonably be desired, whilst among themselves they always appear happy and contented.

The educational progress has been very satisfactory, and I am convinced that the teachers have discharged their duties conscientiously and well; in fact, I do not think I could possibly find a staff of subordinate officers who would as a whole display greater zeal in carrying on their work than do the present officers of this Institution.

Carpentering was commenced as a trade in April last, and being fortunate in obtaining the services of a thoroughly experienced and well-qualified foreman...in time a profitable business will be established, in which the boys will be thoroughly instructed.

There are several alterations, repairs, and improvements required for the main building...

To remove a staircase and make a suitable and respectable main entrance, with hall, etc.

To divide the present visiting-room with folding-doors ...to form a music-room, with entrance from the girls' school-room. At present the girls practise in the visiting-room, but this... is open to great objection, as the work is greatly interrupted, and too great facility is afforded for intercourse with visitors before they are announced.

We are greatly inconvenienced by the kitchen being at one end of the dining-hall and the scullery at the other; the girls working in the scullery are therefore removed from as close supervision as is desirable, and the dining-hall is dirtied by the continual traffic from kitchen to scullery, and vice versa...

10. 30 July 1877   Gilkison

The Mohawk Institute maintains its high reputation, and does its great and good work...nearly ninety children being there. A large addition has been built, affording more comfort to the pupils, and the surrounding grounds are improved and beautified.

...to render such an institution capable of receiving children (in large numbers) at the earliest possible age - even in infancy...such a course would be the effectual means of attaining that change in the Indian people so much desired, and, may thus solve the problem of their real civilization.

11. 1878   NEC Report: R. Ashton

...erecting a play-house for the boys, and of extensive improvements and repairs to the main building.

The pupils continue to make satisfactory progress in their studies and industrial training, whilst there is such a steady improvement in the order and tone of the Institution generally...

Thomas Green, who left this Institution in August last, passed the best examination of the first-year students in applied science at McGill University.

John Elliott, who entered the Ontario Agricultural College in 1877, obtained second-class honours at the recent examination.

Anna Jones passed the entrance examination to the Brantford Collegiate Institute at Midsummer, and on entering the school was immediately advanced to the second form...

All the alterations suggested...have been carried out, and also a large amount of general repairs, leaving the interior of the Institution in excellent order...

The whole of the interior walls of the Institution were thoroughly cleaned, and, where necessary, re-placed; and most of the wood-work received two coats of paint.

The work has been better done, and at very much less cost than could have been done by any one besides our own staff...

...I expressed it as my opinion that it would be greatly to the advantage of the pupils if the Christmas vacations were dispensed with, and the summer vacation proportionately lengthened...I am more than ever convinced of the desirability of such a change in our system, and especially so as each year the number of children left here during the winter vacation is increasing. Very few of the parents would regret the change, if it became the rule, whilst the children would be morally and physically benefited, and a very serious interruption to our training avoided.

12. NEC Report: Six Years Summary

...the Special Committee have steadily in view the recorded desire of the Company to raise to the proper standard of efficiency the Mohawk Institution and the several day-schools...so that the education given there should be sufficient for all classes of Indian pupils.

...great progress has been made since 1872 at the Institution. Important alterations have been gradually introduced in the discipline and instruction of the children, as well as in the arrangements for the comfort and accommodation of the inmates of the Institution...in the building itself, in the outbuildings, in the gardens and yards, and in the manual labour farm...New buildings have in many instances been erected, often, of late, by the resident carpenter and the boys trained under him.

The time-table acted on in 1873 and 1874 was soon slightly altered, so that instead of the boys attending school on alternate days, they were arranged in three divisions, one only of the three divisions being employed out of school in turn. Thus all attend school four days and work two days in the week. Sometimes, indeed, in winter, each division is sub-divided, and thus each boy is out of school one day only in the week. At other times ample employment out of doors is found for the full division, some being engaged in manufacturing hurdles for movable fences, and others in various occupations about the farm-buildings, attending the cattle, etc.

In the year 1873 the number of pupils in the Institution fluctuated considerably, and by the end of the year had dropped to a total of 41-23 boys and 18 girls. In each succeeding year, however, the numbers increased...

Early in 1873 Mr. and Mrs. Griffith, the boys' schoolmaster and the matron, resigned their situations in the Institution. Considering the length and fidelity of their services and their age and failing powers, the Company presented them with eighty guineas, a gratuity which they most thankfully received. Other changes also took place in the subordinate offices in the Institution...Mr. Isaac Barefoot (He was a Catechist for many years, and since been ordained and appointed...to the sole charge of Point Edward) was appointed as teacher of the boys in the Institution, in place of Mr. Griffith. At the same time Miss Jennie M. Fisher was appointed as teacher of the girls there, in place of Mr. Barefoot, from 1st May, 1873. A great improvement was soon made in the Institution by adopting the usual practice in Canadian schools of <u>mixed classes</u>, - Miss Fisher taking charge of the two junior classes of boys and girls, and Mr. Barefoot taking the senior classes of both sexes - Mr. Ashton himself taking some of the subjects in each division, and giving a general superintendence to all the classes. The children, too, are not confined to school work, the boys taking part in the outdoor work, both gardening and farming, and Carpentering, etc.; and the girls being taught to use the sewing and knitting machines and mangle, and assisting in cooking and housework, and making and mending the clothes, etc. worn by the children or used in the house.

Some few, on leaving the Institution, have gone into service in suitable places, and some even, while still resident in the Institution, have been bound apprentice to different trades in or near Brantford.

The testimony of two of the Indians themselves is worth recording. On the 18th of May, 1873, two Indian mothers, Mrs. Smith and Mrs. Davis, visited the Institution and saw the children at dinner. They expressed surprise at various complaints they had heard respecting the food supplied to the children, as from what they saw they considered it excellent both in quantity and quality.

Occasionally visits have been paid to the Institution by benevolent persons interested in the welfare and elevation of the Red race...They expressed extreme gratification... marked improvements in the Institution, and in the appearance and conduct of the pupils. The greater part of the interior of the building had been recently painted (under Mr. Ashton's supervision), by the boys themselves. Mr. Ashton...reporting on 1st August, 1874, that both the teachers (Mr. Barefoot and Miss Fisher), had evinced the utmost interest in the improvement and welfare of the scholars, and that in the pupils themselves he observed rapidly increasing intelligence, energy, and cheerfulness.

Before the Institution closed for the Christmas vacation, in 1874, Mr. Ashton held a public examination, to which parents and guardians of pupils, and friends of the Indians were invited. About forty persons were present...The pupils were examined in reading, geography, grammar, human physiology, and Scripture history. After the examination Lieut.-Colonel Gilkison distributed the prizes awarded during the year. The pupils sang a selection of sacred and secular music, and were afterwards addressed by several of the gentlemen present. The visitors generally expressed themselves as pleased and surprised at the proficiency displayed by the pupils in the various subjects in which they were examined.

After the vacation, and the Institution had reopened, the Hon. David Laird, Minister of the Interior and Superintendent-General of Indian Affairs, accompanied by the Hon. David Christie, Speaker of the Senate, Colonel Gilkison, and Mr. Cleghorn, visited and inspected the Institution, and examined the pupils in their classes. The Minister's entry in the visitors' book was:-

Visited this Institution on the 16th January, 1875, and found the arrangements for the improvement of the pupils almost perfect. The apartments are scrupulously clean, and every effort seems to be made on the part of the manager, Mr. Ashton, and his assistants, to forward the educational interests of those committed to their care. The pupils read tolerably well, write with great ease, and sing very sweetly. Was most pleased with the pains taken to promote the religious and moral well-being of the Indian youths in the Institution.

The Speaker's entry was:-

I am much pleased with what I have seen and heard at the Mohawk Institution to-day. The New England Company deserve the thanks and best wishes of the people of Canada for the good work which they and their officers are doing amongst the Six Nations...

...25th of May, 1878, L. Vankoughnet, Esq., Deputy Superintendent-General of Indian Affairs...spent an hour in the Institution and expressed himself both surprised and pleased at the condition of the Institution, and the attainments and manners of the pupils.

...Mr. Vankoughnet...speaks as follows:-

I had the pleasure last spring of visiting the Mohawk Institution, and gladly place on record the gratification it afforded me to see how efficiently the Institution was conducted under the active supervision of Mr. Ashton, the principal, and his assistants. The children looked healthy, clean, well dressed, and quite contented.

Mr. Ashton was good enough to have them examined before me in their several studies; and I have much pleasure in stating that their proficiency in the several branches of education is remarkable, and would be considered creditable even for white children.

The cleanliness and comfort which characterizes all the different departments of the Institution is exceedingly praiseworthy; and one could not but feel thankful that, outside of the Department, there should be a Company having such a deep interest in the welfare of the Indian race as to found an Institution... for the benefit of the rising generation of Indians.

Colonel Gilkison, a few days later, writing to the Clerk of the Company, mentioned this visit, and added that they were much pleased with the management, and that Mr. Vankoughnet addressed the children in happy terms; and that the improvements in the building and outside are very good and creditable to Mr. Ashton's taste. The Colonel at the same time expressed a hope that it might be in the power of the Company to enlarge the premises, or have another building erected for younger children, which... would be productive of greater benefits to the Indian race.

...20th December, 1878, Canon Nelles, J. Mills M.A... Principal...Brantford Collegiate Institute...and others, were present in the evening at the closing exercises. Principal Mills addressed the pupils, complimenting them very highly on their reading and singing. He considered their exercises equal, if not superior, to any he had ever listened to of pupils of a similar age. He had never visited the Institution before, but, from the two pupils (Green and Jones) who had attended the Collegiate Institution from there, he had been convinced that whoever taught them had done so thoroughly. But he was perfectly astonished at the excellent order they had maintained throughout the evening; he did not believe such discipline could be witnessed anywhere else.

Satisfactory as is this six years' stream of testimony, it must not be understood that there have not been great difficulties to be overcome, and even offences to be deplored, and if possible corrected.

Occasionally the welfare of the younger boys and girls

in the Institution has demanded the expulsion of older children guilty of some aggravated offence or of repeated misconduct, e.g., incorrigible thieves, cheats, or liars. In one instance Mr. Ashton had to report, with deep regret, towards the end of the year 1876, that one of the pupils had been guilty of stealing a prayer-book from a store in Brantford, into which he had gone for the purchase of two hymn books. The boy - an Oneida, and grandson of a native Methodist missionary - had always borne a most excellent character and had evidently yielded to a sudden temptation, for which he was believed to be soon deeply and sincerely penitent. The police magistrate before whom the boy was brought the next day, on investigation of the charge, admonished the boy, and handed the case over to Mr. Ashton to deal with. Mr. Ashton inflicted adequate corporal punishment, and in consideration of the boy's former good character and apparent contrition, did not dismiss him from the Institution. This, it is right to record, is the only charge of misconduct ever brought in a public court against a pupil of the Institution during Mr. Ashton's superintendency, and the magistrate, in admonishing the boy, paid a high tribute to the excellent character generally borne by the lads at the Institution.

Obstruction on the part of parents is still too often an impediment to the Company's efforts to instruct and elevate the young Indians of both sexes. In some cases, however, the parents' consent having been obtained, an arrangement has been made to pay a boy pupil at the rate of 25 cents per week (on good conduct and industry) during the first year of his apprenticeship, half to be paid to the boy monthly, and half to be carried to his account towards supplying him with necessary tools if he satisfactorily completes his term of three years. The apprentice generally boards and lodges at the Institution, and attends evening school there.

A taste for farming, on a methodical and scientific plan, has undoubtedly been fostered in many boys by their training at the Institution...

One object kept in view by Mr. Ashton has been to assimilate the course of instruction at the Institution as closely as possible with the educational system of the Province of Ontario, so that our pupils obtaining the highest certificate awarded in the Institution might be fitted to obtain employment as public school teachers. More than one of the Institution pupils are fairly rivalling their white competitors.

In June, 1875, Mr. Ashton sent Thomas D. Green, one of the Institution boys, to attend the examination of candidates for admission into the Brantford High School, or Collegiate Institute. The boy obtained the highest number of marks of any of the forty-one candidates from the public schools of the County of Brant. His age was then 17½ years. He had been admitted into the Institution, in Jan 1873, and had been a monitor there for the last two years. His superior ability and application had placed him educationally far beyond any of the other pupils then in the Institution, so that the schoolmaster could not devote to him all the attention he required, except of the other children.

On Ashton's recommendation Thomas D. Green was permitted to attend the High School for instruction, - remaining, in all other respects, a pupil of the Institution for one year, and devoting all the time he could spare from his studies to the industrial work of the Institution. Mr. Ashton hoped, in time, to have a class of such pupils in our own schools.

At the end of his first year, July, 1876, he was successful in winning the prizes in his form, for English, Latin, mathematics, and general proficiency, and had proved himself most persevering in his studies, and he received from his masters an excellent character. The special Committee therefore, without hesitation, extended for another year the permission for him to remain in the Mohawk Institution, receiving instruction at the Brantford Collegiate Institute, as before. He successfully passed the intermediate examination held in December, 1876, an examination which is considered to be equivalent to that for a second class Provincial certificate, and is midway between that for admission into Collegiate Institutions, and University matriculation.

In April, 1878, Thomas Green went home for a few months, preparatory to entering the applied Science Department at McGill College...He was prepared to bear the greater part of the expenses of his education by letting his farm, and obtaining some temporary assistance from his friends. His application to the Indian Council for assistance was refused, though the Pagans gave a nearly unanimous vote in his favour, and both Col. Gilkison and Mr. Ashton strongly recommended it. As James Mills...Principal of the Brantford Collegiate Institute, gave the young man an excellent character, and considered his abilities excelled by few, the Special Committee, at Mr. Ashton's suggestion, undertook to pay his fees, (about ten guineas per annum), at the Montreal College.

In the summer Thomas Green matriculated at McGill College, Montreal, and the Secretary reported that the young man had passed one of the best matriculation examinations. He himself expressed, in a letter to Mr. Ashton, his gratitude for the assistance afforded him. The Committee at once gave him a prize, which it was hoped would be a real assistance to him, and would encourage him to continued efforts without injury to his self-reliance.

Soon after Christmas, 1878, the gratifying intelligence reached England, that Thomas Green, at the recent examination, had obtained the first position of his year.

In April, 1877, an intelligent half-breed, John Elliot, was at Mr. Ashton's recommendation, admitted into the Ontario School of Agriculture at Guelph. While there he would be at no expense for board and tuition, and might probably receive from $25 to $50, at the end of the year.

Meanwhile he would require some assistance to provide him with clothing, etc., his interest-money supplying him with pocket-money. Mr Ashton undertook to advance him sufficient to supply necessaries, on the understanding that he returned to the Institution at the completion of his course, and repaid, by his services on the farm, the sums thus advanced; for with the training obtained at the Agricultural College, Mr. Ashton expected the young man would become well qualified to take a position at the Institution, as farm instructor.

Another pupil of the Mohawk Institution, Anna Jones, failed at Michaelmas, 1875, to obtain her certificate at the Provincial Examination of Candidates for school teacherships. She was, however, admitted into the Brantford Collegiate Institute as a student for a second-class certificate, and being a very promising girl, the Committee, as an inducement to greater exertion on the part of other pupils, complied with Mr. Ashton's request...of keeping her at the Institution for a year, the fees being only $16.

For the last four winters the pupils in the Institution have had fortnightly evening entertainments of readings, recitations, vocal and instrumental music, etc., the programme for each evening being provided by the boys and girls alternately. These entertainments are a source of great enjoyment to the pupils, and a very valuable help to the teachers, by conducing to improve the children's reading and articulation of English.

The present staff of instructors at the Institution comprises...Mr. Robert Ashton...Mrs. Ashton, who acts gratuitously as matron, Mr. S. J. Truman, master-carpenter; Mr. J. R. Alexander, farm-foreman; Mrs. F. Cowle, assistant-matron; Mrs. S. Mattingley, laundress; and Miss C. Johnson, sewing-teacher.

Miss Jennie M. Fisher deservedly retains her situation as school-mistress, and the Rev. Isaac Barefoot's place of school-master is now well filled by Mr. Wm Butcher, who received his training in England...He holds a...Provincial certificate in Canada, where he had taught for two years, before undertaking his duties at the Institution in November, 1877.

Through continued attacks of chill fever, Mr. Ashton's health, early in the year 1877, was very indifferent, and Dr. Griffin considered it absolutely necessary that he should take a month or six weeks' sea voyage. The Committee not only granted him at once the requisite leave of absence, but assisted him towards the expense of a visit to England, in July, August, and September, in that year. Mr. I. Barefoot (on leaving Huron College, in June, 1877, and before accepting any parochial work) took charge of the Institution for Mr. Ashton during the latter's absence...everything had gone on well during his absence, but that there had been a great deal of sickness, chiefly ague and low fever, on the Reserve, and that the pupils returned, after the holidays, less regularly and punctually than usual, and that several of them were still suffering from chill fever.

One of the more important subjects of consultation with Mr. Ashton...was a proposal to introduce an Industrial Orphanage for young children in or near the Institution. Another was the question how best to provide against the pupils relapsing into the lower life of their parents on leaving the Institution. A third was the difficulty of interesting the parents in the education of their children...

At present the Committee has not seen the way to opening an Orphanage...

On the second question, the feeling of many of the Red men is, "why teach our girls to be ladies and all that, for when they come home they must learn to be squaws?" This is but too true. For when they marry men too lazy to support them and their children decently, the work of providing for the family falls generally to the lot of the woman. She must plant and hoe the potatoes and corn etc., or lack the necessaries of life. For she cannot find sufficiently lucrative employment in sewing, hand-knitting, straw-plaiting, or basket-work, and so, losing self-respect, she sinks in the social scale. Yet the surest road to Indian improvement is that which will elevate the social and moral condition of young women. The difficulties in the way are many. Few can be employed as teachers among their own people. Still fewer can be induced to enter domestic service among the whites; though there would be little difficulty in providing situations in good families for all we could train. They, however, think this beneath them, and indeed are not happy among strangers. One course may be to interest the Indian girls to manufacture some article of commerce, supply them with the raw material and find a market for the goods when finished, they receiving a settled price for their work. Thus each apprentice might, in two years' time, earn enough to supply herself with a knitting-machine of her own. This experiment is now in progress, and promises well.

13. 29 September 1879 Gilkison

The Mohawk Institute continues its excellent course, with a full attendance of 90 boys and girls...The grounds have been much improved, with a large addition to the main building, rendering it a model establishment.

14. 24 September 1880 Gilkison

...The Institute...continues to flourish, full of children from the Six Nations and from some distant bands. Seven of the senior pupils competed against many whites from schools in the County of Brant, at a late examination; while, at the present time, a majority of the teachers on the Reserve were educated at the Institute. The proposed addition to the Institute for Orphan Infant Children is still undecided upon...95 Pupils on Roll...Teachers J. H. Farlie $400...Jennie Fisher $200...Industrial training twice a week. The boys do farm work; the girls, housework...

15. 26 September 1881 Gilkison

...The Mohawk Institute, with its ninety children, continues to prosper under its efficient management, and in all respects it may be classed as a pattern institution. One highly important feature is the education and training of pupils to become qualified teachers, thus supplying a serious want for Indian schools.

16. 6 October 1882 Gilkison

In the Mohawk Institute the full number, ninety (forty-five boys and forty-five girls), is maintained and the pupils educated in such a manner as to induce numerous applications for admission, which it is to be regretted cannot be complied with.

Among the successful students from the Institute is Thomas D. Green...whose studies carried him to and through...Brantford Collegiate...to McGill College... from which he graduated this year with honors, including the degree of Bachelor of Science...now upon the engineering staff of the Montreal and Sorel Railway Company.

17. September 1884 NEC Report: Carpenter

...I devoted five clear whole days to an exhaustive examination of the work of the Mohawk Institution, and of the condition of affairs on the Reserve...The farm itself, and the stock upon it, appeared to be in excellent condition...most creditable to Mr. Ashton, who is doing better with it than most, if not all, of the surrounding farmers are doing with their land. Mr. Ashton himself attributes part of this success to his thoroughly carrying out, not only with all the inmates of the Institution, but also with all the animals when under cover...the "Dry Earth Sewage System"...every particle of manure...goes to fertilise the ground, and there is no chance of any of the wells or springs being contaminated by sewage...I could not detect the least unpleasant effluvium...

All the farm-work is carried out by the boys, under the guidance, and with the assistance, of two men who act under Mr. Ashton's directions...rough but exact records were kept of stores and materials used...the exact pecuniary condition of the farm could be ascertained at any desired moment. These records are all sent in to the office, and are put into shape usually by Mrs. Ashton, who is of the greatest assistance to her husband in all clerical work, as well as in many ways too numerous to mention...except during the short summer vacation (near harvest time), Mr. and Mrs. Ashton are never off the premises together, is strong evidence of their devotion to their work. Certain slight structural alterations in the farm-buildings appear very desirable...The agricultural machinery appeared good and effective, and very necessary, for the external value of each boy's labour is 50 cents per day, or 12s 6d per week. The thrashing machine...is hired when needed.

Although the pupils had only returned from their

vacation a few days previously, I found the interior of the Institution very clean and in good order, and work was proceeding regularly...the building is fairly well adapted to its purposes, but the worst features are the dormitories, which are badly shaped and very crowded, quite unhealthily so in warm weather. The amount of space available for the private use of Mr. and Mrs. Ashton and their family is really very limited...The laundry, kitchen arrangements, &c., are good, particularly the former. The school-room furniture is susceptible of improvement; but I was glad to observe that the books in use were new and well adapted to their purpose, and that the provision for "object-lessons," and even for a little elementary science, had by no means been neglected. As Mr. Ashton has a good magic-lantern, a few pounds expended in some of the scientific and other instructive series of photographic lantern-slides...would do much good. On the Sunday afternoon I took the whole school, and heard many read and sing, and both questioned and addressed them. The system of teaching in vogue appears good, the teachers being expected to *teach,* and not merely to *hear lessons.* The use of text-books by them and by the pupils during the lessons is discouraged, the pupils being encouraged to write notes of their lessons. I looked over several of these, as well as a large number of examination-papers, &c., and am satisfied that very good educational work is being done, especially by the highest class, in arithmetic, geography, English history, and grammar. The work of this character, however, is much more promising among the girls than the boys, and many of them become teachers in Indian schools on the Reserve and elsewhere, and occasionally even in White schools.

I devoted one evening to a thorough examination of Mr. Ashton's methods of keeping his accounts, school registers, &c...I was prepared to find these very complete, and I was not disappointed...The registers include a record of the character and chief events in the life of each pupil while in school, and of their subsequent career for some years after they leave...the nett cost per head of each inmate is *remarkably low...*
Mr. Ashton...is the Secretary to the small School Board, partly composed of Indians, which manages the Indian schools on the Reserve, and in this capacity he frequently inspects the schools in a very systematic manner. Most of the teachers having been his former pupils, his influence over them is considerable; in fact the Mohawk Institution is fast becoming a Normal School for Indian Teachers. Hence Mr. Ashton practically controls the education of all the children on the Reserve...
...Nelles...and Mr. Ashton concurred in saying that when pupils first went home from the Mohawk Institution, the parental influence was so strong that for a few years they relapsed into Indian habits, and that not until they had homes of their own, did the good effects of the Mohawk training re-appear...

18.   25 August 1885   R. Ashton Annual Report

...Of girls, 3 were sent home through delicate health, 2 left to help their mothers through sickness in the family, 1 to take charge of a school, 1 married, 2 were refused re-admission, their conduct not being satisfactory, and 1 entered domestic service. Of boys, 2 were sent home through ill-health, 1 for habitual lazy and dirty conduct, 2 had completed their course, and left to obtain situations, 4 "Oneidas of the Thames" absconded...

Beyond an outbreak of measles and several cases of malarial fever, the health of the pupils has been good. The general conduct has been satisfactory.

The teachers have worked with skill and zeal, and the classes have made good progress. Five boys and three girls successfully passed the high school entrance examinations, and two girls completed their course of special training as teachers, and have been appointed to the charge of schools. Two boys, who had passed as teachers, but declined the special training, obtained situations as clerks.

Ten scholarships have been established, by means of which deserving pupils will be maintained at the Collegiate Institute, Brantford, to obtain provincial certificates as teachers, &c. All expenses of boarding and clothing of the scholars are provided by the liberality of the New England Company, but I am indebted to the Government for a grant towards defraying the cost of fees, books, &c.

To enable any Indian band in the Dominion to obtain qualified teachers, the New England Company has been pleased to direct that hereafter 30 boys and 30 girls may be admitted from the Tuscarora reserve, and 15 boys and 15 girls from any Indian reserve in the Dominion. Candidates must be between the ages of 11 and 17 years, and able to read fairly in the third reader and work correctly the simple rules in arithmetic. Pupils from other Indian Institutions will not be admitted.

Industrial Department
...The carpenters' shop was closed part of the year, the master being on sick leave. There are four apprentices. One boy is apprenticed to a blacksmith in Brantford, but boards at the Institution.

Condition of Past Pupils
I consider the condition of the 121 pupils [see p. 210] who have left the Institution during the last four years is encouraging, although it does not reach the high standard of our hopes and desires.

I...earnestly request that you will...issue instructions to the managers of Indian Industrial Schools...that "Managers and Superintendents of Indian Institutions are on no account to admit into their respective schools pupils belonging to or who have been in other Indian Institutions without first obtaining the consent of the Superintendent of the school in which the pupil was first received."

The principle embodied in the above suggestion has

been very seriously violated in the past. Pupils who have been dismissed for serious offences or who ran away from this Institution have been readily and without inquiry admitted into others. The effect will render any exercise of discipline as regards the pupils or their parents an utter impossibility, and will encourage both to play fast and loose with their privileges. Another evil to be prevented...is the unwise interference of one institution with the work of another, by which past pupils are diverted from the course for which at great cost they have been prepared. For instance, A.S. was admitted here in 1874 when in his 16th year. He remained 5¼ years, and learned the trade of a blacksmith. I obtained employment for him in one of the largest agricultural machine manufactories in the country. He told me last summer that he was then saving eleven dollars per week over and above his expenses. Now, when he certainly could help himself, he is, at 25 years of age admitted, like a little boy, into an Institution supported in part by the Government. After attending the school 3 or 4 months he successfully passed his examination, and becomes a school teacher, on $250 per annum.

It is very evident that he was qualified to pass his examination before leaving here. However, he did not then wish to teach, so became a blacksmith. Now he expects to teach a year and then enter the ministry. He may, and I certainly hope and pray he will, become a good preacher - he was a good and very industrious blacksmith, and as "example is better than precept" it may be a question in which capacity he might be the better missionary to his brethren.

As a direct result of the case cited above, N.S., a brother of A.S. ran away from this Institution when within two months of completing a course of five years and passing his examination as a teacher. His father came a few days before he left and told him that his brother had entered the other institution and would be sent from there to college, to be prepared for the ministry. Further comment is unneccessary.

19. 15 July 1885 Kelly Report
...visited the *"Mohawk Institution and Indian Normal School,"* the name which the New England Company has recently bestowed...In the school rooms are two large globes...a good supply of maps, Boyd's objects, a chemical cabinet, a library of more than 200 vols, apparatus for illustrating Encyclopedia Britannica, and periodicals such as "The Sunday at Home," "Leisure Houre," "Boys Own Book," "Girls Own Book," "Picturesque Canada...The senior class is prepared for the Entrance Examination. The principal teacher is Miss Watson...the assistant is Miss Jessie Osborne, a great grand-daughter of "Theyendenaga." The New England Company has recently established ten scholarships (value $10 each)...to be chosen from those who shall have passed the entrance

examination. These scholarships are in the Brantford Collegiate Institute...boarding and lodging at the Institute and receiving their clothes free...Last year eight passed the entrance examination...Willis Tobias, standing third in a list of 75 candidates...The widow of...Archdeacon Nelles has donated a silver medal...to be given annually to the pupil...who...obtained the highest...marks at the entrance examination.

Music and scripture history are taught very thoroughly in all the classes. There are two organs...I submitted printed papers prepared by myself to the senior school...arithmetic, grammar, geography, history, literature and spelling...Ashton, prepared a paper in Scripture. The result of the examination was, on the whole, satisfactory... there can be do doubt that the Institution is doing an excellent job...

20. 4 September 1885 R. Ashton to Secretary Education Department
I beg to request a reconsideration of the case of Miss Susan Hardy
a)...That the candidate is an Indian and speaks the Mohawk language fluently.
b) Her attainments are proportionately higher than those of English speaking candidates, as she was examined in a (to her) foreign language...twenty-five per cent would not be an unfair reduction in her favour in the two subjects.
c) As a pupil in this Institution her application & perseverance have been most commendable. She has therefore been permitted to continue her studies at the cost of the New England Company in order that she may become a teacher to her people.
d) It is desired to appoint her as a junior teacher in this Institution as soon as she has completed her training in the Model School.

21. 29 September 1885 R. Ashton to Ross
...Presuming upon a casual acquaintance...I have taken the liberty of making a personal appeal...in soliciting a slight, and in my opinion a reasonable concession on the behalf of Indian candidates brought into honourable competition with their white neighbours in obtaining professional standing as public school teachers.

At the late examination for non-professional certificates Miss Susan Hardy (No.550), an Indian, wrote on both 3rd and 2nd class papers obtaining a pass in the former, and failing in the latter by only two marks in composition and ten in English Literature...
My appeal has been disallowed. During the last thirteen years I have done much to advance education among the Indians, and have personally trained many as teachers, now I am endeavouring to bring them up to the standard of Provincial Certificates...
The only subjects this young woman failed in - English Composition and Literature present almost insurmountable

difficulties to an Indian. This you will more fully realize when you consider that an Indian must translate the question from English to Indian, think out the answer in Indian and then translate it into English.

It is very desirable that we should have a supply of fully qualified teachers for our Indian Schools, and it is necessary that they should have a speaking acquaintance with the language spoken by their pupils - then they must be Indians, but I am afraid that in this generation we shall not get them if the full "pound" is always demanded in composition, unless the examinations are conducted in Mohawk, Ojibway &c. &c.

22. **8 October 1885 Education Department to R. Ashton**
...under the special circumstances...the Minister approves of Miss Hardy receiving II class standing. Please return her III class certificate for correction.

23. **29 September 1886 R. Ashton Annual Report**
During the year the school has been filled to its utmost capacity (45 boys and 45 girls).
...health of the pupils has been exceptionally good... in their general conduct... a marked improvement...especially observable in the cheerful readiness with which they enter upon their appointed duties, and in the pains and pride they exhibit in discharging them.

Educational

All the classes have made excellent progress. Four pupils passed the public examination for entrance to the Collegiate Institute at the city of Brantford, obtaining positions of credit amongst the seventy-one who passed at Christmas.

No. of marks obtainable	755
Highest obtained	519
Matilda Curley, 3rd place	508
Josephine Good, 10th place	465
Phoebe Waddilove 22nd place	430
Susan Hill, 26th place	428

Willis Tobias entered the Collegiate Institute eighteen months ago. He has already been promoted to the fourth form. He is also senior monitor in this Institution, and, as there is no master, he takes charge of the boys and their clothing. He is a painstaking and reliable young man.

John Lickers was promoted to the second form in the Collegiate Institute, but being lame, he had difficulty in walking to and from school, and an opportunity offering, he accepted the appointment of teacher in Board School No. 10. He is doing well; his school having the largest attendance of any on the reserve.

Mary Monture entered the Collegiate Institute at midsummer, 1885, and is now in the third form.

Josephine Good and Phoebe Waddilove entered the Collegiate Institute in January last.

Four other pupils attended the Collegiate Institute for a short time and then left the school; one has since entered the High School at Caledonia.

Industrial Departments.

The farm yielded a good return and profit for the year's work, and proves an excellent source of training for the boys.

The trade shops were chiefly occupied in working for the Institution.

A new residence has been erected for the superintendent. The accommodation for officers has been improved, and the sleeping room for the pupils very considerably increased, so that the boys have just double the dormitory space they had a few years ago. Most of the Carpentering and painting in the above work was done by the boys under instruction.

24. **9 September 1887 R. Ashton Annual Report**
...Of the girls who left during the year, two received appointments as teachers; three others had completed the regular course of studies; and one, a sixth form girl left on account of ill health.

Of the boys, two apprentices (one blacksmith and one carpenter) left before completing their full course, though both are sufficiently advanced to obtain employment at their respective trades, if they wish...four had reached the sixth form, and five the fourth form in the senior school; the remainder had been present only short periods.

Health

The health of the pupils has been generally good, throughout the year. On one occasion there were several cases of varioloid, a mild form of small-pox. The patients were immediately isolated, and when necessary the other pupils were vaccinated. The precautionary measures adopted were effective in preventing any serious consequences. One girl was sent home for change of air, as she was too delicate to continue her studies.

There has been no death here since June, 1880, and only two deaths during the past fifteen years.

Conduct and Progress.

The general conduct of the pupils has been very good.

Education

Excellent progress has been made in all the classes. The work is more rapidly and accurately done, and many of the scholars take great interest in their studies.

Four girls passed the examination for entrance into the Collegiate Institute, taking very creditable marks, though not obtaining positions on the list as advanced as those who passed last year, their average attendance at the institution, three years ten and one-fourth months, being one year and nine months less.

Three girls have accepted scholarships at the Collegiate Institute, and one elected to take her course of training as a teacher at once.

Scholars attending the Brantford Collegiate Institute during the year:

Willis Tobias, 4th form.

Mary Monture, 3rd form. Left November, 1886.
Phoebe Waddilove, 2nd form. Left, December, 1886.
Josephine Good, 2nd form.
Sarah Russell, 1st form. Entered at Christmas.
Sarah Latham, 1st form. Entered at Christmas.
Naomie Latham, 1st form. Entered at Christmas.

Appointments, &c.

Miss Susan Hardy, 2nd Class Provincial Certificate, to be teacher of the junior school here.

Miss Mary Monture...teacher of Board School No.9.

Miss Jessie Osborne attended the Normal School at Toronto, during the first session of 1887, and obtained a Grade A, 2nd Class Professional Certificate.

The Nelles medal for general proficiency was awarded to Josephine Good.

Of the past graduates of this Institution, there are at present actively engaged in their professions: two clergymen, two physicians, one civil engineer and Dominion land surveyor, two civil service clerks, seventeen school teachers, and many others have qualified as teachers but are engaged in other callings. Several are following the trades (carpenters and blacksmiths) they were taught here, whilst a large number are well-to-do farmers and wives of farmers.

25. 30 October 1888 R. Ashton Annual Report

Attendance

...The number entering and leaving this year is greater than the average of the past five years, owing to the railway companies having discontinued allowing Indians to travel at half price, several parents were unable or unwilling to pay the increased charge for sending the children to school. The applications for admission far exceeded the capacity of the institution.

...a majority of the pupils...leave before the completion of their second year and before they can have derived much lasting advantage from the course of training...

It is much to be desired that the Government provide the means whereby institutions of this character might prevent this great waste of labor and resources, by making such regulations as would permit pupils being admitted under a written agreement to remain for specified periods. Without such a system industrial schools cannot successfully fulfil their purpose as few pupils remain long enough to acquire any proficiency in the handicrafts taught. Under the present system a boy will volunteer to learn a trade, but as soon as the school vacation comes he will go home and not return.

At present no means is provided by which Indian youths can be required to fulfil any engagement they or their friends may make, either with the managers of the Industrial School or with tradesmen willing to receive them as apprentices. I could place any number of boys as apprentices in the city of Brantford and would provide them with suitable boarding accommodation if proper

provision was made for holding them to their agreements.

Conduct and Progress.

The conduct and progress of the pupils generally have been satisfactory. Instead of awarding prizes at the end of the year, a system of granting good conduct badges to deserving pupils at the end of each month has been adopted and found to produce excellent results. The well conducted obtain increasing privileges and good conduct pay throughout the year.

Education.

The pupils have made good progress in their school work. Geometrical drawing and music are taught in all the upper forms, and to induce the pupils to greater exercise in the use of English than can be attained in the class room they are encouraged to give frequent readings and recitations for the entertainment of the whole school. The boys and girls providing the programme alternately.

Francis Davis passed the examination for entrance to the Collegiate Institute at 'Xmas.

Five pupils have accepted scholarships and are studying for 3rd class certificates at the Collegiate Institute, Brantford. Two girls attended a session at the Provincial Normal School and obtained professional second class certificates.

26. 1 September 1889 R. Ashton Annual Report

Attendance.

...The institution was filled to its limit (45 boys and 45 girls) throughout the year, leaving many applicants for admission upon our list...

Health.

The general health of the school has been very good. There were several cases of scarlet fever and measles of a very mild character, but beyond these no serious illness of any kind. With a few exceptions, the conduct of the pupils has been satisfactory.

Education.

The school work has maintained its usual standard of excellence in the...branches of the public school course.

Lucy Hill, Lucy Martin, Levi Williams, Jamieson Lewis and Elizabeth Maracle passed the examination for entrance to the Collegiate Institute.

Willis Tobias obtained a third-class professional certificate, and was appointed teacher of a school at Moraviantown.

Josephine Goode and Sarah Russel, having attended the Collegiate Institute at Brantford for some time, and completed a course of six months' special training for teachers in our own schools, received certificates as Indian school teachers, and obtained appointments, the former taking charge of a school at Parry Island and the latter of School No. 7, on the Tuscarora Reserve. Their work has been most favourably reported on.

Lucy Hill and Francis Davis, having passed the necessary examination and completed a six months' course of special training, entitling them to be awarded the graduating diploma of this institution, approved and endorsed by the Deputy Superintendent General, were appointed to the charge of Indian schools respectively at Muncey and No.11, on the Tuscarora Reserve.

The Nelles medal for general proficiency was awarded to Levi Williams.

Two students have partially completed their course of training as teachers, and two others will enter upon their training at the commencement of the coming term. Sixteen past pupils are now teaching Indian schools, and one is teaching in the public schools of the city of Winnipeg. Of these, two hold second, and one holds a third class professional certificates, the remainder having special certificates of qualification for teaching Indian schools.

W. Noah, on satisfactorily completing his term of apprenticeship as a carpenter, was presented with a chest of tools. He is now working at his trade.

27. 30 September 1890 R. Ashton Annual Report
Attendance.

...The applications for admission very far exceed the accommodation of the institution.

Health and Conduct.

The general health of the school has been very good... and the conduct of the pupils has been fairly satisfactory.

Education.

In the education fair progress has been made.

Lizzie Maracle and Jamieson Lewis, who passed the examination for entrance to the High School, are both continuing their studies, the former at Deseronto and the latter at Ridgetown High Schools.

The following ex-pupils have been appointed as teachers during the year:-

Willis Tobias, 3rd Class Public School certificate, to Moravian Town.

Lucy Hill to Muncey.

Frances Davis, to Board School No. XI.

Robert Hill to Board School No.II., in succession to Miss F. Maracle, who taught this school most successfully for eight years, and has been appointed to a clerkship in the Indian Department at Ottawa.

The "Nelles Medal" for general proficiency was awarded to Naomi Latham, who is now attending the Brantford Collegiate Institution.

In September of last year the institution was visited and inspected by a commission consisting of four members of the New England Company, which entirely supports this school...the visit of the Company's Commission will result in the increasing usefulness of this institution, and particularly so through their recognition of the merits of past pupils by the distribution of silver medals to those who, by their exemplary conduct and distinguished services, have done much towards the advancement of

their race, and have proved themselves worthy to form the nucleus of a band of Honourable Past Pupils...

Roll of Honor Past Pupils of the Mohawk Institution to whom has been awarded the Company's silver badge, with the year of their leaving the Institution:-

Rev. Isaac Bearfoot, 1854; Chief Benjn. Carpenter, 1854; Chief Sampson Green, 1862; Chief Alex. Smith, 1867; Mr. Thos. D. Green, 1878; Mr. Nelson Moses, 1878; Miss Sarah Davis, 1880; Miss Lydia Lewis (Brant), 1880; Miss Maggie Maracle (Claus), 1881; Miss Floretta Maracle, 1881; Miss Jessie Osborne, 1883; Miss Susan Hardy, 1886.

28. 11 September 1891 R. Ashton Annual Report
Attendance.

...attendance has become more uniform; only one pupil attended less than a year (she went home sick), and only one remained longer than five years. In 1880 eight pupils attended less than a year, and five more than five years.

The applications for admission continue to exceed the accommodation of the institution.

The average number of pupils boarded and clothed was ninety-one.

The following improvements have been made:-

a) Building a brick basement to the boys' play-house with lavatory, hot and cold shower baths, dressing room, in which each boy has a separate locker, a boot shelf and towel rack.

In the upper floor are a reading room, clothes press, play room and trunk room, forming... a most complete home for the boys...situated as to afford a refuge in the event of a conflagration in the main building.

(b) Putting electric (incandescent) lights into the class rooms and sewing room.

(c) Constructing an officers' dining hall in the basement of main building.

(d) Building a furnace room in boys' department, so as to remove furnace from dining hall.

(e) A new cooking, baking and hot water apparatus in kitchen and scullery.

(f) Adding a third organ for the girls to practice upon. Every girl in the upper school now receives daily instruction in instrumental music.

Health and Conduct.

An epidemic of influenza visited...early in the year and caused interruption to the usual routine, as few pupils or officers escaped its attack. Though in some cases the sickness was severe, no fatality occurred. One girl (a pagan Indian) positively refused to take the medicine prescribed for her, on the ground that "white medicine no good for Indian." I was obliged to ask her friends to remove her. I regret to say she did not recover.

Beyond this the general health of the inmates has been good and no death has occurred in the institution during the last ten years.

The conduct of the pupils has been fair. Six boys absconded immediately on the reopening of the school after the summer holidays, for which, I believe, the system of allowing partially trained lads a period of unrestrained license is responsible, as no others ran away during the previous twelve months, nor have any done so since.

All pupils are now admitted upon written agreements that they shall remain for not less than two years and without any vacation; that those who go home upon the completion of their term must, if they wish to re-enter, make application within thirty days. By this system undesirable characters are eliminated and those only who are deserving are re-admitted. The result is already apparent, and I am convinced that more lasting effects will result from even two years continuous training than from four years attendance under the old system of an annual return to former habits and evil surroundings, which entirely unfit the majority of pupils for further training and in all cases greatly retarded their progress in English speaking.

Education.

The class work has been well done and good progress effected. Four pupils passed the examination for entrance to the Collegiate Institute, and are now taking their special course of training as teachers of Indian schools, viz.:- Francis Styres, Christie Anderson, Reuben Tobias and David Benedict...

Trade Shop.

The balance in favour of this department is small, as there has been very little work done in which profit could be gained, nearly the whole operations being confined to improvements and repairs at the institution, which are charged at actual cost.

It is a great disappointment to me that I cannot induce more lads to remain long enough in the trade shop to gain a fair knowledge of the business. As soon as they obtain a little experience in the use of tools they imagine they are worth more than they get and, are easily led by their friends (?) to seek employment elsewhere, so that few attain to anything like a fair knowledge of their trade.

In reviewing...the year's work I am on the whole satisfied...that substantial progress has been made...

There is great improvement in the condition of the Indian dwellings, but the advance is most marked in the dress and manners of the younger women and girls.

Formerly it was very rarely that a girl came to the institution provided with underclothing and night dresses; these are now becoming necessities. The highly-coloured cotton kerchiefs have been replaced by hats; jackets are taking the place of blankets and shawls, and neatness is considered more attractive than flashy colours and tawdry ornaments.

Increasing necessities demand a wider range of, and more continuous, employment, and this results in a large increase in the number of youths of both sexes seeking occupation away from home, the boys as farm-hands and the girls as domestics; in the latter class the increase is very marked.

29. 20 September 1892 R. Ashton Annual Report

Attendance.

...Of the three pupils who remained in attendance less than two years, one died, one was sent home as being unfit for industrial training, and the other, a boy having no home, was fetched away to attend the funeral of the woman who brought him here, and did not return...

The cost for maintenance is, and will be, somewhat higher than in former years, as the pupils remain throughout the year.

Health and Conduct.

This year has been remarkable for the uniform general good health of the pupils, and also, I regret to say, for the only death which has occurred in the institution during the past eleven years.

The conduct of the pupils has been satisfactory.

Education.

During the early portion of the year the progress of the senior school fell short of that of former years, largely through the teacher's inability to adapt his methods to the special requirements of giving instruction in (to the pupils) a foreign language, and I was obliged to make a change...to the advantage of the school.

One pupil passed the entrance examination to the Collegiate Institute, but through constitutional nervousness failed to successfully pass the six months special training required to obtain our diploma as an Indian school teacher.

Two students will write for their third-class certificates this midsummer, and one for promotion to the second form in the Collegiate Institute, and three for the entrance examination.

In all branches of industrial training the results have been satisfactory. A competent gardener has been added to our staff, a greenhouse has been built and flowers, fruits and vegetables are regularly sent to market. I look upon this as a most promising and instructive industry.

Passed Pupils.

This year is the twentieth of my superintendency, and it is my intention during the year to collect the fullest information possible respecting all pupils who left the institution during that period.

Since 1872, twenty-two boys and thirty-one girls passed the entrance examination to the high schools.

Twenty boys and twenty-five girls have been engaged as Indian school teachers.

Five boys and ten girls are now teaching.

Obtained Professional Standards.

1 B.Sc., D. and PL.S.
1 M.D.
2 2nd class public school teachers
1 3rd   do   do
6 passed Civil Service examination (four hold appointments in the service).
4 are attending collegiate institutes.

30. 14 September 1893 R. Ashton Annual Report
Attendance.

...Of the five pupils who remained less than two years, none were desirable students; two were dismissed for bad conduct, two were physically unfit, and one went to nurse her sick mother and was told not to return.

The average number of pupils boarded and clothed was ninety-four.

Health and Conduct.

Beyond a few slight cases of influenza in the first two months, and one case of pneumonia later, there has been no sickness among the pupils during the year.

The conduct of the pupils has been satisfactory.

Education.

The pupils have made good progress in their studies, though the general standard of attainments is and will be lowered for a time owing to the admission of orphans and neglected children, who are generally quite ignorant on admission; but as this class is admitted for long terms the decrease of numbers in the higher classes will be only temporary.

P.A. and W.P. passed the entrance examination into the Collegiate Institute at midsummer. The former has undergone a course of training for a teacher, and in the early part of last April was appointed to School Board No.11; the latter does not intend to pursue his studies further at present.

N.L. failed...second-class non-professional examination. She will continue her studies for another year.

J.G. passed 3rd class examination, and is now attending the Model school at Brantford.

C.A. completed one year's attendance at the Collegiate Institute, was called home through a death in the family. She has completed her course of training and is in possession of a certificate as an Indian school teacher.

The "Nelles medal" for general proficiency was awarded to Peter Adams.

4 are attending collegiate institutes.

Carpenter's Shop.

Very little has been done in this department...The carpenter resigned his position owing to ill-health at the end of March, and, as no work of a profitable character could be obtained, I did not feel justified in appointing a successor. In September he returned but did not work full time as we had really nothing to do beyond the occasional repairs, etc., necessary for the institution.

It is impossible to induce boys to remain as apprentices sufficiently long to become useful, this renders us unable to obtain work in competition with the large number of machine factories in the neighbourhood, which can turn out all classes of wood work much better and at less cost than we can do.

The difficulty of holding any Indian youths or their parents to the terms of a written contract is, under existing circumstances, practically impossible.

A large addition...in course of erection...will afford a play-room for girls, a large school-room, dormitories, officers' rooms, etc., and raise the accommodation from ninety to one hundred and twenty.

31. 6 September 1894 R. Ashton Annual Report
Health and Conduct.

With the exception of an epidemic of measles, the health of the pupils has been very good throughout the year, though we have to regret the loss of one bright boy by drowning whilst skating.

The general conduct of the pupils shows marked improvement, as under the existing system of admission for definite terms we are enabled to eliminate the badly disposed by refusing them readmission.

Education.

Although admitting as pupils many orphaned and destitute children who are generally totally ignorant, the educational progress has been better than I expected. Good work has been done in both schools, and although our general standard of attainments is somewhat lowered, the foundation has been laid for future advancement.

The applications for the admission of girls far outnumber those for boys. This fact is worthy of note, as formerly the Indians would not readily allow their girls away from home, therefore the mothers of the present generation mostly grew up in ignorance. Now we may hope for rapid improvement, as English will more frequently be the language of the family.

H.B., L.G. and P.W. successfully passed the entrance examination to the Collegiate Institute at midsummer, and are now under training as pupil teachers.

J.G. obtained a third-class teacher's certificate and passed her Model School training examination, winning the highest praise of the Public School Inspector and the Principal of the Model School. She has been appointed to the New England Company School at the Bay of Quinte.

N.L. is continuing her course for a 2nd class certificate.

The "Nelles Medal," for general proficiency, was awarded to Lizzie Goode.

During the year the building has been enlarged by the addition of a wing...three stories high...The whole of the basement forms the girls' play-room, and contains two large furnaces with which the building is heated.

A rearrangement of the older portion of the building is being carried on, and when completed will add greatly to the accommodation ...and comfort of the pupils.

32. Application for Admission

This Institution is established for the purposes of civilizing the Indians and advancing the Christian Religion among them, and imparting a good education, combined with all kinds of useful industrial training, to the youth of both sexes.

Pupils are boarded, educated and clothed free of charge.

Those who are fitted, if desirous, may be apprenticed to various trades, or be trained for teachers of Indian schools.

Candidates for admission must be between the ages of 11 and 16 years, and able to read in the Second Reader, and work the simple rules in Arithmetic.

Orphans, destitute or neglected children of over 9 years of age may be admitted without passing the examination. But in such case an agreement must be signed by the legal guardian, chief of the band, or an agent of the Indian Department, that the child shall remain in the Institution until it is 16 years of age.

N.B. No new pupils are admitted for less than two years continuous residence. At the end of that period they may return home, but will be eligible for re-admission for not less than one year, provided that application for re-admission be made within 30 days.

Pupils are at liberty to write to or receive letters from their relations and friends as often as they wish, but in order to guard against improper correspondence, all communications must be addressed to the care of the Superintendent, who will open and peruse the same should he deem it advisable. Communications in Indian are not allowed.

Pupils may receive visits from relatives once a month - on Saturdays, between the hours of 10 a.m. and 4 p.m.

33. 1894 Benson
...I walked out to the Mohawk Institute...The children had just finished their tea and the girls were walking along the avenue and about the grounds in front of the Institute while the boys were taking their Sunday recreation on the other side in rear of the building...

I was most hospitably received by Mr and Mrs Ashton and upon informing them of the reason of my visit, I was asked to remain for evening prayers, held in the large new school-room, which furnished ample accommodation for the 51 boys and 59 girls then present. Mr Ashton read the Evening Service...and a few additional well rendered hymns were sung, all the pupils taking part in the singing...the harmonium played by Miss Ashton. The singing was sweet and clear, - all knew the words without the use of Hymn-books and the service was joined in by all as if they enjoyed it...none of the mumbling and muffled tones that one might well expect from Indian children. Mr Ashton lead the singing giving the time which was kept correctly as a result of the careful training they receive in this branch. Mr. Ashton assured me that they are able to sing almost any music at sight by simply following him as he beat time for them, and of this I had many opportunities of being subsequently convinced.

After prayers the pupils all filed out of the room in the most orderly manner to their respective recreation rooms... what most struck me during all the time I was at the school was the order, regularity and precision with which all the pupils conducted themselves. This school is as well regulated and controlled as a piece of machinery, going on without stop or hitch from morning to night. The boys have a thorough military organization, being divided into four squads, forming a company, each squad having its corporals and sergeant who act as monitors, and the whole is in charge of sergeant-major, who is the head boy and chief monitor. The discipline of the school is strict and is enforced by the monitors who take pride in their position and the responsibility it entails. This discipline is maintained by a system of rewards and punishments...that this system works well I had ample opportunity for judging while observing the ordinary routine of the school.

The girls are under a modified form of the same system, and I have no hesitation in saying that a system which produces such good results in the way of cleanliness, punctuality, obedience and good behaviour...

While maintaining this strict system of discipline, ample time and opportunity is afforded for healthy exercise and recreation, and although they are at all times under careful supervision, they are not made to feel that they are under espionage. They are treated as reasoning human beings who know right from wrong and are taught to do right for right's sake.

...The chief aim of the Institute is to impart a practical education to the children entrusted to its care, which will be of service to them when they grow up to men and women. Farming is the principal industry taught, and the Institute possess every facility for imparting a thorough and useful knowledge of this most important calling.

The New England Company's Estate...embraces 469 acres...The want of rain was severely felt and some of the crop is almost a total failure. However Mr. Ashton hopes to raise enough to carry him through the winter. A large supply of hay was left over from last year and he will have plenty of fodder corn for his stock. A second crop of roots and a late crop of corn were being put in...Four teams were at work in a large field of about 20 acres. The plowing done by the boys in charge was equal to any seen on the farms of whites.

Mr Ashton drove me all over the farm...the crops were for the most part poor, the fields were remarkably free from weeds. Mustard and thistles were not to be seen, as the boys are kept busy pulling them out when they appear.

No class work was going on at the time of my visit, the children being allowed a month's vacation from studies, but the regular farm, household and industrial work was kept up, pupils working half-time and being allowed the other half for recreation. The barns, sheds, stables, silos, barn-yards and grounds were neatness personified, while everything in and about the building was scrupulously clean and tidy.

A large bell on the end of the implement shed, the central of the buildings is rung at stated times, when the boys all fall in on the parade ground in their proper order, number off and go about their regular duties.

The milking of 33 cows is done by the boys; the yield of each cow is weighed night and morning and a tally kept...The milk after being weighed, is turned into the separator, which is run by two boys...The churning and butter-making is done by the girls in another building, to which a cold storage-room is attached.

The cattle are well cared for fed and cleaned and are brought up regularly from the pasture fields...the stock on the premises:-10 horses (15 working driving and 4 colts), 33 cows, milch, 21 young cattle, [?] sheep and lambs, 55 pigs, 30 poultry
...the work of paving the barn-yard. This was done during spare time, the stone being gathered from the fields. They are firmly and well laid and enable those employed about the stables and farms to get about comfortably, besides carrying off liquid manure to the proper place, instead of leaving it in pools about the yard, as is usually the case, even with well to do white farmers...

While the work goes on regularly there is plenty of time allowed for play and the boys are well supplied with all the necessary requisites for out-door games, such as cricket, foot-ball, lacrosse, base-ball, and gymnastics. The girls have swings, croquet sets, skipping ropes and base-ball. The boys have a larger play-room, about 50 yards to the north of the main building, at the side of the play-ground, where they can amuse themselves in wet or stormy weather. All kinds of indoor games, such as draughts, dominoes, shuffleboard, and magazines etc., are provided and their wooden muskets are stacked here.

Their dressing, lavatory and bath-room is in the basement of this building, which has a concrete floor. Each boy has separate locker, a row of which run around three sides of the room. Their boots and shoes and every-day and working clothes are kept here. Their uniforms are kept in the Store-room and are given out as required and returned to store neatly folded and brushed after use. The Lavatory for the boys...There are nine basins placed in a stationary wash-stand running along one side of the room, supplied with water from taps, with plugs in each basin to let the water off after use. Each pupil has a separate towel marked with his number and no one else is allowed to use it. Nail brushes, combs and brushes, soap, blacking brushes and blacking are supplied, soap and blacking being given out weekly.

The bath is quite original...At one end of the room a raised rim of concrete about a foot high is placed, making a shallow pan about 10 by 15, - hot and cold taps are over the centre and a short hose with a spray nozzle can be attached to either or both taps and played on the boys, who are obliged to take the shower bath at least once a week, unless excused on account of their health...the whole school can be bathed in a very short time. They are sent in squads and are showered in turn. There is no

delay in filling the baths and the water runs off as soon as used. After the shower they file back to their dressing room and the whole thing is over in about half an hour.

The girls have a small bath-room in the laundry. Both these bathrooms are comfortably heated and I consider them a very suitable arrangement...

The girl's play-room is in the basement of the new wing,...cement floor...the arrangements for fire protection are very complete. Each dormitory has two fire escapes which lead to the ground and can be reached at once from all parts of the building. The pupils are all locked in their dormitories at night, but each lock has a pane of glass...which can be broken in case of alarm and the bolt shot back...There is a well-equipped fire department in the centre hall of the main building which communicates with all the passages, and is accessible from every part of the house. There are 12 Ever-ready fire extinguishers...The boys are drilled as firemen and have their regular duties assigned to them in case of danger. The rooms of the staff communicate directly with the dormitories...

Lockers are placed along the wall in the girl's playroom which serve as seats. Each girl has a separate locker marked with her number, in which she can keep her private property and finery. The long tables with benches and an organ are in this room, opening out of which is the girl's clothes and dressing room. The spare dresses and petticoats are hung on hooks, numbered to correspond with the lockers. The girl's lavatory is in rear of this room...A large towel rack with five bars runs the whole length of the room...Towels are hung on this rack after being used and are dry when next wanted. Pupils, on the ringing of the bell warning them to get ready for meals, go to the lavatories, wash their hands and face, and then fall in their proper places and march to the dining room which is on the ground floor in the east wing immediately in rear of the kitchen. There is a separate entrance for girls and boys, the girls entrance being covered from their playroom. This room is divided by an archway 9ft wide separating the boys and girls. There are four tables in each room and all are seated by squads. A sliding window communicates with the kitchen through which the food is handed and placed on the table. Soup is handed round at dinner, but meat, vegetables and bread are placed on the table and the pupil in front of whom the dishes are set helps the others. There is no confusion or hurry in entering or leaving the dining room. A short grace is said the pupils all standing, then all seat themselves quietly and are helped liberally. There is plenty for all and they are taught to eat their meals in a quiet and orderly manner. The matron presides at dinner, sitting between the archway with the pupils in sight. The teachers take charge of the other meals in turn. After dinner all march out to their respective quarters. The dining tables and benches are made of hard-wood and are kept perfectly clean. I think the hard-wood tables are preferable to either zinc or oil-cloth covers which are...greasy. Granite ware is exclusively used. The plates and dishes after being washed are placed in racks...the floors in the dining-room, kitchen and passages on the ground floor are covered with hardwood grating made in sections which can be easily lifted so that any mud or dirt brought into the house by the children's feet would fall through to the floor and not be tramped in. After each meal all the gratings are taken up and the floors swept, the gratings being swept off and periodically scrubbed.

The staff have a private dining room...

The floors, stairs, and most of the furniture are made of hardwood, nearly all this work being done by the carpenter and his boys.

The kitchen is a large square room, the ground floor of the east wing and is filled with every convenience and the cook and her assistants keep everything in the best of order. The utensils were all clean and well arranged. The store-room, pantries, and refrigerators are all near by. Supplies are regularly issued and checked so that no waste can occur. Food supplies are given out daily - stores issued weekly on requisition and the quantity then issued. Most last until the following week. Immediately after dinner on Thursdays the fatigue boys and girls come to the dining-room for their supply of soap, blacking, brooms, scrubbing brushes etc. Worn out articles are brought along with the requisitions and if it is thought that they can be made use of for another week, no new issue is made. The monitors are responsible for the care of these articles and anyone guilty of destruction or waste pays the penalty being placed on the black list. There was a full grown young woman working in the kitchen, who had finished her term in the school. She was fitting herself to become a cook and expected to get a place when she has mastered the culinary art. A well trained cook is always certain of a good place and good wages. Laundry...

Dormitories - girls...The main dormitory...contains 41 beds, being divided into 5 compartments...Eight beds are in each compartment...hardwood...spring wire mattress...no chance for dust or dirt to accumulate under the beds. As the room is always comfortably heated mattresses are not used, but blankets are spread on the springs...Sheets, blankets, pillows, quilt and white counterpane are supplied. The last is removed every evening, folded and put away. These white counterpanes are for show and not for use. The bedding was all clean and the beds neatly made up. The only other article of furniture in the room was a commode, and a dry earth closet, for both girls dormitories in case of necessity. Night gowns are neatly folded under the pillow and when the girls return they undress in this room and fold their clothing on the foot of the beds, putting them on when they get up. Their washing and dressing being finished down stairs in the dressing room and lavatory. The floor is maple, oiled and

was perfectly clean being wiped off every day with damp cloths. Another row of beds could easily be placed down the centre of each partition if required and this would give accommodation for 10 more pupils without overcrowding.

Going down three steps from this room the 2nd Dormitory is reached. Twenty iron beds are in this room, which is large enough to hold 8 or 10 more. Both those dormitories have fire-escapes and outside entrances.

The Infirmary...is completely isolated from the dormitories and has four iron beds. There was no sickness while I was at the school; one of the girls suffering from inflammation of the eyes was kept in a darkened room in the attic for treatment...

Dormitory - boy's...are in the east wing...This wing contains the dining room, kitchen, dormitories, senior school room, dairy, cellar, cold storage room, furnace room (2 hot air furnaces). The dormitories are on the 2nd and 3rd floors. The end room over the extension was being freshly painted. It has 10 iron beds. This leads to what was formerly 3 sleeping rooms, but are now thrown into one...to allow of a freer circulation of air and better supervision of the boys while in the dormitory. There are 8 iron beds in each division of this large room. There is a room in the rear of the centre building with 9 beds and in the rear of the 3rd story of the Principal's house there are 10 beds, making 53 in all, with 3 beds in the sick room, which is at the back of the main building and not connected with any of the other rooms. One of the staff sleeps on each flat, and their rooms communicate with the dormitories. The farm assistant sleeps on the 2nd flat and the junior master on the 3rd flat. They have charge of the boys dormitories. The boys uniforms and clothes are kept in a room next the farm assistant's. The school master has a room off the senior school room on the 1st floor. A few of the bedsteads used by the smaller boys are made of oak, canvas bottoms being used instead of wire mattresses, and are found to be more suitable for young children. The room over the extension is designed for a hospital. It can be cut off from the rest of the building and has a separate outside entrance. A room at the head of the landing leading to the rear of the Principal's house, is set apart for the solitary confinement of very refractory boys with a similar place on the girls side of the building. These two rooms are about 6 by 10 and are only lighted by a barred fanlight over the door. I asked the Principal if he ever had occasion to make use of these rooms, and he replied that he sometimes did so for short periods and that he found that this mode of punishment has a most salutory effect. Confinement in these rooms lasts during playtime and no one but the Principal can order solitary confinement or administer corporal punishment. I was told that, on the whole, the conduct of the children was very good but in this as at all other schools, examples have to be made and resorted to. A milder form of correction and one that usually has the desired effect is to make any children who have been guilty of a breach of discipline do sentry-go on the playground while the others are enjoying themselves. I saw three or four of them doing their solitary march around a well beaten square and they all seemed to be thankful when their turn was up.

Sewing Room

A large sewing room is in the centre of the main building...The sewing for each girl is got ready by the seamstress or one of the older pupils who acts as assistant. All the material required to finish the work is given out at one time, with a card bearing the pupil's number, date of issue, description of garment or work and blank space for the date of completion. There were two sewing machines, pressing boards, cutting boards, table, etc. in the room but most of the work is done by hand. They are all supposed to put the work together properly, after having been shown how to do it. Bad or careless work has to be reported and leads to the black list.

School Rooms.

Senior school-room for Standards 5 and 6...has 30 single hardwood seats and desks screwed to the floor, low in front and getting higher towards the back of the room, ink wells in each desk with shelf under the top. These desks...were made on the premises. The room is well supplied with school material, maps and natural history cards, black boards...an organ...The teacher's desk is on a platform raised...The timetables and Programme of Studies was posted up as well as a conduct board on which is registered the demerit marks of the pupils. This board has a frame and glass cover which is kept locked. It is a very simple contrivance and at a glance shows what the behaviour of all pupils has been for a certain time, any week. The name of each pupil is written on a slip of paper one below the other, this is set in the frame and opposite each name are a number of holes parallel with the name. When a pupil receives a demerit mark, a peg is placed in the first hole opposite his or her name, and for each subsequent mark the peg is moved on one hole. Those without a peg opposite their names have given satisfaction while those who have pegged the most holes are the worst behaved. When the Principal enters the room he can see at once what the conduct of each pupil has been without making any enquiries. A modification of this system runs through the work of the whole school so that the Principal knows exactly what is going on without any tale bearing. The pupils all understand this system and have to govern themselves accordingly. Strict rules are laid down which are to be followed, and Mr. Ashton claims that by impartially enforcing their observance he can so train a child that by the time he is ready to leave the school, he will have formed the habit of doing what has to be done unconsciously, - or to use his own words, he can train an Indian child to work whether he likes work or not.

Junior School for children up to and including the 4th Standard...has 37 desks...seating one pupil in school. This room is also used as a chapel and lectures and other entertainments are given here. At such times two children occupy each seat...It is also used as a music room and has three organs or harmoniums in it...a large numeral frame on a stand, two blackboards, clock, and thermometer, which is heated from the furnaces in the girl's playroom below and is ventilated by registers along the baseboard... A large supply of school material is kept in the book room...I was shown some excellent object lesson cards, divided into kingdoms and illustrated by specimens of raw and manufactured materials which are attached to each card. There was a good supply of kindergarten requisites and geometrical forms and text books...

...three ex-pupils who now are employed as teachers of Indian schools in different parts of Ontario, were spending a portion of their holidays at the Institution, where they had all been trained. They look upon it as Alma Mater and were enjoying the renewal of old friendships. I think it speaks well for the treatment they received while pupils when they will take long and expensive journeys to revisit their old home. One of these teachers, Miss Good, came from the Tyendinaga Reserve, where she has charge of the New England Company's School. Old pupils of the school all speak well of it. Three ex-pupils worked in the Department and are fair examples of the results obtained there. Two of the number enrolled live at the Institute and are attending the Collegiate Institute at Brantford, being fitted for the position of teachers. There were 110 pupils on the roll and present while I was at the School, being 19 over the number for whose maintenance the Department contributes. The present equipment of the school will provide for 120 and accommodation could, without crowding, easily be found for 140 pupils.

The income of the Company has falled off of late years, owing to the depreciation of farming land in England, such lands forming the bulk of its investments, while the poor crops in Western Ontario this and last year have seriously affected the resources of the school. I was shown more than 50 applications for admission to the school which had to be refused for lack of accommodation. If the Department could see its way so as to increase the grant to provide for 100 pupils it would be money well spent...

Drill.

The boys receive regular instruction in drill and were put through their exercises three or four times while I was there, - once in full uniform armed with their wooden muskets. With the ringing of the bell they all fall in on the parade ground, number and are inspected by the Instructor and Sergeant. They wear a neat dark grey uniform, blouse and trousers, with black stripe and glowarry and with polished boots and neatly brushed hair they looked very smart and carried themselves like veterans. They were taken through the manual and platoon exercises, squad and company drill, forming squares, marching in column and line, countermarching and marching in precision. All these movements were gone through correctly and with precision and I have seen very few volunteer companies do better. A son of Mr. Ashton's acted as Instructor. The boys evidently enjoyed the drill and took pride in it.

The pupils at this school come from 10 or 12 different tribes and originally speak as many different dialects, but they understand English and many of them speak it very well; particularly the girls who are not so shy about conversing with strangers as the boys.

Mr. Ashton told me that he proposed having more girls than boys in the school, not because they are less troublesome, but because he is convinced from experience that by educating and training girls in household duties, greater advantages can be made in civilization than by training an equal number of boys. A boy leaves the school, returns to the Reserve, marries an Indian girl who has not had similar advantages and the result is that he reverts to the Indian language, and habits and customs and his children are Indians pure and simple. While a girl who has been thoroughly trained returns to her people, takes pride in her cooking and household duties, and when she marries and has a family, her children are taught to speak English and are brought up to follow her habits of civilization. The man may be the breadwinner, but the woman is the civilizer.

Pupils admitted to this Institution are taken for two years (except in the case of orphans who are retained until they can do for themselves. After the expiration of the two years they are allowed to go home for a month and unless they return their place is filled by the next applicant. This rule applies more particularly to children belonging to the Six Nations - who have been at school previously to come to the Institute, where they are sent for the sake of the Industrial training to be had there...

I was much pleased with this, my first visit to the Mohawk Institute where I found excellent order, perfect discipline and ready obedience the rule...I am now more than ever convinced that the success or failure of such schools depends entirely upon the executive head and not upon subordinates or surroundings. A thoroughly competent Principal will make a success of a school, while a man lacking the ability to direct and manage no matter how well educated, will fail or be content to work on and trust to luck for results.

REGULATIONS for the award of Good Conduct and Black List Badge

(1) Good Conduct Badges shall be awarded under the following Regulations and each such Badge shall be distinguished by a silver star to be worn on the left breast.
(A) Boys shall be eligible for badges 2 months after their admission and every month thereafter.
(B) Boys shall not be eligible for a badge who have had an offence recorded against them during the preceding month, or who have been guilty of theft, absconding, insubordination or gross breach of discipline, during the preceding 3 months.
(2) Good Conduct Badges shall entitle their possession to the following privileges and indulgences:
(A) One Badge, exempts the holder from corporal punishment, except for theft, absconding, direct insubordination or gross breach of discipline, and confers the privilege of going out with friends, and under the charge of a monitor.
(B) Two Badges, in addition to the privileges of those possessing one Badge will entitle holders to go out on their half-holidays.
(C) Three Badges, same as above and to receive 2 cents per week.
(D) Four Badges, as above and to receive 3 cents per week.
(E) Five Badges, as foregoing and to receive 4 cents per week.
(F) Six Badges,   "   "   5   "
(3) Any boy being in the possession of Good Conduct Badges who shall be reported twice in one calendar month shall forfeit a G.C.B. and for every additional report in the same month he shall forfeit a Badge if he possess any.
(4) If a boy being in the possession of G.C.B.s shall be reported for theft, absconding, direct insubordination or gross breach of discipline he shall be liable to lose the whole or any portion of his badges in addition to such other punishment as may be awarded.
(5) There shall also be a 'Black List' for incorrigible boys, who shall be distinguished by a black strap to be worn over the left shoulder, and whoever is in such Black list shall be deprived of all privileges and indulgences, and shall be liable to such other restrictions as the Superintendent may determine.
(6) Any boy who shall not be in possession of a G.C.B. and who shall have 4 offences recorded against him in one calendar month, or who shall be guilty of theft, absconding, direct insubordination or gross breach of discipline shall be liable to be placed on the Black List.
(7) Any boy in the Black List who shall not have more than two reports recorded against him during the period of one calendar month, may be removed from the Black List.
N.B. All boys at the commencement of a school year and new boys from the date of their admission will be granted the same privileges as boys in the possession of 2 G.C.B.s until the completion of the second full month of their attendance, or until they have forfeited such privileges under the foregoing regulations.
The same Regulations are applicable for the girls, with the following alterations however:
Read girl instead of 'boy' whenever necessary, & so on.
(2) (A) Omit: "exempts...and"
(B) Strike out all after the word 'go' and add 'to Brantford or elsewhere for a walk once a fortnight'.
(5) Omit: 'black strap...shoulders' and insert 'black apron to be worn at all times'.

Summer Routine

Bell

5.30 -	Rise, make beds, etc.	1.15 -	Work and prepare for school
6.25 -	Breakfast - Prayers	1.25 -	School (1.30)
7.00 -	Work	4.00 -	Stop school, - recreation.
8.00 -	School Div. Stop Work and prepare for school	5.00 -	School Division to work.
		6.00 -	Stop Work.
8.25 -	School (8.30)	6.15 -	Supper - recreation
(10 to 10.15 - Recess)		8.15 -	Prayers - Bed (Juniors).
(10.15 to 10.30 - Drill)		8.30 -	Seniors (14 years and over prepare lessons)
12.00 -	Stop work and school.		
12.15 -	Dinner	9.30 -	Bed
	All lights out before 11.00 p.m.		

Division A and B attend school A.M. or P.M. on alternate weeks, change

on Friday.
Thursday and Saturday P.M. Holidays until 5 o'clock (School Division only)
Wednesday - Singing 7.15 to 8.15 P.M.
Saturday - Bath and hair cutting 7.30 to 9 P.M.

FARM

Teamsters to clean and harness horses by 8.25 A.M.
Milkers to have cows in stable by 6.25 A.M.
Horses and cows turned to pasture immediately after Supper
Men's dinner hour - 12.15 to 1.15

Daily Routine (Winter)

6.00 - Rise - wash	1.00 - Work (Div)
6.45 - Breakfast	1.30 - School
7.15 - Work (Chores)	4.00 - Stop school

8.15 - School Div. Stop Work	4.30 - Work
8.45 - School	5.30 - Stop work
12.00- Stop work and School	6.00 - Supper
12.15- Dinner	7.00 - School
	8.00 - Prayers
Recess 10.25 to 10.35 A.M.	8.30 - Marks -Bed
	9.30 - Seniors bed

Senior School prepare 2 lessons 8.30 to 9.30 P.M.
Assistant Matron takes supper
Governess takes Junior school 7 to 8 P.M. Mon, Tue, Wed. and Friday
Farm Garden and Trades
Men on duty 7 A.M. to 12 and from 1 p.m. to 5.30
Stock - stables and green house to be visited 8.30 to 9.p.m. for this duty - arrangements may be made for turn about in regular order.
Extra hands to make full time light and weather

DIETARY

To commence Nov.11th 1895
Breakfast:- Changed on May 16th 1895, 3 quarts of pint milk, thick oatmeal porridge ad lib, 4 oz bread and butter with 2 oz addition for boys except twelve younger boys. Reason for this change: all milk now run through the separator, butter fat extracted, and butter given to compensate for the deterioration of milk.

	Breakfast	Dinner	Supper
Monday	8oz bread, 1pt oatmeal porridge, 9lbs oatmeal, 1lb sugar, 12 pts milk	4oz bread. Potatoes unlimited. Soup. Composed beans, carrots, onions, bones ¼ lb meat / pupil	4oz bread and butter. 1pt milk. Cornmeal porridge unlimited
Tuesday	Do	4oz bread, potatoes unlimited. Irish stew unlimited 6oz meat per pupil, potatoes & onions	4oz bread & butter, 1pt tea Potatoes & gravy unlimited
Wednesday	Do	4oz bread, potatoes unlimited, or soup on Monday in winter. summer 4oz bread, 12oz suet pudding & stewed rhubarb unlimited	4oz bread & preserve in syrup 1pt milk. Cornmeal porridge unlimited
Thursday	Do	4oz bread. Potatoes unlimited. 6oz (uncooked) fried pork or boiled meat	4 oz Bread & butter, 1pt tea Potatoes & gravy.
Friday	Do	Same as Monday	4oz bread & butter or 6oz hot bun, milk, cornmeal porridge
Saturday	Do	4oz Bread, Potatoes unlimited, 6oz per pupil of boiled meat and 4oz suet dumpling	4oz Bread, stewed rhubarb, 1pt milk cornmeal porridge
Sunday	Do	3oz Bread, potatoes unlimited. Cold roast meat or boiled ham. (½lb per pupil uncooked) pickled in summer. Rice or bread puddings unlimited, in summer with stewed rhubarb.	4oz bread & butter. 1pt milk. Cornmeal porridge unlimited

34. 1 August 1895 R. Ashton Annual Report
Health and Conduct.

Beyond one case of typhoid fever (imported) and one case (fatal) of inflammation of the brain, there has been no serious sickness. The general health of the school has been and continues exceptionally good.

The general conduct...has been very satisfactory: what misconduct there is, is confined to a few.

Education.

The educational progress of the pupils has been fairly satisfactory.

Mr. E. C. Ashton resigned the mastership in September, and was succeeded by an experienced teacher, well recommended, but who does not readily adapt himself to a class of students so totally different from those he has been accustomed to.

O.P. successfully passed the entrance examinations last summer and is attending the Collegiate Institute. P.W., H.B.. and L.G. completed their course of training as Indian school teachers; the latter is attending the Collegiate Institute.

Two pupils wrote at the entrance examinations this summer (both passed August 1st). N.L. successfully passed the examination for the second class non-professional certificate, but failed to obtain the professional certificate at the completion of the model school course, lacking...only two marks in hygiene.

The "Nelles" medal for general proficiency was awarded to Omer Plante.

At Christmas the classes were rearranged to accord with the excellent "Programme of Studies for Indian Schools" issued by the department.

In future the *pass* examination of this school will be that appointed for the public school leaving examination "Ontario."

Accommodation.

This institution is fully equipped for 120 students, 50 boys and 70 girls and could easily accommodate 135 (5 boys and 10 girls more) without entailing any additional cost except for food and clothes. I have now over fifty applicants whose agreements are signed, and many others are praying for admission.

Owing to the decreased receipts from farm and garden, I have been unable to maintain more than 110 this year.

An increased grant from the department is urgently needed...

35.   26 August 1896   R. Ashton Annual Report

...The class-room work covers the full course of the public schools of Ontario, the public-school leaving examination being the "pass" standard of the school.

The school hours are from 8.30 to 12 a.m. and from 1.30 to 4 p.m. in summer; and in winter, from 8.45 to 12 a.m. and 1.30 to 4 p.m. and from 7 to 8 p.m.

All pupils in standards V. and VI. have private study from 8.30 to 9.30 p.m.

Pupils from two divisions A and B: 1st week - A division attends school in the morning, B division in the afternoon. 2nd week - the order is reversed.

Standards I. and II. are in school full time during the winter months.

Industrial work is carried on by the division out of school, all pupils being employed from 7 to 8 a.m., and 5 to 6 p.m.

The girls are trained in all branches of domestic work, including sewing, knitting, baking, laundrying and butter-making.

Farming and gardening form the principal occupation of the boys, including the management of hot-houses (two), and a dairy of forty cows.

The cultivation of flowers and fruits, and the manufacture of butter are the special industries of the institution.

A few boys are also instructed in carpentry, painting, etc, and under direction of the trade-master, erect and repair all buildings connected with the institution, mission stations and school (nine) on the reserve.

Other boys may be apprenticed to any trade they wish in the city shops, unfortunately there are no legal powers for binding an Indian boy to serve a time.

Religious instruction is given daily in the schools, and on Sunday...9 to 10 p.m., 2.30 to 3.30 p.m...7 to 8 p.m.

Morning and evening prayers are conducted for the whole school daily, and divine service at the Mohawk church, at 11 a.m. on Sundays.

The boys are organized as a company of cadets, divided into four permanent sections under senior boys holding positions as sergeants and corporals...responsible for the dress, cleanliness and order of their respective divisions.

On 1st July last, the corps gave a public exhibition of drill.

"The boys in gray went through their manual-exercise with a spirit which is found nowhere outside of the regular army. The marching was not quite up to the mark of former public performances, but at times the most complicated military movements were done with the utmost regularity...The cadets were halted, and in a few felicitous words, his worship the mayor presented to them the silver tankard, for their excellent performance at the Agricultural Park on July 1st.". - (*Brantford Expositor, July 5th.*)

All boys and girls who do not receive a report in one month, are awarded good conduct badges which, in addition to other privileges, entitle them to receive one cent per week for each badge they possess. A report deprives a pupil of the weekly half-holiday and four such reports in one month, places the offender on the "black-list" with certain penalties until his conduct improves. Corporal punishment is only inflicted for gross *breaches of discipline,* and is seldom resorted to...The conduct of the pupils for the year has been very good.

The health of the pupils has been excellent; five deaths only have occurred in the institution during my superintendency of twenty-four years.

The sanitary condition of the institution is excellent... The water is supplied in a wind-mill, and is of very good quality.

The buildings are heated throughout with coal furnaces, furnishing a constant supply of warm, fresh air, the foul air being removed by heated flues drawing it off the floor.

The building is lighted by electricity, so that there is little danger of fire; every dormitory is furnished with two or more fire-escapes, and for further protection we have one "fire king.", twelve "ever-ready fire-extinguishers," "fire grenades" in all principal buildings, axes, and buckets filled with water in specified places.

The recreation hours are: one hour at noon, two hours in the evening in summer, and one hour in the winter, and for school divisions throughout the year from 4 to 5 p.m.; also one half-holiday each week.

The boys are furnished in their play-ground with swings and horizontal bars, we also have a field where they play cricket, foot-ball and base-ball.

The girls are provided with swings, croquet, etc.

Owing to severe drought last summer, crops were very light, with the exception of corn and potatoes, and consequently there being very little work, the boys gathered cobble-stones from the fields, and paved the whole of the upper barn-yard, an area of seven hundred and ten square yards in all.

Most of our boys on leaving the school work on farms, even those who have learned trades leave them for farm work. A lad of eighteen years of age working at a trade cannot earn more than sufficient to keep himself. At farm work, however he can earn from $100 to $125 a year, with board and lodging. A large proportion engage for a season of seven months, the rate of wages being higher than for yearly engagements. In the winter they live with their friends, doing occasional jobs.

36. 17 August 1897 R. Ashton Annual Report

Class-room Work...during the past term has been thoroughly satisfactory.

Standard I is in school full time throughout the year, and standard II during the winter months.

A band comprising fourteen pieces has lately been formed...

Farm and Garden. -In the farm and garden the result of the season's work has been the most encouraging of the past five years, all crops except hay and roots were good. Apples were so abundant as to be unsaleable. I had a large quantity evaporated and stored...In addition, the farm boys did grading of play-grounds, gravelling of roads, &c., to the extent of $200, in labour alone, which does not show in the accounts.

General Remarks. - Of the pupils discharged during the three years, 1894-96, 72 per cent of the boys were earning their own living, and of the girls 24.4 per cent married and 26.8 were in domestic service and doing well.

37. 4 August 1898 R. Ashton Annual Report

...Class-room Work.- The work during the past year has been thoroughly satisfactory.

One boy obtained a "Commercial" certificate end of second year's course in the Collegiate Institute; he continues his studies at Deseronto. One girl and one boy passed the "entrance" exam...

Nineteen of the boys receive instruction from the bandmaster and form a brass band.

Health of Pupils. - The year has been marked by a very serious outbreak of typhoid fever in August and continuing for several months...There were nineteen cases in all, two of which proved fatal. There was also one death from acute tuberculosis. In the preceding twenty-five years there were but five deaths, none of which were from fever. At the present time the health of the pupils is excellent. No cause could be assigned for the fever, but a complete system of sewers and drains connecting with the main sewer of the city of Brantford has been put in and water-closets have taken the place of dry earth in the girls' department.

There is no school from the 16th July to 21st August, during this time the master and governess take their vacation, each pupil has half a day holiday, the work of the institution goes on as usual.

...The girls are provided with...balls, skipping ropes, &c. Those who prefer to read are furnished with magazines and books from the school library, the boys have their newspapers sent to their reading-room.

38. 25 August 1899 R. Ashton Annual Report

One girl passed the 'Entrance' examination, and another obtained a "Commercial" certificate (end of second year's

course in Collegiate Institute); both have taken six months' special training for teachers' certificates.

Farm and Garden...has been exceptionally successful...

Health and Sanitary Condition. - I regret to say that we had a number of cases of malarial and a mild form of typhoid fever, caused by contamination of our water supply through the high spring floods.

Two girls died during the year, one from pneumonia, the other from blood poisoning from necrotic abscess.

39. 13 August 1900 R. Ashton Annual Report

Accommodation...is provided for one hundred and twenty, fifty-five boys and seventy girls, and a staff of eleven officers.

...educational progress has been satisfactory. Of the thirty-seven pupils admitted, twenty were totally ignorant and eleven were little better, and as few of these could speak any English or understand anything said to them, the teachers' labours have much increased and their patience been tested to the uttermost...

Health and Sanitary Condition...health...very good... no serious cases of sickness...many cases of measles of a mild type. One girl died from cerebral abscess.

40. 7 August 1901 R. Ashton Annual Report

The educational progress has been very satisfactory, as may be seen by comparison of last year's classification... For improvement in English-speaking a kindergarten teacher from the city schools gives three lessons a week... in English conversation upon common things.

One pupil passed the entrance examination and is taking her training as a pupil teacher in the junior school here, another has been appointed teacher at the Bay of Quinte...

Industries Taught.- Carpentry and Painting - Under instruction the boys do all the work for the institution, farm and the mission stations on the reserve.

Brass Band. - The band-master returned from South Africa in November last and re-organized a band of fifteen boys, who have made excellent progress.

...Girls' Work...Those completing the course have no difficulty in finding situations at good wages.

Health and Sanitary Condition. - The health of the pupils has been exceptionally good, though unfortunately two deaths occurred, one from heart disease, the other from meningitis; there were also two cases of typhoid fever, one contracted through a visit to the city with friends, the second was a newly admitted pupil who had not been here a week - both recovered.

41. 28 July 1902 R. Ashton Annual Report

...Three pupils passed the entrance examination...

Brass Band. - The band of fifteen boys continues to make good progress.

Farming, Gardening and the care of Greenhouses...a dairy of over thirty cows, twenty brood mares and their progeny, about two hundred pigs, and the growing of plants and flowers.

Health and Sanitary Condition. - We suffered an extremely heavy attack of...and owing to the unfavourable weather during the spring months...cases of grippe. Three deaths occurred during the year, one from acute Bright's disease, one from pneumonia and one from congestion of the lungs.

The sanitary condition of the institution is all that could be desired...

42. 1902 R. Ashton Journal

July 1. Dominion Day. General holiday. Working at Government quarterly returns.

July 3-5. Continued Government returns.

July 7. Paying accounts...

July 8. Directed work until 10 a.m., then made up School Board accounts to June 30.

July 9. Writing report for May and June.

July 10. Entering up quarterly accounts.

July 12. Attended meeting of the school board at 10.30. to 12.30. A number of the parents took their children out to see a circus.

July 14. Directing work, and fitted boys in their new uniform.

July 15. Commenced harvest; one binder cutting wheat, another rye...

July 17. Summer holidays commenced - no school; working divisions as usual so that each child plays half the day.

July 18. Directing harvest work. P.M. Received Government cheques for Institution and School Board, and paid the same into Bank.

July 19...Beulah Styres, Minnie Maracle, and Edith Monture successfully passed the examination for entrance to the Collegiate Institute; and Lillie Martin, though failing a few marks, has been recommended for a 'pass'.

July 20. Wet day. Conducted Divine Service...

July 22. Posted vouchers. Received notice from the Board of Health to deepen a creek that runs through the Glebe within twenty days...notice was dated the 16th.

July 23. Directed work and inspected the Glebe creek and crops - the wheat is growing in the shocks...

July 24. Mr. Cameron, Indian Superintendent, came to make enquiries about certain children from Cape Croker whose parents wanted them discharged and had, as usual in such cases, made many lying statements...after full inquiry the Department of Indian Affairs fully sustained my contentions that these children should not be discharged. Commenced Annual Report...

July 25. Sent Surveyor Fair to examine the Glebe creek...Re-arranging insurance policy, as I have converted what was formerly a store into a carpenter's shop.

Continued Annual Report as above, and commenced drawing in wheat.

July 28. Directing work. Completed Government

Annual Report...

July 30. A.M. Directing work; P.M. at School Board accounts...

July 31...Heard of the death of the widow of the late Archdeacon Nelles, my predecessor...

August 1. Buried Mrs. Nelles...at the Mohawk Church ...I took fifty of the girls to assist in the church service.

At 8 p.m. with my solicitor I attended a meeting of the City Board of Works, and strongly objected to lower the stream...It was decided that the work should be undertaken by the City, all interested persons paying their fair share...

August 8. I was notified by the Agent of the... Insurance Co. that the insurance rates would be much increased at the expiration of one year. I had applied and paid for an insurance on the Institution buildings for three years, the Company accepted it for one year only.

August 9. Mabel Walker died last night of tuberculosis following an attack of measles; she had been ill for over two months, but as she came from a distance she was unable to be sent home. She was kept isolated.

August 10. A.M. Conducted Special Coronation Service at the Church. P.M. 2.30. Buried Mabel Walker, all pupils attending the service...

August 13-18. All hands threshing grain.

August 19. Sold seven cattle for $296...

August 21. I sold about 600 bushels of rye at 48c. and 568 bushels of wheat at 65c.

August 22-23. Directing, cleaning and sending grain to market.

August 23. Holidays terminated and usual routine commenced.

August 24. Conducted Divine Service at the Church...

August 25. Received cheque for $662.62 for grain sold. Mr. Milligan arrived this evening.

August 26-27. Mr. Milligan inspected the Institution...

August 28. Went to surveyor and solicitors to get the conveyances, but they are not ready yet.

August 29. Superintending work, etc...

August 31. The usual church services and Sunday-schools. At the evening school Mr. Milligan addressed the officers and pupils.

On all days not specified I directed work and schools, and on Sundays conducted Divine Service twice.

Numbers present July, 56 boys, 67 girls, Total 123

Number present Aug., 55 boys, 65 girls, Total 120
The conduct of the pupils has been very satisfactory, and with two exceptions their health has been very good.
...I took advantage of Mr. Milligan's visit to consider with him the...financial position of the parents of children admitted, and I went over each case on the list of my last Annual Report, and also gave him the "application book," showing the order of admission of pupils adopted on my visit to England in 1896, viz. Pagans, orphans, deserted and destitute children, and children who live too far from a day school...our first consideration in selecting pupils

was guided by the moral (or too often the immoral) environment of the child, so that we really admit only such children as in England would be sent to an industrial school.

With regard to the admission of Methodists, such small, neglected, and totally ignorant children as we, for the most part, receive for the reasons given above, would not be admitted into Mount Elgin. It receives children from the best Indian homes as we formerly did.

Then, as suggested above, it is not the particular religious denomination under which the child is classified, but the utter absence of religious life of any kind which marks its surroundings.

As regards the suggestion of the Company that I proceed to Priest's orders, I will interview the Bishop when he returns to the Diocese.

43. 1 October 1902 Milligan to NEC

August 25...I spent the evening...discussing points of administration...third floor used as hospital or isolation ward for contagious and infectious sickness; there were two cases in here.

In the basement of the main block I visited girls' playroom, clothing stores, lavatories, kitchen, men's dining-room, children's dining hall, when I noticed the liberal distribution of nutritious and well-prepared food, also the generous stores. The first floor contains two large schoolrooms, where mixed classes are taught, girls' sewing and cutting-out rooms, officers' quarters, and the offices. The second floor contains the well-arranged dormitories, second to none I ever visited in England, and the Hospital...For use in the wet weather the boys have a two-storey playhouse at some distance from the main building; the clothes-lockers and dressing-rooms, lavatories and baths, are in the brick basement...the boys wear generally for work brown working suits, their neater grey clothing being reserved for cleanly occupation and holidays. The frame upper storey contains band practice room, reading-room, and large play room. Order is strictly maintained here by monitors specially selected for good conduct and character...

...There is ample accommodation for 125 pupils, fifty-five boys and seventy girls, with a complement of eleven officers all told. The teaching and class work embrace the full standard from one to six. School hours 8.30 to 12 noon, 1.30 to 4 p.m. in summer; in winter fifteen minutes later in the morning, with an additional hour in the evening. Scholars, however, in the highest standards always have private study from 8.30 to 9.30 p.m.

The pupils are divided for work into two divisions, which work alternately school and industrially, mornings and afternoons, the order being reversed automatically, to ensure a fair change.

The lowest standard-children whilst such put full time at school classes.

...visited every part of the Institution, at work, at school, at drill...everything satisfactory in its arrangement and condition. The teaching was all I could desire, the method of the teachers good, the discipline excellent...the tone was that of a well-ordered Institution. The children appeared accustomed to a regular systematic condition of order and attention. They seemed all bright and happy, either at work or play. I attended the services at the Mohawk Church, and...evening prayers in the Institution, conducted by Mr. Ashton. I was much impressed by the reverential demeanour of both girls and boys.

I saw the whole of the farming work, gardening, and dairying as carried out by the boys under monitors responsible to their superior officers, also cow milking, weighing-in milk, cream extracting, this work by system being done in an incredibly short time, and perfectly done too. The butter supplied from this farm bears an excellent character and realizes good prices. The 40 cows and the hogs are looked after by the boys...milk, butter, and pork are a very remunerative detail, as these supplies secure good prices.

I went over the whole of the land, grazing and crop. The whole is under cultivation, either grain, roots, or hay; some land had yielded three crops of lucerne this year...The corn (maize) appeared good, some for silo, some for dry food. The silos were being prepared...the farm administration is so arranged as to avoid any waste, and use up everything dead or alive to advantage, the last resource being manure or fuel. Only shorts and bran have to be purchased.

...All the repairing, carpentering, painting, and fencing is done by boys under their proper officer, besides similar work for some of the mission stations.

With regard to domestic work - sewing, repairing clothes, stockings, cooking, baking, laundry, and butter-making - this is done by the girls. This kind of training, with their schooling, causes them to be much sought after as domestic servants, and thanks to Mrs. Ashton's care and forethought they are placed in safe and good situations at $10 per month with board, where most remain. Some few, however, owing to the interference of relatives go back to the Reserve. I inspected the water supply from a new windmill pump...which maintains a constant supply of pure water for tanks and domestic purposes...also sufficient for all flushing purposes.

Chance of fire is well provided for; all dormitories, passages, and halls have extincteurs, hydrants and buckets filled with water...Each dormitory has its fire escape...

The heating is perfect, as is the ventilation of all the building. The lighting throughout is electrical.

Apropos of the working of the schools, Mr. Ashton informed me, each side of the school is divided into sections, each under a monitor or monitress who is responsible for the cleanliness and order of each section, and must report any fault to the teacher in charge, who in turn reports to the principal. The government is carried out with military precision under the best system of rules I ever met with, and of which I submit copy. It is only fair to Mr. Ashton to say much is due to him for the great care he has shown, not only in drawing them up, but also in placing so much responsibility on the boys, as monitors, corporals or sergeants, all subordinated to each other, then to their teacher up to superintendent...

I had many conversations with Mr. Ashton about the admission of half-breeds and the condition of children admitted by him; all except Pagans are admitted conditionally. These latter have the first claim, as have also destitute, neglected, or deserted children or members of large families, or living in vicious environment. Under the latter circumstances the parent must agree to allow the child to remain until the Department permits removal...On no account are children admitted from good homes. Under Indian custom an Indian child who has lost the mother is orphaned. The Indian father will quit the place, the mother's relatives are considered nearer than the father, although he is living. I submit a list dating from November 1895 to May 1902 which shows how ninety-one cases were disposed of. Each child must be properly recommended. Of the number, six were selected right away, forty-six notified to enter, thirty-nine rejected - only one illegitimate on the list, and two were under age.

In going carefully through the school list, I am persuaded we have not a single child whose parents or parent could maintain it properly or who should not be there. The chief difficulty in dealing with the children lies with those twelve and fourteen years of age who cannot read. Such should be detained until eighteen years of age. Another is the interference of relatives...I was deeply impressed by the unflagging energy of Mr. and Mrs. Ashton, in the interest they take in all the industrial, moral, and spiritual phases of the pupils' life, whilst in school and afterwards. The building and grounds showed surprising improvement, so much appeared to have been done. I left with the impression that...we had all that was required in a master and matron...

44. 19 April 1903 Toronto Star
BLAZE AT BRANTFORD; THE MOHAWK INSTITUTE TOTALLY DESTROYED
EIGHTY INDIAN STUDENTS IN BED WHEN THE FIRE BREAKS OUT - ALL ESCAPED
The Mohawk Institute...was totally destroyed by fire tonight. The loss is estimated at $35,000, and this is well covered by insurance...There were about eighty scholars in the building when the fire broke out, and they were in their beds. The spread of the fire was slow, fortunately, and everyone escaped safely. A large part of the contents of the building were also removed to a place of safety from the flames. The origin of the fire was not exactly known. A few days ago there was a blaze in the roof,

due to a defective chimney, and as the blaze tonight broke out in about the same place, the cause was probably the same, although it is supposed that an electric wire had something to do with the fire. The blaze broke out in the roof on the west side of the building, and there was nothing to stop it. An alarm was sent to the city fire department, which responded, but there was no water supply available, and nothing could be done to save those parts of the building which were then remote from the fire. The entire structure was burned to the ground, only the walls standing. Efforts were made to save the creamery, a small building in the rear of the Institution, but were unavailing. There was fortunately no wind blowing at the time, and the large barns were not in danger.

45. 21 April 1903 Benson to Dep. Supt. Gen. DIA
Mr. Supt Cameron of Brantford reports the complete destruction by fire on the night of the 19th instant of the Mohawk Institute. The fire was caused, he says, by a defective chimney...
...The buildings were the property of the New England Company and all that concerns the Department is the disposal of the 121 pupils, who were shown to be on the roll by the last return (31st March). Mr. Cameron says that the Principal is arranging for temporary quarters for the pupils. As, however, as 95 of them come from the Six Nations reserve and 4 from the New Credit reserve, which adjoins it, the Department need not be much concerned about them as they can be easily returned to their homes. The remaining 22 pupils come from the following reserves: 3 from St. Regis, 7 from Tyendinaga, 5 from Newash, 2 from Gibson, 4 from the Moravian reserve, 1 from Cape Croker. These pupils, if not sent home, could be disposed of at the Shingwauk or Mount Elgin schools.
I have understood for some time that it is the intention of the New England Company to withdraw their support from Indian work in Ontario and transfer it to the West. If I am correct, it is not likely that this school will be rebuilt by them and it is a question for the Department to consider whether it would assume the responsibility of rebuilding, even if the site could be secured on reasonable terms. The location is only about one mile from the City of Brantford and contains 410 acres of most valuable property, the Grand river running through the greater portion of it.

The school...has been almost exclusively for the...Six Nations, over 75% of the pupils being taken from that reserve. These Indians are now civilized, well to do and have nine good day schools on their reserve, which should be able to attend to the education of their children.

The last return shows that all the children at the school were young, ranging in age from 8 to 14 years, the average being under 12 years. Farming and gardening are all that the boys are taught in addition to class work while the girls were instructed in general house work, sewing etc. No other industries are taught, two boys, however, helping the resident carpenter.

For over fifty years this school received no assistance from the Government, but it now gets a grant for 91 pupils at $60 each. The Department has never been called upon to contribute anything for buildings and equipment and...it would cost fully $50,000 to replace this school.

46. 6 May 1903 Cameron to Secretary DIA

...the Company decided to rebuild on the old site.

In the meantime the girls are occupying the building formerly used as a Young Ladies College...arrangements have been made for the boys to occupy the old play-house on the Mohawk property, which building is two story and comfortably large enough. This enables the boys to attend the farm work. Classes are formed in each place.

The children are comfortably situated. Mr. Ashton is doing every thing that can be done for the pupils safety and comfort.

47. 11 May 1903 R. Ashton to Secretary DIA

...the Mohawk Institute, was destroyed by fire, on the evening of the nineteenth of April.

The pupils were not for a moment in danger, and left the building in an orderly manner, taking their bedclothes with them. The remainder of the night, they were sheltered in the Boys Play House - a storied building. The girls occupying the upper, and the boys the lower floor. On Monday I secured a large building in... Brantford...the "Ladies College", into which the girls moved in the evening. We have ample accommodation and the usual routine of the school is continued.

I have however been notified to vacate the building, but have no intention of doing so at present.

The boys have been supplied with wire mattresses and occupy the upper floor of their Play House and the Band Room as sleeping apartments. A class room was opened in the Drawing Room of the Mohawk Parsonage.

On the night of the seventh instant, most of the Institutions barns, with a number of horses, cows, pigs and the contents were entirely destroyed by a fire, evidently incendiary in its origins. There has been no class work for the boys...They have been employed in getting out and burying the carcasses of the animals. School will re-commence to-morrow.

I received the following cable from the New England Company on May the sixth - "Company decide rebuild Institution present site...favour erection separate blocks - instead of one building. Send your own plans - write for June meeting - suggestions on rebuilding. Will Government contribute. Hope member of Company visits Brantford shortly".

The Insurance money amounts to [$17000] on...building

and [$3200] on contents...the farm buildings and contents were also well insured. The sum...will not be sufficient to erect suitable buildings for one hundred pupils.

...We had one hundred and twenty pupils present on the night of the fire, but I have allowed between twenty and thirty to go home, on six months leave of absence, or on recall. These consisted of graduates; recently admitted pupils; those having fairly good homes; and a few defective and but little qualified for industrial training...

If we have to leave this building I can accommodate about thirty girls in the Mohawk Parsonage which the Company had recently authorized me to turn into a Junior Institution for the reception of children too young to enter the Institution proper. As there are large numbers of orphan children and children of broken families, who being too young to enter the Mohawk Institute were distributed in other Indian homes, where they were poorly cared for and too often used as mere drudges...[re grants]

48. 20 June 1903 R. Ashton to Secretary DIA

...at the request of the New England Company I have forwarded to them sketch of proposed plans for re-building the Mohawk Institution on the old site, than which none could be found more suitable.

In surveying the site I discovered that the majority of the farm buildings had been erected on land the Company does not own the freehold.

I forward you a map showing the position the school lot of ten acres occupies in relation to the Manual Labour Farm of 200 acres which the Company holds by a License of Occupation dated 17th of April 1850 "the said License of Occupation being granted on the express condition that the New England Company shall hold possession of the same so long as they keep up a Manual Labour School for the use of the Six Nations Indians and no longer."

The Company desires before finally deciding as to re-building the institution to ascertain on what condition they can obtain the freehold of Lot No. 5 Eagles Nest...referred to...as The Manual Labour Farm as they will not authorise me to build on any but their own lands...

49. 24 June 1903 Benson to Dep. Supt. Gen. DIA

I think it is about time the Department instituted inquiries into the causes that have led to the total wiping out of this institution by fire. The first fire may have been accidental, but I very much doubt it. The two later ones were admitted to have been set.

Even an Indian will not set fire to buildings, destroy valuable property and endanger life from pure cussedness. There must have been some real or imaginary grievance which led some of the boys to commit incendiaring and these grievances, as well as the perpetrators of the crime should be discovered.

Mr. Supt. Cameron has been remiss in his duty, to call it by a mild name, in not reporting fully to the

Department what has led up to this climax...the Dept should see that the pupils are sent to their homes on leave until an investigation is held and proper arrangements made for caring for them, if it is decided to continue the school and rebuild.

It is now some six weeks since the first fire and the Department is as much in the dark as to the intentions of the New England Company as it was then and in the meantime some 120 children are so far as we know to the contrary, in a very unsettled condition.

It is years since an inspection was made of this school and even at this late date it would be well to learn how it has been carried on.

If it is the intention to rebuild, it would be better to let the children out on vacation until the school was ready to receive them again, than to go on as at present.
Some of the older boys, if willing to remain to assist in the farm and other work, might be kept on and paid wages for their work. The grant could be allowed for Sept. quarter as was done in the case of the Mt. Elgin Institute, when it was being rebuilt, so that the institution would be at no loss financially for salary of staff, etc.

Before the Department joins in re-establishing the school, the pros and cons for so doing should be carefully gone into. The institution is carried on for the benefit of the Six Nations Indians and if they do not appreciate the work done for them, it is a question whether it should be continued. They are sufficiently civilized to appreciate the advantages of education and if they do not wish to accept the continuance of the good offices of the New England Company in their behalf, they should have the privilege of saying so. At least the question should be submitted to them.

50. 26 June 1903 Rimmild to Dep. Supt. Gen. DIA
Charge of Arson against the Pupils of the Mohawk Institute
...Four boys have been committed for trial on charge of arson. Superintendent Cameron reports that they have confessed and he thinks they may endeavour to implicate innocent pupils. There were about 120 present in the Mohawk Institute...in view of the suspicion which may attach to other pupils the intervention of the Department is necessary. There is probably nothing much to be done for the boys who have confessed. Should others be accused they can of course, if their friends wish and have the means, retain their own counsel. The Department is not interested in obtaining acquittals if there is guilt. The proper attitude for counsel retained by the Department would appear to be that of endeavouring to bring out all facts favourable to the persons accused and acquiring any information which can be obtained as to the reason the buildings were set on fire. If on these terms any of the pupils wish to avail themselves of counsel retained by the Department they should be allowed to do so.

There have been two fires shortly following each other, and it may very possibly be shown in mitigation of the offence of those who have confessed that they had grounds for dissatisfaction arising from harsh treatment.

51. 15 July 1903 R. Ashton
...proposition is that the institution receive a grant for 100 pupils, instead of for 91 as at present.

52. 6 August 1903 Pedley to Sifton
The Mohawk Institute at Brantford was destroyed by fire on the 19th of April and the barns of this Institute and 15 head of cattle and 5 horses were destroyed on the night of the 7th of May, and the building occupied by the boys of the Institute since the destruction of the main building was burned on the night of the 21st of June. The question of rebuilding has been under consideration by the New England Company...

When in this City recently the Rev. Mr. Ashton...on behalf of the Company, made application both verbally and by letter for leave to purchase what is known as the Manual Labour Farm, held by the Company under license of occupation dated 7th April, 1859, from His Excellency the Governor General...and also for a change of tenure under which the Mohawk parsonage property is now held...So far as the Manual Labour Farm is concerned, the title is in the Crown under authority of surrender in 1841, No. 50, and can be disposed of in fee simple to the Institute if so desired...

53. 12 August 1903 R. Ashton Annual Report
Buildings.- The institute, laundry and dairy were totally destroyed by fire on April 19 last; the farm buildings were burnt down on May 7, and the boys' play-house where the lads were temporarily housed was destroyed on June 21, the boys being accountable for the three fires.

Accommodation...provided in temporary buildings for one hundred and thirty five boys and forty-two girls.

Reducing our numbers in the middle of May to ninety-four has very much lowered the average attendance.

Class-room Work covers the full course of the public schools of Ontario. The progress has been very satisfactory.

Two pupils passed the 'entrance' examination last month.

Farm and Garden. - This year has been the best in the history of the farm, showing as it does a favourable balance of $2,258. Products supplied to the Mohawk Institute, $1,667; cash sales, $3,979.

Industries Taught.- Carpentry and Painting - Under instruction the boys do all the work for the institute and the farm. The principal work was building a new cottage for the gardener and improving the Mohawk church.

Brass Band. - The band of fifteen boys continued to make good progress until June 21, when their instruments were destroyed in the conflagration of the band-room and play-house.

...Girls' Work...They make all their own clothing, also that of the boys, with the exception of the best tweed uniform, an issue of which is purchased every other year. The girls completing their training are much sought after, they readily obtain good situations at from $8 to $10 per month from the start.

Health and Sanitation. The sanitary condition of the institution was all that could be desired.

The health of the pupils was very good - two deaths occurred - that of a girl from consumption and a boy from intestinal obstruction, through depraved appetite.

54. 13 May 1904 Benson to Dep. Supt. Gen. DIA

...holidays are not general at the Brantford Industrial school. Class-work is discontinued for six weeks during the months of July and August and very few of the pupils are allowed out of the school during that period. The Principal assumes the responsibility of granting holidays in special cases. It is not the practice to allow all the pupils to go from any of the Industrial schools.

55. 11 August 1904 R. Ashton Annual Report

Buildings.- The main building...is nearing completion. The boys play-house...laundry...dairy...have been rebuilt...

New Buildings. - Barn...with brick basement containing stabling for thirty-five cows; root-house and milk separating room; cement silo...hog pen...ice-house...

Accommodation...has been provided in the new gymnasium for forty boys and in temporary buildings attached to the Mohawk parsonage for forty-three girls.

No new pupils have been admitted since April 19, 1903, when the institution was destroyed by fire.

Class-room Work...The progress has been satisfactory under the circumstances. One pupil passed the 'entrance' examination last month, another has been attending the business college in the city for eight months, taking a stenographer's course. She has not yet tried for her diploma.

...Industries Taught.- Carpentry and Painting...The carpenter and his boys were employed in the erection of temporary and permanent buildings. The farm supplied gravel and sand and the boys mixed all the cement in the construction of the new barn, silo, and pig-pen, besides assisting in all the carpentry work.

Health and Sanitation. The sanitary condition of the boys' department is excellent; that at the girls' home is the best that can be arranged in temporary quarters.

The health of the pupils throughout the year has been very good, no serious illness or death has occurred.

56. 12 May 1905 Benson to Dep. Supt. Gen. DIA

Rev. Mr. Ashton...has been authorized by the New England Company to make application for financial assistance owing to the large amount expended in

rebuilding this institution...he has made arrangements with the Water Commissioners of Brantford to extend their mains to the institution and to put in four hydrants. The cost of this work will exceed $3000 and he asks for a grant of $3000...

The Mohawk Institute was burned down in April 1903 and has since been rebuilt at a total outlay of $32,940.00.

If the Department is disposed to consider Mr. Ashton's application favorably, I do not see that the money could be better expended than in providing adequate water service and fire protection. The last fire was incendiary and attempts to burn down some of the buildings had been made on previous occasions, by pupils who resented the strict discipline maintained at this school. The discipline is still exercised and some of the pupils may again retaliate by firing the new buildings. No Insurance that can be effected will cover the loss of the buildings...

57. 10 August 1905 R. Ashton Annual Report

Buildings.- The new building occupied in October last is in the form of the letter H, built of red brick, with cut stone basement, roofed with shingles, laid on asbestos paper. The main building is 79 x 42 feet, and has two wings 60 x 36½ feet each. The building is two stories high with basement and attic.

The Main Building. - In the basement are the stores, including insulated cold store, officers' dining-rooms, boiler-room, girls' clothing-rooms and lavatory. On the first floor are the offices, sewing-room, and female officers' rooms. The second floor contains the superintendent's residence and two sick-rooms.

North Wing. - In the basement is the kitchen and dining halls; on the first floor, class-room, master's room and farm men's rooms; on the second floor is the boys' dormitory.

South Wing. - The basement comprises the girls' play-room, boot-room and flush water-closets; on the first floor is the class and assembly room, and on the second floor is the girls' dormitory. Each dormitory has an iron fire-escape and door opening into the main building. Boys' play-house...laundry...dairy...barn and cow-stable...silo (cement)...hog pens...horse and cattle stables...with room for sixteen horses and sixteen cattle. Other buildings are: carpenter's shop, implement-house, drive-house, wagon-shed, poultry-house, two greenhouses and an ice-house.

During the last six months, thirty-one pupils have been admitted.

Class-room Work. -This covers the full course prescribed by the department and the first year of high school work. Five pupils passed the examination for entrance into the high school.

Health and Sanitary conditions. The health of the pupils has been very good and the sanitation is excellent...

58. 7 April 1906 **** to Pedley

Dear sir; I wish to ask the Dept to help me; to get my son **** who is now confined at Mimico School in ont; its a prison for boys; he has been confined there about two years; he left home on Cornwall Island about eight years ago to go to the Mohawk Institution School. Shortly their he got into some trouble and was send to prison at Mimico School between Toronto and Hamilton ont; I do not know the exact charge that was made against my son, But however I think my son has been punished enough, and I am quite able to take care of him and look after him if I could only get him home;

So I ask and pray that the Dept give me a help hand and influence to get my son back to my home;

59. 25 April 1906 Cameron to McLean
...in reference to the application of ****...the following pupils of the Mohawk Institution were sentenced on July 20th, 1903, by Judge Hardy...without a Jury, as follows:

****	Mimico Industrial School	5 years
****		5
****		3
****	Kingston Penitentiary	3

****'s sentence expires on the 19th of July next. These were implicated in setting fire to the Mohawk Institution, Mohawk Barns, where several heads of stock were destroyed and the Mohawk play-house where the boys were sleeping after the Mohawk Institution was destroyed. They were also convicted of setting fire to a large barn of one Alexander whose farm adjoins the Mohawk Institution...

60. 1 May 1906 McLean to ****
...asking assistance from the Department to obtain the release of your son, ****, from the Mimico Industrial School...your son was committed to that institution for three years and that his sentence will expire on July 19...

You will have your son with you immediately after the expiration of his sentence...

61. 13 July 1906 R. Ashton Annual Report
Accommodation...provided for 110 pupils...staff of 10.
Class-room Work...Three pupils passed the examination for entrance into the high school...

62. 26 April 1907 R. Ashton Nine months Report
Class-room Work...Three pupils passed the examination for entrance into the high school and three girls who have taken our full course are now attending the Collegiate Institute.

63. 28 October 1907 Smith to Secretary DIA
Since I have occupied this position I have had numerous complaints against the Mohawk Institute. Some parents think that the interest money instead of going to Mr. Ashton should be payable to the children with which to purchase clothing. Others complain that Mr. Ashton keeps the children at the Institute longer than he agreed to do and at the same time they are not being at school but made to work on the farm. I have not been able to advise these parents about these various matters as I do not know the relation of the Institute to the Six Nation Reserve. I would like advice from you fully dealing with the Mohawk Institute and what authority Mr. Ashton has.

64. 9 December 1907 McLean to Ramsden
Mr. Superintendent Smith, of the Six Nation Reserve, states that numerous complaints have been made against the Mohawk Institute, which are as follows:-

Some of the parents...think that, instead of the interest money going to Mr. Ashton, it should be payable to the children, with which to purchase clothing. The Principal is not entitled to receive annuity money for pupils without the consent of parents, and if he does so it should be expended for the children's benefit.

Another complaint is that Mr. Ashton keeps the children at the institution longer than he agreed to and that they are made to work on the farm. The application for admission which is signed by all parents provides for their retention in the school until the age of eighteen years and the Principal cannot sanction their discharge before arriving at that age without the consent of the Department. The half-time system which is in vogue at all the industrial schools should apply to pupils at the Mohawk Institute.

The Superintendent asks to have his relationship with the Mohawk Institute clearly defined. This institution is conducted by the New England Company and is in receipt of a per capita grant, the Agents and Inspectors of the Department are entitled to visit and inspect the school and make reports thereon, the grant being contingent upon the satisfactory reports of those officers.

You will be good enough to visit the school and report fully on its condition.

65. 23 December 1907 Ramsden to McLean
With reference to the complaint that the Principal of the Mohawk Institute receives interest money of pupils...at last fall's pay he received the aggregate amount of $94.50, a large proportion of this amount is taken from pupils with no parents, or with one parent whose home has been broken up. Where the parents are alive and looking after the welfare of their children the Superintendent does not receive any money...The interest money retained from the sources enumerated is placed to the credit of the pupil in a separate account. The pupil is given from time to time any necessary small amounts for holidays and so forth, or for any special material for wearing apparel. These amounts are charged up against the interest money, and on the child leaving the Institution it is given whatever balance is left. This appears to me a good system and well carried out. Occasionally there is a pupil kept beyond the age limit, but there are always good reasons for so doing.

With regard to time given for education - found that the junior forms were given full time at studies, and not required to work half-time until 3rd form was reached. The scholars are making satisfactory progress and are very neat in their general appearance. The school is kept...managed and under good discipline.

I cannot say that I was favorably impressed with the sight of two prison cells in the boys play house. I was informed, however, that these were for pupils who ran away from the institution, confinement being made for a week at a time when pupils returned.

In connection with the discharge of pupils from such Institutions as the Mohawk - I think it worth considering that an amendment should be made to the Indian Act that would permit of the enfranchisement of Indians who have succeeded well at school and whose conduct had been exemplary, and who had received positions to enable them to support themselves, and could be endorsed by the Principal. Then it would appear to me if some such conditions as these were fulfilled it would be much better for these pupils to cease to be Indians and any further wards of the State, and then I take it that these Institutions would be a real benefit to the Indians and the State.

If I were in Mr. Smith's position I would have no hesitation in discussing with the Principal any complaints that came to me, and if not satisfactorily explained, or disproved, report to Department. Mr. Ashton gave me the fullest possible freedom and courts any further inspection.

66. 1908 Webster Report

If the Company are satisfied that this Institute should be carried on as a reformatory I have no criticism to offer. The Indians, however, on the Reserve have little admiration for the education given at the Mohawk Institute. And although their dislike of the system may be largely due to a love of indolence and hatred of discipline, I share their belief that a better use could be made of this fine building.

Mr. Gordon Smith...says that former pupils of the Mohawk Institute are reluctant to send their own children there because they consider the discipline is too strict.

At the Warriors' Meeting...I was told that the boys' education at the Mohawk Institute is not as good as that of the girls, and that the boys could learn farming just as well at home - in fact, that the Institute does little for them beyond feeding and clothing them...the land surrounding the Institute is at present used for farming and for teaching the boys the ordinary work of the farm labourer.

67. 2 April 1908 R. Ashton Annual Report
Accommodation. - Accommodation is provided for 120 pupils and a staff of 12, including 3 farm-hands and a gardener.
Class-room Work...Two pupils passed the examination for entrance into the high school and 4 girls who have taken our full course have attended the Collegiate Institute...

68. 29 April 1909 R. Ashton Annual Report
Class-room Work...Ten pupils wrote on the entrance examination, and 9 passed.

Inspector's remarks...'May I congratulate you on the success of the pupils from the institute this year - the work was very good indeed.' (Signed), J.P.HOAG.'

Two girls who have taken our full course attended the collegiate institute, and the 3 boys who passed last June have been studying type-writing and stenography.
...The boys are organized into a cadet corps, No. 161, for which the Militia Regiment has supplied arms.
ANNUAL INSPECTION REPORT, 1908.
...The Honorable the Minister and members of the Militia Council have been pleased with the good report submitted by the inspecting officer upon your cadet corps, and wish to convey to you and the officer commanding the corps their commendation for the very creditable showing made at the time of the inspecting officer's visit. (Signed) SEPTIMUS DENISON

Health and Sanitation - The health of the pupils has been satisfactory. In June we had an epidemic of mumps and in February of grippe, but no deaths.....

69. 31 March 1910 R. Ashton Annual Report
Class-room Work...Two pupils passed the entrance examination- Mary Latham and Frances Bartram; the former is continuing her studies at the Collegiate Institute. Susanna Latham completed her course at the Collegiate, passing her examination for a 2nd class certificate; she has been appointed assistant teacher here...

Health and Sanitation - The health of the pupils has been excellent, no serious sickness of any kind; we had, however, to discharge one girl with sore eyes, and three with scrofulous glands...

Ex-pupils. - Thirty-one pupils left during the year, 20 being girls. One, with a second-class certificate, has become teacher of the junior department here; 2 are attending the business college in the city; 1 is taking lessons in a dressmaking establishment; Ida Maracle was discharged by the department and given to a woman who promised to send her to school; 1 married, 1 died, 1 is required at home, there being a large family. With the exception of the scrofulous children, all are in good situations as domestic servants, earning from $9 to $15 a month. The girls trained here are in great demand.

Of the 11 boys, 1, who passed his entrance examination here, is continuing his studies at Carlisle institution and working as a printer; another is typewriter and timekeeper for a contractor at Waterdown, N.Y., earning $60 a month; 1 who had passed his entrance and studied stenography, works in the office of a factory in the city. The remainder, with one exception who has not been heard from, are working as farm-hands.

70. 30 January 1911 A. Nelles Ashton to McLean
...correspondence to this institution should in future be addressed to A. Nelles Ashton. The Rev. R. Ashton having retired from the principalship...1st of January 1911.

71. 4 February 1911 McLean to A. Nelles Ashton
...your appointment has been noted...The Department cannot allow the occasion to pass without expressing its appreciation of the excellent results attained by Mr. Ashton, your father, during the period of forty years of his incumbency as Principal of this institution. The Department trusts that you with your intimate acquaintance with the needs and working of the school, will be able to maintain the high standard of excellence attained through the devoted efforts of your father.

72. 31 March 1911 A. Nelles Ashton Annual Report
Accommodation. - Accommodation is provided at the Mohawk Institute for 120 pupils and a staff of 12, including 3 farm-hands and a gardener.
Class-room Work...Four pupils passed the entrance examination. - Jessie Vanevery, Elsie Davie, Pearl Bearfoot and Jesse Moses. The two latter are attending the Collegiate Institute in Brantford...
The boys are organized into a cadet corps, No. 161, and have lately been served with the new Ross rifle.
Health and Sanitation - The health of the pupils has been excellent. One girl was discharged suffering from scrofula; she is now much better and has recently married.
One girl was sent to the city hospital with typhoid for two weeks; she has quite recovered. Her brother spent 7 weeks in the same hospital suffering from appendicitis. As small-pox was prevalent in the city in August, all pupils were vaccinated and quarantined...
Ex-pupils. - Nineteen pupils left during the year, 13 being girls. Of the six boys who left, two were stolen away and sent to the States, the other four are working out for white farmers. Of the girls, two are keeping house for their fathers, one is living in Brantford and attending the Collegiate, one is married and living on the reserve, one is a telephone operator in Chicago, one girl...died suddenly at her home, and six are in domestic service.
General Remarks. - At the suggestion of the department new automatic desks have been installed in the assembly-room....

73. 21 June 1911 A. Nelles Ashton to McLean
...Will you kindly forward "Amended fixed scale for the payment of the Capitation grant for Industrial and Boarding Schools".
The Mohawk Institution will now, according to new agreement receive $200 per head for 120 pupils.

74. 31 March 1912 A. Nelles Ashton Annual Report
Buildings. - The only building erected during the year was a...eleven seated, flush closet...lighted by electricity and heated in the winter with natural gas...
Accommodation. - Accommodation is provided for 125 pupils (70 girls and 55 boys) and a staff of 12, including 3 farm-hands and a gardener.

Class-room Work...Four pupils, Minnie Gibson, Rheva Miller, Arnold Moses, and Andrew Martin, passed the entrance examination into the high school. Three pupils are at present attending the Collegiate in Brantford. Stenography and type-writing were taken up in the senior school (a class of about 8 pupils). A new Underwood typewriter was purchased during the year.
Farm and Garden. - The cash sales in this department amounted to $3,251.90, about $700 less than last year. This was owing to the severe drought. We threshed 868 bushels of wheat, 1,430 bushels of oats, and 447 bushels of barley. Two cars of sugar beets were shipped to the factory. 3,981 lbs. of butter were made and 2,437 lbs sold to the city.
Health and Sanitation - The general health of the pupils has been good, no sickness of any serious nature during the whole year. We have had, however, three or four bad cases of ophthalmia among the girls, which caused us some anxiety. We were obliged to call in a specialist from the city who advised isolation, special dietary...
The sanitation is good, the drainage being connected with the city sewer. New up-to-date closets have been installed on both sides during the year. Both lavatories have been increased and fitted with modern bowls.
In the winter we built a large rink (ice) for the pupils in the boys' yard and both boys and girls enjoyed the skating and hockey.
Ex-pupils. - Twenty-three pupils were discharged during the year, 13 being girls. Of the ten boys who left, 7 are working with white farmers, one returned to the reserve, one is in hospital with a bad leg (tubercular) and one is continuing his studies in Hamilton.
Of the girls, one is attending the Carlyle Indian school, seven are in domestic service, one is continuing her studies at the Caledonia High School, three are at home on the reserve, and one little girl, Cinderella Reid, is dead.
General Remarks. - New laundry equipment was installed during the year, a metallic washer and an extractor, also a steam boiler, and an electric motor. This lessens materially the work of the pupils. Enough washing is kept out weekly for purposes of instruction.
One hundred new white enamelled iron bedsteads have been placed in the dormitories and add much to the appearance of the rooms and the comfort of the pupils.
Our Cadet Corps, No. 161, took first place in No. 2 Military District (Central Ontario), a fact of which we are justly proud.

75. 31 March 1913 A. Nelles Ashton Annual Report
...Class-room Work...Four girls and one boy passed the entrance examination into the high school. Three pupils are attending the Collegiate in Brantford.
Jesse Moses was successful in passing his second year's departmental examination (lower-school entrance to the Normal) at midsummer.
Several pupils are taking up stenography and type-writing...
Moral and Religious Training.- Morning and evening

prayers are conducted for the whole school daily and divine service at His Majesty's Chapel of the Mohawks 11 a.m. each Sunday, weather permitting, by the chaplain, Rev. R. Ashton. On wet and stormy days service is held in the assembly-room, which can be converted into a chapel by the opening of folding doors. Religious instruction is given daily in the schools, and on Sunday from 9 to 10 a.m.(singing); 2.30 to 3.30 p.m. (Sunday school), and 7 to 8 p.m.(singing and prayers).

The Bishop of Huron confirmed a class of 32 candidates on March 28.

Health and Sanitation - The general health of the pupils has been exceptionally good. We were unfortunate in losing a little girl, who died at the Brantford General Hospital of heart trouble. Two pupils were discharged medically unfit (scrofulous). No epidemic of any kind marred the year.

The sanitation is good...Lavatories and closets are up-to-date and disinfected regularly.

...The boys...have a field where they play baseball, cricket, lacrosse and football, swimming and fishing in the Grand river, which is less than half a mile from the school. The cadets spend a lot of time on their new miniature rifle range, under a capable instructor.

In the winter a large rink is built for the pupils, who are allowed on it alternately at given hours.

Ex-pupils. - Twenty-eight pupils were discharged during the year, (18 girls and 10 boys). Of the boys, 8 are working among the whites, one discharged medically unfit is attending school on the reserve, and one who absconded has not been heard from. Of the girls, one is attending the high school in Caledonia, 9 are in domestic service, one is attending school on the reserve and the rest are at present at their homes.

General Remarks. - Our cadet corps passed another excellent inspection in drill, and we hope this year to develop a goodly number of rifle shots.

76. 3 September 1913 Ohsweken Council House
The adjourned Council of the Six Nations opened in due form by Chief David John one of the Fire Keepers.
Upon the complaint of G. W. Miller and Jeff D. Isaac that the children of the Mohawk Institute were being so poorly fed and suffering such indignities at the hands of the officers of this Institute that many of the children are compelled to run away from the School.

The Council after much discussion decided to ask the New England Company to have a thorough and impartial investigation as soon as possible, the Council being under the impression that the Indian Department has no control of this...School, so have deemed it useless to appeal to them in regard to the management of this school, and the secretary of the Council is...authorized to forward the above decision to the New England Company direct.

77. 20 September 1913 Smith to DIA
Complaint was made to the council on the 3rd inst. by George W. Miller and Jeff D. Isaac that their children attending the Mohawk Institute were being poorly fed and subjected to indignities, so much so that they were compelled to run away. The council decided to ask the New England Company to hold an investigation. As far as I can find out the charge of under feeding is that the children are given separated milk and the indignity complained of is that the girl's hair was cut off. Major Ashton the Superintendent told me that he was quite ready to meet an investigation at any time as he did not consider that these charges were well founded. He admitted that the children have been given separated milk and have had it for the past 15 years at least.

78. 24 September 1913 Ohsweken Council House
George W. Miller informed the Council that he had received a letter from the Principal...to the effect that as he had made a complaint against the management of the Mohawk Institute, his two children would be discharged from the School on the 30th instant.
...the Council decided to ask the Department if they could give any explanation for the action taken as they think it hardly fair that only parents who are timorous to make complaints against the said school should be privileged to send their children to the said Institute, as the complaints against the management are pending for investigation by the New England Company; the Council consider that the children of Mr. Miller should not be discharged but that an adjustment might be made if the complaints are established.

79. 29 September 1913 Kelly and Porter to Supt. DIA
On behalf of George W. Miller and Jefferson D. Isaac
...we are writing you in regard to the management of the...Mohawk Industrial School, Brantford.
Our clients say that the children are being punished from time to time in a shameful manner for trifling offences and that they are treated from time to time as though they were criminals. For instances, boys are whipped until they are cut, girls have had their hair cut off close to the scalp, for punishment, and parents are not allowed to see their children if they (the children) happen to be under punishment at the time.
...our clients say that the children do not get sufficient and proper food. Separated milk, spoiled meats...

80. 28 October 1913 Scott to Roche
I have looked into the matters complained of by a couple of Indian clients of Messrs. Kelly & Porter...with reference to the management of the Mohawk Institute. The rules governing the disciplinary action in the case of misdemeanours by pupils, are I think antiquated, and I have set in motion action which I think will result in

benefit. Corporal punishment is not used frequently and the children are whipped with a strap allowed by the Department of Education, Ontario, but I do not believe in striking Indian children from any consideration whatever. If children resident in the school prove themselves continuously so untractable as to require physical punishment, they should be discharged from the school. This school is not a reformatory, and there are at the present time 80 pupils on the waiting list, which is sufficient evidence of its popularity, and with this large number of applicants to choose from it would be folly to continue pupils in the school who are constantly fighting against the rules.

I find that the children are given separated milk to drink, which I think should not be allowed. At least the usual percentage of butter fat should be left in the milk, and it should not be stripped of all its cream as it seems to be at present. The principal tells me that they had a box of oatmeal once which was wormy, and it was served once on the table before this was noticed, but it was not served again...they have too much boiled meat to eat at the school, and we will have a change made...

I have written the enclosed letter to Messrs. Kelly & Porter...the whole trouble has at the bottom denominational jealousy...some time ago the Church of England started a mission at Oshweken, a stronghold of the Baptist Church, and there has been friction ever since. The two complainants...Miller and...Isaac are Baptists.

There is no necessity whatever for an investigation, and if we were to allow it, it would only be considered a triumph, first of these men personally, and second of their faction.

You will observe that I told the lawyers that if their clients wish to take proceedings in the court they are at liberty to do so. Mr. Ashton is quite willing to defend himself against any legal action, and I think if we take this stand we will not hear very much more of the matter.

81. 30 October 1913 Scott to Kelly & Porter
...I...came to the conclusion that no necessity exists for the investigation which is asked for by the Indians mentioned.

That it is a popular Institute is shown by the fact that the waiting list contains the names of 80 children whose parents are anxious for them to attend, but for whom there are no vacancies. This school is under the close supervision of the Indian Superintendent at Brantford and is also inspected by the inspectors of the Department, and any minor improvements in discipline and dietary can and will be made without the formalities of a special investigation.

If your clients wish to take proceedings in the courts they are, of course, at liberty to do so, and the Principal of the Institute will take any necessary steps to defend himself.

82. 30 October 1913 Smith to DIA
...George W. Miller whose children were dismissed by the Principal of the Mohawk Institute asked the council to request the Department to secure an explanation of this action on the part of the Mohawk Institute...these children were sent to the Mohawk at the request of their father and there appears nothing binding on the part of the Principal to receive...or to keep a child unless he desires to.

83. 3 November 1913 A. C. Ashton to Scott
Major Ashton is away having a fortnight's vacation with the hope of improving his health which has been bad lately from nervous dyspepsia. When he returns he will at once forward you our system of Rewards and Punishments the latter being mostly the stoppage of privileges.

He at once acted on your suggestions to give the junior school a recess in the middle of the afternoon. School stops for a quarter of an hour at a quarter to 3.

Mr. Webb, Clerk to the New England Company has forwarded us a copy of Kelly and Porter letter to them at the instigation of Geo Miller and Jefferson Isaac. Major Ashton will have this on his return. I must say it is the most grossly exagerated lying statement I ever read yet there are glimpses of truth in it, for instance the separated milk and the wormy oatmeal (the latter occurred twice only in my experience) and the sending home of the children of the two dissatisfied men - I know they are very angry about this they have gone about the Indians telling them "they took their children from here because they had not enough to eat". I trust it may give them a lesson to speak the truth. There are hundreds of our old pupils who would give this Institution a very different character or why are they so anxious to send their children here.

I enclose our dietary at your request.

84. 19 November 1913 A. Nelles Ashton to Scott
I enclose herewith a copy of our award of Good Conduct Badges and our Black List Regulations as requested on your recent visit. These rules have been in force for many years and have been approved of by the New England Company.

I will further explain our system of reports for misdemeanors.

We will say for instance that Sarah Hill employed in the kitchen department has been checked by the officer in charge two or three times for idling, and when last spoken to has been impudent to the instructress. A report is made out...Nov 10th 1913 S. Hill...continually idling, and impudent when corrected. S. Bonehill. This report is deposited in a box in the visiting-room and remains there until Saturday Morning when it is entered in the report book, and when the punishment is awarded by the Principal, the offence and punishment are recorded in what is called the "Character Book", a book in which every offence and punishment awarded to every pupil is recorded from his or her admission to their discharge.

Thus you will see a pupil is never punished hastily or in anger, and time is given for thorough investigation.

The punishment must of course depend on the crime, but in ordinary cases it is the depriving of privileges, such as loss of play-time or the half-day holiday in the week.

Corporal punishment (the strap) Government authorized, is only used in serious cases, and as we do not have very many it rarely takes place in this school, but when it is used it is done not only for the benefit of the culprit but for the school as a whole.

I have never whipped a girl since my appointment as Principal, nor during my long service under my father as vice-Principal and Boys' Master and never will do as it is always given by the Governess or in her absence by the female officer in charge.

The cutting of girls' hair (but only in the case of small girls) has been ordered on several occasions vis -
Firstly...If a girl will not keep her head clean.
Secondly...In case of absconding, in lieu of a more severe punishment, (for the purpose of identifying the child if she attempted to abscond again) and as an example to the others.

This is done only on rare occasions and is never ordered except in the case of small girls, whose hair usually only reaches to the shoulders. (The Dutch Cut)

No girls hair has ever been cut to the scalp.

No parent or guardian has ever been refused since my appointment, permission to visit their children when on the Black List or under punishment.

Bread and water is given the Black List on Sundays only.

Solitary confinement is generally ordered instead of corporal punishment in cases of gross insubordination, but as this offence is not very often committed, this punishment is seldom awarded.

In regard to the Black List Rules I have modified these in many ways. I very rarely keep a pupil on for more than two weeks, it depending on the spirit of the pupil.

I also take into consideration the temperament of the student.

85. 3 December 1913 Scott to Roche

With reference to the charges which have lately been made against the administration of the Mohawk Institute...I visited the Institute on the 21st day of October and went very thoroughly into the matter with the Principal. I was entirely averse to having a formal investigation made into these charges. It is not a new thing to receive complaints from Indians making various charges against the management of our schools and necessary investigations are always made by our own Inspectors. To have granted an investigation by a Commissioner would only have gratified those Indians whose hostility to the Institute simply arises from personal feeling and is actuated by the hope of giving trouble.

The Mohawk Institute is one of our best conducted schools and I have frequently visited it in the past. On this last occasion I found that the school was doing the usual effective work. No explicit charge was made that the food furnished the pupils was insufficient and that evaporated milk and wormy oatmeal were served to them. The Principal acknowledged that the separated milk had been issued and that on one occasion it was discovered that the oatmeal was wormy when they immediately discontinued the issue. Milk as comes from the cow will from this time forward be used for drinking purposes. Since my return the Principal has forwarded a dietary of the school...it might be varied with good results although it is wholesome and is plenty.

He also sent me a code of discipline; this has been in use so long in the Mohawk Institute that it is difficult to change it. However, I think I left on the mind of the Principal the impression that I considered it too severe. As time goes on it will be possible perhaps to relax it and improve the spirit of the school without weakening the control of the officers. I have visited most of our schools in the Dominion and I find that the pupils at the Mohawk Institute have a less cheerful spirit than those at some other Institutions.

I went over the main building once more and there are two things which I disapproved of, - the location of the dining-room in the basement is very objectionable; the quarters are dull and cheerless, and the officers agree with me in this opinion. The dormitories on the second floor could not be better - they are fine and airy and scrupulously clean. The dormitory on the third floor, where some of the girls have slept for some time is not properly designed for a dormitory. The Department has consented to allow the similar room on the other side of the house to be fitted up for the boys. Both these rooms are objectionable. I have asked the Architect of the Department to prepare a plan for the raising of the walls in order to provide two well-ventilated rooms on the third floor and likewise to provide for the erection of a new dining room. If the New England Company will provide these dormitories the Department will grant funds for the additional pupils...I understand that there are over 50 pupils on the waiting list of this school and there is no reason why the benefits of the Institution should not be extended to a greater number of the children on the Reserve.

86. December 1913 A. Nelles Ashton to McLean

Mr. G. W. Miller's children were discharged from the Mohawk Institution for the following reasons:-
Mr. Miller requested the discharge of the older girl, stating that he thought he could manage her better. (I have

this letter on file).

Both girls absconded from the school, and the conduct of the older one was particularly bad, having been guilty of destroying Institution property, 2 quilts and a sheet, converting them into clothing to run away in.

Mr. Miller then laid complaint against the management of the Institution.

As he lived near one of the day schools (Ohsweken) and as he was able to support his children, I thought it better to let him have them, thus giving him an opportunity of training them as he wished.

Many parents who live a long distance from a school and would be grateful for the privileges of this Institution for their children have to wait on account of lack of accommodation.

It is time the Indians were taught to appreciate the good work done for their children in this school.

It has been a great surprise to me that the Six Nations Council has taken up the matter in the way they have, when they must and do know that this institution has been the greatest assistance to their advancement.

87. 1 April 1914 Brantford Expositor
DAMAGES FOR PLAINTIFF IN MILLER VS ASHTON CASE - GIRLS TOO SEVERELY PUNISHED...
Principal of Mohawk Institute was Mulcted for $400 Because of Treatment by a Subordinate of Two Indian Girls Who Made Their Escape.
Damages to the extent of $400 were awarded to George Miller, a resident of the Indian Reserve, by the jury of the high court...against Major A. Nelles Ashton, principal of the Mohawk Institute, the claim being for $5000. Judgement was reserved by Mr. Justice Kelly on the question of costs and also the question of Major Ashton's personal liability.

The statement of claim of the plaintiff, who was acting as the next friend for his children, Ruth and Hazel, who were inmates of the Mohawk Institute, divided the claim made...and the jury brought in a split verdict.

The first claim was for damages for cutting off the girls' hair, after they had run away from the institution, so that they could later be easily identified. This the jury dismissed...

The second claim was for damages for the two girls, for their being imprisoned, one in a cell, and the other in the sick room, for three days, being fed on water, this being when they made another unsuccessful attempt to get away. In this the jury dismissed the claim of Hazel, who was confined to the sick room, and awarded Ruth, who was kept in a cell without light, $100 damages.

The third claim was for damages for Ruth, who had been whipped, it was alleged, on the bare back, with a rawhide, though it was denied by the defence that a rawhide had been used, the weapon being a strap. On this claim the jury awarded $300 damages.

The fourth claim, that the girls' health had suffered from bad food was dismissed, as it was shown that their health was not injured, and that though the food had been bad on one or more occasions, this was due to the heat of summer, which had turned the meat and caused worms in the oatmeal, which had then been returned to the mill...

TWELVE-HOUR TRIAL
...The evidence was very contradictory on some points. It was conceded by the defence that worms had been found during the hot months in the oatmeal and meat, but as soon as this was discovered the whole order was returned. It was admitted further that the girls' hair had been cut, and that they had been imprisoned, Ruth in a cell, and Hazel, in a sick room, and given bread and water for a day for attempting to run away from Mohawk Institute. It was further admitted that to Ruth had been ministered a strapping, but it was denied that it was too severe, or that it was administered with a whip of rawhide, as alleged...

WITNESS COLLAPSED
Perhaps the most interesting portion of the evidence was that given by presentday pupils of the institution. They were clear and concise, their evidence was direct to the point and they refused to be turned off to one side by the opposing counsel's leading questions or puzzling. One girl, Sarah Hill, bore a gruelling cross-examination unflinchingly, but her physique was not as strong as her intellect, for at the close she collapsed...

ONE CASE PRESENTED
W. E. Kelly...appeared for the plaintiff in the case... brought by George W. Miller...of the Indian Reserve, against A. Nelles Ashton...for cruelty to Miller's two children, Ruth and Hazel, 13 and 11 years of age.
...Mr. Kelly stated that it was the contention of the plaintiff that one of the girls had been mercilessly beaten, being given 12 lashes with a rawhide. The girls had broken away, and being captured, Ruth had been confined in a cell without windows, and with only a small aperture, barred with iron in the door. Hazel had been kept in a dormitory for three days. The plaintiff claimed that this was too severe a punishment for young girls, more befitting a prison institution than a school. It was claimed that the food was unfit for use, that the management was not such as was necessary and proper in this modern age, and that the children were treated very harshly.

FATHER FIRST WITNESS
Geo W. Miller, father of the two girls, on whose behalf action was entered, was the first witness. He stated that on August 7 or 8 the girls had run away and later were discharged from the institution.

Photos were put in showing the conditions of the girls' heads after their hair had been cut off.

Miller continued that Hazel, the younger girl, was in a very nervous condition, but he could not say whether or not it was because of the treatment she might have received at the institution.

Once Pupil Himself.

W. S. Brewster, for the defendant, cross-examined Miller, who stated that he was for three years a pupil of the institute under Rev. Mr. Ashton, when he was a boy. When he grew up he made a written application to have his girls admitted to the institution, this application constituting the principal the guardian of the child during the time that she was at the institution. He knew the rules of the school as they were when he attended. He did not know that there was a rule that any girl who had run away would have her hair cut off. When his girl's hair had been cut he had found out about the rule. There was no objection to whipping unless it was immoderate. In his day there was no solitary cell. This had evidently been built when the new building was put up. He had put the children in the school because they had no mother. His children had run home, and he had telephoned Mr. Ashton that he would bring them back next day, to save the fees of a constable who would be sent after the girls otherwise. He could have sent them to his own school, which was only 400 yards away, but he had no one at home to look after them.

In re-examination Mr. Kelly asked the witness how he had been whipped when at the institution.

Mr. Brewster objected and was sustained.

HAZEL MILLER'S STORY

Hazel Miller, the younger of the two girls, was placed in the box. She was able to take the oath, replying to Justice Kelly's advising her that it was very wrong not to tell the truth. She had been in Mohawk Institute for about a year, before she ran away. "I got out of a window with my sister and two other girls," said she very naively, causing a laugh in the court room. She ran away at 12 o'clock at night, and arrived home at three in the morning, walking all the way. On being taken back, Ruth was put in a cell and the witness and the other two girls were locked in the sick room, from Saturday until Monday, getting bread and water on the Sunday and ordinary food on the other days. Saturday their hair was cut, Mrs. Weatherall taking them to the book room, where Robert Jamieson, a school boy, cut their hair by order of the principal. Nothing else was done to her at this time. There were worms in the porridge and the meat, but not very often. Once it was complained of and the cook said it could not be helped. Separated milk was also given to them. While on the black list the pupils were not allowed to speak to each other and were sent to bed right after supper.

Cross Examination

Cross-examined, the witness said, she wanted a "Dutch" cut, when she went to the school, and her hair was now about as long as when it was clipped off. Her sister had made up a dress secretly at the institution from material belonging to the school and had given it to the witness to

run away in. She and her sister knew that the rules stated that those who ran away would be put in the cell, and have their hair cut. The boy Jamieson, was one of those who cut the hair of the other boys, when they needed it. Mr. Ashton had never touched the witness and had treated her very kindly. She knew she must be punished if she ran away. She had never seen any worms in the meat she ate, and only once in another girl's food. Once or twice the porridge was not done quite right, the pupils themselves doing the cooking as part of their training for a month. She had been whipped on the hands when she had done something wrong. She had not suffered because of the food she got. The black list had been in force for a long time, and she did not complain of that.

Said Whip Was Used.

Re-examined, witness said that a whip was used in "birching". The strap used was put into court, but the witness said there was also a whip. She had not complained of having her hair cut, because it would not have done any good, for she would have been reported.

RUTH MILLER'S STORY

Ruth Miller, 13 years of age, was called. She had run away from the institute because she did not like the food. When brought back she was put in the cell on the third floor, which was 3 feet by 6 feet, with a little hole in the door. There was no light, no bed and no chair. In this she remained for three days, getting bread and water on Sunday. Her hair was cut off on Monday. She was put on the black list, having to walk in a ring in place of playing, and not being allowed to talk to the other girls. She tried to get away a second time, but was caught. She got a birching the next day, receiving 13 stripes on the bare back while laying face downwards on a bed, from Miss Weatherall. The latter had been told to give her 12, but she gave her 13. After that for a week and a half it was hard for her to sit down. She had never received such a whipping before, for it was hard. Her back was black and blue and had red marks. Edith Isaacs, her chum, saw the marks.

She had seen worms in the porridge once, and flies in the bread, which was sour. She had not objected to having her hair cut off for it was of no use.

THE CROSS EXAMINATION

Cross-examined the witness declared that she knew before she ran away that the rules called for the cutting off of the hair of any girl who ran away. On going to the institution she had long hair, but she did not like this and had it cut short. Witness was the only one put into a cell for the escape of the four girls. There had been trouble with the oatmeal in the summer-time, but she made no complaint. Mr. Ashton had treated her all right, and was not present at the whipping. Though Mr. Ashton had said she was to be whipped with a strap, she was whipped with a whip. She had not shown her body to anyone after the whipping. She had taken stuff from the institution to make up clothes to run away in. She had one lock open the day she was caught at the clothes press. She was just as well in two weeks after the whipping as she ever was. She admitted being mischievous, just like the others. Mr. Ashton had never done anything to her himself, but had ordered others to punish her.

EDITH ISAACS

Edith Isaacs, one of the runaway quartet, was next called. She had seen that Ruth had her hair cut. She had also seen the principal hand a whip, which looked like a horsewhip, to Miss Weatherall and tell her to give each of the girls a dozen lashes on the bare back. She had heard Ruth scream. She did not know whether the whip was a rawhide or not. She had not seen anything wrong with the oatmeal or meat. Ruth had wanted the witness to run away the second time.

Cross-examined the witness stated that the principal had not gone up to where the whipping took place.

EMMA ISAACS

Emma Isaacs, the last of the runaway quartet, said that Ruth Miller was put in a cell and her hair was cut. Witness had never seen the whip talked of. She once saw a worm in the meat in hot weather...

GEORGE JOHN

George John...stated that whips were used, but he was not allowed to specify times when they were used. He had seen a worm in the porridge once.

This concluded the case for the plaintiff.

His lordship asked Mr. Kelly if he intended to press the bad food allegation.

Mr. Kelly replied that he could not abandon it.

His lordship asked what he could prove the children had suffered from the "bad food."

Mr. Kelly thought inferences could be drawn.

THE DEFENCE

Major A. Nelles Ashton was first called for the defence...The school was run by the New England Company...the government paying a part of the cost, not a cent of money coming from the Indians. Major Gordon J. Smith inspects the institution every month. A Dominion inspector pays periodical visits. The present building was built in 1904 and the cell was constructed since. The plans were passed by the New England Company and the government had also passed them, as well as passing the solitary cell...

Story of Runaway

...Ruth Miller and the other girls had run away, and Ruth was confined for 24 hours in a cell, while the other three were put in the sick room. The cell was built in the top dormitory, being 5 feet 6 inches long, 4 feet wide, and over 6 feet high. An air pipe hole gives a certain amount of light and there was always fresh air. The punishment was given as a lesson to the girls and to the rest of the school. He did not make the rules, but merely carried them out. It was an unwritten custom of the school for 43

years to cut the girls hair if they absconded. The girls had admitted to him that they tried to get into the clothes press to run away again, and he gave instructions to whip them. He did not mention the whip, the bare back or the number of strokes. He did not give Miss Weatherall a whip, and as soon as he entered the institution he had ordered that the use of the whip be prohibited to any officer. Mr. Miller was not satisfied with the management and wanted Ruth home, and the witness therefore had discharged all four. Miss Weatherall had married and now resided in Medicine Hat. Hence it was not possible to bring her here.

All oatmeal used was purchased from the Wood Mills of Brantford. About August or September he found worms, but had sent the oatmeal back and now used rolled wheat. The housekeeper had nothing else to do but look after the cooking which was done by the girl pupils. There had been no complaints.

Witness stated that he had mitigated punishments, abolishing the whip and cutting down the hours of the "black list".

...Cross-examined, Major Ashton stated that the school was under Ontario public school regulations so far as was possible. He told Miss Wetherall to whip the girls, but did not tell how it was to be done...

"You had plenty of time to get Miss Wetherall here or to have a commission examine her?"

"Yes."

"But you didn't?"

"No."

Mr Kelly asked if Major Ashton did not think a whipping was too severe for such an offence.

Witness did not think it so for the offences committed, as there was a theft case before that.

"Perhaps Miss Weatherall did not know the whip was cut out?"

"Oh, yes she did."

"Rather humiliating for a child to be stripped and whipped?"

There was no answer.

The witness stated that the old whip in use was a rawhide one - a severe whip. He had had complaints of meats being scorched, but not spoiled. The girls had been fed on bread and water, and put on the black list. He had heard that there was a tendency to abolish corporal punishment but it was all a question of who was being dealt with. He felt that he had moderately punished the girls. He assumed all responsibility for his actions. It was true that the children were only fed separated milk. During his incumbency no Indian child had been whipped on the bare back...

DENIED GIRLS' STORY

Geneva Van Every had been at the school for seven years, and had been in charge of Ruth Miller when in solitary confinement. Ruth was in the cell for 24 hours only, and no more, despite Ruth's statement that she had been in for two days. Ruth had had five or six strokes, not more. Three days after the whipping Ruth told the witness that it was not sore at all and she did not care bout the whipping...

MARY HEARNS
...saw Ruth's back after the whipping and testified that Ruth had said it did not hurt her, and she did not care a bit. Ruth had said later that she would run away and tell a lot of lies so she would not have to come back.

EVELYN MILLER
...cousin of the plaintiff, heard the whipping but five or six times. She corroborated the previous witnesses as to Ruth's remarks...

ADA MARACLE
...She saw Miss Weatherall going upstairs to whip Ruth, having a strap, and not a whip, in her hand. The witness had been in the schoolroom at the time, reading.

Cross-examination failed to swerve her a point from this evidence. In four years at the school she had never seen the rawhide. Further, she was positive that the rawhide had never been used since Mr. A. Nelles Ashton became principal...

SARAH HILL
...saw Miss Weatherall bring out the strap from where the whipping took place, and lay it on the table in the sewing room. She did not know where the strap was kept. Conditions had not changed since the cases were brought on. "We get a whipping if we deserve it," said she, adding that there was no need for rawhide whipping for none of them deserved it...

BEATRICE JAMIESON
...had also seen Miss Weatherall with the strap...

LAURA HOWARD
...stated that she had seen Miss Weatherall with the strap...

MILDRED LOTTRIDGE
had had her hair cut at the institution like a boy. She did not want it done, but it was done because she ran away...

ALICE SNAKE
...had also had her hair cut off like a boy's...

ELIZA SNAKE
...had her hair cut to be like her sister...

Helen Clench, recalled, stated that before Principal A. N. Ashton's time Mary Garlow had been whipped with a rawhide on the bare back.

88. 9 October 1914 Boyce to Scott
Enclosed are somewhat lengthy records of some "refractory pupils"....

I am sure if the Department would sanction the removal to another school, in cases where the parents influence is bad, or the dismissal of an occasional pupil who is incorrigible, that we would have much less trouble with the discipline. We have so many really nice children, whose parents are anxious for them to get on, and who

support the rules of the school, that its a pity they have to mix with the hopelessly vulgar, impertinent, and deceitful, whose influence is so harmful.

**** Admitted Oct. 1911 Age 12¾

1914 Oct.		Continually dirty & untidy in parade
"		" out of bounds
"		Throwing stones around buildings
Sept	2	Laziness
"	12	Stealing apples in orchard.
	3	Not going to bed at proper time

21 other reports this year - (1) Using vulgar language to a girl giving out clothes - Mostly for laziness - disobedience - stealing
36 reports in 1913 - (1) Interfering with bad-mark book - crossing off bad marks as if worked off. (2) Bad manners (serious offence) (3) Meddling with books on teachers desk. (4) Interfering with boys supper (stealing) (5) Going out without a badge. (6) Playing football in play house and breaking windows. Constantly disobedient - disorderly, out of bounds - losing clothing - inattentive in school.

**** Admitted August 1913 Age 12

1914 Oct		Talking back to officers - trying to make trouble among boys.
Sept	8	Laziness
	26	Talking during divine service
	13	Disorderly on church parade
	12	Laziness
	3	Throwing bread in Dining Hall
"		Late 10 minutes, ringing chore bell
Aug	1	Misbehaviour in Dining Hall
July	8	Very impudent in school
	3	Impudent to senior girl in charge.
June	25	Disorderly in Dining Hall

Constant reports laziness - lying - rudeness- impertinence - disobedience
This boy is a sneak, continually trying to make trouble with the boys.

**** Admitted August 1911 Age - 14

1914 Sept	27	Neglect of duty
	26	Laziness
	14	Continual neglect of duty
	13	Disorderly on church parade
	3	Throwing stones
		Disturbance in dormitory
	2	Late for parade
Aug	30	Stealing apples
	21	Getting up late
	20	Causing trouble in dormitory
	14	Breaking into cottage garden & stealing
July		5 Reports - June 3 - May 4 - April 4
1913		
Dec	8 "	(1) Beating little calves
Oct	7 "	(1) Stealing onions from greenhouse
		(2) Out of bounds - taping at Dining Hall window to attract girls attention
		(3) Late home from leave - late for dinner
		(4) 50 minutes late ringing bell (All up bell)
Sept	9 "	Constantly leaving clothes out of place, losing shoes - leaving clothes out in rain all night - wearing school clothes to work.

Many reports for late to line - late to school - late ringing bells - for disobedience and laziness. 33 reports in 1912, - 49 in 1913, - 33 in 1914

His mother was an old pupil, her character was bad - talking to her the other day she said "she wished she had been punished more severely while she was here."

Explanatory
The boys have much more liberty than the girls - they are

allowed to go up town or off the place if they have a badge - such reports - as "going out without a badge" - "late home for parade on chores" are frequent with them.

**** - only 3 minor reports in 2 years, none at all in 1⅓ yrs.

**** - age 13½ only six minor reports this year.

****, age 12, is good by fits and starts - Jan 1, April 6. July 2. Sept.1 - total 10 reports this year.

****, age 14, - only 3 reports this year.

**** age 15¾, only pupil absconded since I have been here. (May 19th) except pupils who have only been here a few days - and generally returned at once by their friends.

The parents influence is often very bad - and their visits can be told by the pupils behaviour - for instance - this story was overheard by a teacher last week:

Father visiting son ****, who was some time coming after being called.

Father -"What were you doing - were you working?" Son - "No ma'am." Father "Were you on the walk?" Son "No ma'am". "Why were you so long?" Son "I was playing" (it was recess time) Father "Do they ever lick you?" - Son "No ma'am." Father "If they lick you, you tell me, I'll go for them".

**** Admitted January 1912. - Present age 15

The mother thinks that her children should not be punished - and that we should make exceptions - allow them out without badges etc.

1914 Oct 1	Preparing to run away - out of bounds. Aiding other girls to break into the "private clothes" presses, and steal clothing - lying about it.
Sept. 24	In bed with another girl. (This is considered a grave misdeed with us).
" 18	In the main hall before doors were unlocked in hopes of running away.
" 18	Throwing bread in the dining-hall.
" 17	Climbing over coal, and out of coal house window and running around forbidden parts of the grounds after dark. The coal house was also out of bounds. She was fairly good had had a badge for August and September (until forfeited).
April 8	Reports - 1 - In bed with another girl 2. Out of bounds in farm road.

**** - sister Admitted Jan 1913 Present age 16

Has had badges eight months this year

If the mother would uphold the discipline of the school, there would be much less trouble with the children.

**** Admitted May 1908 Age 15?

1914. Oct. 1	Stealing keys from teachers room - stealing ring pins & other property from teachers room. Breaking 2 locks - stealing clothes from presses. Preparing to run away - lying with others breaking fire-escape lock.
Sept 21	Out of bounds
" 16	Running around sewing room during teachers absence
2 Reports 1914	In bed with another girl - (this
" " 1913	is considered a serious offence
July 25 1913	Getting out of fire escape window, and down fire escape to steal apples at night.
20	Out of bounds - over orchard fence.

Her reports are chiefly for rudeness, impertinence, disobedience and insubordination

**** age 16+

passed her entrance examination to the Collegiate this summer - she also plays the organ well. We can not send her to the Collegiate as her mother is not able to help her with fees, clothes etc.

**** Admitted Nov. 5th 1910 Age 14

1914 Oct. 8	Stealing butter from dairy
2	Preparing to run away
Sept. 23	Stealing apples from vegetable room
20	" " orchard
19	" " , out of bounds, away from her work
12	Wearing school dress at work
11th and 5th	Neglect of work.
2	Impudence in school
Aug. 27	Stealing apples from orchard
23	" cucumbers - leaving work undone
22	Out of bounds - very late for work
July 29	Disobeying orders - hiding in press.

Constant reports for stealing - impudence - out of bounds - disobedience.

**** Admitted July 1912 - Age by our book 12

Looks much older, says she was 14 - July 9 - 1914

1914 Oct. 1	Out of bounds - Preparing to run away. Instigating another girl to run away. Receiving property stolen from officers room & destroying it. With girls breaking into presses, and opening fire-escape window.
Sept 22	Stealing apples in orchard (out of bounds)
12	Neglect of work - wearing school dress at work.
2	" " in sick room, and disobedient.
Aug 20	Telling untruths about an officer.
	Not in bed, after being sent up early as a punishment.
28	Receiving stolen apples - talking while on Black List. Eating apples in school.
25	Stealing apples, climbing orchard fence, while on "the walk" (walking in circles)
23	Impudent - late for sewing class.
	Wearing beads after twice told to take them off.
19	Stealing & wearing monitress dress, preparing to run away.
7	Cutting sleeves out of work dress.
5	Misbehaviour and insolence.
July 29	Disobeying orders; hiding in press.
July 10	Out of bounds - breaking fire-escape lock.

She has many reports for stealing - making vulgar signs - disobedience - out of bounds etc.

1913 Aug. 17 Absconding. (Mother brought her back)

**** Admitted Oct. 1911 Age - 12½

There were three **** children here, the mother encourages them in being defiant.

1914 Oct 1	Out of bounds, preparing to run away. Persuading her younger sister to run away. Attempting to steal clothes. Breaking locks.
Sept 18	Talking in dormitory - after correction.
16	Running around sewing room in teachers absence.
11	Disobedient in " "
4	Breaking wood work in play room.
Aug 28	Noisy on boys stairs - away from her work.
July 27	Idling in sewing room.
June 20	Troublesome, insubordinate in sewing-room.

Many reports for rudeness, impudence - using disagreeable language to other girls - taking blankets from dormitory - insubordination lying - in bed with another girl - "out of bounds." and using bad language.

The mother visits children every month and stirs up

trouble by her rude and impertinent behaviour. She came August 29th -said her son ****'s time was up - "she only put him in for three years." I told her all pupils were entered until 16, and must stay until that age, unless released by the Department. She said "No one could keep her boy, she put him for three years and his time was up." I looked up the application paper, and rang up the Indian Officer - both agreed that he was 15. She then said his birthday was in February - so I told her he could leave the end of March.

He ran away that day. His record was bad, in fact next to **** whose record I reported to the Department with a request for permission to dismiss him, we considered him the worst boy in the school. He had many reports for disobedience, swearing, gross impertinence, teasing little pigs - etc.

When I first came he had a dreadful cough, I built him up on Cod Liver Oil, etc but believed him to have tuberculosis, and sent him shortly before he ran away to the doctor for examination - he did not test for T.B.C.

When he was reported absent - I told the men of his mothers wanting to take him that day but his time was not up until February - and one said "Good Lord, do we have to put up with that lazy fellow until February - he never does any work unless stood over."

After giving time for his mother to bring him back if she had not persuaded him to run away, I wrote her, saying I did not want him back as he was such a troublesome boy, but she was to bring in his clothes. He went in his working clothes but a new pair of shoes. That if she did not bring them back at once I would enter an account against his interest money.

The mother came in a month, was most impudent. I told her I should have sent for ****, and having punished him, have publicly dismissed him. She was defiant, said "no one could punish her children."

I asked why she put her children in the school as she encouraged them in breaking the rules and defying the officers, and she replied - "The school was for Indians; she was going to send her children if she wanted to, and her children know how to behave."

She has not yet returned the clothes. **** was sick off and on all last winter.

**** is a little girl, and so far very little trouble.

I should like to recommend that **** be transferred to the Shingwauk Home, as she needs discipline and to be away from the influence from her mother.

**** Admitted Dec. 1912. Age 13

Oct	1	Stealing keys from teachers room, also jewlery & other property, destroying some. Preparing to run away. With others breaking into presses, and breaking fire-escape lock. Out of bounds.
Sep	19	Out of bounds, away from her work, stealing apples
"	"	In lower corridor before doors were unlocked, preparing to run away.
	17	Out of bounds, climbing over coal & getting out of coal

		house window, after dark, and running around grounds where girls are forbidden.
	11	Stealing apples from orchard.
	2	Impudent and insubordinate
Aug	3	Out of bounds, on laundry roof.
July	29	Disobeying orders - hiding in press.

Frequent reports "out of bounds" - disorderly conduct - theft - lying - Aug 17th 1913 Absconding.

We are not hopeful of improving this girls conduct, a reformatory is the place for her - its too bad to have her contaminating the many nice girls in the school, and we will be glad if you can remove her.

Explanatory

Many pupils have badges all the year - some the highest number obtainable each month. If you refer to the Quarterly returns the character column is marked A, B, & C. A for pupil with a badge - B without a badge - C on Black list. This is not a correct estimate, the pupils having highest number of badges (6 a month) marked A. Another constantly troublesome, might one month obtain a badge, probably given for encouragement, only to lose it at once, yet that pupil is also A. A generally good pupil might have some escapade for which the Black List is punishment, that pupil is marked C - which is hardly fair.

The bad pupils involve others for example - **** admitted March 28th 1914 had not a report until Augst 8th, when she and **** were seen standing naked to the waist in a second story window overlooking boys playground. **** was then cautioned to drop her friendship with **** but continued in spite of warnings.

1914 August	8	Drinking cream.
	19	Stealing girls dress, preparing to run away.
	23	Very late for Sunday school.
Sept	12	Continually standing on back steps watching boys. Wearing school dress to work.
	16	Stealing apples & lying about it.
"		Running around sewing room during teachers absence.
Oct.	2	Preparing to run away with ****

This girls sister admitted at the same time has only had one minor report. The children appear superior and we should do something with them...

**** - age 15½, admitted Jan 18, 1914 has not had a report.

**** age 16½, admitted March 20, 1912, discharged June 20, 1914 had only one minor report - "scorching a towel through carelessness".

**** age 13, has only had ten reports mostly minor in 3½ years.

**** age 12½ -admitted June 1913 - only five reports (minor).

**** age 18 - no report in 2 years.

****, another girl who has made friends with bad girls. Admitted Sept 1913, no report until Jan 20, 1914. This girl belongs to the better class of Indians, and should be a credit to the school. She recently has had several reports for stealing - disobedience, showing temper, and was one of those preparing to run away Oct 1st with her new friends.

****, age 10...here 1¼ years...four very minor reports.

**** age 14½, has not had a report since April.

****, age 10 - only one minor report in a year.

We could give many other instances.

You may notice many reports for "stealing apples" - the pupils are given quantities of apples ever since the first harvest ones came in. Mostly two or three each for dinner, and the same for supper in addition to their proper meal, and they are allowed to take them from the table - but being given the best, they prefer to steal the hard green ones. They throw away fully one-third of each apple.

89. 19 October 1914 Benson to Scott

...Mrs. Boyce, Acting Principal...asks for permission to get rid of some of the refractory pupils of the school, whose records covering fourteen sheets of foolscap she encloses.

I have read these reports and the conclusion I have come to is that the pupils are disciplined to death. What is needed at this school is an entire change of system, as the one inaugurated by Mr. Ashton has been too long in existence and the sooner a change is made the better for the institution.

About allowing the removal of pupils, perhaps they would be better out of the school than kept on the black list all the time and deprived of all liberty.

90. 22 October 1914 S. Stewart to [9 parents] re ****

A complaint has been received from the Acting Principal...that your [son/daughter] is refractory and not amendable to discipline and sets a bad example to the well conducted pupils in the institution.

The Department wishes to inform you that unless it receives your assurance that your [son/daughter] will conform to the rules and regulations of the school and give no further trouble he cannot be allowed to remain there...

91. 5 November 1914 S. Stewart to Smith

The Acting Principal of the Mohawk Institute has made a special report to the Department dealing with the conduct of some of the pupils from the Six Nation Reserve who are refractory and set a bad example to the well behaved pupils in the institution. The parents of the children named in the accompanying list have been written to regarding this complaint and informed that unless the Department is assured that the pupils named will conform to the rules and regulations of the school and give no further trouble they cannot be allowed to remain there. It is further stated...that some of the parents instead of upholding the discipline of the institution actually aid and abet their children in their misbehaviour.

The Department would like you when an opportunity offers to tell the parents or guardians of the children referred to that so long as their children are in the institution they will have to conform to its rules and regulations, which are made in the interests of the children and the proper management of the school.

92. 14 November 1914 Smith to Secretary DIA

...on the 21st inst. I made my monthly inspection... dealing specially with the cases of the refactory pupils ...Before going out I had a call from **** the mother of **** she was very much troubled about the Department's letter to her and thought that if she could not stay in the Institute she will have to place her in the reformatory as she could not control her. I had a talk with the child at the Institute and she promises to behave better and I warned her that I would make enquiries as to her conduct the next time I came out. Mrs. Boyce said that she was doing somewhat better lately. Mrs. Boyce said that one of the other parents to whom you have written telephoned up that she was coming to take the child away as the Department had told her to do so. Mrs. Boyce said that was not the intention that it was merely a warning to make the children behave better.

**** who has two children out there is annoyed because Mrs. Boyce has asked for the interest money of these children because their father gives them hardly any money for spending although he is well off. He now wants to take the children away and place them in good homes which he says he can secure. Mrs. Boyce is willing to let them go if the Department approves. **** told me today that he would let me know by next Saturday where he proposes to place the children...

...Mrs. Boyce informs me that there is no trouble at all with discipline at present as all the children who were unsettled by the Indian Fair have settled down to work and I gathered the impression that the children look more cheerful and contented than usual.

1915 - 1922
Rev. Cyril Turnell 1915-1918 - Ann Boyce 1918-1922

1. 10 February 1915 Webb to Scott
...the Revd. Cyril M. Turnell, M.A. of St. John's College, Cambridge, was appointed as Principal...in place of Major A. Nelles Ashton resigned.

Mr. Turnell possesses high University distinction - taking Honours at Cambridge in Parts I and II History Tripos. He has had considerable experience in dealing with men and boys, and has been engaged in Scholastic work for six years. He formerly held a Commission (as a Layman) in H. M. Army. He is marrying a lady of high educational attainment who would actively interest herself in the work of the Institution. The Company hope that they may have the assurance of the approval of Mr. Turnell's appointment by your Department. They have every reason to believe that Mr. Turnell's appointment will make for the highest efficiency of the Institution. Mr. Turnell proposes to commence work at the Institution on, or about April 20th., -until which time Mrs. Boyce will continue as Acting-Principal. -

2. 13 April 1915 Webb to Scott
...Mr. Turnell left England on Saturday last...He was... only married two days before he left England...Mrs. Turnell...obtained academical distinction at the Universities of Bristol and (I think) Birmingham. She takes considerable interest in social work and has done great things in or near the slums of Bristol among the Women and Girls.

3. 26 May 1915 Smith to Secretary DIA
...this morning I paid a visit of inspection...Major Barker the Inspector of Cadets was also there inspecting the cadet corps. The cadets lined up 46 strong and made a very creditable appearance...there are on the roll at the Institute 58 boys and 67 girls a few of whom will be leaving at the end of the quarter. Mr. Turnell informed me that he believed the New England Company was anxious to increase the size of the Mohawk so as to hold 200 pupils. This would necessitate building an extra dormitory and a dining hall for boys and one for girls...the dormitory in the attic used by some of the girls is not suitable being too dark...Mrs. Ashton is still acting as matron and bookkeeper but expects to retire on pension at the end of August when Mrs. Turnell will take up her duties but without salary. The Principal also informed me that he was gradually relaxing the discipline and he has found no serious breach of discipline since he has taken charge. In reference to the food he says the children are all getting whole milk and he has doubled the supply of butter as he considers children such as he has require more butter fat in their food. I was very favourably impressed with both Mr. and Mrs. Turnell and feel that conditions at the

Mohawk will be quite as good as anything that has existed in the past and probably much better.

4. 21 June 1915 Turnell to Scott
I have been hoping for some time past to arrange a visit to Ottawa in order to confer with you on the proposed enlargement of this Institution and other matters. Unfortunately Miss Hardie our senior teacher met with a bad accident soon after our arrival...I have consequently been compelled to take over the work of teaching the senior pupils myself and this has prevented me from leaving home...Miss Hardie will be fit to resume duty this week. This will make it possible for me to come to Ottawa with my wife. As she takes an active interest in the Institution we should both like to have the pleasure of meeting you. Our teachers start their vacation on the 17th of next month. It will therefore be desirable to arrange an interview before they leave - for during their absence a good deal of the supervision falls upon us.

On my arrival here I found that the School had been admirably managed by Mrs. Boyce and she was good enough to remain for a short time in order to initiate us into the administrative details...

We have however considered it desirable to relax in some respects the somewhat rigid discipline and to improve the dietary arrangements and conditions under which the children take their meals. These changes have been appreciated by the Indians. Also the fact that we are allowing the children living near to go home for a short holiday in the summer.

5. 23 June 1915 Smith
...The Chiefs extended an invitation to the Rev Mr Turnell Principal of the Mohawk Institute to meet them at the Council-house, which Mr Turnell did on the 2nd inst. when several matters in connection with the Institute were discussed. I believe this meeting will lead to a better understanding between the council and the Mohawk Institute.

6. 14 September 1915 McLean to Turnell
...requested by Mr. Reuben Tobias of the Moravian Reserve to write on behalf of his son, Clifford Tobias... who has passed his entrance examination and wants to continue at the Institute three years longer. The Agent states that you are willing for this boy to stay if his tuition is paid.

7. 18 September 1915 Turnell to McLean
...Clifford Tobias. The boy at present is only 14 years old. We are quite willing for him to remain here so that he can attend the local Collegiate Institute subject of

course to his continued good conduct. It is customary for this Institution to pay half the tuition fees and defray the cost of the necessary school books, and the parents are expected to pay the balance which amounts to $15 per annum. They are also expected to provide clothing to take the place of the school uniform as children going into the town daily object to a distinctive dress.

Our chief difficulty is the sex problem. It is impossible to keep the sexes apart when they attend school in the town, and if they give trouble in this respect they have to be dismissed.

8. 25 September 1915 McLean to Turnell

...Clifford Tobias...this boy may remain as a grant earning pupil of this school and attend the local Collegiate Institute, subject, of course, to his conduct and good behaviour...this boy's father will have to pay half the tuition fees and to provide him with clothes to take the place of the school uniform.

9. 29 March 1916 McGibbon to Secretary DIA

...a drowning accident happened at the Mohawk Institute early this morning...the man in charge of the green house took two boys out, without the knowledge and consent of Mr. Turnell, to hunt musk rats in the river back of the Mohawk Church in an old canoe. The canoe upset. ****, went under the ice...Mr. Turnell has the firemen of the City dragging the river for the body. The gardener and the other boy were pulled out of the river.

10. 26 December 1917 Smith to Scott

I inclose...programme of the Bethlehem Tableaux recently given by pupils of the Mohawk institute...the entertainment was a surprise to the people of Brantford, as it was a great credit to the children and to Mrs. Turnell, who designed the costumes and trained the children. All the costumes were made by themselves.

Tableaux lend themselves particularly to Indian stoicism. The same tableaux were put on at Paris the day before, and to make it more realistic, real fire was put in the altar upon which Isaac was about to be slain, but accidently it burnt up too high and scorched "Isaac's" fingers, but Indian-like he never stirred a muscle until the curtain dropped and now he has a badly burned finger.

11. 22 March 1918 Webb to Scott

At a Special Court of this Company...the following Resolution was passed:- That a letter be written to the Indian Department of Canada enquiring whether the Department would be prepared to make an offer to the Company for the purchase of the Mohawk Institution buildings and contents, including the 10 acres of land on which the buildings stand...the Company were influenced by the following considerations:

(1) that by the sale of the Mohawk Glebe Farm, the most profitable land for supplying the produce to the Institute and for farming has been taken away:

(ii) that the expenditure in relation to Agriculture and the upkeep of the Institution is out of proportion to the educational and missionary work of the Company:

(iii) that the farming which the Company is authorized to teach does not include expensive experimental farming

I am directed further to point out that

1. The proximity of the City of Brantford is detrimental to the Missionary work of the Institution.

2. The Agricultural Adviser to your Department has suggested through the Principal...that the Company should lay out money in improving farm stock, in draining the land, and in other farm improvements which appear to the Company to be contrary to the spirit of the terms under which the Charter was granted...

3. The income of the Company would be expended better...in other districts where the Indians are not in the advanced state of civilization as in the districts from which the pupils of the Mohawk Institution are drawn.

12. 1 May 1918 Scott to Webb

I am informed by Rev. Mr. Turnell that you have dispensed with his services as principal of the Mohawk Institute at Brantford, and that you have given him six month's notice...I have received no notification from you directly...at which I am somewhat surprised.

I regret that I cannot agree with your proposal to make a change in the Principalship of the Mohawk Institute. The appointment of Rev. Mr. Turnell we consider has been in the best interests of the Institute... on the 10th February 1915, you used the following words in describing Mr. Turnell: "The Company hope that they have the assurance of the approval of Mr. Turnell's appointment by your Department. They have every reason to believe that Mr. Turnell's appointment will make for the highest efficiency of the Institution."

...your high estimate of Mr. Turnell has been proved by his conduct of the Institute and your belief "that his appointment would make for the highest efficiency" has been amply supported. Those of us who are deeply interested in the Institute and in the welfare of the Indians: namely, Rev. Mr. Turnell, the local Indian Superintendent, and myself, have been giving serious consideration to the position of the school and its future, and it is perfectly clear to my mind that the difficulties which surround the situation will not be removed by the dismissal of Mr. Turnell.

I trust that the Company will not carry out the contemplated action without further consideration. It is my opinion that no change whatever should be made in the administration of the Institute until a properly qualified representative of the New England Company visits Canada and has an opportunity of discussing the present position and the future of the school with me. Unless this is done the Department cannot continue to pledge its financial support to the school...

13. 29 May 1918 Mathews to Scott

...The Court is at a loss to understand your complaint regarding the vacating of his position as Principal of the Mohawk Institution by the Rev. Mr. Turnell. As a matter of courtesy your Department was advised of his appointment and in due course we shall advise you of the appointment the Court makes of his successor.

The Court notes with satisfaction your Department's good opinion of the efficiency and condition of the Mohawk Institute from the point of view of education. But on economic and administrative grounds, the Court considers it necessary to make certain changes.

The Company has appointed General C. E. Ashton, C.M.G. a Commissioner to enquire into the management of the Mohawk Institute. He has full powers as regards the appointment of a proper staff to conduct it for the present and will advise the Company what steps should be taken as to its future.

14. 1 June 1918 Smith to Secretary DIA

...on the 29th of May I made Inspection...Mr. Turnell informs me that he was leaving in August to take up a position under the Bishop of Jamaica, he has no information as to who his successor will be. The work at the Institute is as usual progressing most satisfactorily. There are always more applications for vacancies than can be accepted. At a recent confirmation by the Bishop of Huron 32 candidates were presented. Two of the girls are attending the Brantford Collegiate Institute and one passed the entrance...in April last and proposes to attend Normal in September. Mr. Thomas of the Conservatory of Music has a class once a week in advanced music and Miss McNally of the Collegiate Institute staff conducts a weekly class in domestic science. The cost of the latter is paid by Mr. Turnell from his own income. There are three candidates preparing for the entrance examination.

Mr. Turnell claims to have considerable trouble in running the Institute on account of shortage of funds the staff in particular being ready almost without notice to leave if they do not get the highest wages going. Mr. Turnell thinks that in order to have the farm side of the work looked after better, a Guelph Agricultural college graduate should be in charge but his salary would certainly be far beyond what the New England Company would pay.

There are 20 acres in spring wheat and a considerable area in sugar beets, the balance of the farm is planted for ...raising food for the stock and for the children. The green house is most profitable...the farming land is not large enough to conduct general farming and it would be more profitable were intensive gardening done, but that... would not give the instruction in general farming which

they require.

The general conduct and discipline has been good, no one has been absent without leave since last October and that was merely a case of a boy who went home but was promptly brought back next day by his parents. The parents in every case back up the authorities and insist on having their children punctual and regular. The health is good and there has been no epidemic for a long time.

15. 18 June 1918 Mathews to Meighen

The New England Company, of which I am the Governor, has received a letter, dated May 16th, from Mr. Duncan Scott...in which, referring to a suggestion made by the Company to sell the Buildings and the freehold land of the Mohawk Institute, Brantford, to the Canadian Government, he declines to enter into correspondence with the Company; and suggesting that the Company should send a representative to Canada.

The Company demurs both to Mr. Scott's decision, and to the terms in which it is expressed.

It is impossible for any Member of the Company to go to Canada at the present time. All the Members are very fully occupied in other important work here.

...the Company has appointed General E. C. Ashton, C.M.G. to act as the Company's Commissioner with very full powers. No doubt General Ashton will open communications with you...

16. 28 June 1918 Smith to Secretary DIA

...this morning I made an inspection of the Mohawk Institute. Mr. Turnell seemed very much unsettled and worried about conditions out there as he has made all arrangements to leave in August and has not yet heard whether a successor has been secured. He is also specially interested in the crops this year which he says are extra large and as his farm helpers are engaged only by the month they are liable to leave at any time, unless wages are increased. They have not been asking for increases but if they do he has no funds available to pay them. His barley and spring wheat looks extra good the vegetable garden is good and his stock is increasing very rapidly. He has made over a thousand dollars out of pigs this Spring. The number of pupils is up to the limit and many on the waiting list. There are a few cases of chicken pox of a mild type.

17. 3 July 1918 McLean to Smith

...the Department has had no word of the appointment of a successor to Mr. Turnell. With regard to the farm helpers...the Department appreciates the interest Mr. Turnell is taking in the crop, and, should at any time an increase in wages be demanded, he may meet the current rate and the Department will see that funds are available for the purpose, if required.

18. 22 July 1918 General Ashton to Scott
...the Reverend C. M. Turnell vacates the position of principal of the Mohawk Institution on the 26th instant.

I have appointed Mrs J. M. Boyce to act temporarily as principal...

19. 31 July 1918 Smith to Secretary DIA
...on Friday 26th inst. I inspected...The Rev. Mr. Turnell left for Kingston, Jamaica on the morning of the 25th and I found Mrs. A. M. Boyce in charge. She has no idea how long she is to be there as her engagement is not definite. She complains as did Mr. Turnell that a great many repairs about the buildings are required, for instance the plaster is defaced by the children and broken off in all the rooms and passages where the children have access. She is arranging to have these particular repairs made at once, she complains about a great shortage of blankets and mattresses for the boys dormitory and is to make representations to the New England Company...to reduce expenses she has dispensed with the services of the primary teacher and also the Junior housekeeper. She informs me that her idea of discipline is not that of her father but she thinks that the boys are out of hand as Mr. Turnell was not strict enough with them. The girls she finds to be all right. She evidently bases her ideas as to how the Institute should be managed in regard to equipment and cleanliness on a hospital standard, in which she has had large experience. The day after I was there half of the children were going on their three weeks holidays and on their return the other half will be allowed their holidays. I am informed that two of the male officers have given notice and will leave almost at once.

20. 19 October 1918 Smith
The Board of Health and the Council on the 22nd inst. ordered the closing of the schools for two weeks...The number of cases at the Mohawk Institute has been increasing daily, until today there are 76 children in bed but Mrs. Boyce reports that only 8 are at all serious and even those she thinks will be all well in due course.

21. 24 October 1918 Boyce to Secretary DIA
The school has suffered severely with the influenza...we had seventy-six cases last Sunday - been allowing up a few each day. Most of the staff have been laid up - for days all we could do was to attend to the sick - the farm help have been off duty - and one day only four boys were down - we have only been able to do the chores...

22. 24 October 1918 Smith to Secretary DIA
I regret to inform you that Lillian VanEvery the eleven year old daughter of Noah VanEvery died at the Mohawk Institute this morning of influenza.

She had been delirious for some time but at 8 o'clock this morning appeared no worse. Her father was with her but she suddenly sank and died at 9.15.

Mrs. Boyce is fortunately a trained nurse and is I believe giving the utmost attention to her patients under the advise and care of Dr. Palmer.

This morning there is a reduction in the sick list, there being only 17 boys and 24 girls. Some of them appear to be only run down and amongst those recently admitted to the Institute Mrs. Boyce notices a want of vitality caused by under nourishment...They have no reserve force.

23. 12 November 1918 Smith to Secretary DIA
...30th of October...I inspected...The classes have just started having been closed for some weeks on account of Influenza but the attendance was not large. During the course of the epidemic, every child suffered and every adult...was also attacked except two, consequently work and education of all kinds suffered but they were just beginning to get into working order when I was there.

24. 8 February 1919 Boyce to McLean
...re supplies of military clothing blankets etc...

There are changes contemplated on the management and probably in the disposal of the Mohawk Institution. I could not place an order without consulting my brother, Ge. Ashton...there are so many things the school urgently requires that I hope with his consent we may order blankets, etc. As our boys leave at sixteen years of age and very often younger, its not likely the clothing and shoes can help us much.

25. 19 March 1919 Boyce to Scott
...the Indians were anxious to obtain the "Manual Labor Farm"...to-day - it was flooded up to the stable doors. I hope the New England Company has an option on buying some of the land...We...certainly require more than the freehold ten acres - and would want our present orchard and kitchen gardens - and hog and cattle runs - that only leaves the part flooded nearly every spring.

In Mr. Turnells time they laid out a young orchard, and rows of small fruits in the flooded area - the flood came...and all the young trees and canes were cut off. This land will be of no use for building purposes.

26. 2 July 1919 Boyce to Secretary DIA
...our pupils took a prominent part in the reception to the returned soldiers at Ohsweken.

On the 20th of July we sent 40 girls a governess and two men to drive the team to the Chiefs reception - the girls looked very trim in their summer uniforms - blue serge skirts - buff middies with blue trimmings, blue straw hats with red bands - white stockings and slippers - they went prepared to dance and drill.

Yesterday the Warriors had a great day - we sent 35 boys - all we had in the school - the rest having left for their three weeks holiday on Saturday the 28th. The boys wore cadet suits and scout hats. They had decked the wagons and horses with flags etc and polished the brass harness - as they said -"they were going to show those people in the bush how to do things."

Several of the older girls went in charge of their friends. Miss Hardie - the housekeeper & two men went - and all reported a splendid time.

The boys marched well in the procession - they won in the baseball match - and at lunch sat at the same table as Major Gordon Smith - who reported that they behaved themselves well. Some of our girls helped wait on the tables - which were generously supplied with chicken - hot potatoes - ice cream cakes etc. Our boys were also treated to supper...reached home at 12 o'clock - having also emptied the huge luncheon baskets we had sent not knowing they were going to be so well looked after.

27.   July and August 1919   Report Boyce Acting Principal
...Holidays

The holidays passed very quickly the pupils divided in 3 divisions of 3 weeks each - 18 boys & 14 girls had not proper homes to go to - of these one boy absconded (last year he absconded and returned of his own accord)... Plenty of amusement was provided for those at school...Two circuses each spent a week in town - the pupils all went several times, and were treated by the management to free rides on the merry-go-round, and ferris wheels, and to all the performances.

The pupils attended the Military Tatoo, and fire works at Agricultural Park on Peace Victory Day.

Every week they had a picnic at the Park - the Mohawk Park close here has swings - dancing, pavillion etc - and the girls thoroughly enjoyed it. One evening the accompanist failed to appear, and one of our girls played for the dances. They often went bathing in the River.

School recommenced August 31st - present 73 girls (8 girls lead what I considered undesirable home conditions, were specially asked for by Major Smith, and have overstayed leave) - and 44 boys - 2 on sick leave - and 3 overstayed leave.

Staff

There have been several changes in the staff. Mrs. Hargreaves...is succeeded by Miss Hobbs, fully qualified 2nd class certificate - as junior governess.

Mr. Rogers - artillery lieutenant - competent to teach band instruments and an adept at sports has reported as boys master - we are now appealing for instruments.

Miss Bonehill housekeeper had to return unexpectedly to England.

Mrs. Mathews Matron broke down in health.

Miss Keyes, former teacher, assisted...during the vacation taking girls to the Park etc - and seeing after the house cleaning and cleanliness of the pupils.

Examinations

Four girls and one boy tried the Entrance Examination...

and all passed. Alice Herkimer completed her course at the Business College - and two girls took first class honors at the Conservatory of Music exams.

Three girls can play the church services, and several can play for prayers.

Presents

The militia Department sent us 55 returned mens suits, which we will remake into school and work suits. Also 2 collar badges, and a cap badge for 55 boys.

Gen. Ashton...gave us a quantity of drugs and medical supplies and the school purchased some - we will require more drugs that usual to build up after the "flu".

Health

****, was sent to the hospital for mastoid operation - was there several weeks - made good recovery...one severe case of scrofula...ward of the Childrens aid society - hope to locate her friends and send her home.

Several cases of excema - from impure blood - aggravated condition left by the "Flu"

Farm and Garden

**** left team in field - it got tangled with plough - both horses thrown down - one is badly cut - the vet has treated her over a month. Earlier in the season his brother **** left team with harrows, the horses ran away, smashed the harness and injured both horses.

We threshed 218 bushels of spring wheat - it was shrivelled because of the drought - sold some to the mill at 3 cents a pound...they resold it as chicken feed at 4 cents. So we put add in the paper to sell at 3½ cents at barn, 4 cents delivered. It is selling fast. The oats we sowed in March 288 bushels were excellent - rest have not been threshed but is all drawn in - will be light and the straw short.

We had to buy a new binder - as the old one took 3 times too long to cut - and had frequent breakdowns.

Our pigs have been troublesome - breaking through the old fences...damage to our garden and grounds...

Repairs

We re-roofed the big barn...and painted it with tar. Pitched other roofs - entirely overhauled shingles on Institution roof - Repaired eavestroughing and had new eaves for laundry - also a new copper.

Had all plaster repaired...girls play room was worst.

Built new outside staircase from senior school - new railings and platform and steps from junior school...patched last year when other outside steps were built.

The three furnaces were overhauled and pipes cleaned.

One car of furnace coal was received.

One acre of irrigation completed.

The paint work was all cleaned during the holidays - windows washed - floors and furniture cleaned so no time was lost when school opened.

Allowing children holidays is not altogether a blessing - so many return in dirty condition - we have to use quantities of antiseptics...

28.   7 September 1919   Boyce to Scott

We have a new "boys master" I hope he will prove a success - he is winning the boys interest by sports and games - and would like to start a band. Do you know if we can procure band instruments anywhere? Mr. Rogers is an artillery lieutenant.

29. 15 January 1920   Boyce to Scott
I was in hopes this month that I could afford to buy some books for the childrens library - so wrote the Grollier Society for the rates on "the Book of Knowledge". When I was at the school in 1914 I bought this - and the boys and girls enjoyed it thoroughly - when I returned to the school there was not a volume to be found.

The bills have amounted to more than I expected - the farm was an all round failure last year - so I cannot invest. The last two years before Christmas I have put an advertisement in the papers asking for gifts of magazines and books - and have had a generous response...Could the Department help us...A good library is one of our greatest needs.

The New England Company has also authorized me to apply to the militia for bath tubs - do you think the application would come better from the Department...We need six bathtubs now - and should have more.

30. 23 January 1920   Boyce to Scott
I'm leaving Miss Hardie in charge of the Institute and Mr. Almey (manager) of the farm. We have a competent boys-master Mr. Rogers - in fact a staff I can feel happy about - which is more than I have been able to say since I have been here.

31. 12 April 1920   Smith to Secretary DIA
...30th of March I inspected...there were no complaints of any kind, the children appeared contented and healthy. Mrs. Boyce also reports a large waiting list. Three of the children are attending the Brantford Collegiate Institute and one at the Business College...there are four children preparing for the entrance examination.

A request was made that the school be furnished with a map of Europe a new edition has...been published.

32. 9 May 1920   Boyce to Scott
...I had no idea that the New England Company were in financial straights - have used the strictest economy but tried to live up to their instructions of making necessary repairs and improvements.

Our laundry steam boiler gave out ten days ago, not unexpectedly - got figures for adequate heating system, rendered necessary by failure of gas - accepted one at $450, but have called it off - until I get some idea of how we shall proceed. If we are to close down must make some cheaper arrangement for four months - and if the Department considers taking over the school they might figure on more elaborate system. At present have to carry water from copper to washer - and gas under copper is uncertain.

The holidays are coming and if we have to reduce the number of pupils and staff could do so then without arousing comment.

We have some 75 orphans and destitute children -

about 50 girls and 25 boys - we could carry on with them, and reduce staff by two - saving us $1250 a year (on staff). If we have to keep mostly small children could not reduce on staff.

By reducing number of pupils, present stock of bedding, clothing etc would last some time longer. We have spent considerable on improving farm and orchards and expect results this year.

Rumours have been running around among Indians lately of school closing down - or Department having to pay for it - but Fridays letters were the first I had received.

33. 14 May 1920   Boyce to Scott
Have just received a letter from my brother-in-law, Mr. Cockshutt, stating he had been to see you - about the critical state of the New England Company's affairs...Rev. Brigham of Walpole Island, and Chief Logan of Munsey both old pupils were much concerned at the likelihood of the work being crippled - they both stated they owed their start in life to this school.

I'm enclosing a letter Miss Hardie received to-day from Alice Herkimer - who had her entire education here - and the Indian Department paid half her tuition at the Business College...it was so natural and fluent...

...I had no idea the Company was so crippled. The only word I had from them was "to carry on and to make what repairs and improvements were necessary to carry on efficient work." The per capita cost (120 pupils) for year 1919 was $184.97 - which does not compare badly with 151.72 in 1916 and 164.36 in 1917, when the cost of repairs - and increased cost of living is considered.

34. 17 May 1920   Scott to Boyce
I would advise you not to discharge any pupils at present or take any action looking towards curtailment of the operations of the Institute. We must have a little time to consider what to do, and I will be in a position to write you something definite before very long.....

35. 19 May 1920   Boyce to Scott
This school is to be limited to $5000 a year - we have already had $3100 from the Company and spent it. The estimates for this Quarter are $7000 so I am placed in a difficult position. Several Indians have come for their children as they have heard we are not going to have boys any more - it will certainly create a restless feeling this summer holidays.

The staff could not be cut down and effective work done - unless we reduce number of pupils to 75.
...Over a year ago the Chiefs appointed a committee to visit here regularly -see the pupils meals etc. - and I was asked to name a day a month for them to come - I said no - they could come, and would be welcome, any day they like, and as often as they liked to come - to stay for

dinner if they wanted to - but I would not name a special day as they would think then that we had made a special effort for their inspections. They have never been - we would like them to take an interest in the place - and see the children in school, and the work done.

...I hope you will realize, Mr. Scott, that its the welfare of the school I am interested in - I'm personally not looking for a position...I wish the Department would take the place over...

36. 12 June 1920 Boyce to Scott
I am enclosing list of orphans, and of children deserted by parents - and those with only one parent. The children who have both parents are with few exceptions children of old pupils who are anxious to give them the advantages of a good education...

I can not estimate at all accurately the percapita cost for 120 pupils for the current fiscal year - so much was spent on repairs the last year that comparatively little will be required except on laundry and on heating Boys Play House - but we have not any coal - and food and fuel prices are soaring -hay is very poor - and the insurance should be increased - but I hope estimates will not exceed $200 per head.

37. 29 June 1920 Smith to Secretary DIA
...I saw Miss Hardie who was in charge. The usual summer vacation commences on July 10th, when half of the pupils are given three weeks holidays and on returning the remaining half takes three weeks holidays. A teacher will be in charge all vacation and instruction will be imparted to those who remain at the Institute. The Entrance examinations started yesterday when three pupils presented themselves. Several of the pupils are also taking their examinations in music at the Conservatory in Brantford.

...The market garden has a wonderful showing of early vegetables and from the financial standpoint they should make a success of it. The boys were hard at work in this garden and some of the girls as well, they all prefer out door work to the school. The live stock and poultry appear to be in good condition.

The laundress complained about the ventilation in the laundry saying that the windows in the upper room where the ironing takes place cannot be opened and the heat is excessive...as the building is roofed with metal.

38. 2 July 1920 Brantford Expositor
MOHAWK CADETS PASSED INSPECTION
"Thump thump Thump. I turned over lazily in bed and inquired lazily 'who is there.' Whereupon Cadet Rodman McNaughton opened my door and said "It is a quarter to six, sir, all the boys are up waiting for you to drill them. I pointed out that I had not ordered a parade at such an unearthly hour but the cadet insisted that I had said the

evening before that they would require a great deal more drill in order to come up to standard and consequently they had risen early in the hope that I would get up and drill them. Of course such enthusiasm is infectious and I was soon tumbling out of bed...Lieut. S. Rogers who has been training the Mohawk Cadets for the past year...

On Wednesday...Lt. Col. S. J. Huggins from Toronto arrived to conduct the annual inspection, and the enthusiasm and hard work of the boys produced results that more than satisfied the inspecting officer.

Cadet-Sergeant Major Longboat took command and showed great ability and coolness in drilling the company. The Colonel was so pleased with his work that he promoted him captain at the end of the parades.

During the past year suitable boys have been trained to act as instructors...they were promoted to the rank of sergeant...

The cadets are very proud of their corps and of the service the Indians rendered overseas...

Whilst talking with the boys Master of the Institute it was asked "What is the good of it all?"...Look at those boys running over there. That clumsy fellow is a new boy who has had no training. There is one point in favor of the movement. Then again a boy learns to obey quickly and promptly. They also develop along the right lines physically...

39. September and October 1920 Boyce Report
Church...The girls decorated the church very attractively with oats, wheat, corn, colored vines and fruit for the "Harvest Festival"...
Farm and garden - have had a very busy time - the bridge across the canal had to be finished - oats to draw in - potatoes to be dug. Fall ploughing commenced September 8th...after a welcome rain. We could put on several teams drawing manure and ploughing.
The sweet corn was shocked.
September 11th and 10th the stables were white-washed, inside and out - and the pig-styes and dairy - and again on October 6th.
Threshing commenced Sept. 18th to 23rd - we totalled 2203 bushels - wheat 322 - rye 28, oats 1578 - barley 275 - great quantity of straw.
Then cutting corn and silo filling - took several days.
We sowed wheat Sept 26th and 7th and finished sowing rye October 4th.
The farm drew the gravel and cement for the laundry floor - also the cement mixer to and fro.
Finished digging potatoes October 6th.
Cleaned the wells at the farm cottage.
Dug mangolds and sugar beets - finished October 23rd can not fil car to ship beets.
Drew 45 tons of coal.
We commenced storing apples Oct 6th the girls doing most of the picking. They also stored the onions of which we have a large quantity - pumpkins - citrons etc. They filled the pillows with oat straw. We have very fine apples - thanks to our sprayer. The apple house is full... The pupils have quantities to eat.
We have put in a lot of work on the rhubarb beds, and flowers beds and fruit bushes.
We have purchased four cows, as our milk supply was poor, we are now selling more butter and have good

supply of milk for the pupils.

<u>Staff</u> Mr Almey left to return to College..Mr. Barron the new farm foreman came on duty Sept 7th...

Mr. Richmond left to return to College. Sept 16th, we engaged extra man for silo filling as some boys had measles, and so many were very small.

...Mrs Bilke left on the 22nd and was married...Miss Busch came on as housekeeper Oct. 22nd is doing well

<u>Health</u> - We have had an epidemic of german measles on the boys side.

**** had an accident with a fork, silo filling - fortunately not serious. **** broke his arm on the corn binder, and **** fell on his head - concussion not serious. Many returned from the holidays with scabies.

Measles broke out on the girls side - the real old fashioned kind - ten went down at first and some very very sick - several other cases developed - its now spreading to the boys.

<u>School work</u> - Has been rather interrupted by the measles and several holidays.

Five pupils are attending the Collegiate - 4 girls and 1 boy.

Present 70 girls - 4 on sick leave, - boys 41 - 3 accepted but delayed in coming + 3 on sick leave .

<u>Labor Day</u> was much enjoyed the pupils going to the "trades procession" in town and afterwards to the Park.

<u>Thanksgiving Day</u> was a general holiday - they had great fun over an impromptu concert at night. Several of the pupils act well.

<u>Sports Day</u> was a great success - by way of an innovation the boys paraded their horses and teams - the cleanliness of the horses & harness was decidedly pleasing - the boys must have spent much of their own time and money for cleaning and purchasing brass for decorating the harness. This parade had a marked effect on the daily work of the boys with their horses.

...The All Hallows Eve Concert was a regular scream. The boys pumpkin heads, and the girls as clowns, etc...

<u>Visitors</u> Major Smith looked over the financial affairs - bank statements etc. Sept 9th

Mr Standing...spent October 19th here.

We were delighted October 20th to have Mr. Scott...He looked over the financial affairs of the school - visited the school rooms & laundry - and saw the girls drill.

40. 30 October 1920 Van Loon

I have your letter of the 29th instant with regard to the orphan or neglected children from this band attending the Mohawk Institute and will report as follows;

The **** girls are members of this band they will both be 16 years of age in December and both want to leave the school but it would be much better for them if they can be kept there for about two years more as I know of no suitable place for them, one of them is an orphan, the other, her parents have been seperated since she was about

one year old, the mother has been living with a Six Nation Indian since and has several more children by him, so that it would not be a suitable place for ****, ****'s parents are both dead, her grand parents are not in a position to look after her...money well spent to pay the extra $50 a year while they can be kept there.

41. November and December 1920 Boyce Report

<u>CHURCH</u>

...The Queen Ann Silver was used on these occassions. On December 1st. the Bishop of Huron held a Confirmation Service at which there were 29 candidates... the Schoolroom was prettily and effectively decorated with pink begonias, ferns and other plants...December 23rd...Service of Christmas Hymns and Carols. The School-room was decorated with Cedar, Spruce Bells and Chains and the Chancel was beautiful with its brass Candle-sticks and vases of poinsettas and green.

The remaining pupils on Christmas Day and the following Sunday attended Trinity and St. Judes Churches.

<u>HEALTH</u>

We have had epidemics of sore throats and the grippe. Nearly everyone including the Staff have had the Grippe more or less acutely.

One girl had eryseplas and **** was attended by Dr. H. Bragg for bad sore eyes.

****, a tubercular abscess case was sent to hospital on November 26th.

There were several cases of a very bad rash.

<u>AMUSEMENTS</u>

During December all the girls visited town twice to see the christmas Stores.

<u>The Christmas Concert</u> on December 21st was a great success. The drills, dances, dialogues, songs, recitations, duets and solos were all well rendered and thoroughly enjoyed.

<u>The Song Service</u> with Carols was bright and hearty... Major G. J. Smith presented the prizes won at the Sports and in the Cleanliness Competitions held in the Horse Stable and Cow Barn...he expressed pleasure in the good singing, bright appearance, and smart uniforms of the pupils.

<u>School Closed</u> December 24th, and many went to their homes. 72 remained the night - a few leaving next day.

<u>Forty boys and girls went out as waits</u>...Mrs. Smith asked the party in and entertained them with coffee, biscuits and candies. The children thoroughly enjoyed themselves and the gifts of candy and nuts received "en route". Mr. Cockshutt sent a crate of oranges. The small children were visited by Santa Claus.

<u>On Christmas Day</u> the dinner of roast pork, browned potatoes, mashed turnips, and gravy followed by plum pudding and sauce was so much enjoyed that many suffered next day. The Supper tables were decorated with gay doylies and loaded with oranges, dates, raisins,

biscuits and candy. Many spent the greater part of the next day in bed.

...snow came on Sunday night and we were able to get the bob-sleighs out on Monday and flood the Rink. The skating on the Canal was good. Every afternoon candy or nuts were distributed and each evening the officers joined the pupils in games and dances and more candy.

Many letters were received from those pupils at home saying they were lonely [and wished] they were spending their holidays at the Institute. One boy surprised everyone by refusing to go home with his relations. He declared that he could enjoy himself much better here.

On the 30th December the girls with two officers went on sleighs to the Institution for the Blind to see Mary Was...spent a most enjoyable afternoon.

INCIDENTALS

On Armistice Day all the School and Staff assembled and sang patriotic songs. Various members of the Staff gave addresses. Following a lecture on Fire precautions which included the reorganisation of Fire Drill an Alarm was given. The new Drill was very well carried out and the girls manning all interior hydrants.

The mild weather allowed us to pick apples well on in November. The girls gathered leaves and generally tidied the grounds. On December 24th two boys...stole jack-knives and a hockey stick in town. The goods were returned. This was discovered and reported by other boys.

Miss Hardie and Mrs. Hargreave applied for increase in salary.

Miss Busch, housekeeper, proved a failure.

Miss Hackbourne was engaged November 29th.

Miss Gimby left on the end of November and Miss Keyes, a former officer was engaged for the sewing room. Mrs. Hargreaves secured a position in Toronto December 21st, and asked to be released at the end of month.

GENERAL WORK

...giving out warmer clothing and bedding - putting in double windows and glazing - erecting extra stoves - replacing old stove piping - packing hydrants and cut-off boxes...

42. 1920 Boyce Annual Report

FINANCIAL

...the cost of maintenance of the school, inclusive of supplies from Farm...$20,482.51

The revenue from the Farm was $1,230.66

The cost of the entire establishment was $19,251.86

EDUCATIONAL

Grace MacNaughton completed her course at the Business College, has now a good position and is boarding at the Y.W.C.A.

Three girls passed the entrance examination to the Collegiate - Ethel Green taking honours. They all started on the teachers course after the Midsummer holidays at the Collegiate.

Wilson and Carl Tobias were prepared for the Entrance Examination here...

Ruby and William Smith are in their second year at the Collegiate. William took honours at Midsummer.

Luella Moses left at Midsummer after attending the Collegiate one year. She is keeping house for her father and attending the Caledonia High School.

Alice Herkemer who completed her course at the Business College last year is getting $90 a month at the Goodyear Rubber Co. Akron, Ohio. She was one out of ten retained of a staff of two hundred, when the staff was reduced.

Two girls have been playing the Church organ and several others are qualified to do so. At the Conservatory of Music Examinations:-

Eva Smith passed Grade I - 94 Marks. First Class Honours
Minnie Smith "   "   91 "
Elva Miller   II   81
Luella Moses   III   65

ATTENDANCE

During the year 35 pupils were admitted - 14 boys and 21 girls - and 18 boys and 18 girls were discharged. Of these 4 girls are on sick leave, two boys were enfranchised, 5 absconded and 1 was dismissed.

CONDUCT

The conduct has been good. This year we had to discontinue the Badge Money (that is the rewarding for good conduct) as we were short of money. The boys are taking an intelligent interest in the care of stock, and their farm work. On Sports Day the boys proudly exhibited their horses. There was great competition in the grooming and care of the animals. Many of the boys bought brass ornamentations for their horses harness.

HEALTH

We have had epidemics of Grippe, Mumps, Measles and German Measles, which have not been serious but disarranged the School work. There have been several cases of abscesses. Three girls have had sick leave on this account...One boy with serious tuberculor abscesses has been sent to the Brantford Hospital.

One boy with sore eyes has been under treatment here and was sent home for a time. Several accident cases - not serious - one boy broke his arm. One case of erysciplas.

Our principle trouble is the pupils returning from home with scabies and rashes which do not yield readily to treatment.

RELIGIOUS TRAINING

Mr. Bilkie held classes for preparation for confirmation ...which most of the older pupils attended. The Bishop was very pleased with the examination papers...there were twenty nine candidates...All the pupils attend Sunday services and Sunday school and some instruction is given in school - prayers night and morning. We go to a great deal of trouble in decorating for special occasions such as Christmas, Thanksgiving, Easter, Confirmation, letting the pupils do all the work.

AMUSEMENTS

The severe winter was fine for sports and the girls were often out bob-sleighing on suitable days. Three weeks holiday was allowed at Midsummer but many had no homes and we had from 60 to 65 here all summer, these enjoyed swimming and picnics. Several carnivals came to town and treated the children most generously. The public holidays were observed and Sports Day. Games are encouraged in the Playgrounds and Playrooms. The children can put on very good entertainments - drills, songs, dances, dialogues, solos, recitations, and duets on the piano. They enjoy dancing to the Victrola or piano.

IMPROVEMENTS, REPAIRS etc

During the winter we made fly-screens for the entire lower floor and also cold frames. The latter cost $168.85

One of the officers' bed-rooms was done over as a sitting-room for the officers and another as a study room for older girls. The Mens' Dining Room, walls and woodwork, was painted.

The stair cases were all done over.

Most of the expense went on the laundry. The motor was overhauled in January, a new jacket heater installed with coils for heating rooms and dryers, new cement tubs erected, a new cement floor with drainage troughs was laid and the girls bath was deepened.

CLOTHING

The girls had new flannel uniforms, an issue of school aprons, one of work aprons and heavy drill skirts. The boys had new shirts, jerseys, sweaters and two pairs each of denim trousers for school and work, with the necessary underwear, shoes and stockings. We have gone shabby waiting for prices to drop.

FARM AND GARDEN

We had a severe winter. The frost penetrated our cellars resulting in the loss of a small quantity of apples and potatoes. The pipes were frozen and we had to carry water to the cattle...

Last winter we cut fallen timber on the Glebe and home property. In the fall we cut the avenue of chesnuts at the front entrance and a quantity of brush.

The girls cared for the chickens, the incubator and the young chicks...

The cattle were tested for T.B.C. and the bull was condemned. Two old horses were killed.

All the stables were sprayed inside and out.

We threshed 2,203 bushels of grain and we have quantities of straw but little hay.

We fall ploughed the entire farm, garden and orchard with the exception of the meadows, cut brush and cleaned the fences and ditches.

We completed the fence along the Mohawk Road and repaired line fences. The fences on the flats were removed to avoid loss by Spring floods.

The place is tidier than it has been for six years.

We were forced to repair the bridge across the canal at a cost of $250 and three days labour for men and boys.

We completed irrigation (2½ acres in all) and receipts from the Garden exceeded any previous year by $700.00.

The girls attended to the lawns and flower beds, and the Church Yard, helped in the greenhouse and cold frame work, besides picking most of the peas, beans, tomatoes, small fruits and apples. We had a large quantity of apples which the girls stored besides onions and pumpkins.

We transplanted one rhubarb bed, dug around another, cleaned and pruned the currant and gooseberry bushes.

We bought a large power sprayer, and sold the old sprayer for $5.00 less than it cost four years ago.

We sold quantities of early potatoes at a splendid figure. The late potatoes did not yield well. We have plenty of beans.

43. 25 January 1921 Smith to Secretary DIA
...14th inst...inspection...discussing financial arrangements and the management of the school.

There were six girls in bed sick but nothing serious is anticipated...Mrs. Boyce reports a great necessity for new mattresses and blankets as they have not been renewed for many years and the mattresses in particular are too old and unsanitary for much more service. I mentioned to Mrs. Boyce the transfer of hospital supplies to the Indian Department from the Speedwell Hospital and she expressed a keen desire to secure some of these as when there is sickness it is very hard to properly care for the patients without proper equipment, such as trays, extra dishes, basins and so-on...some hot water bottles, dressing carriages, bed-side tables and some plain chairs, in addition to the blankets and mattresses mentioned above...
...some band instruments also taken over and as Mr. Rodgers the Assistant principal is fully qualified to instruct a band, it was considered that a band could be formed if 12 instruments could be furnished...giving the boys amusement as well as profitable instruction outside of school hours.

During Christmas holidays the water was let out of the boiler in the laundry was again put in use a fire was lighted, but by neglect the boiler was not filled with water resulting in the burst. After several attempts at welding, it was found necessary to buy a new boiler, but the old one has been placed in the boys play house surrounded by a drum, resulting in a splendid apparatus...

44. 2 March 1921 Smith to Secretary DIA
...on Friday the 25th of February I made an inspection of the Mohawk Institute. There is an attendance of 120 of whom one boy young **** who recently returned from the Hospital was in bed, as his health is so undermined that he cannot study or do any work. In the girls

dormitory there were three girls in bed from slight ailments. Both the girls and boys dormitories have had the wood work painted and ceiling and walls white washed making them bright and cheerful in appearance.

In the stables everything appears to be progressing favorably the cows look well are giving a fair quantity of milk and as far as known there is no tuberculosis.

I caused a fire alarm to be sounded but...nobody took any notice except two girls who were working in the green house. There was a strong wind blowing...which accounted for it not being heard...

45. January and February 1921 Boyce Report
CHURCH...As all the services were held in the School-room we have allowed three inexperienced girls to act as organists. They have done remarkably well.
HEALTH During this period we have had several cases of grippe, sore-throat and ear-ache, one of uremic poisoning, two tuberculosis abscesses, and one of scarlet fever. We...sent the case for treatment to the Isolation Hospital. Two pupils are undergoing treatment at the occulist and several have been to the dentist.
**** returned from the Hospital on January 31st. We were unable to fetch him earlier owing to the Hospital quarantine. He requires constant attention and should be in a Sanitarium. We have also one case of hernia which will require an operation.
Amusements. There has been little skating or out-door sports...when we had snow enough we had the bob-sleighs out. The purchase of a few books has helped wonderfully to keep the children amused. The boys are becoming vigorous boxers and the girls have enjoyed dancing.
The Grace A.Y.P.A. gave a Concert that was much enjoyed on February 14th.
A Music Class has been started for the boys.
INSPECTION Major Smith inspected January 14th and February 25th. Mr. Standing inspected in afternoon February 21st and all day on 23rd.
STAFF Mrs. Hargreaves, Governess left January 1st. Miss Keyes, Sewing Teacher, who has had several years experience in teaching was transferred to the Junior School and Mrs. Burnett was engaged to take her place as Sewing Teacher. Both have proved good officers. Miss Hackborn, housekeeper, left the end of January and Miss Davidson came on duty February 1st.

Four boys absconded Sunday February 20th and were all returned by John Lickers, Truant Officer on February 22nd.
INSTITUTE We had plasterers make repairs in the dormitories, the ceilings and upper walls were white-washed and painters worked on the high beams in the girls lower dormitory. The girls have completed the paint work there and have started on the Boys dormitory...
We have been able to purchase from Army supplies factory cotton, sheeting and linen for girls summer dresses at a very cheap figure. We are busy making sheets, pillow cases and shirts besides uniforms...have also bought the winters supply of socks and stockings with a good surplus for next year, at a very low figure...
The Manual Training benches and tools have been of great interest to the boys. Mr. Mutter of the Collegiate Staff commenced classes February 19th. On Saturday the Boys Half-holiday, I found a number of boys in the School-room and...I was told that they were waiting to see Mr. Rogers to ask permission to spend their holiday in the Carpenters' Shop. Several aeroplanes and models are in evidence.

46. 12 March 1921 Standing to Whom It may Concern
I hereby certify that I have inspected the classes at the Mohawk Institution, Brantford for the past three years, and that Miss Susan Hardie during that time has been the teacher, having been trained in the Toronto Normal School, and for a long period she has had successful experience in teaching and guiding the pupils of this school. She is an excellent disciplinarian, not severe, but firm in her control, and I believe, secures the affection as well as the respect of her pupils. In teaching she has been uniformly successful, as is shown by the success of her pupils at the H.S. Entrance Examination.

I feel confident of her worth as a teacher and as one responsible for the care of children in an institution such as that in which she now teaches.

47. March & April 1921 Boyce Report
CHURCH...On Easter Sunday the School-room was appropriately decorated with flowers and plants and the Church brass, by the pupils. On April 10th it was warm enough for us to commence services at the Church...

RECREATION. The boys show great enthusiasm in the Cadet Corps drills and are busy preparing for the Annual Inspection on May 10th. To relieve the monotony of drilling under the same Instructor Mr. Rogers arranged for the Sergeant-major of the local Regiment to train the boys in certain work and they have responded very well. Much time is spent at the river fishing and ball games occupy most of the short recesses. Good Friday was a holiday after service and all Easter Monday...Easter Day all pupils had eggs for breakfast and candy eggs for supper.

HEALTH We have had a troublesome epedemic of "pink eye" with the boys, one case of uremic poisoning, one of erysiplas, and another of Scarlet Fever which was sent to the Isolation Hospital. One girl who had tubercular trouble in hand was sent to Doctors and X-rayed. Amputation was advised below the wrist but the father took the girl away for home treatment. Several pupils have been attending dentist and others the oculist. The changeable weather has given rise to several cases of sore throat and rheumatism...

notes...Mr. Mutter...was delighted with the progress the boys made. Some of the models are excellent. Major Smith inspected both months. We set our incubator in the Hospital with good results...Mrs. Ashton died April 14th, suddenly and the funeral...The Boys acted as Guard of Honour several of the older Girls sang in the Service very sweetly...Mr. Ashton was moved to the Institute...

48. 19 April 1921 J. D. Sutherland to Scott

With reference to the payment by the various bands from the interest funds at their credit, towards the support of orphan and neglected children, members of the bands who are in attendance...a list has been received showing the number of these children who attended during the last fiscal year and the respective bands to which they belong.

It was decided that the increase in grant, viz: $80.00 per capita, which had to be assumed on account of the New England Company having withdrawn the greater part of their financial assistance, would be borne by the bands...As the bands have expressed their unwillingness to have any amount taken from their funds for the above purpose and also as the general vote for Indian Education is ample to pay the per capita grant in full for the maintenance of all the Indian children who are in attendance, I would advise that the full per capita grant be charged to the Vote...

49. 14 May 1921 Jas Mutter Report on Manual Training

A start was made in Manual Training in this school on... February 19th 1921. I was engaged...to take classes every Saturday morning until the beginning of May. Work started with a class of sixteen boys but as the tools supplied were not sufficient the class was divided and came on alternate days. The work taken up was; The theory of timber and tools with notes and sketches of same. Elementary exercises in woodwork. Planing, Sawing, The making of halving and mortises and tenon joints, followed by more advanced work entailing the use of these joints...lessons were given in upholstering (webbing, stuffing, covering, etc). Additional work was taken up in the way of small local repairs.

I attended 12 Saturdays for three hours per day...so that 16 pupils received 18 hours instruction. The discipline and attention of the boys was excellent, they took naturally to the work and made a success of it in every instance and compare favourably with any pupils in this work that I have ever handled, showing fine self-reliance and perseverance...this is an excellent opportunity for a technical department being introduced at the Institute which would work in well with the training in farm work that the boys receive, besides opening other avenues of vocational choice for them. Meantime there are only tools for a limited number. The workshop... could easily be arranged to accommodate a full class.

50. 30 June 1921 Boyce to Scott

All our pupils have gone over to see the circus procession - the tents are not far from here so they will see the horses put in and have first view of everything.

Yesterday Miss Hardie, Mr. Rogers and I motored over to Mount Elgin - we had a delightful day. The McVitees were very good to us and we saw everything. As far as buildings are conserned except for our dining hall we would not change with them. They got a lot of furniture from Toronto which they have put to good use - but Mr. Rogers picked out just the same kind of things and we are hoping to get them before long.

We like our uniforms better than theirs - their girls were not wearing aprons and those working looked very dirty - wet dresses - only one issued a week. We have aprons for each department & others for school. Their grounds and gardens were well kept but we have the advantage there...they have a splendid farm, and their farm buildings and equipment make us green with envy.

Mr. McVitee got from Brandon -uniforms for the boys - new Marine uniforms - black with red stripes - for $1.25 a suit - enough to last for 5 years - and he says Mr. Ferrier has five hundred suits. We require new cloth suits for our boys and would like to get some of them.

51. May and June 1921 Boyce Report

DRESS. On June the 19th the girls wore their new dresses of aeroplane linen trimmed with blue and their new black hats. They looked very nice. The boys wore their summer Cadet uniforms on June 25th.

IMPROVEMENTS. The grounds and buildings look a great deal fresher and brighter of late. The girls painted the windows, doors and verandahs of the center building: the boys doing those parts difficult of access...

HEALTH. Scarlet Fever broke out on May 10th. and as we had five cases we opened our own Hospital and obtained the services of Miss Ward, trained nurse...We closed the hospital on June 27th. and fumigated...

****, suffering from T.B.C. abscesses was allowed sick leave on May 20th.

**** dislocated his elbow on May 18th.

NOTES. The soups and pilchards sent by the Department are very much appreciated.

Manual Training Course finished May 5th.

Cadet Inspection by Lt.Col. Barker May 10th.

Russell Longboat, one of three senior boys who are buglers in the regiment, took first prize in a Battalion Shooting Match on May 9th...

Inspector Wylie, Canadian Fire Underwriters Association passed our wiring...but that unless certain alterations were made in...lighting the basement and dining halls, he would have to render a report condemning the same...

Mr. Rogers went to Mount Pleasant to inspect and select desks for Junior School on June 10th.

On June 15th. we commenced to unload the car of Stores

from Ottawa at 8.30 a.m...By 5 p.m. the goods were checked and stored in addition to the mattresses being carbolized and scrubbed.

**** on June 25th. was allowed out with friends and was apprehended for theft at the local store of Messrs Woolworths.

...During the passed two months all blankets have been washed. The boys have been issued with two new shirts and the girls have had a set of blue aprons. All pupils have had new shoes and stockings...

The pupils have been enjoying strawberries, cherries, red and white currants for their suppers in addition to lettuce etc...

52. 4 August 1921 Smith to Secretary DIA
...the 2nd. inst. I made an inspection...It being holiday season there were no classes of instruction. The plumbers were there putting in the new toilets and the farm section of the Institute was busily engaged in taking in the crops.

Mrs. Boyce has received a very large consignment of hospital supplies from Toronto which cost her nothing but freight, as a result she expects very little clothing will have to be bought for the children for the next two years. Besides clothing a large amount of useful material for the kitchen and other portions of the building were obtained.

Work on the green house extension will be started this week. In the farm, they have sold over $250.00 worth of early potatoes while large returns have been received for green house produce.

Mrs. Boyce has secured the services of Miss Buchanan a farmerette who is possessed of certificates for Social Service Work etc. and is making herself very useful in supervising the girls in light farm work during the holidays, at least for those who stay at the Institute. Her salary will be $25.00 a month. Mrs. Boyce says that without somebody to look after the girls in this manner, no satisfactory work would be accomplished and she feels that they must be employed for at least half the day during the holidays.

53. 2 August 1921 **** Pt. Cunnington to Boyce
I am having a lovely time out hear. But I didn't feel well the first two weeks I was here.

Well how are all of the girls. I hope their all beheaving themselves are they? I wrote to Mrs. Bernett but she hasn't answered me yet. You must tell her to answer will you?

**** told me to send you her love. She said I stole all the news worth telling so she cant write.

I really dont think thats the case, its the case of lazyness dont you? is Mr. Rogers still living? I often think about you all. You couldn't imagine how lonesome I got for you.

Mrs. Cockshutt is very nice to me. Well I must close now tell everybody you see to write ha ha. So good-Bye

from one of your old pupils. I dont think I'll close yet because it will look so silly with only a few words on.

**** is just sitting here laughing for all she's worth. She isnt worth very much what do you think.

Have you any new girls down there.

I suppose the girls are very glad they passed the Entrance Exams. I know **** was, she sang all day and night.

We have an awful time up here with the mice and Bats.

I am so skinny I cant hardly see myself. Well I really must close now.
P.S. Answer soon please.

54. 9 August 1921 **** to Boyce
I will write you this letter in order to tell you that I got home alright last Saturday. And my father is very thankful because you paid my way and gave me those clothes and so am I. **** and I was very glad to get home agin with our father. But I would sooner go back to school again and my father said he thought I better go back again because that was the best place for me because I wasn't very old yet. So please keep place for me. Because I would sooner be at the school than to stay home. But I like it home during the holidays but I don't think I would after. So **** and I will be going back if there is room for me. Please tell us if there is room for me yet.

I will close now please excuse my mistakes.

55. 11 August 1921 Boyce to Secretary DIA
Enclosed is letter from a pupil who is seventeen years of age - Mother dead - father a cripple - last year they did not go home for a holiday - this year I arranged it for them - thinking **** would leave - I even got her a place as maid in London.

I expect this fall to get a tailorers to make over the coats obtained from the Department for our girls - and **** can help here - then I will try to apprentice her to a dressmaker for a few months.

The other letter from Muskoka -my sisters home - where I sent two girls both past sixteen for a few weeks to earn a little money.

One **** has past her entrance - she is illegitimate - deserted by her mother - placed here by the Childrens Aid. She is not clever - but very plodding and ambitious. There is no one to help her. I am going to apply to the Council for a grant to send her to the Business College - but they have never given aid to pupils of this school. Mrs. Cockshutt will help her with clothing - but the girl has no one to help her with fees and sundry expenses.

The writer of the letter is **** who will try her entrance examination this summer. She is very pretty and bright - a talent for music - father paralyzed - mother living with another man by whom she has a large family - neither of them take any interest in the girl. I should like money to further her music lessons - and to fit her for a position next year. She is a Missasauga - have written the agents several times about her - with no result.

Another girl Jessie McNaughton - passed her entrance - is going to study telegraphy this year - I shall apply to the Council to help her - but Major Smith does not think they will.

Could the Department help me with these girls.

56. **July and August 1921 Boyce Report**
CHURCH...During the six weeks vacation we did not have Sunday School but the pupils were allowed to go to City Churches in the evening.
HEALTH We had an outbreak of Chicken-pox during the holidays. **** dislocated a bone in his right wrist whilst home. The doctor has examined this. **** had his arm crushed slightly...
STAFF...A farmerette, Miss Buchanan was engaged...

Holidays commenced July 17th, those having homes were given three weeks. School re-opened August 27th. We had an average of 48 girls and 25 boys here during the holidays. They had a half-day holiday each day with the exception of a few older boys who were employed on the farm all day and were paid accordingly.

Amusements were arranged for them, and Old Home Week in Brantford provided much interesting recreation. The old benches in the Junior School were removed early in the holiday and the pupils had several enjoyable evenings dancing playing parlour games, or boxing.

August 29th. new classifications were made and the clothing issues were checked up making it possible to have school in regular running order on August 30th.

Carrie Crowe and Elsie Clause commenced their course at the Business College.

Flo Elliott took honours at the Conservatory of Music examinations and Creatha Thomas passed.

Carrie Crowe passed the Collegiate Entrance with honours whilst Elsie Clause and Kathleen Maracle passed and Jesse MacNaughton failed in arithmetic.

The boys clothing from Regina arrived August 18th.

The stores from Toronto and the stationery from Ottawa arrived...
***, a student at the Collegiate, went out with a man employed on the farm and as we had had trouble with her before we secured her a place as cook. The man was discharged.

...We were able to buy heavy underwear for girls to very great advantage at the Paris Mills.

**** ran away from the people who have been in the habit of taking him home for holidays and was arrested for vagrancy at Oakville. Mr. Rogers, however, was able to get charge withdrawn and the boy returned.

Instead of the "Badge System" we have formerly used we have now commenced a fresh scheme. Each pupil is allowed 15 cents monthly and this amount is paid into a

fund controlled by a committee of pupils and one officer, who may spend it in any way they choose for the benefit of the others in general: for instance corn roasts, feasts, sporting gear. However, deductions are to be made from this amount in the manner of fines for clothing and articles found out of place, careless smashing of windows, destruction of property, loss of cutlery and any other carelessness which is constantly increasing the running expenses. It is hoped that this method will help to make all careful and that the older pupils will realise that they are in some way responsible for the proper conduct of the younger.

57. **September and October 1921 Boyce Report**
HEALTH...outbreak of Chicken-pox amongst the boys and an epedemic of influenza which kept several of the Staff and many of the pupils in bed. **** met with an accident while threshing. He broke his arm as a result of falling from the mow. **** fell on the stairs and injured his hip. Both boys received immediate medical attention and are well again. **** underwent an operation in the local hospital for double hernia...minor complaints include several cases of sore eyes, the usual outbreak of itch following holidays and one case of acute exema.
STAFF Miss Walker engaged for one month as Housekeeper, on trial, succeeded by Mrs. Neale.

Miss Keyes left October 1st having been ill...

Miss Cummings, teacher, from Reserve School No.5 was engaged at once but could not assume her duties until October 25th. In the meantime Jessie MacNaughton took the Junior School very creditably.

Miss Lee, farmerette, had to leave suddenly, October 6th on illness at home.
NOTES Major Smith inspected September 1st.

Mr. Standing, Public Schools inspector, was here October 17th.

LABOUR DAY. September 5th. The Boys were interested spectators at the Battalion Rifle Matches held on the Ranges of this property. One of our senior boys taking part made a very fair score. The girls went swimming and visited the stores.

SPORTS DAY October 12th. In spite of very cold weather our sports were a great success. This year the local merchants were asked to provide the prizes and a very useful collection of articles was made. Our baker provided the refreshments. The pupils were very enthusiastic in their races and events...The boys Horses were splendid and our visitors expressed their admiration both of the cleanliness of the teams and harness and of the skilled manner in which the teams were driven. The Cattle were also in good condition and very clean. Refreshments were provided in the School-room where we also staged a boxing contest. Mrs. G. J. Smith presented the prizes at the close...

PLOUGHING MATCH. October 26th. It was

considered advisable that our boys should attend the local ploughing match in company of the farm staff who were instructed to use the opportunity from an educational point of view. A marked difference in the quality of the work done by our teamsters since that date shows the benefit derived already.

Ohsweken Fair. October 14th. The boys attended... attracted a lot of attention by their very smart turn-out.

REGIMENTAL CHURCH PARADE The Cadets were specially invited to attend Church Parade on October 24th. with the Regiment. Colonel Colquoun... congratulated the boys on their general smartness in both dress and drill. The girls were present as onlookers.

PUPILS DANCE. October 5th. The girls entertained the boys and gave a Box Social which they financed from their own funds. This fund comes from the new system of rewards which has had a marked effect in the tidiness, care of clothing and equipment.

Mrs Boyce went to Ottawa for two days October 10th.

****, who has caused much trouble and has been guilty of several petty thefts from officers and other boys, absconded in company of a cousin **** and both are wanted by the police for theft. **** has absconded several times being returned each time by the local police. He is absent now.

The girls are now wearing a most becoming set of "tams " made from the blue serge hospital gowns. The necessary issues of warmer clothing and extra blankets have been made...

Mr Coutts of the G.N.W. commenced a class in telegraphy and has expressed his pleasure at the progress made. The D.S.C.R. Toronto were able to provide us with instruments.

Heavy gales blew down a quantity of apples. This year crop was not good...We have not, however, been able to store as many this year as last but the children have been able to enjoy quantities already...

Although we have been exceptionally busy on the Farm and Garden and have accomplished much, we are glad to be able to report that in no single instance has any boy had to neglect his lessons or miss school in order that so much should be done...

We all sufferred from poisoning on October 24th. It is thought that some girl put an irritant (possibly lye) in the baking soda and officers and pupils alike sufferred. The suspected baking soda was handed over to local chemists and we await their report.

It is our intention to kill our own meat this winter. Already we have enjoyed one home-killed calf and chickens are available when required.

...We lifted our geraniums and other stock early and have already several thousand cuttings struck. The greenhouses are a blaze of chrysanthemums of all shades and we have promising beds of ferns, lillies. We expect to place fresh picked tomatoes and lettuce on the market for Christmas.

58. 2 December 1921 Smith Report

Since the terms of the Adolesence Act is to be enforced at the Institute, Mrs. Boyce is somewhat worried as to how the children are to be occupied especially if they pass the entrance examination and are not attending High School. She now has one girl who has passed the Business College examination before she is 16 and their are others who will pass the Entrance examination before they reach that age.

All the teachers and officers are rendering satisfactory services, particularly Miss Cummings, teacher of the junior class, who holds a second class Normal Certificate and has had long experience as teacher. Her salary at present is $40.00 a month but Mrs. Boyce feels that in order to keep her, her salary will have to be increased.

59. 17 December 1921 Boyce to Secretary DIA

...re the advisability of starting a class for those students who are qualified to take High School work. As we are so near the city schools - I think it will cost less to send our pupils to the town. We have not the accomodation for another class room - teachers rooms etc.

As we have to keep our children until eighteen we are making every effort to give them variety and entertainment both in and out of school. The seniors are taking great interest in the class in telegraphy - after passing our standard we hope some will continue the course at the G.N.W. office. When qualified - after six or eight months - they can earn eighty a month in small towns - one hundred and twenty dollars...in the cities.

The boys are interested in their manual training classes - last week they repaired - in some cases upholstered a lot of chairs that had been derelicts for years.

Next summer I entend to give the senior girls a short course in knitting crocheting - embroidery - cooking in small quantities making them write down the receipts and directions.

Meantime we are making a start at an orchestra - we have not found a suitable instructor for the girls - for an Hawaian orchestra.

Our Christmas entertainment takes place next Friday evening. The school room will be decorated - we will close with a few carrols and prayers - as a few are leaving for their holidays on Saturday. I wish you could hear them - we are looking forward to your visit - and the children will enjoy putting on a small exhibit for you.

60. 17 December 1921 Boyce to Secretary DIA

For some years back we have not had a fully qualified teacher in our junior school - the salary offered was $400.00 a year...As the last teacher did not complete a year and we were without a teacher some weeks -I have been paying Miss Cummings $40 a month. When she came here she forfeited her right to the Ontario teachers pension.

We give teachers a large bed-room...board - and washing - they share a sitting room and dining room...We require certain duties...outside school hours.

At the present time teachers are receiving such large salaries - that I think we should give Miss Cummings more - she has had several years experience. On the other hand she is not strong - has lately had to give up teaching for two years - and I'm afraid she may break down again - (but if we lose her I should like to engage a qualified teacher) - she should not have come here only she felt she could not remain on the reserve...Miss Hardie will not be content with her salary long - as some of her old pupils teaching on the reserve are earning more. She has given the best years of her life in her work here - personally I should prefer a younger, brighter teacher - and would very much appreciate it if some system of pension could be arranged instead of a raise in salary...Miss Hardie is a capable teacher - but she has spent her life here since twelve years of age - and her horizon is very limited - and she knows practically nothing of the ways of the world. I think a pension plan would solve our difficulty.

61. 23 December 1921 Smith to Secretary DIA
...on the 20th inst. I made my usual monthly inspection... Mrs. Boyce expects to have all the pupils except about eight present for the Christmas holidays as so many parents have written asking her to keep them during the holidays as times are so hard on the Reserve that they cannot afford any extra expense.

Under the new Instructor which they have for Manual Training a great deal of useful work is accomplished as well as useful instruction given to the boys as all the broken chairs, benches etc. are repaired by the boys, new arms and rockers put on the chairs some have been upholstered, all the benches in the new green houses have been built by the Manual training class...they intend to over haul all the waggons on the farm.

In the stables there were 19 milking cows, besides 10 calves and the bull. The herd is gradually being improved and brought back to a profit basis. Green houses well filled with vegetables to go on the market early when prices are high. Amongst one of the recent purchases of clothing were a quantity of suits...these have to be cut down and altered to fit the boys but Mrs. Boyce cannot get any clothing firm to tender for the work any lower than $7.50 per suit, the ripping to be done at the school which Mrs. Boyce considers too high, there are about 50 suits required at present. She is trying to arrange to secure the services of a tailor or tailoress to do the work at the school on a time basis which she thinks would save considerable cost...

BlackBoards are badly required in both the Junior and Senior class rooms what they have being too high for the children to use...the Inspector has several times called the attention of the Department to the want of blackboards.

Mrs. Boyce is also suggesting that the Department make a beginning on the promised addition...the dinning room is still in the basement and not at all satisfactory and if a new building is built bath rooms and lavatories for both the boys and the girls could be furnished thus doing away with the girls bath tub in the laundry and the boys unsanitary lavatory in the out buildings both of which are not in keeping with a modern school.

62. November and December 1921 Boyce Report
SERVICES...Mr. Bilkie said Good-bye to the children as he was leaving...
HEALTH A few colds with sore throats and rheumatism caused by the unsettled weather were the order. ****'s arm which was broken made a perfect set and he uses it freely now. **** injured his thumb whilst on holidays and **** had a badly impacted fracture of his arm. Both are better. **** whose eye-lids were dreadfully disfigured by burns when she was a baby was operated upon at the local hospital and her appearance is wonderfully improved...
Notes THANKSGIVING DAY...was a general holiday and the girls went for walks and called at the stores. A shooting match was arranged for the boys on the Rifle Ranges. The evening was spent in candy making with a taffy pull as the finale.

ARMISTICE DAY...a service was...attended by all the pupils and staff...Mr. Rogers addressed the school.

All our pupils visited town twice in order to see the stores and the Christmas Displays...

Thursday and Friday before Christmas we spent in decorating the school rooms and the Entrance Hall. We were able to cut the cedar, hemlock and pine from our own shrubbery. This with red wreathing and bells lent a charmingly festive appearance to the whole building which most of our visitors commented upon.

The rink in the boys playground was flooded on December 20th and the hill by the girls playground was put into condition for coasting.

Only those who have been attending over four years were allowed to go home this Christmas. Although over twenty could have gone home only one boy and five girls chose to go. After this we intend to have no holiday leave at Christmas but to give one month during the summer.

All who remained had a most enjoyable time here. The seniors girls had a party on the Principal's flat on Christmas Eve and afterwards played Santa Clause.

Christmas Dinner on the Sunday was a feast of Roast Pork, pickles and Baked Poatatoes followed by Plum Pudding and Sauce. The supper tables were bright and cheery with Christmas doilies, covered with sandwiches, and cocoa, oranges, nuts, candy, dates and fancy biscuits. On Monday we followed much the same program with variations in the way of food and an addition of mince pies to the menu.

ENTERTAINMENTS On the Friday before Christmas the girls gave a Concert and on Monday the boys supplied the program...Every evening of the week we had arranged for some sort of treat. Either a set of games or a dance or a sing-song attended by some of the officers and all the pupils occupied the time between supper and bed-time. During the day there was splendid skating and coasting to be enjoyed. The motor-truck also contributed to the enjoyment of the holiday for trips around the town and to places of interest were made. Over thirty girls accompanied by an officer visited Mary Wassanappe at the Ontario School for the Blind one afternoon and they were shown over the buildings etc. and entertained by the blind girls. The following afternoon a party of blind girls visited this Institution and the girls gave an impromtu concert for their benefit.

November 8th. Mr. Rogers went to Toronto to inspect Motor trucks. He chose one the transfer of which was arranged for by the Department.

November 18th. Mr. Rogers and Mr. Clark went to Toronto and brought it back loaded with office furniture...

November 19th. We sent the truck fully loaded...to the market and made quite a record sale.

Mr. Rogers, Clarke and Cudmore went to Toronto with truck...returned the same day with a load of ladders, drop cloths and painters equipment...

Floretta Elliott commenced taking violin lessons at the Conservatory. We have some instruments for a small orchestra but so far, have not found a suitable teacher.

The Telegraphy Class under Mr Coutts is held weekly and the pupils are making good progress.

Fire Drill was practised on November 15th and December 9th. On the latter occassion the girls were playing in the basement and failed to hear the alarm. To obviate this we are installing electric Alarms. This is being installed by the Manual Training Classes...

November 8th. Mr. Standing inspected Schools.

November 29th. and December 20th. Major Smith inspected.

The Carpenters shop has been re-arranged...equipped as a Manual Training centre. The electric lights were extended and a stove erected. All this work has been part of the Manual training programme which while it aims to teach the finer work also ensures that the pupils learn such carpentering and fitting as will be most useful to those who follow farming as a vocation.

The Manual Training Class has repaired a number of chairs and benches for the School. The benches for the new greenhouse were built by the boys who also made bob-sleighs and cutters for the girls and their own enjoyment. Picture framing has also been taught and the boys are now completing a set of coat hangers.

Great fun was taken by the boys who built a "property"

car which played a great part in the boys entertainment.
CLOTHING A new issue of socks, heavy outside stockings, rubber boots, caps and mits...to the boys.

Pyjamas from hospital supplies were issued to girls - also stockings.

Mrs. Boyce and Mr. Rogers went to the Paris Mills and bought material for the girls heavy petticoats and a quantity of blue stockinette from which has been made a very becoming set of jerseys for school wear.

Mr. Rogers went again in the hope of purchasing boys underwear but bought shop soiled garments cheaper in the city.

All pupils who went home for holidays returned on Saturday 31st December.

Andrew Martin an old pupil who passed his entrance Examination when a pupil here visited us in company with his wife who was a Mount Elgin girl. They had with them their baby in whom we see a prospective pupil.

...We killed pigs for the pupils Christmas dinners and had fat chickens for the officers and men.

We are grateful for many presents McHutcheon the local bakers gave us pumpkins pies for Thanksgiving, jelly rolls which were acceptable after the concerts besides contributing to Santa Clause.

Mr. W. F. Cockshutt gave a case of oranges. Mr. K. V. Bunnell presented us with two games of Indoor golf and a lady sent us a number of childrens books.

63. January and February 1922 Boyce Report
HEALTH We had an outbreak of Grippe three cases of which developed into pneumonia. With one exception all made good recoveries...
**** had tonsils and adenoids removed...
**** was very sick for a time with pleuresy.
We have now however a clean bill of health.
****, (criminal assault case of last summer) was sent to a venereal clinic for examination. At the time we received the Doctor's Reports her father died and she went home to his funeral. We are keeping in touch with her through Dr. Greenwood who reports that she is attending his office regularly for treatment.
STAFF Miss Cummings salary was raised to $600.00... Mr. Barron, farm foreman, and Mrs Neale, housekeeper, both proved unsatisfactory...given notice to leave...
NOTES January 1st...For dinner the pupils had roast pork, roast potatoes, pickles and plum pudding and for supper, bread and butter, dates, cookies, buns and candies.

January 2nd. Holiday. In the morning a party of girls went out in the truck while others went skating on the canal. The stores were visited and there was more skating in the afternoon.

The boys spent part of the day hunting and the remainder skating and playing hockey.

On January 27th the pupils were invited to a concert given by the Brantford Oratorio Society...The pupils were allowed to go and it was surprising to note how many thoroughly enjoyed that class of music.

The boys entertained the girls to a sing-song and dance on February 9th. The supper was provided by the boys.

We have installed a series of fire alarms throughout the building...

The shoe finishing machine has been installed in the Carpenters Shop and the boys are receiving instruction in shoe reparing. They are very interested in this work which is made so much more attractive to them by the installation of the machine...

On February 7th. Mr. Rogers accompanied Major Smith to the Six Nations Council.

Four boys have been giving considerable trouble by absconding. **** who is sixteen has repeatedly absconded but we have had him returned because we had hopes of doing something with him. He is a lad whose father had taken absolutely no interest in him.

****, is a worthless type and very shifty. He has a father and relatives who are capable of looking after him and as he lives near a school we have refused to re-admit him.

**** was returned very promptly by his parents who find very difficult to handle, but as we have the support of his parents we took him back and will probably be able to make something of him.

**** is a constant roamer, he not infrequently returns of his own free will, but he is a disappointment to us all. He is bright and very intelligent but very lazy also. He is strong although undersized and he could do well with his studies if he would only apply himself. As he has only an aged grandmother who ever takes any interest in him we feel that we have to take him back although his presence in the school is harmful to the morale. He could try his entrance this year.

We engaged a tailor at $25.00 per week and he re-made the boys uniforms. This was an excellent opportunity for the girls to work at tailoring and some became quite expert. By this means we have a very smart set of uniforms which have only cost us $4.05 each...

64. 1 March 1922 White to Bishop of Huron

At the last Council Meeting here on the Reserve the question was asked "is it true that a girl of 13, a pupil in the Mohawk Institute, was about to be confined?" The Assistant Principal said it was so, but that the girl was well cared for. After a discussion several of the chiefs advocated the closing up of the school.

...there should be an investigation as to who is responsible for this state of affairs. I understand this is not the first case of the kind that has occurred.

Several of the children have run away from the Institute the last couple of months and could not be induced to go back. There is something radically wrong in the present management.

65. 4 March 1922 Boyce to Secretary DIA

...the farm foreman was discharged - Mr. Rogers is going to take over the entire management of the outside departments so he will not be able to help me with the office work as he has done lately. I think it will save friction in the farm and gardens department and Mr Rogers is most enthusiastic...

66. 4 March 1922 Boyce to Secretary DIA

The copy of letter following may be of interest:
    Dear Miss Hardy,

    I am writing to you because I dont know any of the men officers and I trust you will help me to make a wrong right. When I was a pupil there at school I went to town one thursday and while in town a man (a stranger) stoped me at school. I told him the number there were three and he gave me a dollar ($1) to buy a present for them. But I took the money and spent it for myself. And now I am sending you the money to give it to the boys there now. It is the least that I can do. Please give it to them in any way that you see fit.
    This is all, Yours sincerely for the Best
            Lewis Laforme
Four dollars was enclosed - which we have contributed to our "Honor Roll" fund.

67. 7 March 1922 Scott to Boyce

...Instances of the payment of "conscience money" are not rare, but...speaks well for the training that this boy received while in the institution. Unfortunately the letter does not show where Laforme is now living. I take it... that he is prospering to an extent that he feels he should make good the wrong that he did some time in the past.

68. 8 March 1922 Scott to Canon Gould

...I am somewhat surprised at the tone of the letters from His Lordship the Bishop of Huron and the Reverend James White because they seem to take for granted that the report is true. His Lordship says that it is shown that the condition of affairs at the Mohawk Institute is by no means satisfactory. I consider that the condition of affairs at the Mohawk Institute is highly satisfactory...I trust that His Lordship's letter does not foreshadow a desire to make any change in the management...

The facts...are as follows:- a girl named **** claims that a criminal assault was made upon her when she was at home for the holidays. Mrs. Boyce reported this to me as soon as she knew of it in the autumn, and we endeavoured to prosecute the guilty party but failed to get any corroborative evidence. The girl was watched carefully and has never been reported to me as enceinte. However, we have discovered that she had contracted a venereal disease and last month I ordered that she should be discharged from the school and placed in a hospital in order that she might have proper care. From the moment

I heard of this case it has been under my own observation. I do not want to make any extended comment on Mr. White's letter, further than that the Chiefs of the Six Nations would close up the Mohawk Institute tomorrow if they could do so - not from any reasons of mismanagement or any cause for dissatisfaction but simply from their inveterate desire to thwart the Department in its best endeavours for their progress. The implied idea that, because two children ran away from the school, there is something radically wrong with the management, shows little appreciation of the difficulties with which we have to contend.

69. 14 March 1922 Smith to Secretary DIA

...on the 25th of February, I made an inspection...The Truant Officer mentioned the case of three or four boys who had run away from the Mohawk, were not going to school on the Reserve and were completely beyond the control of those who are supposed to look after them. I mentioned their cases to Mrs. Boyce, one of them **** 16 years of age and has on several occasions run away from the Institute. He is living with his aunt who is a non-treaty Indian. Another case is that of **** who ran away five times in one year, there is nobody to look after him at home and is consequently in danger of turning into a criminal. He is 16 years of age. **** absent without leave and he is wanted by the Brantford Police...it would seem that these boys are entirely beyond the control of either the Mohawk Institute or their own relatives. It has been suggested that they be placed in Mimico Industrial School but as this will impose cost on the Six Nations I have not recommended any motion, in this regard.

The farm foreman Mr. Bauren left at the end of the month also did the housekeeper. Mr. Rodgers is going to assume some of the duties of farm manager and a new housekeeper has been engaged. Preparations for spring work are well under way and the green house is already selling produce on the Brantford market.

70. 18 March 1922 Scott to Smith

...truancy has hurt the attendance at the institute, and it is my suggestion that one or two of the worst boys be committed to the Mimico Industrial School. This action would have a good all round effect on the general discipline, not only at the school but on the reserve. The cost of their maintenance at Mimico can be met from the Vote for Indian Education, if it is thought unwise to charge the account to the Band funds.

71. 20 April 1922 Smith to Secretary DIA

...I made a visit...yesterday...on the roll 69 girls and 43 boys, 7 boys being absent at present. The main part of the halls and corridors have been grained and varnished... the first time this has been done since the building was put up. The upper dormitory on the girls side has been

freshly white washed and painted which makes it look very clean and neat. The whole building inside has now been painted and cleaned up.

Amongst the recent army supplies received from Toronto was a large number of red bed covers, all the beds in the boys dormitory are now covered with these goods which gives it a good warm cosy appearance, They also have enough for the girls beds, but they are not yet in use. One girl was recently discharged as she has developed Tuberculosis following a bad attack of pneumonia. Mrs. Boyce thought she required plenty of fresh air and good food such as eggs and milk and as her father **** a returned soldier is comfortably well off she should be well looked after at home.

A new chicken house with runways is being built as it is proposed to increase the number of chickens...

The Honor Roll prepared at the request of the New England Company just arrived at the Institute yesterday which contains 86 names and is beautifully engrossed, illustrated with a picture of the Institute and the Mohawk Church and surrounded with the flags of the Allies...a similar copy is to be presented to the Indian Department, the cost is $100.00 which is to be raised by subscription...

72. March - April - May and June 1922 Boyce Report

HEALTH We had an epedemic of Grippe in March which developed into Pneumonia in some cases. **** did not make a good recovery and was consequently allowed to go home on sick leave. We had another epedemic of Grippe in June.

OFFICERS Mrs. Myers, housekeeper had a bad attack of Grippe and as she did not get strong again she left on April 5th. Mrs. Hogson was engaged in her place.

Mr. Barron, Farm Foreman, left on March 31st...

AMUSEMENTS In April the boys and girls went to a Dog-and-Pony show in town. Several evenings have been devoted to dances for the boys and girls. The boys joined the local School Lacrosse league and gave a very good account of themselves. We were lucky enough to secure an old pupil, Mr. J Doxdator, as a coach. On May 24th. all the pupils went to Mohawk Park to attend the opening game of the League. Our boys won...On their return supper was served on the lawn and games were played. On June 14th. the children all went to a Circus Procession and...to the show in the afternoon.

VISITORS & INSPECTIONS Major Smith inspected April 19th, May 27th. and June 26th. Mr. Standing, Public Schools Inspector, examined school on March 13th. and 14th. Mr. Abrams visited on April 7th and 8th. and acted as judge for the monthly cleanliness inspection of horses and cattle. Mr. Ferrier inspected April 27th. 28th. and 29th...The Cadets were inspected by Col. Huggins May 18th. and Mr. Edwards of M.D.2. inspected Cadet equipment on June 16th. Mr. Westgate Field Secretary, M.S.C.C. visited April 22nd...

Rev. Owen, our new clergyman visits frequently and takes evening prayers occassionally. He was some years ago in charge of an Indian School out West.

Notes...Wilma Smith, and old pupils, who passed second standard at the Conservatory of Music when here, graduated this Spring. It is claimed that she is the first Indian in Canada with this degree...

...Two typewriters were procured and these are most useful for our advanced pupils who are attending Business College.

73. 19 July 1922 Hazel Elliott to Boyce

I thought I would write you to remind you about money for our clothes and am awful anxious to get back to school again. I was writing you a card, but as I am writing this letter I wont bother sending it. Everybody is well around here.

Was to Church Sunday evening and the sermon & music was real nice.

My Grandma and I went picking raspberries on Monday and got caught in a big storm.

Were having busy times down here. Harrying. Laying etc. Well I hope you are having an easy time.

Miss Hardie has gone I suppose.

How is dear old Happy I suppose she misses the girls awfully bad, its likely she wont know all of us when we get back.

I must close now - have quite a bit of work to do. Tell Carrie I'll write to her when I have a little more time. So good-Bye, Yours for a better girl...Write soon

74. 23 July 1922 Jessie McNaughton to Boyce

Reached home safely on Saturday but I certainly had a terrible day. It was just pouring when I got off the car but my sister was right at the station to meet me. Its rather lonesome down here and I think I'd sooner be up there drawing in wheat. I dont think I'll stay down here for four weeks. I want to go back with George when he goes. I've been coaxing him to go back so he said he would he likes it fine down here and is growing taller every day. Mrs. Boyce will you please try and get some money for me from the department to help me in my course I want to attend the collegiate for about two years and then take up a nursing course. How are all the girls getting along I miss them very much. Well I think I will close now, love to all.

75. 29 July 1922 Smith to Secretary DIA

...on the 14th inst I inspected...holidays were beginning next day the 15th inst...Several changes are being made in the staff. Miss Cummings the junior teacher is leaving and no successor has yet been secured...Mrs. Burnnett the sewing teacher has left on account of ill health, the housekeeper also left on the 12th of July.

Elsie Claus and Carry Crow...have been taken on the

staff in a temporary capacity, one of them will probably take charge of the sewing room and the other some work about the school.

About 30 or 35 children are spending their vacation at the school for various reasons, some have not proper homes to go to and in other cases the parents wish them to remain at the school.

The harvest promises to be a very good one, wheat cutting was commenced on the 15th. The hay has all been cut and drawn into the barn in good shape and... the farm end of the Insitute promises to be very profitable.

76. 22 August 1922 R. Ferrier to Smith

...the Principal...requests that financial assistance be granted by the Department to enable four pupils to take courses in telephoning, telegraphing and high school...

Hazel Elliott, age 17, wishes to study telephoning. It is considered that the Telephone Company in Brantford would give this girl the necessary instruction without charge, as the Company trains girls as operators if they show ability for the work.

Floretta Elliott, age 17, wishes to take a course in telegraphy. The Principal states that the Canadian National Telegraph will take pupils at certain hours. The cost of the course is not stated.

Sylvia Jamieson, age 16, wishes to attend continuation school for two years and then train as a nurse.

Jesse MacNaughton, age 18, who passed the Entrance Examination, desires to attend High School. The Six Nations Council have refused to grant $100 to assist her.

77. 28 August 1922 McLean to Boyce

...the Department will allow a grant at the rate of $100 per annum for each of the four girls...

78. 12 September 1922 Scott to White

...referring to the matter of high school education for the Indian children of the Six Nations Reserve. I have noted your suggestion that we provide accommodation for high school pupils at the Mohawk Institute for children desiring advanced training and, if this is impossible, the establishing of a continuation school at Ohsweken.

...at present there are a total of 37 young men and women of the Six Nations Reserve doing the high school or college work, and that all are being helped by this Department. Four are in residence at the Mohawk Institute and attending classes in Brantford. 29 are attending the Brantford and Hamilton Collegiates and the Caledonia and Hagersville High Schools. We pay our share of the net costs at these institutions and in addition give a small grant to the parents of the children attending so that proper clothing can be provided...The band funds are used for the payment of the tuition and special grants for the 29 Indian children attending the local collegiates and high schools...

...we are doing what we can to provide a higher education for the brighter boys and girls on the reserve. If there is any accommodation in the Mohawk Institute we are always pleased to have high school pupils in attendance there...the matter of providing a continuation school right on the reserve is receiving serious consideration.

79. 28 September 1922 Smith to Secretary DIA
...on the 27th inst. I made an inspection...There are 40 boys present and ten absent without leave of these, five come from the Muncey Reserve. The reason for so many from there Mrs. Boyce thinks is that the Muncey Institute has two months holidays which is much more than the Mohawk has, therefore the boys think that they should have as long as Muncey...

There are 70 girls on the roll. The general work of the Institute seems to be progressing very favourably. The Junior teacher is Beatrice Higginson 23 years of age a graduate of the Ontario Agricultural College and holds a certificate in Physical training but has no professional teaching certificate, although she has done considerable teaching. Mrs. Boyce thinks she is the best junior teacher they have had for some time, her salary is $400.00 per annum.

The new housekeeper is a Scotch woman Mrs. Mavor...Elsie Claus a graduate of the Institute and who has had two years training at the Business College is the sewing teacher. She is doing good service. Another graduate Carrie Crow has a Business College training and is at present living at the Mohawk assisting in anything that may be required and waiting for a permanent situation as a stenographer.

...The fall work is well advanced and when I was there some of the boys were plowing.

80. 30 September 1922 Boyce Report
...GENERAL The pupils returned August 12th. The older boys were in many cases kept back on the farms or where they were employed and some have not yet returned. As Miss Hardie did not return for two weeks after the pupils the older girls were given special instruction in Domestic Science, Fancy Sewing and Knitting for which the supplies from the D.S.C.R. were most acceptable. Many girls are wearing scarfs or sweaters of their own make.

The D.S.C.R. supplies have filled many long felt wants. The pupils now have feather pillows...Our office is now properly equipped and the typewriters are available for pupils who are taking courses. We feel especially grateful for a number of heavy green V.A.D. greatcoats which fit our older girls and are hoping to obtain a number more in order to make them over for our smaller pupils. The blue dressing gowns have been made over into useful and becoming dresses for our girls. We have just completed making the boys a suit of "teddy-bear" overalls for outside wear this winter. This will enable us to issue the hospital clothing...for the boys to wear underneath.

Dr. Westgate, Field Secretary M.S.C.C. wrote July 11th. requesting reports, inventories etc. re taking over school.

Major Smith paid his regular monthly visit of inspection.

Jessie MacNaughton, Sylvia Jamieson and Florette Elliott passed the Entrance Examination...Jessie is attending the local Collegiate; Sylvia is living at home and attending the continuation School at Onondaga; and Florette is taking a course in telegraphy at the offices of the G.N.W. These pupils with Hazel Elliott...accepted for training at the Brantford General Hospital as a nurse, are in receipt of the grant from the Department of $100.

Carrie Crowe completed her course at the Business College, has a good position in town and is boarding at the Y.W.C.A.

Oscar Hess is taking special course in farming and is leaving in the Spring to commence farming for himself...
SPORTS AND AMUSEMENTS July 12th our boys played Lacrosse at Ohsweken.

Football and Base-ball are very popular...with the boys

During the holidays the remaining pupils had a very enjoyable time. In fact several who were not called for at closing decided to remain so as not to miss the fun.

The pupils attended several lectures and entertainments in town. We find that local folks are beginning to take an interest in our work and are often issuing invitations for our children to attend happenings in town.

81. 13 December 1922 Boyce/Rogers to Secretary DIA
I beg to tender my resignation as Principal of the Mohawk Institute - together with the recommendation that Mr. Sidney Rogers be appointed my successor. We were married yesterday, December the Twelfth...

As the Principals wife - I shall assume the duties of Lady Principal.

You may be assured that it will be our ambition to do our best, in every way for the welfare of the School.

1922 - 1929

Sydney Rogers 1922-1929

1. 27 December 1922 Smith to Secretary DIA

...on the 18th inst. I paid a visit to the Mohawk Institute when I was informed that Mr. Sydney Rogers was promoted to the principalship...

The alterations to the building have turned things very much upside down as there is smoke, plaster and dust every place but...there was not a great deal of work required to make it much more habitable...

There was no sickness amongst the children and all the children are to remain in the building during the holidays. Extensive plans have been made to entertain them both with extra food and games and motor rides.

2. 31 December 1922 Rogers Quarterly Report

At the end of October Mr. Owen commenced training the Confirmation Class. This year we caused all children over twelve years of age to attend the classes but left them to decide whether they would offer themselves for Confirmation. We were pleased to present thirty candidates (24 girls and 8 boys)...a boy who was a Diest and had not given any sign of wanting to be confirmed presented himself during the Confirmation Service...on December 11th...prior...baptismal...held on December 3rd.

Clothing. During the quarter we have been able to buy stockings and mits directly from the mills at Paris and were fortunate in securing a jobbers lot of underwear.

The girls have very successfully manufactured sets of one-piece over-alls for the boys. These serve a double purpose in that they look tidy and cover up the ill-fitting and bright couloured clothing procured from the D.S.C.R. with which we...keep our boys very warmly clad.

Staff. Miss Higginson...has been a great success in the Junior School.

On November 1st were engaged Miss Healey O.A.C. Graduate as housekeeper and Mrs. Haythornthwaite as Matron...Mrs Matthews left after being in charge of the laundry for Three and quarter years.

Class-room Work This has been faithfully carried out despite the difficulties due to the presence of workmen.

Amusements. October 4th. 26 girls and Miss Hardie went to Girl Guides Concert at the Collegiate.

October 5th. The Girls were taken to Ohsweken Fair in trucks and the following day the boys attended.

October 30th. Forty pupils attended a Concert at Wellington Street Church to hear Miss Nickawa's recital.

October 31st. Hallowe'en Masquerade. We had a lot of fun made all the more enjoyable by a plenteous supply of cakes and apples.

November 4th. We held our first Plowing Match on that date and were fortunate to secure as judges two very experienced men who claimed that they had never seen better plowing accomplished. We have to thank the Department for supplying the prizes on this occassion.

Thanksgiving Day it rained but...Indoor Games were played and the girls made a quantity of pretty necklaces from the beads sent by the Department and which we afterwards used as prizes and Christmas gifts.

Armistice Day. The pupils attended the Community Service held at the Armouries.

December 4th...our Annual Sports...The Boys horses and cattle were judged from a cleanliness point of view and such good work was general that judging was very difficult.

December 12th. The announcement of the wedding of Mr. and Mrs Rogers was made by Mr. Owen following which the Prizes for Sports day and the Ploughing Matches were distributed. The evening was concluded by a feast of nuts and candy and a dance.

December 19th. The Arcade, a local store, invited our pupils to a reception by Santa Clause and...entertained them to a Punch and Judy show. All pupils had opportunities to visit the local stores before Christmas.

December 21st. The out-door rink was made.

December 22nd. The Senior School-room was decorated for Christmas.

The Christmas holidays were much enjoyed by all. This year no pupils were allowed to go home. From previous experiences we have found that the small number who do go home usually return with some such trouble and the itch or scabies and this leads to a great deal of trouble. Then there is always a section whose parents disappoint them and they are difficult to handle. This year it was announced early that none would go home and consequently all the pupils just looked forward to having a good time at school. We started off by giving every child a present of some sort and as there was a plentiful supply of nuts and candy besides very excellent meals we...able to have a very happy time. Every day some special amusement was planned such as truck rides or sleighing parties. On December 28th. I was able to obtain a free pass for the whole school to the Brant Theatre. Special pictures of interest to children were kindly shown.

Notes. One of our senior girls, Carrie Crowe, graduated from the Business College and was secured a position as stenographer at Bradley, Carrotsons.

On October 20th work on the extensions was commenced.

During the local Teachers Conventions no school was held and we devoted our attentions to general housecleaning and replacing screens with storm sashes. ...On October 30. Mr. Rogers and Mr. Clarke secured a quantity of cooking utensils and cots from the D.S.C.R...

Mr. Orr visited on Nov. 7th. and stayed two days during the commencement of building operations...

Mr. Rogers and Mrs Boyce were married at the Cathedral in Hamilton on December 12th.

Several pupils during this term have applied for admission voluntarily although they were runaways of some time back.

...Colds and sore throats have kept numbers of the children in bed a few days.

Visitors ...Old pupils attending the Fair paid visits...

Mr. Standing, Schools Inspector was here October 17th and 18th...

One of our boys has been taking a course on farm work and has become a very useful hand. He expects to run his mothers farm when he leaves so we have given him every opportunity and so far as he is concerned the experiment is a success.

3. 31 March 1923 Rogers Quarterly Report

...Staff. Mrs. Haythornthwaite left on March 13th...we found that her judgement could not be relied upon.

Miss Higginson left to be married on March 31st.

Amusements On January 1st the children were able to have good skating and truck rides were arranged for the whole school. In the evening the staff and pupils met in the school-room where we had a sing-song and dance with plenty of nuts, dates, candy and biscuits for refreshments.

On January 13th the boys had a sleighing party and the girls used the boys rink.

We purchased a cheap victrola and this has been available for the pupils in their spare time. We have found that this and the Books of Knowledge have had a very good effect on the discipline of the children since it has afforded them much pleasure and amusement and kept them well occupied at times when supervision is more or less relaxed.

Notes. The Steam radiation was connected up on January 4th. and on the 15th we fired the new boiler...

Mr Abrams and Mr Robertson of the Department of Indian Affairs visited...The laundry machinery was installed in the new building on February 19th...We have been able to turn out very fine work since...

Mr. Axford and...representative from the Soldiers Aid Commission visited **** and expressed themselves satisfied with conditions.

Mr. Standing inspected the School-room...March 19th. ...we have discontinued purchasing meats etc. from retail stores and...buy from packing houses and in that manner effect a considerable economy.

Mr. Orr...has paid periodical visits of inspection...

Health. During the early part of the quarter we suffered from much sickness. The alterations caused the building to be more or less draughty and that together with an epedemic of "la grippe" kept many in bed. At one time there were no less than twenty four girls and eleven boys and three of the staff in bed at one time. However, we

were able to get the sick on their feet in a very short time and all made good recoveries. We had one serious case of illness in that of **** who after complaining for a day or two was discovered to be suffering from appendicitis in a very serious stage. She was rushed to the hospital and within two hours of the Doctor's decision she was operated upon. Since the operation she has made a wonderful recovery and is now quite well.

Pupils. This quarter we have experienced considerable trouble with boys absconding. It appears that the children are more or less influenced by the conditions on the Reserve just now, and as there is a scarcity of farm help in this quarter the boys are often made tempting offers. The parents are also very keen to remove the boys from school as soon as they are big enough to be useful but realising the state of morals on the Reserve they are prepared to leave the girls in the safe-keeping of the School until they are older.

In one instance the spirit of rebellion was so very pronounced that two boys armed with clubs openly defied the Principal. They were taken before the local Chief of Police who showed them the seriousness of their conduct and were instantly dismissed from the School after having been provided with sufficient funds to reach their respective homes. One boy, has since expressed his regrets and through a friend has sought readmission. Five other pupils have absconded and two boys have absconded for the third time.

On the other hand, we have just heard from three ex-pupils who have secured very good positions. Grace MacNaughton has been appointed head of the office staff of the Johnson's Floor Wax Company. Eva Curley has been recently elected President of the Girls' Conference an organization of about seven hundred members. Carrie Crowe has also taken a position as School teacher on the Muncey Reserve.

4. 30 June 1923 Rogers Quarterly Report

OFFICERS Mrs. Persall was engaged as Sewing teacher. We had been running short staffed during the building operations.

Mrs. Knowles has been engaged as Junior teacher to replace Miss. Higginson...Mrs. Knowles is not in possession of certificates but is capable, enthusiastic and most interested in her work. Mr. Knowles holds a position in a local office and is living in the Institute, in return for which...he takes night duties with the boys and generally relieves the Principal when and where possible. It was found necessary to replace Mrs. Haythornthwaite with Mrs Martin. Mrs Clark and Mr. Edmondson left at the end of April and were replaced by Mr. W. Dingman and Mr. F. Dingman. Owing to the shortage of big boys it was necessary to engage Mr. Hodge as an extra man. Mrs Martin resigned owing to ill-health and Miss Firth assumed her duties on May 12th.

Miss Clause was on holidays commencing June 16th and her duties were carried out by Jessie MacNaughton a Collegiate pupil.

Miss Elliott was engaged as sub-officer on June 25th.

AMUSEMENTS On Easter Monday...we moved into the new Dining Hall and celebrated...by a special dinner which was improved by a liberal supply of candies. In the afternoon the girls went to stores and to a show. The boys volunteered to start the work of converting the old dining hall and kitchen into a play-room and had a great deal of fun tearing out the old partitions.

Empire Day was suitably observed. The I.O.D.E. sent representatives to present a prize won by one of our pupils for general efficiency and after an address on the Empire, by the Principal the Victrola Record of the King's speech was played. One interesting feature of this ceremony was the manner in which every boy stiffened to attention as soon as the record commenced playing the National Anthem.

On Victoria Day the boys were taken by our truck to Burford and Mr. Brethour, the owner of the largest pure-bred cattle and hog farm in this district kindly devoted a couple of hours to the boys and showed them his entire stock. While the boys were out the girls went to a show in town and to the park. After supper the boys team defeated the girls team at base-ball.

We have made arrangements for both boys and girls to swim in the river and during this past quarter we have greatly encouraged sports between the boys and girls. We find that this opportunity for the boys and girls to get together is reducing the passage of letters and the clandestine meetings which were so troublesome before.

NOTES Mr. Ferrier and Mr. Orr inspected...April 18th... April 26th. Commenced summer routine and a number of girls fitted as farmerettes undertook the milking of herd.
May 26th. Some of the staff and pupils attended Major Smith's funeral.
May 31st. Miss Davis, an old pupil who passed head of the Entrance pupils in Brant County and had since taught on the Reserve for some years, died. Miss Hardie was granted leave to attend funeral.

During the quarter we were able to buy a quantity of white straw hats to match those received from the D.S.C.R. for the girls; all pupils had new shoes and two complete issues of stockings; the girls have made a new issue of aprons for themselves and two sets of overalls and shirts for the boys.

...Cassie Maracle, Irene Longboat, Reta Green and Mary Jacobs were successful in passing the Entrance Examination.

IMPROVEMENTS
...Easter Monday we began to take up our new quarters and to vacate that part of the old building which had to undergo alterations...We had an opportunity to purchase a large butchers refrigerator...With this equipment we can buy meat wholesale or even kill a beast during the hottest of weather without fear of loss.

Our new lavatories and baths are a great aid to health and cleanliness.

FARM
During the Quarter we suffered two losses from our stables. One horse had to be shot and another...became so paralized that she had to be shot. We were able to commence working the land on April 19th. and general farm activities have occupied the male staff since that date...

We have discontinued the practice of making butter... There was always considerable leakage in the poundage through carelessness and extravagance and we find that by issuing a stated quantity of butter per week we are getting bigger returns. We now sell our cream to the local creamery and purchase our butter there. This business also provides us with the opportunity of purchasing large quantities of butter-milk which is invaluable in pig-raising.

We bought a splendid team of mares to replace our losses and one has since given birth to a very fine colt.

Our spare time has been taken up in grading and tidying up after the builders.

On June 20th we cut hay and we were picking strawberries the following day...good crops this year but the prices of farm products are so low that a big profit can hardly be expected this year.

5. 30 September 1923 Rogers Quarterly Report
GENERAL...Mrs Knowles took the Senior School pupils on a course in elocution and memory training while Mrs Rogers gave instruction in embroidery, crocheting and fancy work. Our girls greatly enjoyed this and we discovered some very skilful and artistic workers. A student took charge of the Junior School.

As a result of Mrs Knowles training we were able to stage a Closing Concert which was an undoubted success. Mary Waswanipi...was very well received and her selections on the piano much enjoyed. The following day the pupils left for their holidays on July 14th.

The pupils who were not fortunate enough to leave for holidays were presented with a bathing suit each and the girls were given a pair of white shoes and two pairs of stockings and every boy had a pair of running shoes.

...Through the kindness of General Ashton our Cadet Corps has been presented with some German war trophies.
...Miss Clause left in August and was succeeded by Miss Crowe an old pupil and a Business College Graduate.

At the close of the holidays our pupils returned splendidly. In fact the Roll Call was complete with the exception of those who had for some reason or other not been able to commence their holidays on the right date.

On August 27th. we visited the Paris Wincey Mills and were able to purchase material for repairing our girls work dresses and...for next years summer dresses.

Mr. McVitie visited August 30th.

During the quarter we have made one of our pupils Floretta Elliot a sub-officer, in which position she has greatly relieved our staff generally. She answers the telephone and door, takes charge of girls on walks, teaches music, and relieves other officers.

Miss Firth, housekeeper left and was relieved by Mrs Woods who arrived with a very bad cold and after a few days broke down entirely.

Miss Elliott and a number of big girls decorated the Church for Harvest Festival.

Health has been excellent.

The pupils had some difficulty in settling down after the holiday - especially those who had been berry picking. They were frequently...stealing fruit...impertinent, careless about their dress. Several ran away to be returned very promptly by their relatives.

...succeeded in getting the wholesale houses to fill our orders. The retail houses have been fighting us in this move...we...are hoping to effect considerable economy...

SPORTS & AMUSEMENTS We have been able to give more attention to sports this summer and many games have been played between the different divisions in the school. The best ball games have been those between the boys and girls teams. The boys have the stronger team but our girls have been playing a very sporting game. This scheme of mixing the boys and girls on the playing field has had a very desirable influence on the school and such things as the passing of notes from boy to girl or girl to boy has not been heard of for some time. We find that by making the whole school play to-gether that they soon divide and the boys begin to play alone and the girls play their games, forgetful entirely of the boys.

Swimming in the Grand river has been good and on occasions the City Swimming Pool has been visited. Now the cooler weather has set in our new baths and a plentiful supply of hot water are in great demand.

Strawberries were plentiful and the children had their share. One evening we had a strawberry and ice cream feast at the expense of a Mr. Peters who had been working here.

During the holidays the truck was in use on several occasions taking parties of pupils to the movies.

On July 27th. the children were given ice cream as a reward. They had several times volunteered to help with the harvesting operations when we were badly in need of help when they could have been playing at the river or taking time off.

On August 5th. Civic Holiday the children were taken for truck rides and given a little spending money.

On Labour Day...we had sports in the evening. Mr. Knowles was good enough to supply a good feed of water-melons at the close of the sports.

We were able to send for a load of peaches from Grimsby at a very cheap rate and have a very large quantity preserved besides being able to give each pupil a goodly feast.

On September 29th we had a very successful corn roast closing our evening with a sing-song round a roaring bonfire.

IMPROVEMENTS We are unable to fully express our appreciation of the many improvements that we have had carried out. Our staff Dining Room is greatly appreciated and when the kitchenette is completed will be almost ideal. The new Sewing Room with its large roomy cupboards and lockers is undoubtedly going to mean far greater efficiency in this department. We have a small dressing room in one corner of this room where a pupils may change in order to be fitted with clothing. The hardwood floors throughout the first floor, with the burlaped and painted walls make our corridors and stairways very attractive and sanitary. The New Clothing rooms in the Basement will be of great assistance in keeping the clothing in good condition. Our school-rooms are...without equal for airiness and light and with the new paint and renovated floors they are most attractive. We have just completed a picture framing bee and...succeeded in beautifying the appearance of the whole building.

FARM...prolonged drought which seriously affected the hay crop and...the grain. In August we were badly hampered by an epedemic of Influenza amongst our horses. To arrest this we had every horse inoculated on August 11th. August 18th a terrific thunderstorm at night damaged the standing crops and killed one of our sheep.

On August 20th. we commenced ploughing for Fall Wheat.

Mr. Haworth was engaged on September 1st as Farm Foreman to replace a vacancy caused last Spring when Mr. Edmondson left. He is an excellent man...

6. 18 November 1923 Evelyn Johnson to the Editor, Toronto Sunday World

The people of Ontario and, later, the people of the other provinces, as well as Americans, are continually asking: "What is the trouble with the Six Nations Indians?" Even Brantfordites, who are contiguous to the reserve, ask me this question, and in Hamilton and Toronto I am asked the same question. No one seems to really know what the unrest is about; but everyone seeks for information.

There are many reasons for the present spirit of unrest and rebellion on this reserve. Some of them I have already touched upon in former open letters to the press. Today I wish to draw the attention of the Canadian public to the Mohawk Institution, an educational boarding school, near Brantford, for Indian children of both sexes. The school is somewhat in the nature of an industrial school and is a home for many orphaned boys and girls, as well as for other children whose parents are living.

Practically the whole Indian population in the reserve, however, is at variance with the system of this institution and its executive head. The Indians of both opposing factions in the reserve are asking and begging the Indian department for higher and better education. The New England company, which for many decades conducted the ten day schools in the reserve, together with the Mohawk institution, no doubt believed they were turning out the maximum of educated pupils, whereas, for 40 years not one single pupil from these schools passed the entrance examination to the high schools; yet, the one single school conducted by the Six Nations' council had passed a number of scholars into the high schools. At the present time no less than 30 Indian children are attending high school at various places. A high school is badly wanted in our reserve.

The labor element in Brantford recently passed a

resolution suggesting that the government make a thorough investigation of the conditions and aspirations of the Six Nations. Col. A. T. Thompson, appointed by the government, in September conducted such an investigation in the reserve, and it is to be regretted that the Mohawk institution was not included in the investigation. During the summer more than 20 children have run away from this home-school. All of them claim that they are hungry, and the Indians are angered.

There is something radically wrong when children abandon by wholesale an institution such as this is supposed to be. The Indian department contributes many thousands of dollars towards the upkeep of the Mohawk institution and the New England company also assists in its support. There are at least two hundred acres of productive farm land in connection therewith, plenty of fruit and vegetables, and a large herd of cows, and it is a crying shame to Canada that these children run away in such numbers because of hunger.

One of the missionaries and his wife declared to me that they had met no one in their direct field of labor in the reserve who likes or speaks well of the Mohawk institution. This is suggestive of something rotten in the state of Denmark. The missionary's wife begged me, with tears in her eyes, to use my influence to better these conditions. I told her "I have no influence; the influence lies with the Canadian public."

Why not clean up this sore in the reserve and turn the Mohawk institution into a first-class educational school, teaching trades, nursing and domestic science by qualified teachers of these subjects, and turning out boys and girls fitted to make their way in life, even if they do not wish to or cannot afford to take up higher education?

Members of the family who have, from time to time, become executive heads of the Mohawk Institution, do not bear an enviable record in connection there with. The first of that family, Robert Ashton, was sent out from England by the New England company to take charge of the Mohawk institution in the early seventies. So harsh and overbearing was his conduct that many boys ran away, and when they were found and brought back to the institution they were at once garbed in clothing similar to that of convicts; one leg of the trousers being of blue denim; and the coat was similar in design of color.

In 1903 some of the boys turned, and they burned the Mohawk institution to the ground. The late Rev. Isaac Bearfoot, missionary, and his wife told me it was nothing more than they had expected for a long time. The boys were arrested, tried and sentenced to the Mimico reformatory, which they said they liked better than the Mohawk institution. What a punishment?

My sister, the late E. Pauline Johnson, wrote to me that had she not been leaving immediately on a tour of the northwest and British Columbia, she herself would have taken up the case of these boys.

The Mohawk institution was rebuilt by the New England company. After Rev. Robert Ashton retired as the superintendent, his son, Nelles Ashton, received the appointment. Three of the girl pupils ran away. When these girls were returned to the Mohawk institution their hair was cut off, and they were shut up in the "dark room," or "cell", as some called it, and fed on bread and water.

Chief George Miller brought an action against Nelles Ashton for this treatment of his little daughter. His action was backed by the Six Nations' council. A Brantford jury of twelve men returned a verdict of four hundred dollars damages against Nellis Ashton, together with the statement that "the Mohawk institution is not a reformatory, it is an industrial school."

Mrs. Boyce, now Mrs. Rogers, and who is a daughter of Rev. Robert Ashton, and a sister of Nelles Ashton, then obtained the appointment of superintendent of the Mohawk institution, with the result that over twenty of the children have run away during the summer alone.

The Six Nations are asking why the New England company and the Indian department continue to employ members of this family. Cannot some humane man and woman be found who would take over this work?...And the whole country and the press of the United States is asking, "What is the trouble with the Six Nations Indians?"

7. 19 November 1923 Morgan to Secretary DIA
I attach a cutting from the Toronto World of November 18th. containing a bitter attack upon the Mohawk Institute by Miss Evelyn Johnson, sister of...Pauline Johnson.

Owing to the rumors, much to the same affect as this article which have reached my ears, I have made it my business since I have been in Brantford to particularly note conditions in the Mohawk Institute, which I have visited some 7 or 8 times as well.

It is unnecessary for me to say that there is not one single word of truth in the whole of this article.

I believe Miss Johnson to be actuated by malice on account of the fact that she was obliged to obtain permission to bury her brother in the Mohawk Church yard and in view of the fact that such lying propaganda at the present juncture will have a bad effect on the Reserve and in the Vicinity, I shall be grateful if you will inform me if it is your wish that I should take any steps to reply to this article in the public press.

Both Mr. and Mrs. Rogers are extremely capable and take a keen interest in the management of the Institute and she therefore feels all the more keenly this uncalled for and entirely false attack.

8. 7 November 1923 Standing Inspector's Report
...the attendance of the larger boys has, in many cases been unsatisfactory. After staying a while they run away

to their homes and often no action is taken to send them back. The result is that in the senior school there are three times as many girls as boys.

...while the girls are given some good practical training in sewing, cooking and general housework, and the boys with some work with the gardener and on the farm, there is, nevertheless, no provision for systematic instruction in the principles, either of household science, manual training or agriculture. It would...be most desirable...if the heads of the various industrial departments were also qualified to teach the principles of these subjects...

In the junior division teachers have changed too frequently to admit of steady progress. A well trained primary teacher is desirable for this department, although it may be difficult to retain a suitable one in this position.

9. 31 December 1923 Rogers Quarterly Report

Christmas morning we had a very delightful Carol Service. Some of our older girls are playing for the services. The Children learnt a number of carols for the Christmas Concert and the Christmas tree festivity...

STAFF. Miss Cummings took over the duties of Housekeeper on October 18th. She is an English schoolteacher on leave of absence and due to her enthusiasm and energy we have been able to re-organise the kitchen department with very good results.

Health. Due, no doubt, to the improved sanitary conditions and proper heating we have had a period of eight months during which we have not been in need of a doctor. Several children have had trouble with their teeth and have received attention.

FARM & GARDEN...On October 18th. we killed five pigs for sale. Commenced lifting bulbs for winter on November 1st. We converted the basement of the old Playhouse into a very effective apple and root storehouse. During the alterations one of the soft water cisterns on the North end...fell into disuse so we have run a pipe from it into the green houses...use this water instead of the city water. Full advantage was taken of the mild fall and every field was ploughed hedges trimmed, fence lines cleaned and fruit bushes transplanted. The fences and posts on the flats were taken up November 27th. and 28th.

CLOTHING The boys and girls were issued with new shoes and socks or stockings, while the girls had further issues of bloomers and combinations. Our girls are wearing the blue serge dresses for school and most of the boys are wearing their blue uniforms. Owing to the warm clothing we have been able to make from the D.S.C.R. supplies we have allowed the girls to wear the grey greatcoats for play as they were fast becoming shabby for best. This is the first opportunity we had of allowing our girls coats for to wear in the playground and they look most comfortable in them. We have made a new issue of aprons for the girls but during the winter we do not propose to put them into use. It is our custom to patch and mend through the winter in order to save our new clothing for Spring. A new set of blue uniforms has been commenced for the girls.

NOTES...Oct. 3rd. & 4th. Our girls went by the truck to Ohsweken Fair and the boys spent the 5th at the Fair taking their lunches with them and being relieved of the milking by volunteer girls. It is interesting to note that the girls brought back Lucinda Henry, a girl who had run away the day before and had already repented. She has done well since her return.

D.S.C.R. were closing down and we were able to get a good supply of chairs, lockers for girls playroom, cinematograph and cabinet, kitchen and Dining hall supplied, rugs, bath mats, furniture, an organ and some plants and shrubs.

Oct. 6th...Fanny Jacobs and her brother, old pupils, arrived in two fine cars one morning bringing their respective families to see their old school. They both speak highly of the schools part in their lives.

Colonel Morgan presented the pupils with four baskets of very fine grapes.

Oct. 14th. Mr. and Mrs. Rogers went to Grimsby and brought back a quantity of peaches which the children enjoyed for several suppers.

Oct. 12th. Leo Winnie was foiled in an attempt to make three other boys abscond with him one night. He had persuaded them to wheel him about fifteen miles in a wheel chair. One boy, William Snake, did get away and we have not been able to locate him...

Oct. 26th. Leo Winnie dismissed and taken home...

Oct 31st. Hallowe en. This was celebrated by the officers supplying taffy and lemonade while the school supplied apples and peanuts. During the evening games were played and the boys thoroughly enjoyed making the girls shriek with their ghost parade.

Nov. 7th. Mr. Standing inspected classroom work. Although he expressed approval and satisfaction on the progress here he reported to the Department...that we too frequently changed our junior teacher and that we needed a qualified teacher in that position. In this connection we have been unfortunate. The last four changes have been out of our hands entirely; two left on account of ill-health and two to get married. Our present teacher, Mrs. Knowles, is bright intelligent and most enthusiastic... We find the qualified teacher too ready to confine her interests solely to the classroom whereas the right type of teacher is prepared to take part in the general life of the pupils. Mrs. Knowles is also our Girl Guide Leader...

Nov. 10th. Captain Howarth of the local Fire Brigade organised the boys Fire teams and we had several...Drills.

Nov. 12th. Thanksgiving Day. was celebrated by a feast of meat pies and plum puddings for dinner and apples and pea-nuts for supper extras.

Nov. 13th and 14th. The weather was very mild and we were able to plough the orchards.

Nov. 16 and 17th. We devoted these two days to general work in the Church yard. We removed the broken gate-posts...and replaced them with neat iron posts.

Nov. 19th. The Toronto Sunday World published an

infamous attack upon this School in...a letter written by Miss Eva Johnson sister of Pauline the Indian Poetess.

Nov. 20th. Colonel Morgan wrote to the Department and Colonel Thompson in this connection. We also sent the news-cutting to the New England Company.

Nov. 21st. Colonel Morgan inspected.

A reporter from the Toronto Star visited the school in connection with Eav Johnson's letter. He spent several hours here and returned the next day to see the children at their meals.

Nov. 29th. Colonel Thompson unexpectedly paid a visit of inspection for the Department. He took sworn statements from the members of the inside staff and thoroughly investigated every phase of the school work. He expressed his approval.

Nov. 30th. Fire Alarm Drill. Our Boys team were playing water on the imaginary blaze within 2½ minutes of the sounding of the alarm...

Mrs. Knowles and Miss Elliott with several of the girls commenced a course for Girl Guides.

After the issue of Miss Johnson's letter we experienced a trying time with the pupils. They showed resistance to discipline and one girl became most disobedient and defiant. This girl was in the second year at the Brantford Collegiate and reluctantly dismissed but the effect was immediately shown in the improvement of the general conduct.

Dec. 5th. The pupils went to town to see Santa Clause and to see the Community Christmas Tree...

All the girls went in charge of Officers to town during the weeks preceeding Christmas to see the Stores and to do their Christmas shopping. In addition pieces of cretonne, cords silks and crochet were given to each girl for making into presents for relatives. Some very novel and excellent work was turned out.

December 14th...organised our Girl Guide Corps, No. 6 Brantford. All over twelve years were accepted on four months probation and were formed into the following patrols, Blue Bird, Canary, Oriole, Pheasant and Robin. Colonel and Mrs Morgan were present and their daughter Betty with our gardeners two daughters joined our Corps.

The following two days our guides went to the Y.W.C.A. and the Collegiate for drill.

December 21st. We decorated our Dining Hall and Entrance with cedar and colours and in the evening we staged our Christmas Concert...This was an undoubted success...Colonel Morgan took the chair and many friends and old pupils were present.

Dec 22nd. We killed two pigs for the feast and the weather was so mild that we were able to send the truck to Market with flowers and plants. Many pupils went to town with friends and those who were less fortunate were taken out by officers.

Dec. 24th. We had a wonderful Christmas Tree in the Dining Hall. All pupils were present and the staff brought

their families...By purchasing at wholesale houses we were able to supply every child with a present and a candy bag. Mr. W. F. Cockshutt sent a crate of oranges and Mr. and Mrs. Knowles gave every child a candy cane. One of the delightful incidents...was the number of presents the Children placed on the tree for one another. The pupils had a very enjoyable holiday. There was sufficient snow for sleighing on the hills and for building snow forts yet it was mild. Each evening the whole school gathered in the Dining Hall for games and fun...

Mr. Moule of...Brant Amusements Ltd. gave each pupil an invitation to the local cinema and a box of chocolates.

Dec. 27th. Mr. E. Bearfoot called to see the school...as an old pupil he felt he ought to reply to Miss. Johnson. His father, he was sure, never made the statements as represented in the article. He freely stated that the enemies of the school were to be found almost entirely in the ranks of the Baptists. On referring to the list of runaways immediately before Colonel Thompson's enquiry on the Reserve we discoverred that they were all children of Baptists with the exception of a family of Whites who have an aunt who is very bitter in her attitude towards the school. Although she is an old pupil the reason of her antagonism is that years ago Miss Hardie refused to allow her daughter to sit for an entrance examination for which she was entirely too stupid to write.

We killed another pig for the New Years Day dinner...

10. 10 March 1924 Standing Report

102...39 boys...63 girls...The pupils enrolled are all attending the school classes except when assigned in their turn to certain duties in connection with household or garden or farm, or when illness occurs.

The health of the pupils has been remarkably good...very little time has been lost through illness...The Pupils are fairly well graded and show satisfactory progress in their work. About ten of the Senior Fourth girls will probably try the Entrance Examination this year. This is the largest number for some years.

I am...pleased with the improvement...in the primary Department. Mrs. Knowles has good discipline and does effective teaching...A Map of the British Isles and a new map of Europe are needed. Also supplementary reading... Miss Susan Hardie is teacher of the Senior department and Mrs Eva Knowles of the Junior. Miss Hardie has a second class certificate and has had long and successful experience. Mrs Knowles has not had professional training nor previous teaching experience but she has excellent natural aptitude for teaching and controlling children and is doing good at work supervision and management of the Institution under Mr and Mrs Rogers and the work of the other officers...carried on with energy and efficiency...Since the addition to the buildings conditions have been much more attractive for the pupils than formerly.

11. 31 March 1924 Rogers Quarterly Report

...On Sunday evenings we have had a series of special talks by the Principal some of which were illustrated either by lantern slides or by the Mirrorscope. Once we had a Radio service from the Buffalo Studio. Five of our older girls have taken turns in playing the organ...

Health. With the exception of a slight epedemic of chicken pox we have had little or no trouble this quarter other than a few tiresome coughs and colds...We had only one visit from the Doctor this quarter...to examine a girl who had caught her foot in getting out of bed and fallen and it was feared had received some internal injury.

Staff. Miss Cummings (an English teacher on leave) left in the middle of January. She had done splendid work in reorganising our kitchen department. Miss Wilson took her place and we find her very efficient.

Mrs Knowles and Miss Elliott have taken a very active part in the newly organised Guides and rapidly bringing our girls to the front in Brantford.

Amusements. We had snow all the quarter...so much that we found it impossible to keep our skating rink in good order. However, we sent all pupils out frequently for sleigh rides until the roads became too badly drifted. Then as we found the girls were not playing on their slides we had to send them out for walks to keep them exercised. The pupils have had a great deal of enjoyment this winter out of the victrola, and a radio set which we were able to borrow for them.

January 1st. We had a tea-party with the tables daintily decorated with red baskets containing candies and cake and the evening programme included games and singing.

January 23rd and 25th. The Girl Guides went in sleighs to the Armouries to practice for the Brantford Parade at which they were inspected by the Lieutenant Governor. This parade was on the 26th January and our troup were splendid. Each Guide wore a uniform made from the Blue Dressing gowns we obtained from the D.S.C.R. by themselves since the first of January and a pink kerchief and scout hat completed their outfit...our girls secured the First Prize for their display of needle-work and second prize for first aid work. The drill display by our troup was second to none...afternoon our boys were the guests of the Kiwanis Club at their Annual Minstrel Show.

Mrs Persall, our sewing teacher, was so pleased with the guides good work on the uniforms and their display that she gave them a party at which all the female officers helped to give the girls a very jolly time. On March the fourth, the Principal gave a party to the whole school in the Dining room. We had several boxing contests between the boys and the girls thought it looked so simple that they asked to be allowed to box. We all found their efforts very amusing.

On March the 26th. a Bible class from the Wesley Church staged a play...and it was very much enjoyed...

Mr Peters commenced work on January 16th. and with pupils help has painted several of the rooms on the principal's flat, refinished stairways, scraped several old floors and re-decorated the bath-room.

The pupils have also painted the dormitories which we had previously had white-washed. The mens' Dining Room was also plastered and painted.

Clothing During this quarter our girls have made great headway in their sewing. Beyond keeping every article of clothing in repair they have made a complete issue of new serge dresses and aprons ready for Spring wear. They have in addition...completed two issues of boys shirts.

For the winter months the boys were outfitted with rubber shoes, heavy stockings and new sweaters.

Notes. Colonel McCrimmon of the Cadet Corps visited on January 18th.

Colonel Morgan and an officer of the R.C.M.P. visited on January 21st.

Two boys, possibly old pupils, climbed the fire escape and knocked at the Girls Dormitory window on February 19th. The police were notified and we are keeping a close guard.

Mr. Standing inspected March 5th.

On March 11th. we held a staff dinner in the Principals' Dining Room...It serves to bring the whole staff into closer touch with one another and tends to a more uniform standard for the pupils. The table was effectively arranged by Mrs. Rogers and three of the senior girls waited at table in a very smart manner.

Discipline The disturbing effects of Miss Eva Johnson's newspaper propaganda are no longer noticeable. The introduction of Girl Guides has had the tendency to improve the general discipline of the girls although we had one rather serious case to deal with during the quarter. A number of girls bodied themselves together under the name "Jesse James Gang" and they started out on a regular reign of tyranny over the other girls. However, we became acquainted with the "gangs" activities and were able to break it up. There is a splendid spirit amongst the boys now. Although at times I had feared the honour system was impractical amongst them...at last, I am finding very good results. The senior boy in the school had for some little time been bullying the small boys but the intermediates took the matter up and after severely thrashing him brought him to me and made their report as to his conduct. This is the first instance of its kind to my knowledge...

Farm...has been able to contribute well to the upkeep of the school by sending in plentiful supplies of milk, potatoes, cabbage, other vegetables...

12. 30 June 1924 Rogers Quarterly Report

CHURCH Bishop Williams conducted the...Confirmation ...May 26th. The pupils decorated the church with wild blossoms...eleven girls and three boys presented...

AMUSEMENTS. April 5th. Several requests were made

by boys for a football but this was refused as it was noticed that several boys were using catapaults. Later in the same day a deputation of boys waited on the principal with a basket of smashed catapaults which they claimed to have collected from the remainder of the boys. One boy showed obvious signs of a black eye which he admitted was the result of taking one sling shot forcibly from another boy. Naturally the foot-ball was soon at their disposal. Our girls attended the enrollment of their Girl Guide Officers and we are very proud to state that our Guide Corps is the smartest uniformed in the city of Brantford. On April 11th. we commenced building a playhouse for the girls in their playground. On Good Friday after the service an inspection of the stock was carried out and prizes given for the cleanest. Our Brownies and Guides went for a "hike" on April 19th. This was repeated on April 26th when the evening meal was cooked around the camp-fire. Our Guides were presented with complimentary tickets for the Brantford Oratorio Society's concert on May 1st.

On May 24th. a number of girls surprised the staff and other pupils by staging an entirely original concert. They had made their costumes from crepe paper and their dancing and singing was a revelation to us all. Afterwards they provided a treat of ice cream, biscuits and candy which they had bought with their own savings. So successful was this concert that it was repeated and friends were invited to attend and the principal gave instructions for the school to provide the refreshments.

DISCIPLINE...we are very pleased to report that there is a splendid spirit amongst the pupils. They are beginning to develop an "esprit de corps" and that naturally tends towards better discipline.

STAFF....Mr. Cudmore was discharged on April 5th. and Mr. Hughes engaged in his place...

Mr. Thurlow arrived from England on April 18th. and was taken on the staff to assist in supervision of boys and to take care of machinery, wiring and minor repairs.

NOTES. On April 3rd. The girls reported that a boy had broken into their dormitory. A search was made by the principal but no trace could be found in the dark...

Miss Elliott has commenced training the Brownies. Our small girls are quite enthusiastic and are always ready for their practices on Wednesday and Thursday afternoons.

The Girl Guides practice every Friday evening under the instruction of Mrs Knowles and Miss Elliott in the Dining Hall. There training includes games, country dances, singing and camp fire stories in addition to drill and we attribute the improvement in the girls discipline to be largely due to this training.

April 16th. The Remembrance Chapter of I.O.D.E. presented the school with a picture entitled "Canadian Foresters at Windsor Castle"...

On May 3rd we had an outbreak of measles which lasted until June 7th. many of the pupils were quite sick but all have made good recoveries.

On May 21st we took down the double windows and doors and commenced screening...

May 26th. Bishop Williams and Rev C. Owen had lunch here. The Bishop was some time inspecting the whole school and expressed himself as pleased.

June 10th. Mr Whelan, who is touring Canada lecturing on the League of Nations paid us a visit. He told of listening to Chief Levi General at Geneva and I think had a wrong impression of things when he arrived...he was soon convinced that the Mohawk Institute was far from being as black as painted.

As everything in the garden was late this Spring the Sewing class spent several days on the flower beds...

June 26th. Mr. and Mrs Rogers with Mrs Knowles and Mr. Howarth visited Mount Elgin Institute...

June 27th. Our men and boys hauled a car of coal in seven and a half hours...

June 30th. A garden party for the Girl Guides was held at the Commissioner's house. We contributed four gallons of ice-cream and our Guides danced and helped wait on the visitors.

FARM...Our poultry have kept us well supplied with eggs for setting and the pupils have been plentifully supplied with eggs.

13. 30 September 1924 Rogers Quarterly Report

CHURCH Since the holidays we have made several alterations in the daily curiculum with a view to giving even more time to Scriptural and moral training.

AMUSEMENTS. July 1st. The Principal, Mr. Hughes and seven boys motored to Port Dover to help prepare the Kiwanis Camp for the underpriviledged girls of Brantford. The remainder of the boys went for a truck ride in the morning and the girls...in the afternoon.

July 18th. a closing concert was held in the Dining Hall. Those who were unfortunate enough to miss going away for the holidays were very loyal and cheerful in keeping the work in good order and they were paid according to their merit. This gave them spending money and opportunities were made for them to go to local places of amusement and picture shows. We gave a much more liberal diet in the way of fruit salads and pastries and generally speaking the holidays were a great success.

August 11...a new bridge across the Grand River was opened. General Ashton was an official visitor...all the children went to see the processions...

August 26th. This was a day that some of our pupils will never forget. We were invited to the Toronto Exhibition and arrangements were made for sixty pupils and four officers to make the trip. Due to the kindness of the local Kiwanis and Rotary Clubs we only had to hire one speed wagon as each club supplied the transportation for twenty pupils. We were able to make an early start and had the lovliest weather. The principal followed the trucks with his car loaded with girls who had been especially good during the holidays and we made both journeys without any accidents. Lunches and soft drinks were carried and I think it does our pupils great credit to report that on only one occasion during the day did we have any anxiety on account of a pupil being missing. Through all the great crowds I was able to get in touch with any child any time I wanted that child. The only exception being when a boy was missing for five minutes...he had hidden behind the back of a platform where a sword-swallower was at work in order to find out how it was done.

Sports material and Girl Guide hikes and ordinary recreations have held their usual place in...school life.

NOTES. On July 5th. Mr. McVittie and Mr. McGookin visited the school.

July 7th. The Girl Guides were enrolled by...the local Commissioner...After the ceremony...the Sarah Jeanette Duncan Chapter of the Imperial Order of the Daughters of the Empire presented our Corps with its Colours...After the two events our girls gave an exhibition of singing and dancing. The whole affair reflected great credit upon the hard work of Mrs. Knowles our leader...

July 18th. Colonel Morgan brought down the Musical Director of the Canadian National Exhibition to see the school. He was the gentleman who so kindly arranged for our pupils to gain free entrance to the Exhibition.

July 19th. Miss Hardie and pupils left for holidays; there were only 20 boys and 23 girls left in the building at six o'clock. Mr. Knowles and a few children left the following week.

August 16th. School re-opened and many pupils reported back promptly but a number who were off in the berry fields did not notify us that they were not returning and some delay was caused in filling their places. There were quite a number of applications for admission.

Miss Hardie having six weeks holiday was not back for school opening and consequently the Senior School was carried on by Mrs. Rogers assisted by Mrs Knowles. Special lessons were given in all kinds of fancy work, knitting, embroidery and crocheting. Domestic science and elocution were also taught.

Miss Elliott left on September 1st. She had unfortunately been giving too much time to dances and neglecting her duties in consequence...

September 16th. **** fell off swing and broke her arm. She was sent to the hospital for X-ray treatment before Doctors could discover this and they had some difficulty in setting.

September 24th. Mr Phelan of the Department of Indian Affairs inspected the school and audited the books.

We had an outbreak of measles just before the summer holidays and have had another since. This last attack has been more troublesome and has been complicated with a more or less serious form of ear trouble. The Doctor has been examining all cases.

Two girls named **** aged fourteen and fifteen years were admitted with another girl their own age named **** and after about ten days they absconded. We have since learned that the two **** girls had been very wild and as they had both parents living and well off it was decided that it would not be fair to allow them to return amongst our girls.

September 8th. All beds were issued with two new blankets the summer blankets were all collected and after being washed were re-issued.

We have recently issued sweaters or coats to the boys and heavy underwear. The girls have just completing re-making some homespun dressing gown we received from the D.S.C.R. into work dresses.

All the small girls have been issued with an extra apron so that they have two clean aprons each week.

FARM AND GARDEN...The garden has kept the school very well supplied with all kinds of vegetables and fruits and we have our larders filled with preserves and pickles. The poultry produced eggs so plentifully that we were able to feed the pupils eggs on more than one occassion each week.

14. 25 November 1924 Standing Report
...44 Boys 70 Girls...
Senior Division Miss Susan Hardie $800 & living
Junior Division Mrs Eva Knowles $30 a month & living
Miss Hardie has had good success in general work and in preparing candidates for the Entrance Exam. Mrs Knowles is doing very well indeed with the lower grades.

The teachers are being supplied with the new Ontario Course of Study, which they are recommended to follow...the First and Second Book classes are making good progress in Arithmetic writing and the English subjects reading spelling & composition. The beginners too are getting a fair start...classes in the third and Fourth Books too are doing well. The class preparing for the Entrance Exam is larger than that of last year...all the classes from the First Book up are on the half day system ...None are absent from classes except on account of illness or in some cases for special duties about the building or the farm.

There is a difficulty in retaining the boys long enough at the School to enable them to reach the high School Entrance Standard.

The class rooms are now quite attractive and comfortable and are adequately furnished. Further equipment is desirable in the way of reference books (atlas gazeteer dictionary encyclopaedia) and of books for supplementary reading.

The six girls who tried the Entrance Exam last summer were all successful. Four of them are, I believe, continuing their studies either in the High School or at a Business Collegiate.

15. 31 December 1924 Rogers Quarterly Report
...STAFF. Miss Wilson met with a motor accident which caused her to be absent for one month...we never appreciated the sterling work of Miss Wilson in her department until her absence. She had so drilled her quiet insistent methods in to the pupils that we experienced very little inconvenience by her absence.
AMUSEMENTS. Two motor loads of girls were taken to Ohsweken Fair...The boys went the following day...
On October 25th. we had a weiner and baked potatoe roast in the boys playground at 6 p.m. We concluded the evening by a sing-song around a big camp-fire.
October 27th. We had a corn-husking competition between boys and girls. As is usual the boys finished a long way in the lead. Mrs Rogers suggested that the girls make some corn-husk dolls but we found that that was a lost art.
Our usual Fall Sports Day was a great success. The boys paraded their horses in first class condition.
All Hallo'e en Night was celebrated and the prizes won the previous day at the Sports were distributed.
November 10th. Thanksgiving Day was spent very happily the boys held their annual shooting match and the girls went for a walk in the morning. After lunch the boys and girls met at base-ball and although the girls put up a very good game they were out-classed. Sausages and pumkin pies were added to the days menu.
December 6th. All juniors went to town to see Santa Claus arrive from the North Pole in an aeroplane...all the pupils had an opportunity to visit town and make purchases. We usually sent about half a dozen in charge of an officer.
On December 23rd. we held our Christmas Concert and our pupils were certainly at home with their parts...
Santa Claus arrived on December 24th. and much to the childrens' delight he had a present for everybody and there was a basket of candy and nuts as well as an orange for every pupil.
On Christmas day we had a carol service...and as the weather was very cold we were glad that Santa Claus had been so thoughtful in providing so many games. We had a very special dinner and at tea-time the tables were all decorated with holly napkins and red candy baskets. During the following week there was plenty of opportunity for skating and sleighing. We had our rink in good order and the girls went to Tutela rink nearly every day. Those who could went to the show in town.
NOTES. Mr. McFadden of the local Collegiate conducted some psychological tests upon our pupils...that he might compare children of Indian descent with others.
**** was allowed leave for a few weeks to nurse her sick mother and ****, her sister was allowed home for a few hours to visit the mother. When the mother died we had both girls examined by Dr. Palmer as...**** had died from T.B.C.

Mr. Ferrier...visited on the 14th...15th. of October when the school was inspected and matters of finance discussed. Messrs Rogers and Thurlow motored as far as St. Thomas after the two Fox boys who had absconded.
October 18th. Drs. Palmer and Bragg were called to **** who was rushed to the hospital for operation upon the mastoid.
About this time **** was granted leave as she had her arm in a plaster caste. She failed to return and we tried every possible way to trace her. The Indian offices at Brantford and Hagersville were both notified but no news of her whereabouts could be found. We have lately heard, however that the arm was attended to and is in quite good order...
On November 1st Sergeant Bridger called with reference to runaway boys. He has since given us good help...
**** stole a ride on a tradesman's truck and injured his knee. It was necessary to administer an anesthetic to stitch same and he has had many trips to the doctor since. Mr. Standing inspected the class-rooms on November 25th. and expressed his approval of Mrs Knowles work.
**** and **** were both sent to hospital and have returned in very fine condition after successful operations.
November 30th. Our pupils all began to complain about half an hour after supper and we discovered that they had been poisoned by apple sauce that had been prepared in a boiler that had a new galvanised iron bottom. Emetics were quickly administerred and no ill-effects remained.
Several of our pupils had ear trouble as a result of measles and we have quite a number visiting Dr. Bragg, an ear specialist.
On December 7th. Three small boys went through the ice on the canal after having been warned that they were not to go near the ice. They were put to bed and after we were sure that they would suffer no ill-effects they were punished.
Leave was granted two **** boys to attend their sisters funeral and on their return we found that their mother was in a very impudent frame of mind. She refused to sign a duplicate set of papers to replace those lost in mail and was very rude in her criticisms of the clothing and food given her boys. As she became abusive the Principal decided that she could keep her boys and discharged them forthwith...
The Saturday before Christmas was a very busy day with visitors to pupils.
December 21st. **** sent to hospital. - This boy has complained of earache for some time and we had him under to Doctor practically all the time he has been in the school. Finally he took a serious turn for the worse and an operation was orderred. Fortunately, we were in time for it was discoverred that the trouble was deep seated and long-standing and had it gone much further nothing could have saved him. **** was also sent to hospital. We had been treating her eyes for months as they were

badly ulcerated. Finally the Doctor began to fear for her sight on account of scars and it was decided that she should receive special treatment in the hospital.

On the whole the health of the children has been good apart from the several cases of a serious nature...

Our Dining Hall was used for the Christmas concert and Mr. Thurlow Boys Master took upon himself the work of stage carpenter. He provided a very attractive stage with all foot and head lighting effects.

During October all girls were provided with heavy working dress made from D.S.C.R. grey serge dressing gowns...the girls have blue serge dresses for school and others of a different pattern for best. The girls have all been issued with high shoes and the boys with boots. All pupils have had two issues of stockings or socks.

All girls are provided with heavy petticoats and the boys have sweaters. Our bigger boys are wearing their blue uniforms for school. Every boy has been provided with woolen cap and mitts.

The girls tams were dyed a uniform colour to match their serge dresses.

16. 20 December 1924 Brantford Junior Expositor
BRANTFORD'S OLDEST EDUCATIONAL INSTITUTION

...At the present time there are 120 pupils - 70 girls and 50 boys, mostly of the under-privileged classes. Indian children, who show an aptitude for learning and are located far from the opportunity, are taken into residence as are orphans and deserted little ones, the age limits being from 9 to 18 years.

The instruction given is very thorough. The young folk work on the half-time system, which, though it delays the progress in ordinary school work, makes the instruction far more embracing. Besides the usual public school work, the girls take up and learn thoroughly domestic science, needle work, cooking in all its branches, horticulture and truck farming, fancy work and the art of home-making. The boys learn general stock farming, truck farming, greenhouse work, gardening, shoe repairing and manual training.

HAS STAFF OF TWELVE
The teaching staff comprises the lady principal Mrs S. Rogers, five lady teachers, five men teachers, and Principal S. Rogers.

PINE BUILDINGS
The building is a very fine, solid red brick structure, known among architects as the most beautiful of its kind in Canada. It stands in extensive grounds, approached through an avenue of well-grown maples, with lawns and flower beds, in the midst of 16 acres of orchard. The Institute farm, stretching away over a fertile area comprises 350 acres, including grain land, pasture, fodder fields and there are 6000 square feet of floor space in excellent greenhouses. There are suitable barns, stables, root houses, silos, and pig pens.

The building...was designed and built by Rev. R. Ashton and his son, now Major-General E. C. Ashton. It is most admirably designed for the purpose with a central portion and two wings. The principal's quarters and the administration offices teachers' rooms and the like are in the centre of the building, the boys' dormitories, lavatories, play rooms, etc. occupying one wing, and the girls' rooms the other wing. It is a code of honor that the boys' rooms and the means of communication therefrom with the outer world, are never locked or barred, and put upon their honor, the boys never break faith. The girls' rooms are at all times in immediate touch with the lady principal's quarters...The dormitories are bright, painted pure white, scrupulously clean and airy; there are individual cots for each pupil, lockers, a spacious dining room, a well-equipped kitchen - indeed everything that can be needed in a scientifically run home of this character. The laundry and sewing rooms should be especially mentioned, for not only is all laundry work undertaken by the scholars, but every garment worn by girl or boy is made on the premises, and both sexes, when seen in their ordinary working dress, would bear comparison with any city school scholars.

AN ACTIVE LIFE
The inmates lead a strenuous, active, but healthy life, and are a very fine sample of budding manhood and womanhood. They rise at 6 a.m., and the girls prepare breakfast, the boys doing the morning chores. Breakfast is at 6.45. At 8.15 those whose turn it is to attend school stop work, the remainder carrying on in the various and many occupations that a big household and large farm like this needs. Dinner is at 12.15 and judging from the preparations made by the girls in the kitchen, it is ample and inviting. Samples of their own home-made bread, tea, cakes, and sundry dainties were tempting and really artistic, altogether a fare more substantial and toothsome than that to which city children generally sit down. At 1.30 there is another school session, lasting till 4 p.m., and work in domestic matters and outside chores goes on again till 5.45 which is supper time. The juniors go to bed at 8 p.m., the seniors at 9 p.m. Every pupil gets one half-day off a week, (with the usual Sunday rest as is possible in farm life), and all national holidays.

This vigorous life has its effect for good and, together with the kindly if firm administration, is working wonders for the pupils. A noticeable growing respect for order and cleanliness is observed and the principal and the teaching staff express much encouragement. Music is carefully cultivated, and is so far successful that many of the children are good vocalists, some are excellent orchestral instrumentalists. They sing and play at the ancient church of their reserve...Mohawk Church...

17. 16 January 1925 Morgan to Secretary DIA
...I inspected the Mohawk Institute today during the

children's dinner hour.

I found the dinner, which consisted of liver, potatoes and turnips, followed by buns, plentiful, of good quality, and well and cleanly served. There were 73 girls and 44 boys, of which 8 girls and 4 boys were laid up with slight grippe colds, but there is no serious illness in the Institute.

One boy, ****, is in the Hospital suffering from Mastoids but is better and is expected to come out in about six weeks.

I visited the kitchens, laundry and other outhouses and found them clean and well kept.

The children are warmly clothed and appeared cheerful and happy, whilst the staff is able and efficient.

18. 31 March 1925   Rogers Quarterly Report

Staff...Mrs Knowles, who is a very energetic officer, was poorly and as a nervous breakdown was feared she was granted a weeks rest commencing March 2nd.

Discipline. On the whole we have had very good discipline which has made the work much easier and has enabled the pupils to obtain greater benefits from their school-life. It is most gratifying to note absence of insolence which used to be so common and the children are constantly showing evidence of greater confidence in their teachers. It is felt that the restoration of law and order on the local Reserve has helped a great deal to bring this condition about. While our ordinary pupils are showing improvement, it is regrettable that our students attending the Collegiate and Business College are not so satisfactory. They take no interest in the tasks allotted them at the school and are inclined to be impertinent to the staff. They are frequently quite late in returning from their classes and appear to think that other pupils should be detailed to wait on them. Possibly the lack of discipline in the Collegiate and Business College accounts for their attitude.

Ammusements. On January 1st. sleighriding and skating were the order of the day and a special dinner of Roast pork, baked potatoes, mashed turnip and mince pies. During the evening all the school met in the Dining hall for games and competitions.

On January the seventeenth the girls went for a sleigh ride and took eggs to **** at the hospital they then called for Mary Waswanipi at the Blind School. Mrs Knowles has kept the Girl Guide and Brownie movement active and has had good success despite the fact that the local Commissioner has been out of town and has therefore conducted no Rallies, which always serve to stimulate our girls interest. Outside competition always serve to increase our girls enthusiasm. The boys had a good rink and were allowed to water a hill near the school on which they had some very fine sleighing. A number of boys were given opportunity to build their own sleighs. They used old packing cases and barrel staves for lumber and made some very novel sleighs.

HEALTH. We commenced the quarter with a fairly clean bill of health but in January we had an epedemic of colds with nasty sore throats and in February we had another spell of the flu. It was necessary to call in Dr. Bragg on one occassion as many children that had had ear complications left by the measles were again troubled during the flu epedemic. However, good care resulted in the restoration of our usual freedom from sickness.

****, who was taken to hospital last quarter to be operated upon for mastoid, after recovery, developed tubercular meningitis with fatal results on 17th. February. The Principal wishes to place on record his appreciation of the kindness of both the hospital staff and the Doctors of this town. On one occassion when ****'s condition was puzzling our Doctor no less than four other Doctors came and held free consultation.

Notes. School re-opened on January 2nd. with a full staff. During the quarter Rev. Jones of Ohsweken visited the school often. His visits keep him in touch with the pupils from his Parish and it is felt that this has a good effect.

January 8th. **** visited his brother at hospital who had taken a sudden turn for the worse. We also telegraphed Mr. McGookin to inform father. The father arrived and pleaded poverty so we boarded him for several days for which we got little but abuse.

January 12th. We brought **** home from hospital.

January 15th. Miss Cummings, a former housekeeper here, visited us. She is connected with Childrens' imigration and has experience in that work...she says that our standard of living and accomodation is far better than the average home she visits.

February 19th Mr. Thurlow took ****s body to Middlemiss...

Colonel Morgan inspected monthly.

INDUSTRIES. The Girls have altered Cadet Marine uniforms to fit our boys and made suits for the small boys from jersey cloth purchased at the Paris Mills. They have also made two issues of shirts for boys and one of aprons and combinations for the girls. Besides this they have made new kitchen and Dining room aprons and kept all clothing being worn in repair.

We have commenced a new work with our girls. All scraps of cloth now are being saved and made into very attractive rag rugs.

The boys have renovated the Girls playroom and painted it. This is a great improvement.

19. 5 June 1925   Morgan to Scott

I regret to say that the attitude of Mr Rogers of the Mohawk Institute towards myself, as Superintendent, is such as to leave me no alternative other than to ask you to either absolve me from responsibility regarding him or to definitely notify him that it is your wish that I should continue upon the same lines as my predecessor, Major Smith, and that he must not commit actions, without first consulting me, which may lead to complications of the relations between the Department and the Six Nations.

...since I came to Brantford there has been a systematic lessening of the intercourse between the Institute and this Office. First one thing has been omitted and then another until you were, yourself, obliged to notify Mr Rogers that his returns should be checked by me before reaching Ottawa, and that it was your wish that a monthly inspection should be made by me.

To avoid unpleasantness I have, perhaps, been remiss in these duties and have done my utmost to avoid wounding their susceptibilities in every way I could.

Mr Brant having recently died his son-in-law, Councellor Frank Monture asked me whether his daughter, Dorothy, could leave the Institute to attend the funeral, and I gave him a letter to Rogers, of which I attach a copy (A). I also attach one of Major Smiths letters of a similar nature, selected from his files haphazard (B) to show that my letter was neither discourteous or unusual.

Mr Rogers called here on Saturday afternoon and abused me before the staff saying "That he had never received so insulting a letter in his life, that I had nothing whatever to do with the Institute and that he would allow children to go, or not allow them, regardless of my officious interference".

On May 27th Rogers told me that he had asked the Bishop of Huron to unveil a war memorial to fallen Indians in the Mohawk Church early this month.

Having heard nothing of this officially from the Department...and, knowing that the Council was on the look out for an excuse to accuse the Department of ignoring it...I wrote to Rogers my letter attached...

This formed the subject of a further tirade, during which he called me a liar. "I had nothing whatever to do with the Institute or with the children in it" "He corresponded with and received instructions only from Mr Ferrier and you", and more to the same effect.

On Sunday afternoon he motored out to Mr Hill's, who is my clerk as well as Chief Councellor, and obtained the addresses of the School Board, the Councellors and principal G.W.V.A. to whom he sent somewhat tardy invitations that "He would be honoured by their attendance". The Council, as you know, is divided into two sections, one loyal to the Department and to me, as its representative, led by the Chief Councellor and another, led by Councellor Johnson, with distinctly Mohawk leanings, which loses no opportunity which offers to covertly defy the Department and spread the seeds of dissention amongst the loyal section of the Council whenever possible...

It was into this that Rogers flung an apple of discord by a direct invitation to be present at the unveiling of a memorial of which no one had previously heard.

Several Councellors and members of the School Board asked me why the Department had not asked them to deliberate on the nature of a war memorial to fallen Six Nations soldiers to be erected in the Six Nations Church. I was obliged to admit that I knew nothing about it,* (not true - Mr Rogers called Col's home on May 24 and explained what he was about to do.[written in])* and to add that I did not think that the Department did either, and that not only had I, as representative of the Department received no notice but that also I had received no notice to be present, so I concluded that it had been done by Mr Rogers upon his own authority.

My omission from the list was so obviously, in the eyes of the disloyal faction, an attempt by a white employee of the Department to do what they are constantly themselves striving for, get away from local supervision, that they hailed it with acclamation and voted to attend, and some no doubt will, but the loyal element, being the stronger, voted against attending, on the grounds that they considered that if the Department had any knowledge of the matter they would first have been consulted before the memorial was erected in their church, to their dead, and that the information and invitations to attend would have reached them from the Department through the Official channel of the Indian Office. Some were for wiring to you to stop it but finally they contented themselves with refusing the invitation.

...far from wishing to exercise any authority of officiousness with the Rogers I would far sooner have nothing whatever to do with the Institute. If the Department feels that Rogers can be trusted to be freed from all local supervision and conduct business direct with the Department, it will be a considerable relief to me, although I cannot see how my responsibilities for the Indians can be solely confined to those who are grown up and residing on the Reserve.

...I trust that steps will be taken to prevent any recurrence...and that if Mr Rogers finds it necessary to communicate in future with the Council or others on the Reserve that he may be told to do so through me.

20. 30 June 1925 Rogers Quarterly Report

Staff...Miss Crowe resigned and her place was taken by Miss Allen who promises to develope into a very efficient officer. Miss Hardie has not enjoyed very good health but otherwise our staff has worked most satisfactorily.

Discipline. The three students attending Business College gave us a great deal of trouble and we found that they were in the habit of absenting themselves from classes. They failed in their first examinations and although given an opportunity of an extra months tuition only Effie Montour passed. **** and **** continued to trifle and were consequently dismissed after trying their examination for the second time. Dorothy Montour, who is attending the Collegiate passed her first year and has shown a very marked improvement lately.

Notes. The boys had some good fishing on Good Friday

and Easter Monday.

On May 21st. our pupils were invited to a Band Concert at the local Armouries and were encouraged by the kindly comments made as to their appearance and behaviour.

May 29th. Mr. Ferrier visited and matters pertaining to school advancement were discussed.

May 22nd. The Remembrance Chapter of the I.O.D.E. of which Miss Hardie is a member, presented a prize for the best paper on Hygene...won by Beulah Stonefish.

May 24th. being Bob Rogers birthday was the occasion of a party. We had a large birthday cake and all the staff and pupils shared it.

June 1st. Commenced preparations for unveiling Roll of Honour in Church.

June 9th. A Garden Party was held at St. Peters Ohsweken and several of our girls escorted by Mr. Rogers took part in the programme...due largely to the co-operation of Rev. Jones of that church there is a much more friendly spirit shown towards the school.

June 11th. Bishop Williams unveiled the Roll of Honour in the Mohawk Church. He was assisted by the Reverends Lee, White and Owen. The Brass Band from the Reserve offerred their services and paraded our children to and from the Church. So large was the crowd that many of the pupils has to remain outside...After the service the visitors were entertained on the School Lawn to ice cream and cakes while the band played...

During the quarter the girls were issued with new low shoes and aprons while the boys received two new shirts, new overalls, caps and hats.

Buildings and grounds...to add to the beauty of the school grounds...Mrs. Rogers has taken charge of the flower borders and with a number of girls is giving them the care they need...the gardener...can now bend every effort to production. Large white stones have been placed along the drive and our approach is in very fine condition.

SPECIAL NOTE. On June 30th. we had to call the Doctor to **** a recent admission who had become quite ill. It was discovered that she had been injured by a fall and had been in bed a week before she came here. She is up and appears to be well now.

21. 30 September 1925 Rogers Quarterly Report

Discipline. There has been a decided improvement in the general discipline since the holidays. We have two pupils attending Collegiate and very definite rules have been laid down for their guidance, with quite severe punishments for misdemeanours. As a result they are only too anxious to do their share in maintaining their place in the school. We were also able to dismiss a number of older girls who were not a good influence. We are now, for the first time, able to maintain a Waiting List and as all the parents and pupils know this, there is a very decided effort on everyone's part to retain a place in the school.

Notes. During the holidays the plaster throughout the

school was patched and repaired and the girls re-varnished the stairs, wainscotting and linoleums.

September 16th...one of our boys, was kicked in the shoulder by a horse...First aid was rendered and the Doctor summoned...only a painful bruise...

After the holidays the pupils returned promptly and early in the term we were in the fortunate position of starting our Waiting list...we have not approached any person with a view to inducing pupils to enter the school. Our pupils went home and apparently compared so favourably with other children on the Reserve that before the close of the holidays we were having applications...that we could not accomodate.

Amusements. On July 1st. the girls visited the stores in the morning and played soft-ball. In the afternoon they went in a body to Mohawk Park. The boys spent a good day at the river with the Principal.

A Closing Concert was held on July 3rd.

July 4th. Closing Day. The day passed very quietly and we were left with 30 girls and 20 boys. We gave these children a more liberal diet in the way of fancy articles and generally speaking made it possible for them to have a good time at the school.

Once or twice a week they went to Mohawk Pleasure Park where the management were most kind. Our pupils were allowed to ride the ponies and the merry-go-round free and they made good use of the other amusements... On two occassions we took a number to Grimsby where they picked fruit in the mornings. We provided picnic luncheons and in the afternoons they visited the pleasure Park...and enjoyed spending the money they had earned. One afternoon as a reward for some extra help the girls had given they were taken for a round trip on the town street car. The boys were very willing whenever volunteers were called to help handle a crop and on the whole the summer holiday passed most pleasantly. During the last week all pupils were paid a small sum in proportion to the help they had given and they went to town to spend the same.

On the 17th August, the Monday following School Opening, all the staff and pupils held a Gala at Mohawk Park. This served to settle them all back to school life after which steady work was the order of the day.

Our annual Corn Roast was held on the 24th September...

22. 31 December 1925 Rogers Quarterly Report

Staff During the quarter Mr and Mrs. Knowles resigned and were replaced by Miss McNicoll and Miss Chambers. Both of these have teachers certificates and promise to become good officers. We are attempting to manage the farm work with one man less this winter and conscquently Mr. Roots [?] was asked to resign...

Discipline...improvement in this direction. I find that more and more the parents and relatives are beginning to appreciate the school at its proper value and are more ready to help than to criticise. This attitude is naturally reflected in that of the children.

Amusements On October 1st. the girls motored to the Ohsweken Fair. There were two parties and Mrs Knowles went in charge of one party and Miss Hardie with another. On the following day the boys paid their visit but a very heavy rainstorm caused the roads become impassable and the boys had to trudge to the Middleport Ferry...They were quite late in returning but judging by the way they sang on the trip home I do not think the joy of their days' outing was marred.

...twelth October. The horses and cattle were judged for cleanliness and the boys had a very fine show. The usual races and contests were held and the prizes were distributed in the evening.

Hallow'ene was the occassion of much mirth caused by the various costumes worn by the pupils. The boys had some very good lanterns to display and we had a couple of hours romping and games.

Thanksgiving Day was delightful...the girls visited the stores and in the afternoon played ball with the boys.

November 14th. The girls went to a show in town with Miss Chambers. One of the direct benefits the pupils derive from the extra officer is that on all holiday occassions there is an officer available to accompany them for walks, visiting stores and...places of interest.

During the two weeks preceeding Christmas all the pupils were given the opportunity of visiting town and seeing the window displays and stores. Many of them were fortunate enough to see Santa Claus. The Trinity Dramatic Club very kindly came to the school on 17th December and played Pollyana for the benefit of the pupils. To describe our activities during the Christmas recess I enclose a press cutting. The little girls under Miss Chambers made three rag rugs whilst the senior girls made the officers a complete set of linen luncheon doyleys, trimmed with crochet work. To match this there was also a side table and sideboard runner...

We tried to interest the girls in knitting themselves scarfs and mittens but as the pupils were expected to do this in their own time we failed to get very much work done...

Notes. Girl Guides were re-organised on October 1st. and went for a hike during which they gathered wild flowers and plumage for Harvest Home decorations...

...On October...tenth we had to issue heavy underwear to the boys...By October 21st. all the girls summer clothing had been replaced by heavier wear for winter...On October 26th. Miss Chambers was engaged. She has a second class certificate and teaches the kindergarten children during work hours...other duties she has assumed are those of instructing junior pupils in making rag rugs, elementary sewing, supervision of cleaning and play director.

Mrs Knowles was taken ill on the 25th October so we had Miss Chambers take over her duties until Miss McNicoll arrived.

The Brantford Laundry issued a public invitation for inspection of its plant so Miss Allen, who is responsible for the laundry work here and Miss Chambers took twenty five of the senior girls who were welcomed by the President of the Company who kindly acted as guide throughout the whole of the plant. In addition to this highly instructive inspection the girls were presented with five dollars which they placed in the Radio Fund.

We have now a powerful receiving set with one loud speaker operated in one of the classrooms and we are now trying to swell our fund sufficiently to install a loud speaker in both classrooms. We find the talks to children broadcasted from the various stations are most attractive and the older children enjoy the good music. Of course, the jazz is always popular.

On November 7th. three girls who had absented themselves after the holidays without sending any word applied for re-admission. They and their parents, were quite surprised and indignant when we could not accept them on account of the school being over-full. We are hoping that this action will ensure prompt return from holidays in future.

****, a very naughty small girl, and ****, who is subnormal, absconded on November 23rd in their work dresses with no coats. After searching all morning for them I informed the Mounted Police and the girls were returned the next day. They reported that no one would shelter them and that they were reported to the police as Mohawk Institute pupils...a very welcome change of attitude on the Reserve.

We were offerred a piano very cheaply and as we were in need of another instrument we purchased same on November 27th. Our music class is growing rapidly.

On the 19th. December we fetched a waggon load of evergreens and being the Saturday before Christmas most of the pupils were visited by friends or relatives and went to town with them.

During the week preceeding Christmas everyone was busy. Girls were decorating and boys killing pork and poultry and getting ready for Christmas inspection...

Clothing. In addition to making the seasonal changes in clothing the girls were issued with new high shoes; they made twenty...heavy coats and altered thirty-five heavy great coats in addition to re-making some old grey coats; an issue of new stockings was also made. The boys received new shoes, socks, heavy underwear, overalls, sweaters and were re-fitted with winter uniforms.

Health. Whilst the general health of the pupils has been very good we have suffered one or two severe cases and there has been an epidemic of accidents. **** had a very trying time with pneumonia and as she began to recover another little girl named **** contracted the same complaint. There were also a few bad colds with indications of pleurisy but by careful attention there were no serious results and all the pupils are quite well now.

In the matter of accidents investigation showed that the cause was either purely accidental or else directly due to the carelessness of the victim. **** left his shoe lace undone and this tripped him as he was entering the greenhouse...he fell and broke his collar bone. **** had some snow on his shoes and slipped whilst carrying a plank. This broke his forearm. Another boy walked in front of some wood that was being pitch and was struck in the forehead causing a cut an inch and a half long which bared the bone. Another boy slipped whilst skating and cut his lip on a skate. All these cases were promptly attended to and no ill-effects can yet be seen...

Farm and Garden...the most successful year...On October 13th. I inspected the farm and our Fall crops were all ready to harvest. As the weather was mild I decided to discontinue classroom work until we had the work of harvesting well in hand...we were able to commence operations all over the farm. The school teachers took the very small children out to pick beans; a large squad of boys reported to the gardener in the orchard and as they picked a number of large girls sorted and packed away the fruit in the cellar; other squads were busy pulling the mangels and picking up potatoes. Every morning I called for more effort and I have never witnessed such enthusiasm as the pupils and staff displayed. In about a week we had the work well in hand and school was resumed...By arrangements with the Canadian Packing Company our older boys are visiting that plant chiefly to learn the hog industry. They are allowed to accompany the Government Grader who explains to them all the various features that control his grading. This work is most interesting and the boys are quite enthusiastic. On December 30th. one of our boys was within ten pounds of the correct weight of any pig he saw when estimating weights.

23. 30 January 1926 Rogers to Supt. Indian Education
...It is with great regret that I have to report a very serious breach of discipline on the part of a number of the senior boys and girls of this school. For a period of two or three weeks a number of boys and girls found means of meeting in different parts of this Institute and in fact a party of boys on several occassions made a trip to the Girls dormitory. This was discovered by myself when investigating a report by a junior officer who had had occassion to correct the girls for noisy conduct in the dormitory about 5 a.m. on January 9th. 1926.

I made a very extensive enquiry and caused every pupil implicated to write me a full confession of the whole proceedings and it would appear that serious as I at first thought the matter to be, it was more in the nature of a series of wild escapades. During the period that has elapsed since this occurrence I have had every officer co-operate in obtaining information concerning this affair and to-day I find them of the opinion that the affair was in the nature of a "lark".

Needless to say great care has since been exercised to prevent any possible recurrence and a system of alarms has been worked out to warn of any movement during the night. The culprits have been punished by having leave cancelled and they have also an hours extra work daily.

24. 31 March 1926 Rogers Quarterly Report
Amusements Whenever possible the girls have been taken for walks on fine days. Sleighriding and skating were enjoyed by both boys and girls. During stormy days the children have been able to listen to all kinds of radio programmes. We have found the radio very instructive in entertaining the pupils when in former times it was difficult to keep them out of mischief. We have now a loud speaker for the schoolroom.
1st January...All the girls went for a sleigh-ride and after a supper, very gaily decorated, we gathered in the Dining Hall for games and frolic...
...January Fire Drill and all equipment tested.
...January 27th. As we were unable to purchase chestnut coal we were in great difficulty with the cooking arrangements. The local dealers were asking $14 per ton for coke and consequently were being put to considerable expense. After careful consideration we decided that the installation of the electric stove would help us considerably...Since its installation we have been giving senior girls who will be leaving this year, training in its operation and so it serves a double purpose...
...March Mr. Standing inspected.
During March we worked on picture frames...

25. 3 May 1926 Rogers to Supt. Indian Education
...Could the following girls who have savings with the Department for safe keeping be allowed $25 each?
They are taking music lessons and as they are extras they need a little funds to make their payments. This money would be placed to their credit in the pupils accounts here and would be spent under the supervision of Mrs Rogers.
**** has also a sum of money standing to his credit. He is seventeen years of age and his Grandmother is trying very hard to secure his release but he is very simple minded and I feel sure that the only reason any interest is taken in him by his relatives is that they hope to secure his money. I have refused to allow him home for two years and I am trying to keep him interested in the farm here. If he could be allowed $25 as spending money I am sure he would be much more contented.
...Bessie Maracle... B.Q.M. 45
...Gladys Maracle...B.Q.M. 45
...Eva Jane Lickers..Mississauga N.C...

26. 30 June 1926 Rogers Quarterly Report
Church Three pupils were baptised and the Bishop confirmed twenty-two pupils on May 17th. We were able

to complete a flag-stone path into the Church before the Bishops visit. The Board of Works...gave...flag-stones and the farm staff and boys laid the walk in...six days...

Staff On April 1st. engaged Mr. Foster as teamster but as he was not satisfactory he was allowed to leave at the end of one month. We were fortunate enough to get the services of a neighbour for the spring work...

Mr. Thurlow was given an opportunity to resign as he was not proving satisfactory.

Mrs Persall has on the doctors advice resigned but we are not anxious to loose her so have only made temporary arrangements in the hope that she will recover and return to us. We were able to get Miss Mason daughter of Rev. R. Mason to take her place...

Health. During the quarter the general health of the pupils has been excellent, apart from a slight epedemic of grippe. Several pupils have had to visit the dentist and occulist. On June 11th Dr. Palmer visited the school and examined a number of girls who were giving us a little concern and he pronounced **** as tubercular.

Discipline...a marked improvement in the conduct of the children and a very pleasing spirit is evident.

Notes...During the quarter we have painted the beds and the woodwork in the dormitories...in May we were able to have a spring clean-up outside...and it is generally remarked that the grounds have never looked so trim.

The boys have been fitted out with new overalls, - shirts shoes and stockings and the girls have new summer dresses, underwear, stockings and kitchen aprons.

May 17th. The Bishop of Huron and friends were entertained after Service of Confirmation. Mr. Johnson the famous New York tenor was in town on that day and called to see the Church during the service. It was delightful to see him enter in the singing with the pupils and he was very complimentary in his remarks...

May 18th. Mr. and Mrs Rogers visited wholesale houses in Toronto in search of clothing for boys next winter.

June 22nd. **** and **** again absconded but we had them back in a few hours. Neither of these girls are normal and they give us quite a lot of trouble.

Three girls and three boys wrote their entrance examinations. Two girls dropped out of class, one was sick and the other did not wish to continue...

Amusements. Easter Monday the girls went to the stores and to a show whilst the boys had a good day fishing.

Our pupils attended Miss Frances Nickawa's recital at a city church.

May 24th. Girls went to Mohawk Park and the following day the Remembrance Chapter presented a prize for general efficiency to Norman Lickers. The pupils held a short patriotic concert and the Chapter made a presentation of library books.

June 8th. We had a general holiday and Mr. Rogers took four senior boys to the Agricultural College.

June 22nd. Miss Hardie took a party of girls to help at a

concert at a Reserve Church.

June 29th. Circus Day and all those who had the money were taken in the afternoon...

27. 30 September 1926 Rogers Quarterly Report

Staff. Mr. Thurlow resigned and his services terminated July 15th. Mr. Smith was engaged to fill the vacancy and was on duty July 12th. On July 31st. Miss Chambers, Domestic Science teacher, left to take a position she had secured near her home which was much better paid. Miss Mason, a temporary officer left on the same date.

Miss Wilson resigned on September 1st. She was a very efficient officer but since an automobile accident a year ago her nerves gradually become worse until they renderred her undesirable.

We replaced her with Miss Bates but she showed no signs of becoming a good officer and so was allowed to leave at the end of one week...

Discipline. On the whole this has been good especially amongst the boys but we have had several unpleasant cases of theft and petty stealing amongst the girls.

Notes. On July 1st. the girls went to the River to bathe and to Mohawk Park while most of the boys found work at neighbours.

**** went to the Sanitarium, Hamilton with Mr. and Mrs. Rogers.

On July 8th. all boys were kept from School. Owing to the cool wet weather, weeds were making much more rapid growth than our corn and roots and it was considered advisable to devote a day or two's work to saving the crop. By comparing our corn crop with our neighbours it is easy to see that we were wise in doing this. At the same time the girls tidied the playgrounds under the supervision of the school teachers and some silver spoons and fountain pens that had been stolen were found cached.

The Shrine Club entertained our pupils at a Circus on July 10th.

On July 14th. we ventured a Garden Party and Closing Concert. The grounds were beautiful. This being the result of the work of Mrs Rogers and girls in the flower beds. The weather was ideal and we had a good crowd of Brantford people and interested Indians. The Tennis lawn was gaily lighted and there were booths for the sale of ice cream soft drinks and specimens of the childrens handiwork. We used the front verandah as a stage for the concert and seats were placed on the lawn. The school electrician very kindly loaned us strings of lights and the building was very attractively decorated. During the early evening...visitors were conducted through the school...by officers. During the Concert prizes were given to the pupils who had made most consistent progress during the year and we were able to announce the results of the Entrance Examinations. We had three girls and three boys write this examination and all passed, one boy with honours.

July 17th. the school closed for holidays but we had 42 girls and 28 boys remain. Several were able to leave later when their relatives secured sufficient money to outfit them.

During the vacation the girls were required to work each morning and the afternoons were devoted to amusements such as bathing, visiting park, taking round trips on the street cars and going to shows. We spent the sum of $25 upon these outings.

With the boys it was necessary to hire a number of the older in order to keep the farm work in hand. These boys, however were allowed to attend the moving pictures and sports meets at night with an officer.

On July 25th. **** was suddenly taken very ill and on the following day Drs Palmer and Morrison rushed him to hospital...and operated for appendicitis. He did very well and returned home at the end of two weeks.

The Manager of the local theatre entertained our children on 16th.

Friday August 27th. the last day of the holidays we had a big night ice cream and games on the lawn. During the holidays we varied the diet as much as possible and served ice cream several times for supper. August 28th. the pupils returned from holidays; they were prompt and in good spirits. Some new pupils arrived two and three weeks ahead of time. Some children were even left without papers and had to be sent home.

Monday August 30th. all departments were re-opened in proper order.

August 31st. Mr. Rogers took 12 boys by truck to Toronto Exhibition. These boys had done particularly well during the holidays and spent a very happy and instructive day, witnessing the Grand Stand Performance at its close.

1st. September a car of coal was unloaded on this day and two other were handled during the month.

...September 9th. Mr. Williams of the Department and Colonel Morgan visited the school...

Holiday Improvements. All plaster through-out the building has been patched and the school-rooms and sewing room re-painted...The girls lavatory and dressing room was whitewashed and repainted. Most of this work was done by the girls, men, of course attending to the ceiling and other high work...

28. 31 December 1926 Rogers Quarterly Report

Health. On the whole this has been particularly good with but two exceptions. **** has spent several weeks in bed. He gives a history of falling some two years ago but the Doctor cannot diagnose his case although we have him repeatedly examined. A small girl developed eryseplis.

Discipline This has been good but we found it necessary to dismiss **** and **** as they were guilty of several serious breaches of discipline. Although they were senior girls they were actually teaching younger girls to steal and

behave dishonourably.

Notes...The Daughters of the Empire presented a picture of Brant by Romney.

The pupils gave accounts of various incidents in Brant's life and sung patriotic songs.

October 12th. we engaged Miss Hooper as housekeeper. She is a certified teacher and has also a dietician's course.

The large supply of sheets procured from the D.S.C.R. are worn out and we have had to purchase new.

November 2nd. Dr. Palmer visited and made a general examination of the children.

The Teachers Convention was on November 4th. and 5th. ...the boys cleaned up the farm buildings and the girls worked out on the lawns and in the flower beds.

November 9th. Mr Standing inspected the Class room work.

November 18th. Mr. and Mrs Rogers with **** visited her sister **** at the Hamilton Sanitarium.

On Armistice Day our Girl Guides and the boys were present at the Cenotaph Service...we had some lovely Chrysanthemums and two lovely sprays were placed on the memorial...

Mr. Orr visited on December 9th.

On December 27th Miss Hardie and **** visited **** in Hamilton.

December 31st. Discharged Mr. Smith and engaged Mr. Thurlow temporarily.

The boys have new heavy serge uniforms and caps to match. Both boys and girls have received a new issue of winter shoes, underwear and socks or stockings.

The Dining Hall equipment has been partly renewed.

Amusements. October 1st. Twenty-eight of the senior boys went to Ohsweken Fair by motor truck.

Hallowe'en was celebrated in the usual way and on Thanksgiving Day most of the boys were nutting.

During the Christmas Shopping season all the pupils visited town and saw the various displays under the supervision of officers.

We held our Christmas concert on 22nd December and the pupils were a credit to those responsible for their training.

Many gifts were received for Christmas from the local stores and friends. Santa Claus arrived on time on the 24th. and everyone had a very happy time. Special meals were prepared for the Christmas Day and very pretty effects were obtained by using red candy baskets and napkins for the tables. The weather during the...week was ideal and we had good sleighing and skating.

All the children were entertained at the local Picture Theatre...

...On November 8th the boys had a special holiday to acknowledge their very good work in handling the harvest...

29. 31 March 1927 Rogers Quarterly Report
Health. We have been most fortunate in escaping several epedemics that have occurred in Brantford. There have been no serious cases and but a few sore throats and colds. The only exception was that of **** who stayed in bed for a period without the Doctor discoverring any cause. The boy is, however, about again.
Discipline. We have had several breaches of discipline during the quarter which reflect mostly upon Mr. Smith who was discharged from the position of Boys Master on January 1st. We discovered that he was not sincere in his dealings with the boys and they naturally resented his practices. However, I was able to secure the services of Mr. Thurlow, who had been with us for two and a half years and soon matters were smoothed out and the boys made happy again. With the mild weather this spring three girls absconded but were hastily returned by their parents. We refused to re-accept one girl as she had a very bad record and we found that she was a ring-leader in many of our troubles.
Staff...Miss Allen has been most unwell but has stayed on duty and has developed into a very reliable and efficient officer.
On February 19th. Mrs Persall, who had been wretched for some time, went into the Hamilton Hospital and was operated upon twice...She has been with us some years and as her work is so satisfactory we kept her on full salary and her duties were taken over by Mrs Rogers and other members of the staff. The senior girls also helped by taken charge of the sewing room...
Notes. January 1st was a school holiday. The girls went to the Tutela Skating Rink in the morning and the dinner and supper that day were quite elaborate feasts.
School re-opened January 3rd.
On January 12th. Mr Rogers, Mrs Persall and three girls attended funeral of ****. The school wreath was the only floral token.
January 29th. Miss McNicoll took a large party of girls to the local Cinema.
March 8th. Mr Standing inspected the Class-rooms.
March 18th. The kitchen stove collapsed but the officers responsible for that department rose to the emergency and kept the meals on time in a most satisfactory manner...
The small girls have been busy making rag-rugs for bed-rooms and we were able to sell one or two for the benefit of the radio fund.

30. 30 June 1927 Rogers Quarterly Report
Health. We have had very few cases of sickness. In April there was a slight epidemic of Chicken-pox but this was confined to the girls.
Discipline On the whole this has been very good but early in the term we had a few cases of truancy as is usual at that time of the year. Two of the pupils who tried their Entrance Examinations have been troublesome during their term at the School so their parents were told that they would have to assume responsibility for them should they be successful.
Notes. April 5th...The Salvation Army Band visited the school and rendered a delightful concert after which the senior boys entertained them to light refreshments.
April 18th...Easter Monday was spent in fishing and outdoor sports.
May 4th...two boys Montour were allowed to visit their dying father they returned after the funeral and have since tried their Entrance Examination.
About this time we were able to successfully bid on the uniforms of the Cadet Corps of the Brantford Collegiate and were thus enabled for a very small sum to purchase next winters' clothing for our boys.
May 16th. We had a very serious stoppage of the sewers. After some trouble we discovered some small girls had dropped a book into a toilet.
The Pictures of the Confederation period were very much appreciated by the Staff and pupils. These have been put away and are to be framed by the boys next winter.
May 25th. the Remembrance Chapter I.O.D.E. paid their yearly visit and presented prizes.
June 14th. Mr Phelan...arrived to audit accounts.
June 17th. Mr. Orr visited to inspect the barn in bad condition.
Five girls and two boys wrote their Entrance Examination.
On June 29th we held our Closing Exerises and the prizes were distributed. Each pupils received a Confederation Medal on this occassion.
June 30th. School closed leaving 35 girls and 31 boys...
Grounds...are cared for by Mrs Rogers and the girls...Our grounds are a continual source of comment and congratulations as they have been a blaze of colour since the earliest blooms...

31. 30 September 1927 Rogers Quarterly Report
Discipline. The pupils returned promptly, on the whole and settled down to school work very well. Those who remained during the holidays behaved in a most satisfactory manner.
Health. Several girls who had been causing anxiety were examined at the local Tubercular Clinic...Several children have had to attend the dentist or oculist. We had an epidemic of summer grippe but the most severe cases were only sick two or three days.
Clothing. The boys were issued with new overalls and scout hats whilst the girls received new shoes and aprons.
Notes. On July 1st. those pupils remaining for the holiday attended a big Civic and Military Parade in the morning and went to the Tatoo and Firework Display in the evening. We heard the Dedication of the Carillon over the Radio perfectly.
July 4th. The pupils attended the local Industrial Exhibition.

July 6th. We chartered a street car and the pupils toured Brantford.

July 7th. The Girls were shown over the Kitchen overall factory.

During the holidays many treats were provided for remaining pupils in the form of ice cream suppers visits to parks, motor rides and local shows.

July 29th. Mr. Orr visited...with regard to new barn...

August 8th. The management of the Temple Theatre arranged for a programme free for the pupils.

August 10th. Chartered street car for children to make rounds of city.

32. 31 December 1927 Rogers Quarterly Report

<u>Discipline</u>   There have been no serious breaches of discipline during the quarter.

<u>Health</u>. With the exception of ****, who is in hospital suffering from diabetes, we have had no sickness at all...

<u>Clothing</u>. Winter clothing has been issued and the boys provided with rubber boots and the girls had an issue of new high shoes.

<u>Notes</u>...October 8th. Mr. MacKenzie and Colonel Morgan paid us a short visit, and Mr. Orr was here on the 12th.

On October 16th. Lord and Lady Willingdon opened the new Hospital at Ohsweken. We took a representative party of our Girl Guides and the boys who were inspected by their Excellencies...His Excellency decided to visit the Old Mohawk Church...when the party arrived a number of our girls were on hand as a Guard of Honour. Our Girl Guides were delighted to be presented to Lady Willingdon who is their Canadian Chief.

December 1st. Mr. and Mrs Rogers visited Toronto Wholesale houses making purchase of clothing, equipment and presents for the Christmas Tree.

<u>Amusements.</u> We had our Annual Sports Day on October 11th. It was a wonderfully fine day and the children had a great deal of fun.

On November 7th. the children held a barn dance in the New Barn. The Radio was moved into the barn and five loud speakers were attached.   As reception was particularly good the children were well provided with music.

Our electrician kindly loaned us two or three hundred feet of wire with coloured globes attached and the barn was a very gay...A large number of neighbours came in and all helped to make the evening a riot of pleasure for the children.

Thanksgiving Day...nineteen of the boys were granted leave for the day. Most...visited the scene of the local Militia manoeuvres...that the Principal was commanding the local Artillery Brigade added...a deal to their interest.

On December 23rd. The Trinity Church Choir presented a delightful concert after which the Principal attired as Santa Claus officiated at the Christmas tree. Owing to the fact that kind friends had sent sufficient gifts all the smaller and poorer children awoke on Christmas morning to find that Santa Claus had visited their stocking. The Brant Theatre very kindly entertained the whole school on the 24th. to a showing of Rin.Tin.Tin.

On December 25th. the Dining Room was very gaily decorated and the supper was quite a function for the staff had arranged the tables with gay napkins, coloured candy baskets, fruit and cakes.

The usual Christmas Dinner was served on Monday. During the first days of the holiday the pupils had much pleasure with their sleighs but unfortunately a thaw came and they had to resort to their games and indoor amusements.

Farm and Garden...Many of the girls were out daily gathering leaves and protecting the flower beds for winter. Our Chrysanthemums were very poor this year and our apple crop was not as large as usual...

<u>Improvements</u>. At a very small cost we have built a workroom in the attic which is most useful since all minor repairs can be effected there and hobby instruction can be given.

33. 31 March 1928 Rogers Quarterly Report

Mrs. Huffman resigned to be replaced by Mrs Hamilton as assistant housekeeper.

Mr. Thurlow left March 31st.

<u>Health</u>. Although several of the Staff have been off duty on account of sickness the health of the pupils has been wonderfully good. We have very fortunately avoided the epedemics which have been rather severe in town. **** was operated on at the Ohsweken Hospital and had her tonsils removed as also did ****. **** was in bed several days with pleurisy and as we were concerned about his slow recovery we had him examined and found he was in need of Sanitorium treatment.

We had several cases of rash none of which were at all alarming.

<u>Discipline</u>.   On the whole this has been good but considerable difficulty was met in keeping the boys attending the Collegiate in order. They resent discipline and in some cases are not studying. All have been severely warned that it will be necessary to leave the Institute unless a better example is set the smaller boys.

<u>Notes</u>. January 1st. was celebrated with special meals and a holiday.

January 2nd. School re-opened and those girls who had been on extra duty during the holidays were sent to the Theatre.

January 4th. Mr. and Mrs Rogers motored to the Reserve delivering Christmas gifts. and on the 12th. we visited **** in the Brantford Hospital.

January 30th. The Principal went to Paris to purchase boys clothing and the Tutela Women's Institute visited...

February 2nd.   We transferred **** to the Lady Willingdon Hospital...We found the Hospital sadly in need of help as there had been an unexpected rush of patients and so we left Marjorie Hill, who has passed the Entrance and is taking special domestic training to help. During the period she stayed there she became quite useful in caring for the small baby and taking temperatures and making dressings. We also brought home the sheeting and pillow cases that were not made and our girls volunteered to work during play hours to make these and wash them ready for use.

February Dr. and Mrs Davis had lunch here and took home all the linen we had ready for them.

February 8th. We visited Paris to see a demonstration of Gyptex, and permanent wall finish.

February 10th. The pupils and the Staff were entertained by the local Kiwanis Jollies.

February 12th. Mr. Thurlow went to Ohsweken to deliver Linen and several purchases we had made in town for the Hospital.

February 17th. Mr. Phelan and Father Mackay visited.

February 24th. Mr. VanLoon and Mr. Winger...visited.

34.   30 June 1928   Rogers Quarterly Report

Discipline. This has been quite up to standard...

Health. The health of the pupils has been exceptionally good. There have been, however, a number of spring colds which have been difficult to control.

Staff. Mr. Thurlow left April 2nd. and Mr. Raynor, a returned man...was engaged in his place...On April 29th. Mrs Hamilton, junior housekeeper, was taken seriously ill...She was unable to return and Miss Smith who was engaged in her place collapsed at the end of a week. Mrs. Harrington was engaged on May 5th. and is proving quite satisfactory.

Clothing. The usual changes in clothing for this season were carried out. The boys receiving new overalls and the girls made themselves new issues of aprons.

Notes. On April 4th. the kitchen stove collapsed. We have had considerable trouble and expense with this stove for some time and the quickest replacement was by gas. We have had great satisfaction since replacement and are able to cook all meals for fifty eight cents per diem.

April 5th. Major and Mrs Rogers went to Toronto making purchases.

April 26th. A class from Wesly Church Sunday school gave the pupils a very interesting evening...

May 5th. We had two pupils who had been inmates of Hamilton Sanitarium and as we had to go to Hamilton on business we took them to visit there.

May 17th. All pupils were taken to witness Circus procession and a number of pupils went to the afternoon performances.

Pupils had holiday after service on Good Friday and Easter Monday. The boys were all busy fishing and made some fine catches. Good Friday was exceptionally hot and a large number of the senior girls attended the three hour service held at St. Judes.

May 24th was a holiday for the pupils and some of the staff...**** broke his finger whilst playing. This had to be X-rayed and was a very difficult case to set. Daily visits to the Doctor were necessary but the finger is now healed and doing well.

In the evening...Major Bush and Mr. Chubb arrived and stayed several days making a very thorough inspection.

May 25th.   The Archbishop of Huron arrived for Confirmations the following day on the Reserve and here.

Activities   On April 10th the girls were able to uncover flower beds and generally clean them up. The following day the storm windows were removed and cleaning commenced. During April the girls made a number of rag rugs.

The City of Brantford...gave us the broken sidewalks... These have been laid...from the school to the gate to make better going...and to avoid the lawns being ruined. This has also made a great improvement in appearances.

Notes continue. All the pupils attended the Brantford Industrial Exhibit, as guests of the local Board of Trade.

June 20th. The Elected Six Nations Council visited in a body and had a most interesting time...

We took the gardener and some boys to plant up the flower beds at the Lady Willingdon Hospital.

35.   31 October 1928   Rogers Quarterly Report

Staff. Mr. F. Hughes who has been with us as cattleman for some years left to manage a farm...and Mr. Howard was engaged to fill the vacancy.

Owing to the small number of boys remaining here for the holidays and the pressure of work it was necessary to engage Mr Lunday as extra help.

Discipline. On the whole this has been very satisfactory. This is due in part to the fact that the parents and friends of the pupils are showing a much more friendly attitude towards the school. We find much more co-operation now than we had before.

Notes. School closed on July 14th. for six weeks and we had only forty pupils remain. Most of these were small and it was necessary to hire some of the bigger boys in order to maintain the farm work. All pupils remaining were able to have an enjoyable holiday. It was necessary for all to work part of the time but this work was interspersed with visits to the Cinema, to the Park and the River. While at other times they were given truck rides and minor treats.

School opened in a most disappointing fashion. Had all returned who were expected and the new pupils reported promptly we should have had a full school, but this year there seemed to be a shortage of money amongst the Indians and only those who were near at hand were able to send the children in at the proper time. Several pupils were in the States, five asked for sick leave and others were kept in the berry fields until such time as sufficient money could be earned to pay the return fares.

On August 27th. the Principal and Mrs Persall took a party of pupils who had behaved so splendidly during the holidays to Niagara Falls. This was a most pleasant and instructive day and in addition to the natural sights arrangements were made for the whole party to be shown over the big Chippawa Hydro plant. Lunch was served in Victoria Park and although we had a very strenuous day we all returned home feeling we had had a wonderful day.

August 29th. Mrs Rogers took four girls to the Lady Willingdon Hospital for examination.

September 4th. Three boys started the Fall term at the Collegiate and we were able to find homes for several girls who had passed the Entrance Examination. In the case of the girls we find it much more satisfactory to place them in homes where they may earn a little pocket money than to keep them here and allow them to attend the Collegiate. They have to leave the School early and cannot possibly return before 4.30 or 5.00 p.m. and we find better results are obtained when a girl is so placed that she has to spend her noon hours occupied.

On September 7th. Major and Mrs Rogers left for a holiday during which eight schools were visited.

On September 27th. and 28th. the school for the first time placed some stock on exhibit and the Ohsweken Fair. Our boys were very proud of the results and we were glad to notice the good effect on the school morale. The classroom exhibits were also of a very fine quality.

On September 28th. **** was taken to Hamilton to appear in Court in connection with an assault committed against her during the holidays and whilst in her Mother's care. We lent every assistance in the prosecution of this case and a conviction was secured. It was a matter of satisfaction to us to find the girls mother so willing to take action in this case as unfortunately the Indian mother is inclined to be callous on the question of the daughter's morals.

September 29th. Mr. MacKenzie, Colonel and Mr. Fairchild visited. The Newport Women's Institute visited the school and were entertained to tea. This organisation has been very actively interested in some neglected Indian Children in the school.

Clothing. The girls have been issued with smart new caps of blue, piped with black, with the school badge...

36. 31 December 1929 Rogers Quarterly Report
Discipline. There have been no serious breaches of discipline during the quarter and the fact that our boys have attained some prominence and distinction locally as runners has had a very marked effect upon the boys' general attitude. The girls worked some very nice badges for the boys running suits and every boy running under the school colours is very proud of the ovation the crowd always gives them...this has a most desirable effect in fostering school pride.

Health...we have escaped with only minor sickness. Several of the staff, however, have been sick.

Clothing The usual seasonable changes have been made and new shoes issued.

Notes...October 2nd. Two pupils were taken to Ohsweken Hospital and were operated upon for adenoids and tonsils. Several others who had given us cause for concern were examined and treatments given.

On October 4th. the Church was decorated by the girls for the Harvest Thanksgiving services.

October 19th. Major and Mrs Rogers visited Toronto to purchase supplies.

The School Inspector was here October 25th.

October 31st. All Hallows Eve was celebrated by the pupils with the usual frolics and fun.

His Excellency the Governor General visited officially on November 3rd. and he pronounced the following Monday to be a school holiday.

November 8th. Mr. Phelan...conducted an audit.

November 9th. and 10th. the local teachers held convention; on those two days we threshed.

November 11th. A Community Service was held at the Cenotaph. This was attended by all the Militia Units and every organisation in Brantford. Our pupils were also present and made a very creditable appearance.

November 23rd. The Douglas Seed Company presented the school with a large quantity of imported bulbs which Mrs Rogers and the girls were able to plant in time for Spring flowering.

December 7th. All hands were busy unloading a car of coal.

December 8th...a notable day for the boys. The local newspaper sponsored a Road Race for Indians and there were Five prizes. Present pupils secured three of these and a boy who has recently left won another. This was run over a [7½] mile course against fifty two competitors, of which only 27 finished. Of our thirteen entries there were none who did not finish. Since the Race, the proprietor has presented each entrant with a medal...

December 21st. The children began to decorate for Christmas.

On the 22nd. we had very few relatives visit owing to the bad condition of the roads. All the pupils were taken to town at least once before Christmas.

Santa Claus arrived...and every child had a gift.

On Christmas Day a special service was conducted by the Principal and a most happy day followed. The Dining Hall was very gay and a special feast was prepared for every meal. In the evening we had a large masquerade party and there were many weird costumes improvised.

The pupils were the guests of Mr. Ernie Moule of the local Theatre during Christmas week.

Owing to the kindness of several merchants and friends we were well supplied with fruit and candies.

37. 31 March 1929 Rogers Quarterly Report

<u>Discipline</u>...no serious breaches of discipline apart from the bad influence of ****. He has proved incorrigible and shown a very bad influence. He persistently absconded and always took weaker boys with him.

<u>Health.</u> All the staff had suffered from the epedemic of "La Grippe"...and in most cases were off duty for several days. As we restricted visiting the pupils...were not exposed and we had very few cases amongst them. **** suffered from a bad abscess which required medical attention. **** who was attending the Collegiate and holding a position in town broke her wrist. We have had her in residence but arranged for her to enter service during the Easter Holidays. ****, a diabetic case, complained of a cold and was ordered to bed on January 24th. She was found in a state of coma the following morning and stimulants were administered pending the arrival of the Doctor...she was removed to the hospital and died there. Four pupils attended the dentist and two received treatment from an occulist.

<u>Staff.</u> Mrs Harrington did not recover from the attack of "flu" and resigned. Her post was filled by Miss Gilmour. Mr. John Henderson ceased as an active member of the staff at the beginning of the quarter. Mr. R. Howarth resigned in order to take a course in field engineering...

The Principal, Miss Hardie and Mr. R. Howarth attended **** funeral. Ten pupils were in attendance as pall bearers.

February 20th. Mr. Schuyler who inspected the school farm...in 1918 called on business. He was very much impressed with the improvements in all departments connected with the farm.

Mr. Standing...spent a day in the class-rooms.

A new organ was bought for the services out of contributions received for displaying the Queen Anne bible and silver.

<u>Amusements.</u> January 1st. Miles Isaacs ran eighth in a ten mile Road Race against the pick of Ontario. March 20th. the 91st. Highlanders of Hamilton staged an Indoor-Track meet and for our special benefit a race for Indian boys was run. Miles again led his school chums and was only a few seconds longer in covering the two miles than Pavlo Nurmi. We secured every prize offerred in this race.

March 29th. The Principal and two of the staff took Miles and Norman Lickers to Toronto where Miles ran second in a six miles race and Norman secured the first Junior in a three mile run.

On February 8th. the pupils were the guests of the Kiwanis Club at a matinee performance.

Our senior girls have joined the Lady Willingden Hospital Auxiliary and devote an evening once bi-weekly to making necessaries for the Hospital. They entered a competition sponsored by the W.C.T.U. and we secured several good prizes.

38. 21 May 1929 McLean to Rogers

...The Department is desirous of learning if the older girls at the Mohawk Indian Residential School are being trained in milking cows. As most of the graduates of your school will return to reserves that are largely farming communities, it is very important that the girls be fully competent in this particular. The Department expects that the older girls, under proper supervision, will be given a course of instruction in milking, and I shall be pleased to learn that suitable arrangements have been made.

39. 23 May 1929 Phelan to Scott

...I visited...on the 20th and 21stt...interviewed Mr. Rogers ...regarding the reports that had reached the Department in connection with (a) purchase of farm by Principal and (b) rumours regarding Principal's intemperance.

(a) Purchase of farm by Principal.

Mr. Rogers informed me that, about six weeks ago, he purchased a farm adjoining the Mohawk Institute farm. There are eighty-eight acres of land with a good house and barn. He has already purchased eleven saddle horses and it is his intention to conduct a riding school - as a matter of fact, he has already started and several residents of Brantford have arranged with him to receive riding instruction regularly. On the second day of my visit, (May 21st), he hired a man to conduct the riding school.

About fifty (50) acres of this farm is being cultivated - the seed for this, Mr. Rogers states, has been supplied by himself while the labour from the school (both employees and pupils), as well as school farm machinery and teams, has been used...it was his intention to allow the school one half the proceeds to the crop raised on the acreage cultivated on his farm. He appeared to be of the opinion that this was a profitable arrangement for the school.

From a departmental point of view, I believe that the ownership and the cultivation of the Principal's farm in the manner stated presents very serious difficulty - (1) Principal not devoting his whole time to supervision of school; (2) use of school equipment and school labour, especially the Indian boys, on land owned by the Principal is likely to cause unfavourable criticism and (3) possible profits very problematical. I pointed out this attitude to Mr. Rogers and, while he agreed with me that the proposition is open to the objections just stated, he still seemed convinced that the financial benefit accruing to the school would offset the disadvantages of the scheme.

We discussed the whole matter for some time and visited the farm and I informed Mr. Rogers that the matter would be placed before you for your decision.

(b) Rumours regarding Principal's intemperance.

Mr. Rogers stated quite candidly that he had been arrested on May 3rd on a charge of being under the influence of liquor while in charge of a car. The case has not yet come to trial owing to the absence of Mr. Rogers' doctor, but Mr. Rogers was very emphatic in assuring me that there was no doubt about his innocence. His explanation of the incident is that he had been under the doctor's care for some time and was troubled with insomnia. On the day in question, he had been around the country with two friends in connection with the purchase of horses for his farm. At about three o'clock in the afternoon, they reached a certain farm where the two friends got out of the car and went in, presumably to look at horses. Mr. Rogers remained in the car and says he fell asleep. The County Constable came along and arrested him and Mr. Rogers claims that personal animosity on the part of the Constable prompted this action. He was taken to the police station but was allowed out within two hours.

The Indian Superintendent, Colonel Morgan, appears convinced that Mr. Rogers is frequently using liquor to excess and, as a consequence, is not a proper person to be in charge of the school. At Colonel Morgan's request I had a short talk with (1) Rev. Mr. Owens, (2) County Constable Blakely and (3) Chief of Police of Brantford. Mr. Owens is the Anglican clergyman who attends the Mohawk Institute and he was of the same opinion as Colonel Morgan. The County Constable claimed that Mr. Rogers was drinking to excess, but...I was not very favourably impressed with this man. The Chief of Police stated that, while he had never seen Mr. Rogers under the influence of liquor nor had any charge been previously laid against him, still many rumours had reached him and he felt that Mr. Rogers was not altogether the proper party for the position of Principal of the Mohawk Institute. I had a confidential talk with the Manager of the Bank... where the school account is kept, and he had not heard any serious reports regarding Mr. Rogers' drinking and was unaware of the fact that he had been arrested on May 3rd. I did not inform Mr. Rogers of the above interviews. Financial Condition:

The school finances appear to be improving and...an endeavour is being made to reduce the expenditure...

Mr. Rogers estimated that the expenditures for the balance of the quarter will not exceed $3000. The receipts will be about $2,200., ($1,800 balance of grant and $400 from sale of farm produce). On this basis, there would be a deficit of approximately $1,800 at the end of the present quarter...an improvement.

...some of the hogs have been sold but the team of horses has not yet been disposed of as the Principal stated that he has been unable to secure a purchaser at the price he considers the team is worth.

Including the school farm and the glebe farm, approximately one hundred and ninety-nine acres have been planted, while it is intended to plant sixteen acres more as soon as the latter is sufficiently dry to work.

There are one hundred and twenty-five pupils in the school (71 girls and 54 boys), and all of them are in good health.

40. 28 May 1929 Scott to Rogers

I have before me the report of the officer whom I sent to investigate certain matters pertaining to your conduct as Principal of the Mohawk Institute.

In this report it is stated that some six weeks ago you purchased a farm of 88 acres adjoining the Institute farm, and further that you have undertaken the establishment of a riding school. I need hardly say that these activities are quite incompatible with your status as a full time employee of the department as the responsible head and principal of one of our most important Indian Residential Schools.

You did not think it necessary to advise me of your intention to engage in other employment so that I feel quite free to make arrangements for the future conduct of the Mohawk Institute, as the duties and responsibilities of the position which you occupy require the entire attention of the incumbent.

I note, moreover, that you have been using school equipment and school labour on your own farm land and that you actually utilized the services of employees and Indian pupils for this purpose. I must ask you to let me have a statement of these transactions showing the time spent and the value of the labour at a reasonable rate of wage in order that you may make compensation. You must cease immediately the employment of any equipment or manual labour from the Institute.

I have to advise you that it will be necessary to arrange for the appointment of a new Principal and Assistant Principal at an early date.

41. 29 May 1929 Mrs. Rogers to Scott

We received your letter to-day with deep regret - Mr Rogers has put in several of the best years of his life in the interest of the school - and I have done two persons work for years.

I regret very much the attitude you have taken - with me the Mohawk always comes first and I have put in many years of overtime labor and thought to build up the school. As it is I can be proud to hand it over to a new staff. Dont think I want to take all the credit, but I must take all the blame.

Buying the farm was not premeditated - several English families have settled in the neighbourhood - and we were looking for a location for another friend - he did not buy and it looked to me too good an opportunity to miss. One reason the Mohawk farm does not pay is that there is not land enough. After my purchase in April - the flood covered the property for some weeks. A good deal of the farm is in fall wheat and hay - the Cockshutt Plow Company of which my nephew is sales manager - plowed by tractor the greater part of the remaining land. The middle of March the school ploughed what remained and sewed oats. The school has not touched the fencing. The foreman has kept strict account of all labor - the school to have half the crop - which is more than the usual rate around here. Full reports of actions taken will be in the next quarterly return.

When General Ashton was here last we told him of plan - and asked him to talk the matter over with you - he thought it might not meet with your approval - your wife's death I'm sure made him forget our little plan.

We have not moved the old people off the farm - and a man is managing the care and letting out of the ponies and horses. It is possible a limited stock Company will be formed to manage the riding school when it is built.

When we first bought the farm Mr Rogers thought of sending in his resignation at once - but I thought as the properties adjoin we would be more in the place than usual - we will not be taking afternoons away or any holidays.

Our trip west last Fall gave us many pointers as to the management of other schools - we do not think the Old Mohawk took second place to any of the eight we visited ...we do more in the way of painting wood-work and beds and keeping furniture repaired than any school we saw.

I'm sure Mr. Phelan found the school and grounds in good order - the stables and herd have never been better, the pupils health good and everything running smoothly.

I am sorry we did not write you earlier, but Mr Rogers hates office work and letter writing - and I'm only writing now to explain our view point as I'm sure he will not - I would have liked to remain here a few years longer - You know I lost most of my money during the war - and we could have gradually altered stables - put in electric lights, a furnace, plumbing etc that the house requires - but please be assured that while here we will carry on - and do our best of help our successor -

42. 2 June 1929 Rogers to Scott

...I feel greatly surprised that your inspecting officer should have made any report that would prompt the attitude taken.

One of the chief reasons for purchasing the farm you refer to was that we would enable the Institute farm to make a better showing this year.

I think I would not be asking too much to be allowed to see a copy of the officer's report since I was certainly under the impression that he was convinced of the fairness and the wisdom of the activities to which you take exception. The matter of using school equipment was fully explained and I am sure the Mohawk Institute has by far the better end of the bargain.

Further points in your letter are noted and action is being taken.

Personally, I feel that after devoting the most important ten years of my life to the developement of "one of your most important Residential Schools" your attitude does not impress me that my work has been appreciated.

43. 6 June 1929 SIX NATIONS COUNCIL MEETING
C.E. Morgan

...Moved by Wm. Smith seconded by Ambrose Hill that the following address be presented to Miss Susan Hardy...at Ohsweken on Thursday the 27th inst.

We as members of the Council of the Six Nations... desire to take this opportunity to extend to you our most sincere appreciation and to gratefully acknowledge the inestimable services rendered by you to our people who have had the privilege of being pupils of the Mohawk Institute. This institution, which has accomplished so much for our people, is to be congratulated on having on its staff so competent and conscientious an instructor as you have always been and one who has held the esteem and affection of all who have come in contact with you as pupils. And not alone on our reserve are you estimable qualities appreciated but we know that at other reserves where ex-pupils of the Mohawk Institute reside you are held in grateful remembrance...Carried.

No. 18. The Council voted the sum of $25.00 for the purpose of presenting Miss Hardie with a chair.

44. 18 June 1929 Scott to Mrs. Rogers

...You must understand that it would be only with extreme regret and under real necessity that I should ask for the resignation of your husband and yourself. I have not been very well satisfied with his administration of the Institute and the recent events made it impossible to postpone the change which had been in my mind for some time.

I beg to acknowledge fully your own very excellent services in the interests of the Institute. One reason which made it difficult for me to decide was the old association of your family with the school and your own good record.

I have arranged for successors to Mr. Rogers and yourself and wrote him the other day stating that I would accept your resignations as of the 1st. August. I note in your letter...you state that when you first bought the farm Mr. Rogers thought of sending in his resignation at once.

45. 24 June 1929 Scott to Mathews

...it has been found necessary to ask for the resignation of Mr. and Mrs. S. Rogers...For some time, I have not been at all satisfied with the administration of the School, but matters were abruptly brought to a head a few weeks ago by an extraordinary action on the part of Mr. Rogers. Without giving me any intimation of his intention, he purchased a farm adjoining the Institute and commenced the operation of a riding school on this property...he had even presumed to use the labour of pupils of the Institute and the staff on this farm.

As the importance of the work and the amount of detail which is involve in the management of the Institute is quite sufficient to absorb the energy of the principal, it was impossible to allow this dual arrangement...an immediate change was essential. I...communicated with

...Archbishop Williams...and asked him to nominate a priest in Holy Orders for the Principalship...recommended Reverend H. W. Snell, B.A., Rector of St. Paul's Church, Stratford...I was...glad to approve of his selection..

I have had an interview with Mr. Snell. He is 49 years of age, was born in Canada and brought up on a farm. He has had experience in teaching and in other ways appears well qualified for his new duties. His wife will be the matron...

46. 30 June 1929 Rogers Quarterly Report.

<u>Church</u>...May 26th, we were able to attend service at the church for the first time this year...The girls wore their new blue cloth uniforms and caps and looked very smart.
<u>Discipline</u> Very little trouble. Tom Loft absconded twice - brought back each time by the Mounted Police. Two girls also ran away - the first in years - were rounded up the same day in Hamilton and returned by the Mounties.
<u>Health.</u> Good - several minor accidents and sore eye cases.
<u>Staff.</u> Mr Robert Hawarth left April 15th and Mr Alexander engaged - Mr. Howard left April 30th - and Mr Hughes formerly on the staff was re-engaged.
<u>Notes</u> April 1st - Easter Monday - holiday - very windy and floods were high. Fortunately we had plenty of magazines and games.
April 9th - Mrs Murray Smith gave children an interesting lantern lecture on bulb growing.
May 2nd Dr Palmer vaccinated 80
May 3rd Doctor finished vaccinations - 108 in all of which 99 successfully took...
May 17th Inspectors of Mounted Police visited
May 20th Mr Phelan...looked over place and books...
During May we had all the pianos and organs overhauled
June 3rd - School division had holiday.
June 6th Commenced errection of large ornamental posts at front entrance - took several days to errect and paint...

The Lady Willingdon Chapter had a picnic at Mohawk Park - thirty of our girls and two teachers attended taking sandwiches.
June 11 - Rev Mr and Mrs Schnell went over school, re taking over the management.
June 12th - Inspector of Toronto Public Schools was most interested visitor praised every department.
June 24th - pupils were able to wear summer uniforms - which had all been refitted.
<u>School Activities</u> - Washing and storing away winter clothing - blankets etc. - washing number of pillows - altering and making summer uniforms.

Girls had new issue of hats from England - two issues of new aprons and one of underwear - and new school shoes. Boys new work shoes - two issues of shirts - overalls and belts.

June 27th Mr Rogers barn burned - boys helped firemen put it out - only brick wall & silo remaining...

June 27th Mr Phelan arrived - took inventory...
A picnic was given by the Council at Ohsweken in honor of Miss Hardie. We sent seventy pupils by truck and riding Mr Rogers horses. Miss Hardie was presented with an address by the Council - also one from the past pupils - and a chair. The pupils enjoyed the day - playing ball games and horse racing. They were well treated to sandwiches, cake and lemonade.

The Ontario Historical Society visited June 27th. Mr Phelan left June 29th having taken inventory of farm buildings - stock implements and greenhouse...

Early in April Mrs Rogers bought a farm of 88 acres adjoining the school intending to farm on half shares with the school. There was little ploughing to do and most of that was done by the Cockshutt Plow Co - The school ploughed about six acres...some harrowing and seeding...

The girls did all the work in the flower beds and grounds under Mrs. Rogers.

47. 22 June 1929 Mrs. Rogers to Governor NEC

We are severing - with regret - our connections with the Mohawk Institute, at the end of July.

May I beg to be placed on your pensions list. For many years I helped my parents with the management - care of the sick - class room work etc. without any salary. Then I took charge for one year when my brother had leave of absence.

During the war I lost most of my money in a railroad investment - so was glad to return to the school in 1918 as I could continue the care of my parents. I could have commanded a much larger salary in a hospital but that would have taken me away from Brantford. The school was in such a neglected condition that for four years it was work under a dreadful strain. Now I am proud to say we can hand the school over in as perfect condition as our funds would allow - a competent and contented staff - and healthy and happy children.

The school grounds and flower beds have never looked better. The Government Inspector who in 1918 said it would take at least ten years to build the farm up was here the other day and said he did not think we could have attained so much - he was sure there were not horses or cattle better cared for anywhere - and was full of praises for conditions all over the place.

1929 - 1945
Rev. Horace Snell 1929-1945

1. 4 October 1929 Snell Report for August & September
CHURCH Services have been held each Sunday at His Majesty's Chapel of The Mohawks. The historical interest of the Church attracts a considerable number of visitors. This is good for the pupils as it tends to add importance to their service. The visitors, too, invariably comment most favorably on the reverent attitude of the pupils and the beauty of the service. Chapel Services are held each day in the senior class-room, and the children seem to enjoy them. The readiness with which they respond to the call to chapel is very gratifying. Simple Bible talks are given by the Principal at each evening chapel. The only drawback is the lack of suitable Chapel. The school-room lacks atmosphere and one hundred and thirty-five pupils and teachers crowd the room very much.
DISCIPLINE. On the whole the pupils have been good. There was quite an epidemic of running away when I first took over but they seem to have settled down now that they have found out the reaction of the new Principal. A gratifying development has been the readiness of the pupils to cooperate in the prevention of absconding. Breaches of this rule are making the offender distinctly unpopular.

The most serious breach of discipline has been, also, a moral offence. There have been several instances of theft, most of them by two boys and one girl. Here, too, I have emphasised the harm done to their school and race. The scholars as a whole seem to have responded to this appeal, so that I was able to bring the last culprit, who happened to be the most persistent offender, to trial before his peers. He admitted his guilt and as a punishment was "put through the lines" and deprived of the trip to Ohsweken Fair.
HEALTH. The health of the school has been good...a mild epidemic of MUMPS. Three of the girls...were taken to Lady Willingdon Hospital for tonsilectomies. There are three pupils...receiving treatments for eye trouble...**** and **** suffered fractures of the forearm but are doing well.
STAFF There have been several changes in the staff. Mr. Raynor and Miss Gilmour left Jun 30, Miss Hooper had resigned on June 1, Miss Alleen left Sept 30, as did also Mr. Hughes. All of them resigned to take other positions except Mr. Hughes, whom I had to let go in pursuance of the policy of reducing the male staff. The new members are, The Principal and Matron, Assistant Matron & Nurse, Mrs. Smith; Junior Teacher, Miss MacBurney; Senior House-keeper, Mrs. Jones; Junior Housekeeper, Miss Johnson; Mechanic & Boys' Master, H. B. Jones. The engaging of a man who is a mechanic who can also assist on the farm and act as Boys' Master has abundantly justified itself in the saving of expensive

visits of mechanics from the city. He has more than saved his salary for us in this way...We had 8 women & 5 men on the staff during September. The Senior Junior Housekeepers are both graduates in Dietetics with practical experience.
NOTES...The children, 20 in number, who got no holidays were taken to Springbank Park for a holiday. They were specially interested in Zoo. The picnic was...reward for good behaviour and compensation for the loss of holiday.

A change in the diet from skimmed milk to whole was much appreciated by the pupils and should be good for their physical development.

A number of our boys competed in the races at Ohsweken Fair. Norman Lickers ran first in the five-mile bicycle race. A four year old colt from the farm prepared and exhibited by Harry Lickers was awarded second prize in the general purpose class. Four prizes were awarded to garden stuff...exhibited at the school fair. The whole school were guests at the Ohs. Fair.

We have 6 boys and 1 girl attending Collegiate from here. One other girl, ****, was removed by her parents after spending 16 days. They brought an order from Col. Morgan for her release. I was rather pleased as her removal made room for a needy case.
FARM AND GARDEN. Harvesting is all completed and threshing done. The yield was good considering the season. Our Oats were particularly good. I sold the wheat soon after threshing, realising $532.62 @ 1.30 per bushel. The garden has paid well, but we suffered a severe loss in tomatoes and peppers from the early frost which was most unusual. We estimate that we lost about $400.00. The late potatoes will be very poor owing to the very dry summer.

We have been unable to sell any of the horses...The old brood mare died a few days ago...she was too old to be of any use. Another old horse will have to be got rid of this fall...Two or three old cows will have to be sold.

2. 16 December 1929 Snell to Parents & Guardians
...I am sure you will be interested to hear of some of the doings of the Institute during the past term.

But first let me say how much I appreciate the co-operation of many of the parents in encouraging the children to good conduct and interest in their studies. Parents thus help much in the smooth running of the school and often save the pupil the trouble which must follow disobedience.

There are at present 132 pupils in the School, the largest attendance, I believe, in our history. There are 56 boys and 76 girls...

The conduct of the pupils shows a distinct improvement, and...compares favorably with that of any other school for boys and girls. The...School Inspector gave a very favorable report of the class-room work...

The health of the scholars has been good except for an epidemic of Measles and Chicken pox. There was one case of Infantile Paralysis, but it was taken in time and the boy is back in school with no bad effects. Clinics have been held to discover any defects of eyes throat or teeth, and pupils needing treatment have been, or will be treated.

We are planning to give the children as merry a Christmas as possible. The Christmas entertainment takes place on Dec. 18. The teachers, officers and pupils are working together to make it as enjoyable as they can. On Christmas Eve there will be a tree with presents for everyone, a dramatic club is coming out from the city to present a play on the 26th.; and two or three other entertainments are arranged for the holiday...the children have a jolly time ahead for the holiday.

...I shall be pleased to hear from you at any time I shall be especially glad to have you report to me anything your children may have criticized. We want them to be happy and contented here and if I know I can often remove a grievance and thus help to improve the conditions. Of course children often make unfounded complaints as you know but I shall see that any real or fancied wrongs are righted...I shall also be pleased to hear anything you may have to say in praise of our efforts to give the children a good education and to develope...good, honest Christian Characters.

3. 7 January 1930 Snell Quarterly Report
DISCIPLINE...improvement in the general conduct of the pupils. Absconding notably decreased, probably owing to the unfavourable season of the year. Nine boys left one morning, Nov.5, but three of them returned of their own accord the same evening while the rest were brought back the same night. One new girl tried to run away but was brought back by the other girls. Co-operation of this sort on the part of the pupils is very gratifying. The boys have not yet responded so well. We have had much less petty thieving than in last quarter owing...to a fairly strong public feeling against such offences, among the pupils.
HEALTH   The health of the pupils has been excellent. There has not been a single case of sickness. Twenty-two of the girls who...have diseased tonsils have been taken to Lady Willingdon Hospital for tonsilectomies...
STAFF.   I can not speak too highly of the hearty co-operation of the staff. I only hope I may be able to retain them all indefinitely. There have been no changes during the quarter...I have not required the services of a mechanic from the city once during the quarter. Mr. Jones has been able to make all necessary repairs. This means considerable saving to us.
Notes. The Institute is still well to the front in sports. In a team contest between Brantford and Guelph the first two to finish in a five-mile race were Norman Lickers and Miles Isaac, both pupils of the Institute. These two boys also won good places at the New Year's Meet at Hamilton. Norman was second in the three-mile race,

Junior, being beaten by a step only by the champion mile runner for Ontario. Miles was fifth in the open ten-mile. Other boys also ran well in both these events.

A very enjoyable Christmas was spent by all. The festivities included a Christmas concert which would have done credit to any group of children, a Christmas tree on Christmas Eve, a Comedy and a concert put on by friends from the city, as well as sleigh-rides for the girls and hunting-parties with the Boys' Master for the boys. One result of the hunting parties was that all the children were treated to a rabbit dinner on New Year's Day.

...for the first time in its history, I believe, the Church is taking an interest in the Institute. We have had a few bales, mainly Christmas presents candy etc. with some quilts and clothing. One Girls' W.A. of Grace Church here came down with 14 woollen blankets for pupils' beds. The Secretary for W.A. work among Indians in the Diocese together with a committee...visited the school and are recommending that the Branches contribute to the support of the Institute. I am hoping something may come from that source to help get on our feet...

4. 30 January 1930 Scott to Mathews
...reference to a proposal to sell the Mohawk Institute to the Department. While I am glad to hear from the Company in this connection, I regret that the Department is not in a position at present to make an offer...

I presume the Company's offer to pay the stipend of the Principal is in addition to the regular £1,000 per annum, which is payable under the current arrangement.
...this year, the Department hopes to complete the top storey on the boys' side and to take in twenty more pupils. The Reverend Mr. Snell...has had a very auspicious winter season...Next year, if an item can be provided in the Estimates, I propose to complete the rear wing by the addition of a chapel, etc.

5. 15 February 1930 Morgan to Ex-pupils
The Mohawk Institute having, last year, completed one hundred years of usefulness...Mr. Russell Ferrier, is writing its history which is to be embodied in next years annual report when issued by the Department.

He, therefore, desires me to ask ex-pupils and others interested to furnish short life sketches of ex-pupils who have proved examples of the beneficial teachings at the Institute by outstanding success in such paths of life as they have chosen either in the learned professions, in Military life, in school or on the farm.
...please forward me...any information and photographs in your possession likely to be of service...which will be numbered, registered and returned to you in good order.

It is felt that the people of the Six Nations cannot fail to regard this hundred years of Institute achievement and the outstanding Sons of the Band that it has fostered with pride and the Superintendent of Indian Education looks forward with confidence to the receipt of much useful and interesting information in consequence.

6. 4 April 1930 Snell Quarterly Report
CHURCH...Mr. T. G. Goldsmith has been coming weekly to train the children in singing and there is a noticeable improvement in the musical parts of the services...
DISCIPLINE. The conduct of the pupils as a whole has been good. A few have been in need of punishment, some of them several times, but the great body of them have behaved extremely well. The warm weather brought three or four cases of groups absconding but only one group were away over night. We had one case of a number of girls stealing food and one case of a boy stealing from another boy. He was dealt with by the boys themselves after trial and I doubt if he will repeat the offence. Several boys had to be punished for having catapults after being forbidden and the practice seems to be, at least, in abeyance.
HEALTH. The pupils have been in excellent health excepting two little girls who have swollen glands in the neck. It is hoped they will improve as soon as they can be taken to Lady Willingdon Hospital for tonsilectomies...
NOTES. The principal has been asked to address several organizations on the work of the Institute...Many of these have made or are to make contributions of books for the children's library. They are also given to understand something of what the Department is doing for their Indian wards and how worthwhile it is.
Myles Isaac again brought honour to the school when he stood second in a half-mile race at the Hamilton meet in competition with 43 entries.
The Public School Inspector visited and spoke favourably of the work being done.
A number of most enjoyable concerts were given for the children by city artists. They were also the guests on two occasions of the manager of the Temple Theatre.
A corps of Girl Guides has been organised under the leadership of Miss McBurney, the junior teacher and a keen interest is manifest. It should be a strong force for character building.

7. July 1930 Snell The Eagle
...There are at present 134 pupils in residence; 78 girls and 56 boys...of all ages, from 6 years to 18 years of age. Eight of them residing at the school while attending the Collegiate Institute in the city.
The pupils are drawn mainly from the Six Nations...a number from Moraviantown...Muncey...Bay of Quinte... Caughnawaga...a child must be an unenfranchised Indian. If he is of the Six Nations, the Principal has authority to accept him, but all other tribes and children "not on the list" must have their applications approved by the Department...The first claim upon the school is felt to be that of those who have no homes or worse. There are

probably about 25 of these. After that, pupils are admitted in order of applications as a rule. The financial position of the parents, unless they are very poor, is not taken into consideration. The parents of several of the children are quite well off.
The course taught is partly academic and partly industrial, the aim being to give them a good practical equipment for making a good living. The scholars are divided into two divisions "A" and "B". Each division is in school for one-half of each day, while the other division is engaged in the practical occupations of the house, farm or garden...a staff of twelve besides the Principal. The two school teachers are Normal graduates. One of them, Miss Hardie, is herself an Indian, who received her education at the Institute, and has almost completed her 42nd year as teacher there. Her knowledge of the pupils and her good influence over them are invaluable. The other officers are: Nurse, Sewing Teacher, two Dietitians, both of whom are graduates of MacDonald Institute, Guelph, the other of an English school, the Boys' Master and Mechanic, Farmer, Teamster and Gardener. All the officers are expected to train the pupils in their respective departments of work.
...to give all a complete training, the pupils pass regularly from one department to another. One half change each week. This gives each pupil two weeks at each kind of work at a time. In the course of a number of years they have been many times through the whole round, but at no time are they kept at one thing until it becomes monotonous. The work is light, as many hands make light work. For example: in the cattle barn each milker has to milk and clean off two cows and his task is done.
In temperament and disposition the Indian differs very little, if any, from the white. In school they progress almost as rapidly as...whites in the Public School in spite of the fact that they attend school only half of the day.
Finally, every effort is made to develop good Christian character, and on the whole...the attempt has been successful. The graduates may be found taking their places creditably in all walks of life. Some are leading farmers on the Reserve, others are in business or industry, while many are making good wives in well-kept homes...

8. 2 August 1930 Snell Quarterly Report
...CHURCH...Confirmation...21 girls and 18 boys...
DISCIPLINE. I am very pleased with the improvement in the conduct of the pupils this quarter. There was one instance of two boys climbing to the girls dormitory but the girls gave the alarm immediately and the boys were scared off. I regret to say that the leader was a Collegiate boy who should have been an example to the rest as he comes from a good home. Both boys absconded before I had completed the investigation. The reaction of the pupils, both boys and girls was gratifying. Neither of the boys will be returning after holidays. Another

encouraging feature has been the marked decrease in corporal punishment and the readiness of the pupils to respond to the appeal to their sense of right and fairness...I am very much encouraged as to the conduct of the pupils.

HEALTH...excellent. We...have not had a single case of a pupil being ill enough to be sent to the sick room.

STAFF. I cannot speak too highly of the staff. We are having to make one change. Miss Johnston the junior dietitian has to go home to help her mother. Miss Lydia Smith is succeeding her at the same salary. She is an older woman and should be a very efficient officer.

NOTES. The buildings and grounds present a very pleasing appearance and are the admiration of the many visitors. All the interior of the building except the dormitories has been painted or varnished and almost all of the exterior has been painted so that the building looks very spick and span. All the work has been done by the pupils and staff.

A difficulty will present itself when the school reopens with more pupils. The senior school room is crowded at chapel now. It will be exceedingly difficult to find room anywhere for the larger number which we shall have next term. I hope, therefore, that the new Chapel will not be delayed a moment longer than necessary.

9. 17 September 1930 R. Ashton Obituary

There passed away yesterday at the home of his son, Major A. Nelles Ashton...Rev. Robert Ashton... superintendent of the Mohawk Institute from October, 1872 until 1910, and Incumbent of...the "Mohawk Church," from 1885 to 1915. Born in England...1843...he was associated with the staff of the Middlesex Industrial school, and came to Canada when still quite a young man to assume charge of the Mohawk Institute...

He speedily and most effectively took hold of the position, and for nearly half a century discharged the many difficult duties of the post with unsparing zeal. In exercising supervision over the education of pupils of both sexes, in the school room, and on the farm or in domestic duties, he manifested great skill, and his advice was frequently sought and his methods followed by many kindred institutions...His love of the picturesque led him to beautify the grounds so that they became one of the local show places, and the production of greenhouses and garden flowers was also another most successful hobby. Indeed, his all round management of the property was such as to secure a handsome annual revenue, applied to the expenses of the school, in addition to meeting the wants of the pupils. He took holy orders on June 11, 1903, and his sermons, delivered each Sunday...were models of reasonable brevity and sound reasoning...

Mr. Ashton was a many-sided man, exceptionally well informed...and the possessor of a most logical mind. The military always made a strong appeal to him, and as

chaplain with rank of Major, and member of the officers' mess for a number of years, he took keen participation in the welfare of the Dufferin Rifles.

His favorite sport was...cricket, and many years ago he had a playing field and excellent crease prepared in the rear of the Mohawk Institute property...This was done entirely at his own expense and was his gift to the cricket club...Masonry also enjoyed his very deep interest... occupied all the chairs in Royal Arch Masonry. Meteorological observations...and for a lengthy period he had charge of the Brantford station...To the numerous visitors at the Institute his great knowledge of Indian lore was always most instructive...He was British to the core...

10. 15 October 1930 Snell to Secretary DIA

...decayed teeth in children are not brought to our attention until they are so far decayed as to ache, and that then they are often too far gone to be preserved I would request that all the children should be examined so that both the teeth and the pain may be saved. There would also be a saving of money as the pupils could be sent in groups thus securing the lowest price for the work.

11. 16 December 1930 Morgan

I visited the Mohawk Institute unexpectedly at dinner time, taking Mr. Hilton Hill with me, on account of a report in circulation that the children were insufficiently fed. We found their dinner to consist of an abundance of good and tastefully cooked liver with brown gravy and I am of opinion that there is no truth whatever in the rumour.

12. 3 February 1931 R. Ferrier Memorandum

...I visited...January 29th, 30th and 31st...There were 78 girls and 64 boys in residence and all appeared in good health with the exception of **** and ****.

MAIN BUILDING:

I visited all the rooms in this building and found everything looking very clean.

...the following improvements have been made...(f) The whole of the exterior painted by the boys and whole of the interior, with the exception of the dormitories also painted or varnished by the girls...

13. 18 March 1931 Snell to Secretary DIA

There are at least eight pupils who need attention to their eyes...teachers report that these children cannot see the blackboard...request authority to have their eyes examined...if necessary, to have them fitted with glasses.

14. 17 September 1932 Morgan to Secretary DIA

[Mr. and Mrs. Snell in car accident]...Mrs. Smith, the Assistant Matron, and Miss Hardy, the Senior Teacher are in charge...during the enforced absence of Mr. Snell. The Assistant Matron advised me this morning that everything was going along nicely. They expect that Rev. Mr. Snell will return to the Institute this weekend...Mrs. Snell will have to remain at the Hospital...Mr. Snell was not injured as seriously as was at first thought. Mrs. Snell was injured the more seriously of the two.

15. 29 September 1932 Snell to Secretary DIA
...the conviction of **** on a charge of theft...this last escapade began with the breaking into the room of Mr. Jones, boys' master, and stealing $30.00 in cash and various articles of jewelry...it was a pity that Mr Jones should be called upon to lose this amount of money, and would, therefore, appreciate authority from you to reimburse Mr. Jones...$30.00 from the funds of the school.

16. 25 September 1933 Snell to Secretary DIA
...I have made two changes in the staff, Mr. and Mrs. Jones having left on September 1st. I have filled their places...with selections of officers whom I knew to be particularly adapted for the work. Mr. Jones' position has been filled by Mr. O. R. Pengelley, formerly a teacher of manual training in the Brantford schools and peculiarly adapted for the position of boys' master and mechanic at the Institute...Mrs. Jones' position of Senior dietitian has been taken by Miss Turner, who was Junior dietitian, and the latter position is now held by Mrs. E. Pettigrew who is filling the place admirably.

17. 13 October 1934 Phelan to McGill
I visited the Mohawk Institute...on the 2nd and 3rd instant. There were 137 pupils in residence - 79 girls and 58 boys. This means that the school can accommodate about 13 more boys. All the boys who require institutional care on the Six Nations Reserve have been placed in the school and, consequently, when visiting other reserves in Western Ontario, I informed the Agents that, if they had any boys who should be placed in a residential school, it would be possible to provide accommodation for them at Mohawk.
The Staff:-
The Principal...has a staff of eleven persons. As you are, no doubt, aware, there have been several cases of truancy at this school during the past year and, in addition, I was informed by the Indian Superintendent, Colonel Morgan, that he receives complaints from time to time regarding the conduct of the boys. Some people have reported that boys from the Mohawk Institute have stolen money from their milk bottles, while others state that the boys are allowed to go uptown and they annoy people by asking for permission to do odd jobs and, if they are not engaged, they ask for money.
I discussed all these matters very fully with the Principal and I am inclined to feel that there is some truth in the complaints that have been received. Mr. O. R. Pengelley is in charge of the boys during their leisure time and sleeps in a room close to their dormitory. I am not at all

satisfied that he exerts proper discipline over the boys, although Mr. Snell considers Pengelley a very suitable man. However, in looking over the building, I found the boys' wash room in a very dirty condition and Mr. Snell agreed with me that this showed that Mr. Pengelley did not exercise as much supervision as he should.
As it is inadvisable to lock the doors leading to the fire escapes, I arranged with Mr. Snell to have a wire attached to those doors leading to an electric bell in Mr. Pengelley's bedroom. If any boy, in future, gets up early and tries to leave the building by the fire escape, the bell will ring in Pengelley's room and action can be taken to have the boy kept in the building.
I would recommend that a reasonably firm letter be sent to Mr. Snell, advising him that the Department is not satisfied with the supervision that the boys are receiving during their leisure time and directing him to so advise Mr. Pengelley. Mr. Snell should further be informed that, unless there is a decided improvement, Mr. Pengelley's services should be dispensed with. I also informed Mr. Snell that I did not consider the boys should be allowed to go into town, looking for odd jobs such as cutting grass, etc. There is no necessity for them doing this and it only leads to complaints from residents of Brantford...

18. 26 October 1934 MacInnes to Snell
...the Department has experienced considerable concern during the last year in connection with the many cases of truancy at the Mohawk Institute...I am inclined to feel that the supervision of the boys during their leisure time is not as effective as it might be. While Mr. Pengelly may be well qualified along certain lines, it is doubtful if he is capable of exerting the desired influence over the boys...Mr. Phelan's report showed that the boys' washroom was allowed to remain in a dirty condition. For the next month or so, you should carefully supervise Mr. Pengelly's work, and, if there is not a decided improvement in the conduct of the boys, the Department considers that it would be in the best interests of the school to dispense with his services.
The Department also understands that it has been the practice to allow the boys to go into town and look for odd jobs, such as cutting grass, etc. The Department sees no reason for allowing this privilege, and it should be discontinued immediately.
Except in the case of the older pupils on whom you can place absolute reliance, no pupil should be allowed to go into Brantford without the supervision of some member of the staff...it is necessary for all parties concerned to take every precaution to see that the actions of the boys and girls...reflect credit on the school and not be a cause of complaint...of residents living close to the school.
I trust that you have already arranged for the installation of the electric bell from the doors leading to the fire escapes to the supervisor's bedroom.

19.　12 November 1934　Morgan to Phelan
...I am writing this to you and not to the Dept officially as it is apropos of our talk when you were here and you understand the matter and, also, I hesitate to take up the matter officially although I suppose, as representative of the Dept here, it is my duty to do so.

There has been no improvement, whatever you may have told Mr Snell to do, in the management of the boys and unless they are more efficiently controlled the Dept will be blamed.

Yesterday, at the Cenotaph ceremonial, one of the garbage men, who is an overseas man, said that he thought I ought to know that Institute boys visit the garbage dump early in the mornings, between seven and eight, to collect, and eat, scrap candies and biscuits that have been thrown away by Pattersons factory and this has been corroborated by Mr Attwell...This...may lead to the outbreak of an epedemic in the school, but the point is, how do these boys get out to go there?.

The entire system needs revising and the man employed by Mr Snell to look after the boys should be replaced.

Both the day and night conditions are lax and I think that a man should sleep in each dormitory, in a cubicle if necessary to afford him privacy...

The boys are all over the town at all hours and it will be hard to get them back to normalcy, but not a boy should be in the city or away from the Institute without the man in charge of the boys knowing exactly where he is, when he left, and when he returns. He should report before leaving, when on permit to leave, and upon his return, whatever hour that may be.

...Mr. Snell is a good chap and I do not want to make mischief for him but if he wont sack the man who allows all this and put his house in order himself I have no alternative but to bring it to your attention.

The garbage man says that the boys say that they do not get enough to eat so have to supplement it with garbage candy but this may be taken, "cum grano salis", as they certainly do not appear ill fed.

20.　15 November 1934　Snell to Secretary DIA
I am indeed surprised at the reports...It is true that some boys were at the dump. This is a habit that we have been combating for some time and which recurs at intervals even with the most careful watching. The boys referred were detected by us and were thoroughly punished. But it is certainly not a regular occurence.

As to the boys being seen at all hours in the city I am certain there is no foundation for the statement. The doors are locked at eight o'clock each night and the boys are all sent to bed at nine o'clock, the juniors at eight immediately after chapel. The dormitories are inspected to see that all are in bed at intervals during the evening. The electric bell with switches controlled by the fire-escape doors was installed immediately after Mr. Phelan

visited us and as the bell is in the bedroom of the boys' master, it would be impossible for any boy to leave the building without arousing him. I am inclined to think that any Indian boy seen on the street is thought to be from Mohawk Institute and there are many Indians living in the city.

I have made inquiries from several people living near the Institute as to whether our boys ever gave them any trouble and they have all stated that the boys gave them no trouble. One lady remarked that they were likely to be blamed for much that was done by other boys.

The only times any boys have not been in the dormitory were cases of truancy. In one case the four boys returned voluntarily the next day. In the other we found them near Norwich.

...I am having the fullest co-operation from Mr. Pengelley. He could not give more supervision than he does without leaving undone the mechanical repairs that are part of his duties.

I should be pleased to know who are the people who make these complaints. No one has said anything to me.

21.　16 May 1936　Brantford Expositor
A recommendation that the playground equipment...be inspected every three months...inquest...into the death of Ada Effie Smith, 13...who was fatally injured...when a wheel from a maypole around which she was swinging with four other girls fell off and struck her in the abdomen...

Rev. Mr. Snell described the playground...stating it was equipped with swings, teeter-totters and the "giant stride," or maypole. The maypole was an improvised piece of equipment...an automobile wheel on a shaft adapted to fit into a hole at the top of the pole. It was the breaking away of the wood on one side of the pole that caused the wheel to fall.

"The playground was not under continued supervision...but there was always someone who looked after the recreational periods of the pupils at intervals...It was there when I came, seven years ago, and had been there some two years before"...Pointing to what had been a deep crack several feet along the pole at the spot where it broke, Crown Attorney Wallace asked..."Did you know anything about the crack originally?" "I never knew it was there," Rev. Mr Snell said...stated there were no regulations regarding the method of using the maypole and there was no special grant made by the Government for recreational equipment...

22.　25 May 1936　Snell to Secretary DIA
The newspaper report of the inquest re the death of Effie Smith, while perfectly fair, hardly gives the right impression of the part of my testimony which you quote. The Crown Attorney asked me "Does the Department make a grant for playground equipment?" and, of course,

I answered "NO" but added that the Department did furnish us with equipment such as balls, bats, etc. He then asked if our equipment was sometimes homemade as in the case of the Giant Stride and I answered that it was. No one who heard the evidence could possibly have inferred that the Department was niggardly in its provision for the pupils.

The court did not think Mr. Lager was remiss, inasmuch as he explained that he took it that the ring around the pole had been placed there to strengthen the pole where it was checked. The check, as was shown to the coroner and jury, did not reach completely to the top of the pole. Had the ring been nearer to the top of the pole it would have effectually prevented the split that caused the accident.

...the mother attached no blame to the management. In fact, she made the request that her little boy might be admitted next term if there is room...I have received a very kind letter written on her behalf, thanking us for our kindness in connection with the sad occurrence.

23. 1 June 1936 Snell to Secretary DIA

The boys do get a good deal of manual training under the Boys' Master and Mechanic. All repairs to equipment and plant that can be done by ourselves are almost entirely done by the boys under the direction of the boys Master. This involves considerable training in carpentry, plumbing, painting and repairs to machinery. As an example, the new metallic ceiling in the senior school room last year was done entirely by boys, the boys master merely giving the directions and instructions...In addition to this, the boys are given instruction in the making of models of various kinds, bird houses etc. The excellence of their work is shown by the fact that four of the five prizes awarded at Ohsweken Fair were won by our boys... the boys here get a better training in manual work than they could get in any of our Public Schools where Manual Training is given.

24. [no date] DIA to Snell

...the Department has received...regarding the food served to the children...and the meal served on the occasion of[.?.]officers tends to show that some of the meals are not as appetizing or bountiful as could be reasonably[.?.]at a school possessing the advantages of the Mohawk...

It is, therefore, expected that you will immediately confer with those in charge of the meals and personally arrange for a decided improvement both in the quantity and quality of food served to the children. It is also, expected that all meals be supervised by some member of staff and that you will personally visit the diningroom frequently in order that you may assure yourself that your instructions are being carried out at all times.

The Department desires that whole milk, and not separated milk, be served to the pupils in future. The handling of the milk should also receive great care...

A copy of this letter is being forwarded to Mr. Randle and he is being instructed to visit the diningroom at mealtime whenever he is at the Mohawk Institute. Major Randle is also being requested to confer with you regarding the cost of a new henhouse. If this new henhouse is erected he should at once arrange for an adequate number of hens and fresh eggs should be served the pupils at regular intervals.

25. 29 July 1937 Craig to Snell

I have been consulted by Mrs. ****...concerning injuries sustained by her son, ****, who was a pupil in your school in June last. My client informs me that one of the teachers on your staff called Mr. Logar mistreated her son to such an extent that his body was covered with bruises when her sister...obtained the boy from your school for the summer holidays.

I hope you understand that I appreciate that there is a certain proper form of punishment in case a pupil misbehaves, but such punishment does not allow a teacher to take a pupil into a henhouse, as I am informed happened in this case, and flay him with a belt.

I have advised Mrs. **** to let me know if there is any further mistreatment and in that case I will communicate directly with the Department of Indian Affairs at Ottawa. I also advised Mrs. **** that she is to tell her son that in case of further mistreatment the boy is to go direct to you and also go to a Physician for an examination.

I quite understand the difficulties which there may be in a school such as yours is, so far as the pupils are concerned, but feel that under the circumstances some explanation should be made to the boy's Mother.

26. 11 August 1937 Snell to Secretary DIA

...the matter had been reported to me three weeks before by the boy's aunt and I had made a thorough investigation. A number of other boys were present at the time and they agreed that the boy deserved what punishment he received, that it had been done only with a light strap, and that it consisted of three strokes on each hand and that the boy was hit no place else and did not even cry as a result of the punishment. The boys who were there are entirely reliable (which **** is not) and I have no doubt as to the truth of their statements. None of them had any knowledge of how the boy had received the bruises that his aunt found on his arms.

Mr. Lager, who is mentioned in the complaint is particularly wise and kind in his treatment of the boys and the boys whom I examined testified to his kindness and to the high esteem in which the boys hold him.

...I presume that you have not taken the report as true...

27. 14 August 1937 Secretary DIA to Snell

...In view of the information, which I now have I do not

feel inclined to minimize the situation. Neither in your letter to me, nor in your letter to Mrs. ****, did you make any effort to explain away the bruises and injuries received by **** while he was at your school. Such bruises and injuries do not happen without there being some reason. Your suggestion...that **** "lied" concerning the situation is, in my view, entirely incorrect, and it appears to me that either the boys, which you say were questioned concerning the matter, either did not answer truthfully or did not know and understand the facts. If the boys understanding the situation clearly did not tell the truth I suggest that they did so because of fear. ...you say it is not your practice to administer severe punishment and that you resort to it only when other means fail. Apparently, this practice was not followed in the present case because, as you say in your letter to Mrs. ****, **** cried from repentance after Mr. Lager had talked to him but he did not talk to him until after he had administered punishment.

28.   17 August 1937   Craig to Snell

...You have not attempted to give any explanation as to how the boy received the injuries...injuries, such as he received, do not happen without some cause and those injuries alone are better proof of the truth of his story, than any words written or spoken by you. Apart from the injuries received by the boy, his story is confirmed by your letter in which you admit that the boy was strapped, not by a proper regulation strap as provided for such a purpose but by a belt which belonged to one of your staff; and further that the boy was punished at the hen house in place of being taken by the member of the staff into the office or some other place for punishment.
...in fairness to my client some explanation should be given as to the cause of the boy's injuries.

29.   31 August 1937   Lager to Secretary DIA

Mr. Snell informs me that you desire a signed statement regarding the reprimand and punishment administered to a pupil, ****...by myself...

On the particular day I was supervising some work at the poultry building when I heard a terrifying scream and one of the boys outside directed my attention to **** throwing stones at a little fellow around five years of age by the name of ****, I immediately went out of the building and called to the **** boy to stop but he ignored me and continued to stone the **** child. I distinctly heard two of the stones thud against the child's body and I was roughly one hundred and fifty feet away. I ran up to the boys and asked what **** was thinking about throwing stones with such violence at so small a boy and also explained the serious consequences that may result to this method, I found he was not penitent so I gave him four straps on the palm of each hand to which he smiled so I again spoke to the boy and asked him how he would

feel had he placed **** in a world of complete darkness for the rest of his life by blinding him, and to this end I was successful in making the boy feel sorry, also gaining his assurance that he would not throw stones again. I have gone to great length to find out just how the boy could have received the bruses he is alleged to have...but thus far I have been unable to gain any knowledge.
...I am at a complete loss to understand why the boy should concoct this assertion because **** has given little trouble prior to this cowardly act, and consequently has been treated with the greatest kindness and consideration as do all well behaved children here, and I very much regret to think that a feeling of illwill exists on the part of pupil or parent of any pupil towards myself.

30.   1 September 1937   Snell to Secretary DIA

I am enclosing the signed statement from Mr. Lager... I am also enclosing the belt with which the punishment was administered which you will see is too light to inflict bruises such as were alleged to be on the boy's body. I may say that **** was here last night and I took occasion to question him. He corroborated all of Mr. Lager's report except that he contended that he was told to bend over and touch his toes while he was strapped across the sternum. He identified the strap which I am sending to you as being the one used. He also said that Mr. Lager held the buckle in his hand. He told me that there was a red mark on his groin that night and that it was black the next day. When I suggested that he might have knocked against some obstruction in his play and so caused the bruise he did not seem to sure about it. It was interesting to note that he cried a little and, when I asked him why, he said that it was because he could not return to the school. He also told me that Mr. Lager had always treated him kindly and that he was not held in fear by him or the other boys.

Mr. Lager did not punish the boy in my presence. I cannot find that the principals of any of our public schools require that the staff shall administer punishment only in the presence of the principal. I would not say that it is usual to punish pupils in the presence of other pupils but it does happen occasionally. In this case it was fortunate as I was able to get corroboration for Mr. Lager's report of the incident.

I could not be definite regarding the cause of the boy's bruises as they had not been reported to any of the staff and none of the boys had any knowledge of them. **** told me last night that he had only two bruises, one on his groin and one, a very small one, on his wrist. I am inclined to think that both the mother and aunt exaggerated the boy's story to them and the condition in which he was found.

The lawyer was depending entirely on the story as told by the mother. **** told me last night that he had not seen the lawyer.

I suppose I was a bit curt in my last letter to Mr. Craig but I had sent him a courteous and truthful statement of the matter and I rather resented it when he "suggested" (to use his expression) that I was lying about it.

31. 3 September 1937 DIA to Craig

The Department has secured two reports from the Reverend H. W. Snell...relating to the punishment of the above named pupil. The Principal has also sent forward the belt with which the punishment was administered and a statement, signed by Cyril H. Lager...

The statement signed by Mr. Lager appears to the officials here to be a rather straight forward summary of the events which prompted him to punish ****. The belt sent forward is a light summer belt, much lighter than the regulation strap ordinarily used, and is a belt that might form part of a boy's wearing apparel during the summer months. I am...convinced that no serious injury could be inflicted upon a pupil by the use of this belt.

The reports before us...do not explain how **** received the injuries. Is it possible that the reports of this boy's injury received by you were somewhat exaggerated?

I have failed to discover, in the records here, a single complaint that has reached the Department, with respect to harsh treatment, from any pupil in attendance at the Mohawk Institute or from any individual who might have written on behalf of such pupils. The impression received by the officials who have visited the Institute was that both the Principal and Mr. Lager were exceedingly popular with the boys and girls in attendance at the school. These facts, I feel, should be given due consideration in reviewing the complaint of ****...

32. 3 January 1938 Hoey to Snell

I have given a great deal of thought to the best ways and means of promoting vocational instruction at our Indian day and residential schools. I am convinced...the pupils in attendance at our schools would respond more readily to a course more practical and less theoretical and abstract than the present course appears to be.

It is somewhat difficult to secure capable instructors for this work...we have made no provision whatever for the training of such instructors in the Dominion of Canada until a year or two ago.

I am anxious to submit to you, for consideration, the advisability of employing a capable vocational instructor... If you could...secure the services of such a man and make provision for his room and board, I would...recommend that his salary be paid by the Department...at a salary not exceeding $1,000.00 per annum, plus board and room.

I should like to have, in your reply, information relating to the classroom space that may be available for such work. It is just possible that you may have outside buildings in which instruction in carpentry work, auto mechanics, etc., could be given...

33. 24 January 1938 Snell to Hoey

I have discussed the matter of vocational training with Major Randle and have visited the Vocational department of our Collegiate and the Training School...where I was given every assistance and the assurance of their hearty cooperation as the plan developes.

We have a building which would be very suitable as a shop which could be adapted with very little expense beyond any special wiring that might be necessary.

I am delighted with the prospect of this additional practical training for the boys here. It has been a hope cherished ever since I came but I could see no way of financing it...

34. 21 February 1938 Snell to Secretary DIA

...manual training course, I have to mention a difficulty. The teacher will need to live here I presume and we have no extra room. But we have a small house at present used as a store room for feed that could be moved to a suitable location and put in shape for a dwelling. Our boys' master, Mr. Lager, is a married man and would be delighted to have it to live in if and when a manual training teacher is appointed. This additional privilege would compensate him for the extra work he has undertaken in the care of the hens and make it possible for him to live on the salary we are able to pay. I have fears that we may lose his services unles we can in some way either increase his salary or reduce his living expenses. At present he has to rent an appartment for his wife and child. He of course, lives here and would continue to do so until the extra teacher is appointed...

35. 6 May 1938 Hoey to Snell

...I authorized you to engage a vocational instructor at that time at a salary not to exceed $1,000 per annum - board and room to be supplied by you at the institution.

I am not prepared to authorize the purchase of expensive equipment. I cannot convince myself that the mechanical equipment supplied in the average vocational school would be at all suitable for the purpose I have in mind. The boys in attendance at your school should be taught to undertake vocational projects and complete certain tasks with practically the same equipment that they will have at their disposal when they return to the reserves. This equipment should be authorized by the instructor after he is appointed and after he has had an opportunity to discuss the programme with you and with Major Randle...If you feel that the difficulties surrounding the appointment of this instructor are too great to be easily overcome, I want you to write to me very frankly about the matter. If we cannot appoint an instructor at the Mohawk Institute, it is our intention to make the appointment by way of experiment at some other residential school in the province.

36. 28 May 1938 Randle to Hoey
...Having again seen Mr. Snell, it has now been arranged for him to endeavour to secure a suitable instructor, though on enquiry it appears any one qualified for such instruction expects a salary considerably more than you have authorized, allowing even for the board provided at the Institute.

While appreciating the undesirability of purchasing expensive equipment, it will of course, be necessary to purchase a certain amount, and in this age it would appear wise to include in the instruction to be given, some training in wiring...for the use of electric power...

37. 14 June 1938 Snell to Secretary DIA
...I have engaged Mr. Fruere as manual training teacher for the year beginning September 1st, 1938. He is a capable young man...

38. 26 October 1938 Snell to Secretary DIA
CHURCH...We also have daily chapel services in the school at which Biblical instruction is given. In addition a period of religious instruction is given to each class during school hours and Sunday School is held each Sunday. Confirmation classes in preparation for that rite, attended by all the senior pupils, were carried on for three months and thirty-eight pupils were confirmed. Three of these came to the school from Pagan homes. No attempt is made to proselytise children of other denominations but occasionally they ask for Confirmation and, with the consent of their parents, are presented...the emphasis placed upon religious instruction has much to do with the marked improvement in the character of the pupils.
DISCIPLINE. The conduct of the pupils has been most gratifyingly exemplary. Truancy has almost entirely ceased and there is evident a steadily growing desire on the part of the pupils to follow right because it is right and to co-operate with the staff in maintaining a high standard of behaviour and industry. This is so much the case that I have to resort to corporal punishment only on very rare occasions.
STAFF. Too much credit cannot be given to the very efficient and sympathetic staff of teachers and officers. I feel that it would be very difficult to improve its personel. We have now thirteen members: Principal, Matron, Nurse, Senior teacher, Junior teacher, Sewing teacher, Manual Training teacher, Senior dietitian, Junior dietitian, Boys' Master, Farm superintendent, Gardener and Teamster.
...through the kindness of the Superintendent of Training and Welfare, we have been able to add a teacher specially qualified for Manual Training. About $1100.00 has spent in equiping the shop for teaching carpentry, forging woodwork, farm mechanics etc...
PUPILS. The enrolment has been slightly under our quota of 150. We had 64 boys and 81 girls. The progress was normal. Eight pupils passed the Entrance examination...Five pupils are attending Collegiate from...a uniformly high standing.

39. 27 March 1939 Randle to Secretary DIA
...with reference to Mr. J. M. McKnight's report on the repairs and improvements necessary...

Those outlined in the report are certainly urgently required...and when completed will add greatly to the general appearance of the interior of the building and certainly create a much more favourable impression of the Department's efforts on behalf of the Indians, among the many visitors who pass the building during the...year.

The general appearance of the exterior of the building and immediate grounds leaves little to be desired, and as the interior is kept clean enough, with the repairs...carried out, almost everything will be in good shape and appearance except the bed linen in the dormitories, which generally speaking is old and worn and far from pleasing in appearance...it would be a very good thing if the Principal gave more consideration to it, as it stands out so clearly and gives a particularly bad impression...

On the Principal hearing of the repairs contemplated, he was most anxious to have them carried out by the boys supervised by his own staff. This might be satisfactory judging by some of the work done by them, but it would take considerable time as the boys could not give steady time to carrying it out, so if the Principal writes and suggests it, in my opinion the Department's intention of carrying it out during the summer holidays is preferable.

40. 11 July 1939 Hoey to Snell
...Supt. Randle is being instructed to make the arrangements for painting and redecorating the interior...The Department also intends to supply new single desks for the junior class-room...
In view of the fact that the interior of the building is being totally redecorated, the Department will expect that you will give personal attention to keeping the building in a cleanly condition in the future.

There should be more strict supervision of the Boy's and girl's wash-rooms and toilets, these should be kept in a cleanly condition at all times. All lockers should be promptly repaired when required.

As the beds are now being repainted, it will be a simple matter to keep them in this condition. Only neglect on the part of the school management will cause the beds in future to have the appearance that they have at present...

41. 12 September 1939 Phelan to Snell
...Superintendent Randle and myself went over the whole school...examining the work that has been recently done.

On entering the wash rooms used by the girls in the basement I was extremely disappointed to notice papers scattered over the floor and in spite of the newly decorated walls and ceilings the rooms appeared as if no supervision was being given to the girls.

I feel it is almost unnecessary for me to point out that the Department expects the staff of the Mohawk Institute to see that all rooms in the building are kept in a cleanly condition.

The Indian Superintendent, Major E. P. Randle, is being requested to visit the Mohawk Institute within the next month and to report to the Department any room that is not in the condition in which it should be.

I was especially sorry to see the condition of these rooms in the basement on the day on which I was there because I understand that later in the afternoon a member of your staff accompanied one of the leading members of the American Delegation through the basement. Certainly this gentleman could not have obtained a very good opinion of the training given the girls in the matter of cleanliness of the rooms which they are occupying.

42. 6 November 1939 Hoey to Randle

The Department is in receipt of an anonymous letter from Brantford in connection with the Mohawk Institute. While we do not usually pay attention to such communications at the same time there is one paragraph which I thought advisable to bring to your attention...

"It is a topic of general comment in Brantford that the children are not sufficiently clothed for this weather. It is now November and the boys are still without any underwear. They only received stockings one month ago. Light cotton clothes are worn summer and winter. Even the poor clothes they have are often dirty and ragged."

43. 22 November 1939 Randle to Secretary DIA

...At the time the letter was written the weather was still mild and in fact continued so until just the last few days. Consequently warmer clothing was only being issued at the time the anonymous complaint was written.

However, it is my opinion from what can be seen that the children generally are comfortably clad and look healthy and cheerful.

The boys have both working clothes and better ones, but clad in the former often visit a little store a short distance from the Institute. In these farm working clothes, being boys, they may often look untidy and dirty, no matter how clean they started out earlier in the day, and this may be the reason for some of the comments made.

Otherwise clothes are clean and neat and all the children are watched for cleanliness.

44. 17 March 1941 Hoey to Snell

...there is an acute need of skilled workers throughout the Dominion...we are likely to be called upon in the immediate future to organize and extend worthwhile vocational courses at our Indian residential schools...

45. 22 January 1942 Randle to Hoey

...the Rev. H. W. Snell, is in London in hospital for an operation upon an eye, and during his absence Mrs. Snell has been in charge...while motoring to London to see Mr. Snell last Sunday, Mrs Snell was involved in a serious motor accident and is now in the Woodstock Hospital with a broken leg and arm.

...Mrs. Smith, the housekeeper, is now in charge of the institute, and everything appears to be running smoothly - and the gardener's work and hot-houses are being taken care of by the farm manager.

46. 21 June 1942 Isaac Jones to Hoey

The Company have had under consideration the Lease ...the Mohawk Institution was leased to his late Majesty for a term of 21 years from the 2nd January 1922...the Lessee covenanted for maintenance of the Mohawk Institution...payment of £1,000 per annum towards the stipend of the Principal...

...your Department might be prepared to take over the Institution...acquire the interest of the Company...

47. 9 November 1942 Hoey to McGill

We visited and made an inspection of the Mohawk Institute...Reverend H. W. Snell, was absent, making certain purchases from wholesale houses in Hamilton. Despite the substantial sums spent from year to year on the upkeep and repair of this building, the structure is by no means in first-class shape. The whole atmosphere in the school appears to be somewhat depressing and the rooms, particularly the bedrooms, rather bleak and unattractive. We were particularly interested, however in his farming operations and in his live stock. He appears to have a good farming instructor, Mr Arneil and I questioned this instructor rather closely in respect to his dairy herd, which appears to be somewhat depleted, and to the number of Yorkshire hogs that he is feeding this winter. When we expressed surprise at the small number of hogs in the piggery, he intimated that it was exceedingly difficult to secure the funds necessary to multiply the number of hogs...I...came away with the impression that the cattle and hogs produced at this school during the last two or three years have not been equal to the number consumed at the premises. Mr. Snell is an old man and has never been a good administrator at any time. He never appears to have a good grip on his finances. If this school is to be kept open and in operation, it might very well become a government operated institution, following the withdrawal of the annual grant now made by the New England Company.

48. 29 April 1943 Snell to Secretary IAB

...I have secured an excellent man as Boys' Master and Mechanic. He is experienced, a good mechanic and should exercise a very helpful influence on the boys...Mr.

F. Tuck...now spending a few days here...to familiarize himself with the work and the routine...I did not expect, under present conditions, to get so good a man.

49. 16 June 1943 Cochrane to Minister of Mines & Resources

The Court of the Company...are not at liberty under their Charter to transfer the freehold of the Institute to your Department...wish to facilitate the general scheme which you have proposed. The Company must, however, stipulate that the teachings of the Church of England are and continue to be available for those pupils whose parents desire it...

The Company would be willing to grant a Lease of the Mohawk Institute, apart from the Mohawk Chapel, for a nominal rent, for a term of 21 years, your Department being responsible for maintenance and repairs and for the insurance of the property...

...the Company would not propose to maintain their annual grant of £1000 beyond the end of the current year, but they would pay a salary to a Church of England clergyman nominated by the Bishop of the Diocese and appointed by the Company, to give religious instruction in the School and to serve the Chapel...

50. 20 October 1944 Phelan to Hoey

I inspected...Thursday, October 12. Accompanied by the Principal, I visited all parts of the building and I found everything in good condition, with the possible exception of the boys' playroom. Although the conditions in this room are not perfect, they are much better than I have seen them on former occasions.

Two qualified teachers are employed. This is the second year during which these teachers have been at Mohawk. While the girls are given considerable training in house work, sewing etc., the boys evidently receive little vocational training. The Principal stated that it was impossible for him to secure a qualified vocational teacher this year. At the present time he is employing a man by the name of Bricker. This gentleman is 67 years of age, but appears quite vigorous.

The Principal brought to my attention the necessity for the supplying of a new gas stove in the kitchen at an early date. New tables are also necessary in the children's dining room. Neither of these requires immediate attention, but as soon as such articles are available after the war they should be supplied.

At the time of my visit there were 110 pupils enrolled. The authorized pupilage at this school is 150. The Principal stated that he expected to obtain another 10 or 15 pupils within the next month.

Mr. and Mrs. Snell introduced the question of whether the Department would insist on Mr. Snell's retiring at the end of June, 1945. I pointed out to them that by this time Mr. Snell would be over 65 years of age and that the

original decision of the Department to retire him at that time was still in effect. Mrs. Snell expressed the opinion that other members of the staff were doubtful regarding their future. I pointed out to her that...at the present time, we had no intention of dispensing with the services of any other members of the staff.

51. 6 November 1944 Bishop of Quebec to Secretary of DIA [Anglican Bishops all wrote on the same theme]

...I am informed that the Department is considering the idea of radically changing the whole character of the School by putting it under a layman as Principal and merely allowing the services of a Chaplain for our own children.

I was very much shocked when I heard of this proposal to bring to an end a religious and educational tradition which had been established for so long, and I am sure that Anglicans generally throughout Canada would hear of this decision with regret and amazement.

52. 6 November 1944 Hoey to Archbishop of Quebec

...you express surprise that this Department is considering the idea of radically changing the whole character of the Mohawk...School, by putting it under a layman as Principal and merely allowing the services of a Chaplain for the Anglican children.

...this...is based either on a misunderstanding of the actual facts or a misinterpretation...

In September, 1942, the Governor of the New England Company informed the Chief of our Training Division that it was not the intention...to continue its annual grant of $5,000.00...The Governor did suggest...that the Company would be glad to lease the property to the Government, should the members of the Government feel that the school should be kept open and in operation...

53. 10 April 1945 Dixon to Seager

...Mr Hoey asked...if you would...suggest to him the names of two or three Anglican Clergymen whom he or members of his staff might interview with a view to ascertaining if any of them would be suitable to carry on the work...the new Principal should be between 30 and 40 years of age with some business experience and also reasonably good knowledge of farming...the latter qualification is important as he has been given to understand by the Six Nations Council that in their opinion the agricultural possibilities at the Mohawk Institute have not been used to the utmost extent...

54. 13 April 1945 Seager to Hoey

...I have at least three men here in the Diocese of Huron who...fit in with the qualifications...

In considering the whole situation of the administration of the Mohawk Institute, particularly in view of the possibility of the Church taking it over...it might be very helpful if we set up a kind of administrative Board consisting of able and experienced men, particularly in farming and in business...

If you can give me any information as to the amount of salary to be paid the new Principal together with any other financial advantages the position carries with it, it would assist me in placing the matter before the men...

55. 16 May 1945 London Free Press

A crisis which has arisen in the history of the Mohawk Institute...which "to all practical intentional purposes" may remove the school from the auspices of the Church of England, was yesterday deplored by...Seager, Archbishop of Huron...

The agreement between the New England Company and the Indian Department...has expired and a new one proposed "of a nature to so radically change the character of the school as virtually to destroy it as it is now constituted."

Certain proposals to reorganize the school and change its character from a religious foundation to an exclusively educational one have been made. Through the help of the bishops throughout Canada the Indian Department has stated that it is prepared to continue its per capita grants to the school as soon as arrangements are made with the New England Company, if the M.S.C.C. of the Diocese of Huron will become responsible for its administration...

A delegation from the Indian Department...and the United Church...visited the school with a view of considering changes by which the pupilage...at Mount Elgin might be transferred to the Mohawk Institute. It was proposed that the head of the institution should be primarily an educationalist and one with special equipment in agriculture. Provision was to be made for the religious needs of the children through the appointment of chaplains. This aspect of the proposal has been dropped.

The Anglican Church spent $2,400 in stipend, and $1,521.47 in repairs...last year..."We are not bigoted or selfish since all we desire is the welfare of this people whom we serve...since the school has served in its present constitution for 115 years and that the unquestionable fine results of its work are for anyone to see, that its doors are open to Indian children of every Protestant denomination without any desire to proselytize them, it is far perferable to leave it as it is...

56. 23 May 1945 Dixon to Hoey

...our Society had been asked by the Diocese of Huron to negotiate with your Department with a view to taking over the administration of the Mohawk Institute...You...sent me under cover of your letter of April 17th, 1944, a copy of the draft of the new agreement between the New England Company and your Department providing for the continued operation and administration of the Mohawk Institute by your Department...

...our Executive Committee...reached the following decision:

...the historic connection of the Church of England with the Mohawk Institute is sufficiently safe-guarded by the draft agreement between the Government and the New England Company...

57. 1 June 1945 Hoey to Randle

This will confirm the decision reached at a conference ...this morning...that Joseph C. Hill, now Principal of the two-room Indian Day School (No. 11) in the Six Nations Agency, be offered the Principalship of the Mohawk Institute...Mr. Hill should be paid a salary at the rate of $1500.00 per annum, and that his wife, who has the qualifications necessary to act as Matron, be paid at the rate of $50 per month.

It is the feeling of the officials here that, while Mr. Hill is a capable, fully qualified and experienced teacher, he may nevertheless feel the additional administrative duties and responsibilities at the Institute somewhat exacting. This position is, as you know, an important one. The Mohawk Institute has always occupied a prominent place in the educational program of this Department...Mr. Hill should be assisted in his work by the creation of an advisory board, the members of which board should meet at least quarterly - this board to consist of yourself as Chairman, the Public School Inspector of the district, the Clergyman in charge of the Mohawk Chapel and responsible for religious instruction at the school, the Chief of the Six Nations Band and the Principal of the School, Mr. Hill, as Secretary...this advisory committee should have general supervision of the work of the school and of the farming operations carried on as part of the regular school program. We are anxious that no radical change in the school program or in the operation of the farm or in the work of general administration should be undertaken without first being submitted for review to the advisory committee. While the Principal will be responsible for the employment and dismissal of the members of the staff, nevertheless staff matters might, with advantage to all parties concerned, also be reviewed by the members of the advisory board.

This school, as you are no doubt aware, has been operated since its inception, with two exceptions, under the direction and guidance of Clergymen of the Anglican Church in Canada. The appointment of Mr. Hill, therefore, constitutes a somewhat radical change in policy, but one for which provision is made in the lease sent forward for execution to the New England Company. ...while we are under no legal obligation to consult the Archbishop in this regard, it is, in our judgement, of the utmost importance for the success of the school that he should sanction this change in policy...

58. 15 June 1945 Seager to Hoey
...you having asked for three...nominations...

My second nomination is the Rev. W. J. Zimmerman. He was born in 1905 and ordained to the Priesthood in 1936. He is an exceptionally able and experienced young man who is a specialist in education, particularly Religious Education. He is a Bachelor of Arts of Toronto University and has taken post graduate courses in Education since, working toward his M.A. He was born near the village of New Hamburg...on a farm and has therefore a background of rural experience, increased greatly by having served in entirely rural areas, first in the Canadian Middle West and for the last few years in this Diocese. He has exhibited definite business and administrative ability...Mr. Zimmerman's wife is an extremely capable young woman and has made a specialty of work among children and young people and is possessed with definite administrative ability. She also possesses the wisdom and temperament necessary to deal with a staff of teachers and workers...

...24th May...I cabled the New England Company informing them of the readiness of the Synod of this Diocese to assume financial and administrative responsibility for the Institute under the arrangement with the Indian Department to pay per capita grants...

59. 16 June 1945 Hoey to Seager
...we have not...any authority to administer the Mohawk Institute in the absence of a duly executed lease. The revised lease was sent forward to the New England Company, almost a year ago, but has not been returned...

In the interval, the suggestion has been made that Joseph C. Hill, an experienced teacher, should be placed for the time being at least in charge of the school, under the direction of an advisory committee...

...Mr. Hill has an outstanding record as a teacher...he has had two attractive offers within the last couple of months...It is not at all likely, in view of these offers, that we shall be able to retain him in the two-room Indian Day School on the Reserve, of which he has been Principal for a number of years...his wife seems particularly well qualified for the position of Matron. She is a graduate of Home Economics and has not family obligations. The fact that Mr. Hill has been suggested for this position is in itself a great tribute to the work undertaken and accomplished by the Church on the Reserve over a long period of years...the selection of Mr. Hill would prove popular with the Indians throughout the country...action should be taken immediately if the school is to be kept open and in operation.

60. 21 June 1945 Seager to Hoey
...We had not been informed by the New England Company of this revised lease...To the terms...we offered strong objection, as the effect of them was to radically alter the whole religious character, atmosphere and purpose of the School...I cabled the New England Company...to delay signature as it appeared altogether probable that the Church...would be willing to assume responsibility for the School.

...the proposal stirred practically the whole Church of England in Canada into disapproval...your Department withdrew it...

Under this new proposal the Bishop of Huron was to nominate a Priest of the Church of England properly qualified as Principal of the School, and the Department undertook to continue to pay the per capita grants. In the meantime the assumption of the administrative responsibility for the School by the Church...was still under consideration.

Pursuant to this new proposal I was asked to nominate three Priests...from whom...you might appoint a Principal...Toward the end of May...Colonel Randle interviewed me with the proposal that Mr. and Mrs. Hill should be appointed as Principal and Matron...6th June I met these persons in Colonel Randle's office...

...After careful discussion our committee is of the opinion that the appointment of an Indian as head of the Institution is definitely undesirable. This involves no criticism whatever of Mr. Hill whose qualifications as a teacher, and those of his wife as Matron, are appreciated. The committee believes, however, that the supervision of a staff of teachers and other officers in the School, always a difficult matter as experience as shown, is likely to be much more successful in hands other than those of an Indian, however well qualified he might be...

...the Synod of Huron, is willing and well able to carry on the administration of this Institution...with the undertaking of your Department to pay the per capita grants...

61. 25 June 1945 Cochrane to Minister of Mines and Resources
...it was our intention at first to grant your Department a new lease of the Institute (excepting the Chapel) for a period of 21 years, under the terms of which your Department would be responsible for maintenance, repairs and insurance, and our Company would be responsible for the upkeep of the Chapel and the payment of the Chaplain's stipend.

At this stage the Missionary Society of the Church of England in Canada...intervened and requested that the Institute instead of being under the supervision of the Diocese of Huron (as heretofore) should be placed under the supervision of the Missionary Society, adding that the Diocese of Huron favoured this change...we decided not to execute the proposed lease in your favour at that time, but to await the outcome of negotiations which we understood were progressing between your Department and the Missionary Society. We have now heard from the Missionary Society that in their opinion the historic connection of the Church of England with the Mohawk Institute is sufficiently safeguarded by the draft agreement between your Department and our Company.

The Archbishop of Huron, on the other hand, writes in confirmation of his telegram urging that the Synod of his Diocese should assume responsibility for the administration of the School. As our negotiations were originally conducted with you we would be glad to hear from you as to whether the Archbishop's proposals meet with your approval. If they do, we assume that we should grant a lease of the Institute in favour of the Diocese of Huron...we are still willing and desire to pay the stipend of the Chaplain and to pay for the upkeep of the Chapel...unable to make further financial provision towards the Institute...

62. 9 July 1945 Phelan to Hoey

Mr. Zimmerman is 39 years of age and was ordained to the Priesthood of the Church of England in 1936. Since that date he has held two or three pastorates and, in addition, has spent some months with...the Anglican Missionary on the Big Island Lake Indian Reserve, Onion Lake Agency, Saskatchewan. Mr. Zimmerman possesses a B.A...and an M.A. Degree from Columbia.

Mr. Zimmerman has conducted Children's Camps for three years during the summer months and has always had very close connection with the Young People's Organizations of the Church of England. He was born on a farm and has a background of rural experience, which he claims to have increased by serving entirely in rural areas. He has one child and it is stated that his wife would be capable of carrying out the duties of Matron...

Before making a decision on the principalship...the committee felt that we should again bring to your attention the suggestion to appoint Mr. J. C. Hill...has given several years of splendid service on the Six Nations Reserve, as teacher at two or three of the Indian day schools. Mr. Hill is a Normal-trained teacher, 31 years of age. In addition to his Normal training, he possesses the following special certificates: Manual Training; Agriculture and Horticulture, Physical Training; Recreational Leadership and Religious Instruction. Obtaining the agricultural and horticultural certificates necessitated his attending Ontario Agricultural College, Guelph, for 2 years. He also spent two years at the Teachers' Training College at Hamilton. While attending O.A.C. and college, he devoted a great deal of his spare time and the holiday periods in working for a large grocery firm in the vicinity. For the last three years he did all the purchasing. This work necessarily gave him considerable business experience. Mr. Hill's wife is 26 years of age and spent two years at Macdonald College, where she took the Home Economics course...she was employed by the Department for some time at the Lady Willingdon Hospital.

...we have approved Mr. Hill's conducting social gatherings for the younger people on the Six Nations Reserve during the past three years. These gatherings were both recreational and educational and Mr. Hill has always had a very large attendance of Indian youth, both male and female. It is reasonable to infer, from their interest in Mr. Hill's courses, that he has the sympathy of his own people, and, if he were appointed principal, the committee believe that he would be strongly supported by the members of the Six Nations Band.

The committee feel, from their knowledge of Mr. and Mrs. Hill, that they are capable of carrying out the duties of Principal and Matron...such an appointment would definitely indicate that the Department is prepared to recognize Indians who have ability and training for positions.

Since 1929, Rev. Mr. Snell...has been in charge of this school. He, of course, is an Anglican Minister. Previous to his appointment, however, the principalship of this school had been in charge of lay people for many years. ...the conclusions of the committee comprising Mr. Arneil, Colonel Randle and myself, are (1) If the Department feels that the recommendation of His Grace the Archbishop of Huron is to be accepted, we recommend the appointment of Rev. Mr. Zimmerman, effective August 1, 1945; (2) for the reasons stated above, we feel that it would be preferable to give favourable consideration to the appointment of Mr. J. C. Hill.

63. 10 July 1945 Hoey to Seager

...I still find the proposals now before me for the operation and management of the Mohawk Institute somewhat disturbing and I am anxious to do everything humanly possible to make the position of the Minister and the Government clear and unmistakable, in case this matter becomes a subject of public discussion...

...The financial burden...has been borne almost wholly by the Canadian taxpayers...during the last twenty-year period we have spent approximately $20,000.00 on the repair and upkeep of the school. These figures do not include the $3,000.00 received annually from the New England Company. In addition to this, our per capita grants have amounted to approximately $24,000.00 annually...

The Government too must assume a measure of responsibility for the administration of the school farm. This land is...the property of the Six Nations Indians and is steadily increasing in value from year to year. Just what position the school would be in if the Six Nations Council decided to have this land sub-divided and sold for the construction of houses...Am I correct in assuming that the Diocese of Huron has never at any time contributed to the upkeep or operation of this particular school?

The proposal that came to me first from Lt.-Colonel Randle, that Mr. J. C. Hill be appointed Principal...with the cooperation of an advisory committee - one member of which would be nominated by you - seemed at the time it was made, a rather happy solution to a somewhat involved and perplexing problem...remembering that the members of the Six Nations Council, at an interview with me a couple of months ago, were very critical of the Institution and particularly of the training in farming and agricultural operations provided for the senior boys. Indeed, one member of the Council expressed the view that the time had come when serious consideration should be given by the Council to the withdrawal of the farm lands, which were not, in his judgment, being used to the advantage of the Indians. It is significant that no formal agreement appears to exist between the New England Company and the Six Nations Council, or between the Six Nations Council and the Government, with respect to the use of the school farm.

I...think that our failure to appoint Mr. Hill to the Principalship, in view of his outstanding qualifications... will create an unfavourable reaction on the part of the Indians and one that is not likely to contribute to the success of the Institute.

While I have no desire to comment upon the motion of the Missionary Society of the Church of England, nevertheless in fairness to the Government the position taken by them, namely, that the original lease...sufficiently safeguarded the historic connection of the Church of England in Canada with the Mohawk Institute - will, I feel sure, make the position somewhat embarrassing for the Government when this fact becomes known to the Six Nations Council...for a period of years the Principalship of this school was occupied by a layman, and the Indians are likely to interpret the appointment of a clergyman at this time as discrimination against a man who is exceedingly popular on the Reserve and who has displayed rare gifts of leadership...

64. 14 July 1945 Phelan Memorandum

In addition to interviewing the applicants for the position of Principal...I carefully inspected the buildings...

1. All the farm machinery is in serviceable condition and has received careful attention by the farmer...

2...there is a reasonably adequate quantity of clothing on hand for the girls, the supply of clothing for the boys for the coming academic year, including shoes and rubbers, is very limited...

3. Generally speaking, the school is in reasonably good condition, although some of the rooms require painting... the plumbing and heating were now perfectly satisfactory.

7...Colonel Randle...feels that a new principal could make a better showing by keeping a stricter supervision on the operations of the farm and green-house. The farmer, Mr. Haworth, has been in our employ for several years and has an excellent knowledge of farming. He is a splendid worker...the machinery is kept in excellent condition and the farming operations are carried out efficiently...if the

Principal gave more personal attention...it would be an encouragement both to the farmer and the gardener to put forth extra effort.

8. In visiting the dormitories it was found that practically all the mattresses are in very poor condition, and I strongly recommend...new mattresses be purchased...

9...Reverend Mr. Snell and Mrs. Snell have been instructed to vacate the building on July 31, 1945.

Mrs. Smith, who has been acting as assistant matron, is willing to stay until September 1, at which time she will have to be replaced, as she does not wish to return to the school.

Mrs. Thorpe is only acting temporarily as senior dietitian and another appointment will have to be made to this position by September 1...all other members of the staff...are willing to remain.

10...Dr. R. F. Palmer...has been the medical officer...for a great many years. He has been allowed only $100.00 a year...In case of serious illness, pupils are either sent to the Lady Willingdon Hospital...or placed in the Brantford City Hospital...Dr. Palmer is advancing in age and has not enjoyed good health and, when illness occurs, it is frequently impossible to obtain his services...medical services...should be handled by our Medical Division...it is evident that Dr. Palmer regards the Mohawk Institute as one of his special duties and when he was in good health he visited the school at every possible opportunity.

65. 16 July 1945 Seager to Hoey

It is hardly necessary to recall the fact that as a result of a conference between yourself...the "original lease"... was amended...that the Bishop of Huron should nominate Clergy of the Church of England from whom your Department might make a selection of Principal.

Pursuant upon this understanding, you wrote asking me to nominate such Clergy between thirty and forty years of age. This direction...I followed literally...We here fail to see why this clear arrangement has been followed by a suggestion that a Mr. Hill, whom I did not nominate, should be appointed, which we regard as not in accord with the terms of our understanding. We have, of course, no criticism to make of Mr. Hill who has certain qualifications. The men I nominated, however, particularly the Rev. W. J. Zimmerman, are as well qualified academically as Mr. Hill, and in other vitally important respects have qualifications which he cannot be expected to possess.

Frankly the reason alleged in favour of Mr. Hill, namely that it would please the Six Nations Council but that failure might result in hostile feeling on the part of the latter, while of course reasonably strong, does not begin to weigh with another fact...that among the Church of England people in this Diocese, and...throughout the Dominion of Canada at large, is a rising tide of concern over this matter which at any moment might turn into resentment...We should greatly regret if any embarrassment were caused the Minister through this business...

We are surprised that the Resolution of...our Missionary Society...should have been interpreted as referring to the "original lease"...The reference...is to the "original lease" as amended...It was precisely because the "original lease" was wholly unsatisfactory that Canons Townshend and Dixon interviewed you with the result that it was amended...

It is not surprising that the Six Nations Council should have been concerned over the management of the farm. It is exactly because we recognized this fact and believe that the farm can be made to pay that the Synod of Huron was prepared to assume financial responsibility...

...we have endeavoured to assist you and your Department in every way in this matter. The cable recently received from the New England Company we interpreted as implying a preference for a lease between that body and the Government. We therefore dropped our suggestion that the Synod of Huron should assume responsibility, doing so in the hope that it would facilitate matters...

It is true that the Synod of Huron has never been called upon to make any contribution to the up-keep and management of the Institute but it has built Churches and maintained Missionaries...

66. 26 July 1945 Seager to Glen

...express my appreciation of your kind and considerate reception of the deputation...the Mohawk Institute has always been a religious foundation under the auspices of the Church of England, though not administered by that Church here.

The teaching and influence of the School upon the pupils have been of enormous value in our Missionary work...While the School has always held an open door to pupils of all religious denominations, yet the fact that last school year 72% of the pupils were members of the Church of England is significant, showing...the successful character on the whole of the Church's work upon parents and forbears of the children...you will understand fully our deep desire that the School shall be continued as heretofore...

It was therefore a matter of great satisfaction to us when we understood that a proposal which, as we interpreted it, would radically alter the character of the School, was altered...First, that the Principal of the Institute shall be one acceptable to the Bishop...

...conference in Nov. 1944...this proposal was further altered...that the Principal should be appointed by the Department from nominations made by the Bishop... corroborated by a request from Mr. Hoey that I arrange to send three Clergy to Brantford to be interviewed by his officials...This was done...

...it was not unreasonable that I should expect one of my nominees to have been appointed at once. This, however, has not yet been done

67. 25 July 1945 Hoey to Seager

...In view of the decision reached by the Government and assuming that the New England Company will lease the Mohawk Institute to the Diocese of Huron, as suggested by the Minister, it will be necessary for you to take immediate steps to select a Principal...

We are anxious also to clear up one or two misunderstandings...In your letter of July 16, 1945, you state:

> ...as a result of a conference between yourself...the "original lease"...was amended...that the Bishop of Huron should nominate Clergy of the Church of England from whom your Department might make a selection of Principal.

...the view expressed was completely at variance with the facts. There was no such understanding at any time, nor was the lease now before the New England Company for execution amended, either by the Government or the New England Company...The position of the Government...was that the Principal of the school should be an agricultural college graduate with pedagogical training and experience both in classroom work and farm management...no such man would be appointed to the position unless he was acceptable to you...At...our second last conference, Canon Dixon suggested to me that you would appreciate the opportunity of nominating three or four men...

An additional misunderstanding arose toward the close of the negotiations...it is just possible the Church representatives - though they did not say so - had a feeling that the department was anxious to appoint Mr. Hill to this position. Mr. Hill...is unknown to the senior officials of this department and no attempt was made by the Government at any time, directly or indirectly, to place him at the head of the school. In view of his record, however, as a teacher and leader amongst his people, we felt it was only fair that his case should be very carefully and very sympathetically reviewed...our failure to appoint Mr. Hill without valid reasons would create unfavourable reactions on the part of the Indian population. Our attitude with respect to Mr. Hill was made clear at our last conference...I suggested to Canon Townshend that he communicate...with Mr. Middleton, with the object of securing, if...possible, his services for the school...No pressure of any kind has been exercised upon us and no attempt was made at any time to build up a case on behalf of any particular individual. The success of the Institution and the welfare of the Indian population was at all times uppermost in our minds...

68. 27 July 1945 Seager to Hoey

...The report of the interviewing committee was most favourable, particularly as to the Rev. W. J. Zimmerman.

I trust this clears up any misunderstanding under this head.

As to any misunderstanding that the Department was desirous to appoint Mr. Hill, the only information that I possess on the point is that in your letter to me of 16th July, in which the following occurs:

"In the interval the suggestion has been made that Joseph C. Hill, an experienced teacher, should be placed, for the time being at least, in charge of the School, under the direction of an advisory committee."

My impression is that Lt. Col. Randle, not anyone in Ottawa, was anxious for Mr. Hill's appointment. I take it therefore that there is no serious misunderstanding on this point.

I note the reversion in your letter to the offer of the Synod of Huron to assume financial and administrative responsibility for the Mohawk Institute...when the New England Company, in a cable dated 29th June, 1945, to me virtually declined the offer of the Synod of Huron, the matter, so far as we are concerned, was closed...

In the meantime I am perfectly willing and able, as suggested in your letter, to select a competent Clergyman to be appointed Principal, and I nominate the Rev. W. J. Zimmerman, in accordance with the...recommendation of your officials who...unanimously placed Mr. Zimmerman's name first...can in all probability take charge of the Institute in a fort-night. It will be clearly understood by you, however, that obviously the Synod of Huron can not be responsible for his salary or any other financial obligations of the Institute, as we are necessarily unaware of the mind of the New England Company in the matter, particularly as our offer to them was virtually declined, and as in addition to this I have no authority now from the Synod to assume such financial responsibility.

69. 31 July 1945   Glen to Seager

...the Mohawk Institute and a small parcel of land, approximately nine acres, is the property of the New England Company and that the larger farm, usually referred to as the school farm, is the property of the Six Nations Band of Indians...this school has been leased by the Government over a long period of years and that the entire costs of operation and maintenance, with the exception of an annual grant made by the New England Company, now discontinued, were borne by the Government. The selection of a suitable Principal with the necessary test and experience is, therefore...an exceedingly difficult and exacting task. The Principal in this case occupies a unique position, in that he is not only responsible as well for the employment of the staff, the organization of the classroom work, and the religious instruction provided for the pupils. It is true, the classroom work is inspected by the Public School

Inspector for the County, but the control exercised until now by the Diocese of Huron and by this Department appears to have been more or less nominal. The officials of the Indian Affairs Branch feel that in view of the large annual expenditures involved...the administration of the Institution should be more closely knit...

The Department would be prepared to undertake this direction immediately, but only on the understanding that an experienced agricultural college graduate with pedagogical training were selected for the Principalship. This proposal, however, did not appear at all acceptable to your representatives. Consideration was then given to the operation of the school under your own immediate direction, extending to you full freedom of choice in the selection of the Principal...this Department would continue to pay...the regular per capita grants.

It is altogether likely that the New England Company will be prepared to enter into an agreement with Your Grace for the operation and management of the school. I do feel...the Diocese of Huron should assume this responsibility. The work accomplished at the Institute has not been satisfactory in recent years...operation either by the Government or by the Diocese would...result in more efficient administrative effort and prove more satisfactory to all parties concerned...

70. 17 August 1945   Seager to Hoey

...Friday the 10th, Mr. Zimmerman met Colonel Randall...it was assumed that Mr. Zimmerman was to the appointed Principal by the Government...

The next day...Mr. Zimmerman interviewed Mr. P. Phelan...discussions...included those involved in the management of the School by Mr. Zimmerman as Principal. He was given the keys of the place, introduced to members of the Staff as the new Principal and the matter was apparently finally settled.

At the close of the interview, Mr. Zimmerman naturally inquired as to his position...by whom was he to be appointed, from what source would he get his salary, who was to be responsible for expenditures, etc. etc. Much to his astonishment, he was told by Mr. Phelan that he was to look to the Archbishop of Huron for all these things since the Synod of Huron was taking over the responsibility of financing and managing the School.

...the above statement was made in the face of the facts set forth in my letter to you dated July 27th...we have no authority from the Synod of Huron to assume any financial responsibility whatever...

...it is absolutely impossible for me to transact busines in the face of a contradiction such as the above...

...I therefore find it impossible to continute dircct communication with the Department in this matter. I have appointed the Ven. Archdeacon Townshend of this office to represent me...

1945 - 1970
Rev. John Zimmerman 1945-1970

1. 13 September 1945 Seager to Glen
...The New England Company...propose sending out a representative...to have the matter of the Mohawk Institute administration finally straightened out.

...two matters about which we feel concerned.

The first is the position of the Rev. W. J. Zimmerman, now very busily and effectively engaged in getting the School under way for the season's work...he now has over one hundred pupils enrolled...Your letter to me, however, gives me and him, some concern..."It is my understanding that a Clergyman, Rev. Mr. Zimmerman, nominated by you, has been temporarily placed in charge of the School and will, no doubt, act as principal until a representative of the New England Company visits Canada toward the end of the present calendar year."

...Mr. Zimmerman was appointed Principal before word was received as to the visit of the representative of the New England Company...effective on August 10th last. Finding...that it was the impression of Mr. Phelan, representing the Department, that the Synod of Huron had assumed responsibility for the administration of the School, and knowing that such was not the case, he naturally declined to act until that matter was settled. He resumed the office of Principal, however, under the terms of a Memorandum signed by Mr. Phelan...the decisive phrase in which is "The Indian Affairs Branch would appreciate Mr. Zimmerman taking immediate charge of the Mohawk Institute."...this means that he is appointed Principal, not merely "temporarily placed in charge"...No man of his high ability and equipment would of course accept such an uncertain position...

...the highly important comment..."entire costs of operation and maintenance, with the exception of an annual grant made by the New England Company, now discontinued, were borne by the Government", a statement which I questioned in view of information afforded me by the former Principal...

2. 4 February 1946 Zimmerman to Phelan
I am enclosing a Class Monthly Report for the Manual Training Division.

...we have no instructor at present. I have been very much impressed with the range of work covered by the system...formerly. If our schools could do well all the basic operations necessary for the 10 Badges the time of the children spent here would indeed be very well spent...

3. 7 February 1946 Doucet to Zimmerman
...We are aware that you have no Manual Training Instructor and would suggest that you endeavour to obtain one. I might suggest that you put an add in the paper requiring a man with some teaching experience who would be able to handle elementary woodwork and physical training. You might offer a salary of between $1200.00 and $1500.00, plus room and board. We are prepared to pay one half of the salary...When you have succeeded in securing a teacher...I will be...pleased to go down to the school...to give the teacher the proper start.

4. 22 February 1946 Brantford Expositor
L.C.W. Urges Action to Better Conditions at Mohawk Institute

Recommendations for more clothing and furnishings, better educational facilities and general building improvements...were fully approved...at the meeting of the Brantford Local Council of Women...after they had made an inspection tour.

...the cause for such conditions did not lay upon the shoulders of the Anglican Church, which has supervised the religious aspects...nor of the New England Company ...which owns the land and buildings and which has been forced, through the war, to cease at least for a time, sending over annual grants for the upkeep of the school; nor of the Department of Indian Affairs...

The whole trouble seemed to stem...from the division of authority...and from the entirely insufficient grants which were made annually by the Government...

(1)- The addition of highly trained domestic science teachers so that the young girls might receive training in homemaking, child training, home nursing...

(2)- The addition of highly trained instructors so that boys might be taught woodworking, handicrafts, farming and the basic principles of trades.

(3)- The addition of music and art teachers to the staff.

(4)- The installation of physical education facilities, a recreation room and proper supervision for such.

(5)- The addition of a well-equipped library.

(6)- The addition of a quiet, supervised study room.

(7)- The addition of proper classroom equipment...

Miss M. Milne, R.N., Health Convenor...pointed out that though there were no regular health clinics conducted...it was hoped that suficient dental and medical care would be soon inaugurated...

Members of the present staff...and...Principal were highly commended for their fine efforts despite the dire conditions under which they had to work...

Archdeacon Clarke said...the situation was definitely not the fault of the Anglican Church. He named the three responsible and interested parties who were supposedly taking care of the school, but stated the main trouble was that the whole situation "seemed to be nobody's baby."

Mrs. Willoughby told the members that there was dire need of bedding, clothing, dishes, towels and wash cloths, tablecloths, furniture and various other things.

5. 23 February 1946 Randle to Hoey
...local press reports and comment in connection with the Local Council of Women's action...

...this office would assure you that everything is in normal good order at the Institute. The Principal and his staff have been attending to their duties, and the care, comfort and well being of the children has received first consideration, as far as circumstances and facilities permit. In fact the energy and interest shown by the Principal has resulted in probably the children receiving the best all-round feeding and care in years.

So this office can only express regret that it is not possible to advise you what is behind this sudden interest by an organization who have never previously shown the slightest interest - or why they should have placed the spotlight on the Mohawk Institute in rather an unfair manner.

What is known is that members of the Local Council of Women made a very cursory visit to the school a few weeks ago on the pretence they wished to supply some recreational equipment for the children -but instead spent the brief period of their visit questioning Mrs. Zimmerman on various matters and features concerning the school's administration.

One member also visited this office in my absence and asked for Mr. Moses - and there was a long discussion over the school - but what was said is not known, though Mr. Moses states he said little, as Mr. Hilton Hill, the former Chief Clerk, happened in at that time and did the talking.

On hearing of this incident I informed the Local Council of Women that if they wanted any information from my office it would be preferable if they consulted the responsible person - and they did apologize.

The President also called here, but I was on the Reserve, so finally we only had an unsatisfactory telephone conversation from which it was obvious they had a wrong picture, but were determined to make it public. I suggested they send a written report and recommendation to the Department direct, and see what resulted, - but I was informed that the local Member was attending their meeting and they would accept his advice...Mr. Zimmerman was in the hospital on the occasion of their brief visit to the Institute - but the Local Council of Women never had the courtesy to discuss the matter at any time since with him.

The recommendations made by the Local Council of Women are highly desirable and commendable, and are all ones that have been discussed among us and planned to some degree, but are dependent largely on increased grants by Parliament - and by all-round good management by the Principal.

Had the Local Council of Women taken this action in past years it would have been more understandable, as the then Principal was sadly lacking in every quality to make the Institute a happy home for children, - but to do it at this time when it should be obvious to everyone that the Department in changing the Principal was intent on an all-round improvement, seems rather like an attempt to be sensational and gain publicity rather than be helpful and just, with their case built up on a somewhat limited knowledge and one-sided viewpoint of the Institution.

6. 27 February 1946 Brantford Expositor
       More Information on Institute Conditions
...the Local Council of Women's investigation...came about as the result of a visit to the institution with idea in mind of furnishing and equipping a study room for the students. Mrs. Cockshutt said:

"Every phase of the Institution is in a disgraceful condition. The students have insufficient food and clothes, the rooms are damp, cold and cheerless and recreational facilities are nil.

There is no infirmary or sick room, no regular dental or medical services provided and if an epidemic struck the School results would be disastrous..."

...contributions would be gratefully received...

7. 28 February 1946 Phelan to Hoey
Acting on your instructions, I...spent Tuesday and Wednesday...investigating charges made by the Brantford Local Council of Women...

...the Local Council of Women had arranged a meeting ...it was their intention to have a newspaper reporter present at the meeting...I informed Mr. Macdonald that if a reporter were present I could only listen to what the women had to say and make no comments...a reporter from the Brantford Expositor was present. I told him that I would be unable to make any statement at all to the Members of the Women's Council if he was present. He said that under these circumstances he would withdraw, and he did so. The only publicity that the meeting obtained was an account of the changes the Local Council of Women consider should be made in the conduct of the Mohawk Institute.

The President...is Mrs. George T. Cockshut...
...the Acting Principal, Reverend W. J. Zimmerman, was ill in the hospital for...approximately 3 weeks in...January. During that period a group of members of the Brantford Local Council of Women went to the Mohawk Institute and interviewed Mrs. Zimmerman. They told her that they had approximately $1,400.00 to spend and expressed a desire to assist the Mohawk Institute...they asked Mrs. Zimmerman what was required...Mrs. Zimmerman considered the Ladies were friendly towards the Institute and consequently she pointed out to them several things that could be improved. However, in subsequent newspaper articles they either accidentally or deliberately changed the tenor of her remarks...she evidently told the Ladies that the school was short of clothing and blankets.

This statement was apparently reported by the Ladies to the effect that the children had no clothing and no blankets. These latter statements are certainly incorrect. It is true that the school has not large surplus stock of either clothing or blankets, but...the children are comfortably clad and that sufficient blankets are available for all the children in residence...I pointed out..that a doctor is on call at all times, that there is a trained nurse on the staff of the school and...any child becoming seriously sick...is removed either to Lady Willingdon Hospital...or to one of the local hospitals in Brantford...we hold dental clinics at regular intervals and... any child developing sudden dental trouble...is immediately taken to one of the local dentists...they still expressed the opinion that additional medical care was necessary.

The statement was also made that a member of the staff should sleep close to the dormitories. I pointed out...that the bedroom of one of the male members of the staff is directly beside the boys' dormitory and that the sleeping quarters occupied by the Principal and his wife are immediately outside the girls' dormitory. It would appear ...that they did not inspect the building very carefully.

...I pointed out to them that all the girls are taught cooking and sewing under the direction of a member of the staff. It is true that this staff member is not always a trained domestic science teacher but is a person well qualified to teach cooking. We had a manual training teacher at this school two years ago. Since that time we have been unable to engage a qualified manual training teacher...The appointment of music and art teachers to the staff is a matter of opinion. Certainly, such teachers are engaged at few, if any, of our schools.

The Council of Women complained regarding the general condition of the school. It is true that the building was erected many years ago, but it was rebuilt in 1923. The playrooms available for the children are not as spacious as they might be. The complaint of the Council of Women regarding the size of the dormitories is unwarranted, as these are sufficiently large to provide the necessary air space for the number of children enrolled. ...the 21-year lease of the Mohawk Institute, given to the Department by the New England Company, expired in 1943. One provision of that lease was that the Principal should be a Minister of the Anglican Church. When that lease expired in 1943, the New England Company agreed to re-lease the building, but in their new lease made no mention of the necessity of appointing a Minister as Principal...the Archbishop of Huron took exception to this clause and stated that in his opinion an Anglican Minister should be appointed, in view of the long association of the Anglican Church with the Mohawk Institute. As a result of the stand taken by His Grace, the lease has not been renewed by the New England Company, either with the Department or with the Diocese of Huron. In view of this position, I pointed out to the Council of Women that in

my opinion the Department could not legally spend any money on the Mohawk Institute...if the lease was eventually concluded...the Department would then be responsible for repairs and improvements required to the building. On the other hand, if the lease was concluded between the New England Company and the Diocese of Huron, this Department would only be responsible for payment of the per capita grant. Archdeacon Clarke, of Brantford had given an interview to the Paper, pointing out that the Church of England was in no way responsible for any situation that might arise at the Mohawk Institute...I thought it advisable to have an interview with him...We discussed the whole matter and pointed out to him the situation and expressed regret that he had seen fit to express the position of the Anglican Church. I told him politely that I thought it would have been preferable to make no statement to the Press on the matter unless it was made by either Archdeacon Townshend or Mr Lucas, who were the gentlemen originally appointed by...the Archbishop of Huron to conduct negotiations with the Department. I pointed out to Archdeacon Clarke the amount which we have expended on the building since the beginning of the lease in 1922 and reminded him that general conditions at the Mohawk Institute had deteriorated, due to the neglect of the former Principal, Reverend H. W. Snell, whose services were dispensed with in July last year. Archdeacon Clarke agreed with me that Mr. Snell's services had not been satisfactory. I also reminded the Archdeacon that the present Principal, Rev. W. J. Zimmerman, had been Acting Principal, nominated by his Grace Archbishop Seager...it is hardly fair for the Church to divest itself of all responsibility.

Colonel Randle accompanied me on a complete tour...the building is not modern but is comfortable. It is kept in a very cleanly manner. Probably the worst fault is that the recreation rooms for both boys and girls are in the basement, and while an effort is being made to do so, it is difficult to make these rooms as attractive as all concerned would like to have them. However, Mr. Zimmerman is making an earnest endeavour to improve conditions in this regard. The toilet facilities adjacent to the dormitories are not as extensive as they should be, but owing to the construction of the building, improvements in this particular regard could not be made without very heavy expenditure. Adequate toilet and bathroom facilities are provided in the basement for the girls and adequate toilets and shower baths are provided in the basement for the boys...we found that the doors to the fire escapes were closed with panic bolts, which could be easily opened...

Colonel Randle and myself suggested to the Principal certain improvements that could be made at once in the playrooms...to make them more attractive. The Principal promised to have this matter receive immediate attention.

The public school inspector was interviewed but he did

not know any qualified vocational teacher whose services could be obtained at present. It may be impossible to secure such a teacher before September 1. I instructed both Colonel Randle and the Principal to continue their efforts to secure a manual training teacher. There is a building suitable for manual training and we have a sufficient supply of tools in it. When I told the Local Council of Women that the school was equipped in this manner, they expressed surprise as they had not been shown this particular building. It is a separate building...

Conditions generally at the Mohawk Institute have improved since Rev. W. J. Zimmerman took charge. Many of the complaints made by the Local Council of Women are the result of the unsatisfactory services of Rev. H. W. Snell during the last two or three years of his term as Principal.

A peculiar feature of the whole affair is that Mrs. Cockshutt...has never interviewed Mr. Zimmerman at any time. She visited the school during the Principal's absence in hospital owing to illness and interviewed Mrs. Zimmerman, who of course is new to the work and probably said more than she should have. Mrs. Cockshutt did not interview our Indian Superintendent but instead rushed into print and had the opinions of the Local Council of Women broadcast over the local radio station. Mrs. Cockshutt is a very determined lady and will probably keep up the agitation if she can continue to obtain the support of the other members of the Council... Mrs. Cockshutt's last request was that a committee (presumably including herself) should be allowed to visit the Mohawk Institute at periodic intervals in order to ascertain if the improvements they had suggested are being put into effect. I told her very definitely that we were not prepared to give her any such permission. I pointed out that the school is visited two or three times a week by Indian Superintendent Randle and that other government officials inspected at regular intervals.

8. 15 March 1946 Randle to Phelan

Mrs. Zimmerman this Morning received a phone call from one of the ladies in the city regarding a Sum of $10.00 which was voted to assist the children at the Mohawk Institute. This money has been voted by one of the organizations in the United Church. Mrs. Zimmerman said she would refer the matter to the Principal. As the matter stands the money will be sent to the school. Some decision must be reached respecting this most urgent problem. I have been told that there are few groups responding to the appeal of the Local Council of Women...When asked by the local Council of Women if I would approve a city wide appeal on behalf of the children I said that I could not. I do not believe it is my duty or right to authorize anything of that character. This school is administered by the Department.

One lady who belongs to this United Church group and

who knows the children at the Mohawk Institute was furious at the stories related. The report brought from the local Council was the children are starving. She told me that she has seen the children and she knows that it is untrue. No one has denied these stories in the Press and hence there is much gossip.

9. 20 July 1946 Dr. Palmer to Randle

Having completed three months as acting Medical Officer to the Mohawk Institute I...draw your attention to some of the medical and hygienic conditions...

...my relations with the Principal and Matron have been most cordial, and that I have received the utmost cooperation from all members of the Staff.

...the general health of the pupils has been very good, with a notable absence of respiratory infections.

Forty cases were referred to Lady Willingdon Hospital during this period. They consisted of 36 cases for removal of Tonsils and Adenoids; 2 cases of Acute Rheumatic Fever; and 2 cases of Interstitial Karatitis found to be Wassermann positive and requiring anti-syphilitic treatment.

Two cases of Vincent's Stomatitis were referred to Dr. Bradley Linscott for dental treatment.

Several cases of Impetiga Contagiosa were found and cleared up rapidly with sulphathiazole ointment.

General inspections of all buildings were made and many unsatisfactory conditions were found.

Dishes were being washed in soapy water too infrequently changed, and dried with none too clean dish towels. It was recommended that they be scraped clean, washed in soapy water, rinsed in clear water, dipped in HTH 15 solution and dry racked.

Roller hand towels were found to be in use in the pupils' wash rooms. On several occasions they were found to be very dirty and unsanitary. In my opinion they should be discarded and paper towels provided.

It was found that the female pupils are using cloth sanitary napkins which are washed in the school laundry. It is strongly recommended that they be dispensed with, and disposable sanitary pads be supplied instead.

There are no seats or tables in the boys' recreation room. It is suggested that barrack room benches and tables might be obtained for this purpose.

Flour and sugar were found stored in bags and exposed to mice. It was recommended that such commodities be purchased in one bag quantities and kept in covered metal containers.

Bread was found kept in open baskets, exposed to flies and mice. It was recommended that screened open shelves be built for storing bread.

...the refrigeration space is presently very inadequate, and the equipment is not in good working order.

There is no ice available to cool milk at the dairy, and insufficient refrigeration space for its storage.

The outbuildings are infested with rats, and the Brant County Health Unit has been consulted regarding means to eradicate this menace.

It is hoped that arrangements can be made to carry out the...recommendations without undue delay.

10. [Date?] Brantford Expositor
L.C.W. Reply Re Findings Of Grand Jury

In view of the press report Wednesday of the investigation of the Supreme Court Grand Jury of Mohawk Institute and the report brought in by them that "considerable criticism has been made against this Institute but in our opinion we did not find any evidence to warrant such criticism". Mrs George Cockshutt...told the Expositor today:

The L.C.W. Investigation Committee reported conditions as found at the Mohawk Institute, having in mind the welfare of the Indian children and bringing the School up to present-day educational standards. Some two months of considerable work preceded the drawing up of the recommendations now before the Indian Branch...

Members of the Committee...included...Three former school teachers, one of whom was a specialist in child psychology, two graduates of the Macdonald Institute and who specialized in domestic science and institution management; three child and family welfare workers; a member of the House Committee of the Children's Aid Society for 20 years standing; the President of the Victorian Order of Nurses, and a matron of a children's institute who is a registered nurse...(8) The addition of a supervised recreation room for boys and girls. (9) The installation of better toilet facilities for all children. (10) More dormitory accommodation and teacher supervision at night for the dormitories. (11) A trained dietitian to plan meals and balanced food diets for the children.

...that dental care twice a year and regular medical check-ups, especially for tuberculosis, V.D. and diptheria were extremely necessary, and suggested that the Institution be brought under the County Health unit so that those services might be provided.

It was stated that an infirmary to segregate the children who were ill, from the others, was also needed. Clothing for all children, bedding, dishes and cutlery were immediate needs, they found. They suggested that the War Assets Corporation be asked to turn over to the Institute as soon as possible, mattresses to remedy the bedding situation...

11. 30 September 1946 Neary to Zimmerman
...regarding the employment of a Manual Training Instructor...It was understood from our conversation that you had a fair chance of securing a reasonably qualified man...

12. 11 October 1946 LaVerne Morgan to Neary
...Last night Mr. Zimmerman interviewed Mr. and Mrs. J. Elmer Anderson...his wife is also available for Public School teaching...Between the two of them they could take over the duties of the Senior teacher Mr. Connell who is leaving and perhaps relieve Mrs. Fry of one grade. They seem like a likely couple for the work.

13. 16 October 1946 Neary to Zimmerman
The Department is willing to authorize the appointment of Mr. J. Elmer Anderson as manual training teacher at the Mohawk Institute. A grant of $135.00 a teaching month will be made...towards his salary...

14. 19 February 1947 Zimmerman
Mr. Anderson is getting on with his manual training work. The first project he is tackling is the repairing of the desks in the two classrooms...I prefer to see the boys doing something practical. Mrs. Anderson is doing part-time teaching. They are a splendid couple...

15. 6 December 1947 Zimmerman to Neary
...Last year a special grant was authorized for those going to Collegiate. I have not received the last half of the special grant for Dorothy Jamieson.

This year Pauline Commandant and Lois Claus are attending the Collegiate. Will there be any special grant for them? They are residing at the Institute.

With this matter of food I am running into real difficulty. To maintain the present type of meals being served I cannot remain within the budget. Mrs Davies is trying to give the children a balanced diet. One of the boys said the other day that one of the things which keeps him at the school is the good food. He plainly stated that if there was a return to the former meals as served a number of years ago he would not stay. He is the type of boy who would take to the road. I am concerned about whether if we could make any savings whether we would run into more truancy or not. I am spending a great deal of time on this matter of food.

Last year I bought a number of bags of potatoes at 50 cents per bag. The other day Mr. Haworth was offered $3.00 for all the potatoes per bag. We did not sell any since I do not know what we shall have left over. The bread cost us $50.00 per month alone extra. We use about 1 bag of potatoes alone each day. When you add the extra cost for these items alone you can see what difference it makes.

To illustrate again our problem. According to the Mohawk creamery butter sold to customers cost on March 25/46 39 cents per pound. On November 25/47 butter cost 64 cents per pound. That same month we used 100 pounds of butter and it cost 62.68 as against $39.00 for 100 pounds in March of 46...My records illustrate this rise in connection with one item after another.

I understand that the churches have interviewed the Minister in connection with the matter of grants. Is there any information available?

The other night the Maintenance Man went into the Upper Dormitory and discovered what we have suspected but could not actually discover in the act. Two boys were caught in the act of homo-sex. One lad was holding a younger lad and the third caught in the act while stripped to the skin. The remainder of the boys in the dormitory were watching these disgraceful proceedings. According to the I.Q. test made by Mr. Webster the lad caught in the act is 16 with an I.Q. rating of 7-11 (Mental Age.). What form of punishment will you permit for boys who persist in this filthy business? I have tried to reason with them and employ various approaches. For the lad who will not respond to the normal decencies of life through the normal approaches is there any other way than to resort to the pleasure pain principle?

During this past month we have had some outbreaks of stealing. Colonel Randle sent in one boy during my time here for tampering with the mail on the Reserve. The other week he went up to the store and stole two guns (Toy). He also went through Mr. Barton's home and stole a watch and used a 22 rifle. Another lad went up to the store and stole a purse. He said he wanted money to buy bread. The rule now in force is that boys can go uptown provided they are trustworthy. Needless to say these boys will not be able to go uptown without supervision. I do not want to see this one boy go to some jail eventually. I may belong to the old school but I believe that if we were permitted in these extreme cases to spank their posterior ends it might do some good. If you strap them on the hands they go down to the playroom and say they were not strapped hard. What do you think of it?

All the officers are quite agreed that the type of children coming here has altered. That is the ones who have been here sometime.

16. 15 December 1947 Neary to Zimmerman
...I appreciate your frankness in broaching this matter of corporal punishment. We have corporal punishment regulations which we recommend to Principals who are having difficulty with this matter...These regulations are...

1...Corporal punishment will be used only where all other methods of disciplining a pupil have failed.

2...corporal punishment will be administered only on the hands with a proper school strap (regulation 15" rubber).

3...the maximum number of strokes on each hand in no instance exceed four in number for male pupils of over fourteen years of age and in proportion for boys under that age.

4...all such corporal punishment be administered in the presence of the principal or by the principal.

5...a Corporal Punishment Register be maintained at the school containing the following headings:
a) Date
b) Reason for Punishment.
c) By whom administered.
d) Witness.
e) Signature of pupil punished.
6...this Register be made available for inspection by all Indian Affairs Branch officials visiting the above.

You will find in the long run that it does not pay to strap pupils anywhere but on the hands. The above regulations "systemitize" the administration of corporal punishment and the very form which the pupil has to go through is in itself a deterrent...

17. 10 February 1948 Bishop of Huron to Minister of Mines and Resources
As Bishop of the Diocese of Huron in which the Mohawk Institute...I naturally feel a certain responsibility for its welfare. I am therefore taking the liberty of drawing your attention to its present situation and needs. ...I have asked certain men, including the Principal of the School, to advise me...conditions in the School have notably improved in the past two or three years, both as to the personal welfare of the children and as to farm productiveness and administration...due largely to the work of the Principal, Mr. Zimmerman, to the active co-operation of the Department and the material assistance of the Church. This latter has been very substantial.

The recently developed policy of the Department to strengthen the Day School System on the Reserves, a policy which we cordially welcome, has however...almost completely changed the character of the School...

Until recently the School has served almost exclusively the families on the Mohawk Reserve, whether members of the Church of England or not, many of whose children were trained in the School in the ordinary way and not in the Day Schools. Now, however, the Institute has become a School mainly for underprivileged children, either as a result of broken homes or because of anti-social tendencies in the children themselves. Moreover, they are now drawn from a far wider field than the Mohawk Reserve. Such children require quite different treatment from those under normal conditions such as have prevailed until recent years.

...we regard certain changes as urgent...there are very many children who are far below the achievement of normal children of the same age...These children cannot make satisfactory progress in a regular classroom...survey of the mental ability of these children might be made and if found necessary, special "opportunity classes," similar to those established in the public schools in Ontario towns and cities, be organized. This, of course, would require specially trained teachers, special equipment and above all, an enrolment of not more than twenty for each teacher. This, of course, would increase the cost of tuition, but it is clear that these special children cannot be educated for good citizenship in ordinary classrooms.

With respect to the rest of the children, many appear to have far too much time on their hands owing to the fact that in certain grades they are only taught for part of the day. These include Grades five and six, whose instruction should be, in our opinion, continued throughout the day.

As is to be expected under such circumstances...the average intelligence of the pupils in the School is much lower than it was a few years ago. A few, however, with high intelligence might be trained as "student leaders" to assist in discipline, in games programmes, and in the general supervision of the work of the pupils in the house and on the farm. There is a number of "special or problem pupils" who should not be in the Institute. For example, a boy of sixteen years with a mental age of eight, and children with apparently uncontrollable anti-social tendencies should not...be in the School...the teaching staff would have to be increased to five or six... and made up of persons competent for the special needs...

...reference to the salaries of teachers is necessary. These, in the case of some members of the staff, are very low, and when they retire it will be impossible to secure successors at their present salaries...an Order-in-Council has been passed giving the Indian Day School teachers permanent positions as to status and pensions. We regard it as necessary that teachers in such schools as the Mohawk Institute should be included in this plan...

A leading factor in the altered situation is the vastly increased overhead costs of everything, including food, clothing, salaries and upkeep generally...in 1947 the Department increased the per capita grants in the School by $20.00 per pupil. This increase...would of course not be sufficient for the carrying out of any such plan as is outlined in this letter. As an instance of increased costs, the women's missionary organization of the Church of England found it necessary to spend over $5,000.00 to equip the children in clothing...assistance in this respect on any such scale cannot be continued. The Synod of Huron...made grants which...amounted to $1,000.00 during the past year or so. As the Synod has no administrative authority in the School it is hardly reasonable to expect that body to continue such extensive help...

18. 23 November 1948   Doucet to Neary
Inspection of Mohawk Institute
...The new classroom block is quite an improvement over the former classroom. I am satisfied that this will contribute greatly to the efficiency of the education at this institute provided the proper type of teacher is secured.

My first impression especially when going through the dormitories and the playroom was a sense of depression. It is the old story of noticing children wandering without any purpose whatsoever during their free time. This can have a very baneful effect on their character and on their immediate conduct.

Two of the dormitories are rather badly served by two dormer windows and fire escape door...these dormitories handle as many pupils as wisdom will allow...There is a great deal of space lost in the middle of this school...due ...to the fact that the Principal would be reluctant to have dormitories above his own living quarters...it would be wise to have other quarters for the Principal and to use the school to full advantage. There would be adequate space for bathroom facilities for the boys and girls dormitories if use were made of this space.

...I do not see any possibility with the present set-up of improving the toilet facilities in the dormitories. The present system has nothing in it that is recommendable especially in the boys dormitory. The toilet is open and very close to the beds. This should be eliminated and it could be done by a rearrangement of the beds. Any change, however, would be of a temporary nature and would not rectify the faults that exist...

[Photographs and Comments]
1. The main building...should have the old chimneys removed and the balcony repaired. The central attic should be fitted up as sleeping accommodation...
Boys' Washroom
Showers are situated at far left. Duckboards or rubber mats should be provided to reduce the discomfort of standing on the cold slippery floor. Note the roller towels at the left. There are no personal towels.
One of the three new classrooms. We should add a fourth while army buildings are available. In the desk nearest the door an under-age child is sleeping. We should have a real primary room.
The Principal states that the law requires the fire-escapes to be illuminated. The law may some day focus on the dish-washing, milk-handling, and overcrowding.
Girls' basement.
Three stages in the life of a tissue fixture: a) functioning b) partly dismantled c) vanished. The bowls, seats and valve controls are fine but dignity and decency arent getting much consideration.
Another girls' washroom. Same ration of tissue. Fragments of one seat remain. Partition, but no doors. Strangely enough, the bath-tubs across the room are fully screened, as if there were greater indelicacy in washing.
In the boys' basement there is also a great wastage of toilet seats. The principal was advised to obtain a more durable type.
Something could be done to the floor to make it drain and dry faster after being hosed.
Typical of the way beds are crowded together. This is an argument in favour of "double-deckers" or of opening the middle portion of the "attic" as a dormitory. Both ends of the attic are dormitories.
Girls' end of the attic. A cloth screen is said to be available to draw around this installation. Could it not be

properly partitioned and ventilated? At the boys' end, the toilet is in a recess which has a window.

There was evidence on the ceiling of the dormitory shown above that installations of plumbing like this and others shown over-leaf contribute nothing to the sublimation of "anal--eroticism" (Freud) which is allowed to persist too long and which is too often confused by our principals with sexual manifestations.

The dormitory should approximate more the home bedroom if it is to train pupils in looking after their own things and leaving other people's things alone. "Thou shalt not steal" because everything is locked up.

My purpose in the views presented and expressed over-leaf is to try to create a physical environment which will help rather than hinder the process of conditioning the inmates, many of whom constitute a challenge to the abilities of such staff members as we can attract.

...the conditions are not good enough for a school whose objective is to raise the cultural and moral level of children who have already had a lower-than-average start.

Conditions in the washrooms would by ordinary white standards be called degrading.

In the dormitories, even though there will be [c?], a child should be allowed to keep his clothing and possessions and be trained to look after them.

We should try to add a fourth classroom and equip it in the accepted primary room style.

The sewing room should be set up, equipped, and used as a centre for creative work for regularly constituted classes.

Manual training needs more emphasis. It is a question whether Mr. Anderson should be expected to do all the manual training necessary plus the academic work which only he is available to do.

Physical education and games lack effective direction. The staff should include a person with training and enthusiasm for this work.

19. 10 February 1949 Luxton to Neary

...As Bishop I have again visited the School, spoken to the teachers and children in their class rooms and inspected the farm buildings...I have also had three long interviews with the Principal...I am coming to understand some of the problems that press upon us in this School, and...beginning to see some light on an horizon that has not been in recent years very bright.

Together with Mr. Zimmerman I have gone over carefully the financial records, his records of the pupils and his teaching problems in the School. I have also studied the reports of the District Inspector regarding the I.Q. of the present students and the opportunities of education and development which they now enjoy at the Mohawk Institute. Also I have discussed with Mr. Zimmerman his own future as Principal of the Institute. The progress...during the last four years has been very

remarkable...if we can keep Mr. Zimmerman contented and happy in his work at the Institute, in another four years this School can become a shining example of the concern of the Government, the Community and the Church for the welfare of our Indian wards.

...I have been studying the change in the type of boy and girl now being sent to the Institute, together with the urgent needs this change has brought before the Principal of the School. Most of the children whom we receive at the Institute are from broken homes or difficult home environment...only about 25 out of the whole school have normal I.Q. rating. The average mental age of the whole school is between two and three years below their chronological age. The School Inspector states that forty of the children should be placed in Auxiliary Classes under the care of teachers specially trained for this difficult and exacting work. At present we have three teachers wrestling as effectively as possible with an impossible task. One will be retiring shortly. Her present stipend is $55.00 a month, plus her board, and there seems little likelihood of replacing her except at a stipend equal to that which a teacher would receive from outside schools. Our needs in the teaching end...are...5 teachers... 2 of the 5 to be specially qualified for auxiliary class work - all..to be fully qualified teachers and to be paid at a rate...equal to that received...in Provincial schools...

After school hours we have two supervisors, - one woman in charge of 75 girls and one man in charge of 80 boys. These children need double the supervision and two of the supervisors should be qualified for leadership in sports and games. Also there should be equipment for sports and games and greatly increased equipment for Manual and Domestic Training for boys and girls incapable of sustained academic work.

The Church is profoundly interested in making the Mohawk Institute an important asset in our vexed Indian problem. We lack the means to make any sizable financial contribution to this work. Our contribution must be made through interest, the recruiting of a staff, the loaning of one of our best clergymen for the principalship and the yearly gift of a small amount of money as well as a considerable gift in clothing and other supplies. The Government grant for teaching staff and supervision must be greatly increased without delay or else we must seriously consider withdrawing completely from this specialist area of Indian work...

Since the Mohawk Institute has become almost a centre for the difficult and sometimes incorrigible Indian children its nature has changed radically from the early days of its foundation when it ministered educationally to the boys and girls of the Six Nations. Today our Church responsibility is greatly lessened. Only a small minority of the children are Church of England. Of 11 admitted in the December quarter of last year only 1 was Church of England...we are glad to share in the partnership of the

Mohawk Institute...but unless we have early assurance of increasing aid from the Government in this special sphere of the difficult, subnormal and incorrigible children we cannot continue in the partnership.

The Principal offered his resignation to me yesterday and I have promised to receive him back into his regular ministerial work in the near future unless...we can find a solution to the problems of staff, off-time supervision, sports activities and occupational training...

20. 10 February 1949 **** to Secretary DIA

I want release for my daughter ****, she is at Mohawk Indian school, she is restless at school and seem to lost interest there I have a good place over here for her...

21. 11 February 1949 Randle to IAB

...early Sunday morning, the 23rd of January, it was found that 25 girls had left the building, all in the teen age group, subsequently it was found they had left their dormitories about 4 a.m. that morning, and by picking a door lock and removing some heavy window covering, had made their get away from the basement.

The Principal advised the R.C.M.P. and local police, and also advised the writer, and also immediately contacted the Ohsweken Detachment in order to have them patrol the roads to watch for truants making for the Reserve and to commence calling at homes where the missing pupils were likely to go.

Within a few days...all the pupils were back except two, one from Sarnia and one from Walpole.

Mr. Zimmerman had, of course, previously contacted the Superintendents of outside Reserves - informing them what girls from their respective Reserves were missing.

On the return of the missing pupils they were questioned as to their motives for running away, and their reasons can be listed...

1) Averse to school discipline, and a belief (evidently fostered by outside influences) that they did not have to obey the orders of the Principal or his staff.

2) Some animosity over punishment from our teacher, Mr. Anderson - with allegations of being too rough.

3) Homesickness

4) Went away for no particular reason - other than because the others were going.

The first reason is understandable - as it appears strongly everywhere - the modern child's dislike for discipline - rules or regulations of any kind, and an inclination to disobey and not respect their elders.

There is some evidence that certain elements on the Reserve are encouraging the children in the belief they do not have to obey orders...

Mr. Zimmerman does not credit that Mr. Anderson has in any way exceeded his powers by punishing children, and on my questioning him about using any physical efforts that might look like force - while not intended to

be - Anderson declared he had not done anything of that nature.

There is naturally always some homesickness, and some of it is the parents' fault as many of them that could, often neglect to visit their children for weeks at a time.

This is a matter the Principal could give some attention to - by contacting, in a friendly manner, parents who could and yet do not visit their children.

It rather appears that two or three girls of the fifteen-year-old group were the ringleaders, and more or less led the bulk of the others on.

The Principal is of the opinion that going home for the summer holidays often plays havoc with girls of this age. Their parents or relatives allow them unlimited freedom, and they often - naturally enough - strike up male friendships - and thus come back to school, and are dissatisfied with restraints of life there.

All the runaway pupils were interviewed on their return, and it was hoped that with the kindly but firm talking to they received that they would settle down and conduct themselves in a fitting manner...ten of the same girls ran away again last Saturday, of which five are back.

We are, at the moment, conducting a thorough investigation into this - and may have to lay charges against some families and individuals for contributing to juvenile delinquency, if the facts warrant it.

This office regrets not reporting the first truancy - but as it was all quickly settled, the writer did not wish to burden your division with its heavy responsibilities with a matter it was our duty to attend to and rectify.

...the second outbreak made the matter much more serious, and it was my intention to report the whole matter when all pupils are back and our investigation complete.

22. 2 March 1949 RCMP vs ****

1. On the 5th of February last a total of six young girls left...without permission. On the 7th of February, four more young girls left the Institute under similar circumstances. About three weeks prior to this a total of twenty-five young girls left the Institute without permission...a large number of these girls were making their way direct to the home of **** where they were staying for a few days before leaving for other parts ...successful in serving Rev. Zimmerman and two of the girls with summonses but the other two girls...again left the Institute and to date have not been located...

23. 2 March 1949 Zimmerman to Neary

Mrs. C. Fry informs me that she will not be remaining on the teaching staff...after June 30, 1949...after many years of loyal and devoted service...she has become discouraged because of the reaction of our Senior Girls. I have offered her the Matronship but she has declined. We do need badly a full time Matron. Mrs. Zimmerman can only give part of her time due to Teddy and Jean.

The interest of the school demands a full time Matron. ...I shall be confronted with the problem of a replacement. Mr. Webster strongly recommends the increasing of the teaching staff. I wish to place on record the endorsement of this recommendation. Owing to low I.Q.s, irregular previous school attendance, lack of self-discipline, maladjusted home relations etc. many of our students present difficult educational problems. Small classes are a necessity. We have been delighted with the response of the boys to manual training. I should like to see...a corresponding program...for the girls. The girls I am certain would reveal more interest in the school if there was instruction in cooking, dress-making, hand craft etc. The routine of the school leaves too little time for many of these things...we require 5 teachers. Our teachers must be placed on an equal standing with those in other branches of the service. One must pay a decent salary if we are going to secure adequate teaching. Now that the school is administered by the Department I do not see how we can escape.

...Mr. Pedbisky has begun Cadet training. When he is training the boys up at the Armouries there is no one to be with the little boys. If the boys are to attend the theatre and not pick up things in the stores they must be escorted. This leaves me with no one with the boys at the school.

The Brantford Council of Local Women are purchasing a movie sound projector for use in the Institute. This machine will mean much since we do not possess a gymnasium. I have accepted this offer since this group represents many organizations in...Brantford. I told them of many advances which had been made during the present few years and what the Department had done. I do not feel that one can go on indefinitely ignoring the recommendations of such a group. The Mohawk Institute is too closely situated to the City of Brantford to escape public observation and criticism...

24. 16 March 1949 McCracken to IAB

****, Sarnia Band had three daughters in...during the 1947-48 term. In July, 1948 this man visited the office and informed me that he did not intend to send **** and **** back to residential school in September. He agreed to send his youngest daughter, ****...was supposed to return...in September, 1948 I put considerable pressure on the father to return her at various times throughout the Fall. He tried to persuade his girl to go back to Brantford but she refused and would run away, etc. In January, 1949 the father was successful in getting her back to Brantford, but she remained there only one week and ran away. She returned to Sarnia Reserve...it would be advisable to agree to the discharge of all three of this man's children.

When Mr. Doucet visited Sarnia Agency about one month ago the matter of truancy of three or four Indian

girls from Mohawk Institute was investigated. One of the girls is ****...I have given this girl temporary permission to attend St. Clair Indian Day School...I do not think it would be advisable to force **** to return...as she would no doubt run away again...When **** left...two Kettle Point girls, namely **** and ****...accompanied her. These two girls are running loose on Sarnia Reserve at the present time. I see no use in forcing them to return to Brantford...These girls are about fourteen or fifteen years of age. I recommend that they be officially discharged...

25. 22 March 1949 Neary to Randle
...I presume that these are the children about whom we talked at Muncey recently and that you do not wish to reommend their dismissal from the Mohawk Institute as recommended by Mr. McCracken.

26. 18 March 1949 Leslie to Tuffnell
...concerning the seven children of Mrs.**** Cape Croker Band...The matter of placing the three oldest in the Mohawk...has been referred to the Training Division...You fail to indicate...what effort the father of these children is prepared to make in looking after them...let us have...your recommendations as to where the children should be placed and at what cost...the Interest shares of the parents and of the children will...be deposited in Savings. In the case of the children entering Mohawk...the monies will be retained until they are twenty-one years of age. The shares of the mother might be available to furnish small comforts for her when she is in the Sanatorium. The shares of the father and four children should...go towards the maintenance of the children...

27. 25 March 1949 Randle to IAB
The writer hesitates to interfere in the decision of a Superintendent of another Agency, but...our policy with regard to the children belonging to the Six Nations Superintendency is that if they play truant by running away they must be found and returned.

Otherwise, we should soon have chaos...as any child with a notion that he or she dislikes the school for some reason or other, could make up their minds to run away, knowing that no action would be taken and it was an easy way to rid themselves of the school and its discipline.

Many parents would also be up in arms over such a lax policy, as it is not unknown for a child to run away to some relative, who is sympathetic and stay there, rather than go home to parents who will send them back...

On the other hand...once children arrive at the Mohawk Institute, they become, in a way, my responsibility...when such outbreaks occur, the Principal phones me and on each occasion it has been necessary to institute energetic action as the Principal is inclined to be lost in a fog. ...the action taken in Court against the young men for contributing to juvenile delinquency of the runaways, that each was convicted and given a $50.00 fine or two months in gaol...both the girl pupils and the young men, learned a mighty good lesson...the Principal informs me the girls concerned have been very much subdued since that experience...

28. 9 April 1949 Neary to Randle

We note the action taken by the court against the young men who contributed to juvenile delinquency in the recent truancy case...the **** girls are among the ring leaders in this truancy case and...some consideration should be given to have them committed to a reform institution. The Department can appreciate the extra burden placed on you as Indian Superintendent directly responsible for this school when you are faced with a number of truancies. While the discipline of this school must be maintained, we do not want Indian Superintendents to regard it as a Reform institution to which children can be sent who are giving trouble to their parents.

The Indian parents must also be informed that children can not be sent to the Mohawk Residential School and discharged from it to suit their whims...

29. 25 April 1949 Neary to Dept. Purchasing Agent

...we are limiting each school to a number of labour saving devices each year...Zimmerman...feels that the appliance which will best suit his purpose is the floor polisher requested herewith...this will enable him to have his children spend more time in the classroom and less time on school labour.

30. 7 May 1949 **** to DIA

...I, ****member of the Saugeen Band....am making an application for a transferral of my three children...to the Shingwauck...as soon as possible...reasons...can be stated by me should the Dept of Indian Affairs require...

31. 13 May 1949 Zimmerman to Neary

1 Number of cows milking...May 12/49..23
2. Number of Gallons of milk...May 12/49...966 lbs.
3. Milk supplied to school...May 12/49...375 lbs
4. Number of gallons sold...No milk sold...During Month of April sold 446.9 lbs of butter fat.
One gallon of milk weighs roughly 10 lbs.

The custom at the Institute has been to use skim milk at the school. Besides the skim milk there is sent to the Institute 2 qts. of cream and 6 qts. of milk each day.

32. 25 July 1949 Spence to IAB

...letter...approving of the admittance...of five children of *** widower of the Moravian Indian Reserve.

Mr.**** was married of June 10th last, and he and his wife are prepared to care for the children at their home on the Reserve.

I recommend that these children be discharged.

33. 4 August 1949 Neary to Robertson

...reference to the 3 **** children.

The Department does not see any special necessity for transferring these children to the Shingwauk...at the present time. Even though the father obtains work in Northern Ontario, there is no guarantee that he will be close to the Shingwauk School...

Under these circumstances, the children would be better to remain in the Mohawk Residential School.

34. 13 September 1949 McCracken to IAB

****...was admitted to Mohawk Institute...in September, 1948. His mother, who was divorced, remarried...on July 9th, 1949. She is now able to give her child the proper care in her own home and requests permission to have him discharged...

I have discussed the matter with the Principal of the school and he agreed to the discharge. **** is now attending day school on Sarnia Indian Reserve and I recommend that the Department approve of his permanent release from residential school.

35. 8 February 1950 McCracken to IAB

On or about January 1st, 1950 four children of the Sarnia Agency ran away...aged fifteen...fifteen...fourteen and...fourteen...

**** stopped briefly at Sarnia and then continued on to Detroit, where she is living with an older sister. **** is living in her father's home on Sarnia Reserve. **** and **** are with relatives at Kettle Point.

The two **** children stayed with **** on Sarnia Reserve for about three weeks. I interviewed these children on January 16th. They claimed that the Principal had punished them unjustly and that they were unwilling to return to Brantford. A day or so after my interview ****'s father, ****, appeared at this office. He stated that he was making immediate arrangements to return them...

36. 11 March 1950 Zimmerman to Neary

...enclosed the application form for Mrs. Sharon. She has fitted well into the school...

...as a result of introducing domestic help we have been able to return to the former pattern of A. and B. divisions. The children beyond grade five are receiving their regular half day. The man who works the scrubbing machine has made a tremendous difference...the moral of the children is the best I have seen here to date. We have movies each week.....the children do appreciate them very much.

37. 15 March 1950 Brantford Expositor
Conditions Deplorable At Mohawk Institute, Jury's Report Reveals

The condition of the dormitories and bathroom and toilet facilities at the Mohawk Institute were described as "deplorable" by a grand jury...The grand jury noted that the Mohawk Institute had not been inspected by a similar body during the past four years. "We strongly recommend that this institution be watched closely by succeeding grand juries for the next five to six years... There are 153 kiddies living in this building and this is taxing the accommodation to very serious extent. The conditions of toilet and bathroom facilities were found to be in a deplorable state and we would recommend that this condition be rectified with the least amount of delay ...Condition of the building, particularly the dormitories, is in a very deplorable state. The fire hose and equipment is not of modern design and should be changed immediately as the fire hose was found to be rotten...

The jury praised the work of Rev. W. J. Zimmerman, superintendent, "who has been doing a very excellent job with what he has had to work with."

38. 16 March 1950 Brantford Expositor
Conditions at Mohawk Institute Being Corrected Indian Supt. Here Says
The report of the grand jury...was very one-sided, Lt.-Col. E. P. Randle...said today.

He felt that the force and fairness of the grand jury's contentions were considerably lessened by the fact that the report failed completely to refer to information given the jury by Principal Rev. W. J. Zimmerman, as to major improvements already made and the even more extensive ones shortly to be undertaken...

The superintendent said that funds have been provided this year and tenders from local contractors are already in for the construction of additional dormitories with a considerable addition to the present toilet facilities...

Col. Randle said that the jury was told about the many improvements to be made shortly but it made no reference whatsoever to those in its report.

He said that the Indian Affairs Branch...only took over full control of the Mohawk Institute from the New England Company for maintenance and repairs during the Second World War.

(Until the early years of the war, the New England Company provided directly approximately $6,000 annually for the maintenance and repair of the institute. After the bombing of London when the company lost the revenue from buildings destroyed, the grants ceased and the Indian Affairs Branch then took over full responsibility.)

"Since then, the Indian Affairs Branch has thoroughly appreciated the fact that the buildings needed complete renovation, modernization and the provision of extra accommodation. Some of this has been done, much of it is under way and the rest will be carried out as quickly as various governing circumstances permit," he said.

Wartime and post-war conditions in the building trades had delayed improvements somewhat since most contractors were tied up with larger and more urgent demands, Col. Randle said.

Among improvements carried out since the institute was taken over...was the addition of three more classrooms by moving in a former army hut from Camp 20 in Echo Place. This made two former classrooms available for recreation rooms and replaced former unsuitable accommodation.

These additions took place in 1948, he said, in 1949, the main building and classrooms were completely rewired and more lighting fixtures installed.

Col. Randle said that approximately the same number of pupils have boarded at the school for the last 40 years during which time the accommodation was unchanged.

Other improvements which have been definitely provided for in 1950 are for replastering and redecorating the entire main building. This work had been held over until the rewiring was completed.

Funds are also available this year to provide a principal's residence which will make vacant his present quarters and provide additional staff and pupil accommodation.

...Col. Randle said that a new fire alarm system has also been installed during the last three years and that deficient hose or connexions were replaced.

"We work in close co-operation with the Fire Department," he said. "The new alarm system is directly connected with the Fire Hall."

To criticism of the bedding, Col. Randle said that new mattresses were supplied in the last four years and replacement of worn out bedsteads had already been arranged for this year. Additional laundry equipment has also been provided, he said.

Provision had also been made for the construction of a new silo this year...

...more teaching and domestic staff had been engaged to improve educational facilities and more efficiently administer the institute and lighten the children's duties.

Outlining the increase of government grants toward upkeep of each child Col. Randle said that the per capita increase was from $160 in 1945 to $275 in 1950. The increase...but was allotted gradually year by year, he said.

The per capita grant did not go toward building improvements but was allotted to the clothing, feeding and educational upkeep of each child. Any improvements being made to the buildings and other facilities came from other appropriations, he said.

39. 24 March 1950 Zimmerman to Neary
I am enclosing a rush order for Mrs. Davidson our school nurse. We have had many ill with the 'flu'.

Mrs. Sharon, the new teacher, begun her work on March 6, 1950. She is fitting in very well and appears to be taking a real interest in the Children.

The work has begun in the attic and rapid progress is being made...I do appreciate the increase in salary.

40. 25 July 1950 Gauthier to IAB

...for the past two years we have had thirteen children belonging to six different families attending the Mohawk...All of these children have been taken out for the summer months by the guardians or parents and I am advised and requested by the parents and guardians to ascertain whether these children could be admitted to Shingwauk...

The parents and guardians and the children are not satisfied with conditions at Mohawk...but realize that the return of the children to this Residential School is their responsibility and are aware of the fact that sending them to Shingwauk...will cost more money but still desire to have them attend Shingwauk.

41. 31 July 1950 Neary to Gauthier

...The Department is now prepared to favourably consider allowing these children to change. There are qualified teachers at the Mohawk school and during the current summer we have expended a considerable amount of money in repairs and improvements to the building.

The children of Christian Island who were enrolled at the Mohawk...during...1949-50 and whose parents are unable to support them and send them to a day school... should return to the Mohawk Institute on September 1st.

42. 5 August 1950 Zimmerman to Neary

...the payment of the teachers by the DIA has been a success...during the year 1949-50...The teachers and the remainder of the staff worked excellently together.

The system assures our schools of properly qualified teachers. This is a matter of extreme importance when the future of our Indian People is considered.

43. 12 September 1950 McCracken to IAB

...children of Mr. and Mrs. ****...Sarnia...Two of these children did not remain at Brantford very long. They ran away twice and as the end of term was approaching I could not persuade the parents to return them to Brantford. The parents brought the youngest child home for summer vacation and they are now refusing to return any of their children to residential school.

In view of the truancy of the...children and the attitude of their parents, and also the fact that they are attending day school on the Reserve, I recommend that they be permanently discharged...

44. 26 October 1950 Zimmerman to Neary

...construction of the Principal's Residence is progressing favourably. I am concerned about the matter of a night-watchman after...we move into our new quarters. I believe that with the number of children in the building and since we are using teachers for evening duty who sleep out of the Institute a night watchman is essential.

I understand there is a grant available for the payment...

of a nightwatchman. Mr. George Hawarth, our farm manager for 30 years, is in his 70th year...in view of his many years of service and...there is no superannuation this position would afford a happy solution...the farm and garden is proving too much for Mr. Hawarth.

45. 7 November 1950 Randle to IAB

...this office considers the Principal is wise in endeavouring to secure the provision of a night watchman ...the farm manager is in his 70th year and for the two past years has not been able, owing to failing health, to give the work the supervision or direction it requires.

Consequently, Mr. Zimmerman feels the other farm help are getting dissatisfied over Mr. Hawarth no longer taking his fair share of the work and that a change is necessary in the interest of all concerned, apart from the farm operations which are suffering.

...Barton, who has been his main assistant for many years and is a young capable farmer, would take over the management of the farm.

46. 8 November 1950 McCracken to IAB

**** and ****, aged fourteen and twelve...have run away...They arrived at their parents' home on Sarnia Reserve last Thursday, accompanied by another boy from Tyendinaga Reserve...This is the second time since September, 1950 that **** has been truant. About one month ago he ran away and was escorted back...by the Provincial Police. Mrs. ****... states that the boys told her that they will run away again if they are returned to Brantford and give as the reason the fact that older boys in the school are mistreating them. At the moment the boys do not know that I am aware of their presence on the Sarnia Reserve. I have no guarantee that they will remain at the **** home very long, particularly if they discover that I am aware of their presence.

These two **** boys are entirely out of control, both at home and at Mohawk Instiute. I hesitate to recommend their permanent discharge as I know it will be impossible to persuade them to attend day school on the Reserve...Mr. Zimmerman...states that they are a bad influence on the rest of the pupils at the school. He suggests...Shingwauk.

47. 15 January 1951 Director IAB to Minister

Mr. Hawarth has been employed as Farm Manager at the above school for the past thirty years. He...has been receiving a salary of $115.00 a month...paid from the receipts of the school...For this work we allow at residential schools an amount of $60.00 a month.

...Mr. Hawarth has resigned as Farm Manager and has accepted the position as night watchman, although he was stated to be dissatisfied.

...Miss Susan Hardie...taught at this school for many years. When she retired about 1940, the New England

Company decided...to provide her with a pension of approximately $50.00 a month, in view of her services, and as she was not eligible for any other pension scheme. The Company is still continuing to allow this payment.

It is my intention to communicate with the Company ...with a view to ascertaining if they would be willing to allow Mr. Hawarth a pension.

48. 26 July 1951 Phelan to Zimmerman
...staff for the coming year is complete. The personnel will be as follows:

Mrs. E. M. Henderson   Mrs. Joan Sharon
Miss Nora B. McMeans   Mrs Ruth Arnold
Mr. M. E. Bartley

...With the present salary scale I do not think you need to be diffident about asking your staff to assume some supervisory duties.

49. 15 August 1951 Mingay to Randle
...Will you...forward to us a letter recommending the appointment of Mr. Hanna as full-time Manual Training Instructor, three days at Ohsweken and two days at Mohawk per month...we...have been counting on him to take charge of the Manual Training programme...

50. 16 August 1951 Phelan to Zimmerman
...we expect the staff to be provided with a furnished room or living quarters...Food...is something in addition to this for which the teacher undoubtedly expects to pay. We would urge that you arrange table board for the teachers...This would get over the difficulty of light housekeeping in the rooms which...must be strictly prohibited. Cooking appliances in the room create a fire hazard which simply must not be present.

In connection with the duties of the teachers, we expect that in a residential school they will assist in supervisory duties in connection with the residence life of the pupils. We do not think it is too much to ask a teacher to spend at least one night a week in this manner and one week-end each month. These duties are...in addition to the regular extra curricular activities which one would expect of teachers anywhere, such as the supervision of games in the playground, that is baseball, hockey and outdoor activities that occur at noon and after four o'clock.

The teachers are, as you are aware, responsible entirely to you and we have no desire whatever to interfere in any way with the internal management of the school.

51. 1 July 1952
[Mrs Ruth Arnold resigned replaced by Mrs Neva Leona Williston
Mrs Henderson resigned - replaced by Mrs. Elspeth Grant
Mrs Sharon resigned - replaced by Miss Angela Daeschsell]

52. 9 September 1953 Stallwood to IAB
...need of a vehicle for the transportation of pupils and supplies...

1. There are 13 or 14 Residential pupils attending the Brantford Collegiate Institute. It is...advisable to have transportation to and from the Collegiate for these pupils, not only for...supervision, but also that they may have some time for their duties at the Mohawk Institute.
2...to extend the services of the Home Economics Teacher now employed to serve the Six Nations Reserve to the Mohawk Institute...transporting the class from the Mohawk Institute to the School at Ohsweken.
3...to transport children from the Mohawk Institute to the Dental Clinic at Ohsweken.

53. 28 October 1953 Mingay
...The teachers are somethat restless about supervision after class hours. They feel this is a duty for which they did not contract. In a school contiguous to a large city the Branch cannot expect extra duties from teachers without extra pay. There are too many good positions open in the districts to competent teachers. Teachers will not stay under these conditions. Only two teachers live at the school. The others have their own homes and when the day or week is done they want to be at home...

54. 28 December 1953 Davey to Mingay
...please ennumerate the supervisory duties which are being performed by classroom teachers...

55. 14 January 1955 Mingay to Reid
...the necessity of providing new school accommodation for the children presently attending the Mohawk Institute...We have approximately 165 Indian children, grades 1-8, in this institution and this number has been constant for the past two years. The authorized pupilage for the school is 185.

It has been in the mind of the Branch for some time to make a different arrangement for the education of these children. Instead of erecting our own building, we would very much prefer to have these children taken into the Brantford schools, particularly now that the Institute is within the confines of the city.
...the Indian child makes better progress if integrated with other children, and we think that the association with other children will help us in making the future generation of Indian children independent citizens ready to take their proper place in our Canadian economy...

We have an auxiliary class at present...usually 15 plus or minus. Having in mind the usual figure of thirty children to a class as suggested by the Ontario Department of Education, it would seem that five classrooms and an auxiliary classroom will take care of the 165 children from the Mohawk school...we are thinking in terms of September 1956...

56. 7 July 1955 Davey to Morris
...it is noted that you concur with the Inspector's

recommendation that two persons be engaged for the summer months to give a planned programme for those children who of necessity, must remain at...school.

It was my understanding...it was agreed that one person would be engaged, and it will be in order for you to voucher for payment for Mr. Cecil Montour at the rate of $200.00 per month. I would think that the...school would have staff on hand to assist Mr. Montour, and that it would not be necessary to engage a second person.

57. 12 July 1955 Morris to Davey
...Only one person is being employed at the School. He is Mr. C. H. C. Diltz, who is employed at the rate of $8.00 per day plus room and board at the School.

I visited the...School a week ago and I wish to report that the children are very happy. Mr. Diltz is doing a very fine job. The boys and girls swim regularly at the Brantford swimming pool, under supervision. Mr. Diltz has organized sports, ball games, running races, etc....

58. 15 July 1955 Davey to Morris
...it will be in order to employ Mr. C. H. C. Diltz at the rate of $8.00 per day...until August 31st.

59. 1 August 1955 Zimmerman to Davey
...concerning clothing costs...you stated...that we ought not to depend upon the Church for clothing. I assume that the Church is free to make any contributions she so desires but in the event that contributions are not forthcoming I am in a financial position free to make the necessary expenditures. The Dominion Dorcas Secretary spent over $1,500.00 on clothing and bedding last year. I estimate that $1,000.00 would be required to purchase the clothing that came in the form of bales from the many groups in the Church. The total assistance given by the Church is at least $2,500.00. A pupil increase of $10.00 per year would not provide the money that comes in the form of material from the Church. I never know from year to year the extent to which this amount will vary.

The matter of an increase...is based upon the clothing costs undertaken by the Province of Ontario on behalf of the Training School for girls at Galt...When one of their pupils leaves the school they are outfitted in such a manner that no one can look at them and conclude from their dress that they have been in some institution...

When one bears in mind the home background and utter lack of satisfactory parental relations should we not be...thinking along this same line. Would not better clothing give to the children a sense of dignity and also provide for those who can discern a feeling that someone really cares. We are asking a great deal of human nature when we expect those who have had so little at home to go out into that other world and make good when the very clothes upon their backs set them apart. I wonder what the effect would be if a child could say to himself these

are my clothes and if I do all that I can to take excellent care of them I shall be able to take them with me no matter where I am. The care of property is extremely important and what an opportunity there is for developing a sense of responsibility in this very field. Dress and personal appearance count for so very much in our modern culture.

If the policy is merely to protect the child from the elements of his physical world such as cold and to ignore the social world of which he ought to be a conscious part then the matter of clothing costs assumes another character. I assume that we are seeking to help people to take their place in society with self-respect and dignity.

I am fully aware of the procedure followed in the admittance of girls to the school at Galt. Nevertheless, the Provincial Government feels that they are persons who must take their place in society and I feel that our pupils must do the same. If the process of assimilation is to take place in a satisfactory and orderly manner it must be upon a basis of equality of opportunity. The Pupils of the Mohawk Institute cannot take their place in the City of Brantford, as they are doing in an increasing manner, unless they are clothed as the children are in the City...

60. 5 August 1955 Davey to Zimmerman
...The fact that your School is located in the City of Brantford and that the pupils of your School are drawn from families where the home circumstances are unusually poor will be taken into consideration when I prepare a recommendation for an increase in your per capita grant.

61. 5 August 1955 Mingay to Davey
...you suggested nothing further be done in connection with the admission of the children from the Mohawk Institute to the schools in Brantford. Consequently, although Mr. Reid had asked our Branch to meet the Brantford School Board, this was not done.
...He is quite anxious to proceed with the school in the area of the Mohawk Institute. They will need about five rooms and they wondered if they could purchase a piece of ground on the site of the Institute for a school. If this were done, of course, the problem of supervision to and from school would not arise and this was one of the problems that gave us some concern when this scheme was mooted. It would also mean that the school board would have an asphalted playground contiguous to the school, which would be open to the school at all times for play purposes. Further, it means that they would take all our young pupils up to and including Grade 1 and the auxiliary class. The city's idea is to build a ten-room school with home economics, shops, auditorium, and auxiliary classroom. Of these ten rooms, we would occupy at least five. Mr. Reid's approximation of the cost, furnished and equipped, is $250,000, so that our share would be $125,000. The land on which they would

like to build is now part of the school ground and I expect its sale would be subject to approval by the band council of Six Nations. However, in view of the fact that a good many Six Nations' youngsters are in the school, it might not be too difficult to get the band to consent to the sale of the land for such purposes as an academic centre which would serve the under-privileged Indian youngsters of Southern Ontario.

The School Board at Brantford seems to be well aware of the type of child we have in the Mohawk Institute and does not think this will present any great problem. Mr. Reid tells me that most of the members of the Board are favourable to this...election in December...To me, it would seem that every advantage would accrue to the Branch if a public school were built contiguous to the Mohawk Institute. Even though the children attended public schools, there would be no spare room at Mohawk. Social problems seem to be growing in connection with Indian administration in the South, and it would appear...that the number of pupils that will come to Mohawk in the future will be greater rather than less...

62. 23 August 1955 Davey to Morris
...it was agreed that we would not endeavour to secure the establishment of a joint school to serve all the pupils boarded at the Mohawk Institute. It was agreed, however, that an endeavour would be made to secure the admission of Grades 7 and 8, to one of the existing schools operated by the Brantford School Board. An endeavour will also be made to secure in the 1956-57 estimates funds to replace the three-classroom block which was provided by the conversion of an army hut building. The second building, also a converted army hut, which is located close to the street, will be retained since it is in fairly good condition...Mr. Zimmerman agreed that the proposals... were the most satisfactory solution...

63. 15 November 1955 Davey to Morris
...in our discussion in Brantford last August, it was decided that the approach to the School District should be on the basis of the admission of some of our pupils into the existing schools. The question was also raised as to whether or not the School District would consider the erection of a building for their own purposes which would also accommodate Grades 7 and 8...the opinion was expressed either by yourself or by Mr. Mingay, that the School Board was not interested in this latter suggestion. It was also decided...that we would not consider at this time the sending of any of the children to the Brantford School who are registered in Grade 6 or below...

64. 25 January 1956 Davey to Director
...The committee's recommendation is based on a misunderstanding. The Brantford School Board has not acquired a building site close to the Mohawk Institute, but

is expanding its facilities at existing provincial schools... An approach was made to the school board to have Grades 7 and 8 from the Mohawk Institute admitted to their system. This was refused. The provincial school inspector, in replying to Mr. Mingay's inquiry, stated that the Board was prepared to consider taking in all of the pupils from the Mohawk Institute, but was not prepared to consider enrolling only part of the Mohawk children.

As you know, our residential school is used to care for under-privileged children, a number of whom have delinquency records. The Reverend Mr. Zimmerman... was most apprehensive about exercising control over his 160 pupils, if they were suddenly required to leave the school premises daily in order to attend class in the city...

The 1956-57 estimates provide for the erection of a four-classroom building at the Mohawk Institute to replace an army hut building which is in very bad condition. If the department proceeds with this project, there are still two old classrooms which can serve for a year or two when it is hoped the school board will modify its stand and admit our senior elementary school students in order that this transition can take place gradually.

There is reference to "the rather austere atmosphere" at the Mohawk Institute. This can largely be overcome by... a much broader programme of extra-curricular activities. It is my intention to ask Mr. Barnes to visit the Mohawk Institute in order that the Principal may be given more assistance in developing these activities...

65. 18 March 1957 Morris to Davey
...concerning help for Mr. Zimmerman during the summer, Mr. Mingay advises that there will be approximately 40 to 50 children in residence continuously during the summer months and that additional supervision is urgently needed.

We would recommend that this be provided again for the coming summer. It is suggested that a straight fifty dollars for the whole week be paid...

66. 29 May 1957 Morris to Davey
...each year from 40 to 50 children remain at the Mohawk Residential School during the summer holidays because their home conditions on the various reserves are inadequate. In many cases the parents are away and the children, when they do go home, stay with their grandparents where they receive little supervision...there will be approximately 65 children remaining at the school during July and August. It is hoped that further screening will reduce the number, particularly at Six Nations and Caradoc where the Superintendents indicate that there will be approximately 40 children...remaining at the school.
...we have given a great deal of thought to the advisability of arranging for one month's outing for these children away from the school. It would give the children a much needed vacation and also make it possible for The Reverend Zimmerman to give his staff a holiday and do

any cleaning and painting in the school...required. I suggested at the Homemakers' Meeting at Sarnia last year that the various Homemakers' organizations might...help defray the cost of taking these children to a summer camp. This idea will again be discussed with the Homemakers at this year's convention, and I hope that some definite action will be approved. We have written to the Superintendents in Southern Ontario requesting that the Band Councils vote $20.00 for each child of their Band to assist in defraying the cost of this month's camp...

I was up at Christian Island last week and discussed with the Council the suggestion of a summer camp...The Council there were wholeheartedly in favour of it...

A couple of years ago you...consented to pay the salary of a young man to supervise and arrange sports and entertainment for the children remaining at the Mohawk School. I understand that you have already approved this service again this year. However, for the month of July I feel that we should have approval to engage the services of a woman supervisor who would be with the girls all the time and assist in arranging suitable programs, swimming, running, games, hikes, etc., to keep the children occupied and entertained...

...you may have difficulty in allotting funds to assist this undertaking, but I am sure you will agree...that a month's vacation for these children would be very beneficial. Christian Island was selected after a great deal of thought. There are no traffic hazards there. There are lovely sand beaches and it is a dry, clean location...there is a lovely inland lake which can be used for bathing and picnicking ...it is a pretty sad spectacle to see the expressions of these youngsters who have to remain at the school after knowing that their chums have gone back to homes, mothers and fathers who are concerned about them and kindly disposed towards them, and they have no place to go. These poor children are hungry for affection and need a great deal of organized sports and entertainment to make them feel that they are needed and wanted...they will be better people when they grow up because of this vacation.

67. 5 June 1957 Luxton to Davey
...with a man of Mr. Zimmerman's qualifications and seniority, his present stipend in a parish would be considerably more than he is receiving at the Mohawk Institute...request that you should lay before the Minister my personal request for special consideration for this... clergyman, who has served as Principal...for at least 15 years, and has given...a service that has been...of extraordinary value to both the Indian people and the Indian Department.

He took over a school that was no credit to anyone, and has, by his steady, patient and painstaking care, given it a fine standing and position, not only in Brantford and neighbourhood, but I think among government institutions of learning in the whole district.

68. 3 July 1957 H. M. Jones to Deputy Minister
...Mr. Zimmerman is presently receiving a salary of $2,200.00 per annum...a recently constructed house, light, water and food for himself and family. The total value of these perquisites would be approximately $3,000.00...the equivalent of approximately $5,000.00 per annum...it is intended to set a salary of $4,800.00 for Mr. Zimmerman ...in addition to the perquisites...he presently enjoys, except that there will be a deduction of $25.00 per month for accommodation and an additional $30.00 per month if he consumes food from the school kitchen...

69. 5 July 1957 Morris to Bethune
...with respect to the contributions which are being made by the various Band Councils concerned...this project has been enthusiastically received by all concerned and at this moment the children are enjoying themselves at the camp on Christian Island.

The Six Nations Council has raised funds by holding Bingo and similar affairs and is making their contribution of $200...The Sarnia Band, even though there are no children from that Band, are contributing $100. Likewise, the Kettle and Stony Point Band has voted $25...the Moravian Indian Council passed a Resolution expressing that no money be expended for this purpose even though four of their own children are affected. However, the Homemaker's Club of the Moravian Reserve are contributing $80 of their funds...Chippewas of Thames $100...Chippewas of Saugeen $80...

70. 28 April 1958 Morris to Supt. of Education, Ottawa
...the camp was an unqualified success last summer.

It is hoped that you will continue to provide the salary for a young man to be engaged to supervise the summer activities of the children...You approved this request during the past three years. He will go with the children of course to the Christian Island for the month of July and then will be in charge of the children when they return to the Mohawk School for the month of August. I would suggest that you give consideration to make a salary available to engage a university student...During the month of June he would become acquainted with the children at the Mohawk and be more helpful at the Christian Island camp. Canon Zimmerman in the past selected a Divinity student. I am not satisfied that his selection last year was the best because the boy seemed to be lacking in camp training and athletics...

71. 2 June 1958 Zimmerman to Morris
With the new school likely to be in operation in September and the gymnasium available for activity...the time has come to appoint somebody who will have general supervision over playground and physical training activities.

I should like to see appointed a full time Physical

Training Instructor with proper qualifications who could organize this work and take general charge of the athletic program...a good capable man could do an excellent job for both boys and girls...the playground activities at this school have not been well organized through lack of staff, money and facilities. Now that the facilities are available and more money is available for staff I am sure that a good play program would offset the cost many times in the morale which it would create in the pupils.

72. 6 June 1958 Ottawa [Davey crossed out]

Since the Mohawk Institute is becoming more and more a school for orphans and socially maladjusted children, it would appear to me that the employment of a Physical Education Instructor or Extra-Curricular Activities Supervisor should be seriously considered. The latter term would probably be more suitable, since, as I see it, his responsibility would be not only in the field of sports, but also in the development of a wholesome and interesting social programme for the student body.

With the addition of the gymnasium to the new classroom block...a young man or woman (preferably a man since I feel that the boys will respond to his direction more readily) could be kept busy all the time with the activities mentioned above. The sports programme should include sports and games, physical education, track and field activities, tumbling and pyramid building, etc. The social programme should include hikes, sing-songs, bonfires, drama, music, folk, round and square dancing, etc. A good sports programme of basketball, baseball, volleyball and hockey would do much to improve the morale of the school, as well as to provide worthwhile activity out of school hours.

73. 8 August 1958 Morris to Chief, Education Division, Ottawa

...I am pleased to request that establishment be provided for a teacher-physical instructor to undertake the work of the gym and the recreational program at the Mohawk.

74. 20 August 1958 Zimmerman to Davey

...I approached you in connection with the...provision of Staff for the gym in the new classroom block.

We have on the staff of the school...Sgt. James Rendles who has a certificate for physical and recreational training instruction and who adjusts himself very well with the boys. The children are quite fond of him. In view of the fact that he is or was an army man the feeling and fear has been expressed that he would be too severe with the boys. There is absolutely no ground for such an attitude...

It will be necessary to locate a female supervisor who would be of assistance to Mr. Rendles. These two persons would assume responsibility for the gym work.

I would like to see the immediate provision...of $6,000.00 for this purpose in addition to the establishment

already authorized for the school. We need $3,000.00 for the boys and $3,000.00 for the girl's supervisor. With the coming of the Minister in October and the erection of this lovely school block at such great cost I would feel very embarrassed...to find it necessary to reply that we have no qualified supervision in this very, very important area.

Last year I requested three supervisors for the boys and three for the girls and with this need in mind I have no hesitation in pressing the matter just as strongly as I am able. I have seen very clearly the results of more supervision and direction while at Christian Island not to realize just what can be done. The number of supervisors per person at Christian Island was much greater than what we have ever had at the school.

75. 24 September 1958 Davey to Zimmerman

With the formal opening of the new school building scheduled for next Wednesday, it is hoped that the new motion-picture projector will have arrived. A superior projection screen was sent ten days ago.

It is supposed that the guest list will include some of the older people who are mentioned in the history of the Mohawk Institute which was included with the annual report of the Department for 1930...It is hoped that Miss Susan Hardie's health will permit her attendance. Among many names in the report are Wilma Smith, Elva Miller, Sylvia Jamieson, William Powless, Jesse Moses, Peter White (the lacrosse player) and Tom Longboat.

76. 26 November 1958 Luxton to Davey

...I am most appreciative of all that you have done to bring up the school to the present fine state of equipment and work generally. Canon Zimmerman has said that Mr. Barnes has been discussing staff problems with him at your request, and that your general hope is that through the Church, we may be able to recruit workers of high calibre who will give to our Indian boys and girls the careful, patient and loving attention that they need. I am hopeful that we shall be able to discover for Canon Zimmerman the right type of supervisor, both for the boys' and the girls' side of the school. I...will be most anxious to do all that I can to support you and Canon Zimmerman in the fine work being accomplished.

...what he needs probably more than anything else...is an assistant...who could possibly act as senior supervisor to the boys, and also as assistant to the Principal...Canon Zimmerman is carrying a very heavy load, and...the health and progress of the school depends upon his maintaining his personal contact with the boys and girls, and when necessity arises, with their families...I would have a young ordained man on or about May 1st who might go to the school, and act as senior supervisor and general assistant to Canon Zimmerman, giving the boys out of school programmes and supervision, and also helping generally in the administrative life of the Institute. I am...afraid of

Canon Zimmerman outworking his strength and health, and I think it most important that we should conserve his very great skill and ability in this field...if the stipend were forthcoming...for a senior supervisor - let us say $3,000 a year with the free quarters - I believe that I would have the right kind of man available, one who would give himself with enthusiasm and skill to the promotion of corporate life, teamwork and general happiness among the boys of the institution - and also sub for Mr. Zimmerman in his various responsibilities ...in summer Mr. Zimmerman should have a full holiday away from the school and the children, and that he should not enter into the summer camp on Christian Island. If he had an assistant in whom he had confidence...he would feel freer to take a month off and consequently return to his Principalship in the fall greatly refreshed.

77. 27 January 1959   Davey to Regional Supervisor, Education Division

...extracts from the report of Mr. Barnes...

...the proposal for a four foot chain link fence, I intend to discuss this with one of the Branch's architects to make sure that this...would not detract from the general appearance of the grounds and buildings...the gate-posts should be erected at the same time as the fence...

...we should go somewhat further in respect to the orchard than recommended by Mr. Barnes. If this front area is to be kept mowed and looking presentable, it will, I feel, be necessary to remove more than just the old and dead trees.

...Mr. Barnes has suggested a lay-out for the sports field which includes an enlarging of the girls play area. This seems to be in order although I am more concerned with an orderly placement of the equipment and its location in such a manner that future developments are provided for.

Consideration was not given...to the possible location of the top dormitory to a lower floor. There is no question...that it is preferable to avoid having children sleep in rooms on the upper story...No steps will be taken to install lockers on the upper floors until the possibility of locating the upper dormitory has been carefully considered...there is no intention of making any plans for adding to the classroom block...until we have thoroughly explored Mr. Mingay's suggestion about sending some of the pupils to the Brantford schools.

78. 2 June 1959 Morris to Supts. of Southern Ontario

We shall have a class in homemaking and domestic work...commencing in September. There is space for a limited number of girls and we prefer for this class those who do not wish to go on to the secondary school but who have grade seven or eight standing and who will be at least sixteen years of age by March 30, 1960.

79. 21 July 1959 Davey to Morris

This will...confirm the discussions which were held on...July 19th, at a meeting with Canon Zimmerman...

It was agreed that the salary allotment...did not provide sufficient funds to enable the Principal to secure competent supervisory staff...representation should be made to the Treasury Board for an increase in the salary

allotment...so far as the supervisors are concerned, Canon Zimmerman would have to offer salaries between $3000 and $3600 and...as high as $4000 for the senior supervisor on the boys side...to get someone who is competent to develop a good recreational and sports programme...

It was emphasized that in recruiting staff, Canon Zimmerman should pay particular attention to employing personnel who would be able to establish a good atmosphere in the school. Particular attention was to be given to the personality of the applicants...to ensure that the supervisory staff would have a cheerful disposition... expected that the senior supervisors would be potential housemothers and that one of them would assist the matron in this particular regard...the staff should be capable of providing the care and affection which these under-privileged children so very much need.

...so far as the employment of Indians is concerned... the primary requisites were competence and personal suitability. If people of Indian status having these qualifications could be induced to accept employment...it would be desirable to employ them...

I stated that a careful review had been made of the expenditures for food at all of the Government owned residential schools and that a request was going to the Department of National Health and Welfare to have a qualified dietitian or nutritionist visit selected schools where the expenditures appear to be abnormal...It is also intended to have two or three other school visited to ensure that those schools where the expenditures for food are about average, have adequate funds to offer a proper diet. The Mohawk Institute would be included as one of the schools in this latter group.

...the Principal should pay special attention to the personal appearance of the children, not only in the matter of clothing and cleanliness but also in respect to personal grooming...Canon Zimmerman, several months ago, at your suggestion, arranged for a hairdresser from the City of Brantford to come out to the school to attend to hair styling, especially for older girls...

There was some discussion of the allotment for clothing and Canon Zimmerman expressed the opinion that the present allotment was adequate...there had been an improvement in this regard during the past year...further improvements would be possible and that he has been able to catch up with some of the more urgent needs.

It was agreed that the number of older boys...did not warrant the employment of a full-time industrial arts instructor but that it was desirable to have some instruction in this subject...the Regional office and the Principal would explore the possibility of securing a part-time instructor who could give about a day a week...there would be a great deal of difficulty in securing the services of a competent man for this limited period...

...there was no regular visitation to the school by a qualified nurse or doctor other than the dentist, although the services of pediatrician, resident at Brantford were available on call and the facilities of the Lady Willingdon Hospital could be utilized on the recommendation of the pediatrician...in my opinion there should be regular visits to the Mohawk Institute by a qualified nurse and that I would make representations to the Indian and Northern Health Services in this regard. You emphasized it was your opinion that responsibility for the medical services provided to the Mohawk Institute should rest solely at the unit centered about the Lady Willingdon Hospital...

There was considerable discussion of the use of outside specialists to give advice and direction to the staff of the Mohawk Institute on a variety of phases of the school's work. I pointed out that I was most unhappy about the apparent lack of coordination of direction to the Principal ...more specialists to give advice to the Principal would simply add to the confusion. For example, there are a number of specialists visiting...who might be considered to have an interest in the programme of vocational guidance, the two School Inspectors, the Social Worker, the Placement Officer and representatives of the Children's Aid Society...instructions with regard to this programme should be issued to the Principal, not by all of these visiting specialists, but by the Regional Inspector of Schools and...This does not suggest that these specialists do not have a role to play, but their responsibilities and how they carry them out should be clarified...

80. 24 July 1959 Zimmerman to Davey
...the report covering the recent conversations...this reference "there was no regular visitation to the school by a qualified nurse or doctor other than the dentist."

This statement does not do full justice to the facts...The dentist visited the school last autumn and during the current year we sent to the clinic the most needy cases... I am enclosing a list of the calls...made by the medical health officer during the months of May and June 1959... During the visits of the medical health officer matters of general health were dealt with...menus, sanitation, bed wetting etc...there has been no insistence for inspection visits when this can be done during calls to the school.

No request for service has been made without either the medical health officer coming or sending some M.D. in his place. In my humble judgement Dr. H. Palmer has been a competent children's doctor.

81. 24 August 1959 Morris to Davey
...request that you...review the following suggestions.
1) Medical service of the Mohawk Institute should be the entire responsibility of the doctors and nurses at the Lady Willingdon Hospital...the nurses have been told that they will be expected to provide nursing and public health services to the children located at the Mohawk...it is suggested that officers of the Health Services, Canon Zimmerman and myself sit in on the first discussion and

make arrangements so that their work and visits will not...interfere with the administration of the school...I am very pleased to see that the nurses will make their services available...Dr. Wiebe...mentioned that the nurses were going to make their services available at the Mohawk. I told him I was making the strongest possible recommendation that the doctors at the Lady Willingdon be responsible for health services at the Mohawk. He stated that their nurses and doctors were discouraged by Canon Zimmerman to visit the school.
2) Regarding child welfare services at the Mohawk, I would strongly recommend...approving that the services of the Brant County Children's Aid Society be made available to Canon Zimmerman to assist him with problem cases in the school...Mrs. Fox, present Director, is one of the outstanding persons in this work in Ontario and I am quite satisfied that she could work in that school in harmony and full co-operation with Canon Zimmerman and his staff...these youngsters need all the attention and care that specialists can provide for the reason that they had little or no discipline or understanding as to their social obligations. I know that you have strong feelings with regard to the Social Worker's activities at the Mohawk school...if you approve...arrangements can be made for Canon Zimmerman and myself to...work out the details so that the work of specialists in this school will be accepted by Canon Zimmerman and his staff...
3) With regard to instructions to Mr. Zimmerman in connection with the proposed programs, I disagree with you that they should be issued to the principal by the Regional Office; and instructions to Canon Zimmerman from this office over my signature through the agency office at Brantford. It is therefore important that Mr. Stallwood be present at the various meetings so that he will be fully informed of what decisions are arrived at.
4) Consideration should be given to a committee...to assist Canon Zimmerman in the selection of better qualified help in the kitchen, laundry, as supervisors, housemother, etc. The weakness...is that while Canon Zimmerman is responsible for the running of the school, his wages as well as the wages of the staff are paid by the Department but they are not employees of the Dominion Government. Therefore, they are not strictly under our supervision...The Branch pays the full cost of maintenance, staff salaries, teacher's salaries, etc., and have...full responsibility for criticisms of the school and yet we have no real control over the staff with the exception of the teachers.
5) I again recommend that you...have Mr. J. C. Hill, Supervising Principal, visit this school in connection with inspection work. He is genuinely concerned about the progress of Indian children and...he is doing outstanding work...I am completely satisfied that he will not make it difficult for Canon Zimmerman and that very soon they will be working harmoniously together.
6) I would also recommend...that every effort be made to

arrange for grades 7 and 8 to be integrated into the Brantford school system...

I am quite satisfied that this office, with Mr. Barnes's assistance at conferences between the specialists and Canon Zimmerman, can harmoniously work out all the details so that home conditions at the Mohawk school will be to the complete satisfaction of all concerned. We have come a long way in the last two years and I am quite satisfied that once we receive your blessings on the above suggestions arrangements can be worked out in a harmonious manner and definitely for the betterment of the children. After all, that is our only concern...

82. 11 September 1959 Zimmerman to Morris
...Mr. Leslie Hanna, the Manual Training Instructor on the Six Nations Reserve and a former Instructor at the Mohawk Institute, is willing to come to the Mohawk Institute for two evenings a week for instruction purposes. Mr. Hanna needs no recommendation concerning his ability to do the job.

I hope that something can be initiated shortly in order that the boys can benefit from a much needed program in manual training...

83. 19 December 1959 Zimmerman to Davey
Re: The Farm at the Mohawk Institute
...it is my duty to place on record my conviction concerning the role of the farm......my first responsibility is to the girls and boys of this institution. With the erection of the new school block the program for the curricular and the extra-curricular activity is much more intense and this is as it ought to be. The result is that I do not possess the time to give to farm direction that I was able in the years which are past.

The number of services which the farm can extend to the school is rapidly growing less and less. In the summer the pupils are at camp. We no longer use the fluid milk from the farm for school purposes...I am not interested in operating the farm unless the farm can be of service to the school and is contributing to the welfare of the pupils.

The problems involved in the operation of a successful dairy herd are becoming more complex and technical. The price of fluid milk...is so low that many local farmers are quitting the dairy industry. We are facing each year new problems because of a city that is closing in upon the school more and more. This very morning city children broke into the corn crib and scattered corn over the field.

84. 28 April 1960 H. M. Jones to Dr. P. E. Moore
...Dr. H. Palmer, who provided medical services for the Mohawk Institute, died recently.

I know your Service has been giving consideration to possible changes in the procedures followed in giving medical attention to the Indian pupils enrolled at this

Institute. No doubt the death of Dr. Palmer will have some bearing on the implementation of your plans...

85. 29 April 1960 H. M. Jones to Deputy Minister
Mrs. Fairclough has been interested in the operation of the Mohawk Institute and has requested that certain steps be taken to improve the operation...She has been particularly anxious that the school develop a broader and better programme of extra curricular activities. Among the activities about which she has made specific inquiry is the establishment of a Cadet Corps.

In order to improve the staff employed...arrangements have been made for Mr. Howard Rodine, the Regional Superintendent of Schools...to interview, with the Principal, applicants for positions at the school.

Although the Principal attempted to secure a man who could take charge of the sports and recreational programme, the Regional office is not satisfied with the present employee and an advertisement has been placed in local newspapers...for applicants for...Sports Director.

86. 31 August 1960 Zimmerman to Davey
Last year I requested that consideration be given to a 10% salary increase for certain members of the residential staff...to those other than the matron, boys' supervisors and the house mothers. The proposed increases would come to $3,250.00. For example, the maintenance man started at $3,000.00 and has done a good job and as yet has received no salary increase. We expect him to look after more equipment each year. Many of these people can go elsewhere and receive higher salaries.

I am concerned about the nursing situation...a registered nurse is required. The situation has altered with the passing of Dr. H. Palmer. Many of our children come from a distinctive type of home and these children have certain specific needs. A properly trained person would possess the requisite insights to do the job that the Department of National Health and Welfare expects to be done...We...require another $1,000.00 to secure the type of person needed. Total salary would then be $4,000.00 per year. (Total staff salary increase would be $4,230.00.)

I would like to see the clothing allowance increased $12.50, per child per year. Increased numbers of children are not returning to their parents but to situations recommended by welfare workers. We must provide additional clothing as going away outfits. The appearance of the children means much to all concerned. We appreciated the assistance this June...The extra money was well spent. The children placed in private homes during the summer have done extremely well. Mr. Morris is quite pleased with the comments of those who have had the children.

The health nurse and the doctor have recommended Orthopaedic shoes in certain cases. To date the expense has been borne by the regular clothing allowance.

The matter of fuel costs has been discussed with local experts and with the installation of the new appliances in the kitchen we are faced with certain increased costs... The expected increase is in the area of $500.00 per year.

The household supplies will be affected by the new kitchen, and I hope for an increased standard in this area. It has been difficult to secure the bedding necessary within the limits of the present budget. We require more window dressings if we are to have a homelike effect. To carry out what I have in mind would cost another $1,000.00 per year.

The Miscellaneous item stood at $1,500.00 for 1960. Workmen's Compensation has been put into effect and costs $306.90. I would like to see more money spent on the children's hair. The older girls are beginning to ask for special attention. An increase of $700.00 would be a great help. Total amount required for Miscellaneous, $2,000.00.

87. 20 January 1961 Brantford Expositor
The Mohawk Institute Boasts An Efficient Modern Kitchen

A gleaming, modernly equipped, completely fire-proofed new kitchen, boasting the latest in automatic facilities, now greets approximately 150 resident pupils... when they file in for meals...was added to the back of the building...first phase of a major renovation project...The main building will undergo renovations next summer.

...Zimmerman...explained the installation of the new kitchen, and uncompleted renovation of the children's dining room and smaller staff dining room, is part of a plan to give the institute a "homey atmosphere."

Much of the dining room has been renovated, to provide a larger area, and decorated...The kitchen is equipped with many innovations to take the drudgery out of preparing and cooking meals on a large scale. Formerly much of the food preparation was done manually...Dirty dishes are no longer a problem..an automatic Hobart Dish washer has been installed...The children's dining room has been renovated and repainted in yellow, with brown and yellow patterned tile floors. The scullery and refrigerator areas have been removed and the overhead pipes camouflaged...

88. 22 March 1961 P. E. Moore to H. M. Jones
On March 16th, 1961, Miss Lang...called in...to see their new food service installation. The kitchen is completed and has been in use since mid-January, and the Cafeteria system of service is working like a charm.

The pupils all file into their places, grace is sung, and then the girls go through the Cafeteria line-up, followed by the boys. Since the tables were set with cutlery, milk, dessert and bread, only the main course had to be served, and the service was remarkably quick. All had their meal within ten minutes and still had a hot meal.

The kitchen equipment is very fine, and much appreciated by the staff. There are two walk-in coolers and a walk-in deep freeze unit. The dish washing area is well planned and the machine...is working well. They do not air-dry their dishes, but...plastic ware doesn't dry as rapidly...time is very short when the pupils have to rush back to school.

...they hope to have replacements for the old tables and benches in the dining room before too long. The old kitchen is now an attractive, bright dining room-cum-sitting room for the staff.

Mrs. Davidson has a good three-week menu cycle in effect and the meals appear to be of good standard.   ·

89. 24 April 1961 Davey to Regional Supervisor - Toronto
The Department approves continuation of the employment of five academic classroom teachers... including the Sr. teacher who must teach on a full time basis...the services of a Home Economics and Industrial Arts Teacher are required for 30% of a full time teaching schedule which would be 3½ days weekly for each subject. Accordingly it will be necessary to reduce the full time Home Economics and Industrial Arts positions....

There is no reference to the need for teacher councillor services at this school. If, as you indicated, there will be 35 pupils residing at Mohawk Residential School and attending Brantford City schools, the services of a teacher advisor on a half time basis may be requested. It is possible that the part time Home Economics or Industrial Arts teacher would be qualified to perform the duties of teacher councillor as well, thus permitting the prospective teacher to be engaged at a higher rate of remuneration... only 126 pupils are being retained in classrooms at the...School it might be possible for one of the classroom teachers to devote half time to teacher councilling duties and half time to teaching academic classroom...

90. [Date?] Alice Moore for Deputy Minister
As 35 pupils who formerly attended Mohawk Residential Institute will continue to reside there but receive classroom instructions in Brantford City Schools, the program in Home Economics and Industrial Arts at this school is being reduced from full time to part time.

91. 25 August 1961 Zimmerman to Kaiser
This autumn a certain selected group of pupils will be attending the Belleview Public School in...Brantford. During the discussions between representatives of the City and your own Department, a feeling was expressed that the clothing should be of the same standard as from a private middle class home. The girls, for example, must not be given identical dresses...

I am suggesting that an additional thirty-five dollars be available for these pupils for clothing. The children have a distance of three quarters of a mile to walk...We shall have certain weather problems to attend to...

Mr. H. Rodine...said that any additional expenses would be cared for. There are fees for the Junior Red Cross...

The extra curricular establishment of $2.50 per child per quarter is not adequate. I have found that when these children have a few cents in their pockets that their satisfaction is twofold. There is the pleasure of not only eating an ice-cream cone but there is the additional satisfaction of purchasing the cone by themselves...petty shop lifting decreases if this privilege is permitted.

I have had abnormal cases where they lifted when they had money in their pocket. This is not usual. I would like to see an allowance of $3.50 per child per quarter.

The household supplies establishment did not cover the cost last year and I am having serious difficulty in retaining the costs within the established amount. With the new kitchen and the new classroom block, we have had little latitude in substitute buying since specific items are required. For example, we have been directed to use the soap recommended by the manufacturer of the dishwasher machine secured by the purchasing branch. The machine itself has worked splendidly and the girls love to assist in its operation. I would recommend an additional $650.00.

...I wish to thank the Department for the adjustment in the salary area...it will not please certain employees during these days of constantly rising salary levels. I am pleased since this amount does meet two cases about which I was greatly perplexed.

We have had a very busy but happy year and I do wish to express my gratitude for the wonderful help the Department has been in the financing of this school.

92. 17 October 1961 Bonnah to IAB

...approximately fifteen pupils have now been registered ...from the North. The northern officials feel that they could have had considerable more interest in this had we been able to give them earlier advice.

Inasmuch as the total enrolment at the Residential School is now 140 with forty of these going out to high school and the Bellview Public School, the total enrolment for instruction by our teaching staff is now set at 100. Of this total enrolment of 100 pupils being instructed by the Mohawk staff, twelve are of non-English speaking and are in receipt of special training and remedial work. In addition, about twelve other pupils of the normal Mohawk enrolment are receiving remedial instruction offered by the teachers. Mrs. Byron is giving approximately three half-days to the instruction of Home Economics to the older girls...activity of the local Children's Aids may reduce the demand for residential school enrolment in Southern Ontario by an additional ten pupils next year... I shall be pleased to take into consideration the Northern Affairs possibilities as early as March or April...

93. 25 October 1961 Bonnah to Chief, Education Divison IAB

In response to your memorandum of October 17, 1961 ...in light of low enrolment...it is not proposed to hire the services of Mrs. Chenoweth...this term. The special needs of the classes at this school are such that the existing teaching staff are able to conveniently group the pupils during the time Mrs. Byron is offering Home Economics.

Study is now being given to arranging for the boys to receive limited instruction in the vocational subjects...by utilizing the services of the vocational instructor on Six Nations...We are still weighing the wisdom of this in the light of the special academic shortcomings of the group of boys at Mohawk...more correlation with the academic work is possible in the Home Economics classes than would be with the vocational classes for the boys.

Our decision will, therefore, be based upon the amount of good the vocational instruction can give these boys as in contrast to the time it will remove them from their academic work...

94. 25 January 1962 Zimmerman to Davey

...letter of November 22, 1960, regarding garbage removal, you state, "We would have no objection to you entering into a contract at the prevailing rate of $40.00 a month." I have used the men on the farm and the senior boys to remove the garbage. The $40.00 is credited to the farm with no benefit in salaries to the farm men. During the winter months, I have one farm man. Four boys have offered to assist with the farm chores. These lads are paid $28.00 per month as spending money. The boys have enjoyed helping on the farm under these conditions. One lad was involved in a car accident and given a fine of $50.00 plus costs or a jail term...I have been able to help this lad and he is paying a small part of the fine and is, at the same time, in possession of spending money which he has earned himself. Furthermore, he is continuing his studies in Grade 9...in Brantford...

I have reduced the farm operations for a number of reasons. The encroachment of the City has made farming operations very difficult. Certain groups are seeking to force the installation of costly...milk coolers upon the milk producers. How long we shall be permitted to sell milk under the present conditions is very questionable. The boys are in school all day and their rising time has been put back with the result that the farm labour is a complete charge to the cost of farm operations. This has affected the total cost of operation.

I am spending much more of my time with the children and their problems with the result that I am unable to give as much personal direction to farm operations as I did previously...the time has come when the Department ought to state its position in this matter of the operation of the farm. What is the place of the farm in the operation of the Mohawk Institute?

95. [No date] Davey to Zimmerman
...The arrangements...in connection with the removal of garbage is considered satisfactory. Further, it will be in order to continue to employ pupils on the farm...The question of the payment of farm salaries...must be made in consideration of the finances of the farm operation.

We are somewhat surprised at your request for a statement of policy pertaining to the operation of the farm ...we have indicated that we did not consider that farm operations should be continued in view of the food allowances which were being provided and also the time and effort which was required of the Principal...

It is our understanding that you were to convert from a dairy operation to running a beef herd on the land so as to reduce your operating costs to a minimum...there is no longer any need to conduct a farm operation at Mohawk and that steps should be taken to determine the property actually required by the residential school and the balance disposed of depending upon the ownership.

...please advise...whether you would agree to the complete closing of the farm operation during this coming season.

96. 13 February 1962 Zimmerman to Davey
...The cost of sanitary napkins is a considerable item and with a large number of senior girls enrolled...the expense per annum is about $250.00. Is there any chance that National Health and Welfare would provide this material as they have already done in former years...I have exceeded the allowable amount for Extra Curricular Activities by $37.32 for the year 1961. You will recall the matter of rink rental and the suggestion of charging this cost to the school balance. I desperately needed some skates and assumed that this amount could be deducted from the school balance or the amount for 1962.

97. 7 March 1962 Bonnah to IAB
...concerning Canon Zimmerman's desire to discontinue farming operations...
As the farming operation and the purchase of Parcel 1 containing 9.93 acres from the New England Company, are so closely related, both topics are being dealt with... While we are in agreement over closing of the farming operation, it may not be possible or, perhaps, profitable to carry out this too hurriedly...Canon Zimmerman has not only a Holstein dairy herd but approximately 30 or 40 head of Black Angus as well. The latter herd was being built up, I understand, while the milk herd was decreased. ...consideration must...be given to the purchase, or... retention, of certain Indian owned lands surrounding the Mohawk Institute...Part of the new school is located partially on New England land and partially on Indian owned land. The Principal's residence is not located on New England property, nor is part of the new barn that was built a few years and which is in excellent shape. ...If we are able to move quickly towards a solution...and

can purchase the land required, it will work no hardship on Canon Zimmerman's present farming operation. He has quite a bit of hay on hand and with the land...under our control there would be enough pasture and land available to take care of the diminishing herds until everything was disposed of.

98. 6 April 1962 Bonnah to IAB
...concerning the purchase of Parcel 1 (9.93 acres) in Lot 5, Eagle's Nest Tract, from the New England Company, and the acquisition of additional land from the Six Nations Band adjacent thereto.
...the decision to discontinue the farming operation...is a wise one. The future educational needs of the students at Mohawk Institute would appear to be better served through concentration of our activities towards complete academic training...
...the writer met at Mohawk Institute on April 2, 1962, with the Chief and Land Committee of the Six Nations Council. It was a pleasure also to have Canon Zimmerman and Superintendent R. J. Stallwood sit in on the discussions. The object of this meeting was to acquaint the Land Committee with the reasons why the Branch consider it necessary to discontinue farming operations, and at the same time inform them that to continue our educational program at Mohawk we would require additional land beyond the 9.93 acres in the control of the New England Company. It was also pointed out to the committee that negotiations were underway between the Branch and the New England Company to acquire the old site of the Mohawk Institute since this would be in the best interests of the educational needs of the future students of Mohawk.

While at the Institute, advantage was taken to have the committee visit the site and learn at first hand the boundary of the property the Branch would require...the hospitality of the Institute was extended to the Chief and members of his committee, and a visit was made to the Institute itself and the new day school and gymnasium recently built by the Branch.

The visit of the Chief and members of his committee through the building was somewhat of a revelation. At least two members of the committee were former students of the Institute. The others had never been in the building before and had no idea that such a modern institution existed. Cognizant of the criticism that has been levelled for the past number of years against the New England Company, the Church and the Branch by many of the Indians, I could not help but be impressed by the favourable comments expressed by the committee as a whole. Even the ex-students could hardly believe that such a transformation had taken place since the Branch had taken a more direct interest in the affairs of the Institute. A resurgence of pride was quite evident in the former students and a great measure of satisfaction was shown by the others over the way the interests of the children had been taken care of...

To assume that the Six Nations Indians are not interested in the fate of the Mohawk Institute would appear to be a major understatement. On the contrary, there is considerable interest in the operation of the school itself and activities related thereto. Unfortunately, however, an extremely poor job of interpreting to the Indians the roles of the Church, New England Company and the Branch, has been done over past years.

It was pointed out to the Council that the Mohawk Institute is a historical link in the life of the Six Nations Indians and that when the New England Company came to the Grand River in 1827 there was one thought in mind - to provide education for the Six Nations people so that future generations of Indians might share equally with others in the destiny of the country.

To those members of the council who contended that the Institute was for the sole purpose of educating Six Nations children, it was pointed out that as far back as 1885 the New England Company "decided to accept other than Six Nations Indians". This seemed to satisfy the Council.

The increasing role over the years of Indian Affairs in the life of the Institute was unfolded to the council. Lastly, in the light of existing educational needs, the necessity of considering full-time academic training in preference to coupling education with farming, was explained. All appeared to share the views of the Branch in this regard. There was, however, some thought amongst the female members of the Indian Council that the Branch should make more use of the modern facilities of the Mohawk Institute for training kitchen help and waitresses, since it was felt there were many girls on the reserve who could not even reach grade seven or eight level of education.

I might say that in view of the delicacy of this subject, coupled with the fact that many still have vivid memories of the last sale of land in the Six Nations Reserve that caused such a rift amongst the Indians and eventually landed in the Supreme Court, every consideration in presenting the requirements of the Branch was complied with to avoid any embarrassment to the Council.

It would not surprise me that the ultimate decision of the Council would result in a leasing arrangement of Indian lands required with the cessation of farming activities within one year after reaching agreement, with perhaps a reversionary clause in the interests of the Band, covering the "island" presently under control of the New England Company. It is just possible that no money, or only a nominal amount would be involved. Since earlier title to the New England lot was vested in the Six Nations Indians, such a decision, if reached by the Council should be given every consideration...

99. 22 May 1962 Excerpt from Quarterly Report from Six Nations Agency

The Six Nations Council has been approached regarding the matter of the future of the farm land operations at the Mohawk Indian Residential School. It is hoped that an agreement will be reached with the Council, on whose land the school is situated, whereby the School grounds may be enlarged and the farm area eventually returned to the Band. The Six Nations Council would very much like to see the ownership of the 9.9 acres where the main school building is located, restored to Reserve status. If this could be accomplished, the Council indicated that they would be quite agreeable to grant to the Department, the use of the necessary acreage for school purposes for as long as required...

100. 9 May 1962 Zimmerman to Davey

The running shoes which the girls and boys are wearing in the gymnasium are badly worn. These running shoes were stored in the lockers in the new school block and are used solely in conjunction with the school programme. The cost involved in the purchase of these shoes was met from the clothing establishment.

At the present time, we have fifteen pupils attending the Pauline Johnson Collegiate Institute. In previous years, the parents frequently assumed a portion of the cost of their children's clothing. At the present time, the parents of our high school children are contributing little or nothing toward their clothing. On the present clothing establishment, we do not find that we have a margin. Would you consider...regarding the purchase of running shoes for athletic purposes as a cost to be borne as an educational item and paid directly by the Department?

The standard of dress at the Pauline Johnson Collegiate Institute in Brantford is very high. Our girls are becoming very conscious of their wearing apparel. They wish to be able to wear the latest. For example, they want nylon hosiery and the latest type of footwear, etc.

101. 25 May 1962 Bonnah to Education Division IAB
...some 30 pupils through Grades 6 to high school are in attendance at the City of Brantford Schools...

Current plans include working towards removing all high school age pupils from the residential school to suitable home situations in their local areas...Any resultant decrease in enrolment...will be absorbed through mutual arrangements with the Northern Ontario Region to admit pupils for whom there is not yet regular day school facilities in that region. The expected enrolment...for the coming school term, therefore, appears to be:

a) Attending classes at Mohawk   115
b) Attending Brantford School System   25
c) Total Residential enrolment   140

STAFF RECOMMENDATIONS:
1) Retain present staff:

Retain the present staff because of the disturbed nature of nearly all pupils registered at the Mohawk, making smaller classes essential if the teachers are to do a reasonably good job of preparing the children. In addition to this, the children who enter from the Northern Region enrol with an extreme language problem, and this is better coped with through the smaller classes. I...recommend retention of the present staff of 5 with provision for Home Economics;

2) <u>Services of Manual Training Instructor</u>
I further recommend provisions be made to engage the services of a Manual Training instructor on the basis of 1½ days per week;

3) <u>Interest of Pupils:</u>
It is recommended in the interest of the children...that a young man from the Brantford city system be engaged in the athletic instructional field...after school to give supervision and instruction alternately to the girls and boys...1½ hours per day for four days;

4) <u>Appointment of Teacher-Counsellors:</u>
...the engaging of a teacher-counsellor for service in the Toronto office with attachment to the Mohawk Institute has been approved in principle...to give some time at Mohawk on an intermittent basis. The extensive demand for this service...is reduced in the coming term by reason of the removal of high school pupils.

102. 21 November 1962 Zimmerman to Bonnah

On February 23, 1962, I received a letter signed by Mr. Davey...read in part as follows:

"Please be advised that we are referring the matter of farm operations to our regional office and we are requesting that every effort be made to terminate farm operations at the earlies possible date."

...if farm operations are to terminate...has not the time come when definite plans ought to be made?

One or two members of the Six Nations Council have indicated to me their concern for future use of this land. ..If anything is to be done in the near future in order to be fair to our Six Nation friends, ought not we to begin planning very shortly?

...at the present time the driveway passes through the boys' playground...as you well know, we have had one serious accident...some consideration should be given to another approach to the delivery entrance...

103. 23 November 1962 Bonnah to IAB

...concerning reversion of lands at the Mohawk Institute to the Six Nations Band.

With our submission of March 7th last, a print was enclosed showing the land that would be required for future use in conjunction with the educational program of the Mohawk Indian Residential School. On May 29th it was suggested that arrangements be made to have a surveyor visit the site so that Branch requirements could be properly described, with a view to legalising Branch requirements with the Band Council. The Director...has already approved the Council Resolution of May 3rd last as to the disposition of the lands involved.

While I presume in the intervening months the matter of the 9.9 acres of land involved with the New England Company has not been concluded, the receipt of Canon Zimmerman's letter of November 21st, photocopy attached, prompts me to write you at this time...

When this matter was discussed with Canon Zimmerman and the Six Nations Council, it was understood that Canon Zimmerman would require approximately a year to dispose of livestock and get out of the farming operation in general. Inasmuch as it has been decided to cease farming, both Mr. Rodine and I feel that Canon Zimmerman should take the necessary steps so that the farming operation can be closed out within a year. There should also be no need to wait until the New England deal is completed...to have a survey of the lands required for future educational purposes.

104. 23 January 1963 Zimmerman to Davey

I am in the process of closing out the farm operations...I have always understood that one of the functions of the farm operations was the supplementing of food supplies for the children. Due to government provision, we have a large deep freeze. It is possible to kill and have dressed the carcasses for deep freeze but I would prefer to sell the animals designated for that purpose and place the money in the bank and purchase beef as required. The advantage of this plan is that our meat supply would be fresh and I would not be taking up space in the deep freeze that would otherwise be used.

I assume that this would in no way affect our regular and normal per diem grant for food...

105. 5 February 1963 Zimmerman to Fishcarrier

Farm operations...will shortly be discontinued...the Mohawk Institute will no longer be using the land north of the canal and the land behind the Chapel. In respect to the land between the Chapel and the Institute proper, there are two fields of wheat which I would like to harvest this summer. For the time being, we would appreciate using the field between the Institute and the creek. Part of this land, the Department...would appreciate having for the use of the school. There is one parcel of land...east of the laneway between the barn and the Chapel...that we do not any longer require.

The two fields now in wheat would be returned over to the Six Nations following the next harvest season. In regard to the barns, we are only interested in retaining the metal dairy barn. The old pig stable and the old frame dairy barn are of no further use to the Institute.

106. 19 August 1965   Waller to Jolicoeur
...concerning the purchase of French text books and classroom materials for the two French class-rooms...Mr. Rodine will be in touch with you...as to his requirements...

107. 22 October 1965   Davey to Mrs. Duncan Fraser
...The Mohawk Institute...requires special mention. It is the only Indian boarding school in Southern Ontario and until recently served only children drawn from the reserves south of Parry Sound. Its purpose is to provide hostel accommodation for children requiring special care and attention or those who cannot receive an education while residing at home. Within the last two or three years the need for this kind of service in Southern Ontario has declined...The Childrens' Aid Societies have done excellent work in finding foster homes...The Mohawk Institute has therefore extended its services to a number of the remote reserves in Northern Ontario and Quebec which the Childrens' Aid Societies cannot serve. Students beyond the elementary school level who reside at the Mohawk Institute may receive their education in the Brantford public school system and it is hoped that it will be possible before long to make similar arrangements for the other children residing at the Institute...

108. 12 July 1966   Waller to Jolicoeur
At present a large majority of the pupils...are from northern Quebec. The largest group are Waswanipi children. Within the next year or so the Quebec students will be withdrawn from this school either to graduate or to attend Quebec schools. May I have a brief report from you giving the approximate dates of the withdrawal of the Quebec children from this school...to plan for the future use of the Institute.

109. 8 August 1966   Jolicoeur to Waller
Apparently, you did not read my report...As mentioned in your letter, a large group of Waswanipi children are in the Mohawk Institute; many of them are taught in French. Naturally, if those children were placed in a French environment, better results could be anticipated.
It is impossible...to give the approximate dates of the withdrawal of the Quebec children from Ontario...

110. 27 February 1970   Brantford Expositor
Would Shut Doors To Indian School
With the proposed closing in June of the Mohawk Institute, a way of life will come to an end and a new one will begin for about 90 Indian children.
About 65 children from Northern Ontario and northern Quebec will attend school on their home reserves next fall...The proposed closing of the residential school was announced Thursday by Donald Cassie, superintendent of the Six Nations Indian agency, and Richard Isaac, chief councillor of the Six Nations elected council...only an unexpected increase in the number of pupils from southern Ontario would open the school next fall.
This year there are only 25 southern Ontario Indians at Mohawk, 23 of them from the Six Nations Reserve.
Mr. Cassie and Mr. Isaac said it would be economically unfeasible to keep the school open for 25 children.
There are two reasons behind the proposed closing: it is understood that accommodation is now available for Quebec students in their home province; and the federal department of Indian affairs...feels obliged to meet requests of Indian parents in northern Ontario who want classrooms on their home reserves.
Mr. Cassie and Mr. Isaac said it is anticipated that southern Ontario pupils can be provided for through local child care offices, or through private boarding arrangements.
Operating costs at Mohawk are about $235,000 per year, and are provided by the federal government. A reduction in enrolment would not reduce operating costs proportionately.

111. 10 June 1970   Brantford Expositor
Council to Protest Mohawk Institute Closing
Six Nations Indians who want to save Mohawk Institute may have the last word when the residential school closes June 26.
The band council agreed Tuesday night to let the Brant Historical Society post a plaque at the school. But it wants Coun. Norman Lickers to speak at the unveiling to protest the closing.
The department of Indian affairs announced in February it would close the school because costs are too high and enrolment is too low.
Of the 96 pupils now attending Grades 1 to 8, 59 are from Northern Ontario and 12 from Quebec. They will attend schools on their home reserves next fall. There are 25 pupils from southern Ontario, 23 of these from the Six Nations.
Annual operating expenses are $235,000. The federal government has spent $750,000 on renovations at the institute over the last 15 years.
Edward Oliver, Indian affairs assistant director for Ontario, said this week there has been no increase in enrolment for next September...children from southern Ontario will be placed in homes, probably on the reserve by the Children's Aid Society...
The band council has a committee investigating possible uses for the building and grounds...Lickers suggested the council should use the historical society's plaque project to publicize band wishes to keep the school open...

Facts and Figures - Mohawk Institute

1. Number of boys and girls admitted and left

	Boys Admitted	Girls Admitted	Total Admitted	Total left
1861	20	10	30	15
1862	12	4	16	16
1863	14	9	23	29
1864	11	6	17	16
1865	13	12	25	19
1866	11	12	23	11
1867	7	5	12	15
1868	26	17	43	30
1869	10	9	19	17
1870	11	6	17	
	135	90	225	168

2. 1894
Staff

	Capt. R. Ashton	1200.00 a year
Matron	Mrs. Ashton	
Farmer	J. R. Morrison	400.00
	Miss Hardle	300.00
Asst Matron...	Miss Lathen	150.00
Housekeeper..	Mrs. Hyslop	144.00
Laundress & Dairy Supt-	Mrs Neville	120.00
Music teacher & organist -	Miss Ashton	100.00
Master & farm clerk-	R. B. Harrison	160.00
Garden & groundsman -	J. Kierl	336.00
Farm foreman -	J. Neville	216.00
Physician -	Dr. W. T. Harris	100.00
Carpenter -	D.A. House	$2 a day

The gardener and farmer have cottages with one acre attached, receive one quart milk a day and board themselves.

3. Attendance 1873 - 1896

Year	Boys entered	Girls entered	Boys left	Girls left	Number attending	Cost per head	No. 31/12	Cost of operation	Farm profit/loss	Farm sales	Supplies from farm
1873	4+2R	1R	21	15			41				
1874	29	17	14	11			64	6558.02	807.08		
1875	17	18	17	9			75	6381.89	209.47		
1876	15	15	12	12		92.36	80	7389.51	(108.18)		
1877	14+2R	19+1R	19	15	83	76.50	81	6350.28	1092.00		
1878	19	19	18	18	84	84.93	85	7134.29	368.50		
1879							90				
1885	14	10	12	12			90				
1886							90				
1887							90				
1888	21	21	21	20			90				
1889	16	17	15	19			89				
1890	15	17	14	15			92				
1891	15	13	16	14	91		90				
1892	13	11	12	9	93		93				
1893	12	12	11	11	95		95				
1894	16	26	14	11	110		110				
1895	10	6	5	14	107		107				
1896											
1897									757.73		
1898									1258.85	2293.82	2618.47
1899									1756.29	3353.16	2583.49

4. Showing the present condition of pupils who have left the Institution, during the 4 years ending 31st December...

	1876 Boys	1876 Girls	1878 Boys	1878 Girls	1884 Boys	1884 Girls	1885 Boys	1885 Girls	1891 Boys	1891 Girls	1892 Boys	1892 Girls
Living with Friends	36	21	25	27						3	13	2
Working Farms			17	0								
Farming independently, or on shares					1		1					
Farming at hire or for parents					29		36		42		29	
Working at trades, clerks or in factories					10		5		7	1	7	2
In service (Indian)	0	2	1	1				2	5	3		1
In service (White)	3	1	3	6	1	8		1		15		8
Engaged in teaching			4	2		7	1	4	2	5	2	12
Attending other Institutions/Colleges	1*	0	6	0	4		5		1	3	2	2
Living with friends and attending school					2	5	1	4			8	15
* * girls, also boys under 16					7	17	5	17				
Removed to United States	2	1	2	0	1		2	3				
Re-Admitted	0	1	0	1	2	1	2	1		4		
Married	3	5	2	5		10		10		9		
Unascertained	5	1	1	0								
Doubtful, wandering or idle					2							
Disgraced, dismissed or known to be doing badly	0	2†	3	10	3	1	1	1	1		1	2
Dead	3	0			2	5	2			5		7
Not reported on, having been less than 6 months in the Institution					3	2		1	1			11

* Gone with his mother to Shinwauk Home, Garden River
† Both these girls absconded from the Institution

5. Attendance figures and Standards

Year	Accommodation	Boys	Girls	Grade I	II	III	IV	V	VI	H.S.	Total	Average attendance
1896	125	53	66	13	21	20	21	33	8	3	119	
1897		57	76	18	20	21	19	32	23			
1898		56	71	8	10	24	20	39	26			121
1899		56	77	12	21	19	23	34				121
1900	125	56	69	15	26	29	31	10	14			128
1901		56	69	6	9	51	26	10	23			126
1902		56	69	12	8	46	22	20	22			126
1903	177	57	63	7	13	24	39	12	25			118
1904	83	39	40		5	22	13	23	16		79	81
1905		54	54	15	20	11	16	26	20		108	88
1906	110			8	29	12	19	20	24		112	109
1907	110			7	11	25	22	20	24		109	108
1908	120			12	10	25	22	21	25		115	108
1909				9	14	24	22	22	30		121	118
1910				12	10	14	35	22	31		124	121
1911	120			8	14	12	28	26	34		124	118
1912	125			10	16	16	19	24	44		129	123
1913	125			12	19	14	14	34	36		129	126

6. Statement of Payments made by Department of Indian Affairs towards the Mohawk Institute.

1891-1892	5,460.00	1901-1902	5,460.00	1910-1911	6,000.00	1919-1920	14,514.10
1892-1893	5,355.00	1902-1903	5,460.00	1911-1912	11,922.50	1920-1921	22,830.27
1893-1894	4,092.00	1903-1904	4,715.00	1912-1913	12,000.00	1921-1922	22,329.98
1894-1895	5,892.00	1904-1905	4,951.00	1913-1914	12,000.00	1922-1923	55,340.23
1895-1896	5,460.00	1905-1906	8,981.00	1914-1915	12,003.00	1923-1924	29,185.67
1896-1897	6,825.00	1906-1907	4,500.00	1915-1916	12,006.08	1924-1925	17,926.74
1897-1898	5,460.00	1907-1908	5,597.00	1916-1917	12,002.00	1925-1926	21,258.89
1898-1899	5,460.00	1908-1909	6,000.00	1917-1918	13,231.47	1926-1927	24,616.56*
1899-1900	5,460.00	1909-1910	6,000.00	1918-1919	12,642.44	1927-1928	27,470.06*
1900-1901	5,460.00						

Total   394,132.37 *[handwritten additions Actual Total 446,218.99]

NOTE: On file No. 98411 there is a memorandum of the Deputy Superintendent General of Indian Affairs, dated November 4, 1890. This memorandum states that up to that time the New England Company had wholly supported the Mohawk Institute. The first payment made by this Department towards the maintenance of this institution was during the fiscal year 1891-1892. The above statement, therefore, shows the payments made from that date to March 31, 1926. J.D.S.

7. Cost of Maintenance and Management, Farm Operations, Industrial Departments 1904-1917

Year	Cost of Management	Enrolment	Average Attendance	Cost Per Capita	Farm receipts	Farm expenditure	Farm profits	Farm sales	Supplies to school	Principal
1904							583.82	3271.18	1270.23	Rev. R. Ashton
1905	14,384.30	108	83	173.30	6,510.79	4,755.74	1,755.05	3458.71	1185.75	" "
1906	21,549.59	112	105	205.23	9,981.50	7,739.95	2,241.55	4662.47	1379.25	"
1907	11,091.94	111	106	104.64	4,809.68	3,796.69	1,022.99	2669.92	965.50	"
1908	14,296.46	115	105	136.15	5,524.23	4,619.86	904.37	3526.79	1464.34	"
1909	15,319.37	121	113	135.57	4,846.13	4,096.29	749.84	3420.53	1425.80	""
1910	13,200.75	128	118	111.87	5,316.08	3,258.50	2,057.58	3888.84	1427.34	"
1911	13,099.33	122	117	111.95	5,508.39	3,083.43	2,424.96	3985.16	1523.23	A. Nelles Ashton
1912	15,532.82	129	122	127.32	4,953.18	3,091.35	1,861.83	3251.90		A. Nelles Ashton
1913	18,139.25	127	122	148.68	5,699.74	5,685.49	14.25	4175.64		A. Nelles Ashton
1914	14,996.68	131	124	120.94	7,186.46	3,921.12	3,265.34			Mrs. A.M. Boyce
1915	17,535.50	131	124	141.41	5,246.40	3,779.72	1,466.68			Rev. C.M.Turnell
1916	19,420.62	141	127	152.92	4,550.09	2,447.87	2,112.22			"
1917	26,427.70	140	127	208.10	5,518.96	4,457.86	1,061.10			"
1918 -9 months	21,367.10	134	126	169.58	9,332.38	6,085.00	3,247.38			

8. Maintenance and Management Dec. 31, 1917

Salaries

Rev. C. M. Turnell	Principal	12 months 1000.00	
Mrs. M. B. Turnell	Matron	12 months 240.00	
Miss S. Hardie	Senior Teacher	12 months 500.00	
Mrs. G. Hargrave	Junior Teacher	4 months 133.00	
Miss L. Bell	Junior Teacher	8 months 267.95	
Mrs. M. Goodwin	Housekeeper	12 months 360.00	
Miss J. Reid	Bookkeeper	12 months 240.00	
Miss N. Gilpin	Sewing Teacher	8 months 206.00	
Mrs. D. Reed	" "	4 months 100.00	
Mrs. D. Reed	Assistant Housekeeper	2 months 50.00	
Miss A. Lee	Laundry Dairy Instructress	9 months 235.00	
Miss I. Shaver	Assistant Housekeeper	9½ months 190.00	
Mrs D. Smith	1 week as assistant sewing teacher	5.00	
Mrs. D. Smith	3 weeks...assistant housekeeper	18.00	
Mr. J. West	Boys' Master	12 months 530.00	
C. Tobias	for services rendered	5.00	
Monitors and Monitresses		117.50	
		4197.45	
			10078.35

Provisions

Clothing	3497.93	
Washing, Heating, and Lighting	255.71	
Furniture and House Sundries	1100.54	
Repairs and Improvements	1083.91	
Medical Expenses and Dentistry	417.67	
Office Expenses	120.84	
Sundries, School Requisites, Prize, Library, Telephone	838.70	
Travel and Freight	128.23	
Insurance	591.15	
Gross Cost of Maintenance and Management	24614.48	
Materials and Wages for Farm and Garden	6085.00	
Gross Cost of Institution	30699.48	
Less Supplies from Industrial Departments		
Provisions	3262.85	
Cash Receipts for Sales	5719.53	
Board of Farm Men	350.00	9332.38
		21367.10
Miscellaneous Expenditure (General Account)		79.55
		21367.10

Net Cost of Institution 1917	21367.10
Net Cost of Institution 1916	18220.07
Increase in Expenditure	3147.03
Cost per capita	164.36

FARM BALANCE SHEET
RECEIPTS

Stock in hand Dec.31.1917

Grain	445.00	
Feed	328.00	
Live Stock	5944.00	
Hay, Straw, etc.	450.00	
Vegetables and Roots	670.00	
Tools and Implements	1330.90	
Dairy Implements	125.00	
Garden Stock	527.72	
Garden Tools and Sundries	190.90	10,611.52
Supplied to Mohawk Inst. at Valuation		
Meat and Fowl	187.00	
Vegetables and Fruit	720.40	
Milk, Butter, and Eggs	2355.45	3,262.85
Sales		
Farm Produce	1308.10	
Dairy Produce	418.68	
Garden Produce	1196.50	
Live Stock	2788.25	
Sundries	8.00	5,719.53 18,993.90

PAYMENTS

Wages	2038.56	
Live Stock	423.00	
Seeds and Plants	367.00	
Feed	1548.60	
Tools and Implements	573.02	
Repairs	364.08	
Sundries	415.23	
Insurance	343.80	
Travel and Freight	11.71	6,085.00
To Maintenance Account		
Board of Farm Men	350.00	
Stock in hand Dec. 31, 1916		
Grain	435.00	
Live Stock	5111.60	
Hay, Straw, etc.	830.00	
Vegetables and Roots	75.00	
Tools and Implements	1241.13	

Dairy Implements	127.00		
Garden Stock	517.88		
Garden Tools and Sundries	179.70	8,517.31	14,952.31
Balance in favor of Farm			4,041.59

RECEIPTS

To Cash Receipts from Farm Produce	5719.53		
School Fees from parents of pupils	101.00		
Rent from Gas Company - Glebe	15.00		
Rent from Miss Davis	36.00		
Treasurer's Remittances	4996.75		
Grant from Indian Department	12600.00		
Dividend on Canada Stock	191.53	23659.61	
Balance due Principal's Account Dec. 31,1917		7056.26	30716.07

PAYMENTS

By Maintenance and Management	21351.63		
By Payments on account of Farm	6085.00	27436.63	
General Account			
Insurance on Christ Church Hall	5.25		
Insurance on St. John's Church Hall	6.00		
Repairs to Mohawk Church	6.00		
Insurance on Parsonage at Ohsweken	30.00		
Insurance on Mohawk Church	32.30	79.55	
		27516.18	
Balance due Principal's account Dec. 31, 1916		3199.89	30716.07

9. The cost per head Year ending December 31st

1916 - $151.72	1918 - $137.00
1917 - $164.36	1919 - $184.97

10. 15 August 1920 Salaries A. M. Boyce

Mrs A. M. Boyce	Acting Principal	$1000.00 a year, not paid to date
Miss Susan Hardie	governess	600.00 a year was raised last year
Mrs G. Hargreave	" "	400.00 has little girl with her
Miss M. Gemby	Sewing teacher	30.00 a month
Mrs. L. Matthews	laundry and dairy	30.00
Mrs. L. Bilke	housekeeper	35.00
Mr. S. Rogers	boys master	60.00 a month...here a year should be raised

The above have room, board and washing.

Mr. R. Almey		Farm and garden manager $65.00 a month and extras - is leaving to return to Guelph O.A.C. Has done well with garden, should have a bonus of $100.00
Mr. A. Richmond		Cattleman $50.00 also leaving to return to O.A.C. was promised April 30th, a bonus of $12.50 a month- this has not been paid
Mr. L. Cudmore		teamster $50.00 a month, cottage, garden 2 quarts of milk daily; fuel and keep of horse
Mr. C. Henderson		Gardener, commenced August 16th. $70.00 a month cottage, 2 quarts milk daily, fuel and vegetables and apples
Mr. A. Barron		Farm Foreman, to commence $70.00 a month, house, fuel, milk, vegetables and apples, rough feed for horse

We also pay, monitors, monitress, organist, milk boy, drivers, nurse, chicken girl and often pay on time work each month and sometimes allow money for competitions.

There will be threshing and extra men required next month and also for silo filling. So many of our boys are small.

When the laundress or housekeeper is away, girls are paid who take charge.

Gas, electric light, coal oil and many small bills have to be paid monthly, express, freight, tolls, stamps etc paid as required. Many bills have to settled at once...

11. Year ending March 31st 1921   Orphans, Destitute and those needing protection of a School.

Mother dead x 20

Mother dead, Father deserted family x 4

Father dead x 3

Father killed overseas, Mother nearly blind

Father dead; Mother at Service

Father dead. Mother deserted

Father dead; Grandmother Guardian x 2

Orphan x 9

Orphan Grandmother Guardian x 2

Orphan Step-grandmother guardian

Orphan Grandfather Guardian

Deserted by parents x 5

Illegitimate. Foster father crippled; Grandmother Guardian. Mother living with another man

Mother deserted living with another man; Father ditto; Father now dead

Mother dead;Father crippled

Mother dead Father lately married again

Illegitimate; Placed in School by Childrens Aid; Mother leading immoral life

Father then overseas; Mother led immoral life in New York; Parents now living together

Placed in School when Mother died. Father not seen for four years. He recently married again - took children home for Christmas - kept them on sick leave

Illegitimate; Grandmother Guardian

Mother dead; Father very recently married; Grandmother guardian

Mother dead; Father takes no interest

Father deserted; Grandfather guardian

Mother dead; Father kept her home last summer as she was so useful picking berries

Father dead; Mother living an immoral life

Illegitimate; Grandfather guardian

Illegitimate; Mother dead; Stepfather not a trustworthy person

Mother dead; Father bed-ridden

Mother in asylum 4 years

Father killed overseas; Mother neglects children; Placed here by Council

Illegitimate; Placed in School by step-father

Father deaf and dumb; Mother deserted

Father dead; Mother deserted; No-one takes any interest

Deserted - wandered about Reserve

Mother in Insane Asylum; Neglected

Parents separated; Grandfather guardian

Parents separated x 5

Mother died; Father married again

Parents living but taking no interest x 10

One interested parent x 5

12. 1929 Finances

Deficit - March 31st, 1929	$3,052.43
Expenditures from March 31st to May 20th, 1929	$3,692.26
TOTAL	$6,744.69
Receipts - March 31st to May 20th, 1929	
New England Co. Grant	$1,200.00
Advance on June quarter earnings	$3,000.00
Farm and garden sales	$1,545.58
TOTAL	$5,745.58
DEFICIT	$999.11

13. 1931

Principal	Rev. H. W. Snell	1680.00 a year
Matron	Mrs H. W. Snell	600.00
Nurse	Mrs. A. E. Smith	600.00
Senior Teacher	Miss. S. Hardy	800.00
Junior Teacher	Miss L. McBurney	600.00
Sewing Teacher	Mrs. A. Boyce	360.00
Senior Housekeeper	Mrs. H. E. Jones	480.00
Junior Housekeeper	Miss L. Smith	360.00
Boys' Master	H. E. Jones	720.00
Farmer	Geo. Howarth	1020.00
Gardener	C. Henderson	960.00
Teamster	A. Alexander	600.00

14. Statement of [Government] Expenditures, with the exception of Per Capita Allowance Payments

Fiscal Year	Amount	Fiscal Year	Amount
1920-21	$1,700.00	1932-33	$2,000.00
1921-22	1,600.00	1933-34	1,300.00
1922-23	19,414.00	1934-35	3,000.00
1923-24	14,200.00	1935-36	55.00
1924-25	1,000.00	1936-37	13.00
1925-26	2,000.00	1937-38	68.00
1926-27	2,654.00	1938-39	82.00
1927-28	9,800.00	1939-40	281.00
1928-29	5,500.00	1940-41	100.00
1929-30	5,100.00	1941-42	80.00
1930-31	8,500.00	1942-43	80.00
1931-32	1,800.00	1943-44	97.00

Note:- Since 1935-36 practically all repairs, etc., have been paid from the funds provided by the NEC, during the term of the old lease. During the period that lease was in operation the NEC allowed the Department $5,000.00 a year towards current expenses. This money was placed in a special Trust Account and was expended from time to time, as required.

15. 1945

Rev. H. W. Snell	Principal	1,680.00
Mrs. H. W. Snell	Matron	600.00
Mrs. A. E. Smith	Asst. Matron & Nurse	600.00
Mr. E. W. Yeandle	Senior Teacher	960.00
Mrs. C. Fry	Junior Teacher	600.00
Mrs. Thorpe	Acting Dietitian (Jr.)	520.00
Mrs. L. Ramsay	Dietitian (Jr.)	520.00
Mrs. Bennett	Seamstress	480.00
Mr. G. Haworth	Farmer	1,080.00
Mr. W. A Ramsay	Gardener	960.00
Mr. Thorpe	Boys' Master & Poultryman	900.00
Mr. H. Barton	Teamster	720.00

16. 1948

Financial Statement ---February 1948

Receipts.		
Balance	974.98	
Department	3,172.59	
Farm Sold	237.74	
Farm Contra	563.37	
Garden Contra	75.23	
Other sources		
Church		5,023.9
Expenditures		
Salaries	1,259.10	
Clothing	108.05	
Food	1,400.65	
Phone,Fuel,Light,Water	103.18	
Building & Repairs	150.19	
House Equipment	238.75	
Farm & Garden	261.00	
Transport	.50	
Extra Labour		
Misc.	20.55	3,541.97
Balance		1,481.94
Assets		
Cash on hand		
Cash in bank	2,215.47	
Stock on hand	1,600.00	
Grant earned	4,875.00	8,690.47
Liabilities		
Cheques O.S.	733.53	
Accounts payable	1,165.00	1,898.53
Current surplus		6,791.94

17. 1957

FINANCIAL STATEMENT ---March 1957   September 1957

RECEIPTS.				
Balance	6,399.91		4,423.48	
Department				
Church				
Farm & Garden	482.42		455.93	
Other sources	411.00	7,293.33	1,024.35	5,903.76
EXPENDITURES				
Salaries	1,768.50		1,665.45	
Clothing	168.02		388.27	
Food	1,334.15		1,041.24	
Phone,Fuel,Light,Water	1,433.68		413.14	
Building & Repairs	52.93		136.26	
House Equipment	488.37		376.98	
Farm & Garden	635.83		758.07	
Transport	17.00		68.20	
Capital	111.65			
Misc.	83.20	6,093.33	113.95	4,961.56
BALANCE		1,200.00		947.20
MEMORANDUM				
Farm & Garden produce supplied Inst.	374.71			401.79
Value of Church Clothing				
ASSETS				
Cash on hand	1,058.47		204.05	
Cash in bank	2,505.48		1,863.31	
Stock on hand	1,600.00		1,600.00	
Grant earned	14,580.62	19,744.57	13,112.75	16,780.11
LIABILITIES				
Cheques O.S.	2,363.95		1,120.16	
Accounts payable	3,300.00	5,663.95	3,200.00	4,320.16
CURRENT SURPLUS		14,080.62		12,459.95

18. Indian agents' applications and reports 1949-1950

The home conditions of these children are not satisfactory. The parents are not compatible and live together only sporadically. The father is a veteran and has some difficulty controlling his appetite for liquor...the mother tries to get along but at times finds it impossible so leaves home. The children then lack adequate care. Both parents are agreeable to placing the children in the Institute.

Mrs. **** was admitted to the Freeport Sanatorium...and will have to remain there for some time she having left seven small children to be cared for therefore the Council recommend the three oldest be placed in the Mohawk Residential school...

This child's mother is dead, and since her father re-married the girl has been boarded out among relatives. The child is of a nervous disposition and has developed an impediment in her speech. It is considered the child will receive the proper care and attention to overcome this condition at the School, but is not likely to receive this under the present arrangement.

...very unsatisfactory home conditions...Her father is dead and her step-father does not wish to keep her in his home as the girl's mother is in the hospital with a very serious heart condition.

...you express the opinion that they would not be suitable candidates for a residential school. We are inclined to agree with you in that regard, but we feel it would be difficult if not impossible to place them in any white institution...Our suggestion is that ****, age 10, and ****, age 9, be placed in the Mohawk Institute at Brantford, and that ****, age 12, and ****, age 6, be placed in the Shingwauk...It is realized that in making this suggestion we are separating the family, but we do not feel that this would cause any great difficulty.

Mr. ****, father...was questioned as to why his children should receive institutional care. He stated that both he and his wife are, and have been, working out attempting to save money to build a bigger and better home for their family. The children have been left in the care of an aged lady for whom the task is too heavy and the children are sometimes left more or less on their own which is a worry on the parents. This Office is quite ready to corroborate his statements as Mr. and Mrs. **** are an excellent type of Indian and should be encouraged in their worthwhile ambition.

This child will only be five years of age in November but due to the fact that his mother is constantly moving from place to place and has no means of supporting him, and...the child is badly neglected...

The parents of this child are separated and, as Mrs. **** is in poor financial circumstances...

The mother of these children is having a difficult time in supporting them...her husband died about three years ago in Byron Sanatorium. Since that time all of these children have on one occasion or another been in the Sanatorium...It would certainly be in the best interests of the children if they were enrolled in a residential school as they will be undernourished and neglected if they remain on...Reserve.

...the father of these children, has deserted his family and the mother has no means of supporting them...

...the father...is in jail...and Mrs. **** has no means of support for the child and the other three children...are in the Mohawk...

The mother of these children is deceased and as there is no one to care for them the father wishes them placed in Residential School.

The father of these children is deceased and the mother is continually roaming from place to place deserting her family.

****...is living apart from his wife. There are three children in the family aged ten months, three and five years. Mr. and Mrs **** have never been able to get along together. In the past few years they have had various reconciliations, but none have been permanent. Mrs. **** deserts the family quite often....**** is frequently in jail on intoxication charges. At the present time Mrs. **** is in Port Huron and her husband is trying to look after the three children with the aid of his sister-in-law. It is obvious that the children are badly neglected and undernourished, etc. After discussing the matter with **** I have decided to recommend that the two oldest children be admitted...the home conditions are deplorable...

This boy's parents separated and he has been staying with different relatives for the past 6 months. I believe that his mother took him up to the Institute at school beginning in the hopes that he would be admitted...

The parents of this girl are separated and the mother finds she is unable to control her therefore has requested she be admitted.

Motion No. 1 passed by the Cape Croker Council...July 4th...That the children of Mrs. **** be sent to Brantford Residential school after holidays...Mrs. **** is a widow and has five children which she finds too much of a responsibility...

****'s husband has deserted her and three of their children. A relative is caring for one of these children and by putting **** in Residential School Mrs. **** feels she could go out to work and take the baby with her. As they are in very poor financial circumstances...

Mrs. **** has been deserted by her husband **** and has to support her two children...it is very difficult for her to secure employment but she can get work where she can take the other small child.

...the father is over eighty...and the mother is deaf and dumb...

The parents have a family of seven children, and the mother being sickly cannot properly care for her family. Some children being looked after by some of her relatives. **** frequently missed school last year and was not a good influence while attending, this due to lack of parental supervision; the father being away working often...

...the mother is working and the boy is being cared for in a very unsatisfactory manner in various foster homes...

This child has been living with her grandmother who has become blind and is unable to care for her any longer.

...the father deserted the family some years ago. This girl will be sent to school with her sister who is now home on holidays.

...These children are being badly neglected on Sarnia Reserve as the parents are irresponsible. School attendance has been irregular and it would be in the best interests of the children to be enrolled in residential school.

...the father of these children spends a large portion of his time in jail, and at present their mother has deserted them and the family of six are left at various homes to be cared for. We are now attempting to take action against the parents.

**** lives with an aunt who although married to an Indian spends much of her time at the home of a white man. The conditions are bad and...the child is often left alone at the white man's home. She is a big girl for her age and I am fearful of what the future has in store for her. The boy, ****, does not seem to have any definite home.

Students at the Mohawk Institute

These lists do not include everyone who attended the Mohawk Institute. Names that appear elsewhere in the text can be found in the index. Names of students admitted between 1900 and 1929 are recorded in an Admission Book (to which access is restricted) housed in the Grand River Post Secondary Education Office in Ohsweken.

1. 31 March 1840 Mohawk School...Abraham Nelles

1st Class   Tickets for good conduct

Jacob Hill	10	Rule of Three
John Hill, Jun	6	Compound Multiplication
John Hill, Sen	10	Compound division
Jacob Thomas	9	Compound addition
Jacob Lottridge	5	Long division
Isaac Powlis	10	Rule of Three
David Obediah	5	Compound multiplication
Ellen Smith	6	
J.C.Nelles	7	Simple addition

Read well and spell in Mavor's spelling Book, repeat perfectly the Arithmetical tables, the Catechism in short questions, and several hymns, improvement in writing unsatisfactory in this class, this quarter.

2nd class

Isaac Isaacs	6
George Curly	6
Matthew Nash	0
Jacob Johnson	0
Christian Hill	11
Elizabeth Johnson	10
Mary Case	0

Read tolerably in St. John's Gospel, repeat Catechism, spell in two syllables, write large hand tolerably

3rd Class

Margaret Curly	3
Lydia Hill	6
Mary John	4
Polly Tunis	7
Catherine Clane	7
M.J.Humphrey-Skimmons	

Read in easy lessons of short syllables

John Thomas	Rule of Three
William English	Compound Division
Isaac Doxtater	Rule of three
Baptiste Gibson	Rule of three

Read and spell very well, repeat table and catechism; write pretty well. These four boys only attend school occasionally for a few days, to keep up with what they already know; and devote the remainder of their time to the trades they are learning, the two former carpenters, the two latter blacksmiths.

The improvement of the children generally...is satisfactory. The First class has been very careless in their writing: well pleased with the cleanly manner in which their writing, and cyphering books are kept.

2. 30 June 1859 Institution Report..Thomas Griffiths...

Names	Age	Remarks
John Dixon	19	Reads English History, studies Geography
Thomas Green	18	and Grammar
Henry Green	16	Ciphers in Vulgar Fractions
George Moses	23	" "
		English History, Geography, and
Albert Anthony	19	Grammar, Arithmetic, Proportion.
Susan Jonathan	15	" " Compound Addition
William Smith	18	Reads in Fourth Book.
Josiah Hill	16	Studies Geography and Grammar.
Richard Hill	13	
James Hill	16	Ciphers in Vulgar Fractions
Louis Gibson	15	" "
Peter Douglas	17	" "
Nicolas Williams	18	" Simple Proportion.
Zechariah Hill	17	" "
Alexander Hill	13	" "
George Bombarry	9	" "
Amanda John	15	" Simple Division
Ellen Maracle	16	" "
Augustus Hill	12	Reads in Third Book & Testament.
Charles Jackson	13	" "
John Douglas	11	Ciphers Compound Multiplication.
Sarah Clause	14	" Addition.
Eliza Wampum	11	" "
Christiana Carpenter	15	" "
Magdalen Carpenter	14	" "
Sarah March	12	" "
John Jamieson	16	Reads in Canada Spelling Book and
Cyrus Isaac	12	Testament.
Mark Matthew	10	Ciphers in Compound Multiplication.
James Jacob	11	" Compound Addition
Jessy Douglas	12	" "
James Douglas	14	Reads in Canada Spelling Book and
Philip Hill	11	Testament, Ciphers in Compound
Francis Wampum	10	Addition
Youel Carrier	12	" "
Charles Timothy	13	" "
Alexander Bombarry	11	
Simeon Carrier	11	Reads in Canada Spelling Book, page 50,
Cornelius Seneca	10	writes, and ciphers in Simple Addition.
Stephen Owens	10	" "
Lene Bombarry	9	" "
Mary John	11	" "
Helen Hill	11	" "
Hester Longfish	14	" "
David Carpenter	11	Reads in Second Book, page 17. "
John Hill	11	"
Isaac Hill	10	" "
Abraham Johnson	10	" "
Adam Longfish	11	" "
Peter Beeswing	10	" "
John Green	10	" "
David Hess	14	" "
Ellen Furmer	10	" "
Hannah David	10	" "
Kitty Henhauk	10	" "
Mary Henry	10	" First Book, page 11
Lucy Hill	10	" "

The School opens precisely at 9 a.m. with prayer. We dine at a quarter past 12, and are again in the school-room at 1 p.m. The school closes with scripture-reading, catechism, and prayer, at 4 pm.

3.   31 December 1859   Institution Report...Half-year...
Thomas Griffiths, Teacher

Names	Age	Remarks
Josiah Hill	17	Reads in 4th Book and ciphers in
Richard Hill	14	Simple interest; studies Geography, and
Zachariah Hill	17	the first principles of Grammar
Alexander Hill	13	
Louis Gibson	16	
Albert Anthony	20	Reads 4th Book, and ciphers in
William Smith	18	Practice; studies Geography and
Nicholas Williams	19	Grammar
Augustus Hill	13	
James Hill	17	
Ellen Maracle	17	Reads 4th Book, Grammar, and
Susannah Jonathan	15	Geography; Compound Multiplication.
Christiana Carpenter	15	
Mary M. Carpenter	14	
Alexander Bomberry	12	Reads in 3rd Book, page 101, ciphers in
Youel Carrier	13	Simple Proportion; studies Geography
Charles Jackson	14	
Charles Timothy	14	
Francis Wampum	11	
John Jamieson	16	
Leah Martin	17	Do
Sarah Maracle	13	
Eliza Wampum	12	Compound Multiplication
John Douglas	12	Reads 3rd Book, page 28, ciphers
Cyrus Isaac	13	Compound Mult.
Philip Hill	12	
James Jacob	12	
James Douglas	15	
Jessy Douglas	13	
David Staats	12	
William Doxdater	14	
Mark Jack	11	
Simeon Carrier	11	Reads in 2nd Book, page 114, learns
Levi Bomberry	9	Multiplication Table, ciphers in Simple
John Nicholas	17	Addition
David Carpenter	12	
David Hess	15	Reads in 2nd Book, page 114, learns
Adam Longfish	11	Multiplication Table, ciphers in Simple
Cornelius Seneca	11	Addition
Stephen Owen	10	They sing and read in the English
Isaac Hill	11	language with tolerable ease and
John Hill	11	freedom; but it is a difficult thing to
Abraham Johnson	10	induce them to practise English among
Peter Bunning	10	themselves when alone. They generally
Samuel Hill	8	read and speak English in an under
Henry Jamieson	9	voice, requiring much patience and
Ellen Hill	12	great attention on the teacher's part. All
Ellen Turner	10	that are capable read in the Testament
Hannah David	10	daily.
Kitty Henhawk	9	
Susan Nantichoke	9	
Hester Longfish	14	
Mary L. Davis	11	
Catherine Owen	14	Reads in First Book
Lucy Hill	10	" page 24
Mary Henry	10	" "
Charlotte Coffee	10	" "
Christiana Burning	11	" "
James Green	10	" "
Lucy Green	7	
Kitty Bomberry	7	
Mary Wedge	7	

4. 30 June 1861 Report Half-year...

Name	Age	Remarks
Yeoval Carrier	16	This Class reads in Fifth Book, page 300,
George Bombery	12	ciphers in Simple and Compound Proportion,
Cyrus Isaac	15	Practice, and Fractions; studies Geography and
Francis Wampum	12	Grammar, spells from Carpenter's Spelling-
Charles Jackson	16	Assistant, and reads in Testament.
William Doxdator	16	
Charles Timothy	16	
Jessy Cusick	16	
Simon Carrier	13	This Class reads in Third Book, page 243,
Lené Bomberry	11	studies Geography, and has an exercise in the
Cornelius Senecca	12	Rudiments of Grammar every day, spells from
Peter Booming	11	Carpenter's Spelling-Assistant, writes from
David Carpenter	13	Copies, and ciphers in the Compound Rules
Isaiah Joseph	13	and Simple Proportion, reads in Testament,
Henry Parker	13	and learns Catechism.
Samson Green	19	
David Hess	18	
William Thomas	16	
Isaac Hill	12	
Isaac Doxdator	11	
Samuel Hill	10	
John Nicholas	18	
James Green	13	This Class reads in the Sequel to the Second
Isaac Johnson	18	Book and Testament, writes and ciphers in
Stephen Owen	12	Compound Addition
George Johnson	15	This Class reads in Second Book, page 24,
David Louis	12	writes large Hand, and begins to count.
Abraham Louis	10	
George Aaron	11	
Isaac Hess	12	This Class spells and reads in First Book,
Moses Carpenter	10	page 38, and begins to count numbers in their
Isaac J. Hill	12	natural order.
Daniel Green	10	
James Silver	11	
John Lickers	11	
Peter Bomberry	8	
Jackson Jamieson	12	This Class spells two and three letters. These
Alexander Jamieson	10	last two classes speak very little English.
Abraham Powles	10	
Isaac Hill	10	
Clara Wesley	15	This Class reads in Fourth Book and
Eliza Wampum	14	Testament, studies Geography, and ciphers in
Ellen Hill	15	Compound Division.
Mary J. Davis	12	
Hannah David	12	Reads in Third Book and Testament, ciphers
Catherine Henhawk	11	in Compound Subtraction, studies Geography.
Mary Henry	13	Reads in Second Book, page 101, and
Charlotte Coffee	13	Testament; writes small hand, ciphers in
Mary Wedge	12	Simple Addition, and learns Catechism.
Eliza Jack	10	
Catherine James	9	
Lucy Green	11	
Susannah Crawford	13	First Book, page 20
Hannah Lickers	8	Spells two and three letters.
Lucy Lickers	7	
Mary Hill	12	

N.B. Besides the above exercises the boys are taught husbandry, and the girls, in like manner, housewifery, viz. spinning, sewing, and knitting.
Thomas Griffith, Teacher.

5. 31 December 1861 Institution Report...

Name	Age	Remarks
Yeoval Carrier	17	The boys in this class read in the 5th
George Bomberry	13	Book of Lessons, study Geography and
Simon Carrier	16	Grammar, and cipher in the advanced
Francis Wampum	13	Arithmetical rules
Charles Jackson	17	
Charles Timothy	17	
William Doxdater	17	
Jessy Cusick	17	
Samson Green	20	
Levi Bomberry	13	
William Thomas	17	
Isaac Hill	13	Read in the 3d Book of Lessons, study
Isaac Doxdater	13	Geography and Grammar, and cipher in
Isiah Joseph	14	the Compound Rules, including
Samuel Hill	11	Proportion.
Cornelius Seneca	14	
James Green	14	
Stephen Owens	15	
Peter Burning	12	
David Carpenter	14	
Nelles Timothy	15	
David Lewis	13	Read in 2d Book, page 75, write small
John Anderson	12	hand, and cypher Simple Addition.
George Aaron	12	
George Johnson	17	
Abraham Lewis	11	
Moses Carpenter	12	Read in 2d Book, page 39
Isaac J. Hill	13	
Isaac Hess	13	
John Lickers	13	
William Louis	12	
George Hill	10	Cipher in Simple Addition.
Daniel Green	11	
Peter Bomberry	9	
Abraham Powles	11	Read in 1st Book, page 28
John Knaggs	15	
Isaac Burning	10	
Elliott Jamison	10	
William Statts	11	
John Cusick	10	
Jackson Jameson	12	
Amos Newhouse	11	
Zelba Brigham	17	
Alexander Jamieson	11	
Paul Hendrick	12	
GIRLS		
Clara N. Wesley	16	Read in the 5th Book, study History,
Elsa Wampum	15	Geography, and Grammar; cipher in
Hannah David	12	Decimal Fractions.
Mary J. Davis	13	
Ellen Funn	13	Read in 3d Book, page 143, study
Catherine Henhawk	12	Geography, cipher in Compound Division.
Mary Henry	13	Read Sequel to 2d Book; cipher in
Catherine James	10	Simple Division.
Charlotte Coffee	13	
Eliza Jack	10	
Lucy Green	11	Read in 2d Book, page 15, Simple
Lucy Strong	15	Addition.
Mary Hill	13	
Susannah Crawford	15	1st Book, page 16.
Julia Newhouse	15	
Hannah Strong	10	
Lucy Lickers	9	

Mary Bomberry	9	Spell in 1st Book, page 11
Hannah Lickers	9	
Kitty Funn	9	

N.B. Every boy or girl that can read, reads in the Testament and learns Catechism...Griffith

6. Boys School.
January 1st to June 30th, 1868

No	Names	Age	No	Names	Age
1	Youel Carryer	22	2	George Bomberry	18

Attend the Brantford Grammar School.

No	Names	Age	No	Names	Age
3	George Hill	18	5	Beverly Johnson	15
4	Nelles Monture	14	6	Solomon Anthony	15

These four Boys take Algebra, in addition to the Lessons taken by the other Members

No	Names	Age	No	Names	Age
7	Alexander Jamieson	18	11	James Hill	17
8	John Cusick	17	12	George Martin	17
9	Joseph Monture	16	13	Charles Martin	17
10	Jacob Bomberry	14	14	George Powlass	17

The subjects taught to this Class comprise:-5th Book of the National School Society, Reading, English Grammar, Book-keeping, Geography, Writing, Spelling, Dictation, Arithmetic,

No	Names	Age	No	Names	Age
1	Josephus Cusic	16	5	Elijah Powless	16
2	Dan Thomas	14	6	Edward Martin	11
3	Joseph John	15	7	William Reap	11
4	Abraham Davis	18			

Subjects of Instruction:-Reading 3rd Book a second time, page 18; write small hand; learn Grammatical Definitions, Explanation Catechism, Arithmetic, - Reduction, &c.

No	Names	Age	No	Names	Age
1	Joseph Wedge	14	5	Joseph Murdock	15
2	Francis Bodies	12	6	Peter Hannyeas	11
3	Peter Isaac	15	7	Osceola Loft	12
4	Hiram Jamieson	12	8	Elias Louis	15

Going over the 2nd Book a second time; write Small Hand; learn Catechism; Arithmetic, - Simple Rules.

No	Names	Age	No	Names	Age
1	Matthew Hill	11	6	John Miller	11
2	Louis Benedick	17	7	Nelson Maracle	15
3	Joseph Aaron	13	8	John Skyler	11
5	George Styres	17			

Just begin the 2nd Book; write a little on Slates; do easy sums in Addition; and have begun to learn Multiplication Table.

These last two classes do not understand much English.

No	Names	Age	No	Names	Age
1	George Longboard	15	3	Peter Doctor	10
2	Charles Bell	12	4	Peter Martin	11

1st Book, 2 and 3 letters.

July 1st to December 31st, 1868

No	Names	Age	No	Names	Age
1	Charles Martin	18	5	Jacob Bomberry	15
2	George Martin	18	6	Nelles Monture	15
3	George Powless	18	7	Isaiah Joseph	21
4	Elijah Powless	16	8	John Anderson	20

Read in 5th Book, page 70; study Geography, Grammar, Book-keeping, Arithmetic to Compound Proportion in Sangster's 2nd Book, Catechism, Writing, Spelling, &c.

No	Names	Age	No	Names	Age
1	Abraham Davis	14	8	Osceola Loft	13
2	Dan Thomas	16	9	William Loft	11
3	Edward Martin	13	10	Peter Matthews	12
4	Francis Heweston	14	11	Peter Isaac	16
5	George Styres	18	12	Lewis Benedick	18
6	Hiram Jamieson	14	13	William Reap	12
7	Joseph Hill	15			

Read in 3rd Book, page 104; study Grammar, as far as the Personal Pronoun; Arithmetic, Compound Rules; Catechism, Writing, Spelling, &c.

The Boys of this Class are making a great effort to master the English Language by denying themselves the use of their own language.

No	Names	Age	No	Names	Age
1	Charles Burning	10	6	Henry Powless	11
2	John Miller	14	7	Nelson Maracle	18
3	Gau-ge-ra-ge-ro	10	8	Nicholas Johnson	13
4	John Schuyler	14	9	Allen Johnson	11
5	Joseph Aaron	13	10	Peter Silver	14
11	Sam Maracle	12	13	Matthew Hill	13
12	William Maracle	14	14	Zachariah Burning	11

Read in 2nd Book, page 60; cipher in Simple Rules; learn Multiplication Table, First Catechism, Writing, &c.

The greater number of Boys in this Class understand but little English, but like the other Boys, they promise to give up talking Indian, till they have learnt to speak English with more ease and fluency.

No	Names	Age	No	Names	Age
1	Alexander Loft	11	5	Louis Martin	10
2	Charles Atkins	11	6	Thomas Jacob	12
3	Jesse Jonathan	11	7	Peter Martin	9

1st Book, page 20

1	David Doxdator	12	4	Ca-na-ha-ro-tha	9
2	David Keys	12	5	Elliott Obediah	9
3	Thomas Keys	10			

Alphabet. Talk no English.

Girls' School
1st January to 30th June, 1868.

1	Susan Carpenter	15	6	Eliza Maracle	13
2	Jemima Maracle	15	7	Clara Hill	11
3	Catherine Burning	14	8	Sarah Hill	9
4	Catherine Martin	14	9	Naomi John	15
5	Nancy Wadlove	13	10	Christiana Hendrick	15
11	Susan Turkey	13	13	Mary A. Carryer	15
12	Elizabeth Atkins	13			

5th Book of Lessons; cipher in the Compound Rules, Fractions, Proportion, &c.; study Grammar and Geography; Spelling from Carpenter's Book; Book-keeping; Write from Dictation; learn Explanatory Catechism, Sewing, Spinning and Knitting, with Fancy Needlework, &c.

1	Louisa Miller	17	4	Leah Staats	13
2	Lucy Miller	15	5	Phoebe Snake	13
3	Lucy Thomas	14	6	Sarah Bomberry	12

Read in 4th Book, page 37; write Small Hand; spell from Carpenter's Spelling Book, page 24; cipher in Compound Rules; learn Explanatory Catechism, together with Sewing, Spinning,

1	Susannah Hill	10	4	Lucy Forman	10
2	Christiana John	11	5	Emma Martin	10
3	Elizabeth Owen	16	6	Mary Walker	14

3rd Book, page 103; cipher in Simple Rules; write Small Hand; learn Explanatory Catechism, Sewing, Knitting, &c.

1	Betsy Wedge	12	7	Louisa Cluck	10
2	Rachael Isaac	13	8	Esther Longfish	13
3	Mary George	12	9	Charlotte Miller	11
4	Emily Hill	14	10	Alice Johnson	8
5	Mary A. Cusick	12	11	Eliza Snake	10
6	Susan Maracle	10			

Read in 2nd Book, page 60; cipher in Simple Subtraction; write chiefly on Slates; learn Catechism, Sewing and Knitting.

1	Margaret Venevery	11	4	Charlotte Hope	10
2	Charlotte Powless	11	5	Catharine Duncan	12
3	Julia Carryer	11	6	Margaret Williams	11

Have just begun 2nd Book.

July 1st to December 31st, 1868

No	Names	Age	No	Names	Age
1	Susan Carpenter	16	7	Clara Hill	13
2	Jemima Maracle	16	8	Sarah Hill	11
3	Catherine Burning	15	9	Eliza Atkins	14
4	Catherine Martin	14	10	Phoebe Snake	14
5	Lydia Moses	14	11	Lucy Miller	15
6	Eliza Maracle	13	12	Lucy Thomas	14

Read in 5th Book, page 170; study Geography, Grammar, Book-keeping, Arithmetic to Simple Proportion, Catechisms, Writing, Needlework, &c. **The greater number of these Girl, talk good English with ease.**

1	Elizabeth Owen	17	6	Rachel Isaac	13
2	Christiana John	12	7	Mary George	13
3	Susan Hill	11	8	Lucy Froman	11
4	Emily Hill	15	9	Harriett Goose	14
5	Emma Martin	11			

Read in 3rd Book, page 120; study Arithmetic, Simple Division, Catechism, Writing, Spelling, &c. **These Girls are beginning to talk English with ease and freedom.**

1	Mary A. Powless	11	3	Betsy Wedge	13
2	Mary A. Cusick	13	4	Hester Longfish	14
5	Susan Maracle	10	11	Eliza Snake	11
6	Charlotte Elliott	16	12	Eliza Whoop	12
7	Ida Johnson	9	13	Ellen Loft	12
8	Louisa Clinch	11	14	Julia Carrier	11
10	Margaret Venevery	11	16	Kitty Duncan	10

Read in 2nd Book, page 124; spell from their Lessons; write on Slates; learn Multiplication Table; cipher in Simple Addition and Subtraction; First Catechism; Needlework, &c. These Girls, like the little Boys, are at present scrupulously avoiding the Indian Language, in order to learn English. Both Boys and girls talk more English among themselves than they ever did before.

1	Julia Jonathan	12	5	Esther Martin	9
2	Rebecca Miller	12	6	Margaret Williams	11
3	Sarah S. Crawford	10	7	Christiana Green	13
4	Margaret Burning	9			

1st Book, page 23.

7. 30 June 1872 NEC Report for half-year...

BOYS' SCHOOL

No. Name	Age	
1. Abm. Lewis	20	Boys of this class read in 5th book of lessons, Canadian History, study Geography, English Grammar, Bookkeeping, Cipher in the advanced rules, Scripture reading, etc. etc.
2. Ed. Martin	17	
3. Oseedla Loft	15	
4. Louis Benedick	20	
5. Allen Johnson	14	
6. John Davis	16	
1. Frans. Hewston	17	Read in 4th book, study Geography, English Grammar and Book-keeping (the same as the first class), Cipher in proportion and fractions, Scripture reading, Catechism, etc.
2. Mat Splicer	16	
3. John Schuyler	16	
4. Joseph Aaron	17	
5. Hiram Jamieson	17	
6. Wm. Reep	14	
1. Jesse Jonathan	14	This class are reading the 3rd book over for the third or fourth time. Indian children learn to read and spell as quick as white children, but it takes them a long time before they become good readers, as they cannot speak English words plain, nor understand what they read, therefore they read very little more than their lessons. English Grammar is studied carefully with some good results, Cipher in compound rules, Testament reading, Catechism, etc. etc.
2. Joseph Delisle	14	
3. Chas. Atkins	12	
4. Elliott Obediah	11	
5. Peter Martin	12	
6. Louis Martin	13	
7. George Miller	13	
8. Wm. Staats	15	
9. Mat Hill	15	
10. John Hill	16	
11. Peter Silver	16	
12. Moses Carpenter	20	
13. Michael Longfish	16	
14. John Elliott	14	
1. George Latham	10	Read in 3rd book (page 263); have been going over the rudimentary parts of Grammar during the past year. Their speaking Indian so much among themselves when at play, or when out of school, is one of the greatest hindrances to their progress at school. We do what we can to induce them to talk English, *without compulsion.* Cipher in simple division, Testament reading,
2. Gau-je-ra-ge-ro	12	
3. Albert Hill	12	
4. Abm. Hill	14	
5. Thos. Andrews	12	
6. Joseph Lewis	13	
7. Joseph Portor	13	
8. Henry Powless	13	
1. Samson Jamieson	14	The boys of this class have been reading and spelling in 2nd book during the past year, and are not fit for anything more difficult. We have now introduced the new series of 2nd book. Cipher - addition, subtraction, and multiplication; learn multiplication table, etc. etc.
2. David Doxdater	14	
3. Denis Sero	16	
4. James Hill	10	
5. David Keys	15	
6. George Peters	10	
7. Thos. Jacques	12	
8. Zech. Burning	14	
1. Thos. Keys	12	Second book (page 27), write on slates, multiplication table, simple addition and subtraction.
2. Isaac Clause	13	
3. Joseph Powless	11	
4. Wilson David	11	
5. Dominick Plant	14	
6. Wm. Reilly	9	

GIRLS' SCHOOL

No. Name	Age	
1. Phebe Snake	17	These girls read in the fourth book (new series), page 144; spell in Carpenter's Spelling Book; Grammar - definitions and parsing; Human Physiology; Ancient History; Linear Drawing, Geography - definitions and maps of the world, including all the continents, and Dominion of Canada, including the counties and towns of Ontario; Write; Arithmetic - fractions, decimals, proportion, commission, brokerage, insurance and stocks; Church Catechism.
2. Mary Ann Cusick	16	
3. Christina John	15	
4. Avis Johnson	12	
5. Sarah Jane Davis	12	
6. Julia Carryer	15	
7. Julia Jonathan	16	
8. Mary A. Powless	15	
9. Charlotte Powless	15	
10. Charlotte Hope	15	
11. Louisa Clench	15	

12. Eliza Snake	15	These girls read in the third book (new series) review, page 21): spell in C.S.Assistant; Grammar - definitions; Write; Arithmetic, the simple rules; Exercises in the different tables of weights and measures; Church Catechism.
13. Sarah J. Crawford	13	
14. Rebecca Miller	14	
15. Martha Jamieson	13	
16. Margaret J. Burning	12	
17. Charlotte Johnson	11	
18. Catharine Vanevery	13	
19. Lydia Lewis	9	
20. Charlotte Hill	14	
21. Elizabeth Carryer	11	These girls read the second book (old series), page 62; Spell and answer explanatory questions out of the same; Write; Arithmetic - simple multiplication; Church Catechism, and multiplication table.
22. Mary Jane Hill	10	
23. Sarah Martin	10	
24. Margaret T. Martin	11	
25. Ellen Wedge	14	
26. Sarah Splicer		
27. Susannah Martin	9	
28. Esther Martin	13	
29. Louisa Sero	13	These girls read in the second book (old series), page 9; spell and answer explanatory questions out of the same; cipher in the simple rules; write on slates, study the Church Catechism, and the multiplication table
30. Lucy Douglass	14	
31. Catharine Hill	9	
32. Betsy Hill	10	
33. Ellen M. Garlow	9	
34. Lucretia Jamieson		
35. Mary Jane Butler	13	

8. 1930 Russell T. Ferrier History of the Mohawk Institute
SUCCESSFUL GRADUATES

XRev Isaac Bearfoot - Graduated from the Institute. Taught school on the S. N. Reserve, attended the Toronto Normal School, then taught nine years in the Mohawk Institute, appointed in 1869. Took charge of the Inst. while Rev. R. Ashton went to England for a couple of months. Then attended Huron College London and was ordained a clergyman of the Church of England. He was the incumbent of St. John's and Christ Church on the Six Nation Reserve for years. Now deceased.

Elijah Powless - Left school 1873 - Taught No. 3 School on the Reserve for a time.

William Reap - Left 1873 - Was interpreter for Kahyengah Church for a time.

Joseph Deslile - Left 1873 - Was a clerk in the Indian Dept. Ottawa.

Fredrick O. Loft - Left 1875 - Was bookkeeper in the Asylum for the insane. Toronto - Now on a pension. Enlisted during Gt. War

Lucius Henry - Left 1876 - Taught Ojibway School. Munsey.

Moses Walker - Left 1876 - Taught at Moraviantown and at Chippeway Hill.

John Schuyler - Left 1876 - Taught school at Oneida.

Louis Scanado - Left 1876 - Taught school at Oneida.

Elijah Sickles - Left 1877 - Interpreter to Rev. H. P. Chase.

XJohn Elliott - Left 1877 - Was a reporter for the Mail & Empire. Toronto for a time - was a great orator. He wrote the address of welcome to the returned soldiers from the Gt. War.

Jacob Miller - Successful store-keeper. Worked to bring about the Elective System of Councillors.

Elliott Obediah - Left 1877 - Apprenticed to a blacksmith in Brantford. Worked at his trade.

Scobie Logan - Left 1878 - Taught school at Muncey. Councillor for Muncey.

Adam Sickles - Advanced in his studies - was apprenticed to a blacksmith in Brantford and left in 1879 - taught school at Moraviantown.

John Skinnewa - Left 1878 - Took part in the South African War, with his brother James Skinnewa, or James Dewr.

XNelson Moses - Left 1878 - Very successful farmer.

Clabran Russell - Left 1880 - Taught at No. 5 School for three years on Six Nation Reserve, afterwards went to Chicago.

Isaac Williams - Left 1880 - After being apprenticed as carpenter, and granted a set of tools, obtained employment at Shultz Factory in Brantford, where he was for years.

John Russell - Left 1881 - Successful carpenter in Brantford for years.

(dead)
Harry Jones - Left 1881 - Successful carpenter in Brantford for years. (dead)

XThomas Green - Graduated 1878 - Attended McGill University - New England Co. paid his fees - passed Sr. Matriculation, came first of his year in Applied Science and received a prize of $25.00. Was in the employ of the Indian Dept. - went to Klondike during the gold rush - now on a ranch in Alberta.

XElam Barefoot - Left 1882 - Son of Rev. Isaac Barefoot. Passed Entrance exam. Attended Collegiate. Taught school on Six Nation Reserve for 20 years. Was on fruit farm for 7 years - took total charge of it for 2 years - now in charge of one of the departments in Cockshutt Plow Works, where he has been for 2 years.

William Osborne - Left 1883 - Passed entrance, attended Collegiate, entered Massey Harris Co. office in Winnipeg - went to Klondike during the gold rush. (dead)

Louis Jacques - Left 1884 - Passed entrance. Was a foreman for Bridge Co. Montreal - killed on Quebec bridge.

Daniel McNaughton - Left 1884 - Successful farmer on Six Nation Reserve.

Robert Hill - Left 1886 - Passed entrance attended Collegiate - a successful farmer, on Six Nation Reserve.

Christopher Monture - Left 1885 - Passed entrance - attended Collegiate for short time - awarded scholarship - taught school on Six Nation Reserve - then went working out.

John Lickers - Left 1885 - Passed entrance - awarded scholarship - attended Collegiate - taught school on Six Nation Reserve for years - is now truant officer.

XArchie Lickers - Left 1887 - Successful - farmer on Six Nation Reserve - at present a councillor.

William Noah - Left 1888 - finished his term as Carpenter apprentice. Was presented with a chest of tools. A successful carpenter on the Moraviantown Reserve.

XThomas Whitebeans - Left 1888 - Afterwards became a Methodist Minister - at present on Sarnia Reserve.

XSimpson Brigham - Left-1891- Afterwards attended Shingwawk Home - Graduated from Huron College, London. Became a clergyman of the Church of England on Walpole Island Reserve - recently died.

XFrank Miller - Left 1892 - Successful farmer - at present a Councillor.

XWilliam Powless - Left 1893 - having passed entrance became a successful farmer, and at present secretary to the Six Nation Council.

Peter Adams - Left 1893 - having passed entrance - took training as a teacher and taught in Six Nation Reserve for years.

Cornelius Cusick - Left 1896 - has for years held responsible positions in stores in Rochester, N.Y.

XAlex Leween - Left 1897 - having passed entrance trained as a teacher - taught school on the Bay of Quinty Reserve for years.

James Burnam - Left 1898 - after three years apprenticeship in Brantford, as a blacksmith - now in Niagara Falls.

XFoster Lickers - Left 1899 - worked in Rubber factory in Port Dalhousie for years - enlisted during the Great War, was wounded, and a prisoner in Germany for many months - is now a fruit farmer near Grimsby.

Tom Longboat - Left 1901 - great runner. Won the Marathon in New York.

XThomas Lickers - Left 1906 - worked at farming - enlisted and was killed in the Great War.

Harry Williams - Left 1909 - passed entrance - studied commercial course - was clerk in wholesale dry goods store in Waterdown N.Y. Time keeper and typewriter for a contractor in Waterdown N.Y.

XWilliam Lickers - Left 1911 - killed in the Great War.

Barney Clench - Left 1913 - took part in the Gt. War.

Jacob Silversmith - took part in the Gt. War.

XArnold Moses - Left 1913 - after attending the Collegiate three years - taught No. 7 School - enlisted in the Great War - now a successful farmer on the S. N. Reserve.

XJesse Moses - Left 1914 - after attending the Collegiate four years. Paid as drill Instructor in the school. Taught school on the S. N. Reserve - now a successful farmer and a Councillor.

George Bomberry - Left 1915 - enlisted with the 114th Battalion for the Great War.

XMelville Henry - Left 1917 Has become a Baptist Minister and is at present at Medina Church on the Six Nation Reserve.

XWilliam Smith - Left 1921 - after attending the Collegiate for two years and passing with first class honors. After leaving the Institute he went to the Collegiate but had to leave school on account of weak eyes - is now successfully farming with his father, Councillor William Smith.

Amelia Chechock - Graduated 1876 - Taught school at Muncey Town, at Stonerridge school and at Parry Sound.

Anna Jones - Attended Collegiate - Graduated from here in 1879 - Taught No. 7 Six Nation School for years--married after.

XLydia Lewis - Passed entrance Exam - was soloist at school - graduated 1880--Taught No. 3 Six Nation School for years--married Robert Brant--Their son Lieut. Cameron Brant was the first man from Brant County that was killed in the Gt. War. Now a widow--has a home on the Reserve.

XSarah Davis--Obtained highest number of marks at the Entrance Exam. Brantford Collegiate Institute--July, 1880---Graduated 1880--Taught different schools on the Six Nation Reserve for more than twenty-five years--Her influence was great and example good on the Reserve--A great reader and very well informed woman--died in 1923.

XCatharine Maracle - Passed Entrance Exam. Graduated 1880 --Taught schools at St. Rigis, Cornwall Is, at Bay of Quinte, and at No. 2 Six Nation School - Married Jacob Miller. Has kept a good home on the Reserve and educated her children.

XFloretta Maracle - Passed Entrance Exam, and graduated 1881 - Taught No. 2 Six Nation School - had a position in the Indian Dept. Ottawa for many years -retired on a pension - married Allen Johnson - Now a widow living in Toronto.

XJane E. M. Osborne - Passed Entrance Exam. and graduated 1881 - Became pupil Governess in a Ladies College, Toronto - then Governess in a private family for years - Went to Winnipeg and afterwards married Mr. Donald Kerby of Morden, Manitoba - Now a widow.

XJessie Osborne - Passed Entrance Exam. Attended the Collegiate for three years and obtained 2nd. class Certificate and graduated 1883 - Taught No. 3 S. N. S. - Attended Toronto Normal School - Taught in the Mohawk Institute - Went to Winnipeg and taught school...Married Joseph Young of the Imperial Bank, Brandon, died in Sept. 1928.

XSusan Hardie - Passed Entrance Exam - Attended Collegiate Institute and obtained Teachers' Second Class Certificate - Took a Model School Course - graduated in 1886 - Taught in the Mohawk Institute for a year then attended the Normal School, Toronto, and obtained her Professional 2nd Class Certificate - Has been teaching in the Mohawk Institute ever since.

Mary Monture - Passed Entrance Exam. Attended Collegiate Institute - Graduated 1886 - Taught No. 9 S.N.School for years. Married a Mr. Andrew Scott - now dead.

Pheobe Waddilove - Passed Entrance Exam. and attended the Collegiate Institute one year - Graduated 1887 - Taught Oneida School for a time - Married Sam Muskokaman,

Sarah Lotham - Passed Entrance Exam. Attended the Collegiate - Graduated 1887 - Taught No. 6. S. N. School - Service in Buffalo - Sewing Teacher in the Mohawk Inst. Went to Chicago to go in training as a nurse, but did not complete her course. Now living on the Reserve

XJosephine Good - Passed Entrance Exam. Attended Collegiate and obtained a Teacher's Third Class Certificate - Received the Nelles Medal for general proficiency - Graduated 1888 - Taught school at Parry Sound for four years, then taught at Bay of Quinty and married there - is now dead. .

XSarah Russell - Passed Entrance Exam, and attended the Collegiate - Received the Nelles medal for general proficiency - Graduated 1888 - Taught No. 7 S. N. S. for years - Married Wm. Smith - ex-Councillor - was influential for good on the Reserve - died in March 1929. Having brought up and educated a large family who are all doing well.

Naomi Latham - Passed Entrance Exam - Attended Collegiate - Obtained Teacher's Second Class Certificate - graduated 1895 - taught No. 7   S. N. S for three years then went to Chicago with her sister - Died on the Reserve

in 1929.

Henrietta Hill - Graduated in 1898 - Was Sewing Teacher in the Mohawk Institute for three years - Married Robert Hill of Bay of Quinte - Died of pneumonia in 1903.

Edith Good - Passed Entrance - Attended the Collegiate - Obtained commercial certificate - trained as an Indian teacher - graduated 1900 was Junior officer in the Inst. - Taught Mission School on the Bay of Quinte Reserve for some years - Married Mr. Martin a white man - now deceased.

Bessie Green - Given special training in housework - graduated 1900 after some time at service she took her training as a nurse in one of the State Hospitals in New York for three years - Did private nursing.

Edith Styres - Graduated 1901 - Appointed Jr. Officer in the Institution - Then as sewing Teacher for two years - Married Hardy Miller - Has kept one of the good homes on the Reserve & educated her children.

XBeulah Styres - Passed Entrance Exam - Attended Business College Obtained certificate for short hand and typewriting. Graduated 1905 - Was music teacher and junior officer in the Institution for a time - Went to Victoria, B.C. as nursery Governess to the little girl of Mr. and Mrs. Mackenzie, afterwards became stenographer and secretary to Mr. Hugh Mackenzie, the Manager of the B.N.A. bank, a position she held until she married Onslow Johnson and now lives in Buffalo.

Vera Duncan - Passed Entrance - Graduated 1908 - taught Jr. Department here for a few months. Took a course in dressmaking in Rochester - Was housekeeper and afterwards Sewing Teacher in the Mohawk Inst. for a time. Now married and lives in Regina.

XSusanna Latham - Attended the Collegiate three years - obtained certificate to enter Normal School - Appointed teacher of Jr. School in the Mohawk Institute in 1909. Was organist here for several years. In 1911 entered St. Lukes, Chicago Training School for nurses - did well - came out high in examinations. Went overseas as nurse from U.S.A. Now private nursing in Chicago.

Jesse Vanevery - Passed Entrance - Attended Collegiate for a year and left 1910 - Taught No. 8 School on Six Nation Reserve for two years - Now married and keeping a good home on the Reserve.

Phyllis Jamieson - Left 1916 - Had a position at the Institute for Blind for twelve years. Is now married and living in Brantford.

Gertrude Lottridge - Passed Entrance Exam. Took dressmaking lessons in Brantford - Left 1916 - Worked at the Inst. for the Blind for some time - Is now at Service in Niagara Falls, N.Y.

Ida Curley - Left 1917

XMary Curley - Left 1917

Eva Curley - Left 1918 - Three sisters - All attended the Collegiate for a year or two, then attended the Business College. All have had good office positions in Brantford and in U.S.A.

Rena Davis - Passed Entrance Exam. Attended the Collegiate for a year and left in 1917. Afterwards took a Business College Course and has been a stenographer in an office in Hamilton for some years.

XWilma Smith - Went right through the Teacher's Course at the Collegiate - Was organist for the school - Graduated from here in 1918 - Afterwards attended the Normal School in Hamilton. Taught No. 8 school 1920 to 1929. Did much for the young people of Kahyangeah Church. Was married to Andrew Jamieson in Sept. 1929.

Grace McNaughton - steno Brantford Grad of about 1918

XAlice Herkimer - Passed Entrance Exam. Attended the Collegiate one year and then the Business College. Graduated 1918. Was in an office for some years in Akron, Ohio - now married and lives in Birmingham, Mich.

XLuella Moses - Passed Entrance - Attended Collegiate one year - Played the Church organ here for two years - graduated 1920 - Continued her high School Course in Caledonia for three years more, then went to Toledo, where she was employed in a telephone office for a few years - is now married and lives in Toledo.

XRuby Smith - Passed Entrance Exam. Attended Collegiate for a year - played the church organ here - graduated 1921 - Continued her High School Course in Brantford and obtained a First-Class Teacher's certificate - Attended the Normal School in Hamilton, Taught No. 3 S. N. School for a year, then married Hubert Johnson...lives in Florida.

XElva Miller - Passed Entrance Exam. Attended Collegiate for a year, played church organ-graduated 1921 - Continued High School Course in Brantford and obtained a Teacher's Certificate - is at present teaching No. 4 S. N. School.

Elsie Clause - Passed Entrance Exam - Attended Business College for a year. Graduated in 1922 - Appointed as sewing-teacher and after as Assistant housekeeper in the Mohawk Institution - Now is nursing and housekeeping for Mr. and Mrs. Messacar in Brantford, a position she has held for some years.

XSylvia Jamieson - Passed Entrance Exam. Graduated 1922- Attended Continuation School in Onondaga, then the Collegiate in Brantford - Attended the Normal School in Hamilton and obtained a Teacher's Certificate - is now teaching No. 3 S. N. School.

Carrie Crowe from Muncey Reserve - Passed Entrance Exam. Attended Business College for a year   Graduated 1922   Was in an office in

Brantford for a time - Taught Muncey day School - Returned to the Mohawk Institute for the position as Assistant house-keeper - now married and living in Buffalo.

XFloretta Elliott - Passed Entrance - Took a year's course in telegraphy - played the church organ - Graduated 1923 - Took a position as sub-officer in the Mohawk Institute. She was Lieutenant of the M. I. Girl Guide Co. Brantford, No.5. Then took position in Domestic Service in Toronto - now married and living in Windsor.

Many girls have been trained for domestic service and they have gone out and secured good positions.

(Have marked X opposite those whom I thought were the most prominent...

9.   1919 Attendance: Registration Number, Discharge, Name, Tribe, Religion, Standard, Extras Music Trade, Age, Period in Institution, Parents living. 1920 List of orphans, Children deserted by Parents, Parents Separated, Parents living but taking no interest, One interested parent, age and some personal information. 1921 List of orphan and neglected children belonging to Six Nations Band, for whom a grant of $50 per capita is chargeable to band funds

Howard Aaron	Robert Franklin	Herbert Jamieson	Eliza Maracle	David Seth
Bruce Anthony	Clifford Fraser	Lena Jamieson	Helen Maracle	Maud Seth
John Antone	Reta Fraser	Rosie Jamieson	James Maracle	Fred Shuler
Minnie Atkins	Arlington Frazer	Sylvia Jamieson	Jobie Maracle	James Shuler
Gordon Bardy	Florence French	Vera Jamieson	Kathleen Maracle	Eva Smith
Nugent Bardy	Helen Froman	Willie Jamieson	Reta Maracle	Minnie Smith
Bernard Beaver	Lorna Froman	Adeline John	Marjorie Martin	Ruby Smith
Cecil Bennett	Amson Gibson	Cynthia John	George McNaughton	Willie Smith
Maud Brant	Ethel Green	Matilda John	Grace McNaughton	Ernest Snake
Dorothy Burning	Isabelle Green	Merle John	Jessie McNaughton	Annie Snow
Harrison Burning	Muriel Green	Reta John	Rodman McNaughton	Lizzie Snow
Frank Carpenter	Stanley Groat	Vera John	Elva Miller	Susan Snow
Jacob Carpenter	Clayton Henhawk	George Johnson	George Miller	Ariel Staats
John Carpenter	Leonard Henhawk	May Johnson	Frank Mitchell	Arthur Staats
Elsie Clause	Abbie Henry	Pearl Johnson	Luella Moses	Charlie Staats
Grace Clause	Frances Henry	Agnes Joseph	Cas. Newhouse	Christine Staats
Hazel Clause	Lucinda Henry	Rita Joseph	Evelyn Newhouse	Delilah Staats
Isaac Clause	Mary Henry	Robert Joseph	Gladys Obe	Gladys Staats
Jessie Clause	Wilfred Henry	Theodore Joseph	Orville Obe	George Staats
Norman Clause	Alice Herkimer	Adam Leween	Emily Pheasant	Lenora Staats
Olive Clause	Oscar Hess	Jack Leween	Florence Pheasant	Viola Staats
Lucy Clench	Allie Hill	Bert Lickers	Joseph Pheasant	Coretha Thomas
Nettie Clench	Belva Hill	Gordon Lickers	Laura Pheasant	Cornelia Thomas
Lorne Curley	Cleveland Hill	Grace Lickers	Grace Pheasant	Carl Tobias
Robert Curley	Edna Hill	Harriet Lickers	Evelyn Powless	Wilson Tobias
Francis Davis	Florence Hill	Harry Lickers	Lewis Powless	Melinda Vanevery
Jessie May Davis	Ross Hill	John Lickers	Margaret Powless	Elizabeth White
Josephine Davis	Sherwood Hill	Leo Lickers	Thomas Powless	Lena White
Trellis Davis	John Johnson Hope	Milton Lickers	Ethel Queen	Beulah Wilson
Helen Doxtador	Sandford Johnson Hope	Norman Lickers	Isabel Queen	Evelyn Wilson
Leslie Doxtador	Lily Isaac	Myrtle Loft	Mildred Queen	James Wilson
Flo Elliott	Maggie Jacobs	Ernest Longboat	Chancey Rhodes	Leonard Wilson
Hazel Elliott	Mary Jacobs	Irene Longboat	Jesse Rhodes	Nellie Wilson
Wallace Fishcarrier	Willie Jacobs	Russel Longboat	Mary Sero	Howard Woodruff
Lillian Fox	Dolly Jamieson	Cassie Maracle		

10. 1931 - Dental and medical records: information on dental work, vaccinations, eye examinations

John Anton	Hazel Burning	Della Curley	Earl Doolittle	Hannah Froman
Frank Arkwood	Leonard Carpenter	Frances Curley	Theodore Doxtator	Raymond Garlow
Mabel Batiste	Stanley Carpenter	Alvin Curly	Garfield Doxtator	Phoebe Garlow
Mary Batiste	Ambrose Cayuga	Myrtle Cutcut	Roy Doxtator	Neil Garlow
Alfred Brant	Lorne Cayuga	Orvil Davis	John Doxtator	Clara Garlow
Wesley Brant	Jessie Cayuga	Helen Davis	Joe Doxtator	Helen Garlow
Elwood Burnham	Alva Chrysler	Gertie Davis	Mary Ella Powless	Laura Garlow
John Burnham	Johnny Chrysler	Laura Davis	Clifford Ford	Wilfred George
Rosalie Burnham	Phoebe Clause	Henry Dockstator	Harrison Ford	Queenabel Gibson
Dorothy Burning	Gladys Curley	William Doolittle	Edgar Fraser	Muriel Gibson

Dollie Gibson	Edna Hill	Gladys Johnson	Olive Obediah	Jonas Smith
Hazel Gibson	Cornelius Hill	Howard Levin	Earl Owens	Albert Smith
Marie Gibson	Millicent Hill	Walter Lewis	Earl Peters	Effie Smith
Lottie Gibson	Eva Hill	George Lewis	Ralph Peters	Billy Smith
Russell Groat	Maud Hill	Norman Lickers	Howard Peters	Daniel Smith
Elizabeth Groat	Marie Hill	Orland Lickers	Pharold Porter	Beulah Snake
Catharine Groat	Gertie Hill	Beatrice Lickers	Raymond Porter	Ralph Stewart
Gertie Harris	Arthur Honyust (Hunyas)	Harry Lickers	Alex Porter	Joe Stock
Ford Harrison	Freda Huff	Norma Loft	Morris Porter	Lottie Stonefish
Clifford Harrison	Flossie Huff	Delma Loft	Georgina Porter	Rosa Stotts (Staats)
Herman Henhawk	Vera Isaac	Amid Logan	Thelma Powless	Grace Stotts
Oswald Henry	Ida Isaacs	Sarah Maracle	Alice Powless	Leaman Summers
Donald Henry	Harvey Isaacs	Leo Maracle	Velma Powless	Lula Thomas
Elias Henry	Reva Jacobs	Dalton Maracle	Maud Powless	Robert Thomas
Alma Henry	Oliver Jacobs	Alton Maracle	Elmo Powless	Johnny Turkey
Reva Herkimer	Harvey Jacobs	Herman Martin	Amy Powless	Jim Turkey
Stephen Herkimer	Truman Jamieson	David Martin	Eliza Powless	Amy Turkey
Margaret Herkimer	Wilma Jamieson	Wilma McNaughton	Charlie Sault	David Turkey
Dorothy Herkimer	Sarah Jamieson	Vera McNaughton	Florence Saulte	Emma Turkey
Russell Hess	Orval Jamieson	Calvin Miller	Jennie Saulte	Dorothy Vanevery
Raymond Hill	Esford Jamieson	Elsie Miller	Levina Schuyler	Wilma Vice (Vyse)
Olive Hill	Hubert Jamieson	Lily Miller	Wilson Secord	Orlof Wilson
Onessa Hill	Walter John	Grace Miller	Herman Silversmith	Margaret Wilson
Nettie Hill	Charles John	George MtPleasant	Gilbert Skye	Courtland Wilson
Stella Hill	Norma John	Nelson Murdock	Bruce Skye	Clara Winnie
Ruth Hill	Kate John	Dorothy Murdock	Ralph Smart	Wilkie Wright
Reva Hill	Charlie Johns	Lloyd Nicholas	Harold Smart	Phyllis Wright
Reggie Hill	Pauline Johnson	Grace Obe	Florence Smith	Arthur Wright
Isobel Hill	Nellie Johnson	Edward Obe	Peter Smith	Cecil Wright
Ervin Hill	Morris Johnson	Stanley Obe	Marjorie Smith	

11. 1949-1950 Admissions: No., Name, Date of Admission, Age on Admission, No. of Ticket under which Child's Annuity is paid, Band, Name of Parents and Living or Dead, Religion of Parents, Status of Education upon entering the School, Places and Period of Previous Education. Discharges: No., Name, Date of Discharge, Age on Discharge, Periods in the School, State of Education: On Admission, On Discharge

Admissions 1949

Albert, Lorne	Culbertson, Ellen	George, Bernard	Longboat, Linda	Pedoniquott, Osborne
Ashkewe, Winnifred	Culbertson, Marlene	George, Verna	Maracle, Ethel	Powless, Francis
Ashkewe, Raymond	Culbertson, Ann	Grosbeck, George	Maracle, Joseph	Rice, Vivian
Ashkewe, Evelyn	Elliott, Eulah	Jacobs, Carmen Anne	Marsden, Jesse	Riley, Ernest
Ashkewe, Barbara Ann	Fisher, Anne	Joseph, Ida Matilda	McCue, Caroline	Riley, Patricia
Assance, Merle	Fisher, Donna	Joseph, Elosie	Milliken, Marlene	Sickles, Arnold
Assance, Sheila	George, Vernetta	Joseph, Shirley	Milliken, Edna	Splicer, Joan
Assance, Eric	George, Helen	Joseph, Sally Ann	Milliken, Betty	Turkey, Patsy
Assance, Denis	George, Raymond	King, James	Milliken, Adriann	Turkey, Pelma
Beaver, Orman	George, Carol	Longboat, Mary	Monague, Connie	Turkey, Angeline
Beaver, Russel	George, Marena	Longboat, Elva	Monague, Dorothy	Weeks, Lester
Beaver, Donald	George, Ronald	Longboat, Joseph	Monague, Rena	Weeks, Willard
Culbertson, Russel				

Discharges 1949.

Beaver, Russel	George, Raymond	Johnson, Vivian	Powless, Doris	Thompson, Harold
Beeswax, Sylvia	George, Ronald	Johnson, Verna	Robert, Claus	Watson, David
Beeswax, Robert	Hendrick, Laird	King, Ethel	Schulyer, Alfred	Watson, Thelma
Claus, William	Hill, Karen	King, Ramona	Silver, Orpha	Watson, June
Claus, Gerald	Hill, Larry	Laford, Ora	Snache, Lorne	Watson, Bernetta
Claus, Lucille	Hill, Lylia	LaForm, Marjory	Solomon, Gertrude	Watson, Madeline
Claus, Lorraine	Hill, Clifford	Maness, Kenneth	Stonefish, Marie	Weeks, Lester
Davis, Eleanor	Hill, Ambrose	Maracle, Shirley	Stonefish, Wanita	Weeks, Willard
DeLeary, Marie	Hill, Luella	Maracle, Ronald	Stonefish, Birdine	Williams, Charlie
Elliott, Ronald	Home, Roger	Monague, Berto	Stonefish, Tommy	Williams, Rose
George, Eunice	Home, Mildred	Montour, Robert	Styres, Ronald	Williams, Aileen
George, Helen				

Discharges 1950

Albert, Margaret	Ashkewee, Barbara	Ashkewee, Raymond	Charles, Dale	Claus, Oliver

Davey, Shirley	Henry, Alvin	Maness, Geraldine	Monague, Connie	Thompson Harold
Deleary, Roy	Hill, Sanford	McCue, Caroline	Ryan, Alice	Walker, Ernest
Eliott, Eleanor	Hill, Venora	Monague, Dorothy	Silversmith William	Walker, Herbert
George, William	Hill, Alfred	Monague, Nera	Splicer, Joan	Walker Carol
Grosbeck, George				

Admissions 1950

Assance, Allen	Goose, Jackie	Hill, Barbara,	James, Larry	Riley, Delbert
Doxtator, Dolores	Goose, Donald	Hill, Marion	Petonoquot, Kathleen	Snake, Woodrow
Eliott, Arleta	Goose, Harvey	Hill, Gary	Petonoquot, Ruby	Snake, Cyril
Gibson, Milford	Goose Jimmie	Jacobs, Carolyn	Petonoquot, Ellie	Sturgess, Martha
Gibson, Lorne	Goose, Austin	James, Ronald	Rice, Tommy	Whitebean, Thomas
Goose, Marjory	Henry, Pauline	James, Irwin	Riley, Irene	

12. R.C.M.P. Truancy Reports

Truanted	Name	Found						
5-2-49	Alfreda Schyler	9-2-49	Six Nations Reserve	26-3-49	Jessie Marsden 2/5/34	28-3-49	Six Nations Reserve
	Ramona King			March 49	Ida George 13	9-4-49	Sarnia
	Margaret Laforme				Helen George 14		
	Eunice George			27/3/49	Vernon Hill 19/8/36	28.3.49	Six Nations
	9 others			26/3/49	Watson Winston	28.3.49	
					Roger Seth 17/6/34		
19-2-49	Ramona King	23-2-49	Six Nations Reserve	20-11-50	Milford Gibson	21-11-50	Six Nations Reserve
	2 others				Lorne Gibson		
10-2-49	Eileen Williams	17-2-49	Six Nations Reserve		James Keyes		
	12 others						

13. Quarterly Returns 1952 Register number, Name, Age, Band or reserve, Class, Standing in Class, Date of Entrance to School, Remarks.

Barbara Ann Ashkewee	Sharon Davis	Ruby Greene	Shirley King	Osborne Pedoniquott
Winnifred Ashkewe	Virgil Decaire	Stanley Halfday	James King	Ruby Pedoniquott
Evelyn Ashkewe	Victoria Doxtator	Sandra Halfday	Fred King	Helena Peters
Linda Ashkewee	Margaret Fallis	Mary Harris	Ramona Kiyoshk	Donald Porter
Josephine Ashkewee	Betty Anne Fisher	Helen Harris	Marion Kiyoshk	Minnie Powless
Dennis Assance	Donna Fisher	Elizabeth Harris	Mary Ann Laforme	Lois Powless
Eric Assance	Joyce Forrest	Pauline Henry	Linda Longboat	Frances Powless
Merle Assance	Leah Forrest	Jerome Henry	Deborah Longboat	Doris Powless
Sheila Assance	Grant Fromon	Mervin Henry	Benjamin Longboat	Beverley Powless
Allen Assance	Hannora Fromon	Victor Henry	Lee Longboat	Diane Powless
James Atkinson	Judith George	Lonnie Hill	Leta Longboat	Victoria Powless
Leander Baptiste	Fay George	Mariane Hill	Karen Lottridge	Ronald Proctor
Raymond Bressette	Philip George	Vernon Hill	Shirley Lottridge	Tommie Rice
Richard Bressette	Bernard George	Fred Hill	Linda Maness	Vivien Rice
Benjamin Bressette	Donald George	Gary Hill	Beulah Maness	Delbert Riley
Carl Bressette	Verna George	Frank Hill	Ethel Maracle	Irene Riley
Meritt Charles	Carol George	Lorraine Jackson	Jessie Maradon	Ernest Riley
Diane Charles	Ronald George	Rita Jackson	Howard Martin	Geraldine Rogers
Edward Charles	Leeland George	Leona Jacobs	Eugene Wayne Miller	Lorna Rogers
Lois Clause	Roderick George	Verna Jacobs	Raino Miller	Calvin Sault
Barbara Clause	Priscilla George	Carmen Jacobs	Kenneth Miller	William Sault
Seth Clause	Pauline George	Larry James	Glen Miller	David Sault
Antony Cornelius	Henry George	Ronald James	Dorothy Miller	Donald Sault
Albert Cornelius	Clayton George	Ervin James	Ernest Miller	Robert Shilling
Elaine Crowe	Mary Jane George	Rosemary John	Robin Miller	Arthur Shilling
Phyllis Crowe	Michael George	Roderick John	Manfred Miller	Sylvia Christine Sickles
David Crowe	James George	Beverly Jones	Leonard Milliken	Whitney Sickles
Jean Crowe	Lorne Gibson	Norma Jones	Adrianne Milliken	William Sickles
Marlene Culbertson	Milford Gibson	Norman Jones	Betty Milliken	Betty Sickles
Ellen Culbertson	Donald Goose	Billie Jones	Marlene Milliken	Arnold Sickles
Russel Culbertson	Harvey Goose	Eloise Joseph	Edna Milliken	Irene Simon
Ann Culbertson	Jimmie Goose	Shirley Joseph	Robert Montour	Roderick Simon
Erna Curley	Austen Goose	Charlie Kewageshig	Mildred Nawash	Woodrow Snake
Karen Curley	Marjorie Goose	Garry Kewageshig	Adrienne Patterson	Cyril Snake
Lester Curley	Jackie Goose	Charlie Kewageshig	Janice Patterson	Orlyn Solomon
Ruth David	Robert Green	Linda Kewaquon	Kathleen Pedoniquott	William Solomon
Beverly Jean Davis	Rosie Green	Robert Keyes	Alice Pedoniquott	Madeline Solomon
Marilyn Davis	Gerald Green	Elgin Keyes	Velma Pedoniquott	Andrew Solomon

Beulah Stock
Carmen Stock
Birdine Stonefish
Wanetta Stonefish
Lillian Stonefish

Frederick Stonefish
Marie Stonefish
Verna Stonefish
Tommy Stonefish
Martha Sturgeon

Tommy Thompson
Angeline Turkey
Patsy Turkey
Pelma Turkey

Effie Vanevery
David Watson
Alvin Weekes
Franklin Weekes

Lester Weekes
Velma Weeks
Mary Jane Williams
Douglas Wilson

14. Quarterly Returns 1959, 1960, 1961, 1962. Register No., Name, Date of Birth, Band, Grade, No. of Days Resident.

Diana Abotossaway
Floyd Albert
Gloria Albert
Barbara Ashkewee
Delmer Ashkewee
Evelyn Ashkewee
Josephine Ashkewee
Linda Ashkewee
Winnie Ashkewee
Frances Beaver
Lillian Beaver
Linda Beaver
Alvin Beeswax
Barbara Blackbird
Bertram Blackbird
Ella Blackbird
Jewel Blackbird
Pauline Boucher
Maxine Brant
Gerald Bunn
Stella Bunn
Roy Chapman
Alvin Cook
Donald Cook
Orley Cook
Teleford Copegog
Marlene Culbertson
Leslie Curley
Carol Dale Hill
David Deleary
Donald Deleary
Morrey Deleary
Richard Deleary
Ronald Deleary
Brenda Doxtator
Charles Doxtator
Connie Doxtator
Dennis Doxtator
Gilbert Doxtator
Grand Doxtator
LeRoy Doxtator
Sylvia Doxtator
Ted Doxtator
Victoria Doxtator
Warren Doxtator
Wayne Doxtator
Rosalie Elizah
Velma Elliott
Charity Elm
Raymond Elm
Allan Etapp
Helen Etapp
Juliette Etapp
Simon Etapp
Alice Farmer
David Farmer
Frances Farmer
Harry Farmer
Janet Farmer

Linda Fisher
Ramona Fisher
Raymond Fisher
Ackland French
Brian French
Gerald French
Larry French
Sharon French
Delbert Froman
Geneva Froman
Lois Froman
Louise Froman
Clifford Garlow
Grover Garlow
Hugh Garlow
Norman Garlow
Arnold General
Delores General
Joanne General
John General
Kenneth General
Marion General
Aleda George
Baptiste George
Bruce George
David George
Eugene George
Irma George
Kenneth George
Marshall George
Rachael George
Clara Gibson
Clifford Gibson
Diana Gibson
Frances Gibson
Frank Gibson
Donald Goose
Harvey Goose
Jimmy Goose
Brenda Green
David Green
Joseph Green
Larry Green
Lillian Green
Morgan Green
Robert Green
Russell Green
Gail Grosbeck
Karen Grosbeck
Stanley Halfday
Vereta Henry
Dawn Hill
Janet Hill
Kenneth Hill
Roberta Hill
Sharon Hill
Steven Hill
Charles Hopkins
Gordon Hopkins

Kenneth Hopkins
Leo Hopkins
Gail Isaac
Gary Isaac
Lynora Isaac
Maxine Jacobs
Wayne Jacobs
Mary Jane George
Clifford Johnson
Donna Johnson
Eldon Johnson
Jerry Johnson
Linda Johnson
Philip Johnson
Robert Johnson
Allan Jonathan
Beverly Jonathan
Marion Jonathan
Patricia Jonathan
Ralph Jonathan
Theresa Jonathan
Valeria Jonathan
Anne Joseph
Eloise Joseph
Floyd Joseph
Shirley Joseph
Thomas Joseph
Blake Kechego
Roger Kechego
Eva-Mae Kiyoshk
Marion Kiyoshk
Philip Kiyoshk
Ramona Kiyoshk
Robert Kiyoshk
Mary-Ann LaForme
Arnold Longboat
Benny Longboat
Cecil Longboat
Ginger Longboat
Lyle Longboat
Norma Longboat
Audrey Maracle
Stanley Maracle
William Maracle
Douglas McDonald
John McDonald
Ralph McDonald
Edward Meekis
Aileen Miller
Gary Miller
Glen Miller
Judy Miller
Lenora Miller
Peggy Miller
Raino Miller
Wayne Miller
Adrian Milliken
Faye Nanibush
Ralph Nanibush

Susan Nanibush
Brenda Nicholas
Constance Nicholas
Dale Nicholas
Gregory Nicholas
John Nicholas
John Nicholas
Karen Nicholas
Leo Nicholas
Roderick Nicholas
Susan Nicholas
Victoria Nicholas
Yvonne Nicholas
Erma (Ema) Noah
Ruby Pedonoquot
Velma Pedonoquott
Larry Pinnance
Albert Powless
Donald Powless
Donna Powless
Goldwin Riley
James Riley
Fred Sahguj (Sahjug)
Elaine Sands
William Sands
Hilton Sandy
Phyllis Sandy
Vivian Sandy
Carl Scero
Phillip Scero
Susan Scero
Donald Seneca
Stuart Seneca
David Seth
Gilbert Seth
Larry Seth
Marvin Seth
Steven Seth
Verla Seth
Glenna Shilling
Helen Shilling
Linda Shilling
Wendy Shilling
Arnold Sickles
Betty Sickles
Christina Sickles
Brian Silversmith
Bryce Silversmith
Caroline Silversmith
Garnet Silversmith
Gary Silversmith
Nellie Silversmith
Yuonne Silversmith
Elizabeth Simcoc
Dana Simon
Dwight Simon
Elaine Simon
Irene Simon

Elmer Smith
Leonard Smith
Peggy Smith
Thelma Smith
Barbara Smoke
Cheryl Snake
Cyril Snake
Donna Snake
Wilma Snake
Woodrow Snake
Lorne Sprague
Meldrum Sprague
Sharon Sprague
Alexander Staats
Carol Staats
Frank Staats
Georgina Staats
Wayne Staats
Harold Stevens
Michael Stevens
Cheryl Stinson
Esther Summers
Arnold Taylor
Darlene Taylor
David Taylor
Dorothy Taylor
Elsinor Taylor
Frederick Taylor
Helena Taylor
Iona Taylor
Kenneth Taylor
Lawrence Taylor
Maria Taylor
Maurice Taylor
Rose Taylor
Viola Taylor
Violet Taylor
Arnold Walker
Marilyn Walker
Vaughn Watson
Arland White
Brian White
Colleen White
Daniel White
David White
James White
Jason White
John White
Kenneth White
Linda White
Merle White
Sheila White
Sheldon White
Albert Whiteye
Barbara Whiteye
Enos Whiteye
Robert Whiteye
Georgia Williams

Part Two: Voice of Authority
Mount Elgin

7. Mount Elgin

8. Staff at Mount Elgin ca. 1943

9. Staff at Mount Elgin ca.1943

1849 - 1882

Rev. Peter Jones, founder 1849 - Rev. Samuel Rice 1850 - Rev. Samuel Rose 1850-1857 - Rev. James Musgrove 1857-1863 - hiatus - Rev. R. Tupper 1867-1871 - Rev. R. Gray 1871-1872 - Rev. E. Evans 1873-1875 - Rev. Thomas Cosford 1875-1881

1. 25 July 1849 Christian Guardian

On Tuesday, the 17th inst., the corner stone of the Industrial School...was laid by the Rev. Dr. Richey, President of the Conference, and the Rev. E. Wood, Superintendent of Missions, assisted by...other Ministers, S. Morell, Esq., Ex-Mayor of London, and the chiefs of the Muncey, the Ojebway, and the Oneida Tribes.

The day was delightful and the scene no less so. A deep interest was manifestly felt by the great body of Christianized Indians assembled on the occasion, whilst here and there a pagan Indian...could be seen mingling with the throng or cautiously approaching the outskirts of the congregation...Five or six hundred of the Red men were assembled...for the laying of the corner stone, above which floated the banner of England. The Oneida tribe had marched from their village, preceded by the Chief bearing the national flag, and who, on arriving at the spot placed the banner above the stone. The Ojibways... Munceys...Oneidas mingled together and formed a respectable as they did a numerous, company - their dress and deportment contrasting most strongly with the few pagans in the immediate vicinity.

A number of attached friends in London, anxious to be present with their Indian brethren on so interesting an occasion, duly arrived...The presence of so many ladies and gentlemen...afforded great gratification to all...

At 11 o'clock the Rev. Enoch Wood...gave out the... hymn - the assembly united in singing...The Rev. Dr. Richey...read...parts of the...Scriptures. An appropriate prayer was offered by the Rev. J. Carroll, Chairman of the London District...the congregation devoutly joined...

The Rev. G. R. Sanderson then read the following historical statement, which, with several other documents and publications, was subsequently placed in a copper case, and inserted in a cavity of the corner stone:

The Corner Stone
of this
INDUSTRIAL SCHOOL
was laid

With Religious Ceremony, this Seventeenth Day of July, A.D. [1849] in the presence of the Chiefs and People of the Ojibway, Muncey and Oneida Indians; by the President of the Conference of the Wesleyan Methodist Church in Canada, in connection with the English Conference and the Rev. Enoch Wood, General Superintendent of Missions, assisted by the Rev. Peter Jones, the Rev. John Carroll...The Right Hon the Earl of Elgin, Governor General...The Rev. Conrad Vandusen, Secretary...Dr. Ryerson, Superintendent of Education...

Trustees of the Industrial School and Model Farm
Rev. Enoch Wood,   Rev. Anson Green,
Rev. Peter Jones,   Rev. Samuel Rose,
Rev. John Ryerson,   Rev. John Carroll,
...Accompanying this are printed Circulars and Testimonials, detailing the origin and success of this benevolent enterprise, in which
KAHKEWAQUONABY,
(Peter Jones,)
Indian Missionary and Chief,
took a prominent and successful part

Major E. T. Campbell, Chief Superintendent of Indian Affairs...Colonel J.B.Clench, Visiting Superintendent...

The School is to be maintained by the voluntary Annuities of the Ojibways, at Muncey, New Credit, Sarnia, assisted by the Wesleyan Missionary Society.

KAHKEWAQUONABY...translated the above in the Ojebway language...the documents deposited in their place, the President of the Conference and the Superintendent of Missions laid the corner stone...assisted by the Revs. P. Jones, J. Carroll, R. Phelps, J. Sunday, A. Sickles, A. S. Byrne, G. R. Sanderson; the chiefs of the several tribes; and the Ex Mayor of London.

The corner stone having been laid...addresses were delivered by Dr. Richey and the Rev. E. Wood, interpreted by the Rev. P. Jones...The Rev. John Sunday closed the services by prayer in the Ojibway language.

...the Indians upon the mission had made arrangements for holding a commemorative feast. An ox, several sheep, lambs, etc, had been killed and prepared for the festival. Tables forming three sides of a square, were arranged in a grove and ample accomodation provided for two or three hundred guests. The blessing of the Lord being invoked, the company sat down to partake of the good cheer before them...The day was well advanced ere the feast terminated...No profane jests, no bacchanalian songs, no bursts of over excited passion were there heard to disturb the harmony or to offend the ears of Christian Indians or their white brethren. All things were done decently and in order. Nothing was left to wish for - nothing to regret...Situated on a beautiful elevation, with sloping banks down to the...Thames, the school will be as an agreeable location as it will be a healthy one, while the farm is of the richest quality of soil...

At a general council held previous to the laying of the corner stone it was unanimously resolved to call the new School...THE WESLEYAN OJIBWAY INDUSTRIAL SCHOOL, MOUNT ELGIN. The name of...Lord Elgin, was selected...on account of the deep interest his Lordship

has invariably manifested in the affairs of the Indians...
Lord Elgin has been the friend of our Indians and
missions, and has...pursued a course in relation to them as
honourable to himself, and as gratifying to the true friends
of the Indians as it has been the opposite of...some former
Governors who not only were disposed to withhold from
the Indians their legal rights, but, were prepared to stoop
down to unworthy detraction and wholesale defamation!

2. 1848-9 Peter Jones
The Industrial School Buildings are progressing rapidly,
and will, no doubt, be finished by September next. We
have sown about 25 acres of the School land with Spring
wheat, peas and oats. The produce of which will help to
feed the children who may be taken into the school during
the coming winter.

3. 1849-50 WMMS Report
In the erection of these buildings and the opening of the
school, the Society have experienced some disappointment
in the esteemed agencies by whom the work was expected
to be conducted. The health of the Rev. Peter Jones
failing shortly after the plans were commenced, rendered
it necessary that his wishes to be relieved from the
onerous and responsible duties connected with the position
of Superintendent of the Circuit, etc., should be conceded
...The institution for the past year has had the benefit of
the intelligence, piety, and zealous labours of the Rev. S.
D. Rice, who being called by his brethren to an important
position in the regular work, has also been succeeded by
the Rev. S. Rose, in whose admirable qualifications for
this important charge every confidence is placed, and from
whose judicious plans much success may be ultimately
expected. Such a transformation as an Industrial School
is designed to effect in the mental and social habits of a
degraded people must be a work of years; and
yet...practical proof has already been adduced that the
alterations desired will reward patient and perservering
efforts...Brother Rice reports of this school:

This establishment...was completed in December, at a
cost of about £1,500 Cy...Means have been taken to
provide as far as possible for the children who are
residing, and expected to become residents in the
Institution. The farm now presents an aspect of hope for
a harvest, which, if realized, will go far towards securing
this end. The farm which comprises 200 acres has been
put under fence, and of eighty acres, which are partly
cleared, we have 29 acres Wheat, 10 acres Oats, 2 acres
Beans, 4½ Corn, and 1 acre Potatoes, and the ground is
being prepared for Turnips and Buckwheat...

We have now 13 children as boarders, and 10 are
expected immediately from the New Credit, which, with
the scholars attending, from the Village, will form an
interesting school...

4. 17 February 1851 Wood
Mt. Elgin...is now in successful operation...on the 1st Inst
there were 30 boarders...and 14 more were expected from
St. Clair and Walpole Island. The principal Chief of
Walpole Island is a pagan, but so enlightened...upon the
subject of education, that he voluntarily gave up a fine lad
about 14 years of age to go to Mt. Elgin to be trained to
habits of industry. This boy, himself a pagan, at first
seemed determined to maintain his heathen dress and
distinctions, but by the mild and judicious treatment
adopted by Br. Rose, of his own accord he put on the
clothing suitable to his new position; and altho' for the
first few days he appeared rather wild and irreverent at
domestic worship, yet he suddenly became exceedingly
docile and full of enquiries about this new way.

5. 3 November 1851 Wood
...principal Pagan Chief of Walpole Island...a visit to Mt.
Elgin...favourably impressed with what he saw there...

6. 1851 Rose
...opened...in May, 1850, with 13 children as boarders, and
a number of day scholars, now contains 34 Indian youth,
who are boarded and clothed...Five of these have been in
the School since its commencement; the remainder from
5 to 7 months. They appear happy and contented, and are
making very satisfactory improvement...Some of these did
not know their letters when taken into the School, yet all
can now read; 22 are writing, 16 are cyphering and 10
are studying geography...there have been 20 day scholars
in regular attendance, and some 15 occasionally.

A male and a female Teacher are employed, who have
laboured with very great acceptability and success.
Almost every article of clothing worn by the children has
been made by those connected with the Institution,
amounting to some hundreds.

Regulations. - The bell rings at 5 A.M. when the children
rise, wash, dress and are made ready for breakfast. At
half-past-five they breakfast; after which they all assemble
in the large school-room and unite in reading the
Scriptures, singing and prayer. From six till nine the boys
are employed and taught to work on the farm, and the
girls in the house. At nine, they enter their Schools. At
twelve, they dine and spend the remaining time till one in
recreation. At one they enter School, where they are
taught till half-past three, after which they resume their
manual employment till six. At six they sup and again
unite in reading the Scriptures, singing and prayer. In the
Winter season the boys are engaged in the Evening
school, and the girls are taught needle-work until 9, when
all return to rest. They are never left alone, but are
constantly under the eye of some of those engaged in this
arduous work. Every effort that can possibly be made is
put forth in humble reliance on Divine aid to break up
their indolent and irregular habits, and to implant in them

love of order and industry, for unless this can be accomplished, with all the mental, moral, and religious culture that can possibly be given them, they will leave our schools to resume the chase; and as others have done, wander in idleness, form vicious associations, contract evil habits, and, with their decreased and decreasing nations, fade away before the face of improved and improving society. Your Manual Labour Schools is the last effort in connexion with your Heaven-owned Missionary labours, to save from utter extinction the remnant of a once noble, but now deeply degraded and long neglected race.

7. 1851 Ryerson

...There are now thirty-two children in the Manual Labour School...twenty-two boys and ten girls. They are fine looking young persons, and...are making good progress in learning the practice and habits of industry and economy. The children in the school are taught singing...they have made great proficiency in the study of this branch of science; their voices are like well tuned instruments, and the music they send forth is exquisitely delightful.

8. 1852 Rose

...from an increased conviction of the truth of the concluding sentence in my last year's Report...the education of these youths has been regarded by me as a work of no ordinary character; an education solemnly important in its connection with the future, with unborn periods of time...These youths are to form a class whose history is to be a most important epoch in the history of the nations to which they belong; whose origin is wrapt up in such impenetrable mystery. From this class is to spring a generation, who will either perpetuate the manners and customs of their ancestors, or being intellectually, morally and religiously elevated, take their stand among the improved, intelligent nations of the earth, act their part in the great drama of the world's doing; or through want of the necessary qualifications, to take their place and perform their part, be despised and pushed off the stage of action and cease to be!
...What should that education be, which will qualify them for the great purposes of their being? And while the common and plain answer seems to be, that it should be moral, religious, intellectual, and social; yet...it must...be practical...we meet with many obstructions...to be removed ...We do not get them before they have been educated in all that is evil; until immorality and irreligion have gained a complete ascendancy, and habits and practices the most demoralizing and enervating have been formed, controlling every power or faculty of body and soul. The removal of these obstructions, the disengaging of these faculties, is a work of time...every effort is made to make them believingly and practically acquainted with his word...
There is an increasing desire on the part of those

Indians best acquainted with the workings of the Institute, to have their children admitted, and had we room to receive them, and means to support them, they could be received by scores. Scarcely a week passes by but we are compelled to see them go away, followed by the poor little sorrowful, yet interestingly looking, disappointed applicants. The improved appearance of the children in the Institution, creates in the minds of their old associates a desire to be like them; and when I see the mortality which prevails among them, arising from their ignorance and consequent vice and poverty, and the diminution of their race...

9. 1853 Rose

This institution...received every possible attendance...Its halls have been crowded, and many applicants for admission have unavoidably been rejected. Although restricted to the number of 36, we have, of necessity, 42 boarded and clothed in the Institution, besides 36 day scholars, to whom a meal a day is given. We hope, however, to keep the expenditure as low as the appropriation. Their literary improvement has been very satisfactory. Their moral improvement has far exceeded our expectations, while their religious knowledge is...such as to lead us to the hope...they will become experimentally and savingly acquainted with Christ.

An important epoch in the history of those connected with this Institution, from its commencement, has arrived, -the time for them to leave those to whom they have been wont to listen for daily direction in all things; by whose hands they have been clothed and fed, - the time for them to settle in life, and to provide for themselves. But where shall they go? Back to the wretched abodes of misery and filth, to be again associated with, and influenced by ignorance and indolence? Can those who have been elevated intellectually, morally, and socially, again find companionship in the degraded ones they had left behind - a contented home in the abode of filth? Never. And yet when they leave what, with delight, many of them now call home, where shall they go? This is the question that has occupied my mind till it has distressed it. I have cared for them so long, that I cannot dismiss them without the deepest anxiety about their future welfare. There are means, ample means, by which these youths might be assisted in settling on their own lands, among their own people, follow out the directions and instructions given them in the Industrial School, and prove a blessing to their own people; but these means are in other hands...Meanwhile these youth are waiting and hoping that something will be done...By affording them the means of commencing the world for themselves, the temptation to wander about the country would be removed; they would prove a blessing to their own people, become useful members of Society, and thus at least a remnant of a once noble race would be saved from utter extinction...justice to a long-neglected and deeply injured race would be done...But who will speak for them?

10. 1854 Rose

...Over 42 were maintained in the Institution during the past year; and over 107 have been received since its commencement, who were boarded and clothed...sixty of these have been taught reading, writing, geography and arithmetic, and 13 have made some advancement in, to them, the difficult study of English Grammar, while the remainder, owing to the limited time spent in the Institution, have not advanced beyond the primer. Those who have been longest in the Institution, have made very satisfactory improvement in their literary pursuits. But to break up their indolent, irregular, and vicious propensities, is an arduous task...they have by every possible means, been taught the Holy Scriptures, led to the Cross, made to listen to the warning voice of God - laid under the strictest moral discipline...Deep concern in many has been awakened, and they have been led to pray...but alas, in too many, who had been left too long in the school of corruption...this "goodness" has been too much like "the morning cloud and early dew, which goeth away," and we have been compelled to begin with them again at the beginning. The young are the most hopeful, and should be taken while susceptible of good impressions. Those who can read, are required to commit to memory on the Sabbath, portions of the Holy Scriptures, and it is no uncommon thing to hear them repeat on the Sabbath evening, whole chapters, learned during the day. The portions of Scripture are then explained to them...

In answer to former requests, the Head of the Indian Department has engaged that each youth, on completing the course of instruction given in the Institution, and maintaining a good character, may receive from £15 to £20 per annum to assist them in settling among their own people. This carried out, will do much toward completing the Manual School system.

In addition to the number boarded and clothed...from 38 to 40 day-scholars have received a meal a day in the Institution to enable them to attend the school.

11. 7 January 1855 Rose to Supt. Gen. Indian Affairs

...an extract from a letter under date of 10th May last... from the Hon Col B...stating..."Such Scholars as may have passed creditably through the Institution - in addition to a grant of a lot of land might receive an allowance of from £15 to £20 annually, contingent on their good behaviour and industry". Several of those connected with this institution have entitled themselves...and have been sometime anxiously awaiting to receive it. Without it they cannot settle among their people and become useful members of their community.

Will you...inform me - From what fund are they to

receive it? What steps are to be taken to secure it? And whether they are to receive Deeds of Occupation, as they have been told they would, for the Lots granted.

12. 20 January 1855 Rose to Wood

...One quarter more, and the current year will be ended, and yet not the first "red penny" from the Dept. toward the support of the Institution, or the repairs of the building or the erection of the Wing to the Institution. Is this what the Superintendent General of Indian Affairs calls payment in advance? The parties from whom I purchased the Brick and Lumber for the Wing have not been quite willing to take this kind of payment in advance from me... What do you intend to do to supply Mr. Thompson place when his time is up...31st March - I do not think he could be induced to remain without a considerable advance in salary not even with that. He is a good teacher...

13. 20 February 1855 Rose to Peter Jones

...the vacancies are being filled up, from Sarnia and Walpole Island and this place. One of the leading men from Walpole left here yesterday, having brought his son. He was so well pleased with what he saw, that he promised to return with his daughter and 3 other girls. We are daily expecting another lad from Sarnia - and while there are vacancies I will receive them.

14. 20 February 1855 Rose to Wood

...I wish, much...that Mr Thompson's service could be secured for a longer time. He would do in six months for the boys more than Jack[?] would do in 18...

15. 8 March 1855 Rose to Peter Jones

...The school is doing pretty well. I have not heard a word from the Credit children - this discourages me - when will our Indian friends understand what is for their interests?

16. 21 May 1855 Rose to Nephew

...I have just finished planting about 14 acres of Corn, 6 acres of potatoes, have sowed 67 Bushls [?] and have 50 Bushls sowing of Wheat...I have 19 Indian Boys and 10 Indian girls in my family and we need large crops to supply them with bread...We are trying hard to lead them all to serve God, and some of them are trying to do so.

17. 25 July 1855 Rose to Talfourd

The 3 run away girls were here up to...the close of the Qutr. They left 3d July - What about their return? William Fisher returned and begged so hard to be taken in, that I could not say no. We have 43...I can take the 3 girls...but not an other Boy...28 boys now in 13 beds.

18. 28 July 1855 Rose to Wood?

Mr Thompson tells me this morning, that in two weeks he

wishes to leave. Have you a teacher to fill his place? I have failed to get one. Miss Sanders has left us, and I do not know that she will return. Her daughter has been filling her place but cannot do so long.

19. 20 August 1855 Rose to Talfourd
In compliance with your request I sent Elizabeth Isaac home...and hope that you will be able to send her back in 3 weeks. I have the fullest confidence in her Father, but not in her Mother - who once before tried to take her daughter away. I very much regret that Charlotte Mackaquance[?] had success in getting away and her not being sent. She would have been in d[?]...her sister and [?] people to try it also, but these we caught and brought them back.

We are full - 43 - and wish to remain so. But to have them only a little while, and just as they begin to learn to have them go away discourages us - and has led me to resolve that unless the parents and chiefs put a stop to it I shall give up the work.

20. 28 August 1855 Rose
...Mr German is here; and has gone to work nobly - if he remains...he will do well for the Institution...a Miss Barber...engaging her to teach the boys...

21. 19 September 1855 Christian Guardian Editor[?]
...spent Saturday in examining the operations connected with the School and Farm...The farm...contains two hundred acres...The land is of the best quality, and a large proportion...is under cultivation, and yields nearly all the agricultural products sufficient for the use of upwards of fifty persons...Nearly the whole of the labour on the farm is performed by the Indian youth attending the Institution.

There are at present attending the school, twenty-five boys and sixteen girls, between the ages of about ten and twenty, and more intelligent and active children, in appearance, we have seldom seen. Every day from Monday to Saturday, the children are taught in the school from nine to half-past three o'clock; and during the other portions of the day the boys are employed in the various kinds of work required on the farm; and the girls are taught the different arts of household management. The importance of the influence which the system of training has pursued, is calculated to exercise upon the future condition of the Indian tribes can scarcely be overrated. An objection has sometimes been raised by hasty critics, that very little has as yet been accomplished in connection with missionary efforts, towards the intellectual and temporal improvement of the Indian tribes of our country. We do not know by what mode of calculation such persons are led to expect an instantaneous transition from savage barbarism to the refinement of civilization. Whatever may be the immediate effects of Christianity upon the religious condition of those who receive it, the temporal blessings which it usually confers are the result of the natural laws of progress which are thereby put in operation, and require their proper season to produce their ultimate effects...The effort that is now being made through the Industrial school is the first in which the process of training in the arts of civilization has been commenced at the proper time to secure the desired object. This is the first generation of Indian youth that has been put under a regular course of training in the knowledge and arts of civilized life...Those who have any experience in the education of youth, know how much care and labour are required to train them to habits of order and industry...

...The time which each Indian youth is allowed to remain at the Institution is four years, and though this is by no means sufficient to give them the thorough training which their previous condition renders the more necessary... several of those who have completed their full term, give most encouraging proof, by their industry and economy, of the advantages they have received...

But there is another matter of importance...the Indians, to this day, have no security for the possession of the lands upon which they live; and this means those who are disposed to make improvements, and engage in agricultural pursuits, are prevented by the uncertainty they feel as to the possession of the land, either by themselves or their children...we notice the case of several young men who have been trained at Mount Elgin school, and who are anxious to settle on farms, and yet with abundance of land belonging to their tribe, they cannot obtain that title to a portion of those lands, which is essential to afford them insurance that the fruits of their industry and enterprise will be secure to them and their posterity. Such policy is unwise in the extreme, and tends very materially to defeat one of the important advantages which Missionary labours are designed to confer upon the Indians, which is, not only to make them good christians, but as a secondary benefit, to qualify them for the rights and duties of citizenship in an enlightened community.
...We have pleasure...acknowledging the cordial attentions paid to us by Br. Rose and family, during our visit...and our obligation to him for the opportunity...in obtaining some knowledge of the manner in which the affairs of that Institution are conducted. And while we became more than ever impressed with the good influence it is designed to exert upon the future condition of the Indian race, we were also gratified to witness the high qualifications of Br. Rose for the position he occupies... Nor should we omit to notice the more than her proper share of benevolent aid which Mrs Rose has rendered in the improvement of Indian youth attending the School.

22. 27 September 1855 Rose to Talfourd
...I am much driven with our buildings, farm, etc... Solomon Jackson - one of the Sarnia boys, about 14 years

old, ran away last Sabbath - This is the 2nd time, and unless his father punishes him and sends him back, he is ruined. He was doing well in the school.

I cannot in justice, to the Institution and to the Girl herself, allow the old woman to take her away. We have had no small trouble with her, in cleaning and curing her of her fits. And now that she is well, and doing well; to let her go at large would be her ruin...

We have received 3 girls and one more boy from Walpole. We have over 40 now in the Institution.

23. 3 November 1855 Rose to Waldron
...The Institution is doing pretty well the children are all well - Please say so to the Indians...

24. 14 November (December?) 1855 Rose to Talfourd
...I have been at work, almost night and day, in putting up the addition to and repairing the Institution before the cold weather should set in.
We shall soon have the new school...dining-hall, and kitchens completed. We shall then be fully prepared to receive the Moravian children.
The schools are doing very well. We have 41 children - more than we are allowed to take.

25. 1855 Rose
...The Boys' and Girls' Schools, under...two excellent Teachers, have been in successful operation. Sixty-one names have been entered on the books...during the year as boarders: and though some, who had finished their course, returned home to settle amongst their own people, and others left before the expiration of the time for which they had entered, there are yet 44 boarded and clothed in the Institution; and daily applications for admission for want of room, have to be rejected. In a recent visit to the Institution by the Superintendent General of Indian Affairs, instructions were given to receive the children from Moravian Town, which will require the immediate enlargement of the buildings. An additional wing is now under contract, and is to be completed this Fall.
...Over 11,919 verses of the Scriptures were committed to memory and recited...on the Sabbaths, by these youths...

26. 9 April 1856 Rose to Wood
Mr. German, the teacher has given notice...I know not how to fill his place - the school is doing well, and unless as good a teacher is provided to take his place the Institution will suffer. The demand for good teachers is so very great in these parts, and the Salary so much above what we give, that it is out of the question to get one to take this situation.
We have had no female teacher since December...Mrs Rose...compelled to fill that post...Mrs Rose must be released. And who will take the 21 interesting little girls, for whom she is now toiling by night and by day?

27. 12 May 1856 Rose
It is costing me 15 per cent to meet the demands for the buildings. I take the refusal of the Government to give a decision as a determination not to pay - and if I am to be mulcted to the amount of £921...
...Lord Bury decided I should take the Moravian children ...I told him I could not do until the additions were made. The repairs could not be delayed the floors were worn through, so that I have to patch them - the ceiling was off - the Roof leaked, and to go on these had to be repaired. To do them both together was the most economical. I did them, and that too in the best possible way, and see how I am fixed?
The School is doing well - and with proper support would be a blessing to the Indians...

28. 21 May 1856 Rose to Chesley
...It has now cost me over £20 for the use of money since the accounts were forwarded...ruinous state of matters

29. 23 May 1856 Rose to Talfourd
...One of the Walpole boys by the name of Arthur [?] who was sent here last September with note from Revd Mr Jamieson written at the request of his mother requesting me to use him tenderly as his health was not good; after having been well fed during the winter ran away about 3 weeks ago with a large amount of goods which he stole from the Institution by means of keays which took out of the door while the men were at work in the Building.
Philip [?] one of the young men who left the Institution this spring, with credit, and is now at work on the Island sent me word that he saw the Keays in his Arthur's possession with other things...One is a brass and the other an iron keay I should like much to get the Keays, if nothing more...I was not at home when he ran away or his escape would not have been so easy. I do not know but he would be punished - His mother is one of the company gone to [?] The school is doing well. The Walpole Indians may send one in Arthur's place.
The Moravian Indians want to sent 10 children, and will not be satisfied with less...I could take the 10 provided they can be supported.

30. 22 November 1856 Elizabeth Jones to John Dunlop
...dear P.E. [Peter Edmund] is at the Industrial School at Muncey for which Mr. Jones collected when in the old Country, I rejoice to say it is prospering well now, I have had many inducements to place him there...

31. 1856 Rose
...has been unintermittingly conducted in both the male and female department, giving, during the past year, mental, moral, religious, domestic and civil instruction to fifty-eight Indian youths who have been boarded and

clothed...during their continuance in the schools.

The improvement made by the pupils during the past year has been more satisfactory than that of any former year. In connection with General History as contained in the First Book of Lessons, English and Canadian History has been introduced into the schools, upon the plan approved by the Normal School Toronto. The study of Algebra and Agricultural Chemistry has also been introduced; and the progress made by some of the more advanced boys and girls in these, to them new studies, has quite exceeded our most sanguine expectations. Forty pupils have secured the highest marks for good moral conduct. Over 3,000 verses of the Scriptures have been committed to memory and recited in English on Sabbath evening after the close of the other religious services. Several have been under deep religious concern of mind, and some have found peace in believing. One young man, the son of a pagan Chief, having given satisfactory evidence of his evidence of his faith in Christ, presented himself at our last quarterly service, and in the presence of his schoolfellows, and a large assembly...received Christian baptism. The buildings have been greatly enlarged during the year, and will now comfortably accommodate over eighty children as boarders.

...after six years of strict attention to the working of this Industrial Institution, *it is the one thing needful*, in connection with your general missionary operation, in the recovery and elevation of this once noble, but long neglected, deeply degraded and decimated race.

One of the primary objects...of the Industrial Schools is, *the raising up among the Indians, on Indian lands, of a class of industrious and intelligent people, who would prove a blessing to their race, and a credit to the government, that occupies the position of guardians over them, and to whom they have been taught to look as children to a parent.* Several of these youths, having passed through their course of study with credit to themselves, but not having received the promised aid, and not having the means of settling on lands among their own people, have been compelled to beg permission to remain longer in - what has become a home to them - the Institution.

In giving up the charge of this important establishment, and in taking leave of these affectionate, and promising children, over whom we have watched by day and by night, in sickness and in health - some of them for nearly six years - and whose musical voices we have listened with much profit and delight, - morning and evening...

32. January 1857[?] Rose

...as to the "complaints". I proposed telling you, when at the Institution; but was advised not to do so. The complaints did not come only from the children. But as I have done myself no good telling you what I did, I shall take care in future that I tell less - and save the trouble of

another 'opinion' being, "ventured that the Institution will not be very seriously affected by my absence" or in giving "alarm by fearful prognostications."

33. 11 February 1857 Dignam

...one great institution, fifty children of several Indian tribes, receiving education, food and raiment...a more durable monument to embalm the sacred memory of Jones may yet be seen in the great *Mount Elgin Institution*...The great brick wigwam let loose its students...What ebony hair and ivory teeth - what brawny faces - what pleasant countenances - what amusing jargon - what rapid movements; my old Morpeth horse was soon recognized and got a royal salute. I never saw buckle and tongue dissolve partnership so quick. I stood amazed for a moment, as I viewed the site and size of the building, the appearance and improvement of its inhabitants, the several office houses and their great facilities. I confess I had no conception of its great excellence...

34. 18 February 1857 Dignam

...the sound of the supper bell was welcome music. I surveyed the table with pleasure...I asked...about the excellent dish of buckwheat pancakes...the...answer was "my boys and I sowed 4 acres and raised upwards of 100 bushels after I came to the mission, and I believe all you see, is the produce of the farm, except the coffee"... [we rose up] to pray...The singing was positively charming, carrying several parts without the slightest hesitation.

After prayers they all sat down, every eye is toward the desk for "the order of the day". A motion of the hand and the girls are off in regular procession to the sewing room, while the boys are told off in several companies to their respective duties. School comes on at a regular hour and in they come again...I saw in one room thirteen standing beds with respectable appendages and a pair of white pillows on each bed...the ladies workshop...some of those young seamstresses are ready to leave, after years of attention to cutting, fitting and sewing both their own garments and those of other students...here are made and mended garments for the fifty...just open a window in that mammoth ark and there you will see a great stock of flour - unlid that barrel...superfine beef...pyramids of white dry firm bacon...cakes of tallow...old-fashioned butter firkin... cheese vegetables and honey in order - all the products of the model farm...there is a large washroom, and a large wash trough...there are basins and towels...

35. 11 March 1857 Dignam

...We come into the mess-room. Here stand two large tables *loaded* and *crowded*...At the head of the boys' table stands the teacher, Mr. Faulkner; at the head of the girls' stands Mrs. Faulkner, assistant teacher - every motion watched, and every want well supplied, feasting on the fruits of their own industry...I beg to take leave of the respectable managers and inmates of the Institution... remember the big wigwam with its large family of 50, and room for 30 more; take up your cross, *(I mean your dollar bills gentlemen,)* put a few of them in an envelope ...for I did hear him say, in view of his increasing family, he would want a few barrels of flour - that Christ may say, "Inasmuch as ye have done it unto one of the least of these my brethren" (though they be little Indians)...

36. 1857 Musgrove

The Industrial School has been in successful operation through the year, and the boys and girls have performed their usual amount of labour, both in the field and in the house; and in relation to their literary attainments, Mr. Falkner, the male teacher, remarks: "In addition to paying due attention to, and making considerable advancement in the studies heretofore pursued in the school, the boys, especially the larger ones, have made great proficiency in rhetorical exercises. Some of their original productions, both spoken and written, would compare favourably with...a large class of young white men attending academies and high schools in our country.

On the 31st March, four boys and one girl, who had been in attendance upwards of five years, and whose time had expired, were called upon to give the parting hand to their fellow students, and to sever their connection with the Institution. The boys delivered each an address on the occasion, in English, dwelling at length upon their social and moral state and condition before entering the school, the advantages afforded, the benefits derived, and the grateful feelings they cherished towards those who had the charge of them, and taught them, by precept and example, both how to live, and how to die.

...Two of these young men are now employed as school teachers on our Indian missions, and the other two are also competent to teach the common English branches in any of our schools. The Sabbath school and Bible classes have both been regularly attended to; and I have great pleasure in bearing testimony to the zeal and faithfulness of our excellent teachers, Mr. and Mrs. Falkner...their efficiency in teaching and governing the children in the day school. Mr. Falkner is also the leader of the class among the boys, and Mrs. Falkner among the girls...and to their godly example and teachings...may be attributed, in great part, the good work which has been in progress among the children for the last nine months: many of the larger boys and girls are now meeting in class.

The boys and girls have recited in the Sabbath school 7513 verses, more than double the number committed to memory last year. Elijah McDougal occupies the highest position among the boys, having recited 524, and Clara Wesley among the girls, having recited 375. There are now 40 boarders in the institution. We have not had less during the year, and could as easily keep fifty as forty, the accommodations being provided, and the children desirous

of attending. We have had to reject seven applications for admission lately, the funding not being adequate to support them. How deeply this is to be regretted, when we consider, that these industrial schools form the best ground of hope for reclaiming the Indian race from their roving and indolent habits, and of bringing them into fixed habits of industry and domestic economy.

37. 1858 Musgrove

We have had our full number of children (40) in attendance...They have been clothed, fed and educated. Most of them are young men and women; and, as heretofore have been kept at work on the farm and in the house. Several of the boys and girls have made considerable proficiency in their studies, and are regularly meeting in class. The Bible class and Sabbath School have both been attended...and 6,636 verses have been recited through the year.

38. 1858 Report of the Special Commissioners...

...The buildings at Muncey Town were not completed until 1851, the amount expended being $5,500. In 1856 it was found necessary to enlarge this School at a cost of $3,660, and in 1857 an additional outlay of $640, was made for repairs and improvements...a total sum of $9,800. - This School is appropriated to the Chippewas of St. Clair and Chenail Ecarté, the Tribes on the Thames, and the Mississaugas of the New Credit.

The management of these two Schools [Alderville, Mt. Elgin] having been entrusted to the Wesleyan Methodist Society, the following arrangement was entered into:

The Indian Department agreed to ensure the buildings and to pay to the Society for the board, clothing and education of each child, a certain sum per annum...the yearly average...$64 per head.

The Society...promised to supply the necessary furniture ...books and stationery for the School...the stock and farming implements...support and pay the salaries of the Superintendents and Teachers...provide such assistance as would be requisite to efficiently conduct the Institution.

The produce of the farms was to be applied to the support of the Schools.

It was also stipulated that the Society should receive as day scholars any children who might be willing to attend, belonging to the Reserves on which the Schools were erected, without any charge.

The Schools have now been in operation for about seven years, and although the produce of the farms has somewhat diminished the amount required from the funds of the Society to meet the expenditure, the expectation that by this time they would have become nearly self-supporting has certainly not been realized.

Last year, each farm had nearly seventy acres under crop, and the amount expended by the Society in addition to the sum paid by the Department, was $2,200.

For some time it was found very difficult to induce the parents to send their girls to the Schools, but for the last three years as many as could be accommodated have attended; at present there are...20 Boys and 21 Girls...

The children receive a good plain education; the girls are also instructed in household affairs, the management of the dairy, needlework and domestic manufactures; the boys are employed a portion of each day in working on the farm under the direction of a person specially engaged for that purpose.

If the good effects which were expected to result from the establishment of these schools are not apparent, if they have not fully answered the hopes of those who projected them, no blame can be attached to the Society to whose management they were entrusted.

The different gentlemen placed in charge as Superintendents, as well as their Assistants, have been eminently fitted for the work, and have spared no pains to give the undertaking a fair trial.

We think that the following obstacles have impeded the success of the experiment.

First. The children are too old when they are received into the institutions. They have, before their entrance, acquired idle, filthy, and in some cases vicious habits, and have arrived at an age when it is difficult to attain any control over them, or eradicate the evil practices to which they may be disposed.

Secondly. The children remain too short a time at these establishments to receive much advantage from the training...Their parents have in many cases prejudices against the schools, and remove their children after a very short residence. The pupils themselves too frequently abscond, and return to their homes without permission, finding the wholesome restraint of the school irksome. This evil it is found impossible to prevent.

Thirdly. The system, as now carried out, does not make any provision for the settlement in life of those who complete their education at these schools.

It was originally proposed to give a portion of land to every boy completing his term of study with credit, but this does not seem to have been carried out. The children therefore worked without the stimulus of reward, and learned to regard the establishment rather as a prison than a place where they might acquire the means of advancing themselves, and of improving their position in the country.

Fourthly. It is much to be regretted that neither the funds at the disposal of the Indian Department, nor those furnished by the Society, have been sufficient to enable them to extend the system of practical education so as to include any of the mechanical arts. Many of the boys would prefer acquiring the knowledge of a trade to following the calling of a husbandman.

The expense, too, of establishing some of the most praiseworthy among them in such handicraft pursuits on their quitting the institution, would have been small as compared with that which would have to have been incurred in placing them on farms. It is therefore on every account to be deplored that the want of money has prevented the development of these branches of education. ...it is discouraging in the extreme to see how transient is the impression made upon the children by the training which they have gone through at these schools. They do not seem to carry back with them to their homes any desire to spread among their people the instruction which they have received. They are contented as before to live in the same slovenly manner, the girls make no effort to improve the condition of the houses, nor do the boys attempt to assist their parents steadily on the farm.

...improvement is perceptible in their own personal appearance, but the amelioration extends no farther. The same apathy and indolence stamp all their actions as is apparent in the demeanour of the rest of the Indians.

It is then with great reluctance that we are forced to the conclusion that this benevolent experiment has been to a great extent a failure. It has no doubt, done a certain degree of good, but when we look at the large annual outlay incurred on its behalf, and at the other charges now to be imposed on the Indian Revenues, we cannot recommend that so considerable a portion of these funds should be devoted to the partial education of so small a portion of the tribes, and we proposed that the deductions now made from their annuities (in some cases against their will) with this object, should cease at the commencement of the next financial year.

If these establishments are to be closed however, the interest which the Wesleyan Society have acquired in them must not be overlooked. They have laid out a considerable sum in the clearing of the farms attached to the schools...The establishment at Mount Elgin we should gladly see appropriated as an Indian Orphan Asylum...

39. 1859 Musgrove
The Indian children in the Industrial School have been attended to as usual, and have been employed (out of school hours) in the house, and on the farm; and many of them are making considerable proficiency in their studies.

40. 1860 Musgrove
Our Industrial school has been doing well and is...in a good state. Our number is more than 40 boarders, many of them adults. Their conduct through the year, almost without exception, has been uniformly good. They have applied themselves to their literary studies, and diligently attended to their Industrial and domestic training.

41. 1861 Musgrove
The average attendance of boarders at the Industrial school has been upward of 40. The Bible class and Sabbath School have both been attended to...upwards of 900 verses have been recited during the past 6 months by

one of the boys. As the result of a series of meetings held in the Institution for 2 weeks, 23 of the boys and girls joined the Society and are now meeting in class.

42. 1862 Musgrove

The average attendance of boarders at the Industrial School for the year has been 48. We have kept up the Bible Class and Sabbath School regularly, and upwards of 2,674 verses have been recited by the boys and girls.

43. 1863 Spragge

It appears that the Indians were of opinion that their children did not derive such additional benefits from the instruction there imparted (beyond what could be obtained at the schools in their settlements,) as to reward them for the long continued separation from their children. They objected also to continue contributions to the support of Institutions, in which no adequate provision was made for instruction in the mechanical arts.

The unwillingness of the Bands who sent their children and furnished funds to the Mount Elgin Institute to do so any longer, I found from general enquiry among them during the last summer and autumn, to be, not without sufficient reason. That the children were comfortably cared for, I have no doubt, but to deserve the name of "industrial", other pursuits, than that of farming, ought to have been introduced...

As the Indians are really apt scholars at Mechanical Arts...such employments as Carpentering, Wheelwright work, Shoemaking, Blacksmithing work, etc. etc. might with advantage have been made, especially during the Winter, subjects for instruction.

The farm at Mount Elgin, the property of the Indians, possesses great variety of soils and for experimental agriculture it cannot be surpassed. But...in walking over it last Autumn with the Visiting Superintendent of Indians, I could not avoid the conclusion that the tillage was slovenly to a degree reprehensible.

44. 1863 WMMS Annual Report

The lamented death of the Rev. James Musgrove deprives us of the satisfaction of presenting a report.

45. 1865 WMMS Annual Report

...The deplored death of the Rev. James Musgrove, and the discontinuance of the Industrial Institution, have interfered with the uniformity of our operations, and publication of the report. The Reverend Francis Berry...The unsettled state of the Mount Elgin Institution property has proved detrimental to our interests, and has been used by designing men to our injury. The resuscitation of this Institution is much to be desired, and if reorganized on a proper basis, would do much to benefit this and other bands of Indians.

46. 1866 Francis Berry

...We look with hope to the reorganization of the Industrial Institution under more favorable auspices than ever before...Probably before the publication of the Report of 1866, this Institution which cost our fathers so much labor and means, and which existed, not without its fruits, for sixteen years, but which has been suspended for the last three or four years, will be in active operation as a higher Indian School...to prepare young men for usefulness amongst their red brethren...

47. 16 October 1867 Christian Guardian

We had an interesting formal re-opening of the Mount Elgin Industrial School, Oct. 2nd...R. McKenzie, Esq, of Sarnia, the Indian Superintendent for the western division, gave us the benefit of a short address, expressing himself greatly delighted with the transformed character of the building, the cheerful and neat appearance of the scholars, the gathering of the band, and the promise of much good to the...Indian children, which appeared certain if they industriously availed themselves of it. We had beside our own Missionaries and Agents on this...reserve and that of the Oneidas, the Delegates of the Conference, the Chairman of the Chatham District, and the Rev. Mr. Hough. A very large number of our Indians were away at the camp-meeting on Walpole Island, but...this gathering on the lawn in front of the Institution, where dinner was served to all the visitors, young and old, was very large; the politeness of the Ojibways showing itself by first introducing to the long table, adorned with beef, potatoes, bread, and tea, their friends from across the river - the Oneidas. We gave them one of the largest and fattest oxen we could obtain, and the half of a splendid three year old in addition. Before dinner began, we had a religious service, and when this concluded the Ojibway band of musicians struck up their stirring strains, and throughout the whole of the repast enlivened the scene by suitable airs very well rendered. I was surprised at their proficiency. You might place them at the head of a regiment. We came away just before sundown, and they were still at the dinner-table. Mr. Rose understands the Indian character very well, and both he and Mr. McKenzie were of opinion the Indians enjoyed it marvellously well. The cleanliness and comfort of the internal arrangements are everything we could desire, and the whole farm shows a vast improvement...

There are now thirty boarders under Mr. and Mrs. Tupper's care, and in a few weeks the number will be increased to fifty. The school has now been in operation three months. The weather was beautiful.

48. 1868 Tupper

This Institution was reopened on the 15th July 1867, with only four scholars, but in less than 3 months we had more than forty in attendance; the school has continued to increase, so that during the past three quarters we have had an average of nearly 50 scholars. Our last report shows that we have only seven scholars who are now using the primer, 52 spelling, 50 reading, 34 writing, 29 studying arithmetic, 14 in English grammar, 20 in geography, and one studying book-keeping. At 9 o'clock on each Sabbath morning we have an interesting Sabbath school, in which 48 of the scholars have recited 1,162 Scripture verses during the year.

The progress of the scholars in the various branches of learning is about the same as will be found in the best conducted, and best taught Common schools in the country.

A teacher is employed for the School, who assists us out of school hours, in maintaining good order, and also aids us as we desire, by taking charge of the boys at their manual labour on the farm. We have also a Matron, who takes the oversight of the girls at their work in the sewing-room, where most of the clothing worn by the scholars is made.

The bell rings at 5 A.M. when all the scholars rise. Breakfast at 6 A.M. after which all unite in Family worship. The boys then work on the farm, and the girls in the house till 9 A.M. when the school commences - 9-12 and 1-4; 4-6 work at farm and house. 9 p.m. assemble in the school room for progress and go to bed.

49. 1869 Tupper

The largest number of scholars in attendance at any one time has been 56; the total number receiving instruction in the Institution...has been 38 boys and 28 girls.

Our last quarterly report shows that 46 boys have been taught spelling, 46 reading, 41 arithmetic, 21 English Grammar, 16 have studied Geography.

Our regular hours for teaching are from 9 o'clock A.M. to 12, and from 1 to 4 o'clock p.m., but several of the boys spend about one hour in each evening at study; in this, they are encouraged by the teacher and assisted as they desire. Three of the young men are learning the Carpentering trade, and two are working at shoemaking. In both of these branches, the young men are making satisfactory proficiency. A building...is in the course of erection on the premises for a range of workshops, where the "Mechanical and Industrial Arts" are to be taught.

Our Sabbath-School has been regularly kept up...During the first year, the scholars recited 11,623 Scriptural verses; and in the year now closing, they have recited 18,720 verses...30,343 Scriptural verses in two years.

Our friends are aware that this is an Industrial Institution, and that the boys are required to work on the farm and at their trades out of school hours. The girls are also employed out of school hours at sewing, spinning, knitting, and "house work".

Owing to the want of funds, we have been under the necessity of turning away a large number who have

sought admission as scholars. This lack of assistance from the "Indian Department" is to be very much regretted, especially as we have ample room for a much larger number.

50. 1870 Tupper

During the year now closing we have an attendance of 27 boys and 18 girls, who have received instruction in all those branches usually taught in the common school...

The improvement of the scholars in spelling, reading, writing, arithmetic, geography, English grammar, and history, is nearly equal to...schools generally.

...one of the conditions on which the "Indian Department" affords aid to this Institution, is, that the Department stipulated to assist toward the board and clothing of fifty scholars. In pursuance of this arrangement we have erected a range of substantial workshops, and, as we expected the full number of fifty to be assisted, we have provided ample accommodations for even a larger number. The Department...has reduced the number of scholars to thirty. This is to be regretted, especially as many of the Indians in different parts are exceedingly anxious to have their children educated here.

We have had in the last year three apprentices to the shoemaking, and four apprentices to the carpentering trade, each of whom have made satisfactory proficiency under the instruction of competent workmen.

...a marked improvement in the moral principles and character of most of the scholars under our care: this improvement is manifest in their general conduct, as well as reciting a large number of Scriptural verses, and in learning our Catechism in our Sabbath-school.

Several of the scholars are members of our Church, and others have also expressed a desire to meet in class. This Industrial School should be sustained by the prayers and liberal support of the friends of the Missionary cause, more especially as the Church must look to this Institution principally for the education of its native Interpreters, Teachers, and Missionaries.

51. 29 March 1871 Christian Guardian

...transfer of the charge of the...School, from the Rev. R. E. Tupper (who had resigned the charge) to the Rev. James Gray, late Chairman of the Hamilton District.

On the 28th ult., the Rev. E. Wood...the Rev. J. Elliott...made a formal transfer of the governorship of the Institution...The Rev Dr. Wood addressed the school at some length, giving a review of the establishment and history of the institution. He gave the strongest possible encouragement both to the Indian children and to those appointed to govern and teach them. The Rev. J. Elliott then addressed the pupils and employees...He made the most stirring appeals to the boys and girls to try and excel in all the departments in which they were employed. Dr. Wood then called upon the retiring and installed governors, who each gave short and appropriate addresses. The meeting was most instructive and interesting.

On the following evening, the scholars read addresses to the Rev. Mr. Tupper and the Rev. Mr. Gray, expressive of their gratitude and hope. The Rev. Mr. Gray, made a suitable reply, expressing his sense of responsibility and his hopes for the future. The school is reported in an efficient condition.

52. 10 June 1872 Roberts Journal

...visited the Mount Elgin...Did not like the appearance of things there. In the school-room there were nine Indian boys, two 'white' boys and two 'white' girls. I was told that some of the pupils were away, and that the Indian girls were 'washing the clothes', but I only saw 4 or 5 engaged in that way. There is a workshop attached in which 'cabinet-work' and 'shoe-making' are taught. At the time of my visit there were only two boys there.

53. 1872 Gray

During the past sixteen months there have been times of embarrassment and discouragement, but on the whole we may report prosperity and success. The scholars have made satisfactory progress in their studies, and at the trades; though in consequence of the removal of several of the older ones, we have not, perhaps, so many advanced pupils...Considerable attention has been paid to the improvement of the farm and premises. Several outbuildings have been removed, improved or erected; implements of husbandry provided, a system of drainage introduced, and a good orchard planted, and measures taken for the improvement of the farmstock...

The means of grace have been regularly kept up at the Institution, a small class has been formed, and a weekly prayer-meeting held, a Sunday-school established, and more frequent public religious services maintained. On the Sabbath, after our regular family devotions, all are expected to attend in the forenoon, at the new church erected on the Mission. Our Sunday-school meets in the afternoon, and is followed by the class-meeting. In the evening we have a public service...Those who are now employed about the place are all reliable, and most of them pious persons...

54. 1873 Evans

The year now closing has been upon the whole encouraging. The average attendance of scholars has exceeded the number provided for by the Government. General contentment prevails among the pupils, which is indicated by the fact that none of them have absconded during the last ten months. Gratifying progress has been made by several, both in the school and in the shops in which the trades are taught. I am not without hope that one or two of the boys are destined to fill posts of usefulness among the Indian tribes.

The religious condition of the inmates is not as satisfactory as we desire. The want of a leader acquainted with the Ojibway language, renders it difficult to keep up a class of such as are seriously disposed. This defect we hope to have remedied. The Sabbath-school is regularly conducted, and the results are encouraging.

The general health of the scholars has been good. Two of the girls have succumbed to pulmonary disease. Both gave pleasing evidence of their saving interest in the atonement, and died rejoicing in the hope of eternal life.

The interests of the Indian Bands represented, would be greatly promoted by the Indian Department authorising a larger attendance than at present is provided for. The buildings also require considerable outlay for repairs, and the prevention of decay.

55. 1874 Evans

The work of the year has been steadily prosecuted in the several departments, and generally with satisfactory results. The attendance has been more than ordinarily regular. Marked improvement in conduct has gladdened the hearts of those in charge. The scholars indicated contentedness with the treatment they receive, and we have had no recurrence of the abscondments, which have heretofore been so frequent and painful. The state of health has been unusually good...

Several of the scholars are meeting in class, and of some we have good hope that their hearts are under gracious influence...

We must again express our regret that the Government continues the low limit of attendants, for whom they make provision. The number might be largely augmented without much increased cost to the Society, and with great advantage to the Indians. The earnest desire of the most intelligent of several bands for the rights of citizenship must urge the importance of having the rising Indian generation educated, and brought under more settled and industrious habits than in the past.

In this direction, and in providing for the extensive repairs on the buildings, we hope the movement of the Government will be prompt and effective. The ample funds at the credit of the Indian Department warrant the expectation, both of ourselves and the Indians concerned, that immediate action will be taken...

56. 1875 Cosford

The interests of this institution are promoted with increasing efficiency and success. We have more scholars than the number for whom the Government grant assistance, and might have many more. Their attendance is regular, and many of them are making creditable advancement in their studies; they are contented and happy, and there is also a marked improvement in their conduct and social habits. Their state of health has been very good...More than twelve of the scholars meet in class, and many of the others manifest deep concern for their religious interests...We deeply regret that the Government continues the very low limit of attendance for whom they make partial provision...it is the earnest desire of the most intelligent of the various bands of the Indians that their young people should be educated and more settled, as well as stimulated to more industrious habits...

57. 1876 Cosford

The past year has been one of unremitting toil...with marked and very gratifying success. The school has been in a state of prosperity...The regular attendance of the scholars, their increasing studiousness and desire for knowledge, also their increased and prompt obedience in the performance of the duties assigned them, and more particularly the conversion of most of them to God, are all evidences of that prosperity...the health of the scholars has been very good, and they are contented and happy.

The Institution buildings have been thoroughly repaired. The farm is undergoing a system of proper and efficient tillage and improvement, with a view to remunerative productiveness...we hope to make the whole establishment what its founders designed it should be, the officers and patrons of the Missionary Society desire, and, through the Indian youth who enjoy its advantages, a most powerful means of promoting the stability and success of our Missions among the natives of our country. In a very few years these scholars must become our native agents as missionaries, teachers, local preachers, exhorters, leaders, etc, to carry on their work among their people, if properly cared for, brought to a knowledge of the Truth, and educated in that broad and proper sense, in which they can be only when taken from their old associations and habits, and trained for years, as they are in this Institution.

58. 1877 Cosford

This Institution has been visited with some occurrences of a painful nature during the past year, which have greatly impeded its prosperity. My own severe personal illness, and the failure of all our crops...have very greatly limited our success...gratitude for my wonderful restoration to perfect health, and for the marked prosperity in the work of improving and bringing the farm into a state of remunerative prosperity. Judging from the appearance of our crops we hope to have an abundance of provisions for this year, and some to sell. The school has been in a very gratifying state of prosperity during the year. The scholars have...evinced a thirst for knowledge, and many of them have made very good progress in their studies, and have also been uniformly correct in their deportment and prompt in their obedience in the duties assigned them. About seven-tenths of the scholars meet in class, and the school is in a very good religious state.

59. 1878 Cosford

...The year...has been one of very gratifying prosperity. Our crops were good, and the products of the farm have been equal to all the requirements of the Institution, and have added considerably to its funds. By untiring diligence we have succeeded in bringing the farm into a state of very greatly improved culture and productiveness, and...we intend to make it what it was intended to be- "A Model Farm." The school has been in a very gratifying state of efficiency and success...The moral character of the scholars has very much improved, and a goodly number have manifested pleasing evidence of true devotion to God. Twenty-one are members of the Church, and we frequently have from twenty to twenty-five scholars, and ten whites, at class. The shops are also doing well and in a state of creditable prosperity. One of our most important buildings remains to be renewed, when that is done we shall only have our regular work to pursue...

60. 1879 Cosford

The past year has been characterized by uninterrupted success in every department...The deportment of the scholars has been commendable, and the advancement made in their studies highly gratifying, while the spiritual influence pervading the school has been very good. We frequently have from twenty to twenty-five of the scholars in our class service. The shops have continued with unabated interest and industry, and the results will be found to reflect credit upon those employed in each department. The farm is advancing to a state of gratifying productiveness. We raise not only an ample supply of all farm produce for the Institution, but a creditable amount to sell, even beyond supplying all the employees of the establishment...we shall have as much meat and flour to sell as we require...during the incoming year.

61. 1880 Cosford

This Institution continues in a state of prosperity. The school has been well attended...a good work has been done; its moral state has been commendable, and the scholars have acquired a good degree of proficiency. The farm is in a much better state of productiveness...We raise all the farm produce required for this establishment, the flour and meat for four other families, and also, in part, for three others. The shops are likewise in a state of creditable efficiency. We make first-class work, and can make a large quantity of it - shoes and boots of all kinds, cabinet work and carpenter work - and could make the shops give a nice net profit if we could get sale at moderate prices for our productions. We now have fifty pupils...the least number we ought to have, instead of thirty as hitherto. The prospect of this Institution is now very fair for greatly benefiting and elevating the Indian youth of our country...with very moderate aid from the Missionary Fund, if it is not entirely self-supporting. A very delightful and subduing religious influence rests upon the scholars, which greatly disposes and readily inclines them to receive instruction, and apply themselves in the acquisition of useful knowledge.

62. 1881 Cosford

The six years and a half of my incumbency in this Institution have been years of great anxiety, care, and toil; but...they have been very prosperous, in the advancement of the religious and material interests of the Institution, as well as in the intellectual development and spiritual attainments of the pupils; and the past year has been as much, or more fully marked by these evidences of advancement as any of the former.

The school has been in a very fine state of prosperity throughout the year. The scholars have evinced a growing interest in their studies; some of them are frequently found, during their leisure hours, in groups, studying. They have evinced increased attention to instruction given, promptness and fidelity in the performance of duties enjoined, and greater deference and respect for those appointed to govern and instruct them. The farm is increasing in productiveness - the erection of our large and excellent stock barn...with best arrangements for light and fresh air. For this erection we received from the...Government $1,000. We have also built a very good and commodious carriage house, and have added eighty rods more of good board fence to the farm.

...The building is a large, substantial one, built of brick, two-stories above the basement. It contains eight compartments in the basement - scholars dining-room, kitchen, room for milk pails, pans, crocks, etc.; one for flour bins, working, and furnace; a milk and butter room; one for bread, meat, and all kinds of prepared food for immediate use; one for vegetables; and one for all kinds of fruit...On the first floor there are twelve rooms. In the Governor's apartments there is an ample parlour, a suitable office, and a bedroom...At the front door...stairs lead to upper hall, where there are four good bedrooms...A good-sized school-room... Main Hall...a bedroom for girls...a large dining-room for Governor and family; upper kitchen in second wing...store-room, containing the boys' clothes and new materials. Next is the matron's room...sewing room, where the Indian girls work...dormitories for the Indian girls are upstairs, in three rooms...The boys' dormitory is over the school-room...in main building is the teachers' room, from which he has immediate access to the boys' dormitory...

We have built a new frame outside-kitchen for salting and packing meat, keeping bran, bags, and for general purposes; a brick smoke and ash-house of suitable size; an ice and oil-house; two large sheds...for wood, waggons, etc...planted more than one hundred fruit trees...have added at least twenty-five acres of crop-bearing land to the farm; made...three miles of good board fence; have raised a full supply of farm produce for the Institution, and some to spare, which averages twice as much as was ever raised formerly...

Our Aim...is to educate and elevate the Indian youth of our country, that they become instrumental in the elevation and salvation of their own people.

...The best, most tractable, and successful pupils we get, are the children whose parents, when young, were educated in this Institution. The gentleman who took the census on this Reserve, this spring...when he found an Indian whose home indicated a state of greater thrift and improvement, made it a point to enquire, and invariably found that they had been educated and taught to work in this Institution. Many of our Indian girls have been employed as servants, and have given good satisfaction; some, after spending a year in one place, their employers have parted with them reluctantly, and have applied for others. We have had applications for them from very respectable families, but, at the close of their time, their parents, or some other person, are very anxious that they should return home, and the attraction prevails. Others of our scholars are now succeeding well as School Teachers.

Our fifty Indian pupils recite, with a very good degree of readiness and correctness, from 200 to 600 Scripture verses every Sabbath, generally about 400. We teach the International Sabbath-School Lessons, never urge them to learn more than the lessons, but...to learn them well.

63. Cosford Reminiscences

We bid adieu to our friends in Mount Forest, in the first week in January 1875, and arrived...on the 8th...

A more filthy place morlats never entered - I do not wonder that Rev. James Musgrove and his noble wife, as well as the first Mrs. Dr. Evans died there. We took in the situation and state of things, and resolved that we would renovate, clean and make the whole establishment healthy and comfortable. There was water under the floors of every part of the basement, and a well, full of water and filth of the most offensive nature - the girls indian and white had been in the habit of throwing dirty dishwater, and all sorts of rubish into it, broken dishes, cups and sawsers tea pots &c - Bones, Indian Ruber over Shoes, Spoons, Knives, forks &c. We cleaned it out, put into it a barrol of quick lime, and filled it up with earth. We put in a good lite drain into every compartment of the Basement, with sufficient fall to carry off the water. Having dug a new drain sufficiently low to carry off all the waste water...and connected the drains, from every compartment of the Basement with it. And so placed the Tile around each room within a foot of the walls, and embedded the tile in with sement so that the rats could not possibly make an entrance...Formerly the rats devoured a larg part of our food and left us the refuse. The rats were so bad and numerous, that two men would some times go into the scholars dining room at night when all was quiet, and stop up all the rat holes except one, as soon as the Men would retire and leave the Room in darkness the rats would come in, and soon the men with sticks would rush in upon them and kill a dozen or more at a time. As long as this state of thing continued it was impossible to keep the food from them. ...The last years crop of farm produce was all consumed by the 1st of January, Meat supply was exhausted, and there was no wood, all was consumed. No water to use except as we drew it from the river...We had to buy all our eatables and supply of flour, till the new crop came in...We provided wood for that winter, and also the next year. We had an abundance of old sleighs, waggons, ploughs, harness &c not fit for use. Old horses, 25 old cows...Old cows and sheep dying almost every week.

There was a mud hole on the place called a hog sty. The Barns were tumbling down, an orchard had been planted, but for want of a suitable fence to protect it, was well nigh destroyed. There was not a fence on the farm that would turn the Indians horses. When the wheat was planted out, the men had to chase troops of horses out, at mid night, as a frequent occurrance.

As soon as the Spring opened, we had to re-shingle the Institution. When it rained it not only leaked, but the water poured through it, beds and clothes had to be moved, or the sleepers, if at night, drenched with water, and the beds soaked...After my first year, we raised a fully supply of wheat, and provided also a full supply of meat, besides selling much Four, Meat, and 1600 lbs of Butter yearly, of first quality. During my first two years, I could not increase the stock, because we had not, and could not raise feed enough to keep it, we found it necessary to get rid of the old and very unprofitable stock first. This was no easy task...we soon acquired a good and improved Stock. The value of this arrangement was in these points, it gave good fresh meat for summer, wool for stockings, socks and mittens for winter, and by it, we taught the Indian girls to spin and knit for themselves and friends as well as others.

A knowledge of these arts, made these girls of more value to society, and useful in very many respects.

...When I went to the Institution, the supply of Lumber for the Carpenter and cabinet shop was exhausted.

When I left it, there were about 10, thousand feet of Black wall nut, Cherry, Basswood, Maple, White Ash, Elm...and also of Pine lumber, thoroughly dried and fit for use immediately, properly piled in the ample shed which I had built for this purpose.

When I entered the duties of my office, we were only allowed by the Indian department...to keep thirty scholars, all told, but by proper management, we raised the Reputation of the Institution and were allowed to keep 50. And out to have more.

The Institution did a grand work, in a social, Intellectual, and a moral and Spiral sense. The young women, after spending the time they were allowed there, were highly appreciated as servants. The young men became good mechanics, good and efficient School Teachers, Missionaries, and much better farmers, than they otherwise would have been. At the present time, a large portion of the Local Teachers, Exhorters, Class Leaders, Stewards and Trustees, on our Indian Missions, were educated at our Institution.

While I was Governor of the Institution, we had fifty youths, male and female in constant attendance. I was Superintendant of our Sabbath School...our scholars recited with creditable accuracy, an average of 400 verses of the Scriptures per Sabbath. We had one girl 16 years of age, who committed and recited with great correctness 70 verses per Sabbath, or 700 in 10 weeks and was equally clever in all her other duties and Studies. She has since that active in the capacity of a School Teacher and did also much good work, part of the time she has work as a Servant in respectable families. And is a nice,

devoted and good girl.

In 1849, this Institution was established, at which time the Indians...surrendered this land to the Government, and through it, to the Methodist Church, for the purposes of an Industrial Institution...And the different Bands...Voted certain sums of Money...towards the erection of these Buildings and the Maintenance of this Institution...Sixty Dollars for each boy and girl, educated per year...The Grant of the land was made by the Chippewa Indians on the reserve...For which we bound to Educate, and teach the Girls sewing, knitting, Spinning and General house work. And the boys, 4 or 5 or more the Carpenter and joiner Trade, and also the Cabinet making Business, An equal number were to be taught the trade of Shoe Making, and all the other Boys were to taught the best method of farming. These Children were to be supplied with what clothing, and Boots and Shoes were needful, with good holsome plain food, the supply of Books necessary, and to be taught a good common English education.

By a most unfortunate oversight, the authorities of our Church...allowed the Indian agent, to take these Documents...There they remained in the office of the late Mr. McKenzie...Indian Agent for these Western Bands, and Resident in Sarnia...during about 30 years. During which time, the Government manifested very little disposition to do anything for the Institution. At times they were disposed to close it, and constantly proposing changes, and new conditions, making our circumstances anything but pleasant. There are a few of those still living, who know what ominous threats we received from the Government that they would close the Institution ...About July 1879, I had an intimation that these Documents...were found, and immediatly resolved I would get them...In a short time...I placed those Documents in the hands of the General Secretary...

Prior to this it was almost impossible to secure any aid from the Government...but since these Documents have been in their hands, they are much more liberal...more just. It was after this I obtained a thousand Dollars to erect the Stock Barn...At the same time our Mission work increased so fast...It was almost impossible to grant enough to carry the Institution work with efficiency...I scarcely ever received a remittence, without two thoughts being prominently put before my mind. 1st. The Board were straining its resources to grant what we were getting. 2nd Valued Brethren were suffering More, because of what we were using...Now the Government is much more liberal, and...our Missionary income has increased...

A few weeks before I removed from this important charge, the Rev. Dr. Sutherland came to see us and...said to me. Well, Mr. Cosford, after viewing the whole Establishment, "I do not see anything that I could wish changed. All your successor will need to do, is to step into your shoes and proceed with his work.

1882 - 1909
Rev. W. W. Shepherd 1882-1903 - Rev. T. T. George 1903-1909

1. **6 November 1882 Shepherd to DIA**

...1st...a Standard of Education such as you have mentioned for admission to the Inst. would be a great advantage. It would stimulate to more diligent study before coming. It would create a wholesome competition among the reserve schools. It would be much easier to classify the pupils when they enter the Institution. More work could be accomplished in a shorter term thus allowing a greater number to share the benefits of the Inst.

2nd I am in favor of the limit of four years for the Boys but not any less for the Girls. Those who learn trades with us divide the time about equally between the Shops & School during all of their term in the Inst. I do not think you can improve on that plan.

My experience has led me to the conclusion that it would be well to take the girls when about 13 & retain them for four years. So much depends on the inteligence culture & virtue of the Indian women.

3rd. A primary department would doubtless facilitate the work of the school but would involve the employment of an additional teacher and...an additional building...the extra outlay would be a good investment for the Indians.

The Government Certificate as suggested with the prospect of promotion and the Franchise is a much needed inducement or inspiration to study & work.

2. **22 November 1882 Christian Guardian Viator**

...It was my privilege recently to be a recipient of the hospitalities of the Institute for an evening, as distributed by the worthy and very able governor, Rev. W. W. Shepherd...The school-house is much too small for present necessities, and is furnished with the old-style box-seats and desks, which are generally dilapidated...

OBJECT OF THE INSTITUTE

is to give its pupils a good common English education, and instruct them in agriculture and other industrial pursuits. The boys are taught farming in all its branches, some of them carpentry, cabinet work, shoemaking, etc., and the girls sewing, knitting, spinning, and general housework. The teacher is Mr. Joseph A. Parsons, an undergraduate of Victoria, and is just the man for the situation, whether as teacher in the school or as instructor in the operations of the farm and the care of stock. The matron is Miss Margery Shaw, of St. John, N.B., and is also the lady for the situation. The general average attendance is between fifty and sixty pupils, who come from the various reserves in the western peninsula. The Department of Indian Affairs contributes $60 per head, up to fifty pupils...and all other expenses above that sum are supplemented by the Canada Methodist Missionary Society, at whose expense the Institute was furnished and equipped, and the farm stocked. To give an idea of the

WORKING OF THE INSTITUTE

I cannot do better than append the following programme: - The signal for the day's operations is announced by the loud tones of the bell at 5 A.M. This is a warning for all to get up, not excepting even the Governor; second bell at 5.45 A.M., notice for breakfast; third bell, breakfast; fourth bell, devotion. All to be over by 7 A.M. Then off to work til 9 A.M., when all assemble in the school-room and receive educational instruction till 12, and from 1 to 3 p.m., when another turn is taken at the farm and other industrial pursuits till 6 p.m. At 8 p.m. devotional services, and at 9 all retire for the night's repose. After the morning devotional services the programme for the day's operations is read out, and on Saturdays it provides for a full day's work. I was there on the morning of Saturday, September 30th, and the following

PROGRAMME WAS READ OUT:

To plough, A. McLeod; to cut corn, Peter Otter and J. C. Lewis, twenty-five rows each; to put up corn, W. Peters, J. J. Milliken, and J. Thomas, twenty-five rows each; to plough out potatoes with the horse, Prince, Joseph Sterling; to pick potatoes, Peter Willie, C. Huff, D. O. James, Eastman Albert, A. and J. Brissett, Talford B. Anderson, and T. and A. Fox; to pull rag weed, Peter Muskokomun, F. Fox, and L. W. Lalima; to provide wood and blacken shoes I. Thompson and W. Cloud. The carpenters, shoemakers...as usual. The result of the year's

FARMING OPERATIONS

was - forty tons of hay; eight acres of rye cut green for fodder; ten acres of millet - fifteen tons; forty-two acres of wheat, yielding 1,079 bushels; twenty acres of corn, well matured, and will yield fully 1,590 bushels in the cut; twenty-five to thirty acres oats, good, but not yet threshed; barley, 400 bushels; ten acres peas, good and clear of bugs; and about six acres of roots, consisting of potatoes, carrots, turnips, sugar beets, etc., and three acres of beans. Sixteen bushels of tomatoes were sent to market on that Saturday morning. Fifty-two acres of wheat for next year's crop had already been sown...

THE STOCK ON THE FARM

consists of ten working horses and colts, seventy-five head of cattle, twenty of which are milch cows...with two or three thoroughbreds. Six Leicester sheep, fifty Berkshire pigs, and 100 chickens...The butter for the consumption of the Institute is made on the place, and is first-class...

...I could not obtain a list of the pupils who had received instruction therein since its establishment, but was informed that many had distinguished themselves as teachers, ministers, farmers, etc...the Institute cannot possibly fail in imparting great benefits, and its influence must tend towards the elevation of the rising generations of our red Canadian brethren.

3. **2 April 1883 A. Sutherland**

The suggested changes in the conduct of Industrial Schools appear to be the following:

1.   An Educational Standard of Admission to be adopted.

2.   The time for girls and boys to remain at these Institutions to be limited to three and four years respectively, the last two years, in the case of boys, to be devoted exclusively to learning trades, attending school only at night.

3.   A Preparatory School in connection with Industrial Institutions.

4.   Government Certificates to be granted to those who qualify in the local Day Schools for entrance into the higher School.

5.   Granting Government Certificates to boys who have completed four years at the Institution, and have remained steadily at the trade learned thereat for a period of two years; such certificates to entitle them to enfranchisement and other advantages.

6.   All Institutions and Day Schools to be subject to regular Government Inspections the same as Common Schools among the white population.

7.   The Government Inspector to use his influence with the Indians to make the Indian Children attend the Day Schools, etc. etc.

...In regard to proposal No. 1...any regulation which will induce the Indians to keep their children steadily at the local Schools is highly desirable and it is quite possible an examination test might supply a much needed stimulus. At the same time, the standard should not be made too high and due notice should be given to the various Bands - a year at least - before the rule is enforced. Further, those who pass the Matriculation examination should be permitted to go to the higher School as a matter of right, and not merely of favor.   To hold out the prospect of admission to the higher School, and when the Certificate is gained refuse permission to enter would have a very injurious effect.

2...the time specified is altogether too short.   It would be too short in the case of white children, much more so in the case of Indian Youth, where the habits of years, not to speak of inherited tendencies, have to be overcome. Experience convinces us that the only way in which the Indians of this Country can be permanently elevated and thoroughly civilized, is by removing the children from the surroundings of Indian home life, and keeping them separated long enough to form those habits of order, industry, and systematic effort, which they will never learn at home.

The proposal that boys should spend the last two years exclusively in learning trades, and attend school at night, is...impracticable...Indian lads have no great love for study, and after having wrought at a trade all day it will be very difficult, if not altogether impossible, to induce them to spend their evenings in study.   The present system of giving part of the day to study and part to work is preferable, as it supplies that variety of employment

which is so necessary in the training of Indian Youth.

3.   A Preparatory School...might answer a good end, or at all events such arrangements as would admit of a classification of pupils.

4.   Government certificates to those who reach a certain standard in the Day Schools would have a good effect, provided they carried the right of admission into the Institution Schools.

5.   Certificates to those boys who had completed the Course and learned a trade would also be useful provided opportunity is afforded the boy to continue his trade. When leaving the Institutions they have no money wherewith to start business on their own account, and it is difficult for an Indian Youth to find employment in shops owned by white men.

6.   So far as I am aware all Schools conducted by the Missionary Society are now open to Government Inspection...

..I...submit...the following suggestions:

1.   Increase the number of pupils who may attend from 50 to say 100, and make such provision in the matter of School rooms, etc as will admit of classification of pupils under two separate teachers.   Give prizes for proficiency in the various branches.

2.   Fix the term of residence at <u>five</u> years for girls, and <u>six</u> years for boys, and make attendance for this term compulsory.   The return of the children to their homes, even temporarily, has a bad effect, while their permanent removal after one or two years residence results in the loss of all they gained.

3.   When boys have completed their term and learned a trade, give them not only certificates, but help to start in business, such as a good set of tools, and a small stock of material. If they have learned farming, give them land of their own on the reserve to which they belong, and advance a yoke of oxen and some implements, to be repaid out of annuities.

4.   Increase the number of trades taught at the Institutions, and make provision for the sale of surplus manufactured stock.

5.   Goods are often purchased from the Industrial Institutions by Indians, who give orders on their annuities in payment.   But in paying annuities, these orders are sometimes repudiated by Agents, and the money goes to Independant traders who hold similar orders.   If the design is to encourage these Industrial Institutions, Agents should be instructed to honor all proper orders...

4. 30 June 1883 Shepherd to DIA
...The average attendance of pupils for the year shows a slight excess over the number authorized by the Department.   Judging from the applications constantly coming in from the various bands, it would seem that the advantages afforded by the Institution are becoming better understood by the Indians, and I have no doubt that the

number of pupils could be easily doubled if we had buildings to afford the necessary accommodation. The conduct of the pupils has been, on the whole, most exemplary.

The work on the farm has been steadily prosecuted and shows encouraging results. The yield for the year just closed was the largest yet obtained. Those boys who are instructed in farm work are making commendable progress. One evidence of their efficiency is, that they are in great demand as farm laborers, and can command the highest wages. This, however, increases the difficulty of retaining them the full term in the Institution. The industrious habits acquired here, the method of doing everything at the proper time and season, together with the best appliances for doing so, must have a beneficial influence on their future.

The shoe and carpenter shops are managed by experienced foremen, and the five boys in the former and four in the latter are doing well. But in consequence of having no suitable market for our wares, the net profits are small, and the variety of work not sufficient to give them the fullest knowledge of the business.

The day school, under the able management of an under-graduate...Victoria University, is in a most flourishing condition. The thirst for knowledge awakened in many of the pupils is manifested daily by the eagerness with which they pursue their studies even in leisure hours...the want of a play-house is much felt, especially in stormy weather. Such a building would conduce greatly to the health and cheerfulness of the pupils and would also enable those who desire to study in leisure hours, to use the schoolroom without interruption. A modest expenditure in refitting the school room is also an urgent necessity.

Of the six boys who completed their term in the Institution during the year, four are farming, one is out of health, and the other is now filling the position of teacher on Walpole Island at a salary of $250, and for interpreting for one of the churches, $50. He is also Government interpreter. We have several boys at present who, if we retain, will be capable of teaching, some in one, others in two years. But the difficulty is just at this point. They are competent farmers and are offered quite as much or more to go as farm labourers, at present, as they can get as teachers after years of additional schooling. If the salary for teaching could be advanced to at least $350, it would be an incentive to additional study.

Of the seven girls who completed their term during the year, three went to service among the whites, one married, one has learned millinery and dress-making and the other two are with their friends.

5. 1883 Shepherd
...The produce of the farm this last year was the largest ever obtained in its history...state of things long hoped for by the managers of the Society's funds is likely ere long

to be realized...when all the expenses of the Institution will be covered, or nearly so, by the products of the farm and profits of the shops, together with the grant paid annually by the Indian Department.

To retain efficient officers in all the departments, we pay a little over $3,000 annually in salaries...the cost of boarding and clothing fifty pupils, and the wear and tear of machinery and implements...with the necessary improvements, amounts to a little over $5000 more.

We have been much encouraged in this good work by the strictly moral and, in some cases, devout lives of those under our charge. Of the fifty in attendance over thirty are members of our church, many of them have joined during the year, and nearly all attend class meeting voluntarily; and of those attending this social service we have heard as many as fifteen relate their experience in English at one service. Of the remaining twenty, some are members of other churches...

...it would be a great advantage to this Institution, and to the pupils themselves, if all who are admitted...were required to pass an entrance examination. It would be an inspiration to study before coming, and would enable us to show better results.

6. 1884 Shepherd
...the loss of a most amiable and efficient teacher, by temporary loss of health, which led to several changes, always injurious at the time, but...compensated by the efficiency of the present supply.

A most blessed religious influence has pervaded the establishment most of the year, resulting in the hopeful conversion of many of the pupils. One boy and one girl were forced to withdraw during the year, from failing health, and since have passed to their reward...leaving the fullest proof that they had gone to be with Jesus...

7. 30 June 1884 Shepherd to DIA
...The year will be memorable...on account of the disastrous flood...which swept the flats, taking over seventy acres of a most beautiful and promising harvest, together with a large amount of rail and board fence, which added very materially to the expenses of the year.

The introduction...of a carefully prepared system of marks, promotions and rewards, has proved a great incentive to study and general good conduct. Two pupils successfully passed the entrance examination for the High School at St. Thomas, and out of 103 successful candidates the two were numbers six and seven. Two others failed to pass on one subject. The conduct of the pupils has, on the whole, been most exemplary.

The plan of having all the school in three divisions and only two of them in school at the same time, has worked admirably...a teacher devoting his full time to two classes can accomplish more for them in two days than he could in three with four or five classes to divide his attention.

Although it is a regulation of the Institution that all pupils leaving without the permission of the Principal are considered dismissed and will not again be admitted, yet this is not found to be a sufficient penalty to prevent them from going at certain busy seasons when tempting offers are made or when they become restive over some imaginary grievance. This occurs sometimes when a few months more would enable them to pass for the High School. Could not this difficulty be largely obviated by the Department requiring all parents and guardians (as a conditions of their children being admitted to the advantage of the Institution) to sign articles of agreement binding the parents and guardians to continue the pupils the full time of the agreement?

Would it not be an additional inducement to the pupil to fulfil the terms of agreement if the Department would retain the annuity money during all the years of Institution life, to be refunded to the pupil, with interest, upon the production of certificate from the Principal showing that the terms of agreement had been fulfilled?

Again, if each pupil who succeeds in passing the entrance examination for the High School could have the promise of six months or one year at the school free of charge, would it not be a great incentive to study and to remain at the Institution. This could be accomplished without a very heavy expenditure owing to our proximity to...St. Thomas (twelve miles.) Fifty dollars per half year would settle the account, the pupils returning to the Institution from Friday till Monday of each week.

With these additional inducements to study and the improvements on the building completed, we doubt not but that in a very few years we could supply a large number of teachers for the Indian work.

8. 15 July 1884 S. J. Commego, Joseph White, James Williams, John P. Lewis, Lefontaine Atthill
We the undersigned pupils of the Mount Elgin Industrial School hereby make our statements in relative to the treatment we receive at the said Institution at the hands of those who have the charge of it. We complain that too much work is imposed upon us so that our tuition is limited to only about seventeen hours per week on an average. The board we get is often insufficient and impalatable from the fact of the meat which is given to us sometimes being tainted, and we frequently get stale bread. Upon these grounds we made our complaints to the Principal Rev. W. W. Shepherd and solicited better treatment at least during the harvest. We did this because we were always made to understand by the Principal that if at any time we were dissatisfied in any thing to let him know of the fact so as to enable him to attend the same with a view to rectify any source of dissatisfaction but instead of this being done we were ordered to leave the institution by the Principal at least those of us who had the audacity to make our grievances known to him in

writing. That it is very much against our wish to leave the Institution for we earnestly desire to get an education, and will return to it as soon as this matter is seen into by the proper authorities, and if it were so arranged that our expulsion be not confirmed by the Indian Department, when it originated from so slight a cause as has been in this instance...early investigation being made to the complaints above mentioned...

9. 19 August 1884 Chase
...enclose the Document of Complaints...the Indian Youths the Pupils...felt greived they made the complaints...I hope the Department may think sufficient importance to make the corrections that are made by the Indian Youths...When the Pupils were ordered by Mr. Shepherd then thirteen left. Boys and Girls left the Institute now wandering in Caradoc and Sarnia...
...There are numbers of families of Chippewa Indians in Caradoc bring charges against Mr. Shepherd...he having received Munsee Indian Children into the Institute - contrary to first agreement...made by the Chippewas of Munseytown, to place two hundred Acres of land to erect the Buildings for the use of the Institute...with J.B.Clench...No Indians will have the privillege to the Institute only those Bands of Indians that contribute towards the Erection of Builds and who contribute to the maintances of Pupils...
I do hope the Department may see the necessity of forming a Board of Trustees...to see the better management, to come up fully to the expectation of the Indians...

10. 16 September 1884 Gordon to Supt. Gen. DIA
...I have been repeatedly there at meal time and saw the quantity and quality of food provided the Scholars and thought they got plenty of good wholesome food.
Indians will complain, and as the Department well knows, very often for very little reason.

11. 27 September 1884 Gordon to Supt. Gen. DIA
....on the 20th instant...Revd. W. W. Shepherd...made the following statement to me in reply to the various complaints made to the Department against him by the pupils who left the Institution.
1st, the School hours in the Institution are the same as the hours taught in the public Schools of the Province, with the addition of ½ day on Saturdays. The whole School is in three divisions, two of which are in School, and one out at farm and shop work and the general work of the house, by this arrangement the Senior division of the School, gets four full days or 24 hours a week, the other two divisions get three and one half days or 21 hours a week. It must be obvious, that a teacher having only two divisions to attend to at the same time, must be able to accomplish more good to them than if he had the

three to attend to. When any division is in School, the whole of that division is in, thus keeping the whole division at its work together.

2nd, the Baking is done there 3 or 4 times a week, and bread cannot be much stale; every baking as all housekeepers know are not always equally good, but the effort is to have them as complete as possible and the object is to give all the pupils enough. All the meat of the Institution is put up by the sugar cure method, and as carefully as possible, and that the complaint (giving tainted meat) is unfounded.

3rd With reference of turning any of the Scholars away from the Institution, the facts are as follows.

Lefontaine Atthill, was not a pupil of the Institution then, and had not been for over two years previously but was employed for a short time for farm work, and was dismissed as any other party would be liable to, who might not be giving satisfaction.

James Williams completed his term twelve months ago, is a shoemaker by trade, and received money from Mr. Shepherd to furnish himself with a kit of tools when his time was up, he wished to return to the institution again for a short time, with a view of getting a certificate to teach, and was found when taken back, to be too exacting and unwilling to conform to the rules of the Institution as he had done before. He had the option of conforming to the rules or of withdrawing, and he had done the latter.

Joseph White's time was out and had permission to remain or go as he thought proper. The three so mentioned within, were not properly pupils of the Institution.

James Comego and John P Lewis, made certain untruthful and unreasonable statements in writing to the Principal, which they were required to withdraw or leave. And as they would not do the former, they had to do the latter. There was no dismissal from the Institution in any of the cases, but the rules...must be maintained, and if Scholars will not conform to them, they cannot remain there, as very few unruly and disobedient Scholars would very soon destroy all management in any Institution.

Mr. Shepherd feels that if the School is going to be a success, as he is doing every endeavour to make it such, he must have the rules obeyed, and cannot [sustain] any young man there, who appears unwilling to obey or conform to the rules of the Institution. I [?] now give the Department the [?] of the Revd Mr. Shepherd, of the cause of the five Scholars leaving the Institution, and the Department will see that the chief difficulty lay with themselves.

12. 1884 Carson

June...The room for teaching is not well furnished, the desks are neither adapted to the size nor the comfort of the pupils, and the interior is wanting in that bright cheery appearance so congenial to both the teacher and pupils: a little painting, whitewashing and a few pictures, with the necessary maps would remove the objection.

Thirty-six pupils were present, and others were working on the farm or in the house: during my visit, attention was paid to the character of the teaching in order...I might estimate the probable progress of the pupils...the grand difficulty is to reach the pupils' minds thru the English language. The teacher holds a third class certificate and appears to be energetic and painstaking. In my opinion he does not possess the requisite skill and tact to teach this school well: there should be in charge one of our best second class teachers. If the teachers of the other schools are to be trained here, it is of the first importance that the teaching, discipline, and management be of a high order; these can only be secured by the employment of a thoroughly competent instructor.

December...there were twenty-eight, besides a large class doing work on the farm...the teaching...is fair in the Institution [and very inferior in all the other schools...For the most part, the Indian tongue is used in the play-ground, and by the teacher to give explanations]...to this school we must look for the teachers who will succeed those on the Reserve. This summer two passed entrance to the High School, and at the Christmas Examination others may succeed. If these would spend a few weeks in a good Public School under the instruction of the teacher, they would suit very well to take charge of the schools on the Reserve...

13. 20 December 1884 Whiting

The closing term has been prosperous in every respect. ...class of eight are preparing for entrance examination... A number of improvements have been made, and a new building erected...the lower storey is intended for a playroom for the students during recreation hours, and contains also an extensive lavatory. The upper storey may be used for a schoolroom or for religious services. The whole building...presents a very neat appearance...

14. 1885 Shepherd

...steady growth and prosperity in every part of our work, industrial, educational, and religious. We have rejoiced during the year in the hopeful conversion of more than one-third of all the pupils...

Within a year five pupils have obtained teaching certificates to teach on any reserve in the province. At present two of the five are teaching, and the other three are still at school.

The play-house...now so far completed that the first flat is used for a lavatory and playroom...the second story makes an excellent reading and study room for the boys.

The re-flooring and fitting up anew of the pupils' dining-hall...with an outside entrance from the play-ground, adds much to its comfort.

The school-room is enlarged and much improved by the removal of the lavatory, and by new improved modern desks...

The extension of the south end of the main building...will...supply a much felt want, by furnishing a play-room and lavatory on the first flat for the girls, and on the second flat enlarged accommodation in the tailoring department, and in the third story additional dormitories.

15. 30 June 1886 Shepherd
...average attendance of pupils...only a fraction of the number...who applied for admission during the year.

Within less than two years, nine of our pupils have obtained certificates to teach, and four of them have taught successfully for one year each, while the others have continued their studies in view of greater efficiency.

The pupils, with few exceptions, have made commendable improvement in all their studies, and, in the various branches of industry taught have evinced a desire to be efficient workers.

The moral conduct of the pupils has been highly commendable and inspires hope for the future. The health of all has been such that only one call from a physician has been required during the year...

Every reasonable effort has been made to so increase the productiveness of the farm and the profits of the shop, that this, together with the amount paid by the Department to the society, might cover the annual expenditure, but up to date the revenue has not been equal to the expenditure by some hundreds annually.

16. 1885 Carson
...New desks...have replaced those condemned in a former report. The school room is neat and clean. A good blackboard is required...maps and a large numeral frame...

Fourteen girls and twenty-one boys were studying; ten boys and nine girls were at work on the farm or in the Institution. The studies and work are alternated, four days of the week being devoted to the former, two to the latter. There are three classes, corresponding...the 2nd, 3rd, and 4th classes in our public Schools. At the Christmas examinations in 1884, several passed to a High School.

The pupils are healthy looking and tidy in appearance...

Mr. Whiting, the present teacher, has been more successful than many of his predecessors...he works very hard, and conscientiously endeavors to discharge duties that require rare attainments of both head and heart. He withdraws his services at vacation to enter the ministry...

I was shown through some of the rooms, and found them scrupulously clean. In this connection I urgently request that the Institution be repainted. It is sadly in need of this, and the cost is trifling compared with the cheerful effect it would have on the pupils.

...the work done on the farm and in the Institution is based on a correct principle, and...must have a powerful influence in stimulating the Indians to greater exertion on their farms and in their homes. Boys and girls trained here go back to the reserves with improved characters, and an increased knowledge of farming, handiwork, and housekeeping; they should succeed in teaching those

among whom they dwell, a great deal that makes life happy and progressive...I would advise that as many as possible get their training here...present accommodation would suit sixty instead of fifty children. An increase of ten would add much to the usefulness of the training...

17. 1886 Carson
...Institution is now capable of giving adequate instruction to the children in attendance. The teacher has had three years' experience in a Public School, besides being an undergraduate of Toronto University. The frequent change of teacher is very detrimental to the progress of the pupils...The pupils are healthy, well clad, clean and, so far as I could judge, contented. Their wants appear to be fully met...to be an Indian child in this Institution is to know nothing of the hardships of many white children.

18. 19 February 1886 Sec. Supt. Gen. to A. Sutherland
...the Supt. Genl. has no objection to effect being given to the...recommendations...the standard of education at those Institutions being raised and the pupils passing a matriculation Examination...the length of time the pupils shall remain at the Institutions...a certificate being granted a child who has passed three years at the local Day School and qualified...for entry into a higher school, and...boys who have completed four years at the Institution and have remained steadily at the trade learnt thereat for a period of two years after...presenting a further certificate which...would entitle them to enfranchisement.

19. 17 May 1887 Carson
...School room is very satisfactory...airy, well-furnished, clean and tidy. A few maps are wanted...Good desks. Good board, hardly large enough. Well heated and well lighted. No special yard, but plenty of room for girls and boys. Good closets. Plenty of good water...trees and walks...The accommodation is good. 59 are attending, 43 in school to-day, and 16 at work on the farm. Those pupils examined did middling. There is difficulty in examining owing to language. More attention should be given to English. Pupils are not ready in answering. Discipline, order and management are fair. Teacher is industrious and anxious. I would like more vim or energy in the work...to rouse the pupils. The school promises well, better than in the past. It is very difficult to get a teacher perfectly adapted to the work to be done here.

20. 30 June 1887 Shepherd
...All the classes have made commendable progress... The large number who have obtained certificates as teachers within a few years has been increased by the addition of three more at the late examination.

...thirteen miles from the nearest Collegiate Institute...it is expensive and difficult to send pupils who have passed the entrance examination and are anxious to go.

The work on the Industrial and in many respects Model Farm has been maintained at a right state of efficiency, affording the farm boys an excellent opportunity of becoming acquainted with the best methods of doing all kinds of farm and garden work, and how to manage teams, stock, and all kinds of machinery pertaining to agriculture and horticulture...

For want of a suitable market for what we could manufacture in carpenter and shoe shops and tailoring department, our work in this respect is largely confined to the wants of the institution and those employed by it. This year, however, has been exceptional for the carpenter shop, as the institution had the contract for building the new...council house on the reserve.

21. January 1888 Mrs. Shepherd to Mrs. Parker
...opened under the management of...Dr. Rice, who after a short time was succeeded by...Rev. Dr. Rose, who brought to the work the freshness of early, vigorous manhood, great enterprise, and indomitable perseverance.

The aim of this Institute...has been to educate and Christianize the Indian youth of both sexes from all parts of the Province...in all the subjects taught in the public schools...including more than a year of the High School work, and to give them as accurate a knowledge of our language as the limited time will admit...In addition to this the large industrial farm and shops afford the boys a training in agriculture, horticulture and the different branches of mechanism in which many of them become very efficient. The girls are taught tailoring, dress-making, laundrying, and general house work...

The supreme aim is to compass the pupil during his whole institution life with healthy religious influences and example...more than two-thirds have made a profession of religion...During the six years of our management 264 pupils have shared the benefits of the Institution...

...the Indians gave the land for the Industrial farm...to be under the control of our Church so long as used for industrial purposes, and the Government furnished the money to construct the main buildings, and have made additional grants for enlargements and improvements.... also pays $60 for each pupil annually, while the Church is amenable to the Government for proper management, and is required to give quarterly returns to the Government showing the attendance and the advancement of each pupil...

...what are the conditions under which an Indian boy or girl is admitted to the Institute! They must be able to read in the second book, and work the simple rules of arithmetic. The Institute supplies board, clothes, text-books, etc., so that it is education and training without cost to the pupils. It is very necessary to have a competent officer at the head of each department, and as there are nine departments, beside the principals, the

annual expenses of running the Institute are very heavy.

All the officers...are professors of religion, and a revival meeting just closed has resulted in the hopeful conversion of nearly all the pupils...

22. 30 June 1888 Shepherd
...of those who completed their term and withdrawn during the year, four have attended the High School in Sarnia. Two have received appointments as teachers. One is working at the carpenter business and the rest returned to their homes.

The moral conduct of the pupils has been highly commendable, and about two-thirds of the number have made a profession of religion...

23. 1889 Shepherd
...The removal, by death, of a bright and promising girl marks the first break in the institution during the eight years' term of the present governor. The loss, by fire, of the boys' play-house, including lavatory, clothing-room and junior division school-room, with their contents, placed the work at a great disadvantage for a time. The prospect...of a new building, on a larger and more commodious scale, is encouraging. The advancement made by the pupils in their regular studies, and in the various branches of industry, has quite maintained their former high record. Fully two-thirds of their number have made a profession of saving faith...The new barn...is nearly completed, and is a model in many respects...

24. 30 June 1889 Shepherd
...the industrial...farm has been maintained at a high state of efficiency...furnishing excellent training for the boys and yielding profitable financial results.

The different branches of mechanism have been well managed by skilful foremen, who know well how to communicate instructions, so as to secure the best results for the apprentice boys, and, with many modern appliances and a skilful arrangement of all duties work is reduced to a pleasant employment...

We acknowledge our great indebtedness to the Department for a timely and generous grant to rebuild on a large scale - a play house, lavatory, reading room, and junior division school room, all in one building...we hope to...occupy the new quarters after the summer holidays.

The decision of the Department to enlarge the main building here, at an early date, to accommodate 120 pupils, is anticipated with much pleasure. The plans for enlargement...promise greatly to add to the beauty and attractiveness of the building...the moral conduct of the pupils has been highly commendable.

25. 1889 Carson
First Half-yearly Visit: -The school-room is good, it is neat and clean, but too small for the attendance...School

yard, fenced, closed in satisfactorily. There should be another room or more, also one or more additional teachers employed. Standing of pupils, fair; discipline, order, etc. good. Urban Pugsley, the teacher, does his best, but he cannot do the work of a couple of teachers. *Second Half-yearly Visit*...71 children are now attending... some do very well, the classification is too advanced for attainments of pupils...no satisfactory progress can be made till another teacher is engaged.

26. June 1889 Williams

I will try to write a short composition about this place. It is called Mount Elgin Industrial Institution. First thing I shall say is about farming, because I am one of the farmers, and I like that best, better than any other work. I will leave this for a little while. I will tell you something first. First time I came here it was in 4th of September 1884, A.D. I was very lazy, because I never worked when I was home but just play, play, play day after day. So when I came I was here about two or three weeks, then Mr. William W. Shepherd told me to go in the Shoe Shop and be shoemaker. So I went and I was very glad. When I got there I thought that was very easy work, but afterwards I found out that it is not very easy work always sitting down and sewing, hammering, fixing the old shoes, and I am always watching how am I going to sew. So I got tired of it, and I was very glad when I got out of it too, and now to-day I am one of the farmers. The reason I like to be farmer is because I will be always working outside and be working with the team every day, and sow all kinds of grain such as wheat, oats, peas and barley. And plant some corn, potatoes, cabbage, turnips and carrots, and raise some cattle, and then sell them all for hundreds of dollars; and then when I would get the money I would buy some more land, and some farmer's implements to work with. And while I am here Mr. Shepherd always gives me a team to work with when I am going to work, so as to know how to get started after I'll leave here. And we are doing lots of work in one day, I suppose it would take a man about a week or more to do the same work, as much as we can do in one day. First thing we do in morning is to clean the horses. There are eight horses for working and two for driving, and we always clean them first thing in morning, and then when we get that done we would get ready for our breakfast, and we get up at five o'clock in morning, but on Sundays we get up at six o'clock A.M. And after we get our breakfast we would get ready to go to church, and after we would have our dinner we have our Sunday School in our school room, etc.

27. 30 June 1890 Shepherd

...The pupils, with one or two exceptions, have made commendable progress in all the branches of study. The subjects of study are the same as in the public schools of Ontario, and the examination papers for promotion are from the Educational Department. Pupils after passing the entrance examination for the high-school, who still continue their studies with us till they secure a third class certificate, are promised their expenses while attending the model school...excellent work done in the school, in the shops and on the farm.

Among the repairs and improvements...was the completion of recreation hall...furnishes an excellent play-room and lavatory in the basement. A reading room and study are on the second flat, while the third story is occupied by one division of the school.

28. 1890 H. D. Johnson

First Visit- Mr. Urban Pugsley's Room. The school-room is a good one, and kept neat and clean...The school yard is fenced and kept in good order; it is rather small for the present attendance, but...Mr. Shepherd, told me that it was his intention to enlarge it...The pupils were well dressed and looked comfortable...The standing of the pupils is fair. The discipline, order and general management are good...Mr. Pugsley does his work very satisfactorily, and handles his classes with consummate skill. He is an excellent man for the position.

Mr. Morley Shepherd's Room...He holds a third class non-professional certificate. He teaches very well and shows a good deal of tact in the management of his classes. There are twenty-eight pupils in this room... Everything in the room is in excellent condition...standing of the pupils fair; order, discipline, etc., good...

The pupils attending both rooms speak English with a fair degree of fluency.
Second Visit Miss Hales' Room....is very good. It is well kept...The desks, board, lighting, etc., are all in a very satisfactory state...Miss E. E. Hales, who holds a Second Class Provincial certificate, has had about ten years' experience. She presents her subjects well, and is very thorough in her teaching. The standing of the pupils in this room in writing, drawing, spelling, and the mechanical operations in the simpler rules in arithmetic is very good. The reading lacks expressions. The pupils speak fair English in both rooms. The discipline, order and management are very satisfactory.

Miss H. Rice's Room.- The school room is excellent. It is well kept...Miss H. Rice, holds a Third Class Non-professional certificate, has had no professional training, or experience, except as a tutor. She teaches fairly well and insists on thoroughness in all her subjects. The standing of the pupils in writing, spelling composition, and the mechanical operations in the simple rules in arithmetic is very good; in history and reading, only fair. The discipline, order and management are very satisfactory. The yard, closets, water supply, etc., are all very satisfactory.

Since the Institute re-opened after the midsummer holidays eighty-six pupils have entered the school. At present there are eighty-two in attendance...Ten in the First Part of the First Book; thirty-five in the Second Part of the First Book; twenty-eight in the Second Book; three in the Third Book; and six in the Fourth Book.

All the pupils are taught to work. Some of the boys are taught farming, some shoemaking, and some carpentry. The girls are taught housework as well as plain sewing, knitting and laundry work. Two-thirds of the time each pupil is required to attend school, and the other third is devoted to whatever trade or calling the pupil is learning. The only day that is observed as a holiday during the Christmas holidays is Christmas day, the school goes on as usual during the rest of the time. On every Saturday there is school one half of the day, so that each pupil attends school four days in the week, and is gaining a knowledge of manual labor the other two days.

29. 1891 Shepherd

At the close of the tenth year of our management of this important Institution, it will be proper to review, noting the advancement made during the decade.

We call attention first to the financial gain, although not the most important...in the ten years between 1871 and 1881, in addition to the income from the farm and shops, together with the amount received from the Indian Department, it was necessary to draw on the Missionary treasury to the amount of $12,000 to cover all expenses. While during the last ten years the income from the farm and shops, and the amount paid by the Indian Department, has been sufficient to cover all expenses and make large improvements. During the same period the assets of the Institution have increased a little over $3,000, so that the total gain over the former decade is not less than $15,000.

...During the ten years the average attendance has risen from fifty to eighty, and when the present enlargement is completed we hope to accommodate 120. This enlargement is the more desirable as we have had to refuse a large number of pupils each year for want of accommodation.

Our school hours are similar to the Public Schools, with the addition of Saturday afternoon, and one hour each evening on home work, under the care of a teacher. Our system of having the pupils two days in school and one out, gives all the advantages of a graded school, while it means to the pupil four days each week in school and two days at some branch of industry. The only public holidays we observe during the school year are Christmas and the 24th of May, and the summer vacation is correspondingly extended.

During the past six years some fifteen pupils have obtained certificates entitling them to teach on any Indian reserve in the Province, and most of them have taught or are teaching.

Our pupils have quite sustained their high reputation for good moral character. They have been regular at public worship, and have been largely helped through our excellent Sabbath-school.

30. 1891 H. D. Johnson

Miss E. E. Hall's Room. - The school-room is very good and well kept...The standing of the pupils in reading, writing, spelling, drawing and arithmetic is very satisfactory. A very decided improvement has taken place in the reading...also...in the readiness with which the pupils answered, and in the command of language displayed by them during their recitations...

Miss McKellar's Room.- This room is in excellent order. It is kept neat, clean and tidy. A larger board has been put in since my last visit...Kate McKellar, who now holds a third-class professional certificate; she has had no professional training or experience. The standing of the pupils is generally very good in all the subjects taught, except the reading in Part II, and that is deficient. The work done by the pupils in the Fourth Class will compare very favorably with that done by the pupils in the same form in the Public Schools.

The order, discipline and management in both rooms are very satisfactory.
Second Visit
...2nd November, and found 37 boys and 35 girls registered...Mr. Shepherd, informed me that several others were out on leave of absence for a few days.
Miss E. E. Hales' room...continues to do her work well. The standing of the pupils in writing, drawing, spelling, reading and arithmetic is very good. A very decided improvement has taken place in the oral reading, many of the pupils read now with fair expression as well as understanding what they read...
Miss Annie Campbell's room...well kept...The teacher ...holds a Second Class Provincial Certificate. She had only had charge of the room for a few days at the time of my visit, but from her manner and her methods of presenting her subjects to the pupils as well as her management of the classes, I feel...she will do excellent work.
Two of the pupils passed the High School entrance examination...last July...Alexander Charles, stood third in order of merit in a list of 73 successful candidates.

31. 30 June 1892 Shepherd
...thirty-three have withdrawn during the year; eleven of whom had attended less than one year...12...between 1 and 2 years...6...between 3 and 4 years...3...between 4 and 5 years...1...between 5 and 6 years...

Among the withdrawn during the year was John Case, of Muncey, a competent mechanic who obtained a situation in London...This boy has a certificate as a teacher, but prefers to work at his trade.

Another, Levi Doxtator, of Oneida, who passed the entrance examination, is now living in the home of one of the missionaries, and expects to continue his studies.

Out of the seventeen pupils who during the last few years have taken certificates as teachers, about one-half are teaching or have taught, but the salaries paid on the reserves have not much attraction for our male pupils, some of whom obtained high wages for work in the tunnel at St. Clair, and are now employed on the steamers on the lakes.

Within a distance of ten miles of the reserve, there are not fewer than twenty of our ex-pupils working for white men. The same is true with regard to ex-pupils belonging to other reserves who acquired a good knowledge of farming while here.

The progress made in the schools has been most satisfactory...

The health record of the school for the year has been all that could be desired. We have not required a professional call from a physician during the year. During the eleven years of our incumbency we have only had one death in the establishment.

Since the architect gave his decision that the building is not sufficiently strong to carry an additional story, and cannot with safety be enlarged as proposed, we have been exceedingly anxious to know what will be done. The pressure is upon us for enlarged accommodations, but we are compelled to refuse many applications. A new building with all modern improvements is what we should have with the least possible delay.

32. 1892 H. D. Johnson

First Visit...2nd June...86 pupils registered..

...Miss Hales has charge of the Second and Third Forms. She does her work well. The standing of the pupils in reading, spelling, writing, drawing, composition, geography and arithmetic was good. The order, discipline and management were very satisfactory.

...Miss Campbell has charge of the pupils in the First, Fourth and Fifth Forms...does her work well, especially in the primary classes. The pupils in all the subjects did very satisfactory work. The order, discipline and management in this room were excellent.

The pupils in both rooms speak English with a very fair degree of fluency and as a general rule understand what they read. The reading and oral composition in Part I and Part II classes have improved very much...

Second Visit...November 4th...100 pupils enrolled, 49 boys and 51 girls...Mr. Shepherd...was obliged to decline applications for admission of several...through lack of accommodation.

Miss Hales' Room...all in a very satisfactory state. Miss Hales still continues to teach well...Most of the pupils read with a very fair degree of expression and understand what they read...

Miss Campbell's Room.-Everything about this room is in capital order...Miss Campbell still continues to do very

excellent work...The standing of the pupils in reading, writing, arithmetic, spelling, drawing, history, geography, grammar and composition is good. The work done by the fourth class...would compare very favorably with that done by pupils of the same grade in the public schools...

33. 30 June 1893 Shepherd

...twenty-five have withdrawn during the year, four...had attended less than one year, seven between one and two years, six between two and three years, four between three and four years, four between four and five years.

After refusing more than fifty applications for admission (for want of accommodation) still our average attendance was a fraction over ninety-three pupils. A new building with all modern appliances and accommodation for one hundred and fifty pupils is our great want.

The fact that our pupils come from so many reserves and some of them at a great distance, makes it difficult for us to report just what they are doing after closing their term at the institution.

Three pupils wrote on the entrance examination in June and one on third-class work... We have had very satisfactory results from the industrial farm...

...how the pupils are employed who have left this institution during the last four years.

	Boys	Girls	Total
Hired on farms	24		24
Farming for self	12		12
At service		12	12
Teaching school	2	1	3
Readmitted	3	4	7
At home		6	6
Sailing	4	4	
Married	8	12	20
Unknown	4	3	7
Total	57	38	95

34. 1893 Shepherd

...The fact that the Government has abandoned the idea of enlarging the old building, and decided on the erection of a new one, with accommodation for 130 pupils, is satisfactory to all concerned. The prospect of enlarged usefulness is an inspiration in overcoming the difficulties and discomforts connected with the present building.

35. 24 June 1894 Shaw to the Dep. Supt. Gen. DIA

...to reply to yours relative to a proposed change in vacation of the Mount Elgin...School.

For nearly thirty years there was no vacation, and the pupils were supposed to be in the school every day. During that period not one of them ever obtained a Certificate as a public school teacher.

Eight years ago...it was agreed to adopt the regular industrial system which gave the pupils two days in the school...This carried the advantage of a graded school.

The senior classes were given four full days in the school each week, and two days to the different branches of industry. The junior pupils averaged three and a half days in school and two and a half days at the different industries.

At the same time the summer vacations were commenced, and were limited to six weeks, with two weeks added for Christmas.

It was found however that the winter vacation was impracticable, as the pupils lacked the clothing necessary, and the Christmas vacation was added to that of the summer making it two months. Four years ago the vacation was extended to three months...

To make up for this it was decided to have school every Saturday afternoon, and to have the teachers present for one hour each evening to assist the pupils in the study of the lessons for the following day.

To all these changes, the Indian Department consented, and the results have justified its wisdom. Twenty pupils have obtained Certificates in eight years, while for thirty previously there was none; while there has been an equally marked improvement in the different branches of industry. Before the establishment of a regular vacation the principal and teachers were greatly perplexed with pupils going home without permission, and some times they were almost forced to grant them leave of absence to prevent them from running away. It was difficult to enforce discipline and the efficiency of the school was greatly impaired because pupils were absent. Under the present arrangement these difficulties are largely obviated.

It is well to bear in mind that Mt. Elgin gets its pupils usually from 16 and often from 20 different Reserves. The pupils earn money to take them home and return, and as a matter of course they require time for this purpose.

As the teachers now give nine months unremitting attention it is very desirable that they should be free for the usual vacation.

To make the changes proposed would be a disadvantage to the school and a disappointment to the parents.

36. 1894 H. D. Johnson

First Visit...14th of April...102 pupils enrolled...The general discipline and management of the school as a whole are excellent.

...Miss Hales...continues to do her work thoroughly. The standing of the pupils in reading, writing, drawing, spelling, geography and arithmetic is good, in grammar it is only fair. The pupils generally read with a fair degree of expression and understand the meaning of what they read.

The order, discipline and management are good...

...Miss Campbell is still in charge of the...First, Fourth and Fifth Classes, and continues to do good work.

The standing of the pupils in reading, spelling, writing, history, composition, and geography is good; in the case of the Fourth Class the standing of the pupils in grammar and arithmetic is only fair. The work done by the Fifth Form pupils is generally excellent, especially in book-keeping, writing and drawing.

The order, discipline and management are excellent...
*Second Visit...*21st of November...ninety-three pupils...

Miss Hales's.-The school-room is kept clean, neat and tidy...Miss Hales continues to do her work well; her teaching is thorough, and she possesses the tact and patience required for the work...The standing of the pupils in writing, drawing, spelling, grammar, geography, composition and arithmetic is good. The pupils appear to comprehend the meaning of what they read fairly well, but their expression in many cases is deficient, the result no doubt of their peculiar native accent. The discipline, order, and arrangement are good.

Miss Maggie Smith's-The teacher in this room has been changed...now in charge of Miss Maggie Smith, who holds a third-class professional certificate, and has also passed the Junior Leaving Examination. She has had six months experience in a Public School...She presents her subjects well and is painstaking with her pupils. Her pupils did satisfactory work. Everything about this room is in excellent order and well kept...

It is worthy of mention that a pupil (Miss Melissa Thomas) from this Institute was successful in passing the Public School Leaving Examination held in July...She is still attending and taking up "Primary" work. I was much pleased with her grammar and composition.

37. 30 June 1894 Shepherd

The work of another year has been successfully carried on with less anxiety to the management than in former years. The substantial advancement made by the pupils both in the work of the school and in the different branches of industry has quite maintained the good record of other years. Within the last ten years nearly twenty of our pupils have successfully passed the entrance examination for the high school. We added one to this number this year whose marks placed him as number eleven out of nearly one hundred successful competitors. Our success in the industrial department, especially in making the farm boys competent workmen, has militated against retaining them in the school, as they can command the pay or nearly so of a white man, and would not get much more if they studied for a teacher's certificate...three of our pupils who have teachers certificates are working for farmers quite near the institution and claim they can save more money in this way than they could as teachers. ...The cost of the institution for the year including management was in excess of $10,000. The percapita tax, $60 each for eighty-five pupils, and the income of the industrial farm have nearly settled the bill...

The moral conduct of the pupils for the year has been very encouraging. They have been regular in their attendance at the public services and have been carefully instructed in the great truths of the Bible.

38. 14 August 1895   Shepherd Annual Report

The schools have maintained their excellent record of other years. Three pupils were this year added to the list of those who have teachers' certificates. Thirty new pupils were admitted...an equal number withdrew, most of them having completed the term for which they entered. The average attendance was slightly in excess of the number authorized by the department, which is eighty-five. The health of the pupils has been excellent.

Out of the sixteen boys who retired during the year, one has charge of a school on Walpole Island; another is a student of a French institute in Montreal, and a third is married and settled on a farm on the Oneida Reserve. Eight of the others have had employment as farmers with white men, and are doing well. The other five returned to their homes on the reserves. Out of the fourteen girls who retired three are married, one to a white man; two have since died; and the rest returned to their homes on the reserves.

The two new silos...have proved a complete success... The butter and milk supply of the winter was nearly equal to that of the summer...the beef cattle were in part shipped from the stables.

The year has been one of the most prosperous in the history of the institute. The returns from the industrial farm have amply supplied the institute with beef, pork, milk, butter and flour, also potatoes, turnips, carrots and cabbage, etc., in abundance.

Our returns from the sale of shipping cattle and horses largely supplemented the income from the department, making it possible, in addition to the year's expenses, to pay for fully $500.00 worth of improvements...addition of a first-class steel wind-mill...and a system of piping by which the water is elevated into tanks, so as to supply all departments...

the contractor...is pushing the work of the new institute... The prospect of entering early in 1896 our new home fitted up with all modern appliances is an inspiration that we greatly enjoy.

39. 9 September 1895   Wankey to Reed

...I made the necessary arrangements to send my son to the Mount Elgin School, the local Missionary here having authority from the Principal to get pupils for that Institution. After a time I am told that all the vacancies were filled up.

Now I want to ask your Department that can Non Treaty and illegitimate children who contribute nothing towards the keep of the school supplant rightful owners of the funds supplied by them is right?

40. 17 February 1896   McDougall to Dep. Supt. Gen. DIA

...I have been requested by certain members of the Oneidas of the Thames Band to ask the Department - for information as to whether Rev. W. W. Shepherd...should provide the pupils at that Institution with all necessary clothing and shoes, also whether children from the Oneida Reserve who are attending the Institution as pupils have the same rights as children from other Bands.

...advise me how much money is paid annually to this Institution by the government for each pupil attending. And all that is expected they shall receive in return...

41. 24 February 1896   Dep. Supt. Gen. DIA to McDougall

...all the Industrial Schools furnish maintenance and a certain quantity of clothing to the pupils at such Institutions, but there is no reason why the parents, if able, should not supplement such allowance.

...children from the Oneida Reserve attending the Mt. Elgin Institute are entitled to the same privileges as children of other Bands.

The Department contributes $60 per annum for each of 85 pupils in attendance.

42. 1896   Wadsworth Report

...The staff...Rev. W. W. Shepherd, principal; Mrs. Shepherd, general assistant; Miss Shepherd, M.E.L., first teacher; Miss Hales, second teacher; Miss Kilbert, matron; Louisa Delary (Indian girl, assistant cook; Alfred Lane, cook; John Coulter, shoemaker instructor; Wm. Wilson, carpenter and general overseer of farming; Wm. Price, stockman, (overseer of live-stock); T.H. Boyce, gardener; Samuel Shepherd, farmer; Jno. Kepego, (Indian), farm labourer.

...No holidays are given or allowed to the staff; all days or parts of days lost time are deducted from their wages. Farm hands (pupils included when engaged at farm-work) work from 7 a.m. to 6 p.m. with one hour allowed for dinner. During the long holidays at midsummer, fifteen boys and ten girls are kept in the institute, and work on dairying and the farm, during haying and harvest, also on root crops; to these wages are then paid aggregating $300.

Routine - Winter Rules

5.30 a.m.-First bell for rouse, making fires, and stockmen go to the stables.
6.30 "   Breakfast for pupils and labourers.
7   "   Prayers.
7.30 "   All at work, and principal's and officials' breakfast.
8.40 "   Pupils dress for school.
9   "   School.
10.45 "   Recess.
12   "   Prepare for dinner.
12.20 p.m.. -Dinner.
1.20 "   School.
3   "   Recess.
3.45 "   School out.
5.45 "   All workers stop work and prepare for tea.
6   "   Tea.
7.30 to 8 p.m.-Study
8.45 p.m.-Prayers; then all go to bed, the younger children having been put to bed earlier, and they rise half an hour later than the older pupils in the morning.

The senior pupils have four full days school each week;

the juniors, who comprise nearly half the school, go to school every day, and all day, there being no half-day system here. Every Saturday, from 7.30 a.m. to 12, the children bathe and do odd work, but in the afternoon they attend school, from 1.20 to 3.45.

Every morning, from 7.30 a.m. to 12, washing clothes and cleaning house are engaged in, and in the afternoon the pupils attend school from 1.20 to 3.45...

At the time of my inspection there were ninety pupils ...The eldest girl...is nineteen and the youngest nine, but they are mostly all in their teens. The boys' average age is older, four of them being eleven years, and from that gradually upwards, to the eldest, twenty-one...

I visited the two school-rooms when each one was in session, and was much pleased with the brightness and progress exhibited by the children...

43. 1896 Barrass

Not less than six hundred and fifty Indian youth have been educated at this Institution...They are taken into the Institution, boarded, clothed and educated, under the most judicious and watchful care to promote their happiness, physical health, social habits, and general deportment, while the most untiring efforts are made to promote their moral and Religious interests: and further the greatest care is taken to inculcate habits of industry and frugality, which are essential to the future prosperity and happiness of our Indians. With these they will become well to do, without them, they must remain poor.

The Farm is in a good state of productiveness...All the departments of the Institution are in a state of creditable prosperity. We now supply the Institution with all the farm products required, and have from Six hundred to Eight Hundred dollars' worth to sell...the cost of labour, salaries, farm implements, blacksmithing, clothing, shoemakers, and wages amount with the value of stock, etcetera, to...($27.256.80), towards which...realized from sales of various kinds of work and the present value of stock, etcetera...($21,887.49), making the net expenditure...($5,369.49) The Government makes a grant of...($5,035.)...

44. 29 August 1896 Shepherd Annual Report

The year has been one of marked advancement and will be memorable by reason of the erection and equipment of a handsome new institution...This industrial farm of two hundred and four acres...is in a high state of cultivation.

The new building is 75 x 108 feet. The main tower is 108 feet, with a bell tower on the north end...Counting the basement (which is nearly altogether above ground) the building is four stories with an extensive attic. The building presents a commanding appearance from all sides and is much admired. It is constructed of stone and brick and is of the Renaissance style of architecture. The many-gabled roof is covered with Canadian slate.

It will comfortably accommodate one hundred pupils... when the attic is completed an additional twenty-five... every compartment is complete in itself. The north wing is for the boys and male officers...splendid accommodation for the principal and family. These several departments are amply supplied with lavatories, closets, etc. etc...

...The reading and explanation of the scriptures at family worship is part of the daily programme. The pupils attend regularly one preaching service on the Sabbath and special instruction is given them in the Sunday-school. While all do not manifest that obedience of life which we desire to see, yet there are those who give unmistakable evidence that they are in the path of life. The pupils have access to both religious and secular papers and read them with much interest.

While we have to regret the death of one pupil during the year, it is a matter of congratulation that this is only the third death in our building in fifteen years.

Our industries, - carpentering, shoemaking and tailoring departments - are largely confined to the wants of the institution, and must be while we are prohibited trading with the natives.

45. 14 June 1897 Shepherd to Supt. Gen. DIA

...Our holidays have usually commenced on the third Wednesday of July and for many years have continued till the first of October about two months and a half. Last year however they were reduced by six weeks by the order of the Department. This reduction of time was felt to be a hardship in this way. Many of the pupils had to earn their passage money before leaving the Institute after the holidays commenced. This gave them a very brief stay at home.

If you could...fix it at two months that would be half way between the old and the new time...we have already earned this holiday for all year we have school on Saturday afternoons and an hour's study each evening...

46. 18 June 1897 Supt. Gen. DIA to Shepherd

...as far back as the 5th July 1894, the Rev. Dr. Sutherland was informed that a vacation of eight weeks might be allowed the pupils of the Mt. Elgin Industrial school that year on the understanding that the summer vacation would be reduced to six weeks for the next year and gradually shortened thereafter.

...the two months holidays allowed in 1894 were granted on account of the building operation...it is not the practice of the Department to allow vacations to schools which are in receipt of a per capita grant, such holidays being only allowed in exceptional cases to individual pupils, who are allowed to visit their home as a reward of merit, but on no occasion for longer than one month, for which time the per capita grant is allowed.

Class-work may, however, be suspended for say, six

weeks, so as to give the pupils a needed rest - and allow the employees to have leave of absence.

47. 27 August 1897 Shepherd Annual Report

...we are happy to say at the close of our first year in our new and beautiful institution (with all its modern appliances) that the year has in many respects been the best in the fifty years of the institution in this place...

Farm...two hundred tons of hay, two hundred and fifty tons of ensilage, twelve hundred bushels of wheat, fifteen hundred bushels of oats, an average of one hundred and fifty head of cattle including all ages, with a shipment of sixty to the British market each year. The dairy, poultry and pork departments amply supply the institution... and...only represent a part of the income of the farm.

Improved Machinery. - Our modern appliances for farming make it largely recreation which our boys enjoy and they soon become efficient...and command good wages when they go abroad. This method of supplementing our income has the rare excellency of cultivating self-reliance and is much to be preferred to any source of supply which leads to dependency on others. In nine cases out of ten the Indian youth must depend on the cultivation of the soil, and the sooner he understands that and secures a relish for it, the better.

Carpenter-shop. - Our excellent foreman in the carpenter shop with the assistance of the carpenter boys largely does all the building and repairing and painting, the department only being asked to supply the material. The foreman and boys also make part of our sleighs and wagons, and repair all vehicles and machinery.

Shoe-shop. - The foreman in the shoe-shop, with the assistance of four boys, has largely made and repaired for the institution up to the present...this will not longer be a profitable business, as the price of material and wages would amply supply all with ready-made shoes even if they did wear an extra pair or two in the year. When a fair knowledge of this industry is secured, it is difficult to get profitable employment for the boys thus trained.

Industrial Training of Girls. - Under the instruction of a seamstress and tailoress, the girls make and repair nearly all working and school clothes, the material being purchased in the web. Under the instruction of a male cook and matron, the girls look after the general housework, cooking, baking, laundry and dairy.

*Class-work...*Our long list of successful competitors for the high school examination was increased this year by three who made high marks.

Inspection. - The boys' department, including play-room, lavatory, assembly-room, dormitories and clothing-rooms, is all under daily inspection by the male teacher; while the corresponding inspection of the girls' department is a part of the daily charge of the matron.

Accommodation.- Since the fifteen additional pupils were authorized by the present government, making our number one hundred, our average has been slightly in excess of that number. If the two attic dormitories were completed, we could comfortably accommodate fifteen more girls and the same number of boys.

When the reconstruction of the old building is completed, it will afford ample hospital accommodation, a music-hall and well appointed apartments for kindergarten school, together with two commodious homes, one for the male cook and his family and the other for the watchman and family. These improvements...will make this in many respects a model institution.

Our pupils represent eighteen reserves, so that while we may know their whereabouts for a few months it is difficult to trace them after.

Religious Training.- The regular family worship and Sunday school services are rendered more attractive by the alternate reading of the Scriptures, judicious questions, illustrations with the use of maps, blackboards, charts, and plenty of music.

We are blessed with a missionary and church on two sides of the institution at less than a mile, to which the pupils go once a Sabbath accompanied by an officer. The church that furnishes the best music and brightest service, with plenty of illustrations, is the drawing card.

Drainage.- With a complete system of sewerage carried to a composite pile a quarter of a mile distant for fertilizing the farm, with all outside closets on the dry earth principle together with drinking water in abundance and stored ice from a hard water spring and with a building thoroughly ventilated in every part and plenty of good wholesome food and regular habits, we have but little call for a doctor and have not averaged a dozen professional calls in the year.

48. 25 August 1898 Shepherd Annual Report

...the magnificent new institution...with the extensive improvements now being carried forward in the outbuildings, to bring them up to the level of the new, had drawn out much commendation from the surrounding public. The high state of cultivation and the wonderful yield of the industrial farm...the select quality as well as quantity of live stock, has been greatly admired...

Farm.- With the best of machinery, down to the latest, the corn harvester; grain silos, cold storage, milk separators and steam cooked food for stock, farming is now becoming little more than a recreation. The comparative ease and brevity with which our boys become familiar with all classes of farming machinery and the care of livestock is highly commendable...scores of the boys, who have been trained on the farm, and the girls, who have been trained in general house work, laundry and repairing, have and are now filling good positions...

*Shoes...*has left but little for the ordinary shoemaker but repairing, and that at greatly reduced prices. The wisdom of learning the trade in the old manner is...very doubtful and the trade itself a very unpromising business.

*School...*Our long list of successful competition for the

high school entrance examination was increased this year by two who made high marks...

49. 26 July 1899 Shepherd Annual Report
...the conditions are the most favourable in the fifty years of its history and the prospects are most encouraging.....

Land. - The...land assigned for the industrial farm is all that could be desired in quality but not in quantity. So to make up for the lack in quantity we lease through the department about three hundred acres of the Oneida Reserve just opposite and reaching from the river bank back to high-water mark...annually overflowed and swept by the spring freshets, it is nearly as rich as the valley of the Nile. It is the choicest of pasture land...

...We are subject to the county school inspector. Our long list of successful competition for the high school entrance examination was only increased this year by one pupil, the lowest in years.

50. 26 July 1900 Shepherd Annual Report
...this jubilee report is presented under the most favourable conditions and with the brightest prospects in the history of this school...

Sanitary Condition. - An abundant supply of living water, first-class ventilation, and complete system of sewerage, account in part for the excellent health of the pupils.

51. 14 August 1901 Shepherd to Supt. Gen. DIA
With unabated pleasure and delight in this work, I herewith transmit...my twentieth annual report...this... year...promises to be a record breaker in all but the wheat.

Farm...our jubilee harvest last year gave us about 1,700 bushels of wheat, 2,000 bushels of oats, 3,000 bushels of corn on the cob, 300 tons of ensilage, over 200 tons of hay, and an abundance of roots and fruit for institution purposes...

52. 1901 Shepherd Annual Report
Our jubilee year, just closed, has in many respects been the brightest and best in the history of this institution.

Apart from the accidental drowning of a young boy in the early part of the year, and the death of another by heart failure, the health of all has been exceptionally good. Our location, and flowing water for all purposes, together with excellent sanitary arrangements, are most conducive to health.

...returns from the farm, orchard, garden and live stock were the largest in the history of the establishment...

...The work of the schools, with excellent equipments and two able teachers, is becoming more and more attractive, and is patronized by pupils from eighteen to twenty-two reserves yearly.

...A well-ordered Sabbath School in the afternoon, and a song and catechism service in the evening...Many of our pupils, after from three to six years under these influences

and services, are found among our most intelligent church members and workers.

53. 13 April 1901 Shepherd to DIA
...Our custom is to allow each pupil an opportunity every two weeks for correspondence. This is done in the schoolroom under the supervision of the teachers. All the appliances supplied by the Institute except the stamps. The letters both going and coming are under close sensership and of course have to be intercepted at times. We found it necessary to prevent letters written in Indian from going out and the pupils understand that all must be in English or the letter cannot go...

54. 7 April 1902 Manass to DIA
...My daughter Caroline Manass was a pupil at the Muncey Institution since in October last. She had been vaccinated about 2 years previously. Early in March past she and other girls in the Institution were under orders of the Principal as I understand, and vaccinated by a doctor and in about a week thereafter she was compelled to do or aid in doing the washing and to hang out the clothes to dry. In consequence she caught a cold and one of her arms (the vaccinated one) as also one of her legs became greatly swollen and she was very ill. On Good Friday the 27th ult. my wife went to Muncey and found my daughter very ill, confined to bed and unable to walk. She had written or rather her cousin Ida Manass had for her written a letter to my brother James Manass fully a week before Good Friday stating that she was very ill but the Principal...did not forward the letter nor did he inform me of the severe illness of my daughter, nor did he call in the...doctor or have any attention given to her in her illness. My wife brought my daughter home and she has been ever since under the care of the Sarnia Reserve doctor, Mr. Fraser.

I complain of Principal Shepherd's conduct in withholding the letter referred to in his entire neglect of my daughter in her severe illness and in his not in any way informing me of her illness and especially also in endangering the health and lives of my daughter and others of the pupils by allowing or compelling them to do the work referred to and exposing them to the danger of taking cold so soon after vaccination.

Others of the girls...who were vaccinated at the same time are suffering from the same cause and treatment.

55. 11 April 1902 Shepherd Report
...re the treatment of his daughter Caroline since she was vaccinated early in March. The facts in the case are as follows. She was apparently in her usual health at the time of vaccination. The vaccine sent by order of the Dept was used in her case and that of 54 others who were vaccinated the same date. This was as many as was thought wise to vaccinate at one time. The Dr employed

was one of the prominent and up to date men of the day, and his directions in regard to their safety were fully carried out. The vaccination took place on Friday and the pupils went on with their...duties for about a week without interruption on this account. The vaccination took place on Friday as I said, the first washing was the following Monday. Caroline took her part in the washing on that day the same as the others. Our Laundry is warm and comfortable. On Friday one week from time of vaccination her arm began to get sore and she took a cold which was epidemic among the pupils at the time. Many had had it and recovered, so that we did not apprehend anything serious. The first of the following week some of the pupils were not doing as well as we desired and we called in Dr. Mitchell of Delaware, who is the Dr. of the Chippewa of the Thames, and after the examination of Caroline and a couple of other girls, as well as several boys, he said there was not any grounds for fear, that it would take some time to regain their normal condition.

With several, both boys and girls, it took the form of Absess, under the arm, or in the breast near the arm, but broke and discharged freely, and soon showed signs of improvement, and are now nearly well, with one exception namely one boy whose has not yet broken altho polticed for several days.

In the case of Caroline Manass the girl in question, she seemed affected in one limb, but without apparent suffering when quiet. We thought it a slight touch of rheumatism, and was treated accordingly. While in this condition on Good Friday before the Dr made his next visit, her Mother came as stated, and took her away contrary to our judgement, yet we sent her in a carriage to the station with every prevention against cold. We have been credible informed by her cousin that she is quite improved.

With respect to the care of the pupils and particularly during this trouble, they have been well cared for and looked after, both by Dr and Matron. The latter the vigilent and painstaking of any Matron we have ever had. The rooms are comfortable, warm and well ventilated.

In regard to my refusing to allow any letter to pass this office as stated, I have no knowledge of such a letter having been written, and if I did it was because I did not deem it wise to do so, as there was no danger. Our judgement is if the Mother had stayed away the girl would have been all right in a short time. The Dr said that the scrofulous condition of the blood of these pupils would necessitate a longer time for their recovery.

Our purpose and aim has been, and will be to do the best in our power all things considered, for the pupils placed in our charge, but it looks as though we would never have the approval of some of those for whom we have done the most.

When the girl in question has fully recovered, we think the Dept would do her a kindness, and only do what is

simply due to the Institute by requiring her to return and complete her term, and thus let them know whether we have your confidence or not,

56. 7 October 1902 Shepherd to Supt. Gen. DIA

Farm.- We employ a general foreman over all departments of industry...plans the work, and assigns it, and the boys who are to assist two other foremen on specific lines of the work...farming, gardening, care of live stock, building and repairing. The farm amply supplies the institution with flour, vegetables, roots, fruit, pork, beef, fowl, milk, butter and eggs.

Buildings...The reconstruction of the old institute is so complete that it passes for a splendid new building, and is a magnificent annex to the stately new institution...This annex...furnishes comfortable hospital accommodation and two well equipped school-rooms, which allow the large school-room in the main building to be used as a chapel.

Class-room Work. - The pupils are divided into three sections according to their classes, and two of these sections are in school each day, and the other is employed in the different lines of industry. This plan gives the advantages of a graded school when one pupil of a class is in school all the class must be. In this way the foreman over the different industries knows just what help he will have each day, and can plan the work accordingly...

Accommodation...When application is made for admission...we send the usual blank form...if the questions are satisfactorily answered...the pupils are admitted in the order of the applications. Frequently such applications have to wait for months...before there is room.

Religious Training...the Sabbath school at the institute manned by the officers is the attraction of the afternoon, when there is seldom an absentee.

Ex-pupils. - About twenty-five pupils retire each year. Some return to their reserves, but largely they go out to service among the white people; which latter course we encourage, as we consider it much better for them.

57. 21 November 1902 Shepherd to Supt. Gen. DIA

...First I drew your attention to the utter impossibility of carrying on the work of the Institution in a satisfactory manner with a per capita grant of Sixty Dollars per pupil...we have tried it for a term of twenty years during which time we have been most economical, frugal and almost unwarrantably industrious and yet with all this effort we are seriously in debt today on current account...If we had a larger farm without paying rent it would put us in a different position. Two hundred and four acres is the amount of land belonging to the Institution...the other land we occupy is rented from Indians through the Department, and after paying the rent and making all the fences (as we have to do) and properly tile draining the land the profits are comparatively small.

As far as I know there is no other institution in like

position. Take the Mohawk at Brantford. It is largely supported by the New England Company, so that the Government grant of that institution is supplementary...

You intimated that this being an industrial school we are entitled to a larger grant...If the department can... double our grant we will be able to manage arrears on current accounts and keep out of debt and enable us to lessen the amount of manual labor of the pupils and to more fully instruct and explain the reason for what they do together with increased social comforts which would probably include a library, reading-room, gymnasium shower baths etc.

...the manner and cost of living are greatly increased during the last few years, as well as the expense of the staff which is more than double what it formerly was.

...our out buildings were all constructed of wood...and as they were built from twenty to fifty years ago, it was absolutely necessary if they were to be saved from dilapidation to go on with the work of repairing. This we have done until the cost of material (not labor) slightly exceeds One Thousand Dollars...In regard to this debt you were good enough to say that we need not have any anxiety as the department would provide.

...the shops that have stood for over thirty years and are wooden buildings required foundation, roof, new floors and other repairs which at a low estimate will cost Six Hundred Dollars for material.

The laundry also must have cement floor, new boiler and fittings at an estimated cost of Four Hundred Dollars. ...possibly first in importance...is the erection of an elevated water tank and pipings to give us additional water pressure, as a better and larger preparation against fire. This is very important and should be constructed at the earliest possible date. The cost of this...will not be less than Five Hundred Dollars.

In regard to these items we were delighted to have your encouraging promise.

58. 28 November 1902 Benson to Dep. Supt. Gen. DIA

Rev. Mr Shepherd...calls the attention of the Department to the requirements of this school, referring, first, to the insufficiency of the per capita grant.

This school was established more than fifty years ago and was placed in charge of the Methodist Missionary Society by whom it is still conducted, the Department contributing a per capita grant of $60 per annum to assist them in carrying it on. One hundred pupils are authorized to receive this grant, making the total contribution of the Department $6000.00 per annum...$60.00 a year is not a sufficient sum for the maintenance and education of these pupils and unless such grant is supplemented by liberal contributions from the Methodist Missionary Society, or the earnings of the institute, financial disaster is bound to overtake the school. Mr Shepherd, in his endeavour to make up the required difference has gone very extensively

into stock farming, and...after the most careful economy, he is unable to make ends meet, the deficit on last year's transactions being $86.19. His statement of Receipts and Expenditures for the year ended 30th June 1902, does not show that he received any money from the Methodist Missionary Society, beyond the sum of $6000.00 sent to it by the Department...the Methodist Missionary Society does not contribute anything towards the support of this school, although, so long as it remains under their control, they are bound to make up the deficit...This leaves Mr. Shepherd to rely upon the Departmental grant and what he can make from his farm, which with the land attached to the institution and that rented from the Indians, comprises 504 acres. Mr. Shepherd has to pay rent for 300 acres of this land as well as keeping up the fencing and other improvements, all of which is quite a drain on his earnings, to say nothing of the expenditure of energy on the part of his pupils, who are, as he says, of necessity "unwarrantably industrious". The care of over two hundred head of cattle, which chiefly devolves on the pupils, entails more work than is good for them and leaves no time for other farming operations which they should be taught and in the interest of the school I consider that Mr. Shepherd's stock operations should be largely curtailed, even if it affects the income derived from this source...Mr. Shepherd asks that the present grant be doubled and if the school is to be kept up to a proper state of efficiency, a substantial increase will have to be provided. Experience has shown that it is difficult to finance upon even the largest per capita grant. ...the Principal calls attention to the needs of the school in the way of buildings and repairs and asks for a grant of $2500 which the Minister has authorised...the item of $1000 for material, already expended is, presumably for the construction of a large concrete stable for stock. This was required to furnish accommodation for his extension operations in this direction. The other items appear to be for reasonable expenditure. In fact there are other requirements for which Mr. Shepherd has not asked a grant and which I consider are absolutely necessary. The building set apart for the boys recreation room needs extensive repairs in the way of new flooring and some provision for bathing and ablutions. When I was at the school in September last I found that they had no bathing facilities except the water of the Thames in summer and washtubs in winter, taking their morning wash at the pump. Baths should also be placed in the laundry for the girls: the baths in the main building are not for the use of the pupils. The new building is a very handsome structure but the out-buildings are not at all in keeping with it and certainly want renovating, as a survey of the present premises presents a showy front and a shabby back.

Mr. Shepherd was away when I visited the school...He had then been away two months and during his absence the state of the premises showed the lack of supervision. The teacher who was in charge, was doing all he could to get in the crop with the assistance of the hired man and 24 boys who had remained at the school during vacation. There were also 23 girls at the school...Mr. Shepherd is an employee of the Methodist Missionary Society and the Department had no knowledge of his absence on this occasion, although it has been reported that he is frequently called away on Church Matters.

If the Department intends to make any change in the present arrangement with the Methodist Missionary Society, Rev Dr. Sutherland, General Secretary...is the official to be consulted. Any additional grant...should be conditional upon an entire change of the present system of conducting the school. All the boys attending this institution come from reserves where farming could be successfully carried on and yet I was informed by the teacher in charge that none of them had ever handled a plow or were even allowed to drive a...as time could not be spared to teach them. The boys of this school are...not only working but are being worked, and they as well as their parents see the difference, hence the numerous complaints which reach the Department of ill-treatment of pupils. I saw the meals that were served, and while plentiful, they were not at all inviting and the pupils mode of eating did not speak very well for their training in table etiquette. The supply of clothing on hand was scanty and well worn, but I was told it would be replenished after the Principal's return.

...the system of training pursued at this and other school requires careful revision, as it is little less than a waste of time and money to follow the present methods as there is little use in our educating an Indian if, in our endeavour, we spoil a horn and fail to make a spoon. That our schools have failed in their object is generally admitted...

59. 25 May 1903 Howes to Supt. Gen. DIA
...It is with deep regret that I announce the death of Rev. W. W. Shepherd...who has so ably managed the affairs of that Institution for so many years.

His death was caused by an accident in which he was thrown from his rig...

60. May 1903 A. Sutherland to Dep. Supt. Gen. DIA
...recommend the appointment of the Rev. T. T. George, at present pastor of the Victoria...Church, Chatham...Mr. George is a man forty years of age, has been some twenty years in the ministry, was brought up on a farm and has spent most of his subsequent life in country neighbourhoods. He has good executive ability and in the judgement of the Committee is well qualified for the position in question...Mr. George has been for years on very intimate terms with Mr. Shepherd and known more about the Institute, its work and its management, than any other man in that region...

61. 29 October 1903 George Annual Report
...Grounds.- A beautiful lawn, crossed by a well gravelled driveway, lies southward and westward of the main building, furnishing playground for the girls on the south, and a tennis lawn on the west. To the north...stretch the ample and beautiful grounds used for sports by the boys.

Attendance...I have been compelled to refuse about fifty per cent of the applications presented by parents or guardians in behalf of the prospective pupils...

Industrial Work.- The pupils are instructed according to age and sex in...farming in all its branches, rearing and management of stock, horses, cattle, pigs and domestic fowl, drainage and tilling of land, and carpenter work, and the cutting, making and mending of garments, cooking, baking, general house and laundry work.

Moral and Religious Training. - In charge of an officer the pupils attend public service each Sabbath morning, Sabbath school in the chapel each Sabbath afternoon, song, praise and prayer service in the same place each Sabbath evening. Bible study with the singing of gospel songs is associated with the morning and evening prayer service each day of the week. The conduct of the pupils in general is good...difficulties arise, but pupils are with few exceptions orderly and obedient. In the schools discipline is maintained by the teachers, only grave offences being reported to the principal. In the industrial departments, disobedience and bad conduct are reported to the officer in charge, to be dealt with by the principal as the case demands. No prescribed punishment is laid down, but varies according to the individual case and may partake of the withholding of some privilege or the assigning of an extra task.

Health of Pupils.- The health of the pupils during the year has on the whole been good, three serious cases of pneumonia forming the exception.

Sanitary Condition. - The sanitary condition is not on the whole satisfactory. Certain repairs to plumbing and a supply of pure water are seriously needed.

Water Supply. - The water supply while abundant is not of good quality, as reported by the inspector some time since. This is a serious problem, and demands immediate attention. The confusing of quantity with quality has been too long maintained.

62. 6 June 1904 Macrae
...visited upon May 6 in connection with the rumour that small pox existed in the neighbourhood...The Matron said that two years ago...there had been a general vaccination in the School. The Rev. Mr. George, principal, was very anxious to avoid having any of those children who had entered the School since the general vaccination of two years ago operated upon, as he says that he has seen very bad effects from vaccination. I arranged with him...to isolate the children entirely and prevent strangers who might have infection coming upon the premises.

An examination of the dormitories was made and they were found to be in exceedingly good condition, beds clean and comfortable and the rooms well aired.

The water supply of the School continues to be in every respect bad. I drew attention to the fact of the quality of the water used for drinking purposes a year or two ago. It appears that nothing was done. The present Principal is so keenly alive to the impropriety of using the water... for drinking and cooking purposes that he has obtained water for such purposes from a spring on the River bank. It has also to be carried by hand.

63. 26 August 1904 George Annual Report

Class-room Work...Three pupils successfully passed the high school entrance and one the public school leaving at the examinations held in June and July last.

...Health of Pupils.- The general health of the pupils during the year has been good. One pupil was dismissed suffering from that dread disease consumption. One boy died of spinal meningitis after a sickness of eight days.

General Remarks.- Ready employment is found by pupils (both boys and girls) going out from this institute, the eagerness with which they are sought for bearing testimony to the efficiency of their training.

64. 7 October 1904 Benson to Dep. Supt. Gen. DIA

...I have on several occasions pointed out that the contribution of $60 for each pupil by the Government...is quite inadequate to meet the increased cost of living...the desire of the different denominations conducting these schools to be placed on a better financial basis is only fair and reasonable, and that $100 per capita would not be an excessive amount to allow.

...under management of the late Mr. Shepherd the school was carried on with a very small deficit: it was considerably less than $100 a year. This economical management is accounted for by the methods pursued by Mr. Shepherd who was extensively engaged in stock raising and feeding cattle for the market. To such an extent did he carry on these operations that I have no hesitation in saying that he sacrificed the interests of the school to make both ends meet. Rev. Mr. George...has ...accumulated a deficit of $3,492.40 since he has had charge of this school, and I think it would be well for the Department to examine carefully into his financial transactions and management with a view to discovering how this deficit occurred. My own impression is that he has lost on his cattle transactions and it would take a very skilful drover to carry on Mr. Shepherd's work in this line.

When I was at this school two years ago I found that nearly all the energy of the school was directed to the care of stock, and if Mr. George has let this run down in the interests of the school, he is hardly to blame. I think that if the grant were increased the Church would make no demand on the Department for the payment of the

deficit, and if the cattle transactions were curtailed, it would be an advantage to the school as nearly all the pupils' spare time was taken up in attending to the live stock while their industrial training was neglected.

65. 24 January 1905 George to Supt. Gen. DIA

...Assuming management...on July 1st, 1903, I found it necessary to stock the vacant pastures by purchases made as means and opportunities presented during June, July, August and September...An effort was also made during the year to improve where possible the breeding stock as represented by brood mares, cattle and pigs...by the sale of the inferior and the purchase of the more suitable...

In the item of repairs $3428.80 were paid out while the special grant from the Department was but $2500.00... Every economy possible was practiced in these repairs and the large item above mentioned did not by any means complete them...

66. 27 September 1905 George Annual Report

...The boys lavatory and gymnasium is a frame building of two stories on a brick basement. This building, as also the laundry, is much in need of repair. The outbuildings comprise carpenter and shoe-shops, implement-sheds, carriage-house, horse-stable and pig-pen, together with two grain barns on brick and concrete basements which are used for the stabling of cattle.

Class-room Work...has proved very satisfactory. Four pupils wrote on the high school entrance examination, three were successful, and three senior pupils successfully passed the public school leaving examination. A room for manual training is available and an effort will be made to equip and furnish it as soon as the laundry and boys' gymnasium are placed in condition of repair.

Health.- The general health of the pupils has been good. One boy discharged suffering from tuberculosis, died shortly afterward in the hospital at Sarnia. Another suffering from the same dread disease, but having no home, was cared for in the private hospital of the institute...

Water Supply...having been condemned by the inspector of Indian agencies and also by the public school inspector...an effort was made...The adjustment...proved a serious drain upon the time of the staff and our finances.

General Remarks.- Pupils going out from the institute are eagerly sought for and employers speak highly of the training and ability of ex-pupils in their service.

The extremely severe winter of 1903-4 destroyed all winter wheat in the section, our share of loss being fifty acres. This necessitated the purchase of flour throughout the entire year and at an unusually high price. This added to the increased cost of almost all items of supply, together with the failure of the corn crop of the season of 1904...coupled with unremunerative prices for cattle and pigs, makes the year one of extreme difficulty in matters of finance, especially...the extra cost in placing our water-supply in a reasonably efficient condition...account for the heavy excess of expenditure over receipts...

67.   14 February 1906   George to A. Sutherland

In reply to your personal and private letter of the 26th ultimo, I can only plead, not guilty, in so far as pleading is necessary. I am very grateful for your personal and kindly letter. I have had knowledge of an underground passage leading from the Institute to the Mission Rooms for more than a year past; but this is my first opportunity of meeting them directly, and I am accordingly thankful. I expect rumors and vile fabrications from members of Bands, whose desires concerning their children I have been unable to grant, but these, I expect all who know the Indian character will accept only when verefied. Still there are other stories afloat of such a nature that I am constrained to believe only white men or women would originate. They are mostly of the class to which your third and fourth rumor belong. They may be classed as meddlesome, petty and only harmful when ordinary confidence is wanting in the management. I do not think the person originating and the person transmitting mean any special harm - only that being young I need motherly leading strings. I hope with increase of years to outgrow them. In the meantime I will be grateful for your confidence and for any request for desired information. I need hardly say, that in an Institution of this kind, with its manifold operations that we seldom have the privilege of planning our difficulties so that they may be easily solved...I expect that so long as I try to do my best to make this Institution increasingly more efficient, the more I will be misunderstood and criticized...

Re-rumors:-

I. The stripping off of a girl's clothes and whipping her unmercifully for running away.

First, all correction by way of whipping is done with a regulation rubber strap. I whipped a girl with said strap, not for running away, but for selling her virtue while away to two white men and when caught fabricating a story of assault which led me to have the men arrested and placed on trial. In the court she gave evidence that she sold her virtue with full consent. When taken back to the school she was warned not to tell her experience with the men nor the questions asked her in Court, to any of the pupils on pain of being severely punished. Only a few days after an officer caught her telling the whole story to a group of her fellow pupils. I did not remove her clothes nor whip her unmercifully, but I did whip her and have at no time attempted to conceal it. This was about eighteen months ago.

II The taking of a girl from her bed and beating her for some trivial offense.

This I have never done and do not know to what incident it refers unless it is to the removal from the dormitory of a girl, caught in the early evening in the act of running away. She was placed in the dormitory with the other girls and about eleven the same night tried to make her escape again. The Matron hearing the noise aroused me and together we took the girl and locked her in an officer's room.

The removal followed the second attempt to break from the dormitory where she was placed after her first capture. Mrs. George and the Matron were present and assisted in securing the girl. I did not whip her on that occasion.

I did whip her on another occasion and for another offence. I have never taken any girl from bed or taken the clothes off from any girl at any time or under any circumstances. The two girls referred to were bad girls; the former giving the management a great deal of trouble. I wrote to the Department to secure her release, the correspondence passing through your office. Being an illegitimate, the Department denied responsibility. I kept her until last month - from September 1904 - and then secured her discharge.

The other girl was placed in the Institute by her father because he could not control her. She had been tramping the Reserve until late into the night and at times was out all night. I only learned this after she attempted to get away. I wrote the father and mother to come to my office. I there told them all that had happened and that the girl had tried to get in company with some of her old companions. I told them that I could not keep such a girl at the Institute and they took her home.

III- Inclosed you will find a sketch of the parts affected by the change in the building...

IV - I can sell only when cattle are fit for market and when grass fails to fatten them they must be fed. I sold one car lot in October and three other lots will go out during the coming month.

68.   24-25 April 1906   T. Ferrier Report

STAFF The staff appear to be doing well and working harmoniously together, and it is just a question whether another member shouldn't be added...there being no laundress, nor seamstress and the matron has no assistant.

CHILDREN One hundred and three boys and girls were in attendance, the most of them bright, healthy-looking children. They appear to be well-fed, but their clothing is hardly up to the average.

PROVISIONS A very meagre supply of clothing material and provisions is on hand, far from what it ought to be for the proper equipment of an Institution of this kind...

FIRE PROTECTION The whole Institution is practically without any fire protection, and the main building without any fire escapes....

BUILDINGS <u>Main Building</u> Some changes in the basement affecting the girl's department and portions used for supplies and bakery have been authorized...and when completed will be a decided improvement for convenience in the general work of the kitchen, bakery the keeping of supplies, coal etc., and most important for the privacy, welfare and comfort of the girls...

THE INSTITUTE BUILDING This building is occupied by the families of two employees, and is also used for two school rooms. These schoolrooms are heated by a hot-water plant which is too weak to do the work and has to be supplemented by a stove in each. They have been without ventilation until recently, when two 7 inch galvanised iron pipes have been laced to draw air from the floor to the smoke-flues. This provides an exit for some of the foul air, but no provision is made for a supply of fresh air. While this has been accomplished at a small cost, and is an excellent scheme to the extent of its power and is about as strong as the flues will permit, yet, the fact remains, it is far from being sufficient, since the air, when the windows are closed, becomes stifling. If caging so many children in such, practically, unventilated buildings during the winter months does not break down the general health of the pupils and staff, it is more a matter of good fortune rather than of a good policy...

69. 26 March 1906 **** To whom it may concern
On the 10th day of the month I visited the Mt. Elgin in company with A. Windblow as my interpreter. On the occasion to see my adopted son...whom I adopted when he was one month old from his mother. When the child was given to me I told **** to nurse the child two more months and I would allow her to stay at my place during that time. So she did according to my request and afterwards left the child and place...went off to work at some town in Michigan. And since that time the child has been under my care and support. Nothing was ever given to the child from his mother in clothing or food up to this time. The boy is now over 12 years of age. So I took the boy to the Mt. Elgin Institution after holidays last summer to attend school there. And lately having the understanding from some of the Indians at Muncey Reserve that my adopted boy was sick at school, I therefore at once went to this school in order to see him and with the intention of asking the principal the boy to leave the school for couple days so that I doctor him, afterwards take him back to school again. But, when we arrived there I was not permitted to see my adopted child. Nor ever to come around the school. He said that he had full control of the boy for five years from...the boy's mother. He also said if he found any person attempting to get the boy away from the school would take...I therefore state that **** is my rightful adopted boy...wish to get him back to my home on account of the treatment I have from the principal of the said school.

70. 9 April 1906 Jacobs to Macrae
I have been asked to write to you in reference to a boy who is, at present a pupil at the Muncey Institution whose name is ****. This boy it seems has sore eyes and been that way all winter, and consequently was not taught any, but he had been made to work all the same. This boy belongs to Walpole Island and was deserted by both parents in fact his mother only kept him two months and given up to one Mrs. **** who adopted him and raised

him, and about a year ago his natural mother, unknown to the foster mother, placed him at the Institute, and the foster mother was obliged or thought she was to take him to the institution. & as he has been sick without being attended to properly. This woman wanted to take him home and have him doctored. The Principal Revd T. J. George utterly refused and even refused the woman to come near the building. There has been complaints of that nature by Indians in different Reserves and others complain of excessive punishment of children. I told this woman that I would write to you about it and enclose statements which she brought to me made by her as to the adoption and raising of the Boy. I thought some enquiries might be made as to the condition of things at the Muncey Institution.
The Boy I think if he is not able to be taught, he would not be able to work and should be allowed to go home to his adopted mother.

71. 21 May 1906 George to Secretary Supt. Gen. DIA
...The boy...was placed in the school by his mother who signed the application in regular form. The grandmother... visited him in the early autumn past and called on succeeding days, and on each occasion was allowed to see the boy. Shortly afterward the boy truanted and was found at his grandmother's home Walpole Island. The grandmother objected to the boy's return basing same upon his eyes being inflamed, which was largely accounted for by exposure when a truant from the Institute. The mother wrote me making enquiry as to the boy's health, stating that she had been informed that her son was seriously ill also almost blind. I informed her that the boy was in good health and his eyes alright save a slight inflammation.
She wrote me in reply requesting me not to allow his grandmother to see him as she was endeavouring to influence the boy to leave the school. A short time after this the grandmother called at the Institute and attempted to keep up communication with the boy from day to day visiting him at the playground or at his work. This I refused to allow and informed her that any visitation would required to be made in the office in the presence of an officer and all conversation carried on in english. It is a rule of the Institute that persons other than parents or guardians are allowed to visit pupils only when the pupil is accompanied by an officer and the conversation carried on in English.
The same rule is applied to parents and guardians when there is reason to believe that influence is being brought to bear upon the pupil to create discontent and unrest leading to truancy or removal, otherwise the greatest freedom possible is given to all parents and guardians when visiting pupils, save and except when these visits are made on the Sabbath...

72.   28 May 1906   McLean to Jacobs

...your letter of the 9th ult. complaining that Mrs. ****
was refused permission by the Principal...to see her
adopted son...a report has been received...which fully
exonerates the Principal from any blame...

The school authorities make no objection to parents,
relatives or guardians seeing pupils at certain suitable
times and conditions, but they do rightly object to
clandestine interviews with pupils, which always have a
disturbing effect, and in the instance of this boy a
previous secret interview led to his desertion. Mrs. ****
could have seen her adopted son in the presence of one of
the staff, had she made a direct application to the
Principal.

With regard to the boy's eyesight I may inform you that
there is nothing serious the matter with him. He returned
from his truancy with inflammation of the eyes and has
since quite recovered.

73.   11 July 1906   George Quarterly Report

...I am pleased to report but one case of truancy and he is
an old offender. This happy condition of things I attribute
to the hearty cooperation of your Department and of our
agents on the several Reserves in the work of searching
out and returning the truants of the two previous quarters.
The pupils in attendance seem to be contented and happy
in their work.

Two cases of pneumonia and one of tuberculosis has
called for considerable care and medical treatment. The
pupil No.223 who was afflicted with the latter disease was
removed to his home on the 1st inst. and died on the 5th.
Otherwise the general health of the pupils has been good.
I am experiencing less difficulty this season than formerly
in securing the consent of parents to allow their children
to remain at the Institute during the holiday season.

When holidays are urged I am limiting them to the
required four weeks, requiring parents to sign an
agreement for their prompt return at the stated time.

The progress of the pupils in their work during the year
has been on the whole quite satisfactory.

74.   4 August 1906   George Annual Report

...Laundry - A substantial two-story brick building at
present undergoing repairs...nearing completion. Boys
lavatory and gymnasium...this building is also undergoing
repairs, which when completed will add materially to the
convenience and the comfort of the boys.

Class-room Work...has proved satisfactory. Four pupils
wrote on Part II high school entrance examination with
success, while two senior pupils have successfully
prosecuted the public school leaving work. A room for
manual training is available and an effort will be made to
equip it for use as soon as financial conditions...permit.

Moral and Religious Training. - This is kept constantly
in mind by the teachers and officers in charge. Morning

and evening service, consisting of singing of hymns and
reading of the scriptures and prayers is held in the chapel.
On the Sabbath the pupils attend Divine service at the
Colborne Methodist church, an officer always being in
attendance. Bible study is conducted in the chapel every
Sabbath from 2.45 to 3.45 p.m. and 7 to 8 p.m.

Health of Pupils.- The general health...has been good.
One boy was discharged suffering from tuberculosis of the
lungs, also one girl suffering from a similar affliction of
the glands of the neck. There were three cases of
erysipelas and one of diphtheria, all in a light form.

Water Supply...successful operation of the hydraulic
ram...flow has been ample...

General Remarks.- The work of repairing the boys'
play-house, the laundry, and the girls' lavatory is well
advanced, and when completed will add very much to the
comfort of the pupils. The plumbing in connection with
this work promises to be most satisfactory, remedying a
sanitary condition deplored for years.

75.   5 October 1906   Thackeray to George

I enclose herewith an assignment of all interest moneys
coming to the three **** children until they respectively
attain the age of eighteen years, on condition that they be
taken into your Institute.

We shall not be able to send them for I think about two
weeks, I expect the interest moneys very soon now, and
we shall have to fix them up a bit, will let you know in
due time when to expect them along. Their mother is not
at home, (a bad woman without doubt), and we shall have
to get someone to clean them up, and otherwise prepare
them for their coming.

I am pleased that you are going to take them, for they
are in a bad state on account of their mother not caring
for them.

I have spoken to the Dr. to examine them, and see that
they have no skin disease...

Would you prefer to have all the moneys coming to the
Indian children sent in your name, or in the names of the
individual children, the Dept prefers sending it in the
names of the children as it appears better on the
paysheets.

76.   5 October 1906   ****

I, ****, a member of the Alnwick Band of Indians do
hereby assign and set over to the Mount Elgin Industrial
Institute all interest moneys coming to my sons...until
such time or times as they respectively attain the age of
18 (eighteen) years, on condition that they be taken into
the said institute and treated as other children therein.
[Note on bottom of letter from S.R. McVitty date?]
**** is now about 14 years and I am sorry to say making
every attempt to follow in her mothers steps. **** is a
good boy, will likely leave midsummer. **** was
discharged two years ago, and is doing well.

77. 13 October 1906 George to A. Sutherland
...The general health of the pupils during the Quarter has been good. Some of the old offenders have given trouble by playing truant again. Three truanted on September 2nd, two of whom were returned on October 5th. Four truanted on September 23rd, one of whom was returned October 1st. The other four are still at large. The only reason I can assign for truancy in these cases is a dislike for the confinement of the class room.

The attendance at this date is Forty-eight boys and Forty-nine girls.

Four of our pupils wrote on the July Entrance Examination...and out of a class of one hundred and ten secured the following places according to marks received: Lucy Logan 8th, Marjorie Peters 22nd, Edwin Maness 31st and Florence Silver 32nd.

78. 14 January 1907 George to Secretary Supt. Gen. DIA
...the health of the officers and pupils alike has been good throughout the Quarter. The class work of the pupils has been good and gives promise of a successful year...

The weather...has been abnormally wet...impeding the work in the fields and adding not a little to the cost and care of management.

The stock, both cattle and horses entered winter quarters in better condition than in some seasons past owing to the heavy growth of pasture in the late Autumn.

Handicapped by a lack of skilled labor the repairs under way have progressed but slowly...enlarged the girls' playroom, installed tub and shower baths in the small room adjoining, also a four seat...flush...closet ...improvements...add very much to the convenience and comfort of the girl pupils.

79. 30 May 1907 George Nine Months Report
Class-room Work...quite satisfactory, though interfered with by an epidemic of measles...It is our desire to add manual training as a special department of class work as soon as financial conditions will permit.

Health of Pupils.- While the general health of the pupils has been good, the school suffered from an epidemic of measles of a very severe type, in...February. There were 46 cases, one of which proved fatal owing to complications. One boy and three girls were discharged suffering from tuberculosis of the lungs, and one girl from syphilis. There were two cases of pneumonia and one of diphtheria, all in a light form.

80. 3 September 1907 McLean to Dep. Minister of Justice
...enclose herewith for taxation an account amounting to $29.53 from Constable...in connection with the arrest of ****, a truant pupil from the Mount Elgin Institute

81. 22 November 1907 George to Supt. Gen. DIA
I regret to report the loss last night by fire of the Boys' playhouse. The building was vacated and lights put out at 7.30 and under view by officers at nine and ten, the fire breaking out at 11.20 p.m. The fire originated in the second story, north end, which being used as a boys' clothing room was kept under lock and was not known to have been entered since Monday morning last, when the boys' Sunday uniforms were put away. The first story when entered was found to be free from fire as this room alone contained the smoke pipe of the furnace, said pipe entering the chimney below the ceiling. It is hard to see how the fire could have originated from the furnace.

Fire drills had been practised at 9 p.m. when the fire alarm was sounded, officers and pupils responded promptly...The boys are being cared for in the chapel and laundry. Our principal loss other than the building, is that of clothing to the value of about $500.

82. 28 November 1907 George to A. Sutherland
...loss on building at $2300...requested a grant of $2000 for the immediate rebuilding...

...my opinion points to the presence of someone in the clothing room, to which the pupils had access only when receiving their Sunday uniforms on Sunday mornings and on return of the same Monday mornings. In each case an officer is in charge. I do not imply...that the fire was incendiary but rather arising from a match or matches used or carelessly dropped among the clothing. The boys could only gain access to said room by springing the lock. The real facts may always remain a mystery.

83. 25 January 1908 George to A. Sutherland
I am sorry to report another fire...It broke out this morning at ten minutes to seven in the large barn & had gained considerable head-way - so much in fact that no one had hope of checking it. While the Officers were releasing the Cattle endangered I directed a Bucket brigade of boys & girls & with the help of neighbors succeeded in an hour & a half of hard battle getting the mastery. The wind was from the South West & placed every outbuilding on the premises in imminent peril. Investigation revealed the fact that it was set on fire by a boy sixteen years old taken in on Jan. 1st 1908. The reasoning was that he did not want to stay at the School & thought by burning the building he would be set free. At the same time (he started the fire on Friday evening about 7/30 just after an officer had made his last round) the main building was set on fire in the girls clothes closet. I had thought that some girls had taken a lamp contrary to orders into the room & accidentally set fire to the clothing & dresses hanging on the wall. I now believe that it was started by the same boy by passing a match through the key hole of an inward outside door. I placed the boy in the hands of the Crown Attorney...Officers & Children are very much unnerved but the discovery of the crime will tend to quiet matters again. I cannot say too much in praise of the courage & energy of the pupils in

their work of carrying water &c. If we had not won out our loss would have been exeedingly high - 275 head of cattle, 30 head of horses & 100 pigs with supplies &c.

I trust our danger is over. You will excuse writing as I am not yet in control of my nerves.

84. 27 January 1908 George to Sec. Supt. Gen. DIA

I regret the necessity of again reporting a fire...The loss to the building and straw will not exceed $50. The loss of the cattle owned by the Missionary Society will reach $140. Watching carefully the movements of pupils during the day, suspicion rested on one or other of two boys. After a prolonged investigation the one boy confessed, stating that he started the fire on the main section of the barn just before evening prayers Friday night, within five minutes of the departure of the officer having charge of that building, who makes his last rounds of the building from 7.30 to 8 p.m.

The lad is sixteen years of age and was received into the Institute from the Caradoc Reserve on Jan 1/08 and is a member of the Chippewas of the Thames. The reason given for the deed was that he did not want to stay at the Institute. I immediately sent for his father and after stating to him the entire case, it was thought best to hand the boy over to the civil authorities...

85. 14 February 1908 George to Secretary Supt. Gen.DIA

...****...who set fire to the Institution buildings...plead guilty to the charge and was sentenced...to five years in the Kingston Penitentiary. While the sentence is a severe one for a lad of sixteen, the offence was most serious and the protection of life and property in our exposed position demanded such a penalty as would be a warning to others. The loss on buildings and contents has been appraised, the former at $49.85, the latter at $142.50...

86. 7 April 1908 Kendall to A. Sutherland

As the Indians on this Reserve are complaining about conditions at the Muncey Institute, I thought I, perhaps, ought to report how things stand. Last fall it appeared that the Gibson children there cried and asked to come home whenever anyone they knew went there, and the Indians alleged that the children were beaten too much, chiefly by the matron, made to work when sick, given bad food and were cold in winter. The parents here refused to send any more children and wanted those who were there taken out. This I could not do, but reported to the Revd. Mr. George, who did not reply. I mentioned the matter to Mr. Ferrier and later to Mr. Watch; the latter recommended me to write to the Mission Rooms.

Last week an Indian...died and his daughter and niece were brought home from Muncey on account of his previous sickness. The niece was found to be in poor health, suffering from "itch" and her head "lousy"; the daughter is said to be poorly but I only received

professional information concerning the other child... Dr. Burgess of Bala telling me that the disease was as stated and expressing surprise that "more care was not exercised in the Institution." These parents state that their daughters have been well educated at Muncey and learned good English, for which they are grateful, but they decline to send the children back until sanitary, disciplinary and alimentary conditions be improved. The main point is to re-assure the Indians.

Personally I should imagine that a cottage home system would be suitable for Indian children.

87. 27 May 1908 George to A. Sutherland

I am in receipt of a short note from Brother Shore, dated May 20/08 and enclosed therewith a copy of a letter written by Mr. Wm. Kendall at Bala and dated Bala Apr. 7th/08...the statement is made that the children cried when friends visited them. This is not uncommon in any school and in a measure indicates the affection of child for parent or friend. I have no memory of an occasion when it occurred from other reasons. It is also alleged that the children are beaten too much, chiefly by the matron. In looking up the record of corrections I find that the Bala children have been punished on very rare occasions and in almost every instance the punishment was of a minor character. The matron charged with the instruction of the girls in the sewing room and having under her care from twenty to thirty girls ranging in ages from six to eighteen must of necessity perform the disciplinary requirements of a teacher, but so far as beating the children under her care, it is absolutely without foundation in fact and evidences a resort to new fields for proof of an old charge disproved by the actual numbering of the punishments administered. As to children being made to work when sick, I can only say that such is not the fact concerning any department of the school. So soon as any pupil is known to be unwell, he is examined and placed in the hospital, returned to the dormitory, or released from work as the case may require. To this there is no exception save where a pupil may be assigned work in the morning when he has not reported himself as unwell. If such occurs the officer of the department in charge promptly returns the pupil for examination and treatment. Regarding the character of the food here said to be bad, it would seem an equal disregard for facts was evident. Inspectors from the Department, the local Agent and the Public School Inspector who visits the school twice annually and personally examines all departments of the school work and equipment including personal examination of at least two meals on the occasion of each visit, have without a dissenting voice openly complimented me on the improvement in this department, dissenting only in that two of the above thought that they were supplied with too liberal apportionment of meat. These facts have never previously been reported to me.

Mr. Ferrier when here in the Autumn informed me that Mr. Kendall was finding some fault but in as much as the latter had been at the school on two different occasions and made no mention of these things to me but he rather asked for and received application forms for new pupils, I did not think there was much in it. Later I found a restlessness among the parents of the children in attendance from that Mission and wondered what could be the cause. It soon revealed itself in a peculiar way. Some time previous to Mr. Kendall's marriage I received from the Caughnawaga Agency two little girls, ****, Mrs. Kendall's daughter by her former husband, and **** an adopted daughter. Shortly after Mr. Kendall's visit to the Institute in Autumn last he wrote me requesting the release of these children, that he might send his step-daughter to Alma College and his adopted daughter to the French Institute at Montreal. Against my best judgment as expressed in a letter to Mr. Kendall I unfortunately granted his request. The former has spent the year at Alma; the latter entered the Institute at Montreal and was removed some time about the middle of the Fall term. Learning this, I wrote Mr. Kendall, asking for information as to whether it were true or not that she had returned to the Caughnawaga Reserve and was receiving no schooling. My purpose was to get possession of her with a view to her care and training in our school. I received no reply to my communication. Almost immediately after the discharge of these girls came the indications of the unrest above referred to. These children released from the control of the school seemed possessed of the idea that they were at liberty to say anything they liked regarding the school, its work, equipment, and its officers, regardless of truth or aught else. Some of these letters came into my possession...That they should have done this, I consider it not strange; but quite in keeping with that ingratitude too frequently manifest in the Indian character. That it should be listened to and believed by one of our Indian Missionaries was a very great surprise...

With regard to the specific case of the girls, **** and ****...by examination of the correction roll, I find that **** had but one minor report during the Quarter...and no punishment was attached. In the case of ****, she is reported in January and again in March, both reports being for having a dirty head. Each girl is furnished with a fine comb and her head is examined weekly by a lady officer, who is required to report weekly, all girls having unclean heads. Unfortunately **** gave trouble in this particular from the time of her entrance into the school. Reasoned with at first, afterward punished she was on the eve of having her hair cut close when she was called home on account of the death of her uncle. Knowing well the pride a girl takes in her hair and desiring to cultivate the same, I have removed the hair only in extreme cases. I deem it important that a girl should be held responsible for keeping her head clean, rather than have it maintained

in that condition by an officer. Coming and going as the pupils do, the battle is an almost unceasing one against vermin, not only of the head but of the body. In the case of this girl reported as having the itch, it was certainly not visible on her person when she left the Institute. In some unknown way a number of cases broke out in the school last Autumn but every effort possible was made to confine and destroy it, with the success that it spread to only a few beyond those first afflicted. While a loathsome, so called dirt disease, disliked by all, it is nevertheless hard to destroy and difficult to shut out when, as it has been during the past year, widely scattered in white as well as in Indian schools. So far as reassuring the Indians of the Bala Mission I must rely...upon the good sense and judgment of the missionary. Where the Missionary accepts the fanciful stories of young pupils, almost always anxious for a release from the restraints and kindly though firm discipline of the school, and the re-possession of the free, easy and undisciplined life of the Reserve, little can be done by the management by way of re-assuring parents. Mr. H. D. Johnson...has inspected the school twice annually for some nineteen years. He spends two days on each occasion, examines the class work, dormitories, dining-room, lavatory, sewing-room, barns, stables and out-buildings. He comes at will and is not infrequently here when I am away. He reports in detail to the Department but I know nothing of the nature of his report. I will be pleased if you will write to him direct and ask him as to the condition of the school and its management at his last or any previous visits or at any other time during my governorship.

The suggestion that "a cottage home system would be suitable for Indian children" would be worthy of consideration if we could increase the per capita about four fold. We would be glad to have an adequate increase for the demands of the present system but dream not of such an increase as would make the proposition feasible...

88. 3 June 1908 A. Sutherland to George
...Your letter...seems to cover the whole ground and should be satisfactory so far as the two girls who are named are concerned...I have now good hope that we will succeed in getting such a per capita grant for Muncey as will place the Institution in a much better position...P.S. I return Annie Martin's letter which is certainly a remarkable specimen.

89. 29 June 1908 George to Secretary Supt. Gen. DIA
Institute kitchen set on fire by **** says **** told her to do so. No damage wire instructions here.

90. 29 June 1908 Benson to Dep. Supt. Gen. DIA
Complaints have lately been received from parents of Indian children at the Mt. Elgin Institute, reflecting on the management of that institution, and a short time ago Mr.

Calvert, M.P., forwarded correspondence addressed to him by ****, demanding the return of his daughter from that institution on the ground of ill-health. ****'s letter to Mr. Calvert was accompanied by a medical certificate, which stated that she was suffering from incipient pulmonary tuberculosis and a general weak condition of the system and recommended her removal from the institute for proper care and medical attention.

The Principal was written to for a report...and he sent in a medical certificate from the regular attendant of the school, Dr. Morris, who said that he found her in good health and free from any active disease and taking into consideration the healthy surroundings he was of opinion that her remaining in the institution would be more beneficial than detrimental to her health. Mr. George...gives it as his opinion that, owing to the girl's ability and qualification to earn good wages as a domestic, the father wishes to have her under his control and that he experiences the same difficulty in retaining girls over sixteen on this account.

Another letter was received last week from Mr ****...renewing his application for his daughter's discharge.

From the correspondence it would appear that something more than the alleged illness of the daughter is influencing **** in this case, and a kitchen was set on fire by ****, who says that ****, the girl above referred to, told her to do so. Luckily no damage occurred and Mr. George has asked for instructions...an immediate inspection of this school should be made.

91. 22 June 1908 George Annual Report

Boys lavatory and gymnasium...was destroyed by fire on the night of November 20, 1907. The origin of the fire is unknown...

Health of Pupils.- The general health of the pupils has been good. One girl died from an attack of pneumonia followed by pulmonary tuberculosis. One girl was discharged suffering in a similar way, and one boy suffering from tuberculosis of the intestines.

General Remarks. - Improvements...added much to the appearance and convenience of the institute. We painted all the outside walls of the main building, pupils' dining-room, kitchen, bake-room, corridor, girls' play-room and basement. The walls of the chapel were covered with berlap...with the woodwork was carefully and tastefully painted. The plumbing in the main building was entirely overhauled and put in first-class order, which, together with the improvement to sewers of a year ago, makes the...conditions of the institute of the very best.

Fire, originating from some unknown cause, destroyed the boys' lavatory and gymnasium on the evening of November 20, 1907. This we have as yet been unable to replace, with the result that the boys are not so comfortable as we should like.

The spring was cold and seeding was necessarily late... resulted in the harvest being the lightest for many years..

92. 5 July 1908 McLean to Smith

...request that you will, at the earliest date possible, proceed to Muncey for...inspecting...Mt. Elgin...

Your inspection should deal chiefly with the management of this institution. Complaints have lately been received from the Parents of Indian children attending the school reflecting on the way in which the school is conducted. It is stated that scabies (the itch) has been prevalent and for this reason some parents are not disposed to return their children to the school who have been absent on leave. The Department hesitates to have the regulations put in force until it is satisfied whether there is any truth in this statement or not. Another complaint is that a girl, named **** has contracted tuberculosis while in the school and her father demands her discharge and has forwarded a medical certificate to the effect that she is suffering from incipient pulmonary tuberculosis, while the Principal, who was asked for a report regarding this case, has sent in a certificate from the regular medical attendant of the school to the effect that he found her in good health and free from any active disease and taking into consideration the healthy surroundings he was of opinion that her remaining in the institution would be more beneficial to her health. A telegram was received from Mr. George, the Principal of the school, early this week to the effect that the institute kitchen was set on fire by ****, who says that she acted at the instigation of the **** girl.

The Department would like you to satisfy yourself as to the conflicting statements regarding this girl's health and also to make a searching enquiry into the setting fire to the building. This is not the first incendiary fire that has taken place at this institution and the Department would like you to try to find out what has caused the pupils to take this means of avenging their real or imaginary wrongs. This must be put a stop to or serious consequences may result. It was only last November that the boys' play-house was destroyed by fire and in January another fire was set to the new barn by pupils of the Institute, who believed that they would not have to stay there if the buildings were burned.

In your report you should set forth fully the result of your investigations and give your own personal impressions as to the management of the school.

There are certain needed improvements to put the buildings in a thorough state of repair.

93. 18 July 1908 Smith to Secretary DIA

Pursuant to instructions...to make an inspection of the Mt. Elgin Institute...Feeling that it was better policy to secure all the information I could before calling upon Mr. George i.e. the complaints of Indians themselves, the view of the Medical Officers and Agents. I first interviewed Dr. Lawrence of St. Thomas...formerly practiced among the Indians about Mt. Elgin Institute. He stated that scabies always existed more or less amongst these Indians. There was a predisposition to it where people were housed up in small houses and particularly in the winter time. About two years ago he sent a large quantity of ointment to Mr. George as a remedy for this disease.

He also stated that tuberculosis was very prevalent.

I next interviewed Dr. McEwen of Melbourne, Medical Officer for the Chippewas and Munceys. When Mr. Sheppard was Principal of the Institute, scabies was very bad. Children were taken home and cured and when they went back caught it again. He frequently attended patients in the Institute then and knows of this but cannot speak of conditions under present regime, although he has frequently heard Indians complain still. Dr. McEwen says the drainage at the Institute is good and the water should be good. The situation is very healthy. There is no Doctor nearer than 7 miles.

The same evening I called upon **** the father of ****. **** stated that he had no complaint whatever against the Institute other than as to its management.

His complaints are (1) Pupils are punished by being put to work during school hours when they should be at school, citing the case of **** a Delaware from Six Nations who although at the Institute has not been in school for the past two years. (2) Pupils do not get enough to eat, and the same food is placed on the table day after day until it is eaten or becomes too stale or bad for food, except when visitors are expected when the pupils get an extra good meal. (3) Pupils are made to nurse the sick and sometimes tubercular patients. Said his daughter had to nurse a child who died of tuberculosis and she afterwards contracted the disease. There is no tuberculosis in his family. (4) Parents are not notified if children get sick. (5) Has seen body lice in heads of pupils when at Church. Thinks pupils are left to wash themselves, without sufficient supervision. "There is no body lice in our people at their own homes".

He did not know of any itch but said some pupils had skin diseases on their necks, a sort of scrofula. Knew nothing of the fire or its cause.

I then called on Chief **** a brother of ****'s. He said he had no children at the Institute. Some people will always complain and are never satisfied. He thinks the Institute is well managed and there is no cause for complaint. His brother's child **** won a foot race after returning from her visit to Dr. Cairns (who declared she had incipient tuberculosis) therefore he thinks she could not have been very sick.

Dr. McEwen was with me when I made these two visits and informed me afterwards that **** was a chronic grumbler and Chief **** was one of the most intelligent Indians on the Reserve. He also stated that Dr. **** was not a particularly reliable physician, was said to be a drug fiend, and had little weight in the profession.

Dr. McEwen is of opinion that he should be called in to attend patients from his own Reserve.

Next morning (Tuesday) I saw **** who had a boy at the Institute last year very ill. He alleged that he or some of his family had to go to the Institute every second night to nurse his child while the Matron took a night off to rest. The child got worse and worse and nothing was done for him so that at last he determined to take him home and get his own Doctor to attend to him, but it was too late, for the child died soon after getting home. His charge is that the boy did not get proper attention.

I also saw **** an Indian who was loud in his denunciation of the treatment of the pupils. He had none there himself but knew of several cases. None of these Indians had any complaint about the prevalence of scabies.

On Tuesday morning I met Mr. Sutherland the Agent at Muncey who drove me out to the Institute. Dr. McEwen told me that Mr. Sutherland would not hesitate to fully inform me of any cause of complaint if any existed, but evidently he is well satisfied as I could not get confirmation of any of the complaints above mentioned.

Dr. Morris of Delaware is his own and also Mr. George's family physician and is most attentive to his patients. He has telephone connection between his house and the Institute and can in his motor car reach them in 20 minutes if necessary.

It was about 11.45 before I informed Mr. George of the object of my visit as we were walking from the barn to the house. He asked me if I would like to see the children at dinner and when I said yes we went into the dining room. He said he knew no more than I did what they were going to have. Each child had a plate well filled with potato pie, plenty of gravy and small piece of meat, four half-slices of bread, but no butter, and water to drink. Mr. George said they had milk as far as it would go, at every meal, if there was any, but sometimes they were short. There was abundance of the potatoe pie left over in the kitchen and I noticed that the children got a second supply if desired. I think there was sufficient food.

The first question I took up was the fire in the kitchen. Mr. George showed me statements written and signed by ****, **** and **** respectively. **** stated that she was asked by **** to light the fire in the kitchen. After supper about 7 o'clock she went into the kitchen, took some paper out of a warming closet in the range set light to it through the stove door and placed it among some shingles used for kindling wood against the wainscotting. While doing so **** was watching at an outer door and **** at another door. **** stood at the kitchen door told **** to "hurry up' and after she had done it asked her if it was done and **** said yes. **** confirmed this; the other girl was too far away to hear what was going on. I then had the girls brought in individually and cross-examined them and they all confirmed what they had written, but Mr. George said that **** said more to me than he could get her to admit viz. that she told **** to "hurry up" but **** persisted in saying that she did not ask **** to set the place on fire while the other girls all said they were asked to do what they did by ****. **** is heavy stolid girl, who could probably be easily led, and influenced by fear if necessary, while **** is a small nervous child strong willed and aggressive, and sharp. The girls were told by **** to say if found out that she (****) was in the clothes room changing her clothes. They would give no reason for the fire other than that they wanted to see it burn. I am of opinion that **** was the ring leader, that **** did the deed, but that the other girls...though accessories, were not aware of what was actually going on or what was intended. Mr. George thinks the **** girl was put up to it by her father or some outside influence, but I do not think so, though perhaps she may have heard her father or others say "I wish the whole place would burn down" or something to that effect, which may have suggested the idea to her.

On the other hand I do not think there was anything in the daily surroundings or treatment of the girls to cause them to do the deed. In answer to a question **** told me she was happy at the school did not want to go home, got plenty to eat and did not have to work too hard. I think it was just a sudden attack of wickedness which came over the girl probably caused indirectly by complaints against Mr George and the School which she was no doubt hearing every time she went home.

The fire in the barn last January Mr. George states was started by a boy in the belief that if the place burnt down he would get a holiday. The boy had been punished and was chaffing under discipline.

The fire in the boys play house in November was clearly incendiary, but happened about 3 A.M. when all the pupils were up in their rooms. Mr. George says it cannot be charged to the pupils.

With reference to the charges made by **** I took particular pains to question his daughter closely on these points. She said she had plenty to eat that day, was never hungry. Her food was good and said no bad food was ever given to them. She was not sick and did not feel sick. Admitted winning the foot race after returning from her examination by Dr. Cairns. Had not to work too hard. Some days she worked in the laundry and some days at something else.

Did not have to nurse a sick girl, but only stayed in the room with another girl so that if the sick girl wanted anything she or the other girl could run for the matron. The sick girl, who had tuberculosis was able to attend to her own immediate wants up till Sunday when she died. She had paper cones for her sputa which she wrapped up herself and put in the fire. **** was there off and on from Friday morning till Saturday night. The child died

on Sunday. In view of the circumstances and the standing of the two physicians concerned I think that Dr. Morris' certificate should be received as containing the true statement of facts regarding ****'s health.

None of the children had any sores on their faces or bodies but when questioned further she said there was one...who scratched her arms, but no others. I had this girl brought in, and saw a pretty healthy crop of scabies on her arms, chest and back. The matron informed me that her instructions were that no other child was to use her towels etc but she said it was almost impossible to prevent it. This was the only case in the school and they thought it must have been contracted at the girl's home. There were occasionally cases of it, but nothing more than might happen in any white public school.

With regard to ****'s charge that a boy was two years at the Institute and not once in school Mr. George admitted this but said...the boy in question was a good boy in most ways but when he was sent to school he always ran away, and after recapturing him several times Mr. George came to the conclusion that he would let him go for good the next time as he could not afford to pay out so much Constable's fees and get no returns. He then suggested to the boy that he stay and work in the fields with a team and not go to school, and he has had no further trouble with him, but the moment school is suggested he rebels. Mr. George therefore concludes that it is better to teach the boy farming than have him run away for good.

The boy **** was full of disease when he came to the Institute and shortly after took to his bed and steadily declined despite the Doctor's care. Towards the end the parents persuaded him to let them come and sit with the boy, but as they smoked so much tobacco in the boy's bedroom doing more harm than good, he refused them admission again. They then insisted on taking the boy home, though Dr. Morris said it would be fatal. The case was fatal anyway but he had more comforts at the Institute than at the home.

Naturally when he got home he died soon after and the parents blame the institute for his death, because another Doctor said he could cure him. There is no case against Mr George on this charge.

I stayed at the Institute from Tuesday morning till Wednesday morning and had every opportunity of noting how affairs were managed.

The children appear bright, clean and happy. They have their sports after hours. All the boys take turns at different kind of field work. One group today will be hoeing mangels, while tomorrow they may be helping with the hay. The girls likewise change about. One girl waits on the Principal's dining table for a month, another on the officer's dining table, another helps the cook and so on giving each a turn, and varying their experience and occupations.

The discipline appears good, though not so strict and military-like as I believe is the custom at the Mohawk Institute. Mr. George strikes me as a man of great earnestness and enthusiastic in his work, and is doing his work faithfully and well.

The close proximity of the Reserve is the cause of most of the trouble I think. A boy after four when his duties are over, will skip away home across the fields perhaps two miles away and get back by six. They meet their parents at Church every Sunday, their friends and relations sometimes surreptitiously join them in their walks and if there is discontent it is kept alive by this means of communication. A boy quite clean has returned after one of these short visits infected with body lice. While I was there parents came asking permission to see their children. They join them in the play ground and in fact are hanging around the neighbourhood more or less all the time.

The sanitary condition is good. The kitchens bakeshop, lavatories etc are clean and tidy. The barns yards and stables are clean and tidy and Mr. George appears to spare neither himself nor his officers in the discharge of his duties.

The only recommendation I have to make in regard to the management is that no pupil should be asked, in fact it should be forbidden, to attend any patient, suffering from tuberculosis, or even to enter the room where such a patient is, and...greater precautions should be taken to prevent the spread of scabies by contact with towels, clothes etc than is now done.

As to the fire...some punishment should be inflicted upon **** and **** though it may be difficult to satisfy a Magistrate that the **** girl is guilty. The other girls are practically innocent of wrong doing. **** has been confined to a separate room ever since the fire and the matter should be attended to without delay.

94. 20 July 1908 Smith to Secretary DIA
...report...on the needed improvements...as a result of my inspection last week.

Boys' Play House This building was burnt down last fall and the insurance upon it $2300 was paid to the Department...Since then the boys have no place to go in wet weather except to the Laundry which is of course quite unsuitable. With $700 in addition to the insurance money I think a very suitable building could be erected and it is very much needed...

Work Shop For the purpose of giving the boys more instruction in manual work, better shop facilities are required...A work shop is also required for ordinary every day repairs and improvements...estimated cost of all the improvements required...$5700...Mr. George informed me that if he could choose his own time for doing this work, he could save a great deal in cost of labour...Barn and Play house...should be attended to at once, the former because it has to be ready for the crops and the latter for

the boys in wet as well as in cold weather.

The buildings, belonging to the Department, should be maintained and kept in good repair, and I must say I was surprised at the general appearance of old age which attached to nearly all the out buildings.

Some 300 to 400 head of cattle are wintered there...The cow stables already completed are models of cleanliness and convenience and if those to be built are equal to them, nothing more can be desired...

95. 6 August 1908 Benson to Dep. Supt. Gen. DIA
In view of certain complaints received from parents of Indian children attending the Mt. Elgin Institute reflecting on the management of that school, Mr Superintendent Smith of Brantford was sent there to make an inspection...

Mr. Smith's report...goes to show that the school is in his opinion well managed. He makes one or two recommendations which it might be well to have carried out. The principal reason for sending Mr. Smith to the school was in connection with an outbreak of fire which was said to be the work of an incendiary. Mr. Smith obtained ample proof that the fire was set by one of the girl pupils at the instance of another girl...who is a daughter of ****, one of the strongest opponents of the school. Mr. Smith... recommends that some punishment should be inflicted upon these two girls, although he says it would be difficulty to satisfy a magistrate that the **** girl is guilty. She made a catspaw of **** who actually fired the building and if she could escape punishment there would be very little use in proceeding against the **** girl, who is only a tool in her hands. In fact I do not think it would be a wise policy of the Department to bring either girl before a magistrate; if conviction was secured they would most likely be sent to prison, which would do them more harm than good. In my opinion their punishment should be left to the Principal. The whole trouble appears to be that **** was anxious to get his daughter away from the school and he is more to blame than either of the girls. Fortunately the fire did little or no damage.

Another complaint refers to the prevalence of scabies...Mr. Smith found only one case and it was thought that this must have been contracted at the home of the girl who was affected. There have been occasional cases, but nothing more than might happen in any white public school. On the whole Mr. Smith's report is favourable to the institution and he thinks that the proximity of the school to the reserve is the cause of most of the trouble.

He concludes by recommending that pupils should be forbidden to attend any patient suffering from tuberculosis and it would be well to instruct the Principal to this effect and that greater precautions should be taken to prevent the spread of scabies.

It would be well if the minds of the Indians could be

disabused as to the treatment of pupils at this school. The Gibson Indians, who are all Methodists and have had several children in attendance, are specially bitter against the Principal...Mr. Supt. Macdonald should be instructed to inform these Indians when he next visits the reserve of the result of Mr. Smith's inspection....

96. 21 August 1908 George to Secretary DIA
...It is now nine months since the Boys' Playhouse was burned and we have been seriously inconvenienced during that time for the want of some suitable place for them, and in view of the approaching cold season, this inconvenience will be intensified. Under the conditions following the fire the discomfort of the boys during the day in their temporary quarters had a measure of excuse or justification, but to enter another winter after allowing the entire summer season to pass with out any effort to make provision for their wants cannot be justified in any measure whatever.

In order to make it safe to house the season's harvest I was forced to go on with the repairs of the big barn...I have expended over $700 in material...

97. 2 September 1908 Benson to Dep. Supt. Gen. DIA
...Principal...proposes to utilize the old shop and reconstruct it as a play-house...Mr George is thoroughly competent to carry on the work...recommend that he be authorized to proceed at once....the school cannot be successfully carried on without this building...

98. 7 December 1908 A. Sutherland to Going
...Respecting the matter about which you write, there is probably a slight misapprehension. So far as his ministerial and moral character is concerned, Brother George is responsible only to his Conference and only a member or official of that Conference would have the right to interfere. But as regards his official conduct as Principal of the Mount Elgin Industrial Institute he is responsible to the Board of Missions and its Executive Committee and to no other authority. I assume that if anything occurred reflecting upon Mr. George's ministerial or moral character it would at once be referred to the Conference authorities, but I am not aware of anything of the kind in the present case. The matter will be dealt with, if at all, by the Executive Committee of the Board of Missions, and being now a sense what the lawyers call sub judice it is not open for discussion...it is quite out of the question for me to supply you with documents or additional information touching this case...a statement of financial matters covering the administration of a large institution for a number of years and received...from non-official sources are always unreliable and may be utterly misleading, hence it would be very unwise to base conclusions upon them much less make them the subject

of general discussion. Do not make the mistake of assuming that the Missionary Board, or its Executive, are destitute of a sense of justice, or a feeling of sympathy, and that it is necessary for outside parties to interfere to prevent a Brother from being cruelly treated...the less such cases are stirred up and interfered with, the easier they are settled in a way satisfactory to all concerned.

99. 21 May 1909 George Annual Report
...Class-room Work...very satisfactory....It has been our desire to add manual training as a special feature of class work as soon as the boys' recreation hall is rebuilt...

Health and Sanitation. - The general health of the pupils has been good. One girl was discharged suffering from scrofula. The completion of the reconstruction of the plumbing, together with the abundant supply of water furnished by the hydraulic pumps, has improved very much the sanitary conditions of the main building.

100. 13 July 1909 Shannon to A. Sutherland
...I proceeded to Mt. Elgin Institute on July 2nd...found both the old Principal and the new...during the last two months the most saleable of the horses and cattle...had been sold in order to pay off indebtedness. 280 head of cattle had been carried through the winter, with only feed sufficient for 175...yet at a time when pasture was abundant 150 of the best were sold. Some of the horses were sold for less than cost. What are left both of horses and cattle are mostly of very poor quality and unsaleable.

The stock was carefully taken at a valuation agreed upon between Mr. McVitty and Mr. George, and stands at $18496 as against $26076 a year ago and $17089 when Mr. George took charge in 1903.

During the year the Institute had a revenue of $23459.42 - that is, $10000 from the Missionary Society (which is nearly $3000 more than was ever granted before) $11759.42 from sale of cattle, horses, dairy and farm produce and $1700 special grant from the Indian Department for improvements. And yet there is an overdraft at the bank of $1427.44. Also the following sums are due...$3191.46. Add to this the loan from the Missionary Society made in 1904 - 5000...and you have a total indebtedness unpaid of $9618.90.
...during the last six years, the increased expenditure, provided in part by the loan of $5000 from the Society, has served to increase the value of the assets of the Institute. Now that the live stock has been so greatly reduced and now that the assets stand at a figure little in excess of what they were in 1903 one would have expected that the large sale of live stock recently made would have enabled the Principal to repay the $5000 loan. But the $5000 loan is still unpaid and accounts and notes beside, amounting to over $4000...

1909 - 1934
Rev. Samuel McVitty 1909-1934 - Rev. Oliver Strapp assistant principal 1928

1. 7 August 1909   T. Ferrier Report

I spent from July 29th to August 7th at the school. The time was occupied in stock-taking and assisting Mr. McVitty in his initiation to the many duties devolving upon him as principal of the Institute.

Mr. Shannon has made a careful audit of the books and accounts up to June 30th...the income for the past year was $23,459.42...

Missionary society	$10,000
Government Grant for Repairs	$1,700
Sale of cattle, horses, etc.	$11,759.42

The audit also shows a deficit of $4,618.90. If to this is added a special loan of $5000 from the Missionary Society and the increase of $4000 from the Board over and above the Government grant, we have a total deficit of $13,618.90 all of which has been paid by the missionary society...the grant of $10000 which was made by the Board for last year will have to be the minimum grant for maintenance for the future...the Government grant must be increased from $60 to $100 per pupil.

...a complete inventory of all chattels together with the value of the same is herewith given...the total value of the stock is $12,060.50 which is $6,435.60 less than that given by Mr. George. This difference is accounted for by the following:-

1. I have not included any part of the plant...
2. The former valuation is...much beyond its real value.
3. A number of the farm and garden implements are absolutely worthless and have been so entered.

The live stock has been severely culled and all that were saleable disposed of. The books show that since June 14th, $4,126 for horned cattle and $1,335 for horses have been received.

About one half of the milch cows are not of much use for milking purposes and are too light and poor for beef; only four of them were known to be with calf on July 1st. There were 35 cows milking at the beginning of July, and the cream cheque for the month of June was $17.45, and for the previous month $16. These low returns are partly due to a lack of supervision of the milking. A new man has been put in charge of the stock and the revenue from this source will be increased.

250 bushels of wheat were sold in June with only about two weeks flour on hand.

Potatoes have also to be purchased for immediate use, and with only four acres in crop means that the most of the year's supply and seed will have to be provided.

The selling of so much of the livestock when pasture was abundant is a serious handicap on the chances of profit from the herd for the next year or two.

The sale of $5461 worth of live stock in the latter half of June, reduced the liabilities against the Institute. At the same time it has left the stock in such an unsatisfactory condition that something must be done to replace a portion of it this fall. There will be feed sufficient to winter about 200 head. I...recommend that a loan of $2000 be advanced to the Principal to purchase about 50 stock cattle and some good cows.

The Main Building, the two large barns, stables and hog-pen are in a good state of repair, but all the other out-buildings and sheds are in a delapidated condition and will soon need to be rebuilt.

The bath tubs in the laundry are of wood and are not plumbed with the drain. They are about used up and unsanitary. New iron tubs and two steam boilers should be installed at once, and an additional grant of $500 made for material...

Rev. S. R. McVitty and his excellent wife have taken up the work in an energetic and beautiful spirit.

2. 1 September 1909   McVitty to Secretary DIA

...Mr Ferrier informed me some time ago that your department were willing to put some new wash tubs & plumbing into our laundry here. I hope you can make it possible to have the work done immediately. The laundry is in a dreadful condition. In fact if any sanitary inspector came upon the scene on wash day we would run serious risk of a report for criminal neglect. It is quite usual to have a couple of girls in bed for a couple of days after washing and one mother told me she hadent the slightest hesitation in saying her girl met her death there. I have no authority...to make the change but it ought not to continue...

3. 12 September 1909   McVitty to Secretary DIA

What about the repairs to our Laundry recommended by Mr. Ferrier. It is in a dreadful condition utterly unsafe from a sanitary point of view. This is wash day and a friend of one of the pupils who was present and saw the condition of things told me she would bring in the health Inspector if this thing is not attended to at once. This would be a serious matter for the school...

4. 20 September 1909   McVitty to A. Sutherland

In reply to your request for private memo. would respectfully submit to you the following facts re how I found matters at the Institute July 1st 1909
1. I found a feeling of great unrest among the Pupils. Truancy almost a daily occurence
2. Much disatisfaction among the Indians on the neighbouring reserves, with the treatment the children were receiving at the Institute
3. I am pleased to be able to say this is passing away. We have had no truants since I came here and our school

is full at present and we have refused very many applications from parents of would be pupils. We have the confidence of the Pupils and their parents.

4.   I found the farm almost stripped of stock Mr. George having sold $5445.00 from rising of London Conference until 1st July. This meant that the stock remaining had been culled over so often that there was scarcely a saleable beast on the place, and only one or two sound horses all the rest were more or less blemished 40 Cows having earned for Mr. George 16.00 at the cheese factory for month of May and 17.45 for June. The young cattle were of very poor quality and have been wretchedly cared for during the winter...The stock man, whom I promptly dismissed was guilty of criminal neglect. Most of these cattle we have still on hand some of them those exchanged for cattle of better quality - paying the difference in cash. Owing to abundance of pasture most of them have improved wonderfully. We culled out about 20 cows for Butchers and are fatting them. We are now milking 22 and our cheese AK for August was $77.45 a very marked gain in this department.

5. I found most of the farm implements old and worn out. Had been carried in stock for years but not used, these Mr. Ferrier culled out as useless. Some of the machinery purchased by Mr. George is not very useful. In fact is not being used by successful farmers but we are making the best of it..

6.   I found the children especially the boys much in need of clothing especially shoes. The shoes usually purchased in early summer had not been purchased when we came here. All the wheat in stock about a car load was sold end of June and we were forced to buy flour at 83.20 per cwt. It takes 1 cwt per day. We had no Potatoes on hand and only enough planted to last about Xmas necessitating the purchase of about 300 bags for use and seed until the new ones are ready next year. And about enough wheat this year to run us until Xmas. We have no barley at all & will need to purchase a large quantity to mix the feed for winter use. When Mr. Ferrier called on me...in May I urged him to second Bro. George's continuation. I must say now, having seen for myself it is a pity he was not removed years ago. I say this simply from a business point of view.

All this seems a sorry tale but you ask for facts, and I state them as I would if Mr George was present.

...after all this is said Mrs McVitty and I are pleased with the place & work. We find it pleasant yet arduous. It is many sided, and demands constant care. Things are prospering and we are all happy Pupils Officers, and Principal as a Summer day. All our Bills are paid promptly we save every cent of Discount & are buying at the wholesale. We have a good home atmosphere and are in different ways seeking to advance the moral & spiritual tone of the place...

5. 2 December 1909 McLean to A. Sutherland
...report from the Public School Inspector...unsatisfactory work being performed by Miss Wismer, the junior teacher...it will be necessary to make a change as soon as possible...The senior teacher, Mr. Dowsell, is doing splendid work...a capable teacher should be in charge of the junior room from which his pupils are drafted.

6. 10 December 1909 McVitty to A. Sutherland
...gratified that the Department is moving in the right direction. I am sorry they did not see their way clear to go a little further & make the grant $100 per cap. as Mr. Ferrier recomd. After nearly six months close study of conditions here I am fully satisfied it will take at least that amt to run this school successfully. The school has been seriously handicapped in the past & its usefulness much lessened by lack of funds...It has become almost impossible to get efficient Officers & teachers without paying very large salaries. Our head Teacher is...$600... house heated & milk for use of his family. His hours are from about 7 to 9 seven days of the week. I know he is offered a position in a white school at same salary, hours from 9 to 4 pm...replied to fifteen persons advertising the position of cook etc., not one of them would accept the position even at a good salary. It is too confining and trying. Mrs. McVitty has been forced to take it for past month or more. The price of food has increased considerably and the pupils and their parents are much more exacting than formerly. A five cent meal for a pupil would mean $54.75 per year...leaving $5.25 for clothing, sickness Education & all other necessary expense. To meet this condition pupils have been kept in the school longer than necessary simply for the work they could do and very many of them left it in the end far from being the friend either of the Government or the Missionary Society. It is my conviction that the aim of the school should be to fit boys and girls for farm and domestic work (not by any means for office work or even teachers unless in very few cases) and just as soon as they are well fitted to earn their own living let them go out to good homes and do so. The last couple of years they are kept here after they and their parents think they should go tends to develop all that is sullen and revengeful in the Indian nature besides larger boys and girls in this mood have a most baneful effect upon younger pupils. As a rule pupils should enter the school at ten to twelve years and leave it about sixteen and they should be and would be pupils from the best families & would go out as a real asset to the church and the nation. The pupils would feel that they were kept here until they could help themselves and no longer and in most cases they and their parents would be our friends, and they would early take their place in the nation's life and be a real help to those who so much need farm and domestic helps...We are enjoying the work here and doing our very best...to make this School a great blessing to the Indian people...

7. 7 January 1910 A. Sutherland
...Mr. McVitty...succeeded in engaging a Junior Teacher... she has made a good beginning...Mr. McVitty has succeeded in obtaining the services of a young man from Goderich who has had good experience and the best of references.

Mr. McVitty reports the school in excellent condition. The pupils orderly...punishment very seldom resorted to...

8. 11 January 1910 S. Stewart to A. Sutherland
...acknowledge the receipt...testimonials of Miss M. M. Armour who has been appointed Junior Teacher...the resignation of Mr. Dowswell...is very much regretted...he had been doing most excellent work...

9. 23 January 1910 McVitty to A. Sutherland
...enclose your testimonials of Mr. Williams our Head Teacher...Both our Teachers are doing well I visit their rooms often as possible and think the work being done is excellent. Mr. Williams is a single man about 30 years of age...Both Teachers take a deep interest in the religious life of the Institute...

We are getting along very nicely & find it easy to take a sympathetic interest in the life & work of the pupils. We have some serious difficulties to face but none of them are insurmountable & we are finding the work quite enjoyable...I feel...an ever increasing love for these children...

10. 28 January 1910 McVitty to Secretary DIA
...we awarded the contract for Laundry Tubs...have experienced some trouble in securing tubs so that there has been nothing done as yet.
...in view of the fact that we are likely to have younger girls in the future I have concluded it is a great mistake to put in these tubs at all. The amount of money to be expended $415.00, would be sufficient to install a nice little steam plant, such as they have in most Institutions...

Since our play house was burned we have been using the drying room above the Laundry for boys play house, and in winter weather find it most difficult to get our clothes dried...girls are quite tired after Monday forenoons washing; and almost unfit for school during the afternoon...

11. 1 February 1910 Secretary DIA to McVitty
...your proposed plan would lighten the work for the employees and the girls of the Institution, it has one drawback, that is, the girls would receive probably no instruction in ordinary household laundry work such as they will be required to perform when they leave the Institution, either in their own homes or as servants in the homes of white people. The Department would like to know how...you would propose to give the instruction referred to, which would appear to be most necessary.

12. 17 March 1910 McLean to McVitty
...It must not be forgotten that these institutions are partly conducted for the instruction of the girls in domestic employments. The laundry work of such a large institution would...be arduous for the younger girls, but when they arrive at a certain age they should be taught how to properly cleanse wearing apparel and bedding.

13. 17 March 1910 McVitty to Secretary DIA
...We would retain a number of our best tubs & repair them so that the girls could do the light washing & thus get the desired training but in the steam washer we would do all the heavy work. And there is a great deal of it - The great majority of our girls are very young and really not able to do such hard work...

14. 31 March 1910 McVitty Report
Accommodation. - The main building furnishes room for about 100 pupils and a staff of eight officers. Separate residences are supplied for four officers...

Attendance. - The number of pupils authorized by the department...is 100, and the average attendance is 101.

Class-room Work. - The half day system is followed in case of senior pupils. One week division I is in school in forenoon and division II in the afternoon; the following week the order is reversed.

Division III, composed of about 50 junior pupils, is in school full time. Hours are 9 a.m. to 11.45 a.m., and from 1 to 3.30 p.m. The authorized course of study is followed, and the results are quite satisfactory...

Farm and Garden. - We harvested...30 acres of wheat, 90 acres of oats, 60 acres of corn, 2 acres of buckwheat, 3 acres of potatoes, 6 acres roots, and in the garden all vegetables necessary for our own use.

Industrial Work. - The boys are carefully instructed in all branches of agricultural work, including care and management of horses, cows, pigs, poultry and bees; also Carpentering, fencing and cement work. The girls are taught housekeeping, baking, cooking, laundry and dairy work, also cutting and making of garments, quilting, knitting and fancy needlework.

Moral and Religious Training. - A morning and evening worship...a lady and gentleman officer, attend divine worship at the Colborne church...Sabbath school is conducted under the superintendence of the principal, in the chapel of the institute, each Sabbath afternoon. The school is divided into three classes. Each member of the staff is connected with some branch of the Christian Church, and all are seeking by precept and example to teach the principles of the Christian religion.

Health and Sanitation. - The health of the pupils and staff has been splendid. We have not found it necessary to call a physician during the year. We attribute this largely to an abundance of good food, fresh air, and plenty of outdoor exercise. One boy received treatment at the General hospital, London, for weak eyes. The building is kept clean. The plumbing and ventilation are in a satisfactory condition...

Ex-pupils. - Two pupils were discharged at the request of their parents and are living at home. Four graduated from the school during the year. One of these is studying shorthand and book-keeping, another is receiving three dollars a week as a domestic; the third, four dollars a week as cook in a private home; and the fourth, a salary of $300 per annum teaching school.

All four are a credit to the institution...

General Remarks. - During the year some necessary repairs have been done to the outbuildings, and a new poultry-house is at present in course of erection. It will provide accommodation for 200 fowls, and will be one of the most up-to-date in the country.

We are also installing a small steam plant in our laundry, and hope...to lighten the labour...whilst we retain a number of tubs, which afford ample opportunity for training the girls in domestic laundry work.

The conduct of the pupils, with one or two exceptions, has been excellent; their interest in the different departments of work, is growing. Punishment is our 'strange work', and the atmosphere of the place is home-like.

The officers are efficient and faithful in their work, and seeking to promote the best interests of the school.

15. 11 October 1910 McVitty to Shore

...my salary is only $800. per year. The late Principal had $900 and Essex had promised me a salary of $1000 when I left and are paying it to my successor...if you look over the statement forwarded to your office you will see a deficit of nearly $5000 for previous year has been turned into a gain of nearly $5000 this year. I can say truthfully the school in every Dep. is a success. Order has succeeded chaos. What was practically a penitentiary has been succeeded by a model school and a model home. The good name of the school has been regained & parents are pleading to get their children in. I have dismissed all inefficient officers and raised salaries of present staff about 20/-. We owe no man any thing and are improving stock, implements & grounds, rapidly. Mrs. McVitty has worked in the Institution without pay or reward harder than an officer. My hours have been from 5.30 am to 8.30 pm all summer without a holiday. Found it absolutely necessary to be on hand. Now Mrs. McVitty thinks and I think that my salary should be $1000. I dont ask any additional grant and will guarantee to keep all matters in best of shape...

16. 16 November 1910 McVitty to Shore

In reference to the proposed change in the relationship of the Gov. to Indian Industrial Schools. May I ask to what extent do they wish control? Are you surrendering the authority the Church has had over the staff &c? Will this still be a Methodist school? or nonsectarian...Our Head Teacher is just in the balance as to continuing after present year. He is a splendid man & missionary in his thought and purpose. Would give his life to this work I think under Church auspices but would not remain if the staff is...at the mercy of political parties and the school used as dumping ground for political "hasbeens"...

17. 19 November 1910 Shore to McVitty

...The arrangements made with the Department...affecting Muncey Institute make no changes...increase the Government grant...claims the right of stricter inspection of school buildings...right to insist on the maintenance of a high standard of efficiency in the work...

18. 13 February 1911 Scott to Ogilvie

Schools of the first class must be provided with a sanitary system of water closets. These may be located outside...if a sufficient number are also located inside the building convenient to the dormitories, play-rooms etc., but we could not accept any system of old style outside closets if we are to pay the high per capita grant.

19. 31 March 1911 T. Ferrier Report

BUILDINGS

The main building is kept neat and clean. Considerable furnishings have been put in and some improvements made...new ranges for the kitchens, some good furniture and...an electric light plant, which furnishes light for the main buildings, cottages, laundry, stables and barns. The light plant was put in by the Government...

CLASS ROOMS.

The half day system is carried out for most of the older scholars, while many of the younger attend the class rooms all day.

The teachers are doing good work and up-to-date methods are in vogue, especially in the senior rooms, where a class of nine are in preparation for the Entrance examinations in July...

CHILDREN AND STAFF.

The health of all has been very good, the doctor's bill and drug account being only $35 for the past year and nine months.

The conduct of the pupils has been worthy of praise, and they have greatly assisted the Principal and his staff to create a homelike atmosphere about the entire Institution. There are 102 children in attendance.

FINANCIAL CONDITION.

The business of the institute has been well conducted. All accounts have been settled monthly on a cash basis, goods have been purchased at fair market value and the cattle and products of the farm sold at a fair market price. The management of the milk cows is worthy of mention. The Institute has been kept in meat, butter and milk and the cream sold has averaged over $200 a month. The profits on the sale of the live stock have been good. The Principal has returned to the Mission Rooms the $500 voted...for cattle in 1909, all accounts are paid up to date, and there is a balance of $139.50 in the bank.

THE FUTURE MANAGEMENT OF THIS INSTITUTE

I paid a visit to Ottawa and discussed the basis of a new agreement with the Deputy Minister and the Superintendent of the Education Department. Two propositions were under consideration:-1. The Church to make certain needed repairs to bring the school into Class

"A". This would involve an outlay of about $5000; also to keep the plant in repair from year to year. This would involve about $1000 a year, and the government would give a grant of $100 per pupil for 100 pupils.

2. The Government to make all needed repairs and in so doing provide accommodation for 125 pupils, and keep the entire plant in repair; also pay the rents, which have averaged $900 per year for the last seven years, and give the management $? per pupil up to the number of 125.

...The second proposal was accepted and the contract will be made out by the Department....good management will place the Institution on a self-sustaining basis.

...the needed repairs to place the school in Class "A":-
1. Fire Escapes, - Pole.
2. ...closets in the four dormitories...set in cement and enclosures made.
3. A boys building - to provide class rooms, boys' recreation room - boys' wash room, - bathtubs and shower baths, and lavatory.
4. More bathing and washing accommodation for the girls.
5. Steam plant to supply heat for all the buildings and necessary power.

20. 31 March 1911 McVitty Report

Attendance. - The number of pupils authorized by the department...is 100, average attendance is 102.

Class-room Work...A voluntary study period of one hour is allowed advanced pupils each evening...During the year 13 boys and 17 girls were promoted to higher standards. The pupils are diligent and efficient in their school work...

Industrial Work. - The boys are carefully instructed in all branches of agricultural work...also apiculture, gardening (vegetable and floral), fencing, cement work, and engineering (steam and gasoline).

Health and Sanitation. - The health of the pupils and staff has been splendid, sickness is of very rare occurrence. This is accomplished by regularity and an abundance of fresh air, outdoor exercise and good food.

Recreation. - In winter all outdoor games are indulged in, such as skating, hockey, tobogganing, sleigh-riding, etc. etc. Indoors various parlour games are provided and regular periods allotted for these games. In summer great interest is taken in baseball and basketball. All games suitable for field-day exercise, such as running, jumping, etc., etc., are practised, and regular field-days are held. Hunting and fishing are also provided in season. The boys receive military drill.

Ex-pupils. - Six pupils were discharged during the year at the request of parents. Only two of these were old enough to obtain work. Both are doing well. During the year a few ex-pupils who are really 'making good' visited us and encouraged both staff and pupils.

Conduct...shows marked improvement...Punishment seldom has to be administered; in fact only one serious offence occurred during the year.

21. 8 April 1911 Scott to Pedley

I visited the Mount Elgin School...recommendation I

could make...under the new Agreement.

The Capital expenditures...have been contributed by the Indian Bands interested, the Department and the Methodist Church, the latter having spent over $18,000 in the last 9 or 10 years. If the property were considered to belong to the Church authorities we could pay them $100 per capita per annum, and they would have to make the necessary improvements. But it is clearly impossible to take this view as the land on which the buildings are erected is part of an Indian Reserve, and as both the Indians and the Department were largely interested in the erection of the building...therefore, we should consider that the Government owns the property and made the necessary improvements. By this decision the Church will only be entitled to $80.00 per capita per annum.

We should assume the payment of the rental for farming property...they require about 800 or 1000 acres...

In going over the buildings with Mr. Ferrier and Mr McVeity, we decided that it would be better to rebuild the Boys' Building. This was destroyed by fire and we still hold the insurance which now amounts, with accumulated interest, to $1365.75. In this building will be situated the shower baths which could be used by both boys and girls on special days set apart for their use, and lavatories and closets for the boys as well as a large play-room. It is not necessary to have the lavatories for the boys in the Main Building because they do not wash in the morning until after their work is done, before they go to breakfast.

The school room accommodation in what is called the Annex will be sufficient, as the large room now used for a chapel in the Main Building can be used as a class room from time to time if necessary.

The water closets in the dormitories should have cement floors under and surrounding them and there are some necessary improvements to be made in the girls' lavatories and water closets in the basement...as the accommodation is by no means sufficient.

The Laundry Building also requires...some changes.

All the buildings should be heated by a central steam plant as the present furnaces do not heat the buildings properly in cold and windy weather. There is ample accommodation in the building for 120 or more pupils and if the upper dormitory is used the number to be provided for should be placed at that figure. There are 60 on the waiting list for this school.

Fire escapes should be provided for the dormitories in the Main Building.

When these improvements are made the school will be a credit to the country as the management is everything that could be desired.

22. 19 May 1911 McLean to McVitty

...the proposed building...The Department is desirous of installing shower baths and other bathing facilities which can be used by both the boys and girls...

23. 21 May 1911 T. Ferrier

...we...members of a conference appointed by the General Board of Missions of the Methodist Church...relative to matters pertaining to the Educational and spiritual welfare of the Indian people under the care of the Methodist church...are in receipt of many statements from missionaries and others...that...the work being done in Day schools on the reserves is very inefficient and unsatisfactory...it is almost impossible to obtain a supply of teachers willing to undertake this work, and quite impossible to obtain a supply of competent teachers.

...Mr. H. D. Johnson, I.P.S. for West Middlesex, considers, after a long experience that an Indian teacher can produce the best results in an Indian school.

...Rev. S. R. McVitty, has agreed to a proposition hereinafter out-lined.

We...wish to submit to the Department of Indian Affairs the following scheme...

1...Mt. Elgin Industrial Institution undertake to train a class of Indian students annually for reserve public school teaching, in addition to present work.

2...the government give...an annual grant of $200 per capita for each pupil thus instructed, the institution to be responsible for the education, board and clothing of all such pupils.

3...the limit of the regular course in the main school be Provincial High School Entrance, and that this examination be admission to the special Model Class...

6...all pupils entering this class must possess a certificate of good moral character signed by a clergyman, missionary, Principal or other responsible person...

8...a carefully defined curriculum on Model School work be prepared...

9...a final examination, written and practical, be conducted by the teacher in charge and by the local government inspector of public schools, who shall have supervision of the work done during the term.

10...successful candidates be awarded certificates signed by the local government public school inspector and by the principal of the institution, which will be accepted as sufficient legal qualification for teaching in the Day school on a reserve.

11...the government make provision in the contemplated building...for these school rooms, and such other equipment as may be necessary...

24. 31 May 1911 Shore to McVitty

Brother Ferrier...reports that Mr. Scott was not favorably impressed with the recommendations of our Indian Conference...views of the Department...

1. The Department has never had one Indian as a teacher on a reserve who has been a success.

2. The Indians have no confidence in one another. They are jealous of each other.

3. The Indian needs the stimulation and inspiration of the

white man to hold him at his job.

4. The Indian girls do not like teaching, they prefer nursing.

5. The boys prefer a job somewhere else than on a reserve.

6. The best results in our Day School on reserves has always been by white teachers...

7. The policy favours anything is good enough for an Indian School.

8. The present plan and policy of the government is to give this training by our Normal and Model schools.

9. The Church of England has tried it for years in the north country by sending boys to UCC...

10. How many Indian teachers has Mr. Johnson under his teaching.

11. The statement made that the schools are unsatisfactory is not in harmony with facts. We have at least 75% fair...

12. The Department will give a fair salary for white teachers from $400 up to $460 per month...

25. 20 June 1911 McLean to Shore

...after careful consideration, it is not thought advisable to favourably entertain the proposal. The experience of the Department with Indian teachers has not been very happy and does not tend to show that the educational extension proposed would be profitable. The spirit in which the document is composed is noted with gratification...shows an earnest desire to improve Indian educational conditions.

26. 3 July 1911 McVitty to Smith

...the two Bradley boys truanted from this School yesterday mrg. I am very sorry as they have behaved splendidly since coming here. Will you be good enough to employ a Constable and send them back at once. To alow them to remain away would be ruinous to the order of the school. This matter of truanting is almost a thing of the past here and we want to nip it in the bud.

27. 10 July 1911 Smith to Secretary DIA

...an account of $17.85 being the expenses of Constable Garlow in arresting William and Ernest Bradley...and conveying them to the Mt. Elgin Institute from which they ran away...The reason given by the boys for running away was that they had no money sent to them since they were placed there some few months ago...

28. 5 October 1911 Hughes, McVitty, Gibb, Kingham to Shore

...suggest that a resolution from the Indian Department be forwarded to each council...men and women living immorally forfeit Band privileges...we especially deplore the evil effects a visit to such homes during the summer holidays must have upon pupils attending Industrial Schools, and are of opinion that pupils should not be allowed to visit parents known to be living immorally.

29. 31 March 1912 McVitty Report

Accommodation...Owing to an increase in our authorized attendance, additional accommodation is being provided this summer.

Attendance. - The average attendance for the year was 115. Our authorized attendance now is 125.

Class-room Work...During the year promotions were made, subject to the approval of the inspector, as follows: Standard I to II 12, Standard II to III 5, Standard III to IV 13, Standard IV to V 7.

Five candidates wrote the...Entrance examination and all were successful, two having over 75 per cent...

Moral and Religious Training. - Incidental moral instruction is given from literature, history, etc., and from current local and foreign events...

Health and Sanitation. - Situated upon the high banks of the river, our sewage system works splendidly. We have also an excellent supply of spring water piped to all parts of the building. The health of the pupils has been good except for a serious outbreak of scarlatina last fall. This disease was brought to the school by certain pupils who had been home for holidays. The results, however, were not serious except in two or three cases.

Ex-pupils. - During the year 9 pupils left the school; 4 boys and 5 girls. Two of the boys truanted: the other two returned to their homes. All of the girls went home; one has since died.

Conduct. - The conduct has been the best in the history of the institution. A home-like atmosphere and a mutual sympathy between pupils and staff exist. Consequently reports and punishments are almost unknown.

General Remarks. - This year we added two new departments to our school:-

(a) Music, under the supervision of a competent instructor. The senior girls take this subject and are doing splendid work.

(b) Model class, under the supervision of the head teacher. Three girls and one boy are in training for the work in Indian schools. They are "making good" in every respect.

30. 7 May 1912 T. Ferrier to Secretary DIA

I have made an annual inspection...and found everything in first class shape. The children are happy, well-fed, well-clothed, all in the best of health, and one hundred and twenty five of them present. The entire stock...live stock, household goods, farm implements, dry goods, and food, has increased in value fully six thousand dollars in the three years Mr. McVitty has been in charge. I found all the accounts paid in full and a good cash balance standing to the credit of the Institution...for the amount of work and the class of work that Mr. McVitty is doing for the welfare of that Institution, he should receive at least fourteen or fifteen hundred dollars a year.

31. 23 September 1912 Myers Rama

Resolution in Council...that the Agent write Department and get full information re the Muncy School and who pays expenses in case of Boys being sent from this reserve and what teaching and also whom and how to make application for entrance thereto.

32. 4 October 1912 McLean to Myers

...in the case of a boy being sent from the Rama Reserve to this school the Department will bear the cost of his transport. The prescribed course of study at this school will, if carefully followed fit a pupil to pass the Entrance to High School Examination. In addition to this the girls are instructed in household work and the boys learn farming and kindred occupations.

Application for admission should be made to the Rev. S. R. McVitty, Principal, Mount Elgin Institute, Muncey.

33. 31 March 1913 McVitty Report

...The main building furnishes accommodation for the principal...8 officers...125 pupils. Owing to an increase of 25 in the authorized number of pupils, additional accommodation, consisting of class-room, sewing-room, dormitories and play-rooms has been provided...

Attendance...average attendance for the year was 132...

Six candidates wrote on the high school entrance examination, five were successful, one failing through illness at time of writing.

A class of 17 girls is receiving thorough instruction in piano and vocal music under a fully qualified teacher...

Health and Sanitation...the health of the pupils excellent, save one case of pneumonia which proved fatal.

Recreation. - Pupils in class-room during the forenoon play from 7.30 a.m. to 9 a.m., and those in school in the afternoon play from 3.45 p.m. to 5.30 p.m., and all join in different games during the evening.

Ex-pupils. - Of those who left the school during the year, three are teaching school, several farming, two in factories, one Carpentering, several in domestic service, one has married and gone back to the reserve. All are doing well.

Conduct. - The conduct, with one or two exceptions, has been excellent; punishment of any kind is our strange work, yet we have the best of order. A mutual sympathy exists between pupils and staff.

General Remarks. - This year we have added Blacksmithing as one of the industries taught. Several boys are anxious to learn the trade, and are making a good start. When a boy shows a special aptitude for some particular industry, we usually allow him to specialize on that subject...we think the past year has been one of the very best in its history. We have the confidence and hearty co-operation of the parents of the pupils. They are learning to appreciate the value of the school, and are increasingly anxious to avail themselves of its privileges.

34. 21 May 1913 McVitty

HELPING THE INDIAN: HOW IT IS DONE AT MOUNT ELGIN INDUSTRIAL INSTITUTE

...Many times during the first year or two, when beset with difficulties on every hand and almost in despair...Gradually the difficulties have disappeared...

A most wonderful transformation has taken place in the school. The spirit of rebellion has disappeared, and we have at present in residence one hundred and thirty of as bright and loyal boys and girls as you could find anywhere. And what is also very important, we have the fullest confidence and sympathy of the Indian people around us. Whilst our enrolment is already above our standard, there are still scores of children anxiously waiting for an opportunity to enter.

We are constantly adding to the equipment...three competent public school teachers in charge of our primary, intermediate and senior rooms. Thorough instruction is being given in all the subjects of the Ontario public school course. A year ago we added music to our curriculum, and about twenty girls are receiving a thorough education in piano and vocal music, under a most competent and fully-qualified teacher, who has also developed a splendid choir, composed of boys and girls...

The half-day system obtains; division one is in the classroom in the forenoons, and division two in the afternoons, whilst the primary division is in school full time. When out of the school the girls are taught sewing, knitting, the cutting and fitting of garments, cooking and all kinds of housework. The boys are taught farming... care and management of live stock, gardening, carpentry, Blacksmithing, cement work, fencing, the care and running of all kinds of farm machinery, including steam and gasoline engines. As the pupils advance and show an aptitude for some special line, we encourage them to specialize, and the last year or so of industrial training is usually spent on their chosen subject.

Our buildings are thoroughly modern, and very suitable for the work being done. We have recently installed an electric light plant, which supplies us with 100 16 candle power lights, a first-class hot-water heating system, and an up-to-date steam laundry. Last summer we added two large wings to the main building, besides many minor improvements...we have received most courteous and generous treatment from the Department of Indian Affairs ...who provided the funds and put the work entirely under our care. We are pleased to say it has been carried through to the entire satisfaction of all concerned.

In addition to the per capita grant given us by the Government, it takes at least $10,000 per year to run the school. This amount our Missionary Society is responsible for, and would have to pay any balance not earned by us, but we are pleased to say that for the past two years we have been self-sustaining, not costing our Missionary Society one cent.

In financial matters our success has been really marvellous. We own at the present time $14,000 worth of live stock, $2000 worth of carriages, farm implements and machinery, about $2,500 worth of house equipment, notes receivable $2,500 , and enough cash in the bank to tide us over an emergency, and we "owe no man anything," and yet we have spent each year some hundreds of dollars on extra improvements which properly belong to the Government. We are seeking to farm for profit, and are adopting the most up-to-date methods. We aim at good stock, and are caring for them properly. We recently sold a span of two-year-old Canadian-bred fillies for $1,200, and we own at present an animal for which we have refused $2,000.

We have a dairy herd of fifty cows, which supplies milk and butter to the school and all the families connected therewith, and from which, in addition, we sold last year $2,500 worth of cream, and probably $800 worth of skim milk turned into pork. We had one field of wheat last year which yielded fifty bushels per acre.

But what is vastly more important, our pupils are making splendid progress, and most of them are turning out well. A year ago we sent up a class of five for entrance examination; all were successful. Last year we sent up six; five passed, one failing through illness.

Of our recent graduates three are teaching school, two are bookkeeping, one is a Railroad engineer, one a carpenter, one in a biscuit factory, one in a glass factory, several engaged in farming, two girls are married, and a great many engaged in domestic service. All are doing well. Only one has gone back to Reserve life.

The moral and religious life...is vastly improved. Many of our pupils...leading a good Christian life...

Our matron, Miss McKinley, has served the school faithfully for over twelve years. Her splendid enthusiasm and unswerving devotion to duty are worthy of highest praise. Mr. Kapayo, an ex-pupil, has had unbroken connection with the school for twenty-one years. He is a most efficient officer, and a most trustworthy Christian man; of him as a product of the school we are justly proud. The other members of the staff are all we could desire...We want only the best, and are paying from twenty to fifty percent, higher salaries than were being paid four years ago. We believe every man should be paid according to the character of his work.

We are, further, seeking to develop the moral and religious life of the school by a faithful observance of the following means of grace, viz. family consists of Scripture reading, singing and prayer.

...On Thursday evening a short praise prayer service is held for the pupils...On Sabbath morning we attend the Colborne Church...In the afternoon we have, in the Institute, a fully organized and well-manned Sabbath School, with a full attendance of pupils, officers and their families. A prayer and praise service, in which the pupils join most heartily, brings the Sabbath to a close.

...We have a staff of ten teachers, as follows: Three public school teachers, music teacher, domestic science teacher, sewing-room mistress and laundress, farm instructor, stock-man, mechanic and engineer.

At the beginning of each month the principal hands a list of ten or twelve pupils to each officer; these pupils are composed of an equal number from each division, and remain in that department during the month, so that the instructor in charge would have, say, six pupils in the forenoon and six in the afternoon, and would have the full number for a short time in the morning and afternoon.

Our day, from May to November, is spent about as follows: 4:45 a.m. the "wake-up" bell rings. We roll over once, rub our eyes and jump out. At 6 a.m. the "get busy" bell calls each one to his or her post each pupil immediately reports to the person in charge of his or her department. The officers work with the pupils, teaching them both by precept and example. The morning duties of the girls are getting breakfast, making beds, sweeping and dusting dormitories, and helping to milk. The boys feed stock, help to milk, separate cream, water and clean horses and harness them for the day's work. At 6.45... breakfast and at 7.20 we all meet for morning worship. At 7.45 the work day begins for those at industrial work during the forenoon. Those who are in the divisions attending school in the forenoons play until 9 a.m. At 11.45 we have "cease work" bell, and all get ready for dinner sharp at noon. At 1 p.m. another bell rings calling the pupils who were in school in the forenoon to industrial work and vice versa. The pupils attending school in the afternoon are dismissed at 4 p.m., and then play until 5.30, when "chore bell" rings. Horses and boys come in from the fields, and the milking, feeding of stock, cleaning of horses, etc., goes on until 6 p.m. Then the day's work is finished. Supper bell rings at 6:15, after which the evening is spent in games until 8:30 p.m., when the day is closed with singing and prayer. Pupils then retire, and the lights are put out at 9 p.m. When off duty the older folk of us usually spend the evening visiting, reading, or off for a walk or a drive...days go by quickly.

Time fairly flies. Even the youngest child has something to do. He is made to feel that he is an important part of the concern - in fact, that we could not very well get along without him. The pupils are with us all the time. No two of them are alike. To the student of child life they are a wonderful study as we watch evil tendencies fade away, and the nobler and better instincts spring forth and blossom, giving much promise of splendid fruit in the after days. We rejoice in the work...

35. 1913 Report

Repairs made during the year,

Barns have been painted.

Two wings have been added to the main building. This makes the accommodation sufficient for 130 children. The Principal's apartments have been renovated and well furnished, making very comfortable quarters...

There were 130 children present. The class-room work has been of a high order. Five out of six passed the Entrance examinations. Three graduates of last year are teaching school, two of them in the Institute and one on the Oneida Reserve.

36. 20 June 1914 McVitty to Maxwell

The Department consents to pupils of this School having a Midsummer vacation, not to exceed 30 days, providing the home conditions are such as to warrant it...if you approve, it is our intention to permit the following pupils from your Reserve to go home during July:-

Fred Nahmabin - Florence Brissette - Edna Rodd - Lettie Brisette...

And the following during August:-

Stafford Nahmabin - Cecil Rodd - Isaiah Shawanee...Dora Thomas - Mary Nahmabin - Edith Brissette...Ada Manass - Nancy Shawanee...Lettie Shawanee...

P.S. We have grave doubts as to the wisdom of allowing the following to go home at all, as...we have heard, they have not behaved in a proper manner on former vacations:- **** - **** - ****. Should you sanction their going home you have to accept the responsibility.

37. 20 June 1914 McVitty to Secretary DIA

...a copy of letter sent to the...Agent of each Reserve from which the pupils come...as we are not familiar with the conditions...as to health or morals.

We are justly proud of our pupils, and whilst we are anxious that they should have a vacation, we are more anxious to guard them from evil associations. We further believe that the Agents have a measure of responsibility for these pupils whilst at home, and should therefore be consulted as to who should go. You will notice that whenever we have any special reason to suspect the conduct of a pupil on any former occasion, we mention the fact to the Agent. He is therefore on his guard.

...we believe it has good effect upon the Indians themselves to know that the Department insists upon clean, sanitary homes, and right living as requisite to a visit from their children.

38. 28 July 1914 Mrs. **** to Honorable Dept.

I wish to call your attention to the matter as to the improper care given to my children attending school at Mt. Elgin Institute. When my children came home in March to attend their father's funeral...they were poorly clad in clothing. The underwear they wore were thin. Their heads were neglected, full of lice and nits. I cleaned their heads before returning. Now they are home for a months vacation. They came home the same condition as mention above. I am told matron does not furnish any fine combs to the children to keep clean. I am told parents has to furnish clothes from Sundays. Is this correct? I am told $60.00 is keep out for each pupil out off indian funds & $80.00 from the Government for a pupil's allowance for board. Is it correct parents must aid to clothed their children while attending school at any Indian Institution in Canada? My oldest daughter **** age 15 yrs shoes was not fit to come home with, she asked for a pr new shoes matron refuse her as her old ones were full of holes she was told by matron to put a paper inside to hide her feet. **** is in poor health, is not fit for hard labor only light work. Menstruation is the cause of her sickness. It appears the matron fails to see to this and does not furnish the girls what is required for such at that event. My children says the matron has said time and again **** children were the poorest ones didn't do enough work to pay for their board. If that is the case why can't my children remain at home. They also complain not getting sufficient of food and meat is not fit to eat not being fresh. This school, should be looked into or have some one to inspect everything goes on the table. When my children come home in March 16, 1914 they had the uniforms on they had while attending school at Mt. Pleasant which are now by this time are not fit for Sundays for best. Trusting this letter will convince you to instruct Supt S. R. McVitty to look into this matter at once & oblige.

39. 22 August 1914   McVitty to Secretary DIA

I am in receipt of your letter of the 19th inst., also copy of letter from Mrs. **** of Walpole Island.

In reply would say, I am seldom away from the School more than one day at a time. I seek to make myself, as far as possible, conversant with every detail of the School life, and have not the least hesitation in saying...each and every officer in the School is doing everything for the pupils that could reasonably be expected from them.

Having spent 13 years in the pastorate in different parts of Ontario, and knowing the home life of the people quite intimately, I most solemnly believe that the pupils of this school are furnished better food, better clothing, better sleeping accommodation, and do less work than the average white child in...Ontario.

Since taking charge of the School I have never knowingly done, or permitted to have done to any child in the School what I would not be willing to have done to a child of mine under similar circumstances. I have never, directly or indirectly, asked from, or hinted to the parent of any child that they should in any way assist in clothing their children and I have never known of any officer doing so. Occasionally the parents bring some little articles of clothing for the girls, usually hair ribbons or an unmade dress, which articles the matron accepts from them. We simply do not interfere as it tends to keep a good feeling between parents and children.

Fine and coarse combs, towels, and every other article

really necessary for the comfort and convenience of the pupils are regularly and systematically furnished them, but some of them are so persistently destructive, that, no doubt, there are times when such pupils go without.

As to the **** children in particular, their mother seems possessed of an evil spirit. She has written me some really dreadful letters, and, no doubt at all, she is prompting them to all kinds of evil. When **** used the "napkins" referred to, instead of washing them she puts them in the furnace, and on several occasions in the toilet and stopped the drain, so that on three different occasions it had to be taken up. A few days ago ****'s duty was to place the spoons etc. on the pupils' tables for breakfast. She deliberately put all the large spoons on the small childrens' tables and the small spoons on the big boys' table, save that she put the small spoons at her little sisters' plates. She is not to blame, her mother is, and besides Mrs. ****, and the parents of ****, also from Walpole Island, are telling the most outrageous stories about the School on the Island. I have not the least doubt, that, even Mr. Agent McCallum is influenced by them. His action in not returning pupils would indicate it.

Would it not be a good thing for the Department to instruct Mr. McCallum to visit the School sometime at his convenience, and see for himself. I think that would settle the matter once for all.

I might add, that, in answer to a letter from Mrs. ****, I have stated to her, that, if the Department would sanction it, we would be very pleased to have her children returned to her.

40. 22 August 1914   McVitty to Mrs ****

In reply to your letter of recent date, in which you find so much fault with our School and it's management, would say I am much surprised at your conduct. Surely you know what you say is not true, and also that you are putting your children up to all kinds of evil things. You are not hurting us any, you are destroying your childrens' future.

I have written to the Department saying that if they are willing, it would be a great relief to us to have your children sent home. There are scores of children all around us whose parents know the value of an education who are earnestly seeking to get their children into this School. Mr. Levi Williams teacher of Oneida, whose son and daughter have been here for several years, has put four of his nephews in School this August. He knows what he is doing, you do not, and your children will suffer.

Since coming back from holidays **** has carefully followed your instructions and is making herself hateful as she can. The simplest little thing she is asked to do she deliberately does it the wrong way.

You speak of visiting the School in the near future. We will be pleased to see you, and more pleased if you decide to take the children back with you. Yet, let me assure you, so long as they are here, I will see that they are treated fairly and kindly, no matter what their conduct may be. Our School is better than ever before, and the better class of Indians are seeking to crowd their children in. We have more applications on hand now than we could accept for years to come, so in taking your children out you will not injure anybody, simply make room for others who will be very glad to get in.

You will be pleased to know, that, of a class of seven trying for High School Entrance this year all passed, one girl getting first class honors, and sixth place in the county of Middlesex. Her parents came for her and her sister in an automobile, and were overjoyed at their success. They are continuing High School work here for another year, and taking piano music at the same time.

41. **27 August 1914 McVitty to Secretary DIA**

We find that sixty three boys crowded in the boys' playroom during the winter evenings are too many for the size of the room, so have just put down a new floor in the old playroom over the laundry...as a play-room for about 25 of the smaller boys...it needs some repairs, such as plaster, paint, etc., also a row of "lockers" along...sides which would serve as seats, and also as a place for change of clothing...such lockers were placed in the boys' new playroom, and they are splendid...

We are again to prepared to do all the work if the Department...will supply the material...

42. **6 October 1914   Mrs. **** to Secretary DIA**

Your letter dated Aug 17, 1914, complaint made by me as to management of the Mt. Elgin Institute the improper care received by pupils attending that Institution, I beg to inform you report I laid before you is correct. Believe me I can face S. R. McVitty & the Matron Miss Kinnley in any court in the Province of Canada. Not only my children are neglected. There are other parents has had children sent here & come home with filthy heads not only girls boys as well. One chief **** has two boys attending that school. Their heads were not clean as I asked him myself. **** has had two boys sent to that school both came home unwell during holidays. They claim they are compell to do more work than they are able to stand neither look fit for hard labor or to return to school. The school is O.K. in every respect. Only the management of the pupils. Little ones not able to keep their heads clean. I went after my children upon S. R. McVitty's request before your letter came. My oldest girl **** was strapped on her hand which cause it to swell from strapping for telling me things. My children heads told me the story cause me to ask questions. They came home same as before. McVitty claims no time to keep girls heads clean as they are two many. He also stated he didnt care whether the Walpole children return as he was

better off without them as they were the most troublesome children. More room for others I have wittness heard McVitty say this. He knows better than I do, that my complaint is true while he is trying to blindfold you Dept to cause you to believe his false report. I told him I give him all the chance to take me up he refuse to do anything. Find enclose a letter from S. R. McVitty which is self explanatory.

43. **17 October 1914 McVitty to Scott**

...we have secured a trained nurse as a member of our permanent staff. She will, I trust, be of very great service to the School, and remove any possible ground for complaint as to care of pupils.

The School is quite full and all Departments are in full swing.

44. **15 January 1915 McVitty to Secretary DIA**

...enclosing...a copy of...an agreement furnished the Rev. T. T. George...by the late Mr. Agent Thackeray.

On taking charge of this School I felt that it was not fair to use their money in supporting them here, so left it with the Department. **** drew some of his a year or so ago to take them home. **** has a considerable amount to her credit, which, I understand she is seeking to obtain.

I hope the Department will not forward it, as she would assuredly use it foolishly, or even worse. Nor should it be sent to her father, as he is not entitled to it.

45. **3 June 1915 McVitty to Secretary DIA**

Re our terrible fire...The fire was started by little **** letting off a firecracker under a pile of straw. (Some one had given the pupils fire crackers on Friday, at our pic-nic). He had it in a little tin can, and thought he was hiding where no one would see him. I was at home myself, and every officer was right here. We saw the fire inside ten minutes after it started. Hundreds of people, including almost every Indian in the neighbourhood, were with us in a very short time. The utmost we could do was to save a couple of horses, and a few other animals. We lost about twenty-five head in all, including a very valuable horse.

Our greatest effort was to save the annex and main building...by beating the fire back from the woodshed and laundry, both of which were on fire several times.

I never saw men work harder than the Indians did until every bucket of water was exhausted. We also had a small chemical engine, which we purchased some time ago. It proved of great service in beating the fire out of the laundry and wood shed roof, and a great pile of wood stored in the yard near the shed.

So great was the danger to the main buildings at times that...led us to remove a large part of the contents out into the lawn, but, at the most crucial moment the wind veered from the East almost due North, and this, of course threw the flames in the opposite direction, and so our main building, annex, and laundry are practically unhurt, and school is going on as usual.

The children feel very sorry for what has occurred, (I have sought in every way to impress them with the seriousness of it), and were rejoiced to learn this morning that we hope to re-build our barns right away. They love the animals, especially the cows. I was much touched with the pleading of some boys not to sell the cows. They know them everyone by name, and some boys risked their lives in getting a few out of the burning buildings. The greater part of the cows had just come up to the barns for milking, but were not tied up, so they escaped.

Of course all our implements, machinery, and tools, also harness, hay, straw, and about 1000 bus. of grain were destroyed...

46. 4 June 1915 McVitty to Scott
...You can hardly imagine how it feels in a place like this, not to have even a stall to feed a horse, or milk a cow. Then it is also a difficult task to find any employment for the boys who did this stable work, and when out of School, they are disposed to slip off to the village, or over the Reserve...most important matter is to get under way as soon as possible...Our crops will be upon us soon, and, to lose them would almost drive us to the wall...

...there was no wilful act, or even neglect on the part of anyone in the matter. I called the boys all together on Saturday morning, and had them destroy all the firecrackers I could find, also warned them of the danger. **** had some hidden away. He is a very small boy, and only in school a short time, and I feel sure did not intend any wrong.

47. 16 June 1915 McVitty to Scott
...need of immediate action in the erection of new buildings
1. Because the harvest is almost upon us...if this is not got under cover before the fall rains set in, the loss will be very great indeed.
2. We found it quite impossible to milk the cows outside, and were forced to sell our dairy herd, cutting off an income of about $400.00...per month.
3. Quite a number of boys, too small to handle a team, or work in the fields, found very useful and pleasant employment in caring for the stock. They are quite lost, and inclined to rove all around the Reserve during the half day out of School...

48. 17 August 1915 McVitty to Secretary DIA
For the greater part of the past year the Department has been paying us for supernumary pupils at this School. At present time our registration is away above the standard, and quite a number of Agents are pressing the claims of

pupils on their Reservations.

I think it would be most advisable to increase the capacity of the School to 150, and hold it there. We would then employ a third teacher and assistant matron. As it is, two rooms are crowded, and yet we have not sufficient pupils for three teachers. As to accommodation, we could utilize a second dining room now being used by men working on the buildings. It would accommodate about 20. In this room we could seat senior pupils of merit. It would be an incentive to best things.

We could utilize the attics in both wings of new additions for dormitories. They are nicely finished, and are on a level with the upper dormitories in the main building, are finished with toilet and fire escape, but would need additional radiators for heating.

The prayer room would be a bit crowded, but, by extra seating would accommodate the extra number.

I...heartily recommend this increase, simply for the sake of the children anxious for an education. The extra cost for help would leave about $1200 to feed and clothe these extra 25, so it is not a money making proposition.

Hoping to hear from you soon as possible, as we are turning away a number of children daily. Two very nice little girls from Oneida, both parents dead, came here a few days ago. We were compelled to send them away. Also four others from Muncey.

49. 17 September 1915 Council, Chippewas of the Thames
At the regular monthly meeting of the Council of the Chippewas of the Thames, Caradoc Reserve...it was moved by Chief Geo Fisher and seconded by Myles McDougald that as complaints have been made to this Council in regard to treatment to children at the Mt. Elgin Institute is far from being satisfactory we hereby request the Department to investigate into the matter with no delay whatever, and with no partiality. The chief cause of complaint appears to be the Principal's cruelty to the children, also allowing the children to go very filthy loaded with vermin on their heads. We would like an investigation on the matter at once.

50. 22 September 1915 H. Jones to Secretary DIA
I herewith enclose a resolution from the Council of the Chippewas of the Thames regarding the complaint being made to the Council of the treatment of the pupils...

Regarding the complaints that have been laid I would beg to say that the complaint has come from Mrs. ****, a member of the Muncey Band of the Thames, claiming that her son ****...has been punished too severely. As to the above I would beg to explain that while they were threshing their wheat recently on the Institute Farm, the weather having been very wet the machine was forced to stand in the field for one week waiting for the grain to get dry enough to thresh. When the grain became dry enough to thresh again they had been threshing one afternoon and the thresher being anxious to get through with the job requested them to run for an hour or so after supper, and all hands appeared to agree to do so. As soon as their supper was over they began to thresh again. But they had only been threshing a few minutes when a large stone went through the threshing machine doing considerable amount of damage. The stone flew from the machine nearly hitting one of the men which might have caused his death. At the time it happened it was supposed the stone had been gathered in the sheaf of wheat by accident. But by a short time afterwards sufficient information came forward to prove that it had been placed in the sheaf on purpose by some of the pupils, so that they would not have to work any more than night. Mr. McVitty immediately looked into the matter and traced it directly to the parties who did it. Mr. McVitty having got plenty of evidence to show that **** who was pitching wheat on the waggons in the field got this stone and persuaded another boy by the name of **** who was on the waggon to place it firmly in the sheaf of wheat, saying that when it went through they would not have to work any more that night. When Mr. McVitty had got the full details of how this thing happened, he considered for some time what steps he should take. He concluded that he could not allow such an act go by without some punishment. So he requested me to come to the Institution. He also had all the boys remain in the Dining-room, until it could be looked into. I was present when Mr. McVitty questioned several of the boys as to how the stone was put in the machine. When **** as questioned he stated that **** got the stone and made him put it in the sheaf. When **** was questioned he admitted doing it, and when asked why he did it, he answered that he did it so that he would not have to work any more than night. But since this when talking to his mother he has denied the whole thing after admitting to it, before the whole school of boys. Mr. McVitty strapped both of the boys over the hand for what they had done. Personally I do not think there was any undue punishment administered to either of them considering the serious crime they had committed.

As to allowing the children to be in the filthy condition...on different occasions I have examined the beds of the pupils at the Institution and have always found them clean enough for any person to sleep in. As to the vermin spoken of I have repeatedly heard the officers of the Institution complain that after the pupils have been allowed to go to their homes for holidays that they very often come back loaded with vermin, which soon spreads to the other pupils, causing a great deal of trouble before they can be gotten rid of. I do not think there is any cause for the parents to complain of the way their children are used at this school.

51. **22 September 1915 Fisher to McLean**
A resolution was passed by the Chippewa Council...

asking your Dept to send Inspector to our reserve - we are making a complaint against - Rev McVitty of Mt. Elgin institution of not cleaning the small children - the little boys being full of vermin - 2nd also being cruel to said children by over punishment. Since the resolution was passed by us - the small boys has their hair cut close, and clean underclothing given. If the Inspector is sent - we want one week notice - and want the investigation to be held in our council house.

52. **27 September 1915 McVitty to Scott**
I understand a few of the Chippewa Council here have asked an investigation of alleged cruelty on my part in punishing a pupil, named ****, for putting a stone through the threshing machine.

It happened the day before the Hon. T. W. Crothers visited our School, and I told him every fact as I would on oath. If the Department cares to enquire, I am sure he will be glad to give his mind on the matter. The punishment administered was 6 or 7 straps on each hand with regulation strap, administered in the presence of Mr. Agent Jones and our Head Teacher, Mr. Littleproud. He was not even marked on the hands. He, and the four boys who saw him, all confessed the matter to me personally, each making his separate statement, and all agreeing as to the offence. Then all four confessed the matter, two days later, in the presence of Mr. Jones and Mr. Littleproud.

All four now absolutely deny the confession and I think would sware they did not make it.

My conduct was exceedingly lenient, and instead of punishing the boys at the time, I warned them of the serious nature of the crime, offered to pay the thresher for the damage and cover the matter up. Two days later a threat on the part of one of the four boys to repeat the offense, compelled me to take action on the matter. The presence of Mr. Jones at the time was, I think, quite Providential as he is a magistrate as well as Agent.

In one sense an investigation would please me well. In another, I think to give them the satisfaction of having it would be unwise. They delight to call a man before their council.

I sincerely hope the Department will take very firm ground on the question. It is absolutely necessary....

Mrs. **** went so far as to call Mr. Jones a liar, and use other most abusing language in the presence of a large crowd.

As to any other criticisms of the School management, I don't think there is any just cause. At July 1st. the School was at it's best in every way. Conduct excellent. A few pupils returned after holidays seemingly "possessed", and have no end of trouble since.

Every member of the staff believe the holidays are conducive to great evil, yet I would not like to see them forbidden, but a good warning sent to their Council might do good.

53.   4 October 1915   McLean to Fisher
...Mr. Agent Jones was informed on the 29th ultimo that the punishment inflicted upon **** for putting a stone through the threshing machine was fully deserved and that there was no need for any further investigation. He was instructed to inform the Council accordingly.

...the Department is somewhat surprised that complaint should be made against the Rev. Mr. McVitty for a lack of cleanliness at the...Institution. The Indians can easily satisfy themselves, upon a visit to the Institution, that there children are well cared for and are kept clean and tidy and that the Institution is well fitted for the training of Indian children. You, as Chief, should discourage any groundless complaints against the Institution and should encourage the Indians to send their children there where they can be properly educated and cared for.

54.   16 January 1917   McVitty to Secretary DIA
During the winter weather we are under necessity of drying all pupils bedding and underclothing on the radiators in the sewing room and dormitories, as we have no drying room in Laundry.

We have at present sixteen pupils in bed with colds and sore throat, and our nurse is very emphatic that the dampness from drying clothes is at the bottom of it. Besides it is well-nigh impossible to get bedding etc. as dry as it ought to be before using....we could, for less than $100 build a very suitable drier..

55.   28 February 1917   H. D. Johnson Report
I...recommend...Grade 1 pupils known as "beginners" spend the whole time in the school, one half under the regular teacher and the other half under a monitor.
One of the girls in Standard VI would answer for this purpose and the vacant class-room could be used. If this is done the principal work of the monitor should be to train the pupils to speak english as many of these "Beginners" have little or no knowledge of the English language when they enter the school.

56.   1 May 1917   McVitty to Secretary DIA
In view of the great demand for farm help, and the urgent and repeated requests reaching us from farmers and farmers' wives to permit some of our senior boys and girls to go out to service for the Summer, I appeal...for advice...it is only the larger ones who are wanted. We have about forty capable of rendering fairly efficient service. This leaves about eighty five almost helpless to be cared for.

To permit the seniors to go would, of course, rob us of their assistance, and would also entail much extra labour on the members of our staff in carrying on the work of the school, yet...something ought to be done.
The following seems feasible:-
1. Permit such pupils as are capable, and so desire to go

out to assist farmers, and farmers only, during the Summer.
2. Said pupils to remain under charge of the school, and to receive one-half their wages weekly for spending money, and one-half to be retained for them, and held in trust by the school.
3. The Department to pay the per capita grant to the School as if they were attending...as our expense would be practically the same, and we would lose their assistance.

I would very much prefer matters to remain as they are...but just fear it is not the right thing to do.

57.   3 May 1917   Asst. Dep. and Secretary DIA to McVitty
...the Department approves of your suggestion to allow some of the senior pupils in your institution to engage with the farmers in the vicinity...be good enough to furnish a list of the pupils who go out on service and state the rate of wages they are to receive and the length of their engagement...

58.   19 May 1919   McVitty to Scott
I am enclosing...programme for our closing day exercises...All the others have already promised to be here...we would deem it a great favor if you could...
...About eighty graduates of this school volunteered for active service. One of them, Arnold Logan, was the first Indian to cross the Ocean in defence of the Empire. He sleeps in "Flanders Fields" with about a dozen of his pupil comrades. Could you in any way induce "the powers that be" to present the school with a medium or even small sized German gun, in recognition of their services? And could it be got here by July 1st? How delightful if you could present it, but don't let that in any way interfere with your visit.

59.   1 July 1919   McVitty
PICNIC AND CLOSING EXERCISE
MUSIC
Oneida Brass Band
Muncey Male Quartette
PRESENTATION OF PRIZES
Sunday School prizes; Chief Jacobs, Sarnia
Stock Judging prizes: R. H. Abraham B.S.A. Chatham
Leaving Certificates; Inspector Johnston, Strathroy
WORDS OF WELCOME TO RETURNED SOLDIERS
a) Chief Scobie Logan, Muncey
b) Chief W. K. Cornelius, Oneida
c) Lieut. Col. Emsley, London
GENERAL ADDRESSES - (20 minutes each)
a) Chief Albert Tobias, Moraviantown.
b) Rev. J. W. Andrews M.A. Anglican, St. Thomas
c) Rev. Thompson Ferrier, Inspector of Indian Schools. Brandon.
d) Duncan C. Scott Esq. Deputy Supt. of Indian Affairs
There will be no creed line, no color line, no admission fee.
ALL GOOD CANADIANS ARE INVITED
Bring your lunches, or secure same from booths on grounds.
Lunch at noon.   Baseball 1 to 2 p.m.
Programme 2 to 6 p.m.

60. 2 July 1919 Paragus St. Thomas Times Journal
INDIAN CHIEFS CONFIDENT OF THE FUTURE...

Mount Elgin...chose Dominion Day for its commencement exercises...speakers and honored guests and best of all, Indian mothers and fathers from far and near came to be proud and sympathize with their children...very informal homelikeness which is the keynote of the Muncey Institute...Rev. R. S. McVitty...encourages this home feeling...that the entire population of the reserve regard him as a father. From the boy at the institution whom he addresses as kindly as he might his son, to the chiefs who figured in the program...same commingling of distinctive courtesy and intimate kindliness...

The speeches from the chiefs all centred on one theme, the Indian problem..."Nothing is simpler than the remedy," said Chief Jacobs of Sarnia. "If you train the child you have the man." And he went on suggesting higher collegiate education for the Indian youth. "They leave too soon," he said, "They can scarcely help going back when returning so young to an environment so inferior to that of the institution..."

Sunday School Prizes.
Senior Class - First, Sara Powless, second, Lillian Stonefish; third, Archie Burch.
Bristol Intermediate Boys - First, Harry Ward, second, Percy McGahey; third, David Solomon.
Junior Boys - First, Eddie White; second, Russell Jacobs; third, Albert Martin.
Intermediate Girls - First, Garnett Atkins; second, Vera Jacobs; third, Cassie Deleary?.
Junior Girls - First, Olive Ninham; second, - Lottie Silversmith, third, Margaret Alfred.

Stock Judging Prizes.
...First, Mable Atkins; second, Tom Sandy; third, Hilda Miskokaman; fourth, Willie Ninham
Written Exam. - First, Hilda Moskokaman; second, Edna Rodd; third, Elijah Isaacs; fourth, Archie Burch.
Leaving Certificates- Charlotte Riley, Muncey; Mary Strength, Muskoka; Mary Peters, Muncey; Mary La Forme, Brantford; Susie Fisher, Muncey; Flossie Solomon, Cape Croker; Asa Bunn, Oneida; Dan Ninham, Oneida; Willie Ninham, Oneida.

...Mr. McVitty...takes a most paternal interest in his pupils and made many commendatory notes on their merits as the prizes and certificates were handed out.

"This handsome shield made of copper from Nelson's flagship...is to go to the pupil who wins it three years in succession judging fine stock. Last year a boy won it. This year it goes to Mable Atkins. Let me tell you gentlemen...If any of you want some first class short horns come up here and Miss Atkins will see that you do not purchase amiss, and I'll aid her of course."

"This boy Harry Ward"...answers questions in the Sunday school...the best of any child I have ever met...

"When Miss Johnson left us," he went on, as the graduating certificates were dealt out, "this institution was practically without a kitchen manager. Little Mary La Forme had to take charge and...no cook - no white woman in the Dominion - can defeat her in the quality and

abundance of the meals she prepares for one hundred and twenty-four people per day, mind you!"

And this praise was warmly encored by guests...who were charmed by the menus Miss La Forme, who is little more than a child puts up.

The graduating class were also presented with handsome pocket Bibles. Only to Susie Fisher, whose people are Anglican, was given a pretty Book of Common Prayer, which is a sample of the consideration which marks the management at the institute...

61. 15 December 1919 Scott to McVitty
...no contributions were given by the Government from the public revenues until...1875 and 1876, before that date all the expenditures had been made from...Indian School Fund...I consider the continuous work of the Mount Elgin Industrial Institute to have been a great factor in the present position of the Indians of Ontario, and its continuance under the present enlightened and capable management is necessary for the further development of the race towards its ultimate goal, that is its absorption by the ordinary civil life of the country.

62. 26 April 1920 McVitty to Secretary DIA
I very much regret to make the following very black report. For some time we have been missing oats, potatoes and some other things from the school...two local Indians, according to the sworn statement of several boys, asked said boys to steal this stuff and take it over in the woods for them. Mr. McGookin and I drove over to see these men. They denied at first, then admitted the crime, came to the Agent's office and handed him $25 each in restitution. This I refused to accept, but agreed not to push the matter and give them another chance. Saturday afternoon I gave the boys a half holiday for baseball game. A number of them slipped off to the village and stole a quantity of dry goods and perfume from...the storekeeper there. The ringleaders of this gang are **** who has been a confirmed thief all along. A boy over whom I have spent a great deal of time, and have sought to keep him out of trouble, but to no avail...****, also a confirmed thief, steals from the boys all the time...****, nephew to...**** and an apt disciple for him...**** is an illegitimate, whose father is dead.

I felt after consultation with the Indian agent, Mr. McGookin, that some thing had to be done, so had ****, ****, and **** arrested, and issued a warrant for ****. All will come for trial this afternoon. ****, **** and **** most certainly should be sent to Mimico for a term. It is impossible to handle them here, where they are so ably assisted by our neighbours.

63. 27 April 1920 McGookin to Secretary DIA
**** and ****...& ****...pupils of the Mount Elgin Institute, have been found guilty of theft...and committed

to the Industrial school at Mimico, for an indefinite time.

These boys have been a very bad example to the other pupils, & for their own good as well as for the good of the school, I recommended the above course.

The home influence over these boys has not been of an uplifting nature, & it is felt that if away from the influence of relatives, these boys would have a better chance to make good citizens.

64. April-June 1920 Editor Missionary Bulletin

Mr. McVitty and his loyal staff are to be congratulated upon their contribution to the solution of that yet unsolved problem, the relation of the Indian to our Canadian life.

65. May 1920 McVitty

...In 1909 Mr. George returned to the pastorate and the writer was asked to take charge of the school. In doing so we were under no illusion what ever as to the difficulties of the task awaiting us - the business management of a thousand acre farm, the purchase and sale of all the live stock connected therewith, the judicious expenditure of approximately $25,000 per annum for wages, food, clothing, fuel, light and many other things incidental to the life of the school. Add to these the final responsibility for the health, happiness and discipline of at least 120 boys and girls always in residence, the selection of suitable officers and teachers, and the blending of all these varied interests into something like a happy and suitable community life, and we have a job quite big enough to tax the energies of any one man.

...some people, Indians and white men, who look upon the school as the child of the Government or Church or both, and as such, a legitimate subject for financial amputations. They are unwilling to see that the school exists for the good of the boys and girls within its walls and that slack dealing means less money, and less money means fewer comforts for the pupils (other bills have got to be paid) or else a deficit at the end of the year. We abhor either alternative, so are mostly awake at our post.

...Our bills are paid, our barns are filled with plenty; and what is vastly more important, our school is filled with happy promising children and we have associated with us a staff of officers and teachers second to none in the Dominion. We like the work and the place...The boys and girls concern us most. They are lovable because they are so human; they are perplexing because they are so uncertain, save in doing the thing they want to do and doing it now, irrespective of future consequences.

The doors of the school are open to all Protestant Indian children...We never seek to lead a child away from the church of its parents into the Methodist Church, but we do most earnestly seek to teach them to be true Christians and good Canadians. Many of them are both.

On Sabbath morning our school attends in a body the Colborne Methodist Church...Sabbath School in the afternoon...we select our own course of lessons and have semi-annual examinations. The papers are carefully set, the marking is thorough and substantial prizes are offered. At our recent examination on the lives of Jacob and Joseph about twenty pupils made over ninety per cent. We have morning worship daily and a mid-week service at which attendance is optional, yet about fifty attend.

Besides the different industries taught in the home, the shop and the farm, we have the Ontario Public School course taught by fully qualified teachers, and for the past nine years a large class in music taught by Miss M. C. Cosgrove...We have also a two weeks' special course in agriculture, conducted by Mr. R. H. Abraham of the Indian Department, Ottawa.

Our work is intensive and extensive, reaching out into... the community. During the war eighty-three of our pupils and ex-pupils went overseas and our senior boys rendered splendid assistance to the neighboring farmers.

Amusements do not receive so large a place in the life of this, as some other schools, largely because we are seeking to develop a balanced life. Perhaps the Indian's greatest handicap is his readiness to drop his work and seek amusement. Everyone knows that a job that is worth holding must be held continuously. Here the Indian fails, and we are earnestly seeking by precept and example to break him of this habit. Yet each of the pupils is given several hours for recreation each day; skating and tobogganing in the winter, baseball and basketball in the summer, are their favorite pastimes. Five evenings each week are spent in study, one in parlour games, lantern lecture or talk on suitable subject as deportment, table manners, or some live question of the day...Daily papers and current magazines are supplied regularly.

It is generally supposed that it had been the policy of the school management for many years to utilize all revenue to meet current expenses and consequently farm and buildings were allowed to get out of repair. Of this we cannot say, but do know that the erection of the main School building in 1895, under the Superintendency of the late Principal Shepherd, was a very real step in advance and marked the beginning of a new era. Much was yet to be done. The barns and stables needed attention and were taken in hand by Mr. George. He turned them almost completely around, in fact rebuilt them. He also developed a new water system and secured a good supply of pure water by the use of hydraulic rams. This was a very great improvement, for which Mr. George deserves much credit. He also had the main halls and dormitories of the school building done over in burlap, and this work has proven durable and sanitary.

On taking charge we felt that in matters of "building and repairs" we were going to have a long rest, that all this had been already done. As a matter of fact, in a place like this...they are never done. We found the laundry sadly out of date, wholly out of repair, with the result that the weekly wash day, all work being done by hand, left some lady officers and a large number of girls quite used up. We installed up-to-date machinery and installed up-to-date steam washers, extractor, mangle, steam-drier, and the necessary boiler and engine, and...half a dozen modern tubs at which the girls are taught washing by doing some light work.

Then we found the practice of lighting a building of this size with coal oil lamps both expensive and dangerous, so we installed a really first class electric plant, which is giving perfect satisfaction.

We soon found the building crowded beyond healthy and sanitary proportions and were forced to build two large additions...added much to the appearance of the building as well as providing necessary accommodation.

The heating plant was old-fashioned and leaky and altogether too small to meet our requirements, so a first class hot water system has been installed. At the same time all the officers' rooms and our private residence have been made comfortable and a credit to all concerned. We have never permitted improvements in our part of the school at the expense of others, and invariably the children have come first. But as buildings and number of residents increased, our water supply proved altogether inadequate. Scarcity of water in a school of this kind spells disaster, so we overhauled the entire system and increased its capacity to such an extent that we have tons of surplus water running through the buildings daily and about 50,000 gallons stored for emergencies. We felt surely the end had come; but alas, alas, on a beautiful June day, a new boy, whose friends had supplied him with a bunch of firecrackers which he had most carefully concealed, tried his luck at exploding the whole bunch in an oyster can, with the result that a spark caught in the straw stack behind which he was hiding. A strong wind was blowing, and in less than three minutes the whole yard and buildings were a sea of flames. We did our very best and managed to save nearly all the live stock and the school buildings; the barns and stables were completely wiped out. As we looked upon the smouldering ruins and then upon the fields almost ready for harvest, our heart sank within us. But a "little Scotch" - blood we mean - is quite a help, so we threw off our coats and went to work. When the time for stabling the cattle came we were ready with as fine barns as can be found anywhere in Ontario...we have received the most courteous treatment at the hands of the Department of Indian Affairs, whose practice is to ask the school Principal to furnish a plain sketch...of the building or improvement needed, and a close estimate of the probably cost. This sketch is then turned over to the Department Architect, who endorses or alters it as he sees fit. An amount of money is then voted and tenders called for. In each and all of the buildings and improvements made since coming here we have...supervised the work and certified vouchers for

every dollar paid, and can most truthfully say that in no case has there been one dollar of graft, and...the work has been well and truly done. To-day we have one of the finest school plants in the Dominion...surrounded by a farm of which we are justly proud.

...Are the results...in keeping with the effort put forth?...

RESULTS

Anything like a complete tabulation of results is quite impossible, first from lack of space, second from lack of information. We have written several letters to each of our Indian missionaries in Ontario and Quebec; several replied, some did not...Three generations have passed through the school, but few of the first remain and of these the following are personally known to us.

Of the first generation of Christians:

Albert Tobias of Moraviantown, chief of his tribe, is an able and eloquent man, whose voice is often heard in Annual Conference. He is a true man and heartily in sympathy with every good word and work.

His brother, Walter, a clever business man, although away over military age, went overseas with Moravian men. He now sleeps "in Flanders fields."

Nelles Timothy, ex-chief of his tribe, a natural gentleman, a true Christian, a true friend of the missionary and worthy official of the Methodist Church.

Scobie Logan, able writer and platform speaker, ardent supporter of the Anglican Church, ex-chief and secretary of the Muncey Council, a loyal Britisher and true friend of the Indian.

Job and Mrs. Fisher, honest, upright and respectable Christian folk. Mr. Fisher is an official of the Methodist Church and member of Chippewa Council. To know him well is to trust him much.

Samuel and Mrs. French, good people in the very highest sense, utterly unselfish, their home always open to those needing help.

Chief Samuel Johns, Muncey; shrewd, clever, sarcastic. For years an able and eloquent local preacher. He is truly capable of rendering great service to his church and people.

John Case, ex-chief of the Munceys, calm, courteous, strong, a true Christian, a sincere friend, a capable workman, embodies in himself all the best characteristics of his race.

No doubt there are many others of the old guard unknown to us, and there are certainly many who have already passed through the gate into the City.

Of the second generation of Christians we may mention only a few.

Rev. John Oke, a fully ordained Methodist minister, beloved of his brethren and efficient in service - a man of whom we are justly proud.

Levi and Mrs. Doxtator, Oneida. Mr. Doxtator, for years a successful teacher, is at present in charge of Oneida school No. 2, a chief of his tribe, a devout

Anglican, warden and treasurer of his church, an able champion and true friend of his people.

Mrs. Jake Powless (nee Lilly Isaacs), one of the most efficient and devoted members of the Oneida Methodist Church. Her missionary and his wife feel they cannot speak too highly of her.

Enoch and Mrs. Hill (nee Gussie Green), good farmers, good parents, good Christians, good Methodists. Three of their children are at present in the Institute.

Lyman Fisher, an able and successful teacher, for years in charge of No. 8, Muncey, a good man in the Anglican Church and Secretary of the Chippewa Council.

Eliza French, Muncey, a capable, industrious Christian woman whose services are much sought after.

Chief Charlie Jacobs, Walpole Island, a graduate of Mohawk Institute, married Jane Isaac, a graduate of Mount Elgin. The union has been a most happy one. Blessed with a large family of lean, healthy, happy children, they are a credit to both schools. Their oldest boy, Ashton, has a High School standing from here and is at present filling a responsible and lucrative position in the Wallaceburg sugar factory. Three are with us at present and one waiting an opportunity to enter.

Shortly after graduation, John Kapayo of Oka and Ada Sickles, Oneida, were united in marriage by the late Principal Shepherd. Mr. Kapayo has remained with us ever since. A skilful mechanic, a faithful employee, a kindly man, he has won for himself a large place in the life of the school. He owns a comfortable home in the village of Muncey, where he is giving his family a good education. His boy is at present attending High School. Mr. and Mrs. Kapayo are kind hearted Christian folk, devout members of the Methodist Church, beloved and respected by all who know them.

Of the last generation, two are Railroad engineers, one a fireman, one a brakeman, two are blacksmiths, two are school teachers, many are employed in factories and flax mills, still more are farming - quite a few for themselves under the Soldier Settlement Act - others are helping their parents. About eighty went overseas and many "will ne'er come back again," most of them boys in their teens. Of them, Arnold Logan, Muncey, was the first Indian to cross the sea and give his life for the Empire.

Ralph Monture, Six Nations, served at the front for two years as a runner for the famous 1st Battalion and was awarded the Military Medal for bravery in the field. He is now settled on his own farm and says, "Long may Mt. Elgin live to direct the feet of our young people into those paths, the choosing of which they will never regret."

John Fisher, on leaving the Institute, entered the O.A.C., Guelph. At the close of a most successful year he went overseas, where he spent several years in active service. He joined the Khaki University and with it visited many of the best herds and farms in Great Britain. He is at present teaching school and intends resuming his work at the O.A.C. next fall.

Enos Monture continued his High School work for several years after leaving the Institute. He is now teaching school. He is an earnest Christian and volunteer for life service. The Rev. John Nelson, his present pastor, says, "We look upon him as one of the coming men of the Six Nations, a typical Canadian, capable of holding a leading position in any community, loyal to and proud of the Institute - his old alma mater."

Many of the girls are married and doing well. Many more are engaged in house work, especially in the cities. The scores of letters we receive saying, "My friend Mrs. - has an Indian girl trained in your school. She is really fine. Could you possibly send me one like her?" tell their own tale and please us well...

Norman Manass, Ernie McGaghey, Silas Hill, Annie Leaff, Mary James, Electa Williams, Florence French were exceptionally fine pupils. We loved them much. They early passed over into the land...not very far off. ...Of those at present in the school it will be easily seen that their hearts are right, when we state that on being told of the sufferings of the Armenian children, they promptly subscribed thirty dollars to that fund, some giving practically all the savings they had.

66. 4 October 1920 McVitty to Secretary DIA
We have been fortunate in securing the services of a graduate nurse, who is really an enthusiast in her work. She is anxious to give the Senior girls a thorough course of Saturday evening lectures in home nursing, and needs certain text books for same. As this is work which should be of untold benefit to these girls in the years to come, I hope the Department will...authorize this...We will require about twenty text books in home nursing, at a total cost of $10. These books could remain the property of the school, and serve other classes in years to come.

67. 27 October 1920 McVitty to Secretary DIA
Rev.Mr.Ferrier has given us several days...we both feel that there must be a very considerable expenditure on the part of the church for house equipment, farm implements, carpenter tools and additional breeding stock...total of say $6000.00. We have been doing without things for several years...the fact that we are compelled to turn children away is proof that the Indian is at last appreciating our work...our need for a work shop and boys play house is...imperative...we could get much done this fall and could use the shop during the winter. We have very much repair work to do, and the boys need the training.

68. 13 November 1920 Scott to Lougheed
...I recognize the great need of the combined workshop and play-house, I do not consider this an opportune time to undertake any extensive building...I am disposed... to...make the necessary repairs to the present workshop.

69. 14 October 1921   McVitty to Scott

We are giving our pupils all the whole milk they desire for breakfast, and all the skim milk they can drink at dinner and supper. So pure milk is of vital importance to their health and happiness.

Our school is full and everything going on splendidly.

70. 20 September 1922   H. D. Johnson Report

...six pupils from this school were successful at the recent H.S.Entrance Examinations. One of them headed the list of successful candidates...winning the Rose Prize for Mount Brydges Examination Centre.

71. 4 April 1923   McVitty to Scott

...re heating

(1) I do not think it would be possible to retain our Staff another winter under present conditions.

(2) Our recent "flu" and pneumonia epidemic will cost the Dep. about $400.00, besides the suffering of the pupils and the great tax upon the school staff. It was... intensified, if not...caused by coldness of their dormitories.

(3)...When parents come from a distance to see their children, we have no sleeping accomodation for them... this could be easily remedied by adding two stories above the proposed heating plant...

72. June 1923?   McVitty to *All Parents and Friends of Indian Boys and Girls in Ontario and Quebec*

We are pleased to be able to inform you that our attendance is larger, our health better than ever before. Our promotion and High School Entrance Examinations are fully equal to those of neighboring "White Schools."

The Government and the Church are showing us every consideration, and have already planned large improvements for next year, but what fills our hearts with hope is the really marvelous awakening of the Indian people themselves to the advantages of a higher and better education. Many Indians have seen and felt this for years. All seem to see it now. Several boys who ran away from school years ago have recently returned of their own accord, and are earnestly seeking an education.

The time has come for a real advance; but there must be perfect understanding and agreement as to methods. We have decided therefore to hold a Conference on Indian Education at this school on...June 28th...We hope to have a representative each from the Government and the Church, and most cordially invite each Indian Council in Ontario and Quebec to send a delegate, a forward-looking man, who knows what his people want. We will entertain these delegates well, show them the school as it is, and then sit down together and plan how to make it better.

On Friday, 29th June, we will hold a great School picnic on the School grounds. There will be refreshment booths, games, speeches, community singing, band music, and lots of other good things. Just one whole day of feasting and fun. At its close pupils can go home for Summer holidays.

All "Old Pupils" are especially invited...

73. 6 June 1924   Sexton Report

...generally efficient management of this institution. An atmosphere of comfort and progress is in evidence in every department which I have time and opportunity to investigate. Yet while every attention is being made by the management to secure the intellectual welfare and health of the resident pupils...very inadequate provision for preventing loss of life in case of fire...

74. 15 July 1924   McVitty to Secretary DIA

...we have just...visited the Mohawk Institute...whilst the Mount Elgin Institute is well adapted for the work it is intended to do...is in the matter of "freshness" far behind some of these other buildings. Some parts have never been painted during the fifteen years we have been here...

For sanitary reasons, for economic reasons, and because the visiting public always expects a Government owned plant to be strictly up to date, I must earnestly request...a much more liberal grant...a class of seven pupils sent up for High School Entrance have all passed, several with Honors. Our promotion examinations this year showed marvellous success in class room work, and we have secured the services of a third teacher for next year....

75. 18 September 1924   McVitty to Scott

In the hope of securing a more prompt reply I...approach you personally on a question of vital importance...

1. The tremendous slump in the price of farm produce is cutting our income almost in two. Which means either a less efficient staff of teachers and instructors, or a lower standard of living for the pupils...

2. We have a splendid herd of about 60 T.B. tested dairy cows, and are forced to sell our cream for a mere trifle above cost...I would like very much to start a small creamery of our own...

(1) We would reap the full profit from our herd.

(2) We could afford to give our pupils more butter than at present.

(3) We could manufacture our skimmed milk into cottage cheese, which would make an excellent extra for pupils table.

(4) We could give our girls a thorough training in first class butter making, and would greatly please the hundreds of farmers and...wives who visit the school...

76. 16 January 1925   McVitty to Secretary DIA

...I am pleased to be able to report a full attendance of splendid pupils under three qualified teachers. During the winter months we are sending about 60 backward pupils to school all day. We will, I think, discontinue this about May 1st, returning to half day system...

We have an excellent staff. Wages, clothing, groceries and fuel are all high. Cattle, swine, vegetables of all kinds, and even milk and butter are very low. At least to the producer. So that we find ourselves using up rapidly such little reserve as we accumulated during good times. The balance we have in Capital account is needed to bring our stock up to par, which we purpose doing...

...the time has come when per capita grant should be raised to $150 for this school, the same as others. It is really doing excellent work, and we are exercising every possible care. Personally, I have not been absent from the school over six days all told since September 1st, and am giving the school in all its Departments my full time and best efforts. But inasmuch as it is a stock farm, rather than a grain farm conditions are against us.

77. 31 January 1925 T. Ferrier to Secretary DIA
...need of increasing the per capita grant...

During the past six or seven years the proceeds from the farm, stock etc. together with the per capita grant has not been sufficient to meet the cost of maintenance. The main source of revenue from the farm has been the live stock. The markets have been such lately that nothing can be made in this line. The principal has had quite a large reserve saved in his bank account through years when it was possible to make some profits. This has become about exhausted...I...request the Department to raise the per capita grant from $125 to $150 per pupil.

78. 5 March 1925 McVitty to Scott
...There are certain additional facts...you should have clearly before you when considering this matter.
1. The fact that our school is always filled to capacity, without a solitary canvass, is abundant proof that it is meeting a great need.
2. The record made by our pupils year after year is proof that they are capable, and that our teachers and instructors are efficient.
3. The fact that we seldom ever have a truant or a complaint is proof that the Indian people appreciate what we are doing.
4. This efficiency has been made possible by the fact that although our Per Capita Grant is very low, our Live Stock operations have been unusually successful. We have always been able to greatly augment our grant by our Live Stock profits.
5. Conditions in the Live Stock business have completely changed...We are more attentive to business than ever before, but the more business done the greater the loss...The price of grain makes it impossible to produce beef or milk at a profit.
6. Fuel, clothing, bread and other food we buy, and especially wages are abnormally high...this year we drew from our Reserve Fund about $3500.

79. 15 January 1926 McVitty to Secretary DIA
For several years I have felt that our school is not getting the best results from our milk production...milk in its various forms is not only the ideal, but an essential food. We are at the request of the Department, through its... Agents, refusing strong, well-nourished pupils from good homes, and accepting neglected, undernourished pupils who are orphans or destitute. This will become more and more a necessity as these children must be cared for...it is going to be a difficult task to bring these pupils up to the standard of health and strength so largely forfeited.

They really must have butter, cottage cheese, and other milk products in abundance; but...we have neither churn (Save small hand one), cooling vat, refrigerator, nor even live steam to properly cleanse our pails and dairy utensils. Nor have we any means at present of heating water for girls wash room, save by kitchen stove...I would respectfully solicit the help of the Department in turning the south east basement room of the main building into a nice little modern dairy...

80. 31 May, 1 June 1926 Sexton Report
The school is undermanned at present; there are 140 pupils in attendance with two teachers in charge. I would suggest that the number of qualified teachers on the staff be not less than 3. The discipline in this school is well nigh perfect, changing classes, pupils leaving or coming into school room or dining hall is done with military precision.

The organization is as good as can be expected under present conditions. The number of pupils in any class room at one time does not exceed the number required by the regulations of the Dept of Education for Ontario. The division of subjects among the teachers is fair.

There have been too frequent changes of teachers of the primary classes during the past year.
The present teachers are...Fred Dodson - 47 - Permanent 2nd Ont. Fern Harris - 21 - Interim 2nd Ont... They have been in charge of the whole school since May 15th, 1926

81. 7 January 1927 McVitty to Secretary DIA
During his last visit Mr...Sexton emphasized the need of toning up the building, and at the same time complimented us on the fact that no where in his Inspectorate could be found more healthy, well nourished, promising children; also stated that our senior pupils are well abreast of their respective classes in the Inspectorate.

82. 22 August 1927 McVitty to Secretary DIA
Have just returned from the West, where I visited a number of Industrial schools...We are not a bit jealous, but honestly in necessary things we are greatly behind.

83. 19 December 1927 Sexton Report
...again call to your attention the very inadequate

provision for the safety of the children in the case of fire. The fire escapes are not constructed to meet requirements in cases of emergency.

84. 30 January 1928 McVitty to Secretary DIA
...we have tried a third teacher on several occasions, and the unanimous opinion of our Staff is that it is an unnecessary expenditure of funds at our disposal.

We have two splendid teachers, and neither one wishes less work...Our Senior teacher has 47 pupils in the morning, with four classes; and about the same number in the afternoon with three classes. The Junior teacher has about 45 pupils with three classes. A country teacher will often have as many pupils and about eight classes.

Class room work is an important part of our training, but not by any means the most important. Our experience is that girls who have had a thorough training in domestic work have succeeded much better in after life than those who devoted most of their time in trying to secure High-school Entrance. In the case of the Indian "a little learning is a dangerous thing."

Our school is well organized and well manned. Pupils are not kept out of class room for any reason save sickness and...are well taught in the other Departments.

85. 18 February 1928 McVitty to Orr
...the motor we need is a 7½ horse power...Owing to weather conditions it has been impossible to harvest ice this year...I don't see how we could possibly take care of food for 150 people here without cold storage of some kind...If funds are not available for both motor and Kelvinator...then refrigeration...It is absolutely necessary.

86. 26 February 1928 McVitty to Secretary DIA
...all dormitories are at present furnished with steel fire escapes, and pupils and staff are repeatedly instructed as to how to use them in case of fire.

What we greatly need is some sort of electric alarm system...we can...add one more steel fire escape...

87. 29 May & 15 June 1928 Sexton Report
Nothing has been done to remedy the defective fire escape system.

88. 27 July 1928 MacKenzie to McVitty
...I shall be pleased to hear further as to whether you would recommend that anything be done regarding the fire escapes...an electric alarm system...

89. 6 August 1928 McVitty to Secretary DIA
...I think the building is reasonably well provided with fire escapes, and I assure you every possible precaution is being taken to prevent fire.

As to installation of Electric Fire Alarm system... estimate, which will be forwarded...

90. 6 August 1928 McVitty to Secretary DIA
...a veritable mecca for tourists...our farm, garden, livestock, lawns and grounds are exceptionally fine, and receive most favourable comment from our visitors.

We are...entering upon our 80th Anniversary year, and hope to make it a memorable one. We expect to greatly strengthen our Staff of instructors, and in our sewing room and workshop produce articles of such merit as to win the complete approval of the crowds we expect to visit us at a great Reunion 17th July...Anniversary Day ...never was our attendance as large, or new applications so numerous...

91. 4 and 5 December 1928 Sexton Report
The plan of alternating schoolroom class work, - farm work for the boys and some form of house work for the girls - is an admirable one but is faulty in that there is not enough diversity in the practical work which they do. Indian children, while not inferior in mentality to white children, are particularly clever with their hands: if... instruction could be given them similar to that in Technical Schools, but not necessarily as comprehensive... the problem of Indian Education would be well on the way to a satisfactory solution. Only 3 Senior IV pupils are in the classroom all day. Of the remaining 105 senior room pupils, 53 attend in the forenoon and 52 in the afternoon. Every possible care for the health and comfort of the Indian children in residence seems to have been taken by the Principal and his assistants, as evidenced by their splendid physiques. Wholesome food, comfortable sleeping quarters and wise disciplinary measures have been contributory causes to these results and all reflecting great credit on the management. I would suggest that at least one instructor be added to the teaching staff. Two teachers cannot adequately deal with 148 pupils especially when so many require special attention. Many come here without a speaking knowledge of the English language.

92. 3 January 1929 McVitty
...the mangle...in the laundry...is entirely out of date and very dangerous. It was discarded as dangerous by the New Method Laundry...nineteen years ago, was purchased for a trifle and installed here about that time. There is nothing in the way of modern protection against children getting their hands caught in the rollers. Notwithstanding the greatest precaution we have had several instances of girls getting caught in the roller. Yesterday, a girl got caught and had it not been for the alertness of the man in charge her hand would undoubtedly have been destroyed. Apart from the loss and suffering of the child, it would undoubtedly mean a law suit against the Department or School, or both...

93. 7 January 1929 McLean to McVitty
...the Department does not regularly supply mangles to

Indian residential schools. You might comment on the need of this equipment...

94. 8 January 1929 McVitty to Secretary DIA
...a mangle is absolutely necessary for carrying on the work of the laundry. About 200 sheets, besides towels, pillow cases, girls dresses and other things go through it every week...necessary, not only for appearance sake, but...to get them perfectly dry before putting them to use.

The mangle at present in use is heated and operated by steam, and...is a very old and dangerous one...apart from the very great injury which might come to a pupil through the use of this defective machinery, the Department is taking a very great risk of a suit for damages...
[14 January 1925 McLean to McVitty; 23 January 1929 McVitty to McLean; 26 January 1929 Ferrier to Scott; 1 February 1929 Orr to McVitty; 4 February 1929 McVitty to Orr; 14 February 1929 McLean]

95. 12 March 1929 McVitty to Secretary DIA
...we have beautifully redecorated the sewing room, also a portion of the old sewing room now being used as girls reading room. We have painted girls hall connecting these two rooms, and...decorated an adjoining room which we are fitting up as a worth while library. All this work has been done by our mechanic and his boys...

96. 3 May 1929 McVitty to Secretary DIA
...I am rapidly regaining my health, which was seriously shaken during the winter...I am however asking the Conference for a junior minister as Assistant, and think we have found in the Rev O. B. Strapp, of Oneida Indian Mission, an excellent man for the position. He is an overseas man, thirty seven years of age, thoroughly acquainted with Indian people, and has decided to give his life to work amongst them.

Our School was never in better condition, capacity attendance, health and conduct wonderfully good, and we have an excellent staff of officers and teachers...

97. 31 May 1929 McVitty to Secretary DIA
The mangle...has now been installed. The roller...is not large enough to handle all our work. We are compelled therefore to continue the use of the old mangle, which is wide enough to take in two sheets at a time. My Assistant, Mr. Strapp, who is an expert mechanic has placed on this old mangle a protective device, which makes it much more safe than formerly..

98. 31 May 1929 McVitty to Secretary DIA
...re training of senior girls in milking would say this School has done so for many years. During the past couple of years the practice has been discontinued, largely because few, if any of our girls went to work on farms. Practically all of them take positions as domestics in city homes. We will be pleased...to fall in line with the

Department's requirements, and make arrangements for such training as is suggested.

99. 8 August 1929 MacKenzie to McVitty
The Superintendent of Indian Education visited...the fire protection is not at all satisfactory...The Department insists on fire drill...There is fire hazard in various places in the attic...Mr Ferrier noticed an electric iron...I... request that the use of this equipment be discontinued...the bathing and lavatory facilities for the children are inadequate...

100. 5 October 1929 McLean to McVitty
...you may...purchase...the quantity of slate blackboard required for the junior room...at the lowest possible cost...

101. 8 October 1929 McVitty to Secretary DIA
In compliance with your request...we have opened our school to a crowd of very young and inefficient children, in fact, telling the Indian Agents to pick out the needy ones. This means that our school staff has to be increased, not only to do the work that older pupils would do, but to nurse and care for the little ones who cannot take care of themselves. I am hoping that the Department will assist us...paying an assistant nurse or increasing our Per Capita Grant to $150. The exceedingly dry weather has cut our crops and dairy produce in half.

102. 20 November 1929 McVitty to Secretary DIA
...Mr. Dodson, is anxious to have a Baloptican for use in the senior schoolroom for the projection of opaque objects...exceptionally helpful to the Indian pupils who learn so readily through the eye.

103. 23 November 1929 MacKenzie to McVitty
...no funds...the Department has never furnished this type of equipment to Indian Residential Schools...

104. 29 January 1930 Young to Scott
...last year, in response to the request of your Department, Rev. Oliver B. Strapp was appointed Assistant Principal ...has rendered splendid service...is occupying the living quarters in the institution, this has necessitated Rev. S. R. McVitty seeking a home elsewhere...

105. 15 February 1930 McVitty to Secretary DIA
...The General Council of the United Church meets in London this summer...delegates visit our school...special effort to make our lawn, gardens and buildings as beautiful as possible...we will provide all labor and hereby request a grant from you for...Paint for Girls' Dormitory and Halls, and Pupils' Kitchen...we also need about 1,000 feet of lumber for general repairs...

106. 16 July 1930 McVitty to Secretary DIA
...the cooking range in our Pupils Kitchen is quite worn

out. It is old and unsightly and a real eye-sore when we are showing visitors through...The ovens are so burned out that ashes fall through on to the food being cooked.

107. 4 September 1930 McVitty to Secretary DIA
...the Boiler Inspector has condemned the high pressure boiler used in our laundry for many years and forbidden us to fire it up again...hesitate to ask the Department for a new boiler but feel that is the cheaper and safer thing to do. A defective or condemned boiler is not permissible where so many girls are at work in the laundry...

108. 1 June 1931 McVitty and Strapp to Parents and Guardians, of our pupils, and all other good friends of the Indian people, the Mount Elgin Institute sends greeting.
We are pleased to inform you that the present school year is proving to be one of the "best ever". Attendance largest (154). Health, almost perfect, not a single case of serious illness during the year. Conduct, excellent.

Real progress is being made in every department of our school life. We have a splendid staff of fully qualified officers and teachers who are rendering excellent service in their several departments.

Careful instruction in the best way of doing things is being combined with the necessary duty of getting them done. The result is that at graduation our pupils are well qualified to fill important positions and most of them are doing so.

We are well aware that "Worthwhileness" in an individual depends more on "Moral Character" than a skilled hand or a trained mind. To meet this need we hold a delightful worship period each evening conducted by the Principal or his assistant. All senior pupils and most of the staff join in this service.

Pupils under proper supervision attend Divine Service each Sunday afternoons in the Colbourne United Church.

We have a really wonderful Sunday School with three well organized departments. The lessons are well taught, and an examination is conducted at the end of the session. This year thirty beautiful prizes, donated by Mr. A. P. Campbell, of St. Thomas, will be presented to the successful pupils at a great open air service to be held on the school grounds at 3 p.m. Sunday June 28th...To this service you and your friends are cordially invited.

At the close of the service junior pupils who have been in class room all year may go home for Summer holidays.

The senior room will close on Thursday July 16th. Pupils remaining with us during holidays will be paid just wages for any work they may be required to do.

School will reopen Tuesday September 1st and all pupils not officially discharged by the Department of Indian Affairs will be expected to return on that day.

We earnestly solicit the cooperation of all parents and guardians in caring for the pupils during the holiday season. Take them with you to Church and Sunday

School. Example is more than Precept - they will likely do as they see you do.

...the "financial depression" has reached us. We have been watching it in the offing for some time and governed ourselves accordingly. We owe no man anything. Have splendid farm equipment and a really wonderful dairy herd. We hope to carry on as heretofore.

We wish to express our deep appreciation of the courteous treatment according us at all times by the Department of Indian Affairs at Ottawa,

Be sure to come to the great open air service Sunday June 28th at 3 p.m.

109. 8 June 1932 McVitty to R. Ferrier
As a school we are facing the problem of what to do with a number of senior girls, who have, most of them, gained Entrance to High School. They have had a good training in the simpler duties of house work, but have not had such technical training as would make it possible for them to secure and hold worth while positions as house keepers in good homes. We must look to the Department for help in giving them special training during the next year or two. In many cases you have assisted pupils in going to High School, that is not what these girls need. Help us bear the extra expense of setting up a real Domestic Science Department...where these senior girls can get special training under an expert teacher, one whose duty it will be, to teach rather than to just get work done.
I am enclosing an application from Miss Webster...Can you help us employ her for this special work? We have two good cooks, her work would be extra and special, a real worth while service to these girls.
The public feels that we are not completing our work, I could see that, while making my report to the London Conference on Monday. If you could pay, say $600 toward this special work, it would help us to undertake it.

110. 14 June 1932 R. Ferrier to McVitty
...The Department expects the officer in charge of the kitchen at our institutions to give to the older Indian girls whatever training...is considered desirable. It has not been the practice to pay a special grant if a school undertakes more advanced household training than usual. At the present time, with the Appropriation cut to a minimum, it is impossible for the Department to give favourable consideration to your request...

111. 13 July 1932 McVitty to Secretary DIA
...Attendance has been large, health and conduct excellent and we have with some effort balanced our budget. We have a large staff of well qualified Teachers and Officers who are doing excellent work. A class of eight pupils trying the Entrance Examination were successful 100%. We are quite elated over them and their teacher. We have been able to beautify our school grounds. They are much

admired by our many visitors and must have a worthwhile cultural effect on our pupils. Our great problem is our senior girls, how to bridge the gulph between the Entrance Room and Real Life. High School is beyond most of them, and they are too young to take positions even as cooks or domestics. We are trying to meet the situation this year by adding to our staff a Music Teacher and a University Graduate in Domestic Science, thereby giving a special course in both of these subjects. The girls are very grateful but I do not really know where the extra money is coming from.

...during the year a large number of our pupils have thoughtfully and reverently partaken of the Holy Communion and are giving every indication of wishing to live a good life.

112. 23 July 1932 Dobbin London Free Press
MUNCEY RESERVE RESULT OF KIND AID OF FRIENDS Splendid Work Being Done For Young Indians At West Ontario Institution - REDMAN RETAINS MEMORIES OF PAST - Present Undertaking Is To Fit Him Into Customs of White Brother

...the reporter noted some of the best educational work being done. The pupils write neatly, spell well and give every evidence of sound discipline and of good progress in their general work. One feature of the school exercises is the singing. Each pupil gives evidence of interest in and good enjoyment of the world about them...Boys and girls alike are being fitted for the duties that confront the adult British citizen. And these youths and girls are happy in their environment. Sickness is rare in this residential school of 160 regular pupils.

When Mr. McVittie is asked about the work among the Indians, he uses the language of hope and of restraint. He tells you of results achieved...tells of the difficulty of reading the minds of those whom he tries to lead to better things...

113. 15 January 1933 A. D. Moore to MacKenzie
...I visited this school on Jan 12th and consulted the Assistant Principal, Rev. Mr. Strapp and also had a look over the school proper...
1. Re; Rest Room at the School.
When the pupils are not at work or in the class room or at play they have excess to their locker rooms which are in the basement of the school and are rooms 30′ x 40′ and have cement floors, with a row of locker boxes around the outside of the room which are 18″ high and outside of a small table in the girls part, they are barren of furniture. On account of the cement floor they were not very warm on the day of visit. Two other rooms are also available after supper time, being the prayer room and the reading room, there being school desks in the former and a long table with wooden benches in the latter...The lawn and grounds are used by the pupils in warm weather to lounge about on. The pupils are not allowed in the dormatories only at bed-time or on account of ilness.
2. Re; Bath accomodation.
All pupils of the school are bathed on Saturday of each week and the laundry room is used. Twelve wooden tubs...are plenty small enough to bath children in, as well as being hard to keep in a sanitary condition. The laundry building in which the children bath is a very old structure and not in a good state of repair.
3. Re; Skin diseases among pupils.
...there were 18 boys in bed with colds and sixteen girls and I examined their hands and faces and found two boys and two girls with sores either on their hands or faces and had the assurance of the Assistant Principal and the nurse that there were no other cases in the school. These skin diseases were quite common for some years back and according to Mr. Strapp, the pupils brought a lot of it with them when they returned from their holidays and it was not untill recent months that seperate towels were provided twice weekly to the pupils on the request of the Med. Supt. and this has done a lot to curtail the spread of skin ailments, which is at a low mark at the present. It has apparently taken some considerable time for these skin diseases to clear up on some pupils, as some have large and numerous scars and this fact may have been due to neglect on the part of the school nurse, or some blood disorder in the pupil, or even from diet or other cause.
4. Re Pupils diet.
A little butter is supplied each pupil at Supper, 3 times a week. No eggs have been supplied during the past year, in 4 previous years one egg each was supplied each pupil at Easter time. Dr. McLeod informs me that Mr. McVitty advised him that the pupils were getting an abundance of butter and eggs.
On the day of my visit the following was the Menu.
Breakfast, Rolled oats; cold milk; B. sugar; 3 slices of bread for senior and two for junior pupils; preserved fruit. Dinner. Stew composed of beef, potatoes, carrots, onions & turnips; milk; rice for dessert; 2 and one slices of bread.
Supper. Macaroni and tomatoes; any potatoes or porridge left over is give; milk; preserved fruit and bread the same as breakfast. Occasionally cold meat, pickles, ripe apples and dripping from fried meats are given at a meal. Mrs Blake the cook informs me that she has been at four Indian Residential schools and that Mount Elgin has better food and a larger assortment than the others she was at and the pupils all appear well nourished. The School has a variety of 6 preserved fruits.
5. Re; School sports.
...the pupils have soft balls and foot balls, skating and sleigh-riding in season and they wander around the grounds and woods at the school at will. No lacrosse sticks are supplied as they are dangerous to the pupils without proper padded protection and would be a source

of much ill feeling among the pupils...

8. Re; Unpaid wages of pupils.

In the summer of 1932, Carmen Sickles an older pupil who is at present in the school, had an agreement with Mr. McVitty to work at school during the holidays. Recently Mr. Jamieson, farm foreman informed Mr. Strapp that Sickles had not been paid his wages and Mr. Strapp...took the matter up with Mr. McVitty and the boy did receive a cheque for $20.65 on the 11th of Jan. 1934. This boy was engaged during the absence of Mr. Strapp and he was unaware of the non-payment of wages, and this is the only case that is known of.

9. Re; Graduates of Mount Elgin Institute.

The pupils of this school come from many reserves and many classes of Indians and as an Agent on two reserves I have seen many good pupils and many not so good. Of recent years I have seen many pupils return to their homes on the Oneida reserve of this Agency who have not been a credit to any school and firstly this must be considered from the class of pupil that is admitted and secondly from lack of control on the part of the Indian parents after the pupils return to their homes on the reserve after being discharged.

In speaking to the Assistant Principal and going over the school with him, he brought to my attention several requirements which he maintains are badly needed, but as I had not been asked for recommendations by the Dept, I have not submitted these. Dr. McLeod, Med. Supt. also mentioned the fact that when he asked that fruit be supplied a sick Indian, the Principal would not allow it on account of the cost and the Doctor also has some requirements...with health and sanitary conditions...

114. 30 June 1933 Beaton to McGill

The Executive...on June 28th, nominated Rev. O. B. Strapp as Assistant Principal...Rev. S. R. McVitty...is seriously ill, and it is felt that Mr. Strapp, who has been working under Mr. McVitty for four years, should be in a position to take over and carry the full responsibility...

115. 9 January 1934 MacKenzie to A. D. Moore

A complaint has reached the Department, contained in a letter intended for publication in a Toronto newspaper...

"Wouldn't the general public be surprised to know that these children, who work hard, have nothing softer than a box or table to rest on from the time they rise at 6:30 a.m. till they go to bed at night? (The beds must be kept neatly made up to impress visitors!) That they have not one home-like room for their use? That there is not one bath-tub for the use of the children? That skin diseases and sores are prevalent among the children? That, on a farm where a large dairy herd is kept, last year no more than an average of 1⅓ lbs. of butter for the whole 160 children was allowed daily? That, not once last year did those 160 children receive one whole egg each? That,

where sports should naturally flourish, the school will not provide even lacrosse sticks for the Indians' own game? Don't start thinking of depression. There was money enough this past summer to build stone pillars (to add to the appearance of the school) and to install new bath-tubs for the staff. And wouldn't the public be incensed to learn that some big boys who have worked at the school during the summer holidays never received their promised pay?

The children go to school half a day and work half a day, and are provided with food, shelter, and clothing. Their whole life, day in and day out, is planned for them. They learn to work under direction which doesn't require, and indeed discourages, any individual acting or thinking on their part. Punishment goes to those who don't keep in line. Consequently when they leave school, and this commanding hand is removed, what is the result? The school is not proud of its graduates."

...forward...a report regarding each of the complaints... especially...the diet provided for the children....skin diseases and sores and if the larger boys, who worked at the school during the summer, were paid...

116. 9 January 1934 McVitty to Secretary, Ottawa

Owing to seriously impared health I have tendered my resignation as Principal of above school to the Home Mission Board of the United Church. At the time of doing so, I had not the least knowledge of the fact that an ex-employee of the school had offered to the press a letter seriously reflecting upon the school and its management.

Fortunately an experienced Editor seeing the real purpose of the letter sent a copy to our Mission Offices instead of publishing it - this fact came to my knowledge shortly after I had tendered my resignation.

...for many years we have earnestly endeavoured to give or furnish our pupils with food, clothing, lodgings, nursing, teachers, recreation, vocational training and religious instruction fully equal to if not better than that enjoyed by the children of the great working and middle class white people of the Province of Ontario. I felt that anything less would be unworthy and anything more would be unjust. This standard of equality has been heartily endorsed by the multitudes of white people who visit us from time to time and I am pleased to add by the Indian people themselves who without any solicitation on our part keep the school filled to its doors...

Now that my work at the school is practically ended I fondly hope that my successor may find what I have tried to accomplish, and in the hearty good will of the general public and the Indian people a foundation upon which he can build a larger and better structure than yet has been.

117. 18 January 1934 McLeod to Stone

Information regarding conditions at Mount Elgin Residential School...was recently requested from Mr. Moore, by the Secretary, and as Director of Medical

Services I believe you should have further data from me...the inferences drawn from outside sources looks fairly serious on paper, but generally speaking the medical department and health of the pupils is in good shape.

Regarding the skin condition...on taking over this appointment Dr. Pardy informed me that there was an obstinate condition at this Agency, which he could not name or cure...Several times it has been cleaned up only to re-appear after the children return from visits to their respective homes...At no time was there any great number of children affected, but it is a nasty looking disorder and leaves scars...At present ...there is not a case at Mount Elgin Institute....While its degree of infectivity is low, we had separate towels for all patients, and I have been successful in obtaining separate towels for all pupils...

With reference to food provided pupils at Mount Elgin Institute I have inspected the tables ready for serving several times and concluded that a well balanced ration was provided...you remarked upon the same thing during your visit to Muncey...a letter from Rev. S. R. McVitty Principal, dated May 18th 1932... "An abundance of excellent food such as whole milk (50% Jersey), butter, eggs, meat, bread, and a superabundance of fresh vegetables are served daily, and...the wonderfully healthy appearance of our pupils calls forth the admiration of our many visitors. The usual comment is that white children have no such accommodation. This we know to be true." As for the egg ration I have taken the Reverend Gentleman's word for it, but agree that despite the absence of such food the children are in fine physical condition and have been prior to my appointment...any grievance regarding food is trivial and can be easily remedied.

Regarding bath accommodation for pupils this is in need of improvement, but until financial conditions warranted same, like many other of our needs the end justifies the means. Toilet accommodation is in a similar category, and Mr. McVitty informed me that indoor flush toilets for pupils was an endless source of trouble due to foreign material being thrown in them by ignorant pupils. The outside toilets are kept in a clean sanitary condition and I have inspected them several times.

Aside from the incident reported to you on December 12th, 1932, wherein the Principal refused to supply orange juice to a Pneumonia patient at Mount Elgin...after I had requested same there has been no friction.

I believe that a few recommendations are in order...

1. That all pupils submit to a blood Wassermann test for Syphilis. All new pupils from this Agency examined by me are so tested, but those in the school should have this done as a protection to themselves and others.

2. The system of ventilation in the sleeping dormitories be improved...this is notoriously poor particularly if there are many pupils ill. Mr. O. B. Strapp, assistant principal and myself have repeatedly discussed the situation and...an electric motor and large fan for each dormitory would

make conditions satisfactory.

3. Installation of modern bath equipment when and as finances will permit.

4. Provision of modern flush toilets (to augment one in each dormitory now used at night), either indoors or out for the pupils with a campaign of education and supervision as to management by pupils.

5. A tooth brush for every pupil. Older pupils use them but in my opinion all should for the moral effect if no other goal is attained...

118.   18 January 1934   Executive Committee, Board of Home Missions, United Church of Canada
...this Executive...heard with profound regret that on account of advancing years and declining health Rev. S. R. McVitty has tendered his resignation as Principal...our deep appreciation of the twenty-five years service he has rendered the cause of Indian education. His knowledge of Indian life and character and devotion to the best interests of his pupils have enabled him to exert an abiding and creative influence on hundreds of Indian boys and girls. His executive ability and keen sense of financial values have combined to make the Mount Elgin Institute one of the most efficiently managed residential schools in Canada...we nominate to the Department of Indian Affairs Rev. O. B. Strapp as Principal...

119.   19 January 1934   MacKenzie to A. D. Moore
...With reference to skin diseases among the pupils...The medical officer and the nurse should see that the pupils receive the necessary treatment.

Regarding the diet, it is considered that as there is a fine farm, with a dairy herd, in connection with this school, the pupils should receive an ample supply of whole milk and also butter. The Department is not aware whether the school keeps hens, but, if so...in the case of those pupils who are not robust or otherwise unhealthy, eggs should be included in the diet.
...the Assistant Principal and the Medical Officer brought to your attention a number of requirements for the school, which deal with health and sanitary conditions...

120.   25 January 1934   Stone to McLeod
...all pupils entering school should have an examination for syphilis regardless of where they come from...

I suppose there is no institution in the world with which fault cannot be found, and those in which young children are maintained are particularly open to attack. Knowing the very substantial improvement in our Residential schools in the last five or six years and the earnest endeavour the Department is making to keep up the standard under difficult financial conditions, I really regret to see them publically criticised. My impression from this particular controversy is that the author of it has some private spite vent on the church and the Department.

1934 - 1946
Rev. Oliver B. Strapp 1934-1944 - Rev. S. H. Soper 1944-1946

1. 7 February 1934 McLeod to A. D. Moore
...I have reviewed and inspected conditions at the school..

    1. <u>Sewage Disposal</u> -The present septic tank is inadequate for the needs of the school. Rain water from the roof drains into this tank and in summer storms flood the basement and allows raw sewage to enter the boy's playroom...

    2. <u>Toilet Accommodation.</u>- Two urinals and two flush toilets are required for each of the two boy's dormitories...Two toilets for lower girls' dormitory and three flush toilets in the upper female dormitory. The present toilets a single unit in each floor are antiquated, and the soil pipes are corroded, having been installed in 1895. Outside toilets for both sexes should be entirely rebuilt. In view of the weather conditions and possibility of plugging pipes by children not under supervision the cement vault type are recommended in preference to a flush system.

3. <u>Washing and Bathing Accommodation</u> - A unit of ten modern baths is required for use of the pupils... Present bathing facilities are inadequate. Wash bowls are also required in the boys' and girls' playrooms, and the most modern type would be the most economical. These would serve the children prior to eating their meals.

4. <u>Laundry Building</u>...This floor and sills is in a rotted condition...and is in danger of collapsing. Should this occur during operation of the machinery (due to vibration), there is a danger to the persons working therein and an added menace of injury to pupils due to escape of live steam. While this is not a public health problem it is one of public safety and I would urgently recommend that it be remedied...

5. <u>Ventilation</u>- The system of ventilation in the sleeping dormitories is notoriously poor, particularly if there are any ill pupils there. A large fan and electric motor for each dormitory would made conditions satisfactory.

...cost estimate...this calls for an expert...although I believe that the United Church will undertake to make these improvements for a stated sum. Mr. Strappe... informed me that with a grant to cover these improvements he could accomplish much more than if contracts were let...

2. 10 February 1934 Beaton to J. D. Sutherland
...I have gone carefully over the whole plant and its equipment...and I am...outlining two programmes. The first contains what would be necessary in order to make the plant and equipment worthy of the Government and the Church; the other, the barest minimum of improvements which must be undertaken within the next year if we are to carry on at all.

    Ideally...the following...should be undertaken:

1st.- An extension to the present diningroom and assembly room of about 20 feet. - Under existing conditions, 150 children are being fed in a basement diningroom which is hopelessly inadequate. Apart from the hygenic reasons which indicate larger space, the present fearful over-crowding makes any kind of training in table deportment absolutely impossible. The assembly room...is so small that it is practically impossible to crowd the staff and the student body into it.

2nd.- The annex should be torn down, or...completely rebuilt...the foundation is slipping that an attempt to remodel the present building would be a very difficult proposition - if not utterly impossible.

The little children, who are now climbing rickety outside stairs to their classrooms, should be provided for in classrooms on the ground floor of the new building, and the senior class which now meets in the main building, should also be provided for there. That would also release the present senior class-room for a boys' reading and recreation room - something which is very badly needed.

Upstairs there should be a gymnasium. This would also be used as an assembly room when the students put on plays and demonstrations to which their parents are invited.

The basement of the new building should be a modern root cellar for the storage of vegetables.

3rd. - A new cottage for the herdsman...

4th. - A small annex at each end of the building, running up the three floors, containing bathing and toilet facilities.

5th. - A new laundry...

The <u>minimum repairs</u> which must be attended to immediately are as follows: -

1st.- A new septic tank. -No change has been made in this equipment since the original building was erected...The water from the roof drains into it. The water from the sinks in the kitchen also drains into it. In a time of severe rains, the sewage backs up into both the boys' and the girls' playrooms and flushes through so rapidly that the proper bacteriological action is impossible, polluting the river which runs at the back of the school...

2nd.- If the annex, containing bathing and toilet facilities, is beyond the realm of possibility, then there should be added immediately, in addition to the new drainage pipes, two stands and two toilets in each of the boys' dormitories, and at least five more toilets in the girls' dormitories.

3rd.- The washrooms on the ground floor need to be entirely rebuilt.

4th.- The only supply of hot water in the main building at the present time comes from a tank which is very little larger than the one which is installed in an ordinary eight-roomed house in this city and is heated by a small jacket heater which would be adequate for a family. A new tank and a new jacket heater...should be installed...

5th.- The laundry should be rebuilt...joists are so rotten that one can pick them to pieces with his hands, and we are lucky that the tremendous weight of the cement floor...and the laundry machinery have not broken through into the cellar, precipitating pupils into scalding steam.

6th.- An annex to the laundry should be erected, with dressing-rooms upstairs and bathrooms downstairs.

New laundry tubs, in place of the old insanitary wooden ones which are now in the laundry, should be installed.

7th.- An automatic stoker and fan should be attached

to the boiler which heats the main building. On Tuesday last, in every one of the class-rooms the teachers were using stoves...The cost...would be readily offset by the decreased fire hazard.

8th.- An adequate refrigerator of the walk-in type is very necessary and would add greatly - not only to the quality of the food supplied to the pupils - but to the efficiency of the kitchen staff.

...we ought to have expert advice...Mr. Strapp is an experienced mechanic who understands a good deal about the problems involved in building and equipping a school of this type...improvements...can be carried out without expense so far as supervision is concerned...a considerable part of the work can be done by the school staff.

I have dealt in this letter only with the complaints which Miss Webster made about the building and equipment. The questions which arise in connection with the programme of work and study and play need not be discussed by correspondence...

3. 15 March 1934 McLeod to Stone
    While there is an increase of seven cases of Trachoma...along with several listed as suspicious, there is no cause for alarm as several of these are new pupils and the diagnosis is subject to confirmation.
    ...I would recommend the following;
    1. Services of a dentist for six days....
    2. Permission for extraction of tonsils...ten pupils
    3. A visit by Dr. J. J. Wall as time permits to check up on treatment and diagnosis of Trachoma cases...

4. 9 April 1934 Orr to McGill
    ...owing to the urgency of the situation...advisable to give you particulars about the laundry building.
    The Principal has offered to do as much of the work as possible with his Staff, providing the department will supply the material and one or two expert mechanics...if these changes are not carried out immediately it will be necessary to instruct the school to close the laundry as there is great danger of loss of life if operated under present conditions...

5. 11 April 1934 Orr to McGill
    ...Since 1912 practically no improvements have been carried out to the main building...the Board of Home Missions...outlined a list of improvements, which in their opinion, should be undertaken...and I...submit the following recommendations.
    1. I do not consider it necessary to provide an extension to the building...to increase the accommodation in the dining room and assembly hall...if a rearrangement is made of the rooms in the basement, ground and first floors...it is not necessary or advisable that the Staff dining rooms be supplied from a separate kitchen. There is no reason why all the cooking for the Institute should

not be done in the one kitchen, as this system is followed with success in our other Residential Schools.
    2....the annex...is in a fair state of repair...I would recommend that the rooms be rearranged to provide both classrooms at one end of the building, and an inside staircase built to provide access to the classrooms.
    4....addition for toilets, etc...there is ample space in the building to provide for toilet and bathing facilities...the school is deficient in sanitary appliances in every department except the portion occupied by the Staff. There are no tub baths in the school for the bathing of the pupils, and at present they are bathed once a week in the old wooden laundry tubs in the laundry.
    The only closets available to the pupils in the school are night toilets...in the dormitories. During the day it is necessary for them to use outside closets which are located a considerable distance from the school, and at present are in a very unsanitary condition.
    There is ample space in the rooms adjoining the recreation rooms...and I would recommend that these rooms be fitted up with tub baths, shower baths and closets.
    5. A new laundry building is not necessary...
    6. A new septic tank and drainage system does not appear of any great urgency at the present time...
    7....it will be necessary to provide an adequate supply of hot water when the bathing facilities have been provided. I would recommend that a thousand gallon tank be installed together with a jacket heater...
    9. A cold storage room is needed. This is being provided for in all our new Residential Schools, and it is practically impossible to keep the school supplies of food in proper condition without it.
    I would recommend that proper bathing and toilet facilities for the pupils be provided, including the installation of a new hot water system, also...that the necessary repairs be made to the laundry building. These two items to my mind are the most important and urgent at the present time...It will also be necessary this year to provide a new foundation for the south end of the annex...and if possible the interior should be rearranged as outlined...the kitchen is very poorly located, with practically no light or ventilation...

6. 17 April 1934 McGill to Beaton
    There are no funds provided in this year's estimates to carry out the recommendations made in this report, but an effort will be made to find an amount up to approximately $4,500 in order that the laundry may be put in proper shape and also suitable sanitary conveniences provided in the school for the pupils.

7. 20 April 1934 Beaton to McGill
    ...Your suggestion that the amount of $4,500 be made available to repair the laundry and provide additional sanitary conveniences is quite acceptable...There is no doubt that they are the most pressing needs. I should hope...it would be possible to make a beginning at the

reorganization of the rooms this year, so that the two kitchens can be combined and some enlargement of the present pupils' dining-room made possible.

8. May 1934 McLeod Dental Clinic Report
Total number of fillings -   255
Total number of extractions -   74

9. 10 May 1934 Orr to McGill
...last week I...made arrangements for commencing the work of remodelling the old laundry building...

10. 25 May 1934 Dep. Supt. Gen. to A. D. Moore
...you should visit...as often as is necessary in the conduct of department business. From time to time, you should make a careful study of conditions at this school and report to the Department any matters which you consider should receive our attention. Your inspection of the school should be thorough and complete and accurate information should be supplied...Criticism should be constructive, as suggestions for improving the educational programme are welcomed. It is the Department's aim to keep up the attendance, improve the instruction...To do this effectually requires the active cooperation of the Principal and yourself.

11. 23 June 1934 Strapp to McGill
...I very much appreciate the fact that the courtesy of direct communication with the Department which was enjoyed by...Principal McVitty...is to be continued.
...in future it would greatly help us in the carrying on of the work at the school if an official of the Schools Branch of the Department made a thorough inspection of the school at least annually...we feel that an inspection should be made by someone who is in close touch with the other schools (Residential) operated by the Churches, competent to advise the Principal upon matters of procedure, discipline and general administration...and able to make a comprehensive evaluation of the work being carried on in the various departments of school life.

12. 20 September 1934 A. D. Moore to Secretary DIA
...conditions as a whole in a very satisfactory state, in so far as general management of the school is concerned and the children all appear well nourished and well clad.
There are some repairs that...need early attention so that extra expense will not be incurred in the future...

13. 20 November 1934 Strapp to Secretary DIA
...a matter that, with the onset of cold weather, daily becomes more acute, namely, provision of hot water for the pupils' wash rooms...we have a small jacket heater with a storage tank of approximately 90 gallons capacity...plenty of hot water for perhaps fifteen persons but is hopelessly inadequate for one hundred and fifty...

14. 14 March 1935 A. D. Moore to Secretary DIA
...conditions...are in a very satisfactory state, being little sickness, no truancy, and the management...under the direction of a young and efficient staff...

15. 18 March 1935 Mackenzie to A. D. Moore
...arrangements can be made to improve the teaching of manual training...some equipment is necessary and you may authorize...expenditure not exceeding $275.00 in the purchase of the articles absolutely necessary...

16. 19 March 1935 McLeod to Stone
While there is no increase in Trachoma...definitely established, the increased number of suspects will likely bring up our total when confirmed...some of them are new pupils who have brought the disease in with them from their respective reserves...most of our defective children are senior pupils on the school roll.....
...Strapp is quite anxious that the impaired vision found among his pupils, (and which he has mentioned several times before inspection), be attended to, and I suspect that several of the girls at least have feigned impairment in the test, under the impression that glasses will improve their appearance, which is not original on their part.
...I would recommend;
1. Services of a dentist for six days...
2. Permission for extraction of tonsils of...fifteen pupils
3. Refraction and glasses if necessary...for fifteen pupils ...if done in numbers at $6 per pupils including glasses.
4. A visit by Dr. J. J. Wall to check my diagnosis and treatment of Trachoma.

17. 27 June 1935 A. D. Moore to Secretary DIA
...This school is in bad need of a refrigerator so that fresh meat may be stored, which is now being purchased at a large expense when needed, but which if proper facilities for storage were available, the school could kill their own meat and store the same, rather than sell their animals and have to purchase by small quantity.
...completion of the 3rd class-room should be done as soon as possible, also the repairing and rebuilding of the boys out-houses and additional toilet facilities in the boys and girls dormitories are badly needed.

18. June 1935 A. D. Moore Report
Routine
- At the time of my visit there were 108 pupils in the classroom; 46 pupils in vocational training departments, 8 pupils sick, 1 pupil absent - in Victoria Hospital, London. Total 154.
Health, Sanitation
Appearance of pupils: good, all pupils looking well nourished and clean.
Cleanliness of school: very good
Appearance of school grounds: very clean and orderly

Care of the sick: confined to their beds under the care of the Supt and a registered nurse.

The children's meals: Dinner, roast beef and gravy, buttered carrots, potatoes, rhubarb pudding, bread, butter and milk.

Fire drill, escapes and protection: instructions twice a month. School well equipped with escapes.

Vocational Training

Domestic instruction: lectures and practical work under a graduate dietition

Instruction in farming and gardening: practical work for all grades

Training in the care of live stock: ditto

Manual training: repairs around the school and six benches recently installed...

General Discipline in the school: very good

Efficiency of the staff: young efficient and doing excellent work

General management: very good

Suggestions:...painting...the barns, additional toilet facilities in the dormitories, refrigerator badly needed, completion of the class room, re-building boys out-house.

19. 9 July 1935 MacKenzie to Beaton

...your telegram...reporting an outbreak of measles...and requesting that an isolation ward be prepared in the third storey...a number of the pupils are...home on holidays...it should be possible...to provide proper isolation by re-arrangement of...the dormitories. A dormitory for boys and one for girls who are affected should provide the proper quarters for isolation and treatment.

The Department has not yet definitely decided if the improvements and alterations in the interior of the building will be proceeded with. The Architect of this Department will be visiting the school in the very near future, and the matter will then be given consideration.

The outbreak of measles and the inconvenience caused the members of the staff during the summer holidays is regretted.

20. 16 July 1935 A. D. Moore to Stone

...the measles situation...there has been no increase from the original two cases reported last week.

Immediately upon making the diagnosis July 7th, complete isolation of these two cases, both girls, was affected on the third floor attic. The other female suspect was isolated, and three boys, the latter on the attic of the boys' side of the building...

The measles cases are convalescent and out of bed... but they are still in isolation, partly in deference to Mr. Strapp...they can be discharged from the school on July 17th for vacation...approximately forty pupils who were down with Measles...in 1933...I intend to release to their homes on July 17th school closing day...

21. 18 July 1935 Beaton to J. D. Sutherland

...none of the pupils...had left when the outbreak of measles...occurred...this School has for years followed the practice of carrying on until the middle of July and then opening on September 1st. The Principal...immediately resorted to a re-arrangement of dormitory space...overcrowding some of the other dormitories in order to provide isolation for the pupils who are ill. In the event of fire or panic through some other cause, the fact that 130 pupils were attempting to use exits intended for 100 might easily result in loss of life or injury...We feel that by reporting the matter and asking for immediate action, we have cleared ourselves of responsibility.

The whole situation is exceedingly unfortunate, as it breaks up the arrangements for staff holidays. I hope that long before this Mr. Orr has been able to visit Muncey and made some arrangements for beginning the improvements and alterations. I certainly do not intend the $20,000 in the Estimates for that purpose to be transferred to some other account, if I can help it.

22. 10 March 1936 Strapp to J. D. Sutherland

Some time ago I had a conversation with Mr. J. H. Sexton...with reference to establishing a high school entrance examination centre at this school.

Experience has taught us that the abrupt change to strange surroundings under an examiner who is strange and, at times, apt to be somewhat unsympathetic is frequently responsible for the failure of an otherwise really good candidate. This is particularly noticeable in oral examinations such as reading.

Mr. Sexton is quite enthusiastic about the matter and has taken it up with the Ontario Department of Education...

23. 16 March 1936 Grand Jury of Middlesex County

...March 11th...was the first visit by any grand jury to this institution...This school teaches academic, vocational and dairy work. Their registration is 81 girls and 75 boys, aged from 11 to 17 years. Much credit is due the federal government in maintaining an institution of this nature. We would recommend that the Department of Indian Affairs at Ottawa be requested to supply this institution with adequate lavatory accommodation, also an emergency hospital, capable of taking care of both sexes, with accommodation for six or eight patients. The heating system is at present inefficient, and could be improved at least 30 percent by the Installation of a vacuum pump or air eliminator on the return lines.

24. 17 March 1936 J. D. Sutherland to Greer

...This Department would be pleased if your Department could arrange to have the examination centre conducted at the school, on the understanding that the expense connected with the presiding examiner, etc., would be provided by the school authorities...

25. 15 July 1936 McLeod to Stone
1. The trachoma situation has improved, due to intensive treatment...recommend a visit from Dr. Wall...
2. Would recommend that permission be granted for tonsillectomy in the 11 cases reported.
3. That permission be granted to supply glasses for defective eyes of 10 pupils listed at total cost of $100.
4...services of a dentist be authorized for three days...
General conditions of the pupils is excellent. Toilet facilities were taken up with Mr. Gurney Orr...and since with Rev. O. B. Strapp...and temporary sanitary improvements can be made. Food and diet excellent....

26. 27 July 1936 Strapp to MacInnes
...the desks are required for a class room that was renovated about a year ago. At that time we asked for desks but were informed that there were no funds available...we were using a number of kitchen chairs and some large double desks and have continued to do so during the past year. It is impossible for the pupils to place their feet on the floor and assume the correct posture with the result that they tire very quickly and the work of the class is more difficult to carry on...
The ages in this room will vary from five to fourteen with the majority from five to nine...thirty-five in the room.

27. 6 October 1936 A. D. Moore to Secretary DIA
...it has been found necessary to discharge...**** aged 12 years...admitted...on the 9th of September, 1936.
On October 1st, ****, father of this girl appeared at this office complaining bitterly that his girl was not receiving enough to eat...and that he wished her to be returned to her home. It would appear that this man had visited the school and attended at the noon meal and found that his child had no butter on her bread and no meat in the meal and that her dinner consisted of milk, bread (dry), 4 small potatoes, diced carrots and butter scotch pudding and that in his opinion this was not enough and not to the standard that he fed her at home, when she received meat and butter at least twice a day.
On hearing his complaint, I asked Dr. McLeod to accompany me to the school and did learn that the claim of the man was right as to the meal he attended, but that the girl had not made any complaint to the principal or any of the staff that she had not received enough to eat.
In the presence of the Doctor, the principal and the matron and the dietician, this girl made the statement that she had only received meat at one meal in three weeks, which was denied by the dietician, who maintained they procured meat twice a week, which she did consider sufficient and according to calories, the pupils were getting a well balanced diet and I can vouch that none of the pupils look underfed.
The father could not be convinced that his child was

receiving good enough meals and rather than have further trouble with this parent who was adamant in his demands and at the request of the Principal, I did instruct this girl to be discharged at once, contending that if the father was able to provide at home this was satisfactory and that the vacancy created would allow for another pupil to be placed in the school, as there are many applicants.
There has been a large number of truants from this school of late and in procuring the return of these pupils to the school and on enquiring as to why they ran away, Constable Bella of the R.C.M.P has stated to me that some of these truants on being apprehended complain to him that they are not receiving enough to eat and being made to eat foods that they were not accustomed to and did not like and could not eat.
This complaint of the children can be understood... the foods...are not of the same nature they had received at their homes, where they go in for a considerable amount of salt pork, and other heavy foods...
Dr. McLeod is making a survey of the school as to the health conditions...and pending his report...I will speak to the Principal...to give attention to the feeding of his pupils, as I am informed that the children working in the kitchen are always well fed and it may be possible that these children take foods that should be given to the smaller pupils in the dining room and that these small pupils go short and this would be the result of bad supervision by the officer of the school in charge and should be stopped by her. It is possible these children in the kitchen are playing favourite to friends in the dining-room of other non-friends.

28. 17 October 1936 McLeod to McGill
Generally speaking, the pupils are in excellent physical condition. Food is of the correct type, and sufficient is provided. The buildings, including toilet accommodation are unsatisfactory, but I am informed by the Principal that alterations...in progress will greatly remedy the situation.
Blood Wassermann tests were not undertaken on all pupils, and this will not be done unless directed...

29. 21 October 1936 A. D. Moore to Secretary DIA
...the report requested on health conditions...Dr. McLeod...did submit a full report...I would...recommend that additional meat and butter be given the pupils at this school, who in my mind should at least receive the same allowances of meat that is given in the relief rations, namely 8 pounds of meat per month to all children over 10 years of age and half that amount for children under 10 years, which according to the principal's own statement to the Doctor and myself, they only receive 500 pounds a month for 150 pupils, which is supplemented by the pupils receiving an egg on odd occasions.

30. Specimen Copy of menu Mt. Elgin Residential School Children's Dining Room Oct 12-18

Monday	Tuesday	Wednesday	Thursday	Friday	Saturday	Sunday
Rolled Oats & Bran B & B Milk	Cracked Wheat B & B Milk	Cornmeal & Bran B & B Milk	Cracked Wheat Bread Peanut Butter Milk	Rolled Oats B & B Milk	Cornmeal B & B Milk	Rolled Oats Bran Honey B & B Milk
Roast Beef Gravy Potatoes Cr. Cauliflower Mincemeat Pie Bread Milk	Meat Gravy Potatoes Bkd Veg. Marrow Pumpkin Pudding Bread Milk	Potatoes M. Turnip Tapioca Cream Bread Milk	Potatoes Btd Cabbage Indian Pudding Bread Milk	Veg Stew Potatoes Cd Cauliflower Cottage Pudding Choc Sauce Bread Milk	Potatoes Green Tomato & Onion Fry Creamy Rice Bread Milk	Roast Beef Gravy Potatoes Btd Carrots Pumpkin Pie Bread Milk
Cabbage Salad Sl. Tomatoes Corn Relish Strawberries Bread Milk	Bread Omelet Sl Tomatoes Black Currants Bread Milk	Cauliflower au Gratin Rhubarb Bread Milk	Meat & Vegetable Pie Pumpkin & Raisin Sauce Bread Milk	Convent Pudding (macaroni & eggs) honey Bread Milk	Veg soup Sl Tomatoes Rhubarb Sc Bread Milk	Sunshine Salad Bread Peanut Butter Ginger Preserve Buns Hot Cross

31. October 1936   McLeod Report

1. General health of the pupils is excellent. The skin condition, diagnosed as an obscure form of Impetigo not responding to usual treatment has practically subsided. Concerted effort is being made to eliminate and prevent any return of this condition. All pupils have been vaccinated.

2. There are fifteen children underweight, six of whom are new pupils. Another pupil at six pounds underweight suffered a severe illness about one year ago. No other definite pathology in those underweight, and there is no evidence of undernourishment. Pupils below par are to have special food as arranged with Principal, and they will be checked at intervals...

3. Food. Complaints were heard from the father of a pupil and the pupil, that inmates were not receiving sufficient food. Menus, as arranged each week by a qualified dietitian, were inspected and in my opinion the caloric requirements are being met. Meat in some form is provided twice weekly; eggs are served as a main dish once each week, and at other meals in desserts, and cooked dishes. Butter is served each morning for breakfast with bread and at other meals, in various foods served. Your medical Superintendent visited the school at meal hour several times, and witnessed sufficient food provided for each pupil. Owing to wastage which has been experienced, the individual is served with one slice of bread per meal and one cup of fresh cows' milk. Pupils desiring more may have same on request.

Principal Strapp informs me that the meat account per month is $50.00 for pupils and staff, or 500 pounds of meat. In addition to meat, the protein requirements are augmented by milk and other foods, but in view of the complaint, I would recommend that more meat be provided, particularly in an obvious form for its psychological effect. Mr. Strapp expresses a willingness

to do this, but states that lack of proper refrigeration facilities prohibits proper storing of fresh meat. There is an abundance of fresh vegetables. A more liberal frequency of serving butter might be considered, but with approximately 150 pupils to serve, will cause an appreciable increase in cost. I would report after interviewing several pupils quietly, and witnessing meals served that the food is suitable and sufficient in amount. Some pupils complained that they were served vegetables etc., that they did not prefer, which is natural.

4. Trachoma situation is under control. One case classed x is a new pupil. Recommend that services of Dr. J. J. Wall be made available...to confirm findings. His survey will likely reduce the total of 12 suspicious cases.

5. Would recommend that authority be granted for refraction and glasses to 14 pupils with defective vision. Pupils classed DV? (3), would not cooperate in examination, and it is doubtful if there vision is defective. A conspiracy on the part of some pupils to obtain glasses, particularly girls, is suspected

6. Would recommend that the services of a dentist be engaged for four days to correct defects listed, and those which his examination will disclose.

7. That authority be granted for tonsillectomy on 11 pupils...when written consent is obtained from parents.

32. 22 October 1936   Dep. Supt. Gen. DIA to McLeod
...your...report on the health of the pupils...Please provide the Principal with a copy and discuss with him a suitable diet for the children who are undernourished. I understand the school authorities are willing to provide a separate dining room for these children, and that suggestions regarding dict will be welcomed. I shall be glad if you and Miss McCaig will give some time and thought to this matter and will be interested in knowing the result of your discussion with Mr. Strapp. Please let

me have a copy of the diet list decided upon, as this may be of use elsewhere.

I presume, though you do not say so, that you would appreciate the services of a dentist and specialist for some of these children. It is impossible to provide the necessary funds at present, but, if you will bring the matter up again after the New Year, it may be that the financial situation will be better then.

...it would be advisable to try to furnish an estimate of the number of pupils who require attention, and some outline of the cost at the best rates you can arrange...

33. SPECIMEN DAILY MENU FOR UNDERWEIGHT CHILDREN

BREAKFAST	DINNER	SUPPER	MID MORNING
Choice of; Orange Juice Tomato juice Fresh fruit Stewed fruit Cereal prepared or cooked with milk. Bread with butter, honey marmalade or jam. Choice of; one egg-bacon-ham, Choice of; 1 cup milk. 1 cup cocoa Cereals desired include rice, oatmeal and commeal. Stewed fruits include prunes, figs and apricots. Egg should be soft boiled, coddled or scrambled. Not fried.	Choice of; cream soup - meat broth. Meat such as beef steak, lamb chop, roast beef, chicken, meat hash, fish, or meat stew. Potatoes - baked or mashed with butter or beef juice, meat gravy. one green vegetable or salad. one vegetable with cream sauce. Bread with butter. Choice of stewed fruit with cream or custard or milk pudding, or suet pudding with syrup or jam, or rice, tapioca or junket. Milk 1 cup. Noodles, macaroni or spaghetti may be substituted for meat one or two days weekly. Vegetables desired are asparagus, stewed celery, tomatoes, spinach, peas, beans, carrots and greens.	Choice of; Salmon, herring sardines, mackerel, etc., macaroni and cheese Green vegetable or salad Bread with butter. Preserved or fresh fruit, or baked apple or custard. Milk Peanut butter may be used in lieu of dairy butter occasional. Cold meats are not advisable Foods should not be highly spiced or seasoned. This diet has been designed to provide a maximum of calories, with the aim to build up weight.	Choice of; Milk Cocoa Egg-nog Mid Afternoon Choice of; Milk Cocoa Egg nog One cup of milk is sufficient for each serving This diet should be supplemented by Cod Liver Oil, plain or with hypophosphites.

34. 22 October 1936 Dep. Supt. Gen. to Strapp

...I understand that you are willing to provide a special dining room for...children who are undernourished, and Doctor McLeod has been requested to discuss with you the question of a suitable diet for these children...

35. 14 November 1936 McLeod to McGill

...Miss McCaig and I have prepared a suitable diet for children who are underweight...We have endeavoured to get away from elaborate food preparations, and at the same time to provide a range of choice for each meal, at a minimum of inconvenience.

A copy of this diet was provided Mr. Strapp...some time ago, and he expressed a willingness to cooperate in administering same. He reiterated the fact that absence of refrigeration facilities would curtail the daily serving of fresh meat, but this will be overcome with the onset of cooler weather.

...I will repeat my recommendations regarding the services of a dentist, and tonsillectomy...when financial arrangements may be better facilitated.

36. 29 December 1936 McLeod to McGill

...pupils...who have been underweight, I am enclosing a report on the weights of these children...In a letter to me of October 22nd last, in which you requested a special diet list it was intimated that the school authorities were willing to provide a separate dining room for these children...Miss McCaig and I spent considerable time preparing a suitable diet list...but that this diet has not been followed nor has the separate dining room been instituted. This information comes from the lady superintendent, and the staff nurse.

However, mid morning, and mid afternoon nourishment, including milk, has been given to the underweight children. The results have been very gratifying in that practically normal weight has been reached by all of these pupils. On...discontinuance of extra food several of them lost weight, requiring resumption of feeding between meals.

Failure to provide a separate dining room, and to follow the special diet list of October last was not on my instruction, but was initiated solely by the school staff. Rev O. B. Strapp has been ill, and in hospital, and this may account for the change of plans. He has since returned to duty.

I have not discussed the omission of this diet list with him on the assumption that I should first report the circumstances to your office where the initial instruction on same originated. This passive resistance is typical of the school in relation to this office.

My relations with the staff have been in harmony, with the exception that those in authority manifest a determination to have their own way in rulings of the Department. The dietician on duty did not appreciate preparation of the special diet list when it was discussed with her.

While no controversy on this subject is desired, I feel

that it is my duty to report what has not been done in regard to your wishes.

37.   12 January 1937   McLeod to Secretary IAB
...reference to pupils...who were underweight...I am quite pleased with the results obtained. My motive in writing December 29th, was not of complaint, but more to acquaint Dr. McGill with the fact that proposals made by the Principal to the Department...were not being carried out. I felt that the Department reasonably expected a separate dining room for underweight pupils had been inaugurated as promised, and should be made aware...that nothing along this line had been done.

I do not believe that it would be advisable to write the Principal in view of the improvement made by these children. If under the present system normal weight is not maintained, to be revealed by periodic check-up on my part, a letter could be drafted at a later date.

There have been no major difficulties experienced with the Principal and staff of Mount Elgin Residential School by me. Minor ones include the determination manifested of attempts to safeguard the pupils' health in methods other than those of your Medical Superintendent, the usual objection to the latter and those laid down by the Department being that they prove to be too great an inconvenience. This difficulty mainly involves the treatment of Trachoma, and the opportunity presented by the separate dining room proposal enabled me to bring the situation to the attention of Ottawa.

With the gratifying results obtained with weight production, I would prefer to let the case rest for the present. This in view of the fact that the Principal has been...in hospital, although now completely recovered.

If the occasion should warrant same due to weight loss, proper representation can be made to him both from the Department and myself at the time. Careful observation of the weight of pupils will be made, and it is my opinion that there will not be any great difficulty encountered in view of the excellent recovery of the children involved.

38.   29 January 1937   McLeod to Secretary DIA
...I was informed that owing to lack of funds, recommendations made by me...could not be authorized at that time. I was directed to again submit these recommendations after the New Year in the hope that the financial situation would have improved.

I have visited the school and accordingly make the following recommendations;

1. That authority be granted for refraction of fourteen pupils, and glasses for eyes supplied if necessary at an estimated cost of $140.

2. That the services of a dentist be engaged for four days at an estimated cost of $120.

3. That provision be made for removal of tonsils of eleven pupils, when written consent from parents be obtained by the Principal...

I am mindful of the fact that the financial situation of Medical Department has not improved, but am requesting the recommendations as directed. In the absence of authority for this work I would request permission to proceed with tonsillectomy in about four cases which show marked hypertrophy and disease...

39.   7 February 1937   McLeod to Stone
I have to report one case of Scarlet Fever, and eighteen cases of Influenza...The Influenza at the school is quite mild with no complications to date. Mr. Strapp...set aside an upper dormitory in which the Scarlet Fever case is isolated at one end with screen, and the Influenza at the opposite extremity. He was quite willing to help in the situation but emphatically reiterated that he was taking no responsibility for results owing to the lack of hospital facilities at the school. Since he will not be expected to assume any great burden of responsibility his remarks were passed without comment.

40.   8 March 1937   Strapp to R. Cochrane
...I beg to recommend the following repairs at this school as the necessary minimum.
Basement Rooms and Halls:
Girls recreation and assembly room: Strip loose plaster and re-plaster, Paint ceiling and walls, Screen wash basins.
Hall to dining-room: Strip plaster from ceiling and replaster. Paint walls.
Pupils' bath room; This room was fitted up as an emergency measure when the laundry tubs, in which the pupils had been bathed up until this time, were removed during the remodelling of the laundry building about two years ago. This room was used as a workshop and nothing was done beyond placing eight tub baths along one wall, connecting up the water and drain...The present condition is anything but sanitary and because of the location of the room it is impossible to adequately ventilate it without installing a proper exhaust ventilating system. A new floor should be laid so that proper drainage may be obtained, the walls should be resurfaced...The ceiling should be painted and three electric fixtures installed to give adequate lighting.
Pupils' kitchen; The wainscotting in this room is in a deplorable condition and should be removed entirely. The plaster on the ceiling is loose in a number of places and should be stripped off and the ceiling re-plastered. The walls should be resurfaced and painted. Two extra lights are needed...Proper cupboard space and utensil racks should be provided. A ventilating canopy should be provided above the stove to prevent cooking odours spreading throughout the building.
Pupils' dining room; Strip loose plaster from ceiling and replaster. Paint ceiling and walls, also all woodwork. Remove opaque glass from windows and replace with plain glass.
Boys' recreation & assembly room; During heavy rains the water comes through the walls...the wainscotting has rotted away. A tile drain should be provided to carry off the sewage. The wainscotting should be removed, the walls resurfaced, walls and woodwork painted.
Boys' wash room; Strip off loose plaster, re-surface walls with hard finish, paint walls and woodwork.
Main Floor.
Boys' reading room; Repair plaster, paint walls and woodwork, varnish ceiling, and install one extra lighting fixture.
Manual training room; This room is in fair condition.
Assembly room; At present being renovated.
Domestic Science and Staff Kitchen; Repair walls and ceiling, paint

woodwork and walls, provide adequate cupboards and utensil racks.

Girls reading room; Paint walls, ceiling and woodwork. Install one extra lighting fixture.

Sewing class--room; Paint walls and varnish ceiling.

First Floor...Second Floor

Girls dormitory...Boys' dormitory; Repair plaster. Paint woodwork, walls and ceiling. Install exhaust ventilating fans and intake grilles...

Third Floor.

Centre Room; Strip off plaster from ceiling and replaster. Repair walls and paint woodwork.

North room...is approximately 24 ft. long and 20 ft. wide and at present is not being used. I would suggest that it be fitted up for infirmary accommodation as...we have not a room in which we can isolate a sick pupil.

Stairways from Basement to Pupils' Dormitories.

All these stairways are in poor condition...All treads should be replaced, plaster repaired...and walls painted.

Refrigerator Room.

This is something that does not at present exist. I would suggest that a modern cold storage room be installed in the vegetable storage room in the basement.

Heat Plant.

The heating plant consists of one low pressure boiler with steam radiators and gravity return system. It is hopelessly inadequate as at present installed. I would recommend the following alterations:

1. Installation of a small auxiliary boiler. (On two occasions during the last five years boiler tubes have given out and it has been necessary to draw the fires in mid-winter. Imagine 150 people in the school without a fire in the boiler in February.)

2. Installation of an automatic stoker with thermostat and blower-fan.

3. Installation of a vacuum return pump to promote proper circulation of steam throughout the system.

Main Building Roof.

There are approximately 350 broken and cracked slates on the main roof and towers. During heavy rains the water soaks down through until the main roof timbers are beginning to show sign of decay. The whole roof should be carefully inspected and broken slates replaced. The towers...are really causing much of our trouble as during high winds they sway to such an extent that...it is impossible to prevent the plaster on the walls and ceilings from cracking and falling.

Annex Building.

...the three public school class rooms...

In 1934-5 considerable work was done with a view to remodelling this building. The south wall was badly bulged and in a dangerous condition. It was pulled down and rebuilt. In 1935 the east wall had to be pulled down and rebuilt and now the north wall is badly cracked and needs attention...The senior class room is in good condition but the intermediate and primary rooms have a very patched up appearance and should be completely redecorated.

The architect of the Indian Affairs Branch...made a thorough inspection in 1934...Mr. Orr, proposes to replan the various floors of the building to use up waste space. After giving careful study to the plans of the building he is now convinced that re-planning is utterly impossible and impracticable. He insists that the only solution is a new building in the immediate future.

I find myself in complete agreement with Mr. Orr's decision. This school was in the first place planned for about 75 pupils, the dormitory space was intended to provide for 100 to 125. Our present registration is 154 and we are continually receiving applications from the Indian Agents for more admissions. Our pupilage has so far outgrown our physical equipment that we are working all the while at a decided disadvantage.

I sincerely hope that our Home Mission Board will see its way clear to recommend the building of a new fireproof school in the immediate future. The present buildings would burn like timber if they once caught fire. The strain, upon the staff, of the constant vigilance necessary to prevent fire and the probable loss of life is very heavy. In a new school adequate provision should be made for vocational training in all branches as well as public school work.

41. 12 March 1937   McLeod To Dep. Sec. IAB

Mrs **** been under treatment from this office for some time. She suffers with an unresolved Pneumonia, and possible early Pulmonary Tuberculosis...This woman has a sister, **** aged 17 years...and she has repeatedly requested Indian Agent A. D. Moore and myself to obtain the latter's discharge from school so that the sister may care for her two children, and housework, while Mrs. *** rests in bed as instructed by me.

Rev. O. B. Strapp...is loathe to discharge **** assuming the view that with her domestic science course completed this summer, he will endeavour to place her at suitable employment in a private home. The girl herself is not anxious to leave school, but expressed a willingness to do so as a helpful duty to her sister.

Mr. Moore, Mr. Strapp and myself have discussed the situation, and the Principal of the school suggests that permission be sought for one month's leave of absence for **** to care for her sister...

42. 16 March 1937   Phelan to Strapp

...The Department will approve of your permitting **** one month's leave of absence. She should be returned to the school after that period. No per capita grant can be allowed for her during such absence...

43. 16 June 1937   Strapp to Hoey

The forms concerning pupils graduation are being forwarded to the Agents concerned. It is frequently difficult to predict a year in advance as to whether a certain pupil will graduate at the close of a given year, but, as far as we can we will advise the Agents...

In the matter of certain pupils 18 years of age recommended to continue for another year. These pupils have been placed in the school because of very unsatisfactory home conditions or the death of their parents and we feel that with another year of training it would be possible to place them in positions where they would be able to provide for themselves and not be a burden upon relatives who in most cases would not be able either to control or provide for them.

Because of unsatisfactory conditions we are not permitting [****] pupils to go out for the holiday period...

44. 16 June 1937   Strapp to Parents

TO PARENTS: GUARDIANS & FRIENDS OF OUR PUPILS.

We greet you this year with news that we are sure will be

received with a great deal of pleasure. The Indian Affairs Branch...has extended the time allowed for holidays from six weeks to two months...

Looking back over the past school year we feel that there has been so very much for which to give thanks unto Almighty God. Provision of food and clothing, granting of health and strength, giving of instruction, gaining of experience, and many other things have all made a contribution to our happiness and well-being.

The Academic Vocational and Cultural departments have all had a very successful year. Mention should be made of the winning of the Hon J. C. Elliott Gold Medal for the pupil gaining the highest marks at the examining centre for the Entrance to High School by one of our pupils, Miss Joan Fischer of Sarnia Reserve. We heartily congratulate Joan and her teacher Mr. F. J. Dodson. Two pupils taking the Toronto Conservatory of Music examinations were successful and obtained good marks, their teacher is Mrs. Jamieson.

Parents and guardians are particularly requested to take note of the opening date of school...the regulations provide that pupils returning late may be refused holidays in future. The Indian Affairs Branch has granted the extra two weeks. Let us show our appreciation by cooperating with them to ensure the prompt re-opening...

As usual a number of our pupils will be leaving us this year and starting out in life. We crave for them your kindly interest and sympathetic guidance...

45. 17 July 1937 A. D. Moore to Secretary
...Mr. Strapp...has informed me that he has vacancies for only 3 to 5 pupils when school reopens in the Fall....

46. 13 August 1937 Mrs **** to DIA
I want to write to the Indian Department concerning my daughter ****...also, **** attending same school. **** is past 16 yrs of age, and **** is 14 yrs old.

I am in bad health and I cannot do work at home. My husband is dead and have no one to help me...I have to go out and work and I would like the girls at home where they can help me, they can go to school here as we have a new teacher at our school. The Indian Agent wrote...and Mr Strapp is supposed to answer in return. But either persons dont give me any satisfactory information concerning my girls leave from school.

They are not at present going to school in Mt. Elgin so they may as well be helping me at home. The school here is reopened and pupils are attending thier classes...

...The older girl is dissatisfied in school and it would be best for her to come home...

47. 12 September 1937 Phelan to Strapp
...letter from Indian Agent Trenouth...

"**** has three children at present attending the Mount Elgin Residential School. Since we have a new teacher...

he wishes to have these children returned to his home and attend the St. Clair School.

...**** has a good home and is capable of supporting the children and lives close to the St. Clair School, I would recommend that these children be allowed to return home...

...it would be advisable to discharge these three children at once. We have numerous applications for admissions... there should be no difficulty in replacing them...

48. 16 September 1937 Mrs **** to DIA
I wish to inquire of you to grant me my wish, by allowing my sixteen year old daughter to leave school to come to help me, as I have two little children with me, and I have no other support. I have a chance to go out to work if I had her home and I know she is willing to work also, and help me support us. We also desire to get a home for a reasonable price as we have no home, so there we decided before she went back to school that we would work together and get this home if she is allowed to come home to help.

I wish to have this taken in a kind consideration as we are tired of roaming from place to place...

49. 21 September 1937 Phelan to Strapp
In view of the unsatisfactory results obtained in their classroom work, the Department approves the undermentioned pupils...devoting their full time to vocational activity during the academic year 1937-8...

50. 25 September 1937 Strapp to Phelan
...in the case of the **** girls...it is simply a matter of the mother thinking that they now are old enough to do some work and they could therefore perhaps be of use at home. While they were younger she was quite satisfied to have us look after them and now they are old enough to make a contribution to the life of the school she would like to have them at home...it is imperative that we should have a percentage of pupils old enough to carry on the work of the school without any one of them being at all burdened. These two girls are not yet fitted to go out to work and would only become a liability upon the reservation without any thing to really occupy their time. Mrs. **** mentioned the matter some time ago and when I raised the question it was admitted that there was someone around the house most of time who could do the necessary chores etc. I would strongly recommend against their discharge.

Reference the **** children...Mrs.**** visited the children at the school on Wednesday the 22nd Inst...she informed the Lady Superintendent that she had not known of the application made by Mr. **** for the children to be discharged from school. She stated that she was opposed to their discharge on the grounds that they would not receive the vocational training at the reserve day school and also they would not have the benefit of the discipline of the school which she felt they very much needed...if they are discharged at this time the efforts already expended on their training will be largely wasted and it will have an unsettling effect upon the other pupils in the school. The older girl, ****, has definitely expressed her resentment at the suggestion from her father that she be discharged and the other two are not yet old enough to know what they do want. Mr. Trenouth's letter is merely a matter of following the line of least resistance and...not considering the welfare of the children nor the unsettling effect their removal would have upon other pupils. I...recommend that they be not discharged at this time.

51. 27 September 1937 Strapp to Phelan
...The action of your Agent at Sarnia in the **** and **** cases has led to a wholesale exodus of pupils mainly from that reservation during the last few days. Both the **** and **** families have visited the school and the garbled versions of their interviews with their Agent has given the children the impression that if they run away from school he will give them permission to attend school on the reservation and apply for their discharge from this school. Naturally the life of the reserve, with its freedom to do what ever they may wish to do, is more appealing to the child mind than is the carefully regulated life of the residential school.

I sincerely trust that your Branch will give us all possible assistance to put a stop to this unrest and notify the Agent at Sarnia to have all truants returned to this school immediately.

I beg to report that we have three cases of Chicken Pox and therefore our pupils are at present in quarantine.

52. 27 September 1937 A. D. Moore to Phelan
...Mrs. **** requests her daughter **** to be discharged claiming that she is 16 years of age, whereas this girl is 15 and upon speaking to the principal of the school, this girl is recognised as a good pupil and would be best left there for at least two more years.

53. 30 September 1937 MacInnes to McGill Canadian National Telegram
PRINCIPAL STRAPP MOUNTELGIN REPORTS NOTHING DONE RE BUILDING REPAIRS OR HEATING SYSTEM STOP NO HEAT IN BUILDING PUPILS AND STAFF CONTRACTING BAD COLDS PUPILS TRUANTING AND PARENTS COMPLAINING BECAUSE OF COLD STOP SITUATION SERIOUS

54. 2 October 1937 Highfield to Secretary IAB
****...being discharged from Mt. Elgin...has no home on the Reserve, but Miss **** is a single woman who has a steady position in Detroit Mich, with reasonable good pay, and if nesecary should be able to support her son.

I would consider the boy much better off if it can be arranged to remain in Mt. Elgin Institute untill he is 16 or 18 years old. I have heard nothing of this boy being discharged from Mt. Elgin Institute. It may be personal desire to have this boy transfered to Shingwauk.

55. 20 October 1937 Strapp to Phelan
...with reference to transferring certain pupils...to Chapleau...I have made inquiries in the following cases.
**** Age 15, Sarnia Agency...He generally stays with grandparents or aunt when on the reservation during summer holidays. He was placed in school in 1932 as a neglected child.
**** Age 15, Sarnia Agency. The parents of this child are separated and the mother living part of the time with another Indian...The boy was placed in the school in 1932.
****- Age 10, Walpole Island. This boy was being looked after by an Indian family - as he is a non-band member - and because of extreme neglect was placed in this school in 1934.
****- Age 12, Cape Croker. This girl's mother has been dead for a number of years. She was being looked after by other relatives and on petition of her reputed father, because of her neglected condition was placed in the school in 1930.
****Age 15, Caradoc Agency. Nothing is known about the parents of this girl. She has, however, been looked after partly by two brothers and a sister who usually work out in wood-cutting camps. She has no settled home on the reservation. She was admitted in 1930.
****- Age 13 Walpole Island. This girl's mother, ****, has been separated a number of years from her husband, and is employed in the United States. She has been making her home with a married sister who has been ill for some time. I am informed by Mr. Daley, the teacher at Walpole, that conditions in the home are very unsatisfactory.
I have submitted these names for your consideration as I believe them to be the ring leaders among the truants.
I would appreciate it very much if you could see your way clear to issue definite instructions to your acting Agent at Sarnia with reference to the immediate return of truants from this school and also inform him of the section in the Indian Act providing for attendance at residential school after age 16. Sarnia is still the "Mecca" for runaways. Two from the Six Nations agency and one from Caradoc left us yesterday after informing some of the other boys that they were going to Sarnia, and the Agent there would get them out of school. Much of this I believe is hearsay amongst the Indian children, but from information received from the police, I am afraid there is some basis in fact from their assertions.

56. 30 November 1937 Phelan to Strapp
Enclosed is a statement showing the reports received from the R.C.M.P. in connection with truants from the Mount Elgin Indian Residential School. In several cases since the beginning of October, reports have also indicated that some of those who ran away in September also truanted again on one or two occasions.

As the truancy is apparently continuing, the matter is giving the Department some concern.

I would therefore appreciate if you would write me fully in connection with this matter. No doubt you have very carefully investigated all conditions around this school with a view to determining whether or not there is any real reason for truancy.

57.   2 December 1937   Principal St. John's...School, Chapleau to Secretary IAB

This will inform you of the safe arrival, under escort, of the following pupils from Mount Elgin...

We will do our very best for these children and try to control them so they will not again try to run away as they did from the other school.

58.   6 December 1937   Strapp to Phelan

...the six pupils were transferred to the Chapleau school on December 1st. The only outstanding truant at this date is **** and he is apparently staying with relatives in the U.S.A. He will probably return to the reservation at some later date and can then be apprehended and returned...

Several things seem to have contributed to the general unrest amongst them being the fact that during the holidays so many of the pupils were able to get work and earn money, pupils working for a short while earning as high as $2.50 per day and living with relatives who did not charge them for board. Upon investigating the home conditions of **** I find that she has been in the habit of leaving home at intervals and wandering about the country for a while and then, when she felt like it, returning home and carrying on as if nothing at all had happened and she apparently felt the urge to wander again. I have only received a definite complaint from one pupil, Eddie Noah, and it was to the effect that he had to carry in wood for the fires in the Laundry. As we operate our laundry only one day per week I felt that he certainly was not overtaxed as he had two helpers and was only responsible for the job from 8 a.m. to Noon. During that time the three boys would have to bring in about 2 1/2 to 3 single cords as required.

From time to time we do have complaints that we do not serve meat often enough. Unfortunately we are compelled to purchase all our meat from the butcher as we have no facilities for cold storage. If we had a meat refrigerator we could kill our own cattle and provide meat on the menu more frequently.

May I express my sincere appreciation of the action of your department in transferring the six pupils to another school, it has had a marked effect upon a number of the other pupils who have truanted and I believe has settled the matter at least for this year.

59.   14 December 1937   Strapp to ****

For sometime we have been having trouble with your daughter and on two occasions she has run away...

We would be very glad if you could pay us a visit as soon as possible so that we may talk the matter over and find out where the trouble is.

60.   17 December 1937   **** to Strapp

Yours of the 14th inst...advising me of my daughter, ****'s mis-conduct, this is really shocking to me.

I believed that she was quite contented to stay there at school till she finished her term, and I am sorry she is giving you some trouble and I cannot think of any reason why she would run away. The only thing I can think of, is the rumour I heard early this fall, that a group of girls were punished for something they had done and **** was one of them, and my opinion is this, that she resented being punished for something she was not entirely to blame for, and it is likely that she will never forget the offence given her by some unsuspected offender and I doubt whether I could persuade her to tell me where the trouble lies, I am speaking from my own experience when I was there, more than once I was punished for some things that I didn't do. I will never forget those who gave me the punishment, in spite of my protests, and this is the general experience of most of the ex pupils.

So, I would suggest that you try to win **** by kindness and perhaps she will tell you where the trouble is. You must consider that she is at the age now that she will appreciate a treatment accorded to an older person, and will respond to any confidence given her.

I am enclosing one dollar for her and I am leaving it entirely in your care. Tell her that she is causing me a great deal of anxiety, and ask her if she wants me to be happy, to promise that she will be a good girl. Anxiously awaiting a favourable report.

61.   20 December 1937   Phelan to Strapp

I dislike bothering you again, but we are today in receipt of a report from the R.C.M.P. with reference to...pupils...who have apparently truanted:

Apparently the truancy is continuing and I would appreciate your advising me what reasons have any given for leaving the school.

In view of the unfortunate happening in the West a year or so ago, we are quite concerned about truancy from residential schools, especially during the winter.

I feel certain that you were also concerned about this matter and that you will, no doubt, write me very fully regarding the recent truants.

62.   25 December 1937   **** to Secretary of DIA

Enclosed herewith is a copy of a letter which I received from the Principal of Mt. Elgin Industrial Institute, and also a copy of my letter in reply to his letter, and up to the present I have not received any word from him.

I have decided to ask the Indian Department to have my daughter discharged from that Institution immediately. She is fifteen years old, as she is likely to be troublesome to the staff of officers at the Institute. I hope you will grant my request and oblige.

63. 30 December 1937 Strapp to Phelan
...I have given a great deal of attention to this matter...I am somewhat baffled by the attitude of **** who appears to be the leader in the group. She insists that she 'just took the notion' and 'has been in school too long'. The other girls say that they 'just went with her'. I think that **** was feeling rather blue as since she came to school three years ago her people have not bothered very much about her and have neither arranged for her to go home for her holidays nor visited her at the school. She is rather a moody type of girl and neglect on the part of her relatives does not help her at such times. **** is like a little wild animal and has given us considerable trouble. **** has been an exceptionally well behaved girl and has made good progress in the vocational classes but is at a standstill in her public school work.

Some time ago I wrote to **** suggesting that he pay a visit to the school but he replied that he would leave the matter to me and enclosed a dollar bill for his daughter ****. I felt that if I could get him to pay us a visit and spend some time amongst the pupils he might be able to make some suggestions as to the real cause of the unrest. These girls were absent from the school for about four hours from the time that they left until their return by the R.C.M.P. **** was returned after being absent since September 26th. and informs us that he has been at home at Walpole Island during that time helping his father.

**** and the four girls seem to have settled down and I do not anticipate any further trouble from them.

I beg to make the following recommendations;

Re. ****; This girl very evidently is at the age when she needs sympathetic supervision and kindly but firm discipline. I believe that if we can carry her along until the end of June it would then be advisable to arrange for her discharge. But for the fact that I am afraid of a re-action similar to that following the discharge of the **** girls of Sarnia last October I would be glad to be relieved of any further responsibility for her...her discharge at this time would provoke unrest and possibly further truancy.

****; I believe it would be wise to release this girl from attendance at public school classes and arrange for her to devote full time to the vocational training. If at all possible she should be placed in a position and discharged at the end of this academic year.

****; If at all possible arrangements should be made for this girl to go home to Christian Island for her holidays in 1938.

****; As the home conditions are not at all good we will have to give this girl closer supervision and hope that she will respond a little better as she grows older.

...the children from the Stoney Point Reservation...as **** is 16 years of age and making good progress in her vocational work that she continue to attend this school... the discharge of the other pupils mentioned will help to provide sufficient pupils to warrant the continuation of the Stoney Point School. I...suggest that as the home of ****, **** and **** is not very far from the school they be included with the other pupils listed in your letter. These pupils are the children of Mr. ****.

64. 4 January 1938 Strapp to Phelan
Re. ****...I am still of the opinion that it would not be wise to arrange for her discharge at this time. She was successful at the entrance to high school examination last June but owing to her age and the fact that she did not at that time expect to go on to the high school course I felt it would be better for her to spend a year in the vocational work before being discharged. Her standing in the practical work of the course is good and in the theory is fair...she is at the age when she should have careful supervision and I doubt very much whether, if she went home, her father or her step-mother could do very much to control her. She seems to have gotten over her moodiness for the present and so will probably run along for a couple of months or so without any trouble...perhaps **** would be willing to agree to her staying until the end of the school year and then receiving her discharge.

65. 11 January 1938 Down to MacInnes
...re ****'s request that his daughter **** be discharged ...I have made inquiries as to why **** asks for this girl to be returned, and after careful study I would not recommend her discharge.

At present there is a slight family dispute and he is asking for this child to be returned for purposes which I do not approve of. ****, at present, is living on the Reserve by himself and is planning to have **** keep house for him. I do not think this is necessary. I have the family dispute well in hand and hope to bring about a reconciliation.

At this time I would ask that **** not be informed as to why we are not returning ****, but simply told that we do not think it advisable.

66. 18 January 1938 Strapp to Hoey
...With...the repairs to the heating plant...for the first time since I entered the school in 1929 I have been able to go into the boys' dormitory and feel that they were at least reasonably comfortable...now possible to heat the whole building with very little trouble.

67. 16 February 1938 Mr. and Mrs. ** to Board of Education**
I have a girl at the Mt. Elgin Inst...She has been there for 10 years this Sept coming and 18 years old and is not going to school.

She has been sick with Rheumatism bad and also a bad cough and the doctor has only been to see her 3 times sinse she has been sick and that is in Nov. she took sick. She says she's getting worse all the time. I would rather have her home than to be sent to hospital although I have a small home which contains a bed room and a kitchen.

I went to see the principal yesterday and asked him if he would let me take her home and he said no so I am asking you if you would kindly let her go. I never made no aplication for her to stay any length of time.

68. 24 February 1938 McCracken, to Phelan
...I have discussed this case with the Principal and it is agreed that it would not be to her interest to allow her to return home at the present time.

This girl who is listed on the school records as 17 years of age has been receiving treatment from Doctor McLeod ...for some time for a condition of arthritis. Both her parents have syphilis and the daughter is a congenital case. Doctor McLeod disagrees with the statement that he has seen her 3 times since the onset of her illness and estimates that a dozen attendances would be more in order which statement is borne out by the Principal.

The family reside in a small shack on the Chippewa Reserve which has recently been enlarged with lumber provided by the Department. Sole subsistence this winter has been by relief supplied by the Department. An older sister, ****, discharged from Mount Elgin School last Spring has done no gainful work since and according to a report...is now believed to be pregnant.

In the opinion of this office, including Doctor McLeod and Principal of the school, **** can be much better cared for at the school under a trained nurse and supervisor. She has been placed in bed near a radiator and is being given special food to improve her condition. There is a slight suspicion that this girl may be pregnant following a visit to her home during Christmas vacation from which she returned with an ample supply of cigarettes, seized by the school authorities...

Mr. Strapp informs us that since his refusal to discharge this girl from school she has become unruly disobeying orders and refusing at times to take food. Such action usually follows a visit from her parents whom he blames for the girl's behaviour. Morals in the **** home are open to question and it is no fit place to return a girl whose health is under par.

There is no record here as to whether the application for Residential School was signed and Principal Strapp believes that if there were no signature, such was due to the fact that Indian Agent Thomas McGookin peremptorily removed this child from intolerable surroundings in 1928. Mr. McGookin is quite familiar with the home conditions and could amplify this report...

If this girl is as old as her mother claims, she could be discharged...at the end of...June, in the meantime, she will receive adequate medical attention as heretofore and Mr. Strapp is in favour of this recommendation.

69. 7 March 1938 Chief Deleary to Supt DIA
...concerning Mr & Mrs ****...report to our General Council about her sick daughter...It was decided by the Council that I the chief of the Muncey Indians, Chippewas & Mrs **** to go to the school on Feb 19 and see the sick girl. We found the girl very sick in bed with a very bad cough not a cold - they did not even have a spit box for her she had to swallow back all she coughed up so I told Mr. Strapp to furnish her with a spit box he said he would but it was not done till the next day in the evening. I told Mr. Strapp that she should go to the hospital at once it is very dangerous to have a patient in a dormitory where a good many girls sleep. He promised he would send her to the hospital at once he has not done so. The girl has been sick since November 1st...and she would like to have **** discharge from school June 30th as she is 16 years old and **** is 18 years old and the parents are not under relief...and I wish you would have her removed to her home or to the hospital at once.

70. 15 March 1938 Acting Indian Agent to Secretary IAB
...I have shown the Chief's letter to the Principal of the School and the Medical Superintendent. Both Mr. Strapp and Dr. McLeod have already attempted to assure those interested that the School authorities are acting in the girl's best interests.

Doctor McLeod reports that this girl is suffering from a condition of arthritis and that it would be very inadvisable to discharge her to the deplorable home conditions under which her family exists. With the services of a graduate nurse at Mount Elgin School and constant medical attention she has shown some improvement, although her mental attitude, abetted by her parents, is not one of cooperation in an effort to get well.

Last week when a Dental Clinic was conducted at the School, this pupil was examined by Doctor Ackland, who recommended three tooth extractions and several fillings. This girl, who is practically an adult, refused to permit the Dentist to work on her teeth and carried on to such an extent that Doctor McLeod advised that no force be used in view of the attitude already assumed by her parents. The dental work indicated would assist in combating her arthritis materially.

When shown the letter of Chief Deleary, Principal Strapp affirmed that this girl is receiving every attention both by the Medical Superintendent and the Institute Staff. Although special menu was prepared for her by the dietitian, the girl went on a hunger strike, which was successfully broken by the Principal, who is of the opinion that advice from home has a bearing on her stubborn attitude.

Doctor McLeod states that if this girl were removed to hospital, it would be a long, drawn out and expensive care and that her welfare can be equally protected at the School.

With reference to Chief Deleary's statement that the parents are not on relief, our records show that the father of this girl received, since November, 1937, seven rations. The pension received by him was inaugurated in December and amounts to approximately $3.50 per month. ...this pupil is receiving special care at the hands of Doctor McLeod and the Mount Elgin School staff, I..recommend that no action be taken in this case.

71. 31 March 1938 Strapp to Phelan
....we seem to be in for a real epidemic of Measles with about twenty in bed...I would appreciate authority to engage a special nurse for a few weeks if any more cases develope. It will be impossible for our school nurse to properly care for such a large number and...give attention to her regular school duties...a grant not to exceed $60.00 per month would take care of the matter...

72. 3 June 1938 A. D. Moore to Secretary DIA
While the management of this school is quite satisfactory, the Principal stresses the need of some repairs and alterations and asks that a properly equipped infirmary for handling sick pupils be constructed. This need has been reported to the Department on previous occasions.
   The Principal also asks that a sum in the vicinity of $300.00 be made available for the necessary repairs to a farm house located on the school grounds which has been empty for about three years and which Mr. Strapp now finds necessary to occupy for a further employee to take the place of John Kapayo who is off duty from chronic illness and is occupying the quarters which would be otherwise used by the employee appointed to replace him.
   The verandas at the main building need considerable repair and all exterior wood work badly needs painting... $250.00 would be needed to do this work.
The Principal also asks for the installation of a walk-in refrigerator, estimated cost $800.00, claiming that at present he has to purchase all meats and has no method of keeping the same and that if a refrigerator were installed he would be able to raise and butcher for his own use the meat necessary for the school and in this manner provide meat more often to the pupils from the saving made.

73. 8 June 1938 R. Cochrane to Hoey
...Mr. John Kapayo, who for forty-five years has been mechanic at that institution, is now seriously ill. He has had several operations for cancer...he is not only incapacitated for work, but is not likely to live for more than a year or so.
   Mr. Strapp feels that beyond paying Mr. Kapayo his full salary until the 31st August, there is not much more he can afford to do out of the revenue of the School. It seems to us that, under all the circumstances, the Department might very well consider granting Mr. Kapayo, in view of his long service, a pension on his

retirement, amounting to at least one-half of his pay - which has been $70.00 a month and a house.
   ...the situation is complicated by the fact that Mr. Kapayo claims that his illness is traceable to an injury which he received in the laundry of the School, through the carelessness of one of the girl pupils, who let the door of the drying machine fall on his back some years ago.
   Mr. Kapayo's relatives threaten suit, if something is not done to look after him now. I suppose if the suit were entered, it would be an attempt to recover damages from both the Department and the Church. Mr. Strapp is of the opinion that a moderate pension would satisfy all parties concerned. Will you be good enough to take this matter up and see if something cannot be done....

74. June 1938 Hoey to Teachers
[...1/3 of pupils' time should be in manual training] ...should be Follow-up System - systematic method of supplying the Department, from year to year, with information that will enable us to know exactly what becomes of our pupils after they leave school...by principals...

75. June 1938 Strapp to Hoey
[...anxious to cooperate...suggests regular visits and meetings with department and other principals. Provision should be made for removing pupils from the public school classes who demonstrate their inability to make satisfactory progress at age 15 or attainment of Grade 6....intensive training in a trade, dairying or farming (boys)...and domestic science and gardening (girls)...discharged until properly trained or 18.
...Schools shouldn't be dumping ground for non Band members or problem children.
...Should be full-time Vocational Officer for Ontario...impossible for principals as many responsibilities and extent of territory from which pupils are drawn.] We as staff at Mt. Elgin are intensely interested in the pupils committed to our care, their joys and sorrows we endeavour to share and for their problems we earnestly seek solutions.

76. 15 July 1938 McLeod to Stone
...trachoma situation has improved...recommend that permission be granted for tonsillectomy in the 11 cases reported...permission be granted to supply glasses for defective eyes of 10 pupils listed at total cost of $100... services of a dentist be authorized for three days...General condition of the pupils is excellent. Toilet facilities were taken up with Mr. Gurney Orr on his last visit, and since with Rev. O. B. Strapp, principal, and temporary sanitary improvements can be made. Food and diet excellent.

77. 8 August 1938 A. D. Moore to Secretary IAB
****, 65 year old member of the Chippewa of the

Thames Band, has made application to this office that his son, ****, 15 years of age, receive his discharge as a pupil of Mount Elgin Residential School so that he may be at home to assist him as he is suffering from dilated heart and unable to do any work.

    **** and his younger brother, ****, 13 years of age, were placed in Mount Elgin School two years ago to aid **** as he has three other smaller children but his condition becoming worse, he maintains that he cannot do his work as caretaker of River Settlement School or procure fuel and water without the aid of this boy and while the Medical Superintendent agrees that **** is a sick man, it is a question of whether the boy is to be deprived of a good training at the Residential School or to be let remain at home so that **** can continue as caretaker of the Day school.

    Mr. Strapp...is very much opposed to **** being discharged at the present time and I...would not recommend his discharge although it may mean difficulty concerning the caretaker...

78. 25 August 1938 Mrs ****, Christian Island, to Strapp
    I am very sorry I can't get **** back to School. I havent any money to pay her fares to Muncey. I thought I could have some money before September that's why I took her out of the school. I would of have some money to send her back, but one of my daughters was very sick while we were in Clarkson and I had to come home they sent a telegram where we were. And that why I dont have no money now just because we came home. And I'll be very glad if you could help me out in some way so that she could go back to school. I would be really too glad if you could let her stay there for 2 more years. I want her to learn more things, she doesn't know enough yet. And I wouldn't mind if you could send somebody over to come after her. And I want her to learn more music lessons also how to cook and sewing and everything. She knows quite a bit in music.
    ...please answer soon before its too late for her...

79. 1 September 1938 Strapp to Phelan
    ...thank you for remembering us when the metal working tools were available from Christie Street Hospital. The tools are in excellent condition and make a very welcome addition to our manual training equipment. The increase in our per capita grant has made it possible for me to bring in a graduate of the London Technical School as an instructor this year and we are hoping that it will be possible to do something really worth while in this line...during the past year that my own time was too much taken up with the...supervision of all departments to give the attention that...should be given to this department.
    We have had good average crops this year, our dairy herd is in good shape and we are looking forward to a good year in school...

80. 6 September 1938 Hoffman to Supt DIA
    Mr. ****...has consulted us regarding his son ****. It appears that this boy was attending the Industrial School... for the past two years and that in...July of this year he became ill. The father first became aware of the illness in the 12th of July and after having him examined by a doctor he was immediately placed in Victoria Hospital... and remained there until the 23rd of August...The boy was suffering from an infection of the kidney and was in very serious condition and as yet has not fully recovered.
    The boy has been examined by the resident physician on the Reserve and also by a physician in private practice. When the boy left the hospital the father was advised that he would have to be very careful for a year at least, as the condition might reoccur. The physician on the Reserve wants the father to send the boy back to the Industrial School but the father feels that in view of the fact that half of the day is taken up with work and half with school that the Industrial School would be too much for him in his present condition and he refused to send him back until his physical condition has improved.

81. 15 September 1938 Phelan to Strapp
    ...****. The Agent advises that this girl is now working at Georgina Island...as far as he is aware, the grandmother had no intention of providing the money...necessary to pay the girl's return fare to the Mt. Elgin Institute.
    As the girl is now 17 years of age and is employed, I do not feel that there would be any advantage in having her returned to the school. She should be considered discharged. You will not likely have any difficulty in obtaining another pupil to replace her.

82. 15 September 1938 Indian Agent to DIA
    ...regarding ****, son of ****...it was decided not to return him to the Residential School at the present time.
    This boy suffered a serious attack of acute nephritis or kidney disease in July and was in hospital for several weeks during which time his recovery was not expected. He is still under the attention of the Medical Supt. but has progressed to such an extent that he has been able to walk about daily and there is no trace of kidney infection.
    Dr. McLeod proposed to Mrs. **** that it would be to the advantage of her son to return to Mount Elgin Residential School where he would be given proper rest with no work at all and would have a warm bed and shelter, much more favourable than his home conditions. The proper diet available at the School was also drawn to her attention and the Principal of the School expressed his willingness to cooperate.
    Mrs. **** quite definitely refused this suggestion declaring that she was determined to keep her boy at home.
    In view of the fact that for some time this boy will remain a semi-invalid and that there is a possibility of the

kidney condition returning with tragic results, Mr. Moore and Dr. McLeod concluded that it would be advisable to allow this boy to remain at home and not expose the Department to possible unfair criticism.

At no time was it stated to the **** family that their son would be forced to return to school and the consultation with Mr. Hoffman appears to have been rather premature.

83. 10 October 1938 Strapp to Hoey
...returns for the quarter ending September 30th.
The discharges as noted have been approved with the exception of **** and in this case in consultation with Mr. Agent Moore upon the advice of Dr. Mcleod the discharge of this boy is recommended.
The admissions as noted have...been approved.
...if the Agents of your Branch would arrange for the examination of prospective pupils early in the summer it would be possible to complete our registration at the beginning of September and so lessen the interruption of classes upon the introduction of new pupils.

84. 11 October 1938 A. D. Moore to Secretary IAB
**** of the Chippewa band who has ten children, is protesting the return of his daughters, **** aged sixteen and **** aged fifteen years...after the summer vacation period claiming that **** is old enough to work and had a position and that **** was not receiving the proper medical attention at the School for an infected toe. **** was allowed out in December, 1937, to assist at the serious illness of her mother and...has not returned to the Residential School as promised by her parents.

I did take the case of **** up with the Reverend Principal of the School as I was of the opinion that ****, having a good position in the home of Clarence Trott, ex-reeve of Caradoc Township, could be discharged and allowed to remain there but Mr. Strapp was very determined to have the girl return to the School which she did on October 8th. This girl is sixteen years old and is not nearly ready for her Entrance examination and has not shown any great progress in her book studies and if only returned to the School for domestic training purposes, she would have gotten that at Mr. Trott's home and besides would have been earning money to help her family, also making room for a needy child at the Residential School.

I would ask your opinion and instructions as to this girl being discharged to which Mr. Strapp will not agree, although he admits with her return, he will have exceeded the 150 pupil allowance at his School.

With regard to ****...this girl has an ingrown toe nail and was let out at summer vacation with it now being cured and during her term at the Residential School this toe was never reported to Doctor McLeod although it was treated by the school nurse.

At the time for this girl's return to the School it was

found to be infected and had been opened by an outside Doctor and **** protested his girl returning to the School claiming she was being neglected. Doctor McLeod now knows of this ailment...will have it attended to and if necessary have a surgical operation after the infection has subsided and in Dr. McLeod's opinion this ailment at no time assumed serious proportions. This girl also returned to the school on October 8th and her continuance there as a pupil is recommended.

**** claims he can support his large family but...this man has always received some relief assistance in the way of food, fuel, clothing and building materials every winter in the past and I am doubtful if he can escape again asking for assistance this winter.

85. 18 January 1939 Phelan to Strapp
...During the past two months we have received several reports from the R.C.M.P. regarding truancy. Possibly it is the same children that are truanting but...I have no doubt that you have fully investigated conditions leading up to the truancy of these pupils and that you have taken whatever steps are necessary to prevent it in the future.

86. 24 January 1939 A. D. Moore to Phelan
...concerning the admission of three **** and three **** children who were placed in Mount Elgin School on July 5th and 7th respectively.

Mr. Strapp now informs me that he did not receive any grant from the Department for their maintenance during the holiday period of July and August and he does consider the School should receive grant for these two months claiming he would not have accepted them during this period unless grant were given.

As explained in my letter of July 15th, the mothers of these children were receiving Mother's Allowance and both got into trouble, one being committed to jail and they were emergent cases and would ask your reconsideration of their cases and grants be given as they were all small children and had no earning possibilities at the School and it would have been necessary to supply them with relief during the two months if not placed...

87. February 1939 A. D. Moore Report
Routine
124 pupils in class room
30 pupils in vocational training departments
2 pupils sick
1 pupils absent: Truant whom police cannot locate
157 Total number on roll
Health Sanitation
Pupils appear well dressed
...buildings kept clean and tidy...school grounds well kept
...sick well cared for by the agency Med. Supt., and graduate nurse
The children's meals: Potato soup, peanut butter, fruit

cake, bread & milk
Domestic instruction grades 4 to 8 under direction of graduate dietitian
Instruction in farming and gardening grade 4 to 8 under qualified farm foreman
Training in the care of live stock grades 4 to 8 under qualified herdsman & poultryman
Manual training wood work, brass pounding, weaving and mechanics taught to senior pupils...
Discipline at the school good
Efficiency of the staff...appear quite efficient
General management good...

88. 2 March 1939 Strapp to Hoey

I regret very much to have to report that **** of the Rama Agency has proven very unsatisfactory as a pupil in this school. When she first came to us she said that she only intended to remain here for a month or two and only wanted to take cooking classes, I had a talk with her and suggested that it would be very much better for her to at least stay until the end of the school year and learn all that she could in the practical departments and in the meantime take the matter up with her Agent. She wrote to Mr. Featherstone and he...suggested that she was very much better off in school where she would have an opportunity to learn much that she could not learn at home. Since then despite every effort on our part to make her comfortable and change her viewpoint she has done nothing but complain and at present is proving a very disturbing influence in the school. I very much regret that I have to request that arrangements be made to return her to Rama at as early a date as may be possible.

The **** girls and **** seem to be happy and are proving apt pupils.

89. 17 March 1939 A. D. Moore to Hoey

...A. B. Siskind, Barrister, London, Ontario, had written to the Department concerning the discharge of **** and ****...I would advise that Doctor McLeod informs me that ****, father of these boys, is a chronic case of heart trouble and is unable to do any work. He is in receipt of $15.00 a month soldier pension which has been granted since the children were placed in the school and also receives $6.00 a month as caretaker of the River Settlement Indian Day School which janitor work is done by his wife. Besides the two boys in Mount Elgin School, there are three small children under school age.
...both boys are good pupils and that the elder, ****, is in Grade 8 having a 70% standing on his year's work so far and that the younger boy, ****, is in Grade 6 with a 50% standing which is lower due to his being a runaway truant part of the term.

Mrs. **** is...much younger than her husband who has had a number of affairs with other men and if this woman would remain at home she could well carry on the duties

as janitor of the school and provide the needs of the house with the exception of cutting fire wood.

It is the recommendation of this office that, if ****, the elder boy, passes his Entrance examinations in June when he will be 16 years of age, he receive his discharge and, failing that, to be kept in the school another year. The younger boy, ****, should remain for at least two more years.

Mrs. **** has been very abusive with the Principal of the School in threatening the removal of the children, hence her visit to Mr. Siskind. I would ask that the Department's decision be made known to Mr. Siskind and thereby conveyed to her as I believe this would carry weight and possibly stop her interference at Mount Elgin School.

90. 8 April 1939 Hoey to Siskind
...reference to **** and ****

The father of these boys has a chronic case of heart trouble and is unable to do any work. Besides the two boys in the Mount Elgin school there are three small children under school age at home...Mrs. **** does not stay at home and attend to her household duties as she should...Mrs. **** has been very abusive with the Principal...in threatening the removal of her children.

In view of the progress being made by the boys and the further fact that home conditions cannot be considered totally satisfactory this Department considers that it is in the best interests of these two boys to remain in the Mount Elgin Indian residential school and we are, therefore, not prepared to approve their discharge at the present time.

91. 12 April 1939 **** to Secretary IAB

Kindly consider my circumstances...My wife has been confined in an Institution in...London for a considerable period. I have no housekeeper, with a boy of school age on my hands rendering things very inconvenient since I am a general laborer and have to be absent from home more or less. I have a girl a daughter named **** who has been in the Mt. Elgin Institution for the last eight years and supposed to have been discharged last July and for some reason or other the Principal has not seen his way clear to let her come out. I need her badly at home and would ask you...to confer with Mr. O. B. Strapp regarding the matter...

92. 22 April 1939 A. D. Moore to Phelan
...****...desires that his daughter **** be discharged... so that she may keep house for him.

**** was admitted to this school in September 1930 at which time her age was given as eight years and she must be seventeen years of age at this time. This girl has just been recently promoted to the 8th grade in her classes but will not try her entrance this Summer, which proves that she is not an adept pupil.

Mrs **** is in the Ontario Hospital, London, leaving at home her husband **** and a son about fifteen years of age, **** did for a time have a widow keeping house for him, but she has now left and he claims he is unable to procure another.

Mr. Strapp is not anxious to keep this girl after the present Summer holidays and in keeping her would only be endeavoring to keep her out of trouble on the reserve. As this father has a need of this girl at his home on the reserve I would recommend that she be discharged at the end of the present school term...

93. 17 May 1939 **** Secretary IAB
...I wish to ask your Dept to have my late brother's ****'s children placed in a boarding school. I would prefer to have them in Mt. Elgin Institute and it was also my brother's wish, and also that the ones that were to Muncey School in the past are better educated than the others that were up to the other schools...

94. 25 May 1939 R.C.M.P. Report
It was reported at the Date by the Rev. O. B. Strapp...that two of the girl pupils...aged 17 and 19 years, had assaulted a class mate...Dr. McLeod was called in and the complainant was put to bed for about a week under his care. I consulted the Crown attorney at London regarding the matter and was instructed to have the charges laid...On the a.m. of the 19th instant the complainant was taken to London by the Rev. O. B. Strapp and the accused girls taken in by the writer, accompanied by Miss Stanley...The charge was laid against the above accused by the complainant...and a plea of 'guilty' was entered. Sentence was suspended as noted above, both girls were returned to school by the principal...the action taken in this case will have a decidedly good effect not only on the accused parties, but other pupils in the school...

95. 11 June 1939 McLeod to Stone
Cody Claus age four from Ohsweken in fall from second floor window

96. 12 June 1939 Strapp Statement on Cody Claus's death
...Following an ear infection this boy was being kept in bed for a few days. He apparently climbed onto the sill of the window, overbalanced and fell a distance of approximately thirty feet to the ground. Statements are attached from all who could give any information
McLeod...I do not approve of four year old ill boy being left alone in dormitory. While regulations do not demand screens on windows, had screen removed for repairs been replaced immediately fatality might have been avoided.

97. 13 June 1939 Strapp to McGill
I regret to report an accident which resulted in the death of pupil #791 Courtland (Cody) Claus...
Cody had been in bed for some days following an infected ear which had been discharging pus. On Sunday June 11th. the girls on hospital duty took his dinner up to him at about 12.10 p.m.. One of the girls, Lillian George, removed his dishes at about 12.25 p.m. and the other girl, Vella Seth, saw him in bed at about 12.35-40 p.m..
...three of the senior pupils, Lloyd Nicholas, Christine Henhawk, and Ruth Antone, were standing together at the corner of the girls' play-ground shortly before 1.00 p.m. when they saw him, in mid air, falling. They rushed to where he was lying on the ground, picked him up carefully and carried him into the main building, where they met Mrs. Erratt our lady superintendent and Miss Stanley our nurse. A call was put in for Dr. McLeod. Meantime, our nurse took charge of Cody, and as he was unconscious, treated him for shock until the arrival of Dr. McLeod a few minutes later.
Dr. McLeod advised...Cody's condition was serious and I telephoned Major Randle...to notify Mr. Jesse Claus.
Cody was removed to the Victoria Hospital in London where X rays were taken. Little hope was held out for recovery as it was evident that there was brain injury and internal hemorrhage. Mr. Clause arrived about 9.00 p.m. and remained until Cody died.
I arranged with our local undertaker, Mr. Harding, to provide a casket and look after the body.
I called a Board of Inquiry with Mr. Agent Moore as Chairman at which Mr. Claus was present. The Mounted Police, Crown Attorney, and the Chief Coroner have all made their investigations and the decision was that the case was accidental and an inquest was unnecessary.
Following the Board of Inquiry I accompanied the body to the home of Mr. Jesse Claus.

98. 26 June 1939 A. D. Moore to Secretary IAB
**** of the Chippewa of Thames Band has applied at this office to have his son, ****, who will be 18 years old in December discharged as a pupil...
On taking this matter up with the Rev. Principal, he informs me that this boy is only in the 7th grade and spends only half of each school day in the class room, the balance of the time he works on the farm. His low academic standing is partially blamed on ill health, as he has missed some schooling on this account.
****, the father, is one of the Indians of the Agency to whom we have given a loan for stock and equipment and I do consider that this boy upon his discharge will be of assistance to his father on his own farm, as I can see little benefit of a boy of his age remaining in a residential school and therefore recommend his discharge at the end of the present academic year...

99. 7th July, 1939 A. D. Moore to Secretary IAB
...The Rev. O. B. Strapp...requests that additional space be provided to accommodate his classes in weaving...for $500 he could erect a suitable building and use the present concrete root-cellar for the foundation...

I am not enthused at the idea of building new additions...and do consider that the present buildings being old, will soon need a large expense in repairs and upkeep and that consideration should soon be given to the erection of a new modern school, providing it is intended to go into an extensive manual training programme... through the aid being given Indians to re-establish themselves on their reserves, there should be less need of placing children in a residential school like Mount Elgin in future years...

If a policy of sending fewer children to a residential school like Mount Elgin was pursued and the enrollment cut by a third at least it would leave a lot of space available at the school to use for manual training and technical training, without building additional buildings...

100. 17th July, 1939 Phelan to A. D. Moore
...Very careful consideration has been given to the contents of your letter. The Department feels that vocational training is so important that every possible facility should be provided. The situation mentioned in your letter may eventually occur but in the meantime we will have obtained full value for any expenditure made in providing extra accommodation for vocational work.

101. 25 July 1939 Strapp to Phelan
**** and others who had truanted during the academic year had been warned beforehand that they would be deprived of their regular holiday...remarkable effect on the general behaviour of the pupils concerned...

102. 25 July 1939 Lewies to DIA
...Mrs. ****...has been in to see us concerning her daughter ****. Some time ago Mrs. ****...had her daughter voluntarily placed in the Mount Elgin Indian Residential School through her father **** and the said ****has been attending the Residential School for some time. We believe and are informed that she did play truant from this school on at least two occasions, along with some other girls. This year...Reverend O. B. Strapp, refused to allow **** to return to her home for the summer holidays although the other girls who played truant along with her were allowed to do so. Mrs. **** has told us considerable concerning the treatment of her daughter at this School, which may or may not be true but at any rate she has come to the conclusion that her daughter would be better off with her so that she could attend school and be under her own supervision. This is the desire of both Mrs. **** and her father...We questioned her closely concerning whether there was any

order committing **** to this Institution and she advised that there was not. If this is true, then **** is virtually being kept a prisoner at the Mount Elgin Residential School. We have been in correspondence with the Indian Agent who referred us to the Principal Rev. O. B. Strapp, and we have written him and he denies very strongly that Mrs. **** had been experiencing difficulty in obtaining her release from the school and goes on to say that any proceedings that Mrs. **** may take to obtain the possession of her daughter would only prove embarrassing to Mrs. **** and would without doubt tend to give **** the impression that regulations can be broken with impunity. We would be pleased to...be advised whether there is anything standing in the way of Mrs. **** withdrawing her daughter from the Mount Elgin...School.

103. 21 August 1939 A. D. Moore to Hoey
...**** according to the principal of the school is 15 years of age and at the time of her admission was resident with her grandfather, **** who had her placed in Mount Elgin School, where she has been for the past four years.

****, who is an illegitimate child, did absent herself from the school during the past school term and when she was located by the police was in the home of her mother Mrs. ****, which home the police considered nothing but a bawdy house.

Early in July...****, grandfather of this girl appeared at Mount Elgin School and at the request of the Principal was quite willing that **** remain in the school during the holiday period, as the grandfather claimed he would have no control over the girl if she returned to his home.

Mr. Strapp...informs me that this firm of solicitors had been in touch with him and also with Indian Agent Spence of the Moravian Reserve...both the Principal and Agent had instructed these solicitors that the girl was to remain in school because the grandfather and guardian was willing that she do so and the agitation now being put forward by Mrs. **** would be detrimental to the girl if she was allowed from school in care of her mother.

Mr. Strapp contends that if this girl is removed from the school to the custody of her mother, that he does not wish her to return and that such removal would be contrary to the best interests of the girl.

104. 4 September 1939 **** to DIA
...I wish to ask you a favor by giving a concent of releasing my daughter from Mt Elgin School...my daughter has poor eyesight, and seem be no better since she was in school. So she aint doing much good in school so she could do better at home as I am out working most of the time and I have one boy at home age 9. Somebody has to stay with him when I am away through the day working and she can do the house work alright so you see just how it is..

105. 25 September 1939 Strapp to Phelan
...I have discussed the matter with Mr. Agent Moore and he is opposed to this girl being discharged from school because of her home conditions. I agree...this girl has been under treatment for the past year for an eye condition that requires regular attention and I am perfectly sure that she would not secure the correct treatment if in her own home.

106. 6 October 1939 Phelan to Devlin
...there is no further accommodation available for pupils at the Mount Elgin Institute...unable to consider allowing the daughter of Mrs. **** to be placed in that school...

107. 20 February 1940 McCracken to Secretary DIA
...receipt of a letter written to the Justice Department by Mr. and Mrs ****on behalf of their child...the parents wish their child to be discharged.
...the Principal of the School and he informs me that this girl ran away from the School about a week ago. The R.C.M.P. Police were notified and through their efforts the girl was brought back to the School.
    This girl, ****, upon her return to the School, was questioned by the Principal as to why she ran away and it was ascertained that she had been practically forcing younger pupils of the School to steal things for her. She made various kinds of threats to persuade the younger pupils to obey her in this respect. ****'s age is somewhat in doubt but it is believed that she is 17 years of age. News concerning threats made by the ****girl to make the younger pupils steal for her eventually reached some of the older girls at the School who in turn more or less shamed and ridiculed her to such an extent that she decided to run away. When she was returned to the School in the company of the R.C.M.Police she promised in the presence of the Police and the Principal of the School that she would not steal anything herself nor would she again ask younger pupils to steal for her.
    The Principal of the School accepted her back on the above understanding. Mr. Strapp has advised me that he is not in favour of discharging the girl as it would probably encourage other pupils to adopt similar measures and he is of the opinion that **** should remain in the School and be taught to obey the laws and conduct herself properly. The Principal feels that if the girl were discharged now it would leave the remainder of the pupils in a very unsettled and rebellious mood. In view of the girl's age, the Principal is prepared to recommend her discharge on August 31st, 1940. The home conditions in which this girl would be placed if discharged are decidedly unsuitable and I would strongly recommend that **** be kept as a pupil at the School until August 31st...

108. 22 February 1940 Phelan to Strapp
...the December quarter return...shows the following pupils

over the age of 16: [11]
    Permission was granted last year for the retention of these children in your school until June 30, 1940. However, in view of the fact that the number of children of school age is apparently increasing, and...that due to conditions now confronting us there is no immediate prospect of our securing funds to provide increased pupilage at Indian residential schools, it is considered that in future it will be necessary to adhere more strictly to the provision of the Indian Act requiring discharge of pupils at 16 years of age. Consequently unless there are some exceptional reasons the above mentioned children should be discharged at the end of June next...

109. 22 June 1940 Strapp to Phelan
...what arrangements are being made for a Weaving class...next year...with the cut in the grant...the finances that I proposed to use for this class have just simply disappeared...two of our Entrance class have been granted their certificates...

110. 4 July 1940 Strapp to Phelan
...**** and **** from the Cape Croker Agency, I feel sure that we will be able to take these two children in September. I note that they are ten and twelve years of age respectively.
Because of the large number of older pupils being discharged this year it will not be possible for us to accept more than five or six pupils who are under ten years of age or who have at least grade three standing.

111. 19 October 1940 A. D. Moore to Secretary IAB
...the toilets serving three boys' dormitories...are out of order and need immediate repairs.
...the soil pipe from these three toilets were corroded badly and filled with refuse from the third floor to the basement and that it would not be adviseable to use these old pipes, which have been there since the school was built, forty-five years ago...
    As the toilets are urgently needed and the odour in the building terrific, I instructed Mr. Northcott to proceed at once with the repairs...

112. 28 January 1941 Hoey to Strapp
...a loom be supplied to those who are graduating from the weaving and domestic science course...state if you recommend that all girls graduating from this course should be given a loom or just those who have done especially well. Our experience has been that even though looms are supplied the recipient has to purchase necessary yarn and that when supervision is removed their work is inclined to deteriorate.

113. 5 March 1941 Strapp to Hoey
...it would be advisable to provide all the girls with looms

because of the fact that only with considerable and continual practice will they become competent weavers. A criticism which has filtered back to us through some of the people on this Agency is that the pupils who took the course last year did not have looms to do any work on after they completed their course and arrived at their homes...only perhaps a small number of the girls who are trained will be ambitious enough to do good commercial work but...if a few looms were going into houses on different Reservations the general idea of reviving handicrafts would be given a boost and such things as runners etc, made with cotton carpet warp and using scraps of cotton materials as weft could be made for use in their homes, and no doubt there would be some role for them locally...

114.   7 March 1941   Hoey to Strapp

...With reference to your suggestion that looms should be supplied to the girls of this class, I am not convinced that this is a good thing to do, but as we cannot be certain the girls will neglect to use the looms until we give them the opportunity, I think we are justified in making the experiment when the class is made up of only six girls. This authorizes the expenditure of $50 for the purchase of lumber, and my understanding is that you are willing to arrange to have the boys in the manual training shop make the looms without cost to the Department...

115.   29 April 1941   **** to DIA

I have a girl in Mt. Elgin...I would like to have her in these holidays coming, to come home for good this year.

116.   9 May 1941   Strapp to Phelan

...it may be advisable to discharge this girl as her father is a trouble maker and may involve us in considerable legal correspondence in order to regain control of her this year. He is employed as a casual day laborer and has not had steady employment for several years. On...his last visit to the school he made the statement that "It's time she was working and helping me". This statement reveals his attitude toward his daughter and I have no doubt that he will put up a fight to get control of her.

117.   3 June 1941   Strapp to Phelan

...when I informed the R.C.M.P. of the absence of the four girls I had already received the circular referred to in your letter; I had also, in company with a member of my staff, driven over fifty miles between 1.30 a.m. when the absence of the girls was discovered and 5.00 a.m. "without cost to the Department" as instructed in your circular. If I had been notified by your Indian Agent or the R.C.M.P. when the girls were located I would have sent a car with a matron to return them to the school. On may 18th. three girls truanted, I attempted to trace them and found that they had been seen getting into a car

East of London and then again in Ingersol. I immediately put in long distance telephone calls for the local police in Ingersol and Woodstock asking them to try and locate the girls and if successful to notify me. The girls were located and I sent a car and matron to return them to the school, again, as instructed, "without expense to the Department".

...on another occasion we were informed by a resident of the Oneida Reservation, when we were looking for a truant, that we had "no rights on the reserve when we left the school property". "Only the Indian Agent or Mountie has any authority here". We tried to point out that we were trying to avoid calling in the authorities so as to make as little trouble as possible for the people who were hiding the boy, but...we were powerless to do anything in the face of this attitude and came back to the school.

For the protection of myself and any member of my staff who might have to act under my instructions...I must ask you to define and rule upon any legal right and authority to search for and apprehend any pupil, who may be a truant, upon an Indian Reservation or upon a public highway of the province...under the present circumstances an amendment similar to that appointing the R.C.M.P. as truant officers should be made to the Indian Act, appointing the Principal or his duly appointed representative as a truant officer...If this is not possible or is deemed inadvisable then that Indian Agent be instructed to apprehend truants when notified of the case by the Principal who will then be responsible for providing transportation and escort....

...it is the desire of the Principal and all the members of the staff of this school to cooperate as fully as possible with your Department in any matter in which an economy may possibly be effected.

118.   10 June 1941   Phelan to Strapp

...Indian Agent who, of course, cannot escape responsibility for cooperating with you in the case of truant children.

There is no probability of having the Indian Act amended during the present Session but certain amendments are being considered for presentation to Parliament next year. At that time we will keep in mind your recommendation that Principals of residential schools be given additional authority in apprehending truant pupils. I am rather doubtful, however, that we would be successful in obtaining such an amendment.

119.   4 July 1941   Phelan to Strapp

...your recommendation regarding keeping certain pupils in the Mount Elgin Residential School for another year was carefully discussed with Mr. Hoey. Under present conditions, and on account of the many demands which we receive from deserving pupils for accommodation in residential schools, we feel that it would be a mistake to keep the pupils you mention for a further year...I have discussed this matter with Miss Moodie and she seems to be under the impression that there might be a few of the girls who would profit by a year's special training in domestic science. Miss Moodie intends to write to you in regard to this matter and in the event of your deciding that a few of them would profit by the additional domestic science training we will be prepared to favourably consider their re-admission to the school for the academic year 1941-42.

120. 10 July 1941 Tuffnell to Secretary IAB
...motion...passed by the Cape Croker council at their regular meeting held here July 7th, Chief and all councillors present.

Moved by Wellington Elliott and J. C. Jones that this council recognizes Mr & Mrs **** as the guardians of the two children that are in Muncey Institution namely **** and **** and request the Department to release them for the summer holidays.

...I had a letter from Rev Strapp...some time ago asking about these children and as the home conditions of these two children are not very good I advised him that they be kept at the school for the holidays as they will soon be finished with their courses and will then be sent home.

121. 2 September 1941 McCracken to Secretary IAB
...****...whose mother wishes to have discharged owing to ill health.

Rev Strapp...stated to me that this boy should be requested to remain at the School unless proof is furnished that his health would suffer if such action were taken. As far as can be ascertained this boy did not require any medical attention during his previous term at the School and he appeared to be in good health.

It appears as if the mother of this boy is unwilling for him to go back to the school for some reason, probably due to the fact that he can work now and would be earning money which he would no doubt turn over to his mother. The R.C.M.Police had to visit the **** home last year to get the boy to return to Mount Elgin and at that time the mother caused considerable disturbance.

I would suggest that this boy be re-examined by our Medical Superintendent and if Dr. Jamieson finds him in good health he should be forced to return to the School. This cannot be done until the boy returns to the Reserve as he is now working in some white municipality with his parents. When **** was admitted to the School on September 17th, 1938, he was ten years of age and in my opinion he should return to the School, health permitting.

122. 11 September 1941 Telford & Telford to DIA
We have been consulted by ****...in reference to his two boys, **** 14, and ****, 12, and his daughter, **** 10...The father would like his children discharged from

the Institute as he feels that he can look after them better at home. We would like to get the release as quickly a possible so that the children can live at their home and attend school on the reserve.

123. 13 September 1941 Phelan to Robertson
...Telford & Telford...state that the parents can look after these children and have them attend one of the day schools on the Saugeen Reserve. If this information is correct the Department has no objection to the children remaining on the Reserve provided you feel assured that they will attend one of the day schools regularly. If, however, home conditions are unsuitable we are of the opinion that the children should be returned...

124. 13 September 1941 Robertson to Secretary IAB
...I took ****, ****, **** and **** to the Mt. Elgin Residential School, while at the school Mr. Strapp complained that ****, ****, ****, **** and **** had not returned, on my return I notified the parents that the children would have to return to school, they all objected stating that the food was very poor. Constable Langille got ****, ****, **** and **** and took them back to Muncey. ****, father of **** and **** was away at the time but I am in hopes of having these two boys returned without further trouble.

...**** and ****, these girls are both past fourteen and the home conditions have improved during the past few years, if these two were discharged they could attend the local school for the balance of their education.

125. 16 September 1941 Robertson to Secretary IAB
...**** was returned to Muncey on September 10th, and should remain there as the mother is living with another Indian. Regarding the **** family, this family spent the summer at Wasaga Beach...last week they were at Kintail...during the past three years they have spent possibly six months on the reserve, when a family is moving around like that it is hard to know whether the children are attending or not to any school but when on the reserve we had trouble with their attendance.

...a letter received from Mrs. ****, mother of these children. I did not return from leave until August 25th. and when I got in touch with Mrs. **** she wished to have this application cancelled, so you can see how changeable they are. I would recommend these children be returned to Muncey.

126. 22 September 1941 Phelan to Strapp
...Indian Agent Robertson...has made arrangements for the return of **** and ****...though...they overstayed their leave....home conditions have improved...recommends their discharge...if you have no difficulty in securing pupils this year I believe that it might be advisable to discharge the two girls...

127. 25 September 1941 Strapp to Phelan
...pupils from the Saugeen Agency. When Mr. Robertson was here a short time ago he was emphatic that the children should remain in school because "they would not attend school regularly if at home". I do not understand his changed attitude....I do not think that they should be discharged especially as we are about ten pupils short of our grant earning number.

...that your instruction of last June that all pupils who had reached the age of 16 years should be discharged has worked a real hardship this year as not only have we been faced with the retroactive reduction in the per capita grant...but, we are compelled to do all our buying of clothing, boots, groceries and household equipment on a continually rising market. The discharge of so many older boys and girls and the admission of so many small and helpless children has seriously complicated the problem of doing the necessary work of the school and carrying on the farm program, through which we endeavour to produce as much food as possible for our own use.

An aspect of the situation that I feel has not had the proper consideration is that the policy of replacing older pupils with small children makes more acute the danger of loss of life in the event of panic from any cause. It is imperative that there should be a good number of older pupils who can assist the members of the staff in caring for small children in cases of emergency.

128. 27 September 1941 Phelan to Robertson
...careful consideration has been given to your suggestion that **** and **** be discharged but in view of the circumstances it is felt that it would be in the best interests of these girls to remain in the school.

I doubt very much if the parents' statement that the food is bad at this school is a legitimate one. I have had an opportunity of visiting this school on many occasions and...the food is all that could be desired.

129. 7 October 1941 **** to DIA
COULD YOU RELEASE ****...HAVE WORK FOR HIM AT HOME AS HE WOULD BE MORE SATISFIED AND NOT RUN AWAY...

130. 14 October 1941 Jamieson to A. D. Moore
I beg to report a breakage in the spectacles of ****...I imagine one screw will have to be replaced. Please advise procedure whether it can be done locally or at Ottawa.

The epidemic at the Institute is apparently going to be one of sore throats mostly with two proven Scarlet fever rashes and one other questionable. We have about thirty in bed at the present time...

We were fortunate in obtaining the services of Miss Ruth Hill as our special nurse and I believe she will be able to take all the nursing responsibility off the shoulder of the teaching staff...

131. 15 October 1941 McCracken to Secretary IAB
In the attached letter written by Dr. T. J. Jamieson, Medical Superintendent of Caradoc Agency, he advises the Department that ****...has broken her glasses and repairs are required.

This girl was admitted to the school early in September and was formerly a ward of the Children's Aid in St. Thomas, Ontario.

Apparently the expenditure necessary to repair the glasses would not be large as only one screw has to be replaced which should not cost more that fifty cents.

I would recommend that authority be granted to have these glasses repaired.

132. 21 October 1941 Falconer to McCracken
RE: ****'s Glasses... Authority is granted to have this girl's glasses repaired locally.

133. 29 January 1942 Phelan to Strapp
...your request for the two sewing machines...while I would like to supply them...present regulations prevent our doing so. The argument used is that electric machines do not provide the training for the children that they require in view of the fact that few, if any...will have electric machines when they return to their homes...

134. 1 February 1942 Strapp to Phelan
...I requested the electric model because a survey of the girls who have left this school during the past four years shows that the majority of them have gone into domestic service in homes that are fully equipped with electric machines...A number of the girls who have returned to visit us from time to time have remarked that they were considerably handicapped at first because they had not been accustomed to operating electrical equipment...I have purchased out of school funds an electric domestic sized washing machine and so far six girls here have had a tour of duty with the machine. We have six electric irons and if we had the two electric sewing machines we would be fairly well equipped to give the older girls sufficient training with electrical equipment that they will not feel handicapped when they go into a position.

All of the girls thirteen years of age and over are trained in the operation of the domestic treadle machines...

135. 22 February 1942 Prentice to DIA
From the beginning of September 1941, until the end of that year, I served as the kindergarten primary teacher...while there, part of my many duties was every so often supervising the Indian girls, during the evening hours. Consequently it fell to my lot, to administer medicines of various kinds to the ailing.

I found that many of the girls, big and little, suffered from tooth-ache, because of badly damaged teeth. No dentist ever visited the school, while I was there; and there was no word of one being employed for the coming years. I was amazed at the unchristian - like way these children were treated, and intended writing...longago...

An inspector should visit that school and investigate ...the children's beds and bedding, the clothing or lack of winter clothing which the girls wear, etc - the lack of boxes that can be locked in which to keep personal belongings, which having been broken in years gone by were never replaced, the lack of apples for the children to eat, and which they long for...

136. 26 February 1942 Hoey to Strapp

I enclose...a letter...from Miss Florence M. Prentice...

Dr. Moore has been endeavouring for some time to obtain the services of a dentist but up to the present has been unsuccessful due to the fact that all dentists in London and Mount Brydges seem to be so busy that they do not want to spend the time to visit either the Caradoc Reserve or the Mount Elgin Residential School. If you consider dental work is required...and you know a dentist whose services could be secured during the month of March, please let me know immediately...Dr. Moore has funds available in the current year's appropriation for a three or four day dental clinic...but...the work would have to be done before the end of the current fiscal year.

137. 14 April 1942 Supt. DIA to Strapp

The Indian Affairs Branch has been conducting a nutritional investigation among various sections of the Indian population, and Doctor Moore is anxious to get complete data on the food being consumed in several of our residential schools. Would you be good enough to furnish the following information:

A complete statement of all the food supplied to the children over a given period of time, for example, if the period given were one week, we would require the number of pounds of potatoes and other vegetables, the number of gallons of milk, the number of pounds of meat, butter, etc.

A statement of the menu for each meal for the same period, and the number of children participating of the food, with their ages.

We intend to have this scientifically reviewed by the research department of one of the universities, and be advised by them as to whether the children are getting all the nourishment necessary for their well-being...

138. 3 June 1942 Down to MacInnes

In a report received from Dr. Jamieson re dental clinic ...suggested that two extra days would complete the examining and necessary treatment of the children...

Dr. Jamieson also suggested some form of dental instruction and care of the mouth...

"Now that the Deptment has been so kind as to provide this dental service the pupils should be instructed in

proper care of their teeth. I have been informed that about half the children have not tooth brushes. All should have them and of course all should be instructed as to how and when to use them..."

139. 8 June 1942 MacInnes to Down

It will be in order to employ a dentist for an additional two days at the rate of $30 a day...The Principal of the school should submit to you a requisition for whatever tooth brushes are needed...the children should be given dental instruction and it should be possible to arrange with the doctor, with the possible assistance of the school nurse, to give some such instruction to the children.

140. 10 June 1942 Down to MacInnes

I...request that my duties, if any, in connection with the Mt. Elgin Institute be outlined. This request is brought about through Mr. Strapps apparent resentment at a report that was submitted, at the request of the Department, re dental services and a clinic held at that Institute. He seems to resent suggestions and, I have no desire to tread where others have not, unless it is within my jurisdiction.

Apparently, he is taking exception to Dr. Jamieson's suggestion, that tooth brushes and dental instruction be given the children...I think the suggestion a good one and for the benifit of the children under his care, he should endeavour to co-operate, but it appears Dr. Jamieson, discussed the welfare of the clinic and the children with the school nurse and not with Mr. Strapp. Whether or not this is the correct procedure, does not excuse him from resenting my request.

I would refer to your letter of June 8th, wherein I was requested to ask the Principal of the Institute to submit a requisition for the number of tooth brushes required. He seemed to think I was overstepping my authorities in asking him to submit it to this office.

I have no desire to encroach upon Mr. Strapp's duties or privileges, I was merely carrying out instructions from Head Office. However, it is going to be difficult for me unless I am advised whether or not I have any duties in connection with this Institution. Personally, I am not anxious assume, but would rather leave Mr. Strapp to his own grief and troubles.

141. 16 June 1942 Hoey to Down

...it is our policy to have the Indian Agent visit any residential school in his Agency at least once a month and ...Mr. Strapp will expect you to follow this procedure...it is unnecessary for you to examine the classroom work, as the Provincial Inspector visits this school and submits a report regarding the teaching services...you should inspect the school at least monthly and at a time that will not unduly interfere with the Principal's work. You should examine the building, barns, etc. and if there is any matter requiring Departmental attention you should so advise me.

January 26th to Feb. 1.42

Monday	Tuesday	Wednesday	Thursday	Friday	Saturday	Sunday
R.Oats Bread Butter Milk	C. Wheat Rhubarb Bread Milk	C. Meal Bread Honey Milk	R. Oats Bread Butter milk	C. Wheat Bread C. syrup milk	C. Meal Bread p.Butter milk	R. Oats Bread Butter milk
Meat Loaf Gravy Turnips Potatoes Ginger pudding Bread milk	Meat Pie & veg cottage pudding B. sauce Bread milk	Roast Beef Gravy Parsnips Chocolate Blancmange Bread milk	Veg & meat stew pickles Tapioca cream Bread milk	Meat Loaf potatoes Gravy Fried Onions Rhubarb pudding Bread milk	Minced meat & Gravy Potatoes Beets Prunes Custard sauce milk	Roast Beef Gravy Turnips Potatoes Fruit Gelatine Bread milk
Egg Sandwiches cream cake milk	veg soup Bread milk Rhubarb	macaroni & butter Bread milk Prunes	Bean Soup Bread milk Chocolate cake	Toast creamed eggs milk honey	veg soup Bread milk Johnny cake C. syrup	curried rice meat Bread milk spice Cake whipped cream

February 23rd to March 1st 1942

Monday	Tuesday	Wednesday	Thursday	Friday	Saturday	Sunday
Cracked Wheat Bread Butter Milk	corn meal Bread P. Butter Milk	R. oats Bread C. syrup Milk	C. wheat Bread Honey milk	C. meal Bread Butter milk	R. Oats Bread p.Butter milk	Corn meal Bread Corn syrup milk
minced meat Gravy Potatoes mashed Beets Tapioca cream Bread milk	R. Beef Gravy Potatoes Turnip, pickles chocolate pudding Bread milk	veg & meat stew Date pudding Bread milk	R. Veal potatoes cabbage Rhubarb Gelatine w. cream Bread milk	chopped meat gravy potatoes Beets Rice & raisins Bread milk	R. Pork & Gravy Potatoes Turnip Ginger bread w cream milk	chopped meat Gravy Potatoes fried onions cottage pudding & brown sauce Bread. milk
veg macaroni soup prunes bread milk	Baked Beans Tomato sauce cheese pudding Bread milk	potato soup apple sauce Bread milk	scalloped potatoes sliced pork Chocolate cake Bread. milk	Toast creamed eggs Bran muffins honey Bread. milk	pea soup apple crisp Bread milk	veg. soup Tea Biscuits citron Bread milk

March 23rd to March 29th 1942

Monday	Tuesday	Wednesday	Thursday	Friday	Saturday	Sunday
corn meal corn syrup Bread Milk	R. Oats Bread Butter Milk	C. wheat Bread P. Butter Milk	corn meal Butter Bread milk	R. Oats Bread c.syrup milk	C. wheat Bread Rhubarb milk	Corn meal P. Butter Bread milk
meat & veg stew snow pudding custard sauce Bread milk	R. pork gravy potatoes squash Rice custard Bread milk	minced meat & Gravy Potatoes Parsnips caramel pudding Bread milk	meat loaf scalloped potatoes chili sauce cornstarch souffle Bread milk	R. Beef potatoes onions gravy Bread pudding cream Bread milk	minced meat & Gravy Potatoes Beets Velvet cream Bread milk	Head Cheese fried potatoes cream pie Bread currant buns Butter milk
Rice Fritters custard sponge Bread Butter milk	Fried potatoes prunes custard sauce Bread milk	Baked Beans Rhubarb Bread milk	Potato soup Johnny cake syrup Bread milk	Fried Potatoes cold meat (beef) Bran muffins Bread Butter milk	Bread & Gravy chocolate cake w. cream Bread milk	Baked potatoes Rhubarb gelatine Bread Tea Biscuits Butter milk

April 6th to April 12th 1942

Monday	Tuesday	Wednesday	Thursday	Friday	Saturday	Sunday
corn meal Rhubarb Bread Milk	R. Oats Bread Butter Milk	C. wheat corn syrup Bread Milk	corn meal Butter Bread milk	R. Oats P. Butter Bread milk	C. wheat Corn syrup Bread milk	Corn meal P. Butter Bread milk
Roast veal Potatoes Turnips Gravy Tapioca custard Bread milk	minced meat gravy fried onions potatoes cornstarch pudding & Brown sauce Bread milk	cold roast veal Parsnips Potatoes gravy cottage pudding & Brown sauce Bread milk	minced meat gravy Beets potatoes Rice, raisins pudding & cream Bread milk	veg & meat stew cabbage Bread pudding cream Bread milk	Roast Pork & Gravy Potatoes Squash Date Roly-poly Brown sauce Bread milk	Head Cheese chili sauce scalloped potatoes Rhubarb Gelatine Whipped cream cabbage salad Bread milk
Shepherds pie Bread Butter Date cookies milk	Tomato & macaroni prunes Bread milk	Toast creamed eggs Tea biscuits Bread, butter milk	Fried Potatoes Bread, milk Chocolate cake w. cream	Boston Beans Bread milk butter stewed raisins	potato soup Bread milk Butter Rhubarb	macaroni cheese sauce Bread milk prunes currant buns

142. 10 June 1942 Hoey to Strapp

...Dr. Tisdall comments upon the dietary schedule....

..."A rather surprising point is that these children apparently average 39 ounces of milk a day, which of course is excellent. When the diet is pulled to pieces, it is seen that the protein is adequate, with approximately half the protein obtained from animal sources, namely, milk and meat. The total calories are probably adequate, when you take into consideration the fact that some of the children are no doubt quite young. This would be something which could only be determined however if the exact ages of the children were known. The amount of fat is adequate. Calcium is adequate. The iron is adequate, although there is no surplus. The vitamin A is perhaps a little low. The B1 is a little low, which however would be rectified if Canada Approved Bread or whole wheat bread were used. The vitamin C is markedly low. On paper the 55 mgms. is not bad, but from our experience I am sure you would find that of the 53 mgms. coming from potatoes and vegetables fully two-thirds of this will be lost in the cooking. Due to the large consumption of milk the riboflavin intake is adequate.

"Our suggestion would be to use more green leafy vegetables to supply more vitamin A, and either more tomatoes, tomato juice or citrus fruits - to supply vitamin C."

143. 26 September 1942 Dorey to Hoey

Rev. O. B. Strapp...was in yesterday and brought with him a letter which he had received from the Tire Controller. Mr. Strapp had applied for three retreads and one new tire for his car..."existing tire regulations do not provide for the supplying of replacement tires for the vehicle which is described in your application..."

I hope you will find it possible...to take this up and have these regulations amended. Otherwise, I am afraid we shall be under the painful necessity of closing the Muncey School. You may say that this is an extreme view to take; but...this School is twenty miles from London, which is the nearest town, and you will realize that it is quite impossible to carry on work at the School without having a car to go into London on business and take the teachers and other members of the staff for week-end leave...Mr. Strapp...cannot take any passengers in the truck and it is far more expensive to operate...

Mr. Strapp has also asked me to write about...getting some priority ratings for the Muncey School...He finds it impossible to carry on his work unless he gets something like that. For example, he has a welding outfit which enables him to do many repairs which are necessary. He cannot get supplies for this unless he gets some priority rating...when he goes to buy shoes for the children, he is very much embarrassed because manufacturers cannot give him reasonably prompt delivery...

144. 9 November 1942 Hoey to McGill

...It is now the only residential school operated by the Government in cooperation with the United Church in the province of Ontario. An enrolment of 150 pupils is allowed at this school and per capita grant is at the rate of $160. The cost of operation per pupil, according to the last audit statement, is $241.66 per annum.

The classroom buildings, which are detached from the main building, are the original buildings erected almost a century ago. In addition to the regular classrooms, accommodation is provided on the second floor of this building for certain members of the teaching staff. These residential school buildings are on a mound and subject very much to erosion. This is particularly true of the classroom, one gable of which might collapse at any time, Mr. Dudly had this particular gable strengthened with four or five square timbers. This rendered the wall reasonably safe for a time, but the wall above and below these supports shows signs of bulging and disintegration. The main building was rebuilt in 1895, probably by the Methodist Church, with a contribution from the Government. The records here indicate that from 1896 to 1911 and 1912 $21,000 of government funds have been spent on this school and $11,000 from band funds. In 1912 and 1913 a new addition was built to the main building at a cost to the Government of $17,260.00 This main building represents a style of architecture that has long since been abandoned. The ceilings are at least 12 feet high and the cost of heating from year to year must be enormous. However, the building is of brick construction and from the outside presents a somewhat imposing appearance, but inside it is one of the most dilapidated structures that I have ever inspected.

At the time of my visit the plumbing in the boys' wash-room was in a faulty state of repair, with the result that the wash bowl were full of filthy water and the floor of the wash-room in a filthy condition. The odors in the wash-room and indeed throughout the building were so offensive that I could scarcely endure them. Certain parts of this building are literally alive with cockroaches - this applies particularly to the kitchen. The treads I noticed on the stairway were literally worn away until they are no longer safe. If this were not a government-operated institution, I feel confident it would be closed by the municipal health authorities...this school reflects no credit on either the Department or the United Church of Canada. in my judgment, it should be immediately closed or rebuilt. I consider the principal, the Reverend Mr. Strapp, a good man and a man with a very practical turn of mind. He has experienced the utmost difficulty this year in securing pupils, particularly senior pupils. He had at the time of my visit 120 pupils on the roll and is worried almost to the point of collapse by the financial outlook for the school. The school, he assured me, simply cannot continue to operate with the present allowance. It would appear as Indians become economically better off they display a tendency to keep their children at home and send them to the day schools rather than to the residential school. This may be a rather encouraging tendency but is one that makes it exceedingly difficult for our schools to operate until certain adjustments have been effected, I estimate that it would require the sum of $200,000 to rebuild and furnish the Mount Elgin School with accommodation for 150 to 175 pupils.

In contrast to the school building, the farm operated in connection with this school is a model of efficiency. Mr. Strapp has one of the best pure bred Holstein dairy herds in southwestern Ontario. He has in addition at this time 70 pigs of the bacon type, and has one of the best Yorkshire boars in the province. He has also a good poultry house, well stocked with poultry and his farm buildings are all that one might desire, I...think that we

should cease to operate this residential school and that the place it occupies should be taken by a four-room classroom building, in which we would make provision for continuation classes and vocational instruction. This would enable us to take the pupils from the day schools at Grades 7 and 8 and give them advanced courses in academic subjects in agriculture or auto mechanic, carpentry, etc., and the girls, courses in home-making, domestic science, dressmaking, etc. The principal of this school should, in addition to his duties at the school be made supervisor or inspector of all the schools on the reserve. This would enable us to have an almost ideal experimental educational unit.

145. 25 November 1942 Hoey to Strapp
Re: Priority Ratings......The Purchasing Agent now informs us that it is not possible to secure a rating for your school...I am not at all satisfied with this ruling. If the officials responsible for issuing priority ratings from time to time refuse to give ratings to our schools, I find it difficult to see how we can keep these schools open and in operation...I feel rather helpless in regard to the whole matter. I appreciate very fully, after my visit to your school, the urgent need at the institution for certain supplies and certain repairs. I have intimated to the officials here that they would not tolerate the conditions at your school 24 hours if they were coming in contact with them, as you are, from day to day...would it be possible for you to bring this matter to the attention of the Secretary of the Home Mission Board?...it seems to me that the securing of supplies for our schools - always a difficult matter - has reached a stage when it is almost impossible to secure supplies at all.

146. 3 December 1942 Dorey to Hoey
...Mr. Strapp...says that the repairs authorized at the School have not been carried out...some of these repairs are absolutely essential if the School is to be carried on at all. The unsanitary condition of the playroom and washroom is beyond description. If the condition were due to neglect on the part of the principal or the staff, we could assume responsibility, but it is obvious to anybody with average intelligence that this is due to the fact that the building and everything about it is old and needs repair...

147. 26 May 1943 Hoey to Dorey
...a memorandum from the Deputy Minister...May 22, 1943...states: "It would seem quite clear that we are not justified in permitting the Mount Elgin Institute to be operated after the end of the present school year, not so much because of recent happenings, but because of the unsatisfactory condition of the school buildings.
...the members of the Home Mission board may not be favourable disposed to the closing of the residential school

at Muncey however, I...think that some such action as this will have to be taken, either now or in the immediate future. The present building is in an insanitary and dilapidated condition and the classroom building is apt to collapse at any time...it would cost at least $200,000.00 to build a fully fireproof residential school at this agency...it will be exceedingly difficult for me to recommend such an expenditure, if funds were available, in view of the more urgent needs at Alberni, File Hills and Round Lake...

148. 27 May 1943 Dorey to Hoey
...Naturally such a drastic proposal as you outline will have to receive the consideration of the Executive of our Board...I shall be quite frank in my reaction.

In the first place, I do not think you intend the suggestion that the School at Muncey be closed on June 30th, 1943, to be taken seriously. To ask the Board of Home Missions to consent to this after the School has been in operation "lo these many years," when a notice is sent to us on May 26th - which is just one month and four days' notice - is a good deal more than I think you think we are likely to consider as within the realm of practical politics.

...your proposition involves closing the School now and leaving all these children who are at present in the School without any educational facilities...I do not think that is feasible - and I do not think you do either.

I come next to a very serious feature of the proposition. According to the last Census, there are 5535 Indians in Ontario who are counted United Church. There are 9747 Church of England, and 9862 Roman Catholics. Your proposal...would mean, so far as the United Church is concerned, that there would not be a single residential school in Ontario to which our children could be sent; but it would leave all the Roman Catholic schools, with a total pupilage of 705, in full operation. It would leave the Church of England school, with a pupilage of 520 (I have eliminated the Mohawk Institute), also running. I do not think that this will commend itself to the judgment of the United Church...

...I fully realize that the Mount Elgin School is in a deplorable condition and that it has long outlived its usefulness; but I have not yet come to the place where I would ask the Executive of our Board to urge the expenditure of $200,000 of Government money to replace this old building...situation at Mount Elgin is in a bad way, and...I am quite prepared to co-operate with the Department in making the survey suggested; but we might as well face the fact that, so far as our Church is concerned, we are not going to be pushed around too far nor too fast in connection with these residential schools...

...it does not seem to us to be fair - and I do not think we can get away with it - to notify Mr. Strapp on the 27th May that his ten years' principalship will expire on June

30th. This is what the proposal to close the school would mean; because I do not think that either you or I can envisage Mr. Strapp as a educationist, doing the work which you suggest should be done on this particular Reserve. Some men have some gifts, and others have others...and, quite frankly, I do not think Mr. Strapp's gifts lie in that direction.

The Secretaries of the Board of Home Missions would...be prepared to continue to explore the possibility of radical changes in the educational set-up at Mount Elgin...but I think we should have time in which to do it, and the 30th June...is hardly time enough...I shall try to arrange for a survey of conditions in the Caradoc agency, and to assist in submitting a report on the programme which might be carried forward in the Agency.

149. 31 May 1943 Hoey to Dorey
...I was particularly gratified to note your anxiousness to cooperate with the Department in having a thorough survey undertaken at the Caradoc agency with the object of working out an educational program designed to meet the needs of the Indian population.

...I do not mind admitting to you that the condition of the Mount Elgin Institute has given me a great many anxious hours of late. We have had two memoranda from the Minister's office within the last year, in both of which the opinion was expressed that the institution should be closed. You can easily imagine then the position I would be in, in the case of truancy or in case of fire or the collapse of the classroom building.

I do not suppose that the actual date of the closing should prove to be a serious matter. The Government, having enunciated its policy, is not likely to be unreasonable either with respect to the closing date or the re-employment of the staff...

150. [n.d.] Hoey to Dorey
The Mount Elgin Institute has at this date an authorized enrolment of 150 pupils, for which per capita grant at the rate of $160 is allowed. The actual enrolment is approximately 125 pupils, but a number of these are senior girls who have exceeded the age limit. The pupils are drawn from the following reserves:- Walpole Island 5; Sarnia 9, Kettle Point 17; Oneida 1; Muncey 1; Caradoc 52; Cape Croker 13; Hagersville 1;(New Credit); Moravian 2; Saugeen 4; Christian Island 7; Six Nations 9; Gibson (Parry Sound) 3; Caughnawaga 1.

...there is ample accommodation at the day schools on the reserves from which pupils are recruited and that the closing down of the Mt. Elgin Institute would cause little inconvenience...transportation in one or two cases would no doubt have to be provided...a day school was closed at the Caradoc agency during the present academic year for the reason that the number of pupils available did not justify its operation...17 pupils are recruited from the

Kettle Point agency and yet the attendance at this school has become so unsatisfactory and the number of pupils of school age reduced to such an extent that we are now considering...closing this school. These are facts that confront us, apart altogether from the insanitary condition of the building. From a sanitary standpoint the building has been condemned by the Acting Superintendent of Medical Services, the Inspector for Ontario and a number of Indian agents at the annual conference of Indian agents. The R.C.M.P. in the district have not advocated the closing of the building but have expressed the view that the institution...is no longer necessary.

...There is of course a financial side to this question...I do feel that it is worthy of consideration, in view of the difficulty we have experienced in securing the funds necessary to maintain our Indian day and residential schools in a high state of efficiency. I have before me the last audit statement on the Mt. Elgin Institute. This statement is dated May 26, 1943. The Auditor...states:-

"The cost per pupil per year shows an increase of $34.19 over the previous year...due to the reduction in the average attendance from 141.15 in 1941-42 to 127.76 in 1942-43. The total cost for the operation of the school for the period April 1, 1942, to March 31, 1943, amounted to $37,920.95"...it is significant that the total welfare program on the Caradoc Reserve for the fiscal year, which includes the care of the aged; deserted wives; agricultural operations; drainage; house repair; construction of homes; the purchase of seed; farm machinery, etc., amounted to $10,227.84...we are spending $5.58 per individual on the general welfare of the Indian population and $296.81 on each pupil...at the Institution, and this figure of course does not include other educational costs on the reserve...these expenditures are out of balance. This was the opinion expressed somewhat bitterly by the agents at the conference already referred to.

151. 10 June 1943 Dorey to Hoey

...I went over the Mount Elgin building a week ago, and whilst it is not in good repair, as I have already admitted, it is no different in construction from what it was fifty years ago, and the fire hazards which now obtain have been the same all through the years. In that connection, may I ask if it is to be assumed that the Mohawk Institute which dates from approximately the same period, is to be considered so much superior to Mount Elgin that it is going to be continued? You have the advantage of having visited both - I have never seen the Mohawk Institute and would not presume to pass any judgment on it - but we should like to be sure that the basis on which the proposal is made that all the children go to the Mohawk Institute - which is that the building there is much better - is actually based on fact.

The difficulty at Mount Elgin is very largely with the basement. There is no question that the boys' playroom was wet and dirty when I was there a week ago. The water seeps in from the side walls, and the result is very bad. There is no doubt about that! But, in the meantime, I think that the situation could be remedied if one were to go to the expense of digging a trench all around the building down to the floor level of the basement...coat it with cement; paint it with asphalt; and then put weeping tile all around it...that would eliminate all the wetness in the basement...

...we are ready to assist in a survey of the Reserve; but may I say that there must also be a survey of the Six Nations Reserve...I think it would be apparent to anyone that the place where there is least need of a residential school is the Six Nation Reserve; and, conversely, the place where a continuation school is most likely to be successful, on the basis suggested in your letter, is precisely the same point...I think that it is extremely unlikely that it would be possible to get a sufficient number of children of the secondary school grade to make worthwhile the operation of a school of that kind on the Caradoc Reserve, unless it were fitted up to provide accommodation for pupils from outside Reserves.

...The more I think of your proposition to place all the children of school age who need residential school care in one institution - and that one under the direction of the Church of England, - the less I think of it. We have already had experience in a number of cases of children of United Church parents being sent to Anglican schools... when they come back to the Reserve they consider themselves members of the Church of England, and when our missionary tries to interest them in church work, they reply that they are members of the Church of England - and very often that is simply a cloak for non-attendance and indifference...

I should like to have some further elucidation of the Auditor's report...The total amount which the Government paid to the Mount Elgin School for this period was $22,871.02 and the $37,000 includes the sum of $11,749.33 which Mr Strapp has entered as "Value of produce raised and consumed." I suppose it is fair to include that as part of the cost per pupil, but, if this is done, then I think it could be very materially reduced so as to make a much better showing.

There is no doubt that the total cost of the welfare programme on the Caradoc Reserve is high; but so long as the Government maintains the Reserve system, there is only one thing to be expected - that it will not decrease but rather increase. One cannot expect, on the other hand, to maintain a system, the operation of which saps all individual responsibility from the Indian, and on the other hand, hope that the amount which will be required for the care of the aged, agricultural operations, drainage, etc., will decrease. That is simply impossible.

I should be very glad if you would give further consideration to the matter of having a complete survey of educational needs in Ontario; and also if you could send me a full statement of the cost of operation of all residential schools for the fiscal year 1942-43...

152. 12 June 1943 Hoey to Dorey

...I am anxious to avoid in this correspondence...a discussion of Government policy. Such discussion should really be carried on by the Minister or by the Deputy...I should confine my attention to the task of supplying information and to an interpretation of the educational policy followed by the Department...

...I have never pretended at any time to pass judgment on the general condition of the Mt. Elgin Institute. I did state quite frankly, however, after my last visit, that in my judgment the building was in an insanitary condition. It has, however been condemned by our architects in recent years. These men point out that the buildings themselves are on a mount and consequently subject to erosion. When Mr. Dudley erected supports to protect the gable of the classroom building from collapse, he did so on the specific understanding that he should not be held responsible, did the building collapse at any time in the immediate future...the building is somewhat deceptive in that the outside appearance is not...unattractive...a number of the agents at the recent convention held in Toronto stated quite emphatically that, in view of the insanitary condition of the building they were not prepared to encourage Indian pupils to attend the institution.

...the Mohawk Institute was reconstructed at a cost of approximately $50,000.00 in...1922-23 and 1923-4. In addition to this, the grant of $5,000.00 a year contributed to the Department for the operation of this school has been spent from year to year in general maintenance and repairs...children for the Mohawk Institute are recruited from Tyendinaga, Gibson, Caughnawaga, Sarnia, Moravian, Walpole Island and a number of outlying reserves. The pupils in attendance at this school from the Six Nations Reserve are, with one or two exceptions, orphans or children from disrupted homes...two years ago we made an arrangement whereby high school studies are provided at two or three of the Indian day schools on the Six Nations reserve. In addition to this, we have an arrangement with the Brantford Collegiate Board, whereby the students who complete the Grade 9 course on the reserve with a creditable standing proceed with Grades 10, 11 and 12 at the Brantford Collegiate Institute...it would be very unwise and...pedagogically unsound to modify this program in any sense until it has been given a few years' trial. What I had in mind at Caradoc was a continuation school to which we could send pupils for training in agriculture, home economics, auto mechanics, handicrafts, etc. These children might remain at the Indian Day schools until they were 12 or 13 years old and then proceed to the continuation school. You will be interested to learn that the number of pupils proceeding

with high school studies at the Six Nation Reserve is equal to the number of white pupils proceeding with these studies in the adjoining communities.

...I was intentionally conservative when giving the expenditures involved in the operation of the Mount Elgin Institute. I simply submitted figures showing the actual disbursements. I did not include depreciation on buildings, farm machinery, etc., nor did I include inspection fees or the cost of school supplies, desks, text books, maps, etc., which are supplied from year to year from a distinct and separate appropriation and which are not included in the regular auditor's reports.

I should like you to read again the last paragraph of the memorandum...May 31...I was anxious to point out...the wide discrepancy between welfare expenditures and the annual expenditures at the Mt. Elgin Institute...

153. REPORT RE SURVEY OF INDIAN EDUCATION ON RESERVES IN WESTERN ONTARIO

The Survey consisted of:

(1) Visits to schools and homes on the Muncey, Oneida, Six Nations, Cape Croker, Saugeen, Kettle Point, Sarnia and Walpole Island Reserves;

(2) Conferences with teachers and agents on these reserves;

(3) Visits to the Mohawk Institute and Mount Elgin...

(4) Written reports from five public school inspectors who visit these reserves...

(5) Examination of reports relating to enrolment, attendance and progress of pupils in the schools on these reserves;

(6) Reading of reports of other surveys in Canada and United States.

Points Revealed by this Investigation

(1) Indians who had attended Residential Schools appear to be very successful in later life although the younger Indians appear to drift back into old habits and customs for a time after graduation. They appear to find the progress of changing from a life where all features of it were ordered by the institution to one of absolute freedom on the reserves a very difficult adjustment and naturally so. It is not surprising if for a time they "run wild".

The older Indians who are so successful were usually individuals who entered the residential school about 12 or 13 years of age after having attended Day Schools near their homes. They also report that they were given opportunities of practising leadership among their fellow students and some opportunity of doing some advanced academic work in addition to good training in agricultural and vocational subjects. They prize the religious training received in these institutions. In their day at these schools the proportion of younger children was not so large as today.

(2) There is a tendency today among many families to evade the responsibility of the training and raising the

children by sending, or wishing to send, their children to the residential school.

(3) Indian Agents at several of the reserves believe that the orphans and children from broken homes can be accommodated in Indian homes on the reserve and can receive their elementary education at the local Day Schools.

(4) Your committee believes that for children from Grades I to V or VI depending on the age of the children, a home atmosphere is superior to that of an institution for the natural development of the children, unless the home conditions are very adverse.

(5) The education of Indian children requires teachers who understand these children, who have some knowledge of their back ground, who are sympathetic and who have sufficient training to enable them to adjust the curriculum and management of the school to the particular needs of the children. These teachers ought to be able to conduct elementary classes, at least, in Handwork, Home Economics, Agriculture, Art and Music. They require special K.P. Training and ability to overcome language difficulties.

(6) Generally teachers in Indian schools do not have these qualifications. Frequently they are selected without proper regard to qualifications and occasionally against the advice of the local inspector.

(7) Some of the Daily Schools have a very ample supply of necessary teaching equipment and books for supplementary reading. Many have a very inadequate or unsuitable supply of these things. In a general way the best service occurs where the Indian Agent and the local inspector work in closest co-operation. The Agent has so many other details and interests to take his attention that we should not be surprised when he fails to give this matter the consideration it requires.

(8) Attendance at the Residential Schools is much better than at Day Schools. Attendance Officers with authority to enforce attendance are necessary.

(9) The provincial course of study needs to be modified for Indian schools. We believe that the properly trained teachers with adequate supervision can make the necessary adjustments. Special attention to Art and Crafts, Home Economics, Manual Training, Agriculture, Art and Music should be required.

(10) A Senior School or Senior Room could provide these in more detail for senior pupils and at the same time provide training in leadership, religion, sports and more advanced academic subjects.

(11) This would leave more opportunity to overcome the language difficulty and the retardation in the earlier grades.

(12) Our Residential Schools are planned as Vocational Schools. The enrolment indicates that they are being used in a large measure as orphanages or children's shelters. The large proportion of small children interferes with the other purpose of the school and the younger children receive more and better attention in a school planned for them. The school for older pupils could serve their needs more adequately if a sufficient number of them were present to carry out the plans of the school as they are intended to work. As it is today the pupils who are able to do the work on the farm and in the house are required to do more work than should be required. There is not sufficient emphasis on the training to be derived from this school and too much emphasis on the necessity of producing sufficient to keep the institution running.

(13) The education of the children is linked up with the progress in general on the reserve and thus many other factors on each reserve affect the efficiency of the work of the schools. Where parents are able to work at home on the reserve, the attendance at school is not subject to the same interruption as in the cases where the parents have to leave the reserve for certain periods in order to earn a living.

The progress of the people and their outlook on the future has an important effect on their attitude towards the school. The responses of the children to any educational plans for their improvement is affected favourably or adversely in an important measure by this attitude of the folks at home. Every improvement in the life of the adults will lead to better results in our schools. In this field the Indian Agents generally give good service. Their main efforts appear to be spent in plans for the improvement of living and working conditions among their charges. This work has an important bearing on education: as these conditions improve, the parents will give increasing sympathy and moral support to the work of the schools, creating a more receptive attitude among the pupils. It may be possible to develop a co-ordination of the work of the Agent and the teacher so that each will aid the other in the main objective--to develop good citizens of Canada among our Indian people.

RECOMMENDATIONS

II. Mount Elgin Residential School

(1) The enrolment is too small for continued operation under present plans.

(a) The per capita payment is insufficient to maintain the school;

(b) This forces too much labour on the pupils (profit rather than educational policy becomes the object of this work).

(c) This condition is aggravated by the presence of so many younger children.

(d) The staff has been reduced; schools have been reduced; and the work increased for all.

It is but fair to note that these conditions have been aggravated by the present general prosperity due to war conditions when older pupils find jobs so easily. We doubt that these conditions will be permanently as bad as they are now, but we do believe that they will continue to affect the efficiency and usefulness of the school.

(e) The enrolment has been reduced also by the policy of sending only pupils from broken or disrupted homes.

(2) The main building is still serviceable and can be modernized for the use indicated below. The old school building possibly should be abandoned and removed.

(3) Eventually a new modern class-room building as suggested below should be provided.

(4) Agents on other reserves intimate that the orphans and children from disrupted homes can be taken care of in other homes on the reserve. This leaves a small number from the Caradoc Agency who could be accommodated at Mohawk Residential School.

(5) We recommend that Mount Elgin Residential School be closed as such and used as indicated below.

III. Senior School

(1) We recommend that a Senior School partly Residential and partly Day be established at Mount Elgin.

(2) This school will accommodate Grades VI or VII to X from Caradoc Agency as Day Pupils and from outside agencies as Residential Pupils. Residential privileges may be open to Caradoc pupils.

(3) Pupils from Grades I to V or VI on these reserves to attend day school.

(4) Course of Study--Grade VII or VII to X--Courses of Ontario modified so as to include much vocational training--

Boys: Agriculture, General Shop, Motor Mechanics.

Girls: Home Economics, Home Nursing, Sewing (Dressmaking as well as mending),Gardening and care of Poultry.---

in addition to a good general training in English, Mathematics, Health Practices, Science of ordinary living, Social Studies (including Indian Life and History) Art, Music, Physical Training and Recreation.

For the pupils having the necessary academic ability and ambition, special provision for qualifying for entrance to the higher grades in local High Schools should be available.

The practice in Agriculture, Gardening, Poultry Management, Home Economics, Sewing etc. may be provided by participation in the work on the farm, and in the Residence school dormitories. Emphasis to be placed on the training rather than the profits from the work.

(5) The development of responsibility in the Senior pupils can be obtained or at least encouraged by giving them responsibilities to discharge in connection with work and supervision of younger pupils and as leaders in social and religious activities and in games and in recreative activities.

(6) Day pupils as well as residential pupils will be required to work on the farm on Saturdays and holidays as needed. This work has a double purpose--part of the training and part of the price of the opportunity of attending...

IV. A Voluntary Enrolment

Your committee looked for a change of atmosphere about the whole institution. We hope for the day when Indian parents and pupils will desire to attend such a senior school and count it a privilege to be admitted--one which can be held only by proper conduct and steady progress and application to studies. Instead of having to bring pupils back after they have run away from the institution, the principal may discharge those who refuse to conform to proper school practice. This will be the worst punishment that can be applied to the students of the future.

We realize that this vision involves great and important changes, but do not consider the ideal impossible of attainment.

We further believe that the adoption of this report in its entirety will lead to a new day in Indian Education not only on the Muncey and Oneida reserves but throughout Ontario Reserves and possibly all over Canada. We realize that we have merely indicated the way that others will develop and improve the ideas suggested far beyond either our conception or our ability to conceive means of improving the schools devoted to Indian Education.

We trust that the difficulties lying in the way of adoption may not discourage those in authority from daring to make the attempt to carry out our suggestions.

154. 15 September 1943 Joblin
NOTES ON THE SURVEY OF THE EDUCATION OF INDIAN CHILDREN IN WESTERN ONTARIO
Interviews

Mrs. **** and daughter-in-law; Oneidas

Granddaughter, ****, in Mt. Elgin 2 years, formerly at day-school; other children had been unkind to her at school; more likely because grandparents could not afford to provide for her. Average home, well kept grounds; g-father unable to work out, g-mother hard worker. Invalid aunt upstairs.

Mrs. **** with baby girl. Father labourer; mother little schooling, wants girl to go to day school, so as to have her home. No criticism of Res. school from either.

**** Oneida. Veteran. Schooling at Mt. Elgin, High and Model school both there. Taught on home reserve till the war. Later moved to St. Thomas in order to educate children. Two sons in forces, one a sergeant. Daughter teaching school, now at River Settlement school, Muncey. Younger children now attend Day School. Lovely family. The School should provide an opportunity for any pupils who are capable of taking high school. Favourable; splendid interview.

Mrs. **** grandmother of **** at Mt. Elgin. Very poorly, unable to provide home, though otherwise a good home. **** attended Day school until Mrs. **** too poorly. **** also a pupil of Res. School. Favourable.

****; veteran; older members of family now in army,

attended white schools near reserve. Did better. **** no longer at school; sent to Mt. Elgin because day school teacher so irregular, and too far to go to #3 through wet grass. Wanted to send her to #1. No criticism of Mt. Elgin, but of management of Day Schools, and teachers. Pensioner, able to provide; average home. Should attend Day School.

****; Chippewa. Small one-roomed house; inadequate. Labourer. Critical of School management, but based on rumours. Mrs. ****'s children are content, and no criticism. Girl and boy by former marriage. Likely to send small girl to day school, now that they have a home. No place for pupils to come to from Res. School. Money there wasted if this is necessary...

Mrs. ****; widow. Older sons attended Mt. Elgin, now in army. Father was unable to provide for them. Four small children now, three going to day school. Favourable to both schools; children home if possible.

****; veteran. wife in Ontario hospital. Received education at Mt. Elgin. Praised his training in handling horses; better job. Now good pay. Two girls attended Mt. E. Oldest now going to High School in Detroit. Relatives there. Other girl still at MtE. No criticism of School. Favours vocational training.

Mrs. ****; widow. Large family grown up. younger girl **** at Mt.E. Quite critical of School, but evidence discounted because of her own life. Unfit to make good home for ten years.

Mrs. **** trying to care for four children and three small brothers, though only 20. Untidy; too much for her. Mother ostensibly away working; two small girls at Mt. Elgin. Lovely family until death of father few years ago. Responsibility evidently too much for mother...Should be made possible for mother to be at home.

Muncey Reserves, - on the whole very favourable to Mt. Elgin; ex-pupils especially appreciative of its contribution to their lives. Noticeable that more and more of younger children being sent to Day School, - improved economic conditions make this possible; and improvement in day schools also in recent years. Most of serious criticism is by persons who might be termed professional criticizers; on hearsay, and for personal grievances; very little of it based on first-hand knowledge. Even so, criticism was of management, not of the method of education or the type of school.

Agent, in the main, opposed to Mt. Elgin, or at least not very sympathetic. Tactless in the matter of fostering rumours and criticism. Also to be noted that some white folk contribute to the 'underground' movement, to curry favour with Indians. Fortunately, the Commission was not much influenced by this type of carping criticism.

Sept 16

Visit to Six Nations Reserve at Brantford.

Three Day Schools, -

#2. Two rooms; splendid building, well kept; fitting out a library. Misses Jamieson, capable. Six pupils in grade IX.

#4. One room. Miss Captain. 5 grade VIII. Attractive school and grounds well kept.

#11. Two rooms. Mr. J. C. Hill and Mrs. Lickers. Most efficient, beautiful grounds. 4 grade IX, 3 grade VIII. Mr. Hill highly intelligent, great community worker; married, lives at school; grounds show benefit of summer care. Mr. Hill favours Day Schools; home life possible; learn responsibility there. Recognizes need for Res. Schools for children who have no adequate homes. Would like to have more manual work in Day Schools. Would then make Res. School unnecessary for most of his people. Attendance 85%. Believes this is up to the teacher.

Day Schools here are at their best, and hardly to be compared in some ways with other reserves. No manual work. Many go on to High school in surrounding towns (Receive tuition and $100 a year from Dept). As many as 60 attending in one year. All 16 teachers on reserve are Indian, and all received early training in Day Schools. From one to four attend normal school, and have been so far absorbed by the schools there...General agreement that where homes are suitable and the Day Schools up to their jobs, as here, that this is far better than the artificial situation of the Res. School. But always brought up short by fact of children who have not an adequate home. Some of opinion that many of these could be cared for by relatives, if there were some financial aid; this would be much less expensive than the per capita and administrative cost at a res. School. On the whole it appears that the number of children needing a res.school is steadily diminishing in Western Ontario. No-one has yet agreed that we can dispense with the Res. school entirely.

Some opinions as expressed in discussions.

Colonel Randall.

Disapproves strongly of some aspects of management in Res.Schools; admits that this may be partly due to insufficient grant. Care of buildings should be improved. Nevertheless considers the Res. school indispensable in an improved form.

This improvement could be made at little extra cost as far as management is concerned; repair of buildings might cost a good deal, but should be done. Suggests possibility of smaller schools and higher quality. Same amount spent on smaller plant; about 60% of present number. Strongly in favour of cadet corps in schools; discipline.

Dr. Dorey.

Experience of the church is that most economical school is that with pupils numbering from 125 to 150. This gives rise to possibility of having one school for all of Western Ontario instead of two smaller ones. General agreement that one good school could take care of reduced number of pupils needing Res.school; this the more true if proper method used in sending children to Res, S. Many now who ought to be kept at home. Trying to make up their number.

No difficulty in Western Ontario re denominations. Finest possible cooperation possible with Anglicans.

A few trained persons could easily take place of older pupils in doing the necessary work, and cost no more.

Older children, instead of being released at 16, should remain for two years and be monitors, take responsibility. Possibly being paid for their work. Very important to help them in this period of adjustment. Gradual slackening off of rigid discipline and taking of responsibility.

One school for children needing a home; another for older children and vocational work, to supplement day schools, beginning, possibly, at Grade VI or twelve years. Mr. Hill. Advocates school board for a reserve, so that Indians may take responsibility and become more interested in the work of the school and the education of their children. Six Nations had done this until later years. And done well. Agreed that some Reserves could not do this as yet. But most felt that it was certainly a worthwhile objective. Criticised management, but approved of school in principle.

Sept 21

Cape Croker

Economic conditions excellent...Agent, Tuffnell, of opinion that they are able to care for all their children in homes. Three day schools; C.Croker with Cath.teacher, pupils mixed; present teacher capable; Sidney Bay, Indian Cath.teacher without qualifications; church influence. Port Elgin; large building with residence, Gladys Park; excellent character; inspector's report only fair.

Grade VIII, average one a year from reserve.

Sept 22.

Saugeen

Agent, Mr. Robertson, 16 years on this reserve. Not rated very highly. Believes that children could be cared for on reserve. Band funds quite good. Labourers, much of land worthless at present. Economic conditions fairly good. No relief problem through depression.

Three schools; all with residences, none used.

visit French Bay; Gladys Elder. Favourable report.

Scotch Settlement, Stuart Wells; only fair.

Saugeen; Mr. Knechtel; 17 years; no heart; unsatisfactory Only one or two grade VIII as a rule.

Southampton near enough for High School.

Day Schools have room for many more pupils; present attendance down in almost all schools.

Again, need is for teachers with interest in life of the people, and living on reserve.

Visited Chief Ritchie (?) and Constable Sidney Solomon. Critical of Day Schools; teachers and means of appointing them. Appreciative of Res.School, but inclined to think that Day Schools properly staffed and run would meet their needs

Sept.23

Kettle Point

One School; Miss Fairservice; experienced with Indians in Manitoba; efficient...

Whole reserve apparently solidly behind Mt. Elgin. Many would be sending children now, if permitted. This due in part to inefficiency of past teacher over number of years.

Visited Mrs.****, grandchildren in Mt.E. Lovely old lady, well-kept home. Father, ****, also visited, unable to provide home, Wife... dead...

Mrs. ****...attended Mt. Elgin 1/2 years; most favourable; bright, responsive; with her own opinions; would send her five children to Mt.E. if allowed. Financially able to care for them, as are all at this reserve.

Mrs ****; good home; capable woman; own family grown up and doing well; all sent to Mt. Elgin, after attending day school till about 13 years. Very favourable to Res. School.

****; young ex-chief...capable; 7 children; would like to send them all to Mt. E. But earning big money and able to provide. Need training as tradesmen, so as not to be merely labourers; hard to get children to school in winter; also, some parents do not have adequate lunches for children; affects attendance.

Mr and Mrs ****; very favourable.

Many here have new homes; due to moving from Stoney; Economic conditions excellent.

Sarnia; Morley McCracken, capable agent. Visited school; Mrs. G.E.Thompson, second year; favourable impression on Mr. Young. Class-room well filled. Children alert and well-dressed.

Indians well-off; band funds considerable; employed in U.S. and in rubber plant etc. Splendid homes.

Mrs. ****; **** graduated last year, working in home across line. **** still at Mt. Elgin. Favourable to Res.School; training for domestics.

Mrs ****; poor home; children need Res.school.

Mrs.****; wife of chief...Fine home. Attended Mt.E. Favourable

Can attend H.S. at Sarnia. Tuition $131

Sept 23.

Walpole Island

Visited both schools; Mrs. George, Indian;favourable.

Mrs.Ross and two-roomed school, favourable

Children can attend H.S. in Wallaceburg, and few do.

Economic conditions good; work in Algonac. Great possibilities for farming.

Mrs. ****;...Four children in Mt. E. Quite critical of Principal; but evidence largely discounted. Poor home.

Mrs. ****; 5 children. Small. attending Day School. Mother attended Brandon and Edmonton. Favours Res. School; good example of training received; good personality. New home.

Mrs. ****; attended Mt. Elgin; very capable, fine character. Two daughters attended Res. School, after 13

years, doing well...
Agent, Mr. Daley, former teacher; critical of management of Muncey. Need of vocational training.

155. 20 May 1943 Jessie Seneca

I, Jessie Seneca, of the town of Strathroy...married woman, (formerly of the Muncey Reserve) MAKE OATH AND SAY:

1. That I am the mother of Loraine Tooshknig who was formerly a student at the Mt. Elgin Institute, and she has informed me that the following conditions exist at the said School which is under the principalship of Mr. Strapp.

2. That Mr. Strapp has two storerooms for food; one for himself and staff, and the other for the children of the school. Often the food is poor, the bread being stale and often mouldy, and the cereals, oatmeal and cornmeal often wormy, and the milk often sour. That my said daughter took her turn in the work of the kitchen and has seen these conditions, of which she has informed me. That my daughter was hungry all the time because the food was so unpalatable.

3. That when Miss Smith was at the Institute, who saw that the food was wholesome that was furnished to the children, when she was on kitchen duty.

4. That when Mr. Strapp would punish the girls he would raise their skirts when whipping them. And that my said daughter Loraine has a scar on her wrist which she received when punished by the said Strapp. And that after the girls had retired Mr. Strapp would go to their bedrooms with a flashlight and flash the light in the girls faces.

5. That I understand there was a Miss Prentice teaching in the school who was very kind to the students, and for this reason she was dismissed by Mr. Strapp. And that I believe the school would be much more efficiently conducted if Mr. Strapp was removed from the principalship of the said Institute.

Sworn before me At the town of Strathroy in the County of Middlesex this 25th day of May, 1943. A W. Bixel

156. 7 June 1943 Annie Deleary

I, Annie Deleary, of the Muncey Reserve...Married woman, MAKE OATH AND SAY:

1. That I am the mother of Faye Kechego who was a student at the Mount Elgin Institute...

2. That the food was of such a poor quality that she could not eat the same, and was always complaining of being hungry. The oatmeal and soya beans were not properly cooked, and the milk they had was often turning sour, and she was always begging me to bring bread or other food for her to eat.

3. That while she was at the said School she got athlete's foot which she did not have before going to the said school, and which I have been unable to cure since she has come home.

4. That the children were very severely strapped for very trifling offences, and my said daughter says that she has often seen other girls with swollen wrists after such a strapping.

5. That the clothing supplied to my said daughter was not sufficient to keep her warm in cold weather, and that she was compelled to loan the good clothing which I had purchased for her for special occasions, to other students in the school, and it was often returned much the worse of wear

6. That I believe it would be in the best interests of the pupils in the school if the principal Mr. Strapp were removed from the said Institution and another principal appointed, who would be interested in the welfare of the children in the school, as I feel Mr. Strapp has no interest in them.

Sworn before me...7th day of June, 1943. A.M. Bixel...

157. 7 June 1943 Annie Waddilove

I, Annie Waddilove, of the Muncey Reserve...married woman, MAKE OATH AND SAY:

1. That I am the guardian of Mildred Fisher, who was a student at the Mt. Elgin Institute...

2. That the said Mildred Fisher complained of always being hungry as they never got sufficient to eat, and that the food was cooked so poorly that they could hardly eat what was often put before them, especially the oatmeal and soya beans. And that if they complained about the food they were strapped by the principal, Mr. Strapp.

3. That the milk given the children to drink was often turning sour.

4. That Mildred Fisher informs me that at one time in going to the toilet on the lower floor, as the one on the upper floor was not in working condition, she had to pass through a dormitory occupied by the girls, and that she saw one of the boy students of the school in this dormitory sitting on the side of the bed of one of the girls.

5. That the said Mildred Fisher informs me that the girls are severely whipped or strapped for very trivial offences, and they are warned by him that they must not talk about the conditions at the school when visiting their homes.

7. That the said Mildred Fisher was lousy on several occasions while in the school, and she has athlete's foot which she got at the school and which I have been unable to cure since she came home.

8. That I consider it would be in the best interests of the children who are in attendance at the Mt. Elgin Institute, if Mr. Strapp was relieved of his duties there, as I feel he is not at all interested in the welfare of the children in attendance, and a new principal appointed for the school.

Sworn before me...7th day of June, 1943. A.M.Bixel...

158. 8 June 1943 Charlotte French

I, Charlotte French, of the Indian Reserve at Muncey... married woman, MAKE OATH AND SAY:

1. That my daughter Beulah French was in attendance at the said Mt. Elgin Institute.

2. That during her stay in the said school she often complained of the oatmeal served to them, and was always hungry while in the school and often asked me to bring her something to eat.

3. That during her stay in the school she had a very painful toe caused by an ingrown toe nail. She came home from the school at the summer holidays, but I thought she was given attention at the school and when the holidays were over, she went back to the school hoping to have the toe attended to. The year passed and when she came home at the next summer holidays, her toe was in a worse condition than the year before. I then took her to another Doctor who said she would have to rest before the toe could be operated on. Before this could be done the school authorities sent the Police to my house and insisted that my daughter return to the school. I did not want her to go because I felt that she would not be cared for; however, they promised to give her more careful treatment. When I went to the school with my said daughter, the principal, Mr. Strapp, was extremely rude to me. My daughter should have been given medical long before she received the same, and suffered needlessly and longer than she should have. And that as I believe that Mr. Strapp has not the interest of the children in mind, I am of the opinion that it would be very much better if he were removed from the school and a more sympathetic person in charge.

Sworn before me...8th day of June, 1943. A. M. Bixel

159. 21 June 1943 Mary Seneca

I, Mary Seneca, of the Muncey Indian Reserve...Married woman, MAKE OATH AND SAY:

1. My adopted daughter, Alberta Seneca, has been a student at...Mt. Elgin Institute.

2. That when Alberta asked for a pair of running shoes which she needed very badly, and went up to a teacher, Miss Burnfield...to get the running shoes, several other students went with Alberta, who got the shoes, and Miss Burnfield asked why all the girls came up. She was very cross, and Alberta was the last to leave her room, and as she did so, Miss Burnfield hit her with a clenched fist, leaving a black mark on the child's back.

2. That Alberta informs me that the food is not palatable. The milk is often sour, and lately there has not been any variety in the vegetables.

3. That when my husband and I visited Alberta at the said school, she informed me that afterwards she was called to the office of the principal, Mr. Strapp, who questioned her as to what she told her parents, and what they said to her.

4. That it would be in the best interests of the children at the said school, if Mr. Strapp were removed, and a person of more sympathy and understanding were employed in

his place, who would see that the other teachers were also kind to the children.

..sworn before meE...21st day of June/43...A.M. Bixel...

160. 24 June 1943 Down

RESOLUTION No 1. CHIPPEWAS OF THE THAMES

It was moved by Jason Fox seconded by Wilfred Riley that in view of the sworn statements of complaints made by some of the pupils of the Mt. Elgin Institute against Rev. Mr. Strapp of his illtreatment to the pupils of the said Mt. Elgin Institute that an investigation be called by the Department of Indian Affairs and that all the Bands be notified of said investigation in view of the fact that nearly all the Indians in the Province have children attending said school one time or another and that the investigation be held at the Chippewa Council Hall, Caradoc Reserve.

Carried

...Resolution No. 1, with sworn statements attached, is the result of numerous complaints and continued runaways from the said school. It is thought, locally, that there must be some reason for this condition.

From private information received, I am advised that a circularization of the Bands interested, throughout Ontario, is being made. However, as local resident Agent, I refrain from any further comments, until you have had time to examine the complaints.

161. 12 January 1944 MacDonald to DIA

...have a lot of Indians cutting wood for me & today met in with a Grandchild of one of my employees (who skipped away from the Institution on the threat made by Principle staff.) I heard the boys story & then went up to the institute & heard the authorities story. Then came back and persuaded the boy to go back and then drove him back.

I belive its time for a check up off Mount Elgin Institute Munsey. If half the boys story is right I still am glad I am not an Indian. Will be glad to give you any information I have if you are interested.

162. 12 June 1944 Memorandum from Dorey

The Department intends to implement the Report of the Commission, - certainly so far as the closing of Mount Elgin as a residential school and the establishment of a Senior School are concerned.

This means the building of proper classroom accommodation, but, due to lack of materials, it is impossible to say when this will be done.

This also means the building of a residence, - perhaps not so large as the present one.

...these two things do not necessarily belong together; that is to say, it is absolutely essential that a new classroom be built as soon as possible, but the present building would be suitable, temporarily.

I pass on my judgment as follows:

1st. There would be a smaller number of pupils to be accommodated, and the pupils would be older.

2nd. There would be no very small children, and consequently the present health hazard would be to some extent, at least, mitigated.

3rd. The only reason that I have for even suggesting that the present building should continue is that, to my mind, the first thing the Department must undertake is the replacement of buildings that have been burned; and the next thing is the very much needed extension of buildings. These will certainly take all the money that the House of Commons is likely to vote for some years - even after the war.

4th. It seems obvious that if the whole school were closed now, it would leave altogether too heavy a burden on the present accommodation and a lot of children would be left without schooling at all.

5th. On the basis of the above, it is agreed that we should continue to operate as at present, with the definite understanding that whoever the new man is who is nominated to the Department, he will distinctly understand that it is for a limited period, on the present basis...it would be four years before anything would be done.

6th In the meantime, it is imperative that there be a clear formulation of steps which must be undertaken in working out the policy. It cannot be put into effect all at once; indeed it would be very much better if the changes could be made gradually. In any case, the Indians should be advised of what is proposed.

163. 14 June 1944 Hoey to Strapp
...Inspector Young...reports very favourably on the work of the teachers and also mentions the improvements that have been effected during the year. He recommends....

"The back halls need painting. The window leading to the fire escape should be replaced with doors equipped with a panic-bar. A couple of steps leading up to this door would enable small children to escape safely.

The girls' dormitory now appears dingy in comparison with the boys'..."

164. 16 June 1944 Dorey to Hoey
We beg to nominate for the position of Principal Rev. S. H. Soper, M.A. Mr. Soper is now a minister at Parry Sound but he has had considerable experience in the mission field in West China. On that field he was in charge of a large school for boys, which has many of the same characteristics as our Indian schools in Canada. The training followed agricultural lines, and in this Mr. Soper was quite successful. He graduated from the University of Toronto in 1912, but later took his M.A. in Rural Sociology.

It is our considered judgment that Mr. Soper can do a very fine piece of work, not only in carrying on the work

of the School, but in making possible co-operation between various persons who are interested in the programme of Indian education. It may be of particular interest to you that one of his projects in West China had to do with the introduction of a special breed of goats to provide milk for the Chinese children. He ought to feel at home on the Muncey Reserve...

165. 16 June 1944 Hoey to Dorey
...I must express regret that we were unable, at our conference with the Deputy Minister, to reach a more definite decision on the status and future of the Mount Elgin Institute. I want to state quite definitely that this school has given me a great deal of worry and anxiety, and...the reports on file by officers of this Branch and by public school inspectors, in respect to the general condition of the buildings, fire hazard, etc., are, to say the least, very disturbing.

The condition of this building is due almost wholly to the limited funds at the disposal of the officials of this Branch for the repair and upkeep of residential schools during the last 15 year period. It appears to me to be somewhat difficult, even with the assistance of Inspector Young, to work out an educational program at this school, unless we have definite information with respect to the amount of money that is likely to be placed at our disposal for the construction and upkeep of Indian day schools during the 10 or 15 year period. What I am afraid of, in the case of Mount Elgin, is that it may be kept open and in operation in its present dilapidated condition almost indefinitely. It is my ambition, however, to do everything humanly possible to adjust this particular matter during the brief period I may remain in the Department.

...I would like to work out, with Inspector Arnell, the Indian Agent and the newly appointed Principal, an arrangement with respect to the operation of the school farm and the use of certain farm buildings. I would also like to investigate for myself the suitability of the old building, or part of the old building, for dormitory accommodation, should the money be available to proceed with the construction of an up-to-date, well equipped classroom building...

166. 25 July 1944 Down Survey
..to take you on an imaginary tour
...Building No. 1...is a large barn...in first class condition throughout and fully equipped to house a large number of any type of farm animal.

...Building No. 2...is a T-shaped barn...It is in first class condition and especially equipped with steel stanchions and steel stalls to house approximately 100 head of cattle. It is, without doubt, one of the most up-to-date barns in Western Ontario.

...Building No. 3...an L-shaped building 30' by 50' and 30' by 60'. The

30′ by 50′ is in a dilapidated, unsafe condition and should be demolished. The 30′ by 60′ is an implement shed in a good state of repair.

...Building No. 4...is a brick building...The order here is confusion but at some time it has been used as a general repair for farm machinery. It is in need of major repairs.

...Building No. 5...is an all steel, dirt floor implement shed in A1 condition throughout.

...Building No. 6...is equipped exclusively for horses having fourteen individual stalls and one box-stall. It is in first class condition.

...Building No. 7...is used as a general store house and the raising of early chickens. Some work on the outside brick is necessary to put this building in good repair.

...Building No. 8...frame henhouse in good condition.

The water system, throughout, is supplied from springs located on Indian property and is, I think, under long term lease. It is piped and pumped into pressure tanks and as far as is known, it has never failed.

Root storage facilities consist of two rooms...both dry and suitable for any type of storage; also, one room...the smell here is very bad and the place is musty and wet. However its location lends itself readily to drainage and I think that is all it needs to correct the condition.

This completes our tour and general survey of the farm buildings...they constitute one of the finest and most up-to-date set of farm buildings in Western Ontario. Under proper management and with the leased lands attached they could be made to serve the full requirements of the Mt. Elgin Residential School, not only in the matter of providing food for the pupils and staff but one of the most up-to-date instructional centres for all Indians in Ontario, west of Toronto.

167. 25 July 1944 Down

...The purpose of my visit was to inspect the principal's quarters and make a survey of the farm buildings. My inspection, however, owing to Mr. Soper's desire and his sincere demonstration of will to cooperate, was much more intensive than I had intended. I am therefore, passing on, in the form of a memorandum, a survey of the school buildings used exclusively for the accommodation of staff and pupils together with a few suggestions that would brighten and add to the comfort of all in residence.

In the main building...the girls' dormitory...needs brightening up. Paint will do this but of course it will not repair the floors, ceilings and sanitary system, all of which are major repair jobs.

My particular attention was drawn to the exits leading to the fire escapes. These exits are in the form of double sash windows and in every case, throughout the whole dormitory system, these exits were padlocked. I asked if this were the general procedure when all pupils were in residence and upon whose orders they were locked. I was told yes, upon orders of the retiring Principal; the reason being an endeavour to stop runaways. I registered strong disapproval with such a procedure and pointed out that it would be better to have runaways than have one child burned to death. I also pointed out that responsibility would rest directly with the person giving the order. I also stressed that fire exits and escapes should be unbarred by any obstruction and ready for immediate exit and escape at all times. I would suggest that I be authorized to have these padlocks immediately removed and that in the meantime consideration be given to having the windows removed and replaced with doors equipped with regular panic bars, as suggested in your letter of June 14th.

In the basement I visited the pupils' dining hall. This is one of the most depressing rooms in the main building. The air is foul, the lighting is poor and it is badly in need of brighter decorating. For air circulation, a built-in wall fan...would be a great improvement and have a beneficial effect of relieving the room of the musty staleness. Owing to its location in the basement the lighting cannot be improved by natural light but it can be considerably improved artificially by using larger wattage bulbs and the installing of two more lights. The present colour scheme is both dark and dingy and could be greatly improved by a new paint job. With these suggested improvements it would add new life and could not help but react favourably on the pupils.

Adjoining this hall is the kitchen, also various store rooms, wash rooms and play rooms all in need of various repairs, so much so that only a major repair job could be entertained.

Immediately behind the main building is...a two-story brick, 90′ by 36′, with exterior plastered walls. The north end of this building is bulging to the extent that, at the present time, it is being held in place by a work of art, namely, 2 by 8 planks. On the ground floor there are three classrooms all more or less in need of decorating and all in need of better lighting. Above the classrooms there are three apartments all in need of various repairs and decorating. These apartments are approached by outside, uncovered wooden stairs all in a very dangerous rotted condition. After a final inspection of the exterior and interior of this building I might recommend minor decorating but the logical recommendation would be complete demolition and rebuild.

To the south of this building is the laundry, 40′ by 30′. This is a two-story building in fair repair. The ground floor is equipped with regular laundry tubs and sinks and appears to be in good running condition. The second floor appears to have been used for anything one had a mind to do. It is dirty, untidy and smelly and is a glaring example of neglect.

Immediately south of this building is a frame building'...the Manual Training building. It is literally packed with benches and every type of hand tool and power machinery necessary to establish an up-to-date Manual Training Class. This is in a shameful state of willful neglect and shows an utter disregard for what must have been a sizeable expenditure.

In submitting this report please be advised that it is not in the form of criticism but rather an endeavour to satisfy Mr. Soper's wish for a complete inspection. It is also not without thought that you may consider some of the minor repairs. I have not gone into detail as to approximate cost of the repairs mentioned. There are too many little jobs, and materials would have to be purchased as one proceeded, but a rough estimate for material and labour would likely cover $500.00 This...would only cover minor repair jobs such as painting and papering. The major job...demolition and rebuild would still remain.

168. 11 September 1944 Hoey to Dorey
Re: Enrolment, Mount Elgin Institute

The records here indicate that a number of our residential schools throughout the Dominion are experiencing difficulty this year in securing the number of pupils for which per capita grants are allowed by the Department. This difficulty can be attributed, in part at least, to prevailing economic conditions. At the time of my visit to Brantford a few weeks ago, I was informed that Indians were earning $10.00 a day in the tobacco fields and that a great many teen-age boys were engaged in this work.

In addition to existing economic conditions, there appears to be on the part of certain Indian agents in southwestern Ontario a deep-seated prejudice against residential schools in general and the Mount Elgin Institute in particular. This opposition or prejudice was very much in evidence at the conference of agents held by Inspector Arnell in Toronto early in 1943. As a matter of actual fact, I was the only one at that conference who spoke at all in favour of the courses provided at our residential schools. I did my best, in my own peculiar and awkward way, to remind the Indian agents that we had twelve million dollars invested in residential school buildings and that in this critical period it was their duty and responsibility to see that these institutions...

169. 18 September 1944 Soper to Hoey

...Since receiving your communication of August 12th...I have tried to locate your communications of Jan 29th, Feb 24th and May 8th 1943 re Badges. I am interested in this matter...I have several boys who did splendid service here during the summer who may qualify.

...with the help of one sixteen year old boy and seven 9, 10 and 11 years we have taken in the harvest, 160 tons of hay, 500 bushels of Oats, 350 Bushels of Wheat 200 bushels of Barley, at the same time they have cared for the herd of 55 Holstines and forty hogs. We have taken off three hundred pounds of honey and more to come. We have put up nearly 1000 half gallon jars of tomatoes. It has been hard work, we are desperately under staffed.

Just now we have in residence 65 students. From all the Reserves served by this school ONE NEW STUDENT has been admitted so far, a seven year old girl from the Oka Band sent in by Frs, Brisbois. I am told that there are a number of students who would like to come if permission were granted.

...in my plans for vocational training I must have a larger enrollment of senior pupils. The grant from your department must be supplemented by very large income from the farm. I cannot afford to pay for extra help the work can only be done by boys and girls from 14 years and up. I know that these pupils of that age can now earn good wages and do not wish in many cases to leave their jobs and come to Residential School, but if all the Agents were to be convinced that by sending in here a larger enrollment of students that all students could then get the

training in art, music, machineshop, poultry, bee keeping, animal husbandry and a host of other things then it might be that we could carry out our program. As long as the agents regard this school as a Children's Aid Shelter only we will never be able to do the work we have in mind. Then again it follows that we cannot finance the school at all on less than one hundred and twenty students, nor can it be financed if we have one hundred and twenty, six to eleven years olds. We must have more students and we must have more twelve to seventeen year old students. We can only have these students if the agents are convinced that we are in dead earnest about vocational education.

I have done everything possible in my power to co-operate. The proof that my efforts to cooperate are appreciated is the recommendation of more students.

I have arranged with Mr. Long, our Farm Manager, to allow the Welfare Department of the Caradoc Agency to take over the building known as the Brooder House for the steaming of Willow Wands. This meant that Mr. Long has had to go to considerable trouble and some expense to fit up a Brooder house in our own Chicken House. However, we are more than glad to co-operate as we are assured that when this project is in operation our students will get the benefit of the training in making Willow Furniture. Here again it follows that if there is training to be obtained there must be students to take the training. Just now we have not enough senior students to do the house keeping for this great institution. We have a graduate Dietitian just out from Toronto University but she is so pressed with the actual work that very little time is left for teaching. With another twenty twelve to seventeen year old girls all the girls then could have more training as there would be enough to carry the work and attend school. The half day system demands a large staff and can only be efficient in an institution of this size on a minimum of One hundred and twenty students.

I regret to have taken so much of your time in giving you my rather superficial findings. I suppose that when I am here a longer time I may see things from a different standpoint, in the meantime we will do all we can to make this an efficient and happy home for the little folks entrusted to us.

170. 21 September 1944 Soper to Hoey

...while it is true that during the War Emergency bigger boys and girls will be needed in War Industry there must be a large number of younger children who might benefit by the training this school can give. As things now are the school must face an increasing deficit. We must properly provide for the students we have this will entail heavy percapita expenditures. When the enrollment increases we will be carrying a heavy indebtedness. This will prevent the provision of the equipment needed for their efficient work and will even leave us understaffed until the farm can earn a deficit of six to ten thousand dollars. Even a small enrollment of thirty more junior students would help tide over the present emergency.

We have just completed the cleaning and emptying of the Latrines. This is a job that is increasingly difficult, simply because it is no more the common procedure. The girl's latrine is 90 yards from the dormitory, the Boy's latrine is 120 yards from the dormitory. We must try to visualize just what that will mean in the matter of health of small children in winter weather. There is one bowl and two urinals for 40 boys, and two bowls for fifty girls. This whole matter may have to be held in abeyance for the duration but should be on the immediate post War program.

171. 25 October 1944 Soper to Hoey

...We are in desperate need of help here. Primary Teacher away sick, Mrs Rollins has had no holidays, has gone away for a week, our school cook has to leave can't stand the strain, we have no sewing Instructor. I have spent fifty dollars in advertising, I have written seventy letters to individuals and churches, I have kept the matter before the attention of Selective Service. If we cannot get a cook and a sewing instructor and if we have one more break in the staff we simply cannot carry on. I am desperate. Is there no way that we can get two women! ...I hesitate to worry you about a matter like this but I have done all possible and don't know what to do next...

172. 1944 Extract from Principal's Report

The pupilage of this school is considerably below the economic operating level at the present time, thus creating considerable difficulty in financing and in carrying out a proper training program. At fire drills it has been observed that these are very young pupils have some difficulty in getting over the window sills on to the platform of the fire escapes. I would suggest that the window sash be removed from the openings and that doors with proper panic latches.

173. 14 March 1945 Soper to Phelan

I am very much concerned with the condition of the shoes about here. There are numbers of pairs of shoes that could be repaired and used. I have had several boys working but the equipment is very poor...

174. 24 April 1945 Soper to Down

The outside latrine used by the girls of this school is simply a big cement pit with a house over it. When the pit is full the boys have to be put into it with buckets to dip it out.

In the past, I suppose that did not bother people. Today, with the lack of help and different attitudes of mind to this type of work it becomes increasingly difficult. The boys load and draw barn yard manure all day long without protest, but this other...very difficult.

175. 4 May 1945 Down to IAB

I attach herewith several letters recently received from the Rev. Mr. Soper...No. 1 refers to the installation and repair of the water-system in the main cow barn...If the institution is to continue under its present set-up, or any other set-up in which the cow barn is to be used, the repair job is...very essential...

No. 2...roof of the building...in bad condition but not serious...I suggested to Mr. Soper that if the Department approved of this expenditure, would it not be possible with his farm help and the aid of the older boy pupils to do the work under an educational project. He thought so. If this building is to remain for any purpose at all, the request should be given consideration.

No. 3 refers to the existing condition of the latrines. Mr. Soper explains, but does not know or suggest an answer to the problem. You will have guessed, of course, that he refers to the outside privies which the pupils are made to use during the day. His letter is disgusting in itself as I feel that such places, especially in an institution of this type, should not be left until they are full before emptying. To attempt to remodel or suggest an up-to-date sanitary system for an institution, housing approximately 125 persons, with its present water supply, is a major engineering job; and I would not attempt to discuss the proposition until a competent engineer had explored the possibilities...the system complained of is not out of order, it being obvious that there is nothing to get out of order. It is merely a matter of cleaning out. There are bathrooms available in the main building at all times for the staff, and night latrines for the pupils. Before I would seriously discuss the matter I would want to know the future plans coupled with an engineer's report...

176. 2 June 1945 Dorey to Hoey

...The financial situation...is getting worse. The overdraft has increased...seems obvious that there will be increased difficulty in keeping up...pupilage, and we certainly cannot continue to operate at the present...

177. 7 June 1945 Dorey Memo

1. <u>Mount Elgin</u> - Discussed with Mr. Hoey the financial situation which arises from lack of pupillage. Told him that the School could not possibly operate on basis of 100 pupils, which is present enrollment. Further, that operation of family allowance would probably mean smaller attendance next year. I also pointed out:

(1) That there was an undue proportion of small children who were either orphans or came from homes with undesirable surroundings; that the modern method of looking after such cases was by adoption or by having them taken care of in foster homes, and that, with the operation of family allowances, this could be done in the case of Indians.

(2) That Agents in Southern Ontario were against the School.

(3) That the policy of the Department looked to a radical change at Muncey.

(4) That there was scarcely room in Southern Ontario for both Mohawk Institute and Mount Elgin.

Mr. Hoey more or less agreed with this diagnosis.

He said he thought Mt. Elgin would have to continue for another year and promised to give further thought to the financial situation.

He told me something of the difficulties the Department was having with Archbishop Seager, who had thrown a monkey wrench into the negotiations with The New England Company, who own the Mohawk School but who can no longer support it.

In any event, Mr. Hoey has instructed Col. Randle, the Superintendent of Six Nations, to see Archbishop Seager and say that on the basis of the negotiations with the New England Company:-

1. The principalship has been offered to Mr. Jos. C. Hill, who is now teaching a School on the Reserve, and who is competent to handle it.

2. That Mr. Hill will be assisted by an Advisory Council composed of Col. Randle, a representative of the Indians, and an Anglican Clergyman.

3. That Religious Instruction will be given by an Anglican clergyman.

My opinion is that this is a very sound move.

Hill is an Indian - he is a very good teacher; his wife is a fine woman, they are both qualified teachers.

It will give the Indians a chance to cooperate. If the Archbishop opposes this, the Department may still go on with it, but if he does, he has put the Church in a bad light with the Indians.

In view of the above and that Hill is United Church, it would be my view that, if this goes through, we should during the next year approach the Government -

(1) To put into effect the Young Report

(2) To take all Protestant children needing institutional care into the Mohawk Institute, - at the same time adding a United Church representative to the Advisory Council and making provision for religious teaching by a representative of our Church.

178. 4 August 1945 Soper to Secretary DIA

The following Students have passed the High School Entrance from this chool;

Arlene Mcghey, Caradoc.
Velma Elliott, Cape Croker.
Iris George, Kettle Point.
Vena Monague, Christian Island.
Arnold Henry, Caradoc.
Alma French, Caradoc.

I am expecting some of these students to attend High School, all have to leave home and pay board in distant centres. What grant in aid is given to them? Is that grant received direct from your office or from the Agent concerned?

179. 9 August 1945 Phelan to Soper

Our usual procedure in cases such as this is to have application forms prepared for each applicant...enclosing a supply of the necessary forms which you should have completed and sent to the Agent concerned.

...we require the agent to show what amount the applicant's parents or guardian are prepared to pay...if the Indian parent pays part of the cost he is much more interested in his child's education and will make certain that the child takes full advantage of the High School...

180. 5 September 1945 Soper to Down

...The other estimates for repairs to the steam boilers of the main building, and the furnace for the school building are absolute essentials. I have tried repeatedly to get repairs done before the cold weather sets in...I cannot accept responsibility for the health and well-being of students and staff of this institution unless these repairs...are made with the least possible delay.

181. 19 September 1945 Soper to Bush

...We now have in residence 105 children, the Government grant is $175 per capita. Last year we had one hundred students, giving us an income of $17,500. From this I paid to my staff eleven in all and including my own salary, $10,000 leaving $7,500. From this I had to feed, clothe and light and heat one hundred children for ten months, some of them for twelve months. This means that I have to earn the balance on the farm.

In time past when big boys and big girls came to the school this was possible. Today when we have 45 children under ten and only 3 who are sixteen, three fifteen and five thirteen it is an impossibility. I have just paid out over six hundred dollars for repairs to one tractor. These wee children have to earn that. There is no other source from which it can come. If I were to publish that fact some one would be hurt.

Just now we need potatoe peelers, bread slicers. But we are told that this is impossible. I want to say that something else is impossible. It is impossible for babies of this age to feed, clothe and wash for themselves. I cannot afford to employ help.

The War Assets people have abundance of the things we need and need desperately. But we cannot get them. We have not the money. But the children need just what can be obtained, and without cost, if we could touch the magic spring.

Children have to go out to the barns to the poultry house, out to do chores but I cannot afford proper protection for them.

We need a dental clinic and a throat clinic. Numbers of these children come from back settlements where medical aid is impossible.

The long winter evenings are coming. We have no games equipment. We need a moving picture projector.

Just think of having one hundred and twenty children to amuse seven nights a week for ten months of the year. We need equipment.

After I pay salaries I have just 20 cents a day from the grant to feed and clothe and warm and light the children. On top of that we have to pay all farm equipment repairs and transportation.

182. 3 October 1945 Soper to Phalen

...so many little children need every facility for health and well-being. I cannot see how, with the very insufficient staff that I am able to employ within the grant, we can adequately take care of health and recreation for so many little children...necessity of appointing a nurse...

183. 11 October 1945 Phelan to Dorey

...I am in receipt of the following report from Indian Agent Down:-

"After an inspection and discussion with Mr. Soper, we decided that nothing could be done in the way of temporary repairs. In fact the system is in perfect working order, only it is being used by impracticable people who do not realize that they are not on a city water supply and that the spring supply is very limited... However, the present trouble is caused through the excessive use of Toilet Tissue, and insufficient water under pressure. The first is a matter of common sense and education; the second is a matter for an engineering survey. Mr. Soper first suggested the installation of extra stools but, on the flushing of one stool, it took 7 minutes for the flush tank to refill itself, and in another dormitory, 15 minutes. I pointed out, and he agreed, that extra stools is not the answer. One could install a stool for each individual, but they would be useless without water. He then suggested chemical closets. My comments on such fixtures for an institution of the kind as the Mt. Elgin Residential School are not printable. However, this is his suggestion and is submitted for your consideration.

I feel that this matter is too complicated and involves too many questions, to be intelligently discussed by correspondence"...

184. 15 October 1945 Soper to Secretary, DIA

I have copy of letter written by Mr. Phillip Phelan, on October 11, with regard to the plumbing and toilet facilities in dormitories...in which...is a quotation from the communication sent...by Mr. G. W. Down. The fact of the matter is that trying to work within the grant, we have in residence 75 girls, many of whom are under 10 years of age, and new to the institution. These are all under the supervision of one matron. To say that these are impracticable people is not strictly according to the facts. There are physical limits to the whereabouts of any one person, and no amount of teaching and instruction in the proper use of the toilets will overcome the inadequacy of our water supply. To meet the desperate situation, we have placed ordinary scrub pails in the dormitories for the use of these little children. That may be impracticable, but it is meeting the situation, causing, however, needless work of a very unpleasant character. Now all this may not be printable, but printable or not, it is the fact.

There are a great many things about conditions around this building, and conditions under which little children have to live, which if printed and publicized would cause such a furore of indignation that someone would have to take cognizance of it, and that immediately.

It is impracticable, but also printable that we have here a great number of little children who need attention given to tonsils, adenoids and teeth. We are facing a long winter season, when all of these ills will take their toll of the health of the children, and consequently place an almost impossible burden upon our inadequate staff. I would like some practical suggestions from your department in this matter.

I would also like a clear definition from the Department as to what repairs and equipment may be charged to the Department, and what repairs and equipment must be earned by the labour of 10 and 11 year old boys. In a communication from your department sometime during the summer, I was informed that material for a hay-rack could not be granted by the Department because, forsooth, the wagon upon which the hay rack was to be placed was not the property of the Department. I had to save a crop. Every member of my staff works long hours under most adverse conditions, and the refusal of the Department to even pay for the material to make this hay-rack has brought this whole matter to a head. I wish to say that it is impracticable but it is nevertheless printable, that 8 and 10 year old boys should have to labour in order to pay for equipment to save the harvest.

I am convinced that nothing less than a complete and thoroughgoing investigation into the relationship between the school management, and the Department of Indian Affairs will make for efficiency. It is not asked that any educational institution pay, out of its own labour, for essential equipment. Why, therefore, should their be any distinction in the case of this school? I hope that in the very near future, we may have a clear understanding, in order that the staff may be able to give attention to the moral and academic side of the work. This can only be done, however, if we have the equipment to meet our needs.

185. 18 October 1945 Pratt to Taylor

...you request information regarding the Mount Elgin Indian Residential School, as outlined in a letter received by Mr. J. C. Bush from Reverend S. H. Soper...

The Mount Elgin Residential School is a very old building, having been originally built approximately 75 years ago. In the Fall of 1943 a survey was made of our educational requirements in southwestern Ontario, and at that time the opinion was expressed by the educationists whom we had engaged, that the Mohawk Institute at Brantford could handle all the Indian children from the reserves of southwestern Ontario requiring institutional care. The committee further recommended that the Mount Elgin Residential School be closed. However, the United Church authorities, under whose auspices this school has always been conducted, expressed a desire to have the school remain in operation for a further period, for the purpose of ascertaining if it were serving a real necessity.

In view of the age of the building, it is impossible to keep it in first-class condition, but the Department has endeavoured to keep up the repairs as far as our funds will permit.

I note that the Principal refers to lack of pupils. In the first place, it has always been our policy to have the Church interested recruit pupils, with the co-operation of the Indian agent. In the second place, as intimated in the first part of this letter, this school is not actually needed at the present time, as the number of children requiring institutional care has decreased.

I can assure you that departmental officials will continue to give sympathetic consideration to the requirements of the Mount Elgin School.

186. 22 October 1945 Hoey to Soper

...It is, I feel, unnecessary to state that I appreciate very fully the conditions existing at the Mount Elgin School. These conditions have been to me and, I feel sure, have been to the Secretaries of the Board of Home Missions of the United Church, a source of worry and annoyance ever since I entered the department nine years ago.

You refer in the concluding paragraph of your letter to a thoroughgoing investigation by representatives of the department and a representative of the United Church was held a few years ago. Certain recommendations were made at that time. Inasmuch, however, as the operation of the Mount Elgin Residential School appears to be related to the operation of the Mohawk Institute, it has not been possible for this reason and for a number of others to seriously consider the recommendations made by the members of the Committee of Inquiry. A few weeks ago, we learned that it is the intention of the New England Company of London, England, to send over a representative to study and report upon the future of the Mohawk Institute. It is my hope that immediately following this investigation we shall be in a position to work out a worthwhile educational program based upon the needs of the Indian population of Southwestern Ontario. In the meantime and until such a program is worked out, the operation and administration of the Mount Elgin Institute will require the exercise of the utmost patience and forbearance on the part of departmental officials, the Board of Home Missions of the United

Church and the Principal in charge. I am frankly of the opinion that it is a sheer waste of money to undertake worthwhile repairs at the present school. I have long since reached the conclusion that the school should be either closed or rebuilt.

187. 24 October 1945 Soper to Hoey

...We have now here in residence 124 children, and there are several more to come. This places a great tax upon our physical and spiritual resources. We are indeed glad to have so many little folk, and I am convinced that my present staff has the qualifications of character and ability needed to cope with the present situation. I am indeed fortunate to have such an exceptional group of fine people in the school...It will take time, and a great deal of patience to develop in these little folk the qualities and abilities needed to fit them for life after they leave school.

From my short experience with the people of the various reserves, served by this school, I am convinced that they have confidence in the staff of the school, and in spite of other attractions and advantages, they   are continuing to send to us such large numbers of children.

I want to thank you on behalf of my staff and students for your continued and deep interest in us, and I wish to assure you that now that I am assured that this school has a large place in your plans for the future, we will do all in our power to keep the buildings and equipment in such condition as will tide us over the present emergency.

We desperately need additional members on our staff, in order to keep up with the needs of so many little children, and I hope that within the very near future, ways and means will be found to enable us to have such an increased staff....

188. 14 November 1945 Scott to Phelan

...Yesterday, I had an opportunity to discuss somewhat hurriedly with Doctor Dorey not only the condition of the residential school itself, but steps that might be taken to provide reasonably up-to-date educational facilities for the Indians of the Caradoc Agency. Doctor Dorey feels, and I agree with him, that the department has at its disposal sufficient information to decide on a definite policy and that in fairness to the Church authorities this policy should be clearly outlined and submitted to the Church...He and I are both agreed that it would be a sheer waste of public funds to undertake extensive or substantial repairs to the present building.

189. 23 January 1946 Dorey to Hoey

...our Executive would like to know:-

1. Whether the Department would like to carry through in principle the recommendations of the Special Report made by Inspector Young and submitted February 18th, 1944. These are in general:

(a) The discontinuance of the Mount Elgin School as a

residential school as at present carried on.

(b) The taking care of the educational needs of the Indian people by the establishment of a Senior School on the Muncey Reserve...

(c) The taking care of the children that cannot, for various reasons be accommodated in day schools in a way that would be satisfactory to the Church authorities.

...there are on the Caradoc Reserve some children who would find it very difficult to get to school and for whom transportation should be provided; and that in attendance at the Mount Elgin School there are children whose parents are dead or who come from broken homes. In our conversations at various times, it has been suggested that these would be taken care of either by adoption or by being taken into an already existing school, such as the Mohawk Institute...this would probably entail careful supervision, either through the Children's Aid Society or through the appointment of an officer of the Department...

190. 24 January 1946 Hoey to Dorey

...It is our intention to discontinue the operation of the school as a residential school on or about June 30th. Provision has been made in the estimates now under consideration for the construction of a four-room Indian day school...Provision will be made for the transportation by bus of pupils living beyond walking distance of the school. It is our intention to make provision for orphan pupils either by adoption on the reserve or by enrolment at the Mohawk Institute or by the utilization of both these agencies...The decision reached with respect to the establishment of the consolidated school at Caradoc was based to some extent on the assumption that a fully qualified educationist would be nominated by you to act as principal of the school...

191. 27 July 1946 SCHOOL NEWS

A WEEKLY NEWS SHEET FOR THE CHIPPEWA;MUNCEY AND ONEIDA RESERVES...

Because of the closing of the Mt.Elgin Residential School and the lack of information concerning the plans for the future, there are many questions in your minds. It will be the chief purpose of this News Sheet to answer those question as soon as there are answers available for them. Your Director of Education, Rev E.E.M. Joblin, is particularly anxious that you should have a part in developing and carrying out any plans for the education of your young people. This means that you should have all possible information from time to time. At the earliest possible date, a public meeting will be arranged for the discussion of these matters. In the meantime, the News Sheet will try to fill the gap...

For the new school, the excavating has been completed and we are assured that the new building will be ready for use some time in the fall. The Director has recommended that the senior pupils begin their term at the proper time and carry on in the classrooms of the old building until the new school is ready...Transportation has been promised for those who need it...it is hoped that the new school will be responsible at least for pupils from Grade VII to X. It is quite important therefore that the Director be notified of those pupils who want to attend the school for the work of Grade IX or X...One of the main guiding principles of the new system is that the school programme should be adjusted to the needs of the pupils. You can help us to determine those needs. The Director will welcome your suggestions and opinions as to the educational needs of our young people.

...Mrs. Joblin and I would like to thank you for the warm welcome we have received...We look forward to many pleasant associations with you in...Church, School and Community. Rev. E. E. M. Joblin, M.A.,B.D

Facts and Figures - Mt. Elgin

1. 1911

The staff and salary paid is as follows:-

Principal	Rev. S. R. McVitty	1000.00
Teacher	Mr. J. R. Littleproud	480.00
Stockman	Mr. B. Bentley	400.00
Janitor & Gardener	Mr. C. Willsie	360.00
Farmer	Mr. Geo. Hill	525.00
Carpenter	Mr. J. Kapayo	420.00
Matron	Miss L. McKinley	300.00
Jr. Teacher	Miss M. McLachlin	300.00
Cook	Miss Annie Stover	240.00
Cook	Miss J. Penny	240.00

Financial Statement

	Receipts	Disbursements
Cash on hand, April 1, 1910		1450.21
Missionary Society	10,003.00	
Sale of Cattle	5,222.85	
Sale of Horses	2,117.50	
Sale of Hogs	1,474.53	
Sale of Cream	2,285.53	
Sale from Farm and Garden	1,311.36	
Sale of sundries	600.47	
Annuities	126.65	
Rent for Indians	500.00	
Salaries		4,068.08
Clothing		1,159.85
Food		1,957.66
Fuel and Light		753.24
Building and Repairs		180.71
House Equipment		1,751.96
Farm and Garden Stock		13,881.39
Transport, freight, etc.		123.26
Extra Labor		226.10
Miscellaneous		909.90
Balance in Bank, March 1911		139.50
	25,151.65	25,151.65

2. 1913

STAFF, and Salaries paid

Principal,	Rev. S. R. McVitty,	1,200.00
Teacher,	Mr. J. R. Littleproud	700.00
Stockman,	Mr. Wm. Bomford	600.00
Carpenter,	Mr. John Kapayo,	600.00
Farmer,	Mr. E. J. Witherden,	500.00
Blacksmith,	Mr. E. M. Effrie,	500.00
Matron,	Miss McKinley,	400.00
Music Teacher	Miss May Cosgrove,	275.00
Cook,	Miss Sarah Johnston,	275.00
Teacher,	Miss Mary James,	250.00
Teacher,	Miss Rena David,	250.00
	Total	5,550.00

RECEIPTS

Cash on hand April 1st.,1912	206.62
Government grant	10,000.00
Board bill for carpenters	592.25
Miscellaneous,	209.30
Refund of rent from Government	753.00
Farm and garden,	9,758.86

EXPENDITURES

Salaries,		5586.86
Clothing,		1130.36
Food,		2516.51
Fuel and light,		1108.01
Building and repairs,		609.31
House equipment		1636.48
Farm and garden		6488.31
Transport, travelling, etc.		323.00
Extra labour		473.34
Miscellaneous,		1473.17
Cash balance, March 31st. 1913		174.68
	21,520.03	21,520.03

The live stock consists of: 5 work teams; 4 drivers; 15 colts; 3 imported mares, and 1 stallion. Total value of horses about $7,500. 50 milk cows; 100 two year old steers; 25 yearlings; 2 bulls; 15 calves; Total value about $8,000. 20 hogs.
$2,500 worth of live stock has been sold...The farm implements are in first-class condition.

3. 1921

Receipts:

Cash on hand, April 1st. 1920	219.25
Balance in bank, April 1st.	772.41
Government refunds	556.62
House Rent, Indian Agent	200.00
Per capita grant	12,695.06
Miscellaneous	597.13
Farm and Garden	13,878.00
	$28,918.47

Expenditures:

Salaries and extra labor	$ 9,921.15
Clothing	2,856.74
Food	4,337.59
Fuel and light	2,833.90
Building and repairs	1,268.19
Farm and Garden	6,755.92
Freight and Transportation	406.45
Miscellaneous	274.25
Balance in bank, March 31st	220.14
Cash on hand, March 31st	44.14
	$28,918.47

4. 1922

Receipts:

Balance on hand, March 31st. 1921	264.28
Per capita grant	14,380.70
Government refunds	1,809.01
Farm and Garden	16,050.26
Miscellaneous	200.00
	$28,918.47

Expenditures:

Salaries	$ 9,560.40
Extra labor	56.60
Food	3,894.41
Clothing	3,258.26
Fuel and light	2,924.00
Building and repairs	1,609.01
House Equipment	417.30
Farm and Garden	9,279.55
Transportation	473.08
Miscellaneous	23.42
Balance in bank, March 31st,1922	1,208.22
	$32,704.25

This institution has been maintained on the Government grant together with the profits of the farm, garden and live-stock for the past thirteen years, without aid from our Missionary Society.

5. 1927.

Staff and Salaries Paid

Rev. R. S. McVitty,	Principal	2,000.00 Board & Lodging
Ferne Harris	Junior Teacher	500.00 Board & Lodging
Laura McVitty	Lady Superintendent	720.00 Board & Lodging
Lizzie McKinley	Matron	500.00 Board & Lodging
Kathleen Armstrong	Ass't Matron & Seamstress	480.00 Board & Lodging
Edythe Daniels	Nurse	500.00 Board & Lodging
Stella Liebler	Pupils' Cook	500.00 Board & Lodging
Kate McKinley	Staff Cook	480.00 Board & Lodging
Eliza French	Laundress, 1 Day Per Week	130.00 Meals
Fred Dodson	Senior Teacher	1,000.00 With Perquisites
John Kapayo	Mechanic	1,000.00 With Perquisites
Edmund Waite	Farm Manager	1,000.00 With Perquisites
Chris Fisher	Ass't Farmer (6 Months)	300.00 Board & Lodging

Financial Statement

Receipts:

Cash on Hand April 1st./26	65.22
Per Capita Grant	17,390.00
Farm and Garden	12,860.08
Butter and Cream	1,440.14
Goods Sold	500.61
Rental of House	100.00
Indian Department (Special)	148.04
Miscellaneous	289.51

Expenditures:

Salaries		$ 9,422.30
Clothing		2,961.15
Food		9,152.30
Fuel and Light		2,884.84
Building and Repairs		194.84
House Equipment		1,072.23
Farm and Garden		5,648.84
Travelling and Freight		197.75
Extra Labor		490.75
Miscellaneous		68.18
Cash on Hand March 31st/27		700.27
	$32,793.60	$32,793.60

6. 1935

List of Staff	Occupation	Salaries as at present
Rev. O. B. Strapp	Principal	1500.00
Mrs. M. Erratt	Superintendent	720.00
Miss H. Carlson	Nurse & Girls' Supervisor	540.00
Miss O. Barrberrie	Sewing Teacher	480.00
Miss J. Lind	Dietitian	480.00
" E. Leslie	Asst. Dietitian	420.00
" Currie	Boys' Supervisor	360.00
" N. Heuther	Intermediate Teacher	480.00
" H. Bandy	Kindergarten	480.00
Mr. F. J. Dodson	Senior Teacher	1200.00
" J. Kapayo	Mechanic	640.00
" A. Jamieson	Farm Instructor	720.00
" M. E. Lane	Herdsman	900.00
" Cecil Cady	Utility Man	420.00
Mrs. A. Jamieson	Music Teacher	264.00
		9,904.00

Fiscal Year ending March 31, 1935.

Revenue:-
Grants - Payments received from Mission Board		19,004.15
Farm and Garden Proceeds:-		
Cream	1,442.52	
Miscellaneous	6,848.10	8,290.62
Estimated value of food produced		8,500.00
Sundry refunds and rebates		460.14

Expenditures
Salaries	9,824.08	
Clothing	2,628.52	
Food (actual)	3,500.67	
Estimated value food	8,500.00	
Fuel and light	2,104.60	
Buildings and repairs	323.74	
House equipment	1,548.10	
Farm and garden	5,885.50	
Trans.Trav.Freight & Ex	677.94	
Extra labour	774.30	
Miscellaneous	309.67	
	34,127.24	
Balance March 31, 1934		162.24
Balance on hand March 31, 1935	209.91	
	34,417.15	34,417.15

The number of pupils in attendance as at June 12th was 154...average for the year 153.6.

7. 1936

List of Staff	Occupation	Salaries as at present
Rev. O. B. Strapp	Principal	1,500.00
Mrs. M. Erratt	Superintendent	720.00
Miss H. Carlson	Nurse & Girls' Supervisor	540.00
" O. Smith	Sewing Teacher	480.00
" J. Lind	Dietician	540.00
" E. Leslie	Asst. Dietician	420.00
" Currie	Boys' Supervisor	420.00
" N. Heather	Intermediate Teacher	480.00
" H. Bandy	Kindergarten	480.00
Mr. F. J. Dodson	Senior Teacher	1,200.00
Miss F. Elford	General Supply	360.00
Mr. J. Kapayo	Mechanic	840.00
" A. Jamieson	Farm Instructor	720.00
" M. E. Lane	Herdsman	900.00
" C. Cady	Utility Man	420.00
" Leonard Thomas	Farm Labourer	240.00
Mrs. A. Jamieson	Music Teacher	264.00
		10,524.00

Fiscal Year ending March 31, 1936.

Revenue:-
Grants - Payments received from Mission Board		21,600.00
Farm and Garden Proceeds:-		
Cream sold	843.68	
Hogs "	1,501.42	
Cattle "	335.68	
Misc.	268.89	2,949.67
Estimated value of food produced	4,370.73	
" " Hay, Grain, etc.,	3,934.50	8,305.25
Sundry refunds and rebates		752.76

Expenditures
Salaries	9,996.86	
Clothing	1,776.04	
Food (actual)	3,420.86	

Estimated value food	4,370.73	
Fuel, Light and Telephone	2,892.42	
Buildings and repairs	110.65	
House equipment	1,796.61	
Farm and garden	3,206.81	
Estimated Value of Farm &		
Garden produce consumed by stock	3,934.50	
Trans.Trav.Freight & Ex	644.34	
Extra labour	534.57	
Miscellaneous	352.73	
	33,040.14	33,607.68
Balance April 1, 1935		289.91
Balance on hand March 31, 1936	857.45	
	33,897.59	33,897.59

8. 1937

List of Staff	Occupation	Salaries as at present
Rev. O. B. Strapp	Principal	$1,500.00
Mrs. M. Erratt	Superintendent	720.00
Miss D. Armstrong	Nurse & Girls' Supervisor	540.00
Miss V. Smith	Sewing Teacher	480.00
" J. Lind	Dietitian	540.00
" E. Leslie	Asst. Dietitian	420.00
" G. Joblin	Boys' Supervisor	420.00
Mr. K. Cowan	Intermediate Teacher	480.00
Miss H. Bandey	Kindergarten "	480.00
Mr. F. J. Dodson	Senior "	1,200.00
" J. Kapayo	Mechanic	840.00
" A. Jamieson	Farm Instructor	720.00
" Alex Robertson	Herdsman	900.00
Mrs. A. Jamieson	Music Teacher	300.00
		$9,540.00
Vacant	Farm Hand	420.00
		$9,960.00

Fiscal Year ending March 31, 1937.

Revenue:-
Grants - Payments received from Mission Board		$21,517.73
Farm and Garden Proceeds:-		
Cream and milk	1,062.04	
Hogs	272.19	
Cattle "	382.95	
Seed	206.40	
Sundry sales	229.96	2,153.54
Estimated value of food produced	3,884.96	
" " Hay, Grain, etc.,	3,670.20	7,555.16
Miscellaneous:		
Produce and Groceries	348.08	
Telephone	18.59	
Error - contra	85.00	
Sundry receipts	59.62	511.29
		31,737.72

Expenditures
Salaries		10,078.15
Clothing		1,797.60
Food - purchased	3,221.45	
" produced & consumed	3,884.96	7,106.41
Phone, Fuel, Light & water		2,305.50
Buildings and repairs		237.19
House equipment		1,293.30
Farm & garden-purchased	3,518.21	
" " prod.& cons.	3,670.20	7,188.41
Trans.Trav.Freight & Express		1,439.60
Extra labour		572.35
Miscellaneous		280.41
		32,298.92
Balance April 1, 1936		857.45
Balance on hand March 31, 1937	296.25	
	32,595.15	32,595.17

...the livestock includes 6 farm horses, 50 head of cattle, 12 calves, 1 herd sire, 48 hogs, 600 head of poultry and 20 skips of bees...crops produced in 1936...1936 bushels of oats, 664 bushels of barley, 225 tons of silage, 150 tons of hay, 250 bushels of roots, 13,200 pounds of soya beans, 600 bags of potatoes, 100 bushels of turnips, 225 bushels of carrots, 150 pumpkins, 100 squashes, 41 bushels of beets, 3500 cabbages, 150 cauliflowers, 75 bushels of parsnips and 60 bags of onions...Black currants $10.00, Raspberries $25.00, Citrons $20.00, Rhubarb $40.00, Honey 199.20

9. 1938

List of Staff	Occupation	Salaries as at present
Rev. O. B. Strapp	Principal	1,500.00
Mrs. M. Erratt	Superintendent	720.00
Miss Ada Stanley	Nurse & Girls' Supervisor	540.00

" V. Smith	Sewing Teacher	480.00
" W. Broderick	Dietitian	540.00
" E. Leslie	Asst. Dietitian	480.00
" G. Joblin	Boys' Supervisor	480.00
Mr. K. Cowan	Intermediate Teacher	480.00
Miss H. Bandey	Kindergarten	480.00
Mr. F. J. Dodson	Senior Teacher	1,200.00
" John Kapayo	Mechanic	840.00
" Fergus Wright	Farm Instructor	600.00
" Alex Robertson	Herdsman	900.00
" T. G. Chattoe	Music Teacher	560.00
		$9,800.00

Fiscal Year 1937-38
Revenue:-

Grants - Payments received from Mission Board		$21,275.00
Farm and Garden:-		
Cream and milk	602.60	
Hogs	847.71	
Cattle -including calves	538.17	
Grain	378.00	
Eggs	110.60	
Gasoline Tax refunds	48.06	
Sundry sales	124.30	2,649.53
Estimated value of food produced	3,518.65	
" " feed and grain raised	2,573.85	6,092.50
Miscellaneous:		686.73
		30,703.76

Expenditures

Salaries	9,798.05	
Clothing	1,243.48	
Food - purchased	3,822.60	
" produced & consumed	3,518.65	7,341.25
Phone, Fuel, Light & water	2,247.12	
Buildings and repairs	284.74	
House equipment	1,576.44	
Farm and garden-purchased	3,583.60	
" " " prod.& cons.	2,573.85	6,157.45
Trans.Trav.Freight & Express	1,086.54	
Extra labour	681.96	
Miscellaneous:	184.89	
	30,601.92	
Balance April 1, 1936		296.25
Balance on hand March 31, 1937	398.09	
	$31,000.01	$31,000.01

10. 1939
List of Staff

List of Staff	Occupation	Salaries as at Present
Rev. O. B. Strapp	Principal	$1,500.00
Mrs. M. Erratt	Superintendent	720.00
Miss Ada Stanley	Nurse & Girls' Supervisor	540.00
" V. Smith	Sewing Teacher	480.00
" W. Broderick	Dietitian	540.00
" E. Leslie	Asst. Dietitian	480.00
" L. Baker	Boys' Supervisor	480.00
" H. Bandey	Kindergarten	480.00
Mr. F.J. Dodson	Senior Teacher	1,200.00
" Alex Robertson	Herdsman	900.00
" Fergus Wright	Farming Instructor	660.00
" Wm C. Johnston	Intermediate Teacher	480.00
" Frank Files	Poultryman & Gardener	480.00
" Dickie	Mechanic	540.00
" T. C. Chattoe	Music Teacher (Approx.)	560.00
		$10,040.00
Mrs. J. Lockwood,	Handicraft Teacher - $2.00 per lesson	

Summary of Receipts & Expenditures Fiscal Year 1938-39
Revenue:-

Grants - Received through Mission Board:		
Per Capita Grants	22,951.13	
T.B. Grants	299.00	23,250.13
Farm and Garden:-		
Hogs	722.16	
Milk and Cream	511.43	
Cows and Veal	156.63	
Eggs	52.62	
Gasoline Tax refunds	46.05	
Rebates on Fertilizer	5.40	
Sundry sales	12.80	1,507.09
Estimated value of food raised	5,663.27	
" " Feed and Grain raised	2,931.92	8,595.19
Other Sources:		596.04
		33,948.45

Expenditures

Salaries	10,257.56	
Clothing	1,258.09	
Food - purchased	3,712.23	
" produced & consumed	5,663.27	9,375.50
Phone, Fuel, Light & water		2,810.63
Buildings and repairs		396.38
House equipment		1,540.36
Farm & garden-purchased	3,815.23	
" " " prod.& cons.	2,931.92	6,747.15
Trans.Trav.Freight & Express		991.93
Extra labour		711.49
Miscellaneous:		85.92
		34,175.01
Balance April 1, 1938		398.09
Balance on hand March 31, 1939	171.53	
	34,346.54	34,346.54

...This school appears to be very well conducted. Although the balance of funds on hand is never very large, the school is being financed without any occurrence of overdrafts.

11. 1940
List of Staff

List of Staff	Occupation	Salaries as at present
Rev. O. B. Strapp	Principal	1,500.00
Mrs. M. Erratt	Lady Superintendent	720.00
Miss Leworthy	Nurse & Girls' Supervisor	540.00
Miss V. Smith	Sewing Teacher	480.00
Miss W. Broderick	Dietitian	600.00
Miss Laking	Asst. Dietitian	520.00
Miss Hamilton	Boys' Supervisor	520.00
Miss. H. Bandey	Kindergarten	480.00
Mr. F.J. Dodson	Senior Teacher	1,200.00
Mr. Wm Fraser	Herdsman	900.00
Mr. Fergus Wright	Farming Instructor	720.00
Mr. Wm C. Johnston	Intermediate Teacher	480.00
Mr. Arthur Grange	Poultryman & Gardener	480.00
Mr. J. L. Caverhill	Mechanic & metal worker	1,000.00
Mr. T. C. Chattoe	Music Teacher (Approx.)	280.00
Miss E. LaForce	Weaving Teacher	360.00
Mr. Norman Seneca	Night Watchman (6 months)	240.00
		11,020.00

Fiscal Year 1939-40
Receipts:

Government per capita grants		$24,584.00
Farm and Garden:-		
Sale of Hogs	700.54	
Sale of Milk and Cream	582.19	
Sale of cattle	423.40	
Sale Eggs	50.00	
Sale of machinery	24.72	
Gas Tax refunds	46.05	
Sundry Sales	12.18	2,137.51
Estimated value of food raised	5,377.94	
" " Feed and Grain raised	3,567.50	8,945.44
Other Sources:		835.69
		36,502.64

Expenditures

Salaries	10,551.66	
Clothing	1,655.48	
Food - purchased	3,817.12	
" produced & consumed	5,377.94	9,195.06
Phone, Fuel, Light & water		2,636.94
Buildings and repairs		654.23
House equipment		1,806.42
Farm & garden-purchased	4,351.34	
" " " prod.& cons.	3,567.50	7,918.84
Trans.Trav.Freight & Express		1,559.90
Extra labour		716.89
Miscellaneous:		36,808.97
Balance April 1/39		171.53
Balance on hand March 31, 1940		134.80
	36,808.97	36,808.97

...The appearance of the school is very good, everything appears neat and tidy. The Principal manages to finance the operation of the school with very little difficulty, although this is one of the few schools not in receipt of special grants, such as church grants.

12. 1941
List of Staff

List of Staff	Occupation	Salaries as at present
Rev. O. B. Strapp	Principal	1,500.00
Mrs. M. Erratt	Lady Superintendent	720.00
Miss Leworthy	Nurse & Girls' Supervisor	540.00
" V. Smith	Sewing Teacher	520.00
" W. Broderick	Dietitian	600.00
" May	Asst. Dietitian	520.00
" Gilson	Boys' Supervisor	520.00

* Barker	Intermediate Teacher	480.00
Mrs Parfitt	Kindergarten Teacher	480.00
Mr. F. J. Dobson	Senior Teacher	1,200.00
" McPherson	Herdsman	900.00
" F. Wright	Farming Instructor	720.00
" W. C. Johnson	Mechanic & Metal Worker	600.00
" Long	Poultryman & Gardener	480.00
" T. C. Chattoe	Music Teacher (Approx.)	280.00
Miss E. LaForce	Weaving Teacher	360.00
Mr. Norman Seneca	Night Watchman (6 months)	240.00
		10,660.00

Fiscal Year 1940-41

Receipts:

Government per capita grants		21,712.60
Farm and Garden:-		
Sale of Hogs	1,713.73	
Sale of Milk and Cream	260.19	
Sale of cattle	536.47	
Sale Eggs, chicks, etc	126.98	
Gas Tax refunds	25.04	
Rebates	2.00	2,664.29
Estimated value of food raised	5,522.31	
" " Feed and Grain raised	3,998.35	9,520.66
Other Sources:		1,387.02
		35,284.57

Disbursements

Salaries		10,295.63
Clothing		1,689.89
Food - purchased	3,553.49	
" - raised	5,522.31	9,075.80
Phone, Fuel, Light & water		2,988.32
Buildings and repairs		76.16
House equipment		2,045.70
Farm & garden-purchased	4,345.45	
" " " -raised	3,998.35	8,343.80
Trans.Trav.Freight & Express		995.18
Extra labour		407.46
Miscellaneous:		81.59
		35,999.53
Balance April 1, 1940		134.80
Balance March 31, 1941		849.76
	36,134.33	36,134.33

13. 1942

List of Staff	Occupation	Salaries as at present
Rev. O. B. Strapp	Principal	1,500.00
Mrs. M. E. Rowlins	Lady Superintendent	720.00
Miss C. Burnfield	Girls' Supervisor	520.00
" V. Smith	Sewing Teacher	520.00
" W. Broderick	Dietitian	600.00
" G. Dale	Asst. Dietitian & Nurse	720.00
" Gibson	Boys' Supervisor	520.00
" J. Sibbald	Intermediate Teacher	420.00
Mrs J. Morris	Kindergarten Teacher	420.00
Mr. R. Richardson	Senior Teacher	420.00
Mr. McPherson	Herdsman	900.00
Mr. F. Wright	Farming Instructor	900.00
Mr. H. Rootjess	Poultryman & Gardener	720.00
Mr. N. Seneca	Night Watchman (6 months)	240.00
		$9,660.00

Fiscal Year 1941-42

Receipts:

Government per capita grants		22,111.60
Farm and Garden:-		
Sale of Cattle	1,669.62	
Sale of Hogs	$1,358.66	
Sale of Cream	567.61	
Sale Eggs, chicks, etc	457.71	
Sale of cow hides	34.00	
Provincial Hog subsidies	32.00	4,119.60
Estimated value of food raised	$7,925.82	
" " Feed and Grain raised	3,712.15	11,637.97
Other Sources:		583.12
		38,452.29

Disbursements:

Salaries		9,180.86
Clothing		1,597.50
Food - purchased	4,142.71	
" - raised	7,925.82	12,068.53
Phone, Fuel, Light & water		3,171.52
Buildings and repairs		169.03
House equipment		1,605.32

Farm and garden-purchased	4,350.96	
" " " -raised	3,712.15	8,063.11
Trans.Trav.Freight & Express		1,348.15
Extra labour		502.30
Miscellaneous:		373.59
		38,079.91
Balance April 1, 1941		849.76
Balance March 31, 1942		477.38
	38,929.67	38,929.67

14. 1943

List of Staff	Occupation	Salaries as at present
Rev. O. B. Strapp	Principal	1,500.00
Mrs. M. E.Rollins	Lady Superintendent	840.00
Miss C. Burnfield	Girls' Supervisor	520.00
" E. G. Harding	Sewing Teacher	520.00
" W. Broderick	Dietitian	720.00
" E. Inglis	Asst. Dietitian & Nurse	600.00
" Gibson	Boys' Supervisor	660.00
" J. Sibbald	Intermediate Teacher	420.00
" J. Morris	Kindergarten Teacher	420.00
Mr. R. Richardson	Senior Teacher	960.00
" J. R. MacDonald	Herdsman	1020.00
" F. Wright	Farming Instructor	900.00
" T. E. Staniforth	Poultryman & Gardener	660.00
" N. Seneca	Night Watchman (6 months)	240.00
		9,660.00

Fiscal Year 1942-43

Receipts:

Government per capita grants		21,269.77
Special Grant - 1941		1,381.00
Farm and Garden:-		
Sale of Hogs	1,419.64	
Sale of Cream	530.60	
Sale of Eggs	405.17	
Sale of Poultry	226.02	
Sale of 1 bull	176.80	
Sale of cow hides	16.15	
Hog subsidies	47.50	
Refund on fertilizer	22.00	2,843.88
Estimated value of food raised	7,215.33	
" " Feed and Grain raised	4,534.00	11,749.33
Other Sources:		291.29
		37,535.27

Disbursements:

Salaries		9,834.97
Clothing		2,234.74
Food - purchased	3,202.24	
" - raised	7,215.33	10,417.57
Phone, Fuel, Light & water		2,724.21
Buildings and repairs		296.27
House equipment		1,438.54
Farm & garden-purchased	4,895.97	
" " " -raised	4,534.00	9,429.97
Trans.Trav.Freight & Express		674.15
Extra labour		617.68
Miscellaneous:		352.85
		37,920.95
Balance (Debit) April 1, 1942		477.38
Balance " March 31, 1943		863.06
	38,398.33	38,398.33

15. 1944

List of Staff	Occupation	Salaries as at present
Rev. O. B. Strapp	Principal	1,500.00
Mrs. M. E. Rollins	Lady Superintendent	840.00
Miss C. Burnfield	Girls' Supervisor	660.00
" E. B. Bell	Sewing Teacher	660.00
" E. McKenna	Kitchen Superintendent	720.00
" E. Inglis	Staff Kitchen	600.00
" E. Rogers	Boys' Supervisor	660.00
" J. Sibbald	Junior Teacher	660.00
Mr. R. Richardson	Senior Teacher	960.00
" P. McPherson	Herdsman	1020.00
" P. W. May	Farm Manager	1260.00
" B. A. Strapp	Mechanic & Poultryman	780.00
Mr. Louis Cornelius	Night Watchman (5 months)	250.00
		10,570.00

Fiscal Year 1943-44

Receipts:

Government per capita grants		19,612.00
Farm and Garden:-		

Cash sales: 119 hogs   3,170.05
5 cows   627.95
Eggs, poultry   872.65
4 horses   358.15
Cream   345.18
2 bulls   13.05
Hides   40.11
Hog subsidies   77.50
Grain subsidy   40.11   5,789.99
Estimated value of food raised $7,477.36
" " Feed and Grain raised   2,914.94   10,392.30
Other Sources: 989.80
    36,784.27

Disbursements:
Salaries   9,897.67
Clothing   1,511.09
Food - purchased   3,125.58
" - raised   7,477.36   10,602.94
Phone, Fuel, Light & water   2,711.23
Buildings and repairs   139.01
" expended from advance   491.82
" refunded balance   8.19   639.01
House equipment   1,127.68
Farm and garden-purchased   7,637.67
" " " -raised   2,914.94   10,602.61
Trans.Trav.Freight & Express   613.33
Extra labour   655.05
Miscellaneous: 233.29
    38,593.90
Balance (Debit April 1, 1943   863.06
Balance " March 31, 1944   2,672.87
    39,456.96   39,456.96

This school is in a poor financial condition. The deficit for the year was $1,809.81...reduced attendance...reduced the earnings of the school by $3,048.74 in the per capita grants...

16. 1945

List of Staff	Occupation	Salaries as at present
Rev. S. H. Soper	Principal	1,500.00
Mrs. M. E. Rollins	Lady Superintendent	840.00
Miss C. Burnfield	Girls' Supervisor	660.00
Mrs. E. J. Clarke	Sewing Teacher	660.00
Miss K. Kalbfleisch	Dietitian	720.00
" E. J. Keightley	Asst. Dietitian	660.00
" E. Rogers	Boys' Supervisor	660.00
" J. Sibbald	Junior Teacher	660.00
Mr. S. A. H. Dodds	Senior Teacher	900.00
" D. A. Bowring	Herdsman	900.00
". Gordon Long	Farm Manager	1260.00
" B. A. Strapp	Engineer	780.00
Part time	Night Watchman	250.00
		10,450.00

Fiscal Year 1944-45
Receipts:
Government per capita grants   18,150.00
Farm and Garden:-
Cash sales:-   Hogs   2,319.32
Cream   693.33
Vegetables & Eggs   253.18
Horses   130.00
1 bull   125.00
Hog subsidies   171.00   3,691.83
Estimated value of food raised   4,377.60

" " Feed and Grain raised   1,351.43   5,729.03
Other Sources: 676.55
    28,247.41
Disbursements:
Salaries   10,679.09
Clothing   1,484.94
Food - purchased   3,324.85
" - raised   4,377.60   7,702.45
Phone, Fuel, Light & water   2,547.77
Buildings and repairs   82.99
House equipment   928.90
Farm and garden-purchased   5,065.40
" " " -raised   1,351.43   6,416.83
Transport, Freight & Express   1,080.73
Extra labour   490.40
Miscellaneous: 562.76
    31,976.86
Balance (Debit) April 1, 1944   2,672.87
Balance " March 31, 1945   6,402.32
    34,649.73   34,649.73
...This school is in a poor financial condition. The net deficit for the year was $3,729.45....

17. 1946
Receipts:
Government per capita grants   19,050.66
Church Grants   3,000.00
Farm and Garden:-
Cash sales: Hogs   1,950.59
Cattle   1,964.87
Cream   1,369.06
Eggs and poultry   341.86
Farm produce   264.19
Hog premium   61.50
Hay   53.11
Refunds on chicken crates   12.00
Reimbursement by Dept for fence posts   81.00   6,098.18
Estimated value of food raised   5,560.75
" " Feed and Grain raised   3,401.50   8,962.25
Other Sources: 1,193.57
    38,304.66
Disbursements:
Salaries   10,783.83
Clothing   1,355.48
Food - purchased   4,105.57
" - raised   5,560.75   9,666.32
Phone, Fuel, Light & water   3,249.09
Buildings and repairs   88.16
House equipment   603.20
Farm and garden-purchased   7,091.96
" " " -raised   3,401.50   10,493.46
Transport, Freight & Express   741.20
Extra labour   682.79
Miscellaneous: 965.65
    34,648.58
Balance (Debit) April 1, 1945   6,402.32
Balance " March 31, 1946   6,746.24
    45,050.90   45,050.90

The crop produced in 1945 consisted of Wheat-750 bus...Oats 400 bus...Barley 400 bus... Turnips (feed) 400 bus...Hay 175 tons...Straw 50 tons...Milk 34275 qts...Cream 530 lbs... Eggs 1800 doz...Beef 3430 lbs...Pork 2435 lbs...Vegetables $445.00
...According to the Principal the School will not operate after June 30th. He has been instructed by the Secretary of the Church Mission Board to sell the farm implements and the livestock...no information from Ottawa that the school is closing on June 30th.

18. Mount Elgin Residential School Cost of Operation

COST	1936	1937	1938	1939	1940	1941	1942	1943	1944	1945	1946
per year				34175.01	36808.97	35999.53	38079.91	37920.95	38593.90	31976.86	38648.58
per pupil per year				221.54	241.66	243.98	262.62	204.77	299.06	294.53	
Gov't Grant per pupil				148.78	161.40	147.58	147.58	160.00	160.00	175.00	175.00
Clothing per pupil p.a.	11.84	11.67	8.23.5	8.15.5	10.87	11.45	11.32	17.49	14.07	15.72	12.00
Food per pupil p.a.	51.94	46.14	48.61.7	60.78	60.37	61.50	85.14	81.54	98.77	81.55	85.60
Food purchased per pupil for year	22.14	20.92	25.31.5	24.065	25.061	24.08	22.17	25.06	29.11	35.20	36.36
Number of pupils	155	154	157		152	143	142	128	105	100	126

19. Applications for Admission - information taken from Indian Agents' reports and applications

Mother schizophrenic
Parents separated [x 3]
Parents dead [x 3]
Father dead [x 3]
Mother dead [x 5]
Mother dead - admitted by her father ****
Parents asked as child getting out of control.
Live 2 miles from day school - bush and swamp
Father dead, mother had another child and cut off mother's allowance
Father dead, mother in gaol 6 months for concealment of birth
Children were at Mohawk Institute - mother feels too near reserve and some bad influences
Three other children at Mt. Elgin, father very poor, live too far from day school
Father on relief 5 children
Mother dead - child neglected, runs streets at night
Father unknown, mother dead
Very poor home children getting little care
Mother deserted, girl with grandfather and 11 others
Mother dead, illegitimate
Illegitimate
Transferred from Shingwauk
Transferred from Mohawk Mrs. **** and her children have been abandoned by the husband who is at present away from this Reserve, for the last six months. Previous to his last departure **** had on two more occasions, since a few years, left his wife and children penniless had obtained work but never sent any money to his family. He is a heavy drinker has almost never supported his family, the wife and the children having been helped by her family and also by this office. I would recommend to your consideration the application for ****, 9, and **** 8, as it is considered that it is possible for Mrs. **** to take care of **** 6, this with the help of her relatives...
This little child **** is an orphan, her late Mother...died...January 14th 1937, her father had predeceased the mother...After the funeral of the mother, the Grandfather of the child **** brought the child to his home on the Reserve, with the intentions of placing her in Mount Elgin Residential School this fall, she will be 5 years old in September. Mr. **** has 5 children of his own, the oldest 15 years old, **** has all he can care for, but has done well for this child...
**** is an illegitimate daughter of Mrs. ****, who has younger children. The mother lives alone with her family under very destitute conditions...
****...is the illegitimate daughter of the late Mrs ****, her step father ****had been very abusive to her, and after the death of her mother, June 9th, 1937, I took her to her Grandmother with the understanding she would be placed in a Residential School if possible. This child seems very intelegent, with a noticable personality...
**** has requested me to apply to the Department for the admission of his oldest child, a girl...**** states he is unable to care for this child - as his wife has deserted him, and he wishes her to be placed in a Residential school if possible, although she is only 6½ years of age...
The mother of these children died in December 1934, there are three children, a girl sixteen and these two boys, the father, ****, is unable to care for the boys and send them to school properly...
Father is a white man...was admitted by her mother ****
Illegitimate - father Oneida, mother white?
Father is a white man and whose mother is **** admitted by his guardian
Admitted by her mother
Mother dead - illegitimate, father lives alone
Father is ****non-band Indian, and whose mother is **** was

admitted by his guardian, **** in the absence of the child's mother
The father of these children is a cripple and not able to support them and also the parents are separated...The reason for application for entrance to Mt. Elgin School rather than the Mohawk Institute is because it is felt that at that distance from this Reserve, the children will not receive constant interference from their Mother...
****is an illegetimate daughter of Mrs. ****, who has two younger illegitimate children. This woman supports her family under very destitute conditions...**** is a bright intelligent little girl, and institutional care and training, would no-doubt make her a strong good living woman...
The mother of this girl is in Queen Alexandra Sanatorium, and her father is a shiftless Indian who spends three quarters of his time in gaol. This girl has been sadly neglected since the mother was removed from the home...
This girl is the illegitimate child of the late **** and has been reared by her grandfather, **** who is on permanent relief and is unable to support this child in a proper manner...
The parents of this girl have been living at Dutton, Ontario, and, having a large family and being without property on the Reserve, are finding it hard to make a living...
**** is the illegitimate girl of **** and **** and has been reared by her grandmother, Mrs. **** as both her parents had married and the grandmother was not in a position to further care for the girl..
The parents of **** have a large family and live a long distance from the Day School and the education of this boy was being neglected...
****is the illegitimate child of **** whose father was ****. The mother of this boy is an invalid and unable to give him proper attention and being a needy case....
This boy is the illegitimate child of... whose mother is ****. **** has been living with his grandfather, **** for years and as this man is now unable to work, he could not support or care for this child who was deserted by his parents. He was a very needy case...
Mrs **** wishes to place four of her children three girls and one boy in the Muncey school. The oldest girl is 14 years old and she says she cant manage or control her. The other two girls are 12 and 10 years of age, and the boy is seven years of age. Mrs **** husband has ran away and left her with the care of the children and she feels that the responsibility is too much for her...
...Mrs. **** husband left recently and is there no possibility of his returning? Are there any other children in this family than those mentioned in your letter? It is felt that the mother should assume some responsibility, at least, for her children and we are not prepared to place them in a Residential School unless we receive definite information that no other course is possible. Phelan, April 25, 1938
...children of **** a non-Band member. These children were returned from the above institution at the beginning of the fall term in 1938. I have to report **** and his wife made every effort to care for the girls and send them to school. Quite recently Mrs. **** died (very suddenly). While the father is a fine type of man, he cannot give them the attention they should have...
...while Mrs. **** is a good mother, **** the husband and father, is a good-for-nothing waster. This child is continually being picked up on the Reserve, hungry and poorly clad...
...three children of ****. These children have been deserted by their mother. Their father has been farming them out with various relatives and they have been shifted around from pillar to post in the last few months...
On May 9th **** died...leaving four children with no one to support them, 3 girls and a boy. The boy is old enough to support himself, but the girls will have to be placed where they will get proper care. Their relatives would like them to go to Muncey but I think they should go where there is any opening...

Students at Mt. Elgin

These lists do not include everyone who attended Mt. Elgin. Names that appear elsewhere in the text can be found in the index. The following names have been taken from documents in the RG 10 Series in the National Archives of Canada, which also contain personal information. This information can be obtained from the National Archives of Canada. Names may be spelt incorrectly as there are sometimes several different versions of the spelling of a name.

1. 1877: Name, Age, Tribe, Standing in education: Spelling, Reading, Writing, Arithmetic, Grammar, Geography, Scripture Verses, Moral Conduct, Attendance, [Type of work].

Geo Ayahta	Hester Fisher	Eliza Iyahta	Alex Madwayosh	Lance Smith
John Bablick	Terrence Fisher	Moses Jackdaw	Alfred McCue	Christopher Snake
James Caleb	Ellen French	Lucy Jackson	Isiah Monague	Elias Stonefish
Joseph Clench	James General	Hester James	Charlotte Nahdee	Eliza Tobias
Thomas Elias	Sophie George	Ainson John	Peter Rodd	Hester Tobias
Welden Elias	Phoebe Herkimer	Scobie Logan	Annie Secord	Jane Tobias
Constance Fisher				

2. 1934: from lists of pupils who had Dental work or Trachoma, Defective Vision, Diseased Tonsils, or Vaccinations

Everett Abram	Mildred Doxtator	Alena Huff	Minnie Noah	Wilbert Smith
Lila Abram	Louis Elm	Chester Ireland	Stella Noah	Eli Snake
Tommy Andrews	Susie Elm	James Ireland	Leonard Peters	George Snake
Josephine Antone	Tina Elm	Manson Ireland	Verna Peters	Margaret Snake
Truman Antone	Charity Fisher	Stanley Jackson	Jimmy Plain	William Snake
Wilfred Antone	Clayton Fisher	Hazel Jacobs	Leonard Plain	Pearl Stamp
Leonard Beeswax	Fletcher Fisher	Lilian Jacobs	Phyllis Plain	Bula Stonefish
Marjorie Bigwin	Floyd Fisher	Lorena Jacobs	Ellen Riley	Muriel Stonefish
Mary Bigwin	Gloria Fisher	Vernita Jacobs	Lloyd Riley	Violet Strength
Eleanor Blackbird	Goldie Fisher	Kenneth Jewel	Vera Riley	Stanley Summers
Leila Blackbird	Jennie Fisher	Teddy Jewell	Harvey Rodd	Herman Thomas
Billy Brant	Lily Fisher	Irvin Johnson	Genevieve Rodgers	Leonard Thomas
Raymond Brant	Rosemary Fisher	William Joseph	Virginia Rodgers	MaryLou Thomas
Celinda Bread	Clara Fox	Glen Kady	Gordon Sahnation	Norman Thomas
Earl Bressette	Joe Fox	Clara Kahagob	Louis Sahnation	Rebbecca Thomas
Marven Bressette	Ella French	Nellie Keeshig	Wesley Sahnation	Amy Thompson
Alice Burgoyne	Beatrice George	Shirley Keeshig	Abbie Schyler	Stella Thompson
Leroy Burgoyne	Calvin George	Agnes Kennedy	Alfred Schyler	Albert Tobias
Percy Cornelius	Gladys George	William King	Katherine Schyler	Victor Tobias
Cassy Cornelius	Hilda George	Evelyn Koyoshk	Norman Schyler	Harry Watson
Mary Cornelius	Melva George	Alice Kozeah	Vela Seth	Beatrice Wellington
Douglas Delary	Milford George	Ella Kyoshk	Roy Shanks	Alfred Whyte
Frances Dodge	Howie Greenbird	Lenore Logan	Tina Shanks	Josephine Whyte
Kenneth Doherty	Blanche Henry	Raymond Logan	Carman Sickles	Katherine Whyte
Roy Doherty	Eli Henry	Jennie Lunham	Jimmy Sickles	Myrtle Whyte
Gladys Dougall	Herman Henry	Gladys Madison	Julia Sickles	Simon Whyte
Ainsley Doxtator	Kenneth Henry	Jean Maracle	Nellie Sickles	Garnet Williams
Eva Doxtator	Cecil Hill	Elsie Martyn	Douglas Simon	Lloyd Williams
Freda Doxtator	Evelyn Hill	Peter Myers	Edith Simon	Clayton Wrightman
Gordon Doxtator	Kelly Hill	Matthew Newakato	Rachel Simon	Bernard Wrightman
Isaac Doxtator	Sadie Hill	Roy Newakato		

1935

Ross Albert	William David	Dolly Hill	Gladys McDougall	Bernice Williams
Teddy Bressette	George Henhawk	Virginia Isaacs	Eddie Noah	Harry Williams

3. 1937: Applications for Admission - Forms include Name, Age, Band, Parents Names - living, dead or separated, State of Health of Child, Religion, English speaking, Previous school. Results of Physical Examination. Additional information from Indian Agents' covering letters is reproduced in **Part Two: Voice of Authority** without names. Admitted* September 1st.

Gloria Abram*	Bert Doxtator*	Levi General*	John Ninham	James Proulx*
Dorothy Antone*	Margaret Doxtater	Jenny George	Victor Ninham	Henrietta Snake
Hazel Brown	Abner Elliott*	Eva June Hamilton	Lindy Noah*	Marjorie Snake
Josephine Crysler*	Christopher Elliott*	Levi Hill	Phyllis Noah	Stella Taylor*
Pearl Crysler*	Peter Elliott*	Arlene McGahey*	Florence Oliver	Edna Joyce Williams
Ray Deleary*	Wilhelmina Elliott*	Leona McGahey*	Clifford Peters*	Myrna Ann Williams
Ronald Deleary*	Mildred Fisher	Reta McGugan	Fred Petoniquott*	Orville Williams
Theresa Diabo	Julia General*	Joyce Miskokomon*	Ormond Petoniquott*	

4. 1937: The Department approves the following pupils remaining in the Mount Elgin Residential School for another year:

Wilfred Antone	Charity Fischer	Christina Henhawk	Ellen Riley	Rachel Simon
Amy Cornelius	Milford George	Alice Kozeyah	Gordon Sahanation	Margaret Snake
Tena Elm	Tena George	Lillian Peters		

5. 1937: Recommendations For Discharge 1937. Approved*. Year Entered, Registration Number, Name, Grade, Agency, Remarks

Gordon Antone*	Eva Doxtater*	Jenny Fischer*	Walter Lunham*	Kathleen Simon*
Ainslie Doxtator	Mildred Doxtater*	Shirley Keeshig*	Douglas Simon*	Herman Thomas*

6. 1937: The following pupils, for various reasons, have not returned to school, and I...submit their names for discharge.

Milton Antone	Wilfred Antone	Gladys McDougall	Louis Sahanation	Violet Strength
Trueman Antone	Jenny Lunham			

7. 1938: Applications for admission - information as above (3.).

Wilfred Antone	Nellie Chrisjohn	John Cook	Vanno Doxtator	Dorothy Murdock
Eva Blaker	Shirley Chrisjohn	Earl Cotterelle	Alma French	Franklin Murdock
Margaret Blaker	Courtland Clause	Dorothy Danford	Jennie George	Nelson Murdock
Helen Brant	Ivan Clause	Theresa Diabo	Ina Henry	Clifford Noah
Wilbert Brown	Lucille Clause	Jane Doxtator	Ponty John	Phyllis Noah
Clarence Charles	Elijah Cook	Madeline Doxtator	Mytilda Kahgee	Ruth Waucosh
Marion Chrisjohn				

8. 1938: Recommended for further instruction. Year Entered, No, Name, Grade, Agency, Remarks

Amy Cornelius	Floyd Fisher	Edward Jewell	Ellen Riley	Myrtle White
Tena Elm	Christine Henhawk	Alice Kozeyah	Abbie Schuyler	Katherine Whyte
Charity Fischer	Lillian Jacobs	Lillian Peters	Alfred Schuyler	

9. 1938: Recommendations for Discharge. Year Entered, No., Name, Grade, Agency, Remarks

Truman Antone	Nelson Bressette	Clayton George	Milford George	Genevieve Rogers
Earl Bressette	Theo Bressette	Doris George	Tena George	Maynard Rogers
Eugene Bressette	Francis Dodge	Ellen George	Herman Henry	Virginia Rogers
Hazel Bressette	Fletcher Fisher	Gordon George	Gladys Laforme	Gordon SaHanation
Lloyd Bressette	Anna T. Geroge	Lillian George	Peter Myers	Rachel Simon
Mervyn Bressette	Bernice George	Madeline George	Phyllis Plain	Margaret Snake

10. 1939: Recommended and approved for further instruction.

Everet Abram	Tena Elm	Virginia Isaacs	Doreen Powliss	Myrtle White
Ruth Antone	William George	Lloyd Nicholas	Alfred Schuyler	Katherine Whyte
Susie Elm	Manson Ireland	Jane Ninham	Norman Schuyler	

11. 1939: Applications for admission. Admitted*. Information same as above (3.).

Findlay Antone*	Lambert Cook*	Bernice George*	Faye Kichego*	Vena Monague
Bessie Ashkewe*	Mollie Cornelius*	Iris George*	Audrey Logan*	Howard Peters*
Helen Ashkewe*	William Cornelius*	Wilfred Gray*	Hubert Logan*	Arletta Powless*
Mary Ashkewe*	Hazel Dewasha	Charles Homer*	Alitha Lunham	Bertha Root*
Ferne Bressette*	Jerry Dewasha	Josie Horne	Annette Lunham	Helen Seneca*
Ruby Bressette*	Phyllis Dewasha	Irene Ireland*	Alida Monague	Wallace Solomon*
Doris Birch*	Adelaide Elliott*	Marion Kahgee*	Mildred Monague	Harold Williams*
Alvin Cook*				

12. 1939: Recommendations and approval* for Discharge 1939. Ent'd, No., Name, Grade, Agency, Remarks. Pupils have not returned to school following the holidays...discharge is recommended.

Leila Abram*	Douglas Deleary*	Anna George	Blanche Henry	Martin McGahey*
Annie Anderson*	Helen Dolson	Doris George	Lillian Jacobs*	Lloyd Nicholas*
Mary Anderson*	Abner Elliott	Jane George	Edward Jewell*	Ellen Riley*
William Brant*	Charity Fischer*	Gordon George	Ruth Joshua*	Abbie Schuyler*
Amy Cornelius*	Floyd Fisher*	Madeline George	Alice Kozeyah*	Herman Schuyler*
Cassie Cornelius*	Beulah French*	Howie Greenbird*	Leonard Maracle	Murray Tomigo
Delores Danford	Iris French*	Christine Henhawk*	Clayton McGahey*	

13. 1939: Department approves...remaining in the Mount Elgin School for another year

Everet Abram	Tena Elm	Virginia Isaacs	Doreen Powlies	Myrtle White
Ruth Antone	William George	Lloyd Nicholas	Alfred Schuyler	Katherine Whyte
Susie Elm	Manson Ireland	Jane Ninham	Norman Schuyler	

14. 1940: Applications for admission

Melvin Antone	Marion Doxtator	Jean Summers	Tony Summers	Esther Young
Freida Dixtator	Marietta Nicholas			

15. 1940: Recommendations and approved* for discharge 1940

Ruth Antone*	Tena Elm*	Virginia Isaacs*	Clifford Noah*	Norman Schuyler*
Leonard Beeswax*	William George*	Kenneth Jewell*	Howard Peters*	Muriel Stonefish*
Hazel Bressette*	Manson Ireland*	Leo Nahmabin*	Alfred Schuyler*	Myrtle White*

16. 1940: Recommended and approved* for further instruction 1940.

Everet Abram*	Susie Elm*	Vella Seth*	Isobelle Thompson*	Katherine Whyte*
Alice Burgoyne*	Chester Ireland*			

17. 1941: Applications and admissions*

David Beeswax	Pauline Commandant	Constance George	Donald Hill	Leslie Silver
George Beeswax	Sidney Commandant	Eunice George	Fraleigh Hill	Orpha Silver
Earl Bressette	Helen Day	Harold George	Lorraine Hill	Gertrude Soloman
Eileen Bressette	Mary Day	Helen George	Gerald Ninham	Charles Thompson
Irene Bressette	Rudolph Day	Ida George	Sadie Powliss	Leonard Waukey
Sylvia Bunce	Martha Dolson	Velma George	Carlton Silver	Beverly Young
Kenneth Commandant	Lenly French	James Henry		

18. 1941: Recommendations for discharge. Ent'd, No. Name, Grade, Agency, Remarks

Dorothy Antone	Susie Elm	Eva Hamilton	Joyce Miskokomon	Vella Seth
Kenneth Antone	Rosemary Fischer	Elizabeth Henry	John Ninham	Roy Shanks
William Cornelius	Gloria Fisher	Ina Henry	Norman Ninham	Maitland Thomas
Theresa Diabo	Mildred Fisher	Elizabeth Hill	Floyd Peters	Katherine Whyte
Freida Doxtator	Melva George	Shirley Horne	Leonard Peters	Donald Young
Margaret Doxtator	Emma Gray	Chester Ireland	Helen Schuyler	

19. Recommended for further instruction 1941

Leroy Burgoyne	Emma Gray	Chester Ireland	Helen Schuyler	Stella Taylor
Julia General	Ina Henry	Leonard Peters	Roy Shanks	Donald Young
Lillian George				

20. TRUANTS

Date truanted	Name	Date Found	Place found and Remarks
1937	Ross Albert		
	Herman Henry		
	Herman Thomas		
	Teddy Jewell		
	Clayton Fisher		
	Elsie Martin		
	Garnet Williams		
	Herman Henry		
	Douglas Deleary		
	Herman Thomas		
	Aimslie Doxtater		
	Eddie Noah		
	Ross Albert		
	Gordon Sahanation		
	Leonard Beeswax		
	Alfred Shuyler		
	Murray Tomigo		
	Edward Noah		
14 August 1937	Murray Tomigo		
27 September 1937	Abbie Schuyler		
	Jane Ninham		
	Elsie Martin		
	Susie Elm		
	Melva George		
	Blanche Henry		
	Emma Gray		
	Gloria Fisher		
	Gladys George		
	Velma George		
	Charity Fisher		
	Ervin Williams		
	Virginia Isaacs		
	Katherine White		
	Josephine White		
	Eddie Noah		
	Howie Greenbird		
	Gladys La Forme		
	Julia Sickles		
	Garnet Williams		
18 October	Peter Myers		
26 October	George Henhawk	next day	Glanworth district farmer
November 10	Truman Antone	"	"
19 November	Milford George	"	"
21 November	Cassie Cornelius		
	Murray Tomego	same evening	Melbourne
	Henry Logan	"	"
	Milford George	"	"
	3 others	"	
22 November	Eddie Noah		
1 December	Howie Greenbird		
8 December	Howie Greenbird		
13 December	Phyllis Plain	same evening	Melbourne
	Lillian Peters	"	"
	Tina Elm	"	"
	Melva George	"	"
1.2.38	Gladys La Forme	15.2.38	home - Six Nations
31.1.38	Christine Henhawk	2.2.38	home - Six Nations
	Muriel Stonefish	15.2.38	Ingersoll
13.2.38	Truman Antone	15.2.38	Antone's Grandmother's
	Kenneth Jewell		
27.2.38	Truman Antone	1.3.38	went across border at Windsor
	Kenneth Jewell		
2.10.38	Charity Fisher	11.10.38	Sarnia home of Lawrence Williams
	Muriel Stonefish	23.10.38	Grandfather returned her
	Abner Elliott	13.10.38	Cape Croker
	Leonard Beeswax	11.1.39	Kenilworth
16.10.38	Norman Schuyler	23.10.38	Sarnia
	Leo Nahmabin		Sarnia
3.11.38	Stella Taylor		Cape Croker returned by Verna's father as soon as arrived
	Verna Peters		
24.1.38	Martin McGahey	12.2.39	parents
	Howie Greenbird	2.12.38	Walpole Island
	Raymond Brant		Muncey

Date truanted	Name	Date found	Place found and remarks
1.1.39	Ellen Riley	20.1.39	Chatham
"	Muriel Stonefish		Moravian Reserve
8.1.39	Stella Taylor	same day	Chatham
"	Verna Peters	"	"
"	Edith Simon	"	"
"	Abner Elliott	3.2.39	Scugog
8.3.39	Gordon George		Stoney Point with father
"	James Proulx		
17.3.39	Murray Tomego		returned - left again -
31.5.39	Clayton George	next day	returned himself
7.10.39	Harley Williams	27.10.39	returned by farmer
"	J. Sickles		
29.10.39	Helen Schuyler	31.10.39	returned themselves on 31st after visiting friends in London
	Edith Simon	"	
15.1.40	Virginia Isaacs	19.1.40	Chippewa Reserve
5.2.40	Gloria Abraham	11.2.40	London
"	Edith Simon	10.2.40	
17.2.40	Edith Simon	19.2.40	Chippewa Reserve at sister's
28.5.40	Kenneth Antone	30.5.40	returned themselves after two nights in woods
31.7.40	Kenneth Albert		being allowed to remain out of school until the end of the summer holidays. One month of his holidays were cancelled...He left the school on the 30th inst under the impression that his month was finished
29.9.40	Bernice George	30.9.40	Sarnia
"	Josephine Chrysler	"	
"	Gloria Fisher	5.10.40	Sarnia
"	Emma Gray		
7.10.40	Eva Hamilton	12.10.40	Six Nations
"	Josephine Chrysler		
"	Aleda Monague		
	Jimmy Henry	25.10.40	at father's Sarnia?
	Bob Logan		
	Wilfred Gray	25.10.40	Sarnia
	Kenneth King		
	Kenneth Commandant		
	Joyce Miskokomon		
20.11.40	Clarence Charles	20.11.40	Oneida
"	Tony Summers		
"	Raymond Deleary		
1.12.40	Gloria Fisher		returned voluntarily
31.12.40	Josephine Chrysler		Mohawk
14.13.41	Pauline Gray	16.33.41	Sarnia...visiting with Mr. William Gray...on interviewing Mrs. Gray it was decided to leave the children in her charge until preparations were made to return them to Muncey
"	Viola Henry		
"	Norma Logan		found at home
20.1.41	Freda Doxtator	3.4.41	Oneida
27.2.41	Dorothy Antone		
"	Elizabeth Hill		Sarnia
15.5.41	Pauline Gray	29.3.41	
"	Bernice Williams		
"	Doris Burch		
"	Grace Summers		found ten miles from school
28.5.41	Clarence Charles		
"	Finley Antone		
"	Ivan Henry		Saugeen
9.9.41	Violet Henry	10.9.41	
"	John Pentry		
"	Marian Kahgee		
"	Isabel Root		
18.9.41	Levi Hill		
"	Tony Brackens?		Saugeen
1.10.41	Alvina Cook	4.10.41	
"	Elijah Cook		
"	John Cook		
"	Leo Martin		

Part Three: Voice of Experience
Mohawk Institute

10. Boys Working in Garden, Mohawk Institute 1943

11. Calvin Sault and William A. Sault

12. Farming at the Mohawk Institute 1943

13. Students and Staff at Mohawk Institute ca. 1909

14. Students and Staff at Mohawk Institute ca. 1934

Martha Hill
1912 - 1918

I was born in the year of our Lord 1904, and I went to the Mohawk school when I was 8 years old. So that would have been in 1912. Ashton was getting out when I went in and Rev. Turnell came in.

Ashton - when he was there - he was cruel. When he gave you a licking he used the cat-o'-nine-tails. Until Turnell went in - he took that out. All you could use was a strap, and he couldn't hit you no place - only on the hands. He was a good principal - Turnell was.

My name was Martha John. My father was Elijah Lickers, but he died when I was only nine months old. I was there until the end of World War I. I went there because - it's a silly little thing. My kid sister - she was a half sister by my mother's second marriage, and we couldn't get along. She'd pick at me, I'd pick at her "Mama Martha did this," "Mama, Nancy did this." Well we both got a strapping so she made sure she got the right one. So then her and my Dad talked it over and they decided they'd put me in the school, as I was the oldest of the two. I learnt a lot. I liked the school. The school was all right. There was only one teacher that I ever had any trouble with and that was old Mother Hardy. She was a good teacher but she was strict, believe me. We had Miss Reed - she was like the junior teacher. Miss Hardy, she teached from Book 6 up to the Entrance to the Collegiate - we didn't go by Grades in them days, we went by Books. But I can't really say anything bad about her - she was a good teacher. One thing, we only went to school a half a day. In the morning we went to school. In the afternoon we either went to the laundry, or the kitchen, or we went to the sewing-room or we had to do cleaning. We learned everything about housekeeping there was to learn - cooking and everything. We even learned how to look after a baby when a baby was born. We had a celluloid doll, and we had to dress it, put a diaper on it, pretend we were feeding it. I'll tell you, and this is not a word of a lie, when I come out of there, there wasn't a thing that I didn't know how to do in the house - cooking, ironing, washing, mending, everything. That's why it was a little easier on me having my kids - I knew how to do everything - I could make clothes for 'em, cuz we were taught.

We wore uniforms, we didn't wear ordinary clothes. We had our school uniform that we wore to school, our play uniform that we played around in, and then we had our church - see we went to the Mohawk Chapel, and we had our uniforms for that. We used to look quite nice in our navy-blue trimmed with white, walking down the road - the girls ahead and the boys behind. See, we couldn't mix. You couldn't talk to your own brother. If you was caught talking to a boy you got a penalty.

I never learned to talk my Native language - they didn't teach it at school. Then when I came out of school we never lived on the reserve. We was always on fruit farms from here to Jordan. We worked the fruit belt - my Mother and my Dad and my kid sister. I was thirteen years old when I came out and I was supposed to go to high school, and I missed one subject and I wouldn't go back to the Mohawk school to take that subject up. I said to my Mother, I says "I don't want to go to that school anymore, I don't like it, I want to go home." She said "If you're going to go home you're going to work." And that was composition. I enjoyed the school - I liked the school. I didn't want to go back for that one subject - composition. I said I wouldn't go back and do that because I couldn't do composition - never. You couldn't fool me on arithmetic, spelling, writing, reading - but composition - get out of here! I wanted to go to high school but I was a little monkey and didn't want to go back to school. Of course, if my mother had wanted to she could have forced me and made me go back, but she said to my Dad "If we force her she won't learn, she'll learn nothing. She'll just be stubborn." Because I am stubborn to begin with. She said "She'll just get stubborner and spend the year doing nothing, learning nothing. If she doesn't want to go back, leave her out." If I had taken the composition and passed, then the Nation - the Six Nations would have put me through university. They would have put me as far as I wanted to go in learning. They would have paid for all that. It wouldn't have cost my Mother and Dad a nickel. But as I said, I was just too stubborn, I wouldn't do it.

I would have sent all my kids there. They would have got good training, none of that foolish craziness that they got now. We were never allowed to carry on. The girls played with the girls over here, and the boys played with the boys. The only time you might say we was mixed together was when we went into church, because there wasn't enough seats and we had to mix. But even our dining-rooms - our dining-room was here - the boys dining-room over there. We had to be quiet at meals. If we wanted anything we put our hand up and whoever was on duty would say "Yes, what would you like?" Then you'd tell 'em what you want and they'd get it. The food was good. Between the cook and us, we done the cooking. I had to learn that when I was about this big - how to peel potatoes, how to peel carrots, how to do everything. That's why I say, one thing I was thankful for that school, when I came out there wasn't a thing I didn't know how to do.

I can't say anything about the court case, because 1913 I was only about 9 - I don't know anything about that. I was very fortunate that I didn't have long to contend with Ashton, because me and my stubbornness - he'd have got no place with me. That's one thing, I never took a licking from Miss Hardy. They couldn't whip you - only on the hands and I wouldn't put my hands out. I used to stand there with my arms folded so they couldn't get my hands. I might've slapped somebody or thrown ink balls, or done something in school that I shouldn't, and that's what I was going to get a strapping for. One night I got sent to bed for being a bad girl. I hit another girl - she sat right next to me - and she called my kid sister a "little black crow", because my sister was darker than me. She said "Oh I see the little black crow is here today." I just shut my fist like that, and I hit her right off the bench on to the cement floor. Miss Hardy was on duty and she said "Martha, you go to bed. You're getting no supper." But I stopped and I got some stuff out of my box and I went upstairs and I pulled all the beds apart - every one of them. And she caught me sliding down the banister watching her. You see, on Saturday night they gave the clothes out for Sunday morning to get dressed. My number was 60 and she was calling "60". One of the senior girls said "Miss Hardy you sent No. 60 to bed." "Oh that's right." Just with that she raised her head, and she just caught the tail end of me going back upstairs, so she sent one of the senior girls upstairs after me. So I went down. She said "Put your hands up." There was a great big radiator there in the floor, for the heat from the furnace. She said "I said put your hands up." "Nope." So she give me a shove and I tripped on the radiator and I fell, and I laid there. By the scruff of the neck she shoved me in the seat. She told people after, that I worked for, they were friends of hers - they were having a party and I was working for this woman, getting the party ready - she says "Martha I want to introduce you to somebody." So she took me in the other room and I took one look and I said "Miss Stewart, I'm sorry but this lady and I doesn't need an introduction." I says "We've known one another for years. She was my schoolteacher." Miss Hardy says "Yes I was. She was a good student, she done her work well. Whatever she had to do she done well." She says "There was only one thing the matter with her, she's the stubbornest thing I've ever seen. I never seen anybody as stubborn as she is. She don't want to do anything," she says, "you can't make her." They still can't at this day and age!!

The only thing I got into with the boys was with my brother. I hadn't been there very long, I only just got there, and the teacher was going to give my brother a strapping - Ashton. And when he strapped them, he strapped them right down to the bare butt with the cat-o'-nine-tails. He had to lay on the bench and I'm sitting there and every time he brought the strap down I cried all the harder because he was whipping my brother. He done it right in the schoolroom. But my brother wasn't there long after that - he was just about finished his course. Then my kid brother was there but he didn't get into any trouble. My trouble was just being stubborn. I never caused trouble - not even to fight with other girls, I never fought.

My brother beat the tar out of another kid - a kid his own size - not a little kid. The two of them got in a fight, and of course I guess my brother started it. He had a very bad temper - so did my Dad - he wouldn't take nothing from nobody. So he beat the guy up so Ashton was going to give a dose of it back with this cat-o'-nine-tails. They had one little room - it had just had room to crawl in and go in the bed if you done anything wrong. That's how he'd punish you - he'd make you go in that room. No light - shut the door and lock it from the outside. You couldn't get out of there and you had to stay in there so many hours. Of course, after Turnell took it over he just closed that room up for good. That was never used after Turnell got there - neither was the cat-o'-nine-tails.

I did feel that the rules were rigid. What my mother done - I done something wrong and I wouldn't take the whipping, and of course Saturdays our parents could come and take us out, take us uptown, buy us what we wanted, then we had to be back here by supper. But this day, when my mother and Dad got there, Miss Hardy told my mother I couldn't go out, and my mother turned to the principal and says "What has she done?" She didn't talk to Miss Hardy. So the principal told her and said "She won't take a licking," and he wasn't going to pull my arm out. He says "That's not allowed - they've got to put their arm out and we hit it with a strap." My mother says "Have you got the strap handy?" Turnell says "Yes," and he handed my mother the strap. She laid me across her lap, pulled my skirt up and she walloped my butt with the strap. "Now," she says, "are you going to do it again?" "No Mama, no Mama." I was a good girl for about three months!!! I never forgot that, because all Miss Hardy would have to say was "All right, wait till your mother comes on Saturday." Boy! I'd do anything she told me to do then - I didn't want my mother to whip me.

We got pies and we got cakes, because we baked them. We had a teacher that taught cooking and baking and everything. That's why I said there was nothing in the home I couldn't do when I got out of there.

We had lots of fun. We had swings and teeter-totters, and baseball. We even played hockey - but the girls were a little clumsy at playing hockey. We couldn't get it to go right!! We played ball - we had a basketball team.

After I left there I went to work. I worked at Brantford Cordage when I was only 14. My mother and father said "If you don't want to go to school - you don't want to learn anything - you work." I raised my kids during the Depression. I was going to put the kids in there but my husband kicked against it because he was a white man - "I ain't going to send my kids to no damn Indian school."

We always went to Mohawk Church. I was confirmed in the Anglican Church, but when I came out and went with my mother and my Dad we were Pentecostal Evangelists.

I give them credit, because if I hadn't learned what I learned from the school, I'd have been a dummy. When I was in school, when they had the Canadian Exhibition, they put on for the Indian children at the school - we each had to do something. I had to hem a sheet. Not a great big one, but a bedsheet. And somebody else done crocheting, somebody done knitting, somebody done fancy work, we all done something. I won the prize for hemming the sheet - I don't know who won the other prizes. My mother kept that sheet for years. We were taken down - all those that took something to do - and we all had to stand with that in our hands, and then people come along - the judges - and looked at it. Some done Indian work - moccasins, and a jacket - a little jacket, with the help of their parents, but they got the prize. I've got nothing against the school, nothing at all. I thank them a lot because they taught me a lot, plus what my mother and Dad taught me, and what I taught myself - to be independent. I tried to teach my kids to do the same thing - be independent and live their own lives.

Harrison Burning
1920 - 1928?

I can't remember the dates when I went there. I was there for a long time - eight years maybe. I never kept track - just hoping to get away from there. I was pretty small anyway. I ploughed and I couldn't hardly reach the handles on the plough, and when I first went down there this woman was the principal - Mrs. Boyce was her name before she got married to Rogers. After she married the principals changed hands - it went to Rogers - Ben Rogers - he got fired.

It was a place you could say made you a man before you was - whatever happened in that school you couldn't tell - whatever happened, it was confidential to the boys. If you got in a fight and got all black and blue and everything else, that was as far as it went - it couldn't go any further, because the boys wouldn't let you.

Christmas time come around too, and this here Rogers come up in the dormitory where we slept and he just had a few peanuts with shells on them, and he just throwed them around, and you had to pick your own and somebody would step on your fingers and you didn't even get very much. That was all we got - that was supposed to be Christmas. We didn't get nothing else - just peanuts. If they had put jam on the bread or something - no, we didn't get nothin' at Christmas.

There was a fellow one time too - I think he was farm boss, and he used to buy a pig and fatten it, but we learned to steal - we stole chaff for that fellow - we stole from the school and took it down to his place to grow that pig. It had to be done at night.

Another time too, we went to work and there was a fellow that looked after the playhouse, and I was in the barn and we had all kinds of potatoes in there, and I stole some potatoes and I took them down to him and he made a good mashed potatoes. Me and him was going to have a feast. The only thing was when we come to eat them potatoes there seemed to be something lacking. So he says "Go to the barn and get some salt." The horses had all kinds of salt there, and of course you're in a hurry and don't want to get caught, so I hurried up and just grabbed a pile of salt and took it back to him, and the salt that I picked up was saltpetre. We put that in these potatoes and spoiled it - we couldn't eat it then.

We was hungry all the time we was there. I've seen the time I was at the breakfast table or any table, I was so determined that I'm going to eat it I don't care what it tastes like. Even with that I couldn't eat it - you had to starve. The food - the whole supper or three meals anyway - you couldn't eat it - don't care how hungry you were - how determined you was that you was going to eat it - the taste greets you - you couldn't - you couldn't eat it. We used to take skimmed milk from the cow stable up to the kitchen. I don't know what they done to it, but by the time we got our porridge and tried to put some milk on it you couldn't eat it, they had spoiled the milk. I don't know how they done it, but it was no good any way - you couldn't eat it.

There was one day in particular - these cultivators that we used had wheels on them - two wheels, and there was two of us, and the horses. On our way home after a day's work, or half-a-day's work - we only worked half-a-day, the other half we went to school, or were supposed to - anyway, me and this fellow, we started these horses racing with each other, and just before we got back to the barn, the horsestable officer come out and he said "Right, you two fellows, I'm going to report you to Rogers," and me and this fellow said "He's going to report us," - this was just a conversation between me and him - and we said "Tomorrow morning we won't be here." So we run away that night from the school, and we had one fellow with us, he kept telling us - he was the leader - "Let's go where my mother works" - this was after midnight now. She was working in Ancaster all right and we got down to her and found her, but she took her boy and another boy that was with us, and I don't know where they went, but anyway they left us there. We had nothing to eat and had walked from Brantford down there, but we went to work - "Let's try and get a job." So we called in at the first farmer's there and asked his wife, who poked her head out of way upstairs, if we could get a job. She said "My husband is looking for somebody to help around the farm. Go to the barn and wait for him - it won't be very long and he'll be there - he'll come." In the meantime when we were waiting for him to come back, I told the other fellow, I said "Let's clean the stable out." The horses had a big pile behind them, and we cleaned that all up and took it out. When the farmer come back we asked him for a job. "Well," he says, "yeah, I want to hire somebody." Now we got talking about the wages - how much he's going to pay us. I asked for $25 apiece, and he wouldn't go for that. He says "I'll hire one of yous for $25." I said "You've got to hire the both of us or none at all." He did hire us, but what helped us out was when he seen that his horse stable was all cleaned out and I suppose he thought: Well, I guess those fellows can work. So we got a job, and the other boy stayed there for five or six years. With me, I went home - I stayed about two years. We were lousy as a pet coon. The first thing I know - his own kids, they were all lousy. I suppose it carried from us to them. We were lousy at the school - we was always lousy. In the spring of the year they used to come along with the horse clippers and cut all our hair off. But there was some fellows - big fellows, and they couldn't cut their hair, but I suppose that's where the lice must have come from again, because them fellows never got their hair cut - you couldn't make them cut their hair, because they were pretty well like men. That's how come we were lousy - we never even thought about giving it to this other fellow's kids.

We never went back - they didn't know where we was. We thought we was a thousand miles away from the school, and a long time ago they used to have them booths along the road, and farmers and people driving their car would drive up to that place, up to these booths, and you could buy ice-cream and pop, all along the highway. I thought we was way away from the school, but one night me and my buddy went out to this booth and had ice-cream and pop, and I turned around and by jeez, there was my uncle!!! sitting there on the bench. That was the funny part, we thought we were so far away from the school and Brantford that they couldn't never find us anyway, even if they come out.

There was another time we run away from school. My uncle lived up the other end of the reserve there. One day we seen Rogers go past, on the road, and I stopped right away my job and ran to hide, because we didn't know how far we were. What happened - this fellow got to the next house and we run and hid in the barn. Them days farmers had about that much hay on the one side - anyway we were covered with hay, and Rogers come out there looking for us and he was just standing on the other side of the pile of hay - we were standing on the other side - that's how close he come to getting us. But that same night this fellow - they called him John Lickers - he come into my grandfather's place and they had supper. After supper - they were talking in Mohawk - which we didn't understand - he borrowed a horse off my grandfather to go back to Brantford. After supper we were sitting around and he come along and said "All right boys, we're going to take you back to the school." But as I say, he borrowed my grandfather's horse to do that, because he had his horse pretty well tired going up and down the road looking for us. We had to put the old hand out there and get 'er. Rogers was the fella that strapped us.

Another time too, Rogers, in the winter there, had us dig a hole - like a grave. The ground was froze and we weren't very fast digging this hole. We might have been out there ten days or so, trying to dig a grave. One day he fetched this horse - I think he said it was 31 years old. Rogers led that horse out, standing beside the grave, and after a while he come out and he had a great big pearl-handled revolver - BANG - and the horse just shook his head and started for the barn. He never killed him - he had to go to work and put two or three more shots in him, before he finally killed him. All we had to do was just push him over and he was in that grave we was digging. I think that horse deserved his board till he died himself.

We used to hate to go to the greenhouse - it seemed to the rest of the boys that that was a suckhole place. There was one time we went out there and there was Lawyer Lickers - he wasn't lawyer Lickers at that time he was only one of us kids. They put us pulling carrots, and Norman ate so many carrots that he upset his stomach. Every chance we got we ate something.

We didn't spend enough time at school to get an education - you'd go to school half-a-day, and half-a-day work. One thing I will say, it made men out of us. You didn't run around asking your parents for any money - it kinda made you earn your own way - you was independent of your parents. Right away - you was growed up right away. There was no running over to your Dad and asking for money. You earned it yourself.

I deserved to be sent there. My mother died when I was 7 years old, and I had nobody to look after me. My father caught pneumonia - they called it consumption and in fact, in all of his life he never really overcome that - but my uncle come down after my father was too sick, and he took us - me and my sister. Well, he went to work and he left this muzzle loader standing beside his rocking chair, and me and my sister used to come home from school and we had no toys, nothing to play with. This muzzle loader was standing there and I used to take a match and put matches in this gun, and I'd pull the trigger - there was an enjoyment to it. One time I was doing that, and if the thing didn't shoot - shot right through the upstairs - up on the next floor. I think over that - that was the way I wasn't trusted now, and I think that's what made them take me to the school.

When I first went there I cried and I cried and I cried, but it didn't help any. That's what I say about the kids - one day you're a boy, the next day you're a man - look after yourself. None of the rest of the kids are going to pity you or nothing. You looked after yourself, you don't look after the other fellow, because as I say, you can't tell anybody, you can't, because the rest of the school is going to get you anyway, if you told what happened. So they can't be good to you, the rest of the kids they'll take your bread away from you, and all what you had to eat. I don't know how some of us didn't starve. I can't understand that, because they'd take your bread away from you maybe two or three days at a time, and you just didn't have anything to eat, because the rest of the kids just got your food. I think there was two dry pieces of bread for breakfast, and you had this porridge which you couldn't eat, and for dinner they gave you one slice of bread for dinner, and it didn't matter you could cry to the Principal, you cried and they never even heard you. For supper we had two more dry pieces of bread, and as I say we couldn't eat the potatoes and stuff like that what they put out for you. We went into the dining-hall, the dining-hall was a nice looking place and everything, you'd never think that some kids were starving there - I don't know if you'd call it starving, but anyway they were pretty hungry. You never got no chance for a second helping - like bread - that was it. When you had that you was finished.

I was there when they renovated the buildings, and put up the new barn. Anyway they used to heat the school real good - as far as heat went they looked after you pretty good that way. It was the meals that hurt.

One time one of the bigger boys had a stye come on his eye. This fellow come along and kicked at him, like he was going to raise his feet over the top of this little boy, and it worked all right but the third time he done that I'll be darned if he didn't kick the little fellow right in that stye.

Then I seen them too - we used to call it 'putting them through the gang'. If a big fellow lost something, they managed to take someone out of the schoolroom to blame. It didn't matter what you done, the rest of the boys can't help you. But what they used to do - you had to stand with your legs apart, and they give you them cylinders that had a great big brass ring on there, and this fellow that they accused would have to crawl between everybody's legs and you hit him with that belt till he was out of your reach - some would just fall right over. I never got into it but I seen it - that's what made you a good boy. You wouldn't steal, you wouldn't care how easy it was to get somebody's money or something like that. How easy it was, but you paid for it by this here, they called it 'through the gang'. That was really hard to take, but still you was in there with the rest of the boys hitting him too, because if you sympathized with the guy crawling through your legs, you're liable to be next - the first chance they get they'll get you that time, accusing you of something. It was rough, it was rough, but you growed up a man overnight and there was nobody there to help you.

I believe it when people say they didn't learn to love in there. Like me - I often say "I have no heart" - I have no heart. I might look like I got a heart, but I don't. And another thing, that Principal, maybe he took after me, because one time he come in there and he had wire-haired terriers, two of them. He took that dog and put the dog's tail on a piece of metal, and one of the boys held that dog's tail, and this Rogers went and got a coal chisel, and he - bang! - cut that dog's tail right off, and then he had a pail of turpentine, and after he done that he stuck that dog's tail right in the turpentine. Then he done that to the other one. He musta had no heart doing that. I didn't like him much.

There was one time - the Fair used to be on the first, second, and third of October. Well, they went to work and took us kids down there, and we went down there with a team of horses and an old-fashioned wagon. I don't know if it was any use them taking us down there because we never got any money. What's the use of going to the Fair with your hands empty? I even asked one time - I was standing behind the booth where they were making hot dogs - and I asked the fellow who was making hot dogs if he would give me one, and he fixed 'er up and handed it over to me, and he put his hand out and wanted money. I said "I told you to give it to me, that's what I asked for," and he took it back. One time when I was a grown man, I was to Beamsville Fair and there was a small girl running around and it looked like she couldn't have had any money. But anyhow, I put my hand in my pocket and I gave her some money, but then if somebody would have seen me, they might say "Look at that fellow bribing that girl." I pitied her and they could have said "Look at him trying to bribe that girl." Just the same at the school, I often wished that somebody would have done that when I was at the school. They never gave you a cent, and then they took you down there in a wagon. What good is that going to do you when you're starving to death? You wanted to have something to eat, but they took you down there anyway, and I don't think there was anything to eat. They was our horses anyway, our wagon. He had one of the boys drive the horses and wagon down there.

You was learning self-defense - if you want to fight don't fight with an Indian from the Mohawk school, because he's going to get you. You bet your hat we learned to fight. Rogers had a special man for me to fight - he was big. He was also dumb. If he hit you you knew you was hit. That was the trouble with Rogers, I think we was the best boxers to watch - me and this fella. He enjoyed that. After he seen us two boys go at it he was satisfied.

We used to cut ice down at the river and there was these shoes we had on - just ordinary shoes - like leather shoes. That's all we had on when we were cutting ice. I used to have sores on my feet all winter long - chilblains. We cut ice, he never gave us any different shoes - we wore them day in and day out.

I didn't speak my language when I went there. It was just at the change - they wanted children to speak English. I've seen fellas come in there and Rogers made 'em, regardless of whether they could talk English or not, but they made you there. I don't think Rogers done anything for that school, but as I say he got fired and then turned right around and got another goverment job. I was too small I didn't know if he was drunk or if he wasn't.

It made a man of you. One day you was a baby, the next day you was a grown man.

Peter Smith
1926 - 1935

I went in '26. I was there with Rogers and Snell. I went in September 1st - the fall of '26, and I stayed there till the spring of '35. My father died when he was very young. My mother was very young, she was at the Mohawk too. My sister, brothers and I - we were very young, very small when my father died, so my mother - there was nothing to do, no work, and she had no money - she took care of my grandmother who couldn't do the work any more - so she helped my uncle keep house, and we stayed with my uncle. We had no place to go, nobody could afford to keep us - though people were generous, they'd take any child - a child would need some place to stay and they'd keep them. Anyway, we ended up at the Mohawk. After I thought about it for a while I thought: Well, I'm very happy with this deal because at least I had three meals a day, I've a bed to sleep in, clean clothes, hot water, baths and everything else - all the conveniences. We got three meals a day - maybe not the greatest, but they kept us alive. We grew most of our own food - most of it. I think Reverend Snell said at one time they had something like 32 cents a day to keep us kids - pay all the heat, pay all the help, pay everything - the entire operation. We did all the work - it was good training. All we did was farm work. I think the educational opportunities were there if one was smart enough to take advantage. The only thing I regretted in a way - we only got three hours a day schooling. We'd work in the morning - half of us worked in the morning and half in the afternoon, and if you worked in the morning you followed a team behind a plough, and that was hard work for a young boy - you were tired when you came down to go to school, and you couldn't take advantage of the schoolwork there. So we fell behind. I worked on the farm and in the summertime I worked all day. Only when I was real small did I go home for summer vacation, but as I grew older, I didn't get my mother to come and pick me up so I just stayed there. But I learned to work hard - I think it made an honest kid of me. Living in large groups like that - you had to get along with the others. To some extent there was bullying - I think you'll find that. I asked a very well-educated person one time, various things about the harshness of the schools and stuff like that, and he said that extended from England - that's the way they taught in England. They were very hard on them - a lot of the strap.

In the over-all picture I'm very happy I went there. As I said, I don't know what would have happened to me if I didn't go there. Nobody could afford to keep me down there - nobody was working. People were just getting by themselves. There was no relief down there - no nothing at the time. I remember a man living across the road from my uncle there - all by himself. He got 50 cents a day - the Nation gave it to him, so he could live.

I remember a lot of kids who were really good kids. One thing I always tell everybody - the small boys that would come into the school - we weren't allowed to talk Indian - we weren't allowed to talk Indian at all, we couldn't say a word in Indian, just speak English, and these children would come in and maybe have no English at all and they would get in groups like cattle, trying to understand English, because they would give them a licking - or they'd give you a scolding or something like that for not being able to say it in English, and they just wiped out the entire Indian language. It's just the one thing I felt sorry - because you'd see a group of ten or twelve small boys standing in a group and trying to learn a little English. Some of them never heard English. I didn't speak any Indian - but it was all the way around us. If we could have utilized our language, probably we would still have our language today - but we don't have a language. The seniors today are dying off on the reserve and taking the language with them. Sure they teach it in the school, but we had children in the school and they came home and we can't talk Indian with them. This is what I like about the people in the Longhouse - they teach their children the Indian language before they learn to speak English. I think this is great today.

They gave you a minimum of education. If you were a very intelligent person you could get over this. Some boys they would go to school. I didn't go to high school. E G had no guidance - well, they didn't have guidance counsellors at that time. Rev. Snell said afterwards they should have prepared him for college, but he never gave the person any direction. He was never given guidance saying: This is what you can do, and this, and this. He just became a mechanic. You were looking to survive - grab what opportunities you can. I felt lucky - after I left the school I got into the ironwork. Drifted around the country and the U.S. I always worked - found jobs. I was on the road a lot when the children were small. I served in the US army overseas in the war.

We had a Dr. Kenneth Kidd who was a teacher - when he taught at the Mohawk he was waiting for a job - he'd graduated and he couldn't get a job. He used to take us kids out for a walk on a Saturday, some place. Everybody liked him - he was just a prince - he'd talk to them. Then there were others - you had to walk the line - military - speak when you're spoken to - you'd hide when they came. It was an individual thing. Reverend Snell himself, I thought, was a good administrator, from our point of view. We thought he didn't have any troubles. We had some tough ones and we had some nice ones. They changed quite often. Mr. Pengelly was a bachelor. I think in discussion with the staff - he wasn't tough enough on the children. He didn't believe in it. He spent most of his time trying to invent things.

He'd spend hours working on things, drawing things and trying two or three things while we were at the school. I remember one boy took something out of his room one time, and we were in the dining hall at mealtime. And he came down and he asked the boy "Did you take it?", and the boy said "Yeah." And he said "Can I have it back?", and the kid handed it to him and he walked away and never said no more! He got the thing back and he never said a word - just said "Thank you," and walked away. So you can see he wasn't very tough. Another thing he did for us kids while he was there - we built boats. He'd tell us how to build a boat. Nobody else would ever do anything like that for us. How to make the ribs for a boat. He really didn't associate with the boys that much - he spent most of his time in his room inventing things. If you went into his room for something you'd see all kinds of drawings on paper.

Most of us didn't go out at night from the dormitory. If you wanted to get out all you had to do was go downstairs. They never locked the basement doors. We could always go outside - there was a ledge - you could go up there. People were always going up and down - but there were very few accidents. We never really got sick. We used to go to the dentist - Dr. L. They used to cut the boys' hair when they had lice. They used it as a punishment if the girls ran away at one time, to embarrass them. The girls were kinda restricted - in a fenced-in playground. If they went out some place they took 25 of them in a bunch. They had music lessons for the kids.

You know what the hardest time was? When it came time to leave for the summer holidays and no-one came there. I used to look out the window and look out the window, waiting for someone to come. But it never happened to me. I was very disappointed. I never really blamed anyone.

Mr. Rogers would go out drinking, but I didn't think he was an alcoholic. I often wondered if he was a non-commissioned officer in the army, or if that was just a title they gave him to give him some rank. When Rogers was there we used to have wiener roasts. Snell was a very intelligent guy, he was very very intelligent, and he would take us out for a walk in the evening, and he'd explain the stars in the sky, and sometimes when he had the energy, he would recite things and do things for the kids. I think Snell was great on account of being a priest, because in church he would talk to us, his sermons weren't up and above us. They were for the children. He used to do a wonderful job of preaching.

They just worked us all the time. We did our own harvesting, all the planting and ploughing - all the work. Mr. Howe had one assistant. If the boys got out of hand, Rogers wasn't afraid. I'll tell you, when I first went there some of those boys were almost men - they were big and strong. He'd wade into them. He'd put the boxing gloves on and I think the boys respected him. That's why he didn't have too much trouble, because he wasn't afraid of the boys. Only once I remember, he hit a boy. He didn't pound on him, he just hit him. He told him to do something and the kid didn't do it. Maybe he'd been drinking - I wouldn't know - I wouldn't be able to tell at that time, I was just a small boy. We didn't get personal care at all, that's another thing, they didn't have the staff to give care. The small kids were neglected - nobody bothered with them.

I ran away once, but they picked me up.

The girls would bring the boys food. We often went to the dump. We used to scrounge for everything. In the wintertime there was no work. In the summertime we didn't go, because you could go out and work in the gardens. If a guy wanted his lawn cut, or weeding, they'd give us a quarter or 50 cents if we'd go and do these jobs. A lot of us worked around the school - there were some big gardens around there and they'd pay us 5 cents a row, or 25 cents. If you earned 50 cents you earned a lot of money, two or three times a week, and it kept you in spending money. But in the wintertime you'd scrounge - you'd scrounge for things to get money with. You'd get a bowl of porridge and a slice of bread in the morning, then at noon time you'd get bread and soup, and at night biscuits and potatoes. It was a treat if you got meat. They'd kill a hog. We worked on the farm, we were hungry all the time. We had a team of horses - you had to clean all the stock, clean the stables - you had to work all the time. We got up at 6 in the morning and worked until 6 at night. After supper - one nice thing about it - in the springtime we'd choose up sides and play hide-and-seek. One night half the boys would play and the next night the other half. I thought that was great. It's the one time we all got together. Right after supper you'd take right off and you had till 8 o'clock. We'd run right off and go some place. The kids were honest - when they were caught they wouldn't go out the next night. As soon as everybody on that team got caught then the other team would take off. One night we were playing by the Mohawk lake, and we were being chased and they saw them coming from all three sides, and we jumped right in the Mohawk Lake, and there were water snakes, and everybody swam right across the lake - with all their clothes on!!! We really laughed about that. We used to swim back of the chapel at noon time. At the weekends we'd go right back on the Henry property, and the water was deep back there.

Some of them went to the high school from the Mohawk. Only a few, but the potential was there if you were really determined you were going to do it. When I came out of the Service, I went back to school to get my high school education, I stayed there for a couple of years. I went to welding school - earning money was more important. I found out later the recommendation they gave me was "a very good farmer."

Edward S. (a.k.a Russell) Groat and Marjorie J. Groat (nee Smith), Ruth Jamieson Seneca
1930 - 1939 and 1928 - 193?, 193?

Edward: We were watching this video and the people that were there giving their representations really gave some hideous accounts of the things that were happening there, and after the video was over I made mention of the fact that I had been at the Mohawk Institute for nine years and I never saw anything like that. But then there was a lady there and she said when she was there things were terrible. The same man was Principal - Snell was there - but all the time that I was there Snell was never - shall I say - vicious to the children to my knowledge. My biggest complaint about him was his lack of caring really - he didn't put enough into the job that he had there.

They did have one Indian teacher there when I was there - Miss Hardy. She was there with my grandmother as a student and she stayed on and went to Normal school. She graduated in 1886, and then she came back as a teacher until she retired in 1936. I think she died in 1951, so she was at the Mohawk except for the last 15 years of her life. My grandmother was born in 1856 - she was Lucy Thomas when she was there. M went there in 1920 something when Rogers was there and he was there until 1929.

Marjorie [wife]: I went as a little wee kid - I don't remember how old I was. I was Marjorie Smith.

Ruth [friend]: I don't remember the year I went there - when Auntie put me in - I've got the paper at home. I was young when I was there - about 7 or 8. I was there 3 years.

E. A thing called Depression put us there.

R. Same with me.

M. Poverty.

E. My grandmother raised me. Her bachelor son lived with her and when the Depression came along there was just nothing any more, and the only thing they could do was put me in the school.

M. They came from different reservations - all over.

R. Some of them I remember - they were just little - they weren't three years old and they couldn't speak English.

E. You won't find my name in any records. For some unknown reason when my grandmother put me in there she put me in there as Russell - Russell Groat.

R. Snell was there when we were there.

M. I had Rogers and Snell. I heard that Rogers drank, but I don't know anything about that. I never saw him that way - of course I was small. He was good to the kids. I can remember when the winter came and he'd take the car and we had sleds and he'd fix it up some way and drive us around the circle and down the lane pulling us on the back of the car in the sleds - he was good to the kids in my estimation.

R. You couldn't tell what was going on anyway.

M. I thought Rogers was very nice. I liked him, and she

was a little on the cross side - she'd get out and work in the flower beds. The flower beds were all kept nice - at the side of the school and down the lane. When I first went we went to school all day in the first and second grade, and then when we got bigger we went to school just half-a-day. There was the sewing room - clothes to be mended from both boys and girls. There was the laundry to be done and the kitchen work..

E. They had a setup there where they only had two classrooms. They didn't have the grade system - 1 thru 8 - that they have now. They had first, second, third and fourth, and there was junior first, junior second, senior first, senior second. They had the first class and the fourth class in the A division, then they had the second class and the third class in the B division. Well, when the A division was going to school the B division was working, and then they'd switch at noon, and those that went to work in the morning went to school in the afternoon, until the end of the week when they flipped over again. It was a little bit involved, but I never had all-day school until my very last year before I went to high school. The first class - it would be first and second grade now I guess, worked in the greenhouse area. The seventh and eighth graders, or fourth class, worked on the farm. The same would be true of the other group - the second class, or third and fourth graders, worked in the greenhouse and the fifth and sixth graders, or the third class, worked on the farm.

M. You mean the little wee ones had to work in the greenhouse too?

E. Oh yes - well, the primaries no. When I went there I was in the first class, so I never had the privilege. Schoolwork wasn't really that important to them I guess, as we only went to school half-a-day. The first class - the first and second graders - let's say they went to school in the morning - the junior teacher had that group to teach. In the afternoon they switched over - he had that class which would be third and fourth graders and then they flipped back and forth again.

M. Did you have to go to school all day Ruth?

R. Half-a-day.

M. And you were small. What did you do in the other half?

R. They made me work - we used to have to clean the dorms - you know how you'd be assigned a job.

M. Well, we cleaned the dorms before school - before we went to class, didn't we, in the morning?

R. When I was there we had to do it in the half-day - Mrs Smith was the supervisor - she'd come around and inspect and if it wasn't done right we'd have to do it all over again. That's why I learned very young - when you do something, you do it right the first time, so you don't have to do it twice.

E. So you learned your lesson well, believe me.

R. Then I worked in the dining-room and then in the scullery.

M. When I was smaller I worked in the dining-room a bit and the laundry and the kitchen, but of course when Snell come and I was one of the bigger girls, I worked upstairs in the Principal's department. She [Mrs. Rogers] did her own work, I think, unless some of the girls went up and did the work and took care of the third floor. When Reverend Snell and his family came it became with the girls.

E. They had built-in servants.

M. Yes. 'Built-in servants' is right.

R. Oh yes, that was like priority - you had to be really good - know what you were doing. That's where J worked - she used to work in the officers' dining room. She used to steal me food.

M. I don't think I ever worked in the officers' dining room. I was there when the Snells had the car accident, and that's when I worked upstairs a great deal. I had to take care of upstairs and attend to their meals and keep everything right. There was definitely a difference in the food we got.

R. Even that thing they called the cold room - you'd see all that butter and everything else in there - we never got butter.

E. It wasn't the best food.

R. At least you ate.

M. You got three meals a day.

E. It wasn't the best but you got three meals a day - kids, you know, they've got hollow legs when it comes to eating - you can eat all day. We got enough to sustain us - probably not enough to satisfy us, but there was enough. Not too much but enough.

R. I can remember that the kids went down to the dump.

E. They had Patterson's candy factory - they used to clean out some of their areas and great big chunks of candy would get thrown out and that's what the boys used to go after. It wasn't just any food - they wanted that candy and they used to get big chunks of it and bring it back and clean it up and break it up and everyone had some candy.

R. I know when I had to do the boys' dorm I'd find candy up there - like chocolate.

E. I know we wouldn't have had much to eat at home.

M. Welfare came in after that to help the Indian families.

E. In the 1950s they probably had enough to eat on the reservations, whereas in the '30s - before I went to the school - I can remember my grandmother going out into the back shanty and grinding the corn, bringing it in and making cornmeal mush out of it, going down the cellar and getting a jar of fruit, putting fruit on the mush to make it palatable. We had no milk, we had no butter. If we had any bread it was home-made bread that my grandmother had made, and sometimes if we were badly enough off or hungry enough my uncle would take lard and put that on the bread with salt. I never did like it so I never did it. We had plain dry bread with cornmeal mush with fruit on it.

M. They put syrup and honey on our bread.

R. We had a lot of stew but I suppose that was to make it enough to go around. I could never say that there wasn't enough, but I remember when J used to work up in the officers', she used to cut big slices and put a lot of butter on it and jam, and she'd put it on the lift and send it down. It was like a treat, not because you were hungry because you did get fed - you got cereal every morning - the idea is that it was something different.

E. Something that was good.

M. The girls had to learn to make the biscuits - they bought the bakers bread but we got biscuits at night. I remember doing that.

E. You could tell they were learning - sometimes they were real good and sometimes they weren't. But when you were hungry you ate them anyway. As far as the food was concerned we could find fault with it, but that wasn't the worst problem. I don't know if there was any real bad problems. I never got a beating. Sometimes I should have. One time I broke into the storeroom where they stored the apples - it was down in the cellar. There were about three or four of us boys - we found a way of opening a window. Broke through the floor and got our apples. I never even got a spanking for that - nothing. That would be the time you would get something like that - but I didn't. I never really got banged around. I got the strappings - Miss Hardy was my biggest problem there, and it's only because she tried to make me into an artist and I am not an artist. When I was in this Entrance Class readying for high school, part of the work we had to do was art work.

M. The grapes we had to do!

E. She insisted I was going to be an artist, and I'd draw something and it would look terrible, and it got so that every time I ruined a piece of this art paper I got a strapping - so this was almost every day after a while. This wasn't a beating - it was just to let me know I wasn't supposed to do it any more.

M. She was getting so old she couldn't hit hard any more - if she really wanted to punish you she would go and get Mrs. Boyce, the sewing teacher, to do the strapping.

E. I never got that - it wasn't that she was trying to beat me up or anything. It was just to remind me - just to get my attention - that's all.

R. You can't say you were abused. I got strapped a couple of times from the boys' master because I run away - I was just following my sister - we'd run away because we were homesick. Not because we were so abused we had to get out of there, but because I wanted to go home.

M. You're not used to it and it's hard. It's not like the video that we saw as they talked - this has affected their lives later on in life - it didn't bother me for some reason.

E. Now, we were handicapped in that we didn't mix with the general public so that we knew what was going on. When I went to high school in 1936 - going into high school the first year I didn't even know what the world news was.

Once in a while somebody would get a paper but the only thing we looked at was the funnies, and the sports page and that's about all. So we were never told anything at the school - we were never encouraged to find out what was going on - never told how we should act. Once in a while they would tell us you are supposed to say "yes sir", "yes ma'am", and when you meet a lady you're supposed to tip your hat - little things like that. But never our relationship with other people - how we should treat them, how we feel we should be treated - we never got any of that, so when I came out of that school I was lost - I didn't have any idea what the world was like.

M. I think that's the only thing that made it really hard on them - when they had to go.

E. I spoke English when I went there, but when I was there there were three boys who came down from Bala and they spoke very very little English. And the smaller boy - the two older ones were brothers - and the smaller boy was just another one from the reservation - he couldn't speak English at all. His worst experience was from the boys themselves teasing him. Because he was so small they would pick on him, and he wanted these other boys to help him. And that was one of the first things I learned in the Mohawk language - "help me". They weren't beating up on him, they were just teasing him - tormenting him just to hear him holler - but he got to the point in the end where he learned the English language and they didn't pick on him any more. I speak some Mohawk - not as much as I'd like. I'm trying to learn. My biggest problem now is trying to remember what I'm learning! One of the things we heard on that video was that they were not allowed to speak the Native language - that was not true at the Mohawk.

R. Not at all.

E. As a matter of fact one of the fellows there was trying to teach me the Mohawk language - we were just a couple of kids - we'd get on to something and we'd find something funny about it and it would sound like something funny in English and we'd make fun of it, and we never got very far. But nobody stopped us. As a matter of fact, whenever we had any doings going on this fellow - K S - he could speak six dialects - all six of the Six Nations - and whenever anything came up that we were entertaining ourselves, or entertaining somebody else, K was asked if he would sing an Indian hymn. But we also had some boys and they were from Caughnawaga I think, and they were influenced by the French up there and so they sang French. And so Mr. Snell would get these boys together and he'd have them sing something in French, and he'd say "Now this is what I want you to do - I want you to hear K sing Mohawk, and it's so nice because K sings hymns whereas these others sang Alouette and so on." He would encourage K to sing Mohawk hymns, so K would get up there and sing - it was good. There were never any arguments and yet S was saying when she went there she could hardly speak English and they wouldn't let her speak Indian. Didn't she say that

one time they even stuffed her mouth with rags?

I guess the three things they had most problems with were the food, the mean treatment, and not being allowed to speak their own language, and at the Mohawk when I was there, we didn't see any of that.

R. They claim it got bad after we left.

M. But there was getting to be smaller and smaller kids too coming in - not bigger kids; because when I went I was just small and here were these big kids - I thought they were awful big kids - they'd tease the little kids.

E. I think Zimmerman went into this not allowing them to speak the Indian language, but I don't think Snell would have done this because he wouldn't change all of a sudden, because I was there until 1939 and I think he was there until 1945.

M. He was still there in '42 - because he married us in '42!! I guess we were the only ones that Snell married - up to that time - that had both been at the school. He married different ones where one of the boy or the girl had been there. He said it was just like marrying his own kids.

E. I left in 1939. I graduated from high school and went to New York City with my aunt and lived with her there for a while. Then in summer of 1940 I came back to Buffalo and stayed with my mother, and I then had a stepdad. So I stayed with them - we were married then. In November of '42 I went into the American airforce - was in there for three years - came out in 1945 and went to work to support my family. By then we had a son and a daughter.

I started working as a machinist and I got tired of that. In '53 I went to work for Sylvania, but 1957 the big change came, and they put me into the industrial engineering department and I had to learn to be an industrial engineer. They brought people in from Cornell to teach certain things, and they sent some of us to UB. I went on to do more and more things in the plant improving my experiences. So when I left Sylvania after 15 years, I was an industrial engineer in electronics - I had no trouble whatsoever finding work - as a matter of fact they would come after me - I eventually went to work for Moog Music - the synthesizer people. I worked for them for 5 years where I was head of the industrial engineering department. I just kept on working my way up. From there I went to work for Sierra as an industrial engineer. Then I retired from there. Then a friend of mine called -"You're not working, I want you to come and work for me." So I worked about seven years for him as a design mechanical engineer, until I retired.

Back in 1960 we as a family started this little church [Indian Church of Buffalo] in a storefront, over on what was called at that time Indiantown (Buffalo). We outgrew that and this building became available, so we bought this building and we've been here since then.

M. I didn't graduate from high school - I wasn't one of the bright ones. I couldn't spell to save my neck. I left the Mohawk and went up north of Toronto and worked with a couple. I stayed up there for about three years then I had a friend living here in Buffalo and she says "Come on, I'll get you a job," so I came on over to Buffalo and I've been here ever since. I did housework. If I'd have went to high school I could have got something else - if I'd had the education. I think I've done all right for myself when I consider that I've got along, I haven't got into any problems.

E. It wasn't really expected of them. I had a sister that left the year I went to high school. She didn't go to high school either - she left and came out and she became a beautician, which couldn't be considered domestic. And I had a younger sister and she came out of the school and she went to work in an office. In the '20s maybe and the early '30s that was an expectation - that they'd go into domestic work.

R. I think it was up to the individual.

E. When I went there in 1930 I don't remember how many boys there were going to high school, but I know there were three of them specifically - N L went on to become a lawyer. A lot of them came out of there and became iron workers. I was an iron worker for a while - for about five or six weeks - then I got hurt on the job and when I got well again she says "NO. You don't go back there."

R. I didn't get any education there.

M. Well, did they encourage the girls that much?

R. Well, the girls when I was there was divided. For a while we'd go to school in the morning and then we'd switch and then we'd go in the afternoon. I remember Miss Hardy was our teacher, then I remember Mr. Pitts being our teacher afterwards whenever we alternated. I was too young anyway - when I came out I went right to No. 2 school, and I think I must have got lost there before that, because when I come out I wasn't interested much in school. I can remember when they would have got close to Entrance Class we didn't have to go to school - us younger ones would have to work. It didn't mean we were allowed to go and play or anything - but they'd give them all day - they was the ones that were important and had to be pushed.

E. We went to school all day, but the problem with that was when everybody else had days off I had to go to school.

R. We made our own play - played baseball - a swing.

M. There were swings when I was there.

E. Thursday afternoon there was no school, so the kids that were supposed to go to school Thursday afternoon had the afternoon off, and there was no school Saturday afternoon. The dividing line was Friday - Thursday/Friday. You went to school, in the morning let's say, until Thursday. Then you went to school in the afternoon on Friday, but there was no school Saturday afternoon so that group had the afternoon off. But those in the afternoon went to school until Wednesday afternoon. Thursday there was no school, so they had that off, but they went to school Friday morning and Saturday morning. So you got your five half-days of school again, but those two half-days you were free to find your own source of amusement most of the time. Of course the boys had it a lot better because they could go down to the river and go fishing, or they could go for hikes, or they could go swimming.

M. We just had the playground. Once in a great while if you had money you could go to a show Saturday afternoon. Miss Hardy would walk us up to the show.

R. Then of course we were allowed to go out - our parents were allowed to come once a month and take us out for the day on a Saturday. My mother didn't come every month. Whenever she had money she'd take us out to eat - buy us something.

M. Auntie used to come and get me. She took me out in the summer for the six weeks vacation that they'd close the school down, and she'd come and get me for the summer - and when I think about it - just to get clothes for that five or six weeks and then back into uniform. We left the uniforms there. My father died when I was small, and so an aunt had me, and uncles and aunts took the rest because my mother couldn't take care of us. My aunt would come and get me but she couldn't take all of us, so Billy, Pete, and Harvey stayed there the year around, the years they were there.

I can remember when the Fall Fair come down at the reservation, they'd put the benches in the truck and they'd pack us in and take us all down to the Fair for the day.

E. One year the boys would go Friday and the girls would go Saturday, and the following year the girls would go Friday and the boys would go Saturday - so that each one would get the good day, which was Saturday.

M. More parents were out that day. I can remember them taking us down to the hospital on the reservation and getting our tonsils out, and adenoids. I got quite sick with it - I didn't care for the anaesthetic they gave me.

R. Everybody had a number - my number was 15.

M. I was 63.

R. You worked, and if you didn't work then you went into the sewing room - remember we had a sewing room in the afternoon.

M. We used to sew in the morning and the afternoon too.

R We made all the aprons.

E. They didn't make the overalls for the boys - that was about the only thing they bought though, and the stockings.

R. But if they got holes in them we were taught how to darn them - we didn't get a new pair because they had a hole in them.

E. But they made the boys' shirts and the girls made their own uniforms.

M. We did a lot of work - but I think it was good for us, I really do, it was discipline.

R. And the appreciation - they'd make you do it over. I know I had the awfullest time learning how to darn - I don't know how to yet, but then they'd put you on something else. But you know it's a funny thing - I think from it all what you learn, or at least I did, is appreciation. When you get something you appreciate it - you really really appreciate it - you take nothing for granted. Another thing was the discipline - like Marge said.

M. We had to get up, we had to go to bed at a certain time.

Our meals were regular - once the school bell went you came along and you did these things.

R. And it never leaves you - other people eat any old time - I like my schedule, and it started when I was young.

E. The biggest advantage that I find is that I never would have gone to high school had I stayed on the reserve, I'm positive of that. I have no idea what my life would have been. My grandmother didn't have any money to say that I could have done anything I wanted. So if I had to evaluate my residence at that school I would say it was a very positive thing, because I got to go to high school. I didn't get to do what I wanted in high school - again because Snell was lax in showing us what to do. I wanted to become an engineer even then. I'm always doing things - I can't draw and I don't like sitting in an office doing that kind of work. But to make things and do things - that I can do and I like to do. So when I went to high school they asked me what course I wanted to take. There was a fellow there two years ahead of me - Charlie John. He said "Take the technical course and that prepares you for entrance in the college into engineering" - because he knew what I liked to do. So when it came time to choose the course I chose the technical course; and so they put me in a class, but I didn't know it, I didn't get the technical course, I got the industrial course where they taught you how to run machines and how to be a carpenter, how to be an electrician. We had machine shop, motor car, electrical shop and drafting. Those are the things that I had to learn. Fine, I didn't have any problem with it but that's not what I wanted. And I didn't know that until I was in the second year - into the tenth grade before I realised it and we didn't know anything about the outside world - nothing - and Snell didn't even care. When I was ready to leave at the end of three years - and I got a diploma, and I told everybody I was leaving that year - he called me in and he said "I understand you're leaving high school" and I said "Yeah, I graduate this summer." He said "I thought you were going to be another Norman Lickers." Well, Norman Lickers was the attorney. He had to sign my report cards. He knew exactly what courses I was taking. Well, you don't take woodshop, you don't take electrical shop, you don't take motor car shop, you don't take drafting to become a lawyer. It wasn't until I was at the end that he even took an interest in what I was doing in high school. So for me to go and say then - "Well I'll go on" - I would have had to start right over again and take all those courses that I missed by taking the industrial course. But of course being a kid I didn't want to do that, so I left.

R. You didn't have the counsellers like they do today - you didn't have any guidance telling you this is what you should do, this is what you should take. You just went to school and that was it - you figured it out for yourself.

E. We had some bullying - not a great deal - one boy in particular that was really brutal. He had a bunch of probably half-a-dozen smaller boys who were his slaves. They had to do what he wanted to do all week, and then come Saturday night he would go to the store and buy a little bit of candy and give them each one candy, and that was their pay for the whole week. He had a very appropriate nickname - they called him Satan. But he was mean to those kids - fortunately I was not one of them. If they didn't do exactly what he wanted he'd beat them up. And it came time one time that he beat up somebody a little too much, and there was a boy, and he stepped and took the side of the little boy and he beat up on old Satan, and Satan didn't have his slaves any more. He was the worst one - there were others - L M - he was nasty to some of the kids, but I wouldn't say there was any great deal of picking on other kids. I remember one of the boys got up and got ahold of another boy and put his hand over his nose and his mouth, and he held him until he passed out. And so they called Mrs. Smith, the nurse, and she came out and took him into the sick room and left him there for a couple of days, and he was all right after that.

R. I had a sister who is thirteen months older than I, but when we were young I was about this much shorter than her, like I was small, and there was only thirteen months between us, and she was always so much more mature than I was, so if I ever got into a fight everybody abused me. They had to answer to her - she'd beat them up - so they were kinda on the scared side. So if anyone would go after me I'd just run through the schoolrooms, playrooms, hollering for my sister and she'd come out wherever she was and take over. So then they just left me alone - they didn't dare, because they knew they were going to get beaten. My sister was tough.

E. I was never beaten by any of the boys - I mean I had my fights - boys are going to be boys and have their fights.

R. That's right with me. I can't say I was ever abused.

E. But to say I got beaten up from any of the bigger boys - I never had that.

M. We used to have our quarrels. One of the girls - I thought she was such a big girl when I was there, and I thought: Oh boy!, when I get big - and when I went to Stoneridge Church before we got married - there she was at church one Sunday when I was there. I looked at her and she talked to me and told me who she was and I thought: Well, you're not so big now! But when you're small you think everybody else is so tall.

R. I guess there was a lot of bad things went on after we left, because when I remember some of the people talking about Zimmerman - how terrible it was. I can't say it was like that when I was there - it wasn't the best, but kids fighting - that's only natural wherever you are.

E. One of the things S said was the girls were given shock treatments - they were lined up and given shock treatments - I don't know what it was for - bed-wetting maybe. But that was after I was there.

R. I remember them doing that - you remember the toilet? The toilet room - there was that black cord hanging down - with a thing that had no bulb in it. I never got in on that - I think it's because I had my sister to protect me. But that's what they used to do - they used to line up, and the first one had to stick her finger up in that socket, and it would go right through everybody

E. The teachers made them do that, or the kids?

R. No, no, the teachers didn't make them do that - it was the kids themselves that did that. In fact they got punished when they were found out they were doing this, because they could have killed themselves. But I remember that bathroom down in the playroom - I can remember that yet. I was afraid to do anything.

E. We had a boys' master, Roy Pengelly - he was only there a couple of years. But there was a man who I wish had been there all his life, and all my life too. He had done so many things, and I think that's maybe what got me interested in doing things. Some of the boys wet the bed and he wanted to do something about it. So where he ever got these moulds I don't know. But he had about three of us boys go with him into the blacksmith's shop. He had a forge in there and our job was to turn the crank on the forge and we had to melt aluminum. And he had these moulds - poured the molten aluminum in the moulds - and we had to polish them. And he actually made spoons - or paddles - and he hooked those to a transformer and he had the boys who wet the bed would have to massage themselves across the groin. Now this wasn't 110 volts - it was through a transformer very low. You couldn't actually feel anything, you couldn't feel a tingle because I tried it myself just to see what it was like. There was no tingle there, but he said that by passing this current through the muscles that it was strengthening the muscles. There may have been something to this, because about 12 years ago I had an operation on my back and that's one of the things they did to me in the hospital - one of the big hospitals in Buffalo - they put these things on my back and I could feel the tingling - the voltage was higher there than he used. He also made combs out of aluminum, so that people could comb their hair, and that was supposed to stimulate hair growth, because he was sort of losing his hair. But that was one of the things he did - no it wasn't a punishment it was a therapy. It didn't hurt - you couldn't feel anything. He made a wind generator to charge a car battery for instance, and he made that and some of the bigger boys helped him build that, and this was a great thing that he did for them. Then he brought his brother down - his brother lived up near Rice Lake - and he spent a month or two there. He brought all his tools and all his forms and everything he needed and the boys - and I helped on this one - we built a canoe. We actually built a canoe. When that canoe was finished we could borrow it - he got a cart for it someplace - a four wheel buggy - took the body off it - and we'd put the canoe on there and take it down to the Mohawk Lake and he taught us how to paddle a canoe. Here's a white man teaching Indians how to paddle a canoe! But I have never forgotten that. He was never harsh but he taught us things. I think if he'd stayed longer than that we'd have learned an awful lot more.

M. He probably did a lot more for the boys that way than punishing them.

R. He done a lot - I know they all felt so bad when he left.

E. I thought Mr. Lager was pretty good to the boys.

R. I thought he was pretty good to the boys. How was Mr. Jones to the boys?

E. He was fine. He had his room in the boys sick room - just off the dormitory and he put a lathe in up there - a wood lathe. You can imagine what a mess there was - but he had some of the boys --I didn't help on any of those projects - he was teaching them how to do lathe work.

As far as the sexual offences were concerned there wasn't any of that while I was there either. There was some between the boys - it wasn't that blatant either - I could name two or three of the boys that were guilty of that.

I don't know anyone who sent them there for strictly educational reasons - I think it was always economic. For me it's the way it turned out, and I'm happy for that, but I don't think it was a primary reason for any of them.

I suppose if I really dug I could find some bad things to say about it. But I see so many good things.

M. That's what I see - the good part, and I think it's best to remember the good part. Because if they're going to remember the bad things, that's what's making them depressed, and making their lives miserable. Remember the good things and be happy about it.

E. One thing I thought about at the Mush hole - if you fell down and skinned your knee for instance - you could go in and Mrs Smith would wash it and put some iodine on it, and put a bandage on it and say "O.K. you're all set." Whereas if you did that at home your mother would come along and hold you until the crying stopped, and then bandage up the knee, You missed that and I think that part's more important than the bandage. But we never got anything like that. We never got a pat on the back even for anything that we did. Nobody said "That's a nice job you're doing. Gee! that was great." Every year Miss Hardy's chapter of the I.O.D.E. used to come to the school and present something to the most deserving student. And in 1936, her last year there, which was my year in the entrance class, we were all sitting there expectantly wondering who was going to get the prize - we all thought it would be S - she was a smart girl. It came down to the presentation and I got the prize - I've got it at home yet - it was a book - of English-type boys' stories - things that happened in England. But I treasured that book. Nothing was said then, but the following week Miss Hardy told me that she was disappointed that I got the book - she didn't think that I deserved it. She thought S should have got the book. My marks were higher than hers were apparently.

M. That's where the put-down was - you were made to feel that you were not worthy. And that's what a lot of them - in that video we saw - were put down so that they just felt that they were unworthy - didn't make anything of their lives - they just felt like nothing.

Raymond Hill and Hilda Hill
1929 - 1937 and 1938 - 1941

Raymond: I liked it there - it was all right. My parents didn't go there, but some of my brothers did. We got three meals a day. I lost my language. They threatened us with a strapping if we spoke it, and within a year I lost all of it. They said they thought we were talking about them.

I didn't have too much to complain about. But when I turned 16 I was eager to get out of there. I didn't like being cooped up there. Some of them had hard times.

When I got out I bummed around for a year or two, then I worked in a canning factory in Brantford. I was there for 42 years and I retired 8 years ago. I was a good worker at the school. I worked in the greenhouse and I still grow flowers for the Church.

Hilda [wife]: I was 13 the day I went there - 1938. I was there for three years, and I was out for a year, and after that I got married. Mr. Snell was there. I was so used to having the freedom to go out around here and eat any kinda fruit that was on the trees growing around the place, but when I got there I didn't have that privilege, although the orchard was right over the fence. I wasn't able to go there and get any apples, and yet the apples were so tempting, and so the girls went over - climbed the fence - and they asked me to go with them. So I climbed over the fence too and we got some apples - we had aprons on and I tied a string around the apron - I never had a belt, and I pushed them down into my apron - it was something like a jumper - and the officer, Mrs. Smith, yelled out from the verandah "Come on you girls, get out of there. Come on get up here." So I crawled over the fence and I went up and I dumped all my apples in a little box we had - it was supposed to be a cupboard, but it was a long box about 10 or 15 ft long, and each one had a little door in it, and you put your stuff in there - I put all my apples in there and I went up. I didn't get a strapping. I wasn't punished because I was a new girl and I didn't know I was not supposed to go over there, but the other girls all got punished. They got a report - a black mark - they had to scrub on a Saturday - either morning or afternoon - whatever time they didn't go to school.

I was very skinny when I went there, but we ate three meals a day, and I put on weight while I was there. The food was good - I didn't mind it - because I had three meals a day there. That was something different, even if it was the same thing once a week. In the morning we had porridge - oatmeal, and then we had milk, and then we had just two slices of bread. Some mornings there was jam on it, and other mornings there was syrup. Noontime we'd have potatoes - whole potatoes with skins on. Sometimes there'd be liver - ugh! - I don't like liver that way. The liver was put in great big pans - 12-14 inches wide and long, and they basted it in flour and they put it in a pan with water and they put onions on top of it and they baked it. They took

the liver out and they made gravy with the rest. I don't like liver like that to this day - ugh!! Our dessert was bread pudding and that bread that was in there was so stale, but we still ate it. And sometimes we would have turnip as a second vegetable - I never liked turnip. And then another time we'd have soup - and that's where I didn't like the turnip - in the soup. That was at noontime. At suppertime if there was any potatoes left over, we would have them cut up and fried in the oven.

When I first got there I was allowed to more or less do nothing - as a child. Later on they put me to work. They had girls work in the kitchen and they made biscuits, and if there was any left over they got them for supper - but the boys usually got it. The senior boys got it - they got all the extras. The little boys didn't get much - they got their meals, but they didn't get as much as the senior boys did.

R. The boys were always hungry - that's for sure!

H. On Tuesdays and Thursdays we got a cake, and in the wintertime sometimes we'd get an apple on a Sunday night. On Easter we got one egg - that would be on a Sunday night, and we saw butter I think once a week -

R. - Sunday.

H. Sunday was usually our special day. If there was any milk left over the senior girls got that - skim milk -

R. Half the time it was sour - especially in the summer.

H. There was a dairy down in there - they sold the cream. They'd use about a pound of butter for the girls - maybe a pound and a half, and a pound for the boys to butter their bread. They had lots of eggs and lots of apples, but we got one apple. There were 83 girls when I was there so that wouldn't even be a bushel, plus the boys got an apple. And they weren't the biggest ones either - they weren't the nice big ones - they were the left overs.

R. I think in the fall they would take all the apples to market, like all the rest of our vegetables. Onions and tomatoes, carrots, all that stuff went to the Brantford market.

H. The boys worked and the girls worked. First I worked in the sewing-room. I had to go there and I learned how to iron and sew and patch things. That was my first encounter with hydro - electricity. They had a big outlet there and they put our irons in there and we had to iron, and I wondered how come they shove that thing in there that makes it hot. The power was on and I shoved my thumb in there!! I got it!! It scares me now - electricity - when I shoved my thumb in that outlet - WOW!! I learned to use the sewing machine, and I went from there to the kitchen and I would have to wash the potatoes in the morning for dinner and have everything on at 11 o'clock. And in the morning we'd have to make some biscuits and have that for dinner, and then you'd have to go in at 5 o'clock and butter the bread - we'd eat at six. Butter the bread - or whatever we'd have on our bread - peanut butter or something. Sometimes there wasn't anything on it - it was just dry. After that we'd have to clean up the kitchen. I also worked in the dining hall where we'd set the table and wash all the dishes - they were all granite things - plates and cups. I went from there to the laundry room where I washed and ironed and mopped the floor. They had a great big machine there for all the clothes - great big thing. We'd put them all in there and turn the water on, drain it and rinse it, and put them in a dryer, and iron our clothes - most of the time we didn't have to iron them - just the officers' things they'd send down. I went to work - as I got older - I worked in the officers' - cleaning their room. And you would get a tiny - about an inch square - of cake, that they brought, leftover from their supper, or a little piece - about a quarter of a sandwich, or maybe sometimes they'd give you a piece of candy - depends on who you worked for. If they were really nice to the girls they gave you something nice. You had to fix the bed and dust and do the floors, and that was it, and that was every day. Another time you had to work in the dormitory - fix the beds. They were supposed to have been all fixed but you had to straighten them out. Each child had to fix their own bed but then you had to straighten them all out and sweep the floor - you swept, you didn't have a dust mop. I didn't think I was doing a lot of work because I never had that to do at home - all this was new to me. We changed work every two weeks - we got something new to do, and I never had to do these things before, so I learned to do that and I didn't mind it. And I learned to scrub too, because if you misbehaved - we went to school half-a-day on a Saturday - then I had to scrub the top of a flight of stairs down to the bottom. We were supposed to scrub but I never did - just wash 'em - and if I heard the officer coming I'd start scrubbing. I'd done something bad - maybe if I sassed the officer back - mostly it was just sassing back. I got to the point where I got sassy. I don't remember ever getting a strap.

R. I got the strap until I was big enough to take care of myself and then they didn't dare strap me. I fought back and that was it - that ended the strapping I got. I got a talking to, but I didn't get a strapping.

H. I got in a fight with one girl once in the kitchen. She was always mouthing off to me - saying things to me - and I just give her a black eye and that ended her!! That was the only fight I had. I never had problems with the girls - I never had that problem with them. When the younger girls come in, the older girls would have - we called 'em slaves: "Fix my bed for me," "Do this, do that for me," but we always gave 'em a cake that night. "I'll give you a cake" - you never worked for nothing. Maybe that's why I got along with them - they'd ask me to do things for them and they'd give me their cake, so it wasn't a bully thing - not when I was there. One of the girls - she was going to high school and she asked me to write a composition for her - I just liked to write stories like that and I wrote one for her and

she got good marks on it. A lot of them knew my sister - she was there before me - so I was not a newcomer. And I liked to play ball - I got along good with the kids - I played with them. We played together - we played on the maypole together.

R. Most of the time you had a lot of good friends. The odd time you had things you didn't get along with, but you'd still call 'em friends. It was the bigger boys that bullied us. You had to do as they said, or else. I got a few lickings from the bigger boys. But as you got older, things began to change and you didn't have to do the things you had to do before when you was a small boy. I was about 9 years old when I went there - I was there till I was 16 - 7½ years I was there. I used to go home in the summers.

H. When I was there they told me - one of the older girls told me - they says "Hilda, you're not going home this summer." I says "Why?" She says "Cuz your mother and Dad have separated." And I didn't know that - Mum and Dad put us there because things were really hard at that time - there were 5 or 6 of us home. My Dad was cutting wood, and when they got welfare they had to pay it back, so then they finally put us to the school - three of us. They said my Mum and Dad had separated, and I didn't know this, but yet they came after us. Another year - the final year I was there - my sister lived in Toronto and she had a job for me there - I didn't know about this though. I was packed up to come home that Saturday, and my Dad come after me, and the officer said "Hilda, you're not going home, you're going to Toronto - you've got to go to work in Toronto." I didn't know nothing about this, and I just looked at her and I says "I'm going home." I just grabbed my little bag of clothes and I ran right out the door and got into my Dad's car. My younger sister went to Toronto, and I never saw her - one summer she came back - and I never saw her again for 18 years. I was 16 when I left there. I went as far as Grade 9. I never went to high school - they never encouraged you there to do anything. I went to work as a maid in Galt, and I went from there and met my husband and I've been working for him ever since!!

R. I worked in the greenhouse - for the last 4½ years I always worked in the greenhouse. I could have worked on the farm but I didn't want to do that, so I started in the greenhouse and I liked it, and I still like it - so I worked in there until the time I left when I was 16. At that time pretty near everybody left when they were 16. A few stayed on that wanted to go to Collegiate, and College after that. They stayed on and had their room and board - they'd eat and sleep at the Mohawk, and they went from there. Everybody knew who you were as soon as you walked in there cuz you still had the same Mohawk Institute clothes on. They didn't dress you up to go to school or anything, they'd just dress you in what they could afford.

H. When I was there, one year there was no children to try for exams, because there were three teachers that year -

they'd let teachers come and go. I had Miss Frame, Mr. Yeandle and Mr. Paxton - and they couldn't write their exams because they had no teachers stay long enough for a year, to get them through - so there was no children to try their exams.

R. I think when Miss Hardy was there she had a lot to say as to where you went, if you were gonna stay on and go to school, and what course you would be taking, cuz she was familiar with the courses that you were taking at school, and what you wanted to be when you started at the Collegiate. At that time you went from what was called the 9th grade to Collegiate. You had the choice of whether you wanted to stay from there on, or leave, but they didn't give you much encouragement. Now I remember Bob Lickers (Norman) - he went on to be a great lawyer - he had the brains, and I imagine he had something pushing him that he wanted to go on. I guess we could have had the same thing, but our eagerness was to get out of there as soon as possible. We found out in later years some of us regretted - well, I do - I regret leaving there at that time cuz I could have went on. My hardest time was being one of the younger boys cuz that's where we got bullied around, but as you got older - when I was 16 - nobody bothered with you cuz you were one of the bigger boys. I mostly ran away when I was younger, through getting beat up by the bigger boys, and one thing and another. I was punished a few times because I run away. I was locked up in the dormitory after the Mounties brought me back. I climbed down the wall and I was back on the reserve in 1½ hours. I ran away 6 or 7 times because I was fed up, but they must have liked me - they took me back!

H. When did you quit running away?

R. When I was 12 - 13 - somewhere in there - well, when I could handle myself and look after myself - that's when I quit running away. They didn't bother with you when you started taking your own part, and could take your own part, but when you submitted to them it was a different story.

I didn't get along with the staff too good until I was older. I wish I had stayed and got an education. We went to school half-a-day - but it was equal to the schools down here. Miss Hardy and Mr. Pitts the senior teacher were good teachers. We got a good education. You got along with Snell as long as you were honest and catered to his wishes.

When I got out of school I thought I could do great - get a job and work. There were no jobs to be found. I went and stayed in Buffalo with my brothers for about 2 years, and I must have visited every place in Buffalo to look for a job. Nobody would hire me - I was either too young, too small in build. I remember my brothers working as sandhogs - under the streets of Buffalo making tunnels for the sewer outlets - they were working for 50 or 75 cents an hour. Where could I get a job - at 16? Then I decided to come home and I worked around here the odd time for about two years till I got on at a canning factory in Brantford. I

worked there all summer for three years, then I got on steady.

H. I wasn't there when Miss Hardy was there, but my sister was. Mr. Pitts was there. The first year I went there they said "Mr. Pitts is coming here." and their voice was in terror when they spoke that. He had been there before and he was coming back. He was over 6 foot and a big, solid man. They were afraid of him and I was in Grade 6 when I went there, but he had such a big battering voice. We had to write something in math - and I was the only one who did it. He just blasted the other ones, and I was so afraid, that when he asked me what grade I was in, I lied, in fear, and said I was in Grade 5. I was the only one that got those things right and he said "Here's a new girl come in here, and she knows the answers to that." And I never did tell him I was in Grade 6, so I put myself back that time, just because I was so afraid of him. He was mean - a girl had a sleigh and she lent it to a girl going down a hill, and they put water on it to freeze it overnight and they went down it, and too many of them got on it and they broke the sleigh. But the one who broke it blamed the other girl and she got a strapping. She didn't cry - you can imagine the pounds that come down on her hand, and she would not cry and her hand puffed right up. She went upstairs and the next day her hand puffed so high. She cried after, but we were all crying cuz she wouldn't cry, and he got more - the harder he hit - she wouldn't cry - I don't know how she did it. But that hurt him - made him angry because he couldn't make her cry. It was right in front of everybody, and she went up to the dorm and she cried up there, but her hand was so puffed up. I think that was an abuse if there ever was one. He apologized the next day. He told us the next winter that he was going to marry one of the farmhand's daughters and there was complete silence in the school. This girl came from high school and they said "Mr. Pitts is going to marry Bessie, he told us in class this morning." She said "Did yous congratulate him?" They says "No." She says "Well you should have." I think that really hurt more than anything to him, cuz they never said a thing to him. He stayed there that one year and he was gone, but oh! he was mean. He strapped and strapped. And another fellow was there and a girl didn't do her work - she didn't answer the questions right - and he come right down and he just jumped on her and just shook her in her seat. She just cried and she said "I'll tell my Grampa on you." He said "Go ahead, tell him." There was a couple of mean teachers there - they'd do it right in front of the class - not alone. Mr. Snell was the Principal - I'd keep away from him. He used to come around the big girls - we'd be walking in the hall and he'd come around after chapel. If he met us in the hall he'd put his arm right around your shoulder and say "Hallo, my dear." I just kinda edged away cuz I was never used to hugging. Nobody ever hugged me - but he put his arms around me - "Hallo dear." He did that to the senior girls and they just kept out of his way. I never heard of any sexual abuse when I was there. The girls usually kept to themselves - away from the officers. He was the only one there - Mr. Lager was there but he lived next door - he never stayed there. I think Mr. Snell was too busy with his jugs of wine. My sister and I helped carry up two jugs of wine for him. We didn't drink that all for communion.

R. We seen him bringing in wine a lot of times - like she said, I'm sure we didn't drink that all for communion. When you have two or three jugs at a time, that would have lasted a couple of years for communion, cuz there wasn't too many of the older boys taking communion. I can remember about 12 of us, and I'm sure he didn't give us a pitcher of wine and we drank it all - though sometimes we used to push it up to get more than we should have got!!

H. Mr. Pitts would say "We're going to have a confirmation." He says "I want yous to learn the catechism," and I had to learn the catechism. He says "Who all are baptized?." I was baptized - immersed in water at Medina Baptist Church when I was ten - so I put my hand up. He said "Well the rest of you'll have to be baptized." So we had to learn the catechism and we had to be confirmed. We had a white thing over our heads and we went to the Mohawk Chapel and there was a man there and he touched us on our heads - the Bishop of Huron I think - and said "This my child, this my child," and sprinkled us with something and made a cross. I was confirmed then.

R. We had no choice whatsoever. They told us "This year you're going to be baptized and confirmed, and I think we were baptized and confirmed at the same time, but this you were told to do - you didn't have any say in it.

When I was baptized down here, about 8 or 10 years ago, I remember me asking him "Is it right to be baptized twice? I was confirmed and baptized at the Mohawk - is it right for me to be baptized again?" I said "I had no say when I was at the school, that I could be baptized or not - they just baptized me whether I liked it or whether I didn't." The pastor up here told me "I think it's right for you to be baptized on your own accord, not to be told you had to be baptized." So I was baptized twice.

H. There was a girl on the maypole and the thing fell off - she got killed.

R. It was while I was there - it would have been about 1937.

H. There was a friend of mine - a neighbour. After I went to the school he wanted to come up with us - he lived across the road. And he come up there and I was working in one dorm and I heard he was sick. So no matter what they had for dinner they'd take his plate up there - one big cold potato, your bread, maybe you had some milk there left over, and whatever meat you had. You took that up to them - whatever their meal was at dinnertime, you got that, even at supper you got that. He was sick up there 3 or 4 days, and on a Saturday I took his food to him and he said "You tell my Mum I'm sick up here," and she came up to see him and she took him to a doctor in Brantford. He had an

appendix and he had to have an operation, and they took him home and he never come back. So I don't know how long he'd have been laying there, or what would have happened if he'd stayed there. They'd give you an aspirin if you had a sore throat or a cold or something, or a stick with a swab with iodine or something and rubbed your throat with it - that was a cure-all - for a sprained ankle, or whatever you had - a sore toe. They had a dispensary, but all I could see in there was iodine.

At Fair time down at Ohsweken here they'd hire a cattle truck - take us all in a cattle truck - and oh! would they ever call us names when we got down here. But the man who had the Feed and Seed factory here in Brantford gave us a dime apiece. We didn't have any money of our own - we just had that dime. We used to enter some things in the Fair for the school, and I made fudge as an entry in the Fair. And the teacher told me what to put in it, and I did what I was told, and I got First Prize on it, and I might have got a dollar or 75 cents which I shared with my sister, and I went down to the kitchen and she said "Hilda, here's your candy." It was in a chocolate box, and there was three pieces left out of the whole thing. I got three pieces out of all I made. They didn't care about us. There was no love shown, nothin', for us. The Principal's wife come down there in the mornings or at noon time, and she always had a little white dog, and she was a short lady, really heavy set, and she carried that dog with her, and she'd say "Good morning girls" and she'd turn around and the smile was wiped right off her face. When I do that my husband calls me Mrs Snell!!! Artificial smile just turned right on.

R. It seems so funny that all the good people that they had there for the children, they all seemed to disappear over the year.

H. Less than that - six months.

R. Mr. Kidd - he was a boys' master - the same as Lager and Jones. He was a school teacher and boys' master. We liked him - he didn't stay there too long. Before he was leaving he took pictures of every kid that was there, and I remember him giving us 3 cents apiece for taking our pictures - for every boy that was there. You remember that, cuz nobody else ever gave you anything - none of the officers anyway.

H. We had a lady there - her sons were in the Air Force - Mrs. Fry. She was a short grey-haired lady. She was very good to the girls, and she told us - one night up there before we went to bed "Now girls," she says, "I'm going to tell you this" - maybe she knew she was going to leave - "When you leave here," she says, "I want yous to be able to be your husband-to-be's - your first kiss, let it be your husband's." I think she meant more than kissing, I think she meant sex, but sex wasn't mentioned then. She would take us for a walk way round the Mohawk lake there after school - on her days off. She'd take us to the show - the other officers would never - we had to beg them to take us to the show, if there was a show we wanted to see. But she would always take us - she didn't last long. Anybody was good to the kids was gone. But the mean ones they stayed - they stayed their whole year. I liked it when Mr. Merriman came in - he was a music teacher. Oh, he was a nice person - he and his wife. He's the one that put on plays - he put on beautiful plays.

R. There wasn't anything for us to do. We were there - they had about three pair of roller skates and about the same thing in ice skates for 79 boys. That was pretty near the only activity we had. They never put us in a group to play ball. A lot of the boys played ball but they would never let us join a league or anything. We were good at playing ball. Bob Lickers used to be a great runner, and Miles Isaac.

The only time they let the girls come over when I was there was for ice skating. They let 'em come around cuz they never had no ice on the girls' side, so they had to come around to the boys' side, and that was once in a great while.

H. We played ball on the boys' side once in the three years I was there - that was on the 24th May.

R. My sisters were there when I went there. We could ask to see them and I think there was special nights for that - on a Tuesday night, you could talk to your brothers or sisters, but that didn't last long cuz my sisters left two years after I went there. I think it was allowed once a month, or every three months, something like that.

H. My Dad was in the first school, before this one. I think he said he helped burn it down!!

R. They used to really have some real bad boys' masters, and as I said before, the ones that we liked, they wasn't there very long. They just got rid of them and brought in somebody that was really mean. And I don't think us boys were that bad that we really needed a bad boys' master to make us come to terms?

H. They wanted to show their authority - because we're Natives.

R. Mr. Kidd, he was a nice one. We all liked him - that's why they let him go. Nobody liked Mr. Lager - I never liked him. I used to always keep my hair in good condition, and just to be mean one time he got two or three of the boys to catch me and take a hold of me, and he shaved off all my hair. For no reason at all. I always kept my hair clean and combed. He said "The rest of the boys got their hair cut - you've got to have yours cut too." I cried, and I asked "Why? I keep my hair really neat and clean." But, just to be a bully he had to come and cut it off.

H. When he was there, any kid come into the school, they were all shaved right to the skin - skinheads. The girls had to have their hair cut short. If you wanted it long you had to keep it in braids.

R. There was three of the boys' masters there that I didn't care for: Mr. Jones, Mr. Lager and Mr. Pitts. They were really mean. Mr. Pengelly, we liked him too. I used to go to the dump. He helped us make canoes. We had some nice boys' masters there. They didn't like Mr. Kidd on account of he wouldn't be mean to us or slap us around, or

give us a strapping for hardly any reason at all. He was nice to us and so was Mr. Pengelly. There was two canoes that he built for the boys - well, we all helped build the canoes - and we'd go around the Mohawk Lake and up and down the canal. Most of the time Mr. Pitts and Bessie had them boats in the summer - they would paddle around the Mohawk Lake, and we never got to use them. We could have them after supper, but how long could we have them, we had to be in bed by - the juniors 8 o'clock, and the seniors 9 o'clock? So we didn't have very much time. I don't think Mr. Pengelly liked that either. There was a bunch of boys jumped Mr. Lager one night after supper. He did something to the boys, and this was all made up before suppertime, before we got into the supper hall, that they were gonna jump him. They knocked him down and they all dispersed, and one or two got a couple of licks in at him. Really I don't think they found out who it was, because they all clammed up and nobody would tell what happened. He was mean to the boys and they were gonna get him one night, and that's what happened.

They just strapped us on the hands. I remember one of the boys one time, he got strapped by Mr. Snell, and when Mr. Snell come down with the strap, he closed his hand on him and he yanked it from his hand and he hit him back with it. I don't think they ever got the boy back again, because I think at that time he run away too. I don't know if he were brought back, but he didn't do it because of what the boys said they were gonna do if he did.

H. I don't regret being there -

R. - I don't either -

H. - because I learned to scrub, I learned to sew, and learned to cook what little I did do. I learned a lot there. So there's no regrets of me being there. I had my clothes, roof over my head, my schooling, and food. I didn't have to worry about that. I had to eat three times a day. Even if it was kinda wormy and ugly, that was better than really sometimes what I had at home.

R. At that time there were a lot of kids. Your family wasn't making no money and there was no work to be found, so it was a hard time keeping you. A lot of them didn't put you there for spite. They put you there cuz they couldn't keep you. I can go back in time and I can remember a lot of the people - our people - saying they called it the dirty thirties. There was no work, and there was nothing hardly to eat, and what you did get - you maybe got - well I started work for 22½ cents an hour, and that was factory work, so you can imagine what it was like for them, before us.

H. My Dad used to cut wood, and my Mum used to make baskets for a living. We had nothing - no clothes to go to school in, no shoes, especially for winter. It was all right in the summertime, but not in the wintertime - we had no shoes at all. We had macamaws - rubbers with high heels on 'em - and we'd take an old pair of shoes and cut the heel part off - the back part of the heel, and stuff it in there, and that was what we wore. No shoe in there - just that heel, to make sure that heel would stick in that high heel. No shoes in our rubbers - the low ones - just cardboard. But we still went to school. We made fun of each other. There was others poorer than us, but we still had one meal, or three meals a day even - just a piece of bread or something. But we still ate. I don't regret going there cuz our Mum and Dad really couldn't afford to keep all of us home, with the little he had to work on. We were very poor, but we still ate, we still had a roof over our heads, we were still warm.

R. I wonder about that time myself, cuz I remember the kids when I went to school after I was there a few years. We went to school half-a-day - we were ahead of these schools down here and they were going to school all day, and we were going to school half-a-day. We'd work half-a-day and go to school half-a-day.

H. Maybe it was because our one class down here was all the classes together, whereas we just had two classes in school - Grades 5 and 6. The juniors were in the other school.

R. That was divided between only 2 teachers though.

H. When I went to school down here, they was from beginning right up to Grade 8 and she had to teach all those. Whereas at school we were just the senior kids, then they had to divide the juniors. They just went half-a-day so they were able to complete all our chores.

R. A lot of it had to do with how poor they were. I had an idea that's why I went to the school but they never told us "We're putting you away cuz we can't afford to keep you." You heard it mentioned once in a while "How are we gonna get this, how are we gonna get that?" Then when they did put you away then we practically knew why they were doing it. There they was sure you was gonna get three meals a day and a place to stay where it was warm, and an education along with it, so they didn't have any alternative.

H. My parents were at odds with each other at that time, because of her struggling, and she was the main bread winner of the family. She's the one that was able to look after us, and my father, all as he did was cut wood, and that was hard for them at 50 cents a cord, and he cut by himself. With all the family to keep there it was hard for them at that time, so the thing to do would be to put 'em there. I know they was arguing all the time, so I think there was problems there. Not that there was anybody else involved, but the atmosphere - the burden of trying to keep them in the home. When we went to school that was when she was able to go with him to cut wood and help out.

R. When I was small I never had no parents. I went to my Aunt's and I moved over to my Uncle Edward's. My parents had parted - I never had no mother or father. In fact when my Dad come up to the school one time, I just knew him and that was about all. I was over to my Uncle Edward's, staying there, and from there I went to the Mohawk, but when my mother came to see me, I didn't even know her - she'd been away that long out of my mind. I went and hid in the barn cuz she said she was coming to see me and I

didn't know who she was. I hid in the barn and I wouldn't see her, and it was a long time before I got to know her. She came occasionally over to my Uncle Edward's and that's how I got to know her. Gramma Kate was my mother and Uncle Edward was my father - to us they were my parents, and when he got rid of us to the Mohawk, I didn't know what to think. "Why is he sending me there?" I guess he couldn't afford to keep us.

H. My Dad and Mum used to come after us - early Saturday morning - 8 o'clock and they'd take us back. They'd come out to see us at Christmas, or Easter and in June. Christmastime they'd take us uptown, then my sister'd come up to see me at Easter. A lot of the children were from way up north where their parents couldn't come down - they never saw them, they stayed there year round. I felt sorry for them.

R. There was no money for the parents to travel. At one time they said the Indians used to get half-fare wherever they'd go, which was supposed to be inherited by them - wherever they travelled they got half fare.

I earned my money when I was at the Mohawk, working out in the farms around about the Mohawk. They used to let us go and work out there, weeding. But these parents - if they could afford a dollar they'd send it to their children - maybe once or twice a year and that's all the money they had for a year or so. So a lot of times I don't really blame the school, and I don't blame my parents. But something they did - at least we never starved, or got into trouble. We could've got into trouble like they do today, but we never ever did. We were afraid of the jails.

When we grew older - 14, 15, we were able to look after ourselves, nobody bothered with us. But when you were small, if a bigger boy told you what to do, you had to do it, there was no alternative. You did it or else you got slapped around.

H. I came from a home - we may have been poor, but we had Biblical teaching and we had parents. So when I left there at that age I was more or less developed into knowing right and wrong. I had parents. I knew who cared about me, even though they couldn't really afford, they did their best for me. So my sister and I both had that background. We had it instilled in us, so we were able to handle the situation at the school. As for other children who come in from up north, way farther out, who come in there small - I don't know what their home life was like - but they come into another place where they couldn't talk to each other in their own language, and that was taken from them, so they lost that there - like "What can we do, we can't talk no more?" Getting into something all strange to them, no parental guidance at that tender age, and I think a lot of children have come up like that - you've got to fend for yourself. If you want something and you couldn't get it, then you stole for it. We wanted apples, we had to steal for them. We got punished for something we wanted to eat - we were hungry. They'd break in the kitchen and steal for something to eat, and you got punished for that, so that goes from there - you want something you're gonna steal for it.

R.   It's true we learned to steal.

H.   I didn't speak my Native language. My Dad couldn't speak Indian but he could understand it.

R.   I could speak some of my Native language, and what little I did know I wasn't long forgetting it. My Dad - he spoke 6 languages. I think our parents had a lot to do with it too. If they were speaking seriously about something and you come in the room, they sent you out. They didn't want you to know what they were saying. They were talking Indian amongst themselves. What little my Dad said to me - he never tried to speak Indian to me - I had to catch on by myself what he was saying. My uncle did talk Indian to me, that's where I learned. He explained a little bit in his broken English what it was. I knew some Cayuga and some Mohawk. Those that came from up north and from

Montreal, they talked both Indian and French, but they weren't allowed to speak any of it.

H.   There was a brother and sister came from Montreal - they didn't need to be there. They were well-dressed and they were there for two weeks and she cried every day she was there, and her parents came after her. She must have been from a home that she was well-loved. She wouldn't take part in nothin', she just cried. And that was when I was there and the children wasn't mean to nobody.

R.   We were punished for a lot of petty things - we shouldn't have been punished at all.

H.   I remember working in the dairy and I had to take all the stuff out of the fridge and scrub it down good.

R.   We didn't dare write home to our parents about what was going on - our letters had to go through the officer. Our mail was censored. Sometimes we wrote letters and took them to the Post Office ourselves.

Emmert General
1932? - 1938?

I was there from '32 or '33 to '38 maybe. I think I left the same year Miss Hardy left. She was quite an old lady when she left, but she taught me. I was there when Mr. Snell was there - I didn't think very much of him - he took away our language - he carried it on. I spoke my Native language when I went there but if you tried to speak to someone in your own language you'd always get the strap or something - they figured we were talking about them. We got disciplined for that.

I was sent there because my mother and father were separated when my sister was just a little baby. My aunt sent me and my sister there. In 1939 - '41, '42 I joined the army and went overseas.

I was 14 or 15 when I went there - they made me one of the senior boys. I was in charge of the playroom where the boys stayed. I was the playroom boss - I had to see the boys got up and done their chores. It was quite hard for me - then I had to get myself ready to go to school. I had to take care of one little guy - he was about three years old, I used to have to carry him to Church, and carry him back. That was my job.

Sometimes I'd go to school in the morning, sometimes in the afternoon. We'd work on the farm half-a-day. Not very often I'd go to the greenhouse, but I milked cows and looked after horses. I didn't look after the pigs, but I had to feed the horses, and harness the horses and get them ready to go out in the field, and helped milk the cows and drive the cows to the pasture, and at 5 o'clock we had to go after the cows and drive them back again, and milk them again, separate the milk. They sold the cream, and gave us the skim milk. Not very often we got whole milk - never, that I can remember.

All the time I was there I worked on the farm - I stayed all summer until the year I left, I went to Tillsonburg and worked on a farm there. I worked on the farm up there winter and summer - all summer, getting in the hay, getting in the grain; and we got paid for that. I worked all day long during the summer. We just got paid in the summer. In the spring there used to be a whole bunch of gardens around there - on Erie Avenue and that; they used to call the school and I used to go and weed gardens for these different people. Then on Saturday I would go to the show or something. Three or four boys would get together and we'd go to a show. One gardener had a bunch of bees and they got into my hair...I was playing hockey one time on the street between the church and the school and one guy got me right in the eye with his hockey stick and knocked me right out. So they took me up to the school and put me in bed and left me there for two or three days. They treated me all right when I was sick. That was the only thing I had against them was they took away our language. I spoke Cayuga - I'm Upper Cayuga.

I ran away once and when I got back there I really got the strap - right to [forearm] - cut my wrist open. I seen a lot of them like that, getting the strap, and they wouldn't even cry. They punished us for practically nothing. You'd do something - I couldn't even go and talk to my sister - they'd want to know what you were talking about - "We were just talking." They'd say "Go to the Principal, go to the Principal" and I'd get the strap just for talking to my sister. It was only the Principal who gave the strap. George Howarth - he was the foreman on the farm, and I think Henderson was the greenhouse foreman - they treated us pretty well on the farm. Lager - he was kinda mean - he was the boys' master.

I was a ploughman - I belonged to the ploughman's association on the Reserve, ever since I was 12 years old. I got first prize at the ploughman's match in Ohsweken here when I was 12 years old - I was the youngest. When I went up there and worked on the farm I got to use the horses, plough and everything.

The porridge was just like glue in the morning - when I was up in the dormitory, when I got hit in the eye, one of the senior girls used to sneak me sandwiches - if they would have got caught they would have been punished.

That girl that got killed up there - they had a wheel on a pole with chains down from it, and they'd swing around on this thing, and this wheel come off and hit her.

I went to Tillsonburg and got a job on a farm out there, they were the ones got me the job out there, but I didn't stay there too long. I forget what happened out there - I didn't get along with the people. I left at almost midnight and I got here on the Reserve the next morning. Boy! was I ever tired - that's a long way. I had to walk, I started hitchiking but I couldn't get a ride - took me about five hours. My aunt used to live next door here - she's the one that sent us here.

It wasn't perfect - I shouldn't even have been sent there - I was dead against anything like that - the residential schools. They should have been building a high school here. A lot of the Natives don't want to take French as a second language, they want to take their own language. I hear they

are going to start teaching Native languages in these high schools now. When I'm among older people I talk my language - trying to get it back, but I have to mix my own language with English.

I was unhappy because of the way they treated everybody, making them speak English instead of their own language. I had to learn English. I imagine in the early days my aunt who sent me - she was there before me - she would have talked her language all the time.

As far as having a vacation - I never had a vacation - I stayed there and worked all summer. The food there in the summertime was as terrible as in the winter.

As far as discipline and abuse - it was all right in the summertime, because we were practically on our own - the ones who stayed. We went out and weeded gardens and stuff.

I got along good with all the boys there.

My parents didn't come and visit me because there was only my Dad anyway. He didn't come and visit me - my aunt came once or twice. That didn't bother me because I was working on the farm, and at the weekend I could go out and go to the show. I didn't need to have my parents take me out. I could go on my own - with the boys, for a quarter, so that way it was all right. It didn't bother me about my family, on account of I could go out to a movie. I was one of the senior boys, I was in charge of all the boys - they kept me there in the summer to take care of the cows and horses, and I'd look after the younger boys.

Lorna
1940 - 1945

We don't have the government that we had then. Looking back at the government - it was so interwoven with our way of life - the whole thing of our lives was governed by what the creator had given to us - the way of life that we should go, giving us discipline and a way of disciplining, and giving us a way of government and a way of life. By that I mean our own personal - deep inside - way of life. Things that harm us and things that are good for us and things that you shouldn't do, and along with that was all the stories - scary stories - that would keep a person from wanting to do those things, because of the damage that would result from the bad things. There was always a story for the bad things that you did, so that kinda kept you in line. And then undermining all of that was the residential school. We had the opposite - no more government, no more mama, no more daddy, no more uncle, no more sisters, no more Longhouse, no more way of life. The whole thing was disrupted and the people who were put at residential schools were molested. So there was a mental as well as physical abuse that went on. I come from the later years. I wasn't strapped for speaking Indian, I couldn't speak Indian. They had already taken the Native

language away, so there was no problem being beaten for speaking Indian, but there still was that white authority - a trauma that affects me yet - things that will probably always be there. Maybe that's as far as I can go - with just an awareness of it. I haven't come to the answer!!

I think the real terrible thing that happened for me - I'm trying to figure out what was the most terrible thing than just being there without a family. That's painful. There was this young woman - she was 19 in Grade 5 because she was epileptic and slow I suppose. She went up into the dormitory during the day when you weren't supposed to be up there. She went there for privacy because she was having her period, and the nurse caught her and reported her to the principal. The nurse brought her down to the playroom and the principal came down - he had sent for her and she said she wasn't going to go. She said she would take her licking right in the playroom, if she had to. So she didn't go and he strapped her until she had an epileptic seizure. The kids tried to protect her but we couldn't, because he was starting to strap her and lick her and he just kept on, and the girls were standing around and one of the girls pulled the strap from his hand from behind and kicked it, and all the girls tried to kick it away, and he shoved everybody aside and that - even brutally shoving everybody aside and knocking girls down. So everybody ran out of the lavatory and into the playroom, and that's when he got the strap and came after everybody and started strapping everybody wherever he could swing the strap. And then he got to her, because the kids backed away - nobody wanted to get hit, so they sort of got stood up against the wall and she was left alone, and he strapped her and strapped her until she had this seizure. And the next time at line-up, I think it was on the Saturday - it must have been because all the girls were there - anyway, the principal's wife came down at line-up and told the girls not to talk about what had happened. She said if we talk about it one to another, or if we talk about it to anybody, and if they find out, we would get worse. That really affected me in my counselling. I found it very very hard to talk about that experience. I was a child and seeing all that happen.

He was strapping her all over - anywhere he could reach her. After she had collapsed and he went back upstairs, we went to the faucets and tried getting water. In our playroom we didn't have no toys, nothing. Just the clothes we had on and empty boxes all round for storage - I don't know what they expected us to store in them - and cupboards. We kept our one towel in the cupboard - we didn't have much else of anything else in there, and if we had soap or something it would soon be gone because kids would steal them and hide them in their cupboards and we couldn't look in anybody else's cupboard. And we went and got the water with our hands and put it over her on her face. She came to after a while, and we helped her up and took her to the old lavatory, and that's where she showed us her back - how many times he had hit her. I was surprised that her whole back wasn't bleeding. It looked like as if there was blood just under the skin, and her head - where he had strapped her on the head there were these big welts, so that she couldn't comb her hair, and she had a black eye and there was bruises on her face, and her legs - all over her legs and buttocks. She was just a beaten pulp. We said "Why did you do this?" She said "I don't know, but I didn't want to get raped." I didn't even know what the word was, and I was going to school - I must have been about nine years old. I didn't know what the word was until later, and I thought it must be pretty terrible for her to take a beating like that. But then I didn't really realise then until I got older, what it really meant. Snell used to drink wine. You could tell when he was high, his face used to be just red, and he'd be smiling all the time!!!!

My brother was at the Mohawk too, and I'm thinking now, maybe that's why the boys wet their beds so much, because the men were sodomizing them. But the boys' dorm was just a big stench up there - mattresses were rotting. We used to work up there and have to do the boys' dorm and fix their beds in the morning, and we'd have to take the mattresses off and drag them out and dry them on the fire escape every day. The boys had to go up and fix their beds at 5 o'clock when they'd got through their chores.

And my brother got sick - he must have had the flu or something and it turned to pneumonia. The principal wouldn't let my father see him, and so my father insisted that he see him, and he pushed past the principal and the nurse hurried us, and my father went up to the boys room with her, and he reported to the Council what a terrible mess the boys' dorm was, and he went to see a lawyer, and there was a union he had to go and see, and when he went there they told him he could sue, because his son was half dead. He was so bad with pneumonia that the doctor said another week and he would have died. They said that we could sue - he said "No, he didn't want to sue, but they should just make sure that they had another principal come in," and that's when they changed and Mr. Zimmerman came. We were there when Mr. Zimmerman came, for a couple of years after that, and then we left. Things got a little bit better with Mr. Zimmerman, we had Brownies and Girl Guides, and we could go for walks, and in the spring we changed from our winter dress to our summer dress. That was about the only thing that was changed. There wasn't anything done about not having any toys - nothing changed very much.

We were really terrible. Being in there we were - I wouldn't say animal-like - we were worse than animals. They had the orchard there and after Mr. Zimmerman came they said that the children should have apples, because before we never had apples - that the children should have apples. So they were bringing a bushel basket of apples for the girls, and we got one apple each. And they'd do that about once a week. Anyway we said "Why should we just get one apple when they've got the whole orchard and they've got bushels of apples?!!" They would give us one apple each and then he'd go and take the rest of the apples around to the boys' side and we never knew what they did with them. We wanted them and they were very good apples, so the next time he came to give us the apples, we knocked him down!!! and the apples were rolling all over the place and the girls were gathering them in their aprons and we got as much as we wanted!!! Actually the bigger girls got the most and the younger girls went without so some of us ended up with no apples at all, but because of that they said they wouldn't give us apples any more, and that was a big thing for us. I guess we were all hungry - every child was hungry. You could buy a loaf of bread from the baker, but the other girls would try and get it.

We lined up for everything, we'd line up by number before we'd do anything - before you'd go to school, before you were dismissed for the duties. It was divided into two groups: A division and B division. If A division was in school, then B division would be doing the work and it varied mornings and afternoons, for one week, and then the next week B division would be in the morning and A division would be in the afternoon. We had to make beds and do all the work. I'd do laundry - I guess some of the girls were up in the laundry room for the staff, and they'd do all the ironing - they ironed all the staff clothes. They didn't do any of their ironing at all. They cooked their meals - the kitchenette girls were taught to cook meals for the staff that were different from our meals. They got a lot better meals and food. I didn't get to work in the kitchen. I used to make the beds and weed the garden, and learned how to make shirts. They made all the boys shirts. I think I was 12 when I left there. I was about 6 when I went there and my father put us in because my mother had passed away when I was three. We weren't lousy when we went there - we had long hair and all our hair was cut, and we got lice. They said "One good thing, they're not lousy." And I wondered what that word meant, I'd never heard that before, and anyhow it was good, but it didn't last very long, because we went downstairs, and we were stripped first in the sewing room, and given clothes to wear, but before that we had our hair cut. After they stripped us they cut our hair and put these clothes on us, and we were sent downstairs. They said "If you need anything, come up and knock on this door and the nurse will answer, and she'll tell you what to do." So we went downstairs and hardly had a need to knock on the door. We never got sick for some reason. We had to take cod-liver-oil every morning.

Looking back on it now, seeing this man beat up this girl, I lost my identity. I think not only seeing her get beat up was a denial of my own self, but not having a role model.

There was a lot of feelings of abandonment - aloneness. Aloneness every day. That feeling of not having anybody, of being so lonesome. We knew our Dad and we knew our sister, and we knew what it was like to be with them, and how we felt, and the difference of being there with nobody was really traumatic. My father wasn't allowed to visit for the first few months, because they said it would be unsettling, and we didn't see our brother for two months after we went to the school.

The more counselling I've had, the more I realise the traumas - the effect the residential school had on me. I'm thinking that people who really don't know - really haven't been counselled - because before this I never realised how much the residential school had affected me.

My sister was there too with me when I was there. To hear her lonesome cries - my goodness!- it would have been better if I was there by myself. She was my father's baby. She had turned five when she went. To hear her cry and to hear her holler "Daddy", was worse than my lonesomeness. I used to put my arms around her and say "Don't cry, don't cry," and I'd be crying. Then we'd both be crying. She was very much a baby. She was babied a lot and spoiled, and she found it difficult to be there.

We did things mostly on our own, being left alone in the playground and in the playroom. We had developed - over the years the girls had certain slang words and actions, and certain things that was always done. And the bigger girls would pick on the little girls, and we were always afraid of being slapped. We'd look at somebody just in a certain way, and they'd say "What are you looking at me like that for?" and slap you. So we were in fear a lot of one another. We didn't have toys, as I said, but I learned to play hopscotch there. We had broken pieces of glass and sticks to write with. We'd draw in the hopscotch diagram on the ground and we'd do that a lot. As soon as the snow went away we started to play hopscotch and we'd have two or three diagrams going where the girls were playing hopscotch, and we'd play about five or six to one diagram. When you'd miss you'd get out and somebody else would play, until everybody went through and you got your turn again, and you'd go where you left off. A couple of girls had jacks and a ball. That's one thing we had. Another thing we had - they'd bring us old uniforms and old dresses, and we'd tear them up and tie them together, and to get them weight we'd dip them in the bath and toilet, and we'd swing that around and we'd skip. The thing was the water would get all over the floor, and we'd have to wipe it up afterwards, but we didn't mind mopping up the water because we had so much fun skipping, and that's when we made our rope really long and played with all the other girls - everybody would skip. Probably would be on a Saturday afternoon.

We used to play hide-and-go-seek - but we didn't have too much places to hide - behind the trees that was all, but nevertheless we used to play. We gathered up all the leaves and laid them underneath the porch walls, and we used to hide there. I was hiding, and I was running and I jumped over these leaves, and I fell and I hit my head on the brick. And I had this big cut in my head, and I bled and bled and bled and I passed out. When they finally found me, they said "Where were you?" They said "You fell asleep." Then when they saw I was laying in my blood, they picked me up and carried me to the lavatory and somebody went and got my towel, and they used my towel to wash out my hair. We couldn't get the blood out of the towel, and there was a high fence there and I hid my towel over there. I threw it over the fence because I didn't want to report that I had gotten hurt. I was afraid of the strap so I threw my towel over there, and forgot about it. It must have been in the spring some time, but before the holidays I got the strap for losing my towel. They kept saying "Find your towel," but there was no place to look for my towel - in the bathroom - kids were helping me look around - but it was no good at all!!! I didn't remember at all, until recently when I was in counselling - in the last eight years - what happened to my towel. I was really weak, I just didn't have any energy at all. I just lay on the boxes for about three days!!! It was just the fear of telling. The older girls said "Don't tell" - they told everybody not to tell. I never thought about telling anybody.

Mrs. Fry was nice. She was a young person's teacher - the junior room teacher, who had replaced Mrs. Boyce.

When I left I went to No. 8 school here on the reserve, and when we went back to school we were with the other kids in our grades. We learned how to write - how to read and write and arithmetic. They gave me - the I.O.D.E. Chapter - the ladies up in Brantford - in each of the grades they had given a book, to honour people I guess, and they gave me Anne of Green Gables when I was in Grade 4. I must have been 11 at the time, and would have rather they didn't give the book because it just made the other girls mad that I got the book. I never read it, I never read the book at all. They'd say "You think you're smart because you got the book." I didn't even know nothing, or think about it you know!!! I just made a mess of my life in the worst way!! They all thought another girl should have it, but the I.O.D.E. ladies said it was because I couldn't see and I had good marks, so I had kept up my grades in spite of my not being able to see, so they gave me this book for encouragement. I used to have to go from my seat to the board to see what was on the board.

They used to give us shock treatments for bed-wetting. A lot of us never wet our beds but we still had to do it anyway. They said it worked for the girls but it didn't work for the boys. They couldn't really ever find out why, but I think it was because of the sexual abuse that went on there - bed-wetting is a result of sexual abuse. They used to bring in a battery - a motor of some sort or some kinda gadget, and he'd put the girl's hand on it and it would jerk us and it would go all the way through us from end to end - it would travel. And we would do that about three times. The girls who were brave enough would put their hands on that flat thing. We always had an outhouse, and hearing that toilet flush was a shock, because then you'd remember where you were in the night, and you'd have that knotted feeling about being away from home. But that was the realisation - hearing the toilet flush - where I was at, and I used to feel awfully isolated and rejected and alone, and abandoned. I can name those feelings now, but I didn't know what I was feeling when I experienced them being there - I didn't identify my feelings.

We always knew when the government inspectors were coming. We had to clean up. We used to have to scrub the cement - scrub down everything - when we knew that they were coming. They would tell us when we were going to be inspected - "You have to clean up." They'd give us chores to do and we'd have to do them. We'd have to scrub that cement floor, and when they came down we'd all be smiling!!! We had to make it clean for them to come in eh! My father said for them to come by surprise. My father went to Six Nations Council and told them what a terrible place it was for them, how the boys' room was so messy. But they never ever went to the boys' dorm. They would take them all over and spend time in all the other places, and then when they got to the boys, it was always too late to go to the boys' room. So they'd inspect the barns and all that, but they just never inspected the boys' room. And when my

father told them "Go there unexpected, pay them a visit, go and see for yourselves. The reason it's clean is that those kids are cleaning up before you go."

My brother didn't go back - he wouldn't go back. My father wouldn't let him go back - this was my father's only son. To see him so near to death - he didn't want to send him back. So we went back for two years after that, and it was better, because my father said "If you go back now, it will be better, and when you come out you'll be older, and you'll be able to take care of yourselves. Go back for a few more years" - and that's what we did. It was nearly the same - we had spring dresses for spring. I know we wore winter dresses all year with Snell. They were dark blue with red collars and cuffs. And we had an apron to go over it, and we wore that all the time. We never ever changed our dresses, or our combinations. We were given one combination and we wore that all year. We took a bath and we put on the same combinations, and our same dress, and our aprons was the same. They'd wash our aprons - once a month, I think, they'd change our clothes - our stockings, and we'd hand in our towel. You see we had a place for our aprons, a place for our towel, and a place for our stockings, and the kids who did the dorms would do the sheets. But in our box was two single sheets, an apron and socks rolled up, and a towel. That's what we'd have in our little pile. The towel was just a little one, but quite long. So on maybe a Thursday, evening some time, we'd go to our boxes and get our clothes, and then we'd put them on and hand in our dirty clothes. Then we'd sit in our seats with our aprons and our stockings and our towel!!!. Then we'd form a big round and we'd go round the school and as we came by we'd drop them in the pile. And when I didn't have my towel they said "No towel, Lorna General, No. 57"!!!!!

I had the strap for losing my towel, finally. But I think the fear of the strap was the most terrible thing and I suffered it for so long! I did get a strapping three times on each hand for not finding my towel. My sister met me at the bottom of the stairs and she said "What did they do to you?" I said "I got the strap." I didn't cry until she cried and then we both cried. I showed her my hands and I was trying real hard not to cry but it was sore. She said "Let me see" and I showed her, and she cried. It was really sore. I couldn't hold her, my hand was so sore - halfway up to my elbows. We got the strap for singing that song *There is a boarding-school far far away* during our chapel time. The girls, because we were mad, because this man did this to this girl, and we said "Let's sing this song, we'll really sing it out loud," so when chapel time came we sang that song. The boys were dismissed and the girls got a strapping. Everybody got a strap then. And we all got strapped for stealing - for going on a walk and we'd stolen turnips and we carried them in our aprons. We held up our aprons and piled in the turnips and then we were going to eat them all - we ran to the playground and tried to bury them, but it was too hard to dig with nothing. We brought them to the thing and they cooked them for us and we had turnips three times a day. We had to eat them till we ate them all up!!!! All of us got sick, we all had real real bad diarrhoea and stomach-ache - oh it was bad, it must have been food poisoning!!!!

I'm hoping with counselling and talking about it, and sharing - I've never shared so much about the residential school as I have in the last two years. Everybody wants to hear about it. I went to speak to the Executive Council of the Anglican Church, and I told them about the traumas I suffered there, and what it was like for me, and how I couldn't talk when I came into counselling, because they had said "Don't talk about it" as a child, and it was interwoven into my whole being, and it was very difficult for me to talk about what had happened. First of all there was a lot of fear, but then I realised I didn't have to be afraid to tell my story, and it wasn't my fault. To be free to talk and to tell was a release and a healing. If I had a story to tell, I'd better tell it, and I really feel I do have a story. The things that have affected me and the traumas that I suffered there are still affecting me. You see on our reserve now - our Family Violence centre, you see now - it's just terrible - how much has been handed down from generation to generation, from the residential school. I was drinking and leaving my children and neglecting them. I beat them and shook them up - I felt I had to control my children to have good children. Then when I was 31 I heard a sermon in church and I repented. Maybe some people feel that I'm a bit prejudiced against the school - I think I have a right to be. And as I said before, with counselling, I realise the softness that I'm coming into - it's not always been there!!! It's only come with talking about it and getting it out - the feelings about the experience.

A reality just hit me that I am the way I am, because I'm changing in my inner self - changing is healing for me. My counselling has been one of trauma, and my healing has been one of love. Love of people who will listen to my story. I've had the opportunity to tell my story all over the country, so it's not the first time. And the other time I was crying - even when I had my interview at the Mohawk Institute - at the Cultural Centre. We were sitting on the lawn. The Anglicans made a video of it and they showed it to their Executive Council. But a couple of years ago I was there with the Executive Council, and I think that happening really helped me to heal. It was the most helpful thing. They said "What can we do? We want to know."

I've always felt that I wanted to be a Minister from a very young child; because I was there at residential school, I came in and I forgot about it. Then later on through my counselling as I got rid of the traumas and began to heal, the same calling - the same feeling came back that I wanted to be a Minister. I never really had the authority to say I wanted to be a Minister!! - low esteem and self-worth and all of that. From the United Church I learned that they were having this Native Ministry for Natives, and I said "Could I go?" and they said "Yeah." But I didn't have a Church because of my eyesight too, and when the Minister left Grand River United, they called me. The ANCC - the All Native Circle Conference okayed my licence for baptisms and sacraments and for marriages. That's the most I ever hoped for - that's my far-reaching star.

Everything that intertwines in my life, the main fibre is the residential school, where I can go back to find the source. But it's always the residential school. I had no other experience. That's it. I never had no experience except the residential school in my forming years - I mean six and those years. We didn't learn an appreciation of the importance of any person - the uniqueness of a person!!

Lorna's Sister with Lorna
1940 - 1945

Lorna's Sister: I was one of the five youngest there. I was 4½. I didn't know what was going on - I knew later on. All I remember is a great big building with great big walls. I remember crying. I was confused - scared - I remember jumping up and down, but I don't know what I was jumping up and down for!!

When we were there, working in the Principal's office wasn't such a good place to work. Mr. Snell beat one girl till she fell over on the floor and had an epileptic seizure. He stepped right over her - in fact he stepped right on her and he said "She'll get over it." Because I was so small then, we were afraid of her, because we knew she had these seizures. At the time we didn't know they were seizures, we just thought they were something sinister about her - she took fits - that's what they used to tell us. So when he beat

her that time, they had us little girls all scared and they were telling us "Hurry up, get water for her, get water for her," so we'd give her water to drink but we didn't know what with. So all us little girls would go running into the bathroom and we'd get our hands cupped full of water and we'd run towards her and by the time we got to the doorway, of course it would be out of our hands, and we'd turn around and run back and get some more. We were scared and we had to do what the older girls told us to do. We just kept doing that. It was senseless when you think about it now. We were scared, and we were scared of her - she was an older girl - about 19. Today when I think back about it, I think she was just a severe epileptic and she wasn't being treated at the school. She had these seizures every so often which would scare the daylights out of the younger ones.

Like I say, I was one of the five youngest - we were "the five."

The senior room teacher, his name was Mr. Yeandle - every month they used to gather up the youngest kids and take us up to the senior room and line us up and give us electric shocks. They used her as the grounder - she actually held on to the thing, and those shocks were supposed to prevent us from wetting the bed. I don't think it helped because we was always wetting the bed!! I don't know if it hurt her, but it sure did feel like somebody was jerking our arms out when it went through us - it must have. They made us hold hands - we'd all be lined up around the classroom in a circle and he had some kinda machine, and she had to touch it, and when she touched it it would go right through all of us.

Lorna [sister]: I think he made her touch it - she'd be strapped to the machine and he'd turn it on and the shock would go all the way down.

S. How it felt to me, it was just as if someone was jerking my arms out and the backs of your knees would hurt. At the time we didn't know why they were doing it - they'd just line us up and do it to us. I was only four, for crying out loud, it would just be time to go and line up and hold on hands and everybody just automatically did it, because that was the time to do it and that's what happened at that time. There was no mention of why, or anything, we just had to do it and it was part of being there.

I remember being thrown in the clothes closet with Gramma - she was the youngest one, and I was the next one to her. They used to call her Gramma because the uniforms were so long on her - they'd come down to her ankles. I remember being thrown in the clothes press with her, where all the Sunday 'go-to-meeting' uniforms were. There were rats in there and I remember crying, and I remember wondering: Why was I in there? Why did they put me in there? And even then I didn't know. We were both sitting there crying and afraid that these mice were going to get us, or these rats. I guess we were thrown in there for speaking Indian. I don't remember speaking Indian but my aunt says we used to speak Indian fluently before we went. I don't remember, but I remember being thrown in there. I don't know who did it - all I remember is being in there - whether it was one of the bigger girls - whether they were told to put us in there. There was this bunch of girls from Walpole Island that used to speak Indian all the time, and they were always getting thrown in there, but they used to go and hide after a while and speak Indian. My older sister - she always said if I tried hard enough I could speak again. I know what I want to say, in my mind I know what I want to say, but it just won't come out. I talk a little bit of Indian now and then, but apparently we used to be fluent before we went to the Mush hole.

Little as I was I always felt I had to take care of my sister, and she always felt she had to take care of me. We had these uniforms with numbers on them - I was 63. She

lost her towel - and they only give you two or three days to find it if you misplaced it. So we went around looking for that towel of hers and of course she couldn't see very well. We looked and we looked. We looked in all the boxes, we looked in all the lockers, we looked all over and we couldn't find it. So the day that she was supposed to turn it in, she couldn't, so she had to go and see the sewing room teacher, Mrs. Bennett. So I walked with her to the stairway, and just now when you go to that place and you see the stairway, it's just an ordinary stairway, but when I saw her going up there it looked like a mountain, I'm telling you. She went up so damned slow, I thought she'd never get to the top!!! I heard the knock and I heard that door open and I heard them take her in. I didn't hear any talking but I heard the swats. I counted, and don't quote me on this because I may be wrong, but I think I heard 24. But I was 4½ - maybe I said 1, 2, 24, I don't know!! But to my mind at that time it was 24. Then the door opened and there she was, and she looked so tiny coming down and she was crying. She come down and she was crying and I never thought she'd get to the bottom, and I was crying. She come down and she just stood there and she was crying and I was crying, and she showed me her arm and right up to her elbow was crimson red from the strap. When I think of it now I still want to cry and I think it must have been more than 24 whacks to make it that red!!

L. I thought it was three on each side, but it could very well have been 24!!!

She gave me more time than three days, but it was in the last three days we looked for it. It was in the fall until spring, and every week, or every time we handed in our clothes, I had to go in this room and she'd ask me if I'd found it. Sometimes she'd call me from the school, and I always waited - I was never ever able to relax for that day, because after she'd ask me for my towel - during school hours she would bring me out of the room and ask me - I always felt that she had the strap ready and I'd get the strap right there in the hallway, and I'd have to go right back into school. When the time for me to get my strap came, she did it in the sewing-room. I was in school and she brought me out of school. Sally was in A division and I was in B division - that's how we were able to be together because she wasn't in school.

The reason why I lost it was because we were playing hide and seek and I jumped and hurt my head. They brought me in and somebody ran and got my towel and they used it to wipe my head. It was all bloody and we couldn't get out the stain. Somebody said "Throw it away so they don't see it" so they rolled it up all small and lifted me up to that high fence, and I dropped it over. You know I had forgotten all about that - forgotten what happened to it until I went for counselling.

S. You mean all this time you'd done away with it and you had me searching for it?!!!!

L. I bled a lot and I imagine that's why I forgot.

S. J ran away from the Mush hole one time, and I remember when he was running away - we were in chapel and everybody was telling us "Don't look out, don't look out. J's running away - he's crawling through the leaves." So we made sure we didn't look outside, because if you looked outside or anything the officers in charge would try to see what you were doing. He was crawling through the leaves, and I guess he wasn't old enough to know his way home, and he got lost and hid in the dump. I don't know how many days it was before they found him. But when they found him they brought him back to school, and at chapel time again, they brought him into the chapel room again - which was the senior room - and they sat him in front of us and he had all that impetigo all over him, and his tongue was all swelled up where he couldn't close his mouth, and it was all white hanging out of his mouth.

L. A rat bit his tongue and he was sick and feverish, and he hadn't been allowed to sleep.

S. And they told us to take a good long look at him. This is what would happen to us if we decided to run away. To this day when I hear that hymn *Onward Christian Soldiers* I think of J, and I get all weepy inside when I think how cruel it was of them to make him sit there in front of us in chapel, and make us sing Christian songs. I mentioned this to him one time and I reminded him what happened to him when he ran away from the Mush hole, and you know, to this day he denies it. He said it didn't happen - he must have blackened this out, because I know it happened - I was there, I saw it. Yet for him to say it didn't happen - I had the wrong J - but there was only one J at the school.

Mr. Yeandle was supposed to be one of the better teachers - him and Mrs. Fry. Mr. Yeandle was the one who give us the strap. He was a good teacher. Mrs. Fry was a good teacher - she didn't stay there very long, probably because she couldn't take what was being dished out. The worst person there to me was Mrs. Pettigrew - she was in the kitchen. She was the worst person to me - because she gave me a strapping. We were going for lunch and it was on a Saturday when the Women's Auxiliary used to make corn soup for all the kids and you could eat as much as you wanted. The salt was sitting near my girlfriend and she didn't want it near her so she pushed it over to me, and you know how kids are - she pushed it to me and I pushed it back to her, and Mrs. Pettigrew saw me and she singled me out, and I hated her for the rest of my life! Because she only gave me the strapping, she didn't give my girlfriend the strapping. We were both doing it!!

L. They had a strap in every drawer - wherever they were stationed, they would have a strap. In the scullery there was a drawer with a strap where you'd do the vegetables. All they had to do was open it up - it was right there. They didn't have to go looking all over for it.

S. When I first went there I was too young to go to school. I was even too young for the bunny class - they had a bunny class. So they took us five that were the youngest and they made us go under this longer table in the sewing room, and they used to have hampers of black stockings in there - the black stockings we used to wear. So they used to make us five go under that table and we were supposed to roll those stockings up. That's how they made us work - rolling black stockings up into a ball and putting them in bags. Because we were so young we used to play ball with them, and they used to reach under the table with those big yardsticks and hit us with them so that we would get to work. And not only that, they used us with the older girls. Whenever the older girls got in problems and they didn't want to tell on anybody - we'd have to have assembly or lineup - and the whole staff would come down and they'd threaten to beat us or put us through the mill, if the girl behind it didn't own up to what they were doing. That's how they would get them to tell on each other. But the one time I remember, that day your division was going to drown Mrs. Bennett when she tried to drown M. I don't know what happened because I wasn't up there, but your division was in the sewing room. We were downstairs and all of a sudden we heard this great commotion from upstairs, and everybody comes running down, and everybody's howling "Run! Water, water!" In fact I wrote a story about it and it's called *Water, Water, Everywhere* And they come running down howling "Water, water" and they're trying to tell us what's happened, and here we are, us young little kids again. So Mrs. Bennett was trying to get them back in the sewing room and she come downstairs, and the bigger girls - I don't where they got pails of water - but as she came round the corner they threw the water in her face, and no matter where she went everybody was throwing water on her because she tried to drown this one kid upstairs.

L. I think the water bucket was there to do that because when a person did something they weren't supposed to, she'd duck their head in the water and hold it under the water. That was a form of punishment. She was trying to put M's head in the bucket and this was just too much for the other girls, and they saw the opportunity to take off, so they took off, and she lost interest and started to chase them. I don't know where the other buckets came from either. Maybe one of the girls was a matron and they knew where to get the buckets, but we never ever had buckets, and we never ever had containers of any kind.

S. The next morning - they had assembly and you had to count off your numbers - and they wanted B Division to step out. So they had to step out and they wanted them to step forward and confess to who was doing what - who were the instigators, and no-one would. So then they made us step back and they threatened them with us again - the little kids. That if they didn't tell who was responsible for what happened, then they would punish us by putting us through the mill. So then they asked again "Will the guilty parties step out," and, I don't know what it was about - or maybe it was because we were just used to it, but all five of us stepped out - the little ones. We must have looked at each other, or we must have had some sort of unity about us where we would step out like that, because we never stepped out before. But when she asked us to step out or they'd put us through the mill, all five of us just stepped out, to show them that they could do what they want with us!! Or maybe it just took that time - everything that had happened before - we weren't afraid of them now.

L. That was the hardest thing - seeing them step out. For me - I didn't want to step out. I didn't - I really didn't want to step out. And I wasn't the first to step out - I must have been about the last. It really did something. Finally everybody that was in B division stepped out, yet I was still trying to hold back. But where would I be if I didn't step out? So I had to step out. I had run out - I left the room - left the sewing room while it was in session. Everybody left. I didn't have a bucket. There was older kids that had the buckets - or more aggressive.

S. They couldn't do nothing. They'd have had to give everyone the strap. I think they took away visiting privileges. That's what they'd do when they couldn't prove anything. Like you could visit your brother once a month.

L. It wasn't once a month - it was quite a while, by the time everyone had visited and your turn came up again. We only visited about 4 times in the whole year. We didn't see my brother for two months after we went there.

S. I remember being sick - all us little kids had mumps. I remember the top dormitory where they used to put us. This medicine the nurse would give us - it was chalky and so one of us got the bright idea that the plaster tasted just like this medicine they give us and we started eating this plaster from the wall. The nurse came up and found out about it and she came up there and she turned us all over and gave us a spanking!!. But in our minds we thought that if it tastes like the medicine we were going to get better. I suppose we were hungry too!

We used to have fire drills.

L. When someone would step on the fire escape it would go down, and so we could only be out there so long, and we'd all have to get out there, because if it went down before everybody was out there then they'd have to jump or stay up there. We just had so much time to get out of our beds and get out there.

S. I'm afraid of fire escapes to this day. I thought that's how it was at the Mush hole - that the whole thing went down - like the steps.

They put me on this maypole when I was little and swung me around till I fell off. You can't even get me on a ferris wheel!! This was like a ride - you'd go round on it. But they put me up there and they'd tie you on it and swing you around till you'd fall off, when I didn't want to do it. There was an apple orchard there and our playground used to be right next to it with a fence going through. Us little five - because we were so small - the bigger girls would make us crawl under that fence and steal apples. If we got caught by Mr. Lager, who was the boys' master, then we'd get a

strapping. If we didn't do it for these bigger girls, then we'd get beat up, or I was put on the maypole for that reason. You knew right away which side your bread was buttered on - what you had to do - you had to go and steal those apples. And we had these big aprons on with belts, and we used to put the apples in our aprons and come back with an apron full of apples. You'd get back on the other side of the fence and the big girls would take them all - you wouldn't even get one!! If you had one for yourself you had to take that risk.

L. If you took a bite they'd slap you.

S. Being a smaller person you didn't get anything. You had to be afraid of the staff, and you had to be afraid of the older girls. Probably because of everything that happened to them when they were younger, when we got there they just turned around and did it to you - the older ones when we were there that were big enough to get away with it.

L. Nobody tattled on anybody.

S. They used to make us fight too because we were sisters. We must have been kinda close, but the bigger girls would put us in a circle and make us fight. Then if we didn't fight each other they'd beat us up!! I don't know why that was. By the time you came out of the Mohawk you were a scrapper. Your culture was taken away - you were nothing. All you knew how to do was fight. You had a chip on your shoulder.

Mrs. Turner, she was all right wasn't she? She had a kind face.

L. If she was on duty, everybody realized that she was good, so they were good. The ones that were mean inspired us to meanness.

S. I used to get scolded. I remember Mrs. Smith - she was the nurse - used to threaten me - to this day I don't know what it was to do with me and my shoes. She always got after me because I ran the heel down on my shoes.

There was the song we used to sing in Church:

There is a boarding school far far away
Where we get mush 'n' milk three times a day
Oh how the huskies run
When they hear the dinner bell
Oh how the huskies run
Three times a Day

and the other one - on the Queen's birthday we all used to stand by the steps, waiting for the driver -

24th of May is the Queen's birthday
If you don't give us a holiday we'll all run away!!

An hour and a half later a great big cattle truck would pull up and they'd pile us all into the cattle truck and bring us down to the reserve to get our Bread and Cheese. When we were up there we were all so eager to come down here and get our Bread and Cheese. When we got down here all with green uniforms, and our bald heads and everything, and we'd be just like cattle. They'd drop us off the trucks and we'd stand there all huddled together, because the other kids from the reserve would come around and point at us and stare at us. So we weren't happy - we couldn't go anywhere or do anything, because they said "Look at the Mush hole kids - with no hair", and stuff like that!! We had our bald heads because of the bugs that used to come in there - body lice. That was one of the reasons why we were taken because they said our father couldn't take care of us properly, but I never got body lice and I never got head lice while I lived with my father. But I sure got 'em at the Mush hole. We had bugs, and we didn't want to have bugs so we got into the kerosene, and I put some on my girl-friend's head and she put some on my head, but I guess we put too much on and we got blisters. When her sister found out about it - we were crying - she asked her who did it and she pointed at me, so her sister slapped me up, and then when she realized I had blisters in my hair too, she felt so sorry that she hugged us both.

L. For a long time they couldn't comb their hair because of the blisters. If the nurse or the staff had found out that they had blisters they would have got strappings, and so they didn't tell them.

S. One time we ran away from Mrs. Bennett when she took us to Mohawk Park and we stole all those turnips. We had turnip soup all week!!!

We learned to survive - it was a good survival course for a 4 year old!!! Hopefully if I go and get hypnotized I'll be able to speak Indian again - maybe it's there!! I can't remember speaking Indian. But I remember the day we came home. I remember that day as if it were yesterday. The day we came home we were standing out there when my Dad came out and he was speaking Indian to us. Lorna and I looked at him - we couldn't figure out what he was talking about, and he got angry with us - really angry. Or maybe not so much angry as disappointed. He said "Even my dog could understand." That was true, his dog could understand Indian!!! That's what the Mush hole did to me - it took away my language, and to this day I don't want to speak Indian. It seems that if I speak it there's something - a dark shadow will come over me - something ominous will happen to me.

There were those awful combinations we used to have to wear - every two weeks we got to change them - the same time you'd change your bedclothes. I imagine there must be a lot of mental blocks - so much happened there. The boys if they used to run away too much they used to hang them by their wrists from the water pipe and give them lashes. I imagine it was probably the boys' master.

When my brother was sick, my father finally forced his way up there. The bed right next to my brother had faeces in it.

L. One girl ran away. When she came back she was put through the mill in the playroom. She had to crawl through a line of legs and everyone would hit her with a board. She had a broken nose and was badly bruised. She didn't go to a doctor. I met her after and she told me she vowed she'd get everyone of us and kill us!! We almost killed her.

S. When they'd put them through the mill they started out with us five youngest and our legs couldn't hardly spread apart.

L. They started with us bigger girls - at the end she was just laying there. They were saying "Hit her, hit her," and she couldn't go through there, they were too small. I didn't realise until after that it wasn't our job to help the officers punish runaways - that this wasn't the way to treat runaways.

The boys that they used to hang up - they'd probably get the older boys to do it too.

S. That's where I learned how to fight.

L. We couldn't visit with our brother during visiting time, because we would probably tell what had happened. They took away our visiting privileges so we couldn't talk about it.

S. When we did see him he would give us old slabs of bread. My brother wasn't bad looking and the girls that worked in the scullery used to like him and they would slip him extra slabs of bread, or else he'd trade something for something. I'm wondering how it could last till the next time he saw us - these old crusty slabs. Girls used to slip out slabs of bread, or once in a while we'd get those hot biscuits, and once in a while they'd sneak out biscuits by putting them in their stockings - under their garters, and they'd give it to us to give to him.

L. We used to sneak out bologna and have a picnic - with bread - and we used to share it with him.

S. My husband was in there - he used to say he was 64 lbs when he went in. Four years later when he came out he was 1 lb lighter.

They thought my father couldn't take proper care of us, but I'm here to tell you I never got bugs when I was living in my father's house, but sure did get them within a week after I was at the Mush hole. I changed my underwear more than once every two weeks when I was at my Dad's too!!

If you wet the bed your mattress and your bedclothes weren't put out to dry or anything. They had to dry by themselves and it was still damp when you went to bed. You'd find a dry spot and lay there, or else jump in bed with your sister after the matron made her last rounds. We always knew when it was her last rounds because as soon as she left Lorna'd say "Come on"!!

L. We'd wait until the last rounds were made and then she'd come over. She never peed once she was in my bed!!!

S. I still never eat apple pie - I had to go and steal these apples and if I got caught by the boys' master I'd get a whipping, but if I didn't go and steal these apples for these big girls I'd get a whipping too. And the one time that I was put on the maypole by these older girls I fell off, so to this day you can't get me on a ferris wheel. That's what they'd make us do, the bigger girls, they'd make us steal apples, and we'd fill our aprons up with apples. We'd have to crawl on our belly, because the boys' master's house was right there and he was watching for apple stealers. We'd have to crawl on our belly and get those apples and crawl back under the fence. The only thing the big girls did for you was hold the fence up!!! You'd have all these apples in your apron.

L. I was too big to go under the fence.

S. I still remember us as 'the five'. We were always together all the time I was there, but why I remember 'the five smallest' is because when I first went there I was one of the five smallest. But as time went on I wasn't one of the five smallest, but I was still one of 'the five'. We were a unit more or less - when we were older we stuck together because we had been through hell, we might as well go through more all together!! - we were always one. There's one I didn't want to keep in touch with because we used to fight like cats and dogs. She and I used to fight - as soon as we'd look at each other we'd fight - for no reason at all, only that they made us fight all the time. It was terrible. Today I don't think I want to meet her because I might want to fight her!!!!

L. There was a meeting in Ohsweken with the Aboriginal Justice and L asked me to come because they were talking about the injustice of the residential schools and I was talking, and because I can't see, I didn't know who was there. But afterwards - I was talking about things that happened and about my brother - one of them said she had forgotten about the things that had happened, but when I talked about them, then she remembered. Then the others - they all remembered that and they were laughing about that!! But they all said they had forgotten, different things. I guess I remember them because I went to counselling, because I

realised there were things wrong with me.

It was like a prison. We were locked in - imprisoned. When I think about that it makes me feel jittery inside - like I want to get out, and there's no way out. When I think about how we were there without nobody coming for us.

S. One holiday we came out and went straight to the Blind Institute and we were still prisoners. My sister worked there, and she brought us out, because my Dad wasn't going to bring us out, so she brought us out for the summer, but she had to take us to the Blind Institute to be with her. All the kids had gone home for the summer.

My Dad had this little car - this Model-T car, and we knew that he'd only come to see us every two weeks. But faithfully, faithfully, we stood out by the steps to the driveway every week. Early in the morning, as soon as we went through what we had to do, we stood there and waited all day, knowing that he wasn't going to come, but hoping that he would come. And then when he did come we'd get all excited, and he'd either visit us or take us out. He'd take us to Brantford and we had to stay in the car while he got us this fish and chips. I swear today, if I can get fish and chips - if I see somebody selling fish and chips and wrapping it up in newspaper - oh gee! I think I could eat all the fish and chips!! because that's how he'd bring it back to the car - wrapped in newspaper, and we just spread it out on the seat and have a feast. That's something though, when you know within yourself he's not going to come, and you stand there anyway hoping. Maybe it was hope that helped us in life!

Marguerite Beaver
1940 - 1948

My family was there and it burned down [1903] and they had to come home. We went there voluntarily, because we wanted to, not because we had to. We were treated well - very well. One girl did have a child - she said it was one of the teachers - but he used to go to her house all during the summer - everybody said it was his, but you can't probably prove it, but there was nothing like sexual abuse went on while we were there - ever. We always got a lot to eat - well, see Mr. Zimmerman came in there and then Mr Peguis and Mr. Hough from the No. 20 camp came - that closed down - and the cook, and the engineers, come over from there and they were really fantastic - we used to get eggs and bacon - they used to make everything. They'd get up at 4 o'clock in the morning and be down there cooking. We got a lot of things to eat - good stuff like everybody else - after Zimmerman came. It was a man who cooked for the army camp and he was good.

I enjoyed it there - I really enjoyed it because my two brothers and sister went at the same time, and I was there seven years. In fact I wrote my Entrance exam for going

into Grade 9. They didn't let us write it there because we only went to school half-a-day all year, and every one of us that went up there to Echo Place School to write, every one of us passed really high. The ones from the Mohawk Institute were the highest ones that graduated, and yet we only went to school half-a-day, and we had to work the other half. I went to B.C.I. - I graduated in 1951. We couldn't stay at the Mohawk Institute - not when I was there. When you turned 16 you had to get out, but I got out before. I went to the Mohawk when I was 7 or 8, so I must have went in 1940 to 1948. The ones that didn't have no parents could stay at the school for high school - there was people from all over the place. When I was there there was ones that went to high school from there, but when you were 16 you had to get out. There was a lot that used to stay there in the summer too - that didn't have no place to go. Peter and Betty Smith used to take some of them in the summer - they lived in Buffalo.

We sewed, we had to do everything, we learned to scrub floors. It was so funny, not long ago somebody asked me if I wanted to go up and see the Queen Anne Silver, and I said "No I don't. I cleaned that silver so many times." We had to because we used to take communion out of it every Sunday. We went to church twice on Sundays - in the morning and in the afternoon. We dressed up in our best clothes and marched down there. My Dad was Longhouse and my mother's side was more or less Anglican. I went to the Longhouse with my Dad when I was small, but then I started going to Sunday school at St. Paul's Church.

I didn't know how to speak Mohawk when I went there - none of us did. That's why a lot of them said they couldn't talk it when they were there, but I don't think there was any from this reserve that knew how to talk it anyway. I understood it at home and I think if my Dad didn't die when he did, I'd be able to talk it now. I couldn't carry on a conversation or anything, but I never learned to talk it.

I was there when Snell beat K S - I was one of the ones that was going to go after him. They took her to the doctor and she never come back. He was hitting her with the strap and she just stood there, and he just kept hitting her on the arms, and stuff just came out of her mouth and she just fell. At the time I didn't know she was epileptic. I didn't hear anything about her saying she didn't want to get raped. I don't think there was any sexual stuff there, not that I heard of or knew of, and I was one the older ones when I left, and I'd never ever heard of anything. One of the girls got pregnant - but she got pregnant when she went home for the holidays. It was funny because the boys - she worked in the kitchen and they used to come through with the milk, and we had to wash everything in the laundry room - well, we had pinafores we used to wear, and everybody was proud about their belts, that our boyfriends gave us, with big buckles, and all of a sudden we noticed she wasn't wearing a belt. And the boys would come in and say - and they used to call her 'Rama hag' - "Rama hag's going to have a baby." But she was the only one I remember. She was sent home. We could speak with our brothers - on Thursday nights, in turn when your name came up. After Mr. Zimmerman came we could play ball - we used to come down here to the different schools and play ball. We could talk to our brothers - we used to have to go up in the front - we used to call it the Visitor's Room and I think we could talk to them three minutes, or five minutes on Thursday nights. Other than that we couldn't even go on the boys side or nothing when Mr. Snell was there. Then they built a rink - the Rotary Club and different clubs in Brantford - they gave us skates and they built a big rink and we used to be able to go and skate at nights, and go on the boys' side and play ball. When Mr. Snell was there we couldn't even go talk to them - you'd get a licking, you'd get a strapping if you were caught talking to the boys. But I was lucky, me and my sister, because my brothers - when they could go out they used to go and work at Passmore's - and we always had money and they'd give us chocolate bars and apples and oranges. My Mum and Dad used to come up and see us

every Saturday anyway, and bring us home once a month for the day. My family - we didn't *have* to go there, but we wanted to because all the others had gone there. My Mum had gone there and my older brothers. I had one older brother who didn't go, but all the rest of us went. We'd go out once a month - they'd come at 8 o'clock in the morning and we'd have to be back at 6 o'clock at night. That's probably why I liked it there. We had everything - we'd never want for anything. We'd get our own toothpaste, and body powder and soap and all that, because what was supplied there wasn't - it was castile soap. Now I use castile soap because it's so good germwise!! I don't know what kinda toothpowder they had up there, but my family we always had our own toothpaste. We could keep it because we had "bigger sisters" that looked after us when I was there. They had to look after you and make sure your hair was done, and your teeth was washed and all that.

I liked it there. I learned a lot. I learned to cook - I'd have been taught it at home too, but not like - we had to make the boys' overalls, and the boys' shirts, and the yokes were the hardest things to do. I used to shove that on my sister, because she was a real good sewer!! We made everything, and we darned the boys' socks and our socks. We did the laundry, and changed the beds once a week, and we changed our clothes once a week, and we had our different uniforms. Then after a while we were able to wear some of our own clothes, but when my sister was there they were able to wear all their own private clothes. My mother used to take her clothes and shoes and everything. But not when I was there - we had to wear uniforms. The clubs in Brantford used to donate all these clothes - new clothes and everything after Zimmerman came.

I'll never forget when Mr. Snell was there and my brothers - one of them used to work in the chicken house, and they used to get - my heavens, I don't know - 1700 eggs a day, and we got one egg at Easter. Can you imagine that? One egg, and all them eggs that they got a day, and we'd have to candle them and everything, and they sold them. They used to sell all the cream - they had cows and pigs and chickens and horses, and they grew all their own potatoes and turnips, and vegetables, and they had the big orchards. We got good food when I was there, after Mr. Zimmerman came. In fact the officers - when he was the principal - they ate what we ate. Before that they'd have their own roast beef and everything. They used to cook all that down in the kitchen and you'd have to take it up. As you got older you got to work different places, you got to work up in the officers, then up in the principal's. We used to have to take them bacon and eggs and everything we never got, until after Zimmerman came and they ate what we ate. Mr. Snell's daughter used to live there - she used to make us so mad. She used to come around with her suckers and all that, and we could not go past this line of trees up from the girls' playground to where the cars park now. We couldn't go past that and she'd come around with her ice cream cones and her suckers and just make us wish we had some. Like I say we were never in want, not just my family, there was a lot of different ones from down home that their Mum and Dad came to see them and took them stuff. I know when Snell was there my mother used to bring us up roast chicken, and she used to bring us everything - roast chicken and cake, and they always brought us fruit and that. My brothers used to have to go and get the cows, and as they'd be coming back they'd give us stuff through the fence - which we'd have got a licking if they ever knew. But they always used to make sure we had everything. And at that time half a quarter was a lot!! My brothers used to go work at Passmore's and they used to go and cut grass after supper, and they used to give us money, they always had money. I can't complain, but there are some who never ever seen stuff like that, and they didn't have family to go and see them really. There was one little girl from Walpole Island and she was tiny - maybe she was five years old - she was so tiny they used to have to put her to sleep in the afternoon, because she couldn't stay up all day. We used to have to get up at 6 o'clock in the morning, and after chapel at night the little ones would have to go to bed, but when I was a senior we could stay up to 9 o'clock, but that was it. And I think that was why we were all so smart in school, because there was no TV, and I think there was one radio - a battery radio - what was there to listen to then? That's all there was to do was to study, and that's all we used to do. We couldn't go down in the playroom, we had to stay up in the senior schoolroom until 9 o'clock, and then we all had to go to bed. In the afternoons - say after school - well we went to school in the afternoons till 4 o'clock - well then, at 5 o'clock, the ones that had to work had to go to the kitchen - the older ones - but we used to play ball and that out in the yard. Another thing we really liked - they had the Brownies and Girl Guides. Shirley Stern was our Captain and Barbara Boddie was the Lieutenant and we used to look forward to that. And Lady Baden Powell come down there and we all went to the Tutela Park and the ones from the Mohawk Institute - I'll never forget, oh we were so proud - we won everything - the inspections for the Brownies and the Girl Guides, out of all the Troops in Brantford. They used to take the ones that stayed there in the summer, they used to take them camping. I went with them one time when they went to Chiefswood and we had a fabulous time.

I liked the teachers - there was a music teacher there, but she didn't stay long - she was an Indian girl - was she? We used to look real forward to her coming there. When I first went there Mrs. Boyce was the first sewing-room teacher and then Mrs. Bennett. We used to tell my Mum and Dad everything that happened to us. I got my hair cut for smoking. My Mum - she worked for the Crown Attorney - and they were going to sue them that time - he said they could be in jail if they cut your hair, and I had real long hair and they cut it up to here [ears]. They cut our hair for punishment that time. I got a strap a lot of times - for

smoking, going over in the orchard and stealing apples!! I run away once - there were seven of us that run away once, and we had no reason to because we had just been to the fair the day before that. Mother and Dad were so mad at me - she said: "They were good enough to bring you down here - what are you running away for?" My sister was so mad at me, she was screaming at me. We were getting down the fire escape - we knew how to stick this thing in the door so it would hold that button so the alarm wouldn't go off. We were bad - bad. I got a licking once for pushing Miss Bennett in a hole in the dormitory. I didn't push her - she come up there and she started picking on me anyway - well I gave her reason to I guess, me and these three girls. There was a big hole in the floor, and she just come marching up that top dormitory accusing me of being out of bed or something. You could get up and go to the bathroom, but I forget what - she come in and I wasn't even out of my bed and she come around there, and she said that I was going to get a strapping, and I said "What for?" She said because I was out of bed and I was laughing at her. I wasn't laughing at her, and I wasn't even out of my bed, and she come to the one side of my bed, and she had the strap in her hand, and I don't know whether she was going to hit me with it. I jumped up and as she leaned on my bed I pushed it, knowing there was a big hole by my bed, and I pushed the bed and it fell and of course it hit her leg and knocked her over. She didn't get hurt - she fell on the bed. She always used to say "Oh your sister would never think of doing this." My brothers were always so good when they were there too. I guess I was the bad one - I had a lot of fun.

I worked at Sears and Roebuck in Rochester right from high school in 1951. Then later I took my mother's place and now I do cooking and housekeeping.

I think the education has been useful to me - not just reading, writing and arithmetic. At the Mohawk School we were taught everything - how to cook, how to clean, how to scrub floors, how to make clothes, how to knit - just everything. How to do laundry. We used to have to do all the laundry - iron the boys' shirts and pants - we had to do it just right. Clean the silver, do the dishes right. We had to darn the socks - put a ball in there. I liked it there - a lot of them I know didn't - they were orphans, they didn't have anybody. There was always my brothers and my sisters there, and after my two brothers left, my younger brother came back. I can understand the ones that didn't that were orphans. My younger sister and my two cousins - they were sent home because they had one parent, and they sent all the ones in from Quebec that couldn't even speak English. If you had one parent you couldn't be there and everybody was up in arms about it because that was built for the Six Nations, not everybody else.

Mr. Zimmerman, when he came there he had the one daughter, Joanie, and Mrs. Zimmerman not long after got pregnant and had Barry, but my sister had more personally to do with them because she worked with them up there. I never got that privilege, I wasn't old enough. It was just the older girls that got to work. As you got older you worked your way up, and that was the highest you could go, was to work up there for them! He was always really good to me, and he was good to our family. And even after that we used to go up there and he used to say "Oh, my children." My mother got to know him through the church, and my mother was involved in a lot of different things in Brantford. So he was just a really really good friend, right until the day he died. If one of our family passed away we'd always get him to come down and speak - he was always really close to us. He wasn't that strict with me - I mean there's rules and regulations, and sure I broke the rules a lot but I took my punishment for it. As far as hating him and that for it - I could hate my Mum and Dad because they had to discipline me too. But we had both a Mum and a Dad, and my mother was very well known in Brantford, knowing the big shots because she worked for judges and different ones up there. We were very fortunate. I always got along with the other kids - I'm a joker from the word go! I was always in sports and that.

When No. 20 camp was still there, this J C and M L, they sneaked out and went over to No. 20 camp and they got caught. And at that time I was a senior, because they would punish us by not letting us go to the show. See, we used to go to shows on Saturdays, and so when they got caught doing that we put them through the mill. All our privileges was cancelled, we couldn't go to the show on account of them getting caught, and so that was the only time I remember them putting anyone through the mill. They were big girls then, and we put them through the mill, and that was all of us standing there with our legs apart, and they had

to crawl through there and we'd hit 'em on the bum - that's all we had to hit 'em on because that's all you could see go through!! That was the only time - no they weren't beaten up - how could they get beaten up when we were hitting them on the bum? But that was the only time they ever snuck out to the army camp!! No, they weren't beaten up at all, because a lot of the ones that lined up to do it - and everybody wouldn't line up, it was more or less just the older ones - us older ones that was deprived of our privileges - a lot of them didn't even hit them as they crawled through. A lot of them did hit them. But that was the only time we put them through the line, that I remember, when I was there.

I'm not saying that the teachers were afraid of my Mum and Dad, but they knew very well that if they did anything to me I was going to go back and tell my Mum and Dad, and I mean nothing like that was allowed. I don't care how many times they gave me a strapping on the hands, because as we got bigger we just didn't cry no more, and they just got madder because we didn't cry. They'd get tired before we did. They'd strap you four or five times and if you didn't cry they'd know - I remember getting strappings from Miss Turner and Miss Pettigrew - they were the kitchen people. I even forget what I did wrong then but I remember getting a strapping from them. Because they'd hit you on the hand and you only take so much till it numbs - so it don't hurt. The strap was about a foot long and about four inches wide, and they'd hit you with that and naturally it stings for the first two or three times and after that it goes numb. They'd hit you on the hand so that the strap curled round and got you going down and coming up, and it would flip and hit you twice.

Jennie Blackbird
1942 - 1946

Because of the poor living conditions as I was growing up on Walpole Island, at an early age before I was a teenager, I went one evening to the Indian Agent's residence here on the Island. I told him of my wish to be sent to an Indian Residential School in order to get an education and he complied. During those years there was no welfare or government assistance to be obtained, which meant children had to walk for miles to and from school.

Thus in the fall of 1942, myself, and three others from here were boarded on a train by the Indian Agent to Brantford. Though I knew it would be lonely being away from home, I had good thoughts about where I was being taken. I knew I would no longer have to walk to school, and I would have food and shelter while there, which I really looked forward to.

When we arrived we were picked up by Mr. and Mrs.

Snell, the principal and matron of the Mohawk Institute. For some unknown reason, I had a scared feeling about Mr. Snell, not so much Mrs. Snell. By that I mean "first impression is a lasting impression." He told us that the policy of the school was to go to school half-a-day and work half-a-day. We had to put on navy-blue uniforms, black stockings and new boys' black leather shoes. We were eyed curiously by other Native girls from different reservations, but mainly from the Brantford area. Girls were on one side of the school and boys on the other side.

My new way of life started off learning how to scrub cement floors on my knees, and sewing and working in the laundry room, and kitchen. There were two women (not Native) who were in charge of the kitchen and laundry room. In the kitchen I learned how to bake biscuits and make soup, which we had every day. And mush every morning with skim milk. The school had a farm which provided vegetables. The boys had to milk the cows and work on the farm. I also had to learn how to operate a big huge round washing machine in which we did all the laundry, including linen and all the school students' clothes.

Meals were always the same. Girls who worked in the kitchen and staff dining room had to wake up half-an-hour earlier to prepare meals. Boys had to wake up half-an-hour earlier too, to milk the cows.

The children were always hungry because of the limited amount of food we were given. If one child was extra hungry, one of us would sacrifice our food. Especially those of us who worked in the kitchen who had access to the food prepared. It used to make me wonder, yet never questioned, that the staff ate food fit for kings and queens. There was always two girls who worked in the staff dining room, who wore black dresses (different from the rest) and fancy white aprons and white crowned caps. The girls who worked in the food area would steal food and shared with others. We used to steal salt from the kitchen, then we would take raw potatoes, raw turnips. At the time I did not feel it wrong to do this. After all, the school was our shelter and food provider. It used to confuse me as to why the staff ate so good and plenty, yet we were always hungry. At the time I understood the school was from Indian funding. And all staff were non-Native who got the benefit of good food.

The thing that shocked me most was when I was told I could not speak my native language. I was birthed into this language, yet, was told I was being rude. This really pierced me. Because my native language was all that was spoken in the home, the English language was the first foreign language I learned. And we weren't allowed to speak our Indian language?!! My inner emotions could not accept this, but I could not express myself enough to say what was in my heart in the English language - what little I knew then.

I knew in my heart that this was wrong and so unfair to us Native children. The emotional shock tremors that I suffered then I still feel to this day, but through this mental anguish I made up my mind that I would endure while there. But this did hurt deep inside.

Anyway, I made good friends while there, which was very important to me. We accepted one another and got along as best as we could. And they had Brownies and Girl Guides. We had to accept what we were taught. I had no problem with this.

The sewing room teacher was very nice and was so patient with me. It was through her I learned how to sew and master the sewing machine. Though I broke ten needles, yet I was determined I was going to learn how to make girls' uniforms and the boys' shirts. And I did. I used to sneak into the sewing room when she wasn't around, and practised sewing on scrap patches. Even though she gave up on me many times, I would try all the harder. When I admitted sneaking in the sewing room, breaking ten needles, and showed her my practised patches, she did get angry.

She did give me a shaking up, and I did push her away from me. Results? I became one of the main sewing girls. I was happy after all that. We became close friends though a lot of the girls didn't like her.

One day I confided to her I was always hungry and times I didn't have the money to go to the movies. She felt sorry for me and bought me peanut butter and marmalade which I kept locked in my locker. She at times gave me money for a movie if I didn't have it. To me this was a real treat, so different. The other girls didn't know about this. Of course there were those who were more fortunate.

We used to march uptown to Brantford to the Capitol theatre. This was when we had the opportunity to sneak and mail letters home - because every letter that came to the students was opened and read by the principal and matron. If there was anything in the letters that wasn't to their liking, it was erased. This was another shock - to get letters from home and find they had already been opened. That's another reason why we all felt like prisoners. It seems like the white rulers who took us to these schools weren't satisfied enough, but I felt we didn't deserve this invasion of privacy. It was done anyway, and was still done the day I left.

My school teacher, Mr. Yeandle, was very nice. Through him I learned more of reading, writing, spelling and arithmetic. I only went to Grade 7, but took a bit of Grade 8. At least we were taught a bit of what to expect in the next grade. The school had Grades 1 to 9. The three high school girls went to downtown Brantford Collegiate. They walked from the school to the end of the laneway to the street (Mohawk) to catch the bus.

I do regret not furthering my education. Mainly because there was no government assistance, if memory serves me right, at that time. The native people really didn't have no choice when children were taken from homes to these boarding schools.

Family values soon disappeared because of this. Native customs before I went to the school were strictly taught in love. Deep down inside I did feel robbed because of this European way of discipline. I remember laying in bed at night, thinking about my culture and this white man's culture. Why? Why? I realized I had to accept this culture shock because it was a reality happening to the Indian people on reservations around.

So I knew while here I had to take orders. Later, when we communicated with other girls who were there longer, they warned us to never cross Mr. Snell's path or you get the strap. In other words, his orders was the law we had to abide by. Mrs. Snell was a more kind person. He was harsh to my recollection. I used to think at the time he looked domineering.

During his time, girls would run away for amusement, just to have a story to tell. Maybe because we felt cooped up. Finally, even though I never had no intentions of running away, I went along with the other girls. We got as far as the orchard. Guess what? We got caught. We got strapped on each hand from Mr. Snell. Next day we went to school though we all had swollen blue marks on our hands. The strappings were always in the visiting room.

The second time I ran away I got as far as the train station. That was when Snell really strapped us, and then my hands all swelled up. The third time I made it home. I was influenced by this girl. I had no intention of running away but she made the school sound real bad. I was already 16 and I immediately went to work, and the only time I ever went back to the school was at the reunion. We just about froze but we made it home. We hitchhiked and I remember being really afraid, but it didn't seem to bother her. They were just running away left and right - then they would tell what happened - it was something to talk about. So, running away was our "current event."

While there I did hear of rumours, if some child did something really wrong, they was put in solitary confinement and was locked up for three days, no lights in the room. A room - I believe four by four? - with only water three times a day. It was a dark room. Again, we were not taught how to cope with situations such as this. To some extent I did experience emotional injury that cannot heal like a physical wound. I was afraid of Mr. Snell. I do believe most of the girls were, or so it seemed.

This one particular girl who was about sixteen years old at the time, used to have seizures, even before we arrived at the school, so I was told. And anyone who provoked her, she would have a seizure. She was noted as the strongest girl in the school. And she did have big muscles - Big Muscles!

Because there were only seven of us from Walpole, we were small in number. Some of the girls from Six Nations and nearby reservations challenged "muscle girl" to fight, and anyone who dared from Walpole, even though this other girl from Walpole didn't want to scrap with "muscle girl" because she was much bigger in size.

The girls cheered for "muscle girl" because they were large in number. After pushing them, the war began. So, we Islanders had to cheer for our side. As a result, Walpole won a great victory that day. We had a champion, a hero! Boy, we girls from the Island was proud of her.

From then on, we were not threatened. We got along. But, when the principal got wind of this and found out who instigated the fight, poor "muscle girl" was taken into the visitors' room and got the strap. By the time I seen her in front of the dispensary room, her face was flushed. She fell on her face and down a flight of stairs. She was immediately taken to the dispensary room to recover, which was several days. The seizure was brought on after the strapping, so she said later.

During Mr. Snell's term there, we didn't get too much of anything. He was later removed. Then, Mr. and Mrs. Zimmerman took over. There was a quick change for the better. For the first time we started eating cornflakes and homo milk. Food was so much better. We even got ice cream which we never had before. There sure was a lot of grateful hearts, though the staff still ate better. Schedules were still the same - we worked half-a-day, went to school half-a-day.

Most of the clothes that the children wore were made by the sewing room girls with instructions from our sewing room teacher. Bless her heart. Girls' uniforms and boys' shirts were made from scratch. We mended the boys' denim pants. We also darned all the socks. The girls wore sharp-looking boys' shoes. The girls also wore thick long black stockings.

The girls were on one side of the school, and the boys on the other side. Times the boys would sneak over to the girls' side after lights were out. One of the staff would check to see if all girls were in their beds and sleeping. Some of the girls would stuff blankets in their beds to appear one was in bed. The boys managed to sneak in the top dormitory to bring us pop, chewing gum and just talk. To my recollection, they never got caught. Nothing else happened. This was just another "current event."

Once a month the brothers and sisters were allowed to visit in the visiting room on a Wednesday night. I was allowed to visit with the three I went there with, which was nice.

The Christmas concert was the highlight of the year. We had a school Christmas play which I was always involved in with others. We received candies, oranges, and flannelette nightgowns which we could not bring home on summer holidays. My grandfather would mail my homecoming clothes for me, and my train ticket. But there were children more fortunate than others, whose parents came after them.

I enjoyed walking to church every Sunday in the Mohawk chapel, and I used to look forward to the chapel service every evening after supper in the senior room. And my favourite sport was baseball. Both girls and boys played this sport. And this did break the monotony.

While there, I never heard, to my knowledge, of any sexual abuse on children. Truthfully, I liked the school except for two things: not being allowed to speak the First Nation Native Language which was already here when Christopher Columbus arrived in North America - being stripped of this language and losing family values. I had to learn all over again to love and to speak my language when I got home to stay. Although I eventually got my language back, emotional damage was done, and once emotional damage is done it's severed and the tremors from the emotional shock I endured are still with me to this day. It's really, really sad to think about it. The very foundation of our culture is love, and God's love was strongly taught. This helped me in my determination to overcome some of the emotional shock from my experience at the school and develop positive life skills. I thank God I have a brighter outlook on life now.

Vera Styres
1942 - 1943, 1946 - 1947

One thing that the Mohawk Institute took away from our people was a sense of family, because there you were taught survival of the fittest and the individual - the 'me', the 'I', was the most important thing. Because we didn't operate or function as a family there, we didn't learn the values of being a family, and so we didn't learn how to be parents because we weren't parented. And they wonder about the lack of parenting skills now in our Native communities and how the parents seem to be more concerned about their own well-being, rather than the children. It's what we learned there - we didn't learn how to be parents. Maybe some people don't agree with me, but it was not a good time.

One of the things that comes to mind is not being taken care of when you were sick. You were punished if you were ill because it was an inconvenience to the officers if you were sick. I had fallen and probably had concussion because I lost a day after bumping my head. I remember crawling into a great big cupboard that was in the girls' playroom, and I had lost a day and I got punished for not being accounted for, and I got the strap when actually I was sick - unconscious for a day and a couple of nights. They had a nurse there, but if you said you had a headache or your stomach was upset, they didn't do anything about it. They said "You'll be all right - forget about it - you'll get over it." My younger sister fell down and skinned her knee and it got infected, and they wouldn't take care of it until gangrene set in and she was falling down and they sent her to the hospital here in Ohsweken. They never even informed my mother about it until she was ready to go back to the school - things like that. Another time I remember getting the flu and getting sick and almost delirious from the fever, and throwing up, but still being forced to get up out of my bed and clean up the mess I made, and got strapped for making a mess.

There are some good points about having been there - there are a lot of things I never would have learned if I hadn't gone there. At home we were kinda poor, my Mum and Dad had split up - so I knew why I was there because my mother explained why we were going there and she said it would only be for a little while, and she kept her word. It was just a little while. We stayed one school year, and then five years later things got bad again and some of us had to go back to the Mush hole again.

When I first went there I was seven, so I went to school half-a-day and got to play half-a-day - that wasn't bad. Five years later when I went back again, it was school half-a-day and work half-a-day, and I got to work in the sewing room, and I got to work in the laundry, and I got to work in the kitchen, and learned how to mend socks, learning how to patch clothes, learning how to mend blue jeans and all that kinda stuff. I really appreciate having learned that because

if I was home my mother did all that, because it was easier for her to do it than to teach us how to do it, and at least I got to learn those things. I had never experienced central heating or running water and I really appreciated that - learning about the different things that were available - because when I was there the second time, when I was in Grade 5, the different church groups or other groups in the city would invite 12 little girls to go to a Christmas party, or a Valentine's party or something like that, and I got to go to those things. That wouldn't have been available to me if I had been home, so I got to find out about those things. I got to learn about people, I got to learn about how other people lived other than just being on the Reserve, and just knowing the people in my own neighbourhood. So those kinds of things I do appreciate, and going to school half-a-day was not bad. I think I learned as much in that half-a-day as going to school full time - maybe not the variety of things you learn going full days, but the basics of an education was there.

I got to belong to Brownies and Girl Guides. That was something I wouldn't have had if I had stayed home, or rolling skating, which we did quite a lot of in the playroom. That was one - maybe the only - pastime we had, but I did learn to rollerskate. The regimentation was kinda hard to take. Either a bell would ring or a whistle would blow, and you had to line up according to your number. Saturday morning you had to line up, and I'll always remember, after giving out all the orders, they would say "Six little girls to the bath," and away we'd run, and we had to take a bath two or three in the tub at a time, and then go and line up for our clean clothes. These are just incidents I remember that was part of the routine, but one of the bad things is I can't eat mush to this day - I just can't eat it. It feels terrible in my mouth and I gag on it.

My mother came to visit us once a month, so she kept in contact with us, and we did go home every summer, and she would also take other kids with us for the summer as well. She even took the principal's dog one time for the summer as well.

There's good times and there's bad times. Going to church and getting dressed up - I don't know why they called those army shoes 'dress shoes', but they were hard on the feet. At least through the week we got to wear some broken in ones that were not quite so stiff. The black stockings we had to wear didn't stay black too long, because they turned a greenish-grey after a while. We had special shoes, stockings, tunic, blouse and that, to go to church. We also had to wear a tam - one of those beret sort of things with a tail on it. That was our Sunday outfit. Through the week we had these aprons - you know the striped material that engineers' outfits are made of. The tunic that we had to wear through the week was made of denim. The one that was for Sunday was of different material - a navy blue sort of thing with pleats all around, from the yoke down. Some had a belt, some didn't. If you lost your belt, you just didn't have one after that. The shoes were kinda awkward, and they always made you wear one size larger, so it never failed, you had blisters constantly on your feet, because the shoes didn't fit. Some of the clothes were handmade. Me and my sisters were fortunate - we had our own underclothes. Those who didn't have their own underwear - they were made - a combination boxer shorts and vest sewn together, with buttons down so you could get in to it, and it was made out of old sugar bags and flour sacks - real stiff cotton - kinda scratchy. I was glad I didn't have to wear those things. Another embarrassing thing for the girls who were having their menstrual period, they had folded up cotton diaper sort of things that they would wear, then they had to wash them out and constantly recycle. There was no such thing as sanitary pads for the girls then. Again I was fortunate I hadn't reached that point, but the idea of them being collected in a laundry bin and having to be washed, so you got to wear these stained things again when your time came around, that was not very nice. So there was incidents that were blaringly embarrassing, not very nice anyway, but there were other things that were not too bad. I can't eat cereal to this day because of what we were given to eat there, and I remember how it was cooked. It was put in a great big vat and soaked overnight, not cooked, it would barely get warmed - kinda like you make wallpaper paste I guess.

Mr Snell was the principal the first year I was there - '42-'43, and then Zimmerman was there in '47-'48 when I was there the second time. There was an improvement in the food in the two times I was there, but I still lost a lot of weight. My mother came there to see us - we must have been there a couple of months, and she came there and she got so upset at how skinny I was that she punched Mr. Zimmerman in the face. But I suffered as a result of that because he force-fed me after that, but nothing stayed down, and he was wearing my breakfast just about every day that he fed me. That was not very nice.

But again, we understood why we were there, because my mother explained why we were there, because she couldn't afford to feed us. She was true to her word. She had a home for us in '47 when we came home, and we never had to go back again. I was there two years '42-'43, '46-'47, so it wasn't straight through. But I do know a lot of women who were there from the time they started school until they were old enough to be out on their own. I see these women, talk to these women now, and we are doing the best we can.

I hate to think what I might have been like if I had been there all that time, instead of just the two years that I was there.

I've talked to some girls - there in the late fifties, early sixties - and I don't know if Zimmerman was getting tired of his job or what, but some of the students there were exercising their rights a little more forcefully. One girl has a kidney problem to this day as a result of being kicked in the back. We have never gotten together specifically to talk about the Mohawk - just if the subject happens to come up we relate different incidents that happened - but not to really talk about it in depth, to say how we felt about it and what effect it had on us, or things like that. It probably would help to talk about it. I try not to remember the sense of abandonment - that bothers me. The lack of having someone there to comfort you when you were feeling like that. That's what was so despairing when I think about it. I recall writing a letter to my mother. All our mail was censored in and out anyway, so the letter never did get to my mother, telling her how lonesome I was and how badly I wanted to go home, and the reason for wanting to go home was put in the letter as well, and that was probably why it couldn't be sent out. It was explained to me that if I tried to write again, or if I ever wrote anything like that again about the school, I would be punished. We were told things we could do, and things we couldn't do, and any kinda initiative was discouraged, so you had to be very creative in initiating any kinda entertainment or anything that would make you happy. Once girls got together and they were talking or laughing, they were dispersed immediately, so you couldn't get together and have girl talk. I don't know why, maybe they thought any group of kids getting together were planning on running away. Speaking of running away - if anyone ran away and they were brought back to the school, the other students had to punish them, and the punishment was putting them through the mill, which meant that the runaway had to crawl through a line-up. We'd all have to get in a row with our legs spread apart and the runaway would have to crawl through and each of them would have to give them a whack on the behind as they crawled through.

I don't know too much about what happened on the boys' side, as the boys and girls were kept separate. Even in the classroom the girls sat on one side and the boys sat on the other side. Through my experiences as a social worker I've found the kids who were in need of protection were often the grandchildren or the great-grandchildren of people who had been at the mush-hole, so the lack of parenting skills - if you don't learn them, you can't pass them down to your children eh? So if you don't learn what a family is about, how can you practice being a family?

Sylvia Soney
1943 - 1947

I went to the Mohawk Institute in the fall of 1943. I was 9 years old and we stayed there to June of '47, when I was 13. The reason I went there is that the Reserve I come from is comprised of several islands, and my Dad got a job at a hunting club on one of the islands that was then only accessible by water. So we could not get up to the main reserve where most people lived and go to school. So when I went there my older sister went - she was about 12, and my older brother who's about 1½ years older than me, and I think some other kids went at the same time, but there were other kids from Walpole Island who had gone there before us. Three of us went to boarding school and the younger kids stayed home with my parents as they weren't in school yet. We got driven by the Indian agent and my Mum to Chatham and then we caught a train there and were met in Brantford by the principal. I can't remember too much about going there except I was sad to leave my Mum at the train station. I didn't mind the train ride and I wasn't alone so I wasn't scared - I had my two older siblings. When we got to the school I remember getting an orientation - going into the visitors' room and being told what the rules were. The principal talked to us and told us about the school, and then my sister and I were taken over to the sewing room and my brother went wherever he went, and there was a lady there and she gave us our number and showed us where our little box would be where every Saturday we'd get clean clothes, then showed us to where we were going to sleep in the top dormitory, and we were given school clothes - I think we turned in our clothes at that time. When we got to our dormitory there were girls from the Island there and they were glad to see us.

You lived by bells, you woke up by bells - everything you did was by the bell - you lined up. We went to school half-a-day and worked the other half-a-day - you had chores. We spent a lot of time that was unsupervised, just entertaining ourselves in the playroom or outside. Whatever we did there we basically entertained ourselves. There was nothing down there - it was a cement floor playroom and there were lockers around the edges, or boxes, but there was really nothing there - you know how a basement looks with those columns. We'd play tag and hide-and-go-seek, and go into another room and tell ghost stories. You kinda broke off into your own age groups. When I first started there I was in the junior school which was on the other side of the building, and right above our playroom was the senior school room and I think that started at about Grade 4 or 5. You had to learn very early to get along with other kids. Basically you were on your own, and if you didn't have very good social skills or someone to help you out - it was kinda like a little pecking order - and you quickly learned how to look out for yourself. You had to develop different ways of

coping, and my way was - I didn't cause a lot of waves. I tried to get along with people, and you learn not to talk about other people, because if you did you could be fighting or getting into some type of conflict or be threatened. But I think that was more something that happened with the boys. Whether they wanted to or not they were fighting from the first day on. The girls weren't that physical, but we could have our differences. I never got in a fight in my four years I was there. My sister took care of me to make sure I kept clean and combed my hair, and tried to mother me, so I wasn't fearful, but I definitely knew how far to go with somebody - say the monitor's kid sister might take advantage. I think I did fairly well. I had my little run-ins every once in a while but nothing major - just like every normal kid does - but I think you were probably a lot more fearful because you knew you were on your own if it got out of hand - it was just you, alone. Basically you were powerless and what could you do but endure it?

Did I like it or hate it? I didn't really make a judgement on it. When I got there that was the situation I found myself in and I got along the best I could. I didn't really think about do I hate it or do I like it. There were some things I liked about it. I liked having a lot of other Indian kids to play with and go to school with. We were all Indians - it definitely confirmed who I was. It was just something you endured. I always heard regularly from my mother - my mother was a great letter writer and she wrote to us regularly and she sent us boxes at the holidays - we got parcels. And when we got parcels we got a lot of friends temporarily! Anything that came in and out they [the school] read. My mother would send us spending money and - my teacher, Mrs. Fry, was a pretty good teacher - and sometimes when she'd go to town, you'd tell her what you'd want - toothpaste, BB gun candy - she'd get us little treats. I had my own circle of friends - my sister kinda looked out for me but she had her own circle of friends.

I wasn't at that age where my language was taken away. English was my first language, but my parents went to boarding school, and people of their generation - that's the generation mostly that really was punished severely - and probably that's why they never taught me or my siblings to speak Indian. They got the message.

Did I get an education? I think I got an education in a lot of ways!! I quickly, early on learned to be independent - as much as I could in a very controlled situation. It made a big difference to me because I was 9, not 5 like some people were, because when I went there I knew how to behave, having been raised in a family, and my interpersonal skills - I feel I did fairly well for 9 years old, to get along there. The academic education I got was pretty good, considering we only went to school a half-a-day. I think I could match that up with what our current kids are getting. You were educated differently in those days - you got strong basics. I came out of there in Grade 7 - I was 13, and I had no trouble fitting back into the regular school system. I went to high school in Algonac, Michigan, because my parents were still down the river and rather than come up here, it was easier for us to go across the river, but we would have had to pay tuition, so rather than do that we moved over.

I was kind of scared of the principal - I didn't really know him. We started out with Snell and we probably didn't really know who he was. I heard the name and kinda knew enough that I didn't want to get into trouble and see him, because I knew people got strappings. The next guy was Zimmerman, I remember him, and probably the same thing - just like any authoritarian figure in a school, you don't want to get into trouble with them. I couldn't say that I liked or disliked him - probably I just didn't want to interact with him too much. I didn't want to get into trouble. He was also our preacher - we had regular services every night and then on Sundays. I never personally got a strapping from him, but I know of other students who did.

Mrs Fry was a dedicated teacher and she always treated me with respect. I had a difficult time with math but there was no-one I could call on to help me - I probably faked it a lot - but I felt she was a real good teacher. The next teacher I had was Mr. Yeandle and he was in the senior school. I'll never forget either one of them - I learned a lot from her and I certainly learned a lot from him. My favourite subject with him was social studies - but whatever he was teaching us whether it was science, social studies or history he would involve drawing. We'd get our notebooks and drew from the board where he'd draw our lessons- whether it was fur traders in snowshoes, or the parts of a flower, or a rabbit or whatever. He was really good - I learned a lot from him. He was even-tempered - you didn't get away with anything - he was a teacher. He was pretty reasonable. I learned a lot in the sewing-room - I can't remember that lady's name - Mrs. Bennett? I remember her eyes went out. I learned how to darn and sew dolls in the sewing room, and I hated it but I did learn how to mend - we'd get boys' underwear or socks with great big, gigantic holes so you'd have to mend half at a time. I was too young to make clothes - my sister sewed boys' shirts or made our aprons, but our thing was mending holes. We got to make rag dolls.

One of my duties was to scrub either the dormitory or a section of the boys' dormitory, and when I was over there I could look out of the dormitory window and see the boys a couple of storeys below, and oftentimes in the spring or fall they would be like little dustballs, fighting, and they would push each other into each other, and make each other fight. I used to always be glad at least I wasn't a boy because I'd have to be fightin' all the time. Another job I had was to scrub a row in the junior schoolroom or senior schoolroom. Another time I had to get up early in the morning and fill a

laundry tub full of cold water and then load it up with potatoes, and then stick my hands in that cold water with a scrub brush and scrub potatoes. That's basically it, we were either washing the floor or doing something - also working in the scullery, doing dishes. I never really worked down there to really be bossed around by the cook. Some of them were kinda nice and some of them weren't very nice - there's not too much directions you had to give me about doing potatoes, so I didn't really get yelled at. I never worked in the laundry room.

I learned how to make my bed as soon as I got up in the morning. I learned to do sewing - I learned not to be afraid of that. I could survive it, I didn't like it, I hated it, but I did it. The skills I learned were how to get along with people - I don't think I learned them there. I'm not sure I learned anything to help me get a job. I think what they were trying to train you for was either to be a farmer's helper or a domestic.

The food was horrible. We never got meat. We used to get soup with a big piece of fat in it - it was gross - and they'd take this piece of fat and put it on the hot water pipes to cook. I don't remember getting any fresh vegetables or fruit. There was an apple orchard next to our playground, and the only way you'd get any of them was to climb the fence, and then it was considered stealing and you'd get into trouble. But they were the Mohawk Institute's orchards. Some of my brave friends would go over and chuck some apples back - I'd be a party to it but I didn't go over the fence. I remember going up in the attic - I was supposed to be cleaning eggs - right near the principal's stairway, just outside of his apartment. He was on the second floor - there was a third floor - and between there a couple of girls and I used to clean eggs there - we had a lot of eggs, but we never seen eggs to eat ourselves, but we had to clean them. Sitting there we got the brilliant idea - probably not a new idea! - but some supplies were kept in the attic and we went up there and stole jam. The food was not only terrible but you didn't get enough of it and we were probably very malnourished. When I came home I was 13 years old and I weighed 79lbs. When I came home I just couldn't get enough to eat. I hate milk - I always have - and I would drink canned milk just straight, and peanut butter. I gained 20lbs that summer we got home to stay. We were malnourished, some of us were starving. You could get a bit more if you worked in the kitchen and even there kids stole food, or if you had friends in the kitchen they would give you extra supplies. If my sister was there she would give my brother extra bread, or what she could, under the table - put a knife under there and stick an extra piece of bread under there - if you had friends in the kitchen. My brother was in a similar condition - he was malnourished.

I had fun with other students - my little group. I remember on one occasion going for a walk to a park with Mrs. Fry, with all the students - it was either spring or fall. I think I went to the movies once. One other time we were going to go shopping, around Christmastime, and I walked part way and my feet were getting tingly - I was freezing - and we weren't dressed properly, and I went as far as a store along the way and several of us younger ones went back.. Basically we were on our own as to how to dress. I don't think we had any snowpants. It was basically our shoes and black stockings, and probably our Sunday coat. It was good learning - there was some friendly competition - I had fun with other Indian kids.

I remember my 10th birthday - it was in June, 20 days before we were to go home. My mother made a big deal of birthdays, but I never expected anything at school. My sister came and took me down the hill, and the girls had made a kinda tent, and they took me in there and they all sang Happy Birthday, and they gave me a little present - It was a little birdcage with a little tiny bird in it.

We led a very disciplined or structured life - according to the bells. Everything we did we had to line up for. I got a strapping once from a teacher for mocking him. He was a rather effeminate man and talked with a lisp, and he came out and spoke to me, then he shut the door and went back in. I was coming right back and as soon as he shut the door I mocked him. Very shortly he came out and I got a good strapping. I think that's the only strapping I got, but I know sometimes it could be pretty harsh - especially if a student would resist breaking down or crying. Whoever was strapping them then was harder on them because they wanted some reaction. I would hear about kids getting strapped and their hands were all swollen, and they wouldn't just hit their hands but right up their arms. Towards the end of our stay I remember an incident in the cafeteria. When we ate our meals the boys were on one side and the girls were on the other side. There was a younger staff person, but he and an older male student got into a fight. I don't know if he was going to strap that young man, but kids as they got older would be more reluctant to accept corporal punishment - they would stick up for themselves or other students. It was probably upsetting for that man because I think the other kids were ready to come to that student's aid. It was kinda scary to see that happen, but on the other hand it was exciting to see that student stand up for himself.

I have no idea if there was sexual abuse - there may have been, but nothing I could say happened.

We had a standard set of clothing. When you first went there in the fall you got a pair of boys' black shoes, and you got black stockings, bloomers and some kind of a dress, and then on top - we called it an apron but it was more like a jumper - and both those things were made out of denim. The dress part of it was a solid colour and the apron was striped. I don't recall having a coat - except our Sunday coat. We had a Sunday outfit - a navy-blue dress with trim, and later on we got a pleated skirt and a white blouse. I think we had a tam - but never really anything to keep you warm. I don't recall them giving us gloves. If you got something from home like a sweater - if that's what you got,

that's what you had. Sometimes things got stolen. When I think about it now it seems quite inhumane that they could have allowed children to be so ill-fed and so ill-dressed. When I had to run around to the junior school room in the wintertime, I ran around in my shirtsleeves. I didn't have a sweater or a coat - or if I did I mighta lost it - but I remember clearly running around there and freezing when I got there. When we got our recess I would run around to the girls' side and go in the girls' room and turn on the hot water and I would stick my arms under it to warm up, and my hands. Then of course we had to go back out so I often had chapped skin. We'd play outside sometime but you just went out with whatever you had. I musta had something or I borrowed something. The junior room was on one side [of the Institute] and our room was on the other side, so we'd line up and go out here to class, and then at recess we had to run back.

The health [care] was pretty dismal. If you were fortunate enough to have good health and didn't get sick, you were OK. If you got sick I don't think too much happened - you might be sent to your bed. There was a little sick room off our dormitory and if somebody got really sick, or had one of the kid diseases, they might go in there. Once when I was working on the boys' side - this was probably the year I left, or the year before - and I had a girlfriend, and her brother - I don't know whatever happened to him - he was laying in bed - it seems like that's all he did all day, laying in bed, and there was a white mucus coming out of his eyes. I don't think he was ever cared for medically. I've often wondered if he ended up blind, or what happened to him. Another little girl - we had a kitten, or cat - and she used to really like this cat. She was playing with the cat one time and she moved a little too slowly and the cat scratched her eye, and after that the eye looked funny and she couldn't see out of it. I don't think she got any medical attention. Every once in a while there'd be an outbreak of cooties. The girls would be having to help clean each other up. In the springtime they'd sit out on the backsteps - one step at a time - and they'd be cleaning each other's heads. I didn't really have to worry too much because I always had my hair cut short.

We had a nice clean bed. We each had our own beds. There weren't enough blankets and those big dormitories were very draughty. We only had one blanket in the winter. Sometimes the bigger kids would take blankets from the little kids. We only had to bath once a week - that's when you got clean clothes. My sister made me bath more often - between after-school and suppertime we had some time. I know I would never leave my kids, or grandchildren alone for an hour, and there they were leaving 80 kids pretty much by themselves, except perhaps with a monitor - a lot of things could happen. Or if you had an older sister who was kinda the mothering type she'd try to keep you in order.

Now, as an adult looking back, I look back on it as - some parts were good, and some parts are really hard to understand, especially how the Church and the Government were in cohoots to help us not be little Indians, help to Anglicize us. I understand now what they were doing - it was one of the assimilation strategies that Indians had to suffer, had to endure. But even though I understand it now, it seems really inhumane to me, how they could do this to little children. For me I don't think it was bad because I was 9 years old and had my older sister to look out for me. For those kids who went there when they were very young and stayed for many years without going home, I would wonder if they would ever recover from it. With us, we went there when we were 9 thru 12 and we came home every summer, and if you have a strong family...those people who didn't have a family or who were orphans, I think it would feel like abandonment, and powerlessness and often their self-esteem was way down or they got into alcohol.

I had two brothers. The brother who's older than me - he ran away six months before we were due to come home - and he made it home. He ran away with a boy from Six Nations and they got to some place where this boy's father was working near Brantford, and then that man was kind enough to give him enough money for busfare to Chatham. He said when he was on that bus he didn't really notice another Indian guy. When he got off the bus at Chatham this man said to him "Where are you going?" My brother said he was going to Walpole Island. This man says "Well I'm going there too. I'm going to Bill Soney's house - do you know him?" My brother said "Yes, that's my grandfather." So the man got a taxi and they came out here to the river - the Chenail river - and the river was almost frozen, but there was a boat there. So they took that boat and came across the river and walked up to home. When my brother got home he was in terrible, terrible shape. I think he was about the same size as me, even though he was a year and a half older. When he got home he just layed around and ate and ate and ate. He was just very lazy and after a while they found out that he'd had a touch of TB. He was in really bad shape. I don't know when the Indian agent found out my brother made it home, but he found out and he said he wanted to send him back, and my Dad said "If you send him back, I'm going there too." So nothing ever happened - my brother stayed home, then a few months later we came home. My parents must have made a decision not to send us back. By that time another brother of mine had - first of all he'd gone to Mt. Elgin by himself when he was six and he stayed there one year and it closed and he came to Brantford. When he came home he wouldn't

eat on the train or anything, so my mother found out - took him to the doctor - that he had a sore mouth, and he had trench mouth. So that's probably why we didn't go back.

I just think it was pretty inhumane. I'm glad I went though! I'm glad I went. I have some understanding of what some people go through, and I have met some casualties of the boarding school - some people who when they get out of there have trouble coping. There you're told what to do every minute - all the time, as far as working, getting in line and stuff like that. Then to be let loose and if you've been told all those years that anything Indian is no good, a person would have some questions. They would come out of there and be unable to fit on the Reserve, and they wouldn't fit out there - they were marginalized. People who were probably at school same time as I was - whether it was Mohawk Institute or Shingwauk - they don't really care to come back here - they were away so long - to them it's just another place on the map. They may have gotten into alcoholism - all that stuff has to do with that. Parenting skills - that's one of the casualties - you can't pass on what you havn't experienced if you've been in an institution for ten years. How can you parent effectively if you havn't experienced it? I don't think staff would be good parenting roles. That's one of the things that still affects us. Being just one of eight, with a caring mother and Dad - that certainly helped. I can remember my mother wrote to us when we first got there, and she had gone to boarding school in Michigan. My Dad had too - they're both from Walpole. She said that at Mt. Pleasant - she liked the school - they had movies and they had dances and this and that. Her experience was good and so she figured ours would be good too. When she was over there she didn't want to come home and she came home once and she didn't like it because it was remote. That school over there was pretty modern. It had modern conveniences even around when she went - probably in the teens or twenties. She wrote to us, probably in May, and said if you don't want to come home, that's fine, because we were way down - we were quite isolated - and she said if you don't want to you don't have to. No Way! We're going home! There were a couple of years when we didn't get our train tickets right away and we'd be all in a dither. Where we lived was like an Eden. On our side of the Island there was a great big beach.

I liked it, but at the time what can you do, you just endure.

Lonnie Johnson
1948 - 1956?

I went there in 1948 till 195? - I was in there about 8 or 9 years.

I thought we were treated lousy - in every way you could think of. Sometimes we'd be in taking a shower and if the boys' master didn't like somebody he'd start swinging the strap. He'd hit guys all over and there was nothing we could do about it. He was about half-cut half the time but we never said anything. This was with the younger guys, the older guys they'd shower first, and we had about ten towels between maybe 100 of us. If you could imagine 35 guys drying on the same towel ahead of you - when you'd get it it was just like a washcloth.

It was awful treatment around there - I could tell you things you wouldn't believe. One time they brought us cereal in the morning and the darn stuff was moving - it had maggots in it. They expected us to eat it. Zimmerman threatened the boys with a strap if they ever told - if it ever got out. But he's dead now and can't argue. We'd have squash and they'd cook it and leave it out, and the flies would get at it. We'd find the odd maggot in it.

Some of the guys are darker than others, and they had this one boys' master - his name was Mr. Williston - and everybody hated him with a passion. You had to turn your hands with the knuckles up and he'd whack you with the strap if you didn't wash good enough. A lot of the guys were dark, and you can't wash tan out.

Zimmerman was nice when there was other people around, but when you was there by yourself you were the bottom of the barrel. I got to know him better after I came out. My father-in-law was head of the ministerial association on the Reserve, and now and again when I used to get laid off - I'm a union card member - I'd go up there and do some work at the Mohawk Chapel, and Zimmerman was running that. He was drinking a lot of wine and he was about half cut now and again. For a preacher - he drank and smoked - for me, I thought that was wrong. He was strict - he had his ways about him. If he didn't like you, he'd let you know - just like all the rest. If the staff had something in for you they let you know - me and five other guys. They figured I was a bad guy - I don't recall ever doing anything bad, but I used to like to scrap - fool around. One day they caught me fooling around with this other guy - they thought we were fighting, and they caught a couple of other boys, and there was four of us had to pick up 20 acres of potatoes. The others would load it on the wagon - you try picking that up by hand - it takes you a week. We were just young kids. I was born in '43 and I went in '48 so that would make me 5 when I went there - 5 to about 12 or 13. I was there to Grade 5 and I did 6, 7 and 8 on the reserve. The education was pretty well the same here. We went to school 9 to 4. The older guys, like my brother Frank - he used to have to look after the cattle - they'd let them out a little early sometimes, to get the cattle and that. We had to work on picking vegetables, then do all the haying.

The food was awful. They used to give us what they called raisin cake. You could take it and you could throw it 50 ft and it would splatter on the wall and it would stick like glue. There was Christmas and Easter we got treated - we'd get porridge all the other times, except Christmas we got shredded wheat or rice krispies or puffed wheat. We never got toast or anything like that. We got bread and most of the time it didn't have nothin' on it - 99% of the time.

I never ran away. I seen what they did to the other guys - it wasn't worth it. You lost what privileges you had - in the summertime you could go and cut grass uptown, and make ourselves the odd spending money - if you were bad you never got none of that.

I got the strap - I thought my hands were made out of the strap!! I must admit I wasn't an angel - I got quite a few strappings. I used to do a lot of fighting. I got along good with everybody. Some of the older guys used to work the younger guys. If you were a single brother the old guys would pick on you, but I had an older brother - they didn't bother me.

Both Frank and I when we went there we used to talk Mohawk, and when they caught us talking our own language they'd give you a strapping and you'd end up losing it - at a young age. You never got to talk it to nobody else. The boys' master, the teacher, it depends where you were. If you got caught talking your own language, you got it.

It was a time of your life and you went through it. I don't hold no grudges against anybody. It's over, it's over, but if I could have had my own way I would never have went there. I don't really know why I went there - I was just young and all of a sudden I was there.

I suppose in a way we had some fun - we played ball and we played hockey.

There wasn't any sexual abuse that I knew of.

Later on after I come out of there they got TV rooms and everything. When I was there we didn't have nothin'. We had a pair of boxing gloves and you'd be careful of your buddy or he'd beat you up. I don't think nobody really liked it there, as far as everybody I've talked to. Some boys - they were for ever running away from there. I think there was three or four brothers from Sarnia - they got a bad deal. They would strap you on your bum sometimes, or around the back of your hand, or wherever they took a liking to hittin' you. If they thought they were going to correct you - they must have thought that's the way to correct you. I knew a couple of guys there - you could strap 'em all day on the palm of your hand and they wouldn't cry - just the type of guy who wouldn't give in.

I never seen homosexuality or anything like that.

They used to bring us to Bread and Cheese, and the Fair and that. They'd give you a quarter and expect you to get two meals out of that and have a good time - I think we got a quarter once - once in 7 years. Once in a while they would take all the guys and take 'em to the show in Brantford, and we'd dress up like a bunch of freaks to go up there. We used to have these pants - they'd call 'em breeks - like riding pants - they came in tight below your knees and had laces up the sides, and a red chequered shirt. Either a red chequered shirt or a green chequered shirt. They looked the same but one was red and one was green.

When we had to brush our teeth they used to give us this chalk we had to use - chalk like you write on the blackboard with - that's what we had to use for toothpaste. They wouldn't let you use your own toothpaste - you had your own toothbrush - they supplied that. And I think everybody was lousy there pretty well. They used to put this stuff on our head that they called pickle juice. You'd smell it a mile away, but I guess it did the job and cleaned people out. I never ever had the lice at home.

I can remember my teachers - they weren't too bad, but they used to have one woman down there - she used to be the cook. They used to call her 'giant woman' - everybody had a nickname! She brought you spinach or something and you didn't eat it, she'd make you sit there till you ate it, and she'd twist your ear. And man! she could twist! She'd make you eat it whether you wanted it or not. She was English. The guys they seemed to get to go there were something like an old army sergeant - they'd yell and holler and carry on. They had this one guy - Mr. Williston. I looked for him for a couple of years after I got out. If I'd ever met him I'd probably have done him in. He was the meanest. Then they had another guy there - his name was Nugget Clark. I can still remember this Nugget Clark saying "Maybe Mr Williston's scared of you, but I'm not." When Williston would come on duty he'd say "Maybe Nugget's scared of you, but I'm not." They both liked to show that they had the authority over you - especially this Williston - he used to go out of his way to - I mean you would hate him if you met him - but on the outside I don't know what he would be like.

He never had a good word for anybody. He's the guy that if he didn't like the colour of your hands - you could wash for an hour and you showed him and he didn't like 'em, he'd get carried away. He used to get really mad at me cuz I wouldn't cry, cuz I could tire him right out from getting a strapping. My hand would be really hard and he'd jump right off the floor and bring that strap down. I just wouldn't let him have the enjoyment of thinking he could beat me.

There was a pretty good teacher named Mrs. Newman. She was a little short lady. Then there was a nurse used to be in there - I don't know her right name - and she used to treat everybody pretty good. We had a teacher named Mr. Watson and he was a nice guy - you don't find too many of them. They had the sewing woman Mrs Boyce. She must have been 300 years old!! She was quite an old lady - they just had one woman looking after all the clothes for all the boys and girls - she did the patch work and all that, and tried to stretch everything that she had - that would be enough to drive anybody mad - but if you sat down and talked to her, she proved all right. She always treated me good anyway.

The farm masters - Mr. Baker and Mr. Howard - they weren't bad fellows - if you did what you were told. This Williston fella - his wife was a teacher. She matched his description - she didn't have anything nice to say about anybody. They were meant to be together. There was one real good teacher - I can't remember the name. We had a teacher there - her name was Mrs. McMeans - she used to put lipstick on and she never used a mirror - she'd miss both ends of her mouth and she was some sight!! She used to teach what they call the 'opportunity class' - the guys who didn't want to learn. The teacher we had up there - they had down here. He was a pretty good fellow - his name was Mr. Hanna. We had one real nice school inspector used to come around, by the name of Mr. Webster. He knew everybody in the county by their name - fantastic man. He was nice to everybody.

The school was really what you made of it yourself. I seem to have survived and I think everybody else had the same chance. You were there and there wasn't much you could do - you had to live it.

Name withheld
1948 - 1956

I went there when I was about 8 or 9. My mother and Dad parted and my Mum couldn't support us on her own. I was 16 when I left. I left in '56. I didn't go to high school. I just wanted to get out of there - when I turned 16 I decided to leave.

It was all mixed - bad times and good times and sad times. I got on OK with the other girls.

I ran away from there once and I went back on my own.

When I got back Zimmerman gave me a strapping. He made me pull my underpants down - right on my bare...I was about 14. I didn't like that. One of the other girls that came back - she didn't get a strapping. That was the first time I ever got that. A few other girls - they all got a strapping. We had to go in the office one at a time. It was embarrassing. I just ran away for something to do!! My best girl friend was going so I went with her. Then we got her home to Muncey Reserve and that's when we turned around and came back. Her mother brought her back.

There was one man supervisor there - he didn't like me too good either. I was a supervisor in the dining room that year and he was always picking on me. He said if he ever had a chance to give me a strapping he was going to do a damn good job of it. I didn't like him either - he was mean. I wouldn't listen to him - he was the supervisor and he'd tell me to do something and I wouldn't do it. He was supervising the boys and I was the supervisor in the dining room. He never got a chance to give me a strapping. The supervisors - most of them were OK if you kept in line. If you didn't you just got a strapping. I never got a strapping from the supervisor. I behaved myself - did what I was told. This one lady - she worked in the sewing-room - I remember when I first got my monthlies I went up there. I didn't know what to do, and one of the girls told me to go up there and I told her what happened, and she just said "Damn bleeding Indians anyway." That's what she said - I never ever forgot that. Some of them were prejudiced - they probably worked there for the money. They never checked into things like they do now. If one of the kids complained nobody would believe them anyway.

I finished Grade 8. Our teacher we had in the eighth grade - she taught 6, 7 and 8 - she was real good. She was excellent. She never raised her voice to us and I never seen her strap anyone. She had patience - Mrs. Newman.

We got the strap on our hands in school - I think that has a lot to do with the children listening and minding. I got a strap in school once and I never ever did anything to get another strap. I behaved myself after that. I was so embarrassed - I didn't want to go up there in front of everybody and get the strap. We had to stand in front of the whole class and he would strap us. That was a man teacher we had - he was there before Mrs. Newman - he was just young.

Having sisters there helped you from being lonesome. You'd miss your Mum and Dad - you didn't see 'em much. Even though they were there though you'd still get lonely for your Mum and Dad. They'd visit and they wrote letters. It must have been awful for the ones who never saw their parents once in a while. I missed a few summers - I stayed all year. Mum would come and get us whenever she could - she cared about us. We were disappointed if we had to stay - lonesome.

They took the boys - the boys could go to a show every Saturday, but the girls couldn't. They wouldn't let the girls do anything. The only place we marched was back and forth to church on Sunday. Once in a great while they'd take us to a show, and then we had the Bread and Cheese down here, and they'd bring us down here for that. Other than that we just stayed in the playground or the playroom. Then they got a television for us - we could watch that in the evenings until it was bedtime, and on weekends. When I got older I was in the Girl Guides. Somebody would come

to the school for us and we would stay there - I liked the Girl Guides. I liked it best when I carried the flag - it was blue and gold.

I didn't know my Native language when I went there. Some of the children couldn't even speak any English, but they couldn't speak their own language - if they came there, they'd get mean to them if they spoke it.

When I got to be in Grade 6 I had to make beds up in the dormitory, and keep the floor clean. And then when I got into Grade 7 - we just went to school half-a-day, in the afternoons, we had to work in the kitchen in the mornings - I had to do vegetables. Then when I got into Grade 8, that's when I was a supervisor in the dining-room. I had to make sure everything was on the table - dishes, knife and fork - silverware. Everything depended on the girls from Grade 6-8 - that's when they started us working. I worked in the dining room too one year - I remember scrubbing the cement floor. That was one thing I liked about the place - it was mostly kept clean. We had to scrub on our hands and knees with a scrubbing brush and pail.

I had two brothers there. The only time I'd see my brother was when we had meals - I think we were together at noon. We weren't allowed to talk to the boys - they didn't want us talking to boys. It was bad for them - one night we were all up in bed and all of a sudden I heard this - one boy was up there just screaming - like somebody was killing him. We could hear right through the whole dormitory. They said one of the bigger boys was getting after a little guy. My brothers would never talk to me much about that - I never really had a chance to talk to them about it. He was screaming anyway - I was just scared. I didn't hear about any sexual abuse until after I got out. I didn't hear about it when I was in there. I was talking to this one lady and she was in there, and I don't know if it was one of the supervisor men that got after her, and she got raped when she was up there. There was a lady who worked in the kitchen who looked like a man. She used to like putting her arms around us - holding you and touching you if you walked by. She didn't look like a woman to me - she had whiskers - she shaved all over. Nobody bothered me like that. There were some that were picked on.

I'm grateful for my education I got there - what I know now - I'm grateful for that.

The boys used to get it really bad if they did something wrong. There was no love there - you'd get love from nobody there - just from your brothers and sisters if they were there.

You got used to the food - it's all you got - you had to eat it. I didn't like that oatmeal they gave us in the morning. I had to sit there one day till noon - until I ate it. I couldn't eat it - I never used to eat it cuz it was slimy - it would make you gag. One of the girls came in and they got my dish and they threw it away when the officer wasn't looking!! The only thing I didn't like was oatmeal. I don't know why the oatmeal tasted like that - oh it was awful. I used to always give mine away - I wouldn't eat it. If you could find somebody that ate it you'd give it to them. They had another one - tapioca - it was like fish eyes - that was terrible tasting. We had some good meals - maybe you just get used to eating that. We always had a dessert around noon and supper. That's how I learned to like vegetables - I had to do vegetables when I worked in the kitchen - a great big pot of buttered beets, or buttered carrots - different things. I don't know if it was real butter, but it was in squares. They had cows there - I wonder if they made their own butter. Skim milk - that's all we got - every meal. They sold the cream - we never got no cream. The officers got cream on their table but the children didn't get none. They got eggs.

I went to Buffalo after I left school. My Mum had a baby and I stayed home and babysat while she went to work. Then when I was 19 I met my husband and we got married. I had a good life after I met my husband - he was good to me. We had five children and that was my life - I stayed home and watched the children.

Albert Sault
194?

The only thing I could think about was how to get out of there - to escape - wipe out that part of my life. My mother dropped us off there and that was the last I saw of her until just before I went in the Marine Corps.

I was just a slave - getting up at 4 a.m. - milking the cows. We learned to do a job right. It was like a concentration camp.

We had to march down to eat and sit at attention until they told us we could eat. The meals were skimpy. If we ever had bread we had to give it up to the big boys - they would beat us. The bigger boys took everything - our money, our food, our clothes. One time they took our clothes when we were swimming and they made us swim across the Mohawk Lake - we ran away in our swimming trunks. There were a lot of bad boys. There were bullies who would make us late so we would get the strap. There was one little guy - they would hang him on the steam pipes. I remember one time on the riverbank they had guns and were shooting at our feet.

'Skin' was a nasty character - he flogged us. I stayed clear of him. If we were late we were flogged by the personnel. Another boy and me we worked on a farm - the farmer brought us back 10 minutes late and he explained that it was his fault, but after he'd gone they flogged us anyway. We'd be made to drop our pants and lie across a table and we were beaten with a strap this wide. I heard he was as bad with the girls.

The barn master was Baker. The Maintenance man taught me about the boiler - he was the only one that was decent - except for Anderson the school teacher.

I ran away and never returned. We camped out in the park. We were sitting on the railroad tracks and they suddenly came out of the woods - Zimmerman and the boys' master. They were in the ditch so we took off down the tracks and they were chasing us all the way down the railroad track. They were yelling "You're gonna get a beating if you don't stop. Stop - we just want to talk to you."

I was apprenticed in a tailor's shop. I worked for five years, and I took night courses - went to school every chance I could get. I love machines. I did electronics. I took all the brothers in Rochester, where I had a collision shop for 15 years. I was in the U.S. Marines for seven years - I got out just before the unit was sent to Vietnam. The Mohawk Institute was good training for the Marine Corps.

Calvin Sault
194? - 1953

I lost ten years of my memory - I didn't lose it - I just obliterated it from my memory because of the bad experience I had. Even after this I had a lot of bad experiences - worked it right out of my mind. I had a lot of aggressions and bad feelings to the school and to society - I didn't really know where to accept any help or get any help. Every time I run away and got a beating I got the skin ripped right off my leg by Mr. Wilson - the boys' master. When I did run away they sent the boys after me - of course they helped me get away - I finally got smart and stayed between the railroad and the Queen Elizabeth Highway and made it to Niagara Falls and made it across with the tourists - I found a quarter - I don't know what it was to get across the bridge and they helped me there.

It was good for some people because they had nowhere else to go. But we owned land in Dunnville - my mother - for a long time I had to get that in my head that she was married real young and didn't know what to do with the kids. She didn't know how - I don't know if they were too proud, or didn't know how to accept or ask for help, or what it was. For fifteen years I never spoke to my mother - not till after my father died. My grandmother gave me a partial home and even then - even though my mother was just around the corner I never went to see her - she didn't seem to want us. I don't know what it was - I never had the nerve to sit down and figure this all out. This whole experience in - I'll say the Mohawk Institute - the Mush hole - they boiled the oatmeal so hard sometimes it was even green - they just threw in the sugar and it was just like a glue. The only time we got any decent food was when the government officials come there - we took advantage of that and we got seconds and thirds. We got cakes and we got cornflakes and all the good stuff when they came, but soon as they left we went back to the same old garbage - potatoes, turnips, cabbage, and mush. Hardly ever did we get any meat and they would sit over there with roasts on their table - they'd eat like kings.

They called him 'Skin' - he'd sit over there like a big fat king and enjoy himself - Zimmerman - on our food. I never started to gain weight until the last three or four years. I would walk into a restaurant and I couldn't stand the smell of cabbage, turnips, or liver, which was what they had. In order to get good food we used to go over to the dump - there was two of them - we used to call it the 'D'. - the black D and the city D; and they would find food in there - bales of hay and straw. I was lucky, I had a cousin there - there was bread - we used to call them slabs - with jam on them - and they would put it on the table and make sure that we sat there.

I constantly had to fight - I learned to fight in the outside society for what I wanted - I set a goal and went after it. It was a learning experience. I made sure my kids and my grandchildren never had to do that - of course I didn't know they were going to stop it. I was afraid to come back here for a long time - I was afraid they would put me in jail, because they chased me down at least once or twice a week - and each time I got a beating.

The only one that talked halfway decent to us was the farmer, Mr. Baker, and if we didn't find aggressiveness from the school personnel we got it from a gang that was there - they called themselves the Robin Hood Gang. Some of the experiences we had with this Robin Hood Gang - down in the basement, we had a game. I learned real fast that you watch certain ones getting near the light switch - the heaters were on the ceiling down in the basement there - they were steam heaters - one particular one I used to throw up there - he was real small. I would throw him up on the steam heaters and jump there myself, because they used to turn the lights off and then throw skates. Or if I wasn't near there when they turned the lights off there was a hole into the bathroom just big enough for me to dive through. I'd dive into the bathroom. We had constantly to be on guard of something or other. From my part I had a very bad time there and there came a point I wasn't going to put up with it. I didn't know what I was going to do, but it wasn't helping me.

We weren't allowed to talk about our native ways. I couldn't speak the language - I hadn't been able to speak the language till I was 48 years old and I started going back to school and learning it. My father knew it - they said it wasn't any good - to get along on the outside world you had to learn English - to this day I'm still in disagreement. You have to know who you are and what you are - your culture, your ways, to identify yourself. Later in life - when I was up in my 40s and 50s - I'm the first Pipe Carrier on this reserve in 150 years. Which is quite an honour to be accepted into the Elder cultural ways and traditional ways. I still live in my traditional ways. When I'm on the outside I live by standards of the outside society. It can be done. You have to understand and recognize a man's individuality. You have to constantly forgive a man for what he does, and you have to look at things with respect for everything about you. Being in the Mohawk Institute stiffened me to what I want in life. Although I had a bad time there - not everybody did have a bad time in there. Some were favourites - one particular teacher, she was wonderful - Mrs. Newman - and she would help me with my work. I was looking for somebody to release my things to and unload, and she was a very good teacher - one of the best that I had there. And Mr. Baker of course - he was a good man.

Of course - back then you had to abide by certain rules. Several times they picked me up - the police picked me up in Hamilton, or Burlington, or Stony Creek or somewhere - I never knew where I was half the time. When they picked me up - I don't even know how they found me some of the time - I thought I was hid real good.

This experience was a learning experience - no matter how bad it is. It took me a while in a State hospital to figure out and to get rid of all these aggressions. I was in a State hospital - now I'm completely sane - I have the papers to prove it. By their standards I'm sane. I tried alcohol for a while - but only for three or four years. I'd drink for two days and be sick for four. I knew right away that wasn't for me. I never did try drugs.

I was basically a loner after that. I achieved what I had by setting a goal and going after it. So even though I had bad times there and I blanked a lot of it out of my memory, for everything bad there's a good. Every sickness has a medicine, if we go look for it. I knew I was restricted there, even though I was fairly young, I knew I was restricted of what I had an idea of. We basically did not know anything about any life at all as - all we knew was the farm - we worked.

My education consists of Grade 5 - even to this day. Even though I had a bad time there it was a learning experience, but I made sure my kids didn't see that. I was glad to hear that they wiped them out of existence. I thought I was the only one that had the bad experience, but it wasn't so. Some had worse experience than I did. One brother, he's almost a recluse because he thought we left him there - we wouldn't go back and get him. But we had no way of getting him out of there. My mother wouldn't sign the papers. I did years later come back through the States and I got my Grandmother to sign the papers so I could get my brother out of there, and I got him a job in Smithville - well, he worked there a couple of days. He was free, he was alone and there was nothing I could do about it.

Once around Christmas, the Kiwanis club or one of them, gave a Christmas party and we were elected to go, and we were given toys. When we come back they stood up there, took the toys away from us and gave us socks - thin socks not work socks. Zimmerman and his wife and Miss Chisholm - she was the nurse - they would line up there and take them all away from us and give us thin socks. Dress socks - they were no good for work. They were useless, literally useless to us. They said the toys were no good to us, but they were - they were given to us. Even if we lost it to one of them other people, we could see it. If I lost something through a bet, and I could see it every now and then, it would still in my heart belong to me, whether somebody took it from me or not. I wish I wouldn't bet, but even if one of the other people took it from me, the bigger ones, it would be mine. When the Queen became Queen, the Government give us medals - they took 'em away from us. They were sent from the Government for us and they took 'em. I don't know what they did with them, but by rights they still do belong to us. What Skin and his wife or those other people did with them, whether they give them away or sold them; his children played with them - they might still have them. I don't know if they were gold plated or what but they were pretty anyway. Today the Church is not owning up to the problems we had there - an apology. Rather than an apology they could give me back my toy. I wouldn't be happier than if they'd give me my toy back and my medal. An apology is like a voice on a windy day. Some of them were real bad - they were hurt for life. I talked to one in particular and there are times when he's

drunk he talks about that and he goes back in time so to speak, and it's ruined his life.

By the time I was 29 I owned two homes. I went out and I worked, and I worked at three jobs, and I tried to go back to school, but by then I was 18-19 and I was in Grade 5. I think I run away in '52 - '53 or something like that. My brother A, he run away and went to the States. And my brother B - he came back to the Reserve.

Like I say, we didn't get enough food in there -we'd eat raw turnips. I couldn't stand turnips, literally. Cabbage - my wife loves cabbage and I wouldn't allow it in the house.

Although we had bad experiences there was still a little fun. I broke my arm and my leg and cracked my skull a few times. We had a very good nurse - Mrs. Doxtator. She's retired now but she remembers me clear back to 1952. I splintered my leg rather than breaking it so they couldn't put a cast on. It was stretched out. I enjoyed that, she used to come and read to me. Every child needs someone - you pick upon a figure - and she would read to us.

I go to prisons and talk to Native inmates there and Guelph College. That's pretty good for a man with only Grade 5 education. I fill my life even though I can't work no more - this is all volunteer and I work on a ball of tobacco. I usually don't talk to people unless they bring me tobacco. I have to tell the truth when my pipe is together.

I was not sexually bothered - I was a fighter, so anything I didn't want to do I didn't do, or I tried not to do. I was literally beat up many times because I didn't do things to their liking. If it was done in there, it was by the other boys - the older ones. They did disappear for a time - it's possible that this did happen - I don't know. In talking with some of them that I knew - they weren't. As mean as I was, I protected several of the boys from getting a beating - I'd get right in there and fight. I wasn't going to allow nobody to walk over me or the friends that I played with.

John Martin
1949 - 1954

I was there from '49-'54 - as soon as I turned 14 they shipped me to training school. The first day I was there I ran away. I ran away about a hundred times - had to be a hundred times - I literally hated that place.

I got a scar on my back where that guy - Reverend Zimmerman - strapped me. It was on my hands and he couldn't make me cry so he hit me on the back. He even strapped the girls and he wasn't supposed to do that - he would strip them and strap them. I know for a fact because we ran away with four or five girls - me and B L and he strapped them right in front of us. He's not supposed to do that, but we were kids and we didn't know any better. I told him one day I was going to kill him, when they sent me to the training school. But he's dead now - I said "One day I'm

going to get you - I don't know how, but I am." He got away with a lot of things - a few of the guys threatened to kill him, but nobody ever did I guess, he just died of old age. My stepfather said the guy before him was even worse than that - I said nobody could be worse than Skin.

My mum and dad split up and his barns burned down and he started drinking and he just didn't want looking after anybody. In the summer holiday my grandpa and grandma used to come and get me cuz we were gone for the summer holidays when school was over.

I was so bad I didn't even know what my name was - I went to school under John Hill. When I went to the Mohawk Institute - the Mush hole - I was under John Newhouse. When I wrote for my birth certificate they sent it back under John Martin. I didn't even know who I was for a long time - my stepmother raised me since I was about a month old.

I learned how to steal - learned how to steal pretty good - you had to steal to eat - to get full. All the boys - all the guys who lived on the farm - they would run down to the dump to get full before they did their chores - the city dump was just down the path from us. We used to go uptown and steal in the bakeries. Anything we could find that was eatable we would eat out of the dump. We got up at 5.30 and all they'd give you was a little bit of mush with a little bit of brown sugar in the middle of it - that was your breakfast. I know they had milk because I used to deliver the milk to the kitchen. If you didn't have a girl in there you were in lots of trouble. I had a girl friend, I was lucky. She just liked me and she used to steal me sandwiches and stuff out of the kitchen.

All them animals they had there - 90 cows - we never seen milk. 800 chickens - we never seen eggs. They sold them to make money and pocketed it.

When you went to school you could talk to girls, but other than that we weren't supposed to talk to them.

We had uniforms - red sweater and pair of pants. They took us to the fair in Ohsweken and the Bread and Cheese in Ohsweken. Once a month they'd take us down to the show. That was terrible - lined up with girls on the one side and boys on the other, to take you uptown to the show.

We had to go to church every Sunday whether you liked it or not. You were baptised and confirmed - didn't even know what it meant. My Dad was a preacher at Bethlehem mission - they never teach you what you know today about God and Jesus. We were baptised - my wife and my daughter - Pentecostal church.

I actually believe he was a sadist - I really do. He used to get his kicks strapping people - you could tell. There was a lot of guys so used to it he couldn't hurt them. That day he was strapping me I was black and blue way up to here. He says "You're not going to cry, are you?" I said "You ain't big enough to make me cry any more." He said I could go, so I turned and walked away and he hit me right across the back. I just turned around and looked at him and said "I still ain't going to cry." I've still got a scar there. About a month later they shipped me to the training school. I was one of the few that went from bad to worse to terrible, cuz I wound up in penitentiary - and I blame that place. We were a herd of animals - there was no love there - there was no love whatsoever. I never knew what that word meant when I was a kid.

And when you first went there the bigger boys used to beat up the little boys, and if you told on them the bigger boys would beat you up. So you learned you didn't squeal on them. After I went back - I ran away to my Dad's and they took me back, and my uncle says "If you strap him I'll be back to see you," so he strapped me anyway - they didn't care. That night the bigger guys tied me up to a post and

were bouncing a ball off my head. Then he strapped me again for being late getting in bed - I was tied to a post and he never took me off and untied me. That's what turned me off Christianity - the guy's supposed to be an Anglican minister - head of a church and this is what they do. It's pretty hard to believe it. You learned to be tough there I'll tell you - you learned to be tough.

I learned how to work there - but they do make you work hard.

I used to like Mrs. Davies - she was the nurse - she was pretty fair. If you were sick she was pretty fair. It's funny, I can remember pretty nearly all their names. Mr Wilson's not still around - he was boys' master.

The staff didn't do it to the boys, but I know the guys used to rape each other - I know that for a fact - I've seen it. To me it was a miniature penitentiary. A lot of them girls got pregnant - don't ask me how, cuz we weren't allowed to get near them. But I know this one guy - he was there - they hired him to work on the farm and he said he used to go to bed with a lot of them girls. He said they used to climb out of the dorm and come to his room.

Some of the guys done pretty good. I knew four guys who went to high school, but most of the guys I know turned out to be alcoholics. I was just talking to J B when my nephew got married - and I said "Do you remember the bad old days?" - most people say the "good old days." When I found out it was closed I was glad. When they had that reunion I didn't even know they had it or I woulda gone. I used to sleep right next to the fire escape on the second floor. We'd put a piece of metal in the door and we would cross over the top to the girls dorm - we got pretty good at that.

There was a fire - a big one - when all the barns burned down, and they tried to blame the boys, but how could they blame us when we were all sleeping - it happened at 3 o'clock in the morning. They tried to say the boys done it so they wouldn't have to work.

We just had holidays in the summer - but 9-4 if parents came to get you they would let you go out for the day. My dad came a couple of times. It's terrible when you see kids standing at the fence waiting for their parents to come and they never show up. I used to be one - I used to stand there. I'd say "Dad, I'll see you in a couple of weeks," and he'd never show up. It's a terrible feeling. He did show up one day and I'd ran away that very morning before he got there. They caught me about three weeks later and they says "Your father was here to visit you."

I ran away to Buffalo - I had an uncle there and he took me in. I got sick of living on the streets over there so I come back by myself.

It took me until just about six years ago to turn around - just since I met my wife. I didn't care about nobody or anything - that Mohawk was filling my mind. I just could never forgive that guy and what he had done to us. And when I found out he was dead I was mad that I hadn't done it. That's a terrible way to live your life you know - trying to get revenge.

All along I thought nobody cared - but my sister did, because when they sent me to the training school I was there for a few years, and after I got out they sent me to a service station to work - '58-'59. I worked there for $30 a month and my room and board. Wasn't very much - only a dollar a day - I was seventeen. I phoned my sister and she said "We're coming to get you." I guess she always did care - but she couldn't do nothing about it - she wasn't much older than I am. She and her husband married and she got pregnant. My other sister is a head nurse - but she was smart. When my mum and dad split up she lived with my mother and she went to a high school.

They didn't care if you passed or not - when you went to school there - they didn't care. As far as I'm concerned those teachers were there to get a pay cheque. They didn't teach you nothing. They had a grade system - I went to Grade 8 there. I went to the training school and I took correspondence courses on my own. From the training school I wound up in Guelph - '64 I was in the penitentiary and I took more correspondence courses - vindicated myself.

When I was in the penitentiary I talked to some of them - they said they were better off in the penitentiary than they were in the Mohawk school - that's hard to believe isn't it? There's more freedom in the penitentiary - in your cell. Not as much abuse, no, but that stays with you. I still dream about that place once in a while. I'll never forget the time he hit me in the back - because when I walked downstairs my friends said "You're bleeding." I said "I know, he strapped me in the back." I have the scar - my wife can see it and she asked where I got it - I said the Mohawk Institute. He strapped the back of my legs black and blue. I says "You'll never make me cry. That thin strap - you can't hurt me." He was so tired I think he was just about ready to cry, but he couldn't make me cry. My dad come to visit me in the morning - they had just caught this guy from running away, so they sent him up to the dorm and while they were dressing me to go out with my dad, he escaped. I came back and they strapped me because he got away again. That wasn't my fault. I'll never forget that because I come back and I said goodbye to my dad and I walked downstairs and he said "D S got away cuz of you." I said "Why me?" He jumped out of the fire escape while I was dressing that morning. That wasn't my fault. Then they wonder why people hate that place. I told my dad and he said "There's nothing I can do about it. We talked to them and we were just told to mind our own business." "We'll discipline the boys."

When I used to deliver milk I'd steal apples - I used to go through the orchard and steal apples so we could eat - and they'd strap you every time - even if you took one apple.

All I learned in there was to hate people - I learned you never have friends, because I had two friends and all they do is squeal and get you in trouble, and I learned you never

have friends. I keep telling my daughter - it's not any better today. Your friends will shit on you - they're out to hurt you. They're out to get what they can out of you - that's it. I really believe that - even today. I keep telling her - the more you do for people the more they'll use you and then they shit on you.

I did farm work - it was all farm work. We were all day in school - when the haying season come you'd do half-a-day in school. All that stuff they grew there and the little food they gave us - they sold that stuff to the white people. The potatoes they grew - they grew fields and fields and fields of it - we never seen that much potatoes and stuff.

That's where you got trench mouth and that from - they got so bad they were using their shirts to wipe the silverware off - there was stuff from the morning on the supper dishes. I still check my dishes - my wife checks them now before she gives them to me.

We got up at 5.30 and we'd eat at 7. In the meantime we put in a lot of work and you're hungry. That's why we called it the Mush hole - we'd get a bowl of porridge and a little bit of sugar - no milk. The guys at work had to be last to eat, and if there wasn't enough it was too bad. Then they'd wonder why we used to run down the dump to get full. It looked kinda funny - you'd get up early in the morning and see about 20 guys heading down to the dump.

They used to send us out to work for people in Brantford - we never saw the money - I know they got paid. We used to cut grass, rake for other farmers.

C (Sister). Grandma put him there because he wouldn't listen - it was "I'll send you to the Mush hole." He says "I don't care - I can get out." Then he begged to get out: "I'll be good, I'll behave, I'll do what I'm told if you let me come home." He had a place to go and she put him there and she could take him out any time she wanted.

J. Kids who were bad went there - I was bad.

C: John went there because he had a discipline problem. My father and mother parted and neither wanted John because of his bad habits. My mother couldn't afford to keep him and my father went to the States to work, and my sister and I had a place to go, but because John stole - John stole - John did bad things. You're talking about a nine or ten-year-old boy who went to the neighbour's barn, turned all his cows out of the barn - not just turning them in the barnyard, but opening up the gate and chasing them down the road - now that's the things John done. Now that's bad. What he done to another neighbour - he went to their house and nailed him in - he nailed the door shut. John knows he done these things - that's why John went to the Mush hole.

J. This is the sister who took me out of that place in Hamilton. Her and her husband took me in.

C. We had you home for Christmas to our house. I get this knock on the door - "You know John Martin - he can get out for Christmas if he has a place to come." I says "Well, I have to talk to my husband first. I can't say yes if my husband doesn't like it." He had a three day pass - I had four children. While John was there he said if he had a place to live he could get out. He was in Bowmanville so after he went back my husband said "Well he can come and stay with us." His Dad had a couple of acres. "Dad's got a lot of work and John can earn his keep working for my Dad." My husband used to quit his job and come home and farm. So we got John out, but he had to come and help. So John had to go and get himself in trouble again and we had to let him go back. Things just happened and my father-in-law said "I can't have him around here," and I couldn't handle him by myself as my husband was away working.

I'm working at a place right now and the woman was in there, and I asked her how she liked it. "Oh," she says "It wasn't too bad." She had a twin sister and her sister was always getting in trouble and she got the strap and she said the strap had tacks in it. They had a leather strap and they put tacks in it and they'd hit kids with it. The lady I work for is a schizophrenic so I can't really know if what she's telling me is true.

J. I know they had two kinds of straps - they had one that was smooth and one that was really rough. Oh god! that hurt. Guys used to cry on purpose after a couple of hits so that he'd stop.

Delbert Riley
1950 - 1955

I went in around 1950. I think I went there because my parents were very poor, with 8 kids in the family. Whatever it was at the time - I don't remember. But they weren't very wealthy at the time, even though my father was one of the few people who had cars.

The boys lived on one side, the girls on the other, and in the centre was the church - in this case the Anglican church

The Anglican system was much different from the Catholics - we didn't have a bunch of nuns teaching us. The teaching was very good - I can't really fault the education system.

Probably the biggest problem at the time in there was the lack of control, and also the food.

The kids in there ranged in age from high-school to little ones. I myself was six at the time I first went to the Mohawk.

It was called the Mush hole for very obvious reasons - this was the breakfast meal six days a week - the preparation of this particular mush was terrible - they must have boiled it for at least ten hours, and of course it came out like a very sticky paste. It just tasted bad. Along with that we had skim milk - the school was essentially a large farm - a large field. Budgets weren't very large - most of the goods and things from the farm were sold off.

The food you got was very little - very small portions. Most of the good food was eaten by the older kids. You didn't get a lot of food, and of course you were hungry all the time. There was a lack of organization on the part of the administration - I'm not saying this was the case in every school but it was the case at this time in this school.

We used to steal food - in the fall we used to steal vegetables. We got a couple of eggs on Easter Sunday, and cereal from a box. Two slices of toast that's all you get - there were no seconds. Noon meals were probably a bit better, but not much - desserts were taken by the older boys. The storage of foods couldn't have been very good - there were various other residents shared it with us and when it was cooked of course we seen all these bugs as well. Christmas was the one time of year we got full - we got presents and candy. The staff had separate meals.

The worst thing about it was the cold. Our dress consisted of overalls, longjohns and a plaid shirt and that was it. Probably for three years we didn't have coats.

I was probably lucky - I got sick - they didn't bother me cuz they thought I was going to die. I was in bed a few months and nobody bothered me after that - they thought I wouldn't survive.

The strap was the most severe punishment you could get for running away. I can recall a lot of times in the middle of the night being herded outside for roll call. Each of us was assigned a number and we had to identify ourselves and it was reported to somebody. This roll call was used to identify who was absent. If they were caught - and in most cases they were as they were young kids, they were brought back, and of course they would get the strap on the rear end. It was administered by the Reverend Zimmerman - we used to call him 'Skin' - and it was given to boys and girls alike. They would be stripped down, and the marks left on them, of course, were all black and blue. Your hands were rather long - they extended up to your elbows - you were black and blue - five or ten on each side. The toughest thing about that was - if you were given the strap the older kids would make sure you didn't cry or yell out - you had to take it and not make a whimper, and most of the kids did - that is tough.

One of the more severe things, other than the psychological thing of being away from your family, was from the treatment by the older kids. For whatever reason this wasn't checked. The boys' masters - they were supposed to be in control. A lot of the abuses - sexual - came from the older kids. A lot of the older kids would steal from the younger kids, and make the younger kids steal. If you didn't come back with what you were sent out to get, or if you were to tell, you'd get worse. A lot of the younger kids lived in fear and terror of the older boys - it was a way of life to us. You had to do a lot of fighting. The first night, I got in a fight. I was very strong - I scared them - didn't realise how strong I was - I threw them all over the place. I was scared of them but you soon learned how to fight. The younger kids - the toughest part - some of the things they were forced to do were pretty violent. They were forced to ride young calves, until they fell off. Some of them were forced to hold onto hot pipes, and if they didn't hold on long enough they were strapped. Some of the things I can't even mention.

There was a nice yard - they would have picnics on the other side of the fence.

To supplement our food there used to be a couple of dumps. Most Sunday mornings kids would be up at four o'clock in the morning - to get out and get back before they marched us to church, dressed in our uniform of red sweater, white shirt, tie, special shoes. Usually by 7 o'clock we were in bed - up by 6 unless you worked in the barns - you were up by 4. We usually got lots of sleep.

It wasn't until 1953 that changes came about - we got TV. In 1953 I got my first coat. There were some real young kids, and older kids were given responsibility for the younger kids - help them in the bathroom, dress them, wash them up, and to look after them until they were in the classroom.

I was on my own from age 13, and worked my way through high-school. It was lucky I liked school. I worked as a machinist, and made lots of money in the States, came back to Canada and went to university. I became an activist in the '70s in the Indian movement.

I had difficulty interacting with other people and this was hard when I was raising my family.

Karen Hill
1951 - 1958

I went when I was 7, in 1951. All I know is my Mum couldn't look after us. I was too young. I was there seven years. We went when we were seven and we started right in Grade 1, and I came out when I was in Grade 8. I went to BCI - I didn't finish high school though, but that's where I went.

Well, I don't think it ruined my life. I guess I enjoyed it. I didn't at the time, but looking back there wasn't anything bad about it that I can recollect - a lot of discipline. I mean discipline - you get up in the morning at a certain time, you eat a certain time. You get used to that. Of course doing that for seven years, it's good for a person. At least I think it is - discipline in that way. Of course you got the strap when you needed it. I don't think anybody got the strap for no reason, and I don't think it was bad - you weren't abused or anything like that. If you knew you weren't supposed to be running and you were running in the hall, or something like that, and that was a rule - you weren't supposed to run in the hall, and you did it, then you got the strap. Then you knew not to do it again. The first time I did it was the first day I was there and I didn't know the rules. I shouldn't have got punished that time because I did not know the rules. I mean maybe it's posted, but when you're first there you're not looking for rules, you're doing other things. I don't hold it against them - I'm not scarred for life. It was something you had to do - you got sent there - what could you do? Seven, eight, nine, ten, eleven - what could you do - you got sent there, you made the best of it, right?

I liked the education there. You went to school every day, except when you were really, really sick, and I liked that. There was one teacher - she was in Brantford - Mrs. Cripps. I remember her because one time in Grade 3 or 4,

I remember her mentioning that I got 100 on spelling and 100 on arithmetic, and I was the only one in the whole class who had got that, and I didn't think I would on arithmetic, but spelling I was good at, and I thought that was nice of her to mention it, and I remembered that. Sometimes it only takes one line to change one's life for the better for the future. I don't know if I did well, I did my best and I got by. I wasn't a brain or anything. The teachers - they were fine, but you see this was such a long time ago that I can't remember too much.

We had to learn housekeeping skills. There was a point that you had to make all the beds in the dorm, and clean floors, and then you got to a point where you had to work in the kitchen, then a grade up you had to work in the scullery. Then you got to work where the nurse was - so you got to learn some skills there. You know the first time I made a cake they entered it in the fair at Ohsweken and it won first prize. But I didn't like that because - I liked the idea of winning first prize, and they did give me the ribbon - but they didn't let me eat the cake. The ones who looked after you - the supervisors and the housemothers - ate the cake. In the dining room the kids sat in two rows, and they sat up here, and they got to eat the cake. I didn't even get a taste of it, but I remember it. I felt even if they had given me a taste - I didn't care if they gave all the other kids a taste - but I felt that I should have had a taste. But I was OK - I got the ribbon, if that was any consolation. I would have rather had the cake.

I wasn't unhappy. There were times when you got the strap - you weren't happy about that, and there was one time I got the strap really bad, and my sister, she was the one that cried. I didn't cry. But the lady lives in Brantford that gave me the strap, and I see her walking on the street and I go to the other side. I don't even acknowledge her. I don't want to give her name - she's still living. But she gave me the strap really really bad, and I see her and I don't even speak to her, even though I know who she is, but I don't know - I don't know how I'd feel about her if I spoke to her. I'll tell you what happened. She gave me the strap to my wrist - one of those sort of razor straps - she gave me the strap to here and I vowed I wasn't going to cry. I was in Grade 4 or 5. I wasn't supposed to be up there helping the older kids - like a certain age you did the dorms, and the younger kids they didn't do it till they got in the next grade. Well, I was up there where I wasn't supposed to be and I was helping them make beds and I got caught. So she gave me the strap, and there was about seven of us girls and she gave the strap to my wrist, and I didn't cry. I vowed to myself I wasn't going to cry, so she said "Get to the end of the line." So she strapped two and she got to me, and she strapped me up to the elbow, and I still didn't cry. "I'll get to you later." So she strapped all the rest of them, and it was just me up there, and she strapped me up to my shoulder, and it was just a dreadful sight. And I got downstairs determined I wasn't going to cry, and my sister saw it and she started to cry. That's when I started to cry. I thought that was a little bit too much, you know, for just being in a dorm. And it was really red, and it was just all swollen, but to this day I don't want to talk to this supervisor. But it didn't scar me - I used to spank my kids when they needed it, but I didn't go to that extreme. That's not a happy story is it? I wasn't unhappy, that's just one incident.

The food was OK - you got three meals a day. I have a good story but I don't want to tell it. I don't remember anything like trench mouth because I used to work in there and the dishes were clean, they had to be or they'd get sent back. The lady would come and inspect everything - you'd sweep the floor, and if it wasn't clean you'd have to do it over. There was a supervisor who'd watch.

On our side it was just girls, there weren't any boys. It was sort of like family, because on the reserve you see the ones who went to the Mohawk, and even though you don't see them for three or four years, when I do see them, and they only live like two roads from here or something, it's like you haven't seen your family for a long time. It's like a bond is formed with the ones that lived there when I lived there.

Sometimes we were too poor that we had to stay there all summer. Sometimes my Mum brought us home, so that was our vacation. My Mum did come and take us out sometimes - she came once in a while, but she not only visited with us,

she visited with all the kids there. She used to play guitar, so she'd come and sing songs and all the kids liked her. She didn't come too often, but I guess she was supportive of us.

I had one lady, she used to always get after me, like when I'm 7 and she was 11 - older, and I used to hate it when we used to play house and she used to say "I want her for my daughter." "I don't want you as my mother." I liked playing the game, but I didn't like her and she always picked me - she was mean. And I thought about it years later, and I thought maybe she was mean at home - she had been mean to at her own home, because she was always mean to me. I remember when I was about 10 or 11, I went into the girls' washroom and she was in there, and she said "Who's out there?" and I said "Me," and I thought: Oh brother! Now I'm going to get it - because she picked on me all the time. So she needed toilet paper, so she said "Come here," and I went in there and she said "Bring me some toilet paper," and she grabbed me and said "Bring me some paper," and she pulls me like this, and I looked at her and I said "No way" and slapped her right across the face. And I said "No," and I left and ran away - hid behind my sister. But she never was mean to me after that, so I think I just had to stand up for myself. Then there was another girl, she lives in Ohsweken, but I liked her so it was all right when she picked me. The total difference, but I think it was how they were treated at their own home.

I remember the good times - like anything you don't remember the bad times. I probably would have been a different person if I wasn't there, because like I said, you learned discipline.

I don't remember whether they [the boys] had to make their own beds - I think maybe the girls had to go over there and do it. You're there seven years, you only see the boys when you're done eating - you didn't eat together, the boys come in after you're all done. I don't remember eating together. I just remember where we sat down to eat and the boys had chores to do and when they got done their chores they had to look after, and you had chores to do, and you see them in the classroom, but you couldn't play with them or anything, you were on your own side.

There was a time my sister did something and I told on her, and the teacher said "You wouldn't do that would you ****?" and she said "No," and I got the strap for lying. But I wasn't lying, and **** to this day, she'll tell you that story and she'll laugh. She thought it was funny, but it wasn't funny at the time, because I wasn't lying. I probably told on her because I would have got the blame for something I didn't do.

Name withheld
1953 - 1960

I was there from 1953 to 1960 - for about eight years. I got out in June '60 - it seemed to me I was about 8 when I got sent there, and my brother was only about 6.

In a way I'm kinda glad I went there. It taught me a lot of things - for one thing, how to work and be responsible - not just for myself, but for other people too, like my family. We used to get up about 6 o'clock in the morning - the older girls - and we'd have to go down and get the breakfast and set the tables, clean up the tables. The girls used to eat first - we ate downstairs in the basement. We had about four long tables, there was two rows, with the benches attached right to the table, so we didn't need chairs. We used to have to set up the tables anyway, cook the breakfast for everybody. You had mush every day - that's why they call it 'Mush hole' We used to eat at 7, and I think the boys used to eat at 7.30 or 8 o'clock. But they used to always eat after we did anyway, except at noontime we all had our meals together - the boys and girls. We weren't allowed to talk, we just had to sit there and finish our meal, and you couldn't just get up and walk out, you had to wait until everybody was finished and march out. You had to march in and march out. They used to give us tin dishes and tin cups, to eat out of and drink out of. We just used to get whatever they put on our place - that's all you got, we didn't get seconds or anything. Sometimes the food was eatable, sometimes not. I remember we used to get milk at every meal, and it used to be that skim milk - I couldn't look at it today, I had so much of it. You had to eat everything, your plate had to be clean, and we had to drink whatever they gave you. Fridays we used to get fish - but ugh! I don't think it used to be cooked half the time. Hardly anybody would touch it anyway, and we'd all get in trouble for that - for not eating it. At every meal we were supposed to eat everything up that they gave us. But the staff - they used to have a table in there too, just for the staff, and you should see the meals they used to get. They had the very best of everything. Sometimes even the principal used to come down and eat with them once in a while, but he used to live right by. His house was right down the driveway. Soon as we'd see him coming we knew there was going to be trouble. If he came down during the lunch hour he'd call somebody out - he'd single them out in front of everybody - then he'd give them a strapping, in front of all the boys and girls and staff. If he couldn't catch 'em any place else, that's the place he would get them. The principal seemed OK. Every place has rules, and if you break them you have to be punished. Somebody has to do it. In there, there was a lot of rules: you had to go to bed at a certain time, get up at a certain time, go to school, come back.

We couldn't even talk to the boys. I couldn't communicate with my brother too much - they told us where the barrier lines were - how far we could go, and if we got caught past that then we'd get a strapping. So I couldn't talk to my brother too often. I remember at nights - at suppertime - when us girls would go down and have our meals, somebody would be banging on the basement window, and I'd look up and there would be my brother standing up there. He'd be signalling - and I knew right away what he'd mean: he wanted me to sneak out some bread for him because he was hungry. So I'd have to sneak it out and then get it to him somehow. I was lucky I didn't get caught at any time. We used to get two slices in the morning, two at night and one at noon. Instead of eating my bread I'd take it out for my brother - I know he used to be so hungry.

A couple of years before I left from there I got to be supervisor in the dining-room. We checked the tables after they were set. We used to have to sit at the same spot every time, and I knew where my brother used to sit, and I just heaped his plate way up - when I was supervisor - made sure he got lots to eat. I was taking a chance with that too. If I got caught I would have been in trouble for that too.

We used to have to have our lights shut off at a certain time at nights, and we weren't allowed to talk or run around after the lights went off. The housemother used to come up and check on us every hour or so, and if we were caught out of bed, then we'd get into trouble for that too. It seemed that any way you turned you were in trouble anyways! I didn't really get in trouble that much. I didn't get that many strappings, I think just about twice when I was in there. When I first went there, this girl came up to me and she asked me, she says "Do you know how to fight?" I said "No," and she said "Well you'd better start learning." I said "Why?" and she said "Well, these girls'll pick on you whether you fight or not." She said "It happens every day. Especially if you don't fight, they really pick on you." That was one of my first lessons I learned. The way that girl told me - she said they beat somebody up every day in there, and you just had to watch out for yourself, or get somebody that was older than you to more-or-less look after you - try and be friends with them or something. It was one of those things you had to learn in there. The first time somebody tried to fight with me I wouldn't fight back, but the next time I did fight back. We got caught and we got sent up to the office, and the principal told the girl - he said "You're always up here, you're always causing trouble all the time." He turned round and he gave her a strapping, but he just told me "Don't let it happen again." That was my first time up there so after that they didn't seem to bother me too much any more, when I started fighting back. I suppose it was just the idea that if they did it once they would do it all the time. Some of those poor girls - a lot of them used to bully some of them girls around, some of them would have a black eye all the time. You couldn't complain - you'd just get sent up to the office and get a strapping and you'd be on your own again.

We used to have to wear certain clothes - they called them uniforms, but they were like dresses - sort of a blue-coloured dress. We used to have wear these big shoes - they looked like men's shoes to me. They were real heavy shoes. We used to have to change three times a week, and that was another thing - we had to line up again to go up and get our clothes, and we had certain numbers - I can't remember what my number was. We used to have to go up there and get our clothes out of a certain box - whatever our number was, that's where our clothes would be in. It was our responsibility to make sure that all our clothes were in there. If there was anything missing then you had to go without.

Everything we did we had to march - line up, one at a time. Even when we used to go to Church on Sundays, we used to have to march again - two by two down the road. I used to feel kinda embarrassed when all the cars would go by us, everybody looking at us. The one time - we used to get Communion every Sunday, and some of the crazy girls got into the wine!!! They drank it and they got drunk I guess - they were falling all over, and they wondered what was wrong with them - the housemothers - and we had to more-or-less cover up for them. We were just saying they were sick, and we tried really hard to keep them away from them so they wouldn't get into trouble. It's funny because there was only a little bit of wine in there, and those girls were falling all over.

After I was there for about four years I started liking it there. The two best times of my life I remember back then was at Christmas time. We'd all line up - the bigger girls - and we'd walk right downtown Brantford, and we'd go to that Hotel Parsons that used to be there. He used to put on a big dinner for us every Christmas. We'd have a big turkey and all the trimmings. They'd give us candy - I used to just love that. Another time I used to like was in summertime. At the end of June they used to let us come home for a couple of months, July and August, then we used to have to come back in September again when school started. By then my mother had broken up with my stepfather and was living by herself - I imagine that's why we were allowed to come home. I used to really look forward to June - counting the days off - oh boy! I'll be going home pretty soon.

But after a while I really started liking it there, and it seems to me I would have preferred it to being at home. My sister and other brother were only there for two years. When we first went there we just felt like we were being rejected by my mother. Well, my stepfather, he was the one that didn't want us around. It's not that we were bad or anything, it's just that he didn't want us around. My stepfather was really mean to us too. He used to give us a spanking. We used to have just ordinary shoes, and we'd walk to school in the wintertime. Every morning he'd get up

and he'd say "You kids come home with your feet wet, you're going to get a spanking." Every night - we couldn't help it, all we had was shoes to walk in the snow - every night we got a strapping. Then he'd go away sometimes, and he'd go for two or three days, then he'd come home really late at night and he'd start beating up on my mother, so my mother would just wake us up and we'd have to run through the fields - sometimes with no shoes on. We'd go over to this old lady's who lived near us, and we'd spend the night there. This was before we went in there, this was all happening, so this is why I was kinda glad to get out of there - at least I didn't have to run away at nights or get hungry, like I did at home, or be really abused like I was at home. So I think that last year - 1960 - the Children's Aid told me I didn't have to go back, and I was supposed to start high school that year, and they said I didn't have to go back, but my brother had to go back, and I started thinking to myself, and I told my Mum "If [my brother]'s got to go back, I'm going back too," and she said "Why? You don't have to," and I said "I know I don't have to, but I want to because [my brother]'s going back there. If he's there all by himself he's going to be hungry all the time." That's the first thing I start thinking about and I said "At least if I'm with him, I can sneak some stuff out for him." They just let me go to school half-a-day just to more-or-less help out in the classroom, and in the afternoons they used to teach me how to use a typewriter, like the Grade 8 teacher. I was supposed to go to high school the following fall, but I didn't go. I went for about three weeks then I quit. It seemed like it was having so much freedom - after being locked up so long. It just seemed like I didn't want to be locked up any more. I would have been 15 that year. The cops were always after me and they said if I didn't go to school they would send me some place else, so I just kept running away till I was 16.

In 1970 I took this course down in Syracuse, and I graduated and I've been pretty well working ever since - I got Grade 8 and they let me in with that - health care aide. Then I took another course in St. Thomas in '78 and I graduated from there, and I've been working ever since. I worked down here for about six years on the reserve, and I worked in St. Thomas for about 9 years, and now I'm working back down here again. I work for the Band Office.

Even my brother says that "I'm glad I went there. At least it's taught me how to work and I don't have to live on welfare." I used to drink but I quit. I drank for about six years and I just all of a sudden quit. It's sad when you think about these people that were in there that end up like that.

I think - this is what makes my family special - at least I got somebody, and I care about them, and I show them - which wasn't shown to me. I think that's why I think my family's more precious to me than if I wasn't sent there. I don't know, it might be different. When I raised my kids I always thought back to how I was raised, and I thought: Well, I don't think I'd like to raise my kids like that - being mean to them, and chasing them outside in the wintertime. Sometimes my husband thinks I'm too protective of my children but I just can't help it.

I wonder how things would have turned out if I didn't go there - the Mush hole. I remember my brother crying really loud that night they took us, and even at that young age I was, I just told him "There's no need to cry - they don't care about us. If they did they wouldn't be sending us away." They took us from my mother's and they took us over to Mt. Elgin and they had a big place set up where they took kids - foster kids I guess - and we had to go for two or three days till they took us to Brantford. I remember my little brother crying all that time.

The housemothers were pretty good - most of them. I remember there was one I used to really like - she was from Germany and I can't remember what her name was, but they used to call her 'Sputnik' because she was from Germany! Our teachers were really good too - I remember Miss Newman - she was my Grade 7 and 8 teacher. She was just a little short fat lady, but she was really nice. Mrs. Cripps - I think she was Grade 5 and 6 teacher.

There was a lot of bullying going on. I suppose you were lucky if you had an older sister or brother to stick up for you.

That one time we ran away from there - me and some other girls. There must have been about five of us, and we were heading the wrong way because we went down the tracks and ended up in Mount Pleasant. We ended up at this little wee run-down house, so we went in there, and we looked outside and all of a sudden there was a whole bunch of cruisers out there. I said "Oh oh! Here they come," and they got us all and took us back to Brantford. When we got back we all got a strapping - it must have been about 2 o'clock in the morning and we all got a strapping. We had to go downstairs and scrub the floors with a toothbrush - like cement floors, concrete floors!! They had this little wee room that was full of vegetables like carrots and potatoes, and we had to peel all that stuff that was in that little room, carrots and potatoes. We got punished for about a month that time, we had to scrub that floor with a toothbrush and peel all them vegetables. Some of them used to be rotten and it would smell really awful in there. I just ran away to go with my friends, I guess - you see, I didn't have no place to go anyway. They started calling me 'Chicken', so I thought: I guess I'll go with them.

Zimmerman - they used to call him 'Skin'. When I think back about then, I just kinda laugh about all the crazy things we done. I always seem to remember the good parts about it, not the bad parts. Like I say, I didn't mind it in there after a while. I suppose I could say I called it home - it seemed like it was the only place I had really. I had a lot of friends in there. I keep in touch with a few of them, not too much any more.

I'm just wondering who paid for the schools - for the meals we used to have - it wasn't up to par you know!

I remember too we used to all have our hair cut really short - just like a boy's hair cut. Maybe because there was so much of us and it was easy to get something - like head lice. Somebody did come in there with lice, they'd get them to clear it up right away before they spread it around. I think the nurse that used to work there was kinda mean. She wasn't really that old - I'd say she was in her 30s, and she was one of them kinda people that was a closet alcoholic. She'd drink by herself and she'd take it out on us - she was really cross with us, yet we could smell that booze on her all the time. I remember my brother was sick there once - he got blisters on his head. I don't know what caused it - I didn't even know he was up there. They had two rooms up there - they used to call them sick rooms. They figured if someone was really sick they'd put 'em in there, and somebody musta went up to the nurse's office and she came back down and she said "Did you know your brother's in the sick room?" I said "No." You see they wouldn't tell you anything, and she said "I just came by there and I seen him in there." So I tried to sneak up there and I didn't see anybody around so I snuck down to the room where I thought he'd be in, and he was in there and I said - I kinda had to whisper to him - "What are you doing in here?" and he said that there was something wrong with his head - he had blisters all over. I had to sneak back out and sneak back down to the playroom, and you know I could just hear him screaming up there sometimes - I don't know if they were busting the blisters on his head or what - it was awful to hear that. I guess it musta got infected because they had to send him right out to the hospital in Ohsweken. He was there for about a week. It was funny because they didn't tell you things like that - if your brother was sick - they wouldn't let you know. There were so many little things like that that happened, and you try so hard to forget about those things. It seemed like I can't remember the bad times, I only remember the good times I had in there, with all my friends. I think that's the only thing I really used to miss, was talking to my brother - communicating with him more or less. It seemed like I didn't even miss my mother - maybe I was so angry with them I didn't even want to think about them.

It was nice when my sister came there, and my other brother, but again I couldn't talk to my other brother, just my sister and I all the time together. And she was older than I am anyway, so she used to hang around with the older girls. Then she wasn't in there too long. She didn't like it very much in there. She always hated that place - she's always telling me - she wouldn't put her cat in that place.

We used to get a strap and the strap was really big, and it was rounded on the ends - it used to come way up on our arms.

We were only allowed to watch the TV for about an hour or so at nights and we had to go to bed at 9 pm. I thought they had a radio but I guess we didn't. You just had to think of something to do on your own.

My brother doesn't talk about it too much, but he's got his

own business and he's doing really good for himself, and that's what he always says - "I'm glad we went there, we knew how to work." I think that was one of the main things, like I say we got three meals a day. They weren't the best but it was better than we were getting at home before we went there. Another tale my brother used to tell me - he and his friends would go down to the creek and catch frogs, and they'd make a little camp fire and they'd fry the frog legs - just for something to eat, they were so hungry!!! I don't know if he feels bitter about going there or not. It seems so silly, but that last year I didn't have to go back, but I went back for him, and I was in there two weeks by myself, and I didn't know - apparently he had taken off with my mother and my sister and her husband, because they lived in the States, and my brother had taken off with them, because he didn't want to stay. Yet I was there for two weeks and I didn't know!!! We can't even talk to them, we can't see them, we go past the one line and that's it, we're in trouble. There was an old school behind the building there - it was the school before they built the new one - it must have been this high off the ground. Somebody had taken the boards off of the outside and you could crawl in there and sit right under there. And that's what we used to do, we'd go in there and we'd smoke. There used to be a girl - she used to work out from the Mush hole, and she used to go out every day, and we asked her to get cigarettes and she would. Anyway, this one day we went under there and we were sitting there smoking. We used to do this every day and somebody must have seen us and they told on us, and we were sitting under there smoking. All of a sudden from the other end one of the girls called "Sputnik's coming around there!" So we started crawling on our hands and knees to the other end, and there was another hole at the other end and we come out there, and as we were crawling out she was standing there watching us. She could move so fast eh!! Oh!! Besides that, we had our aprons on and we were just all covered with dirt, because we were crawling on our stomachs to get

out the other end. She reported us to the principal, and he came down right at lunchtime and gave us a strapping, right in front of everybody. He used to just jump up like that with all his might. I think he used to enjoy it. I've heard of the principal being really mean, but I've never actually seen it myself. But when you get a strapping with a big long strap, and it leaves a mark way up your arm here, and you could see the shape of the strap on your arm, after he'd get through, then it would be just swollen and purple. I think my mother said something to him - she came up there that one time and she noticed that my arm was like that - I had just gotten the strap, and she asked me what happened and I told her, and she raised heck with Zimmerman that time. He still continued - right from when I first went there to when I left, it was still the same.

Sometimes I think about that place, and I got a nephew that was taken away from his mother and father and he was raised in a foster home, and the stories he told us about them places - they were twenty times worse than what we had to go through.

Another thing we used to do over there - they had an apple orchard directly in front of the place, and we used to sneak over the fence and get a whole bunch of apples to have something to eat, to stay full, and we'd hide some, we'd bury some or put it where just us could find it, if you got really hungry or something. We used to have to sneak over cuz they got a fence around it and this was as far as you were allowed to go. If you went past it we'd be in trouble.

Even the dorms where you used to sleep - they've got that all changed around. When we went to that reunion we still ate downstairs where we used to eat before - at least we had a chair instead of sitting on them benches. There used to be bars on the windows. We used to sneak down through the toilet and through the rafters onto the boys side. The boys came over to our side one time. I was asleep and all I could smell was the toe jam!! When they got back the house father was waiting for them.

Kenneth George
1953 - 1960

I think I went in 1953 when I was six years old - I was there for about 8 years.

If you had a friend in there it was all right. It was pretty rough in there - you got three squares a day but it was just enough to keep you going I guess.

The older guys would try to bully you, but if you fought back they wouldn't bother you. They'd slap you around but so long as you fought back you were all right. So I didn't really have much trouble - I learned that when I went in there. I used to wonder why I'd always be crying when I first went in there - I could never figure that out - so later

on some of the older guys from the reserve told me that I used to speak fluent Oneida. So I thought back and I finally realised, when I got there I remember this teacher, she had a big clock and she was asking me what time it was, and I must have been speaking my language instead of English, and she really smacked me around with a ruler. I finally realised I was speaking my language, so after that I didn't speak my language. Now I can catch a few words here and there. A few guys around here remembered me when I was growing up and they said I never spoke English, I just spoke Oneida. That's what I lost - that's what made me mad.

Quite a few times I seen these young people come in for the first time and as soon as they talked between themselves in their own language, this officer would come along and would smack them. They must have thought we were talking about them. The older I got the worse it got for that - the Cree kids started to come in there - it was really bad, because that's all they knew. They were terrified - they were really scared, because all they knew was Cree. Us older guys would kinda pull them aside and try to help them speak English. I always wondered why I ended up getting this ruler across the hand. I didn't know why I was being hit. Now I know why - these guys told me about it. I can't make a sentence in Oneida, but I can pick out words here and there, and that's really sad.

It wasn't a good place, but it wasn't a bad place. You had to do certain things at certain times - there was a schedule you had to follow. I worked on the farm when I was about 11. Certain guys worked in the chicken coop, certain guys milked cows, certain guys fed the pigs, and certain guys fed the calves. Everybody had their chores to do. The older you got the earlier you had to get up. For about a year I had to start waking up early and going out to milk the cows - about 5.30 or 6.

I know we grew our own vegetables - everybody had to work in the gardens. There were certain guys that looked after the vegetables. The older you were the more chores you had to do. I think that was good - the work ethic - that was the good part. At least your day wasn't long and boring. I passed to Grade 9, but there were too many things to do, so I never went on to high school. I started working as soon as I left. I tried everything and anything I could think of - carpenter's helper, carpenter, bricklayer's helper, bricklayer, electrician's helper - whatever. I tried driving trucks, growing crops, helped grow tobacco - there was so much to do. Back then you didn't need your Grade 8, or higher education in the '60s and '70s. Now it's different. At least they gave you that - your education.

There was discipline - you had to do certain things, and if you didn't you paid for it. The discipline was kinda heavy for that time. I remember I got a strapping on my hand. If you were really extra bad they tied you to a bench and beat you on the backside - that was even worse. That happened to me a couple of times. But it wasn't my fault - the other guy did it, I never helped - he kept it for himself and said don't tell on me.

Towards the last part there - I don't know what happened - it seemed like it flipped right over - it just amazed me that it happened. I recall a couple of men - I don't know who they were, but they come down - two men to check everything - the food and the discipline. I just got the strap that time and they asked "Any of you guys ever get the strap?" They all pointed at me. So I had to unbutton my shirt and they saw my arm - they were so mad - it was all bruised.

It seemed like after about two months they switched right over. We had to line up to go to supper in our usual way - we were sitting there and it was funny because they set it up so different - before, your food was already sitting on the table, already served. This time they handed it to us. This man stood up again and he said "Boys and girls, I want to tell you something, you can come back for seconds"!!! Oh my god! you could hear the crashing and banging, and then we had to calm everybody down. We calmed everybody down, and everybody went back for seconds. It was really amazing. After that I remember it getting better. I can hardly remember getting meat - boiled fish we had on Friday. We'd milk the cows but we'd still end up drinking skim milk.

When I went to school it was down the lane. There was a swimming pool - it was right behind the kitchen, for the kids that stayed in the summer. We went home for part of August. I went back there for that reunion - it seemed so strange to be back. I said "If I ever get out of here I'm never coming back"!!! I tell my kids if they talk back - you should be in that school that I was in and you wouldn't talk back!

The discipline was strict - you just had to accept that you were in there, and if you left they'd just bring you back. Once I ran away with my brother - when I first went there. He just told me "Come on, let's go for a walk," and we ended up out on the road. I was pretty tired. That's when I got my first strapping. My brother was going to take my strapping but they wouldn't let him. I just thought I was going for a nice walk, and we ended up running away!! That's the only time I ever ran away - I was too far from home. It seemed like it was a long ways. Some of them - they'd keep trying to run away, and they'd send them to that other place - Bowmanville.

We didn't see too much of Zimmerman - just on Sunday when he would preach, or when we got a strap. We just seen those ones they called 'officers' - that took care of the boys. He didn't even come down to the playroom. I remember he had an office - he'd take you in and give a whipping. You'd see him once in a while - maybe on a Saturday he'd be at the school.

Sometimes I thank my Mum for sending me there. That work thing - anything they wanted done, you had to do it. They worked you. You always worked, then on Saturday these guys would complain about being bored. I don't know what they'd do, somebody'd get bad and they wouldn't tell, and all of us would have to pay. There was an officer - I think he was a Sergeant Major. I remember our yard - he used to mark a square - it was a great big yard, and he'd square it all out and each guy would have to clean a square, until they told whatever they did. But nobody would tell so we did lots of cleaning. We didn't know who did what, but they made everybody pay - bottles, bottle caps - whatever was in that square we had to clean up.

It seems like that school was a long ways away to me. I don't hardly think of that place. It seems like it was someplace else. When I went back to that reunion I was almost sad - I had so many friends there, but I seen hardly any of them. They were from all over the place.

I went to Church all those Sundays - I never knew what religion they were. I know they used to try and wake you up when you went to sleep - they poked you really hard. I don't know what happened to them after Church, but I know they used to get real violent if you went to sleep on them. He was terrible when he was trying to do his speech up there and you went to sleep. He'd come right down the aisle and he'd point at you and holler right at you. That woke you up for a little while. He was pretty violent that guy. Zimmerman - he was the one that would be up there, the minister.

There was a teacher from Australia - she was a nice lady. The gym teacher was nice too. We had Mrs. Ingram for Grade 8. They tried to make us do home economics - that didn't go over too good - not with the boys.

They'd take us out to the movie-house at Christmas time. There was a television room, but mostly we stayed outside until dark. On Saturdays we had to scrub the playroom. We went to church on Sundays. We had our chores to do, and school. After school we went outside - our playground was bigger than the girls' - theirs was just a little square. There wasn't really much to do in there - just watch TV. It seemed like the day was full though, except Sundays. There were bounds around where you could go. I remember we used to have fire-drills and us older guys had to look after the little guys, check up and make sure they were all outside. It was more fun there when you were older - you had a rough time when you were little.

Alice Bomberry
1953

Reverend Zimmerman was the principal when I was here, and also the chaplain of the Mohawk Chapel. Every Sunday we'd all go over for Sunday School and Church and come back.

Everybody had chores to do - the girls were responsible for kitchen work and for caring and looking after the little ones. I remember coming down into what is now our rare books room and doing sewing for the clothing that needed repair, washing the clothing, cooking meals - a lot of the housekeeping skills.

When I was here in 1953 we were in school all day and at that time I was only nine years old, so my responsibilities weren't as much as the older girls who would be going down to the kitchen early in the morning and helping prepare the meals, or staying later to clean up the kitchen and do all these other things. The younger girls - we had to make our own beds and those kinda chores. I don't ever recall going down into the kitchen or doing anything in terms of preparing a meal. I don't recall going out into the farm - it was mainly the boys who looked after that part - the farming and the gardening. But the girls were more responsible for indoor type of chores - cleaning and sewing and washing - those kinds of things. At 9 years old I wasn't as responsible for those kinds of activities as the older girls were. I don't ever recall anyone complaining, but then, 9 years of age, and that many years ago, it was hard to recall. I was just here for one school year. My knowledge would not be as in-depth as some people who stayed here over a number of years. Some of them were here from the time they were 5, until they were of age to leave, and there was a girl who was here from the time she was three, so she was quite small. I was lucky, my parents were quite close by, although they couldn't afford to keep me. We got to go home once in a while - it was more the case that they would come and visit here whenever they could. It was heartbreaking though to leave - like when they had to go, and you had to stay - it was heartbreaking. I can imagine what it was like for the ones who had to stay here year round, because they didn't have family to go to, or maybe their family wasn't there at the home - maybe gone somewhere. But I was quite lucky I think.

My experiences here, I would say, would be positive. Though I was lonely, as a little girl of 9, it wasn't a bad experience like some of the children had. In my opinion, though I don't know if you'll get this from anyone else, but I think it depends on one's own attitude coming into the place, whether it worked for you or against you. I didn't mind being here - I had a roof over my head, I had clean clothes, warm clothes. I had cousins here who more or less oversaw me - there were a few times that other girls tried to hit me or be mean to me and they would be there to get people away from those kinda things.

But I would say for the most part it was a good experience for me. I don't have any bitter memories of the place. The only thing that shook me when I came back after many many years was being able to go in and out of that front door. It was like you could stay on this side of the door, but if you went out in the hallways, or tried to go in and out of the front door, without permission, you were in trouble. Or if you went beyond the treeline - that was another experience I had - walking round the yard, just being out there after many many years. You felt like screaming "I can go past this line here." It was a weird feeling - very emotional.

I have Grade 12, and I've taken university courses - I have one more to get a B.A., and I've taken college courses. Two different kinds of certificates that I went through for - Business Management, and Supervisory Studies, at Mohawk College. So I have gone on, and I had a lot of encouragement from my mum and from my grandmother, to go on and get a good education. I don't know that it all stemmed from here, but I always did like school since I can remember. The teachers that I had when I was here were quite nice - I can remember some of them quite well. I

really think it boiled down to one's attitude. If they chose not to like it here then it would reflect on their attitude and they would be getting into problems, whether it would be with their classmates or with their supervisors. That's my opinion anyhow. You weren't necessarily bad in order to come here. It was maybe because you had one parent or no parents, or two parents who couldn't afford to look after you at home, and felt this was the best for you at the time.

Peggy Hill
1955 - 1957

I was at the Mohawk from 1955-57, aged 13-15. I left when I didn't go back after visiting my mother. I ran away to the States. I met the man who became my husband. Even when I came back - I had a child - I heard they were still looking for me.

I feel I could have had a proper education if I hadn't gone to the Mohawk Institute, and would have been able to make more of my life.

My mother couldn't take care of us - there were nine in our family. My brother and I had a white father, but we didn't lose status as they were not married. I don't blame the Mohawk Institute for ruining my life - but I blame the Indian Agent on the reserve who sent me there when I wanted to go to school on the reserve. I didn't like being confined - but they threatened to send me to reform school if I didn't stay.

The things that were bad were the lack of food, the fenced-in yard, and we couldn't talk to boys. We only had two changes of clothes - we wore the same ones for a week. Saturdays we had our weekly bath and weekly change of clothes. One week we'd wear baggy blue jeans with long-sleeved turtlenecks, and the next week we'd wear dresses - they were plaid with green, red and white. Breakfast was skim milk, mush, two slices of bread with jam - no butter. We didn't get second helpings unless there was macaroni left over, but you had to be an aggressive child to get any, or beets - but who's going to ask for more beets - and mush, and that used to be so slimy because they left it cooking on the stove all night long. No radio; TV - we were only allowed to watch for an hour or two in the evening. There was nothing to do. The playroom was a dungeon-like room in the basement with a picnic table - there were no books or toys to play with. The dormitories had bars on the windows and were padlocked shut. They had fire drills - usually in the winter at night.

There were a lot of strappings. There were two little boys who ran away - not very far - and hid in a pipe - a drain that goes under the road, and the other boys would get them food - boys would go to the dump and get food. They were caught and Zimmerman took them into the classroom and

put them in front of the class. They were covered in sores from hiding out - he strapped them in front of the class. He slapped the one little boy around and the scab on his face came off and was bleeding all over the place - Zimmerman didn't care. I left with some other girls once, but I came back. It was too cold and I was afraid of the beatings kids got when they ran away.

My husband was also there for two years, but he ran away and was sent to Shingwauk, where he got terrible beatings.

I wouldn't send my cat or my dog to that place. Our only crime was being poor - our parents couldn't feed us the way the Indian Agent thought we should be fed.

I was in a foster home with my brother. We had nice clothes and decent food, but I had a feeling the man was going to start to sexually abuse me, and I was homesick for my family and I wanted to go back to the reserve. The agent, Mr. Morris, wanted to put me in another foster home in Toronto, but I was afraid to do that after the previous experience.

After my husband died in 1986 I went to Fanshawe College to take upgrading courses, but it was too soon - I didn't have time to grieve for my husband - we were married for 29 years. He didn't want me to work - I worked because I wanted to as a Nurses Aide. We lived in London. I run a tree service - not on welfare - I want to work. I learned to work hard - my grandparents raised me until I was ten years old. We lived 5 miles from the store and I would take this sack and walk to the store in all weathers to buy groceries - potatoes and things. My grandfather would chop wood in the bush and I would help him haul it back to the house - we had no hydro. So I can't credit the Mohawk Institute with learning to work.

We only were in school half the day - I had to work doing the baking half the day. If the idea of sending me to the Mohawk Institute was to get an education, then why was I put in the kitchen or the laundry-room at least three half-days a week? I got too good at the baking so mostly they kept me in the kitchen.

There were a lot of fights. The second day I was there I got in a big fight. I had beautiful long hair and because I was new they hadn't cut it off, and the other girls were jealous and pulled my hair. The day they cut my hair - short like a boy's - I cried. I remember this one winter - it was during the wintertime, there was this Mrs. Milligan - she worked in the sewing-room as a supervisor there, and she had a lot to do with taking care of the sewing and things like that - she knitted me a sweater and she knitted one for my brother. They were both the same colour, only mine had the buttons so I could wear it like a coat and my brother's was a turtleneck shape. I remember someone taking a pair of scissors and cutting the back - a big piece out of the bottom part of the sweater. I remember being taken to the office over this, cuz they thought I didn't appreciate the sweater and tried to destroy the sweater myself, and that wasn't the case. Why this person would do this - it was more out of jealousy I guess, maybe they thought Miss Milligan was playing favourites or something, I don't know. The only thing I could think of was just it was plain jealousy. I got the strap at that time cuz I couldn't tell 'em what happened to the sweater - I didn't know. I was surprised when they confronted me with it and showed me the sweater - I didn't remember it being in that condition..

I got along all right with the two teachers - Mrs Newman, the teacher, was OK. But the inside staff - Mrs. Bunt[?] - she was a big lady - she was quite mean; Mrs. Davies, the supervisor, was really one of the meanest people - I don't think she had any feelings. I worked in the kitchen. The cook was a middle-aged lady nicknamed 'arkbone'. In the dining-room the staff sat up at their table and they got all the good food. I got first prize too for a cake - a date-nut loaf - but I got to eat it - I didn't get the ribbon. My sister and I used to sneak food - bread - out for our brothers, so we were always hungry. I got the strap once - I was looking after some soup in the kitchen and my brothers were picking up garbage near - and they asked for something to eat. The only food there was the soup so I gave them some in a jam can. They took it and were drinking it behind the building, but one of the staff looked out of an upstairs window and saw them. I got the strap for stealing soup.

Life on the reserve was hard, but better than the foster home or the Mohawk Institute. It was like being in gaol - we couldn't go to the store, or leave the grounds - there was nothing to do. We had to walk everywhere if we did go anywhere. We got to see Elvis in his first movie. We had to walk to Church every Sunday rain or shine. Once we went camping to Christian Island - I had to do the laundry.

I still feel bitter about what the Indian Agent did. I would have liked a decent education to help me in life - particularly in the custody battle for my adopted son.

Jo-Bear Curley and Frank Hill, with Karen Hill
1955 - 1958, 1962 - 1964 and 1947 - 1958

Jo-Bear: I went there from 1955-1958 and 1962-1965. I don't think I liked it there when I was there, but when I think about it now, I think I probably liked it. I took off when I was in Grade 8. The principal from down here came out to see me and said "You either go back to the Mohawk, or you go to school down here, or we'll send you to Reform school." I had a choice of three so I went down here till I was 16. It wasn't the Mush hole itself, it wasn't bad, it was school that I didn't like. Even when I went down here - I didn't want to go to school. Actually there was nothing about that school that I did mind - I guess I liked it. And if it was still open I probably would have sent my kids there. The only thing I didn't like about being up there was nobody would ever come and see me. Karen would pop in once in a while, E would pop in once in a while - Ma she'd pop in once in a great while. It was lonely up there, so I had to learn to deal with not being with my family. My Ma, she just lived down here - it's only a 20 minute drive to Brantford.

I had a couple of fights up there, but nothing that wasn't ironed out the next day. It was pretty good. The only thing I didn't like was the schooling part of it and the fact that my mother would never come and see me. I remember the last few years I was there - they used to let the senior girls go to the show on a Saturday, and I wouldn't go because I thought my mum would come up and see me and I'd miss her. I would stay there and my mother wouldn't come and see me and I'd miss out all around. So after a while I just decided, If she comes she comes, and if she doesn't come she doesn't. Big deal. I think that's the only thing I didn't like - being lonely there.

You got a licking if you needed it. I don't think you got the strap for no reason. I always used to get the strap mind you - but I was a bad girl. I used to do everything to try and get in trouble. Maybe I thought they'd call Ma and she'd come after me or something. Maybe they wouldn't have me there and she'd take me home to live with her- But I was always trying to get into trouble. But it was trouble like sneaking downstairs after I was supposed to go to bed at 9 o'clock, and we'd sneak downstairs and have girls watch for us so we could watch TV. It's stupid now when you think about it, but it was fun in them days. I didn't always get caught. I remember scrubbing the playroom floor with a toothbrush - actually I didn't scrub the whole floor. When the supervisor was there I'd pretend I was doing it but as soon as she went out I'd use a rag and wipe over it - there was things you could get away with. I was caught by the Principal out behind the school necking with my boyfriend there. That's why I had to do it - well - that's the truth!! At that time I think I was 15 years old. I had a boyfriend - all the girls had boyfriends - we never done anything bad bad - just a kiss on the cheek.

Karen [sister]: I didn't have a boyfriend.

J. Well, that was back in the early sixties - you're talking about the fifties. You didn't do stuff like that - unless you were bad like me. Actually I wasn't bad.

They used to have dances - they never had dances when you were there did they Karen? - they used to have dances once or twice a month. The girls would have the boys over - we could never dance the waltz with our boyfriends, but we had fun with them. I remember the time E was over the fence - these boys and girls - they weren't doing nothing, they were just gabbing, but they had to sneak around to be together, and I went over the fence, and E found me and she said "You get over on the other side of the fence," and I said I didn't want to, I wanted to be with E. She wouldn't let me, so I went and squealed on her and she got a licking. I still get pleasure out of it after all these years!! I remember being in the apple orchard one time and we got caught, trying to steal apples. I was only about eight. We got caught and I tried to hide behind one of the trees so they wouldn't see me, but I was too chunky I guess!!

When I first went there I was only five years old, and there was little things that I done like stealing apples - I got caught for that. When I went back there I was eleven and everything had changed from the time I was eight. By the time I left there when I was fifteen, a lot of things had changed. We got to wear our own clothes - we didn't have to wear their clothes. We didn't have much clothes - we could wear our own clothes if we went to Belleview, or High School kids. Then they changed their shoes - remember the shoes they used to have? We got decent looking shoes. The kids used to be able to go to the store on Saturday and Sunday. They could earn money, or get whatever money there was in the office, and go to the store and get whatever they wanted. It never used to be like that when Karen and E were there. Then they finally started letting the kids come home on the weekend - down here, on this reserve. There was only five or six of us from this reserve. All the rest were from Thunder Bay or Whitefish Bay and up there. There were a couple of kids from Sarnia - not very many though. They let us come home for the weekend, and the first weekend I came home, I didn't go back, and I thought that was funny too. I was 15, and they let us out on Friday nights and we went back on Sunday nights, but I stayed home. I don't know why they didn't come looking for me or anything - maybe they didn't want me. But anyway I lied about my age and I said I was 16, and I worked in Dunnville for three weeks before the Principal came out and said to me "You've got a choice of three," and I went to school down here for three weeks, and I just quit, and then when I was 24 I went back to school again at Mohawk. I got my upgrading, then I was going to

go in for commercial art, and I didn't do that, that's when A was born. I went to work on the roads instead. Then I quit that after a few months and stayed home with my kids. Then I went back to school again and took that course they had up there - Women and Trades. I didn't do nothing - I went back - just an educated bum I guess! I went back and I took an offset printing course. I remember Miss McMeans. Mrs Newman - she used to be a really good teacher, only she used to get on my case all the time.

I kinda liked that school - now when I think about it. But when I was there I didn't like it, probably because I didn't have the freedom I wanted. Still don't have the freedom I want!! We couldn't even go and play ball on the boys' side. They wouldn't even let us chum with the guys. We used to have secret meetings - only there'd be a whole group of us. There were four or five of us girls who always hung around together and we would hang around all these guys who hung around together - "He likes me and he likes her etc." and we were all just a bunch, but we were always all together. Yeah - I kinda liked it.

K. When you think about it you forget about the bad times and only remember the good times.

J. Actually I don't think there were any really bad times.

K. At the time they were bad, but now thinking about it -.

J. I think running away and getting caught - as far as the cornfield. I ran away when I was about five years old, or six years old - just got out the door and in the cornfield and got caught. Didn't get as far as the road.

K. How come you ran away?

J. Probably because there was me and [3 others]. We got caught and sent to bed with no supper. I never ran away again till I left. I don't know - I probably ran away to see what it was like to run away. L [brother] used to run away all the time.

K. They'd just bring him back and he'd be gone again.

J. He wouldn't even stay and eat. In the last couple of years I was there you could even go along for seconds - they would even give you seconds. Mostly the boys would go up. If you took your dish up and if there was some left you could get in line for more.

K. That's pretty good, because I think they did give you all the good meals - and you got people there that barely got three meals a day. The mush wasn't that great.

J. You had clothes on your back, you were warm all the time. I think a lot of people were more lonely than anything else - they wanted their parents more than anything.

K. You went to school every day. The discipline - you got a sense of discipline - you got up at a certain time, brush your teeth, eat, everything at a certain time.

J. You got very independent - you learned how to make a bed, cook, clean floors. I didn't like to go to Church on Sundays, but we had to do it. A lot of Sundays I faked sick.

K. We never learned anything did we?

J. One time we had a test and I didn't want to go to school, so I faked sick, so I went up to the dispensary and the nurse said to me "What's the matter?" and I said "I'm sick." So she stuck the thermometer in my mouth and went out to the sick bay where the kids were sick, and when she went out I took the thermometer and rubbed it on my clothes. When she come back she looked at the thermometer and "Jo-Bear Curley, YOU'RE DEAD!" Then she tried again.

Frank: I went there when Zimmerman was just new. I didn't feel he was very just in his thinking, because the supervisors that were there - if they had it in for you they'd say "Having a hard time with that student" - Zimmerman he'd come along and he'd strap the one. There was a couple of occasions that I had gotten a strap - I would figure our supervisor was just half blind I guess. I have a birth mark on my neck - it's still there today. So we were standing in line getting checked after we had taken a wash to go to school in the morning. He said "Your neck's dirty, go and wash it" - he never knew that the birthmark was there. So I went and washed again. I thought: Well, I'll be a little late for school. It didn't wash, so there I was getting another strapping, and I was wondering: What for? I did take a wash. One day I happened to look - I thought: "I got a strapping because I happen to have a birthmark back there." After all these years it's still there, it doesn't wash off. Another time I remember I had a key to the barn - I was more or less the cowboy - I'd go to the pasture and bring the cows in, and open up the barn and put them in; and the farm boss said that I had broke in the barn. Now I said "That wouldn't be very smart, you know, I had a key to get in the barn." He said "You made it look like somebody else got in." I thought: Boy! this is silly. I got a strapping for that. I don't know - some of the finer moments I guess, I didn't really care to remember them.

J. You just got the strap if you were bad!! I didn't care - I didn't care about nothing. I didn't care about school, about nothing. Actually, one year I went back there and at the end of the year before all the kids went back up north for the summer, I remember them getting gifts for being the most improved kid, or smartest, and I got a gift for being the most improved kid in one year, and I got a big lump in my throat and the tears come down because I thought I was bad!!

Sally English - she lives in Ohsweken - she was a supervisor when I was there. In fact she was the one gave me this - I forget what it was - but it was for being the most improved kid of the year. I must have improved there for a minute!! But she was telling me - we get talking there sometimes - she told me "I remember when you first came there and you thought nobody was going to push you around." She said "I never seen a kid so stubborn as you."

F. I went to high school - while I was still there - but I don't think it really helped. I think after getting out of school there you still got to prove yourself outside the Indian group. But I had to seem to know a lot more than the other people that I was working with - other nationalities - not Indians, whites mostly - that I had to prove myself against those in order to get a better paid position. And once I was in that position everybody wanted to work for me, because of what I knew and how to do it. I was what you might say lazy - I just used my head. I was an ironworker - I was ? engineer at the farm, but the school hadn't taught me that.

There was this little guy - I remember the older kids hanging him up on these hot pipes - it was just for their kicks, their enjoyment - to see how long he could hang there.

J. We used to choke ourselves !! We used to put our scarves around our necks. We used to go to the schoolroom from 7 o'clock to 8 o'clock at night. And I remember sitting there one day waiting for the kids to get ready to go over to the school because we all had to go over together - I don't know why I did it - I think I was mad and I think I wanted to kill myself or something!! But I was sitting on a table and I pulled my scarf like this, and my head just went - and when I come to I was on the floor, with my head between my knees!! It was funny. G G did that one time and she freaked right out, so we decided not to do that anymore.

F. You know those towels we used to have - those big circular ones - we had a pipe hanging across there and we had about ten of those towels hanging on it. B G must have got a high out of it or something - he used to hang there with his head in the towel. After a while he'd pass out - from banging his head on the wall from being unconscious!!

J. You could only watch TV for an hour or something.

F. I think they had teeter totters and swings - outside of that there was no activity. You made your own fun - you did whatever made you happy. As far as organized ball there was nothing like that. Just now and again one of the supervisors would take interest in the talents of the boys - see what they could do. I don't remember anything faring out of that.

J. We used to have talent shows in the gym.

F. What gym?

J. When I was there they had a gym.

F. It wasn't even built when I was there - just in the planning stage. They were ready to close the place by the time they had that built.

J. I remember one girl, she got the strap one time so bad - her arms and shoulders were so bad - just black and blue, and she wouldn't cry.

K. That's like me - that happened to me.

J. And they just kept hitting her and hitting her and hitting her. The supervisor - Mrs. Morgan - she was a supervisor from up north - she was an Indian but she was a supervisor. But E wouldn't cry - no way - and every time she hit her, E would just get madder, but she wouldn't cry. Her poor arms - I can still see them - and she's dead. After I left - some of the boys beat up this guy. I remember hearing a couple of the boys beat him up really bad and he was in the hospital for three or four days, and he died. I don't know who the boys were who beat him, these were stories I got from people who were there after I left.

F. Being the cow boy there - I would say 5.30 in the

morning we'd be awake, and there used to be this dog ended up with the boys there - a collie dog. And rather than me going out in this 20-acre field out behind the Mohawk Chapel and look for cattle in the fog where I wouldn't know where I was going, and the grass was high enough where I'd get wet all over - this dog had come there one time - we looked after it and it was nice. It followed me to the field - we'd say "Go get 'em Lassie." Lassie would get all wet but it didn't bother Lassie, and I'd wait for them to come to the gate - the way they were supposed to come. They shot that dog on me and that hurt me. It was the guy in the boiler room - they just did it out of sport. That's when I was given the strap. A lot of times I felt like running away, but then again I stayed. One Sunday all the boys must have taken off - and here I had gone down by the glue factory. There was an orchard down there - this was in the wintertime - we had gotten there and this guy - maybe we were trespassing - but what I was punished for rather than picking the fruit that was there - who was going to do it - it was frozen and we hadn't taken anything - was trespassing, as well as taking whatever that was there - it wasn't for us. I got the strap across the behind for that. Everybody else was getting everything. You could see guys - he used to grab their hand like this - it ended up here, so what? They're only the kids there and he's laying the punishment. I guess it was mostly justified what he had done. I seen kids who got strapped up here [upper arm]. That other one too - Miller - he worked in the boiler room but every now and then he would be on supervisory capacity. He was half in the bag all the time, drinking all the time. I guess he took his miseries out on the boys because he couldn't drink because he had to do that. That's what he'd do. Didn't matter where - if it would be on the hands - that was tough luck for the boy.

You know the orchard in front of the place - nobody could go there either. That fruit was just made to bear and fall on the ground. Nobody could pick it - unless at night or early in the mornings. We went to the dump quite often - there were four dumps - and they got candy there. Westons was a big factory.

J. And the guys used to take their girlfriends cowsalt!!!

F. We used to have this rocksalt - cowlicks, and they'd want some, because they used to be in the orchard too, eating these green apples and they'd rub them around on the salt, beccause they didn't have no shaker - rub it on a green apple. These are things you had to do for yourself. In the winter D T used to open up the root cellar to take the vegetables for the meal that night, but he'd take the raw vegetables down to this place. But while he had the root cellar open taking things down to this place, some of the guys would go down - when he'd come out we'd go down and grab carrots, maybe even a cabbage, potatoes and everything because we were hungry. It seemed like the three squares weren't square any more - there just wasn't enough there.

J. We used to steal big things of icecream out of the deep freeze and throw them out the back door to the boys. I was bad. Never got caught.

F. If you had a girl friend you would eat pretty good too - you had a friend in the kitchen. I had this milk machine and I would go and pick it up, and while I was putting it together she'd give me this loaf of bread. While I was milking the cows I'd be eating this loaf of bread. That more or less tided me over. Sometimes I'd be eating my loaf of bread, and F, he'd grab my milk pail and he'd be eating my bread. The baker used to come early in the morning, and if he couldn't get downstairs, he'd leave bread piled up there. Needless to say, the boys who knew it was there would have two or three loaves of bread apiece, and the order would go in as being short. That was survival of the fittest I guess - you learn young and remember it when you are old. I don't know that it was stealing - it was a matter of survival. But in order to be able to survive to the next meal you would take something.

J. When Miss Reid used to be on duty, and the girls would finish their work in the kitchen and they'd steal an apple or something, and they'd get the strap from her; and I'd go out and I'd say "Miss Reid can I have an orange?" or "Can I have an apple?" and she'd say "Yeah go and help yourself"!! And she'd always let me have an apple or an orange because I'd ask, but if Miss Winter was on duty - forget it! I used to steal everything. I'd always try to get caught from her. I never worked in the sewing room or the laundry room.

F. One time - the old lady Mrs. Boyce - she had to be 110 years old - but I used to take care of the clothes I had, and I had gone just about the whole year, and I had gone to pick up my clothes in my little cubby-hole to take, and she says "If you get by one more week without us having to mend it" - because she didn't have to do anything - she didn't even have to sew on a button, just fold it amd put it away, where I picked it up. I was playing around, feeling pretty good that I had made it just about the whole year without having a tear in my clothes, so the things were getting threadbare. So I ran away from this guy - playing tag or something, and he grabbed me - and I thought: There it goes - there goes a whole year's worth of good feeling - all tore up. I think they just discarded that shirt and give me another one.

I don't know why I was sent there - probably because of my stepfather - my stepfather couldn't get along with me. You had to make your own good times - that's what holds some of the kids together now - remembering the good times. Some turned out bad. I don't know who all ran away - but it seemed to be the thing to do at the time.

Sunday morning there was a different feeling - the boys - they were gone. The girls had to stay in - there was a fence around them. We'd just go. Even at night sometimes we'd climb trees to watch car races by Mohawk Park in Brantford. They used to have car races on Friday evenings - we'd climb trees and watch - we had no money to get in. The big boys took the Coronation medals. The teachers gave them out.

Bob White Eye
1955 - 1964

I was in Brantford from 1955 to 1964, and it was the most drastic time of my life. We were abused, we were hungry, we were neglected and we were assaulted. As far as getting an education, I think we learned the education of survival. When I went there in 1955 all we got for breakfast was a bowl of molasses and some crackers and some kinda powdered milk or something, and we were sent to school half-a-day and into the garden the other half of the day. Things did eventually get a little better in the 1960s, but not a whole lot. They were abusive to all the children - the supervising staff, the ones who were supposed to look after us all day. The teachers weren't too bad, they had a job to do. The farmers, they were wicked, they'd beat you for anything. But I often wondered why we had chickens, and we had cattle, and we had pigs and we had all those things, but we never got none of that stuff set on the table. I don't know where we got meat from, we never killed any chickens or cattle. When they did give us cereal you could put your spoon in it and turn the bowl upside down, and they wouldn't fall out - that stuff was like glue.

I was kidnapped by the Childrens' Aid Society from my parents. My Dad didn't even know where we were for a whole month at least. I think Children's Aid had a quota to fill at that time, and they took my family and that satisfied the government and that kept Brantford in existence.

Love - we didn't get none of that. Hugs and squeezes were non-existent - not even between brothers and sisters. We couldn't see our sister - she had to stay over there on the either side. There was a flower garden in front and we'd work there and we'd work over that way and she'd stand close enough so we could talk to her, but that was about the only way we could talk to her.

It was like a small prison camp. We were there only two days and we didn't know that the barn was off limits - we had no idea. Right behind our house there was a stables and we used to make trails through the hay and straw and slide down there into the calf pen. When we got to Brantford we seen this huge barn - biggest barn we ever seen in our lives, and it was filled with straw. So we said "Let's go and play there." We went and played there for only probably about ten minutes, and no-one had told us it was off limits. They just shoved us out into the yard with all these other people that were completely strangers, so we went together as brothers and went to the barn, and the next thing we were being beaten - so severely beaten that it was just pathetic. I was only seven and my brother was only five. One was close to ten and the oldest brother close to 13. But to beat us that way and not tell us why. They made us drop our drawers and took a leather strap and beat us. To a youngster that's murder - what can you do, you can't defend yourself!

I spoke my language when I went there, but I got beat so bad to speak English, that that's all I know now is English. My sister was only two or three years old when we were there. She was in diapers and my older brother had to go and put her to bed at night. All he spoke was Indian and he got the tar beat out of him. So they beat us into submission to do what they wanted us to do. We lost our Native culture. I didn't even know where I lived in 1964 - I didn't even know where I was going to. I had no idea where I had come from. When I decided to leave the school I picked up a map and looked for Thamesville, that was the closest I could remember, and someone had to help me.

We spoke a little English, but mostly Delaware, and they wouldn't allow us to speak any of that. We had to learn English right from Day One. When we spoke on the playground we had to speak English. That was difficult to do because as a little person you don't know all the English interpretation as you would speaking the language. The reason we spoke Indian was that Grandmother - that was all she ever spoke, she spoke no English at all. Dad spoke English so we had English and Indian, but not fluently. When I was there in the sixties, the Cree children started coming in and they spoke no English, and they literally beat this one child into submission, that he is in fact mentally retarded today, and that is from this beating in Brantford. Were we educated? Maybe some people were glad they got to Grade 8. There was a girl from Cape Croker going to high school, 2 from Six Nations, 1 from Moraviantown - they went to Pauline Johnson. They had to walk. I think that might have been all right - going to high school, no-one supervising you. When we first went there we went to school only half-a-day, and we were in the fields the other half, but that was probably only the first two years. After that we started going all the time - the older boys they still had to do the harvesting. Where the cutoff was I don't know, but I know my brother and I, we had to go and gather eggs early in the morning. To us it was a long ways back then - it isn't today, it's only a few feet now, but then it was miles!! It was dark and it was always a frightening experience - for a little guy. There was this time we went there and this man had his hand sticking through the wall, trying to grab a chicken. We walked in and we seen this hand and it was really frightening and we ran. We got hold of the farm guy and he made us go back there - whether he believed us or not - a hand sticking through! Someone was probably more hungry than I was. But we would steal eggs and we would boil them in a coffee can, and then we got brave and stole a chicken and boiled him in a coffee can. We were hungry. Many times we'd go to the city dump. There was a Weston's candy truck that would take excess candy, or too old candy, to the dump, and we'd go and dig it up just to survive. In 1959 or '60 they started spraying the dump with chemicals, but we don't know what they put on it. About that time things were starting to get a little on track, they wanted us to be more like family. I don't recall the cafeteria, I think something that interesting [second helpings] - I would have remembered that. I don't remember a new cafeteria - if it's something erased from my mind. The dining facility - you marched down into the lower part and you sat at tables and your plate was already set there. Maybe that's the only picture I remember. I was the last one there - my brother got sent to Bowmanville. He punched Mr. Zimmerman, and the reason he punched Mr. Zimmerman was - he was going with this girl - his girl friend. They were fooling around in the yard in front of the Principal's house - there was a school there and they were fooling around. They brought her in and they made her take her clothes off and they really beat her. They stripped him down and put him in a room and they stripped her down and beat her - in front of their staff. Even though we were brothers we had our different areas. He was fast and I was quiet and shy.

I was beat one time - I fell asleep in church. Zimmerman was preaching, and they dragged me back to the school and threw me in the dressing-room, and they just beat me like a - if my older brother didn't jump in, I imagine they would have killed me. A man by the name of the Mr. Harding - his first name was Jerry - I'll always remember that - he must be in his 60s or 70s by now - if he's not passed on - but he beat me so bad that if my brother didn't jump in, I know I would have been dead. He was a man and he picked me up and he threw me clear across the room. We had boxes on the walls and in these boxes is our change of clothing and it had numbers on it. I flew into that and came back and he kicked me and picked me up and threw me again. My brothers jumped in. If they hadn't jumped in I don't know where I'd be. I'll tell you one thing about Mr. Zimmerman - we knew every sermon - they were always the same, they never changed and we memorized every one!! But he'd be preaching and someone was falling asleep and he'd come down to them and he'd poke them right in the chest and say "Why aren't you paying attention?" Then he'd snap his fingers - where we took our beating was called the Press Room - he'd snap his fingers and say "You to the press room, you to the press room," when we'd get back to the school. It was a long march back to the school, it seemed like for ever, and it got longer when you knew you were going to get a beating!! It was really something because every Sunday - there wasn't a Sunday that didn't go by when someone wasn't getting beat. So you were trying to keep your neighbour awake - but it was hard to stay awake - it was boring. It was a challenge to go to church even. You had to survive to go to church. Church shouldn't have been like that.

There was an apple orchard there and you couldn't touch the apples. There was no way you were going to get an apple. Of course we did get in there - we'd go in the middle of the night - climb down the wall of the building. There were bricks that were jutted out at the school - you can see them. You'd come out of the second floor, and you'd reach over and hang on, and if you fall you know you're going to get a broken leg or a broken back, but you hung on and you just went down and picked apples and put them in your shirt and climbed back up. But you wouldn't give 'em away. You'd sell 'em to your neighbours: "If I give you an apple now, you'll give me a slice of bread." Or there was a dessert that they always made - date turnover - and we called it 'mushtop' because it had oatmeal on top - but that was a pretty decent dessert so we said "I'll give you two apples now for that dessert." It was generally on Friday that we had that dessert so we had the dates all scheduled to make a deal with somone!! Everybody was bargaining every which way they could, and if you didn't pay your dessert you were in for a licking from the guy that you made the deal with. I guess you learned to bargain. Everyone had their own deal. There was times when somebody would have something special - maybe one of the parents would send a package, and the negotiating would start: "I'll give you this now, if you'll give me this at a later date." Ritz crackers was a bargaining issue. Ritz crackers was only a quarter a box or something. "I'll give you 5 Ritz crackers if you give me your dessert for the next 3 Fridays"!! That sort of thing. The Ritz crackers were good for the moment, but the dessert, it was hard to give it up, but you would have to pass it down and give it to him. It didn't necessarily have to be an older boy, maybe somebody your own size. You made the deal and if you didn't you were going to get in a fight, and a lot of them had older brothers!!

There was a lot of bullying when we first got there. Every Saturday we had to get inside the ring and box with somebody that was first our size and then move up, and just keep fighting. There was many Saturdays I had a bloody nose and was crying because I had to take a licking, because I didn't know how to fight!! I remember my oldest brother fought for two hours with a boy from Saugeen. They were beat but neither one of them wouldn't give up. They fought between the root cellar and another building - there was very limited space, but they fought in between there. It was an all out war between them. There was a lot of bullying - especially if they knew you were timid. There was one man from Cornwall Island. He only had one eye - he had an artificial eye. Everybody, I mean everybody - he wouldn't cry, he just wouldn't - they'd come by and they'd punch him as hard as they could. He would be angry because you could see it in his face, but he'd just stand there and look at them, he'd never swing back. He took more punishment from the time that I knew him to the time he left, than anybody I've ever known. Because everybody just punched him to see if they could make him cry, but he wouldn't cry. He just stood there. I often think of him because we got to be really good friends. I couldn't befriend him because I didn't know how to fight. I could take a good licking but it wouldn't have mattered. But him and I were really close. We could talk about different things. We adventured in our minds what we wanted to be, we had our own little secrets. We always shared if we had anything. He had a brother and he was quite the opposite. He'd cry in a moment, but everybody picked on him anyway!! Everybody that I know got the strap cried, except one girl. They beat her. They put out her hand and they give her about 20 smacks on it with a leather strap. She'd put the next one out, and when she'd finished she'd say "Thank you", and they would start again. All she would say was "Thank you." She was a tough kid. Most of the guys that took a whipping - everybody knew they were getting a whipping and there was a hush. The big guys, they'd try not to come out crying, but you stayed out of their way when they got a whipping because they're going to take it out on somebody. Some of them they just wouldn't cry - they'd just take a beating. But they'd be mad. They used to tell us "Tough it out. Just tough it out," but when you're five, or six or seven or eight, and they take this leather strap out, no matter how tough you wanted to be you broke down.

There was one incident - well there was more than one incident, but this is one I know was concrete - they took my brother and they held his feet and they held his hands, and they laid him across the picnic table and they took his drawers down and they whaled him. They beat him, but they always made people take their pants down. I don't know when they started hitting us on the hand - I think maybe only the teacher did that when we went to school.

The teachers weren't bad. There was one funny incident, and Zimmerman even laughed at this. There was a lady by the name of Mrs. Cripps, and she was the science teacher and she had false teeth. She was standing in front of the class and she was mad at us - either because we hadn't done our assignment or we weren't paying attention. But she started yelling, and while she was yelling her plate fell out and hit the desk, then it hit the floor and rolled across the floor. And we all fell out - we just thought that was the funniest thing. She was still trying to talk without it and she wasn't making any sense, so that made things worse. So she went out - she was crying now - she went out and picked up her teeth on the way out the door, and we knew she was going after Zimmerman. When Zimmerman came we told him what happened "She was yelling and her plate fell out and rolled across the floor." He bowed his head and he smiled and said "Somebody has to go out and apologize to her. I'm not going to whip you for this - it's sort of funny." So we had to take the head of each class to go and apologize to her before she'd come back in!!! But her choppers went flying across the room. But that was a funny moment and nobody was punished for it. But that's about the only funny thing that happened. Nothing else was funny. We went to Victoria Day celebrations at Six Nations - it was good to go, we were free there - of course you don't know where you are so you can't run away, cuz where are you gonna go?!

After a while they took us to a place called Christian Island for the summer - that was a relief. At least you got away from the school and you sorta got away from the environment. You got to mingle with Native people on Christian Island - that was pretty good. That didn't happen until the sixties.

I ran away one time and I almost froze to death - because I didn't know where I was going!! I ran away with my friend from Moraviantown. We made preparations - we thought: Let's get out of here. But we didn't make proper preparations. We were just two knotheads going somewhere. It must have been about 20° below zero when we took off. He had a lighter - this was to light our fire. We got up behind Burford or somewhere, in amongst the trees and we said "Let's build a fire here before we go on." The lighter wouldn't light and it was getting dark, so we decided to get back on the road. He said he knew the way home. This car picked us up, but we didn't know at the time that if they picked up anyone from the school they had a reward for them to bring them back. The guy took us back to the school and got the reward - and we sure got our reward. We were cold and they didn't give us a chance to warm up or nothing, they just threw us in the Principal's office and Mr. Zimmerman bent us over this chair and took our trousers down and just whaled us. You get the strap when you're half frozen - it's a killer. It's worse than anything you want to have happen to you - to get the strap when you're cold. After that I figured that's where I had to stay. But I did run away earlier than that. I went to Six Nations to a family there. I didn't know where I was then. They called the police and brought us back to Brantford and we were beaten again - and the family - it was their son - I don't know if he was a bad son!!

Sexual abuse - we witnessed it - we seen it take place. But what can you do about it? What can you say about it, who do you tell? You can't tell the staff - they're not going to believe you. But it did occur. It did happen. One that we know of. One of the staff members and one of the men who worked in the boiler room - the heating men. But they must be both gone now. It did happen. Not Zimmerman to our knowledge. He was just the boss - how mean he was. He was mean - he was one mean man. There was one Minister there - he was some sort of help, but he was very abusive - I mean sexually abusive - to little children. I seen him in the middle of the night, you know, he'd go to these little guys, and if there hadn't been four brothers, we'd have been in trouble ourselves. There was other staff members that abused the children, and if we'd had any sense back then we would have ganged up on them, and just tore em up. Sometimes I think about it, but I've gone to different counsellings to straighten out my head. I'm a graduate from Los Angeles, and an engineer, so I kinda reflect back on it every now and then when I see abuse, hunger and neglect, default. Their educational system wasn't what it should be.

I think a lot of people came out of there dissatisfied with their education, and you see a lot of them now pursuing a higher education. You see some seeking out counselling now because of things that happened to them over the years.

I don't know if any of these people have been charged - I don't even know if they are alive. I went to look for some records of the school and nobody could find any records of the school. Nobody could find an attendance sheet, or any medical records. I'd like to see medical records and find out what kinda medicine they doped us with. One time they sent me to the sanitarium in Brantford because of malnutrition - I fell down three flights of steps, before they realised I was sick. I told them I was sick and they didn't do anything. They stuck me in a hospital bed for a while, up in the nursery there, and sort of fed me, but I almost died - it was pretty close. I think we were guinea pigs because they gave us shots in our arm that swelled our arms up and made us sick. Sometimes we just got to sit in the corner and cry because it hurt so bad, but everybody was hurting. The playroom was bad at times but mostly we tried to hang out together, because that was all you had, that was your only resource of strength, that was to lean on one another. The staff was out to destroy you.

One guy when he was in charge he'd come in and say "Are you all right boys?" and we wouldn't see him till morning. He'd get one of the boys to take care of the boys. He was all right - his name was Mr. Nolan - he'd come in and say "Shower up boys", and you'd want to shower because he's not pushing you in there. It was maybe a three day shift and they had other ones in there that were monsters. One guy by the name of Mr. Lawrence - he had a cat-o'-nine-tails and he wouldn't think twice before beating you with it. You couldn't go to the bathroom. If you did he'd beat you all the way back to bed. You couldn't wet your bed because you had to drag it around in the morning. So what were you going to do? You'd hang on as long as you can till you think you're safe. They'd rub your nose in it. Poor little boys. You're scared to go to the bathroom in case you get beaten.

They never did tell you what the rules were. If they thought you were doing something wrong they just beat you. One time I was milking a cow. I'd never milked a cow before. I got my stool and I set it there - they only had one machine at the time - it was just an experimental milking machine - so everybody had their little stool and their own cow that they'd be going to. I guess I had grown up to the point where I was old enough to milk a cow. The cow stuck its foot in my bucket and gave my bucket a kick and it went flying, and the farmer came over there and he beat me up and down the aisle and threw me out of the barn. Then I got sent back to the school and I got beat for missing school. So I don't know whether I was missing school or missing farming!!! You couldn't learn getting beat down the aisle. His name was Mr. Papple. My brother laughed when he seen that bucket go flying and Mr. Papple go flying after

me.

I was in the root cellar one time, and we were cleaning it up. It was spring and there was old rotten potatoes. I picked an old rotten potato up and threw it across the room at one of the guys. I missed, but I didn't see the staff had seen me. He dragged me out of there and beat me half to death - for throwing a rotten potato across the way when I was supposed to be working! It reminds me of a Japanese prison. You could be doing a project with one of your fellow students, and if you talked to them - well I mean how are you going to do a project with someone without talking to the person - you'd get beat half to death for talking in school. I make no excuses for them - they beat me, and I know they did.

All the guys had a bad time - and the girls, though I can't speak for the girls. I think a lot of people have erased it, or put it in the back of their minds. I think if they sat down with a counsellor, it might bring an anger out that they don't want to show, because there's nothing they can do about it now, and there's nothing going to be done about it, because the people have mostly passed on and the school is now a cultural centre, and most people would probably rather forget the school ever existed.

I've had counselling, but I still don't think like an Indian. I'm still living in a white man's world, thinking like a white man. Now I'm a minister - non-denominational - through the Pentecostal in the U. S. I was in the Marine Corps for 13 years, as an engineer, then I was in the Navy. Eventually I came back to Canada and now I'm in University.

The residential school is to blame for my generation of Native culture being gone. I see things at a different perspective than most people do, and it's because I know what the Bible says, and I base a lot of my interpretation of what is going on about me on the Bible. I don't think as a Native, because I don't have that.

We were so poor the mice moved out! But we survived, we were happy here. Sure Dad drank when he could, but there were plenty of times when he couldn't. I knew how to play cribbage when I was 7 - it was something to do. We played euchre. We knew Native ways, we knew Native medicines because Grandma always took us to the woods and she'd point out what was good for us. I couldn't do that today.

I think it created in me the real value of having a dream, and making that dream come true. From a world of ugliness - of being an educator - a help - and to bring people together as a community and as friends. Because it was every man for himself - survive one way or the other. Use whatever was available to you, even if it means hurting someone along the way, and I couldn't live with those values. I still dream of helping. I have visions of great things. I never want to be famous, I just want to be able to be there - to help somebody - no matter what colour, creed, whatever. I don't want anybody to go through what I went through. If I knew a child had to go through that, I would do everything

I could to adopt that child. Teach home values, not only to the children but to the parents. I have control of my thoughts, they don't have control of me. I'm not upset. I think my bitter days - I drank them away. I just want to be able to know that I'm Indian and still face whatever challenges are out there.

My dream goes on. I think it started when I first went to Brantford - I was always thinking about getting out of there. I'd always want to be somewhere else. I'd run in the fields at the Mohawk and dream of being elsewhere. I think that helped. Did I learn anything in Brantford? I learned to dream. It helped me escape. I could erase things from my mind really easily. That's why I can't remember a lot of things about Brantford. Good times - I can't really remember them - Christmas, Easter.

Because nobody came to get me I just walked away from the school. I told the Principal that I'd had enough of the school and I was leaving, and I walked down that long roadway - it's not long now but it was then - and I walked away from there. They never sent the police after me, and they never came after me, so I just stayed away.

Lee Snake
1963 - 1965

I didn't like it too good. The lining up for everything. It seemed like you lined up for everything - you lined up to get a beating. I got 52 beatings, that I counted - from Zimmerman - whoever. They strapped me on the hands. I remember they used to blow the whistle and you had to be in line in a certain period, when you were playing. So if you weren't there on time you'd get the strap for being late. Nothing that I could see that I did wrong - I came late, or you weren't paying attention in Church or talking to your neighbours. They wouldn't pick you out right in Church - what they would do is make a note. After we'd get back from Church they'd line us up downstairs and call your name out. If your name was called you knew what you were in for. If you weren't, then you knew you weren't in for a beating that day. It was every day too. Maybe I did something wrong an average of once every two weeks!

My father disowned me. He used to drink. Back then the RCMP were hard on people that did drink. If you got caught drinking, or drunk, very likely you'd end up in jail. If there was a white guy and an Indian, they would take the Indian to jail. That caused a lot of family breakups. I blame it more on alcohol - he used to beat my mother, and after all those years she just said "To hell with this - I don't need it." Actually she was one of the first women to get up and leave her husband and kids, on the reserve. She had 9 kids. I was the baby when she left. It was '62, so I was 5 years old. I must have went when I was 6 - I remember I was 8 when I left.

Well, it did me a lot of good too. I guess one of the biggest things was I learned - no matter what - you can't abandon your kids, and let somebody take them that really don't know how to raise kids.

We were beaten for speaking our own language. I picked up a lot of Cree - there were a lot of Cree kids there - I knew basic words. We were beat for speaking the language - that's one thing I tell my kids now - they go to a Native school at Oneida - their mother is Oneida. Being from Muncey there's no way I can hear my language (Delaware) - it was beaten out of them when my mother was at residential school. Everyone from Muncey didn't have a language like the Oneida or Cree from up north, so we learned bits and pieces of their language.

I was there with two brothers, but my oldest brother was in a separate dorm and I rarely seen him. Maybe where we played. I got along good with the other boys. My brother was bullied - my oldest one. Maybe it was how you acted - they tested you as soon as you got there. If you took the bullying you were bullied all along. If you stood up and fought for yourself, you weren't bullied as much. They pushed you up and took what you got. I remember even older guys getting us younger guys to fight each other - making us fight.

They had Cubs for the older kids - you had to be 9 years old. They had Scouts. But mostly you were just let out into the playground. There was floor hockey. They were kinda behind - the year before I left I remember them bringing boxes of skates. But that wasn't until May and what good are skates in May? I remember all the boys getting skates and either burying them in the field for next year, so they could dig 'em up and use 'em - so other boys wouldn't steal 'em on you. That was kinda stupid. It was a nice gesture but maybe it coulda happened in November or December!

I remember **** [staff member alleged to have sexually abused the boys]. I remember him beating me. He was a priest, I guess, or preacher. But I ran into him again when I was 15 years old. He was working at the Corrections. That was him. The boys would talk. He never tried nothing with me - I knew enough to stay away from him. I was at training school when I was 15 and I met him again. There was boys in there - that was '72-'73 - there was boys in there claiming that he was touching them improperly. Why open up a can of worms? Eventually they'll have to pay for their misdeeds. Probably people in Ottawa are waiting for these people to die out - they won't do anything. It's frustrating because we know what happened. You'd have to get the boys that were abused, but even if they do tell, what's going to be done? They're more embarrassed about it than anything. If it comes out that all this was true, how are they going to compensate me? Look at what they took from me. They tried to take our language. They took my freedom. All in the name of God.

I definitely had problems later, from being at the school. My kids don't go to regular school to learn English because I feel - people conquer another nation they have to take their language. When they take their language you take their ceremonies and their dances, and their religious ceremonies. That's what they tried to do. How I explained it to some people who tried to talk me out of sending my kids to the Native school - I says "You can be the most educated person, you can have Ph.Ds, you can go to university, but you are no good to nobody, you're no good to yourself if you don't believe in yourself. If you don't believe in your people. If you're a fall-down drunk, if you beat your kids - you're no good to nobody." It's the young people - we've had enough - we've seen what our people have been through. The white man always controlled us - they always tried to say "Our way is better. You'd better go to school and learn - you can't get along without English, you can't get along without math." But we can get along without it and still live in the two worlds. That's what I'm preparing my kids for - to live in those two worlds, but respecting the other society's motivations, but not participating in them.

Bill Monture and Kelly Curley
1963 - 1969 and 1969

Bill: I didn't like it - I don't think anybody did. My grandpa passed away and my mother and dad were working in the States. He would look after us and after he passed away we ended up in the Mohawk Institute - I call it the Mush hole. I still remember the first day I went there. They took me downstairs and into the boys' playroom, and it was just like they put a cereal bowl on everybody's head and shaved right around it. That really scared me. It was 1963 and I'm 38 now - I was probably 7. My brother and my sister went with me.

They started getting pool tables. I remember one time they had a barber's shop from Hamilton - like a school. They'd take us up into - like a rest-room area and they had all these chairs set up, and these guys would practice on your hair.

You ate porridge every day!! That's how it got its name. One of the things I didn't like was they had all that beef and stuff there, and they had that orchard right in front, but you never seen any of that stuff. They still had beef when I was there. You used to walk into this dining area - they had this great big room and their [the staff] table would be there, and french doors - and their table would be all nice and they'd be getting all this great food. On Friday you'd get fish and oh my god! you could smell it all over that place!! The staff - they were strict. I remember one time getting a licking for swearing and I got 25 on each hand. It was just like somebody took a whole bunch of pins and just stuck them in my hands. The welts came up about four or five inches up on my arm. Mr. Boyce did that. He felt kinda bad after - what he did, but I don't think it was right - what happened. After a while when he got done strapping me - I was on my knees, crying - I was hurtin', I was sore. After it was all over he come over to one side and he said he was sorry. I think of the people that was there I liked him the best - he was a good staff.

Kelly: I liked Boyce the best. There was one guy named Christiansen and he was there the last year. I remember one time we were leaving the playground and going in the playroom in the basement. I was the first one in, and there was a couple of other guys behind me, and he says "Kelly, close that door." I says "I wasn't the last one in." The last one in was supposed to close the door. He says "You opened it. Close the door." But there were rules that were laid down before. I says " I'm not closing the door." And he walked up to me and he slapped me across the cheek, and he says "You go close that door." I says "I'm not closing that door," and when he hit me I got mad and I says "I'll get my brother, I'll go home and tell my brother, and he'll come up here and kick your ass." He slapped me again and I ran outside, and he followed me outside and he slapped me once in the parking lot. He told me to go and see Mr. Zimmerman. "You go up and see Mr. Zimmerman and tell him why I'm sending you up there." And I did and I told Mr. Zimmerman that he had no right hitting me cuz I wasn't the last one in the door. I got the strap - five on each hand. Like there was rules that we had to follow, and I followed the rules, but he didn't. I think it was just an authority - I don't hold a whole lot of animosity towards the person, but it was wrong what he did - beating us - making up rules as they went along. They had rules, but it seemed that the housefathers could make up their own rules and you had to obey them too. Each housefather would have a set of different rules - little things they liked. So you knew who was going to work that night, that week, and you acted accordingly because it was - how you'd act towards one housefather, you couldn't act that way towards another one. Every two weeks you'd change your acting.

B. I think Mr. Boyce was a little more easy going

K. I think most people liked him the best. I found Christiansen to be strict and Mr. Helen to be just a sicko!! I don't want to say nothin' bad against these guys, but that's my feelings that I had as a kid. I don't wish any bad luck -

I don't want to see them go to jail or nothin' like that. There was good times, but there was those bad moments. And sometimes the bad moments wasn't because we was being disciplined - but we weren't being disciplined in a constructive form. We weren't being disciplined as to the rules and regulations laid down by the institute, we were being disciplined in how them people were disciplined. However they were brought up, that's how they treated everybody in there - maybe even a little worse. I don't want to say nothin' bad about anybody cuz I'm not supposed to - that's my beliefs - you say good things. You tell the truth and that's it. But I don't want what I say to be taken and have somebody go to jail. There's a lot of stuff[abuse] that would warrant criminal charges, but it's over and done with. I'm healing my life - that was a big part of my life. It was only one year, but it was still a big part of my life, and I've taken a lot of treatment for it. Not specifically for that institution, but for my problems in general. And that's all part of it. It's shit we carry for all this time. I can remember laying in bed wondering when it was my turn, at night. One of the staff was gonna come around, and I was wondering when it was my turn to take me down that aisle and back. My turn came but I never went. I wouldn't get out of that bed, and I kicked and screamed and cried, and the guy just left. There was one guy that I knew of.

B. It never happened to me.

K. I can also remember laying in bed and hearing someone crying across the room.

B. It seemed that they just downgraded you - they thought that just because you were in the Mush hole you were bad.

K. I have a lot of good memories about it - I had 3 square meals a day - and when I was home we were lucky if we ate once a day. So there's a positive side - I had clothes on. We lived in a two-room house. We didn't get hydro till '73. Before, we had a wood stove and kerosene lamps and no fridge. Being in there was a lot better than being home - I don't mean it was better, just that we had more material things. We didn't have that love and that sense of belonging, but we had food and we had clothes and shoes - albeit second-hand or used - but at least we got to change our clothes every day and shower. I never had that as a kid before, and even after coming out of there it was a good number of years before I got that stuff again. So in a way it was good. I was thirteen.

B. We all dressed the same. I think the Mohawk Institute made me very independent.

K. I don't know if it made me so much independent - I think it made me rely on other people. I think I was more independent before I went there. If anything it taught me to rely on other people.

B. I had an older brother - he fought my fights for me.

K. I went through alcohol and drug treatment and I need that regimental sort of a thing in my life.

B. You'd fend for yourself - I used to go over and steal apples from the orchard.

K. We used to find morels and ask the kitchen staff to cook them. I took them a 6 quart basket and they wouldn't cook them - "You can't eat those, those are poison!"

B. That's what I couldn't understand - why they had the orchard there and you couldn't eat an apple. Before we went there they had chickens and pigs and cows, and all the stuff they grew - vegetables and stuff. We used to have to go out in the garden and pick those potatoes. Where does it all go? To pay for some of the bills at the school.

K. Another thing I hated was they made you go to church. You could either go to the Anglican Church or the Catholic Church. There was no in between - you had to go.

B. Yeah. That's why I don't go to Church today.

K. I think if a person wanted to go they should have been allowed to go, but if they didn't want to go it shouldn't have been forced on them. I don't have anything bad to say about the Church, because to each his own, but I thought I was in touch with my Creator back then, trying to be a spiritual being and giving thanks. When I went there I got away from that. When I come out of the Mush hole I went into a foster home - my foster parent - he taught me more about my native ways. Today that's what I do. I believe in that spirituality - being honest and just talking, and don't have to worry what people think of you - cuz before, I was always caring what people thought of me, and putting on a front to people. Today I'm me, and if you like me, fine, and if you don't like me it don't matter. If you believe me, fine, and if you don't believe me that don't matter either, cuz I know, and I'm the one I gotta be truthful with.

B. His Mum used to bring me home from the Mush hole sometimes. I think farther up north they was rougher on kids than they was here - that's the way I look at it. I seen Zimmerman taking a whatyoucallit to somebody for running away. I ran away from there too. I was right across the road laying over there in the reeds watching the cops over here. After they left I go home and the next thing I knew I was going back!!! I ran away cuz I didn't think I belonged there. I ran away twice, and the second time I remember we left and we were heading down the tracks - you could go for miles. All of a sudden, about 3 o'clock in the morning I was getting real hungry, so we went up to this one house to get something to eat and they put out alarms??

K. It would be like putting a rat in a room full of cats - that's how I felt. You didn't belong.

B. I got a licking when I got back. Zimmerman had - it wasn't a belt - it was like a cord - like an extension cord.

K. Like a razor strap - that the barber sharpens a razor with - that's what it reminded me of.

B. He'd strap you on the back of your legs - anywhere he could. He'd hold you and spin you around. I felt sorry for that one guy who came with me got it worse than I did. Just to hear him holler. One guy got killed running away - he got hit by a train trying to cross the tracks.

K. I think if it was a very nice place - there's positive and negative things about it - but if it was a very nice place people wouldn't want to run away from it. And each person runs away they have their own little reasons.

R [friend]. It's not only one generation, it's the next generation down, because they didn't speak Indian when they come out of there. My grandfather was in there and he was beat for speaking his language.

K. I'm just glad I was there the last year when it closed down - I'm not glad I was there - but I'm glad that it was the last year!! Cuz - my kids today - there's a lot of negativity I have, and it's breaking that cycle of how we were taught and treated. If we don't do something about it we're going to teach our children the wrong way of life. I'm getting back to my Native ways - that's the right way for me. Some of it was good - that regimental sort of stuff that was taught to me - that schedulized daily routine - I did learn from that. The good things I kept and the bad things I threw on the back shelf - never touched it again.

You got up, you had your breakfast, you went to school, then you come back, you did your chores, got ready for supper, and after that you got to go outside and play. I guess it was better because the stories I heard from before I went there. Everybody looked after everybody else. If you were from one Reserve you tend to look after all those people from that Reserve, like the younger ones. You became the younger ones' parents from your own community. You still made friends with the other students, and sometimes you even became closer to them students than you would to people from your own community. But it seemed like everybody had their own groups too. A lot of it had to do with language too - these people over here spoke Cree, they'd speak Ojibway - although they were the same, or close - you could understand a little bit, they tended to hang out with family groups - that's what they were - family groups. If there wasn't a family group there was a community group.

For me it was good - it taught me structure in my life. But it was bad because it took away a lot - in the most impressionable years of my life - early teens. A lot of freedoms that I should have been allowed to have, or see, or do. For people that were there for longer than me - they wouldn't know the difference between the right and the wrong. They would have nothing to compare that experience to. If you had asked me three years ago you'd have got nothing but negativity, there was so much hurt and hate inside me. Today I'm more open minded - that's just with dealing with a lot of my problems.

The reason we went there - it was probably financial. There was six of us and mother and stepfather living in a 2-room house, and the house was 12ft by 18ft. One room was a kitchen/living/dining-room and bedroom at night, and the other room was a bedroom, and there was just a curtain between them. No hydro and outside washroom. For me that was a normal way of life. It was probably normal for our grandparents. Looking back I think I had a pretty happy childhood, but there was a lot of things I went without.

As a child I felt abandoned. Why do I have to be here? Doesn't my mum love me? Those thoughts went through everybody's head who ever went in places like that.

B. I had my brother and sister. I was too young to realize.

K. I had my brothers and sisters too. I think age has a lot to do with it - to me just turning a teenager I think I had a good understanding of what society was trying to tell me, and it was a big conflict right off the bat.

When I got the strap the one day when the housefather sent me to Zimmerman - I got 5 on each hand and that was nothing. And that was for being disrespectful. I learned something too. If you go there and you try to tough it out you're going to get a licking till you cry, but if you go there and get one hit and start bawling...

B. They'd ease up on you.

K. I cried right away!!

B. I didn't cry right away - not till after a while. Sometimes you'd wait till the strap was coming and then pull your hand away and they'd hit themselves - oh gee! they'd get mad!!

R. That was a whole issue for future generations too because people would come out of there and they'd start abusing their children. My father put me in the hospital when I was young, cuz he was in the Mush hole and he got the strap. That was the only way of disciplining that they learned.

K. That's what I found when I went to treatment. I put a look in my little girl's eye one day. I was standing there reading the newspaper and she come up to me and she said "Daddy can you read me this book?" I yelled at her "Get the hell away from me! Goddammit, can't you see I..." and right away this tape clicked in, Where did you hear this before? and I says "Come here babe, I'll read you that story." She kinda looked up at me, out of the corner of her eye - she gave me that look "Daddy I don't love you any more." When she give me that look that was the feeling I had when I went to the Mush hole, when my parents left me there - I could identify with the hurt. I said "There's something I gotta do", and I went to treatment. It turned my life around from being a negative asshole to just being me.

B. I guess I'm a strong-minded person. When I left there I went to Niagara and I was there for a while and I got sent away for a year in the States in Rochester. It was the same - you marched in pairs, we wore the same clothes - only there you had to cut the grass!! Me, it made me very independent - it made me a better person. I didn't go to high school. I was kinda bad when I was young. After I left from Rochester I went to Buffalo and I belonged in the gangs. That's the difference between Kelly and me - after I moved home from there I was only 16 years old and I probably changed my life around.

K. But we're still brothers!!!

B. His mum - I'd call her Mum. My mum and dad were in the States. She was like my ma - when she'd come and take her kids home for the summer and I'd go along for the weekend. I'd be standing and watching. That's the part I didn't like - standing and watching people leave to go home, and never getting the chance. Their home was small and for them to take me in too - it's something I'll never forget for the rest of my life, what she did for me. Sometimes I'd sit there for hours in the drive. Then when I did leave - I was the last person to leave the mush hole - the very last. There was nobody else. I remember Mrs Gibson telling me "Is there any place we can take you?" I said "I think I've got a brother," and I was trying to remember where my brother lived cuz I didn't know. I tended to forget my brothers and sisters - the older ones, cuz they had all moved to the States. Coming out I remember going down Frog pond - dropped me off there that night, and coming down here - this place was all boarded up and the grass really high.

There was some bullying - I had my grievances - but I had my older brother there so I wasn't worried. I'd just go along to him and tell him and he'd do my fighting for me. But I think if I was there by myself it'd probably be a different story. They did breed some good fighters. That's how I am - I don't give a shit for nobody and I won't take none from nobody. You learned to protect yourself. You can live by their rules, but they'll never change me. I am who I am. I'm Native and I'll always be Native.

I remember the kids from up north would come down earlier, before we would go in there, to get adapted to the food system. They'd always be on medication and you could go up to them and pull their ear lobes away from the side of their face. They had sores on them.

K. I don't know how long that swimming pool was there, but that was one of the things we looked forward to in the summertime - was going swimming once a week.

B. In the sixties they put the new wings on. Some of the older boys would run over to the dump and get the candy that was thrown away. Across from the dump there was this pond and we'd go swimming in there, and you'd come out dirtier than what you went in. It was full of leeches too.

We used to smoke. That time I found some money in front of the building, and this one guy they called Igor - he was older - and I had him sneak over to the store and I bought all this candy. I ended up getting caught with it and they took it away from me. They said I'd get it back when I was ready to go home - I never did get it back!!! They ate all my candy.

Part Three: Voice of Experience
Mount Elgin

15. Mildred Monague, Loretta Riley, Violet Henry, Nettie George

16. Bernice George, Emma Gray, Melva George

17. Vena Monague and Phyllis Noah

18. Pearl Chrysler and Bernice George

19. Pupils doing the laundry at Mount Elgin

20. Students at Mount Elgin

21. Boys gathering the grain sheaves at Mt. Elgin

22. Boys at Mount Elgin

Kathleen Kennedy
1922 - 1930

I went there in 1922. I didn't have to attend classes the first year I was there because I was too young. I was just at the school there and then I started classes in 1923. I was born in 1914. My name was Kathleen Abram.

It was a wonderful school and it was a good Christian school. And nobody was abused like you hear all these different things going on at the different schools - how they were molesting. We never, never, never, had any molestation of any kind. We had a good principal and good teachers that really cared for us Native children. Mr. McVitty was a good principal. He did take an interest in the kids. We used to have chapel every evening before we'd have our study hour. Whenever we were having an ailment of some kind we had a doctor and a nurse to look after us. We had to be clean!!! That's one thing - we had to be clean. I remember getting down on our hands and knees and scrubbing the floor. They had those white hardwood floors and they had to be just perfect too, so we had to be clean. We had different jobs that they'd appoint for us each month. We worked down there in the lower kitchen - that was where the cook worked for the pupils, and then there was the upper kitchen where they worked for the staff - the principal and the teachers. I worked up there the last six months I was there - I guess I was so good!! I left school in July 1930. I guess they liked me so well they kept me there!!

There was three dormitories apiece for the boys on one side and then the girls on the other. We used to have sports - we'd play softball or volleyball. On Sunday mornings one of the teachers would teach Sunday school, and in the afternoon we used to march to that Colborne Church. We had to stay in line and we daresn't chew gum. We had to listen to Mr. Dodson - he was our senior teacher, and he was our preacher for the school. He was good. He was there quite a while. Then we had a Miss Harris that was a teacher. Then we had a Miss Armstrong that used to teach the music lessons. Then when Mr. McVitty left there was a Mr. Strapp come in. I was there with Mr. Strapp - he got to be the principal. There was a Mr. McKenzie there - he was the vice-principal. Mr. Strapp was good - we just kept up the same ritual when he got in there. But they weren't mean at all with us kids - you know how mischievous us kids could get - we were never thrashed or beat up. I got a strap because I ran away from there!! There was three of us got together and we had these girls sit on our bed - we took the sheets off our bed and tied 'em together and put 'em out this window!!! When we got to the corner up there - at the railroad crossing - who should be standing there but my Dad. I told these girls "Oh my gosh!" I said, "There's my father standing there. Come on, let's get going." So we just turned around and went back. They wouldn't have found out about us, but some girl snitched on us. So then we had to go to Mr. Strapp - so what he did was - he had this strap, but he made us hold our hands way up, and he just came down like this [lightly], one stroke on each hand, and that was it. It wasn't a thrashing of any kind. There was no meanness, nothing. No prejudice either. I really enjoyed it. Because that's where you learned discipline. You learned respect. You learned how to sew. They used to have cattle, and they used to have chickens, so we had that to look after, and they had some swine. I didn't look after them - the boys did that. My job was to work in the kitchen.

My brother Harvey went to the school too. We were allowed to speak to each other - they didn't restrict us from talking to our relatives. We used to get out there and play ball against each other - the girls against the boys!! We had the fence there too, but we used to go over on the boys' side - at that time. The staff used to play tennis and we'd get behind them and we'd be the ones to chase the balls!! We had good food - because everything was planted there. We used to have to pick tomatoes. And just another patch over they had watermelons, so about 5 o'clock when the staff was having their evening meal, one of us would go over there and steal some watermelons!!! Then the last one this girl went and picked here turned out to be a citron!! We used to go in the apple orchard and steal apples. Then they used to have honey bees. We had three meals a day - breakfast, dinner, supper.

We used to have to sing every evening too. We had chapel hour and if we didn't know the hymn that they selected, then we'd have to sing it over and over again until we learned it. If you wanted to take music lessons they had teachers there to teach - everything was provided.

I took my Entrance, but I didn't go to Continuation School - it was only if you could afford it. So I just continued on working. I had to go out and work - I went on my own when I left school. Of course when I was in school, I'd come home for the holidays and we used to have to go and pick berries, and cucumbers and beans. We had to earn money so my grandmother could buy us some new clothes before we went back to school. 1st September we had to be there no matter what day it was.

My Grandmother was the one that entered me. At that time they used to call it 'ration' and she was getting $4.80 a month. And that was just to buy food, and if she went over that then they took it off her next month's cheque. That's the only reason why she entered my brother and I in the school, because in the wintertime you can't supply the right clothing, so that's why we went there. We had to wear their clothing - what they supplied - the uniforms. But in the summertime our parents had to supply the clothing. I can remember going out pulling flax, picking berries - one year we got 1¼ cents a box. We had to go to school because they wanted us to learn.

The school was very helpful because that's where you learned obedience, and you learned respect - because we used to have to say "Yes Ma'am," "No Sir." I did domestic work. I remember I worked in St. Thomas at that Empire Hotel there. I used to have to help the kitchen cook and I had to help the upstairs maid and I got $5 a week!! But in them days you could buy a pair of shoes for $1.95.

Mr. McVitty had two girls - Helen and Laura. Helen died when we were still at the school - she had an appendectomy operation and she didn't come out of it. Laura died after they moved to St. Thomas - she had a brain tumour. We got to know them because they lived right there.

We were raised by my Grandmother - I could speak my language. I can still speak it - I never give up my Native language. We used to speak it when we were downstairs in the playroom, or when we'd go to bed, or when none of the teachers were around. They used to just tell me to speak English, so when a bunch of us would get together then we'd speak it. No, I never gave it up - no way!

Elizabeth (Lizzie) Grosbeck
1924 - 1927

I was born September 12th, 1909. My mother died when I was 4 months old, I was taken in by a woman my father hired. My stepmother promised to give me back to my father when I was seven - she said that was the hardest thing she ever had to do. I went to live with my father when I was seven and started going to school. My father, Lyman Fisher - he was at Mt. Elgin too - was a teacher but stopped teaching around that time when they brought in qualified teachers. He worked on the next farm and that brought in butter, eggs and milk. He died in 1948.

Mr. McVitty knew I didn't have a mother and he came to my home to see if I wanted to go there, and he asked my father if he would consent to send me there. I was glad to go and I worked all summer picking cucumbers to get money for clothes. I took the train to St. Thomas and went shopping.

After I left at the end of the summer term, I went to help a lady in Strathroy for the summer, then I came home and worked in Mt. Brydges for the winter, then I came home with my Dad.

I was only at Mt. Elgin from 1924 to 1927 - for 2½ years. I liked it so much I stayed there in the holidays. It was a nice place - they took in a lot of children and helped people. I liked Mr. McVitty and his family - I liked them all. The children all got along.

I did domestic work. At the school they did cooking but I never worked in the kitchen. I worked in the sewing-room, cleaned the school-rooms, then I worked upstairs for the officers. You learned how to do laundry, ironing, washing. They had a nurse, cook and senior and junior teachers, and a teacher for small children. Mr. Kapayo looked after the lights etc. - he had two boys working with him, and he was good with them.

We went to school all day when we were trying our Entrance - to go to school in Melbourne. I didn't go to high school - I could have gone to high school in Strathroy when I was with the Sextons, but I stayed and helped the lady. I couldn't do the algebra. I used to fall asleep in school.

I never ate the porridge the whole time I was there - or drank the milk. That was all we had for breakfast every day - porridge. I didn't like it, or the skim milk..

We walked to the church every Sunday and then we'd come home at 1 p.m. and have our dinner. They had Christmas trees at the Church.

Nellie Stonefish
1924 - 1928

My mother went to Mt. Elgin. She was a natural born cook - she worked out west in Saskatchewan and all over on the railroad - she must have decided to sell her restaurant and come back and look after her elder sister - the one who raised her. Homer was her name - but people didn't really know her because she'd been off the reserve so long. Anyway she went to St. Thomas. Shortly before we left Saskatchewan some lady said something about a big school, and she asked if I wanted to go there. I knew my skin was darker than other children, but I didn't know why. I said "Yes." When I come down here I found out I was an Indian. After about a year of living in St. Thomas she said "If you don't behave yourself I'm going to send you to Mt. Elgin." I said "That's where I wanted to go in the first place." Anyhow in 1924 she signed me up. The first year I went there the kids used to call me "white girl" because my accent was different from theirs. But at school the kids were not allowed to speak their own language, and when children would be playing outside playing ball - I think the word was "hanyah"[?] - "Catch it" - but if the matron heard them say anything they'd get a strapping. And those strappings were pretty healthy too. Our arms used to be black and blue from the elbow down. The matron would give us the strap, but mostly Mr. McVitty, and he was over six feet tall - a heavy duty man - mostly he did. I think the first year I must have got about eight - I wasn't smart!! I don't exactly know what we did because we didn't dare sass him back.

The reason children went to school as I understood it, wasn't necessarily because they were bad - maybe a single parent. Not all parents on the reserve approved of going to the school - a lot of people didn't. Two or three kids at the school - they must have been fairly well off cuz maybe they'd get some presents - candy or something. We were sorta always hungry - sometimes I'd get something.

When I was out west I had a very smart teacher - I was 8th or 9th at this other school I went to. Anyhow, at the Mt. Elgin I didn't learn beans - I didn't know what grade I was in - at Mt. Elgin it was Junior 1 - first grade, Junior 2 - second grade, and so on. Then they had an Entrance Class - they were allowed to go all day. Then you have to try your exam in Melbourne. Trouble is - Daddy Dodson - we figured he favoured the Chippewa people - a little bit prejudiced. Mr. Dodson was a little short man. If there was a little boy that didn't go to school walking outside with his hands in his pocket or something, he'd make us all get up - all the grades - and watch that little boy. Trying to tell us how useless we are! He tried to make me a teacher's pet - I didn't want any of that. He had a way of being sassy sometimes. What he used to do - we had to go to Colborne Church on Sundays for service - so if there was a small child went to sleep or whispering or chewing or spitting gum, he spent all the next morning talking to us and we never read till June. We only read that one time in all the year - in class. E W and I were always tied pretty well head of the class - even though I didn't study.

We'd go to school half-a-day and then we worked half-a-day. The girls in the kitchen - they changed the work list every month - the kitchen girls did the dishes and stuff - they'd be allowed to walk around, while we in the sewing room might have to stay there till 5 o'clock. I got to work up in the kitchen after a while. They had one girl work in the principal's apartment.

The school sure as heck taught us discipline. We had to make beds every day after breakfast - 20 beds on each side. There's two girls in a dormitory and you make 'em when you came back from breakfast, and you'd sweep up. Saturdays you'd scrub the floors on your hands and knees. But if you got smart and decided to make the beds before breakfast, then Miss McKinley come along and see them, she rips them all apart. They had to be made neat - like hospital beds - she rips them and it makes more work afterwards than before you start. Same way if you scrubbed your floor early before noon and they caught you, you had to do it over.

I don't remember if we had hot water or not. We had Lifebuoy soap. The towels were on rollers. We had to line up - really small children went to school in another building. We used to call it the Hospital - it wasn't much of a hospital! We had plug shoes - boys' shoes. By Christmas time they had strings in for shoelaces. And black stockings, denim petticoat, bloomers, we wore, and cotton uniforms -

stripes. We were allowed to wear our own clothes on Sunday when we'd go to church - Colborne Church - we had to walk down there and back. We had Sunday School in the morning and Church in the afternoon, or vice versa.

In the wintertime us girls were not allowed to go outside after dark. We had an outside toilet - we were allowed to go out there to the toilet - then we went to the prayer room and had a prayer service for an hour, and an hour for studying.

When you went there as a small child - I was about 10 or 11 by the time I went there - a 'big sister' - would take you under her wing. If a big girl went there - Boy! she really had a hard time. The girls that stayed there a long time - the odd ones, they weren't all like that - were real bossy. When we get lined up and ready to go to eat - we line up starting with the bigger girls going down to the little girls. There was usually a teacher - Miss Harris was one - we paid attention to her pretty good because "Right Nellie Morrow, don't do that no more" - I didn't like my name being called out if I did anything. She could control them, but another little lady came there - a Miss Armstrong - she was kinda small. I think she was a Christian lady. She wore those boots that clip across the front and somebody saw her outside and because she was kinda small in them they called her 'Puss-in-Boots'! Everybody had a nickname - some weren't very nice. People used to say she used to cry - there had to be a teacher come in at night around 10 o'clock to check on the dormitories - poor Miss Armstrong, when she would come in, somebody would say "Miaow, miaow."

There used to be worms in the cornmeal!! They weren't alive but they were little and round and brown - you could see 'em. So when I got to work in the kitchen - I was 13 or 14 - when they make up the list - that bin was empty once. Boy! did I get up there! Well, we scrubbed, scrubbed - we always had to have a scrubbing brush. Boy! did I clean that. You learned how to use a scrubbrush there. I remember my legs sticking out and my head down in there, scrubbing that bin. Of course you were always hungry so you wanted to eat everything. They'd give you some syrup and two slices of bread and a cup of milk. The big girls got the cold milk and the little girls got the warm milk that just came - that didn't taste very good. Sometimes you'd see blood streaks in it too. Sometimes we'd have a candybox and we'd swipe some oatmeal and put salt in it and eat that.

In the mornings two older girls that worked in the kitchen - the cook would come up and get them and they had to make the oatmeal - great big pots. When H and I got a bit older we'd sneak out when these two girls did, and there was tall trees there and we'd play softball. You'd hear the girls groaning and hoping we'd keep quiet - they wouldn't get up for another hour. We weren't working in the kitchen.

We worked in the sewing room - we did some knitting, but the socks weren't darned - the black stockings - we'd just cut up old ragged ones and put a patch on them. They did have a big sewing machine. We had to make the shirts.

After a while I got to do that. The yokes - you sew them together first before you put the sleeves on. It's already cut out. Sometimes white people would go through the sewing room and they said "Don't you wish you could sew like that?" Before that I used to knit socks. There were around 83 girls - we all had our own number on account of our uniforms, socks and stockings, bloomers.

Miss McKinley was about 67 - she was the matron - girls' matron. She was kinda lame. They had one girl called a playroom girl. Our playroom consisted of a big place and it had wooden boxes all around, and the girls had to use those for their own use. That girl would have to get some coal oil and comb the girls' hair with a fine comb, because they'd come with them or sleep together - with lice. I remember once I went out there - just off the upper kitchen and there were these two cans out there and I got what I thought was coal oil. Miss McKinley yelled out "What're you putting in those girls hair?" I says "Coal oil." She says "It smells like gasoline to me."

The new dormitories were just above there. We had great big tanks of water along there for the water supply - and toilet. We had to go to bed around 9 o'clock - and the toilet - the box was way up high and we'd climb up there if we wanted a drink of water. And of course the girls always got the dickens for being noisy - they said we were worse than the boys. We'd pillow fight and you couldn't tell who your friends were or not because we all had white nightgowns on.

The old dormitory was the medium size girls' and the upper dormitory was where the little kids slept - 'old dormitory' they called it. The new dormitory had a lot of windows, but the old dormitory just had two little windows. The matron - they switched the light on when they'd come in about 10 or 11 o'clock - the same light worked in both dormitories. Sometimes McVitty would come in - we didn't think that was quite right. You weren't allowed to sleep with another girl - sometimes we did though. I remember this E J - she was sleeping there and Miss McKinley saw her and Boy! she'd just strap her. E was laying there as if nothing happened and she was strapping her on the bed. I don't know about the boys - I heard they used to strip them down to the buttocks when they strapped them.

One time in the prayer room Mr. McVitty said "If you see something on the floor, pick it up. Don't say 'I didn't put it there'. Or you see a sheet torn, take it down and get it sewed." I went down to the sewing room - this sheet was ripped - so meantime this girl's sister had come in and was helping me. I got the dickens for I'd got a young girl doing my work for me while I'm gallivanting around not doing anything. Here I'm trying to be conscientious and I get it. Kathleen once - Miss McKinley sent her up to clean this girl - she had real shiny black hair - a lot of hair and a lot of nits. So after breakfast she sent her up to the dormitory - Kathleen. I was playing hopscotch downstairs by myself and after a while I got tired and I thought I'd go up the back steps and help her out for a while. Then I got tired of the job and I went back downstairs and Miss McKinley come from somewhere "Where are you going? What are you doing?" I said "I was up helping clean T's hair." Just then Mr. McVitty come along. He said "Here, here. What's going on?" and he takes the strap from her. She said "I sent her up to clean T's hair and here she is sneaking out." OK, you're supposed to put your hands out and get a strapping - and you don't dare - I should have called Kathleen to come down that she'd made a mistake. Maybe she thought we looked alike, or she forgot - I don't know, but anyway I was going to get a strapping. Anyway he swings the strap and I moved my hand a little bit and it hits his knee. Boy! did I ever get it then - he just strapped you right around your body. I had black and blue spots on my legs. I went home with black and blue spots but I never complained cuz my mother was strict too.

When somebody's two years older when you're 14, 16 year old girls seemed like - old ladies. R and L were friends and they started pushing H and I around. You learn quite a bit about peoples' attitudes. We knew R was scared of getting the strap and we sat across from her. We were up there [office] for something too and we were rubbing our hands and putting on Lifebuoy soap, and R's sitting over there. She'd rather have somebody preach to you, talk to you - lecture. We'd sooner get a strap and get it over with. We knew that, so we were rubbing our hands and sitting there and saying "We just know we're going to get the strap and it really hurts." She was nearly in tears and we were getting a kick out of it. They just pushed us around in a good-natured way. Once I had a cup of water and L - she was really nice but we just wanted something to do - she didn't want it thrown on her, so I started chasing her. There's an orchard not far and here I'm running behind her - of course there wasn't any water in it by the time I got there, but she thought there was! This other girl, A, had done something - she wasn't a bad girl, but she'd swiped something maybe - they decided they wouldn't send her to reform school - at the age of 17 or 18. The girls really give her a hard time - the bossy ones. In the wintertime a bunch of girls formed a gang - they picked on one person. You're cooped in all winter downstairs - you had to make your own fun. Another one, O - she had brothers at Brantford and she was quite a scrapper. I remember A was laying there - there was a table there covered with upholstery - and I don't know what she was punching her for. A just laying there relaxed and not doing anything. We couldn't figure out whether she was chicken and didn't put up a fight, but I guess nobody did, because every time some girl got into trouble Miss McKinley would say "Yes, I know, O told you to do it." That A girl - she was older - she was playing with a ball and it got caught in the eavestrough above the girls' dormitory. There was a fire escape but the ball was right out in the middle of the eavestrough, and that O made her climb way out there. Boy! if she ever fell down - there was a ton of cement at the bottom.

There were more girls - about 83 girls and roughly 60 some boys - you weren't allowed to mingle. They had great big boys in Grade 1 - I used to think that was pretty bad - why should they be in Grade 1 - nearly men, 16, 17 years old. There was a big laneway where you drove in. When we first went there - on Sunday - they never did that till the last year we were there or so - us girls were allowed to walk down there and back, but the boys were fenced in. So they could speak to them. Otherwise your flirtation consisted of - when the boys go out their door they smile at some girl when she goes out. When we worked in the kitchen - if some girl liked some boy - we had to cut our bread by hand - they'd give them - and the bigger boys were like men - 17, 18 - they'd cut them big slices and the rest of us would just get normal slices. I remember H and I, and this E - she was very nice and very quiet - we got the idea - we says "So-and-so really likes you. Why don't you smile at him?" In the meantime we'd write a note and put it in his bread and it said "I really like you. Why don't you ever smile at me?" We sat back and played cupid - laughing away. The Walpole Island girls used to save their syrup - get a jar and hide it away. On Saturday they'd make taffy and we'd come along and steal it, and they didn't dare tell on us!!

The last year I came home - when they made us stay there they finally said we couldn't go home till the middle of July - we'd only get six weeks holiday. H - she lived there all the time - we get into little troubles here and there. Inside downstairs there was this big long hall, it was quite dark because there's dark windows, and storerooms. As you go straight ahead there's the dining-room, and as you go upstairs there's the prayer-room. I remember the girls - it was nice and warm lying outside - there was these steps that lead up to the staff - they called it annex - where the boys brought in the milk and stuff. So we'd get a cup of water and one of us would stand in this dark hall. They called me Buttercup because I used to be twisting my hair all the time. So I'd say to some girl who was walking by "Did you see Smitty? She's looking for you down in the hall there." So she'd go down there and she'd throw water on them!! And then we'd change around. Now I don't know why Mr. McVitty was walking through there. Boy! was he tempting - I sure felt like it. I still think I should've, but we couldn't run out and lay down beside the girls, because they'd say "Who was the last one came here?" I didn't know whether he'd take roll call or not and find me. It wouldn't have mattered because we were used to getting a strapping anyway. Anyway I was really tempted to throw the water on him - but I didn't - because he couldn't see who did it - just retaliating because they made us stay there.

The boys had a matron - she was English - Miss Daniels, and she spoke very [English accent]. We kinda didn't like her cuz we thought she favoured the boys. Well, she probably did because she was their matron. Sometimes she would have to be a matron at night when we'd have to go to bed. She come in this night - and I'd gone to sleep with my cousin T P. I took my black socks and put them for my head on the pillow, and put my clothes there for an image. She wanted me to get up and turn on the light - when you turned on the one light it turned on the one in the other dormitory and the big girls were making too much noise. She says "Nellie, Nellie." She pulls the bed apart and I wasn't in there!! So she sent me out in the hall and I had to stay there till - a long time - maybe 10 or 11 o'clock - then she let me go back. Maybe she was conscientious cuz she came in there to check on me and see if I was all right and there I was gone again!!

Another thing H and I done - somebody forgot to turn the light on when they come upstairs - it'd be dark and we'd lay down on the floor, the first person'd trip over us and somebody else, and soon there'd be a whole pile - and nobody'd know who was the original who did it!! What I didn't like was when you'd go to sleep and somebody decides to take a pillow and come along and hit you on the bed - if I was awake I'd crawl under the bed, I didn't like getting hit when you were half asleep!!

Our main fun was - we did play softball, but I wasn't very good cuz my fingers were short - and hopscotch, and the swing. Then walking up and down the avenue - there was this place we could walk back and forth - we called it the avenue. We'd play tag and we'd play what we called "Institution." A bunch of girls lined up - every morning we had to sing something about 'Lord be present at our table' - a Grace - so a whole bunch of us would line up where the big tanks were on both sides - Boy! they were big, and that toilet with the box way up there. We'd be sitting there - then maybe the lights would go on - and holy cats! everybody heads for their beds. I can remember jumping in - you'd run into somebody trying to get to your bed fast before they'd catch you. There was one small window and that was all the light. I used to get a book or something and try to read - otherwise we'd tell stories - we'd continue it on and on - a few of us. We'd look out and imagine we saw something - we saw lights - we made up stories. Just up here was this - K E - there were three of them and she used to cause trouble - but she couldn't scrap so the other girls would get after the rest of them - they were scrappers. That's how you learned a little bit. Naturally there was one or two girls used to push me around a lot. A few years ago - maybe 20 years ago - this A D used to push me around a lot - I said "Remember how you used to push me around at school?" "Just try it now!!" I said!!!

It gave you kinda an idea how to get along with people, and judge people by their actions - what they're like. B - we used to tease her - she must have got some candy, and I was in bed one night and she gave me a couple of pieces of candy - I liked her anyway - but I never forgot it. About second year when I was chumming around with this R R - and her sister was younger - she was a bit hard of hearing - the one that was helping me when I got the sheet fixed. They had an older sister M - she was nice too - but all the big girls seemed to get mad at her - so other ones kinda picked on us too, taking it out - it was a cousin of hers - G - she might have been 14 and we were just young 11 or 12 - she'd take snow and put it down our backs, and do mean things to us. Before spring happened things changed around - M was OK and they started picking on her. Boy! did we ever get after her - the two of us - and make up for it. There was another girl - I and L - we used to like to wrassle with them. She had an older sister. She used to get that Christmas paper - that red paper and put it on for lipstick. One morning we were all lined up for breakfast, and McVitty was coming down and making her go to the sink - making her go past all the girls and strapping her all the way along - she must have called him 'a damn flirt'.

I must have liked it. I pretended I didn't, so after I'd been there two years - see my mother and I weren't really close - it wasn't like when a child is with her parents all the time - I said "How much longer do I have to stay here?" She said "Well, you wanted to go there - I signed you up for three years." The third year I was there I said to my mother "I think I'll stay at Mt. Elgin during the summer holiday - not go home. She said "Don't you think I want you home?" So I didn't stay. So I guess I really liked it there - a lot of kids didn't. Everybody said they didn't and so I suppose I said so. So the second or third year - Mr. Dodson said if he had his way there'd be no holidays at all because kids forget everything what they learned. So, one year - I was 15 when I left, but I'd be 16 when school started in September - there was 14 in our class and he said we gave him such a hard time that he was going to put us in Junior Fourth, Senior Fourth and then Entrance Class. That meant three years for Grade 8 - I thought "Oh my gosh, I'll never get my Grade 8." When we'd do our homework we wouldn't really study we'd practise writing - that's why I can tell if anybody writes me a letter now, our writing is different. We'd practice writing big words in the dictionary - write them out. So when I first went to Buffalo I told my mother I couldn't stay there another year because I'm going to have to never get my Grade 8. I heard about child labour over there and I'd be 16 in September so I thought I'd get a job. I didn't know what gymnasium meant, I didn't know what algebra meant - their history was different - I had to go to school until I was 17. There was an Indian school over there. This other school was down in the Allegheny Mountains. They made arrangements for me to go. Mr. Sampson said "Don't run away here - there's a lot of bears!!!" There you could wear your own clothes all week long, we got ice cream on Sunday. It was run by the Quakers. We didn't get the strap. What I didn't like about their dormitories is the beds were too close together - when you had to make the beds. I studied hard - arithmetic. Boy! was I ever lonely and the

girl I chummed up with - she was very quiet. They had a little library and we'd just sit and read - you wouldn't know I was the same person. I wasn't bad, but at least at Mt. Elgin I was always active - liked to play ball and so forth. I wrote back and forth - that's when Mr. Strapp became the principal - R tells me he didn't strap so much but my friends told me he was just as bad. I was so doggone lonely - we were allowed to go on wiener roasts, and go to the store on Saturday afternoons, and the girls never got into trouble. They played ball but all they had was a sponge ball - we used to use a softball. That was the only time I joined in something. I kept writing to my mother to come and get me - but she was out cutting grapes and didn't get my letter. Two of us ran away - we went to her sister's place - the principal took me back but he expelled her. He didn't give me the strap but I had to stand in the hall all the time.

H and I tried running away from Mt. Elgin but we gave up. There were some girls mad at us, and on Sunday we went to Church - we went to the toilet and we stayed in there when they went down to church. When they got to Colborne they told Miss Harris - "Where's Nellie and H?." She had to come all the way back and Mr. Waite hooked up the buggy. I only just lived across the river - my aunt and uncle up there. We didn't have any money or anything, but I was going to go to Buffalo because my mother was living there. We got on to the river all right but we didn't get off it cuz it crack! crack! crack! We were scared and we said "I guess we'll just go back." We were going back across the river when we met Mr. Waite and Miss Harris. We said "How much for the buggy ride?" (there was a song). And they said "Oh you'll pay dearly"!! We knew we were in for a strapping. It was nice and neat - arms black and blue.

We always pretty well had a tooth ache - Dr. Woods used to be the doctor and sometimes they'd pull a tooth out. I thought: When I leave here, if I ever get a toothache the tooth is gonna come out. There was a H A - she was kinda nice quiet little girl, but oh boy! she used to sit and cry and cry. I could tell she came from a pretty good family. She'd sit and cry and cry and she had something wrong with her tooth. She was so lonely she couldn't get adjusted - she was a little younger than I was - she must have been 11.

As I understand it there was a teacher come from Toronto to teach there, and she didn't like the conditions. In the laundry room they had a mangle. Along the wall there there were these stationary tubs, and in the afternoons - I guess the kids had to take a bath once a week - we older girls had to climb up in these tubs and take a bath. There were quite a few other things this lady didn't like - she wrote to the newspaper in Toronto and they looked into things. So it improved a bit from the time I left in June 1928. I'da probably went back if I coulda been in Grade 8.

Dorothy Day
1929 - 1930?

I forget the year - but I know it was the year Mr. Strapp was there. He was meaner than Mr. McVitty was, so they tell me. I didn't like the school at all. They wouldn't let you talk Indian. The ones that was there - like the Oneida girls - if they caught you talking Indian they'd take you out and give you the strap. He tried to give me the strap. Well, it wasn't really over talking Indian - it was a hymnbook. You know how young kids get together - and one of the girls had a hymn book and we said "Let's sit over there and sing a few hymns." So we did - we sat and sang hymns, and one of the girls from Cape Croker she said "Here Dorothy, you can have it," - each one take a turn picking out a hymn. So I did, and all of a sudden one of the matrons come running around the corner and she said "What are you girls doing?" I guess she heard them singing - making all this racket. "Who's got the Hymnbook?" And I had it of course, looking through it!! "Give me that hymn book Dorothy." She says "Where did you get it - up in the prayer-room?" There was this prayer room up there - we used to have to go up for prayer every evening. I said " No, I didn't get it out. It doesn't belong to me." And [the girl] whispered "Don't tell her who give it to you - she'll give me the strap." I said "Gee, I don't know the girl's name - she just handed it to me." "Go up and see Mr. Strapp," she said. So I went to see him and I got up there and he locked the door, and he said "I hear you stole a hymn book from out of here." I says "No, I did not steal it." So he says "How come it was in your possession when the matron found it and brought it up here to me." I said "One of the girls decided we would sit in the shade and sing a few hymns or whatever to pass the time away until suppertime." He says "I think you're lying so I'm going to give you the strap." So I said "I don't think you will." He says " I think I will. I make the strap decision and I'm going to give you the strap, because we don't permit people to steal hymn books and take them out." "As I told you before I didn't steal it, I don't steal - I was taught not to steal." So he went up to the front there and took the strap out of the desk, and I got up and I went to the opposite side of the room. I thought "Boy, you're gonna have to catch me before you do it." I was only 12 going on 13 at that time. So he come over and he says "Come over here and hold your hands out." I says "If you can catch me you'll strap me, but if you can't...!!!" He tried for half an hour to catch me and I'd wait till he came close and then I'd just jump on the desk and on to the other one. There were desks along there - like a schoolroom where you sit. He chased me for a good half hour until he got so tired, and he was fat you know, and he was perspiring all over. He says "I'll report you," he says, "you'll be punished another way for this. I'll get you sooner or later." I says "Oh no I won't, because I'm going to get out of this school as quick as I

possibly can." Finally somebody was rapping on the door, and it was Mrs. Barnett. She was the sewing teacher and she had heard that he was going to give me the strap, and she didn't believe that I would steal. She was pounding on the door and she said "If you don't open this door Mr. Strapp I'm going to report you to the officers." So he opened the door and he was just sweating from running around there, and he was puffing and his face was all red, and by this time I was down the opposite side of the room again, ready to go again!! She says "Did he hurt you Dorothy?" I says "No, he couldn't catch me. It would only happen if I tripped and fell. He couldn't catch me - I jumped on the seats and that." And she says "Well, I'm taking you back up into my room." So I went back with Mrs Barnett, but that was my first encounter with Mr. Strapp. He was a miserable old coot - he wouldn't believe you - even on a stack of Bibles, and he was a minister. We were only having a bit of fun singing hymns. We weren't even singing the whole hymn - just the choruses. You couldn't live with him.

There was a lot of things I recall that I didn't think was right - especially the meals. The food was terrible. In the mornings we would get oatmeal and it would be half-cooked, no sugar, skim milk to put on that - just like water - white water - after they took the cream off it they gave it to the children. You had a glass of milk to drink - that same stuff, but I never drank it. One slice of bread - no butter, nothing else on there. One big slice of bread - that's all you were allowed for breakfast, and that age you're always hungry. We never seen two slices of bread - the odd Sunday - but there'd never be anything on it. Just bread - you never got no butter or nothing else to put on it. There was one great big slab of bread, and then that bloody old skim milk - I never did like milk. I like chocolate milk but I never could drink that skim milk. Dinnertime we'd get one egg, one piece of potato, and a piece of vegetable and that's all we got there. We never got dessert. The only time we had a good meal was when guys came from Ottawa to visit the school, and then we'd have a good meal. We'd have juice and a boiled egg - we'd have a wonderful meal. I didn't know about this the first time they came down, and all of a sudden we were all lined up and they said "We're having a visitor today." And I looked down at where I was supposed to sit and I said "Gosh, how come we've got all this nice food today?" Someone said "Sh - you'll get the strap again." He says "We're having a guy from Ottawa come down and see how well cared for these children are fed and clothed and everything. He's going to take a tour of the school and go through all the rooms." He said the grace and we sat down and I couldn't believe it, we even had a glass of orange juice. We never had that before. I had a boiled egg - it was nice - and we had toast for a change. I said to the girl next to me "It's too bad they don't come once a week." And then after that we were filing out and he was standing there - Mr. Strapp, and the guy from Ottawa was on the opposite side of him - and he said "Dorothy, I want you to behave for a change" - like I do this every morning - I didn't - "or else I'll phone Ottawa - see what punishment you should have." Then I says "Well, I only said what was true, that it's nice we had one good meal for a change." I went on and he followed and then he said "Go on." So he let me go and I went on with the rest of them and did the chores we had to do. That's why he didn't like me - old Strapp - nobody would say a word, they were so scared - I says "Gee! How come we're getting all this stuff today and any other time we get nothing - one slice of bread and oatmeal that's not cooked." The other kids said "Dorothy, be quiet." I thought to myself: Well, whether I get the strap or not, this guy should know what's going on.

I had to make the beds up there on the third floor. That was another thing - when you went to bed you only had two sheets - in winter time even - two sheets and one blanket, and a pillow, and you were supposed to take all your clothes off and just wear that skimpy nightdress they had. We used to push those beds together we'd be so cold, and all sleep together, before we could go to sleep, to be warm. All the Oneida girls would sleep together, and the girls from Cape Croker would all get together!! It was just like the League of Nations. We'd hear the staff before they come up. I think the only true friend we had in there was Mrs. Barnett, and she was really good to me - good to a lot of us. If she knew they were coming up, she'd come over. She'd come to the door and rap and she'd say "Girls, get back in your own beds - they're coming up the stairs." And of course we'd fly around there and push the beds back where they belonged, and back in like we were sleeping. But she was the only one that was on our side. If it wasn't for her we'd have had some pretty rough times. Lots of times she'd say "I'm taking Dorothy up to clean my room," and I'd go up there and her room didn't need cleaning. She had meals she'd brought up from the upper kitchen and we'd eat them. And she looked in my hair, because I had long curly hair and she'd say "I don't want you to get anything in your head Dorothy because they'll make us cut that hair." And naturally I didn't have too many friends because they all had to get their hair cut and I didn't. They were quite jealous of that, but I never did get anything in my hair. She'd comb my hair out every time I'd go up there to make sure there was nothing in my head. That was quite the place to be.

We got the strap for talking Indian - I thought that was terrible. Because they couldn't understand what we were saying I guess, they thought we were talking about them, but we weren't really. We kept our language because we'd talk when they weren't around. We'd go out behind where the rhubarb was grown - you're not supposed to - but we used to jump over the fence and get on the other side, and sit

around there and talk and talk in Indian. I never lost my language, and then when my mother come to see me, my mother talked Indian to me all the time. They didn't object if your people come to visit you - if they talked Indian, then you could talk Indian, but if they ever caught you talking Indian inside of the school after she was gone, then they'd take you up and give you the strap. "Don't you know this is an English school you're going to - you're not supposed to talk Indian." That's why a lot of them were running away all the time - nearly every day they'd be looking for somebody.

Just once I ran away, but I didn't go inside where the rest of them was so I didn't get caught. But I let them have my sheets to get downstairs - we tied the sheets together and we'd swing down. But I got back before the rest of them did, along with a couple of other ones that thought we should go back because they send the Mounted Police after them. We got back before they rounded the rest of them up. The girl that worked in the upper kitchen had the key to the upper kitchen - we could go through there and up the high way up to the dormitory. She went with them too and she left that door unlocked and all we had to do was climb up the stairs up to the upper kitchen and go on through. Boy, I even had all my clothes and I just got into bed when they brought them in and put the lights on. They counted the beds - how many wasn't there. We were frightened I'll tell you. That's the only time I went with them. They went to a dance at the New Hall. They had a dance down there and they all wanted to go so they went - for a little excitement. They all got the strap - ten times on each hand they said, for running away.

You had five minutes to get up when the first bell would ring, five minutes to get up and put your clothes on, five minutes to run two flights of stairs and be downstairs and stand in line for the second bell to go in and wash your hands and face. And that's all they give you - five minutes to wash your hands and face and brush your teeth, and comb your hair and stand in line again. We'd be running over each other to get down those stairs - it was good exercise - no wonder nobody ever put on any weight. They'd be standing at the bottom of the stairs with a watch to make sure you were down there in 5 minutes. You should see the girls coming down there - we had those boots that laced up high and they'd tie them together and lace them when they got to the bottom. If you weren't down there - up you would go to get the strap. They would give you the strap for being late - you were supposed to be down there when you were supposed to be.

In a way when you look back it was good training. I never did very much sewing when I was at home. I did some things for my mother, but I was never sitting down and having to make your own bra and things like that. You had to make your own bra and your own underwear in there. But I do know how to put a bra together!!. Mrs Barnett would cut them out for us but we had to sit at the sewing machine and put them together.

The nurse, Mrs. Daniels, she was mean, but if you didn't cross her she was all right. But Mrs. Barnett she would lie for us even, to keep us out of trouble. There was a Mr. Dodson - he was the teacher there. I was the youngest one in the class there. We only went to school half days. In the morning we'd do the chores and we went to school half-a-day. They'd have a certain amount in there in the morning, and a certain amount in the afternoon. Usually it was the small kids that were too young to be doing housework - they were in the morning, and the rest of us that was scrubbing the floors. You had to scrub the bloody old stairs that we run up and down on, every day - not the same girl - they used to take certain ones that had to do that, and different ones to have to make the bed, and they had this all worked out. I hated scrubbing that floor - steps - way up two flights - you had to scrub all that - you had to do it. Some of those girls used to rather work in the lower kitchen where they cooked - some of the girls used to have to go down there and cook. I was lucky I always managed to get out of that - going to cook. I'd sooner scrub floors than go up there and cook. What you could do with the supervisor - you could say "Could I exchange - instead of going down to cook, could I do something else?" She'd say "Well, if the girl - whoever's doing it - is agreeable." But I don't think he ever knew about that - old Mr. Strapp. There was a lot he didn't know, I'll tell you!! Oh! he was mean for a minister. Everybody said that Mr. McVitty was not like that. If you did wrong he'd give you a chance the first time - but don't do it again. He wouldn't take you up there right away and give you the strap.

They couldn't keep me there because my father was from the States. Mrs. Barnett helped me get out of there. I got blood poisoning in my hand from a rusty needle, so she negotiated with the people - she knew who to talk to - tell them that I wasn't really all Oneida, I was half Onondaga Indian, my father was from the States and she couldn't see why I had to be at the school. My mother put me there. We used to have to go to the post office for our mail. This one day I went after the mail and it was a heck of a long walk from where we lived over to Muncey. My mother used to get mail from my sister over in Detroit, she was looking after her little boy, and my sister would send her money every other week. She sent me out to get the mail and I get over to the post office and there was a whole bunch of people and my cousin was there and she said "Gosh! it's getting dark, you'd better get back." My mother did have a couple of letters and I said "Yes, I'd better get back with these letters." When we come out a great big blizzard come up - god! it was awful, and I didn't have boots on. I just had shoes because it wasn't bad when I left. She says "Stop in my place till it stops." So I stopped in there. It was getting on - it was about 10 o'clock and her mother says "It's stopped snowing now. Maybe she could wear my boots on top of her shoes, and we'll walk her

home." Her brother and her walked me home, and it was close to 11 by the time I got home. My cousin told my mother, she said "It was so bad she couldn't come home right away so she stayed at our place." My mother didn't believe it - I don't know where she thought I'd be. Anyway she ended up putting me in Mt. Elgin school. When I came out of school I stayed at my Granny Danford's because my mother had moved into town to St. Thomas. I was 12 going on 13 when I went there and I stayed 2 years. I never would have got out if it hadn't been for Mrs. Barnett - my hand was all swollen. I had to go to the nurse every day to dress that hand of mine. They had the Doctor come in and look at it. He was going to cut it open because it was all swollen up. But instead of that he took all the pus out of it and bandaged it up and give me a shot. He said the poison was gone "You won't lose your arm!" he says! They used to have him just come down every two weeks - the doctor that used to come down and look at us ones that were sick.

I did go to school, but later on I never did get back. I was in Grade 7 when I was there and Grade 8 when I left. But you couldn't get a good education for going just half-a-day. You didn't learn too darn much there I'll tell you. My brother used to come down and bring me soap - decent soap - they used to have that Lifebuoy soap - it was horrible. He'd give me money, and we'd go up to Muncey once a week if you had money to spend when you'd get there.

The girls got along pretty good. A couple of times that A - she'd grab my hair from the back when we were standing in line - jealous cuz I had long hair I guess! I tried to avoid her as much as I could. K, she says "Dorothy," she says, "why don't you just slap her a couple of times. She'd cut out pulling your hair." I says "Well, you know what would happen. I would be the one go up to Mr. Strapp and getting the strap. He wouldn't touch her." He was always after me. Waiting for me to make one mistake. When I was sitting down sewing she come from behind and grabbed my hair and I slapped her that time. I threw her half way down the stairs. If it hadn't been for Mrs Barnett I would have got the strap that time. But she knew it wasn't my fault - I didn't start it. That put a stop to the pulling hair. You either fight for yourself or you get beat up. The Oneida girls used to hang around together.

I don't remember anybody making repairs the two years I was there. Some of those rooms upstairs - the floors was creaky. And the baths they had - they had little tubs - I think there was six all lined up on the one side, and you could just stand in there. You couldn't sit right down in there, and all the girls had to take turns. And towels - there was one dinky towel - that was supposed to dry you? That Lifebuoy soap - you could open the door and smell it - that medicated stuff - it was something else.

We used to have a lot of fun - they used to have a sort of a garage down there - the car never was in there. We used to go in there and some of the girls would play the mouth organ and we'd square dance down there. All the girls would get a partner and we'd square dance!! We had to make our own fun. I never seed them taking you anywhere to a circus or anything. We used to get groups together and sing, steal rhubarb and eat it out there - we'd be so hungry!! It tasted good if you put salt on that thing - it took the bitter taste away. We used to steal that rhubarb. They had a stack of it that one side of the building. We used to steal the green apples. Some of those girls that worked in the lower kitchen, they used to bring the raw oatmeal up there, and we used to eat that too - just the way it was - not cooked. We had fun as far as that goes - companionship anyway.

I think Mr. Strapp was just there for the bloody money he could get out of it. I don't think he had an affection - he should never have been in there with children. He was mean - you'd never think a minister would be, but he was. He was mean. Mr. Dodson was good to the kids - the schoolteacher - he was nice to the children. He'd never report you to Mr. Strapp even if you couldn't do what he told you - where arithmetic and that was concerned. He never said "I'm going to send you to Mr. Strapp." I never heard that from Mr. Dodson while I was there, though a lot of them said he did. He told me that time "Dorothy," he says, "I don't think you stole that book." I says "No, I didn't steal it, but I had it, because I wouldn't squeal on the girl that give it to me to look at." Nobody liked him in that school down there - he was a minister but he was miserable. He didn't have anything kind to say to any of the children in there. I sure was glad to get out of there.

I didn't have anything like any sexual abuse - nothing like that. One thing I will say about old Strapp - I don't think he bothered the girls. I don't know how he could, because all of them hated him - they all did. None of them had a good word for him, cuz he was mean, mind you, that guy. He enjoyed punishing the children, I'll tell you that. I know some of the girls that were brought up in there and given the strap - if he missed and hit you on your arm, some of them would have great big welts on their arm where he'd hit them with the strap. I never heard anybody say a good word about him. I went to his church before I went to the school, and he seemed to be all right with the church, as far as the church was concerned, he was preaching up there. I never thought he'd be that mean.

He'd catch us talking Indian. He'd come around "If I find out who's talking Indian is going to get the strap. Do yous hear that? This is an English school and you must talk English." We used to get together and talk Indian - the Oneida girls. Mrs. Daniels used to say "These Oneida girls are the instigators of all the trouble in the school."!!! They had to have a reason to take us up and give us the strap but you had to watch it. They caught us eating that bloody rhubarb one time and we thought we were going to get it, but they couldn't prove who went over the fence first - nobody would squeal on the other ones, so they punished us all. We had all this salt we got from one of the girls who worked in the kitchen - they were supposed to be cooking the meals for us. We got this salt from her, to put on our rhubarb. And green apples. You have to wonder why we never got sick from all those green apples.

They made sure we got a decent meal when they come to visit - that was the only time we got what you would say a decent meal. I guess he questioned some of the people - the guy that was there that day - he said one of the girls was saying "How come we got such a good meal today?" that you never have eggs here. They said "Yeah, we never have eggs any other time." I often wonder why they didn't investigate that - why he didn't go ahead and report it. When we were going off to Church he says "I'll get you for that crack." I says "What crack?" Like I didn't know!! I think he knew damn well he couldn't punish me cuz he'd never catch me. I can just see him like yesterday - his face would get so red, he'd get right down to the end and almost catch me, and then I'd jump on top of the desk and come all the way down the side, and he went back along this side again, and his face was just beet red, he was so mad. Strap in one hand - he would have hit me with it if he'd ever caught me, but he couldn't catch me.

It was a bright sunny day when they told me I could go home. A beautiful spring day. I still had my hand in a bandage and I was walking across that bridge from Muncey to the Oneida side. The birds were singing and it was just a beautiful day. I used to pray every night before I'd go to bed that I'd get myself out of there - something would happen and I could go home.

Susie Doxtator
1930 - 1941

I was an orphan so I liked it there. But if I'd had a father and mother I don't think I would have liked it there. It was a good school - we learned a lot. We learned how to keep house and be clean and look after ourselves. I went there when I was about seven, but I only came home for a holiday one year and I stayed there the rest of the time. When we stayed there all summer it was nice because we got paid for

doing all the work. In the summer holidays all the ones who had fathers and mothers came home and we had to do all the mending of the clothes that they left. We did learn all about cooking and to keep ourselves clean. I guess it was all right if you didn't have no mother and father. They both died when I was a baby. I lived with my aunt. When I was old enough to get out of the school they got me a job in St.

Thomas as a housekeeper in a home, where I stayed right in. I just went as far as Grade 7. I would have wanted to go to high school but I wasn't that smart. I didn't like school anyway.

We done all the laundry, ironing - whatever had to be done. We had to scrub way upstairs - we had to go up the steps to get there, with pails of water. I was 18 when I left - old enough to know better!! I did the domestic science and weaving course - I liked that, but I forgot how to do it now. We learned how to can and cook different things. We done a lot of canning - strawberries. We used to get the strawberries just on Sundays. The meals weren't too bad either, but on Mondays was the lousiest meals, and that's the day we worked the hardest. We done all the laundry - sometimes we didn't get too much of a meal there and we'd go hungry. We just got simple meals - potatoes - mostly stew. We used to get two slices of bread at noon, and again at suppertime. We made our own butter - homemade butter but it wasn't very good butter - the kids didn't know how to make butter. We always had special meals on Christmas and New Year's, Thanksgiving. We always had a lot of chickens - we'd get about 23 chickens to do everybody.

The staff were - well, some of them were nice, but some of them were kinda mean. They would slap us. One lady tried to do that to me - I just slapped her right back. Nothing happened to me. I was all right after they found out I wouldn't take it. I just couldn't see anybody doing that to anybody.

The ones that had a father and mother there could come home at Easter and Christmas for the day.

We had to wash out our rags - when we had our periods. That was an awful job. We had to wear uniforms - one for everyday and one for Sundays. On Sundays we'd get to wear our own clothes to go to Church. A lot of girls came from pretty wealthy families and they'd get big parcels of stuff. I never got nothing.

McVitty had just left and old Strapp was there. He was all right after he knew you wouldn't take the dirt from him. I think they were glad to get rid of me because I used to stick up for everybody and I got heck from the staff.

One bad thing - the worst thing I know about that school, is that they wouldn't let us talk our own language. If they heard us talking our own language we'd get punished. I didn't know how to speak English. I didn't forget it, but a lot of people didn't understand me when I did speak my own language, because I didn't speak it quite right. I speak it now. I got the strap a lot of times for speaking my language. Strapp would do it - that's why I came to hate him. I worked for him and his wife the last year I was there. I just worked for him in the staff kitchen. The staff kitchen was good because you ate whatever the staff ate - the good meals. Their meals were a lot better. They didn't take notice of us - they were just there for the money.

I had two teachers - I got to be their pets - a couple of teachers. We used to have a choir there that sang at Church

every Sunday, and we had a man come from London and teach on piano lessons, which I took and didn't do me no good!! It was fun at the time but I wasn't good enough to play piano.

We learned how to cook all kinds of dishes - but that was for the staff. They really had the top meals. There used to be two girls that looked after the stove and it was their job to cook porridge in the morning. It was yukky because they didn't know how to cook it. It was like somebody spit in it. I never could eat it. Everything was watered down - even the syrup. We'd get whole milk and that would be watered down.

One time an Inspector come without telling the staff he was coming, and it was suppertime, and everybody was eating, and he come downstairs to where the dining room was, and he walked around. Then he asked the big boys if they were getting enough to eat, and they all said "No." The bigger boys were working on the farm and they should have got enough to eat but they didn't. So they told him that their meals weren't good enough and the next day they got a whole loaf of bread!! We had everything there to have good meals, because they planted everything, and they made a great big hole and stored it under the ground. If we wanted potatoes, turnips, whatever, we just had to go and get it under the ground. I know we got a lot of stew. We had cows and pigs there to kill for food - we never got too much eggs but we had a lot of chickens. Just at Easter I think we got one egg. They used to sell them out - we should have got them. We used to make our own cottage cheese. We used to get kinda angry - we'd see them cows and they used to take it out of the school and go and sell it.

In the winter time I didn't like it either because we didn't have no quilts to be warm, for the bed. We used to sneak up to the attic and they had great big fur rugs up there and we used to bring those down to cover us. When you got sick they didn't believe you - you had to be half dead before they believed you were sick. You didn't get the very best of care. There was supposed to be a nurse, but if anything was wrong all she knew was vaseline - if you had a headache she'd give you vaseline.

Actually it wasn't bad there - we used to have a place to stay, and three meals a day, and a place to sleep. I wouldn't want to go through that again - not what I know now I wouldn't! There wasn't any sexual abuse that I know of.

I ran away once and I came home to my aunt's, but they were so poor they couldn't look after anybody else either. Anyway we got caught and sent back to the school. They didn't punish us. When we sassied the staff back, we'd get punished for that.

The place where I worked I had every other weekend off, so I could come down on the reserve and visit with my sister and my aunt. I always did domestic work - I worked for a lawyer in St. Thomas for about two years.

Four of my kids went to Mohawk for 2 years. They didn't like it there - then I got 'em out.

You had to be tough in those days. We used to have to scrub that old school on our hands and knees. I remember one morning I had one more piece of floor to scrub, and the bell rung to go to breakfast, and I wanted to finish this one little piece. That's when the staff came along and she said "Didn't you hear that bell?" I said "Yeah, but I want to finish this piece," and she slapped me. I was big enough to stand up for myself, so I just grabbed my scrubrag and gave it to her across the face. I had to go to the office that time, but I told the principal why I hit her. I said "I'm not little any more, I'm big enough to stand up for myself." So he told me not to do that any more. I says "I won't if they leave me alone." If they ever tried to strap me they'd get it right back. They was nice sometimes but they could be pretty damn mean too.

We did get special meals on Sundays - we got a special supper - pickles and potatoes and meat and a cinnamon bun. It wasn't too bad when we had the real dietitian take over - she used to balance all our meals. What we should have got [looking at menus], we never got. I know we got a lot of stew - I don't remember getting meatloaf - maybe there was hamburg some days. We never got pie too often - maybe once a year.

There was a lot of staff there that cared for us, but there was some staff that would rather beat us up. I was so glad when I got big enough to stand on my own feet. I got in trouble sometimes hitting staff back, but they always asked for it - they always hit me first and I hit 'em back. That's where my trouble was. Mrs. Erratt - I was her pet! She was going to take me with her when she left, she was going to sorta adopt me. I really liked her. Miss Lind - she was another nice one. She was kinda young and she'd never let us go inside at recess, she'd always make us stay out and do

exercise. Joblin - he was nice - he always took the children's part, if we were nice. Miss Stanley - she was sort of a nurse - she was the one that was always giving us vaseline.

I was sorry they pulled that building down - it was a beautiful building, they could have used it for something. We had three dormitories, the new one, the little one, and the old one. They all had plumbing. In the night we shouldn't have been in the kitchen - but you turn the lights and ooh!! it was black with cockroaches. We'd get cold milk to drink. There was an orchard and they had great big Spys, and when we knew the staff was in eating their lunch we'd quick go in this orchard and steal apples. They wouldn't let us eat them - we had to steal them.

They were good to my kids at the Mohawk, because my husband went there to school and the principal knew him. They knew what he'd do if he beat up on my kids. He was good to them. My husband got expelled from Brantford school because he got in a fight with the principal. Cuz they saw him - they beat up on a little kid this big - one of the staff claimed that he was the one that stole this car blanket that go in the car. They blamed this little boy and he beat him something awful - they didn't even recognize him when they got through with him. My husband stepped in and he beat the principal up for that. He says "I'm a big boy and you're not going to beat up a little boy around here." So when that summer came they expelled him.

I was always in a fight - with the staff. I got along good with the girls. You had to learn to fight.

I don't know why I ran away - getting bored, I guess. I ran away with A.S. - ended up in Tillsonburg - we walked there. They didn't even punish us - it wouldn't do any good if they did punish us.

Lila Ireland
1931 - 1939

I don't know if anybody liked it. I wanted to go there. My Dad was there with W. W. Shepherd, and my Mum was there with Mr. McVitty. McVitty was still there when I first went to school but all I remember about him is he was big. I think I went there in the fall of 1931 - cuz I was 9 and I turned 10 in December. I was there 7 years I think. I was 17 when I left there. O. B. Strapp was Vice-principal. There were young men and women there when I went there - some were in their twenties - they were going to school - I don't know why they didn't let them go. I stayed there one summer - the kids that had homes to go to went home in the summer - but a lot of kids didn't have homes to go to. But they needed the bigger kids - if we had all left, there would have been just little kids.

I don't know if anybody liked Strapp - I didn't like him. His name was Strapp and he used his name. He didn't have

that type of personality either - he wasn't the kinda person who attracted kids. You can't really say he didn't have an interest in the kids - he tried - he had visions of having the young people have their own band. The only thing we did - the girls had music lessons, we had a choir.

I don't know why [the Indian agent] said [This girl is recognised as a good pupil]. I was not "a good pupil" - I was pretty dumb!

I ran away - four of us. We got caught - we weren't really hiding anyway. We were just over here [Oneida] - we had no intentions of going any place - this was our home. We were here three or four days. Then we decided we wanted to go to the store and somebody reported us. Anyhow they caught up to us and took us back. We were punished by being restricted in our activities - if there were some special things going on we were curtailed. It was punishment enough just to be there! Yet I wanted to go there - I was dumb - 9 years old. My older sister had been there. Really it was a haven for a lot of children. We got three meals a day and clean bedding, clean clothes once a week. Saturday was bath day and clean clothes day.

When I first went there the cook couldn't even cook beans. We had soup that was just beans and water - no meat. Eventually it got better. Strapp let all the old officers go and they got young officers. We got porridge every morning, and we got a substantial lunch and supper I guess. I don't recall getting any meat - I worked in the kitchen but I don't remember serving any meat. Maybe we didn't have meat because I recall one girl going there and she complained that we didn't have any meat. She left - her father did take her away. I know we got butter on our bread in the morning cuz we used to butter the bread. They made their own butter there. Maybe we didn't get butter all the time. What I recall most is the milk - it was so skimmed it was blue. Then there'd be a change in the spring when the cows would be let out and they'd eat grass - and the milk would be horrible. They used to sell the cream to Silverwoods. They planted fields of grain, corn, they had a big barn of Holstein cattle, and two great big bulls, two teams of horses, and chickens and pigs. They had a garden with strawberries and raspberries, rhubarb, watermelon and muskmelon. I got so sick of tomatoes. The girls in the kitchen did an awful lot of canning - we ate the tomatoes, and we'd get a small bit of strawberries sometimes.

We had classes - they called it domestic science then - those were good. We learned everything - serving tables - serve from the left and clear from the right! - your linens and all your silverware. In that way it was good and helpful later on. We did sewing - the girls made all the girls' uniforms, and we made quilts and even pillowcases. When I first went there Mrs. Barnett was the girls' supervisor. The beds had to be made just right and lined up so that the cuffs of the sheets were all turned over exactly the same - there was even a board to measure them with. You had either 8 or 10 beds to make. So then you come along and look at it and every one of those cuffs had to be absolutely straight and all even or she'd rip them all out, and that would maybe make you late for class cuz you had to do them over. She was good to the girls - not if you were bad though. If she thought you weren't toeing the line she could be downright miserable. She would bring a cup of tea to class and she would share it with the kids - she must have had more than one cup of tea! She taught knitting. She wasn't all bad - after she left she came back periodically to visit the girls. She had a Model T Ford - one boy was privileged to look after her car - he'd get it out for when she went somewhere - they must have got one weekend off a month.

I liked the teachers - they were all likeable. When I graduated from Grade 8 Mr. Dodson said they only let us pass because we were all too old!! That was really something - but he was just joking. It was difficult for me

to learn math - it just wouldn't sink in - the teachers really tried. I don't know how I ever did pass Grade 8!! I wanted to go to high school - my earnest desire would have been to become a nurse, but my father said "You'll be a good cook" - I suppose meaning all I'd ever do is get married and cook. I worked in a nursing home. Some of the pupils went on to high school - I know of two - they were exceptionally bright students. A few of us they called graduates - they made us stay a whole year before we were allowed to leave there. I took the weaving course - I just hated that class. We never got to keep anything that we made. We made scarves and bags. They were in a pretty pattern - one girl made a pretty lining and put wooden handles on thinking she could buy it, but they wouldn't let her keep it.

I got the strap on occasion - if I did something. I don't know what I did. I guess I got the strap for running away. Or being in the wrong place at the wrong time - if you were in the main hall when you weren't supposed to be, or up in the dorms.

There were a lot of advantages - the only disadvantage really was you couldn't be home with your folks. I don't know why I ran away - I just wanted to come home I guess. Or else I couldn't come home for the summer. Well you'd just get - nowadays they call it burnout - fed up - you wanted some freedom - when you're doing the same thing constantly day in day out.

Everyone had their chores to do and you knew what time they had to be finished, so you accepted that you had to do the work - I never really thought I had too much work to do. There was one nurse - every time somebody did something wrong, she made them scrub somewhere as a punishment. We used to call her Miss Scrubheart.

They used to have recreation days - field-days. We had recitals when everyone who had music-lessons would play, or someone would come in and entertain us. We had sing-songs which Mr. Dodson led, and we'd do a play at Christmastime. We had CGIT - Canadian Girls in Training - like Girl Guides - once a week. At Hallowe'en and Christmas we'd have special activities - recitations and drills. It wasn't all dull!! We had a music teacher from Six Nations - Mrs. Jamieson - her husband looked after the horses. Then there were Mr. and Mrs. Kapayo - and he had a helper - they looked after the chickens. We must have had pigs - because when they killed them we heard them screaming. I don't know what they did with them.

The school was well run - well organized. They had the girls picking tomatoes and carrots. We'd steal food - that was part of being at Mt. Elgin!! We didn't steal it out of the kitchen - they used to have the carrots piled for the winter in a big pile of earth and we'd dig them out. If you eat too many carrots you get terrible indigestion - then they'd holler for the nurse. Miss Daniels would come and she'd be angry cuz she'd know what's causing the indigestion. Sometimes there'd be an epidemic - chicken-pox, measles - and everybody would be sick and there'd only be a few left to serve the people. The only thing that wasn't really looked after was if you had something like an appendix - it was hard for them to take it seriously. Dr. McLeod would come but all the medication they ever had was aspirin and cough medicine. If you ever got sick Miss Daniels gave you a cup of fruit juice and castor oil. Then you had to drink a glass of cold water - you had to take it - she just saw that you took it. Then you'd just have to run out to the outhouse - the longhouse we called it. They did have indoor toilets in the dormitories but you weren't allowed to go there during the day. You even had to find your own paper.

They had a dentist about once a year.

Manson Ireland
1932 - 1939

My Dad died August 28th, 1932, when I was 12 years old, and that's when they sent my brother Chester and me to school there - on September 15th 1932. I didn't have any schooling before that. Well, I went to school the odd time before that, but that's about it, and the only reason I went was because my mother used to give me an egg sandwich to take!! I was 18 when I left in 1939 - they kicked me out!

McVitty was there when I arrived. He was really tall. He was bending over and I was looking straight up at him to talk to him - that's how tall he was. He was talking to me, and my mother was there, and whatever he said my mother would tell me in Indian, and I would answer. I didn't speak a word of English when I went there. They never really told us not to speak our language - we had to learn English, but we spoke Oneida to each other right through. I can still speak Oneida fluently - I didn't lose it.

McVitty was there for a year or so after I got there. He was all right - from what I know of him. Then we got the Reverend Oliver B. Strapp for principal. He was very strict - he was an Englishman. He was in the First World War. When I came out of that school and I went in the army there wasn't any difference, because he was just as strict as the army. We had another supervisor - Mrs. Erratt. She was very strict in her own way but she wasn't mean, she was nice to us. She wasn't nearly as strict as the principal was. He'd come and bash you over the head if you didn't do what you were told, but then two of the boys socked him one and that fixed him - he didn't hit anybody after that. There were these two guys who were already almost adults and they had girlfriends. He had a strap and he was going to strap them. He went to swing and they grabbed the strap and clipped him on the jaw and knocked him on the stairway. When he came to, he went back into his office and called the RCMP. Early next morning - 7 o'clock - the RCMPs were there, and they made them go back into their own civilian clothes. Eight o'clock they gave them their marching ticket - they kicked them out of that school.

The farm instructor's name was Robertson and he was also a captain in the First World War - he was another strict guy. Everything was 1, 2, 3. He corrected the guys and he would give them a slap on the head or something, but some of these guys came down with pitchforks and they said -"Hey - don't do that again." He understood it. He had boys there that were school age and if they'd fight, some of the senior boys would step in and take over.

When we first went there, we never had pyjamas or anything to wear, so whenever we got up we were bare - going to the washroom. Miss Daniels would be in charge of us and she'd spot us, so we'd go running into the washroom and stay there till she closed the door. Eventually after a couple of years the principal got us pyjamas, but it was terrible before that with that woman supervisor there. She'd come in there with the strap - BANG! BANG! BANG! you got it if you were running around. Her last visit would be at 9 o'clock, but that didn't stop her running in there if she knew something was wrong.

There were six or seven long tables in the dining room, and the seniors sat on the ends of those tables, to correct the other fellas - us young guys. Chester and I were sitting together and we couldn't speak a word of English - this was a couple of weeks after we got there. We were sitting there talking back and forth and laughing, and suddenly this woman, Miss Barnett, hit us BANG! BANG! with a ruler right on the head. One of the girls sitting right across the aisle spoke up for us and had a few words with that woman, and she quit hitting us. That was about all that happened when we spoke our language. Anyway, it wasn't really our language that they were after, it was to be quiet. You couldn't talk in the dining-room when you were eating. It was discipline. It was an English discipline. We had army men to look after us. Everybody had to stand up and our seats went back together. Everybody stood up, and faced the way they were going to go, and they marched out. That's the army all over again. Some people say that they were hard on people - on the children, but it wasn't bad for me. We didn't see any sex abuse in our time - of course the guys and girls had girlfriends and boyfriends. One guy fell in love with the boys' supervisor, and he was one of the seniors. We knew something was going on, but we never could find out just what it was, until one day the principal found out something about it and she was told to pack up and leave at the end of the month. I went down to the barn and this guy was feeding the calves, and he had tears running down his face. He was in love and his woman had to go away!!

We went to school half-a-day until Grade 8. I was three

years in beginners. My math was up and everything else I could do, but the grammar held me back. It was training for survival rather than book work. The school gave us training in carpentry, and we had training on livestock and poultry and horses, and we also had a chance to go and work in the fields. I had to work on the farm - milking cattle and working on the machines. We raised Leghorns - white Sussex and we used to sell the eggs. We candled all the good eggs and sold them to market. We had approximately 50 head of cattle. We had butter - we were churning it ourselves. By the time we got the cream churned there wasn't that much butter left, and so what butter there was we ate it right there at the school. There were at least 20 staff and 150 pupils, and if we ate butter every day there wasn't much left.

The difference between today and those days is like the difference between night and day. What they trained us for in those days was how to get along in the world, without too much reading and writing. You went out and you learned how to feed chickens, you learned how to get the rations right when you're feeding hogs - feeding the weaning ration, then the growing ration - mash - then the fattening mash. You've got to mix those things so you've got the proper protein supplement in the grain - that's how you get your bacon. Those times were pretty tough. You only got one cent per pound of grain that you fed. They used to tell us all this stuff. The same with poultry - I was in charge of poultry and the first year we raised 1000 Leghorns, and out of 1000 I lost 350 chicks. They got coccidiosis. So I told the principal how many I lost and he was mad. I thought he was going to fire me. I said "Well, next guy that takes over, I hope he does better." He said "What other guy. You're going to stay." He sent for some books and articles on poultry from the OAC at Guelph. I studied them and worked at those books trying to teach myself, and also the principal was there to help me out and he would ask me about them. The second year I lost 18 chicks and actually I learned a lot. That's the difference between knowing and not knowing.

I stayed at the school in the summer of 1936 to work. They had this old International 10/20 tractor with the steel lugs, which was really hard to ride on. They used it to run this new combine they had gotten. It was the first combine that ever came out, and we were all kinda green on this thing - even the principal and the farm instructor - as to how ripe the grain had to be before you could combine it. In the early days it had to be quite right, because if it wasn't right the wheat would green-heat. After the first cutting we put the wheat on the granary floor and in two or three days it was green-heating all the time because it was too green to pick, and we'd have to take the shovel and shovel it one way one day, and shovel it the other way the next day. It meant that you had wait another week or two weeks, and then you'd combine and it didn't green-heat. I used to stay there all summer when I was on the machine - we got paid for it -

there were no jobs out of the school anyway. We had a 700 acre farm there, on land that was leased from the Chippewas. When the school terminated in '46, everything was turned over to the Chippewa band - the barns and everything.

Really I think the school was worthwhile for me. Towards the end I had four years of four hours a week training. Tuesdays and Thursdays I went up for manual training for two hours - we had a class of copper working - we made copper chandeliers, and I learned silver soldering, and blacksmithing, and learned to temper stainless steel so we could sharpen knives so they kept an edge, so for me it was all right. They were showing us how to do lathe work with metal, and lathe work with wood to shape spindles. Well, I went up there and I was going to make a plenishing hammer for taking up copper. So I put a slot in there with a hacksaw blade; and there's this other hole for the drill and I put this point in there, and this is the one that turns. I got the dog for the steel and I put this big machine on there, and I went along and I just tightened that thing and it cut the steel. I was trying to make a bulky hammer but I was going to get it polished for a plenishing hammer. Well, I didn't have the right dog on this end where I put the slots and it really tightened up like the bits on a drill, and these dogs on the end curled up when I tightened it. The principal was away when I was doing this. I left the thing on one side and I went out to the farm to clean the stables and get ready for milking. In the meantime he came back, so at suppertime he already knew what went on and he was asking people who was up there and spoiled the lathe. To tell the truth I didn't know I spoiled it. I went up there to look but it looked to me like nothing happened. So I went up there to the principal and I asked him "What really happened to that?" So he started telling me, because I told him "I was up there, I'm trying to make a plenishing hammer." Well, he agreed that it was all right for me to make a plenishing hammer, but he said "You should have consulted us for what you wanted to do." I said "I thought I knew already." But apparently I didn't. So you know what? He said "You tell your teacher I want to see you 10 o'clock tomorrow morning up there." I thought: Manson Ireland, you're going to get a real good licking. They took me up there, and strict as he was he said "Tell me what you were doing." So I showed him I wanted to make a replenishing hammer for my copper work. So then he showed me this other big gadget that he put on the slide on the lathe. He said "This is what you're going to do: this holds it there, then you can work that thing back and forth." Then he said "It's not that bad, I can fix it and we can still use it. But next time you'd better let me know what you're going to do." He made me make that hammer - that same morning. He made me go at the lathe, and I put a new one on the handle, and he was there all the time showing me how to do it, and helped to shine that thing up. He took the time - instead of beating me up - he took the time to teach me to do that. But I guess you could say I was in trouble till then. Strapp himself - he knew about all these things. I was running the laundry - back in 1938 - during the summer months when the staff was on holiday. One day the thing got overheated and there's a safety thing in the back with a hole in it and that was full of lead. When it got overheated it melted that lead and the water started pouring out of it, so we had to stop the laundry until the next day when the principal was there. I said "That thing at the back was leaking - that's how the water was getting out and the steam." So he looked in there with a light and said "OK, take it out." So we took a pipe wrench and we took it out and took it upstairs, and he made me clean all that out and he plugged one end of it and he lifted the lid. First of all we had to put flux in there so it would really stick to the side of it, then we filled it full of lead again and put it back, and that's all there was to it. Our principal was teaching me all this stuff. I don't know why I was the only one getting taught, but I know there were others learned a lot there.

We got plenty to eat. We used to roll our own oats. We ate cracked wheat - oatmeal. It wasn't as bad as people said. The one blame thing I never liked was parsnips. Do you remember when they had a dry season out west - they couldn't grow anything - in Saskatchewan? We sent about four carloads of turnips, potatoes, carrots and parsnips. I was in charge of loading and I told the boy "Load up them blame parsnips."

I gained their trust at the school. One time one of the guys had a girlfriend and she ran away from there with another girl because she was having trouble with her boyfriend. This guy wanted to come after her - he knew where she was. Mrs. Erratt said "No." "Just a minute," she said, "if Manson goes, then you can go, but you can't go if Manson doesn't go." So he came running down to the playroom and said "Manson come on. We've got to go across the river and get the girls." We had to walk over here - we had shoes that were all right for the weather, but the girls were wet through - they only had leather shoes. I knocked at the door. We opened the door and walked right in and there they were sitting behind the stove with their stockings off - they were hanging up drying. The girls were drying their feet, so we talked to the woman there while they sat there and then we left. They came with us but that one

darn girl was stubborn. We got to the corner, and my mother lived down there. We had come that way and I had said to my mother "I want some hot biscuits." But we couldn't get our hot biscuits although my mother said she had them made - she was standing at the door. So I yelled to her "We can't go, these girls are ready to run." When they got down to the road they went running up towards St. Thomas. We went running after them and they fought and we couldn't get near them. I said "You'd better get back here. You're really going to get it," and I went running up there, and I managed to turn them and head them back this way. But they were running up that way again. We finally got them home. We went right through to the principal's office, right away, to get in through the front door. Mrs. Erratt talked to the girls - I left right away, I figured it was her job after that, so I left. I don't know if they got a strapping or what.

One time they told me I couldn't go home, so I walked across the river. We used to get some canned goods out of the storeroom - strawberries or something - and go back. We'd walk right across the river. We used to go all over, but we had to be back by a certain time. We never tried to be late - if you were late it was too bad.

I took carpentry in that school, and I used to do some carpentry work around, and I worked in the kitchen upstairs and I put that arborite in it with the metal edges. I put the hardwood floor in the chapel - I did that all alone - it took me two days to do that - I was kinda a lone ranger - doing carpentry. I remember the winter of 1940 I joined the army. After I came out of the school I couldn't get a job as a carpenter, so I worked as a farmhand. When I went into the army they said they wanted carpenters. They gave me a test and I passed it to be a carpenter like the rest of them. The Sergeant Major said to the Captain "That guy's too young to be a carpenter." I had only just turned 19. However the Captain said "That guy answered every question I gave the others, and if they can become carpenters, why not him?" Finally they came out of there and said they had a carpenters' refresher course coming up. So they asked me to go on that course in Guelph and there were 22 guys there for that class, and I was the second highest out of that bunch. Out of 500 marks I got 410. They gave us IQ tests in the army and I got 125.

Ruth Ninham
1933 - 1939

I was put in there by my aunt when I was 12. She did me a favour. She didn't really keep me, but when she did she was very stingy of what I ate. She was mean.

I didn't like it there at first but it was all right after I got to know some of the girls.

The food wasn't the greatest - we didn't get too much.

The only time we got good food was when the principal knew that the guy was coming from Ottawa to check - then it was all hunky-dory. It all depends who worked in the kitchen. In the officers' kitchen it had to be the best, so when you worked up there you ate good. We ate what they ate because we had to serve them and you couldn't come down, so when you worked upstairs with the officers you ate up there too - you ate what they ate and it was definitely better. We used to find worms in the mush. We took the worms out and gave it to the little ones!!! The worms weren't in it any more, but once you see a worm in your porridge, you're not going to eat it are you? We didn't anyway. It was a long hall and the officer would walk down and we'd pass the dish down after she'd gone so she wouldn't see - same way passing the dish back. Sometimes we'd get caught. We had to eat everything up, so we either had to give it away or smuggle it out somehow if we didn't like it. We had to keep pretty quiet in the dining room - we only had so long to eat.

In the back yard - it reminds me of a race track - we used to walk round and round all day. There was a fence and an orchard on the other side. We used to steal apples - if you got caught you got sent up to the office. The boys used to give us some carrots or whatever it was from the garden.

One time I was working down in the kitchen. I had to cut the bread - and I had the keys to the pantry. Another girl had the keys to the store-room where they kept the butter. I was really hungry for pan bread. There was a whole bunch of us and each one took what we needed - we stole it - and we said "On Saturday let's make some pan bread." So we made it, and I was taking music lessons and I asked this girl to see when it was cooked - to watch it. I was just coming downstairs and there was Mr. Strapp coming down there just as the girl was taking the bread out of the oven. So he followed her into the dining-room - it was a great big pan. He asked her what she was doing, so I said "I made it." He said "What's she doing with it?" I said "I asked her to take it out." He told her to take it upstairs and put it in the garbage - of course it didn't go in the garbage!! So he sent me up to the dormitory. He knew I wasn't in it alone, but I wouldn't squeal. The girls were so scared - they thought I was going to squeal on them. I said "I'm not a squealer." They thought I was going to get a strapping on my bum. He came in the dormitory and asked why I did it - he was as nice as pie. I said "You know, we're poor, and we're used to pan bread at home - we get hungry for it." Well, he said "Every month, whoever works in the kitchen - once a month - they can make it." So that's what they done after that!! I never did get the strap.

And if you were punished you couldn't go home for Easter or whatever holiday was coming up. On Saturday, when we knew everybody had gone to town, we'd go to this girl's parents or we go to my grandfather's, and we'd get back before everyone came back from town. One time we got caught - we were coming back up the hill and there was Mr. Strapp standing waiting for us!! We didn't get the strap - we got privileges taken away - but we still went home again, cuz they'd always go away for Easter or whatever. If there was a holiday he'd always go away and there was only one officer. We didn't live close but we'd go and my uncle would bring us back.

The work that we were made to do - in a way it was nice. I wouldn't say nice - but at least we had an idea what the outside world is going to be like. Maybe that's why people have different feelings about it, but the way I look at it, it's a hard world out there, so more or less they were preparing us for the outside world. I went to work in Port Stanley, and then in Toronto and Detroit. I did domestic work.

When I finished I was going to take up for a dietitian, but there was no help to go to high school. My grandfather would have helped me if he could. I was going to go to Preston but they closed it and made an army camp out of it. Either a dietitian or a nurse. We were trained up to a certain point what to do when people were sick - so basically we had a knowledge of it. I was there when Cody Claus fell out of the window. The screen was out of the window - up on the third floor. That should have been replaced right away - it was out for quite some time. I happened to look up - and you know how you push yourself up on the window - he was pushing himself up and I was just going to say "He's going to fall down," when he came right down. I ran around the building but I couldn't catch him - he was on the ground by the time I got there. For the longest time I'd close my eyes and I'd see him falling - so for a long time I was scared to go to sleep.

One time I was put up in the attic - we had to scrub the whole attic for a punishment. There was two of us. I never ran away further than Oneida - we just really went for a walk. We used to even go and help look for girls that run away. We knew where they were but we'd go some place else just so we'd stay out longer!! We'd go to the other end of the reserve to look for them, and so many girls would go that way and then we'd all meet back, and see if we found them. If we didn't find them then the police would step in, or the Agent.

Mr. Dodson used to put us to sleep. He was a good teacher to a certain extent but he used to kinda put us to sleep. Mr. Johnston was a teacher up there too.

Strapp said that if we were caught talking our Native language we'd get the strap. He had a nickname - [Indian word for strap] - and we used it to tell if he was coming. Some damn fool went and told him and he knew - he said "Never mind [nickname] - I'm coming." He knew what his name meant - someone told him. I could speak my language - I still speak it. Some of them - they'd start September and go home in June, and "Oh - they can't talk Indian, they forgot." They were full of shit - how can you forget your own Native tongue?

The school had its bad points and its good points.

I got on all right with the other kids - though they had gangs. They got mad at one another - they came to blows once in a while I guess. There wasn't really any bullying - but M and I kept to ourselves.

There used to be a dance-hall up the hill, and the girls used to run away and go up there - that was after they took the locks off the dormitory window to see if they could trust us!! M and I would go out during the week. We had to put our clothing at the foot of the bed, but we'd get some extra clothes and pillows and put them in the bed as dummies. We never went on the weekend when the other girls went to the dances cuz they'd always get caught! We just went for a walk, or we went to her place - we'd get something to eat. Then we had a night watchman - he knew, but he never told on us - he helped us get back in.

I went home in the summers - but one time somebody stole something - stole some money from an officer maybe - and we couldn't go home for half the summer till they found out who did it. There was an old man on the reserve and he was a big tease. One time I told him to "Go to heck" and he told my aunt I swore at him and told him to "Go to hell," and she sent me back to school two weeks before school started. One time I went home for a month to look after my

grandma, but then I had to go back to school.

We had some fun - I was in a choir and we'd come to London to sing, and we'd have Christmas concerts. We'd go sleighriding, skating with those funny skates you put on your shoe. We played ball sometimes with the boys on their side. If there was extra bread we'd put it under the table to the boys, or if there was any buttered bread left over we gave it the boys at dinnertime. We didn't get that much to eat. On Saturday we'd put our money together and the baker used to come and we'd buy bread. We did get hungry sometimes. The only time we got good food was when they were checking on the school from Ottawa. And parsnips - this one time almost everybody must have got turned off parsnips - this one kid had scabs on his head and it looked so bad, and the way the parsnips were fixed - nobody could eat it. We did canning - rhubarb - they taught us the basics.

Melva George
1933 - 1940

I was there 8 years. I graduated when I was 15, and I went back for a weaving course.

The school was at a time when there was no welfare, and if you didn't have parents and you didn't have enough food gathered to last you all year, you were in trouble. That was one thing about us - we lived down the road here, and everything was grown - right from here to the hill. And below the hill was our pasture. We had cattle and pigs, horses, chickens. And then he [grandfather] looked at the women too hard, and that's when they split up and everybody ended up with nothing. The fences started breaking down - to keep the cattle in. But my sister was there, and two brothers from my family.

We came home for holidays, but we didn't have much of a holiday one year. We had the red measles, and we had to stay at the school until it went through the kids. There used to be Silverwoods down the road, and I used to go there every day and wash the separator - for a dollar a day. That was my spending money - that was like $100 today.

It must have been 1940 when I left. I got married in 1943. I think it was 1933 when I went - I was seven anyway. McVitty was there when I first went - just when I was getting acquainted - when they told me I couldn't speak my own language.

When I graduated, I graduated with 86%, and I thought I was the highest in the class, but this L N beat me on art, that's where he pulled up his marks. I didn't go to high school - I would have had to go to Brandon Manitoba if I would have wanted to go to High school at that time. I wanted to work in Detroit, but I couldn't get my birth certificate. I just did housework - babysitting.

My language started coming back. When my husband died, I thought that's what I'd do. I go to Thunder Bay - I

take a course in methods of teaching. It keeps coming out - the different ways of saying words, but my trouble is I don't know if I'm speaking Potawatamie or Ojibway. I would ask a fluent speaker "Is this the way you say that?" Little things like the way you say the word for 'ear'.

That school was better than starving to death. At least we got to eat something, even if it wasn't the best. I remember being so hungry I jumped the fence to get a frozen cabbage.

One of the nice things that happened - we always got a Sunday bun for supper. We appreciated the Sunday bun - it was our sweet for the week. The staff - they got the best of everything and the butter, we just got dry bread. We had skim milk - they had to have the butter for the staff. One time we were having cornmeal for breakfast, and my cornmeal wasn't cooked. It had a great big lump of dry oatmeal - the size of my bowl. And that old Strapp, he seen that I didn't eat it, so he came and stood there over me, and made sure I ate it - raw cornmeal. You couldn't say anything - I had to eat it. And then to top it all off, I used to hate parsnips, and this boy came to the dining-room with his hat on, and Mr. Strapp came and really got after him "Take that hat off," and his head was full of scabs, and I didn't like to eat with somebody like that.

One time I went in the store-room and I was so hungry for peanut butter, I put my hand in the peanut butter pail, and I put some peanut butter in my mouth, and I could hear Mr. Strapp coming - jiggling his keys. And he came in the storeroom and he says "What is there to eat?" I was surprised I was able to answer because my mouth was full of peanut butter!!! So I guess I was troublesome!! I worked in the kitchen and I had to start putting desserts on the table. And that tapioca - ugh! That tapioca looked like fish eyes.

The school was more or less self-supporting - they planted all the vegetables. We worked half-a-day. I was always small, and there was always older girls that would make the porridge and that. I wouldn't be allowed near the stove, so even in the sewing room I'd be darning socks where the other ones would be allowed on the sewing machines. There was always older girls.

We had to clean up the building before we went to school. The outhouse cover was on hinges. There were about ten seats in there. The boys'd get in there and they'd have to shovel that out and take it away.

The boys' dorm was on one side and the girls' on the other, and in the centre was the principal's apartment. The staff had rooms on both sides - supervisors. We used to have our clinic way up in the middle attic, and we had to do the dishes up there when there was chicken pox or something. The ones that had to stay in bed, we had to sterilize the dishes they used.

Behind the main building was another building and it was the classrooms. Then there was barns.

One time I was sliding - we were all able to go sliding that one day, and I head for the post down below the hill and broke my collarbone. My arm was in a sling for quite a while. Another time I got chills and we went for a walk, and I was so cold I couldn't warm up no matter how fast I walked. When I got home I started throwing up and I got sent to bed, I couldn't eat - I can't remember if I drank water. Here I had jaundice and they took me to hospital in London. I turned yellow when I was in the hospital and I couldn't see. I was so skinny and they'd give me extra bread. I remember my ribs were showing. Then after school I'd get a glass of milk or something, two slices of bread with nothing on it.

"Melva George is like a little wild animal and has given us considerable trouble"!!!! [reading report from Strapp to DIA] 'A little wild animal' - that's really something. They must have struck me so hard, to strap me. I had to get my regular treatment. I was a bad girl!! The principal was ready to give us the strap - he really lived up to his name - it suited him!! I think Strapp carried the strap around with him - he always had it handy. McVitty didn't carry the strap around with him - I didn't see it.

I ran away that time because I was so bored. We were having a practice for Christmas carols, and we were nudging each other "Oh, it would be a nice night to go sleighriding - play on the hill eh?" So we snuck out of there - we were by the door to the hallway, and we snuck out of there thinking they wouldn't miss us. We just got out of the door and we went through the upper kitchen, and we looked back, and here the night watchman had seen us, so he come after us with his bedroom slippers on!!! It was a nice night but we thought they were going to catch us over on the hill, so we didn't go to the hill, we went over towards the village at Muncey. We circled around the Mounties' building and got onto the railway tracks. We got as far as Melbourne before

they caught us. We were glad to get caught because it was so cold. The wind and the snow came up and it was really snowing. The Mounties caught us and bring us - we went by a sign with a checkerboard on it and I said "Let's play some checkers." The Mountie said "They're going to play checkers with you when we get you back"!!! Anyway I thought: What's the use of singing Christmas carols? They'd give Bibles to the kids and I always missed out on them. They either give them to the ones in the group ahead of me or the group behind me, so I always missed out. I thought: What's the use of being a Christian, and I always believed in what my grandmother always did - the Ojibwa religion. She had the tobacco.

One time when I was little - we used to have to go to that outhouse before we went to lunch. All the bigger girls went first and I had to wait at the end, so I was late for getting in line for lunch, and that Tilly Barnett, she had her yardstick up high all ready to hit me. She yells at me - she says "Where were you?" "I was in the shithouse," I said. All the girls started laughing at her, and she had to laugh too, and put her yardstick down!!! The shithouse saved me that time.

One of the boys when we were working in the clinic, up in the central attic - one of the boys was coming over - I don't know if he was coming to give us a hand - they used to travel on the roof and the eavestroughs. They were made out of slate, and one of the boys was coming across, and one of those slates come out, and he went sliding down to the eavestrough, and he would have fell over, only there was a nail there, and his jacket caught on there, so he was saved by that nail!!!

Well, they let me take music lessons, which I appreciate, and they musta done that because I was bad eh!! Our music teacher that used to come to Mt. Elgin - he was organist at Metropolitan - his name was T. C. Chattoe. We used to call him 'furry ears' - he had hair growing over his ears!!! I got to play a few hymns, and songs at a concert. I remember this Chief Os-Ke-Non-Ton - he was a Mohawk from Caughnawaga - he musta been a pupil here. He was an opera singer, and he sang at Carnegie Hall in New York - he used to be the usher there and they let him take lessons so he could sing - he had a nice voice.

They had this inspector - his name was Sexton. My brother C - he didn't answer him - and he knocked C right out of his chair - just because he didn't answer him.

I laughed one time - we got sent to the board - we had to do a great big table of multiplying by four, and I hurried up and got my work done and went back to my seat. I made this one little mistake, and this L - I was always competing with him - he just copied my answers. So after he took his seat I went back up and corrected my mistake, and did he ever just roar!!! One time, it was going on Valentine's Day, and he was making valentines. He had one special one that everybody wanted to get from him, and he wouldn't give it to anybody, but I never bothered with him. I knew I'd never get anything from him, but I was the one he chose. I suppose because I didn't bother him.

We used to have our good times. I remember lining in front of the camera. They had Micky Mouse skates - you just strapped them onto your boots, and they were skating around there, they made a pond special beside those trees. Anyway we had this nice skating piece of ice there, and here I am skating in front of the camera, and that was really funny when they showed it to us, everybody was laughing at me. T A was really good on his skates - he'd do all the figures you see on TV - he skated just as well as the champions. And we used to go down and cheer for our local teams in the sports - the ball teams for all the area. Even in wintertime they'd have a team to come be near the river there. We'd go down and cheer for them.

Clyde Peters
1934 - 1941?, 1943? - 1946

I went in 1934 when I was 5. It was hard times and my brother and sister were there. I left in '46 - it closed down the year after I graduated. I missed a couple of years - I didn't go steady all the time cuz my Dad had broken both his wrists and I stayed home to help around the house. To bring money in I got a job cutting grass at peoples' houses. That was for about two years. My Dad couldn't do anything - he was all tied up. When I was absent I was going to school here at the back end of the Island. Then I went back to the mush hole and finished up.

When I first went I was too small to do any work, so all I did was play. I began working in the horse barn. After I got a little bit bigger and began to do things I used to take the horses out for a drink of water at the trough and bring them back in and clean their stalls. I was guilty of taking the horses out at night!! We done it a couple of times. We had a democrat and they'd hitch the team up to the democrat and they'd take off with it, riding the horses. And the other fellas would come a few minutes later and try to locate the democrat right out the back of the reserve there. I went out a couple of times. Then the one night we were gonna go again, and the boys - my bed was right beside the fire escape window, so everybody had to come through that way to get out - and when they came by they grabbed my jeans and tied the legs up in knots. So after the last ones went out, I got up to put my jeans on and I had to unravel all the knots they'd put in there, and by the time I got that done the lights come on, and the staff came in, so I just simply crawled back into bed and pretended I was sleeping. They come and checked everybody and got all the names of the guys that were out, and somebody had actually done me a favour!!! They lost a lot of privileges and they got the strap, and if I remember rightly they got a lot of memory work to do - a couple of poems and whatever they had to memorize to get their privileges back - so it cost them quite a bit.

I did run away - it was during Mr. Soper's reign. I felt that I was not being treated fairly in the system. I had difficulty with a teacher. I don't know - whether we all go through it or what I don't know - but it seems to me, through the years I found different ones that I had difficulty with at one time or another - learning. Maybe for a year or two, then this seemed to pass and you were back to your old standards of learning real quick and well. But at the particular time it happened I was going through some difficulty - the teacher used to get on me about it - and finally it just got to the point where I wasn't going to take it any more. So after lunch one day I walked down to the cow pasture and up the hill to the road, along the road right out through the reserve to No. 2 Highway, stuck my thumb out and got a ride right off the bat. Came home [Walpole Island] and surprised my Dad, he didn't expect me back for another few weeks. He said "You've got to go to school. Why don't you stay for a day and we'll get you back for Monday." He took me back on the Sunday. We had a discussion about it with Mr. Soper in his office, and my Dad said that I had come back willingly - he had brought me back - and seeing that I had come that way I shouldn't get punished or get the strap or anything, and Mr. Soper agreed. 20 minutes after my Dad left I got the strap. I just felt that at that time I was again dealt with wrongly, but I didn't have any notion of running away again. I had my say as to what I felt was going on and he heard it, but it was just one of those things that happened, I guess. I just didn't see how it could be, because he was a minister and gave his word that he wouldn't give me the strap, but he did, and it took a little bit off of his shine as far as I was concerned. After that I really didn't associate with him much - I used to before then, he was fair in many respects, we got along good, but it just stopped the whole thing as far as I was concerned. I don't remember exactly but it seemed like I had 7 or 8 on each hand. It was the only incident really that upset me - other than the school classroom bit. I don't recall who the teacher was. There were two boys from Saugeen and they sat one seat behind me on a row each side. The one guy was always into trouble - he'd do something, and when he'd do something then he'd tap me on the shoulder and I'd turn round. Of course when I'd turn around the teacher saw me and he'd assume I was the one causing all the commotion. He'd tell me to "Come on up here," and I'd go up there and I'd get the strap. I tried to tell him a couple of times that it wasn't me, but he wouldn't pay any attention to that. So I got disturbed about that too. To me he was taking someone else's word and I wasn't the one that was doing it, but I was the one getting caught, when I'd turn around. These two guys were always doing something - they'd throw an eraser at someone or something like that - and when the teacher looked around they'd be just sitting there and everyone else would be looking around wondering what was going on. I don't know - you'd think the teacher could put two and two together when it happened three or four times - he'd get the picture. Usually somebody else was punished.

I spoke my Native language until I found out you couldn't without getting a licking. I never got the strap for it but I was warned enough that I didn't do it. When we'd go up in the dormitories in the evening I had a friend from Sarnia who I could talk with. We'd sit there and talk and a couple of other boys would come over and talk. I pretty much kept my language but I lost quite a bit over there cuz we weren't able to talk it. Then when I came back home, most of the ones that I chummed around with didn't use it steady, so then I lost some more. The only time I got to use it really was visiting old folks - I'd go over and help someone - help them bring in wood, or help them around their home. If they carry on a conversation I can understand it.

When I left I was too young to join the army. I went to Wellesley barracks to join up in 1943. I was gonna to quit school and join the army cuz my brother was in it. I was a good size and I filled out the application and I was just about to sign the papers when who should walk in but my brother. He says "He'd not old enough to sign up." So they sent me back home and back to school.

I look back at it, and other than the two incidents that I mentioned, it was OK. I remember when I first went in there we went down to our noon meal. There was meat and potatoes and boiled onions. The boiled onions were just simply thrown in a pot and boiled and put on the table. They had no appeal for me and I tried to eat 'em, but when I started to eat them I knew I was going to throw up. So I left them on the plate, and whoever was on duty in the dining-room at that time, they came down and checked the plates on every table before they let you go, and I had eaten everything except my onions. The teacher told me to stay there until I cleaned 'em up, but I didn't touch 'em any more. So when class resumed the teacher came and said "You can go over to the school." So I came into the classroom, and sitting on my desk was my plate with the onions. The teacher said "You're gonna have to eat those onions." I said "I'm not eating it." She said "Well, if you don't, you're gonna get a strap." "Well," I said, "I guess I'll have to take the strap." Anyway they vowed they were gonna keep the plate in front of me. My sister was in the senior classroom - this was the primary classroom - somebody went out and into the senior room and told my sister what was happening, and she come in and she went physically at the teacher. She said "He's not gonna eat those onions," and she just spilled them all on the floor, and that ended that situation there.

I got to see my sister every day. It was a simple situation that the boys' and girls' areas were at each end of the main building. The girls had their playground at the end of it, and

the boys' playground was out to the front more. The boys' playground - if there was anything doing - like the 24th May we had races - the boys' playground was where it would happen. In the middle of the back side of the main building was the kitchen area. The bathroom was right down on the lower floor, just outside of the girls' area, and when everybody went for their Saturday bath, there was no fence right at that point outside, and we could sit on the steps and visit with each other. If the boys had a girlfriend they could stand there - it was like an imaginary line that was on the ground. A lot of times - there was a lawn out in front - sometimes the girls would be allowed to come out and sit in the shaded area.

The food was substantial enough to get along. We done all our own farming. We grew our own vegetables there. We had a 600 acre farm with horses and cows, pigs and chickens. When I started to work the first year, I was too small to do any of the physical work so I spent all my time playing. When I did get work I did minor things like watering the horses, cleaning the stalls. I did that for one year. The next year I went to the cow barn and learned how to take care of the animals there. One year in the pig barn, another in the chicken coops, then by the time I got back around to the horse barn, I understood what had to be done. I was big enough to take teams out and work with them. Then I learned how to run the tractors and I did the major part of the spring farming before I come home in June for the holidays. I took from that experience - I guess the ability to work with tractors kinda helped because when I come out I went into just general labour and there was nothing much available at the time. I took care of people's yards, make a lawn if you had to - whatever had to be done - cut the grass. I did that for a couple of years, then I went into factory work. I didn't like being inside - I was kinda an outdoor person. I wanted something where I was outside so I went and signed up on the steamboats. After that I worked as a construction labourer, then I got into heavy equipment.

I found Strapp overbearing - he seemed to want to let the kids know that he was still the authority. If you were doing something, minding your own business out there, he'd come by. If he didn't like what you were doing out there he let you know about it. He says "If I catch you out here again you're gonna get the strap." I think Strapp was more feared than hated - if you'd see him coming along you simply got out of his way. The boys were pretty well allowed to roam at will. You got your chores done - in your free time you could sit down in the playroom and visit, or go up to the reading room and sit quietly there. Or you could go out - maybe go down by the river and toss flat stones, go for a walk along the road or back in the woods. It was free - you could choose your friends and go for a walk. The boys got along fine. I remember when I first went in there were two boys - they were about the same size and had pretty much the same idea in their head. They'd have a fight a couple of times a week and they'd come out about even - they were both pretty well matched. That was about the only ones that I saw that would do this.

I don't recall any mention of sexual abuse - I never saw any.

The work that I did - I was always handy with machines, and I wound up, the last two years I was there, out of the classroom the whole day, getting the fields ready for the spring planting. After breakfast I'd load up my equipment that I needed, ploughs and all that stuff, and I'd be out there on my own all day. After breakfast I'd start out and by 8.30 I'd be on my own. I'd plough all day and disc, then I'd go and get the seed - go and plant the corn and wheat, whatever had to be in. I was alone out there. The girls would pack me a good big basket of lunch - milk, sandwiches, fruit, and I was out there all day till after supper. Sometimes I'd get back for supper, sometimes I wouldn't - they'd have a big plate set out for me.

I remember the incident with the tractor [see p.] Somebody tried to start it up and shifted the gears and ruined the gears. I was always pretty handy with machines - checked my oil and water. I'd grease and oil it before I'd go and I always carried a grease gun with me. I was pretty

much able to maintain the equipment.

We had an instructor there - there were times he'd come down if we were doing a field, and tell us how to plough and how to disc it, and where to start. Once he saw that you were doing all right he'd leave you. We had some acreage on the Oneida side and you had to go round by the old bridge - it took an hour to get around there to that field, and we worked in there. They trusted me to take the equipment - I suppose they could see from the school across the river! But I enjoyed it - being outdoors, and I was handy with machines.

Then of course we rolled our own oats for mush. We basically prepared all the equipment. We'd go out in wintertime and take the manure out and spread it in the fields.

Towards the last I was able to come home for Christmas holidays. My Dad would come to the school and get me. It was hard times - the Depression was still on. My Dad worked hard to get money to come up and visit. My mother passed away when I was quite young. My brother and sister were there and my Dad asked if I would go. I said I'd go - I went willingly to the school.

Emma Soney
1935? - 1941

I didn't like it there. I went there because my mum and dad separated so they came and took us. My brother was 4 years old and I was 6 - there were four of us that went. I got used to being away from home, but I didn't like it because it was the teachers that was mean at times - according to their mood I guess. They hit the kids - they would hit them anywhere they wanted.

We learned to work! We learned to make beds, mend clothes, mend socks, make uniforms. The uniforms were blue and red - blue denim material with a red bias around the neck. We had long black stockings and black top shoes. Those shoes were hard and they never fit - never - especially the little ones.

We didn't learn very much in school. We were only in school for 3 or 4 hours in the morning. We went in at 9 am and you'd get out at noon. So I didn't learn much and I only went to Grade 7. When I got out I looked for a job for myself. I went across the river to the States and worked in a little factory over there - that was seasonal work and I did take some domestic jobs for summer cottagers over there.

I ran away from there. I got home too, to Sarnia!! My dad took me back. Nothing happened to me because my dad told them not to touch me. I ran away because the teachers were getting too mean - you were always getting a licking till I was black and blue. If you didn't eat all your food up, or if you're late for school, you'd get a licking.

When the staff knew there were school inspectors coming

they'd clean the place up and serve us a good meal. The food was often half-cooked. We learned to steal. We'd steal cream and brown sugar and raw oatmeal and mix it all together and eat it. One time my friend was getting cream and I was in the corridor with a pail of soapsuds and a mop. The staff had these bunches of keys and they'd jingle so you could hear them coming. So I hollered at her and she came running around the corner - she was wearing running shoes - she came running around and she slipped in the water and fell and spilt all the cream. So I just dumped my whole pail over the cream to hide it!!!

The discipline was too harsh - they could have talked more instead of hitting you. Strapp - he lived up to his name.

My mum and dad were there too. If they [the staff] were kinder - it would have been different. Mrs. Erratt - she was nice - she had a rumble seat - we used to say "Here comes Rumble"!! But when anybody was too good to us they got rid of them.

The porridge was half-cooked - cornmeal, cracked wheat - the wheat was still hard. When we got big enough we started to cook. I worked in the kitchen - the staff kitchen. That was better - they got better meals. I'd eat whatever I could eat - anything that was spare, that wasn't needed, but the help had to eat somewhere else. They had a lot of eggs there but we never got them. The boys would get eggs and they used to go in the bush and make fires and cook eggs.

Those old napkins - that was rotten -ugh! They were just rags with old, black dried blood on them and you had to wash them. You had to put 'em in the bag - ugh! They'd have you work in the laundry. I was playing on the monkey bars and I fell off. I thought I got hurt - I ran to the bathroom. They were outhouses - outhouses! I sat there for the longest time, I was just crying and crying. They didn't tell us anything about it - I didn't know what was happening. The older girls would just tell you "Get away from here." They didn't talk about those things in front of people in those days. The Indians in those days wouldn't eat with women having their period - they had separate dishes, and they'd wash their own dishes and then pack them away for the next time.

I spoke my Native language when I went there - that was all I knew. I kept my language. A lot of them used to get a licking for speaking their language, but I never forgot it. The staff wouldn't have lasted if they hadn't been mean - Strapp, Smith, Broderick, Cowan. I might have finished school if the staff weren't so mean. It was getting so all the kids were starting to hit back - it was terrible there for a while. There used to be fighting all the time - even in the schoolroom. Whenever a teacher got nice or gave help, they'd be let go - as soon as the staff found out that someone was nice to the kids.

I know how to work anyway!! After I got married I had a restaurant - I used to make 18 pies a day. The work at the school helped - I learned to cook and clean.

I got along good with the other girls. Melva and I was always around together. It would have been good if it hadn't been for the staff. I used to wish somebody would come and do something about it. My dad caught Strapp hitting my sister. We just happened to come in the front door and he said "Where's your sister?" I said "That's her hollering in there." He went in there and pushed him down. He said "Don't ever touch my kids again." That's why nothing happened to us after we ran away.

We had a fence around the playground - we couldn't go out. There were monkeybars. We made our own fun. We played baseball. We had a ball team - of course we didn't go anywhere. We used to be in relay races.

I was there for seven years - I was there for a long time. I was small and I remember there were big girls - they seemed like big ladies to me. My family used to own a pool-room in the house there, and there would be Camp-meetings at the back of our house, but I blame it on drink. After my grandfather died, everything went haywire. My mother left us and went to live somewhere else.

On the third day after we went there we had to have our tonsils out. I don't know why - we weren't sick, but it was the rage then I guess. They made us eat tomatoes and corn on the cob right after we had our tonsils out.

I just wished someone would come and do something about the school. It was like a concentration camp.

Kenneth Albert
1935 - 1940

I was born in 1924, I went to Mt. Elgin in 1935 and left around 1940 when I was 16.

The school did good for the children - I wouldn't have got an education if I'd stayed home. I could handle a job and I learned discipline. We did learn - the hard way - by doing it - agricultural methods - how to farm.

The school only went to Grade 8. I didn't go to high school but I went to a trade school in Windsor and got my own education.

The food was nourishing but there wasn't enough.

The problem was a sense of being confined. There were privileges but these were restrictions. There was no time for play - no talking after lights out - if you laughed you got beaten.

We got up at 6 a.m. and went down to do the milking - we had 4-8 cows each to milk. We had to weigh all the milk - could be from 40-45lbs. We were just small boys. One boy had a cow gave so much milk that he had to milk it three times a day and weigh all the milk and some days it was 40-45lbs. We only got the skim milk - it was separated and the cream sold. We farmed 450 acres and we did it all - harvesting and threshing wheat, silos. We picked all the potatoes - maybe 50 acres. We grew all the wheat and corn for the livestock - a large herd of prize Holsteins, we looked after the teams of 8-10 horses, 500 chickens, but we never had a boiled egg for breakfast - not even at Easter. We had to shovel all the coal off the cars and into the storeroom.

I got strapped - on the bum - for riding a horse after hours. I didn't get the strap when I ran away because my father took the principal by the shoulders and told him he'd whip him if he touched me. Some of the teachers would beat the kids - but there were younger teachers there who would hug a kid after he was beaten - out of sight of the teacher who did it.

The kids would run away because they didn't like being confined - they were lonely for their parents. They didn't get any love in the school, and they didn't get enough to eat - so no matter how poor their home they wanted to get back home for food and love.

The food [on the menus] sounds good, but there wasn't enough of it. We used to trade food. The girls used to hide bread in their bloomers. If you had a girlfriend in the kitchen they would stick extra slices of bread on a knife under the table. You were hungry when you came in from working all morning on the farm, and one or two slices of bread wasn't enough.

I got along fine with the other kids - they were a pretty good lot of kids.

There was a playground, but you were restricted. We only had something like an hour before supper to play. We had to make our own fun - there were no toys, no teeter-totters - nothing. We could go fishing in our spare time - we used to sell the fish. We walked to the Methodist Jubilee Church every Sunday.

Strapp never came back to visit - there was no compassion or kindness - it was prejudice. We did get some good - we got training.

Mrs. Albert: My sister was strapped - she had exzcema on her hands - they were really sore and bleeding - and she wouldn't do the wash. Strapp strapped her on the sore hands. When my mother heard she took a buggy whip and came after Strapp, but she didn't manage to hit him.

Lloyd Doxtator
1935 - 1940

I ran away from there early 1940 so what went on after that I couldn't tell you. It was all right. I was there in 1935. This friend of mine wanted to take off so I took off with him. The place was all right but he wanted to get out so I went with him. We never went back. We wound up in Niagara Falls - I was born in 1926 so I was about 13.

I was there with Strapp - not too much could get out of place with him. If you done anything wrong you'd get the strap. I got the strap a couple of times - I don't remember what I did - it must have been something bad. It's hard to remember that far back.

Milking cows - they had quite a few cows, ploughing the fields, hoeing the fields, planting the potatoes and carrots, cabbage and onions and stuff like that. I liked the staff. We cleaned out the barns - cow barn, the horse barn, cleaning the manure out. We went to school from 9 to 3 - something like that. Everybody done their share of the work. Maybe one day I done something, the next day someone else done it - we took turns. I liked the farmwork - I couldn't learn nothing with my blockhead in school!! I never did learn much. When I got back on the reserve after about a year I lived with my grandmother. She had a little farm so I helped her. After she died I went back with my mother.

My mother put me there.

Sometimes we didn't get enough to eat - not always. That's why I had a girlfriend - she'd sneak me a couple of sandwiches or something. Most of the time we had porridge for breakfast - porridge and toast and a glass of milk. The food wasn't too bad I guess, but at that time my stomach wasn't up to anything anyways. I always had kinda an upset stomach. I was supposed to eat mostly warm milk and dry bread broken up in the milk. That was all right. When I got to eat vegetables it took me a little time to get used to that.

I just knew about the farming part - hoeing the garden, ploughing, milking the cows - that's all I ever did that I know of. I liked it all right. I got along pretty good with everybody.

We used to let the horses out in the pasture - we used to ride them sometimes - couple of times at night - I never got caught. Sometimes they let us ride them during the day. I didn't do an awful lot of it.

I don't really remember the names of the teachers. I can't remember too much anyway. You used to get a scolding when you tried to look over the shoulder of somebody and copy what they had!!

As far as I'm concerned the school was all right - not that I learned anything. Though I done a lot of farming after that - I liked that. It's hard work though.

We had a little baseball team - not a team but a little baseball once in a while in the summertime. I came out in the summer holidays. We used to play hide and seek, or tag, or we'd go swimming - a lot of swimming in the river. And fishing - a lot of fishing too. We didn't see too much of the girls. We had separate dormitories - women on one side, men on the other. Some used to sneak down the fire escape and go into the women's dormitory. Sometimes the women would come back to the men's dormitory. Sometimes they got caught and sometimes they didn't. It would happen around 1 or 2 o'clock in the morning. I don't think I ever did that. In wintertime we built a sleigh - six of you could ride on it. There were runners on the bottom of the sleigh. We had a big steep hill and we'd wet her down during the night. Next day we'd go down on that sleigh, and we'd go for about a mile - going real fast. Go down for about a mile - pull the sleigh back up and go down again. We didn't have to look after the animals too much in the winter - the animals were pretty well locked up. There was a lot of snow at that time so you couldn't let em out. You'd feed 'em hay there in the barn. You'd just clean out the manure - it wasn't much of a job - in a couple of hours you were finished. We had more free time in the winter to have a good time.

Donald Young and Esther Lewis
1935 - 1941 and 1940 - 1943

E. We had our duties to do. Don did the barn and gardening.

D. I think up to Grade 6 you went half-a-day to school and worked the other half. Sometimes you were in the dairy part, or farming, or poultry. They changed around every three months. You worked in the dairy for three months, then you went somewheres else.

E. I went in 1940. I can't remember how long I was there - it wasn't very long anyway. Two or three years? I wasn't there when Soper came.

D. I went in 1934, and I was there maybe about seven years. I don't know what year I came out.

E. It was Strapp and Mrs. Erratt who were the head honchos at that time.

D. I don't remember her too well. Strapp was pretty strict - this guy - he was really strict and he was supposed to feed us better. They didn't feed us what they should have fed us.

E. That was one thing about it - the food. It was OK, but why could you not have homogenized milk instead of skim milk? Where did the cream go? We had strawberries - we'd never have cream on them. Apple orchards - you were lucky if you seen an apple.

D. We only got butter once a day and that was in the morning. Then the cereal was made out of field corn - they ran it through a grinder.

E. That's why we called it the mush hole.

D. We had the same old thing every morning.

E. Every morning.

D. Then we had dry food, no gravy - nothing. No butter.

E. Suppertime you got that old pudding that they called blancmange - wasn't that awful stuff - tapioca.

D. They called it fish eyes.

E. Oh gross!!

D. He could have fed us better than that. They used to kill a beef every so often - we never seen any of that - it was for the staff or something.

E. We never had beef.

D. Every so often they killed a pork or a beef, and we never saw any of that - it went to all the staff. They ate really good.

E. I know, because I worked in the dining-room for the staff. They had salads. What was her name - Willow Broderick - the dietitian.

D. You had to be on time for your meals.

E. You used to have clean your plate - that's for sure.

D. Sometimes you'd try and stick it in your pocket or something, if you didn't like it. But it was him - they could have fed us better.

E. [Looking at menus] Get out of here! Roast veal, meat loaf, scalloped potatoes - get out of here!

D. Who put that on there? We never seen any of that.

E. Cornmeal - breakfast - oatmeal.

D. It was generally potatoes and parsnips. I still don't eat parsnips. Dry - no butter to put on them or anything. What did we have at suppertime? That was a dull meal too. We never seen meat - never. We never seen eggs - no eggs either. We had our own chickens. I don't know where that went. That was supposed to run itself that farm, you know. The beef and the eggs and everything. They must have sold a lot of that stuff. They couldn't eat it all. We never had no meat, no chicken.

E. That baker that used to come - my heavens! How many loaves of bread he dropped off there - that'd be three times a week. Then if you had money on a Saturday you bought goodies from the baker.

D. We just had about two slices each meal - of bread.

E. I think just one.

D. The boys would get this field corn and shell it, and they'd go out somewhere far away and they'd cook it - so they had enough to eat. It wouldn't pop - it would just cook. There was an orchard about a mile away and they'd go over there and get apples. Strapp, he was an awful man I think.

E. and D. We never spoke our Native Language - our grandfather he was Scotch.

D. Yeah - we got an education. To Grade 6 you went to school half-a-day. Sometimes you'd go in the morning, sometimes in the afternoon. You'd have to work the other half. I never went to high school - I went to Grade 8.

E. After that you were supposed to be old enough to go out on your own.

D. You were 16, and after 16 you went. They couldn't force you to stay there.

E. I remember those stairs coming from the upper regions to the playroom. We used to have lockers in the basement - locker boxes - and we'd put our little goodies in there. They curved, and I fell down them things. That's how I chipped that tooth. You know why I fell down? I'd got issued a new pair of boots, and I was running down to show N my new boots, because they were still new. When I got them before, they were always somebody else's hand-me-downs. I had a black eye. I can't remember the name of the nurse.

D. You all had a number too - for your clothes and that. I still remember my number - it was 9. We had those little boxes for our clean clothes.

E. In the shower-room - the bathroom.

D. It was something like the army, something like a gaol.

E. Rules and regulations.

D. I never ran away.

E. He was a model student. He never used to even have to write exams - he passed on his year work. I never ran away. I was too small to think about running away.

D. I don't think there was too many runaways - they had

Mounties and they'd catch you. That old farm manager - he used me good, but he was mean. He was Scotch - he fell off his motor cycle and broke his back, and he went over there as farm manager - oh! he was a mean son-of-a-gun, but I got along good with him. But he'd slap them guys around. Mean, that son of a gun!

E. They used to stand out back because it was separate corners - one guy'd be on a porch - he'd be playing the mouth organ and somebody else had a guitar and H W would stepdance. It wasn't all drudgery.

D. There was the odd time like Hallowe'en when we got these peanut butter sandwiches.

E. We used to go on these paper chases - remember that? This was for the smaller kids, and at the end of it we'd have a wiener roast, or sandwiches. I know I got a shock trying to climb over a fence, and it was an electric fence, and boy! did my whole arms just quiver.

D. We had a field day and they gave you chocolate bars. About two or three for first, second was one. That was the way they paid you for winning, was chocolate bars. I suppose a chocolate bar would be about 5 cents. It was a big deal to get a chocolate bar!!!

That Strapp was a bad, bad man. He didn't do any good to us.

E. Look at the big wedding he put on for his niece. There was food galore. They put up a trellis with roses. The boys had to have the lawn just immaculate for her. We were all just gawking because she was so beautiful.

I got strapped one time for being in the main hall. He come out opened the door - their dining room was right across. Somebody asked me to go and see the time, and I wouldn't go downstairs and around, I just went straight through, and he just nabbed me. That was the only time I got the strap - it was just two whacks on each hand. My nickname was Sassy!!

D. It may have been pretty good there if they had had a different principal. If we'd used all the beef and pork and eggs that we were supposed to get. They either sold them or did something with them, because we never got it. I don't ever remember eating meat or eggs.

E. Porridge for breakfast and I don't remember what we used to get for lunch.

D. It was a dried old potato and mostly parsnips or something. I don't remember having carrots. They didn't have nobody to watch them - the schools - at that time. If somebody come in and see what was going on, but I don't think they ever had that.

E. Personally I don't think Strapp liked Indians. He shouldn't have been there to start with because I think he was a bigot. We were dirt. We were just little Indians.

D. They had a farm manager, running the farm, and a manager for the dairy.

E. What did Johnson do?

D. He was a teacher.

E. In the workshop - manual training

D. There was all this meat went to the farm manager - they must have lived all right.

E. We used to go for walks. I remember this one teacher - she was quite great for doing that, and we had apple orchards, apple trees, and we'd find this apple tree - it was down a long old road - and get these wild apples and eat them. If you went into that store room there was bushels and bushels of apples sitting in there, and canned food - peaches. We never seen a peach.

When I came out of school I knew how to be a waitress. I knew how to be a chambermaid, so it wasn't all that bad. They made you wait on these people from left to right, how to set a table, and they had good silverware too. When I left school I took a course in being a furrier - Harry Rubens in Toronto, and I was a furrier. But that went belly-up - they don't sell fur coats any more!! Then I got married. I worked at hotels in London. The school didn't help me get a job, but it helped me in the sense of knowing how to wait on tables. When I went one year to school, I worked at the Home Dairy in London after school, 4.30 to 7 o'clock, in the cafeteria, carrying trays up and down stairs, so knowing how to meet the public and be polite to them, I think that's half your education to start with. We didn't live too much on the reserve.

D. I did jobs around for a while then I got into trucking. I drove for a trucking company, then I had my own trucks for about 30 years. The school didn't help me in that way. We had a couple of old tractors and the rest was horses. I think we had four teams of horses. We had a real old tractor, then they got a little newer one - just a small one. Everybody liked to drive that thing, but most of it was done by horses. They shifted me around every three months. You'd all get in a big room and they'd read out your name, where you were going to be, what you were going to do for three months. You might be in the dairy, or farming with the horses - doing the planting. Then they had the pigs.

They used to ride the horses at night - I went on it. They'd get these horses out of the barn and go way across the river on Oneida. We'd go way out in the dirt riding those horses real fast - they was work horses. You'd go in the barn and there would be old Strapp and everybody would just take the horse and jump off and put them in the barn and nobody would know who had them.

E. Nobody would squeal on them. That was one thing about it, every student - well maybe there was the odd one - but if anything went wrong or you did something, nobody would report it, or if they were investigating they would not squeal on you.

We were pretty confined. Once a month was it, we used to be able to walk up to Muncey store. You'd get your money that was in your cash box and buy a chocolate bar and walk back. I thought that was great. Going to the fair - that was something different too. You had to line up.

D. They used to get their coal coming in at Muncey too - railroad cars - and we'd go up from the school as a team, and pitch it all in the waggon or sleigh, bring it back and unload it.

D and E. I don't think there was any sexual abuse there.

E. Mrs. Erratt was a gracious lady. She could be stern too. I can't remember half the teachers' names. Our nurse was Gibson, and I know if you got any dental work done, it all had to be done again when you were older. I can remember the dentist came in and I had dental work done.

D. That Strapp - he was always there. He was really strict and he was supposed to be a United Church minister. He always had his outfit on, you never seen him without it. He'd only go out Saturday nights. He always had a new Studebaker car and somebody had to wash his car Saturday morning. He'd go to London or someplace and he'd never wear his regular outfit, he'd just have a suit on when he'd go. He was mean this son of a gun - he was mean. I got along with him, but other ones - boy! I seen him strap other guys. I never got the strap.

E. Those two little girls that came from Sarnia - they were in the dining room, and they were protective to each other, and they were talking in Indian. And he said "You don't talk like that here. You talk English." And he cuffed them up. I remember that.

D. Some of the older ones went and hit him and he had the Mounties right there. The Mounties lived right on the Reserve about a mile from the school. The first thing he'd do is call them.

Doris King
1936? - 1938

When I first went to this residential school it was in the Depression era and a lot of our Native people had to take their young children over there. My name then was Doris George. I went there with my sister Madeline. I was there for just a couple of years. I was very young - around the age of 9 or 10.

I only spoke English when I went there - I didn't know how to speak my own language.

I remember my first day, going down that long drive. It was strange for me when I went, but I admired it because it was so clean looking. The grass was all neatly cut and there was a long line of big maple trees each side of the road. Everything looked good to me. We were introduced to Mr. Strapp, then someone showed us our beds where we were to sleep. There were two big dormitories. I was afraid - in that great big school.

As for the principal there - he was there to do his job, and he did his job. I never really got to know him that well but I heard about him all around the school. They used to say "You'd better watch out - if you have to go to Mr. Strapp, you're really getting the strap!!" I seen it just once, where someone got a strapping and he put their hand out flat and he really hit it. He gave them a good one. Mr. Strapp was OK I guess, but everyone talked about him because he was the one that disciplined them. I never got the strap.

I only went to Grade 5 there. We went to school in the back part of the building. I was only there a couple of years and I don't remember too much about the teachers or the staff. The staff and the teachers, as far as I know, they were just like teachers of today. I didn't really learn any skills because I was there just two years, so I didn't get involved in any of that. We were young when we went there so we just played around when we weren't in school. Some were old enough that they learned to sew - I remember the sewing room. The boys used to go and milk the cows and feed the chickens. I worked in the kitchen. We used to wash dishes and put the food away.

I was always hungry - we didn't seem to have enough food. For breakfast we would get a glass of milk, a slice of bread and porridge. That's why they gave it the name "Mush Hole". That sounds like a good meal here [looking at menus] - roast beef, carrots. I can't remember those kinds of good meals.

When we were working in the kitchen we used to help ourselves to a sandwich or something if we were hungry and hide them under our clothes. We had these long navy bloomers with elastic round the bottom of the legs and we used to hide bread and things in them. The girls would say "Jiggers on the track" if someone was coming. One time someone yelled "jiggers on the track" and I grabbed two eggs that I thought were hard boiled and stuffed them in my bloomers. We went outside and were sitting against the fence talking. I had forgotten about the eggs and I drew my legs up under me and Crack! the eggs broke. They were raw! Oh! what a mess. The food - it could have been a little better, or a little more of what they served. I wouldn't have stolen those old eggs if I got enough food!!

One day we were all dismissed from class and out in the playground there was a crowd of people all looking at something on the ground. When we got there, there was this young boy lying there. He was up in the dormitory and he was eating something, and he might have lost his spoon or something and he fell out of the window.

We used to go to the Fall Fair. We used to walk there - about a mile or so. We went in groups and each group had someone to look after them. I didn't have much money to go to the Fair - maybe just enough for a drink and a hot dog. It was one of the enjoyable times. I never ran away. I lived way down here at Stony Point so it was a long way for a young person to try and go, and you wouldn't know the dangers awaiting you on the road. But there was a young boy there - he was about 12 - he used to run away about once a month. He ran away so many times that after a while they took his clothes away at night when he went to bed. It was all right the first night, he was there the next morning, but then he must have started thinking what he could do, so he just went around and gathered clothes from the boys his age, got himself dressed, and out he went. He wasn't there the next morning, but the other children missed their clothes, because Murray already had them!! He was somebody else!

We used to go for sleighrides during the winter down the hill, and they'd hook up a team of horses and take us for another sleighride. They'd load the sleigh up with straw and everybody climbed aboard and away we went. There was a lot of fun times. Another fun time - they used to let us go swimming in the River Thames. The water was quite deep there. I couldn't swim but we'd get out into the water there and this one time my sister went out too far, and I was in a safer place. The first thing I knew she grabbed ahold of me and tried to get me to carry her out cuz she got into the deep waters and she could have drowned. She pretty nearly drowned me too cuz I kinda went down a little bit. We both could have drowned. We had a big playground but it was kinda boarded in. We used to talk to the boys sometimes over the fence. They'd come to the fence and we were on the other side and we'd talk to them - I never got into trouble over that.

I don't know too much about the discipline either, but I know we had to get in bed at 9:00 pm so that was all right. We wouldn't be tired the next day if we had our rest - so it was good there. I can't remember any sexual abuse. There wasn't anything bad that I know of happened while I was there. There was no evidence of anything bad. It was all right being there. It was something new for me cuz I used to live in the bushland and we used to walk to school at Stony Point. I didn't see anything wrong with it - I kinda enjoyed being there. My Dad and Mum used to come and visit us. This one Christmastime they brought us a big box of goodies, with walnuts and mixed nuts and oranges and

apples. That was nice, receiving them on Christmas. I can't remember them doing anything special for us at the school - I guess if I remembered it would have been special!

When we arrived there was lots of the kids from different Reserves - Sarnia Reserve, and Kettle Point and Stony Point, Muncey - all around. It brought out a lot of our shyness, meeting people. But for the longest time I was really shy - I didn't like to face people - even when I came home I was shy. I think I got on well with the other kids. We used to go down in the basement - when we were kids we didn't have money. When our Dads sent us there we didn't have everything like toothpaste and toothbrush. There was some powder that you clean the basin with. I used to get that and get a kleenex and I used to brush my teeth - not knowing any better, just a young girl, and I wanted nice clean teeth. So I cleaned my teeth with it and rinsed my mouth real good, and I felt really good about it. Maybe that's why I don't have any teeth today. The ones whose parents could afford all this were all right, but I didn't have it. They had boxes down in the basement - each one had a box where they could keep their belongings. We had navy-blue uniforms.

The language shouldn't have been taken away - it should have been learned in the school because it was our heritage. I feel that they shouldn't have taken it from them, it should have been taught to them more than anything cuz it was a Native school. But I didn't learn any language so today I don't know how to talk our Native tongue - just a few words that I learned around here and there. At that time I was just a young person, but when I think back on it today, as an Elder, I think it was very wrong.

I think you get an education just learning different ways - not only in the classroom but out of the class too - you educated yourself in different ways at the school - learning the different ways of kids from different Reserves, and how people get along and how they feel. You learn about the treatment of the staff - whether it's good or bad. They had a sewing room so you learned how to sew. It wasn't all bad, there were some things you got educated on.

Ronald Deleary
1937 - 1942

I went in September 1937. I was 8 years old. They just come and got us - it must have been around bedtime, this Indian Agent came, and they gave my brother and me a couple of beds - the other boys were in bed.

My dad had left, and my mum and my brother and me were living with my grandmother. We went to the day school. I was at Mt. Elgin for 5 years - it was an improvement on the day school in that we didn't have to walk to school in the winter and come home in the dark.

I was in Grade 3 and they gave us a tour of the Grade 7, 8, and 9 schoolroom one time, and on the way out I grabbed a Grade 9 math book from the pile, and I hid it in my desk. So E H, and L G, and I, we used to look at this book and do the math problems. One day the teacher was putting problems on the board and she looked round too quickly and caught me putting the book back in the desk. She came running down and looked at the book, but she said nothing. Then she asked me to stay after school and I got scared I was going to get a whipping. But she called in the instructors and they made me do some of the questions, and I did this for about ten minutes, getting all the answers. They asked me who the others were, and the next night they called them in and the Principal came too. When we got to equations they were asking how we did it, but we did it in our head. So when we went into Grade 5, we had to catch up on social science, though our spelling was right on. We were kept in Grade 5 for three weeks, and we had to do an hour's homework every night. Before Christmas we were jumped up to Grade 7. My brother skipped a grade too. In Grade 7 we were younger and we were at the bottom of the totem pole. In one month we were at the top of the class again. They had these social things on Friday nights for the boys and girls from Grade 7 with coffee and cookies. The three younger ones of us in the same class were allowed to go. - we weren't into the social side of it with the bigger kids, but we went and filled our bellies with the goodies.

The principal was Strapp - Oliver B. Strapp - he sorta lived up to his name. I got it a couple of times for running away. My home was close by on the reserve and it didn't take much on a Saturday afternoon to run off to my grandmother's. I was strapped a couple of times - on the hand and the rear end.

Seven of us took off one Sunday afternoon. We took our clothes from the attic and took off down the railroad tracks. The first night we stopped at a farm near Appen and asked them for something to eat. But they knew where we were from and they went to get their coats so we ran off down the tracks. They came after us in trucks and tried to cut us off. I remember I was wearing a white sweater, but we hid down beside the tracks and they passed the flashlight right over us, but they didn't find us. We came to a dairy barn and stayed in there. The hay was warm and we were used to playing in the barns, in the hay. When the farmer got up in the morning he knew something was fishy. We said we'd clean out the barn for them and milk their cows - there were only four of them. We knew how to milk cows and do all that from the school. They fed us breakfast and the farmer said "Tonight I'll give you a meal and money, but I won't say nothing." We stayed another night then we took off again and kept on the tracks. We had these pole vaults - we did a lot of pole vaulting at the school, and they came in handy. We were crossing this field and we saw an OPP car, so we pole vaulted across the stream. We stayed in barns and we'd knock on the door and ask if we could stay, so we got fed. We got to Alvinston and we couldn't find a place to stay so we tried to sleep in the bandstand. There was a hotel there and the owner got up early and he found us. He asked us "When did you eat last?" and he brought us in and fed us; he put mattresses on the floor and we had a bath. We stayed a couple of days and he said "I'll take you back, but they've got to promise not to touch you." So when we got back he made them promise, but as soon as he'd gone they took our clothes away and made us go to the dormitory, and

they kept us there for about three weeks. We got a strapping on the rear end. The reason we ran away was because one of the farmhands - Fraser - was mean. He would hit guys with a cane. He never hit me, but some of the other boys he did.

We did learn. But instead of making farmers out of us, or domesticates out of the girls, we all knew how to steal. There was no lock we couldn't get into. We put nails on the tracks and flattened them - all the boys had them and we could use them to open any lock. The officers had all these canned goods in a big room - rows and rows of it, but we never got any of it. One fellow said "Want some berries"? There was this huge verandah under Strapp's office and he showed us how to go in under this verandah and get into this storeroom to get the fruit. We never got caught - I introduced my brother to it too.

From Grade 6 on we went to school half-a-day. We worked in the pig barn, and with the chickens, horses and cows - we all took a shot at it. We all learned farming and how to take care of animals.

There were some good people. There was one took care of the horses - Wright. Everyone liked him. If you were in trouble he never told anyone else - he kept it to himself and and dealt with it. There was another man who took care of the poultry and he was well respected. Fraser took care of the cows but when the boys all started running away he was replaced.

I ended up doing manual training. We'd fix the furnaces and do all the repairs. It was the best place to be. We'd sneak up to the girls' dormitory carrying wire and pliers so we'd look like we were fixing the beds or something, and we'd get the comic books from under their beds. Or we'd go in the officers dining room - the brown sugar was the best - we'd carry these little candy bags and fill them with brown sugar.

There was no way to get to high school from there. I went to school in Byron - I was three years older than the Grade 8s.

Some of the kids weren't scared of Strapp. One time Strapp grabbed I Y by the collar to shake him up, and the kid just stood and looked at him. He didn't do nothing. One time my uncle came with this car and took us for a ride to my grandmother's. When we got back Strapp was standing there and he pulls out his strap. He was going to start on me but Uncle Don said "Don't you ever touch that kid." Strapp was going to give my brother a strapping one time, and I seen him, and I ran and jumped on him and grabbed his arm. I got hit across the neck and my brother grabbed his legs, but he left us alone. That was in the boys' playground. Towards the end Strapp spent a lot of time in hospital - there was no discipline. He just sorta quit and the boys had to discipline themselves. We'd sneak away down the fire escape.

Cowan was one nice teacher. He'd come and tell stories to the big boys, and he even gave them a cigarette once in a while.   Johnson, the teacher, had a room over the classroom and I'd go up there to look over the books. He had a girlfriend and they used to take me to London to the movies. I was Johnson's pet!! I learned a lot - he helped me with everything I did in school. Even after I got out he had openings for me. Mrs. Erratt was another teacher - she was well-liked by everybody.

We had to box every day. I used to fight too. There was a definite pecking order. I would get in a fight with the bigger boys and beat them up. One morning I got in 5 fights and - one really big boy - I beat him up and I never got in fights again - nobody bothered with me after that, but I had to lose a lot of fights to get there.

I stayed there a couple of summers and worked - it paid well, I think we got $60. I had the job of keeping the furnace for the water heater stoked up. We were treated so good in the summer - they took us places. I think the regular officers had the summer off and they had fill-ins.

You made your own athletics - hockey, football. Some nights they took all the boys and you'd have 50 on one side and 50 on the other, so you never got a chance to kick the ball. We used to fish - and we learned to fish and cook them. They had these Trail Rangers. We'd take needles, pins - anything - and go fishing. People from off the reserve would buy them off us.

They showed us a lot of movies - Westerns. We made bobsleds and iced the hill every night. Most of the boys were in very good health. We'd go in the woods and find food - wild potatoes, onions, and hazel nuts. The bigger boys used to have cigarettes - roll your own, and chewing tobacco - we'd go off in the hills and ravines and smoke. The girls had cigarettes too - there were lines of smuggling.

There was a trio of boys that used to sing - Manson Ireland, L P, R S, and they'd go places and sing. I got a strapping one time for singing 'Silent Night, Hallowe'en Night' and everyone laughed; then I felt Dodson's rag around my neck. He used to carry this long limp rag and hit people but it didn't hurt nobody.

I often wonder what happened to all the looms the girls had in this big room. When we were on manual training we'd hide out in there and sleep.

I couldn't speak my language when I went there.

We had no toothpaste, no toothbrush - the older boys would make charcoal sticks and toothpicks. We all had jackknives and we made everything - all our toys.

The food was bad - we had mush every morning with bugs in it - we only ate down to the bugs! We never had any eggs though they had thousands of chickens. We did have a bun every Sunday, but when I first went there I never got my bun, because I had traded it away and always owed it to someone. We had whole milk once a year and we never got any meat. The officers ate good though. The girls would cook a roast for the officers and we'd steal it. Christmas was the only time we got meat - then we got chicken. We became good peach and pear pickers at night.

We'd get one slice of bread - the bigger boys had girlfriends and they'd get more. The baker would bring extra bread - and we'd buy it for 7 cents a loaf. We'd share it with the guys who didn't have anything. We'd have parsnips and beets boiled till they had no flavour. I hated those beets - the beets would disappear in the root cellar, when the boys were moving them around. We had to move them and chuck out the spoiled ones and the beets would always go first. We ate a lot of vegetables raw.

If you were sick you had to sleep in your vomit until the next time they changed the beds. We had to soak our heads with kerosene, and use this fine comb for lice. I got lice in the hospital.

I learned metal smithing too and we went to the Toronto Exhibition with our stuff. We did wood shop and made birdhouses and things. We had to take care of three furnaces and the hot water heater, the classrooms and the laundryroom. I did that for one year - the last year I was there.

One Hallowe'en we got all these pipes and joined them together and we put one end under the wall of the girls' outside toilet and ran the pipes around the garden. When the girls were in there smoking we made ghost noises "oooooh" down the pipe, and the girls were so scared they ran right out of there - one of them even went through the wall I think. The next morning we hid all the pipes and we never said a word about what we did.

We went up to the attic and got shoes and hid them around, then the day we left we got our clothes and ran away, and I never went back.

I never heard anything or knew anything about any sexual abuse. Sometimes it would get cold and people might share beds.

The two summers I stayed there we had to paint the school and some of the bigger guys, 16 and 17, had girlfriends. Some of them worked in the kitchen and they would hang slices of bread on a knife and pass them under the table. We would take a can of paint and creep under the table and paint these slices of bread with this black paint.

We'd steal horses at night and ride them, though the bigger boys would get the good horses. They cooked all this beef one night for some do in London and we stole most of it - we'd go and take great handfuls of it.

They gave us caps with ear flaps on, underwear, socks and boots. I don't remember getting really cold - there was always a building to duck into. The basement was cold.

Muncey was about 1¼ miles away and we'd run to the store after supper. At 6.50 the first bell for prayers would ring, and we had to run hard to be back and line up in time, but we'd never be late. The older boys would go out to dances at Muncey - we did that a couple of times, but we were younger than the other boys so we were just kids hanging around looking in the windows.

It was a good learning experience - we learned to cope, to handle ourselves.

Mildred Riley
1937 - ?

I went there in the fall of 1937 I think. I wasn't happy about being there. It was all right - there were kids my own age. I got to know different girls - people from different reserves I probably would have never met. I could have just been with the other kids - was great to me, but what I didn't like was - as I understand it now - the cruelty. When you saw people with all their faults, pettiness, jealousy - the little things. We had one officer - one woman there, I remember, she didn't stay very long - they got rid of her because everybody liked her. Her name was Miss Bowman? I don't know where she lives now, I haven't saw her in years. The others - the rest of them - I don't keep in touch with them, I don't care if I ever see them. Hopefully I'll never see them. There was our matron - Mrs. Erratt, I can't remember her first name - she was good - sort of an older woman, the motherly type. The kids had a nickname for her - Jiggy Erratt, whatever that meant. I remember a lot of them too. Helen Bandy - she could really play the piano. Another one - Smith - she taught sewing to the girls. She was a great needlewoman, she wasn't much for compassion or kindness. Then we had a teacher whose name was Ken Cowan. He used to like playing the guitar and singing gospel hymns. If we could get him interested in playing his guitar, he got carried away on it and we got out of a lot of work if we could get him singing, and playing on his guitar.

It's odd how you think back over things - what you remember.

We were going to Church all the time - three times on Sunday - whatever it was it seemed an awful lot. You couldn't get out of going - it was compulsory to go. If they'd had something interesting like Sunday School or something instead of sitting there and having to listen to somebody reading the scriptures, then they preached a while, then you sang a hymn. This was United, and no matter what you were, you went to the United Church and you sat there every Sunday. Service in the morning, and then lunch, and then we walked to Church in the afternoon, and then after that we went back - there was a certain amount of play time, then we had our supper and then there was a service after supper - for crying out loud! Three services on Sunday! I vowed: When I get out of here I ain't never going to Church again. My family were churchgoing - but Church of England.

I worked in the storeroom wrapping clothes and all that - I more or less knew people by their number - and every week we had a bath, and in your bundle of clothes would be the uniform for the week, the underwear, the black stockings, and you'd wrap them up and put them in the pigeon-hole. And everybody had their number on the pigeon-hole, and if you didn't like somebody you gave them ragged socks or ragged underwear. Underwear that was too small or too big, or whatever. You'd better be friends with the girls that worked in the storeroom or you were going to regret it!!! There were different ways to get back at people. We all got along because a lot of people were related. Even Sarnia isn't that far away - there's Rileys at Walpole, I have relatives at Sarnia, and Six Nations.

We did get to talk to the boys - not too much - usually if you were in their class. Some of these kids had a poor grasp of English when they came to the school, and certain ones were put with them, more or less to talk English to them, and P J couldn't make out even what his name was. I didn't speak my language when I went there - I could understand, but as far as speaking it - not too good.

I didn't do a lot of sewing - they got other people - like B A - she could really do fine stitches. She used to do mending for the officers. We made all the uniforms.

I don't like to think about the school, but I did like some of these kids.

I don't know too much about people who ran away - keep in mind I was one of the younger ones. I never ran away.

There's another one don't like to see me either - he tried to get out of work one time. He told the woman in charge he was sick. "What's wrong with you?" "I got heart trouble." So every time I see him I put my hand on my heart - I don't say a word! Boys didn't get crushes on me - I was too mean!! He don't like to see me - even yet - and that was 30 years ago, you'd think he'd forget.

No dentist ever visited the school that I can recollect, and we never saw a doctor, God forbid, unless we were sick. I remember being very very sick and they got scared because I lost so much blood, and they finally called the doctor - Dr. McLeod. At least I didn't have to work. I just more or less fell over. I came out of the dining-room, and sick or not you had to clean up everything on your plate, and I went weaving, staggering down the hall to go to the playroom. I just fell in the hall. I lost a lot of blood - somebody must have cleaned it up - my nose bled, and blood was coming out all over, and they must have called the doctor. I remember having my nose packed. But as far as having a doctor come in every so often, they never did that. We never saw a dentist or anything like that.

The only apples we ever got were ones we picked up off the ground, or frozen ones when they used to take us for walks - if we found any frozen apples or anything along the way. It depends who took us. Some officers were kinder and would let us pick the wild apples. Some of the food was pretty awful. I remember their rhubarb yet - it was terrible! Bitter! They used to have two kinds of rhubarb and I think they kept the red for the officers and we got the green. And rhubarb is actually quite good if it's prepared right. We never saw any of this stuff they're talking about [looking at menus]. I never seen no meat pie - oh yeah, their tapioca. Their rhubarb pudding was all right. Sometimes we got the red rhubarb, but mostly we got the green with a sauce. Rolled oats. I don't recall ever seeing any tomatoes either, tomato juice or citrus fruits. How those Christians can lie.

A lot of this stuff wasn't really cooked. The beans would be hard, and whoever cooked it hurried. I know this for myself, when I cook food and I hurry it, it don't taste as good as if I had taken more time with it. The milk was often turning sour.

I don't know if anything came of the complaint we made, but they sure quit chasing me around over that. They just never bothered me any more. We must have got together - I only remember one other woman. Strapp must have spanked them on the behind - I don't know, he never spanked me. He got too much enjoyment out of hitting me on the hands. There was this girl, her name was P - I'll remember to my dying day!!. I don't know what we done, but there was this P, J, and myself. We had to go to Strapp's office, we were going to get a strapping then. Mrs. Strapp used to always come in the office when her husband was going to punish somebody. She'd come in and she'd be moving things in the desk sat right by the door, and she'd sit there. P had the damnedest laugh you ever heard, it was more like a cackle. Mr. Strapp was strapping her, hitting her on the hands, and she'd keep moving back. She'd put her hand out, and he'd hit this hand and she'd step back and he'd hit this hand, and she kept stepping back. We were all three standing in a circle - I was wondering what she was moving back for. And he was so mad his eyes were just rolling up - you could just see the whites. I thought he was going to fall over. We were all looking at her, moving back, moving back, and she moved right back by this Mrs. Strapp. And he hit her so hard on the wrist that she just bent right over, and she let out a god-awful fart, right by Mrs. Strapp's ear!! P was kinda a tall girl, she was older than me. Mr. Strapp looked at her, gathered his strap together and he said "Get out of here you dirty thing." She ran out laughing, not the least bit remorseful. We got out of that strapping - he never called us back. She never apologized to Mrs. Strapp, she didn't do anything, she just ran out laughing!! We probably stole something to eat - that's about all we ever did. I'll tell you after I got friends with that J, I never went hungry again. Never mind we stole something we got so blamed tired of. We stole a great big container of peanut butter - I hate peanut butter right to this day. I never eat it. We gave it to the rest of the kids we thought could keep their mouth shut, after we had all we wanted. Sure the others would have told on us.

They didn't always exactly run away - if there used to be something going on, the kids would go out of the window and go to the dances. They didn't do no harm - it depends which way you look at it whether it was harmful. Every time J and I got together we talked about that P L and wondered what happened to her. J said "Boy! she did save

us from one god-awful strapping that time!" I guess it wouldn't be funny to anybody else but it was funny then. It was darn funny then. I've seen kids that were strapped that bad that their wrists used to be just puffy. And they had one man there - he was a teacher, Mr. Johnston - god! I just hated that man with a passion. His name was Cloyd or something - Cloyd Johnston and when they really wanted to punish somebody, they got him to strap 'em. He used to just jump off his feet - jump in the air - and bring that strap down. I used to swear if I ever got a chance I'd run that man over, and I wouldn't think twice. I guess he gave me the strap once or twice. You didn't have to do anything - you just look around and boy! you got it. I didn't enjoy it but I learned how not to treat my children, I can tell you, and how not to treat anybody else's kids. Right to this day I can't see a kid hungry. That Joblin - he was another Christian. They'd come over there and they'd pray and they'd preach. I don't know how those kids could sit there, present a face that was interested. I bet if they were to ask them, their thoughts were miles away. We'd sit there and look so interested - I learned that there.

Can't say that I learned anything that was positive - I learned to be good to people, to be kind, and to help people - that way you'd survive. Yeah, that was one thing I learned - survival. It's stood me in good stead all these years - how to survive. One thing I did learn there - kids that were from the longhouse - they didn't believe but they were taught - you had to believe in the United Church.

Strapp never took an interest in the children, no. His quarters were in the front part of the school, and he more or less stayed in there. It must have been like an apartment - I never went in his part except to get the strap, because his furniture was pretty nice and I guess he just didn't want any of the children coming in there - afraid they would touch something, knock something over and break it. No, I didn't have much to do with him - didn't see much of him at all. Didn't see really very much of any of them. Just more or less ones my own age I knew better - naturally they were my friends.

What did we do for fun? We'd go out and get something to eat probably. I had a cousin - he was there - it was easier for the boys, they could always sneak away - get away. He used to go home to his mother and she'd send me bread and stuff back to the school. If you wanted to talk to anybody, you'd just go out in the yard, because there was a big fence dividing us. You'd be walking around, around the fence, but you'd better not be there too much because somebody'd ask what you're doing there - a teacher. Some of them'd come through there and they'd happen to see you, they'd want to know what you were doing, and heaven help you if you were delivering a note or something. We used to have a little fellow - he used to carry that little pail of cream up to Muncey - they sold it up there. That was his job - just to carry the cream up there. He was from Kettle Point.

After I left the school I stayed on the reserve and went to

school - got enough to eat. I worked in Detroit - a lot of us did. I think the boys - they just got as far away as they could and never looked back. Most of those guys were kind. L N - I didn't care much for him when he was at school. He'd come in the room and he'd detour - I sat in the very last seat in the very last row - and he'd tour around and he'd look around and make sure no one was looking at him and he'd grab my ears and shake my head. I got even with him - I gave him one big sock and one little sock, and he come up to the storeroom to complain and say "I can't wear these socks - look at them." "There ain't no more," I said to him. I could sew real fast and they always had numbers stitched on the clothes in red, and I always used to carry a needle and red thread wrapped around it inside of my uniform. I could rip that number out real fast and sew it real fast - a new number in there. One thing I did learn in there was to be devious - sneaky. So L N he quit grabbing my ears and shaking my head.

The food was mighty bad.

[re personal information in the archives that anyone can see?} Well, it's not a lie and a lot of people when they write history - they put what sounds good? Now this by no stretch of imagination sounds good. In fact I could add a little to it. Say you had two dresses - two nice dresses and for any special occasions like the Christmas concert or something like that, you had to lend your dress to someone else that it would fit. A lot of people didn't like that. To this day I don't like lending. My daughters - I never permit them to wear each other's clothes when they were growing up, or my sons either. Never - I don't believe in it. But we had to lend our clothes - our dress as it was in my case - to someone else that didn't have as nice a dress. We didn't have any choice, we were told to do it. I think that's really why I'm like that. That's one rule I made when my kids were growing up - they would not wear each other's clothes.

I wasn't at the school for the long haul - when times got better I wasn't there. My mother died in '36 and my father - I don't know, work wasn't that plentiful. It got better - I hate to say it - after the war. There was more work, and my father did work. He had a steady job then. My mother was very close with my father. I didn't get along with my father till I was over 25. I disagreed with him - he'd say something and I'd contradict him. I never did believe how right he was until I was 35.

I think the boys found it harder to talk - maybe I'm wrong. A lot of these guys were loners.

Some of these people would have liked to keep their kids but they couldn't - they didn't have the means to do it. We always ate quite well - but then again, my folks were different. They planted a garden and preserved fruit. I can remember drying apples and corn. Corn on the cob - cook it up, cut it off, and dry it. I can remember my grandfather gave us a big darning needle and we'd pull it through whatever he was drying - squash or stuff like that. Apples - didn't matter you didn't grow apples - you'd get wild apples. I can remember them putting stuff away for the winter. My husband used to do this too. We had tomatoes, the guy up the road maybe would have cabbages. One year we grew our own cabbage - I got so tired of coleslaw, cabbage rolls. A lot of times back on the reserve water was scarce.

I felt closer to some of these kids than I do my own relatives. You can talk and laugh about certain things with them that you wouldn't think of telling your own relatives - you wouldn't even bring it up. These guys were your brothers. The guys used to walk over the roof. There were two dormitories - with the upper dormitory the boys could walk across the upper attic and come down. The girls used to go up in the attic, and they had the clothing storeroom on the one side - you were allowed to go in there on Sunday and get your coat, or hat, or whatever - and I think the boys storeroom was on the other side. They had their dispensary up there - it wasn't very handy anyway. You had an awful time getting up there. First you had to get up there - you had to get permission mind you, to get up there. Before you'd get in the dormitory there'd be one bedroom and that's where the officer slept. The ones that wet the bed would have to dry it and make their own beds - nobody else would do it. They weren't exactly mean people I guess - they did the best they could. They assigned a girl to sleep beside this other girl - whoever wet their bed - and you had to wake up them up. I never did - I let them sleep over, I didn't care. For that many people there wasn't much bedwetting. I think it was more emotional. This one girl who wet the bed - her mother got sick very suddenly and they took her mother away and they put her and her sister in Mt. Elgin, and I think she was too small. She was just a little kid - you wake up a little kid and make them go to the bathroom. Usually it wasn't the older ones that wet the bed - it was the younger - I think maybe being brought from their homes and all that was familiar...

I do know there wasn't any fat people there. I knew about drinking water long before it was advised - for a diet. I don't think there was any excuse for giving us skim milk. They had a farm instructor and he had the big boys working under him, and he more-or-less was supervising - the kids were doing the work. Go to school half-a-day and work half-a-day. They took so many of the big boys out. There was big boys when I was there - '38-'39, and they were working. In fact I can't remember seeing any of those bigger boys in school.

Ina Henry
1937 - 1941

This record says I went there in 1938, but I was there when the war broke out, and I stayed there one year after and I was there four years.

To me I went in a good year, I have nothing to say against my Mt. Elgin training. That's where I learned things. If I was punished, it was my own fault. I don't say I asked for it, but I was never punished just to give somebody the thought that they strapped me - for their own order. Everything I wanted - all I had to do was write to my two brothers - my grandmother's sons - one was just two years older than me so we were more like brothers and sisters - and say I wanted a new sweater, or I'd like some hairdos, I'd like a watch, my shoes are wore out and I don't want to wear these hightop shoes. If your parents could afford it you could wear your own things, that's why I say I went in good years. I was able to have a perm, that's when I started having perms. You could have your own socks - sockettes, you didn't have to wear them big black long ones. You could wear your own sweaters for chapel if there was something going on in the chapel, you didn't have to wear their sweaters. Things were good.

I was born and raised in Strathroy. Then when my grandmother came and married - she was Mrs. Fred Elm - I lived in Oneida two years when I went to Mt. Elgin. So I was way ahead having gone to Strathroy school. They didn't put me in a low grade, they put me right up with the seniors. I left Mt. Elgin when I was 16, so I was only 12 when I went there.

We went to school half-a-day and worked the other half. I went in the morning and worked in the apartment in the afternoon. The principal's apartment was where I got all my training to go out and work. It helped - I was a live-in student in the summer times when we went on our holiday. I was 13 when I first went out in St.Thomas and babysat. Every summer I went to work some place and stayed right there. I didn't have to stay at the school - my mother lives in St. Thomas and she knew people. I worked in London two summers. We learned how to set a table - fancy too - the silver, china and the crystal. The Strapps had their own apartment and dining-room, and I looked after that dining-room. You didn't have to house-clean their apartment because somebody else would come in and do all that - like painting. They did have better food - well you couldn't make a fancy dessert for 75 boys, 85 girls. You'd get a little better dessert up there because there'd be only Mr. and Mrs. Strapp and sometimes their niece stayed with them. On the other side of the wall was the staff dining-room, where I think there'd be 10 people, so they could get a little better dessert. We ate just what they ate in the upper kitchen when you were working there - you didn't have to go downstairs and eat with the rest. You'd stay right there in case they'd

ring that little bell if they wanted something, to go in the dining-room. We all had turns - we weren't in that kitchen the whole term. Other girls had to have a chance to learn too. I think they got more cut-up meat in the lower kitchen. Chicken, I remember, we had to prepare from scratch. The boys would kill the chickens and bring them in and we'd pluck them and clean and wash them, and that wasn't just one chicken. Each girl had about 16 chickens - that's why I don't like chicken today. It wasn't very often you'd have a roast chicken with stuffing downstairs, but you'd have it upstairs. Downstairs you'd have cut up chicken - the legs and the thigh, maybe not the breast; and chicken soup with rice with all the other bits. But I'm pretty sure I didn't starve while I was there. The food that was served - if you didn't like it - I sat on the end of a long table, and generally there was little ones sitting down on the sides of the table - say eight, and another bigger one at the end - so naturally if you didn't want to eat this funny looking meat you'd say "Who wants my meat?" There was always someone who'd say "Yes, I'll have it." You couldn't talk during meals but you could make motions. If everyone had spoke, with 75 - 100 children, think of the noise that would make. You could put up your hand and say something about the meal - something that you seen that shouldn't have been done. She'd come over - the one that was looking after the dining-room - and see what your complaint was. There was nothing to talk about anyway. Right after dinner you had twenty minutes to wash your face and change your uniform to get to work or go to school.

I have nothing against it - if it wasn't for there - I don't say my grandmother and aunts didn't teach me, they were the ones that taught me how to sew and knit and crochet.

I never ran away. I didn't have to run away. I could just go out of the door and sneak down the hill and go up the road and take the short cut to where my grandmother lived, and four miles and I'd be home. I'd visit there for a half hour and go back to school. We did sneak away, but I never got caught. That would be on a Saturday when you're not supposed to be someplace. You'd walk fast and skip along and in no time you'd be there. All you'd got to do when you got there "What you got to eat?" and get a piece of nice pie or cake. They never told me not to do it - I guess it was up to me whether I was going to get caught and punished. I wasn't the only one - a lot of them used to do that.

I got punished once. They asked me to go down in the main cellar. It was a little wee room, dark and narrow with one light, to go and sort apples. One bad apple would ruin the whole bunch. If someone were going by the basement door, they could see a light. If they rapped you'd say "Who is it?" Instead of just asking who it was on the other side of the door, I opened it, and it was my girlfriends. "What are you doing?" "Sorting apples." "Give me one." So I threw a not very good one. "Throw a better one than that." So I started throwing good ones. Right up here Mr. Strapp: "What do you think you're doing?" "Passing out apples." "Shut the door." So I went up those back stairs and in his office and he asked what I was doing, and I said I was supposed to be sorting apples. "How come I had the door open?" "Giving my girl friends apples." So I got the strap that time, but he let me go down and finish the job. As soon as my friends heard him holler with that big voice they were gone. He was a big man but you couldn't hear him coming.

We didn't have to be at work till 9 o'clock in the morning, till a quarter to one, then you had your dinner and on to school in the afternoon, or reverse. It was just light duties - make the bed, gather up their coffee cups and take them to the kitchen to get washed - you didn't have to wash them. Finish their laundry - it was mostly small stuff. I found him all right. Another time in winter we were going down Muncey Road. It was rough till you got to Muncey, but it was kinda a nice road - it wasn't paved but it was hard gravel - dirt. It was winter-time and I think there were three sleds that time, but they let us mix. They let boys and girls mix wherever you got on the sled, and we pushed Mr. Strapp off, so he had to walk. But one sled driver - they knew what we did, so they stopped and picked him up. But everybody got a lecture that evening at prayer - it happened that he 'accidentally' fell off, but they knew very well he got pushed off. It was in fun - it wasn't meant to harm, but it seemed like he looked right at us - he must have known who did it!! He didn't deprive us - he didn't say no more sleigh rides - I guess he liked the sleigh rides too.

When I went to Mt. Elgin I didn't have to walk a long way to school any more, and I had lots of girlfriends. Between that year when I was 16-17 I went to visit the school, and it did just happen that Mr. Strapp did come by and he said: "Ina, when you make up your mind, you can come back any time, your bed is waiting." But he didn't say "You're compelled to come back," which I didn't, which I should have. I might have got my Entrance. I was in Senior Fourth, but they didn't compel you to write your exams and I didn't think I was ready. I said "Give me another year to think it over," but I didn't go back. So I didn't write my exams, but I was in Senior Fourth. I thought I knew it all. My bossy brother, John - he was in the army, I was scared of him - told me I should go back, but Ken told me I could do what I liked. So every principal wouldn't give you that chance "Your bed is waiting for you to come back." He didn't like us to go because he knew what was ahead of us - that's why.

In 1982 I went to Fanshawe to get my nursing certificate, and that's what she told me - my reports and everything was done up good in the book, and everything she'd talk about she'd say "Ina, how come you know? Where did you learn that from?" I said - like making beds "I went to school for four years and learned how to make my own bed" - and that's a hospital bed. She said "I can't do nothing for you Ina, you know everything we talk about, even the cooking." I was 13 when I found out my grandmother had sugar diabetes. I was raised with diabetics. My aunt - she went blind, I worked with her - she was diabetic. I went through the course halfway and she said "You can come back at the end of the course and get your certificate," but I thought: Why go back? I was going to come home anyway and retire.

I didn't have a bad time, and if I did, I brought it on myself, but I wasn't strapped until I was blue, I wasn't put in detention. I've read all the stories, and heard a lot of stories from other residential schools and they don't compare with my life there at all.

Phyllis Hopkins and Vena Missauba
1938 - 1944 and 1939 - 1945

Vena: In the picture[p. 427] we were about 12 or 13.
Phyllis: Must have been - I think we left when we was about 14 didn't we?
V. I had my 15th birthday in June and we left right after that and I went to work. First my age wasn't correct and she was older than me and she was always ahead of me. She was in seniors and I was in intermediates when she left, and we wanted to be together, and my age was down. I didn't know exactly how old I was till I sent for my birth certificate when I was 21.
P. What I don't understand is how I got in here without a birth certificate. There's no way there was ever a birth certificate - in Toronto or anywhere. We searched in every church for a baptismal certificate - then they told me I was just born in the bush on a stump!!!

I had a whole bunch of brothers and sisters - nine of them, but none of them went there but me. M - my sister, she was there way before me. I went there because nobody didn't want me. We didn't have any money. I didn't know of anybody else that was going but me. I went through it all and I mean I had everything - all the checkups and everything, just to get here.

K - he's a minister - he told us the way he got in there - his Mum took him for a walk and walked him all the way up there, and that was the end!!!! He said: "I don't even know what I was doing there - all I knew was I wanted to go home"!!! We all wanted to go home!

V. Al [husband] was supposed to go there too and he took off for the bush I reckon.

P. He was a smart kid - we weren't!!

Al. They never caught me!

V. But if we hadn't gone there, what would have happened to the lot of us? There was no future at all - nothing doing, and the government never gave anything.

P. There was no such thing as welfare.

V. I got my education myself - I worked for a lawyer and I took care of their kids every evening. Their mother was an actress - they were really nice people. It was rich living - it wasn't my money naturally. I went to school in the daytimes - I had a bike. I had some interest money and I took that out. I wasn't supposed to have it till I was 21, but they took it out when I needed it - the government official came to see me - came to see Mr. Ross to see if I was really going to school, and they said if I was I could have my own interest money. I went to school there and I went to work in Detroit for a year, and I came back and went to business school. By this time I think the government paid my fees for the business school, and I went to work, and one day my interest money ran out and I had $8. Then I said "Oh my money's gone," but I was working by then. I just stayed with those people all those years and looked after their kids. I did a service for them and I needed a place to stay. They were very kind people.

P. She was one of the lucky ones - I wasn't that lucky.

V. The only way I got in there was, when we got through with the Entrance, they said "Who wants to go on to high school?" I just put up my hand. I was the only one that put up my hand. The United Church found a place for me, and then the first place they found the father died or something and the woman had to take the mother in, so I was without a place, so she phoned this Mrs. Ross. She said she wasn't particular about taking in a 15 year old girl, but they'd give it a try, and I was with them for nine years - even a year after I was married.

P. Well, Strapp placed me with a family after working for him, but they wanted me to work, they didn't want me to go to school, so I just had to work. Finally after a while I left and came home, because school was a thing that you wanted to do, but if nobody helped you, you couldn't get any place.

V. Like you say I was one of the lucky ones, but living with a family you're always on the outside looking in. I was quiet enough not to really be bothered. It did bother me, but not that much. They wanted to go to the cottage and I'd go with them, and after a couple of days the water would get to me. Coming from Christian Island I'd get lonely for the water - at that time I did. You were so alone. A few of the kids came to visit me, but it's not your own home to bring your family or kids into or anything. We had to give up certain things in order to do this - it wasn't easy.

V. and P. The loneliness at the school at first was terrible - really bad.

P. Who else did we have but her and I? That's all you have. There's nobody. Nobody comes to see you. We were just two people that nobody ever bothered with. You were just put there and that's it. We stayed there all year.

V. There was maybe only six girls there in the summertime, and all the rest went home.

P. That's where I learned to milk cows and feed the pigs and everything. It was good experience and a way of getting out of doing the same old thing.

V. I guess they left me inside - I never milked any cows. We worked in the kitchens - upper kitchen or lower kitchen, or the sewing room.

P. You only went to school half-a-day anyway. When you got to Grade 8 you went all day.

V. My young sister was there with Soper - it was a lot easier for them the year Soper was there. The principal at Muncey when we were there - Baldy - we were out west and we were in a park - my husband was stationed there. We went to church and who do you think was the speaker - but him. In Manitoba we met him. I didn't mind - it doesn't bother me.

Al. The Church was open and we were walking by and I said "Do you want to go to Church?" The Service had just started and we walked in.

V. They invited us for dinner - they were very nice. It depends on the people you talk to how bad he was. I don't think I ever got the strap. Did you ever get the strap?

P. No.

V. We were kinda lucky. Some of us - they did get a strapping. But it all depends what you did. I ran away - I was going out to a dance. I was thirteen then.

P. We all did it. I ran away too.

V. We all tried. One girl knocked her shoe off the fire escape, and the nightwatchman caught us so we just kept on going - she was without a shoe. When I ran away that time, like I said, I didn't mean to run away. We had to scrub the wall for about a month afterwards, after school.

P. I worked for Strapp. Remember when we first went there, they all used to call them big girls - they were all older.

V. Some of them were 19.

P. Some were up to 21 - guys too. That's all I can remember about them - big girls and big boys - that's what they were called. But they were all older ones.

V. They had nowhere else to go. They'd get through their entrance and they wouldn't have nowhere to go so they'd come back and take weaving class - they used to make our scarves and things like that. They had a teacher for that.

We always cleaned. There was a bunch of us elected to do the cleaning every morning, so it wasn't really filthy. We went over the boys' side. There wasn't any bathrooms - just one on each floor in the dormitory, we had to go outside. Do you remember how they used to clean out the old outhouse - the boys? They used to put that big cover off and get in there and dip it out. I don't know how they dipped it out, but they had to do the 'longhouse' as we called it. We had one inside toilet. They cleaned it out somehow - they wouldn't allow us round there when they were cleaning it out.

The food was sufficient, but I don't imagine we got all that much, because when we went to live with these people I couldn't eat all that they ate.

P. Fish-eyes - we used to get this tapioca - oh, I couldn't eat that stuff. It used to make me nearly throw up just to look at it.

V. I couldn't eat my vegetable marrow - it'd just slide down my throat, so we'd exchange, her and I.

P. Otherwise you'd have to sit there till you eat it up. You're going to sit there boy!, and you're going to eat it.

V. So we'd just eat each other's things.

P. That's the only thing I really couldn't eat. I just had to look at those things and oh...!

V. It didn't bother me at all, but I just couldn't stand that vegetable marrow - it was so slippery.

P. I could eat that. That was one thing they couldn't really complain about was the food - it was there. We got enough. A lot of them when they got a dime used to go buy bread from the baker.

V. It was sufficient - but if it was somebody who always liked to eat, they probably didn't get enough.

P. The boys never used to get enough to eat - we knew that - a lot of times we'd steal a loaf of bread or something and give to them, and they'd eat it.

V. We'd have to get rid of it in a hurry. I don't know if I ever stole anything.

P. We did - I know I did.

V. If we craved for something we must have had apples. Applesauce - we canned a lot too. We canned the strawberries, the rhubarb, and everything they could put down. I ate rhubarb. We used to have a contest, we'd sit there and you weren't supposed to make a face, and we'd have to eat this rhubarb. We must have made those teabiscuits, because Charles Ross used to say I made teabiscuits for them, so I must have learned to make them somewhere. We had butter and cream - the officers got the butter. I don't know what we ate. Probably we got some butter but we can't remember it, it was so small!! If we stole a little bit of food when we were up there and we didn't get caught, we'd get a little bit of fat on us.

P. One thing I learned at that school that helped me out was being independent. You can't depend on nobody else - you got to do it yourself. Being in that school like that - there were a lot of people there - you just have to make your own living, make your own way - make everything for yourself.

V. It was kinda good in a way. Remember how we used to make our own fun. We'd get in these old gunny sacks. When Al was in the Service out west - they said "All the ladies get in a potato bag" and we had a race. So I knew I could do it and I went, and I got in this potato bag, and I was the first one over there. I even beat the PT teacher.

Her husband says to Al "How come your wife can do all this?" It was just from having to make our own fun when we were young. They didn't provide too much. We just prayed. Every night they had service and we took turns even, running the service. They taught us that too. Sometimes somebody would get the giggles up there.

P. I never was sorry that I went there.

V. No - where would we be if we didn't? They taught us to sew, and taught us to cook.

P. They taught you to take care of everything for yourself.

V. Take care of the younger kids - we were maybe even 12 years old, cutting other kids hair - you know the other little kids. There was nobody else to do it - you had to do it.

I don't know what our life would have been, but there was nobody to look after us after my father died. My uncle looked after us, but there were 12 of them. I learned to take care of myself and go where the work is. It's not going to come to me - I have to go where it is. No matter where it is, I'm going to go there.

P. You could hardly talk to the boys. You were really separated - the boys from the girls. They got their own side.

V. I don't think they ever found out about the roof idea did they? Because some of the boys used to come and visit some of the girls but I don't think too much went on though - they didn't stay very long. It was the boys looking for girlfriends, but I don't know what actually went on - I never had a boyfriend come and see me.

P. But they used to let us talk to - remember that little Cody Claus - he was about the only one we could talk to. He fell out of the window and he died.

V. He was only 5 or 6 - very young.

P. Younger than that wasn't he? Wasn't he 4?

V. They left him alone in one of those big dormitories.

P. That L was up there that's why they left him. He was sick in bed that time - they didn't even see him - it was on a Sunday morning. I think he died by Monday morning.

V. H S - she died there too at the school. She was from Muncey. She went to the hospital in London and first thing at the service the Principal told us that she had died.

You must have went a year ahead of me because I never met that Cody. I heard the story, you must have went ahead of me one year and come out a year ahead of me. We went in October '39.

P. I was there when he died. Remember on Sunday mornings you used to go outside and wait for that bell to ring at 10 o'clock to go to Church. There was one at ten-to-ten and the other one rung at ten. The one at ten-to-ten was to get in line and I remember we were all outside - it was a nice sunny day, and that little boy was looking out the window there. He had this spool of thread - an empty spool but he used to tie it on a string, so he had something to play with, and he was leaning it out the window. There was a little itty-bitty hole in the screen - just a little one, and that's where he would stick his hand and play with it and he dropped it. So he tried to reach for it I guess, and that's when he went through.

V. A lot of the guys ran but they couldn't get there in time.

P. Whoever was in that dorm at the same time, he was sick, or that little boy would never have been up on the fourth floor if there was nobody in there.

I'm sure Cody was just 4 when he died - he was just an itty-bitty baby, and that little girl, Lucille, she used to cry all the time cuz she wondered what happened to her brother. We used to save every kinda junk for him to play with cuz we had nothing. And you know what I did when I had Janet, I went out and bought dolls for her and everything, because I always wanted one - I used to see the kids with them at school.

V. I still buy dolls.

P. She would not take that doll - no way she wanted a doll - she liked plush animals.

V. With Susie, I used to make doll clothes for her and everything - even with fur collars.

I don't think some of these girls even told their husbands they were in that school - that's how badly they feel. So I just leave them alone and I never talk about it.

P. I never had no trouble.

V. No - I guess we were young enough not to have any problems. We had bullies - but whoever was getting bullied the rest of us watched them.

P. What was your number - mine was 44?

V. Mine was 65.

P. We were all numbers.

V. M's was 48 - I checked her in; she had nice clothes.

P. That's something we never had. We never had clothes at home.

Some had alcohol problems - I met a girl in Detroit -ooh she was real bad.

V. A lot of them blame the school for their restlessness. Some of them - maybe the loneliness of the younger years might have got to them. They don't talk and tell you these things, if we see them. What do they intend to do about it if anything? They can't do nothing.

P. There's no schools anymore.

V. But you never know. It helps to understand.

With us as parents - we can look after the little ones and love them, but we can't take it very well ourselves.

P. That's hard to do.

V. D says the same thing too - you can give it out, but you can't take it. You just can't accept it all that easily.

P. You not only learned to be independent but you never had another's love when you needed it.

V. When you needed it - in your younger years. We never went home in the summer time. They used to take us to town - a few of the officers. They tried to do little things for us, or either buy us little things in town if we had any money of our own.

P. There used to be a lady and her husband - they're dead now, they were from this reservation [Moraviantown]. They used to go around to all these little fairs they have in summer selling things, and they were the only people I can ever remember coming to see me up there. They used to sell stuff at Muncey fair - remember we used to walk up to the Muncey fair. Those are the only people that I can ever remember all my life - that I knew anybody from our reservation. They didn't come and see me - we seen them at the fair.

V. Some people used to come in like that Os-Ke-Non-Ton - he was from Caughnawaga. He'd been over England singing - he was a great singer - opera singer. I read about the ones from out West about how down they were and I said "Well we can't really say that we were that bad." We were watching one from Cape Croker, so these were like rapes - the ministers or the priests would come and get the children with no mother, just the father there and they'd take them up and put them in these residential schools. These kids were badly treated - well we never seen any of that. We got to be in Entrance Class.

P. And our cod-liver-oil. We were just talking about that in Florida - they said "People are always sick around here - how come you never get sick?" I said "Cuz I went to that Mt. Elgin School and they made us take cod-liver-oil. They had a strap in one hand and a spoon with cod-liver-oil in the other. You either drink it or else - they had a salt shaker too - you could put salt on it if you wanted.

The officers that looked after us - some were good and some were bad. Remember Mrs. Erratt - she was one of the nice ladies we had. The one I was scared of all the time was that Mr. Johnson, remember - he was six-toed.

V. This [photo p.   ] was a kind lady.

P. She was the one we called CFRB - she was loud like CFRB.

V. Yeah - she had a voice, boy!!

P. When she hollered you jumped. Mr. Dodson - he was one - he used to make me laugh - he was just an itty bitty guy you know. He could do something with that strap when he hit you. But it never bothered me. There was one teacher - remember that last one I had - Richardson? There was only four of us that were going to graduate that year. I could do the work - I was always up with it, and I always kept my books - made sure my books were neat and clean. I **never** ever made any other mark on it. Mr. Richardson used to make me go and sit in the next seat and help N R. Oh, I didn't like helping her. No way I didn't like doing somebody else's work. And I'd help her from day to day. I used to have to sit in the same seat with her. I used to get so disgusted with it. Mr. Richardson said "Well Phyllis, I don't care if you pass on your work for the year or not - you'll never pass, I'll make sure of that. You'll never get out of Grade 8. You're going to stay for another year." So I just figured I guess I'm here for another year, cuz I just couldn't handle doing her work and mine too, but he made me do it, so I did it. When that Inspector came my book was perfect. It was clean and neat and he could read everything in it and I passed without even having to write an exam. Boy! I was the happiest person that ever was.

V. He probably just told you that to get N to try and get through the grade. It looks bad on the teacher - one child didn't pass in the class when she should have.

P. Mrs. Erratt was one for being nice to all of us, then there was Miss Broderick in the upper kitchen, she was another one who would be real nice.

V. Yes I remember her coming and asking if there was anything I needed from town when I was making something in my books, like cooking.

P. The vaseline lady - she was another one that was kind..

V. I know who you mean, but I've forgotten the name. Our hands used to be so chapped.

P. She wouldn't give you nothing else either - everything was vaseline.

That guy that used to take the boys out all the time. He used to holler "Roll out!" He'd tell the boys when they had to get up in the morning to milk the cows and that. It would be 5.30 in the morning. We didn't have to get up till 6.30. In the springtime you'd be looking out the window and you'd see the boys bringing the cows up from way back in the pasture. I never did get to do that, but I did get to go and milk the cows and feed the pigs. That's when I got scared of the pigs. I was told that if you'd fall in there they'd eat you up too. I don't know if they were just telling me or what, I don't know.

V. I don't think they were that hungry!!

P. I don't think so either, but that's what they used to tell us - the boys wanted to scare us. That's where I learned that when I wanted to work, I could work outside, I could work inside, I could do anything.

V. Did you know those boys used to get up through the night and go after those horses and race them?

We were quite self-sufficient with the vegetables and that. We even made our own brassieres and everything. We made all our clothes.

P. We sure did. The only thing we ever got I guess, or anything that was worthwhile, was those black stockings. I remember that Mr. Dodson - everyone used to roll their stockings down below their knees. You can see in that picture she did. I always kept mine up. He never did want that - he wanted them always up - and there's your 'army boots' you wore.

V. See how dirty our uniforms would get from working in the kitchens. We would have one a week.

They discouraged us speaking our own language - I guess I could speak it when I went there - yes I think I could, because I learned English after. We lived in Germany for two years - all the languages came to me easily. When I was in high school there - Central Collegiate - I sent for my records one day, I was going in for a course - I had made

96% in Latin. Who learns Latin any more? I laughed - I thought that was funny. I can understand a little bit of Chippewa - like "shut the door" - just the little things, but if anyone speaks for a couple of hours I have to concentrate and translate everything in my mind to English and I get so tired at the end of that time. It's difficult - Indian language - you've got to live with the people to talk it. People can learn their language back again.

P. With all the white schools now, none of the kids know it but the little kids. They have a girl that teaches up there [Moraviantown] - she teaches these kids words and they learn their Native Language. When they go out to the white school they never hear these things again, so their language is gone again. These are day care kids - we have a small school of kindergarten kids - so they have two years, day care and kindergarten and that's it, they never hear it again. My aunt when she died even, she couldn't speak a word of English. Every time she'd come and see my mum, she'd talk Indian to her of course, but she had the same little words for us all the time, and we always knew she'd talk with her hands, she knew we couldn't understand Indian.

V. S - that was the only home she ever knew - she was so small being sent to Muncey.

P. That was the only home I ever knew too. It was good and it was bad. To me it was like - you do the best you can. Make the best of it - you're going to be there anyway. There's no way you are going to get out. Just go ahead and live your life in there and do what you have to do.

V. You didn't know what was ahead of you, what was going to happen to you or not.

P. My mum never was one for welfare. There's no way that she wanted welfare, and I can remember when my sister was small, and I don't know who it was came around, but she always said "You don't do those things, you work for a living, and if I can't work for what I got, I don't want it." It wasn't exactly welfare, it was sort of like a church. They gave her diapers, but she wouldn't take them. My oldest brother used to wear her shoes to school. They had one pair of shoes between them. How many would do that now? That's all my mum had. I found a letter my aunt wrote for my mum. She was asking for her two weeks work - to earn 25 cents to buy a pair of shoes, because my mum and my brother never had a pair of shoes. She never wanted nothing for free - she wanted to work for it. I don't know if that's where I learned it, but I think the Mt. Elgin school had a lot to do with me being independent - I sure do. Although at that time we would have liked someone to come and hug us, but we never got it, so now we don't even want that. I don't know why - it's always been like that.

That's what I learned there anyway - to be independent.

Lorraine Brigham
1939 - 1942

Moses Seneca - he got addresses and he went about and he approached all the students that were there and got their complaints. Like with me, he took me to a lawyer in Strathroy - this was a woman lawyer, which I liked because you could talk to her easier. I would have been afraid to talk to a man. Moses Seneca - that's what he did on his own - he didn't have children there. He must have been in his late seventies at this time - but he had heard of so much abuse that he didn't think this Strapp should be there for all the years he was, so he wanted him moved. I don't know whether he was removed at the time or what happened. At the time - that's what I remember hearing - that he was going to be removed from the school - that there was too many complaints. Then I didn't hear any more about it because we moved away from that area. We came to Walpole and then I worked in Michigan. The other thing he never liked - I don't know if anything was ever said - was the school time. See when you got out of these boarding schools you couldn't compete with the other students - you only had half a year's work. And when you got out and you're 14-15, you're ashamed to end up with the 10-11 year-olds - that's how far behind you were in school. They never made no move to make sure you did your homework. They made sure you did your work in the school - keeping the place clean.

I was 12 when I left. I was there when World War II started. My oldest brother, before he went overseas, came to visit me, and I was there four years. Of course I made it home every summer - my mother made sure of that. But there was kids in there - when they got in there they never got out till they were 18. When I went away to school my father had died, and it was just the general practice - when the father dies they take the children, whether the mother wants to let them go or not - they were gone. When I got there I well remember that too - when they take your clothes - your own clothes - and then they give you the uniform - black socks, high-topped boots, bloomers - I always had to roll them up cuz none of the clothes ever fit right - and they threw me a nightgown - I mean threw it at me. All the children were crying that arrived there about the same time - it was in the evening - I don't know what day it was. Anyway, all the kids were crying and I thought: Never! I'll never cry! I just got into it. I did what I was told to do. I got along - you have to survive. You have to survive against the staff and you have survive against the kids because they're from different tribes. I didn't have anybody to talk to and I made up my mind - and I knew this from hearing my great-grandfather - I was away at school when he died, and he died at 105 - Austin Sands. I sat by his feet and he told me "When you grow up, never marry a Oneida," he said, "never. And don't hang around those people

because they won't treat you well. They don't like us - because of the Indian wars." So when I got to the school I find out there's a lot of Oneida, and I thought: What am I going to do? Grandpa told me they wouldn't like me, so I decided then and there - I think I stayed up all night, I couldn't sleep - I'm gonna make friends with them and I'm gonna learn their language. And I did. They lived close by, and when we were told not to speak our language - they did - behind everybody's back. I spoke my language and I kept it. My brother was on his way overseas and he came and told me "If you don't speak the language, don't forget it. Before you fall asleep remember the words you learned - remember - don't ever lose it." So that was OK and I can speak it fluently and now I'm teaching my little grandson.

Now that I'm older - it was like being in a prison. There's no happy memories. And the other thing I always griped about - I seen the boys - and there's fields and fields they planted. I worked in the strawberry fields and picked - gosh! I don't know how many crates of strawberries. Well, for the whole season we might have got a little wee dish to say we had strawberries, but we worked at that. We'd go out there - we were made to pull weeds, and big trucks would roll in from London and pick up all the strawberries that were harvested. There was no jam or jelly made. They had chickens - chicken coops - maybe three times the length of this house - great big chicken coops and we got one egg Easter Sunday and that's it. And yet there was a lotta eggs - crates and crates of eggs - and then when I worked - after I got to work, I made some friends with the staff and they trusted me and they had me clean their room. I did hear - they were griping too - they weren't getting enough eggs - Mrs. Strapp - that was her pocket money. She sold the eggs, and she sold the strawberries. It was the staff talking that I heard and they didn't think it was fair - she never really became friends with the staff. She stayed in their quarters - she didn't mingle with the staff that much. These boys that had to work in the fields - and it's easier to farm now than it was in those days - with horses. They were still using horses and that's a slow job - I could see that the boys weren't fed enough - the workers.

I worked in the kitchen - and the one for the staff. And I learned I could pick their locks. I'd see the boys - they're still hungry - I used to hand bread out the kitchen window and get peanut butter - they ordered peanut butter by the buckets. But I never got caught at that. Even if you got money from home - when they were going to give money out you could get - maybe 25 cents - maybe not that - it just depends how they feel. When I was there bread was 5 cents a loaf - the baker used to come there. I'd get bread - I'd save my money. I mean, living with a bunch of students that way you had to be looking out for yourself always - I don't care who you were with.

I did learn - if I knew something had gone on, I never opened my mouth, because I'd be punished a couple of times. I'd get punished from the staff or Strapp, and then kids'll deal with me. So I knew enough to keep my mouth shut - at all times. [re Complaint - Strapp lifting up the girls' skirts] That didn't happen to me - I was kinda a kid that wouldn't take it - I'd take it on the hands. The girls told me - they warned me. You always warned each other what happens when you go up to the office. And they told me "You know he's going to lift your dress and you're going to get that strap on your seat. I said "Not me. He's not doing that." They said - you know you argue back and forth - "Yes he will." If I was wrong I would have had to do work for these girls, and I wasn't going to do that either. I didn't want no control from them. So I said "No, you just watch" I said, "I'll take the strap on my hands." Well, they said "Girls have to bend over - on a chair or something, and that's the way he punished them. It's only boys that get the strap on the hands." I says "Well, I don't care," I says, "I'll take it on the hands." I'm telling you - red face - he was a madman. You know I can still see the face when I talk about him - what happened that day, and I was in the room all by myself with him that day. The matron was out in her office. And I refused - I was going to fight. I could fight, I could kick! He had a mad child too. I made too much noise. He asked me to bend over - you were given orders, and I refused those orders because I didn't think he should be able to do that - he's a man. Oh no! He couldn't make me do it. I do have a scar yet - you can see it on my wrist. And you know the strap that they used - it was that wide and that thick, and there was wires in that strap and it was the wire or whatever else was in it, that cut me. Some kids - I forget now what they did - but they included me because I knew and they thought I would be forced to tell - but I never did tell. I never even talked about it. I never told my mother until we went to that lawyer - why I got strapped. I was just taken in with these kids. Thinking back - there was so many times - if you see something, you're included. You didn't have to do it, but you're included - you got punished too. I took the strapping rather than tell what happened. See they never took the time to find out what maybe happened. If they got the wind of something - punishment - whether it was the kids that did it or not. They never took the time to talk to anybody. And then I remember this one time - I think I went back two years - the last Sunday I was there he told us "Come back clean you savages." Those were the words - I never forgot those. What upset my mother - the times that she'd come and see me - she'd see Mr. Strapp - he always wore his collar - he was a Minister - and she couldn't believe how cruel he could be, and the language he used. People didn't know what he was like when he got into the time for punishment - his face was all red, and we knew the look!! It was beyond what it should have been. But you know, what the boarding school

taught me - I made a vow to myself: If I have children, they will never be taken from me! My oldest daughter - when I'd go to work - she must have been about 5-6 years old - I'd tell her "You hide if you see the Indian agent coming." Whoever was babysitting I said "You just make sure you hide." And then when sisters came along I told her "Hide them," and the babysitters never understood why I gave those orders they were to be hidden. But that's what it was - I was afraid somebody would just pick them up and just place them in a foster home. I just had that fear, I guess.

When you come out of there you don't have any trust in anybody - that's what it does do to you. I'd talked to my older brother and I said "How did you feel?" and he said "Right to this day I don't trust anybody." He was at Shingwauk. We'd compare stories, and the time I was in a boarding school and the time he was in Shingwauk, I don't think it was half as bad [Shingwauk]. My understanding is the staff had a better way of talking to the kids. It wasn't this slamming - they never took time to talk to you that it was wrong - you know - how you should talk to children.

That's what I didn't like - the way I was treated when I got there, and then hearing Strapp say "Come back clean you savages."

I knew how to stay out of trouble. I did my work. If you were ambitious - it didn't matter if you did your homework as long as your work was done - what you were wanted to do. Any time a staff was leaving and we got somebody that was kind - they weren't there very long. They were gone.

[re Complaint - Mr. Strapp coming around the dormitory with a flashlight] That was supposed to be making sure everybody was in their beds - making sure somebody didn't decide to leave the place. And what I never could understand was - why would they have fire escapes and have the window locked? That was the other thing. I used to think about: What would I do? and I slept by the window where the fire escape was, so I figured out what I would do. I would have to lift my bed at one end and push it against the window. There was a bunch of us girls and we would teach each other how we should tie our sheets if we broke another window. They had storm windows - so there were actually two windows you'd have to break.

I never ran away. After I knew how to get along with the kids that I didn't trust I got along with them, and the staff - same thing. The feeling you get - the way you're spoken to - I think they forgot we were human. That's how I felt. I came from a Christian family - my grandparents. They were strict - but as long as you obey orders you're OK. You learned how to get along with people.

They hired a person - a dietitian, but I'm telling you, the staff - they did their own thing - they'd be crocheting - they didn't have their eyes on what the kids were doing - they were just told to do it, and you know you're cooking with great big pots, and some of the oatmeal wouldn't even be cooked, and then they made their own cereal most of the time, and you'd see blades of grass in it. That was the other thing. After a while I started thinking they were feeding us the stuff they ground up for the pigs. It was bad. And bread you sometimes had to peel off the mould. The big eaters - you're sitting at the table - kids next to you and the ones across from you - you had to watch. I'm talking about when I first entered the school - they'd reach over and take food out of your dish. So what I did - I spit on my food and nobody took it!!! That's how I hung on to my food!!! We did trade food - if it's carrots you didn't like - maybe the next meal - next time something that they didn't like - we'd trade. With me I liked all vegetables cuz my mother always had a garden. My mother always put food away for the winter. My grandfather - he had pigs, ducks, you name it. Every Sunday - the kids that could understand - we'd have to sit on the floor and fold our legs and arms, and he'd tell us how he would plant, when to plant. And of course when you're anywhere from 18 and up, until you have your own kids, you start thinking back how you can survive if you have to. I remembered - when I had to do it here - I filled this garden myself - my husband didn't have no interest in having a garden, so I did it. And I was working same time. Every day - as soon as I get home - out there. Before I'd go to bed I have to clean my house, I have to wash diapers. I could do all that that time - I'm still doing it! Mt. Elgin helped me because I think you get something out of something you hate even. But I made up my mind no child of mine was ever going to be taken from me.

I had a step-father - we lived in Ailsa Craig, we lived in Strathroy, we lived in London - it was a lot of moving. He was just that kinda person - he didn't want to be in one place. So by the time I was 15 I was fed up with it - I couldn't be in school any length of time, and I left and I told my mother I said "I'm not getting anywhere, and I'm going to Walpole where I know my way around, and I had an older sister here, and she was working in the States doing housework. And I said "If I can just support myself," and I had aunts who lived on the island and I got along with them, and I never lacked for a place to live. And I knew enough - you buy food wherever you're at. So I always had a place with my aunts, and cleaned their house.

I went the same year as Vena and her sisters - 1939. The reason I was put in the school was because my father died. A parent died - a father died - all the kids went away to school at the time that I went in. When I got married, my mother-in-law, she was white - she was from Michigan - Simpson's mother. I got to know her real well - she was like my second mother - and she told me a lot of things why children were shipped off like that. My mother would have got the word today to have me ready tomorrow. There was no warning. The reason they did that - he got paid for every head he put in the school. She was married to an Indian agent and she knew what went on, and she said "There was nothing I could do - I didn't like it." Because she was

married to an Indian before - Simpson Brigham's father, and when he died she married the Indian agent - Highfield. The parents didn't have a say. Indian agents at the time they had control of everything. It wasn't a question that my mother couldn't support me - not at all.

The work was the main thing - it didn't worry anybody if you got behind in school. It never mattered.

You'd sit in the chapel - to this day I don't know what I heard. I just thought: When I get of here! I think the only comfort that I had - if I could get outside - sit outside, I'd hear the mourning doves. Then come Christmas you know you're going to get something from home, but you didn't really look forward to it because if you get a box of fruit or something, you know it's going to go in the storeroom and get locked up. You'd maybe get one apple or a little bunch of grapes they'd just hand out to you, and the rest of the stuff would spoil before they'd give it all out.

Another thing I never liked - you could take a good warm coat back to the school and you wouldn't see it until you got out of school in the summer the next year. We only had sweaters and winters were harsh. Anybody that went to Muncey they never wore a winter coat.

If someone was in to visit Strapp you'd get a little more decent food. Maybe you got fruit on the table. But that's the only time, and he didn't have too many visitors, so I don't remember ever seeing fruit. We'd be taken for walks just in back of the school and there was walnut trees. We'd pick walnuts and bury them - we'd do what the squirrels do. You'd get so hungry you can always eat walnuts. We could see apple trees - if you could get over the fence you could eat them. I seen a little girl eat toilet paper.

My father-in-law, Simpson Brigham, was at the Mohawk Institute. My mother-in-law said he went into the ministry because of his age, and because there was no other kinda work he wanted to do, or would be able to do - he didn't have a choice. But then, when he got into the ministry he loved it. But he had a brother - he would have been younger. The parents were told that the boy ran away - but he was never found - to this day.

About sexual abuse - the only thing that I knew about - there was this girl - she had the flu and she was in bed, and Strapp was around inspecting the dormitory. And when he seen her alone - he yanked her out of bed. Of course she fought back and she tore his shirt off of him. That was common knowledge with the kids - she told all the kids - never be in the dormitory when he comes in alone. That's the only thing I heard. She was one of the senior girls.

These uniforms were nice after they got all frayed and everything - but if you got a new one [it was stiff] under the arms. I didn't do any sewing - except mending socks.

All you're waiting for is for summer to come. You didn't look forward to the holidays either - like Christmas. Summer holidays - you lived for those days.

Bernice (George) Jackson
1939 - 1944?

This is a picture of me and my girlfriend [p. 427]. The school was a big place - these windows here are where we used to sleep - the dormitories, and below here, the little windows, used to be the lower part of the whole building and that's where we used to go down to wash up, wash our hands and brush our teeth - there was a whole row of basins.

I liked it at times - you had to get used to it. You were there for years and we were allowed to come home during the holidays - the two months. There was a lot of children that didn't get home because they lived possibly too far for their parents to come after them - there was a lot of them that came from a long way, the Quebec area and Brantford. I was able to come home during the summer, and then when we had to go back 1st September and the first thing we'd see this great big school - it was on top of a hill and we used to try and hide - "Oh no, we don't want to go back." But you sort of had to get used to it and like it, but there were times when you didn't like it. Sometimes they treated you a little rough.

We lost all our Indian language and culture for being there. We weren't allowed to speak our own language. If they heard us talking in our language to someone they wouldn't like it and they'd tell us not to talk like that. I used to speak it and understand it. I knew English and our own language when I went there, but we used to **like** talking in our own language, but we were never allowed to do that. And if we done anything that wasn't suitable to the staff we would get strapped. They had these great big heavy straps and in fact I got a strapping maybe a couple of times. One reason was I ran away from the school - me and a bunch of girls. I guess it was just a spur of the moment thing to take off. I knew we'd get caught to come back. We didn't even get right home before we got caught and got taken back. We got good strappings when we got back and the principal - he was a big guy and he just came right down on our hands - 10-15-20 times on each hand with a big strap - it must have been about a yard long and ½ inch thick. He would take us into his office one by one, and not only me got a strapping - different kids would get sent to the office if they had done some little thing wrong that didn't agree with the staff - you'd get sent to the office and get the strap. I got the strap in school one time - you know how kids like to fool around. I poked the girl in front of me with my pencil - jabbed her - and of course she squirmed and the teacher told me to stand up and go out in the hall and he gave me another big strapping. I wasn't bad or anything but you'd get caught doing these little wee tiny things and you'd get a big strap. We didn't really do anything out of the way - nothing that you hear goes on today, just little minor things.

Was it 1940 I ran away? I was with a few girls. We just started hitchhiking and then we got a ride one time with this great big transport truck, and then we got off in Chatham. We were just kids that didn't know actually where we were going, and we got back to Chatham and we hitchhiked to Sarnia Reserve and that's where somebody told on us that we were around, and they came and picked us up again - the staff or somebody did - and took us back, and that's when we got big strappings. Plus we were deprived from certain things for a long time. But there were fun times too. The teachers used to take us on little hikes, and we used to have baseball games. We used to get to slide down that great big hill. We used to go down into the river behind the barns. They used to let us go down there and slide.

All my sisters were in this school. My older sister wasn't there too long and she came home and she took sick and she passed away. But then I had another sister go there, she isn't living no more. Then my younger sister she was there too, but I had left by then. My sisters were still there, but I was old enough to leave school. I must have been there six to seven years. I think I left the school when I was 16. I was there during the war I know, because my brother used to come and visit me in his uniform. He was stationed in London. I was home when the war was over, I know that, because I was waiting for my brothers to get home. I think Strapp was still there when I left, because I don't remember the name of the new principal, and then I heard they were shutting the whole school down. I was there quite a while anyway - too long.

I was old enough to come home, but I didn't come back on the reserve, I came to Forest - that's where my Dad was working - he got me a job at this basket factory and that's where I worked and boarded in town, so I didn't come back on the reserve to live. That's why I lost all my Indian language and culture - from not actually living on the reserve too much. I just got the education I got when I was at the school - I went to Grade 8. After that I started to work. They had Grade 8 and after Grade 8 you went into Entrance. We used to all go to school half-a-day, and the other half we had to work, but when you got into Grade 8 you got to go to school all day. There was girls sometimes that were 18 years old.

I did learn discipline there - it was just like army. You had to line up for this - line up for that, and go to bed a certain time, wake up a certain time, get a bath certain time - exactly like being in the army. We had to line up to go to church off the school grounds - a little church on Muncey Reserve. Every Sunday we'd line up and we had to march to the church - it must have been about a mile and a half-two miles away, and then we had to line up when we got back. We were able to wear our own coat or clothes if we wanted to, to Church. We had to go way up on the top of the building - that's what they called the attic, and that's where our dress clothes were hung up. We weren't allowed to wear them through the week, we had to wear uniforms. When you went there you never took a lot of clothes because you knew you were going to be wearing uniforms, and we never really had a lot of clothes there - maybe one oufit - just what you wore there - and it was hung up and you could get to wear it if you wanted to, to Church. A lot of kids never wore their own clothes, they just wore the dress uniform. It was like a heavy denim. It was a dark blue with little red trim around the sleeves. The jackets - I can't remember whether they supplied us with jackets or not. Our stockings were black, in the wintertime. We used to wear heavy black boots for winter, and in the summer they gave us high-top running shoes to wear, but we still had the old uniforms. When we worked half days, we used to have to make the uniforms. They taught us how to make the uniforms. We never made the boys' clothes - they just wore an overall and they had those sent in - but we made all the dresses that the girls wore. The half day you had to go to school, and the half day you either went to the sewing-room or you went into the laundry room. On Mondays - there was a big laundry room and some of the girls worked in there. Some of the girls worked in the kitchen, some done the scrubbing of the dormitories. You'd have to get down on your knees and maybe there'd be three girls would come down in a row and scrub the floors. They were great big long rooms. Some made beds, and some were assigned to clean the staff rooms where they slept - their own bedrooms - we had to clean those out too for them. And we had to clean the hallways all down. They put up a sheet - a bulletin - and every month they'd change over, where you had to work for that month, and that's what you done for the whole month. The other half day you'd go to school and work at this place what they told you to work at. You could be sent to the laundry room, the sewing room - different jobs, the kitchen and staff room. They ate in their own dining-rooms, and they got better meals than we did. We used to get oatmeal in the mornings with worms in it and we were made to eat it up. You sat there until you ate it whether you liked it or not. Then while we were eating they would have a staff going up and down watching - walking up and down in the middle. The boys ate on one side and the girls on the other side. The staff - they weren't all teachers, but they just worked there - and if you didn't eat everything up, they would make you eat it up. You sat there till you did. [looking at menus] You know what we used to call tapioca? 'Fish eyes'. Date cookies? When did we ever get date cookies. I don't remember eating too much meat. Roast pork? I don't remember eating any of that stuff. We had mashed potatoes, and stuff like that, macaroni, and prunes - I remember eating prunes. Rhubarb. They used to do a lot of their own canning too. They had a big garden of rhubarb and we had to put it down. Certain girls would be working in the kitchen and they would have

to put the rhubarb down with the dietitian that showed us how to do all this. When you worked in the kitchen you had to get up real early.

We didn't have much to do with Mr. Strapp - he had his job to do and sometimes it was with the strap.

When you're young you don't see the conditions of it - you just have to live with it. Where we slept they always had one inside toilet, only one, for I don't know how many kids in a dormitory - maybe 50 kids in each place and only one toilet, for each place. We weren't allowed to run upstairs to use them, we stayed mostly down here all the time, and if you wanted to go to the washroom you had to go outdoors to the outhouses. You were only allowed to use the indoor one at night. We weren't allowed to be on the boys' side either. This fence here separated the boys from the girls, so a lot of our fun was just doing things - playing ball and that. Brothers and sisters weren't allowed to talk to each other - the only time you seen them was in the dining area.

They took people too that were poor - too many to actually raise. The family didn't have a lot of money to come and see you all the time, you may have seen them just maybe two or three times a year. My own family - my dad hired somebody to drive him in - some Scots who had a farm across from us at Stony Point, so he could come and see us. We used to get all happy to see them. My mum died - she was living when we went there, but she died later - I remember my mother coming to see me.

It was an all right place while you were there, but it was a place you wouldn't want to be, but you had to live with it and get used to being there.

I didn't find anything wrong with the teachers - so long as you were behaving yourself. Like I say I got a strapping just for poking the girl in the next seat. They used to strap a lot in those days - teachers had the strap too in the classrooms. There's a lot of kids that were abused you know by different teachers - it depends on your actions. A lot of kids ran away all the time - they'd get caught and be brought back. I think the children ran away because they were unhappy, you never got to see your family for months at a time. It was lonely. Or they got punished and they just said "Enough," and they took off - I think that's why a lot of them ran away. You would be brought back to the school and punished again. We didn't get to do too much of anything really. They took us for an outing, like a walk, or a sleighride. As the years went by I think they used to take a group of girls to a play in London. I didn't go, but I remember them all going to a play. Sometimes you had fun with the staff - they weren't always mean!! Like holiday time they would have things for us to do. They would arrange parties for us in the classrooms. We stayed there at Christmas, and I can't remember too much of anything for Christmas, I really don't. I think we did have a tree, but nothing on it, maybe they gave us a bag of candy But the teachers would learn the kids plays, and we would go out onto the reserve and put it on. On Muncey Reserve there was a little hall and we used to go there and put on a Christmas play - like a pageant. A lot of kids used to run away and go to that building. They used to hold dances there during the Fair, and the kids would run away and go

there, just to be amongst their people. If you got caught you got punished for it. But I must talk about some good things, I learned how to scrub well, sew, can fruit, how to set tables, and learned discipline.

Mildred George with Bernice Jackson
1939 - 1945?

Bernice [friend]: You'd feel really bad when you'd see all the parents coming. You used to see them coming over this big hill, and you used to wonder if that was your parents coming to pick you up - it would be late afternoon.

Mildred: You'd wait all day. I was 12 years old when I went home for six weeks. My uncle came and got me or he sent money for me to go home on the train. After that when I did go home I always worked, because I wouldn't have anything to spend or to buy new clothes with when I went back on the reserve.

I wouldn't say they were mean or anything.

B. Well, I did! They were only mean if you did something wrong.

M. They would scold you - you wouldn't answer you wouldn't get a strapping from any of your teachers, it was the superintendent that gave the strap - the boss.

B. I got a strapping from the teacher.

M. You were a bad girl!!!

B. You know how I got the strap? I just poked a girl sitting in the next seat to me in the classroom.

M. We were bad girls - we used to pass notes back and forth - we were bad - you know, typical kids.

My kids - if I tell them a few things - they say "Oh Mum, you're telling stories again" - they don't believe things were that bad.

I never had the opportunity to run away - I probably would have. My sister did though.

My father was very good-hearted. My grandfather was a preacher. My brother was more like a father to me than a brother, he took care of me and my three sisters. I think I felt more lonely after my father died. Sheer loneliness.

After lights were out I'd go to sleep with my next sister up - Vena. After lights were out they told stories and the place where I slept right by the window - they said a girl had died there. I was just a little girl and it scared the heck out of me, and after lights were out and the last check made, I'd go and sleep with my sister. I was that scared to sleep in that corner. I still sleep with the lights on to this day. I have the kitchen light on when I go to bed.

B. We used to have a staff member come in to make sure everyone was in bed, and when she left everybody would run around again. Pretty soon she'd come in again - just yelling. Remember that one little short lady - they called her CB.

M. The one I remember was a big huge lady, and they used to call her CBL.

B. That was a radio station - because she always hollered.

M. There was some really good ones - like my Grade 8 teacher, he was hardly any older than we were, and we always went for walks. He was full of energy - not like the older ones - Bill Jamieson - I don't remember where he came from. I have a picture somewhere because I must have torn my uniform that day because I have a big old pin in the front of my dress. After we got our studies done we used to be able to go out for a walk. The teachers had to go too - they were in charge no matter what.

B. If you left that fenceline they thought you were running away and made you go right back.

M. They taught us how to can - we had rhubarb, raspberries and strawberries, and there used to be an upper kitchen and a lower kitchen. The upper kitchen was staff members that we learned how to serve properly.

B. And they ate better food than us.

M. Yeah.

B. We had mush with worms in it - they served us oatmeal for every breakfast, or rolled oats or mixed oats. Cornmeal and cream of wheat too. They used to store it in these big wooden bins for days and days, and that's why they got wormy. I can remember when worms would float up in your bowl, I had worms float up in my bowl.

M. We used to have meat - to this day I like peanut butter because I never got enough as a child. We used to go into what they call the storeroom, and there were these bigs things of peanut butter, and we'd get a big spoon and run away with it down the hall. It was stealing more or less.

B. The bakers used to bring all the bread in this big bakery truck, and if you had money you could buy a loaf of bread and go hide it in our lockers, and we'd snack on that when we got hungry.

M. I remember that.

B. You'd buy a loaf of bread for 10 cents. When your parents came to visit they'd leave you a little bit of money in the office.

M. Every Saturday you used to line up and you'd get 50 cents or so.

B. If you had it they used to let you have 20 cents or a dime from your little account. Your parents left you - maybe $5 - there was nowhere to spend it. The staff used to go to London Friday evening and you'd send for a little bag of candy with your money. They would bring you a bag of candy - 10 cents worth, and they would write down what you had spent. If your parents left you $3 they'd write it down and you could get something once a week. Or you'd buy a loaf of bread and put it in your locker. They had these wooden lockers - all lined up on the floor, and maybe two would have a locker.

B. They were like boxes.

B. They were wooden, and there'd be two girls to a locker. They'd be all lined up.

M. We always had a lot of milk because they had their own cows and horses.

B. They used to have those great big cans of milk, with the cream on top, and they'd take the cream for the staff people. There was a store we used to go to on a Saturday. One of the staff would take us for a walk down to the store.

M. It was a couple of miles. Sunday we used to go to Church about three times - 11 o'clock in the morning and then 7 o'clock in the evening. In the afternoon we used to line up and go about a mile-and-a-half away and go to church in the afternoon. When they ask how I know all the hymns, I say it's because I had to go to church so much as a child.

B. Mr. Strapp used to play that great big horn.

M. I remember one teacher she played the saxophone. They were all quite musical. For Easter we used to have to practise for weeks and weeks to sing two or three songs. We'd be up in the choir singing.

We put on plays for Christmas and put up a tree, but I don't remember too much about gifts - they maybe gave us a little candy. We put on a play - we must have been pretty good if we went somewhere else to put it on, and I remember practising for weeks and weeks.

It's a good thing I had older sisters, because I just wouldn't have made it otherwise.

B. We didn't have boyfriends, because boys and girls couldn't mingle.

M. They were separated - yes.

All I knew was my Native language before I went there. If somebody was talking today I could understand, but if I had to answer back in Indian I couldn't.

B. We lost all our Indian language and our culture.

M. I don't really feel bitter about the school, because we learned a lot. Except that we missed - my grandmother used to sew, make baskets, work with porcupine quills - I don't know any of that, I'm bitter about losing all that. She'd work with sweet grass and make baskets - that was their living.

B. My dad made chairs, and when he got a whole lot made he'd pile it all on this old car, and he used to go to the white community to farm homes and little towns, and then he would buy a lot of groceries and come home. That's how we used to make our living. We never learned to do all that when we were sent away to school.

M. I can remember when we scrubbed our dormitories - how big were they? Anyway there used to be about seven or eight girls all with a scrubpail and all done it at the same time, and you'd scrub one strip all the way down.

B. Those were big dormitories.

M. They probably held about 50 beds. I just remember those floors were always real clean. We learned to do laundry and to iron, and to sew. The beds used to be on each side and in the centre - maybe 30 - there were lots.

B. They were those single iron beds with a mattress.

M. We'd go one month into the cooking down in the kitchen, and from there we'd go to the laundry one month, and we just rotated.

B. We'd have a big bulletin there and every month you looked to see where you'd have to work, and you'd be happy - sometimes you wouldn't be - where you were placed. The other half day we'd go to school.

M. Yeah - wonder we learned anything.

B. I didn't - only went to Grade 8. All we learned was arithmetic and just basic things.

M. You know there are kids these days in Grade 8 that can't do what we did. I think we were well taught. I got to Grade 8 and I was supposed to go on to high school, but I never had any money - always a lack of money. There was no-one to give you any.

B. I never heard of anyone going to high school from Muncey.

M. Strapp was a big built man - Soper was kinda small - at least as I remember him. I think Strapp went to Manitoba to be principal of another school.

B. He liked to strap.

M. And his name was Mr. Strapp!! Kids would be sent to him, and he would strap you. He was in charge - there was no-one else to do it.

B. He would strap you all right. I got a big strapping from him the time we ran away.

M. I was 12 when I first went home - my uncle paid for us to go home. I was 8 when I first went there. My sister went to work in Ottawa and she used to send money and hats and mitts for us.

They helped people to find jobs doing housekeeping. It's so different when you have parents - that's what made me so tough.

B. In those days girlfriends used to hold hands, and put their arms around each other and walk around the fence.

M. We used to have ringlets and we'd curl our hair. Vena had earaches and I had to heat her pillows.

I remember one time two or three boys crawled along the eavestroughs and came down and in the window. They got caught by one fat little lady - they were trying to hide under the bed and she was kicking them. She marched them off to the principal. I was just little. The staff would do rounds with a flashlight. There were staff on each floor and a staff member had a room next to the dormitory.

We used to play baseball with the boys. We had tube

skates we put on over our shoes.

We used to take baths with two in a tub, then we'd get our clean clothes - a dress, shirt, underwear and socks. They'd be rolled into bundles and shoved into our cubbyholes. Everyone had a number.

I don't remember any fighting - I had sisters to look after me. One time I was sleepwalking and I went to A's dormitory and bit her - all the way downstairs and upstairs. We all looked after one another.

B. Though we used to get mad at one another.

M. There was one girl who used to boss the others, and she would beat the others up if they wouldn't do what she wanted. She was really mean.

I don't remember too much about the food. We had cod liver oil every morning.

When we had our periods - the older girls did - they got a square knapkin folded up, then they threw them in a bag on the door. Then they'd be soaked in cold water and the girls had to plunge them in this water before they went to the laundry to be washed. You had to ask for a napkin every time you wanted to change it.

Anita Bressette
1939 - 1946

My name was Anita George. I was there probably about six years - '39 to '46. I was there when Soper was principal. I was approximately seven when I went there. My grandmother was taking care of me.

I liked Muncey, it was good, it was educational for me - I learned a lot. We had no electricity so I learned how to vacuum a floor. Everything we did we did good. We worked in the kitchen helping to set up the meals, and I also worked upstairs with the officers, served them and worked in the upper kitchen as well. The boys down in the barns - when the boys got sick there wasn't enough boys to work down there and we had to also go down there, and I learned how to milk the cows, feed them, and also the horse stables - we fed the horses and mucked out the horses. We were busy all day, we had to scrub the steps with a scrub brush. We made the beds - the first thing we got up in the morning the beds were made, we ate, we had to help in the kitchen with the dishes. We were hard workers but it prepared us for a family - prepared me for the big family I had.

We had chapel time - Wednesday nights. Sundays we marched to church when it was nice. I was in the choir and we got invited out to different churches in the area around London as a choir. Christmastime we had real nice plays that we put on and there was lots of practice preparation for putting the plays on - I don't know how many nights, but we'd get together and practice. It was always a big thing - Christmastime - Hallowe'en - every special occasion. There was decorating, and hot chocolate and sandwiches in the evening.

I worked in the sewing room as well and I got to make the uniforms. You had to learn how to run the machine and make uniforms and the purple pants - bloomers. I was a senior after and we had to help the girls. All of us had some kids that were lousy and we had to put the larkspur on their hair and clean them. I got to work in the dispensary helping - with toothaches, putting toothache drops in - learning how to bandage. I worked right in there along with the nurse that was in there, so when the boys got sick

sometimes and there was several of them that were sick, I had to go help her take care of them - learn how to read the thermometer, take the temps, and help her give out the cough medicine and everything. I was very busy - not only me, everybody else would take turns too - but I don't know why I seem to be picked to do everything, but I enjoyed doing what I did, and it helped me a lot cuz we were taught to do everything good - we didn't do anything sloppy. I worked in cleaning the staff bedrooms - Mrs. Erratt - I had to clean her bedroom. We had to go work in the fields as well - picking strawberries. When we worked down with the cows we had to bring the milk up - they made their own butter. We worked right along in the kitchen with whatever they did - slicing meat or bread, setting up the tables.

The school teachers were very good - all the teachers we had were good. I never was mistreated in any way that I could say. I never knew of anyone being molested or anything like that. I couldn't say anything bad about the school myself, because I enjoyed what I did. We went home for the summer holidays. At the end of June before we left the school they had a big programme - singing and everything. We had good music teachers, and we sang - lots of singing. We'd get around the piano and we'd all sing. When I was a senior - on Fridays I got to go in with the little kids. One of the teachers would go home early and I had to take the class - mostly reading to them. I had lots of responsibility. When I came out of school it helped me a lot because I was taught to do everything good - to vacuum, dust, do dishes. We learned how to cook as well. So it helped me because the only jobs I could get was to babysit, and so that helped me to get jobs babysitting, and they'd like me because I could work, and I did a good job at my age. Where if I'd stayed home I wouldn't have learned how to run a vacuum cleaner or anything like that. You learned to run the sewing machine. I couldn't say anything against it, I couldn't. The conditions at home - we didn't have electricity, running water, and they had all this there - indoor toilets - that was luxury. During the day we had the outhouse, but at night we didn't have to go out, when we went to bed. We'd jump in the bathtub every Saturday. We didn't have anything at home, we had to draw our own water and everything. There I was taught everything, so for me it was an asset that I went there. I think your teachers and everything mean a lot, discipline as well.

I might have ran away a couple of times but I got a strapping for it. You had to take your clothes off and put your nightgown on, and there was a stool and they'd put you over that stool, pull your nightgown up and give you the strap. They took down your underpanties and they smacked you - you got about five or six - you got a good strapping on the bum. This was a high stool - you weren't going to do that again. I got caught running away.

I got caught stealing. You could learn how to pick locks, we had very patient tutors. You know that big storeroom - I went in there and took some dates and raisins, in our old purple pants - stick them up there, and we got caught and taken up the office. "What are you stealing for?" I said "Well, because I'm hungry. Well, it's something to eat, that's why I stole." So every day they took me in for a glass of milk and a sandwich, at ten o'clock in the morning. So they fed me because I told them I was hungry. We would eat raw turnips, and potatoes and carrots, whatever was there we'd eat that. And we'd get that old mush 'n' cream. We'd mix it with cream and eat it raw.

Mr. Soper - he had an invalid wife. I worked up in the staff kitchen then and served the staff. You had to learn how to go in - they'd ring the bell - what to take in, what to serve next, how to set the table properly, and to serve all the staff. They had good food. I liked working up there. You only got to work there for so long - maybe two weeks, then you'd get switched around back to downstairs. There were lots of cockroaches. Everything in the building was scrubbed down.

If we got high marks - we got marks for everything we did - and if you got good marks you were able to go into London and they'd take us roller skating or to a movie, or we'd go shopping, or looking around, so that kinda encouraged us to do good in everything. In school I was an A student, I had excellent marks, and when I passed Grade 9 I got recommended in a lot of subjects and I didn't have to write exams. But I didn't go back to school after I left because I would have had to go to school in Sault St. Marie - to Shingwauk - to go to high school, but my grandfather wouldn't sign for me to go there. Oh well, I couldn't really complain. I couldn't really complain about the school either - I had lots of fun. Everything we did we made fun. We had to go down and feed the cows - we'd throw bales of straw down there and throw somebody else with it. I don't know how dangerous it would be because we had pitch forks and we'd throw the straw down there and somebody would go right along after it. We lived dangerous.

We had a reading room where you could study, and we had another room with a piano in there - if you wanted to go

in there and play the piano, you could. Were you there [Vena] when Mr. Jamieson was there - he was a music teacher?

I don't remember Mr. Strapp that good. I think Mr. Strapp used to do the strappings. I saw him spank someone else. In the classroom if you got a strapping they'd strap you and that strap was long and you'd have marks on your wrists. If you behaved yourself you didn't get into trouble. When I ran away - I guess I just wanted to come home. We were seniors at that time and we were just seeing how far we could go. We didn't really know the danger of going away and walking and walking, but our uniforms would give us away. We did get pretty close to home, and they came with a staff car and picked us up and brought me home to Grandma's and told Grandma I ran away. I did almost make it home.

We were able to speak our language amongst each other. When I went there all I spoke was Indian - so when we went to school we had to learn to speak English, so it was kinda difficult. Some of the kids they couldn't speak English at all, so we had to interpret. I picked up English pretty good. It wasn't hard once you got away from home - cuz that's all you spoke at home was Indian. So it wasn't much of a problem for me - I picked it up as I went along, and when we were with each other we'd speak the Indian language. But once you left the reserve you weren't speaking your language. Today I can understand some but I can't carry on a conversation and I can't speak it fluently, but I understand if anybody speaks to me - that never did leave me. Lots of people can't understand it today, but I still understand it. It's very difficult to listen to your language - especially when you don't know what they're talking about, but I can understand and I can appreciate the hymns, or a preacher.

A lot of them didn't like it - well the food wasn't the best. If I sat beside someone who liked the food I didn't like, I could give it to them. We grew our own vegetables - fields and fields. Chickens too - eggs. I remember we used to have rhubarb crisp - that was good. But I didn't pay no attention to the meals. When I got caught stealing that was really good - I got hot chocolate and a peanut butter sandwich every day - they called that nourishment.

One thing I found very good - before we'd eat, we'd always have grace. The officer - she always used to tell us to bow our heads and give thanks for the food, and before we went to bed we knelt down beside our beds. In the wintertime if it was cold we could sit in our bed and we said the Lord's Prayer. It was a must, to say the Lord's Prayer. So I thought that was very good. We didn't know the meaning of Communion, but we took Communion. So there was a little Christian background, and Mr. Strapp used to read out of the Bible. We used to get to go to the store.

My sister went to the Muncey too. I couldn't stand her because she was always on at me to clean her hair all the time!!

You had your own friends. Once in a while you felt lonely, especially when you first went back in September, but you got back into the swing of things. You looked forward again to the end of June to get out again in the summer. Maybe some of the kids - the boys - just didn't hit it off. My brother went to school there and he didn't care for it at all. Myself, I had lots of fun. We played ball, did sports, and in the summer time we'd go swimming in Mud Creek. Wintertime we went sliding. I learned how to iceskate, how to roller skate, play ball, wheelbarrow racing -

we did all the sports - we ran. We ran right around this whole thing here. I learned how to ride horses there even. I was a senior. I liked to work with the horses. I knew nothing about horseback riding but I was the person who would say "Hey, get on and ride." I would do that, I wasn't afraid of anything. We'd grab a potato sack and throw it on, grab its leads, jump astride of the horse, and go clumping along. The officers - they've got real beautiful riding horses.

I don't have no regrets. It gave me a good start.

Sophia Albert
1942 - 1945

A lot of them didn't enjoy their stay there, and the reasons they were there varied too. It may have been that the reason they were there was the reason they didn't like their stay too. I didn't really mind it - I must have been 9 - 10. My sister is two years younger than I am, so we must have been 8 and 10 went we went there. I was 13 when I came back out. Mr. Strapp was there when we went in, and Soper came just before we left.

I didn't notice things about the buildings because I was younger - some of the people noticed the conditions - some of it was pretty bad. I remember the classroom building being braced up at some point - was that when we were still there or when it was a day school - because we did use the same classrooms for the day school.

There were places we weren't allowed to go - they were restricted to us. We just had certain areas to play in, and the dormitories where we slept. We always entertained ourselves - it was fun for the smaller children, because the older ones would help - those longer evenings when we were shut in. The older ones took the younger ones to look after - the way we were taught to do it in our house - look after the younger children. We always had an older friend to look out for us, and help us with things we couldn't manage ourselves.

I don't know if I learned anything there - because we'd done everything for ourselves at home. My mother worked out - doing housework for other people all around the area here - and we had to look after each other at home - everybody had to help. On Sundays we always went to Church, so it was the same thing when we went to the school - we picked up on what chores we had to do, and again on Sundays we went to Church.

Our age group didn't have to do much work, but at times everybody had to help. I remember scrubbing the floors in the dormitory, which they did every Saturday morning. There would be a whole row of brushes across the floor - on our hands and knees with scrub brushes washing the floors down. Everything was done by hand of course.

At the time of our school reunion I went around asking a

lot of these questions of the older people who were at the school, and conditions at the school at the time we were there weren't too bad, because they weren't any better at home, or they were even a little better than at home.

I never remembered going hungry at home, we always had something to eat. My mother worked out to keep food on the table - she worked hard. She did all her own sewing and made our clothes - I always thought we were dressed pretty well!! Even my older brother's dress shirts - she made those - but I wonder what we looked like going to Church on Sunday morning. She did a lot of sewing for other people too. We came back here with my mother after I left and went to day school.

I went to high school - after they changed Mt. Elgin into a day school I went there - I finished Grade 8.

We ran away - I don't know what our reason was, but one Sunday evening we decided we were going to come home. Well, we headed in this direction and we got just down over the hill, when the Principal and one of the older boys caught up to us - we were just across the hill from home!!! Probably about six miles. We were taken into the chapel and everybody was gathered there - I don't know if they had to go for that purpose or what - we got a strapping, and I guess that was all. I believe it was Soper there at that time. That was the only time that I remember getting a strapping there - that was because we decided to go home without anybody's permission - we just walked away.

I was probably too young to notice what was going on with the older ones - it seems to me the older ones had their own dormitory. I believe it was one floor - the one above us, and then the floor we were on was divided into the intermediate and the junior. Then I remember some of the older girls being in that same dormitory - whether they were latecomers during the year, or why they were in our dormitory - or maybe they were put there to keep an eye on us - I do remember a couple of older girls being in that same dormitory where we were. It must have been all mixed on my floor because I think when we first went there we were put in beds side by side - and we were in a smaller area to start with, where our beds were very close together, and then there was the aisle around the beds and these other beds next to the wall. Then later on we were moved into another section where the beds were just lined up from the wall and there was an aisle down the centre - but it was all on the one floor. I don't remember anything unusual happening except for the times when they went out at night. They would use the fire escape to go out, but this was just to go out, and probably go for a walk somewhere and go to bed. This was quite late at night. I think the doors were probably locked - at one time I remember them talking about a smaller child falling out of the windows from quite a way up - that probably caused them to lock windows, and they probably had more precautions from that time on. I think that's about the worst thing I ever heard of happen. I remember I gave the welcoming address at the school reunion, and after I finished a lot of them said "You didn't mention this, and you didn't mention that," and I said "Well, I was trying to keep it on the cheery side!" They would mention things like the lice that went through the school and different things like that - the more unpleasant things. I would think that perhaps some children came in that had them already - and probably did bring them from home. I remember one family right here that always seemed to have lice all the time - they'd send them home to be cleaned up but they'd come back a few days later just as bad.

I don't think they cut our hair when we went into the school, but if someone did have lice really bad and didn't seem to get rid of them, then I think they would cut their hair. I know we only had one thorough bath a week - the rest of the week we took sponge baths and tried to keep ourselves clean and wash our hair and take a sponge bath at the sink. I remember when I first went there - the first time I had to go for a bath - thinking that's a little more private for you. There was a toilet outside, but we did have indoor toilets.

Wasn't the school operated through the church? I think that's probably why we were sent there - because the minister probably suggested this to my mother - to have us sent there for training and that. My mother sent us - I think it was for the educational part of it. It didn't turn out as well as we thought it would I suppose, but of course they closed it down the year after we came back home. I suppose we were getting to dislike it or something!!! I can't really remember why!! I think that would have been the bigger part - that she wanted us to get the training that she thought the kids were getting there. But I learned just as much at home as I did there. I remember we went to school for half-a-day - or at least the intermediates and seniors went to school for half-a-day, and they worked the other half. We all had jobs to do - the cleaning and the cooking - we did a little bit of everything. I believe when we were there they had one of the older girls as sort of a supervisor over us, to see that we did the work that had to be done at the time.

When we were home we were sharing, and with everything that had to be done at home we were learning just as much - the only difference was other girls the same age and getting to know all the other kids from all over Ontario - Christian Island, Cape Croker - all the northern reserves. The ones that came from those places spoke their language too, though it wasn't really permitted, we did. To me that was good, that people were speaking different languages - we got to hear a bit about other languages.

Some of the kids who ran away sort of had no home, but they didn't want to be at the school and they would go with someone who knew they had a home to go to - that's one of the reasons they would have just went with someone who was heading home.

Walter Summers
1942 - 1946

I went there in 1942 - January 1st, and I must have been 11 years old because I turned 12 in March. I was treated OK - it's just that sometimes everybody gets out of step - everybody I guess goes through that. If you had reason to be strapped then you're going to have to be, but other than that I enjoyed it. There was children in there older than the rest of us, that looked after us - they were 17, 18 and they didn't leave because they had no place to go. Then they found a place for them. They started to close down in 1946 - that's when they started selling livestock - horses, cows. It took 'em six months and they started in January until June when the school was completely closed. I was there in 1946 and after they closed they turned it into a day school and you went on a bus to get there, and I went there two years after to the day school. I was 18 when I quit - I didn't finish, I quit because I was getting too old. My parents were getting older and they had their farm that they couldn't look after any more so I helped when I could. And in the meantime I got a job working in construction, and then I'd go home at night and do the work there too. Then I'd get up the next morning - 4 o'clock in the morning - and do the chores, and do the planting till my ride came about 7 o'clock to go to London to go to work.

I didn't really learn much at the school that helped me as a construction worker. It's just that we learned how to speak English. I didn't learn too much in school - mathematics - I never did learn it. I couldn't get the hang of it and there was no teacher to show me. They didn't have the time - there was too many children in there to teach everybody individually. And you only went to school half-a-day at a time. When I got there they put me in the Intermediate Class, then I went up to Senior. Then I started working in the barns - looking after horses and looking after cows. We had evening classes - I think it was every Monday and Friday for about an hour-and -a-half. The bigger boys - they tried to help us do the math - but I just couldn't get the hang of it!! After I quit school and I did a couple of things here and there, that's how I learned my mathematics. Other than that I was satisfied with what I learned. At least when I got out I knew how to go about doing work here and there.

We learned English. I spoke very little English when I went there - my parents they spoke Indian. They weren't really that strict about speaking Indian, but of course we'd never speak Indian anyway when they were on the grounds. As long as we knew that there's nobody close by to hear us, we spoke Indian. There was more than a dozen children at the school spoke the same language as I did. When you'd go home for the summer holidays you were right back into speaking Indian again. These other children from different reserves - they'd never get a chance to go home.

My brother went there in 1939 and I wanted to go with him, because we were close - we were together. When he left to go I said I wanted to go with him. But it was hard for me to go because I had some kinda sickness with my heart and the doctors wouldn't let me go right away. It took me that long to clear up whatever was the problem. I did have parents and it took me a few years before I could get in there, but I insisted that I was going to go! My parents didn't have too much money - there was others in the family, and the two sisters that I have went to the Shingwauk school. They left when they were 8 or 9 years old and they never got home till they were 18 or 19. It took us a long time before we got used to each other again because I never knew them - I knew them before - but in that time that they were gone. They didn't speak any Indian at the time they came back - they had to learn over again.

Mr. Strapp was principal at the time I went there. As I say, you made it bad for yourself or you made it good - it was up to you - it's not that he'd just come out and strap for no reason. If there was a reason you'd get a strapping for it. If you were in an area you were not supposed to be in at such and such a time. You'd get out of the boundary now and again. I only got a strapping three or four times. But it must have been my fault - that's why I got the strap. I didn't think he'd strap me of his own free will. It was something that I'd done wrong to get a strapping for it. One time one of the teachers - they had little garages for their cars and they always had it locked - accused me of breaking into his garage and that I played around with some papers in his car. That was another time that I got strapped. I didn't do it - they didn't believe me. There was another boy with me that got it too. It was the same thing - we both got a strapping. I wasn't even near the place. So that was one time I got a strapping for something I didn't do. I got a strapping for things I did do too - being out of bounds from

where I should be. We used to be late for supper and stuff like that. We went to the store - we never got a licking for that. We'd lose privileges - like staying up for half an hour to listen to the radio. We didn't have TV so all we had was radio that we listened to after supper from 7 o'clock to 9 o'clock. We went to bed at 9 o'clock. We'd get up about 6 o'clock in the morning - then I looked after the cows - they'd get us out of bed to have the cows ready. It took about half an hour to get them ready before everyone else came to do the milking. We took turns every two weeks - somebody else changes over.

Mr. Soper was pretty good. I liked him better than Mr. Strapp. He was better for me - he'd listen to you first before going any deeper and giving the strap. He'd try to get the true story before giving any punishment. I got along with Mr. Soper pretty good myself - there was a couple of times we'd have discussions. He'd talk to you first before he'd see if he believed me or not. I don't remember getting the strap from him. We talked things over first. As I say you made it yourself what you wanted to be. You could be bad you could be good. Just like being in the army. You could make it tough or you could make it easy.

I ran away one time when Mr. Strapp was there - I was away for about a week. Then again I ran away for a second time when he was still there - again for about a week. The first time I ran away - I used to know a farmer on the first concession in Delaware - that's where I ended up. This lady that lived there - she used to be a school teacher there years back and she knew what the school was like, she used to teach there. She let me stay there until someone else came along and found me, and they hauled me back to the school again. Her husband was a farmer and I helped him in the barn. I was only 14 at the time.

The second time I started off to go to Chatham and I got part ways there and then they caught me. Some of my own people happened to be driving by and I was hitch-hiking and they recognized me right away, and they knew where I came from. The man gets out of the car and says "Where are you going?" I says "I'm going to Chatham." "What are you going to do there?" "I'm going to get a job in a factory." "Well," he says, "I think I'd better call the principal and have you picked up." I didn't want to go back. Finally the police came, then Mr. Strapp came and got me. He didn't give me a strapping the first time I run away, but the second time he made me go up to the dormitory and take off all my clothes. About an hour later he came up and gave me a strapping on my behind - my hands and behind. He said "That'll teach you not to run away again." I was grounded for about 3 days. After that him and I got along pretty good. He just wanted to show me that he was the boss, I guess. Quite a few ran away - even the girls used to run away. I just went along with another fellow because he ran away!! The second time I ran away I was on my own. I was getting older and I could see why the older children kept running away. After I was about 16 - my mathematics was real bad

- I just couldn't stand it any more. No matter what kinda figures came up I couldn't figure it out. The teacher didn't have time to show me. When I went to work I watched the other guy measure things and that's how I learned.

We used to have a school teacher - a mechanic - and we had this one motor and we stripped it right down and rebuilt it again. He showed us piece by piece how it fit together. We used to do it some evenings. I was interested in what they were teaching us - I wished we had done more.

When the bigger children left - they used to look after the smaller children - if you see something that's not right you were elected to correct them. A lot of children learned through the older children. We had the odd fights now and again but five minutes and they're friends again. We always got along good.

We played baseball and hockey - snowball fights. The older children they made bobsleds, and sliding down the hillside out there. In the summertime we used to go Boy Scout camping. We didn't go any great distance - we'd go back to the old cow pasture - there was running water back there - and we'd camp out there. There used to be about 15 or 20 of us. The best part I liked about it was when we ate.

The food at school - well - it was good. Well, they had different cooks - some was good and some was bad. An Oneida cook come there for two years - Sara Cornelius - and we got pretty good decent food. We always had enough to eat, but some of them didn't know how to cook.

As I got older then I didn't enjoy it that much any more.

Douglas Doxtator
1945?

I was about 9 or 10 years old when I went over there. We were up early in the mornings - about 6 o'clock in the morning, and we went to work in the barns with the livestock. Then we had breakfast, then you went to school for half-a-day, then the rest of the day you were working in the barns, cleaning them up, looking after the cattle and the horses. Saturdays we used to do the same thing. We didn't have to go to school on Saturday, but we worked - worked in the barns and the fields all day. On Sundays we had Church service in the morning, and the afternoon was pretty well free time - to fool around - till 4 o'clock and we had to go back in the barns and work again. Then we came in for our supper. You had to stay around unless you got permission, or one of the parents wrote a note - but they had to be there to bring us out and take us back.

It wasn't too bad but they had a curfew. You couldn't stay up - you had to be in bed by 9 o'clock. You couldn't leave the grounds.

Mr. Soper - he was there when I was there. I wasn't there a full year. Soper wasn't too bad - he was fairly strict with the students. They couldn't get away with much. While I was there I never got the strap, but I seen different ones get it - that were bad. Some of them would sneak out at nights and they'd come back in and get caught, and they'd get the strap. They'd have bed checks. They were in there at 9 o'clock when you went to bed., and they had another bed check around 11 or 12 o'clock, to make sure everybody was in bed. After the last bedcheck they'd sneak out - some of them in shop made keys and they'd come back and unlock the doors. The kids were fairly young - there was a few that were around 16. It was very difficult - the shoes weren't that good, because when somebody left they would have to turn their shoes in, and the next one that would fit them, they'd give them to. You were very lucky if you got a new pair of shoes.

When I was there it wasn't really that bad - I don't know what it was like before that. I didn't mind it. Of course on Sundays I'd get permission to come home - I just had a little ways to go. We spent most of our time working - working out in the fields. They had different crews - a crew working in the horse stables, they had ones that worked in the cattle barn, doing the milking and all that. I did the milking - feed the cattle, clean the stalls.

We had a fair amount to eat - of course I didn't eat that much anyways. Soper made it go as long as he could. I didn't have nothing against Soper - he was good with the children.

To me it wasn't that bad. Of course it was easier for me than a lot of the children who were from quite a ways away, and they couldn't get home. I got along fairly good with the other boys - there might have been the odd one who was a bully but we had older guys that I was friends with, and if they tried to pick on me they'd look after me.

Notes

Part One: Voice-over

Citations that appear elsewhere in the book are referred to that appearance. Documents: MI = Mohawk Institute, ME = Mt. Elgin; e.g. MI 1827:1 refers to Part One: Voice of Authority: Mohawk Institute 1827-1872, No. 1. Former students: Name and page number. Other citations see Bibliography.

1. ME 1934:184
2. ME 1849:63
3. Lorna's sister p.380
4. Fitzgerald 1993:xx
5. Peter Jones, Missionary Bulletin Vol. XVI, No. 2, April-June 1920:169
6. Hodgins 1894-1910, Vol.4:129
7. NEC Letter Book 1872-6 Vol.1:382 Venning to Chance, 12 November 1874
8. Jones 1860:264
9. Jones 1860:277
10-11. Hodgins 1894-1910, Vol.5: 296-297
12. Hodgins 1894-1910, Vol.4:126
13. Hodgins 1894-1910, Vol.5:297
14. Hodgins 1894-1910, Vol.5:302
15. Hodgins 1894-1910, Vol.2:348
16. WMMS 21st AR 1846:viii
17. Peter Jones Nov. 27th, 1848. The Colonial Intelligencer Jan. & Feb. 1849, Nos. IX. & X. New Series. pp.146-148
18. MI 1827:17
19. MI 1827:51
20. MI 1827:53, 63
21. MI 1827:24, 101, 108, 119
22. MI 1827:115, 131
23. MI 1827:127
24. MI 1827:124, 135-137
25. ME 1849:6, 8
26. see Graham 1973, 1975
27. ME 1849:9-12, 21, 31
28. ME 1849:38
29. ME 1849:43
30. ME 1849:49-50
31. ME 1849:57
32-33. ME 1849:62
34. MI 1872:2, 4, 32
35. MI 1872:4, 7
36. MI 1872:27, 31
37. MI 1872:4
38. MI 1872:32
39. MI 1872:48, 55, 62-65
40. MI 1872:75-86
41. ME 1882:2
42. ME 1882:3
43. ME 1882:54-55, 58
44. ME 1882:67-72, 81-90, 92-93, 95
45. Missionary Bulletin Vol.XVI, No.2, April-June 1920:162
46. MI 1915:19
47. MI 1915:3-4
48. see Titley 1986
49. MI 1915:12
50. MI 1915:27, 39; MI 1922:4, 5, 9 All reports from 1919-1929 contain sections on the farm and improvements, but only some representative samples appear in the book
51. Marjorie Groat p.362
52. MI 1915:41, 62
53. Harry Burning pp.359, 357 vs. MI 1922:2
54. MI 1922:9, 11, 12
55. MI 1922:6

56. MI 1922:3
57. MI 1922:39-42, 44-45
58. Peter Smith p.361
59. Edward Groat p.362
60. MI 1929:11, 18, 19, 40-43, 47
61. MI 1929:47
62. MI 1945:5
63. ME 1909:4, 15
64. see Montour 1985:44
65. ME 1909:6
66. ME 1909:39
67. ME 1909:101
68. ME 1909:84, 109
69. ME 1909:112
70. ME 1909:116
71. Christie 1976:212
72. Lorraine Brigham p.469
73. Manson Ireland p.443 Ruth Ninham p.445 ME 1934:27-37, 144-152, 155-159,
74. ME 1934:153
75. ME 1934:50
76. ME 1934:169-170, 181, 187
77. MI 1929:46, 49, 51-70; 1945:1
78. MI 1929:60
79. MI 1929:65
80. MI 1929:68
81. MI 1929:67
82. MI 1945:4
83. MI 1945:17, 19
84. Name withheld p.410
85. Speech by Staff Member honouring Canon Zimmerman, 1966. Thanks to S. English
86. MI 1945:107
87. ME 1909:65
88. Lonnie Johnson p.396
89. Clyde Peters p.448
90. MI 1827:45, 48
91. MI 1915:14
92. MI 1929:17-20, 25-32; Peter Smith pp360-361, Edward Groat p.367, Raymond Hill p.372
93. MI 1945:79
94. personal communication
95. ME 1849:26
96. ME 1909:48
97. ME 1909:84
98. ME 1909:91, 101
99. MI 1827:8
100. MI 1827:85
101. MI 1827:133
102. MI 1915:32-35
103. MI 1929:46-47, 49
104. MI 1945:4
105. MI 1945:19
106. ME 1849:38
107. ME 1849:27-28, 43
108. ME 1882:64
109. ME 1934:6, 32
110. ME 1934:169-170, 181
111. MI 1827:92
112. MI 1827:108, 125, 137; p.43

113. MI 1872:30, 41, MI 1945:17, 31
114. 1960s: New Credit, Nawash, Oneida, Chippewa, Tuscarora, Lower Cayuga, Upper Cayuga, Moraviantown, Parry Island, Mud Lake, Walpole Island, Oneida of the Thames, Chippewa of the Thames, Upper Mohawk, Lower Mohawk, Muncey of the Thames, Bay of Quinte, Mistassini, Waswanipi, Fort William, Long Lake, St. Regis, Kettle Point, Chippewas of Beausoleil (Christian Island), North Seneca, Deer Lake, Trout Lake, Scugog
115. ME 1882:3, 21; 1909:101
116. see ME Facts & Figures:19 for Reports. Children and Agents from: Muncey of the Thames, Chippewa of the Thames, Oneida of the Thames, New Credit, Walpole Island, Gibson, Saugeen, Caughnawaga, Kettle Point, Stony Point, Christian Island, Newash, Caldwell, Six Nations, Sarnia, Moraviantown, Cape Croker, Rama
117. ME 1934:41, 43, 50-51, 54, 63-64, 105, 122, 128
118. ME 1934:169
119. MI 1827:22, 47
120. MI 1827:115
121. MI 1827:115, 118
122. MI 1827:131
123. MI 1872:29
124. MI 1945:55, 61-64
125. ME 1849:48
126. ME 1849:62
127. ME 1882:20
128. ME 1909:23-24, 29
129. ME 1934:22
130. Vena Missauba p.464
131. MI 1827:24
132. MI 1827:127
133. MI 1872:4
134. MI 1872:27, 29
135. MI 1872:32
136. MI 1872:63
137. MI 1922:8
138. MI 1929:1, 23
139. MI 1945:4
140. MI 1945:23
141. MI 1945:82
142. MI 1882:8
143. ME 1882:58
144. ME 1909:6
145. ME 1934:58
146. ME 1934:181, 184
147. MI 1872:23
148. MI 1872:27
149. MI Students:8; p.219; MI 1929:5
150. Peter Smith p. 361
151. ME 1849:9-11
152. MI 1827:14
153. MI 1827:75, 88, 131
154. MI 1872:4
155. Emmett General p.374

156.   Name and interview withheld
157.   ME 1849:54; 1882:12
158.   ME 1882:53, 71
159.   Montour 1985:18-19
160.   Susie Doxtator p.439
161.   Emmert General p.374
162.   MI 1827:43-44
163.   MI 1872:32
164.   MI 1872:43, 46, 48, 65, 75-86
165.   MI 1872:79, 87-88
166.   MI 1915:3-4; Martha Hill p.355
167.   MI 1922:6
168.   MI 1922:3, 11, 21
169.   MI 1922:23, 27
170.   MI 1929:1, 38; see p.383 for description
171.   MI 1929:17-21, 25-31, 38; Lorna pp.375-376; Lorna's sister 379, Marguerite Beaver p. 385, Jennie Blackbird p.389
172.   MI 1945:15-16
173.   Bob White Eye p.420
174.   Albert Sault p.399
175.   John Martin p.401
176.   ME 1882:67
177.   ME 1882:81-95
178.   ME 1909:14
179.   ME 1909:29, 42, 49-53
180.   ME 1909:62-63
181.   Name and interview withheld
182.   ME 1934:27
183.   ME 1934:56, 94, 107, 157-162
184.   Dorothy Day p.436
185.   Manson Ireland p.442
186.   Frank Hill p.417
187.   MI 1827:89, 131; 1872:12
188.   MI 1872:32
189.   MI 1872:75, 79; 1915:3-4
190.   MI 1922:13, 16-17
191.   MI 1929:11, 24
192.   MI 1945:15
193.   Edward Groat p.363
194.   Hilda Hill p.372
195.   ME 1882:8, 58, 86, 93
196.   ME 1909:6, 20, 30, 38, 69
197.   ME 1909:113, 116-117; 1934:18, 27, 29, 31
198.   ME 1934:30, 33, 58, 72, 87
199.   ME 1934:137, 142, 155-159
200.   Dorothy Day p.435
201.   Montour 1985
202.   ME 1934:27
203.   MI 1945:15
204.   Montour 1985:28-32
205.   Bob White Eye p.419
206.   MI 1945:4, 6-7, 9
207.   ME 1882:54-55
208.   ME 1882:90-93
209.   ME 1934:67-69, 80, 82, 95-97, 135-136
210.   MI Lorna p.377; Vera Styres p.390
211.   ME 1934:130-132
212.   Lorna p.376
213.   Hilda Hill p.371
214.   NEC Conference 1908:9-10; see also Titley 1986; ME 1882:68
215.   MI 1945:7, 9, 18
216.   MI 1945:71
217.   ME 1909:65

218.   ME 1934:181
219.   Anita Bressette p.477
220.   Karen Hill p.406
221.   MI 1827:131
222.   MI 1872:43-56
223.   MI 1929:39-41, 47, 50; 1945:9, 18
224.   ME 1849:62-63
225.   ME 1882:56, 58, 66, 68, 81-85, 89
226.   ME 1934:1-2, 4-7
227.   ME 1934:40, 66, 72
228.   ME 1934:111, 144
229.   ME 1934:146, 148, 165-167
230.   Manore 1992:17
231.   MI 1872:12
232.   MI 1872:12
233.   MI 1872:41
234.   MI 1872:42
235.   MI 1872:87
236.   MI 1915:14, 27, 42, 57
237.   MI 1922:2
238.   MI 1922:15, 22, 25
239.   MI 1929:2; 1945:21
240.   Vera Styres p.391
241.   MI 1827:23-24, 68, 87, 112
242.   MI 1872:2
243.   MI 1872:62-64
244.   MI 1872:65
245.   MI 1872:75-86
246.   MI 1929:25-31
247.   MI 1827:22
248.   MI 1827:42
249.   MI 1827:68; 1872:8
250.   MI 1872:86
251.   MI 1929:2
252.   MI 1945:19
253.   MI 1945:23
254.   MI 1945:59, 66, 79
255.   Name withheld p.398
256.   MI 1872:48, 55; 1915:73-74; 1922:9
257.   John Martin p.401
258.   Marguerite Beaver p.384
259.   Peggy Hill p.413
260.   Name withheld p.408
261.   ME 1882:53, 55
262.   ME 1882:67
263.   ME 1882:71-73
264.   ME 1882:93
265.   ME 1909:28, 36-37
266.   ME 1909:38-40
267.   ME 1909:50, 52
268.   ME 1934:89-90
269.   ME 1849:8, 43
270.   ME 1882:54, 90
271.   ME 1882: 67, 69, 86, 90, 92-93, 95; 1909:38
272.   ME 1934:67-69, 155-159, 161
273.   ME 1849:8
274.   ME 1909:29; Montour 1985
275.   ME 1909:65
276.   Esther Lewis p.454
277.   Lorraine Brigham p.469
278.   ME 1849:36; 1882:8
279.   Montour 1985:5,7
280.   Kay Kennedy p.429
281.   Melva George p.446
282.   Vena Missauba p.464

283.   Phyllis Hopkins p.467
284.   MI 1827:53, 63, 112
285.   MI 1872:62-64
286.   MI 1915:35; 1945:98
287.   ME 1934:153-154
288.   MI Facts & Figures:18; p.214
       ME Facts & Figures:19; p.347
289.   ME 1882:69-70; 1934:67-70, 80, 82; Lorna p.376; Hilda Hill p.371
290.   Vera Styres p.391; Ronald DeLeary p.457; Emma Soney p.450
291.   Martha Hill p.356
292.   Peter Smith p.361
293.   see Graham 1973, 1975
294.   Martha Hill p.356
295.   MI 1872:79
296.   Lorna p.375-376
297.   Harry Burning p.358-359
298.   Emmert General p.374
299.   Name withheld p.410
300.   Lorna p.377
301.   Vera Styres p.390
302.   Lorna (personal communication)
303.   Calvin Sault p.401
304.   Edward Groat p.367
305.   ME 1849:8
306.   Jennie Blackbird p.388
307.   White 1991
308.   Kelly Curley p.424
309.   Del Riley p.405
       White 1991
310.   Ronald DeLeary p.458
311.   Sylvia DeLeary p.394
312.   Doris King p.456
313.   Dickens 1839:219
314.   Hughes 1857
315.   For a discussion and overview with bibliography of English boarding schools see Gathorne-Hardy 1977. For Canadian Indian Residential Schools see Miller 1996, 1995, 1994, 1990, Johnston 1988, Haig Brown 1988, Knockwood 1995, Cheechoo 1993, Montour 1985
316.   see Gathorne-Hardy 1977
317.   ME 1934: 153
318.   Foucault 1979:228
319.   Foucault 1979:303
320.   Foucault 1979:203
321.   Karen Hill p.406
322.   Lorna p.383
323.   Karen Hill p.405
324.   Walter Summers p.479
325.   Ina Henry p.462
326.   Jo-Bear Curley p.414
327.   Martha Hill p.356
328.   Dorothy Day p.435
329.   Ronald DeLeary p.457
330.   Emma Soney p.451
331.   Johnston 1988:137
332.   Kenneth Albert p.451
333.   Marjorie Groat p.365
334.   Emma Soney p.450
335.   Emma Soney p.451
336.   NEC 1829:8-9
337.   MI 1827:64

Part Two: Voice of Authority
Mohawk Institute 1827 - 1872

1. NEC 1829:6-7
2-3. NEC 1829:10-11
4-5. NEC 1832:5
6. NEC 1832:6
7. NEC 1832:7
8. NEC 1832:14
9. NEC 1832:18
10. NEC 1832:14
11. NEC 1832:19
12. NEC 1840:5-6
13. NEC 1840:8
14. NEC 1840:139-140
15. NEC 1840:14-15
16. NEC 1840:16-17
17. NEC 1840:147
18. NEC 1840:20-21
19. NEC 1840:24-25
20. NEC 1840:26
21. NEC 1846:1-2
22. NEC 1840:62-63
23. NEC 1840:175-177
24. NEC 1840:219-220
25-28. NEC 1840:87-91
29. NEC 1840:95-96
30-33. NEC 1840:105-108
34. NEC 1840:131-132
35-38. NEC 1846:2-4
39. NEC 1846:95
40. NEC 1846:4-5
41-42. NEC 1846:5-6
43-44. NEC 1846:9-11
45-48. NEC 1846:16-19
49-51. NEC 1846:21-23

52. NEC 1846:27
53. NEC 1846:102-103
54. NEC 1846:25
55. NEC 1846:30
56. NEC 1846:33
57. NEC 1846:36
58. NEC 1846:39-40
59. NEC 1846:108
60-61 NEC 1846:41-43
62. NEC 1846:45-46
63. NEC 1846:133
64-7. NEC 1846:150, 153-160
68. Hodgins 1894-1910, Vol.5:292
69. NEC 1871:81-2
70. NEC 1874:67-69
71-72. NEC 1859:2-3
73. NEC 1859:7
74-75 NEC 1859:10-11, 16-17
76. NEC 1859:4-5
77. NEC 1859:8-9
78. NEC 1860:2; RG 10, Volume 2771, File 154, 845, pt.1
79. NEC 1860:56-57; " "
80. NEC 1860:10-11; " "
81. NEC 1860:14-15; " "
82-86 NEC 1861:2-8; " "
87. NEC 1874:69-71
88. NEC 1869:6-13
89. NEC 1871:91-2
90. NEC 1874:71
91-92. NEC 1871:122-3
93. NEC 1871:101-103
94. NEC 1871:123-124

95-96. NEC 1871:99-101
97. NEC 1871:72
98. NEC 1874:104
99. NEC 1871:103-104
100. NEC 1871:352-353
101. NEC 1871:124-125
102. NEC 1874:72
103. NEC 1871:126
104. NEC 1871:281
105 NEC 1874:72
106. NEC 1871:126
107. NEC 1874:73
108. NEC 1871:327, 329-333
109. NEC 1874:77
110. NEC 1874:268-269
111-116 NEC 1874:86-96
117. NEC 1874:299
118. NEC 1874:98-100
119-120. NEC 1874:96-98
121-122. NEC 1874:102-104
123-124. NEC 1874:100-102
125. NEC 1874:107-112
126. NEC 1874:116-117
127. NEC 1874:112-114
128. NEC 1874:125-126
129. NEC 1874:106-107
130. NEC 1874:124
131. NEC 1874:120-122
132. NEC 1874:115
133. RG 10,Volume 1906, File 2301
134-136. NEC 1874:132-133
137. NEC 1874:136-137
138-140. NEC 1874:150-1

Mohawk Institute 1872 - 1914

1-3. NEC 1874:152-165
4. NEC 1879:136-148
5-6. NEC Letter Book 1872-6 Ms 7928 vol 1
7. NEC 1879:148-155
8. DIA AR, CP Sessional Papers (11) 1877:15
9. NEC 1879:155-158
10. DIA AR, CP Sessional Papers (10) 1878:18
11. NEC 1879:158-162
12. NEC 1879:16-31
13. DIA AR, CP Sessional Papers (4) 1880:18
14. DIA AR, CP Sessional Papers (14) 1881:14
15. DIA AR, CP Sessional Papers (6) 1882:2
16. DIA AR, CP Sessional Papers (5) 1883:2
17. NEC 1884:4-30
18. DIA AR, CP Sessional Papers (4) 1886:16-17
19. Report Minister of Education OLA SP5 1886:130-132
20-22. RG 2-N2-0-595-2
23. DIA AR, CP Sessional Papers (6) 1887:22-23
24. DIA AR, CP Sessional Papers (15) 1888:22-23
25. DIA AR, CP Sessional Papers (16) 1889:122-123
26. DIA AR, CP Sessional Papers (12) 1890:27-28
27. DIA AR, CP Sessional Papers (18) 1891:114-115
28. DIA AR, CP Sessional Papers (14) 1892:24a-25
29. DIA AR, CP Sessional Papers (14) 1893:23-25
30. DIA AR, CP Sessional Papers (14) 1894:21-23
31. DIA AR, CP Sessional Papers(14) 1895:22
32. RG 10, Volume 2771, File 154, 845, pt. 1
33. RG 10, Volume 2006, File 7825-1A

34. DIA AR, CP Sessional Papers (14) 1896:21-22
35. DIA AR, CP Sessional Papers (14) 1897:304-307
36. DIA AR, CP Sessional Papers (14) 1898:222-223
37. DIA AR, CP Sessional Papers (14) 1899:255-8
38. DIA AR, CP Sessional Papers (14) 1900:290-1
39. DIA AR, CP Sessional Papers (27) 1901:308-310
40. DIA AR, CP Sessional Papers (27) 1902:298-300
41. DIA AR, CP Sessional Papers (27) 1903:292-294
42. RG 10, Volume 2771, File 154,845, pt.1; NEC 1902:125-130
43. RG 10, Volume 2771, File 154,845, pt.1; NEC 1902:140-151
44-52. RG 10, Volume 2771, File 154,845, pt.1
53. DIA AR, CP Sessional Papers (27) 1904:326-328
54. RG 10, Vol 2771, File 154,845, pt.1
55. DIA AR, CP Sessional Papers (27) 1905:304-306
56. RG 10, Volume 2771, File 154,845, pt.1
57. DIA AR, CP Sessional Papers (27) 1906:282-284
58-60. RG 10, Volume 2771, File 154,845, pt.1
61. DIA AR, CP Sessional Papers (27) 1907:282-284
62. DIA AR, CP Sessional Papers (27) 1908:282-284
63-65. RG 10, Volume 2771, File 154,845, pt.1
66. NEC 1908:12-13
67. DIA AR, CP Sessional Papers (27) 1909:291-293
68. DIA AR, CP Sessional Papers (27) 1910:285-288
69. DIA AR, CP Sessional Papers (27) 1911:418-420
70-71. RG 10, Volume 2771, File 154,845, pt.1
72. DIA AR, CP Sessional Papers (27) 1912:521-522
73. RG 10, Volume 2771, File 154,845, pt.1
74. DIA AR, CP Sessional Papers (27) 1913:509-511

75.   DIA AR, CP Sessional Papers (27) 1914:534-536
76-86.   RG 10, Volume 2771, File 154,845, pt.1
87.   Brantford Expositor, 1 April 1914; RG10, Volume 2771, File

154,845, pt.1

88-92.   RG 10, Volume 2771, File 154,845, pt.1

Mohawk Institute 1915 - 1922

1-46.   RG 10, Volume 2771, File 154,845, pt. 1A

47-81.   RG 10, Volume 6200, file 466-1, part 1

Mohawk Institute 1922-1929

1-9.   RG 10, Volume 6200, file 466-1, part 1
10.   RG 2, P-3 1924:132/9-2 Box 132
11-13   RG 10, Volume 6200, file 466-1, part 1
14.   RG 2, P-3 1924:132/9-2 Box 132

15.   RG 10, Volume 6200, file 466-1, part 1
16.   Brantford Junior Expositor, 20 December 1924, p. 23
17-23.   RG 10, Volume 6200, file 466 -1, part 1
24-47.   RG 10, Volume 6200, file 466 -1, part 2

Mohawk Institute 1929-1945

1-8.   RG 10, Volume 6200, file 466-1, part 2
9.   Brantford Expositor, 17 September 1930
10-11.   RG 10, Volume 6202, file 466-13, part 1
12.   RG 10, Volume 6200, file 466-1, part 2
13.   RG 10, Volume 6202, file 466-13, part 1
14-20.   RG 10, Volume 6200, file 466-1, part 2
21-22.   RG 10, Volume 6202, file 466-23, part 1
23.   RG 10, Volume 6200, file 466-1, part 2
24-31.   RG 10, Volume 6200, file 466-1, part 3

32-37.   RG 10, Volume 8605, File 451/1-13, Pt.1
38.   RG 10, Volume 6200, file 466-1, part 3
39-40.   RG 10, Volume 6201, file 466-5, part 4
41-45.   RG 10, Volume 6200, file 466-1, part 3
46.   RG 10, Volume 6200, File 466-1, part 4
47.   RG 10, Volume 6200, file 466-1, part 3
48.   RG 10, Volume 8605, File 451/1-13, Pt.1
49-52.   RG 10, Volume 6200, file 466-1, part 3
53-70.   RG 10, Volume 6200, file 466-1, part 4

Mohawk Institute 1945-1970

1.   RG 10, Volume 6200, file 466-1, part 4
2-3.   RG 10, Volume 8605, File 451/1-13, Pt. 1
4.   Brantford Expositor 22 February 1946
5.   RG 10, Volume 6200, file 466-1, part 4
6.   Brantford Expositor, 27 February 1946
7-8.   RG 10, Volume 6200, file 466-1, part 4
9.   RG 10, Volume 6200, file 466-3, part 1
10.   RG 10, Volume 6200, file 466-1, part 4
11-14   RG 10, Volume 8605, File 451/1-13, Pt.1
15-19.   RG 10, Volume 6200, file 466-1, part 5
20-28.   RG 10, Volume 6202, file 466-10, part 6
29.   RG 10, Volume 6201, file 466-5, part 6
30.   RG 10, Volume 6202, file 466-10, part 6
31.   RG 10, Volume 6201, file 466-5, part 6
32-35.   RG 10, Volume 6202, file 466-10, part 6
36.   RG 10, Volume 8606, File 487/1-13-001
37.   Brantford Expositor, 15 March 1950
38.   Brantford Expositor, 16 March 1950
39.   RG 10, Volume 8606, File 487/1-13-001
40-41.   RG 10, Volume 6202, file 466-10, part 6
42.   RG 10, Volume 8606, File 487/1-13-001
43.   RG 10, Volume 6202, file 466-10, part 6
44-45.   RG 10, Volume 8606, File 487/1-13-001
46.   RG 10, Volume 6202, file 466-10, part 6
47-48.   RG 10, Volume 8606, File 487/1-13-001
49.   RG 10, Volume 8605, File 451/1-13, Pt.1

50-54.   RG 10, Volume 8606, File 487/1-13-001
55.   RG 10, File 32/25-1-1
56-66.   RG 10, Volume 7188, File 451/25-1-004
67-68.   RG 10, Volume 8606, File 487/1-13-001
69-70.   RG 10, Volume 7188, File 451/25-1-004
71-73.   RG 10, Volume 8606, File 487/1-13-001
74-76.   RG 10, Volume 7188, File 451/25-1-004
77.   RG 10, File 32/25-1
78-81.   RG 10, Volume 7188, File 451/25-1-004
82.   RG 10, Volume 8606, File 487/1-13-001
83.   RG 10, Volume 8798, File 479/25-13-001, pt.2
84.   RG 10, File 32/25-1
85.   RG 10, Volume 8606, File 487/1-13-001
86.   RG 10, Volume 8798, File 479/25-13-001, pt.2
87.   Brantford Expositor, 20 January 1961
88.   RG 10, Volume 8798, File 479/25-13-001, pt.2
89-90.   RG 10, Volume 8606, File 487/1-13-001
91.   RG 10, Volume 8798, File 479/25-13-001, pt.2
92-93.   RG 10, Volume 8606, File 487/1-13-001
94-100. RG 10, Volume 8798, File 479/25-13-001, pt 2
101.   RG 10, Volume 8606, File 487/1-13-001
102-105. RG 10, Volume 8798, File 479/25-13-001, pt.2
106-109. RG 10, File 32/25-1
110.   Brantford Expositor, 27 February 1970
111.   Brantford Expositor, 10 June 1970

Mohawk Institute - Facts and Figures

1.   NEC 1871:331
2.   RG 10, Volume 2006, File 7825-1A, Benson 1894
3-5.   NEC 1879:139, 143, 148, 152-153, 155, 158, 162
           and from DIA AR (Annual Reports)
6.   RG 10, Volume 6200, file 466-1, part 2
7-11.   RG 10, Volume 2771, File 154,845, pt. 1A

12.   RG 10, Volume 6200, File 466-1, part 2
13.   RG 10, Volume 6200, file 466-1, part 2
14-15.   RG 10, Volume 6200, file 466-1, part 4
16.   RG 10, Volume 6200, file 466-3, part 1
17.   RG 10, Volume 7188, File 451/25-1-004
18.   RG 10, Volume 6202, file 466-10, part 6

Mohawk Institute - Students

1.	NEC 1846:95
2.	NEC 1859:10-11
3.	NEC 1859:16-17
4.	NEC 1861:13-14;RG 10,Volume 2771
5.	NEC 1861:18-19; " "
6.	NEC 1869:6-13
7.	NEC 1874:126-127

8.	RG 10, Volume 6200, file 466-1, part 2
9.	RG 10, Volume 2771, File 154,845, pt.1A
10.	RG 10, Volume 6202, file 466-13, part 1, part 2
11.	RG 10, Volume 6202, file 466-10, part 6.
12.	RG 10, Volume 6202, file 466-10, part 6
13.	RG 10, Volume 6200, file 466-2, part 1
14.	RG 10, file No. 32/23-26-466

Mt. Elgin 1849-1882

1.	Christian Guardian Wednesday, July 25th, 1849
2.	WMMS 24th Annual Report 1849:xi
3.	WMMS 25th Annual Report 1850:ix-x
4-5.	MMN
6-7.	WMMS 26th Annual Report 1851:xi-xiii
8.	WMMS 27th Annual Report 1852:x-xii
9.	WMMS 28th Annual Report 1853:x-xi
10.	WMMS 29th Annual Report 1854:xiv-xvi
11-20.	S. Rose Copying Book 1854-62 UCA
21.	Christian Guardian Wednesday, September 19, 1855
22-24.	S. Rose Copying Book 1854-1862
25.	WMMS 30th Annual Report 1855:xxiii
26-29.	S. Rose Copying Book 1854-1862
30.	Elizabeth Jones to John Dunlop, November 22, 1856, National Library of Scotland, Dept of Manuscripts, Dep 360/102. Thanks to Donald Smith
31.	WMMS 31st Annual Report 1856:xix-xx
32.	S. Rose Copying Book 1854-62
33.	Christian Guardian February 11, 1857
34.	Christian Guardian February 18, 1857
35.	Christian Guardian March 11, 1857
36.	WMMS 32nd Annual Report 1857:xxii-xxiii
37.	WMMS 33rd Annual Report 1858:xviii
38.	CR 1858
39.	WMMS 34th Annual Report 1859:xiii-xiv

40.	WMMS 35th Annual Report 1860:xv
41.	WMMS 36th Annual Report 1861:xviii
42.	WMMS 37th Annual Report 1862:xx
43.	DIA AR CP Sessional Papers (5) 1863:Appendix No.44
44.	WMMS 38th Annual Report 1863:xvi
45.	WMMS 40th Annual Report 1865:xviii-xvix
46.	WMMS 41st Annual Report 1866:np
47.	Christian Guardian October 16, 1867:166
48.	WMMS 43rd Annual Report 1868:xxvi
49.	WMMS 44th Annual Report 1869:xxix-xxx
50.	WMMS 45th Annual Report 1870:xxxiv
51.	Christian Guardian March 29th 1871:51
52.	NEC 1874:312
53.	WMMS 48th Annual Report 1872:xxii
54.	WMMS 49th Annual Report 1873:xxxi
55.	WMMS 50th Annual Report 1874:xxxiv
56.	WMMS 51st Annual Report 1875:xxxvii
57.	WMMS 52nd Annual Report 1876:xxvi
58.	WMMS 53rd Annual Report 1877:xxvi
59.	WMMS 54th Annual Report 1878:xxvii
60.	WMMS 55th Annual Report 1879:xxv
61.	WMMS 56th Annual Report 1880:xxx
62.	WMMS 57th Annual Report 1881:xxxiii-xxxv
63.	Cosford Papers pp. 29-44

Mt. Elgin 1882-1909

1.	RG 10, Volume 6205, file 468-1, part 1
2.	Christian Guardian November 22, 1882:375
3.	RG 10, Volume 6205, file 468-1, part 1
4.	DIA AR, CP Sessional Papers (4) 1884:16-17
5.	WMMS 59th Annual Report 1883:xxxi
6.	WMMS 60th Annual Report 1884:xxx-xxxi
7.	DIA AR, CP Sessional Papers (3) 1885:17-18
8-11.	RG 10, Volume 2269, File 53,978
12.	Report Minister of Education OLA SP5 1885: 173-174
13.	Christian Guardian December 31, 1884:441
14.	WMMS 61st Annual Report 1884-5:xxxviii
15.	DIA AR, CP Sessional Papers (6) 1887:16
16.	Report Minister of Education OLA SP5 1886:140
17.	Report Minister Of Education OLA SP7 1887:100
18.	RG 10, Volume 6205, file 468-1, part 1
19.	Report Minister of Education OLA SP7 1888:153
20.	DIA AR, CP Sessional Papers (15) 1888:21-22
21.	The Missionary Outlook February 1888:24
22.	DIA AR, CP Sessional Papers (16) 1889:19
23.	WMMS 65th Annual Report 1889:
24.	DIA AR, CP Sessional Papers (12) 1890:19
25.	Report Minister of Education OLA SP 6 1890:227-230
26.	Our Forest Children Vol III, No. 3. June 1889
27.	DIA AR, CP Sessional Papers (18) 1891:17
28.	Report Minister of Education OLA SP4 1891:227-230
29.	WMMS 67th Annual Report 1891:xlvii-xlviii
30.	Report Minister of Education OLA SP11 1892:170-173
31.	DIA AR, CP Sessional Papers (14) 1893:20

32.	Report Minister of Education OLA SP3 1893162-164
33.	DIA AR, CP Sessional Papers (14) 1894:17-18
34.	WMMS 69th Annual Report 1892-3:lx
35.	RG 10, Volume 6205, file 468-1, part 1
36.	Report Minister of Education OLA SP3 1894:200-202
37.	DIA AR, CP Sessional Papers (14) 1895:25
38.	DIA AR, CP Sessional Papers (14) 1896:17-18
39-41.	RG 10, Volume 6205, file 468-1, part 1
42.	DIA AR, CP Sessional Papers (14) 1897:365-368
43.	Hodgins 1894-1910, Vol 8:295
44.	DIA AR, CP Sessional Papers (14) 1897:303-304
45-46.	RG 10, Volume 6205, file 468-1, part 1
47.	DIA AR, CP Sessional Papers (14) 1898:260-261
48.	DIA AR, CP Sessional Papers (14) 1899:294-296.
49.	DIA AR, CP Sessional Papers (14) 1900:294-296
50.	DIA AR, CP Sessional Papers (27) 1901:312-313
51.	DIA AR, CP Sessional Papers (27) 1902:301-302
52.	WMMS 77th Annual Report 1901:lv-lvi
53-55.	RG 10, Volume 6205, file 468-1, part 1
56.	DIA AR, CP Sessional Papers (27) 1903:294-295
57-60.	RG 10, Volume 6205, file 468-1, part 1
61.	DIA AR, CP Sessional Papers (27) 1904:328-329
62.	RG 10, Volume 6205, file 468-1, part 1
63.	DIA AR, CP Sessional Papers (27) 1905:306-307
64-65.	RG 10, Volume 6205, file 468-1, part 1
66.	DIA AR, CP Sessional Papers (27) 1906:284-286
67.	Sutherland Papers
68-73.	RG 10, Volume 6205, file 468-1, part 1

74.   DIA AR, CP Sessional Papers (27) 1907:284-285
75-76.   RG 10, Volume 6205, file 468-1, part 1
77-78.   Sutherland Papers
79.   DIA AR, CP Sessional Papers (27) 1908:284-6
80-81.   RG 10, Volume 6205, file 468-5, part 1
82-83.   Sutherland Papers
84-85.   RG 10, Volume 6206, file 468-5, part 2
86-88.   Sutherland Papers
89.   RG 10, Volume 6206, file 468-5, part 2

90.   RG 10, Volume 6205, file 468-1, part 1
91.   DIA AR, CP Sessional Papers (27) 1909:293-295
92-93.   RG 10, Volume 6205, file 468-1, part 1
94.   RG 10, Volume 6206, file 468-5, part 2
95.   RG 10, Volume 6205, file 468-1, part 1
96-97.   RG 10, Volume 6206, file 468-5, part 2
98.   Sutherland Papers
99.   DIA AR, CP Sessional Papers (27) 1910:293-295
100.   Sutherland Papers

Mt. Elgin 1909-1934

1.   RG 10, Volume 6205, file 468-1, part 1
2-3.   RG 10, Volume 6206, file 468-5, part 2
4-6.   Sutherland Papers
7.   RG 10, Volume 6205, file 468-1, part 1
8-9.   Sutherland Papers
10-13.   RG 10, Volume 6206, file 468-5, part 2
14.   DIA AR, CP Sessional Papers (27) 1911:421-422
15-17.   Shore Papers
18.   RG 10, Volume 6206, file 468-5, part 2
19.   RG 10, Volume 6205, filc 468-1, part 1
20.   DIA AR, CP Sessional Papers (27) 1912:522-523
21-22.   RG 10, Volume 6206, file 468-5, part 2
23.   RG 10, Volume 6205, file 468-1, part 1
24.   Shore Papers
25.   RG 10, Volume 6205, file 468-1, part 1
26-27.   RG 10, Volume 6206, File 468-5, part 2
28.   Shore Papers
29.   DIA AR, CP Sessional Papers (27) 1913:511-513
30-32.   RG 10, Volume 6205, file 468-1, part 1
33.   DIA AR, CP Sessional Papers (27) 1914:536-537
34.   Christian Guardian May 21, 1913:9-11; RG 10, Volume 6205, file 468-1, part 1
35.   Joblin Papers
36-40.   RG 10, Volume 6205, file 468-1, part 1
41.   RG 10, Volume 6206, file 468-5, part 3
42-44.   RG 10, Volume 6205, file 468-1, part 1
45-47.   RG 10, Volume 6206, file 468-5, part 3
48-52.   RG 10, Volume 6205, file 468-1, part 1
53.   RG 10, Volume 6205, file 468-1, part 1
54.   RG 10, Volume 6206, file 468-5, part 3
55-59.   RG 10 Volume 6205, file 468-1, part 1

60.   RG 10, Volume 3207, File 520,486, pt.1
61.   Joblin Papers
62-63.   RG 10, Volume 6205, file 468-1, part 2
64-65.   The Missionary Bulletin Vol XVI No. 2, April-June 1920:159-207
66.   RG 10, Volume 6205, file 468-1, part 2
67-68.   RG 10, Volume 6206, file 468-5, part 4
69-70.   RG 10, Volume 6205, file 468-1, part 2
71-72.   RG 10, Volume 6206, file 468-5, part 4
73-75.   RG 10, Volume 6206, file 468-5, part 5
76-78.   RG 10, Volume 6205, File 468-1, part 2
79.   RG 10, Volume 6206, file 468-5, part 5
80.   RG 10, Volume 6205, file 468-1, part 2
81-82.   RG 10, Volume 6206, file 468-5, part 5
83.   RG 10, Volume 6207, file 468-5, part 6
84.   RG 10, Volume 6205, file 468-1, part 2
85-90.   RG 10, Volume 6207, file 468-5, part 6
91.   RG 10, Volume 6205, file 468-1, part 2
92-95.   RG 10, Volume 6207, file 468-5, part 6
96.   RG 10, Volume 6205, file 468-1, part 2
97.   RG 10, Volume 6207, file 468-5, part 6
98.   RG 10, Volume 6205, file 468-1, part 2
99-100.   RG 10, Volume 6207, file 468-5, part 6
101.   RG 10, Volume 6205, file 468-1, part 2
102-103.   RG 10, Volume 6207, file 468-5, part 6
104.   RG 10, Volume 6205, file 468-1, part 2
105-107.   RG 10, Volume 6207, file 468-5, part 6
108-116.   RG 10, Volume 6205, file 468-1, part 2
117.   RG 10, Volume 6210, file 468-13, part 1
118-119.   RG 10, Volume 6205, file 468-1, part 2
120.   RG 10, Volume 6210, file 468-13, part 1

Mt. Elgin 1934-1946

1-2.   RG 10, Volume 6207, file 468-5, part 6
3.   RG 10, Volume 6210, file 468-13, part 1
4-7.   RG 10, Volume 6207, file 468-5, part 6
8.   RG 10, Volume 6210, file 468-13, part 1
9.   RG 10, Volume 6207, file 468-5, part 6
10-11.   RG 10, Volume 6205, file 468-1, part 2
12-13.   RG 10, Volume 6207, file 468-5, part 6
14-15.   RG 10, Volume 6207, file 468-5, part 7
16.   RG 10, Volume 6210, file 468-13, part 1
17-19.   RG 10, Volume 6207, file 468-5, part 7
20.   RG 10, Volume 6210, file 468-13, part 1
21.   RG 10, Volume 6207, file 468-5, part 7
22.   RG 10, Volume 6210, file 468-22, part 2
23.   RG 10, Volume 6205, file 468-1, part 3
24.   RG 10, Volume 6210, file 468-22, part 2
25.   RG 10, Volume 6210, file 468-13, part 1
26.   RG 10, Volume 6207, file 468-5, part 7
27-39.   RG 10, Volume 6210, file 468-13, part 1
40.   RG 10, Volume 6207, file 468-5, part 7
41-52.   RG 10, Volume 6209, file 468-10, part 1

53.   RG 10, Volume 6207, file 468-5, part 7
54-65.   RG 10, Volume 6209, file 468-10, part 1
66.   RG 10, Volume 6207, file 468-5, part 8
67-70.   RG 10, Volume 6209, file 468-10, part 1
71.   RG 10, Volume 6210, file 468-13, part 1
72.   RG 10, Volume 6207, file 466-5, part 8
73.   RG 10, Volume 6205, file 468-1, part 3
74-75.   RG 10, Volume 6033, file 150-60, part 1
76.   RG 10, Volume 6210, file 468-13, part 1
77-86.   RG 10, Volume 6209, file 468-10, part 2
87.   RG 10, Volume 6207, file 468-5, part 8
88-93.   RG 10, Volume 6209, file 468-10, part 2
94.   RG 10, Volume 6205, file 468-1, part 3
95-97.   RG 10, Volume 6210, file 468-23, part 1
98.   RG 10, Volume 6209, file 468-10, part 2
99-100.   RG 10, Volume 6207, file 468-5, part 8
101-110.   RG 10, Volume 6209, file 468-10, part 2
111.   RG 10, Volume 6207, file 468-5, part 8
112-114.   RG 10, Volume 6210, file 468-11, part 1
115-129.   RG 10, Volume 6209, file 468-10, part 3

130-132. RG 10, Volume 6210, file 468-13, part 1
133-134. RG 10, Volume 6210, file 468-11, part 1
135-136. RG 10, Volume 6210, file 468-13, part 1
137. RG 10, Volume 6205, file 468-1, part 3
138-141. RG 10, Volume 6210, file 468-13, part 1
142. RG 10, Volume 6205, file 468-1, part 3
143. RG 10, Volume 6207, file 468-5, part 9
144. RG 10, Volume 6205, file 468-1, part 3
145-146. RG 10, Volume 6207, file 468-5, part 9
147-149. Joblin Papers
150. RG 10, Volume 6205, file 468-1, part 3
151-154. Joblin Papers
155-161. RG 10, Volume 6205, file 468-1, part 3
162. Joblin Papers

163. RG 10, Volume 6207, file 468-5, part 9
164. RG 10, Volume 6205, file 468-1, part 3
165. Joblin Papers
166-167. RG 10, Volume 6207, file 468-5, part 9
168-171. RG 10, Volume 6205, file 468-1, part 3
172. RG 10, Volume 6207, file 468-5, part 9
173. RG 10, Volume 6210, file 468-11, part 1
174-175. RG 10, Volume 6208, file 468-5, part 10
176. RG 10, Volume 6205, file 468-1, part 3
177. Joblin Papers
178-179. RG 10, Volume 6210, file 468-22, part 1
180-188. RG 10, Volume 6208, file 468-5, part 10
189-191. RG 10, Volume 6205, file 468-1, part 3

Mt. Elgin - Facts and Figures

1. RG 10, Volume 6205, file 468-1, part 1. Reel 7937. Report of the Mount Elgin Institute Year Ending March 31, 1911, T. Ferrier
2-5. Joblin Papers

6-17. RG 10, Volume 6210, file 468-24, part 1
18. from DIA AR (Annual Reports)
19. from RG 10, Volume 6209, File 468-10, parts 1 2 & 3

Mt. Elgin - Students

1. RG 10, Volume 2269, File 53,978
2. RG 10, Volume 6209, file 468-13, part 1
3. RG 10, Volume 6209, file 468-10, part 1
   Strapp to Hoey October 7, 1937
4-5. RG 10, Volume 6209, file 468-10, part 1
6. RG 10, Volume 6209, file 468-10, part 1
   Strapp to Hoey October 7, 1937
7-9. RG 10, Volume 6209, file 468-10, part 1
10. RG 10, Volume 6209, file 468-10, part 2
11. RG 10, Volume 6209, file 468-10, part 2
   Strapp to Phelan October 11th, 1939

12. RG 10, Volume 6209, file 468-10, part 2
   Phelan to Strapp 4 July 1939. Strapp to Phelan, 11 October 1939
13-14. RG 10, Volume 6209, file 468-10, part 2
   Phelan to Strapp 4 July 1939
15-16. RG 10, Volume 6209, file 468-10, part 2
   Phelan to Strapp 26 June 1940
17. RG 10, Volume 6209, file 468-10, part 3
   Strapp to Phelan 13 October 1941
18-19. RG 10, Volume 6209, file 468-10, part 3
20. from RG 10, Vol 6209, File 468-10, parts 1 2 & 3

Photographs

Bibliography

Books, Articles and Theses

Abbott, Frederick H. *The Administration of Indian Affairs in Canada.* DOC USI DI 1115A35

Cheechoo, Shirley. *Path With No Moccasins.* Box 59, West Bay, Ontario P0P 1G0 1993

Christie, Laird. *Reserve Colonialism and Socio cultural Change.* Ph.D. thesis, University of Toronto 1976

Curtis, Bruce. *Building the Educational State: Canada West, 1836-1871.* The Althouse Press, London, Ontario. 1988

Dickens, Charles. *Nicholas Nickleby.* Penguin Books, Harmondsworth. 1839

Ferrier, Russell T. *The Mohawk Institute.* Report of the Superintendent General of Indian Education, 1930

Fitzgerald, James. *Old Boys: the powerful legacy of Upper Canada College.* MacFarlane Walter & Ross, Toronto 1994

Foucault, Michel. *Discipline and Punish.* Vintage Books, New York 1979

Gathorne-Hardy, Jonathan. *The Public School Phenomenon.* Hodder and Stoughton, London 1977

Graham, Elizabeth. *The Uses and Abuses of Power in the Mohawk Institute and Mt. Elgin Residential Schools.* Paper, Laurier III Conference on Ethnohistory and Ethnology, Walpole Island, 1994.

- *"Shades of the Prison House begin to close": two Indian residential schools.* Paper, Northeastern Anthropological Association Annual Meeting, Waterloo, Ontario, 1991.

- *Medicine Man to Missionary.* Peter Martin, Toronto 1975

- *Strategies and Souls.* Ph.D. thesis, University of Toronto 1973

Grant, John Webster. *Moon of Wintertime; Missionaries and the Indians of Canada in Encounter since 1534.* University of Toronto Press, Toronto 1984

Haig Brown, Celia. *Resistance and Renewal.* Tillacum Library, Vancouver. 1988

Hodgins, J. G., ed. *Documentary History of Education in Upper Canada.* 28 vols. Toronto. 1894-1910

- *The Establishment of Schools and Colleges in Ontario 1792-1910.* L. K. Cameron, Toronto. 1910

Hughes, Thomas. *Tom Brown's Schooldays.* Collins, London 1857

Jaine, Linda, ed. *Residential Schools: The Stolen Years.* Saskatoon: University of Saskatchewan Extension Press 1992

Johnston, Basil. *Indian Schooldays.* Key Porter Books, Toronto 1988

Jones, Peter. *Life and Journals of Kah-ke-wa-quo-na-by (Rev Peter Jones) Wesleyan Missionary.* Published under the direction of the Missionary Committee, Canada Conference. Anson Green, Toronto 1860

Knockwood, Isabelle. *Out of the Depths: The Experiences of Mi'kmaw Children at the Indian Residential School at Schubenacadie.* Roseway Publishing, Lockeport 1995

Lambert, Royston. *The Hothouse Society; An exploration of boarding-school life through the boys' and girls' own writings.* Penguin Books 1968

Manore, Jean. *A Vision Of Trust: Chief Shingwaukonse, E.F. Wilson and the founding of Shingwauk Hall.* Paper, Annual Meeting of the Canadian Historical Association 1992

Miller, J. R. *Shingwauk's Vision.* University of Toronto Press, Toronto 1996

- *Native Residential Schools in Historical Context.* Paper, Annual Meeting of the Canadian Catholic Historical Association, Calgary 1994.

- *Owen Glendower, Hotspur, and Canadian Indian Policy.* Ethnohistory Volume 37, Number 4. 1990

Montour, Enos. *Brown Tom's Schooldays.* Edited by Elizabeth Graham, 105 Allen St. W. Waterloo, Ontario N2l 1E6 1985

Nock, David A. *A Victorian Missionary and Canadian Indian Policy; Cultural Synthesis vs Cultural Replacement.* Canadian Corporation for Studies in Religion, Wilfrid Laurier Press, Waterloo 1988

Pettit, Jennifer. *From Longhouse to Schoolhouse: The Mohawk Institute, 1834-1970.* MA thesis, University of Western Ontario 1993

Rogers, Edward S. and Smith, Donald Eds., *Aboriginal Ontario.* Dundurn Press, Toronto 1994

Shortt, Adam, and Doughty A. G. Eds. *Canada and Its Provinces.* 22 Volumes. Toronto 1914

Smith, Donald B. *Sacred Feathers; The Reverend Peter Jones (Kahkewaquonaby) and the Mississauga Indians.* University of Toronto Press, Toronto 1987

St. Louis, E. A. *Education.* 8 April 1952, DIA library. 1952

Titley, E. Brian *A Narrow Vision.* University of British Columbia Press, Vancouver 1986

White, Vicki. *Breaking the Spirit.* Brantford Expositor, July 6, 1991.

Wober, Mallory. *English Girls' Boarding Schools.* Allen Lane The Penguin Press, London 1971

Woodland Indian Cultural Educational Centre. *Schooldays.* Woodland Indian Cultural Education Centre, Brantford 1984

Manuscript Collections

Cosford Papers
United Church of Canada/Victoria University Archives, Methodist Church (Canada) Missionary Society fonds, Thomas Cosford fonds, Reminiscences fonds 3064, PP COS 86.073C Tr File 1 of 1

Joblin Papers
United Church of Canada/Victoria University Archives, Methodist Church (Canada) Missionary Society fonds, Elgie E. Joblin PP JOB Vol III Box 1, File 3 Mt Elgin Industrial Institute, Mt Elgin Residential School 1849 - 1946

MMN
United Church of Canada/Victoria University Archives, Wesleyan Methodist Missionary Society Collection Series 2, Correspondence from Missionaries, Statesmen, Lay Readers and others in Mission areas. 78.128C Reel 25

National Library of Scotland, Dept. of Manuscripts, Dep 360/102 (Eliza Jones)

NEC
New England Company Letter Book 1872-6. Guildhall Library, London. Ms 7928 volume 1.

RG2
Ontario Archives of Ontario, Toronto.
RG 2 Indian Affairs, N2-0-595-2;
RG 2 - P-3 1924 132/9-2 Box 132 Mohawk Institute
RG 2-42-0-595 P-2 Box 15 Mohawk Institute

S. Rose Copying Book
United Church of Canada/Victoria University Archives, S. Rose Copying Book 1854-62 83.065C

RG 10
National Archives of Canada Records Relating to Indian Affairs
Volume 1906, 2006=C11133, 2269, 2771=C11.276, 3207=C-11340, 6033, 6200=C7933; 6201=C7934, 6202=C7935, 6205=C7937-8, 6206=C7938, 6207=C7939, 6208=C7939, 6209=C7940-1, 6210=C7941, 7188=C-9697, 8605=C-14229, 8606, 8798= C9718

Sutherland Papers
United Church of Canada/Victoria University Archives, Methodist Church (Canada) Missionary Society fonds, Correspondence of the General Secretaries, Incoming Correspondence of the General Secretary, Alexander Sutherland. --1900-1910, fonds 14/2/4, 78.092C-box 8

Shore Papers
United Church of Canada/Victoria University Archives, Methodist Church (Canada) Missionary Society fonds, Correspondence of the General Secretaries, Correspondence of T.E. Egerton Shore, fonds 14/2/5, 78.093C-box 4

Missionary Society Publications

Christian Guardian [Methodist]

Missionary Bulletin (Methodist

NEC New England Company:

1829   Report by a committee of the Corporation commonly called the New England Company of their proceedings for the civilization and conversion of Indians, Blacks, and Pagans, in the British Colonies in America and the West Indies.

1832   Report by a committee of the Corporation commonly called the New England Company of their proceedings for the civilization and conversion of Indians, Blacks, and Pagans, in the British Colonies in America and the West Indies, since the last Report.

1840   Report by a committee of the Corporation commonly called the New England Company of their proceedings for the civilization and conversion of Indians, Blacks, and Pagans, in the British Colonies in America and the West Indies, since the last Report in 1832.

1846   Report by a committee of the Corporation commonly called the New England Company of their proceedings for the civilization and conversion of Indians, Blacks, and Pagans, in the British Colonies in America and the West Indies, since the last report in 1840. London

1859   Report

1860   Report

1861   Report

1869   Report

1871   History of the New England Company from its incorporation, in the seventeenth century to the present time including A Detailed Report of the Company's Proceedings for the civilization and Conversion of Indians, Blacks, and Pagans in the Dominion of Canada, British Columbia, the West Indies, and South Africa, During the Two Years 1869-70. London 1871.

1874   Report of the Proceedings of the New England Company, for the Civilization and Conversion of Indians, Blacks and Pagans in the Dominion of Canada, South Africa and the West Indies, During the two years 1871 - 1872. London 1874.

1879   Six Years' Summary of the Proceedings of the New England Company, for the Civilization and Conversion of Indians Blacks and Pagans in the Dominion of Canada and the West Indies 1873-78. London 1879.

1884   Report to the New England Company of A visit to two of their mission stations in the Province of Ontario, Canada, in the year 1884. by Wm. Lant Carpenter, B.A., B.Sc.

1902   Report

1908   Report

1908   Conference on Indian Education in Canada. Convened by the Company - The New England Company. April 15, 1908. Printed by Spottiswoode and Co. Ltd., London England.

WMMS

Wesleyan Methodist Missionary Society in Canada: Annual Reports

Government Publications

DIA AR

Canada, Department of Indian Affairs, *Annual Reports*

Canada, Parliament, *Sessional Papers*

Canadian Welfare Council

1967   *Indian Residential Schools. A research study of the child care programs of nine residential schools in Saskatchewan.*

CR

Province of Canada, *Report of the Special Commissioners appointed on the 8th of September, 1856, to Investigate Indian Affairs in Canada,* Journals of the Legislative Assembly of the Province of Canada, Vol.16, Appendix 21, 1858.

Canada, Indian Department, *Report on the Affairs of the Indians in Canada, laid before the Legislative Assembly, 1845-1846.* (2 volumes, Montreal, 1846-47) Gov.Doc Can (Prov) I

OLA SP

Ontario Legislative Assembly, *Sessional Papers*

RCAP

Report of the Royal Commission on Aboriginal Peoples. Volume 1: *Looking Forward, Looking Back*; Part Two: *False Assumptions and a Failed Relationship*; 10: *Residential Schools,*. Ottawa: The Commission 1996

Magazines and Newspapers

Brantford Expositor

Brantford Junior Expositor

The Colonial Intelligencer; or, Aborigines' Friend London: Printed and Published for the Aborigines' Protection Society;

Our Forest Children

St. Thomas Times Journal

Correspondents

Dates refer to term in office where known, or to time period in which they appear in the records.

DIA = Department of Indian Affairs, IAB = Indian Affairs Branch, Dep. Supt. Gen = Deputy Superintendent General, NEC = New England Company

Ashton, A. C.	Mohawk Institute 1913
Ashton, A. Nelles	Principal Mohawk Institute 1911-1914. Son of Robert Ashton
Ashton, Robert	Principal Mohawk Institute 1872-1911
Ashton, Maj. Gen. E. C.	Teacher Mohawk Institute 1895; Commissioner NEC 1918
Bagot, Sir Charles	Governor General of Canada 1842
Barefoot (Bearfoot), Isaac	Student then Teacher Mohawk Institute 1869-1876
Barrass, Rev. Dr. Edward	1896
Beaton, Rev. Kenneth	Associate Secretary Board of Home Missions United Church 1934-1935
Benson, Martin	Indian Department 1894-1918; Clerk of Schools 1909
Berry, Rev. Francis	Methodist missionary Muncey 1865
Bethune W. C.	IAB 1957
Blake, Oliver	Senator of Canada 1872
Blomfield, C. J.	NEC Report on Mohawk Institute 1872
Bonnah, T. L.	Regional Supervisor, Toronto
Botsford, Hon. A. E.	Commissioner of the NEC 1870
Bouslaugh, Mr & Mrs	Superintendent and Matron Mohawk Institute 1868, 1871
Boyce, A. M., (Mrs. Rogers)	Acting Principal Mohawk Institute 1914-1915, Principal 1918-1922. Daughter of Robert Ashton. Married Sydney Rogers 1922 became Principal's wife.
Bush, Mr. J. C.	Scotland Ontario 1945
Busk, Jacob H.	Treasurer of NEC 1838-1858?
Cameron, E. S.	Superintendent Six Nations 1903-1906
Carpenter, Wm Lant	NEC 1884
Carson, J. S.	School Inspector West Middlesex 1885-1889
Case, Rev. William	Founder of Indian Missions Wesleyan Methodist Church 1849
Chance, Rev. James	Missionary Six Nations 1872
Chase, Henry	Interpreter Sarnia 1884
Clause, Hazel	Student Mohawk Institute 1921
Clench, J. B.	Clerk of Indian Affairs 1827
Cochrane, Arthur	Governor NEC 1945
Cochrane, Rev. Robert B.	Secretary, Board of Home Missions, United Church of Canada 1937, 1938
Cosford, Thomas	Principal Mt. Elgin 1875-1881
Craig, H. H.	Lawyer for parent Mohawk Institute 1937
Davey, R. F.	Superintendent of Education IAB 1955, 1963
Deleary, Chief	Muncey 1938
Devlin, Samuel	Indian Agent Parry Sound 1939
Dignam, W.	Writer in Christian Guardian 1857
Dixon, Canon L. A.	Missionary Society of the Church of England in Canada, 1945
Dobbin, Tom	Reporter, London Free Press
Dorey, Rev. George	Associate Secretary Board of Home Mission United Church 1942, 1946
Doucet, A. J.	Supervisor of Vocational Training 1946-8
Down, George W.	Indian Agent Sarnia 1938-42
Elliot, Rev. Adam	Missionary at Six Nations 1859, 1870, 1872
Elliott, Floretta	Student & Staff Mohawk Institute
Elliott, Hazel	Student Mohawk Institute 1922
Elliott, Rev. J.	Chairman London District Methodists 1871
Erratt, Margaret	Supervisor Mt. Elgin 1939
Evans, Rev. Ephraim	Principal Mt. Elgin 1873-1874
Falconer, Dr. W. L.	Assistant Superintendent of Medical Services, DIA 1941
Ferrier, Russell T.	Superintendent of Indian Education 1922-1932
Ferrier, Rev. Thompson	Superintendent of Methodist Indian Schools and Hospitals in Canada 1906, 1911, 1919, 1925
Fishcarrier, Mr. H.	Secretary, Six Nations Council 1963
Fisher, Chief George	Chief Chippewa of the Thames 1915
Fraser, Mrs. Duncan	Burlington club member 1965
Gauthier, H.	Indian Agent Christian Island 1950
George, Rev. T. T.	Principal Mt. Elgin 1903-1909
Gilkison, Col. J. T.	Superintendent Six Nations 1870, 1872-1882
Givins, James	Superintendent of Indian Affairs 1827
Glen, Hon. J. Alison	Minister of Mines and Resources 1945
Going, Rev. A. H.	Methodist Minister Exeter 1908
Gordon, Thomas	Indian Agent Muncey 1884
Gould, Canon	Diocese of Huron 1922
Gray, Rev. James	Principal Mt. Elgin 1871-1872
Griffith, Thomas	Schoolmaster 1872-73 Superintendent of Mohawk Institute
Hardie, Susan (Hardy)	Student 1886; Teacher Mohawk Institute 1886-1935
Highfield, Roy	Indian Agent Walpole Island 1937
Henderson, Rev. Dr.	Methodist Mission Rooms 1908
Hoey, R. A.	Superintendent of Welfare & Training 1938-42; Director IAB 1942-46
Hoffman, W.	Barrister 1938
Howes, R. G.	Staff Mt. Elgin 1903
Jacobs, F. W.	Chief Sarnia 1906
Jamieson, T. D.	Medical Superintendent Caradoc 1941
Joblin, Rev. E. E. M.	United Church Minister Caradoc 1943; Director of Education Muncey 1946
Johnson, H. D.	School Inspector Middlesex West 1890-1922
Johnson, John	Chief Six Nations
Johnson, Evelyn	Six Nations 1923 (Pauline Johnson's sister)
Jolicoeur, A. R.	Regional Superintendent of Education, Quebec 1966
Jones, Elizabeth	Wife of Rev. Peter Jones
Jones, Henry	Indian Agent Delaware 1915
Jones, H. M.	Director IAB 1953, 1960
Jones, Isaac	Treasurer NEC 1942
Jones, Rev. Peter	Methodist missionary; Founder of Mount Elgin 1849
Kaiser, S. W.	DIA 1961
Kendall, Rev. William	Methodist Missionary Gibson 1908
Kelly, M. J.	School Inspector County of Brant 1885
Kelly and Porter	Law Firm Brantford 1913
Lager, Cyril	Boys' master Mohawk Institute 1937
Leslie, A. G.	Trusts and Annuities Division DIA 1949
Lewies, W.	Wilson, Pike, Stewart, Lewies lawyers Chatham 1939
Lister, Henry John	Member of NEC 1868
Lougheed, Sir James	Senator, Government Minister 1920
Lugger, Rev Robert	Founder Mohawk Institute, NEC missionary 1827-1836
Lumsden, G. A.	Indian Agent Christian Island 1939
Luxton, Bishop George	Bishop of Huron 1949, 1957
MacDonald, R. W.	Farmer near Mt. Elgin 1943
MacInnes, T. R. L.	Acting Secretary DIA 1934, 1936; Secretary Indian Affairs 1942

People and Places Index

More names can be found in the alphabetical lists of students on pp. 221-242 (Mohawk Institute), 348-352 (Mt. Elgin). One name may refer to different individuals. Names of people who attended the schools are in italics.

Aaron, George 216-217
Aaron, Joseph 217-218
Abraham (Abrams), R. H. 135, 139, 284, 286
Ackland, Dr. 310
Adams, Peter 89, 219
Akwesasne (Cornwall Island, St. Regis) 100, 103, 419
Albert, Eastman 241
Albert, Kenneth 451f; Mrs. 452
Albert (Jamieson), Sophia 477f
Alderville 6-8
Alexander, Mr. A. 164, 213
Alexander, J. R. 81
Alfred, Margaret 285
Allen (Alleen), Miss 151, 153, 157, 165
Almey, Mr. R. 122, 124, 212
Alnwick 5, 262
Anderson, Capt. 6
Anderson, Christie 88
Anderson, J. Elmer 187, 190-191, 399
Anderson, John 217
Anderson, Talford B. 241
Andrews, Thos. 218
Anthony, Albert 60, 215-216
Anthony, Solomon 217
Antone, Ruth, see *Ninham*
Armour, Miss M. M. 273
Armstrong, Miss D. 343
Armstrong, Kathleen 342, 429, 431
Ameil, Mr. W. S. 175, 179
Arnold, Ruth 196
Arthur, Sir G. 47
Ashton, A. Nelles 9-10, 13, 32-33, 35, 105-113, 115, 117, 168, 211, 355-356
Ashton, General E.C (C.E., A.C.) 95, 108, 119-121, 140, 146, 149, 163
Ashton, Robert, 9, 13-15, 17, 19-20, 22-23, 27-29, 31, 33, 40, 65, 69-71, 76, 78-90, 93-107, 111, 116, 128, 142, 149, 168, 210-211, 219; Ashton, Mrs. 20, 71, 81-83, 90, 99-100, 117, 128, 210
Atkins, Charles 217-218
Atkins, Elizabeth 218
Atkins, Garnett 285
Atkins, Mabel 285
Atthill, Lefontaine 244-245
Bagot, Sir Charles 50
Baker, Mr. 397, 399-400
Baker, Miss L. 344
Bandy, Miss Helen 343-344, 459
Barber, Miss 230
Barker, Miss 345
Barrass, Dr. Edward 253
Barrberrie, Miss O. 343
Barnes, Mr. 198, 200-201, 203
Barnett, Mrs/Miss 20, 435-437, 441-442, 447

Barron (Bauren), Mr. 124, 133, 135, 212
Bartley, M. E. 196
Barton, Mr. H. 188, 195, 213
Bartram, Frances 105
Bates, Miss 155
Bearfoot, Elam 144, 219
Bearfoot (Barefoot), Isaac 9, 14-15, 55, 58-59, 61, 65, 69, 71, 75, 79, 81, 87, 93, 142, 219
Bearfoot, John John 52
Bearfoot, Pearl 106
Beaton, Rev. Kenneth 295, 297-298, 300
Beaver, Marguerite 384f
Beeswing, Peter 215
Bell, Charles 56
Bell, Miss E. B. 345
Bell, Miss L. 212
Benedick, Lewis (Louis) 217-218
Benedict, David 88
Bennett, Mrs. 213, 381, 383, 386, 393
Benson, Martin 9-10, 16, 23, 26, 30, 33, 40, 90, 100-101, 103, 116, 257, 259, 265, 269-270
Bentley, Mr. B. 342
Berry, Francis 235
Bethune, W. C. 199
Bilke, Mrs. L. 124, 212
Bilkie, Mr. 125, 132
Bishop of Huron 2, 12-13, 15, 32, 99, 107, 119, 124-125, 134, 151, 154-155, 159, 176, 178-180, 185, 188, 371
Bixel, A. W. 332-333
Blackbird, Jennie 39, 387f
Blake, Mrs. 294
Blake, Oliver 64-65
Blomfield, C. J. 61-62
Bodies, Francis 217
Bomberry (Bombarry), Alexander 215-216
Bomberry, Alice 412f
Bomberry (Bombarry), George 215-217, 220
Bomberry, Jacob 217
Bomberry, Kitty 216
Bomberry (Bombarry), Lené 215-216
Bomberry, Levi 64-65, 216-217
Bomberry, Mary 217
Bomberry, Peter 216-217
Bomberry, Sarah 218
Bomford, Mr. Wm. 342
Bond Head, Sir Francis 6
Bonehill, S. 108, 121
Bonnah, T. L. 205-208
Botsford, Hon. H. E. 59
Bouslaugh, Mr. and Mrs. 56-57, 59, 61-63, 68
Bowring, Mr. D. A. 346
Bowman, Miss 459
Boyce, Mr. 423

Boyce, Mrs. A. 213, 363, 377, 386, 397, 417
Boyce, Mrs. A. M. (Miss Ashton, Mrs. Rogers) 9-10, 13, 23, 27, 31-33, 116-117, 120-137, 139, 142-149, 154, 157-160, 162-164, 210-212, 357, 363
Boyce, T.H. 252
Bradley, Ernest 276
Bradley, William 276
Bragg, Dr. 124, 148, 150
Brant, Henry 51
Brant, John 5, 44
Bricker, Mr. 176
Brigham (Tooshknig), Lorraine 332, 468f
Brigham, Rev. Simpson 122, 219, 470
Brigham, Zelda 217
Bressette (George), Anita 427, 475f
Brissett, A. 241
Brissett, J. 241
Brisette, Edith 279
Brisette, Florence 279
Brisette, Lettie 279
Broderick, Miss Willow 344-345, 451, 453, 467
Bryce, Dr. 28
Buchanan, Miss 129-130
Bunn, Asa 285
Bunt, Mrs. 414
Burch, Archie 285
Burgess, Dr. 264
Burnam, James 219
Burnett (Burnnett), Mrs. 127, 129, 136
Burnfield, Miss C. 333, 345-346
Burning, Catherine 218
Burning, Charles 217
Burning, Christiana 216
Burning, Harrison 357f
Burning, Isaac 217
Burning, Margaret 218-219
Burning (Boorning), Peter 216-217
Burning, Zachariah 217-218
Bury, Lord 231
Busch, Miss 124-125
Bush, Major 159
Bush, J. C. 338-339
Busk, J. H. 46
Butcher, William 81
Butler, Mary Jane 67, 219
Byrne, Rev. A. S. 226
Byron, Mrs. 205
Cady, Cecil 343
Cairns, Dr. 267-268
Cameron, E. S. 98, 100-101, 104
Campbell, Miss Annie 249-251
Campbell, A. P. 293
Campbell, Major E. T. 226
Ca-na-ha-ro-tha 218
Cape Croker 98, 100, 192, 214, 285, 307, 317, 319, 325, 327, 331,

338, 351, 418, 435-436, 466, 478
Caradoc 198, 244, 264, 282, 307, 320-321, 325-327, 329, 333, 336, 338, 340-341
Carlson, Miss H. 343
Carpenter, Chief Benjn 87
Carpenter, Christiana 215-216
Carpenter, David 215-217
Carpenter, Joseph 57
Carpenter, Magdalen 215
Carpenter, Mary M. 216
Carpenter, Moses 216-218
Carpenter, Susannah (Susan) 57, 60, 218
Carpenter, Wm. Lant 82
Carrier (Carryer), Julia 67, 218
Carrier, Simon (Simeon) 215-217
Carrier (Carryer), Yeoval (Youel) 68, 215-217
Carroll, Rev. J. 226
Carryer, Elizabeth 219
Carryer, Mary A. 218
Carson, J. S. 245-247
Case, John 249, 287
Case, Mary 215
Case, Rev. William 6
Cassie, Donald 209
Caverhill, Mr. J. L. 344
Chambers, Miss 152-153, 155
Chance, Rev. James 61, 64-65, 68, 73, 76
Charles, Alexander 249
Chase, Henry 244
Chattoe, Mr. T. C. 344-345, 447
Chechock, Amelia 220
Chenoweth, Mrs. 205
Chesley, S. G. 231
Chippewa of the Thames 7, 16, 24, 33, 199, 226, 233, 235, 240, 244, 256, 264, 267, 282-283, 287-288, 310-311, 313, 315, 330, 333, 341, 352, 431, 443
Chisholm, Miss 401
Christian Island 4, 13, 29, 195, 199-201, 309, 312, 325, 338, 414, 420, 464, 478
Christiansen, Mr. 423
Christie, David 79
Chubb, Mr. 159
Clane, Catherine 215
Clark, Mrs. 139
Clark, Nugget 397
Clark, Richard Edward 53
Clarke, Archdeacon 183, 185
Clarke (Clark), Mr. 133, 139
Clarke, Mrs. E. J. 346
Claus, Cody 315, 445, 465-466
Claus, Mr. Jesse 315
Claus, Lois 187
Claus, Lucille 466
Clause (Claus), Elsie 14, 130, 136-137, 140, 221
Clause, Isaac 218
Clause, Sarah 215

Subject Index

There is a boarding school far far away

Where we get mush 'n' milk three times a day

Children at the Mohawk Institute risked the strap for singing their own words to the old hymn. In one week in 1895 oatmeal porridge was on the menu for breakfast every day, and cornmeal porridge for five suppers. Generations of children fed on mush 'n' milk used the nickname *mush hole* for The Mohawk Institute and Mount Elgin.

The Mush Hole tells the story of two Indian Residential Schools through three voices. *Voice-over* is an analytical overview of the history of the schools from an anthropological perspective. *Voice of Authority* is a collection of documents including principals' reports, Indian Affairs Department correspondence, newspaper stories, and letters from parents, in the original words. In *Voice of Experience* 60 former students share their memories of life at the schools.

Mohawk Institute Students

Heffle Publishing   ISBN 0-9683179-0-1